PRAISE FOR *A PRACTICAL GUIDE TO RED HAT® LINUX,* *SECOND EDITION*

"Since I'm in an educational environment, I found the content of Sobell's book to be right on target and very helpful for anyone managing Linux in the enterprise. His style of writing is very clear. He builds up to the chapter exercises, which I find to be relevant to real-world scenarios a user or admin would encounter. An IT/IS student would find this book a valuable complement to their education. The vast amount of information is extremely well balanced and Sobell manages to present the content without complicated asides and meandering prose. This is a 'must have' for anyone managing Linux systems in a networked environment or anyone running a Linux server. I would also highly recommend it to an experienced computer user who is moving to the Linux platform."

—Mary Norbury
IT Director
Barbara Davis Center/
University of Colorado at Denver
from a review posted on slashdot.org

"I had the chance to use your UNIX books when I when was in college years ago at Cal Poly San Luis Obispo, CA. I have to say that your books are among the best! They're quality books that teach the theoretical aspects and applications of the operating system."

—Benton Chan
IS Engineer

"The book has more than lived up to my expectations from the many reviews I read, even though it targets FC2. I have found something very rare with your book: It doesn't read like the standard technical text, it reads more like a story. It's a pleasure to read and hard to put down. Did I say that?! :-)"

—David Hopkins
Business Process Architect

"Thanks for your work and for the book you wrote. There are really few books that can help people to become more efficient administrators of different workstations. We hope (in Russia) that you will continue bringing us a new level of understanding of Linux/UNIX systems."

—Anton Petukhov

"Mark Sobell has written a book as approachable as it is authoritative

—*Jeffrey Bianchine*
Advocate, Author, Journalist

"Excellent reference book, well suited for the sysadmin of a Linux clu
ter, or the owner of a PC contemplating installing a recent stable Linu
Don't be put off by the daunting heft of the book. Sobell has striven
be as inclusive as possible, in trying to anticipate your system admin:
tration needs."

—*Wes Boudville*
Inventor

"*A Practical Guide to Red Hat® Linux®* is a brilliant book. Thank y
Mark Sobell."

—*C. Pozrikidis*
University of California at San Diego

"This book presents the best overview of the Linux operating system th
I have found. . . . [It] should be very helpful and understandable no ma
ter what the reader's background is: traditional UNIX user, new Linu
devotee, or even Windows user. Each topic is presented in a clear, co
plete fashion and very few assumptions are made about what the read
knows. . . . The book is extremely useful as a reference, as it contains
70-page glossary of terms and is very well indexed. It is organized
such a way that the reader can focus on simple tasks without having
wade through more advanced topics until they are ready."

—*Cam Marshall*
Marshall Information Service LLC
Member of Front Range UNIX
Users Group [FRUUG]
Boulder, Colorado

"Conclusively, this is THE book to get if you are a new Linux user ar
you just got into RH/Fedora world. There's no other book that di
cusses so many different topics and in such depth."

—*Eugenia Loli-Queru*
Editor in Chief
OSNews.com

PART I
INSTALLING RED HAT LINUX

A PRACTICAL GUIDE TO RED HAT® LINUX®

THIRD EDITION

A PRACTICAL GUIDE TO RED HAT® LINUX®

THIRD EDITION

FEDORA™ CORE AND
RED HAT ENTERPRISE LINUX

MARK G. SOBELL

PRENTICE HALL

Upper Saddle River, NJ • Boston • Indianapolis • San Francisco
New York • Toronto • Montreal • London • Munich • Paris • Madrid
Capetown • Sydney • Tokyo • Singapore • Mexico City

Many of the designations used by manufacturers and sellers to distinguish their products are claimed as trademarks. Where those designations appear in this book, and the publisher was aware of a trademark claim, the designations have been printed with initial capital letters or in all capitals.

The author and publisher have taken care in the preparation of this book, but make no expressed or implied warranty of any kind and assume no responsibility for errors or omissions. No liability is assumed for incidental or consequential damages in connection with or arising out of the use of the information or programs contained herein.

The publisher offers excellent discounts on this book when ordered in quantity for bulk purchases or special sales, which may include electronic versions and/or custom covers and content particular to your business, training goals, marketing focus, and branding interests. For more information, please contact:

U.S. Corporate and Government Sales
(800) 382-3419
corpsales@pearsontechgroup.com

For sales outside the United States, please contact:

International Sales
international@pearsoned.com

This Book Is Safari Enabled

The Safari® Enabled icon on the cover of your favorite technology book means the book is available through Safari Bookshelf. When you buy this book, you get free access to the online edition for 45 days.

Safari Bookshelf is an electronic reference library that lets you easily search thousands of technical books, find code samples, download chapters, and access technical information whenever and wherever you need it.

To gain 45-day Safari Enabled access to this book:

- Go to http://www.prenhallprofessional.com/safarienabled
- Complete the brief registration form
- Enter the coupon code P9KM-KSMJ-9RNK-IUJ9-8I4M

If you have difficulty registering on Safari Bookshelf or accessing the online edition, please e-mail customer-service@safaribooksonline.com.

Visit us on the Web: www.prenhallprofessional.com

Library of Congress Cataloging-in-Publication Data:
Sobell, Mark G.
 A practical guide to Red Hat Linux : Fedora Core and Red Hat
Enterprise Linux / Mark G. Sobell. — 3rd ed.
    p. cm.
 Includes index.
 ISBN 0-13-228027-2 (pbk. : alk. paper)
 1. Linux. 2. Operating systems (Computers) I. Title.
 QA76.76.O63S59485 2006
 005'4'32—dc22
                            2006014003

ISBN 0-13-228027-2

Text printed in the United States on recycled paper at Courier in Stoughton, Massachusetts.
First printing, June 2006

For my uncle,
David Z. Levitov (1920-2005),
who gave me the world.

Brief Contents

CONTENTS

CHAPTER 7: THE SHELL   201

PART III   DIGGING INTO RED HAT LINUX   231

CHAPTER 8: LINUX GUIs: X, GNOME, AND KDE   233

CHAPTER 9: THE BOURNE AGAIN SHELL   265

CHAPTER 10: NETWORKING AND THE INTERNET   343

PART IV   SYSTEM ADMINISTRATION   387

CHAPTER 11: SYSTEM ADMINISTRATION: CORE CONCEPTS   389

CHAPTER 12: FILES, DIRECTORIES, AND FILESYSTEMS   447

CHAPTER 13: DOWNLOADING AND INSTALLING SOFTWARE   475

CHAPTER 14: PRINTING WITH CUPS   503

CHAPTER 17: CONFIGURING A LAN 567

PART V USING CLIENTS AND SETTING UP SERVERS 577

CHAPTER 20: **sendmail**: SETTING UP MAIL CLIENTS, SERVERS, AND MORE   627

CHAPTER 23: SAMBA: INTEGRATING LINUX AND WINDOWS   695

CHAPTER 24: DNS/BIND: TRACKING DOMAIN NAMES AND ADDRESSES   719

CHAPTER 25: iptables: SETTING UP A FIREWALL   763

CHAPTER 26: APACHE (httpd): SETTING UP A WEB SERVER   785

Appendix D: The Free Software Definition 1007

Appendix E: The Linux 2.6 Kernel 1011

PREFACE

The book   Whether you are an end user, a system administrator, or a little of each, this book explains with step-by-step examples how to get the most out of a Fedora Core or Red Hat Enterprise Linux system. In 28 chapters, this book takes you from installing a Fedora Core or Red Hat Enterprise Linux system through understanding its inner workings to setting up secure servers that run on the system.

The audience   This book is designed for a wide range of readers. It does not require you to have programming experience, but having some experience using a general-purpose computer is helpful. This book is appropriate for

- **Students** who are taking a class in which they use Linux

- **Home users** who want to set up and/or run Linux

- **Professionals** who use Linux at work

- **System administrators** who need an understanding of Linux and the tools that are available to them

- **Computer science students** who are studying the Linux operating system

- **Programmers** who need to understand the Linux programming environment

- **Technical executives** who want to get a grounding in Linux

Benefits   *A Practical Guide to Red Hat® Linux®: Fedora Core™ and Red Hat Enterprise Linux, Third Edition,* gives you a broad understanding of many facets of Linux, from installing Red Hat Linux through using and customizing it. No matter what your background, this book gives you the knowledge you need to get on with your work. You will come away from this book understanding how to use Linux, and this book will remain a valuable reference for years to come.

Overlap   If you read *A Practical Guide to Linux® Commands, Editors, and Shell Programming,* you will notice some overlap between that book and the one you are reading now. The first chapter, and the chapters on the utilities, the filesystem, programming tools, and the appendix on regular expressions are very similar in the two books, as are the three chapters on the Bourne Again Shell (bash). Chapters that appear in this book but not in *A Practical Guide to Linux® Commands, Editors, and Shell Programming* include Chapters 2 and 3 (installation), Chapters 4 and 8 (Red Hat Linux and the GUI), Chapter 10 (networking), all of the chapters in Part IV (system administration) and Part V (servers), and Appendix C (security).

THIS BOOK INCLUDES FEDORA CORE 5 ON A DVD

A Practical Guide to Red Hat® Linux®, Third Edition, includes a DVD that you can use to install or upgrade to Fedora Core 5. Chapter 2 helps you get ready to install Fedora Core. Chapter 3 provides step-by-step instructions for installing Fedora Core from this DVD. This book guides you through learning about, using, and administrating Fedora Core or Red Hat Enterprise Linux.

WHAT IS NEW IN THIS EDITION?

The third edition of *A Practical Guide to Red Hat® Linux®* covers Fedora Core 5 and Red Hat Enterprise Linux version 4. All the changes, large and small, that have been made to these products since the second edition of this book have been incorporated into the explanations and examples. The following list details the sections of this book that have undergone the most major changes.

- **Access Control Lists** (ACLs; page 185)   A security feature that provides finer-grained control over which users can access specific directories and files than do traditional Linux permissions.

- **SELinux** (Security Enhanced Linux; page 400)   A security feature that enforces security policies that limit what a user or program can do.

- bash (the Bourne Again Shell; Chapters 7, 9, and 28)   These chapters have been reorganized and rewritten to provide clearer explanations and better examples of how bash works both from the command line in day-to-day work and as a programming language to write shell scripts.

- yum (page 476)   A program that keeps Fedora Core systems up-to-date. The yum utility downloads software from repositories on the Internet. It can upgrade existing software and install new software. You can run yum manually or have it run automatically every night.

- pirut (page 483)   A graphical software package management utility. The pirut utility is similar to yum except that it works with groups of software packages. For example, you can use pirut to download and install the entire KDE desktop environment with one command.

- parted (page 65)   A command line utility that reports on and manipulates hard disk partitions.

FEATURES OF THIS BOOK

This book is designed and organized so you can get the most out of it in the shortest amount of time. You do not have to read this book straight through in page order. Once you are comfortable using Linux, you can use this book as a reference: Look up a topic of interest in the table of contents or index and read about it. Or think of the book as a catalog of Linux topics: Flip through the pages until a topic catches your eye. The book includes many pointers to Web sites where you can get additional information: Consider the Internet an extension of this book.

A Practical Guide to Red Hat® Linux®, Third Edition, is structured with the following features:

- In this book, the term **Red Hat Linux** refers to both **Fedora Core** and **Red Hat Enterprise Linux**. Features that apply to only one operating system or the other are marked as such using these indicators: FEDORA or RHEL.

- **Optional sections** enable you to read the book at different levels, returning to more difficult material when you are ready to delve into it.

- **Caution boxes** highlight procedures that can easily go wrong, giving you guidance before you run into trouble.

- **Tip boxes** highlight ways that you can save time by doing something differently or situations when it may be useful or just interesting to have additional information.

- **Security boxes** point out places where you can make a system more secure. The **security appendix** presents a quick background in system security issues.

- Concepts are illustrated by **practical examples** throughout the book.

- **Chapter summaries** review the important points covered in each chapter.

- **Review exercises** are included at the end of each chapter for readers who want to further hone their skills. Answers to even-numbered exercises are at www.sobell.com.

- This book provides resources for **finding software** on the Internet. It also explains how **download** and **install** software using yum, BitTorrent, and, for Red Hat Enterprise Linux, Red Hat Network (RHN).

- The **glossary** defines more than 500 common terms.

- The book describes in detail many important **GNU tools**, including the gcc C compiler, the gdb debugger, the GNU Configure and Build System, make, and gzip.

- Pointers throughout the text provide help in obtaining **online documentation** from many sources including the local system, the Red Hat Web site, and other locations on the Internet.

- Many useful URLs (Internet addresses) point to sites where you can obtain software, security programs and information, and more.

- The comprehensive index helps you locate topics quickly and easily.

KEY TOPICS COVERED IN THIS BOOK

This book contains a lot of information. This section distills and summarizes its contents. You may want to review the table of contents for more detail. This book

Installation

- Describes how to download from the Internet and burn a Fedora Core installation DVD or CDs.

- Helps you plan the layout of the system's hard disk and assists you in using Disk Druid or parted to partition the hard disk.

- Explains how to use the Logical Volume Manager (LVM2) to set up, grow, and migrate logical volumes, which are similar in function to traditional disk partitions.

- Describes in detail how to install Red Hat Linux from a DVD, CDs, a hard disk, or over a network using FTP, NFS, or HTTP.

- Covers responses to the **boot:** prompt and explains how to work with **Anaconda**, Red Hat's installation program.

- Covers the details of installing and customizing the X.org version of the X Window System.

Working with Red Hat Linux

- Introduces the graphical desktop (GUI) and explains how to use desktop tools including the panel, Panel menu, Main menu, Window Operations menu, Desktop menu, Desktop switcher, and terminal emulator.

- Presents the KDE desktop and covers using Konqueror to manage files, start programs, and browse the Web.

- Covers the GNOME desktop and the Nautilus file manager.

- Explains how to customize your desktop to please your senses and help you work more efficiently.

- Covers the Bourne Again Shell (bash) in three chapters, including an entire chapter on shell programming that includes many sample shell scripts.

- Explains the command line interface and introduces more than 30 command line utilities.

- Presents a tutorial on the vim (vi work-alike) textual editor.

- Covers types of networks, network protocols, and network utilities.

- Explains hostnames, IP addresses, and subnets, and explores how to use host and dig to look up domain names and IP addresses on the Internet.

- Covers distributed computing and the client/server model.

System administration

- Explains how to use the Red Hat system-config-* tools to configure the display, DNS, Apache, a network interface, and more. You can also use these tools to add users and manage local and remote printers. (See page 415 for a list of the tools.)

- Describes how to use the following tools to download software and keep a system current:

  - yum   Downloads and installs software packages from the Internet, keeping a system up-to-date and resolving dependencies as it processes the packages. You can run yum manually or set it up to run automatically every night.

  - **BitTorrent**   Good for distributing large amounts of data such as the Fedora installation DVD and CDs. The more people who use BitTorrent to download a file, the faster it works.

  - up2date   The Red Hat Enterprise Linux tool for keeping system software current.

- Covers graphical system administration tools, including the Main menu, GNOME and KDE menu systems, KDE Control Center, and KDE Control panel.

- Explains system operation, including the boot process, init scripts, emergency mode, rescue mode, single-user and multiuser modes, and steps to take if the system crashes.

- Describes files, directories, and filesystems, including types of files and filesystems, **fstab** (the filesystem table), automatically mounted filesystems, filesystem integrity checks, filesystem utilities, and fine-tuning of filesystems.

- Covers backup utilities including tar, cpio, dump, and restore.

- Explains how to customize and build a Linux kernel.

Security

- Helps you manage basic system security issues using ssh (secure shell), **vsftpd** (secure FTP server), Apache (the **httpd** Web server), iptables (firewall), and more.

- Presents a complete section on SELinux (Security Enhanced Linux), including instructions for using system-config-securitylevel to configure SELinux.

- Covers using system-config-securitylevel to set up a basic firewall to protect the system.

- Provides instructions on using iptables to share an Internet connection over a LAN and to build advanced firewalls.

- Describes how to set up a chroot jail to protect a server system.

- Explains how to use TCP wrappers to control who can access a server.

- Covers controlling servers using the **xinetd** superserver.

Clients and servers
- Explains how to set up and use the most popular Linux servers, providing a chapter on each: Apache, Samba, OpenSSH, **sendmail**, DNS, NFS, FTP, iptables, and NIS (all of which are included with Red Hat Linux).

- Describes how to set up a CUPS printer server.

- Describes how to set up and use a DHCP server.

Programming
- Covers programming tools including the GNU gcc compiler, the gdb debugger, make, and CVS for managing source code.

- Explains how to debug a C program.

- Describes how to work with shared libraries.

- Provides a complete chapter on shell programming using bash, including many examples.

DETAILS

Part I
Part I, "Installing Red Hat Linux," discusses how to install Fedora Core or Red Hat Enterprise Linux. **Chapter 2** presents an overview of the process of installing Red Hat Linux, including hardware requirements, downloading and burning a DVD or CDs, and planning the layout of the hard disk. **Chapter 3** is a step-by-step guide to installing either version of Red Hat Linux and covers installing from a DVD or CDs, from a local hard disk, and over the network using FTP, NFS, or HTTP. It also shows how to set up the X Window System and customize your graphical user interface (GUI).

Part II
Part II, "Getting Started with Red Hat Linux," familiarizes you with Red Hat Linux, covering logging in, the GUI, utilities, the filesystem, and the shell. **Chapter 4** introduces desktop features, including the panel and the Main menu; explains how to use Konqueror to manage files, run programs, and browse the Web; and covers finding documentation, dealing with login problems, and using the window manager. **Chapter 5** introduces the shell command line interface, describes more than 30 useful utilities, and presents a tutorial on the vim text editor. **Chapter 6** discusses the Linux hierarchical filesystem, covering files, filenames, pathnames, working with directories, access permissions, and hard and symbolic links. **Chapter 7** introduces the Bourne Again Shell (bash) and discusses command line arguments and options, redirecting input to and output from commands, running programs in the background, and using the shell to generate and expand filenames.

Experienced users may want to skim Part II

tip If you have used a UNIX or Linux system before, you may want to skim over or skip some or all of the chapters in Part II. All readers should take a look at "Conventions Used in This Book" (page 17), which explains the typographic and layout conventions that this book uses, and "Getting the Facts: Where to Find Documentation" (page 102), which points out both local and remote sources of Linux and Red Hat documentation.

Part III Part III, "Digging into Red Hat Linux," goes into more detail about working with the system. **Chapter 8** discusses the GUI and includes a section on how to run a graphical program on a remote system and have the display appear locally. The section on GNOME describes GNOME utilities and explains how to use the Nautilus file manager, including its spatial view, while the section on KDE explains more about Konqueror and KDE utilities. **Chapter 9** extends the bash coverage from Chapter 7, explaining how to redirect error output, avoid overwriting files, and work with job control, processes, startup files, important shell builtin commands, parameters, shell variables, and aliases. **Chapter 10** explains networks, network security, and the Internet and discusses types of networks, subnets, protocols, addresses, hostnames, and various network utilities. The section on distributed computing describes the client/server model and some of the servers you can use on a network. Details of setting up and using clients and servers are reserved until Part V.

Part IV Part IV covers system administration. **Chapter 11** discusses core concepts such as Superuser, SELinux (Security Enhanced Linux), system operation, general information about how to set up a server, DHCP, and PAM. **Chapter 12** explains the Linux filesystem, going into detail about types of files, including special and device files, the use of fsck to verify the integrity of and repair filesystems, and the use of tune2fs to change filesystem parameters. **Chapter 13** explains how to keep a system up-to-date by downloading software from the Internet and installing it, including examples of using yum, BitTorrent, and Red Hat's up2date utility. **Chapter 14** explains how to set up the CUPS printing system so you can print on the local system as well as on remote systems. **Chapter 15** details customizing and building a Linux kernel. **Chapter 16** covers additional administration tasks, including setting up user accounts, backing up files, scheduling automated tasks, tracking disk usage, and solving general problems. **Chapter 17** explains how to set up a local area network (LAN), including both hardware (including wireless) and software setup.

Part V Part V goes into detail about setting up and running servers and connecting to them with clients. The chapters in this part of the book cover the following clients/servers:

- **OpenSSH**   Set up an OpenSSH server and use sh, scp, and sftp to communicate securely over the Internet.

- **FTP**   Set up a **vsftpd** secure FTP server and use any of several FTP clients to exchange files with the server.

- **Mail**   Configure **sendmail** and use Webmail, POP3, or IMAP to retrieve email; use SpamAssassin to combat spam.

- **NIS**   Set up NIS to facilitate system administration of a LAN.
- **NFS**   Share filesystems between systems on a network.
- **Samba**   Share filesystems and printers between Windows and Linux systems.
- **DNS/BIND**   Set up a domain nameserver to let other systems on the Internet know the names and IP addresses of your systems they may need to contact.
- **iptables**   Share a single Internet connection between systems on a LAN and set up a firewall to protect local systems.
- **Apache**   Set up an HTTP server that serves Web pages that browsers can display.

Part VI   Part VI covers programming. **Chapter 27** discusses programming tools and environments available under Red Hat Linux, including the C programming language and debugger, make, shared libraries, and source code management using CVS. **Chapter 28** goes into greater depth about shell programming using bash, with the discussion being enhanced by extensive examples.

Part VII   Part VII includes appendixes on regular expressions, helpful Web sites, system security, and free software. This part also includes an extensive glossary with more than 500 entries and a comprehensive index.

SUPPLEMENTS

The author's home page (www.sobell.com) contains downloadable listings of the longer programs from this book as well as pointers to many interesting and useful Linux sites on the World Wide Web, a list of corrections to the book, answers to even-numbered exercises, and a solicitation for corrections, comments, and suggestions.

THANKS

First and foremost I want to thank Mark L. Taub, editor-in-chief, Prentice Hall, who encouraged and prodded me (carrot-and-stick approach) and kept me on track. Mark is unique in my 25 years of book writing experience: an editor who works with the tools I am writing about. Because Mark runs Linux on his home computer, we share experiences as I write. His comments and direction are invaluable. Thank you, Mark T.

Thanks also to the folks at Prentice Hall who helped bring this book to life, especially Julie Nahil, full-service production manager, who gave me guidance and much latitude while keeping me to schedule in producing the book; John Fuller, managing editor, who kept the large view in check; Noreen Regina, editorial assistant, who attended to the many details involved in publishing this book; Heather Fox, publicist; Dan Scherf, media developer; Sandra Schroeder, design manager; Kim Spilker, marketing manager; and everyone else who worked behind the scenes to make this book happen.

I am also indebted to Denis Howe, the editor of *The Free On-line Dictionary of Computing* (FOLDOC). Denis has graciously permitted me to use entries from his compilation. Be sure to look at the dictionary (www.foldoc.org).

A big "thank you" to the folks who read through the drafts of the book and made comments that caused me to refocus parts of the book where things were not clear or were left out altogether: David Chisnall; Chris Karr, Northwestern University; Jesse Keating, Fedora Project; Scott Mann, IBM, Systems Management and Integration Professional; Matthew Miller, Boston University; and George Vish, Senior Education Consultant, HP US Linux Program Manager, Hewlett-Packard Company.

Thanks also to the following people who helped with the first and second editions of this book: Carsten Pfeiffer, Software Engineer and KDE Developer; Aaron Weber, Ximian; Cristof Falk, Software Developer at CritterDesign; Steve Elgersma, Computer Science Department, Princeton University; Scott Dier, University of Minnesota; Robert Haskins, Computer Net Works; Lars Kellogg-Stedman, Harvard University; Jim A. Lola, Principal Systems Consultant, Privateer Systems, LLC; Eric S. Raymond, cofounder, Open Source Initiative; Scott Mann; Randall Lechlitner, Independent Computer Consultant; Jason Wertz, Computer Science Instructor, Montgomery County Community College; Justin Howell, Solano Community College; Ed Sawicki, The Accelerated Learning Center; David Mercer, Contechst; Jeffrey Bianchine, Advocate, Author, Journalist; John Kennedy; and Jim Dennis, Starshine Technical Services.

Thanks also to Dustin Puryear, Puryear Information Technology; Gabor Liptak, Independent Consultant; Bart Schaefer, Chief Technical Officer, iPost; Michael J. Jordan, Web Developer, Linux Online Inc.; Steven Gibson, owner of SuperAnt.com; John Viega, founder and Chief Scientist, Secure Software, Inc.; K. Rachael Treu, Internet Security Analyst, Global Crossing; Kara Pritchard, K & S Pritchard Enterprises, Inc.; Glen Wiley, Capital One Finances; Karel Baloun, Senior Software Engineer, Looksmart, Ltd.; Matthew Whitworth; Dameon D. Welch-Abernathy, Nokia Systems; Josh Simon, Consultant; Stan Isaacs; and Dr. Eric H. Herrin II, Vice President, Herrin Software Development, Inc. And thanks to Doug Hughes, long-time system designer and administrator, who gave me a big hand with the sections on system administration, networks, the Internet, and programming.

More thanks go to consultants Lorraine Callahan and Steve Wampler; Ronald Hiller, Graburn Technology, Inc.; Charles A. Plater, Wayne State University; Bob Palowoda; Tom Bialaski, Sun Microsystems; Roger Hartmuller, TIS Labs at Network Associates; Kaowen Liu; Andy Spitzer; Rik Schneider; Jesse St. Laurent; Steve Bellenot; Ray W. Hiltbrand; Jennifer Witham; Gert-Jan Hagenaars; and Casper Dik.

A Practical Guide to Red Hat® Linux®, Third Edition, is based in part on two of my previous UNIX books: *UNIX System V: A Practical Guide* and *A Practical*

Guide to the UNIX System. Many people helped me with those books, and thanks here go to Pat Parseghian, Dr. Kathleen Hemenway, and Brian LaRose; Byron A. Jeff, Clark Atlanta University; Charles Stross; Jeff Gitlin, Lucent Technologies; Kurt Hockenbury; Maury Bach, Intel Israel Ltd.; Peter H. Salus; Rahul Dave, University of Pennsylvania; Sean Walton, Intelligent Algorithmic Solutions; Tim Segall, Computer Sciences Corporation; Behrouz Forouzan, DeAnza College; Mike Keenan, Virginia Polytechnic Institute and State University; Mike Johnson, Oregon State University; Jandelyn Plane, University of Maryland; Arnold Robbins and Sathis Menon, Georgia Institute of Technology; Cliff Shaffer, Virginia Polytechnic Institute and State University; and Steven Stepanek, California State University, Northridge, for reviewing the book.

I continue to be grateful to the many people who helped with the early editions of my UNIX books. Special thanks are due to Roger Sippl, Laura King, and Roy Harrington for introducing me to the UNIX system. My mother, Dr. Helen Sobell, provided invaluable comments on the original manuscript at several junctures. Also, thanks go to Isaac Rabinovitch, Professor Raphael Finkel, Professor Randolph Bentson, Bob Greenberg, Professor Udo Pooch, Judy Ross, Dr. Robert Veroff, Dr. Mike Denny, Joe DiMartino, Dr. John Mashey, Diane Schulz, Robert Jung, Charles Whitaker, Don Cragun, Brian Dougherty, Dr. Robert Fish, Guy Harris, Ping Liao, Gary Lindgren, Dr. Jarrett Rosenberg, Dr. Peter Smith, Bill Weber, Mike Bianchi, Scooter Morris, Clarke Echols, Oliver Grillmeyer, Dr. David Korn, Dr. Scott Weikart, and Dr. Richard Curtis.

I take responsibility for any errors and omissions in this book. If you find one or just have a comment, let me know (mgs@sobell.com) and I will fix it in the next printing. My home page (www.sobell.com) contains a list of errors and credits those who found them. It also offers copies of the longer scripts from the book and pointers to many interesting Linux pages.

Mark G. Sobell
San Francisco, California

1

WELCOME TO LINUX

The Linux *kernel* was developed by Finnish undergraduate student Linus Torvalds, who used the Internet to make the source code immediately available to others for free. Torvalds released Linux version 0.01 in September 1991.

The new operating system came together through a lot of hard work. Programmers around the world were quick to extend the kernel and develop other tools, adding functionality to match that already found in both BSD UNIX and System V UNIX (SVR4) as well as new functionality.

The Linux operating system, developed through the cooperation of many, many people around the world, is a *product of the Internet* and is a *free* operating system. In other words, all the source code is free. You are free to study it, redistribute it, and modify it. As a result, the code is available free of cost—no charge for the software, source, documentation, or support (via newsgroups, mailing lists, and other Internet resources). As the GNU Free Software Definition (reproduced in Appendix D) puts it:

Free beer

"Free software" is a matter of liberty, not price. To understand the concept, you should think of "free" as in "free speech," not as in "free beer."

THE GNU–LINUX CONNECTION

An operating system is the low-level software that schedules tasks, allocates storage, and handles the interfaces to peripheral hardware, such as printers, disk drives, the screen, keyboard, and mouse. An operating system has two main parts: the *kernel* and the *system programs*. The kernel allocates machine resources, including memory, disk space, and *CPU* (page 1026) cycles, to all other programs that run on the computer. The system programs perform higher-level housekeeping tasks, often acting as servers in a client/server relationship. *Linux* is the name of the kernel that Linus Torvalds presented to the world in 1991 and that many others have worked on since then to enhance, stabilize, expand, and make more secure.

THE HISTORY OF GNU–LINUX

This section presents some background on the relationship between GNU and Linux.

FADE TO 1983

Richard Stallman (www.stallman.org) announced[1] the GNU Project for creating an operating system, both kernel and system programs, and presented the GNU Manifesto,[2] which begins as follows:

> GNU, which stands for Gnu's Not UNIX, is the name for the complete UNIX-compatible software system which I am writing so that I can give it away free to everyone who can use it.

Some years later, Stallman added a footnote to the preceding sentence when he realized that it was creating confusion:

> The wording here was careless. The intention was that nobody would have to pay for *permission* to use the GNU system. But the words don't make this clear, and people often interpret them as saying that copies of GNU should always be distributed at little or no charge. That was never the intent; later on, the manifesto mentions the possibility of companies providing the service of distribution for a profit. Subsequently I have learned to distinguish

---

1. www.gnu.org/gnu/initial-announcement.html

2. www.gnu.org/gnu/manifesto.html

carefully between "free" in the sense of freedom and "free" in the sense of price. Free software is software that users have the freedom to distribute and change. Some users may obtain copies at no charge, while others pay to obtain copies—and if the funds help support improving the software, so much the better. The important thing is that everyone who has a copy has the freedom to cooperate with others in using it.

In the manifesto, after explaining a little about the project and what has been accomplished so far, Stallman continues:

> **Why I Must Write GNU**
> I consider that the golden rule requires that if I like a program I must share it with other people who like it. Software sellers want to divide the users and conquer them, making each user agree not to share with others. I refuse to break solidarity with other users in this way. I cannot in good conscience sign a nondisclosure agreement or a software license agreement. For years I worked within the Artificial Intelligence Lab to resist such tendencies and other inhospitalities, but eventually they had gone too far: I could not remain in an institution where such things are done for me against my will.
>
> So that I can continue to use computers without dishonor, I have decided to put together a sufficient body of free software so that I will be able to get along without any software that is not free. I have resigned from the AI Lab to deny MIT any legal excuse to prevent me from giving GNU away.

NEXT SCENE, 1991

The GNU Project has moved well along toward its goal. Much of the GNU operating system, except for the kernel, is complete. Richard Stallman later writes:

> By the early '90s we had put together the whole system aside from the kernel (and we were also working on a kernel, the GNU Hurd,[3] which runs on top of Mach[4]). Developing this kernel has been a lot harder than we expected, and we are still working on finishing it.[5]
>
> ...[M]any believe that once Linus Torvalds finished writing the kernel, his friends looked around for other free software, and for no particular reason most everything necessary to make a UNIX-like system was already available.

---

3. www.gnu.org/software/hurd/hurd.html

4. www.gnu.org/software/hurd/gnumach.html

5. www.gnu.org/software/hurd/hurd-and-linux.html

What they found was no accident—it was the GNU system. The available free software[6] added up to a complete system because the GNU Project had been working since 1984 to make one. The GNU Manifesto had set forth the goal of developing a free UNIX-like system, called GNU. The Initial Announcement of the GNU Project also outlines some of the original plans for the GNU system. By the time Linux was written, the [GNU] system was almost finished.[7]

Today the GNU "operating system" runs on top of the FreeBSD (www.freebsd.org) and NetBSD (www.netbsd.org) kernels with complete Linux binary compatibility and on top of Hurd pre-releases and Darwin (developer.apple.com/opensource) without this compatibility.

THE CODE IS FREE

The tradition of free software dates back to the days when UNIX was released to universities at nominal cost, which contributed to its portability and success. This tradition died as UNIX was commercialized and manufacturers regarded the source code as proprietary, making it effectively unavailable. Another problem with the commercial versions of UNIX related to their complexity. As each manufacturer tuned UNIX for a specific architecture, it became less portable and too unwieldy for teaching and experimentation.

MINIX Two professors created their own stripped-down UNIX look-alikes for educational purposes: Doug Comer created XINU (www.cs.purdue.edu/research/xinu.html) and Andrew Tanenbaum created MINIX (www.cs.vu.nl/~ast/minix.html). Linus Torvalds created Linux to counteract the shortcomings in MINIX. Every time there was a choice between code simplicity and efficiency/features, Tanenbaum chose simplicity (to make it easy to teach with MINIX), which meant that this system lacked many features people wanted. Linux goes in the opposite direction.

You can obtain Linux at no cost over the Internet (page 35). You can also obtain the GNU code via the U.S. mail at a modest cost for materials and shipping. You can support the Free Software Foundation (www.fsf.org) by buying the same (GNU) code in higher-priced packages, and you can buy commercial packaged releases of Linux (called *distributions*), such as Red Hat Linux, that include installation instructions, software, and support.

GPL Linux and GNU software are distributed under the terms of the GNU General Public License (GPL, www.gnu.org/licenses/licenses.html). The GPL says you have the right to copy, modify, and redistribute the code covered by the agreement. When you redistribute the code, however, you must also distribute the same license with the code, making the code and the license inseparable. If you get source code off the

---

6. See Appendix D or www.gnu.org/philosophy/free-sw.html.

7. www.gnu.org/gnu/linux-and-gnu.html

Internet for an accounting program that is under the GPL and then modify that code and redistribute an executable version of the program, you must also distribute the modified source code and the GPL agreement with it. Because this arrangement is the reverse of the way a normal copyright works (it gives rights instead of limiting them), it has been termed a *copyleft*. (This paragraph is not a legal interpretation of the GPL; it is here merely to give you an idea of how it works. Refer to the GPL itself when you want to make use of it.)

HAVE FUN!

Two key words for Linux are "Have Fun!" These words pop up in prompts and documentation. The UNIX—now Linux—culture is steeped in humor that can be seen throughout the system. For example, less is more—GNU has replaced the UNIX paging utility named more with an improved utility named less. The utility to view PostScript documents is named ghostscript, and one of several replacements for the vi editor is named elvis. While machines with Intel processors have "Intel Inside" logos on their outside, some Linux machines sport "Linux Inside" logos. And Torvalds himself has been seen wearing a T-shirt bearing a "Linus Inside" logo.

THE LINUX 2.6 KERNEL

The Linux 2.6 kernel was released on December 17, 2003. This kernel has many features that offer increased security and speed. Some of these features benefit end users directly; others help developers produce better code and find problems more quickly. See Appendix E for a description of the new features in the Linux 2.6 kernel.

THE HERITAGE OF LINUX: UNIX

The UNIX system was developed by researchers who needed a set of modern computing tools to help them with their projects. The system allowed a group of people working together on a project to share selected data and programs while keeping other information private.

Universities and colleges played a major role in furthering the popularity of the UNIX operating system through the "four-year effect." When the UNIX operating system became widely available in 1975, Bell Labs offered it to educational institutions at nominal cost. The schools, in turn, used it in their computer science programs, ensuring that computer science students became familiar with it. Because UNIX was such an advanced development system, the students became acclimated to a sophisticated programming environment. As these students graduated and went into industry, they expected to work in a similarly advanced environment. As more of them worked their way up the ladder in the commercial world, the UNIX operating system found its way into industry.

In addition to introducing students to the UNIX operating system, the Computer Systems Research Group (CSRG) at the University of California at Berkeley made significant additions and changes to it. In fact, it made so many popular changes that one version of the system is called the Berkeley Software Distribution (BSD) of the UNIX system (or just Berkeley UNIX). The other major version is UNIX System V (SVR4), which descended from versions developed and maintained by AT&T and UNIX System Laboratories.

WHAT IS SO GOOD ABOUT LINUX?

In recent years Linux has emerged as a powerful and innovative UNIX work-alike. Its popularity is surpassing that of its UNIX predecessors. Although it mimics UNIX in many ways, the Linux operating system departs from UNIX in several significant ways: The Linux kernel is implemented independently of both BSD and System V, the continuing development of Linux is taking place through the combined efforts of many capable individuals throughout the world, and Linux puts the power of UNIX within easy reach of business and personal computer users. Using the Internet, today's skilled programmers submit additions and improvements to the operating system to Linus Torvalds, GNU, or one of the other authors of Linux.

Applications   A rich selection of applications is available for Linux—both free and commercial—as well as a wide variety of tools: graphical, word processing, networking, security, administration, Web server, and many others. Large software companies have recently seen the benefit in supporting Linux and now have on-staff programmers whose job it is to design and code the Linux kernel, GNU, KDE, or other software that runs on Linux. For example, IBM (www.ibm.com/linux) is a major Linux supporter. Linux conforms increasingly more closely to POSIX standards, and some distributions and parts of others meet this standard. (See "Standards" on page 8 for more information.) These developments mean that Linux is becoming more mainstream and is respected as an attractive alternative to other popular operating systems.

Peripherals   Another aspect of Linux that appeals to users is the amazing range of peripherals that is supported and the speed with which support for new peripherals emerges. Linux often supports a peripheral or interface card before any company does. Unfortunately some types of peripherals—particularly proprietary graphics cards—lag in their support because the manufacturers do not release specifications or source code for drivers in a timely manner, if at all.

Software   Also important to users is the amount of software that is available—not just source code (which needs to be compiled) but also prebuilt binaries that are easy to install and ready to run. These include more than free software. Netscape, for example, has been available for Linux from the start and included Java support before it was available from many commercial vendors. Now its sibling Mozilla/Thunderbird/Firefox is also a viable browser, mail client, and newsreader, performing many other functions as well.

Platforms   Linux is not just for Intel-based platforms: It has been ported to and runs on the Power PC—including Apple computers (ppclinux), Compaq's (née Digital Equipment

Corporation) Alpha-based machines, MIPS-based machines, Motorola's 68K-based machines, various 64-bit systems, and IBM's S/390. Nor is Linux just for single-processor machines: As of version 2.0, it runs on multiple-processor machines (SMPs). It also includes an O(1) scheduler, which dramatically increases scalability on SMP systems.

Emulators Linux supports programs, called *emulators,* that run code intended for other operating systems. By using emulators you can run some DOS, Windows, and Macintosh programs under Linux. Wine (www.winehq.com) is an open-source implementation of the Windows API on top of the X Window System and UNIX/Linux; QEMU (fabrice.bellard.free.fr/qemu) is a CPU-only emulator that executes x86 Linux binaries on non-x86 Linux systems.

Xen Xen, which was created at the University of Cambridge and is now being developed in the open-source community, is an open-source virtual machine monitor (VMM). A VMM enables several virtual machines (VMs), each running an instance of a separate operating system, to run on a single computer. Xen isolates the VMs so that if one crashes it does not affect any of the others. In addition, Xen introduces minimal performance overhead when compared with running each of the operating systems natively.

Using VMs, you can experiment with cutting-edge releases of operating systems and applications without concern for the base (stable) system, all on a single machine. You can also set up and test networks of systems on a single machine. Xen presents a *sandbox,* an area (system) that you can work in without regard for the results of your work or for the need to clean up.

Fedora Core 5 includes Xen 3.0. This book does not cover the installation or use of Xen. See www.fedoraproject.org/wiki/FedoraXenQuickstartFC5 for installation instructions.

For more information on Xen, refer to the wiki at wiki.xensource.com/xenwiki and the Xen home page at www.cl.cam.ac.uk/Research/SRG/netos/xen.

WHY LINUX IS POPULAR WITH HARDWARE COMPANIES AND DEVELOPERS

Two trends in the computer industry set the stage for the popularity of UNIX and Linux. First, advances in hardware technology created the need for an operating system that could take advantage of available hardware power. In the mid-1970s, minicomputers began challenging the large mainframe computers because, in many applications, minicomputers could perform the same functions less expensively. More recently, powerful 64-bit processor chips, plentiful and inexpensive memory, and lower-priced hard disk storage have allowed hardware companies to install multiuser operating systems on desktop computers.

Proprietary operating systems Second, with the cost of hardware continually dropping, hardware manufacturers could no longer afford to develop and support proprietary operating systems. A *proprietary* operating system is written and owned by the manufacturer of the hardware (for example, DEC/Compaq owns VMS). Today's manufacturers need a generic operating system that they can easily adapt to their machines.

Generic operating systems   A *generic* operating system is written outside of the company manufacturing the hardware and is sold (UNIX, Windows) or given (Linux) to the manufacturer. Linux is a generic operating system because it runs on different types of hardware produced by different manufacturers. Of course, if manufacturers can pay only for development and avoid per-unit costs (as they have to pay to Microsoft for each copy of Windows they sell), manufacturers are much better off. In turn, software developers need to keep the prices of their products down; they cannot afford to convert their products to run under many different proprietary operating systems. Like hardware manufacturers, software developers need a generic operating system.

Although the UNIX system once met the needs of hardware companies and researchers for a generic operating system, over time it has become more proprietary as each manufacturer added support for specialized features and introduced new software libraries and utilities.

Linux emerged to serve both needs. It is a generic operating system that takes advantage of available hardware power.

LINUX IS PORTABLE

A *portable* operating system is one that can run on many different machines. More than 95 percent of the Linux operating system is written in the C programming language, and C is portable because it is written in a higher-level, machine-independent language. (The C compiler is written in C.)

Because Linux is portable, it can be adapted (ported) to different machines and can meet special requirements. For example, Linux is used in embedded computers, such as the ones found in cellphones, PDAs, and the cable boxes on top of many TVs. The file structure takes full advantage of large, fast hard disks. Equally important, Linux was originally designed as a multiuser operating system—it was not modified to serve several users as an afterthought. Sharing the computer's power among many users and giving them the ability to share data and programs are central features of the system.

Because it is adaptable and takes advantage of available hardware, Linux runs on many different microprocessor-based systems as well as mainframes. The popularity of the microprocessor-based hardware drives Linux; these microcomputers are getting faster all the time, at about the same price point. Linux on a fast microcomputer has become good enough to displace workstations on many desktops. Linux benefits both users, who do not like having to learn a new operating system for each vendor's hardware, and system administrators, who like having a consistent software environment.

The advent of a standard operating system has aided the development of the software industry. Now software manufacturers can afford to make one version of a product available on machines from different manufacturers.

STANDARDS

Individuals from companies throughout the computer industry have joined together to develop the POSIX (Portable Operating System Interface for Computer

Environments) standard, which is based largely on the UNIX System V Interface Definition (SVID) and other earlier standardization efforts. These efforts have been spurred by the U.S. government, which needs a standard computing environment to minimize its training and procurement costs. Now that these standards are gaining acceptance, software developers are able to develop applications that run on all conforming versions of UNIX, Linux, and other operating systems.

THE C PROGRAMMING LANGUAGE

Ken Thompson wrote the UNIX operating system in 1969 in PDP-7 assembly language. Assembly language is machine dependent: Programs written in assembly language work on only one machine or, at best, one family of machines. The original UNIX operating system therefore could not easily be transported to run on other machines (it was not portable).

To make UNIX portable, Thompson developed the B programming language, a machine-independent language, from the BCPL language. Dennis Ritchie developed the C programming language by modifying B and, with Thompson, rewrote UNIX in C in 1973. The revised operating system could be transported more easily to run on other machines.

That development marked the start of C. Its roots reveal some of the reasons why it is such a powerful tool. C can be used to write machine-independent programs. A programmer who designs a program to be portable can easily move it to any computer that has a C compiler. C is also designed to compile into very efficient code. With the advent of C, a programmer no longer had to resort to assembly language to get code that would run well (that is, quickly—although an assembler will always generate more efficient code than a high-level language).

C is a good systems language. You can write a compiler or an operating system in C. It is highly structured but is not necessarily a high-level language. C allows a programmer to manipulate bits and bytes, as is necessary when writing an operating system. But it also has high-level constructs that allow efficient, modular programming.

In the late 1980s the American National Standards Institute (ANSI) defined a standard version of the C language, commonly referred to as *ANSI C* or *C89* (for the year the standard was published). Ten years later the C99 standard was published; it is mostly supported by the GNU Project's C compiler (named gcc). The original version of the language is often referred to as *Kernighan & Ritchie* (or *K&R*) C, named for the authors of the book that first described the C language.

Another researcher at Bell Labs, Bjarne Stroustrup, created an object-oriented programming language named C++, which is built on the foundation of C. Because object-oriented programming is desired by many employers today, C++ is preferred over C in many environments. Another language of choice is Objective-C, which was used to write the first Web browser. The GNU Project's C compiler supports C, C++, and Objective-C.

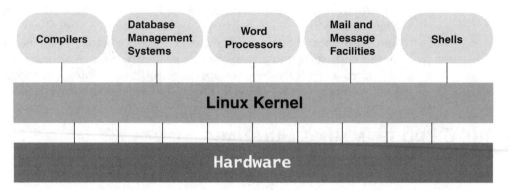

Figure 1-1   A layered view of the Linux operating system

OVERVIEW OF LINUX

The Linux operating system has many unique and powerful features. Like other operating systems, Linux is a control program for computers. But like UNIX, it is also a well-thought-out family of utility programs (Figure 1-1) and a set of tools that allow users to connect and use these utilities to build systems and applications.

LINUX HAS A KERNEL PROGRAMMING INTERFACE

The Linux kernel—the heart of the Linux operating system—is responsible for allocating the computer's resources and scheduling user jobs so that each one gets its fair share of system resources, including access to the CPU; peripheral devices, such as disk, DVD, and CD-ROM storage; printers; and tape drives. Programs interact with the kernel through *system calls,* special functions with well-known names. A programmer can use a single system call to interact with many kinds of devices. For example, there is one **write**() system call, not many device-specific ones. When a program issues a **write**() request, the kernel interprets the context and passes the request to the appropriate device. This flexibility allows old utilities to work with devices that did not exist when the utilities were originally written. It also makes it possible to move programs to new versions of the operating system without rewriting them (provided that the new version recognizes the same system calls). See page 1011 for information on the Linux 2.6 kernel.

LINUX CAN SUPPORT MANY USERS

Depending on the hardware and the types of tasks that the computer performs, a Linux system can support from 1 to more than 1,000 users, each concurrently running a different set of programs. The per-user cost of a computer that can be used by many people at the same time is less than that of a computer that can be used by only a single person at a time. It is less because one person cannot generally take advantage of all the resources a computer has to offer. That is, no one can keep all the printers going constantly, keep all the system memory in use, keep all the disks busy reading and writing, keep the Internet connection in use, and keep all the terminals busy at the same time. A multiuser operating system allows many people to use all the system resources almost simultaneously. The use of costly resources can be maximized and the cost per user can be minimized—the primary objectives of a multiuser operating system.

LINUX CAN RUN MANY TASKS

Linux is a fully protected multitasking operating system, allowing each user to run more than one job at a time. Processes can communicate with one another but remain fully protected from one another, just as the kernel remains protected from all processes. You can run several jobs in the background while giving all your attention to the job being displayed on the screen, and you can switch back and forth between jobs. If you are running the X Window System (page 15), you can run different programs in different windows on the same screen and watch all of them. This capability ensures that users can be more productive.

LINUX PROVIDES A SECURE HIERARCHICAL FILESYSTEM

A *file* is a collection of information, such as text for a memo or report, an accumulation of sales figures, an image, a song, or an executable program. Each file is stored under a unique identifier on a storage device, such as a hard disk. The Linux filesystem provides a structure whereby files are arranged under *directories,* which are like folders or boxes. Each directory has a name and can hold other files and directories. Directories, in turn, are arranged under other directories, and so forth, in a treelike organization. This structure helps users keep track of large numbers of files by grouping related files into directories. Each user has one primary directory and as many subdirectories as required (Figure 1-2).

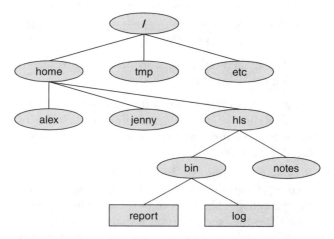

Figure 1-2   The Linux filesystem structure

Standards   With the idea of making life easier for system administrators and software developers, a group got together over the Internet and developed the Linux Filesystem Standard (FSSTND), which has since evolved into the Linux Filesystem Hierarchy Standard (FHS). Before this standard was adopted, key programs were located in different places in different Linux distributions. Today you can sit down at a Linux system and know where to expect to find any given standard program (page 176).

Links   A *link* allows a given file to be accessed by means of two or more names. The alternative names can be located in the same directory as the original file or in another directory. Links can make the same file appear in several users' directories, enabling those users to share the file easily. Windows uses the term *shortcut* in place of *link*. Macintosh users will be more familiar with the term *alias*. Under Linux, an *alias* is different from a *link;* it is a command macro feature provided by the shell (page 318).

Security   Like most multiuser operating systems, Linux allows users to protect their data from access by other users. It also allows users to share selected data and programs with certain other users by means of a simple but effective protection scheme. This level of security is provided by file access permissions, which limit which users can read from, write to, or execute a file. Access Control Lists (ACLs) have recently been added to the Linux kernel and are available in Red Hat Linux. ACLs give users and administrators finer-grained control over file access permissions.

THE SHELL: COMMAND INTERPRETER AND PROGRAMMING LANGUAGE

In a textual environment, the shell—the command interpreter—acts as an interface between you and the operating system. When you enter a command on the screen, the shell interprets the command and calls the program you want. A number of shells are available for Linux. The three most popular ones are described here:

- The Bourne Again Shell (bash), an enhanced version of the original Bourne Shell. It is one of the original UNIX shells.
- The TC Shell (tcsh), an enhanced version of the C Shell. It was developed as part of BSD UNIX.
- The Z Shell (zsh). It incorporates features from a number of shells, including the Korn Shell.

Because users often prefer different shells, multiuser systems can have several different shells in use at any given time. The choice of shells demonstrates one of the advantages of the Linux operating system: the ability to provide a customized interface for each user.

Shell scripts   Besides performing its function of interpreting commands from a keyboard and sending those commands to the operating system, the shell is a high-level programming language. Shell commands can be arranged in a file for later execution (Linux calls these files *shell scripts;* Windows call them *batch files*). This flexibility allows users to perform complex operations with relative ease, often with rather short commands, or to build with surprisingly little effort elaborate programs that perform highly complex operations.

FILENAME GENERATION

Wildcards and ambiguous file references

When you are typing commands to be processed by the shell, you can construct patterns using characters that have special meanings to the shell. These characters are called *wildcard* characters. The patterns, which are called *ambiguous file references,* are a kind of shorthand: Rather than typing in complete filenames, users can type in patterns and the shell will expand them into matching filenames. An ambiguous file reference can save you the effort of typing in a long filename or a long series of similar filenames. For example, the shell might expand the pattern **mak✳** to **make-3.80.tar.gz**. Patterns can also be useful when you know only part of a filename or cannot remember the exact spelling.

DEVICE-INDEPENDENT INPUT AND OUTPUT

Redirection

Devices (such as a printer or terminal) and disk files appear as files to Linux programs. When you give a command to the Linux operating system, you can instruct it to send the output to any one of several devices or files. This diversion is called output *redirection.*

Device independence

In a similar manner, a program's input that normally comes from a keyboard can be redirected so that it comes from a disk file instead. Input and output are *device independent;* they can be redirected to or from any appropriate device.

As an example, the cat utility normally displays the contents of a file on the screen. When you run a cat command, you can easily cause its output to go to a disk file instead of the screen.

SHELL FUNCTIONS

One of the most important features of the shell is that users can use it as a programming language. Because the shell is an interpreter, it does not compile programs written for it but rather interprets programs each time they are loaded from the disk. Loading and interpreting programs can be time-consuming.

Many shells, including the Bourne Again Shell, include shell functions that the shell holds in memory so that it does not have to read them from the disk each time you want to execute them. The shell also keeps functions in an internal format so that it does not have to spend as much time interpreting them.

JOB CONTROL

Job control is a shell feature that allows users to work on several jobs at once, switching back and forth between them as desired. When you start a job, it is frequently in the foreground so it is connected to the terminal. Using job control, you can move the job you are working with into the background and continue running it there while working on or observing another job in the foreground. If a background job then needs your attention, you can move it into the foreground so that it is once again attached to the terminal. The concept of job control originated with BSD UNIX, where it appeared in the C Shell.

A LARGE COLLECTION OF USEFUL UTILITIES

Linux includes a family of several hundred utility programs, often referred to as *commands*. These utilities perform functions that are universally required by users. The sort utility, for example, puts lists (or groups of lists) in alphabetical or numerical order and can be used to sort lists by part number, last name, city, ZIP code, telephone number, age, size, cost, and so forth. The sort utility is an important programming tool and is part of the standard Linux system. Other utilities allow users to create, display, print, copy, search, and delete files as well as to edit, format, and typeset text. The man (for manual) and info utilities provide online documentation for Linux itself.

INTERPROCESS COMMUNICATION

Pipes and filters Linux allows users to establish both pipes and filters on the command line. A *pipe* sends the output of one program to another program as input. A *filter* is a special kind of pipe that processes a stream of input data to yield a stream of output data. A filter processes another program's output, altering it as a result. The filter's output then becomes input to another program.

Pipes and filters frequently join utilities to perform a specific task. For example, you can use a pipe to send the output of the cat utility to sort, a filter, and can then use another pipe to send the output of sort to a third utility, lpr, that sends the data to a printer. Thus, in one command line, you can use three utilities together to sort and print a file.

SYSTEM ADMINISTRATION

On a Linux system the system administrator is frequently the owner and only user of the system. This person has many responsibilities. The first responsibility may be to set up the system and install the software.

Once the system is up and running, the system administrator is responsible for downloading and installing software (including upgrading the operating system), backing up and restoring files, and managing such system facilities as printers, terminals, servers, and a local network. The system administrator is also responsible for setting up accounts for new users on a multiuser system, bringing the system up and down as needed, and taking care of any problems that arise.

ADDITIONAL FEATURES OF LINUX

The developers of Linux included features from BSD, System V, and Sun Microsystems' Solaris, as well as new features, in their operating system. Although most of the tools found on UNIX exist for Linux, in some cases these tools have been replaced by more modern counterparts. This section describes some of the popular tools and features available under Linux.

GUIs: GRAPHICAL USER INTERFACES

The X Window System (also called X or X11) was developed in part by researchers at MIT (Massachusetts Institute of Technology) and provides the foundation for the GUIs available with Linux. Given a terminal or workstation screen that supports X, a user can interact with the computer through multiple windows on the screen, display graphical information, or use special-purpose applications to draw pictures, monitor processes, or preview formatted output. X is an across-the-network protocol that allows a user to open a window on a workstation or computer system that is remote from the CPU generating the window.

Desktop manager   Usually two layers run under X: a desktop manager and a window manager. A *desktop manager* is a picture-oriented user interface that enables you to interact with system programs by manipulating icons instead of typing the corresponding commands to a shell. Red Hat Linux includes GNOME (Figure 1-3, www.gnome.org) and KDE (www.kde.org), the most popular desktop managers.

Figure 1-3   A GNOME workspace

Window manager   A *window manager* is a program that runs under the desktop manager and allows you to open and close windows, run programs, and set up a mouse so it does various things depending on how and where you click. The window manager also gives the screen its personality. Whereas Microsoft Windows allows you to change the color of key elements in a window, a window manager under X allows you to customize the overall look and feel of the screen: You can change the way a window looks and works (by giving it different borders, buttons, and scrollbars), set up virtual desktops, create menus, and more.

Several popular window managers run under X and Linux. Red Hat Linux provides Metacity (the default under GNOME) and kwin (the default under KDE). Other window managers, such as Sawfish and WindowMaker, are also available. Chapters 4 and 8 have more information on GUIs.

(INTER)NETWORKING UTILITIES

Linux network support includes many utilities that enable you to access remote systems over a variety of networks. In addition to sending email to users on other systems, you can access files on disks mounted on other computers as if they were located on the local system, make your files available to other systems in a similar manner, copy files back and forth, run programs on remote systems while displaying the results on the local system, and perform many other operations across local area networks (LANs) and wide area networks (WANs), including the Internet.

Layered on top of this network access is a wide range of application programs that extend the computer's resources around the globe. You can carry on conversations with people throughout the world, gather information on a wide variety of subjects, and download new software over the Internet quickly and reliably. Chapter 10 discusses networks, the Internet, and the Linux network facilities.

SOFTWARE DEVELOPMENT

One of Linux's most impressive strengths is its rich software development environment. You can find compilers and interpreters for many computer languages. Besides C and C++, languages available for Linux include Ada, Fortran, Java, Lisp, Pascal, Perl, and Python. The bison utility generates parsing code that makes it easier to write programs to build compilers (tools that parse files containing structured information). The flex utility generates scanners (code that recognizes lexical patterns in text). The make utility and the GNU Configure and Build System make it easier to manage complex development projects. Source code management systems, such as CVS, simplify version control. Several debuggers, including ups and gdb, help in tracking down and repairing software defects. The GNU C compiler (gcc) works with the gprof profiling utility to help programmers identify potential bottlenecks in a program's performance. The C compiler includes options to perform extensive checking of C code that can make the code more portable and reduce debugging time. These and other software development tools are discussed in Chapter 27. Table B-4 on page 982 lists some sites that you can download software from.

CONVENTIONS USED IN THIS BOOK

This book uses conventions to make its explanations shorter and clearer. The following paragraphs describe these conventions.

Red Hat Linux   In this book, the term *Red Hat Linux* refers to both Fedora Core and Red Hat Enterprise Linux. Features that apply to one operating system or the other only are marked as such, using these markers: FEDORA or RHEL.

Text and examples   The text is set in this type, whereas examples are shown in a monospaced font (also called a *fixed-width* font):

```
$ cat practice
This is a small file I created
with a text editor.
```

Items you enter   Everything you enter at the keyboard is shown in a bold typeface: Within the text, **this bold typeface** is used; within examples and screens, `this one` is used. In the previous example, the dollar sign (\$) on the first line is a prompt that Linux displays, so it is not bold; the remainder of the first line is entered by a user, so it is bold.

Utility names   Names of utilities are printed in this bold sans serif typeface. This book references the emacs text editor and the ls utility or ls command (or just ls) but instructs you to enter **ls −a** on the command line. In this way the text distinguishes between utilities, which are programs, and the instructions you give on the command line to invoke the utilities.

Filenames   Filenames appear in a bold typeface. Examples are **memo5**, **letter.1283**, and **reports**. Filenames may include uppercase and lowercase letters; however, Linux is *case sensitive* (page 1023), so **memo5**, **MEMO5**, and **Memo5** name three different files.

Character strings   Within the text, characters and character strings are marked by putting them in a bold typeface. This convention avoids the need for quotation marks or other delimiters before and after a string. An example is the following string, which is displayed by the passwd utility: **Sorry, passwords do not match.**

Buttons and labels   Words appear in a bold typeface in the sections of the book that describe a GUI. This font indicates that you can click a mouse button when the mouse pointer is over these words on the screen or over a button with this name.

Keys and characters   This book uses SMALL CAPS for three kinds of items:

- Keyboard keys, such as the SPACE bar and the RETURN,[8] ESCAPE, and TAB keys.

- The characters that keys generate, such as the SPACEs generated by the SPACE bar.

---

8. Different keyboards use different keys to move the *cursor* (page 1027) to the beginning of the next line. This book always refers to the key that ends a line as the RETURN key. Your keyboard may have a RET, NEWLINE, ENTER, RETURN, or other key. Use the corresponding key on your keyboard each time this book asks you to press RETURN.

- Keyboard keys that you press with the CONTROL key, such as CONTROL-D. (Even though D is shown as an uppercase letter, you do not have to press the SHIFT key; enter CONTROL-D by holding the CONTROL key down and pressing **d**.)

Prompts and RETURNS   Most examples include the *shell prompt*—the signal that Linux is waiting for a command—as a dollar sign (**$**), a pound sign (**#**), or sometimes a percent sign (**%**). The prompt is not in a bold typeface because you do not enter it. Do not type the prompt on the keyboard when you are experimenting with examples from this book. If you do, the examples will not work.

Examples *omit* the RETURN keystroke that you must use to execute them. An example of a command line is

```
$ vim memo.1204
```

To use this example as a model for running the vim text editor, give the command **vim memo.1204** and press the RETURN key. (Press ESCAPE ZZ to exit from vim; see page 152 for a vim tutorial.) This method of entering commands makes the examples in the book correspond to what appears on the screen.

Menu selection path   The menu selection path is the name of the menu or the location of the menu, followed by a colon, a SPACE, and the menu selection(s) separated by ⇨s. The entire menu selection path is in **bold** type. You can read **Konqueror menubar: Tools⇨Find** as "From the Konqueror menubar, select **Tools**; from **Tools**, select **Find**."

Definitions   All glossary entries marked with ᶠᴼᴸᴰᴼᶜ are courtesy of Denis Howe, editor of the Free Online Dictionary of Computing (www.foldoc.org), and are used with permission. This site is an ongoing work containing definitions, anecdotes, and trivia.

optional   OPTIONAL INFORMATION

Passages marked as optional appear in a gray box and are not central to the ideas presented in the chapter but often involve more challenging concepts. A good strategy when reading a chapter is to skip the optional sections and then return to them when you are comfortable with the main ideas presented in the chapter. This is an optional paragraph.

URLs (Web addresses)   Web addresses, or URLs, have an implicit **http://** prefix, unless **ftp://** or **https://** is shown. You do not normally need to specify a prefix when the prefix is **http://**, but you must use a prefix from a browser when you specify an FTP or secure HTTP site. Thus you can specify a URL in a browser exactly as shown in this book.

Tip, caution, and security boxes   The following boxes highlight information that may be helpful while you are using or administrating a Linux system.

This is a tip box

tip   A tip box may help you avoid repeating a common mistake or may point toward additional information.

This box warns you about something

caution A caution box warns you about a potential pitfall.

This box marks a security note

security A security box highlights a potential security issue. These notes are usually for system administrators, but some apply to all users.

CHAPTER SUMMARY

The Linux operating system grew out of the UNIX heritage to become a popular alternative to traditional systems (that is, Windows) available for microcomputer (PC) hardware. UNIX users will find a familiar environment in Linux. Distributions of Linux contain the expected complement of UNIX utilities, contributed by programmers around the world, including the set of tools developed as part of the GNU Project. The Linux community is committed to the continued development of this system. Support for new microcomputer devices and features is added soon after the hardware becomes available, and the tools available on Linux continue to be refined. With many commercial software packages available to run on Linux platforms and many hardware manufacturers offering Linux on their systems, it is clear that the system has evolved well beyond its origin as an undergraduate project to become an operating system of choice for academic, commercial, professional, and personal use.

EXERCISES

1. What is free software? List three characteristics of free software.

2. Why is Linux popular? Why is it popular in academia?

3. What are multiuser systems? Why are they successful?

4. What is the Free Software Foundation/GNU? What is Linux? Which parts of the Linux operating system did each provide? Who else has helped build and refine this operating system?

5. In what language is Linux written? What does the language have to do with the success of Linux?

6. What is a utility program?

7. What is a shell? How does it work with the kernel? With the user?

8. How can you use utility programs and a shell to create your own applications?

9. Why is the Linux filesystem referred to as *hierarchical?*

10. What is the difference between a multiprocessor and a multiprocessing system?

11. Give an example of when you would want to use a multiprocessing system.

12. Approximately how many people wrote Linux? Why is this unique?

13. What are the key terms of the GNU General Public License?

2

INSTALLATION OVERVIEW

Installing Red Hat Linux is the process of copying operating system files from media to the local system and setting up configuration files so that Linux runs properly on the local hardware. You can install Linux from many types of media, including CDs, a DVD, the local hard disk, or a hard disk and files on another system that is accessed over a network. Several types of installations are also possible, including fresh installations, upgrades from older versions of Red Hat Linux, and dual-boot installations. You can perform the installation manually or set up Kickstart to install Red Hat Linux automatically.

This chapter discusses the installation process in general: planning, partitioning the hard disk, obtaining the files for the installation, burning CDs or a DVD if necessary, and collecting information about the hardware you will need when you install the system. Chapter 3 covers the actual installation.

Red Hat developed Anaconda, an installation tool that performs an interactive installation using a graphical or textual interface, to automate and make friendlier the process of installing Linux. To install Linux on standard hardware, you can typically insert the first installation CD or the installation DVD, boot the system, press RETURN a few times, and change CDs a few times if you are installing from CDs. However, you may want to customize the system or you may be installing on nonstandard hardware: Anaconda gives you many choices as the installation process unfolds. Refer to "Booting the System: The **boot:** Prompt" (page 44) and "The Anaconda Installer" (page 47) for information about customizing a Red Hat Linux installation.

MORE INFORMATION

Local   **lvm** man page including the "See also" pages listed at the bottom

Web   SELinux FAQ   people.redhat.com/kwade/fedora-docs/selinux-faq-en
X.org release information   wiki.x.org
memtest86+   www.memtest.org
Hardware compatibility   hardware.redhat.com
Partition HOWTO   tldp.org/HOWTO/Partition
LVM Resource Page (includes many links)   sourceware.org/lvm2
LVM HOWTO   www.tldp.org/HOWTO/LVM-HOWTO
BitTorrent   www.bittorrent.com
PXE   www.kegel.com/linux/pxe.html
PXE and Kickstart   www.stanford.edu/~alfw/PXE-Kickstart/PXE-Kickstart.html

Downloads   *FEDORA*   Download instructions   fedora.redhat.com/download
FEDORA   BitTorrent trackers   torrent.fedoraproject.org
FEDORA   Download server   download.fedora.redhat.com/pub/fedora/linux/core
FEDORA   Mirrors   fedora.redhat.com/download/mirrors.html
RHEL   ftp://ftp.redhat.com/pub/redhat/linux/enterprise

PLANNING THE INSTALLATION

The major decisions when planning an installation are determining how to divide the hard disk into partitions or, in the case of a dual-boot system, where to put the Linux partitions, and deciding which software packages to install. In addition to these topics, this section discusses hardware requirements for Red Hat Linux, Fedora Core versus Red Hat Enterprise Linux, and fresh installations versus upgrades.

CONSIDERATIONS

SELinux   If you plan to use SELinux, turn it on during Firstboot (page 56). Because SELinux sets extended attributes on files, it can be a time-consuming process to turn on SELinux after you install Linux.

GUI On most installations (except for servers), you will probably want to install a graphical desktop environment. GNOME is installed by default. You can also install KDE or both GNOME and KDE.

Chapter 4, "Introduction to Red Hat Linux," uses examples from KDE to introduce the graphical desktop. Install KDE if you want to follow these examples. You can remove KDE later if you like.

On a server, you normally dedicate as many resources to the server as possible and few resources to anything not required by the server. For this reason, servers rarely include a graphical interface.

Software and services As you install more software packages on a system, the number of updates and the interactions between the packages increase. Server packages that listen for network connections make the system more vulnerable by increasing the number of ways the system can be attacked. Additional services can also slow the system down.

For a system to learn on, or for a development system, additional packages and services may be useful. However, for a more secure production system, it is best to install and maintain the minimum number of packages required and enable only needed services.

REQUIREMENTS

Hardware Red Hat Linux can run on many different types of hardware. This section details installation on 32-bit Intel and compatible platforms such as AMD, Cyrix, and VIA as well as 64-bit platforms such as AMD64 processors (both Athlon64 and Opteron) and Intel processors with Intel Extended Memory 64 Technology (EM64T). Refer to the release notes if you are installing Red Hat Linux on PowerPC (PPC) hardware. Within these platforms, Red Hat Linux runs on much of the available hardware. You can view Red Hat's list of compatible and supported hardware at hardware.redhat.com. Although these lists apply to Red Hat Enterprise Linux, they serve as a good guide to what Fedora Core will run on. Many Internet sites discuss Linux hardware; use Google (www.google.com/linux) to search on **linux hardware, fedora hardware,** or **linux** and the specific hardware you want more information on (for example, **linux sata** or **linux a8n**). In addition, many HOWTOs cover specific hardware. There is also a *Linux Hardware Compatibility HOWTO*, although it becomes dated rather quickly. Red Hat Linux usually runs on systems that Windows runs on, unless the system includes a very new or unusual component.

Memory (RAM) You need a minimum of 128 megabytes of RAM for a 32-bit x86 system that runs in text mode (no GUI) and 192–256 megabytes for a graphical system. For a 64-bit x86_64 system, you need at least 128 megabytes for text mode and 256–512 megabytes for a graphical system. Linux makes good use of extra memory: The more memory a system has, the faster it will run. Adding memory is one of the most cost-effective ways you can speed up a Linux system.

CPU   Red Hat Linux requires a minimum of a 200-megahertz Pentium-class processor or the equivalent AMD or other processor for textual mode and at least a 400-megahertz Pentium II processor or the equivalent for graphical mode.

Hard disk space   The amount of hard disk space you need depends on which version of Red Hat Linux you install, which packages you install, how many languages you install, and how much space you need for user data (your files). The operating system can occupy from about 600 megabytes to over 9 gigabytes.

BIOS setup   Modern computers can be set to boot from a CD/DVD, floppy diskette, or hard disk. The BIOS determines the order in which the system tries to boot from each device. You may need to change this order: Make sure the BIOS is set up to try booting from the CD/DVD before it tries to boot from the hard disk.

CMOS   CMOS is the persistent memory that stores system configuration information. To change the BIOS setup, you need to edit the information stored in CMOS. When the system boots, it displays a brief message about how to enter System Setup or CMOS Setup mode. Usually you need to press Del or F2 while the system is booting. Press the key that is called for and move the cursor to the screen and line that deal with booting the system. Generally there is a list of three or four devices that the system tries to boot from; if the first attempt fails, the system tries the second device, and so on. Manipulate the list so the CD/DVD is the first choice, save your choices, and reboot. Refer to the hardware/BIOS manual for more information.

WHICH ARE YOU INSTALLING: FEDORA CORE OR RED HAT ENTERPRISE LINUX?

This book describes two products: Fedora Core and Red Hat Enterprise Linux. This section briefly highlights the differences between these products.

FEDORA   The Fedora Project is sponsored by Red Hat and supported by the open-source community. With releases, called Fedora Core, coming out about every six months, this Linux distribution tests cutting-edge code; it is not a supported Red Hat product and is not recommended for production environments where stability is important. Fedora aims to reflect the upstream projects it incorporates, including the kernel. In contrast, Red Hat Enterprise Linux includes many changes introduced by Fedora Core. Architectures supported by the Fedora Project include

- **i386**   Intel x86-compatible processors, including Intel Pentium and Pentium MMX, Pentium Pro, Pentium II, Pentium III, Celeron, Pentium 4, and Xeon; VIA C3/C3-m and Eden/Eden-N; and AMD Athlon, AthlonXP, Duron, AthlonMP, and Sempron.

- **ppc**   PowerPC processors (found in Apple Power Macintosh, G3, G4, and G5, and IBM pSeries systems).

- **x86_64**   64-bit AMD processors including Athlon64, Turion64, and Opteron; and Intel 64-bit processors that incorporate EM64T technology.

RHEL   Although you can download the code for free (refer to "More Information" on page 24), Red Hat Enterprise Linux is typically sold by annual subscription that includes the Red Hat Network (page 498) and technical support. It is more stable but less cutting edge than Fedora Core.

Red Hat Enterprise Linux AS (advanced server) and Red Hat Enterprise Linux ES (enterprise server) function identically and are designed to run servers. ES is licensed for x86-compatible, AMD64, Intel EM64T, and Intel Itanium2 systems with one or two CPUs and up to 16 gigabytes of memory. AS is licensed for servers of any size and supports IBM zSeries, POWER series, and S/390 series systems in addition to the systems that ES supports.

Red Hat Enterprise Linux WS (workstation) supports the same architectures as ES on the desktop/client side, running office productivity and software development applications. WS supports systems with one or two CPUs, up to 4 gigabytes of memory, and does not include all the server applications that come with AS and ES. It is not designed for a server environment.

INSTALLING A FRESH COPY OR UPGRADING AN EXISTING RED HAT SYSTEM?

Upgrade   An *upgrade* replaces the Linux kernel and utilities on an already installed version of Red Hat Linux with newer versions. During an upgrade, the installation program attempts to preserve both system and user data files. An upgrade brings utilities that are present in the old version up-to-date but does not install new utilities (you can install them later if you like). Existing configuration files are preserved and new ones added with a **.rpmnew** filename extension. A log of the upgrade is kept in **/root/upgrade.log**. Before you upgrade a system, back up all files on the system.

A fresh installation yields a more stable system than an upgrade

caution   For better system stability, Red Hat recommends that you back up data on a system and perform a fresh installation rather than an upgrade.

Clean install   An *installation*, sometimes referred to as a *clean install*, writes all fresh data to a disk. The installation program overwrites all system programs and data as well as the kernel. You can preserve some user data during an installation depending on where it is located and how you format/partition the disk.

GRAPHICAL OR TEXTUAL INSTALLATION?

There are several ways to install Red Hat Linux. You can choose a graphical installation, which displays graphics on the screen and allows you to use the mouse, window buttons, and scroll lists to choose how you want to configure the system. If you have a smaller system with less memory or a system with an unsupported graphics board, you can run a textual installation. This type of installation performs the same functions as a graphical installation, but uses a pseudographical interface to step you through the process of configuring the system. The Anaconda utility controls both types of installations.

SETTING UP THE HARD DISK

Formatting and free space Hard disks must be prepared in several ways so an operating system can write to and read from them. Low-level formatting is the first step in preparing a disk for use. Normally you will not need to low-level format a hard disk, as this task is done at the factory. The next step in preparing a disk for use is to divide it into partitions. The area of the disk that is not occupied by partitions is called *free space*. A new disk has no partitions: It is all free space. Under DOS/Windows, the term *formatting* means writing a filesystem on a partition; see "Filesystems" below.

Partitions A *partition,* or *slice,* is a section of a hard disk that has a device name, such as **/dev/hda1**, so you can address it separately from other sections. During installation you use Disk Druid (page 58) to create partitions on the hard disk. After installation you can use parted (page 65) to manipulate partitions.

LVM Disk Druid can set up logical volumes (LVs) that function like partitions. When you set up LVs, you can use the Logical Volume Manager (LVM, page 32) to change the sizes of volumes. It is much more difficult to change the sizes of partitions.

Filesystems Before most programs can write to a partition, a *data structure* (page 1028), called a *filesystem,* needs to be written on a partition. The mkfs (make filesystem) utility, which is similar to the DOS/Windows format utility, writes a filesystem on a partition. Many types of filesystems exist. Red Hat Linux typically creates **ext3** filesystems for data, while Windows uses FAT and NTFS filesystems. Apple uses HFS (Hierarchical Filesystem) and HFS+. OS X uses either HFS+ or UFS. Under DOS/Windows, filesystems are labeled **C:, D:,** and so on (sometimes a whole disk is a single partition). Under Linux, typical hierarchical filesystem names are **/** (root), **/boot, /var,** and **/usr.** You can have different types of partitions on the same hard disk, including both Windows and Linux partitions. Under Linux, the fsck (filesystem check) utility (page 470) checks the integrity of filesystem data structures.

Filesystem independence The state of one filesystem does not affect other filesystems: One filesystem on a drive may be corrupt and unreadable while other filesystems function normally. One filesystem may be full so you cannot write to it while others have plenty of room for more data.

PRIMARY AND EXTENDED PARTITIONS

Partitioning allows you to divide an IDE disk into a maximum of 63 separate *partitions,* or subdisks. A SCSI disk can be divided into 15 partitions at most. You can use each partition independently for swap devices, filesystems, databases, other resources, and even other operating systems.

Unfortunately disk partitions follow the template established for DOS machines a long time ago. At most, a disk can hold four *primary partitions*. One of these primary partitions can be divided into multiple, *logical partitions*; this divided primary partition is called an *extended partition*. If you want more than four partitions on a drive—and you usually do—you must set up an extended partition.

A typical disk is divided into three primary partitions and one extended partition. The three primary partitions are the sizes you want the final partitions to be. The extended partition occupies the rest of the disk. Once you establish the extended partition, you can subdivide it into additional partitions that are each the size you want.

PARTITIONING A DISK

During installation, Anaconda calls Disk Druid to set up disk partitions. This section discusses how to plan partition sizes. Although this section uses the term *partition*, the planning and sizing of LVs (page 32) is the same. For more information refer to "Using Disk Druid to Partition the Disk" on page 58 and to the *Linux Partition HOWTO* at www.tldp.org/HOWTO/Partition.

Under Red Hat Linux, druid means wizard

tip   Red Hat uses the term *druid* as part of the names of programs that guide you through a task-driven chain of steps. Other operating systems call these types of programs *wizards*.

PLANNING PARTITIONS

Simple setup   It can be difficult to plan partition sizes appropriately if you are new to Linux. For this reason many people choose to have only three partitions. The first partition holds the information the system needs to boot: the kernel image and other files. This partition is mounted as **/boot** and can range in size from 50 to 300 megabytes. A second partition is the swap partition, which can be any size from 512 megabytes to 2 or more gigabytes. The last partition is designated as root (**/**) and contains the remainder of the disk space. This setup makes managing space quite easy. But if a program runs amok or if your system receives a *DoS attack* (page 1030), the entire disk can fill up, and system accounting and logging information (which may contain data that can tell you what went wrong) may be lost.

When you ask Disk Druid to set up the disk with the default layout, it uses the scheme described above, with the root and swap space set up as LVs.

PARTITION SUGGESTIONS

This section discusses additional partitions you may want to create. Consider setting up LVM (page 32) *before* you create partitions (LVs); LVM allows you to change partition sizes easily after the system is installed.

(swap)   Linux temporarily stores programs and data on a swap partition when it does not have enough RAM to hold all the information it is processing (page 458). The size of the swap partition should be twice the size of the RAM in the system, with a minimum size of 512 megabytes. For example, a system with 1 gigabyte of RAM should have a 2-gigabyte swap partition. Although it is not required, most systems perform better with a swap partition.

/boot   This partition holds the kernel and other data the system needs when it boots. Red Hat recommends that the **/boot** partition be 100 megabytes, although the amount of space required depends on how many kernel images you want to keep on hand.

This partition can be as small as 50 megabytes. Although you can omit the **/boot** partition, it is useful in many cases. Some older BIOSs require the **/boot** partition (or the root [**/**] partition if there is no **/boot** partition) to be near the beginning of the disk.

/var   The name **var** is short for *variable:* The data in this partition changes frequently. Because it holds the bulk of system logs, package information, and accounting data, making **/var** a separate partition is a good idea. In this way, if a user runs a job that uses up all the disk space, the logs will not be affected. The **/var** partition can occupy from 500 megabytes up to several gigabytes for extremely active systems with many verbose daemons and a lot of printer activity (files in the print queue are stored on **/var**). Systems that are license servers for licensed software often qualify as extremely active systems.

/home   It is a common strategy to put user home directories on their own disk or partition. If you do not have a separate disk for the home directories, put them in their own partition. These partitions are often named **/home** or **/usr/home**.

Set up partitions to aid in making backups

tip   Plan partitions around what data you want to back up and how often you want to back it up. One very large partition can be more difficult to back up than several smaller ones.

/ (root)   Some administrators choose to separate the root (**/**), **/boot**, and **/usr** partitions. By itself, the root partition usually consumes less than 30 megabytes of disk space. However, **/lib**, which can consume more than 200 megabytes, is part of the root partition. On occasion, you may install a special program that has many kernel drivers that consume a lot of space in the root partition. Allot 1 gigabyte to the root partition at a minimum.

/usr   Separating the **/usr** partition can be useful if you plan to export **/usr** to another system and want the security that a separate partition can give. The size of **/usr** depends on the number of packages you install.

Where to put the /boot partition

tip   On older systems, the **/boot** partition must reside *completely below cylinder 1023* of the disk. When you have more than one hard disk, the **/boot** partition must also reside on a drive on

- Multiple IDE or EIDE drives: the primary controller
- Multiple SCSI drives: ID 0 or ID 1
- Multiple IDE and SCSI drives: the primary IDE controller or SCSI ID 0

/usr/local and /opt   Both **/usr/local** and **/opt** are also candidates for separation. If you plan to install many packages in addition to Red Hat Linux, you may want to keep them on a separate partition. If you install the additional software in the same partition as the users' home directories, for example, it may encroach on the users' disk space. Many sites keep all **/usr/local** or **/opt** software on one server and export it to other systems. If you choose to create a **/usr/local** or **/opt** partition, its size should be appropriate to the software you plan to install.

Table 2-1 gives guidelines for minimum sizes for partitions used by Linux. Size other partitions, such as **/home, /opt,** and **/usr/local,** according to need and the size of the hard disk. If you are not sure how you will use additional disk space, you can create extra partitions using whatever names you like (for example, **/b01, /b02,** and so on).

Table 2-1   Example partition sizes

Partition	Example size
/boot	50–100 megabytes.
/ (root)	1 gigabyte.
(swap)	Two times the amount of RAM (memory) in the system with a minimum of 512 megabytes.
/home	As large as necessary; depends on the number of users and the type of work they do.
/tmp	Minimum of 500 megabytes.
/usr	Minimum of 1.7–5.5 gigabytes, depending on which Red Hat Linux programs you install. These figures assume **/usr/local** is a separate partition.
/var	Minimum of 500 megabytes.

RAID

RAID (Redundant Array of Inexpensive/Independent Disks) employs two or more hard disk drives or partitions in combination to improve fault tolerance and/or performance. Applications and utilities see these multiple drives/partitions as a single logical device. RAID, which can be implemented in hardware or software (Red Hat gives you this option), spreads data across multiple disks. Depending on which level you choose, RAID can provide data redundancy to protect data in the case of hardware failure. Although it can also improve disk performance by increasing read/write speed, RAID uses quite a bit of CPU time, which may be a consideration in some situations. Fedora Core 5 introduced support for motherboard-based RAID chips through the **dmraid** driver set.

Do not replace backups with RAID

caution   Do not use RAID as a replacement for regular backups. If your system undergoes a catastrophic failure, RAID will be useless. Earthquake, fire, theft, and other disasters may leave the entire system inaccessible (if your hard disks are destroyed or missing). RAID also does not take care of something as simple as replacing a file when you delete it by accident. In these cases, a backup on a removable medium (that has been removed) is the only way you will be able to restore a filesystem.

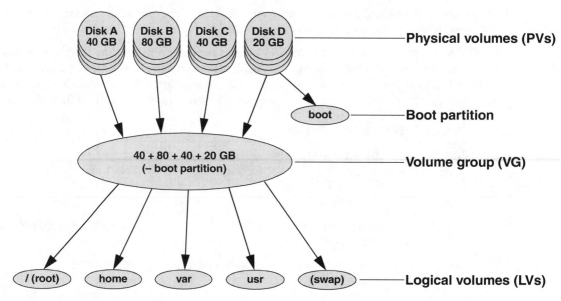

Figure 2-1 LVM: Logical Volume Manager

Disk Druid gives you the choice of implementing RAID level 0, 1, 5, or 6:

- **RAID level 0 (striping)** Improves performance but offers no redundancy. The storage capacity of the RAID device is equal to that of the member partitions or disks.

- **RAID level 1 (mirroring)** Provides simple redundancy, improving data reliability, and can improve the performance of read-intensive applications. The storage capacity of the RAID device is equal to one of the member partitions or disks.

- **RAID level 5 (disk striping with parity)** Provides redundancy and improves (most notably, read) performance. The storage capacity of the RAID device is equal to that of the member partitions or disks, minus one of the partitions or disks (assuming they are all the same size).

- **RAID level 6 (disk striping with double parity)** Improves upon level 5 RAID by protecting data when two disks fail at once. Level 6 RAID is inefficient with a small number of drives.

LVM: LOGICAL VOLUME MANAGER

The Logical Volume Manager (LVM2, which will be referred to as LVM) allows you to change the size of logical volumes (LVs, the LVM equivalent of partitions) on the fly. With LVM, if you make a mistake in setting up LVs or your needs change, you can use system-config-lvm to make LVs smaller or larger easily without affecting user data. You must choose to use LVM at the time you install the system or add a hard disk; you cannot retroactively apply it to a disk full of data. LVM supports IDE and SCSI drives as well as multiple devices such as those found in RAID partitions.

LVM groups disk components (partitions, hard disks, or storage device arrays), called *physical volumes* (PVs), into a storage pool, or virtual disk, called a *volume group* (VG). See Figure 2-1. You allocate a portion of a VG to create a *logical volume*.

An LV is similar in function to a traditional disk partition in that you can create a filesystem on an LV. It is much easier, however, to change and move LVs than partitions: When you run out of space on a filesystem on an LV, you can grow (expand) the LV and its filesystem into empty or new disk space, or you can move the filesystem to a larger LV. LVM's disk space manipulation is transparent to users; service is not interrupted.

LVM also eases the burden of storage migration. When you outgrow or need to upgrade PVs, LVM can move data to new PVs. To read more about LVM, refer to the resources listing under "More Information" on page 24.

How the Installation Works

The following steps outline the process of installing Red Hat Linux from CDs or a DVD using Anaconda. Installation from other media follows similar steps. See Chapter 3 for the specifics of how to perform the installation.

1. Insert the first installation CD or the installation DVD in the computer and turn on or reset the computer.

2. After going through computer-specific hardware diagnostics, the computer displays the initial install screen with the **boot:** prompt at the bottom (page 44).

3. You can enter commands and press RETURN following the **boot:** prompt, press RETURN without entering commands, or wait for a minute without entering anything; the computer boots Red Hat Linux from the CD or DVD.

4. As part of the boot process, Red Hat Linux creates multiple *RAM disks* (page 1051) that it uses in place of a hard disk used for a normal boot operation. Tools required for the installation are copied to the RAM disks. The use of RAM disks allows the installation process to run through the specification and design phases without writing to the hard disk and enables you to opt out of the installation at any point before the system warns you it is about to write to the hard disk. If you opt out before this point, the system is left in its original state. For more information refer to "Begin Installation" on page 54.

5. You can check the installation media at this point.

6. Anaconda starts, usually probing the hardware before starting the X Window System for a graphical installation.

7. Anaconda collects information about how you want to install Red Hat Linux.

8. When Anaconda is finished collecting information, it displays a screen that informs you it is about to begin installation (Figure 3-9, page 55) and writes the operating system files to the hard disk.

9. When you reboot the system, Firstboot ask you some questions that are required to complete the installation (page 56).

10. The Red Hat Linux system is ready to use.

THE MEDIUM: WHERE IS THE SOURCE DATA?

When you install Red Hat Linux, you copy operating system files from a source—frequently CDs or a DVD—to the target computer's hard disk. There are two formats and many possible sources for the files.

FORMATS

Red Hat Linux operating system files can be stored in two ways: as directory hierarchies on CDs, a DVD, or a hard disk; or as CD images or a DVD image on a hard disk (called *ISO images* after ISO9660, the standard defining the CD filesystem). Although the format is different, the content is the same. You can install Red Hat Linux or burn CDs or a DVD from either format, although most people use the ISO images to burn CDs or a DVD because it is more convenient.

SOURCES

This chapter and the next provide information about installing Red Hat Linux from CDs containing ISO image files or from a DVD containing a single ISO image file. The procedures are identical with one exception: When working with a DVD you do not have to change media during installation. These chapters do not cover installing from directory hierarchies; you use exactly the same techniques to install from a directory hierarchy as from an ISO image. Directory hierarchies are more cumbersome to work with than ISO images because they contain many files; each ISO image is a single file.

You can automate the installation using Kickstart (page 63).

CDs OR DVD

RHEL Red Hat Enterprise Linux CDs are sold by Red Hat and its distributors. ISO images for Red Hat Enterprise Linux are available from Red Hat Network. To download these images, go to rhn.redhat.com, create an account if you do not have one, log in, click **Channels** on the menubar at the top of the page, click the name of the product you want to download, and click **Downloads**. The page that you download Red Hat Enterprise Linux from has instructions on how to download the installation or source disks. See also "Checking the Files" (page 39) and "Burning the CDs or DVD" (page 39) for more information.

FEDORA This book includes the DVD necessary for installing Fedora Core. Alternatively, you can purchase Fedora CDs or DVD from third-party vendors or you can download the Fedora ISO image(s) and install from the images or burn CDs or a DVD (next section).

HARD DISK

You can store ISO image files on the target system's hard disk if it is already running Linux. You need to burn only the first installation CD, the rescue CD, or the DVD (page 40) to boot the system for a hard disk installation.

NETWORK

You can use ISO image files located on a server system that the machine you are installing Linux on can connect to over a network during installation. You can use FTP, NFS, or HTTP for network installations. Unless you have a fast Internet connection, however, it is not advisable to perform an installation over the Internet because it can take a very long time; downloading ISO files is a more reliable and possibly less frustrating option. You need to burn only the first installation CD, the rescue CD, or the DVD (page 40) to boot the system for a network installation.

You can also perform a remote network boot using PXE. See "More Information" on page 24 for sources of information on PXE.

DOWNLOADING, BURNING, AND INSTALLING A CD SET OR A DVD (*FEDORA*)

You can download and burn Fedora Core CDs. Although you will not get the customer support that comes with Red Hat Enterprise Linux, you will not pay Red Hat for the software. One of the beauties of free software (Appendix D) is that it is always available for free. Red Hat makes it easy to obtain and use Fedora Core by providing ISO images of its CDs online. These files are large—almost 700 megabytes each—and there are five of them, so they take days to download using a 56K modem and hours using a broadband connection. The DVD ISO more than 3 gigabytes.

You must use 700-megabyte CD-ROM blanks

tip When you burn Fedora Core CDs from the ISO images you must use 700-megabyte blanks. The smaller 650-megabyte blanks will not work because there is too much data to fit on them.

This section tells you how to find the files you need, download them using a couple of different techniques, check that they downloaded correctly, and burn them to CDs or a DVD.

FINDING A SITE TO DOWNLOAD FROM

The Fedora Web site maintains the ISO images you need. Other (mirror) sites also maintain these packages. You can use a Web browser or ftp to download the files from one of these sites. Alternatively, you can use BitTorrent to download the ISO images; see page 39.

Figure 2-2   The Fedora download server, **core** directory

You can download and burn the CDs or DVD on any operating system

tip   You can download and burn the CDs or DVD on any computer that is connected to the Internet, has a browser, has enough space on the hard disk to hold the ISO files (about 3 gigabytes), and can burn a CD or DVD. If you do not have enough space on the hard disk for all five CDs, you can download and burn them one at a time (each requires slightly less than 700 megabytes). You can use ftp in place of a browser to download the files. For more information refer to "JumpStart: Downloading Files Using ftp" on page 604.

To conserve network bandwidth, try to download from a mirror site that is close to you. Failing that, you can download from the Red Hat site.

Mirror sites   Locate a mirror site by pointing a browser at the following URL:

```
fedora.redhat.com/download/mirrors.html
```

Scroll through the list of mirror sites to find a site near you and click that site's URL. The display will be similar to that shown in Figure 2-2, which shows the Fedora download directory. To display this directory, point a browser at fedora.redhat.com, click **Download** from the tabs at the left side of the screen, and then click **Download Server** from the expanded Download tab. FTP and HTTP sites look a little different from each other.

Red Hat site   To download files from the Red Hat Fedora site, point a browser at the following URL, which locates the Red Hat Web page at the top of the directory hierarchy that holds the Fedora Core files (Figure 2-2):

```
download.fedora.redhat.com/pub/fedora/linux/core
```

When you have located a site to download from, continue with the next section.

Figure 2-3   The iso directory for Fedora Core 5

FINDING THE RIGHT FILES AND DOWNLOADING THEM

The pathnames of the Fedora Core ISO image files differ from site to site, as shown in the following examples:

```
/pub/linux/fedora/core/5/i386/iso
/fedora/core/5/i386/iso
/fedora/linux/core/5/i386/iso
```

All sites share a common path following the **core** directory (bold in the preceding list). Table 2-2 shows the hierarchy below the **core/5** directory, the directory hierarchy that holds the Fedora Core 5 release. If you are downloading other than Fedora Core 5, go to the directory hierarchy below the appropriately numbered directory (**3**, **4**, and so on). The structure of these hierarchies parallels that of the Fedora Core 5 directory.

Click (open) directories until you get to the **iso** directory for the release you want to download (Figure 2-3). To download the CD ISO image files, click the five files listed below, one at a time. Replace **FC-5** with the name of the release you are downloading. To download the DVD ISO image file, click **FC-5-i386-DVD.iso**.

```
FC-5-i386-disc1.iso
FC-5-i386-disc2.iso
FC-5-i386-disc3.iso
FC-5-i386-disc4.iso
FC-5-i386-disc5.iso
SHA1SUM
```

The five large *.iso files hold the ISO images of the Fedora Core CDs. The short SHA1SUM file holds the SHA1 checksums that you can use to confirm the downloaded files are correct (page 39). You may want to download the rescue CD image (FC-5-i386-rescuecd.iso) as well (page 40). The FC-5-SRPMS-disc*.iso files hold the source code for Fedora Core; you do not normally need these files to install Fedora.

Table 2-2 Relative locations of Fedora Core files (Fedora Core 5 shown)

Location in the */fedora/linux directory hierarchy	Contains
core/5	Fedora Core version 5 directory hierarchy.
core/5/source	Fedora Core source files.
core/5/source/SRPMS	Individual Fedora Core source RPM files.
core/5/source/iso	Fedora Core source ISO image files.
core/5/i386	Fedora Core files for the 32-bit architectures. See the list of processors under "Which Are You Installing: Fedora Core or Red Hat Enterprise Linux?" on page 26.
core/5/i386/debug	Fedora Core debugging program RPM files.
core/5/i386/iso/FC-5-i386-disc*.iso	Fedora Core installation CD ISO image files 1 through 5.
core/5/i386/iso/FC-5-i386-DVD.iso	Fedora Core installation DVD ISO image file.
core/5/i386/iso/FC-5-i386-rescuecd.iso	Fedora Core rescue CD ISO image file (page 40).
core/5/i386/iso/SHA1SUM	SHA1 checksums for the ISO files in the same directory.
core/5/i386/os	Individual Fedora Core rpm packages.
core/5/i386/os/RELEASE-NOTES-en	Fedora Core release notes in English. For an HTML version, download RELEASE-NOTES-en.html. See the copy at fedora.redhat.com/docs/release-notes for the most up-to-date version.
core/5/ppc	Fedora Core files for the PPC architecture. This directory hierarchy is almost the same as the i386 hierarchy.
core/5/x86_64	Fedora Core files for 64-bit architectures. See the list of processors under "Which Are You Installing: Fedora Core or Red Hat Enterprise Linux?" on page 26. This directory hierarchy is almost the same as the i386 hierarchy.

Depending how fast the Internet connection is and how busy the site you are downloading from is, it may be better to wait until one download finishes before starting the next. (Using ftp [page 604], you can queue the downloads so they proceed sequentially without intervention.)

Once you have downloaded the five installation ISO files or the DVD ISO, the SHA1 checksum file, and optionally the rescue CD ISO file, the next step is to check that the files are correct. See "Checking the Files."

USING BITTORRENT TO DOWNLOAD THE ISO IMAGE FILES

You can use BitTorrent (page 484) to obtain the ISO images. Because BitTorrent is available for both Windows and Mac OS X (www.bittorrent.com), you can download and burn the Fedora CDs or DVD on a Windows machine or a Macintosh. See page 484 for information on using BitTorrent from Linux. You can obtain BitTorrent for Fedora and the tracker for the ISO files from torrent.fedoraproject.org.

CHECKING THE FILES

The **SHA1SUM** file contains the *SHA1* (page 1054) sums for each of the ISO files. When you process a file using the sha1sum utility, sha1sum generates a number based on the file. If that number matches the corresponding number in the **SHA1SUM** file, the downloaded file is correct:

```
$ grep i386-disc1 SHA1SUM; sha1sum FC-5-i386-disc1.iso
43546c0e0d1fc64b6b80fe1fa99fb6509af5c0a0  FC-5-i386-disc1.iso
43546c0e0d1fc64b6b80fe1fa99fb6509af5c0a0  FC-5-i386-disc1.iso
```

Check each of the ISO images you downloaded in the same manner. Computing an SHA1 sum for a large file takes a while. The two long strings that the preceding command displays must be identical: If they are not, you must download the file again. *RHEL* uses an **MD5SUM** file instead of **SHA1SUM** and the md5sum utility instead of sha1sum.

Test the ISO files and test the CDs or DVD

tip   It is a good idea to test the ISO image files when they are downloaded and the burned CDs or DVD before you use them to install Red Hat Linux. A bad file on a CD may not show up until you finish installing Red Hat Linux and have it running. At that point, it may be difficult and time-consuming to figure out where the problem lies. Testing the files and CDs or DVD takes a few minutes, but can save you hours of trouble if something is not right. If you want to do only one test, test the CDs or DVD.

BURNING THE CDs OR DVD

An ISO image file is an exact image of what needs to be on the CD or DVD. Putting that image on a CD or DVD involves a different process than copying files to a CD or DVD. The CD/DVD burning software you use has a special selection for burning an ISO image. It will be labeled something similar to **Record CD from CD Image** or **Burn CD Image**. Refer to the instructions for the software you are using for information on how to burn an ISO image file to a CD or DVD.

You need only burn the rescue CD for a hard disk or network installation

tip   If you are installing Linux from files on a hard disk on the target system or from files on another system on a network using FTP, NFS, or HTTP, you need a way to boot the system to begin the installation. The rescue CD, the first installation CD, or the installation DVD can serve that purpose. Once the system is booted, you have no need for the CDs or DVD.

Make sure the software is set up to burn an ISO image

tip   Burning an ISO image is not the same as copying files to a CD or DVD. Make sure the CD/DVD burning software is set up to burn an ISO image. If you simply copy the ISO file to the CD or DVD, it will not work when you try to install Fedora Core.

RESCUE CD

The rescue CD cannot do anything the first installation CD cannot do. However, it holds less information so you can download and burn it more quickly than the first installation CD.

Rescue mode   You can use the rescue CD, the first installation CD, or the installation DVD to bring the system up in rescue mode. Bringing a system up and working in rescue mode are discussed on page 397.

Hard disk or network installation   You can use the rescue CD the same way you use the first installation CD or the installation DVD to boot the system to begin a hard disk or network installation: While booting from either CD or the DVD, give the command **linux askmethod** in response to the **boot:** prompt. See page 45 for more information.

GATHERING INFORMATION ABOUT THE SYSTEM

It is not difficult to install and bring up a Linux system, but the more you know about the process before you start, the easier it will be. The installation software collects information about the system and can help you make decisions during the installation process. However, the system will work better when you know how you want your disk partitioned rather than letting the installation program create partitions without your input. The screen will be easier to use if you know what resolution you want. There are many details, and the more details you take control of, the more pleased you are likely to be with the finished product. Finding the information that this section asks for will help ensure that you end up with a system you understand and know how to change when necessary. More and more, the installation software probes the hardware and figures out what you have. Newer equipment is more likely to report on itself than older equipment is.

It is critical to have certain pieces of information before you start. One thing Linux can never figure out is all the relevant names and IP addresses (unless you are using DHCP, in which case the addresses are set up for you).

Following is a list of items you may need information about. Get as much information on each item as you can: manufacturer, model number, size (megabytes, gigabytes, and so forth), number of buttons, chipset (for boards), and so on. Some items, such as the network interface card, may be built into the motherboard.

- Hard disks.
- Memory (you don't need it for installation, but it is good to know).

- SCSI interface card.

- Network interface card (NIC).

- Video interface card (including the amount of video RAM/memory).

- Sound card and compatibility with standards, such as SoundBlaster.

- Mouse (PS/2, USB, AT, and number of buttons).

- Monitor (size, maximum resolution).

- IP addresses and names, unless you are using DHCP (page 431), in which case the IP addresses for the system are automatically assigned. Most of this information comes from the system administrator or ISP.

  - System hostname (anything you like)

  - System address

  - Network mask (netmask)

  - Gateway address (the connecting point to the network or Internet) or a phone number when you use a dial-up connection

  - Addresses for nameservers, also called DNS addresses

  - Domain name (not required)

FINDING THE INSTALLATION MANUAL

The definitive resource for instructions on how to install Red Hat Linux is the Red Hat Installation Guide for the release you are installing and the platform you are installing it on. You can view or download installation guides at the following sites:

- *RHEL*   Go to www.redhat.com/docs/manuals/enterprise. Additional installation, setup, and troubleshooting resources are available from Red Hat at www.redhat.com/apps/support. You can also search for a keyword or words using the Search Red Hat box at the upper-right corner of most Red Hat Web pages.

- *FEDORA*   Go to fedora.redhat.com, click **Documentation** from the tabs at the left side of the screen, and then click **Installation Guide**. Additional help is available at fedoraproject.org.

CHAPTER SUMMARY

When you install Red Hat Linux, you copy operating system files from media to the local system and set up configuration files so that Linux runs properly on the local hardware. You can install Linux from many types of media, including CDs, DVD, or hard disk, and from files on other systems that are accessed over a network. Operating system files can be stored as directory hierarchies on CDs, a DVD, or a hard disk, or as CD or DVD (ISO) images on a hard disk. You can use a browser, ftp, or BitTorrent to download the ISO images. It is a good idea to test the ISO image files when they are downloaded and the burned CDs before you use them to install Red Hat Linux.

The major decisions to be made when planning an installation are how to divide the hard disk into partitions and which software packages to install. If you plan to use SELinux, turn it on during Firstboot, after you install Linux. Because SELinux sets extended attributes on files, it can be a time-consuming process to turn on SELinux after Linux is installed.

The Fedora Project is sponsored by Red Hat and supported by the open-source community. Fedora Core is a Linux release that tests cutting-edge code; it is not recommended for production environments. Red Hat Enterprise Linux is more stable than Fedora Core.

EXERCISES

1. Briefly, what does the process of installing an operating system such as Red Hat Linux involve?
2. What is Anaconda?
3. Would you set up a GUI on a server system? Why or why not?
4. A system boots from the hard disk. To install Linux, you need it to boot from a CD. How can you make the system boot from a CD?
5. What is free space on a hard disk? What is a filesystem?
6. What is an ISO image? How do you burn an ISO image to a CD or DVD?

ADVANCED EXERCISES

7. List two reasons why you should not use RAID to replace backups.
8. What are RAM disks and how are they used during installation?
9. What is SHA1? How does it work to ensure that an ISO image file you download is correct?

3

Step-by-Step Installation

Chapter 2 covered planning the installation of Red Hat Linux: determining the requirements; performing an upgrade versus a clean installation; planning the layout of the hard disk; obtaining the files you need for the installation, including how to download and burn CD and DVD ISO images; and collecting the information about the system you will need during installation. This chapter focuses on installing Fedora Core. The process of installing Red Hat Enterprise Linux is similar. Frequently the installation is quite simple, especially if you have done a good job of planning. Sometimes you may run into a problem or have a special circumstance; this chapter gives you tools to use in these cases.

INSTALLING RED HAT LINUX

To begin most installations, insert the first installation CD or the installation DVD into the CD/DVD drive and turn on or reset the system. For hard disk- and network-based installations, you can use the rescue CD (page 40) instead of the CD or DVD.

The system boots from the CD or DVD and displays a screen of instructions with a **boot:** prompt at the bottom. Refer to "BIOS setup" on page 26 if the system does not boot from the CD or DVD.

You cannot boot from a floppy diskette Because most kernels have grown too large to fit on a floppy diskette, you cannot boot from a floppy. Specifically you cannot fit a standard Fedora Core or Red Hat Enterprise Linux kernel on a floppy diskette. Fedora gives you the option of booting from a USB pen drive using the **diskboot.img** file.

BOOTING THE SYSTEM: THE boot: PROMPT

Normal installation You can supply many different parameters following the **boot:** prompt. You must press RETURN after entering any of these parameters. If you are installing from CDs or a DVD, you can generally press RETURN without entering anything to start installing Red Hat Linux. Or you can just wait—if you do not type anything for a minute, the installation proceeds as though you pressed RETURN.

CD and DVD installations work the same way

tip On the installation screens, the term CD means CD or DVD. Aside from changing CDs during an installation, there is no difference between installing from CDs and installing from a DVD.

Display problems If you encounter problems with the display during installation, supply the following parameters, which turn off video memory, in response to the **boot:** prompt:

```
boot: linux nofb
```

Non-CD/DVD installation If you are installing from other than CDs or a DVD—that is, if you are installing from files on the local hard disk or from files on another system using FTP, NFS, or HTTP—supply the following parameters in response to the **boot:** prompt:

```
boot: linux askmethod
```

See page 45 for information on using the **askmethod** parameter.

Booting As the system boots, text scrolls on the monitor, pausing occasionally. After a while (up to a few minutes, depending on the speed of the system), the installer displays a graphical or pseudographical display, depending on the system you are installing and the commands you gave at the **boot:** prompt.

The balance of this section covers the parameters you can supply following the **boot:** prompt. Unless you are having problems with the installation or have special requirements, you can skip to the next section, "The CD Found Screen," on page 46.

BOOT PARAMETERS

All of the parameters (except for **memtest86**) you can supply following the **boot:** prompt consist of the word **linux** followed by an argument that is passed to the kernel or to the Anaconda installer. Many of these parameters can be combined. For example, to install Linux in text mode using a terminal running at 115,200 baud, no parity, 8 bits, connected to the first serial device, give the following parameters (the **,115200n8** is optional):

> boot: `linux text console=ttyS0,115200n8`

The next set of parameters installs Red Hat Linux in graphical mode (by default) on a monitor with a resolution of 1024 × 768, without probing for any devices. The installation program asks you to specify the source of the installation data (CD, DVD, FTP site, or other).

> boot: `linux resolution=1024x768 noprobe askmethod`

Following are some of the parameters you can give at the **boot:** prompt. A set of parameters must be terminated with RETURN keystroke.

RETURN   Without entering a parameter, press RETURN in response to the **boot:** prompt to perform a graphical installation from CDs or a DVD. This installation probes the computer to determine as much as possible about the hardware.

memtest86   Calls memtest86+ when you boot from a CD or DVD only. The GPL-licensed memtest86+ utility is a stand-alone memory test for x86-based computers. Press **C** to configure the test; press ESCAPE to exit. See www.memtest.org for more information.

linux askmethod   Presents a choice of installation sources: local CD/DVD or hard disk, or over a network using NFS, FTP, or HTTP.

- **Local CDROM**   (Use for both CD and DVD installations.) Displays the CD Found screen, which allows you to test the installation media (the same as if you had pressed RETURN without entering a parameter at the **boot:** prompt).

- **Hard drive**   Prompts for the partition and directory that contains the ISO images of the installation CDs or DVD. Do not include the name of the mount point when you specify the name of the directory. For example, if the ISO images are in the **/home/sam/FC5** directory and **/dev/hda6** holds the partition that is normally mounted on **/home,** you would specify the partition as **/dev/hda6** and the directory as **sam/FC5** (no leading slash).

- **NFS, FTP, or HTTP**   Displays the Configure TCP/IP screen from which you can select DHCP or enter the system's IP address and netmask, and the IP addresses of the default gateway and primary nameserver.

  When using NFS, the remote (server) system must export (page 685) the directory hierarchy that holds the ISO images of the installation CDs or DVD. The NFS Setup screen requires you to enter the NFS server name and name of the Fedora Core directory. Enter the server's IP address and the *name* of the exported directory, not its device name.

linux lowres Runs the installation program at a resolution of 640 × 480 pixels. See also **linux resolution**.

linux mem=*xxx*M Overrides the detected memory size. Replace *xxx* with the number of megabytes of RAM in the computer.

linux mediacheck Tests the integrity of one or more installation CDs or DVDs using an SHA1 sum. This option works with the CD, DVD, hard disk ISO, and NFS ISO installation methods. For more information refer to the "Test the CDs or the DVD" tip on page 47. You are always asked if you want to perform this test during a normal CD or DVD installation.

linux nofb **no framebuffer** Turns off the framebuffer (video memory). Useful when problems occur when the graphical phase of the installation starts. Particularly useful for systems with LCD displays.

linux noprobe Disables hardware probing for all devices, including network interface cards (NICs), graphics cards, and the monitor. Forces you to select devices from a list. You must know exactly which cards or chips the system uses when you use these parameters. Use these parameters when probing causes the installation to hang or otherwise fail. These parameters allow you to give arguments for each device driver you specify.

linux rescue Puts the system in rescue mode; see page 397 for details.

linux resolution=*WxH* Specifies the resolution of the monitor you are using for a graphical installation. For example, **resolution=1024x768** specifies a monitor with a resolution of 1024 × 768 pixels.

linux skipddc Allows you to configure the monitor manually; see **linux noprobe** for more information.

linux text Installs Linux in textual (pseudographical) mode. Although the images on the screen appear to be graphical, they are composed entirely of text characters.

linux vnc Installs over a VNC (Virtual Network Computing) remote desktop session. After providing an IP address, you can control the installation remotely using a VNC client from a remote computer. You can download the VNC client, which runs on several platforms, from www.realvnc.com.

THE CD FOUND SCREEN

The first screen that the installation process displays is the pseudographical CD Found screen. Because it is not a true graphical screen, the mouse does not work. Instead, you must use the TAB or ARROW keys to highlight different choices and press RETURN to select the highlighted choice. This screen allows you to test as many installation CDs or DVDs as you like, in any order. Choose **OK** to test the media or **Skip** to bypass the test. See the following caution box.

Test the CDs or the DVD

caution   *FEDORA*   Because Red Hat does not manufacture Fedora disks, during a CD- or DVD-based Fedora installation, Anaconda displays the CD Found screen before starting the installation. From this screen, you can verify that the installation CDs or DVD do not have any errors. Testing the CDs or DVD takes a few minutes and can save you hours of aggravation if the installation fails due to bad media.

RHEL+FEDORA   You can force the display of the CD Found screen by supplying the parameters **linux mediacheck** in response to the **boot:** prompt (page 46).

A CD or DVD may fail the media test if the software that was used to burn the disk did not include padding. If a CD or DVD fails the media test, try booting with the following parameter:

```
linux ide=nodma
```

If the CD or DVD passes the media test when you boot the system with this parameter, reboot the system without this parameter before installing Red Hat Linux. If you install Linux after having booted with this parameter, the kernel will be set up to always use this parameter and the installation and operation of the system may be very slow.

THE ANACONDA INSTALLER

Anaconda, which is written in Python and C, identifies the hardware, builds the filesystems, and installs or upgrades the Red Hat Linux operating system. Anaconda can run in textual or graphical (default) interactive mode or in batch mode (see "Using the Kickstart Configurator" on page 63).

Anaconda does not write to the hard disk until it displays the Begin Installation screen

tip   While you are installing Red Hat Linux, until Anaconda displays the Begin Installation screen (Figure 3-9, page 55), you can press CONTROL-ALT-DEL to abort the installation process and reboot the system without making any changes to the hard disk. However, if Anaconda displays the initialize warning dialog box (page 49), when you click **Yes**, it writes to the disk immediately.

Exactly which screens Anaconda displays depends on whether you are installing Fedora Core or Red Hat Enterprise Linux and which parameters you specified following the **boot:** prompt. With some exceptions—most notably if you are running a textual installation—Anaconda probes the video card and monitor and starts a native X server with a log in **/tmp/X.log**. (This log is not preserved unless you complete the installation.)

While it is running, Anaconda opens the virtual consoles (page 113) shown in Table 3-1. You can display a virtual console by pressing CONTROL-ALT-F*x*, where *x* is the virtual console number and F*x* is the function key that corresponds to the virtual console number.

Table 3-1   Virtual console assignments during installation

Virtual console	Information displayed during installation
1	Installation dialog
2	Shell
3	Installation log
4	System messages
5	Miscellaneous messages
7	GUI interactive installation

At any time during the installation, you can switch to virtual console 2 (CONTROL-ALT-F2) and give commands to see what is going on. Do not give any commands that change any part of the installation process. To switch back to the graphical installation screen, press CONTROL-ALT-F7.

USING ANACONDA

Anaconda provides a **Next** button at the lower-right corner of each of the installation screens and a **Back** button next to it on most screens. When you have completed the entries on an installation screen, click **Next** or, from a textual installation, press the TAB key until the **Next** button is highlighted and then press RETURN. Select **Back** to return to the previous screen. Click **Release Notes** at the lower-left corner of the screen to display the release notes for the version of Red Hat Linux you are installing.

ANACONDA SCREENS

Anaconda displays different screens depending on which commands you give and which choices you make. During a graphical installation, when you leave the CD Found screen, Anaconda starts, loads drivers, and probes for the devices it will use during installation. After probing, it starts the X server. This section describes the screens that Anaconda displays during a default installation and explains the choices you can make on each of them.

Logo   Anaconda displays the Logo screen (Figure 3-1) after it obtains enough information to start the X Window System. There is nothing for you to do on this screen except display the release notes. Select **Next**.

Language   Select the language you want to use for the installation. This language is not necessarily the same language that the installed system will display.

Keyboard   Select the type of keyboard attached to the system.

Monitor   Anaconda displays the Monitor screen only if it cannot probe the monitor successfully. Select the brand and model of the monitor attached to the system. Select a generic LCD or CRT display if the monitor is not listed. You can specify the Sync

Figure 3-1   The Logo screen

frequencies in place of the monitor brand and model, but be careful: Specifying the wrong values can ruin some older hardware.

Initialize warning   This warning is displayed if the hard disk has not been used before. The dialog box says that the partition table on the device was unreadable and asks if you want to initialize the drive. When you initialize a drive, all data on the drive is lost. Click **Yes** if it is a new drive or if you do not need the data on the drive. Anaconda initializes the hard disk immediately.

Install or Upgrade   Anaconda displays the Install or Upgrade screen (Figure 3-2) only if it detects a version of Red Hat Linux on the hard disk that it can upgrade. Anaconda gives you the choice of upgrading the existing installation or overwriting the existing installation with a new one. Refer to "Installing a Fresh Copy or Upgrading an Existing Red Hat System?" on page 27 for help in making this selection.

Figure 3-2   The Install or Upgrade screen

Figure 3-3   The Partition the Disk screen

Partition the Disk   The Partition the Disk screen (Figure 3-3) allows you to specify partition information and to select which drives you want to install Red Hat Linux on (assuming the system has more than one drive). Specify which drives you want to install Linux on in the frame labeled **Select the drive(s) to use for this installation.** Anaconda presents the following options in a combo box; click the box and then click the choice you want:

- **Remove all partitions on selected drives and create default layout.**
  Deletes all data on the disk and creates a free space the size of the disk to work with, as though you were working with a new drive.

- **Remove linux partitions on selected drives and create default layout.**
  Removes all Linux partitions, deleting the data on those partitions and creating one or more chunks of *free space* (page 1033) on the disk. You can create new partitions using the free space. If there is only a Linux system on the disk, this choice is the same as the previous one.

- **Use free space on selected drives and create default layout.**   Installs Red Hat Linux in the free space on the disk. Does not work if there is not enough free space.

- **Create custom layout.**   Does not alter disk partitions. This choice causes Anaconda to run Disk Druid (page 58) so that you can preserve the partitions you want to keep and overwrite other partitions. It is good for installing Red Hat Linux over an existing system where you want to keep **/home**, for example, but want a clean install and not an upgrade.

The default layout that the first three choices create includes two logical volumes (LVs: swap and root [**/**]) and one standard partition (**/boot**). With this setup, most of the space on the disk is assigned to the root partition. For information on the Logical Volume Manager, see page 32.

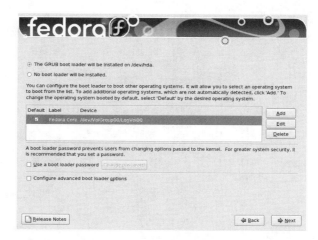

Figure 3-4 The Boot Loader Configuration screen

If you put a check mark in the box labeled **Review and modify partitioning layout** or if you select **Create custom layout** in the combo box, Anaconda runs Disk Druid (page 58) so that you can verify and modify the layout before it is written to the disk.

The disk is not partitioned until later

tip With one exception, Anaconda does not write to the hard disk when you specify partitions. Instead, it creates a table that specifies how you want the hard disk to be partitioned. The disk is actually partitioned and formatted when you click **Next** from the Begin installation screen (page 54). However, if Anaconda displays the initialize warning dialog box (page 49), when you click **Yes**, it writes to the disk immediately.

Disk Druid Anaconda runs Disk Druid only if you put a check mark in the box labeled **Review and modify partitioning layout** or if you select **Create custom layout** from the combo box as described in the previous section. See page 58 for information on the Disk Druid disk-partitioning program.

Warning Displays a warning if you are removing or formatting partitions. Click **Format** or **Yes** to proceed.

Boot Loader Configuration Anaconda displays the Boot Loader Configuration screen (Figure 3-4) only when you put a check mark in the box labeled **Review and modify partitioning layout** or select **Create custom layout** in the combo box in the Partition the Disk screen. By default, Anaconda installs the grub boot loader (page 533). If you do not want to install a boot loader, click the radio button next to **No boot loader will be installed**. When you install Red Hat Linux on a machine that already runs another operating system, Anaconda frequently recognizes the other operating system and sets up grub so you can boot from either operating system. Refer to "Setting Up a Dual-Boot System" on page 68. To manually add other operating systems to grub's list of bootable systems, click **Add** and specify a label and device to boot from. For a more secure system, specify a boot loader password.

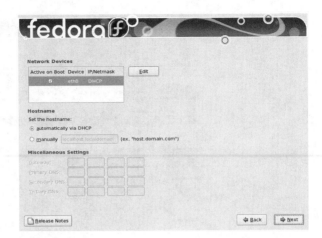

Figure 3-5 The Network Configuration screen

Network Configuration The Network Configuration screen, which allows you to specify network configuration information, has three parts: Network Devices, Hostname, and Miscellaneous Settings (Figure 3-5). If you are using DHCP to set up the network interface, you do not need to change anything on this screen.

The Network Devices frame lists the network devices that the installer finds. Normally you want network devices to become active when the system boots. Remove the check mark from the box at the left of a device if you do *not* want it to become active when the system boots.

To configure a network device manually (not using DHCP), highlight the device and click **Edit** to the right of the list of devices. Anaconda displays the Edit Interface window (Figure 3-6). Remove the check mark from the box labeled **Configure using DHCP** and enter the IP address and netmask of the system in the appropriate boxes before clicking **OK**.

If you are not using DHCP, click **manually** under **Set the hostname** in the Network Configuration screen and enter the name of the system. When you turn off DHCP configuration in Network Devices, Anaconda allows you to specify a gateway address and one or more DNS (nameserver) addresses. You do not have to specify more than one DNS address, although it can be useful to have two in case one nameserver stops working. Click **Next** to continue.

Time Zone The Time Zone screen allows you to specify the time zone the system is located in. Click a location on the map to enlarge the selected portion of the map and then click a city in the local system's time zone. Alternatively, you can scroll through the list in the combo box and highlight the appropriate selection. Put a check mark in the box next to **System clock uses UTC** if the system clock is set to *UTC* (page 1062).

Root Password Specify the **root** password twice to make sure you did not make a mistake typing it.

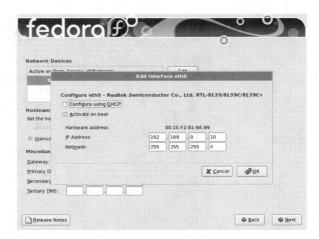

Figure 3-6   The Network Configuration: Edit Interface window

Install KDE to follow the examples in Chapter 4

tip   Chapter 4 uses examples from KDE to introduce the graphical desktop. Install KDE if you want to follow these examples. You can remove KDE later if you like. To install KDE, click the radio button next to **Customize now** on the Software Selection screen and follow the instructions in the text.

Software Selection   As the Software Selection screen explains, by default Anaconda installs a basic Fedora Core system including software that allows you to use the Internet. See Figure 3-7 (next page). The screen has three boxes that you can put check marks in to select additional categories of software to install:

- **Office and Productivity**

- **Software Development**

- **Web server**

Toward the bottom of the screen are two radio buttons:

- **Customize later**   Installs the default packages plus those required to perform the tasks selected from the list at the top of this screen. If the system can connect to the Internet, you can easily install other packages using pirut (page 483) after the system is up and running.

- **Customize now**   Calls pirut (next section) after you click **Next** on this screen so that you can select specific categories of software and package groups that you want to install. If you want to set up servers as described in Part V of this book, select **Customize now** and install them in the next step. See the preceding tip about installing KDE.

In most cases it is a good idea to customize the software selection before installation. The examples in Chapter 4 are based on KDE. If you want to follow these

Figure 3-7   The Software Selection screen

examples, click the radio button next to **Customize now** and follow the instructions in the next step.

When you select **Customize now** in the preceding step, Anaconda runs the pirut utility (page 483), which allows you to specify the software you want to install. Regardless of the software you select now, you can use pirut to change which software is installed on a system any time after the system is up and running (as long as the system can connect to the Internet).

The pirut utility displays two adjacent frames toward the top of the screen (Figure 3-8). Select a software category from the frame on the left and package groups from the frame on the right. For example, to install KDE, which is not installed by default, click **Desktop Environments** on the left. The pirut utility highlights your selection and displays a list of desktop environments you can install on the right. Click the box next to **KDE (K Desktop Environment)** so there is a check mark in it; pirut highlights KDE, displays information about KDE in the text frame toward the bottom of the window, displays the number of optional packages that are selected, and activates the **Optional packages** button. To get started, accept the default optional packages. See page 484 for information about installing other optional packages. If you will be running servers on the system, click **Servers** on the left and select the servers you want to install from the list on the right. Select other package categories in the same manner. When you are done, click **Next**.

Begin Installation   Clicking **Next** on the Begin Installation screen (Figure 3-9) begins the process of writing to the hard disk. First Anaconda partitions and formats the disk as necessary; next it installs Red Hat Linux based on what you have specified in the preceding screens, placing a log of the installation in **/root/install.log** and a Kickstart file (page 63) in **/root/anaconda-ks.cfg**. Clicking **Back** allows you to step back through the installation screens and make changes. To completely change the way you set up Fedora Core, you can press CONTROL-ALT-DEL to reboot the system and start over. If you reboot the system, you will lose all the work you did up to this point. Click **Next** to install Red Hat Linux.

Figure 3-8   The pirut package selection utility with KDE selected

This is when Anaconda writes to the hard disk

caution   You can abort the installation by pressing CONTROL-ALT-DEL at any point up to and including the Begin Installation screen (Figure 3-9) without making any changes to the system. Once you press **Next** in this screen, Anaconda writes to the hard disk. However, if Anaconda displayed the initialize warning dialog box (page 49), when you clicked **Yes**, it wrote to the hard disk at that time.

Installing Red Hat Linux can take a while. The amount of time it takes depends on the hardware you are installing the operating system on and the number of software packages you are installing. If you are installing from CDs, Anaconda will periodically prompt you to switch CDs.

Installation   When Anaconda is finished, it tells you that the installation is complete. Remove
Complete   the CD or DVD (if that is the medium you were installing from) and click **Reboot**.

Figure 3-9   The Begin Installation screen

Figure 3-10   The Welcome screen

FIRSTBOOT: WHEN YOU REBOOT

When the system reboots, it is running Red Hat Linux. The first time it boots, Red Hat Linux runs Firstboot, which asks a few questions before allowing you to log in.

Welcome There is nothing for you to do on the Welcome screen (Figure 3-10). Click **Forward**.

License Agreement After the Welcome screen, Firstboot displays the License Agreement screen. Select **Yes, I agree to the License Agreement** if you agree with the terms of the license agreement and click **Forward**.

Firewall Next you are given the opportunity to set up a very basic firewall. First select **Enabled** or **Disabled** from the Firewall combo box (Figure 3-11). If you enable the firewall, select the services that you want the firewall to allow to pass through to the system. These services are the ones that the system is providing by means of servers you set up. For example, you do not need to enable WWW to browse the Web using Firefox; you need to do so only if you want to set up an Apache (HTTP) server. Selecting **WWW (HTTP)** does not allow HTTPS (secure HTTP), which is used for secure browser connections to financial institutions and when giving credit card information, through the firewall. Select **Secure WWW (HTTPS)** to allow secure HTTP to pass. In the Other Ports text box, list other ports and protocols you want the firewall to pass. The Firewall screen is the same as the one displayed by the system-config-securitylevel utility. For more information refer to "JumpStart: Building a Firewall Using system-config-securitylevel" on page 768. Chapter 25 on iptables has information on how to build a more complete and functional firewall. Click **Forward**.

SELinux SELinux, which stands for Security Enhanced Linux, enforces security policies that limit what a user or program can do. On this screen you can choose one of two policies, Enforcing or Permissive, or you can disable SELinux. If you enable SELinux, you can also modify its policy. The policy defaults to Enforcing, which prevents any user or program from doing anything that is not permitted by the policy. If you will

Figure 3-11   The Firewall screen

never want to use SELinux, disable it. If you do not want to use it now but may want to do so in the future, establish a Permissive policy—it issues warnings but does not enforce the policy. It can take a lot of time to turn on SELinux on a system where it has been disabled. For more information refer to "SELinux" on page 400. Click **Forward**.

Date and Time   The next screen allows you to set the date and time. Running the Network Time Protocol (NTP) causes the system clock to reset itself periodically from a clock on the Internet. If the system is connected to the Internet, you may want to enable NTP by clicking the Network Time Protocol tab and putting a check mark in the box next to **Enable Network Time Protocol**. Click **Forward**.

Display   Next Firstboot displays the Display screen, which allows you to specify the type, resolution, and color depth of the monitor. For more information refer to "system-config-display: Configures the Display" on page 70. Click **Forward**.

System User   The next screen allows you to set up user accounts. You can set up user accounts either now or after the system is fully operational. For more information refer to "Configuring User and Group Accounts" on page 538.

Sound Card   The Sound Card window identifies the sound card(s) and has a button that can play a test sound. You can specify the default audio card and PCM (digital audio) device from the Sound Card screen. Click **Finish**.

When the Sound Card screen closes, you are done with the installation. You can now use the system and set it up as you desire. You may want to customize the desktop as explained in Chapters 4 and 8 or set up servers as discussed in Part V of this book.

INITIALIZING DATABASES AND UPDATING THE SYSTEM

After booting the system, log in as or su to **root**. Update the **whatis** database so that whatis (page 146) and apropos (page 145) work properly. Next update the **locate** database so that locate works properly. (The locate utility indexes and allows you to search for files on your system quickly and securely.) Instead of updating these databases when you install the system, you can wait for cron (page 547) to run them overnight, but be aware that whatis, apropos, and locate will not work until the next day. The best way to update these databases is via the cron scripts that run them daily. Working as **root**, give the following commands:

```
# /etc/cron.daily/makewhatis.cron
# /etc/cron.daily/mlocate.cron
```

These utilities run for several minutes and may complain about not being able to find a file or two. When the system displays a prompt, the **whatis** and **locate** databases are up-to-date.

If the system is permanently connected to the Internet, you can set up yum (page 476) to update the system software and utilities nightly. If it is connected to the Internet periodically, you must run yum manually to update the system. Working as **root**, give the following commands:

```
# /sbin/service yum start
# /sbin/chkconfig yum on
```

See page 482 for more information.

INSTALLATION TASKS

This section details some common tasks you may need to perform during or after installation. It covers using Disk Druid to partition the disk during installation, using parted to modify partitions after installation, using Kickstart to automate installation, and setting up a system that will boot either Windows or Linux (a dual-boot system).

USING DISK DRUID TO PARTITION THE DISK

Disk Druid, a graphical disk-partitioning program that can add, delete, and modify partitions on a hard disk, is part of the Red Hat installation system. You can use Disk Druid only while you are installing a system: It cannot be run on its own. You can use parted (page 65) to manipulate partitions and system-config-lvm to work with LVs after you install Red Hat Linux. As explained earlier, if you want a basic set of partitions, you can allow Anaconda to partition the hard disk automatically.

Anaconda runs Disk Druid when you put a check mark in the box labeled **Review and modify partitioning layout** or if you select **Create custom layout** in the Partition the Disk screen (page 50).

Clone and RAID   Disk Druid includes Clone, a tool that copies the partitioning scheme from a single drive to other drives. Clone is useful for making multiple copies of a RAID

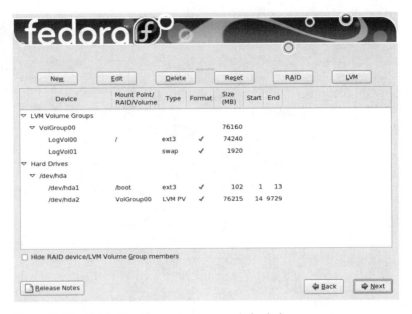

Figure 3-12   Disk Druid: main screen, default layout

partition/drive when you are creating a large RAID array of identical partitions or identically partitioned drives. Click the **RAID** button to access the Clone tool, which is active only when at least one unallocated RAID partition exists. For more information on RAID, see page 31.

Figure 3-12 shows the Disk Druid main screen as it appears when you have chosen the default layout for the hard disk (see "Partition the Disk" on page 50). This screen has three sections (going from top to bottom): a graphical representation of the disk drives showing how each is partitioned (not shown Figure 3-12), a row of buttons, and a graphical table listing one partition or LV per line.

The following buttons appear near the top of the screen:

- **New**   Adds a new partition to the disk (page 60).
- **Edit**   Edits the highlighted partition or LV (both on page 61).
- **Delete**   Deletes the highlighted partition or LV.
- **Reset**   Cancels the changes you have made and causes the Disk Druid table to revert so it matches the layout of the disk.
- **RAID**   Enables you to create software RAID partitions and to join two or more RAID partitions into a RAID device (page 31).
- **LVM**   Enables you to create physical volumes (PVs), which you can then use to create LVs (page 32).

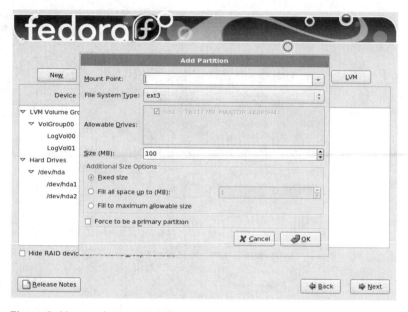

Figure 3-13   Disk Druid: Add Partition window, **ext3** filesystem

The Disk Druid table contains the following columns:

- **Device**   The name of the device in the **/dev** directory (for example, **/dev/hda1**).

- **Mount Point/RAID/Volume**   Specifies where the partition will be mounted when the system is brought up (for example, **/usr**). Also used to specify the RAID device or LVM volume the partition is part of.

- **Type**   The type of partition, such as **ext3**, **swap**, or PV.

- **Format**   A check mark in this column indicates the partition will be formatted as part of the installation procedure. All data on the partition will be lost.

- **Size (MB)**   The size of the partition or LV in megabytes.

- **Start**   The number of the block the partition starts on.

- **End**   The number of the block the partition ends on.

At the bottom of the screen is a box that allows you to hide RAID device and LVM volume group members. Do not put a check mark in this box if you want to see all information about the disk drives.

Add a new partition   To add a new partition to a hard disk, the hard disk must have enough free space to accommodate the partition. Click the **New** button to add a partition; Disk Druid displays the Add Partition window (Figure 3-13). Specify the mount point (the name of the directory that the partition will be mounted over [page 466]) and the filesystem type; use the arrow buttons at the right end of these text boxes to display drop-down menus of choices. If there is more than one drive, put a check mark in the box next to the drive you want the partition to be created on in the Allowable Drives frame. Specify the size of the partition and, in the Additional Size Options frame, mark **Fixed size** to create the partition close to the size you specify. Because of block-size constraints, partitions are not usually exactly the size you specify. Mark **Fill all space up to (MB)** and fill in the maximum size you want the partition to be to create a partition that takes up the existing free space, up to the maximum size you specify. In other words, Disk Druid does not complain if it cannot create the partition as large as you would like. Mark the third choice, **Fill to maximum allowable size**, to cause the partition to occupy all the remaining free space on the disk, regardless of size. (If you create another partition after creating a **Fill to maximum allowable size** partition, the new partition will pull blocks from the existing maximum size partition.) Put a check mark in the box labeled **Force to be a primary partition** to create a primary partition. Click **OK**, and Disk Druid adds the partition to its table (but does not write to the hard disk).

Edit an existing partition   To modify an existing partition, highlight the partition in the Disk Druid table or the graphical representation of the hard disk and click the **Edit** button; Disk Druid displays the Edit Partition window. From this window, you can change the mount point of a partition or format the partition as another type (**ext3, vfat, swap,** and so on). You cannot change the size of a partition from this window. To do so you must delete the partition and create a new partition of the desired size.

LVs: LOGICAL VOLUMES

When you ask Anaconda to partition the hard disk with a default layout (see "Partition the Disk" on page 50), it uses LVM (page 32) to set up most of the hard disk, creating LVs instead of partitions. It places **/boot** on the first partition on the drive, not under the control of LVM. LVM creates a VG (volume group) named **VolGroup00**. Within this VG it creates two LVs: swap (**LogVol01**) and root (/, **LogVol00**). The swap LV occupies up to a few gigabytes; the root LV takes up the rest of the drive. This section explains how to make the root LV smaller so that you can add additional LVs to **VolGroup00**.

If you click the **LVM** button with the default setup (with the root LV occupying all of the disk that is not occupied by the swap LV and the **/boot** partition), Disk Druid displays a dialog box that advises you that there are not enough physical volumes and suggests that you create a new partition. Because the existing partitions occupy the whole disk, you cannot create a new partition.

To make the root LV smaller and make room for additional partitions, first highlight the root partition (**LogVol00**) and then click **Edit**. Disk Druid displays the Edit LVM

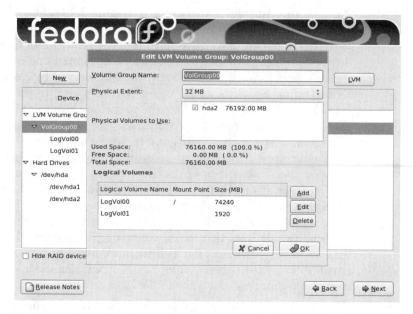

Figure 3-14   Disk Druid: Edit LVM Volume Group window

Volume Group window (Figure 3-14). The figure shows that **VolGroup00** has no free space (see the line in the middle of the window). It shows two LVs: swap, which does not have a mount point, and root, with a mount point of **/**.

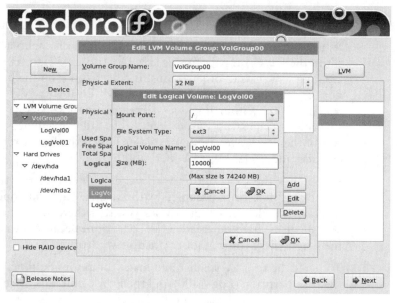

Figure 3-15   Disk Druid: Edit Logical Volume window

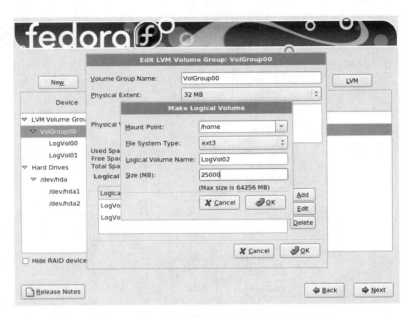

Figure 3-16   Disk Druid: Make Logical Volume window

Highlight root (**LogVol00**) in the Logical Volumes frame and click **Edit**. Disk Druid displays the Edit Logical Volume window (Figure 3-15), which allows you to change the size of the root partition. Replace the numbers in the Size (MB) text box with the number of megabytes you want to assign to the root partition. Figure 3-15 shows the size of the root partition being changed to 10 gigabytes (10,000 megabytes). Click **OK**.

Once you decrease the size of the root partition, the Edit LVM Volume Group window shows that the VG has free space. You can now add another LV to the VG. Click **Add** in the Edit LVM Volume Group window to display the Make Logical Volume window (Figure 3-16). Select a mount point, filesystem type, and size for the LV. You can change the LV name if you like, although Disk Druid assigns logical, sequential names that are easy to use. Figure 3-16 shows a **/home** LV being created with a size of 25 gigabytes. Click **OK** when the LV is set up the way you want.

Figure 3-17 (next page) shows the modified Disk Druid main screen with the new **/home** LV.

USING THE KICKSTART CONFIGURATOR

Kickstart is Red Hat's program that completely or partially automates the same installation and postinstallation configuration on one or more machines. To use Kickstart, you create a single file that answers all the questions that are normally asked during an installation. Anaconda then refers to this file instead of asking you questions. Using Kickstart, you can automate language selection, network configuration,

Figure 3-17   Disk Druid: main screen with the new **/home** LV

keyboard selection, boot loader installation, disk partitioning, X Window System configuration, and more.

The system-config-kickstart utility (part of the **system-config-kickstart** package that you can install using yum [page 478]) displays the Kickstart Configurator window (Figure 3-18), which creates a Kickstart installation script. On *RHEL* systems you may need to download the package that contains Kickstart using Red Hat Network (page 498).

Figure 3-18 shows the first window the Kickstart Configurator displays. To generate a Kickstart file (**ks.cfg** by default), go through each section of this window (the

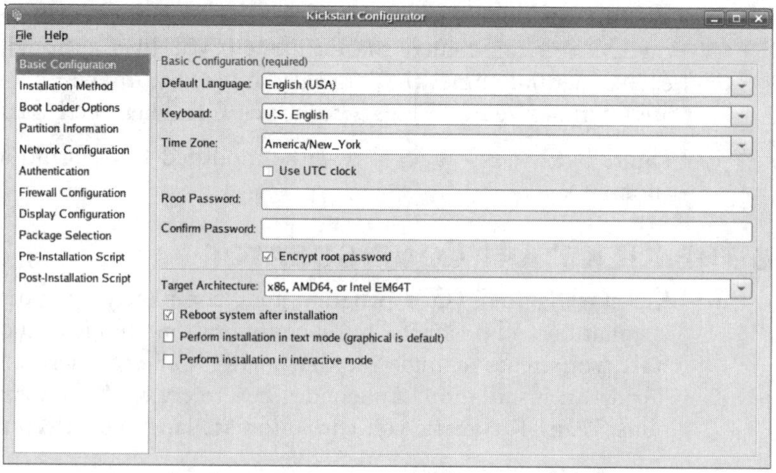

Figure 3-18   Kickstart Configurator

items along the left side) and fill in the answers and put check marks in the appropriate boxes. Click **Help** on the menubar for instructions on completing these tasks. When you are finished, click **File⇨Save**. The Kickstart Configurator gives you a chance to review the generated script before it saves the file.

parted: REPORTS ON AND PARTITIONS A HARD DISK

The parted (partition editor) utility reports on and manipulates hard disk partitions. The following example shows how to use parted from the command line. It uses the **print** command to display information about the partitions on the **/dev/hda** drive:

```
# /sbin/parted /dev/hda print
Disk geometry for /dev/hda: 0kB - 165GB
Disk label type: msdos
Number  Start    End     Size    Type      File system  Flags
1       32kB     1045MB  1045MB  primary   ext3         boot
2       1045MB   12GB    10GB    primary   ext3
3       12GB     22GB    10GB    primary   ext3
4       22GB     165GB   143GB   extended
5       22GB     23GB    1045MB  logical   linux-swap
6       23GB     41GB    18GB    logical   ext3
7       41GB     82GB    41GB    logical   ext3
Information: Don't forget to update /etc/fstab, if necessary.
```

Figure 3-19 graphically depicts the partitions shown in the example. The first line that parted displays specifies the device being reported on (**/dev/hda**) and its size (165 gigabytes). The **print** command displays the following columns:

- **Number**   The minor device number (page 463) of the device holding the partition. This number is the same as the last number in the device name. In the example, **4** corresponds to **/dev/hda4**.

- **Start**   The location on the disk where the partition starts. The parted utility specifies a location on the disk as the distance, in bytes, from the start of the disk. Thus partition 3 starts 12 gigabytes from the start of the disk.

- **End**   The location on the disk where the partition stops. Although partition 2 ends 12 gigabytes from the start of the disk and partition 3 starts at the same location, parted takes care that the partitions do not overlap at this single byte.

- **Size**   The size of the partition in kilobytes (kB), megabytes (MB), or gigabytes (GB).

- **Type**   The partition type: primary, extended, or logical. See Figure 3-19 (next page) and page 28 for information on partitions.

- **File system**   The filesystem type: **ext2**, **ext3**, **fat32**, **linux-swap**, etc. See Table 12-1 on page 464 for a list of filesystem types.

- **Flags**   The flags that are turned on for the partition, including **boot**, **swap**, **raid**, and **lvm**. In the example, partition 1 is bootable.

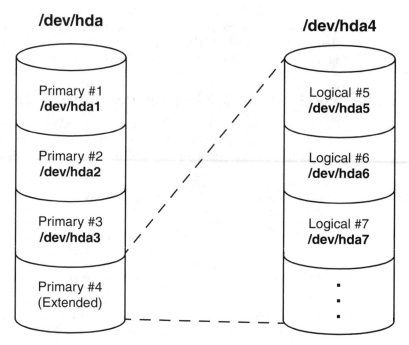

Figure 3-19   The primary and extended partitions from the example

In the preceding example, partition 4 defines an extended partition that includes 143 gigabytes of the 165 gigabyte disk (Figure 3-19). You cannot make changes to an extended partition without affecting all logical partitions within it.

In addition to reporting on the layout and size of a disk drive, you can use **parted** interactively to modify the disk layout. Be *extremely* careful when using **parted** in this manner, and always back up the system before starting to work with this utility. Changing the partition information (the *partition table*) on a disk can destroy the information on the disk. Read the **parted** info page before modifying a partition table.

parted **can destroy everything**

caution   Be as careful with **parted** as you would be with a utility that formats a hard disk. Changes you make with **parted** can easily result in the loss of large amounts of data. If you are using **parted** and have any question about what you are doing, quit with a **q** command before making any changes. Once you give **parted** a command, it immediately makes the change you requested.

To partition a disk, give the command **parted** followed by the name of the device you want to work with. Following, after starting **parted**, the user gives a **help** (or just **h**) command, which displays a list of **parted** commands:

```
# /sbin/parted /dev/hdb
GNU Parted 1.6.25
...
Using /dev/hda
(parted) help
  check NUMBER                         do a simple check on the file system
  cp [FROM-DEVICE] FROM-NUMBER TO-NUMBER   copy file system to another partition
  help [COMMAND]                       prints general help, or help on COMMAND
  mklabel LABEL-TYPE                   create a new disklabel (partition table)
  mkfs NUMBER FS-TYPE                  make a FS-TYPE file system on partititon NUMBER
  mkpart PART-TYPE [FS-TYPE] START END     make a partition
  mkpartfs PART-TYPE FS-TYPE START END     make a partition with a file system
  move NUMBER START END                move partition NUMBER
  name NUMBER NAME                     name partition NUMBER as NAME
  print [NUMBER]                       display the partition table, or a partition
  quit                                 exit program
  rescue START END                     rescue a lost partition near START and END
  resize NUMBER START END              resize partition NUMBER and its file system
  rm NUMBER                            delete partition NUMBER
  select DEVICE                        choose the device to edit
  set NUMBER FLAG STATE                change a flag on partition NUMBER
  unit UNIT                            set the default unit to UNIT
(parted)
```

In response to the (**parted**) prompt you can give the command **help** followed by the name of the command you want more information about. See the following example. When you give a **print** (or just **p**) command, parted displays current partition information just as a **print** command on the command line does.

The parted utility will not allow you to set up overlapping partitions (except for logical partitions overlapping their containing extended partition) and it will not allow you to create a partition that starts at the very beginning of the disk (cylinder 0). Both of these situations can cause loss of data. Following are guidelines to remember when defining a partition table for a disk. For more information refer to "Partitioning a Disk" on page 29.

- Do not delete or modify the partition that defines the extended partition unless you are willing to lose all data on all of the logical partitions within the extended partition.

- It is a good idea to put **/boot** at the beginning of the drive (partition 1) so that there is no issue of Linux having to boot from a partition too far into the drive. When you can afford the disk space, it is desirable to put each major filesystem on a separate partition. Many people choose to combine root, **/var**, and **/usr** into a single partition, which generally results in less wasted space but can, on rare occasions, cause problems. Although it is not recommended, you can put the contents of the **boot** directory in the root filesystem.

- Although parted can create some types of filesystems, it is usually easiest to use parted to create partitions and then use mkfs and mkswap to create filesystems on the partitions.

The following sequence of commands defines a 300-megabyte, bootable, Linux partition as partition 1 on a clean disk:

```
# /sbin/parted /dev/hdb
...
Using /dev/hdb
(parted) mkpart                                (create new partition)
Partition type?  primary/extended? primary     (select primary partition)
File system type?  [ext2]?                      (default to an ext2 filesystem)
Start? 1                                        (start at the beginning of the disk)
End? 300m                                       (specify a 300-megabyte partition)
(parted) help set                              (use help to check the syntax of the set command)
  set NUMBER FLAG STATE          change a flag on partition NUMBER

      NUMBER is the partition number used by Linux.  On msdos disk labels, the primary
      partitions number from 1 to 4, logical partitions from 5 onwards.
      FLAG is one of: boot, root, swap, hidden, raid, lvm, lba, hp-service, palo,
      prep, msftres
      STATE is one of: on, off
(parted) set 1 boot on                         (turn on the boot flag on partition 1)
(parted) print                                 (verify that the partition is correct)
Disk geometry for /dev/hdb: 0kB - 250GB
Disk label type: msdos
Number  Start   End    Size   Type     File system  Flags
1       1kB     300MB  300MB  primary  ext2         boot
(parted) quit
Information: Don't forget to update /etc/fstab, if necessary.
```

When you specify a size within parted, you can use a suffix of **k** (kilobytes), **m** (megabytes), or **g** (gigabytes). After creating a partition give a **print** command to see where the partition ends. Perform this task before defining the next contiguous partition so that you do not waste space or have any overlap. After setting up all the partitions, exit from parted with a **quit** command.

Next, make a filesystem (mkfs, page 419) on each partition that is to hold a filesystem (not swap). Make all partitions, except swap and **/boot**, type **ext3**, unless you have a reason to do otherwise. Make the **/boot** partition type **ext2**. Use mkswap (page 458) to set up a swap area on a partition. You can use e2label (page 418) to label a partition.

SETTING UP A DUAL-BOOT SYSTEM

A dual-boot system is one that can boot one of two operating systems. In this section, *dual-boot* refers to a system that can boot Windows or Linux. The biggest problem in setting up a dual-boot system, assuming you want to add Linux to a Windows system, is finding enough disk space for Linux. The *Linux+WindowsNT mini-HOWTO* covers installing Linux first and Windows NT second (or the other way around). The next section discusses several ways to create the needed space.

CREATING FREE SPACE ON A WINDOWS SYSTEM

Typically you install Red Hat Linux in free space on a hard disk. To add Red Hat Linux to a Windows system, you must provide enough free space (refer to "Hard disk space" on page 26) on a hard disk that already contains Windows. There are several ways to provide or create this free space. The following ways are ordered from easiest to most difficult:

Use existing free space If there is sufficient free space on the Windows disk, you can install Linux there. This technique is the optimal choice, but there is rarely enough free space on an installed hard disk.

Resize Windows partitions You can use Windows software, such as Partition Magic, to resize existing Windows partitions to open up free space in which to install Linux.

Add a new disk drive Add another disk drive to the system and install Linux on the new disk, which contains only free space. This technique is very easy and clean but requires a new disk drive.

Remove a Windows partition If you can delete a big enough Windows partition, you can install Linux in its place. To delete a Windows partition, you must have multiple partitions under Windows and be willing to lose any data in the partition you delete. In many cases, you can move the data from the partition you will delete to another Windows partition.

Once you are sure a partition contains no useful information, you can use Disk Druid to delete it when you install Linux: From the Partition the Disk screen (page 50), choose to create a custom layout with Disk Druid, highlight the partition you want to delete, and click the **Delete** button. After deleting the partition, you can install Red Hat Linux in the free space left by the partition you removed.

INSTALLING RED HAT LINUX AS THE SECOND OPERATING SYSTEM

After creating enough free space on a Windows system (as discussed in the previous section), you can begin installing Red Hat Linux. When you get to the Partition the Disk screen (page 50), choose **Use free space on selected drives and create default layout** to have Anaconda partition the free space on the hard disk automatically. If you need to delete a Windows partition, you must choose **Create custom layout**, which calls Disk Druid (page 58) so that you can delete the appropriate Windows partition and create Linux partitions in the free space. When you boot, you will be able to choose which operating system you want to run.

THE X WINDOW SYSTEM

If you specified a graphical desktop environment such as GNOME or KDE, you installed the X.org (x.org) implementation of the X Window System when you installed Linux. The X Window System release X11R7.0 comprises almost 20 rpm packages; the easiest way to install X.org on an already installed Linux system is to use pirut (page 483) and choose **Base System**⇨**X Window System**. The X

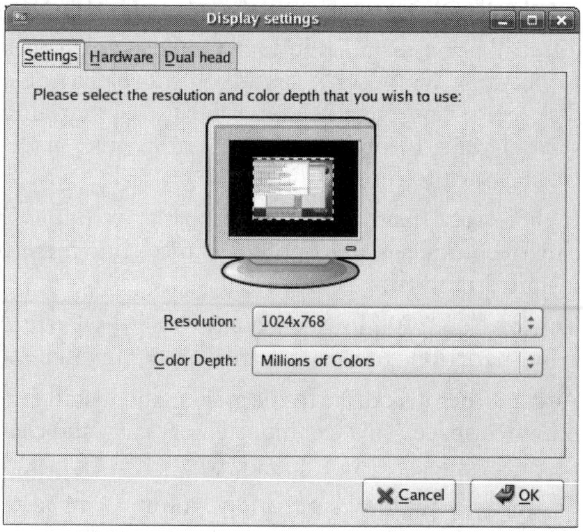

Figure 3-20 The Display settings window, Settings tab

configuration files are kept in **/etc/X11**; the configuration file that guides the initial setup is **/etc/X11/xorg.conf**.

system-config-display: **CONFIGURES THE DISPLAY**

The system-config-display utility displays the Display settings window (Figure 3-20), which allows you to configure X.org, including the monitor type and video card. To run this utility, enter **system-config-display** on a command line. From KDE select **Main menu: Administration⇨Display** or from GNOME select **System: Administration⇨Display**.

Figure 3-20 shows the Settings tab of the Display settings window, which allows you to specify the resolution and color depth for the monitor. Normally the system probes the monitor and fills in these values. If these values are missing, check the specifications for the monitor and select the appropriate values from the combo boxes. No harm is done if you specify a lower resolution than the monitor is capable of displaying, but you can damage an older monitor by specifying a resolution higher than the monitor is capable of displaying. A color depth of 8 bits equates to 256 colors, 16 bits to thousands of colors, and 24 or 32 bits to millions of colors.

Next click the Hardware tab. The system normally probes for the monitor type and brand as well as the model of video card; these values appear next to the words **Monitor Type** and **Video Card**. You can manually select a monitor or video card. Figure 3-21 shows the Monitor window on top of the Hardware tab of the Display settings window.

Specifying a monitor To specify a monitor, click **Configure** across from the words **Monitor Type**; system-config-display displays the Monitor window. Scroll down until the name of the manufacturer of the monitor you are using appears and click the triangle to the left of

Figure 3-21   The Display Settings window, Hardware tab, Monitor window

that name; system-config-display opens a list of models made by that manufacturer. Scroll through the list of models. Click to highlight the model you are using and then click **OK**. If an appropriate model is not listed, scroll to the top of the list and click the triangle next to **Generic CRT Display** or **Generic LCD Display**, depending on the type of monitor you are setting up. From one of these lists, select the maximum resolution the monitor is capable of displaying. Click **OK**.

Specifying a video card   To specify a video card, click **Configure** adjacent to the words **Video Card**; system-config-display displays the Video Card window. Scroll down until you see the manufacturer and model of the video card in your system. Click **OK**.

Specifying two monitors   The Dual head tab allows you to specify a second video card that can drive a second monitor. Specify the monitor type, video card, resolution, and color depth as you did earlier. You can choose to have each monitor display a desktop or to have the two monitors display a single desktop (spanning desktops). Click **OK** to close the Display settings window.

The system-config-display utility generates an **xorg.conf** file (discussed in the next section) with the information you entered.

THE xorg.conf FILE

The **/etc/X11/xorg.conf** file comprises sections that can appear in any order. The format of a section is

> *Section "**name**"*
>   **entry**
>   *...*
> *EndSection*

where *name* is the name of the section. A typical *entry* occupies multiple physical lines but is actually just one logical line, consisting of a keyword followed by zero or more integer, real, or string arguments. Keywords in these files are not case sensitive; underscores (_) within keywords are ignored. Most strings are not case sensitive, and SPACEs and underscores in most strings are ignored. All strings must appear within double quotation marks.

The Option keyword provides free-form data to server components and is followed by the name of the option and optionally a value. All Option values must be enclosed within double quotation marks.

Boolean Options take a value of **TRUE** (**1, on, true, yes**) or **FALSE** (**0, off, false, no**); no value is the same as **TRUE**. You can prepend **No** to the name of a Boolean Option to reverse the sense of the Option.

The following sections can appear in an **xorg.conf** file:

ServerFlags	Global Options (optional)
ServerLayout	Binds Screen(s) and InputDevice(s)
Files	Locations of configuration files
Module	Modules to be loaded (optional)
InputDevice	Keyboard(s) and pointer(s)
Monitor	Monitor(s)
Device	Video card(s)
Screen	Binds device(s) and monitor(s)
VideoAdaptor	Configures the Xv extension (optional)
Modes	Video modes (optional)
DRI	Direct Rendering Infrastructure (optional)
Vendor	Vendor-specific information (optional)

This chapter covers the sections you most likely need to work with: ServerLayout, InputDevice, Monitor, Device, and Screen. See the **xorg.conf** man page for more information.

ServerLayout SECTION

The ServerLayout section appears first in some **xorg.conf** files because it summarizes the other sections that are used to specify the server. The following ServerLayout section names the server **single head configuration** and specifies that the server comprises the sections named Screen0, Mouse0, Keyboard0, and DevInputMice.

The term *core* in this file means *primary*; there must be exactly one CoreKeyboard and one CorePointer. The AlwaysCore argument indicates that the device reports core events and is used here to allow a non-USB mouse and a USB mouse to work at the same time. The result is that you can use either type of mouse interchangeably without modifying the **xorg.conf** file:

```
Section "ServerLayout"
        Identifier  "single head configuration"
        Screen    0  "Screen0" 0 0
        InputDevice "Mouse0" "CorePointer"
        InputDevice "Keyboard0" "CoreKeyboard"
        InputDevice "DevInputMice" "AlwaysCore"
EndSection
```

Refer to the following sections for explanations of the sections specified in Server-Layout.

InputDevice SECTION

There must be at least two InputDevice sections: one specifying the keyboard and one specifying the pointer (usually a mouse). The format of an InputDevice section is

Section *"InputDevice"*
  Identifier *"id_name"*
  Driver *"drv_name"*
  options

  ...
EndSection

where **id_name** is a unique name for the device and **drv_name** is the driver to use for the device, typically **keyboard** or **mouse**. The system-config-display utility typically creates three InputDevice sections. The following section defines a keyboard device named Keyboard0 that uses the **keyboard** driver. The keyboard model is a 105-key PC keyboard. You can change **pc105** to **microsoft** if you are using a U.S. Microsoft Natural keyboard, although the differences are minimal.

```
Section "InputDevice"
        Identifier  "Keyboard0"
        Driver      "keyboard"
        Option      "XkbModel" "pc105"
        Option      "XkbLayout" "us"
EndSection
```

To change the language the keyboard supports, change the argument to the XkbLayout Option to, for example, **fr** for French.

The next InputDevice section defines a mouse named Mouse0 that uses the **mouse** driver. The Device Option specifies a PS2 device. The ZAxisMapping Option maps the Z axis, the mouse wheel, to virtual mouse buttons 4 and 5, which are used to scroll a window. For more information refer to "Remapping Mouse Buttons" on page 239. When set to **YES**, the Emulate3Buttons Option enables the user of a two-button mouse to emulate a three-button mouse by pressing the two buttons simultaneously.

```
Section "InputDevice"
        Identifier  "Mouse0"
        Driver      "mouse"
        Option      "Protocol" "IMPS/2"
        Option      "Device" "/dev/psaux"
        Option      "ZAxisMapping" "4 5"
        Option      "Emulate3Buttons" "no"
EndSection
```

The next InputDevice section is similar to the previous one except the Device Option specifies a USB mouse. See "ServerLayout Section" on page 72 for a discussion.

```
Section "InputDevice"
# If the normal CorePointer mouse is not a USB mouse then
# this input device can be used in AlwaysCore mode to let you
# also use USB mice at the same time.
        Identifier  "DevInputMice"
        Driver      "mouse"
        Option      "Protocol" "IMPS/2"
        Option      "Device" "/dev/input/mice"
        Option      "ZAxisMapping" "4 5"
        Option      "Emulate3Buttons" "no"
EndSection
```

Monitor SECTION

The **xorg.conf** file must have at least one Monitor section. The easiest way to set up this section is to use the system-config-display utility, which either determines the type of monitor automatically by probing or allows you to select from a list of monitors.

Do not guess at values for HorizSync or VertRefresh

caution   If you configure the Monitor section manually, do not guess at the scan rates (HorizSync and Vert-Refresh); on older monitors, you can destroy the hardware by choosing scan rates that are too high.

The following section defines a monitor named Monitor0. The VendorName and ModelName are for reference only and do not affect the way the system works. The optional DisplaySize specifies the height and width of the screen in millimeters, allowing X to calculate the DPI of the monitor. HorizSync and VertRefresh specify ranges of vertical refresh frequencies and horizontal sync frequencies for the monitor; these values are available from the manufacturer. The dpms Option specifies the monitor is *DPMS* (page 1030) compliant (has built-in energy-saving features).

```
Section "Monitor"
        Identifier   "Monitor0"
        VendorName   "Monitor Vendor"
        ModelName    "Dell D1028L"
        DisplaySize  360 290
        HorizSync    31.0 - 70.0
        VertRefresh  50.0 - 120.0
        Option       "dpms"
EndSection
```

A Monitor section may mention DDC (Display Data Channel); DDC can be used by a monitor to inform a video card about its properties. If you omit or comment out the HorizSync and VertRefresh lines, X will use DDC probing to determine proper values.

Device SECTION

The **xorg.conf** file must have at least one Device section to specify the type of video card in the system. The VendorName and BoardName are for reference only and do not affect the way the system works. The easiest way to set up this section is to use the system-config-display utility, which usually determines the type of video card by probing. The following Device section specifies that Videocard0 uses the **tdfx** driver:

```
Section "Device"
        Identifier   "Videocard0"
        Driver       "tdfx"
        VendorName   "Videocard vendor"
        BoardName    "Voodoo3 (generic)"
EndSection
```

Screen SECTION

The **xorg.conf** file must contain at least one Screen section. This section binds a video card specified in the Device section to a display specified in the Monitor section. The following Screen section specifies that Screen0 comprises Videocard0 and Monitor0, both defined elsewhere in the file. The DefaultDepth entry specifies the default *color depth* (page 1025), which can be overridden in the Display subsection.

Each Screen section must have at least one Display subsection. The following subsection specifies a color Depth and three Modes. The Modes specify the screen resolutions in units of dots per inch (dpi). The first Mode is the default; you can switch between Modes while X is running by pressing CONTROL-ALT-KEYPAD+ or CONTROL-ALT-KEYPAD–. You must use the plus or minus on the numeric keypad when giving these commands. X ignores invalid Modes.

```
Section "Screen"
        Identifier   "Screen0"
        Device       "Videocard0"
        Monitor      "Monitor0"
        DefaultDepth    24
        SubSection   "Display"
         Depth          24
         Modes          "1024x768" "800x600" "640x480"
        EndSubSection
EndSection
```

If you omit or comment out the Depth and Modes lines, X will use DDC probing to determine optimal values.

MULTIPLE MONITORS

X has supported multiple screens for a long time. X.org supports multimonitor configurations using either two graphics cards or a dual-head card. Both setups are usually configured the same way because the drivers for dual-head cards provide a secondary virtual device.

Traditionally each screen in X is treated as a single entity. That is, each window must be on one screen or another. More recently the Xinerama extension allows windows to be split across two or more monitors. This extension is supported by X.org and works with most video drivers. When using Xinerama, you must set all screens to the same color depth.

For each screen, you must define a Device, Monitor, and Screen section in the **xorg.conf** file. These sections are exactly the same as for a single-screen configuration; each screen must have a unique identifier. If you are using a dual-head card, the Device section for the second head is likely to require a BusID value to enable the driver to determine that you are not referring to the primary display. The following section identifies the two heads on an ATI Radeon 8500 card. For other dual-head cards, consult the documentation provided with the driver (for example, give the command **man mga** to display information on the **mga** driver):

```
Section "Device"
        Identifier   "Videocard0"
        Driver       "radeon"
        VendorName   "ATI"
        BoardName    "Radeon 8500"
EndSection
Section "Device"
        Identifier   "Videocard1"
        Driver       "radeon"
        VendorName   "ATI"
        BoardName    "Radeon 8500"
        BusID        "PCI:1:5:0"
EndSection
```

Once you have defined the screens, use the ServerLayout section to tell X where they are in relation to each other. Each screen is defined in the following form:

Screen [ScreenNumber] "Identifier" Position

The *ScreenNumber* is optional. If it is omitted, X numbers screens in the order they are specified, starting with 0. The *Identifier* is the same Identifier used in the Screen sections. The *Position* can be either absolute or relative. The easiest way to define screen positions is to give one screen an absolute position, usually with the coordinates of the origin, and then use the **LeftOf**, **RightOf**, **Above**, and **Below** keywords to indicate the positions of the other screens:

```
Section "ServerLayout"
        Identifier    "Multihead layout"
        Screen     0  "Screen0" LeftOf "Screen1"
        Screen     1  "Screen1" 0 0
        InputDevice   "Mouse0" "CorePointer"
        InputDevice   "Keyboard0" "CoreKeyboard"
```

```
            InputDevice    "DevInputMice" "AlwaysCore"
            Option         "Xinerama" "on"
            Option         "Clone" "off"
        EndSection
```

Two options can control the behavior of a multimonitor layout: Xinerama causes the screens to act as if they were a single screen and Clone causes each of the screens to display the same thing.

gdm: DISPLAYS A GRAPHICAL LOGIN

Traditionally users logged in on a textual terminal and then started the X server. Today most systems provide a graphical login. Red Hat Linux uses the GNOME display manager (gdm) to provide this functionality, even if you are bringing up a KDE desktop.

CONFIGURING gdm

The gdmsetup utility configures the login presented by gdm by editing the heavily commented **/etc/gdm/custom.conf** (*FEDORA*) or **/etc/X11/gdm/gdm.conf** (*RHEL*) file. By default, **root** can log in both locally and remotely. It is a good idea to disable remote **root** logins because, when a user logs in remotely using gdm, the password is sent in cleartext across the network. From GNOME you can select **System: Administration⇨Login Screen** to configure gdm.

USING kdm

The kdm utility is the KDE equivalent of gdm. There is no benefit in using kdm in place of gdm: Both perform the same function. Using gdm does not force you to use GNOME.

The configuration file for kdm, **/etc/X11/xdm/kdmrc**, is heavily commented. You can edit the kdm configuration using the KDE control panel, but doing so removes the comments from the file.

MORE INFORMATION

Web   X.org   X.org, freedesktop.org

X.org documentation   ftp.x.org/pub/X11R7.0/doc/html

CHAPTER SUMMARY

Most installations of Red Hat Linux begin by booting from the first installation CD or the installation DVD. When the system boots from the CD or DVD, it displays a **boot:** prompt. You can respond to this prompt by entering a variety of commands, by pressing RETURN without entering a command, or by not doing anything. In all cases, the system boots Red Hat Linux from the CD. If you are installing from files on the local hard disk or over a network, give the command **linux askmethod** in response to the **boot:** prompt.

The program that installs Red Hat Linux is named Anaconda. Anaconda identifies the hardware, builds the filesystems, and installs or upgrades the Red Hat Linux operating system. Anaconda can run in textual or graphical (default) interactive mode or in batch mode (Kickstart). Anaconda does not write to the hard disk until it displays the Begin Installation screen. Until it displays this screen, you can press CONTROL-ALT-DEL to abort the installation without making any changes to the hard disk.

The Disk Druid graphical disk-partitioning program can add, delete, and modify partitions and logical volumes (LVs) on a hard disk during installation. The parted utility reports on and manipulates hard disk partitions before or after installation. The system-config-lvm utility works with LVs after installation.

A dual-boot system can boot one of two operating systems, frequently Windows and Linux. The biggest problem in setting up a dual-boot system, assuming you want to add Linux to a Windows system, is finding enough disk space for Linux.

Fedora Core 5 uses the X.org X Window System version X11R7.0. Under X.org, the primary configuration file is named **/etc/X11/xorg.conf**.

Red Hat Linux uses the GNOME display manager (gdm) to provide a graphical login, even if you are using a KDE desktop. The gdmsetup utility configures the login presented by gdm by editing the **/etc/gdm/custom.conf** (*FEDORA*) or **/etc/X11/gdm/gdm.conf** (*RHEL*) file.

EXERCISES

1. What is the difference between Xinerama and traditional multimonitor X11?

2. Which command would you give in response to the **boot:** prompt to begin an FTP installation?

3. Describe the Anaconda installer.

4. Where on the disk should you put your **/boot** partition or the root (/) partition if you do not use a **/boot** partition?

5. If the graphical installer does not work, what three things should you try?

6. When should you specify an **ext2** filesystem instead of **ext3**?

7. Describe Disk Druid.

8. When does a Red Hat Linux system start X by default?

ADVANCED EXERCISES

9. If you do not install grub on the master boot record of the hard disk, how can you boot Linux?

10. Why would you place **/var** at the start of the disk?

11. Assume you have configured four screens, **screen0** through **screen3**. How would you instruct X.org that your screen layout was a T shape with the first screen at the bottom and the other three screens in a row above it?

PART II

GETTING STARTED WITH RED HAT LINUX

4

INTRODUCTION TO RED HAT LINUX

One way or another you are sitting in front of a computer that is running Red Hat Linux. This chapter takes you on a tour of the system to give you some ideas about what you can do with it. The tour does not go into depth about choices, options, menus, and so on; that is left for you to experiment with and to explore in greater detail in later chapters. Instead, this chapter presents a cook's tour of the Linux kitchen; as you read it, you will have a chance to sample the dishes that you will enjoy more fully as you read the rest of the book.

Following the tour are sections that describe where to find Linux documentation (page 102) and offer more about logging in on the system, including information about passwords (page 111). The chapter concludes with a more advanced, optional section about working with windows (page 119).

In the next section, be sure to read the warning about the dangers of misusing the powers of Superuser. Heed that warning, but feel free to experiment with the system: Give commands, create files, click icons, choose items from menus, follow the examples in this book, and have fun.

CURBING YOUR POWER: SUPERUSER/root ACCESS

While you are logged in as the user named **root**, you are referred to as *Superuser* or *administrator* and have extraordinary privileges. You can read from or write to any file on the system, execute programs that ordinary users cannot, and more. On a multiuser system you may not be permitted to know the **root** password, but someone—usually the *system administrator*—knows the **root** password and maintains the system. When you are running Linux on your own computer, you will assign a password to **root** when you install Linux. Refer to "System Administrator and Superuser" on page 391 for more information.

Do not experiment as Superuser

caution Feel free to experiment when you are logged in as a nonprivileged user, such as when you log in as yourself. When you log in as **root** (Superuser) or whenever you give the Superuser/**root** password, however, do only what you have to do and make sure you know exactly what you are doing. After you have completed the task at hand, revert to working as yourself. When working as Superuser/**root**, you can damage the Linux system to such an extent that you will need to reinstall Red Hat Linux to get it working again.

"System Administration" on page 99 describes tasks you may want to perform working as **root**.

A TOUR OF THE RED HAT LINUX DESKTOP

GNOME (www.gnome.org), a product of the GNU project (page 4), is the user-friendly default desktop manager under Red Hat Linux. KDE (www.kde.org), the K Desktop Environment, is a powerful desktop manager and complete set of tools you can use in place of GNOME. This tour focuses on KDE. This full-featured, mature desktop environment boasts a rich assortment of configurable tools and features. After you log in, this section discusses several important features of the desktop, including the Main panel and the Main menu, and explores how to use some of the unique features of windows under KDE. Along the way, you will see how to roll up a window so only its titlebar remains on the desktop, how to move easily from one desktop or window to another, and how to configure the desktop to please your senses. As the tour continues, you will learn to work with files and browse the Web using Konqueror, one of the primary KDE tools. The tour concludes with coverage of the KDE Control Center, the key to customizing your desktop, and a discussion of how to use the Panel menu to modify the panel (at the bottom of the screen) to best suit your needs.

As Red Hat Linux is installed, when you log in, you use GNOME. Because the examples in this section are based on KDE, you must tell the system that you want to run KDE before you log in. The following section explains how to log in to a KDE desktop environment.

Starting with "Getting the Facts: Where to Find Documentation" on page 102, the chapter covers both KDE and GNOME.

LOGGING IN ON THE SYSTEM

Typically, when you boot a Red Hat Linux system, it displays a Login screen on the system console. This screen has a text box labeled **Username** with four word/icon buttons below it. These buttons allow you to work in a different language (**Language**), specify a desktop manager (**Session**), reboot the system (**Restart**), and turn the system off (**Shut Down**). For more information refer to "The Login Screen" on page 111. Click **Session** and the system displays the Sessions dialog box, which allows you to choose whether you want to run GNOME or KDE, or make another choice. To follow the examples in this section, click the radio button next to **KDE** and then click **Change Session** to close the dialog box. If the KDE radio button is not visible, KDE is probably not installed; refer to the "If KDE is not installed" tip on page 84.

Enter your username in the text box labeled **Username** and press RETURN. The label changes to **Password**. Enter your password and press RETURN. If you get an error message, try entering your username and password again. Make sure the CAPS LOCK key is not on; your entries are case sensitive. See page 112 for help with problems logging in and page 114 if you want to change your password.

RHEL   The change you make in the Sessions dialog box affects only the current session. The next time you log in, you revert to your default desktop environment (KDE or GNOME). Use switchdesk (page 116) to change your default desktop environment.

FEDORA   Once the system has determined that you are allowed to log in, it displays a dialog box that asks, **Do you want to make KDE the default for future sessions?** It displays this dialog box because you elected to change your session to KDE before you logged in. The dialog box has three buttons that allow you to make the change effective **Just For This Session** (until you log off), **Cancel** the change, or **Make Default** (make the new desktop manager your default desktop manager). To work with the examples in this chapter, choose **Make Default**.

The system takes a few moments to set things up and then displays a workspace with a panel along the bottom and some icons at the upper left (Figure 4-1).

Figure 4-1   The initial KDE screen (*FEDORA*)

If KDE is not installed

tip   The KDE desktop environment should be installed on the system to follow the examples in this chapter. You can use the GNOME desktop environment, but some of the examples will not work the same way. To install KDE, log in on the system as described earlier, omitting the step that has you click **Session** (do not click the **KDE** radio button).

This procedure works only if the system is connected to the Internet. Without an Internet connection, it is easiest to reinstall Red Hat Linux with KDE.

RHEL   Use up2date (page 494) to download and install the following packages: **kdeaddons**, **kdeadmin**, **kdeartwork**, **kdebase**, **kdegraphics**, **kdelibs**, **kdemultimedia**, **kdenetwork**, **kdepim**, **kdeutils**. Now you can log in to the KDE environment as described in "Logging In on the System" on page 83.

FEDORA   Once you are logged in under GNOME, click **Applications** at the left end of the panel at the top of the screen. GNOME displays a drop-down menu. Slide the mouse pointer until it is over **Add/Remove Software** at the bottom of the submenu and then click. Supply the **root** password when the system asks for it. After a pause, the system displays the pirut Package Manager window (Figure 4-2).

Click **Desktop Environments** in the left frame and pirut displays GNOME Desktop Environment, KDE (K Desktop Environment), and XFCE in the right frame. Click the small box next to KDE so that a check mark appears. Click **Apply** at the bottom right of the screen and pirut displays the Package Selections window that asks you to confirm which packages you want to install. Click **Continue** and pirut displays various windows as it resolves dependencies (checks whether the system needs any other software to support the packages you are installing), downloads the KDE packages from the Internet, and installs them. When it is finished it displays a dialog window that says **Software installation successfully completed**. Click **OK** and you are finished installing KDE. Click **System** from the panel at the top of the screen, select **Log Out** from the drop-down menu, and click **Log out** from the window that GNOME displays. Now you can log in to the KDE desktop environment as described in "Logging In on the System" on page 83.

See page 483 for more information on pirut.

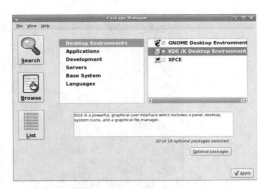

Figure 4-2   The pirut Package Manager window

Click and right-click

tip   This book uses the term **click** when you need to click the left mouse button and **right-click** when you need to click the right mouse button. See page 98 to adapt the mouse for left-handed use.

Getting the Most from the Desktop

When you are working in a complex environment and using many windows to run a variety of programs simultaneously, it is convenient to divide the desktop into several areas, each *appearing* as a desktop unto itself and occupying the entire screen. These areas are virtual desktops. The *workspace* comprises what is on the screen: buttons/icons, toolbars/panels, windows, and the *root window* (the unoccupied area of the workspace). Typically GNOME and KDE are set up with a desktop that includes four workspaces.

Desktop theme   In a GUI, a *theme* is a recurring pattern and overall look that (ideally) pleases the eye and is easy to interpret and use. To view a wide variety of themes, go to themes.freshmeat.net, www.kde-look.org, or art.gnome.org. Using themes, you can control the appearance of KDE, GNOME, and most other desktop environments.

Is it a desktop, a workspace, or what?

tip   Confusion reigns over naming the subcomponents, or divisions, of a desktop. This book, in conformance with GNOME documentation, refers to everything that usually occupies the display monitor, or screen, as a *workspace; desktop* refers to the sum of the workspaces. Put another way, the desktop is divided into workspaces.

KDE documentation and windows use the term *desktop* instead of *workspace*.

The Power of the Desktop: Using the Main Panel

When you log in, KDE displays a workspace that includes the KDE Main panel, which is essential to getting your work done easily and efficiently. The Main panel is the strip with icons that act as buttons (Figure 4-3) along the bottom of the workspace. A panel does not allow you to do anything you could not do otherwise; rather it simply collects things in one place and makes your work with the system easier. Because the Main panel is easy to configure, you can set it up to hold the tools you use frequently, arranged the way you want: application launchers to start, for example, email and word processing programs, menus (including the Main menu, represented by the red hat or Fedora logo), *applets* (applications that are small enough to be executed within a panel), and special objects (such as a **Logout** button). You can create additional panels, called *extensions* or *extension panels,* to hold different groups of tools.

Figure 4-3   The KDE Main panel

Figure 4-4 The Firefox tooltip

Tooltips Tooltips (Figure 4-4), available under both GNOME and KDE, is a minicontext help system that you activate by moving the mouse pointer over a button, icon, window border, or applet (such as those on a panel) and leaving it there for a moment (called *hovering*). When the mouse pointer hovers over an object, GNOME and KDE display a brief explanation of the object.

Icons/buttons The icons/buttons on the panel display menus, launch programs, and present information. The Web browser button (the mouse with its cord wrapped around the world) starts Firefox by default. The email button (the stamp and letter) starts Evolution, an email and calendaring application (www.gnome.org/projects/evolution). You can start almost any utility or program on the system using a button on a panel.

Panel Icon menu Each icon on a panel has a Panel Icon menu, which allows you to move the icon within the panel, view and change (configure) the icon's properties, and remove the icon from the panel. It also contains the Panel menu (page 100) as a submenu. Some icons have additional context-based selections whereas some applets have a different menu. Right-click an icon on the panel to display its Panel Icon menu.

Pager Each rectangle in the *Pager,* the group of rectangles labeled **1–4** on the panel, represents a workspace (Figure 4-5). Click a rectangle to display the corresponding workspace. For example, click the rectangle labeled **2**. This rectangle becomes lighter to indicate that you are viewing workspace 2. While you are working with workspace 2, click the Firefox icon on the panel. KDE opens the Firefox window and a small window with the Firefox logo in it appears in rectangle number 2 in the Pager.

Now click the rectangle labeled **3** and open the OpenOffice.org Writer by clicking the Main menu icon (the red hat or Fedora logo), clicking **Office** from the pop-up menu, and then clicking **Word Processor** from the submenu. With Writer in workspace 3 and Firefox in workspace 2, you can click the rectangles in the Pager to switch back and forth between the workspaces. GNOME calls this tool the *Workspace Switcher.*

Taskbar To the right of the Pager is the *Taskbar,* a group of skinny, horizontal rectangles with an icon and the name of a program in each one. You can use the Taskbar to display a specific window regardless of which workspace it appears in. Click one of the rectangles and the corresponding program/window appears on the screen; KDE switches to a different workspace if necessary. If the window running the program you clicked on is not visible because it is buried under other windows, you can click

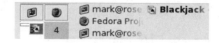

Figure 4-5 The Pager (left) and the Taskbar (right)

a rectangle on the Taskbar to pop the window to the top of the stack of windows. GNOME calls this tool the *Window List*. If you have a lot of applications running on various workspaces, you can configure the Taskbar to show only those applications on the current workspace. See "Configuring the panel" on page 101 for more information on configuring the Taskbar.

LAUNCHING APPLICATIONS FROM THE MAIN MENU

The red hat or Fedora icon at the left end of the KDE Main panel has a function similar to that of the **Start** button on a Windows system; click it to display the Main menu. From the Main menu and its submenus, you can launch many of the applications on the system. This menu differs under GNOME and KDE.

KNotes   You can use the Main menu to launch KNotes, a reminder system that displays windows that look like Post-it notes. After you display the Main menu, slide the mouse pointer over the Main menu until it is over **Utilities**. The system displays the Utilities submenu. If you click **Utilities**, KDE freezes the Utilities submenu. With or without clicking **Utilities**, move the mouse pointer until it is over **Desktop** and KDE displays another submenu. Now slide the mouse pointer until it is over **KNotes** and click to display a small, yellow window that you can type in (Figure 4-6).

You can use these windows to leave yourself reminders. Although KNotes may seem trivial, it offers many things to experiment with. Click and drag the titlebar at the top of a KNote to move it. Right-click the titlebar to display the KNotes menu. When you start KNotes, it puts an icon toward the right end of the panel. Right-click this icon and see what happens.

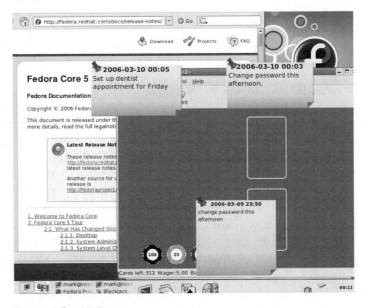

Figure 4-6   KNotes

Copy icons to a panel
To copy a selection from the Main menu to a panel, left-drag the item from the Main menu to a panel. To remove an icon from a panel, right-click the icon and choose **Remove** from the pop-up menu.

Logging out
At the bottom of the Main menu is **Log Out**. Click this selection to dim the workspace and display a window with four buttons: **End Current Session** (log out), **Turn Off Computer**, **Restart Computer**, and **Cancel** (do not log out). Log out or continue experimenting as you please.

Feel free to experiment
Try selecting different items from the Main menu and see what you discover. Many of the submenus provide submenus with even more selections (such as KNotes). Following are some applications you may want to explore:

- OpenOffice.org's Writer is a full-featured word processor that can import and export Word documents. From the Main menu, select **Office⇨Word Processor** (*RHEL* uses **Office⇨OpenOffice.org Writer** [only with the **openoffice.org** package installed]).

- Firefox is a powerful, full-featured Web browser. Click the panel icon of the world with a mouse wrapped around it to start Firefox. You can also select **Main menu: Internet⇨Firefox Web Browser**.

- The gaim Instant Messenger (IM) client allows you to chat on the Internet with people who are using IM clients such as AOL, MSN, and Yahoo! To start gaim, select **Main menu: Internet⇨Instant Messenger**.

  The first time you start gaim, it opens the Accounts window and the Add Account window automatically. In the Add Account window, put check marks in the boxes next to **Remember password** and **Auto-login** if you want gaim to log you in automatically when you start it. Click **Save**. In the main gaim window, enter your IM password if necessary and click **Sign on**. Go to gaim.sourceforge.net for more information, including gaim documentation and plugins that add features to gaim.

CONTROLLING WINDOWS

On the screen, a *window* is a region that runs, or is controlled by, a particular program (Figure 4-7). Because you can control the look and feel of windows, even the buttons they display, your windows may not look like the ones shown in this book. (Select **Main menu: Settings⇨Desktop Settings Wizard** to customize windows in your account [*FEDORA* only]. You can further customize windows by selecting **Main menu: Control Center** and then clicking either **Appearances and Themes** and selecting one of the subtabs or by clicking **Desktop** and selecting **Window Behavior**.)

Resizing a window
To resize a window, move the mouse pointer over an edge of the window; the pointer turns into a double arrow. Click and drag the side of the window as you desire. When you position the mouse pointer over a corner of the window and drag, you can resize the height and width of the window at the same time.

Titlebar
A titlebar (Figures 4-7 and 4-8) appears at the top of most windows and in many ways controls the window it is attached to. You can change the appearance and function of a titlebar, but it will usually have at least the functionality of the buttons shown in Figure 4-8.

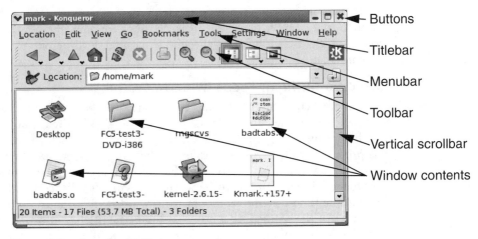

Figure 4-7   A typical window

The minimize button collapses the window to its rectangle in the Taskbar on the panel; click the rectangle on the Taskbar to restore the window. Clicking the maximize button expands the window so it occupies the whole workspace; click the same button on the titlebar of a maximized window (the button has a double-window icon) to restore the window to its former size. Clicking the maximize button with the middle or right mouse button expands the window vertically or horizontally. Use the same or a different mouse button to click the maximize button again and see what happens. Clicking the close button closes the window and terminates the program that was running in it. Left-click the titlebar and drag the window to reposition it.

Window Operations menu   The Window Operations menu (Figure 4-8) contains most of the common operations that you need to perform on any window. Click the Window Operations menu button or right-click the titlebar to display this menu.

Toolbar   A toolbar (Figure 4-7) usually appears at the top of a window and contains icons, text, applets, menus, and more. Many kinds of toolbars exist. The titlebar is not a toolbar; it is part of the window decoration placed there by the window manager (page 121).

Context menu   A context menu is a menu that applies specifically to the window you click. Frequently a right-click brings up a context menu. Try right-clicking on the icons on

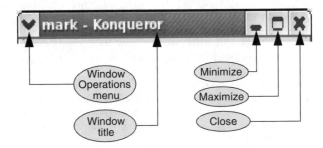

Figure 4-8   A titlebar

the desktop. Depending on what the icon represents, you get a different menu. For example, the context (icon) menu is different for the Trash, CD/DVD, and folder icons. Try right-clicking with the mouse pointer in different places; you will find some interesting menus.

CHANGING THE INPUT FOCUS (WINDOW CYCLING)

The window with the input focus is the one that receives keyboard characters and commands you type. In addition to using the Taskbar (page 86), you can change which window on the current workspace has the input focus by using the keyboard; this process is called *window cycling*. When you press ALT-TAB, the input focus shifts to the window that was active just before the currently active window, making it easy to switch back and forth between two windows. When you hold ALT and press TAB multiple times, the focus moves from window to window, and KDE displays in the center of the workspace a box that holds the titlebar information from the window that currently has the input focus. Under KDE, you can hold ALT and SHIFT and repeatedly press TAB to cycle in the other direction.

SHADING A WINDOW

When you double-click a KDE titlebar (Figure 4-8), the window rolls up like a window shade, leaving only the titlebar visible. Double-click the titlebar again to restore the window. If the window does not roll up, try double-clicking more quickly.

CUTTING AND PASTING OBJECTS USING THE CLIPBOARD

There are two similar ways to cut/copy and paste objects (e.g., icons and windows) and text on the desktop. You can use the clipboard, technically called the *copy buffer,* to copy or move objects or text: You explicitly copy an object or text to the buffer and then paste it somewhere else. Applications that follow the user interface guidelines use CONTROL-X to cut, CONTROL-C to copy, and CONTROL-V to paste.

You may be less familiar with the *selection* or *primary* buffer, which always contains the text you most recently selected (highlighted). You cannot use this method to copy objects. Clicking the middle mouse button (click the scroll wheel on a mouse that has one) pastes the contents of the selection buffer at the location of the mouse pointer (if you are using a two-button mouse, click both buttons at the same time to simulate clicking the middle button).

With both of these techniques, you start by highlighting the objects or text you want to select. You can drag a box around objects to select them or drag the mouse pointer over text to select it. Double-click to select a word or triple-click to select a line.

Next, to use the clipboard, explicitly copy (CONTROL-C) or cut (CONTROL-X) the objects or text.[1] If you want to use the selection buffer, skip this step.

---

1. These control characters do not work in a terminal emulator window because the shell running in the window intercepts them before the terminal emulator can receive them. You must either use the selection buffer in this environment or use copy/paste from the **Edit** selection on the menubar or from the context menu (right-click).

To paste the selected objects or text, either position the mouse pointer where you want to put them (it) and press CONTROL-V (clipboard method) or press the middle mouse button (selection buffer method).

Using the clipboard, you can give as many commands as you like between the CONTROL-C or CONTROL-X and CONTROL-V, as long as you do not use another CONTROL-C or CONTROL-X.

Using the selection buffer, you can give other commands after selecting text and before pasting it, as long as you do not select (highlight) other text.

You can use klipper, the KDE clipboard utility, to paste previously selected objects. See page 262 for information on klipper.

CONTROLLING THE DESKTOP USING THE ROOT WINDOW

The *root window* is any part of the workspace that is not occupied by a window, panel, icon, or other object. It is the part of the workspace where you can see the background.

Desktop icons   Icons on the root window respond appropriately to a double-click: A program starts running, a data file (such as a letter, calendar, or URL) runs the program that created it (with the data file loaded or, in the case of a URL, with the browser displaying the appropriate Web page), and a directory brings up the Konqueror file manager (page 94). Within Konqueror, you can move, copy, or link a file or directory by dragging and dropping it and selecting **Move/Copy/Link** from the resulting pop-up menu; you can run or edit a file by double-clicking it.

Icon context menus   Display an Icon context menu by right-clicking an icon that is not on a panel. The Icon context menu is the only way to perform some operations with icons on the root window. Figure 4-9 shows the Icon context menu for the Trash icon.

Desktop menu   Display the Desktop menu by right-clicking the root window. You can open a window or perform another task by making a selection from the Desktop menu. Both KDE and GNOME have Desktop menus, although each presents a different set of choices.

Configure Desktop   The Configure Desktop selection on the Desktop menu opens the Configure window (Figure 4-10), which presents many choices for you to experiment with. Each

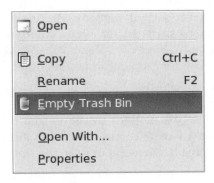

Figure 4-9   The Icon context menu for the Trash icon

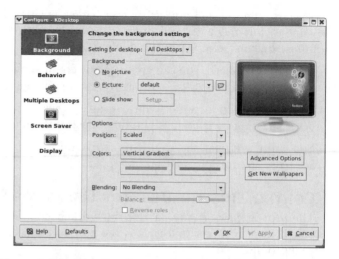

Figure 4-10   The Configure window, Background selection

icon in the vertical panel on the left of this window displays a different set of choices. Some choices, such as Behavior, display multiple tabs on the right, with each tab displaying a different set of choices.

Desktop background — Click **Background** on the left panel of the Configure window to change the desktop background settings (Figure 4-10). Near the top of the right side of this window is a combo box labeled **Setting for desktop**. Initially the box says **All Desktops**, meaning that whatever changes you make to the desktop using the rest of this window apply to all (four) workspaces. Click **All Desktops** and choose a single desktop from the drop-down menu to have the settings apply only to a single workspace. Using this technique you can make each of your workspaces look different.

Click the radio button next to **Picture** and choose a file that contains an image to use as wallpaper from the combo box to the right of this button. Alternatively, you can click **No picture** and choose a pattern and color(s) for the desktop background. Choose a pattern from the combo box adjacent to **Colors** and click one of the two color bars under the combo box. KDE displays the Select Color window. This window presents several ways of selecting a color. Click the palette icon, move the resulting crosshairs cursor over a color you like anywhere on the screen, and then click again to select the color. Click **OK**. Refer to "kcolorchooser: Selects a Color" on page 260 for more information on the Select Color window.

Experiment with the choices in the Background and Options frames to create a desktop background that pleases you. Click the **Get New Wallpapers** button under the picture of a monitor to choose and download new backgrounds that you can select in the Picture combo box. Select **Picture**, choose **default**, and then click **Apply** to return the background to its initial state.

GNOME and KDE — The Configure window presents numerous choices for how you can set up the appearance and functionality of the desktop. This abundance of choices demonstrates a major difference between KDE and GNOME, the two major Linux desktop

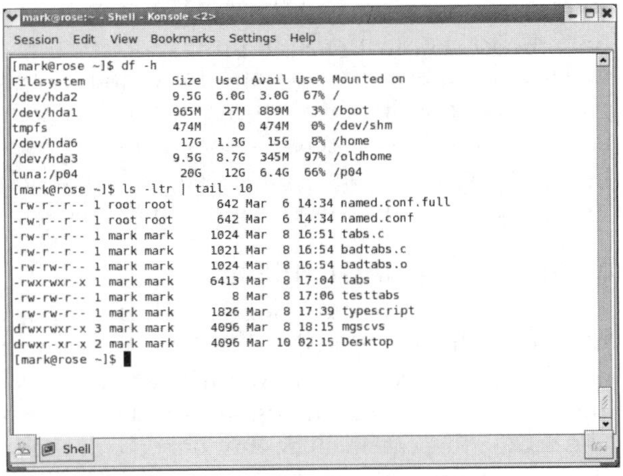

```
mark@rose:~ - Shell - Konsole <2>
Session  Edit  View  Bookmarks  Settings  Help
[mark@rose ~]$ df -h
Filesystem            Size  Used Avail Use% Mounted on
/dev/hda2             9.5G  6.0G  3.0G  67% /
/dev/hda1             965M   27M  889M   3% /boot
tmpfs                 474M     0  474M   0% /dev/shm
/dev/hda6              17G  1.3G   15G   8% /home
/dev/hda3             9.5G  8.7G  345M  97% /oldhome
tuna:/p04             20G   12G  6.4G  66% /p04
[mark@rose ~]$ ls -ltr | tail -10
-rw-r--r--  1 root root      642 Mar  6 14:34 named.conf.full
-rw-r--r--  1 root root      642 Mar  6 14:34 named.conf
-rw-r--r--  1 mark mark     1024 Mar  8 16:51 tabs.c
-rw-r--r--  1 mark mark     1021 Mar  8 16:54 badtabs.c
-rw-rw-r--  1 mark mark     1024 Mar  8 16:54 badtabs.o
-rwxrwxr-x  1 mark mark     6413 Mar  8 17:04 tabs
-rw-rw-r--  1 mark mark        8 Mar  8 17:06 testtabs
-rw-rw-r--  1 mark mark     1826 Mar  8 17:39 typescript
drwxrwxr-x  3 mark mark     4096 Mar  8 18:15 mgscvs
drwxr-xr-x  2 mark mark     4096 Mar 10 02:15 Desktop
[mark@rose ~]$
```
```
    Shell
```

Figure 4-11   A konsole terminal emulator window

managers. While GNOME has moved toward simple sophistication, giving the user a standard interface with fewer choices, KDE has emphasized configurability. If you try to configure the GNOME desktop manager, you will have fewer choices but each choice is well thought out and powerful. Some users prefer one approach; others prefer the other.

RUNNING COMMANDS FROM THE TERMINAL EMULATOR/SHELL

A *terminal emulator* is a window that functions as a textual (character-based) terminal and is displayed in a graphical environment (Figure 4-11). To open a terminal emulator window under KDE, right-click the root window (the desktop) to display the Desktop menu and select **Konsole** (*RHEL* uses **Main menu: System Tools⇨ Terminal**). Under GNOME, select **Applications: Accessories⇨Terminal** (*RHEL* uses **Applications: System Tools⇨Terminal**). Because you are already logged in and are creating a subshell in a desktop environment, you do not need to log in again. Once you have opened a terminal, try giving the command **man man** to read about the man utility (page 104), which displays Linux manual pages. Chapter 5 describes utilities that you can run from a terminal emulator.

You can run character-based programs that would normally run on a terminal in a terminal emulator window. You can also start graphical programs, such as xeyes, from this window. A graphical program opens its own window. When you run a program from GNOME or KDE, you may be asked whether you want to run the program in a terminal. When you answer **yes**, the program runs in a terminal emulator window.

When you are typing in a terminal emulator window, several characters, including *, ?, |, [, and], have special meanings. Avoid using these characters until you have read "Special Characters" on page 126.

The shell   Once you open a terminal emulator window, you are communicating with the command interpreter known as the *shell*. The shell plays an important part in much of your communication with Linux. When you enter a command at the keyboard in response to the shell prompt on the screen, the shell interprets the command and initiates the appropriate action—for example, executing a program; calling a compiler, a Linux utility, or another standard program; or displaying an error message indicating that you entered a command incorrectly. When you are working on a GUI, you bypass the shell and execute a program by clicking an icon or name. Refer to Chapter 7 for more information on the shell.

SESSION MANAGEMENT

A session starts when you log in and ends when you log out or reset the session. With a fully compliant GNOME or KDE application, these desktop managers can *session-manage* your data. When you run a managed session, the desktop looks much the same when you log in as it did when you logged out the previous time. The data in this case includes not only the data that the application manipulates but also information about the state of the application when you end your session: which windows were open and where they were located, what each of the applications was doing, and so forth.

USING KONQUEROR TO MANAGE FILES, RUN PROGRAMS, AND BROWSE THE WEB

Konqueror is the desktop tool you will probably use most often (Figure 4-12). It is similar to but more powerful than Windows (Internet) Explorer and easily morphs into a file manager, browser, and executor of many programs, both within and outside the borders of its window. Even though Konqueror is much more than a Web browser, its name indicates its place in the evolution of browsers: Navigator, Explorer, and now Konqueror, spelled with a K because it is part of KDE.[2]

Konqueror provides network transparent access, which means that it is as easy to work with files on remote systems as it is to work with local files. With Konqueror, you can copy files from or to a remote system, using the same techniques you use for copying files locally.

Because it opens an application within itself, Konqueror makes the process of clicking and viewing almost any type of file transparent. Click a PDF (Acrobat) file icon within Konqueror, and it opens the file within the Konqueror window.

The most important feature of the Web browser, the file manager, and the other faces of Konqueror is that each of these separate tools is seamlessly integrated into the same window and shares the same appearance, tools (such as bookmarks), menu system, icons, and functional characteristics. As a result, you can browse from a Web site to an FTP site, copy a file from the FTP site to the local filesystem or desktop as though you were copying it locally, and run, edit, or display the file within Konqueror or in another window.

---

2. Apple used KHTML, Konqueror's HTML rendering engine, to create its browser and continued the tradition, naming the browser Safari.

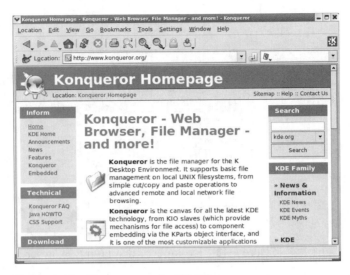

Figure 4-12   Konqueror the Web browser

Getting started   You can bring up Konqueror as a browser or a file manager, and you can switch from one to the other while you are working with it. Double-click the Home or Trash icon on the workspace to open Konqueror the file manager. Once Konqueror is open, enter a URL, such as **fedora.redhat.com,** in the location bar and press RETURN to switch Konqueror to browser mode. You can toggle the Navigation panel (the narrow subwindow on the left; see Figure 4-14 on page 97) on and off by pressing F9 or selecting **Konqueror menubar: Window⇨Show/Hide Navigation Panel.**

Because you can change the appearance and functionality of Konqueror, what your system displays may not match what is shown and described in this book.

Konqueror works with many different kinds of targets: plain files (including executable, sound, and graphical, among others), directory files, and URLs, including HTTP and FTP addresses. You select the target by clicking the target's icon within Konqueror or by entering its pathname or address in the location bar. Konqueror's reaction reflects the kind of target you select:

- **Plain file** (local or remote): If the file is executable, runs the file (see "MIME/executing files," on the next page). If it is not executable, tries to find the appropriate utility or application to open the file.

- **Directory file:** Displays the contents of the directory in a Konqueror File Manager view.

- **HTTP address:** Opens the URL in the HTML (Web) viewer, which has been loaded and embedded within the Konqueror window.

- **FTP address:** Treats a file obtained by FTP just as it would treat a local plain or directory file.

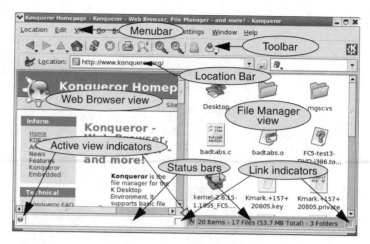

Figure 4-13   Konqueror displaying browser and File Manager views

MIME/executing files

MIME (Multipurpose Internet Mail Extension) types were originally used to describe how specific types of files that were attached to email were to be handled. Today MIME types describe how many types of files are to be handled, based on their contents or filename extensions. Both GNOME and KDE use MIME types to figure out which program to use to open a file. An example of a MIME *type* is **image/jpeg**: The MIME *group* is **image** and the MIME *subtype* is **jpeg**. This MIME type is associated with the kuickshow KDE image display utility. (Many MIME groups exist, including application, audio, image, inode, message, text, and video.)

When you click a file whose name is **sam.jpg**, KDE examines the file's *magic number* (page 1042) to determine its MIME type. If that technique fails, KDE looks at the file's filename extension—in this case, **jpg**. When KDE determines the file's MIME type is **image/jpeg**, it calls kuickshow to open the file.

optional   From the **Main menu**, select **Control Center.** When the KDE Control Center window opens, click **KDE Components** and then **Fle Associations** to display a complete list of the MIME types that KDE can work with. Be careful when making changes in this window as changes here can affect how Konqueror and other programs work with files.

Running a program

In the Konqueror location bar, enter **/usr/bin/xclock**, the pathname of an executable file that runs a graphical program. Press RETURN. After checking that you really want to run it, Konqueror runs xclock.

When you want to run a textual program, select **Main menu: Run Command** or press ALT-F2 to open the Run Command window. This window is part of KDE, not Konqueror. After entering the name of the program you want to run, click **Options**

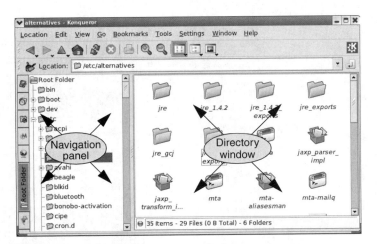

Figure 4-14   The Konqueror file manager displaying icons

and put a check mark in the box adjacent to **Run in terminal window.** For more information refer to "Run Command" on page 261.

Views   The term *view* describes a subwindow within the Konqueror window (Figure 4-13). Choose **Konqueror menubar: Window** to add and remove views in the Konqueror window. The choices in this menu always work in the *active view,* the one with a green dot at the lower-left corner (or the only view). For more information refer to "More About Views" on page 256.

Toolbar   The Konqueror toolbar (the bar with the icons in Figure 4-13) is straightforward. A right arrow at the right end of the toolbar indicates that not all the icons fit in the width of the window. Click the arrow to display (and choose from) the remaining icons.

File Manager   The Konqueror File Manager view allows you to work with the filesystem graphically (Figure 4-14). Press F9 to display the Navigation panel, which helps you navigate the filesystem. Try clicking either the root or home folder icon in the vertical stack of icons at the left of the Navigation panel. Then click a directory in the Navigation panel to display its contents in the Directory window. Double-click a file in the Directory window to execute it, display its contents, and so on, depending on the contents of the file.

CUSTOMIZING YOUR DESKTOP WITH THE KDE CONTROL CENTER

The KDE Control Center and the GNOME Desktop Preferences window present information on and allow you to control many aspects of the desktop environment. Each tool works differently. This section discusses the KDE Control Center. The gnome-control-center utility displays the GNOME Desktop Preferences

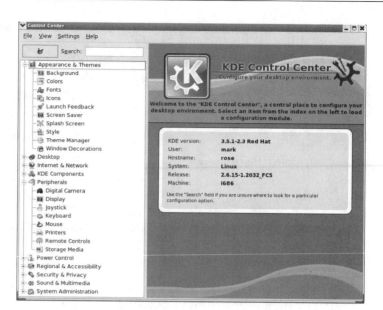

Figure 4-15 The KDE Control Center

window. Display the KDE Control Center (Figure 4-15) by choosing **Main menu: Control Center**.

The column at the left side of the KDE Control Center window displays a list of categories such as Appearance & Themes and Power Control. You may have to click the clear button (the broom and dustpan) at the top left of the column to display this list. Click on a category to expand it and display the topics within that category; click on it again to hide the topics.

When you click a topic, the KDE Control Center displays information about the topic on the right side of the window. Frequently tabs appear at the top of this information. Click the tabs, make the changes you want, and click **Apply** at the lower-right corner of the window to make your changes take effect.

Left-handed mouse | For example, you can change the setup of the mouse buttons so it is suitable for a left-handed person by clicking the plus sign in the box next to **Peripherals** to expand this category and then clicking **Mouse** (Figure 4-16). On the right side of the window, click the tab marked **General**. Under Button Order, click the radio button next to **Left handed**. Finally click the **Apply** button at the lower-right corner of the window. Now the functions of the right and left mouse buttons are reversed. See page 239 for instructions on how to perform the same function under GNOME.

If you change the setup of the mouse buttons, remember to reinterpret the descriptions in this book accordingly. When this book asks you to click the left button or does not specify a button to click, use the right button, and vice versa.

Help | Select **Help▷What's This** from the menubar; KDE adds a question mark to the mouse pointer. If you click the item you want more information on, KDE will display a brief message about this item.

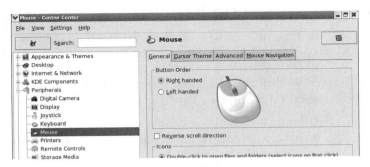

Figure 4-16   The KDE Control Center mouse topic

Administrator mode   Some topics, such as those in the System Administration category, control system functions and require Administrator mode (Superuser) access to the system to make changes. When the KDE Control Center displays the **Administrator Mode** button at the bottom of the window and items in the window are grayed out, click this button and enter the Superuser (**root**) password to display and work with these topics.

Following are brief descriptions of some of the categories and topics in the KDE Control Center.

Appearance & Themes   Controls how information is presented to the user, including desktop elements (background, colors, fonts, and icons), the screen saver, and window decorations.

Desktop   Controls how the desktop, including panels and windows, works.

Internet & Network   Controls file sharing and desktop sharing. This category includes a subcategory for setting up Web browsing with Konqueror (page 95); the subcategory controls the use of cache, cookies, plugins, stylesheets, browser identification, and other Konqueror-specific settings.

KDE Components   Configures file associations (refer to "MIME/executing files" on page 96), Konqueror's File Manager mode (page 97), KDE sessions (page 94), and KDE spell checking.

Peripherals   Controls the system monitor (display), the system keyboard and mouse, system printers, and an optional digital camera.

Power Control   Controls battery operation and monitoring for battery-powered computers.

Regional & Accessibility   Controls accessibility for disabled users, country- and language-specific settings, and the keyboard layout and shortcuts.

Security & Privacy   Controls how passwords are displayed and remembered, privacy settings, and cryptographic settings, including configuring SSL and managing certificates.

Sound & Multimedia   Controls the sound system, playing of audio CDs, the system bell, and system notifications.

System Administration   Many of the topics in this category require you to click **Administrator Mode** and enter the Superuser (**root**) password. Working as yourself, you can modify your password and perform some other tasks. Working as Superuser, you can change the system date and time, install fonts, and change the way users log in on the system.

CUSTOMIZING THE MAIN PANEL USING THE PANEL MENU

Handles   Right-clicking an icon displays the Panel Icon menu for most icons. Some icons, such as the KNotes icon and the Pager and Taskbar, display Icon context menus (page 91) when you right-click them. This type of icon has a handle. Right-click or middle-click the handle adjacent to the icon (not the icon itself) to work with the Panel Icon menu.

KDE does not display a handle until you position the mouse pointer over an icon. The handle appears to the left of its icon as a narrow vertical space with a triangle at the top and hatchmarks on its left (Figure 4-17). With the mouse pointer hovering over a handle, KDE displays a tooltip that includes the word **handle**.

Icons that display pop-up menus when you click them have an indicator that is similar to a handle. However, this indicator does not have hatchmarks and the triangle is not filled in. In addition, the tooltip displays the name of the menu and does not include the word **handle**.

Adding icons   The Panel menu provides tools to customize the panel. Right-click an icon or handle on the panel and select **Panel Menu** or right-click an empty space on the panel to display the Panel menu (Figure 4-18).

From the Panel menu you can add and remove applets and applications and configure the panel. You can also add different types of panels to the desktop. Feel free to experiment by adding icons to the panel—you cannot do any harm.

Adding applications   You can an add an application from the Main menu by clicking **Add Application to Panel** in the Panel menu, selecting an application category, and then selecting an application. For example, **Panel menu: Add Application to Panel⇨Office⇨Word Processor** adds an icon for the OpenOffice word processor to the panel.

At the top of each menu that you display by selecting **Add Application to Panel** is an **Add This Menu** selection; click it to add the entire menu to the panel. When you click the icon that adding a menu places on the panel, KDE displays a pop-up menu.

Removing icons   To remove an icon from the panel right-click the icon or handle to display the Panel Icon menu and then select **Remove**. You can also remove an icon by selecting **Remove From Panel** from the Panel menu, selecting **Applet** or **Application** from the resulting pop-up menu, and clicking the name of the icon you want to remove.

Moving icons   You can move a panel icon by clicking the icon with the middle mouse button and dragging it. For icons with handles, click and drag the handle. To cause an icon to shove aside bordering icons and not jump over them, hold the SHIFT key while dragging.

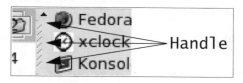

Figure 4-17   A handle

Figure 4-18   The Panel menu

Configuring the panel   The Configure Panel selection on the Panel menu displays the Configure—KDE Panel window, which determines the location, appearance, and functionality of the panel (Figure 4-19). Click the icons on the left side of the window to display pages where you can modify the panel. One icon selects the Taskbar (page 86) for modification.

Try changing the appearance or arrangement of the panel. Click **Apply** to make your changes take effect. Click **Defaults** and then **Apply** to return things to the way they were when the system was installed.

When more than one panel appears in the workspace, KDE displays a combo box labeled **Settings for** at the top of the Arrangement page. Use this combo box to specify which panel you want to work with.

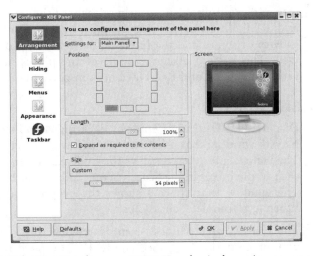

Figure 4-19   The Configure—KDE Panel window, Arrangement page

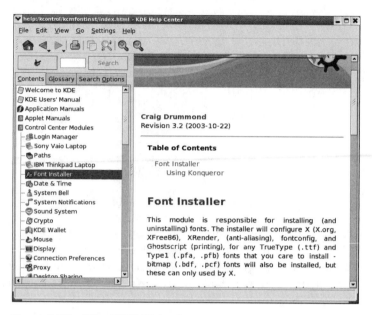

Figure 4-20   The KDE Help Center

GETTING THE FACTS: WHERE TO FIND DOCUMENTATION

Distributions of Linux, including Red Hat Linux, typically do not come with hard-copy reference manuals. However, its online documentation has always been one of Linux's strengths. The manual (or man) and info pages have been available via the man and info utilities since early releases of the operating system. Both the GNOME and KDE desktops provide graphical Help Centers. Not surprisingly, with the growth of Linux and the Internet, the sources of documentation have expanded as well. This section discusses some of the places you can look for information on Linux in general and Red Hat Linux in particular.

THE KDE HELP CENTER

Display the KDE Help Center by clicking **Main menu: Help.** If the Help Center displays a window that asks whether you want to create a search index, click **Create.** The Help Center then displays the Build Search Index window. Put a check mark in each of the boxes in the Search Scope column of this window and click **Build Index.** The window that appears shows the progress being made in building the index. When it is complete, click **Close.**

The Help Center window contains two vertical sections separated by a thin bar with hatchmarks on it. (See Figure 4-17 on page 100 for an example of a bar with similar marks.) Click the hatchmarks and drag the bar left or right to adjust the sizes of the two sections of the window.

The left side of the Help Center window contains three tabs: Contents, Glossary, and Search Options. Click the **Contents** tab to display a list of the Help Center contents

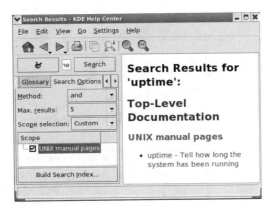

Figure 4-21   Result of a search for **uptime** in the KDE Help Center

on the left. This list includes the KDE FAQ, the KDE User's Manual, Linux (UNIX) man pages, GNU info pages, KDE Control Center modules, and more. Click an item on this list to display a list of subitems available for further exploration. Click a subitem to display that item on the right. Figure 4-20 shows the Help Center, Contents tab, displaying information on the **Control Center Modules**⇨**Font Installer**.

Clicking the **Glossary** tab displays definitions of words related to Linux sorted either alphabetically or by topic. When you click the **Search Options** tab and select one or more items from the Scope column, you can enter a word to search for in the small text box just above the tabs. Click **Search** to display the results of the search in the right portion of the window. Figure 4-21 shows the result of a search of the Linux (called UNIX in this window) manual pages for the word **uptime**.

GNOME HELP

To display the GNOME Help window (Figure 4-22), select **System: Help** (*RHEL* uses **Applications: Help**) from the panel at the top of the screen. Click topics in this window until GNOME displays the information you are looking for. Click **Command Line Help** to display man and info pages.

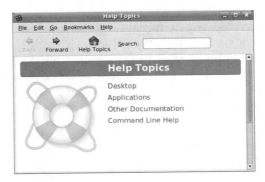

Figure 4-22   The GNOME Help window

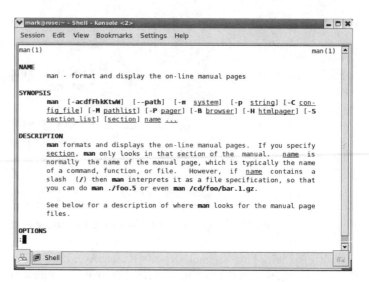

Figure 4-23   The man utility displaying information about itself

man: DISPLAYS THE SYSTEM MANUAL

In addition to the KDE Help Center and GNOME Help, the character-based man (manual) utility displays pages (man pages) from the system documentation. This documentation is helpful when you know which utility you want to use but have forgotten exactly how to use it. You can also refer to the man pages to get more information about specific topics or to determine which features are available with Linux. Because the descriptions in the system documentation are often terse, they are most helpful if you already understand the basic functions of the utility.

Because man is a character-based utility, you need to open a terminal emulator window (page 93) to run it. You can also log in on a virtual terminal (page 113) and run the utility from there.

To find out more about a utility, give the command **man**, followed by the name of the utility. Figure 4-23 shows man displaying information about itself, after the user entered a **man man** command.

less (pager)   The man utility automatically sends its output through a *pager*—usually less (page 128), which displays a file one screen at a time. When you access a manual page in this manner, less displays a prompt (:) at the bottom of the screen after each screen of text and waits for you to request another screen by pressing the SPACE bar. Pressing **h** (help) displays a list of less commands. Pressing **q** (quit) stops less and causes the shell to display a prompt. You can search for topics covered by man pages by using the apropos utility (page 145).

Based on the FHS (Filesystem Hierarchy Standard, page 176), the Linux system manual and the man pages are divided into ten sections. Each section describes related tools:

1. User Commands

2. System Calls

3. Subroutines

4. Devices

5. File Formats

6. Games

7. Miscellaneous

8. System Administration

9. Kernel

10. New

This layout closely mimics the way the set of UNIX manuals has always been divided. Unless you specify a manual section, man displays the earliest occurrence in the manual of the word you specify on the command line. Most users find the information they need in sections 1, 6, and 7; programmers and system administrators frequently need to consult the other sections.

You can use Konqueror to view man and info pages

tip You can view man and info pages by entering, for example, **man:cat** or **info:cat** in Konqueror's location bar (Figure 4-13, page 96) or in the Run Command box (page 96). The KDE Help Center also offers direct access to these pages as UNIX manual pages. GNOME Help refers to them as Command Line Help.

In some cases the manual contains entries for different tools with the same name. For example, the following command displays the man page for the write utility (page 150) from section 1 of the system manual:

```
$ man write
```

To see the man page for the **write** system call from section 2, enter

```
$ man 2 write
```

The preceding command instructs man to look only in section 2 for the man page. Use the –a option (see the adjacent tip) to view all man pages for a given subject (press **q** to move to the next man page). For example, give the command **man –a write** to view all man pages for write.

Options

tip An option modifies the way a utility or command works. Options are usually specified as one or more letters that are preceded by one or two hyphens. The option appears following the name of the utility you are calling and a SPACE. Other *arguments* (page 1019) to the command follow the option and a SPACE. For more information refer to "Options" on page 203.

man **and** info **display different information**

tip   The info utility displays more complete and up-to-date information on GNU utilities than does man. When a man page displays abbreviated information on a utility that is covered by info, the man page refers you to info. The man utility frequently displays the only information available on non-GNU utilities. When info displays information on non-GNU utilities, it is frequently a copy of the man page.

info: DISPLAYS INFORMATION ABOUT UTILITIES

The character-based info utility is a menu-based hypertext system developed by the GNU project (page 2) and distributed with Red Hat Linux. The info utility includes a tutorial on itself (go to www.gnu.org/software/texinfo/manual/info or give the command **info info**) and documentation on many Linux shells, utilities, and programs developed by the GNU project. Figure 4-24 shows the screen that info displays when you give the command **info**.

Because the information on this screen is drawn from an editable file, your display may differ from those shown in this section. When you see the initial info screen, you can press any of the following keys or key combinations:

- **h** to go through an interactive tutorial on info

- **?** to list info commands

- SPACE to scroll through the menu of items for which information is available

- **m** followed by the name of the menu you want to display or a SPACE to display a list of menus

- **q** or CONTROL-C to quit

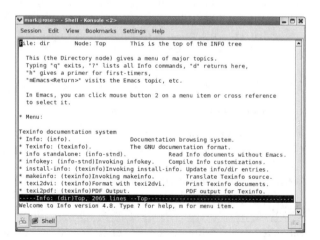

Figure 4-24   The first screen that info displays

The notation info uses to describe keyboard keys may not be familiar to you. The notation **C-h** is the same as CONTROL-H. Similarly **M-x** means hold down the META or ALT key and press **x**. (On some systems you need to press ESCAPE and then **x** to duplicate the function of META-x.)

You may find pinfo **easier to use than** info

tip The pinfo utility is similar to info but is more intuitive if you are not familiar with the emacs editor. This utility runs in a textual environment, as does info. When it is available, pinfo uses color to make its interface easier to use.

After giving the command **info**, press the SPACE bar a few times to scroll through the display. Figure 4-25 shows the entry for sleep. The asterisk at the left end of the line means that this entry is a menu item. Following the asterisk is the name of the menu item, a colon, the name of the package (in parentheses) that the menu item belongs to, other information, and a description of the item on the right. In most cases the package name corresponds to the name of the rpm package (page 487) that contains the item. Figure 4-25 shows that the sleep utility is part of the **coreutils** package.

Each menu item is a link to the info page that describes the item. To jump to that page, move the cursor to the line containing the menu item and press RETURN. Alternatively, you can type the name of the menu item in a menu command to view the information. To display information on sleep, for example, you can give the command **m sleep**, followed by RETURN. When you type **m** (for *menu*), the cursor moves to the bottom line of the screen and displays **Menu item:**. Typing **sleep** displays **sleep** on that line, and pressing RETURN displays information about the menu item you have chosen.

Figure 4-26 shows the *top node* of information on sleep. A node is one group of information that you can scroll through with the SPACE bar. To display the next node,

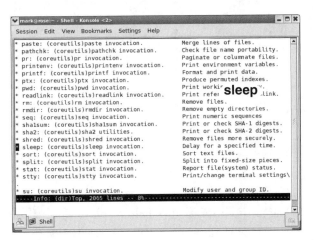

Figure 4-25   The screen that info displays after you press the SPACE bar a few times

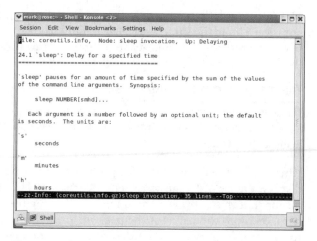

Figure 4-26   The info page on the sleep utility

press **n**. Press **p** to display the previous node. You can always press **d** to display the initial menu (Figure 4-24).

As you read through this book and learn about new utilities, you can use man or info to find out more about the utilities. If you can print PostScript documents, you can print a manual page with the man utility using the **–t** option (for example, **man –t cat | lpr** prints information about the cat utility). you can also use a browser to display the documentation at www.tldp.org, fedora.redhat.com/docs, fedoraproject.org/wiki/Docs, or www.redhat.com and then print the desired information from the browser.

THE ––help OPTION

Another tool you can use in a textual environment is the **––help** option. Most GNU utilities provide a **––help** option that displays information about the utility. Non-GNU utilities may use a **–h** or **–help** option to display Help information.

```
$ cat --help
Usage: cat [OPTION] [FILE]...
Concatenate FILE(s), or standard input, to standard output.

  -A, --show-all          equivalent to -vET
  -b, --number-nonblank   number nonblank output lines
  -e                      equivalent to -vE
  -E, --show-ends         display $ at end of each line
  ...
```

If the information that **––help** displays runs off the screen, send the output through the less pager (page 104) using a pipe (page 52):

```
$ ls --help | less
```

HOWTOs: FINDING OUT HOW THINGS WORK

A HOWTO document explains in detail how to do something related to Linux—from setting up a specialized piece of hardware to performing a system administration task to setting up specific networking software. Mini-HOWTOs offer shorter explanations. As with Linux software, one person or a few people generally are responsible for a HOWTO document, but many people may contribute to it.

The Linux Documentation Project (LDP, page 110) site houses most HOWTO and mini-HOWTO documents. Use a browser to go to www.tldp.org, click **HOWTOs**, and pick the index you want to use to find a HOWTO or mini-HOWTO. You can also use the LDP search feature on its home page to find HOWTOs and more.

GETTING HELP WITH THE SYSTEM

KDE and GNOME provide similar Help facilities. Each provides tooltips (page 86), a context-sensitive Help system, and the Help systems discussed on pages 102 and 103.

FINDING HELP LOCALLY

The **/usr/src/linux/Documentation** (present only if you installed the kernel source code as explained in Chapter 15) and **/usr/share/doc** directories often contain more detailed and different information about a utility than man or info provides. Frequently this information is meant for people who will be compiling and modifying the utility, not just using it. These directories hold thousands of files, each containing information on a separate topic.

USING THE INTERNET TO GET HELP

The Internet provides many helpful sites related to Linux. Aside from sites that carry various forms of documentation, you can enter an error message that you are having a problem with in a search engine such as Google (www.google.com, or its Linux-specific version at www.google.com/linux). Enclose the error message within double quotation marks to improve the quality of the results. The search will likely yield a post concerning your problem and suggestions about how to solve it. See Figure 4-27 on the next page.

The Red Hat Web site The Red Hat and Fedora Web sites are rich sources of information. The following list identifies of some locations that may be of interest:

- Manuals for Red Hat Linux through Red Hat Linux 9 and *RHEL* are available at www.redhat.com/docs.

- Various types of support documents and support are available at www.redhat.com/apps/support.

- You can query the Red Hat Knowledgebase (requires free registration) at kbase.redhat.com.

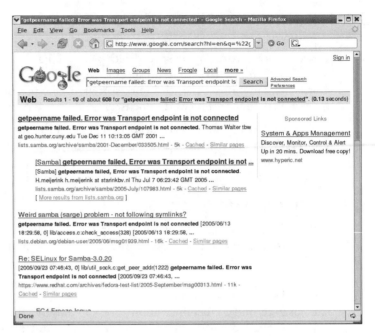

Figure 4-27   Google reporting on an error message

- *FEDORA* documentation is available at fedora.redhat.com/docs, and fedoraproject.org (click **Documentation**).

- *RHEL+FEDORA* The home pages (www.redhat.com, fedora.redhat.com, and fedoraproject.org), have a wealth of information.

- *RHEL+FEDORA* support forums are online discussions about any Red Hat–related issues that people want to raise. One forum is dedicated to new users; others to Apache, the X Window System, and so on. Go to www.redhat.com/mailman/listinfo to browse the lists. Another site that has similar, useful information is fedoraforum.org.

- *FEDORA* information is available at fedoranews.org.

- *RHEL* hardware help is available from the Red Hat hardware catalog at hardware.redhat.com. The hardware that *FEDORA* supports is mostly a superset of that supported by *RHEL*.

GNU   GNU manuals are available at www.gnu.org/manual. In addition, you can visit the GNU home page (www.gnu.org) for more documentation and other GNU resources. Many of the GNU pages and resources are available in a wide variety of languages.

The Linux
Documentation
Project   The Linux Documentation Project (www.tldp.org), which has been around for almost as long as Linux, houses a complete collection of guides, HOWTOs, FAQs, man pages, and Linux magazines. The home page is available in English, Portuguese,

Figure 4-28   The Linux Documentation Project home page

Spanish, Italian, Korean, and French. It is easy to use and supports local text searches. It also provides a complete set of links (Figure 4-28) that you can use to find almost anything you want that is related to Linux (click **Links** in the Search box or go to www.tldp.org/links). The links page includes sections on general information, events, getting started, user groups, mailing lists, and newsgroups, with each section containing many subsections.

More About Logging In

Refer to "Logging In on the System" on page 83 for information about logging in on the system and changing your default desktop environment (KDE or GNOME).

Always use a password

security   Unless you are the only user of a system; the system is not connected to any other systems, the Internet, or a modem; and you are the only one with physical access to the system, it is poor practice to allow any user to log in without a password.

The Login Screen

Four icon/word buttons appear below the Username/Password text box on the Login screen. Click these icons to change aspects of the session you are about to log in to. You can also press F10 to display a pop-up menu with similar choices.

- **Language**   Displays a window from which you can select the language for the session you are about to start. This change affects window titles, prompts, error messages, and other textual items displayed by GNOME, KDE, and many applications. Just after you log in, the system asks whether you want to make this change in languages permanent or if it is a one-time change.

- **Session**   Displays the Sessions dialog box, which presents several choices concerning the session you are about to start. Choose one of the following, click **OK**, and continue logging in:

    - **Last Session**   Brings up the same desktop environment you used the last time you logged in.

    - **Default System Session**   Brings up the default desktop environment.

    - **GNOME**   Brings up the GNOME desktop environment.

    - **KDE**   Brings up the KDE Desktop Environment.

    - **Failsafe GNOME**   Brings up a default GNOME session without running any startup scripts. Use this choice to fix problems that prevent you from logging in normally.

    - **Failsafe Terminal**   Brings up an xterm terminal emulator window without a desktop manager and without running any startup scripts. This setup allows you to log in on a minimal desktop when your standard login does not work well enough to allow you to log in to fix a login problem. Give the command **exit** from the xterm window to log out and display the Login screen.

RHEL   Any changes you make in the Sessions dialog box affect the current session only. The next time you log in, you will revert to your default desktop environment (KDE or GNOME). After you log in, use switchdesk (page 116) to change your default desktop environment.

FEDORA   Just after you log in, the system asks whether the change made in the Sessions dialog box is just for this session or if you want to make it permanent. The failsafe logins do not ask this question.

- **Restart**   Shuts down and reboots the system.

- **Shutdown**   Shuts down the system and turns off the power.

WHAT TO DO IF YOU CANNOT LOG IN

If you enter either your username or password incorrectly, the system displays an error message after you enter *both* your username *and* your password. This message indicates that you have entered either the username or the password incorrectly or that they are not valid. It does not differentiate between an unacceptable username and an unacceptable password—a strategy meant to discourage unauthorized people from guessing names and passwords to gain access to the system. Here are some common reasons why logins fail:

- **The username and password are case sensitive.** Make sure the CAPS LOCK key is off and that you enter your username and password exactly as specified or as you set them up.

- **You are not logging in on the right machine.** The login/password combination may not be valid if you are trying to log in on the wrong machine. On a larger, networked system, you may have to specify the machine that you want to connect to before you can log in.

- **Make sure your username is valid.** The login/password combination may not be valid if you have not been set up as a user. If you are the system administrator, refer to "Configuring User and Group Accounts" on page 538. Otherwise, check with the system administrator.

Refer to "Changing Your Password" on page 114 when you want to change your password.

LOGGING OUT

To log out of a KDE graphical environment, click the red hat or Fedora logo at the lower-left corner of the display and choose **Logout** from the pop-up menu. From GNOME, select **System** or **Actions** from the panel at the top of the screen and click **Log Out**. From a textual environment, press CONTROL-D or give the command **exit** in response to the shell prompt.

USING VIRTUAL CONSOLES

When running Linux on a personal computer, you frequently work with the display and keyboard attached to the computer. Using this physical console, you can access as many as 63 *virtual consoles* (also called *virtual terminals*). Some are set up to allow logins; others act as graphical displays. To switch between virtual consoles, hold the CONTROL and ALT keys down and press the function key that corresponds to the console you want to view. For example, CONTROL-ALT-F5 displays the fifth virtual console. This book refers to the console that you see when you first boot a system (or press CONTROL-ALT-F1) as the *system console* (or just *console*).

By default, six virtual consoles are active and have text login sessions running. When you want to use both textual and graphical interfaces, you can set up a textual session on one virtual console and a graphical session on another. No matter which virtual console you start a graphical session from, the graphical session runs on the first unused virtual console (number seven by default).

LOGGING IN REMOTELY: TERMINAL EMULATION AND ssh OR telnet

When you are not using a console, terminal, or other device connected directly to the Linux system you are logging in on, you are probably connected to the Linux system using terminal emulation software on another system. Running on your local computer, this software connects to the Linux system via a network (Ethernet, asynchronous phone line, PPP, or other type) and allows you to log in on the Linux machine.

Make sure **TERM** is set correctly

tip No matter how you connect, make sure you have the **TERM** variable set to the type of terminal your emulator is emulating. For more information refer to "Specifying a Terminal" on page 984.

When you log in via a dial-up line, the connection is straightforward: You instruct the emulator program to contact the computer, it dials the phone, and you get a login prompt from the remote system. When you log in via a directly connected network, you use ssh (secure, page 585) or telnet (not secure, page 363) to connect to the computer. The ssh program has been implemented on many machines, not just on Linux systems. Many user interfaces to ssh include a terminal emulator. From an Apple, PC, or UNIX machine, open the program that runs ssh and give it the name or IP address (refer to "Host Address" on page 353) of the system you want to log in on. For examples and more detail on working with a terminal emulator, refer to "Running Commands from the Terminal Emulator/Shell" on page 93. For more information about logging in from a terminal emulator, see "Logging In on a Terminal" on page 116.

CHANGING YOUR PASSWORD

If someone else initially assigned your password, it is a good idea to give yourself a new one. A good password is seven or eight characters long and contains a combination of numbers, uppercase and lowercase letters, and punctuation characters. Avoid using control characters (such as CONTROL-H) because they may have a special meaning to the system, making it impossible for you to log in. Do not use names, words from English or other languages, or other familiar words that someone can easily guess.

For security reasons none of the passwords you enter is displayed by any utility.

Protect your password

security Do not allow someone to find out your password: *Do not* put your password in a file that is not encrypted, allow someone to watch you type your password, or give your password to someone you do not know (a system administrator never needs to know your password). You can always write your password down and keep it in a safe, private place.

Choose a password that is difficult to guess

security Do not use phone numbers, names of pets or kids, birthdays, words from a dictionary (not even a foreign language), and so forth. Do not use permutations of these items.

Differentiate between important and less important passwords

security It is a good idea to differentiate between important and less important passwords. For example, Web site passwords for blogs or download access are not very important; it is not bad if you choose the same password for these types of sites. However, your login, mail server, and bank account Web site passwords are critical: Never use these passwords for an unimportant Web site.

To change your password from a terminal emulator or other command line, give the command **passwd**. To change your password from KDE, select **Main menu: Settings⇨Password** (*RHEL* uses **Main menu: Preferences⇨Password**). From GNOME select **System: Preferences⇨About Me** and click **Change Password** (*RHEL* uses **Applications: Preferences⇨Password**).

The first item the system asks for is your current (old) password. This password is verified to ensure that an unauthorized user is not trying to alter your password. The system then requests the new password.

A password should meet the following criteria to be relatively secure. Only the first item is mandatory.

- It must be at least six characters long (or longer if the system administrator sets it up that way).

- It should not be a word in a dictionary of any language, no matter how seemingly obscure.

- It should not be the name of a person, place, pet, or other thing that might be discovered easily.

- It should contain at least two letters and one digit.

- It should not be your username, the reverse of your username, or your username shifted by one or more characters.

- If you are changing your password, the new password should differ from the old one by at least three characters. Changing the case of a character does not make it count as a different character.

Refer to "Keeping the System Secure" on page 556 for more information about choosing a password.

After you enter your new password, the system asks you to retype it to make sure you did not make a mistake when you entered it the first time. If the new password is the same both times you enter it, your password is changed. If the passwords differ, then you made an error in one of them. In this situation the system displays an error message or does not allow you to click the **OK** button.

If the password you enter is not long enough, the system displays the following message:

```
BAD PASSWORD: it is too short
```

If it is too simple, the system displays this message:

```
BAD PASSWORD: it is too simplistic/systematic
```

If the password is formed from words, the system displays this message:

```
BAD PASSWORD: it is based on a dictionary word
```

If the system displays one of these messages, enter a longer or more complex password in response to the **New UNIX password:** prompt.

When you successfully change your password, you change the way you log in. If you forget your password, Superuser can change it and tell you the new password.

switchdesk: CHANGES YOUR DEFAULT DESKTOP

RHEL The switchdesk utility tells the system which desktop you want to log in to by default: KDE or GNOME. Initially your account is set up to log in to GNOME by default. To use switchdesk, give the command **switchdesk** followed by the name of the desktop you want to be the default (**gnome** or **kde**).

FEDORA The switchdesk utility is not installed by default because it is not needed. It is part of the **switchdesk** package.

LOGGING IN ON A TERMINAL

Before you log in on a terminal, terminal emulator, or other textual device, the system displays a message called *issue* (stored in the **/etc/issue** file) that identifies the version of Red Hat Linux running on the system. A sample issue message follows:

```
Fedora Core release 5 (Bordeaux)
Kernel 2.6.15-1.2054_FC5 on an i686
```

The issue message is followed by a prompt to log in. Enter your username and password in response to the system prompts. If you are using a *terminal* (page 1059) and your screen does not display the **login:** prompt, check whether the terminal is plugged in and turned on, and then press the RETURN key a few times. If **login:** still does not appear, try pressing CONTROL-Q. If you are using a *workstation* (page 1064), make sure it is running. Run ssh (page 585), telnet (page 363), or whatever communications/emulation software you have to log in on the system. Try logging in, making sure that you enter your username and password as they were specified when your account was set up; the routine that verifies the username and password is case sensitive.

Did you log in last?

security As you are logging in to a textual environment, after you enter your username and password, the system displays information about the last login on this account, showing when it took place and where it originated. You can use this information to determine whether anyone else has accessed the account since you last used it. If someone has, perhaps an unauthorized user has learned your password and logged on as you. In the interest of security, advise the system administrator of any circumstances that make you suspicious and change your password (page 114).

Next the *shell prompt* (or just *prompt*) appears, indicating that you have successfully logged in; it indicates that the system is ready for you to give a command. The first shell prompt line may be preceded by a short message called the *message of the day,* or **motd** (page 453), which is stored in the **/etc/motd** file. The usual prompt is a dollar sign ($). Red Hat Linux establishes a prompt of *[user@host directory]$*, where *user* is your username, *host* is the name of the local system, and *directory* is the name of the directory you are working in. For information on how to change the prompt, refer to page 293.

BRINGING A GUI UP FROM A CHARACTER-BASED DISPLAY

By default, Red Hat systems present a graphical interface when they first come up. If the system comes up with a textual interface, you can log in on a virtual console and start a graphical display by giving the following command to bring up your default desktop environment:

```
$ startx
```

If startx does not work, run system-config-display (page 70) to set up the graphics card and monitor configuration for the X Window System.

CORRECTING MISTAKES

This section explains how to correct typographical and other errors you may make while you are logged in on a character-based display (either a virtual console or a terminal emulator). Because the shell and most other utilities do not interpret the command line or other text until after you press RETURN, you can readily correct typing mistakes before you press RETURN.

You can correct typing mistakes in several ways: erase one character at a time, back up a word at a time, or back up to the beginning of the command line in one step. After you press RETURN, it is too late to correct a mistake: You must either wait for the command to run to completion or abort execution of the program (page 118).

ERASING A CHARACTER

While entering characters from the keyboard, you can back up and erase a mistake by pressing the *erase key* once for each character you want to delete. The erase key backs over as many characters as you wish. It does not, in general, back up past the beginning of the line.

The default erase key is BACKSPACE. If this key does not work, try DELETE or CONTROL-H. If these keys do not work, give the following stty[3] command to set the erase and line kill (see "Deleting a Line" on the next page) keys to their default values:

```
$ stty ek
```

DELETING A WORD

You can delete a word you entered by pressing CONTROL-W. A *word* is any sequence of characters that does not contain a SPACE or TAB. When you press CONTROL-W, the cursor moves left to the beginning of the current word (as you are entering a word) or the previous word (when you have just entered a SPACE or TAB), removing the word.

---

3. The command stty is an abbreviation for *set teletypewriter*, the first terminal that UNIX was run on. Today stty is commonly thought of as *set terminal*.

CONTROL-Z **suspends a program**

tip   Although it is not a way of correcting a mistake, you may press the suspend key (typically CONTROL-Z) by mistake and wonder what happened (you will see a message containing the word **Stopped**). You have just stopped your job, using job control (page 280). Give the command **fg** to continue your job in the foreground, and you should return to where you were before you pressed the suspend key. For more information refer to "bg: Sends a Job to the Background" on page 281.

DELETING A LINE

Any time before you press RETURN, you can delete the line you are entering by pressing the *line kill key* (or *kill key*). When you press this key, the cursor moves to the left, erasing characters as it goes, back to the beginning of the line. The default line kill key is CONTROL-U. If this key does not work, try CONTROL-X. If these keys do not work, give the following command to set the erase and line kill keys to their default values:

```
$ stty ek
```

ABORTING EXECUTION

Sometimes you may want to terminate a running program. For example, you may want to stop a program that is performing a lengthy task such as displaying the contents of a file that is several hundred pages long or copying a file that is not the one you meant to copy.

To terminate a program from a character-based display, press the *interrupt key* (CONTROL-C or sometimes DELETE or DEL). When you press this key, the Linux operating system sends a terminal interrupt signal to the program you are running and to the shell. Exactly what effect this signal has depends on the particular program. Some programs stop execution immediately, some ignore the signal, and some take other actions. When it receives a terminal interrupt signal, the shell displays a prompt and waits for another command.

If these methods do not terminate the program, try stopping the program with the suspend key (typically CONTROL-Z), giving the **jobs** command to verify the job number of the program, and using **kill** to abort the program. The job number is the number within the brackets at the left end of the line that **jobs** displays ([1]). The **kill** command (page 395) uses **–TERM** to send a termination signal[4] to the job specified by the job number, which is preceded by a percent sign (**%1**):

```
$ bigjob
^Z
[1]+  Stopped                 bigjob
$ jobs
[1]+  Stopped                 bigjob
$ kill -TERM %1
$ RETURN
[1]+  Killed                  bigjob
```

---

4. When the terminal interrupt signal does not work, use the kill (–KILL) signal. A running program cannot ignore a kill signal; it is sure to abort the program (page 395).

The **kill** command returns a prompt; press RETURN again to see the confirmation message. For more information on job control, refer to "Running a Program in the Background" on page 219.

Killing a job that is running under a GUI is straightforward. At the upper-right corner of most windows is a button with an **x** on it (the **close** button in Figure 4-8 on page 89). Move the mouse pointer so that its tip is over the **x**. If you leave the mouse stationary for a moment, instructions on how to kill the window appear. With the mouse pointer over the **x**, kill the window by clicking the left mouse button. You may need to click several times.

Repeating/Editing Command Lines

To repeat a previously given command, press the UP ARROW key. Each time you press it, the shell displays an earlier command line. To reexecute the displayed command line, press RETURN. Press DOWN ARROW to browse through the command lines in the other direction.

The RIGHT and LEFT ARROW keys move the cursor back and forth along the displayed command line. At any point along the command line, you can add characters by typing them. Use the erase key to remove characters from the command line.

For information about more complex command line editing, see page 304.

optional

Controlling Windows: Advanced Operations

Refer to "Controlling Windows" on page 88 for an introduction to working with windows under Red Hat Linux. This section explores changing the input focus on the desktop, changing the resolution of the display, and understanding the window manager.

Changing the Input Focus

When you type on the keyboard, the window manager (page 121) directs the characters you type somewhere, usually to a window. The *active window* (the window accepting input from the keyboard) is said to have the *input focus*. Depending on how you set up your account, you can use the mouse in one of three ways to change the input focus (you can also use the keyboard; see page 90):

- **Click-to-focus** (*explicit focus*) Gives the input focus to a window when you click the window. That window continues to accept input from the keyboard regardless of the position of the mouse pointer. The window loses the focus when you click another window. Although clicking the middle or the right mouse button also activates a window, use only the left mouse button for this purpose; other buttons may have unexpected effects when you use them to activate a window.

- **Focus-follows-mouse** (*sloppy focus, point to give focus,* or *enter-only*) Gives the input focus to a window when you move the mouse pointer onto the window. That window maintains the input focus until you move the mouse pointer onto another window, at which point the new window gets the focus. Specifically, when you move the mouse pointer off a window and onto the root window, the window that had the focus does not lose it.

- **Focus-under-mouse**   Same as focus-follows-mouse (KDE).

- **Focus-strictly-under-mouse** (*enter-exit*)   Gives the input focus to a window when you move the mouse pointer onto the window. That window maintains the input focus until you move the mouse pointer off the window with the focus, at which point no window has the focus. Specifically, when you move the mouse pointer off a window and onto the root window, the window that had the focus loses it, and input from the keyboard is lost.

GNOME   Under GNOME select **System: Preferences⇨Windows** (*RHEL* uses **Applications: Preferences⇨Windows**) to change the focus policy. Put a mark in the check box next to **Select windows when the mouse moves over them** to select the focus-follows-mouse policy. When there is no mark in this check box, click-to-focus is in effect. Click **Close**.

KDE   Under KDE use the KDE Control Center to change the focus policy: Select **Main menu: Control Center**; from the KDE Control Center select **Desktop⇨Window Behavior** and choose the desired focus policy. Click **Apply**.

To determine which window has the input focus, compare the window borders. The border color of the active window is different from the others or, on a monochrome display, is darker. Another indication that a window is active is that the keyboard cursor is a solid rectangle there; in windows that are not active, the cursor is an outline of a rectangle.

Use the following tests to determine which keyboard focus method you are using. If you position the mouse pointer in a window and that window does not get the input focus, your window manager is configured to use the click-to-focus method. If the border of the window changes, you are using the focus-follows-mouse/focus-under-mouse or focus-strictly-under-mouse method. To determine which of the latter methods you are using, start typing something, with the mouse pointer positioned on the active window. Then move the mouse pointer over the root window and continue typing. If characters continue to appear within the window, you are using focus-follows-mouse/focus-under-mouse. Otherwise, you are using focus-strictly-under-mouse.

CHANGING THE RESOLUTION OF THE DISPLAY

The X server (the basis for the Linux graphical interface, see page 234) starts at a specific display resolution and color depth. Although you can change the color depth only when you start an X server, you can change the resolution while the X server is running. The number of resolutions available depends both on the display hardware and on the configuration of the X server (see page 70 for details). Many users prefer to do most of their work at a higher resolution but might want to switch to a lower resolution for some tasks, such as playing games. You can switch between different display resolutions by pressing either CONTROL-ALT-KEYPAD-+ or CONTROL-ALT-KEYPAD--, using the + and - on the keyboard's numeric keypad.

Changing to a lower resolution has the effect of zooming in on the display; as a result, you may no longer be able to view the entire workspace at once. You can scroll the display by pushing the mouse pointer against the edge of the screen.

THE WINDOW MANAGER

A *window manager*—the program that controls the look and feel of the basic GUI—runs under a desktop manager (typically KDE or GNOME) and controls all aspects of the windows in the X Window System environment. The window manager defines the appearance of the windows on the desktop and controls how you operate and position them: open, close, move, resize, iconify, and so on. It may also handle some session management functions, such as how a session is paused, resumed, restarted, or ended (page 94).

A window manager controls *window decorations*—that is, the titlebar and border of a window. Aside from the aesthetic aspects of changing window decorations, you can alter their functionality by modifying the number and placement of buttons on the titlebar.

The window manager takes care of window manipulation so that the client programs do not need to. This setup is very different from that of many other operating systems, and the way that GNOME and KDE deal with window managers is different from how other desktop environments work. Window managers do more than simply manage windows—they provide a useful, good-looking, graphical shell to work from. Their open design allows users to define their own policy down to the fine details.

Theoretically GNOME and KDE are not dependent on any particular window manager and can work with any of several window managers. Because of their flexibility, you would not see major parts of the desktop environment change if you were to switch from one window manager to another. These desktop managers collaborate with the window manager to make your work environment intuitive and easy to use. Although the desktop manager does not control window placement, it does get information from the window manager about window placement.

RED HAT LINUX WINDOW MANAGERS

Metacity, the default window manager for GNOME, provides window management and starts many components through GNOME panel commands. It also communicates with and facilitates access to other components in the environment. The kwin window manager is the default window manager for KDE.

Using the standard X libraries, programmers have created other window managers including **blackbox**, **fluxbox**, **wmx**, and **WindowMaker**. Under *FEDORA* you can use yum (page 478) to install any of these packages.

USING A WINDOW MANAGER WITHOUT A DESKTOP MANAGER

It is interesting to see exactly where the line that separates the window manager and the desktop manager falls. Toward this end, you can run the Failsafe Terminal from the Login screen: Specify **Session**⇨**Failsafe Terminal** and log in. You should see a clean screen with an undecorated window running xterm. You can give commands from this window to open other windows. Try xeyes, xterm, and xclock. Give the command **exit** to return to the Login screen.

CHAPTER SUMMARY

As with many operating systems, your access to a Linux system is authorized when you log in. You enter your username on the Login screen, followed by your password. You can change your password anytime while you are logged in. Choose a password that is difficult to guess and that conforms to the criteria imposed by the utility that changes your password.

The system administrator is responsible for maintaining the system. On a single-user system, you are the system administrator. On a small, multiuser system, you or another user may act as the system administrator, or this job may be shared. On a large, multiuser system or network of systems, there is frequently a full-time system administrator. When extra privileges are required to perform certain system tasks, the system administrator logs in as the **root** user by entering the username **root** and the **root** password; this user is called Superuser or administrator. On a multiuser system, several trusted users may be given the **root** password.

Do not work as Superuser as a matter of course. When you have to do something that requires Superuser privileges, work as Superuser for only as long as absolutely necessary; revert to working as yourself as soon as possible.

Understanding the desktop and its components is essential to getting the most out of the system. The Main panel offers a convenient way to launch applications, either by clicking icons or by using the Main menu. The Main menu is a multilevel menu that you can use to maintain the system and to start many of the most common applications on the system. A window is the graphical manifestation of an application. You can control its size, location, and appearance by clicking buttons on the window's titlebar. A terminal emulator allows you to use the Linux command line interface from a graphical environment. You can use a terminal emulator to launch both textual and graphical programs.

Konqueror is a multipurpose tool—one of the most important on the desktop. You can use it to run programs, browse the Web, and manage files. Konqueror is transparent to the network: You can work with local or remote files and not be aware of the difference. Konqueror's power derives from the seamless integration of its functions.

The KDE Control Center provides a way of setting and changing many characteristics of KDE and kwin, the KDE window manager. Using the KDE Control Center, you can control Web and file browsing with Konqueror, the look and feel of your desktop, the sound component of the system, network aspects of the desktop, and personalization of the desktop, including options that make it easier for people with special needs to use. For Superuser, the KDE Control Center contains a system administration module.

The man utility provides online documentation for system utilities. This utility is helpful both to new Linux users and to experienced users who must often delve into the system documentation for information on the finer points of a utility's behavior. The info utility helps the beginner and the expert alike. It includes a tutorial on its use and documentation on many Linux utilities.

EXERCISES

1. The system displays the following message when you attempt to log in with an incorrect username *or* an incorrect password:

   ```
   Incorrect username or password. Letters must be typed in the correct
   case.
   ```

   This message does not indicate whether your username, your password, or both are invalid. Why does it not reveal this information?

2. Give three examples of poor password choices. What is wrong with each? Include one that is too short. Give the error message displayed by the system in each situation.

3. Is **fido** an acceptable password? Give several reasons why or why not.

4. What is a context menu? How does a context menu differ from other menus?

5. What appears when you right-click the root window? How can you use this object?

6. Where is the **Main menu** button, and what does it look like? Why is it an important tool (KDE only)?

7. What is the primary function of the Main menu?

8. What is the input focus? When no window has the input focus, what happens to the letters you type on the keyboard? Which type of input focus would you prefer to work with? Why?

9. What are the functions of a Window Operations menu? How do you display this menu?

10. What is the Main panel? What does your Main panel show you, and what can you do with it? What do the Pager and Taskbar applets do?

11. What are tooltips? How are they useful?

ADVANCED EXERCISES

12. What change does the mouse pointer undergo when you move it to the edge of a window? What happens when you right-click and drag the mouse pointer when it looks like this? Repeat this experiment with the mouse pointer at the corner of a window.

13. Try the experiment described in "Using a Window Manager Without a Desktop Manager" on page 122. What is missing from the screen? Based only on what you see, describe what a window manager does. How does a desktop manager make it easier to work with a GUI?

14. When the characters you type do not appear on the screen, what might be wrong? How can you fix this problem?

15. What happens when you run vim from the Run Command window without specifying that it be run in a terminal? Where does the output go?

16. The example on page 105 shows that the man pages for write appear in sections 1 and 2 of the system manual. Explain how you can use man to determine which sections of the system manual contain a manual page with a given name.

17. How many man pages are in the **Devices** subsection of the system manual? (*Hint:* **Devices** is a subsection of **Special Files**.)

5

THE LINUX UTILITIES

When Linus Torvalds introduced Linux and for a long time thereafter, Linux did not have a graphical user interface (GUI): It ran on character-based terminals only. All the tools ran from a command line. Today the Linux GUI is important but many people—especially system administrators—run many command line programs. Command line utilities are often faster, more powerful, or more complete than their GUI counterparts. Sometimes there is no GUI counterpart to a textual utility; some people just prefer the hands-on feeling of the command line.

When you work with a command line interface, you are working with a shell (Chapters 7, 9, and 28). Before you start working with a shell, it is important that you understand something about the characters that are special to the shell, so this chapter starts with a discussion of special characters. The chapter then describes five basic utilities: ls, cat, rm, less, and hostname. It continues by describing several other file manipulation utilities as well as utilities that find out who is logged in; that communicate with other users; that print, compress, and decompress files; and that pack and unpack archive files.

> **Run these utilities from a command line**
>
> tip   This chapter describes command line, or textual, utilities. You can experiment with these utilities from a terminal, a terminal emulator within a GUI (page 93), or a virtual console (page 113).

SPECIAL CHARACTERS

Special characters, which have a special meaning to the shell, are discussed in "Filename Generation/Pathname Expansion" on page 221. These characters are mentioned here so that you can avoid accidentally using them as regular characters until you understand how the shell interprets them. For example, it is best to avoid using any of the following characters in a filename (even though emacs and some other programs do) because they make the file harder to reference on the command line:

& ; | * ? ' " ` [ ] ( ) $ < > { } # / \ ! ~

Whitespace   Although not considered special characters, RETURN, SPACE, and TAB also have special meanings to the shell. RETURN usually ends a command line and initiates execution of a command. The SPACE and TAB characters separate elements on the command line and are collectively known as *whitespace* or *blanks.*

Quoting special characters   If you need to use a character that has a special meaning to the shell as a regular character, you can *quote* (or *escape*) it. When you quote a special character, you keep the shell from giving it special meaning. The shell treats a quoted special character as a regular character. However, a slash (/) is always a separator in a pathname, even when you quote it.

Backslash   To quote a character, precede it with a backslash (\). When two or more special characters appear together, you must precede each with a backslash (for example, you would enter ** as **). You can quote a backslash just as you would quote any other special character—by preceding it with a backslash (\\).

Single quotation marks   Another way of quoting special characters is to enclose them between single quotation marks: '**'. You can quote many special and regular characters between a pair of single quotation marks: '**This is a special character: >**'. The regular characters are interpreted as usual, and the shell also interprets the special characters as regular characters.

The only way to quote the erase character (CONTROL-H), the line kill character (CONTROL-U), and other control characters (try CONTROL-M) is by preceding each with a CONTROL-V. Single quotation marks and backslashes do not work. Try the following:

```
$ echo 'xxxxxxCONTROL-U'
$ echo xxxxxxCONTROL-V CONTROL-U
```

optional   Although you cannot see the CONTROL-U displayed by the second of the preceding pair of commands, it is there. The following command sends the output of echo (page 137) through a pipe (page 136) to od (see the od man page) to display CONTROL-U as octal 25 (025):

```
$ echo xxxxxxCONTROL-V CONTROL-U | od -c
0000000   x   x   x   x   x   x 025 \n
0000010
```

The \n is the NEWLINE character that echo sends at the end of its output.

BASIC UTILITIES

One of the important advantages of Linux is that it comes with thousands of utilities that perform myriad functions. You will use utilities whenever you work with Linux, whether you use them directly by name from the command line or indirectly from a menu or icon. The following sections discuss some of the most basic and important utilities; these utilities are available from a character-based interface. Some of the more important utilities are also available from a GUI; others are available only from a GUI.

Folder The term *directory* is used extensively in the next sections. A directory is a resource that can hold files. On other operating systems, including Windows and Macintosh, and frequently when speaking about a Linux GUI, a directory is referred to as a folder. That is a good analogy: A traditional manila folder holds files just as a directory does.

In this chapter you work in your home directory

tip When you log in on the system, you are working in your *home directory.* In this chapter that is the only directory you use: All the files you create in this chapter are in your home directory. Chapter 6 goes into more detail about directories.

ls: LISTS THE NAMES OF FILES

Using the editor of your choice, create a small file named **practice**. (A tutorial on the vim editor appears on page 152.) After exiting from the editor, you can use the ls (list) utility to display a list of the names of the files in your home directory. In the first command in Figure 5-1 (next page), ls lists the name of the **practice** file. (You may also see files the system or a program created automatically.) Subsequent commands in Figure 5-1 display the contents of the file and remove the file. These commands are described next.

cat: DISPLAYS A TEXT FILE

The cat utility displays the contents of a text file. The name of the command is derived from *catenate,* which means to join together, one after the other. (Figure 7-8 on page 212 shows how to use cat to string together the contents of three files.)

```
$ ls
practice
$ cat practice
This is a small file that I created
with a text editor.
$ rm practice
$ ls
$ cat practice
cat: practice: No such file or directory
$
```

Figure 5-1   Using ls, cat, and rm on the file named **practice**

A convenient way to display the contents of a file to the screen is by giving the command **cat**, followed by a SPACE and the filename. Figure 5-1 shows cat displaying the contents of **practice**. This figure shows the difference between the ls and cat utilities: The ls utility displays the *name* of a file, whereas cat displays the *contents* of a file.

rm: DELETES A FILE

The rm (remove) utility deletes a file. Figure 5-1 shows rm deleting the file named **practice**. After rm deletes the file, ls and cat show that **practice** is no longer in the directory. The ls utility does not list its filename, and cat says that no such file exists. Use rm carefully.

A safer way of removing files

tip   You can use the interactive form of rm to make sure that you delete only the file(s) you intend to delete. When you follow rm with the **–i** option (see page 105 for a tip on options) and the name of the file you want to delete, rm displays the name of the file and then waits for you to respond with **y** (yes) before it deletes the file. It does not delete the file if you respond with a string that does not begin with **y**. The **–i** option is set up by default for the **root** user under Red Hat Linux:

```
$ rm -i toollist
rm: remove regular file 'toollist'? y
```

Optional: You can create an alias (page 318) for **rm –i** and put it in your startup file (page 170) so that rm always runs in interactive mode.

less Is more: DISPLAY A TEXT FILE ONE SCREEN AT A TIME

Pagers   When you want to view a file that is longer than one screen, you can use either the less utility or the more utility. Each of these utilities pauses after displaying a screen of text. Because these utilities show one page at a time, they are called *pagers*. Although less and more are very similar, they have subtle differences. At the end of the file, for example, less displays an **EOF** (end of file) message and waits for you to press **q** before returning you to the shell. In contrast, more returns you directly to the shell. In both utilities you can press **h** to display a Help screen that lists commands you can use while paging through a file. Give the commands **less practice** and **more practice** in place of the **cat** command in Figure 5-1 to see how these commands work. Use the command **less /etc/termcap** instead if you want to experiment with a longer file. Refer to the less man page for more information.

hostname: DISPLAYS THE SYSTEM NAME

The hostname utility displays the name of the system you are working on. Use this utility if you are not sure that you are logged in on the right machine.

```
$ hostname
bravo.example.com
```

WORKING WITH FILES

This section describes utilities that copy, move, print, search through, display, sort, and compare files.

Filename completion

tip   After you enter one or more letters of a filename (following a command) on a command line, press TAB and the Bourne Again Shell will complete as much of the filename as it can. When only one filename starts with the characters you entered, the shell completes the filename and places a SPACE after it. You can keep typing or you can press RETURN to execute the command at this point. When the characters you entered do not uniquely identify a filename, the shell completes what it can and waits for more input. When pressing TAB does not change the display, press TAB again to display a list of possible completions. For more information refer to "Pathname Completion" on page 314.

cp: COPIES A FILE

The cp (copy) utility (Figure 5-2) makes a copy of a file. This utility can copy any file, including text and executable program (binary) files. You can use cp to make a backup copy of a file or a copy to experiment with.

The cp command line uses the following syntax to specify source and destination files:

> cp *source-file destination-file*

The *source-file* is the name of the file that cp will copy. The *destination-file* is the name that cp assigns to the resulting (new) copy of the file.

The cp command line in Figure 5-2 copies the file named **memo** to **memo.copy**. The period is part of the filename—just another character. The initial ls command shows that **memo** is the only file in the directory. After the cp command, a second ls shows two files in the directory, **memo** and **memo.copy**.

```
$ ls
memo
$ cp memo memo.copy
$ ls
memo memo.copy
```

Figure 5-2   cp copies a file

Sometimes it is useful to incorporate the date in the name of a copy of a file. The following example includes the date January 30 (**0130**) in the copied file:

```
$ cp memo memo.0130
```

Although it has no significance to Linux, the date can help you find a version of a file that you created on a certain date. Including the date can also help you avoid overwriting existing files by providing a unique filename each day. For more information refer to "Filenames" on page 167.

Use scp (page 583) or ftp (page 601) when you need to copy a file from one system to another on a common network.

cp **can destroy a file**

caution   If the ***destination-file*** exists *before* you give a cp command, cp overwrites it. Because cp overwrites (and destroys the contents of) an existing ***destination-file*** without warning, you must take care not to cause cp to overwrite a file that you still need. The cp –i (interactive) option prompts you before it overwrites a file. See page 105 for a tip on options.

The following example assumes that the file named **orange.2** exists before you give the cp command. The user answers **y** to overwrite the file:

```
$ cp -i orange orange.2
cp: overwrite 'orange.2'? y
```

mv: CHANGES THE NAME OF A FILE

The mv (move) utility can rename a file without making a copy of it. The mv command line specifies an existing file and a new filename using the same syntax as cp:

mv existing-filename new-filename

The command line in Figure 5-3 changes the name of the file **memo** to **memo.0130**. The initial ls command shows that **memo** is the only file in the directory. After you give the mv command, **memo.0130** is the only file in the directory. Compare this result to that of the earlier cp example.

The mv utility can be used for more than changing the name of a file. Refer to "mv, cp: Move or Copy Files" on page 179. See the mv info page for more information.

mv **can destroy a file**

caution   Just as cp can destroy a file, so can mv. Also like cp, mv has a –i (interactive) option. See the caution box labeled "cp can destroy a file."

```
$ ls
memo
$ mv memo memo.0130
$ ls
memo.0130
```

Figure 5-3   mv renames a file

lpr: PRINTS A FILE

The lpr (line printer) utility places one or more files in a print queue for printing. Linux provides print queues so that only one job is printed on a given printer at a time. A queue allows several people or jobs to send output simultaneously to a single printer with the expected results. On systems that have access to more than one printer, you can use **lpstat –p** to display a list of available printers. Use the **–P** option to instruct lpr to place the file in the queue for a specific printer—even one that is connected to another system on the network. The following command prints the file named **report**:

```
$ lpr report
```

Because this command does not specify a printer, the output goes to the default printer, which is *the* printer when you have only one printer.

The next command line prints the same file on the printer named **mailroom**:

```
$ lpr -P mailroom report
```

You can see which jobs are in the print queue by giving an **lpstat –o** command or by using the lpq utility:

```
$ lpq
lp is ready and printing
Rank  Owner   Job Files                Total Size
active alex     86 (standard input)      954061 bytes
```

In this example, Alex has one job that is being printed; no other jobs are in the queue. You can use the job number (86 in this case) with the lprm utility to remove the job from the print queue and stop it from printing:

```
$ lprm 86
```

You can send more than one file to the printer with a single command. The following command line prints three files on the printer named **laser1**:

```
$ lpr -P laser1 05.txt 108.txt 12.txt
```

Refer to Chapter 14 for information on setting up a printer and defining the default printer.

grep: SEARCHES FOR A STRING

The grep[1] utility searches through one or more files to see whether any contain a specified string of characters. This utility does not change the file it searches but simply displays each line that contains the string.

---

1. Originally the name grep was a play on an ed—an original UNIX editor, available on Red Hat Linux—command: g/re/p. In this command **g** stands for global, **re** is a regular expression delimited by slashes, and **p** means print.

```
$ cat memo

Helen:

In our meeting on June 6 we
discussed the issue of credit.
Have you had any further thoughts
about it?

                        Alex
$ grep 'credit' memo
discussed the issue of credit.
```

Figure 5-4   grep searches for a string

The grep command in Figure 5-4 searches through the file **memo** for lines that contain the string **credit** and displays a single line that meets this criterion. If **memo** contained such words as **discredit, creditor,** or **accreditation,** grep would have displayed those lines as well because they contain the string it was searching for. The **–w** option causes grep to match only whole words. Although you do not need to enclose the string you are searching for in single quotation marks, doing so allows you to put SPACEs and special characters in the search string.

The grep utility can do much more than search for a simple string in a single file. Refer to the grep info page and Appendix A, "Regular Expressions," for more information.

head: DISPLAYS THE BEGINNING OF A FILE

By default the head utility displays the first ten lines of a file. You can use head to help you remember what a particular file contains. For example, if you have a file named **months** that lists the 12 months of the year in calendar order, one to a line, then head displays **Jan** through **Oct** (Figure 5-5).

This utility can display any number of lines, so you can use it to look at only the first line of a file, at a full screen, or even more. To specify the number of lines displayed, include a hyphen followed by the number of lines in the head command. For example, the following command displays only the first line of **months**:

```
$ head -1 months
Jan
```

The head utility can also display parts of a file based on a count of blocks or characters rather than lines. Refer to the head info page for more information.

tail: DISPLAYS THE END OF A FILE

The tail utility is similar to head but by default displays the *last* ten lines of a file. Depending on how you invoke it, this utility can display fewer or more than ten lines, use a count of blocks or characters rather than lines to display parts of a file,

```
$ cat months
Jan
Feb
Mar
Apr
May
Jun
Jul
Aug
Sep
Oct
Nov
Dec

$ head months
Jan
Feb
Mar
Apr
May
Jun
Jul
Aug
Sep
Oct
```

Figure 5-5   head displays the first ten lines of a file

and display lines being added to a file that is changing. The following command causes tail to display the last five lines, **Aug** through **Dec**, of the **months** file shown in Figure 5-5:

```
$ tail -5 months
Aug
Sep
Oct
Nov
Dec
```

You can monitor lines as they are added to the end of the growing file named **logfile** with the following command:

```
$ tail -f logfile
```

Press the interrupt key (usually CONTROL-C) to stop tail and display the shell prompt. Refer to the tail info page for more information.

sort: DISPLAYS A FILE IN ORDER

The sort utility displays the contents of a file in order by lines but does not change the original file. For example, if a file named **days** contains the name of each day of

```
$ cat days
Monday
Tuesday
Wednesday
Thursday
Friday
Saturday
Sunday
$ sort days
Friday
Monday
Saturday
Sunday
Thursday
Tuesday
Wednesday
```

Figure 5-6   sort displays the lines of a file in order

the week in calendar order, each on a separate line, then sort displays the file in alphabetical order (Figure 5-6).

The sort utility is useful for putting lists in order. The **–u** option generates a sorted list in which each line is unique (no duplicates). The **–n** option puts a list of numbers in order. Refer to the sort info page for more information.

uniq: REMOVES DUPLICATE LINES FROM A FILE

The uniq (unique) utility displays a file, skipping adjacent duplicate lines, but does not change the original file. If a file contains a list of names and has two successive entries for the same person, uniq skips the extra line (Figure 5-7).

If a file is sorted before it is processed by uniq, this utility ensures that no two lines in the file are the same. (Of course, sort can do that all by itself with the **–u** option.) Refer to the uniq info page for more information.

```
$ cat dups
Cathy
Fred
Joe
John
Mary
Mary
Paula
$ uniq dups
Cathy
Fred
Joe
John
Mary
Paula
```

Figure 5-7   uniq removes duplicate lines

```
$ diff -u colors.1 colors.2
--- colors.1    Fri Nov 25 15:45:32 2005
+++ colors.2    Fri Nov 25 15:24:46 2005
@@ -1,6 +1,5 @@
 red
+blue
 green
 yellow
-pink
-purple
 orange
```

Figure 5-8 diff displaying the unified output format

diff: COMPARES TWO FILES

The diff (difference) utility compares two files and displays a list of the differences between them. This utility does not change either file, so it is useful when you want to compare two versions of a letter or a report or two versions of the source code for a program.

The diff utility with the **–u** (unified output format) option first displays two lines indicating which of the files you are comparing will be denoted by a plus sign (**+**) and which by a minus sign (**–**). In Figure 5-8, a minus sign indicates the **colors.1** file; a plus sign indicates the **colors.2** file.

The **diff –u** command breaks long, multiline text into *hunks*. Each hunk is preceded by a line starting and ending with two at signs (**@@**). This hunk identifier indicates the starting line number and the number of lines from each file for this hunk. In Figure 5-8, the hunk covers the section of the **colors.1** file (indicated by a minus sign) from the first line through the sixth line. The **+1,5** then indicates that the hunk covers **colors.2** from the first line through the fifth line.

Following these header lines, **diff –u** displays each line of text with a leading minus sign, a leading plus sign, or nothing. A leading minus sign indicates that the line occurs only in the file denoted by the minus sign. A leading plus sign indicates that the line comes from the file denoted by the plus sign. A line that begins with neither a plus sign nor a minus sign occurs in both files in the same location. Refer to the diff info page for more information.

file: TESTS THE CONTENTS OF A FILE

You can use the file utility to learn about the contents of any file on a Linux system without having to open and examine the file yourself. In the following example, file reports that **letter_e.bz2** contains data that was compressed by the bzip2 utility (page 140):

```
$ file letter_e.bz2
letter_e.bz2: bzip2 compressed data, block size = 900k
```

Next file reports on two more files:

```
$ file memo zach.jpg
memo:      ASCII text
zach.jpg: JPEG image data, ... resolution (DPI), 72 x 72
```

Refer to the file man page for more information.

| (PIPE): COMMUNICATES BETWEEN PROCESSES

Because pipes are integral to the functioning of a Linux system, they are introduced here for use in examples. Pipes are covered in detail beginning on page 216.

A *process* is the execution of a command by Linux (page 300). Communication between processes is one of the hallmarks of both UNIX and Linux. A *pipe* (written as a vertical bar, l, on the command line and appearing as a solid or broken vertical line on keyboards) provides the simplest form of this kind of communication. Simply put, a pipe takes the output of one utility and sends that output as input to another utility. Using UNIX/Linux terminology, a pipe takes standard output of one process and redirects it to become standard input of another process. (For more information refer to "Standard Input and Standard Output" on page 208.) Most of what a process displays on the screen is sent to standard output. If you do not redirect it, this output appears on the screen. Using a pipe, you can redirect the output so that it becomes instead standard input of another utility. For example, a utility such as head can take its input from a file whose name you specify on the command line following the word **head**, or it can take its input from standard input. Thus, you can give the command shown in Figure 5-5 on page 133 as follows:

```
$ cat months | head
Jan
Feb
Mar
Apr
May
Jun
Jul
Aug
Sep
Oct
```

The next command displays the number of files in a directory. The wc (word count) utility with the **–w** option displays the number of words in its standard input or in a file you specify on the command line:

```
$ ls | wc -w
14
```

You can use a pipe to send output of a program to the printer:

```
$ tail months | lpr
```

```
$ ls
memo   memo.0714   practice
$ echo Hi
Hi
$ echo This is a sentence.
This is a sentence.
$ echo star: *
star: memo memo.0714 practice
$
```

Figure 5-9   echo copies the command line (but not the word **echo**) to the screen

FOUR MORE UTILITIES

The echo and date utilities are two of the most frequently used members of the large collection of Linux utilities. The script utility records part of a session in a file, and unix2dos makes a copy of a text file that can be read on either a Windows or a Macintosh machine.

echo: DISPLAYS TEXT

The echo utility copies anything you put on the command line after **echo** to the screen. Some examples appear in Figure 5-9. The last example shows what the shell does with an unquoted asterisk (*) on the command line: It expands the asterisk into a list of filenames in the directory.

The echo utility is a good tool for learning about the shell and other Linux programs. Some examples on page 222 use echo to illustrate how special characters, such as the asterisk, work. Throughout Chapters 7, 9, and 28, echo helps explain how shell variables work and how you can send messages from shell scripts to the screen. Refer to the echo info page for more information.

date: DISPLAYS THE TIME AND DATE

The date utility displays the current date and time:

```
$ date
Thu Jan 20 10:24:00 PST 2005
```

The following example shows how you can choose the format and select the contents of the output of date:

```
$ date +"%A %B %d"
Thursday January 20
```

Refer to the date info page for more information.

script: RECORDS A SHELL SESSION

The script utility records all or part of a login session, including your input and the system's responses. This utility is useful only from character-based devices, such as a terminal or a terminal emulator. It does capture a session with vim; however, because vim uses control characters to position the cursor and display different typefaces, such as bold, the output will be difficult to read and may not be useful. When you cat a file that has captured a vim session, the session quickly passes before your eyes.

By default script captures the session in a file named **typescript**. To use a different filename, follow the script command with a SPACE and the new filename. To append to a file, use the –a option after **script** but before the filename; otherwise script overwrites an existing file. Following is a session being recorded by script:

```
$ script
Script started, file is typescript
$ date
Thu Jan 20 10:28:56 PST 2005
$ who am i
alex      pts/4    Jan  8 22:15
$
$ apropos mtools
mtools               (1)  - utilities to access DOS disks in Unix
mtools.conf [mtools] (5)  - mtools configuration files
mtoolstest           (1)  - tests and displays the configuration
$ exit
Script done, file is typescript
$
```

Use the exit command to terminate a script session. You can then view the file you created with cat, less, more, or an editor. Following is the file that was created by the preceding script command:

```
$ cat typescript
Script started on Thu Jan 20 10:28:56 2005
$ date
Thu Jan 20 10:28:56 PST 2005
$ who am i
alex      pts/4    Jan  8 22:15
$
$ apropos mtools
mtools               (1)  - utilities to access DOS disks in Unix
mtools.conf [mtools] (5)  - mtools configuration files
mtoolstest           (1)  - tests and displays the configuration
$ exit
Script done on Thu Jan 20 10:29:58 2005
$
```

If you will be editing the file with vim, emacs, or another editor, you can use dos2unix to eliminate from the **typescript** file the ^M characters that appear at the ends of the lines. Refer to the script man page for more information.

unix2dos: CONVERTS LINUX AND MACINTOSH FILES TO WINDOWS FORMAT

If you want to share a text file that you created on a Linux system with someone on a Windows or Macintosh system, you need to convert the file before the person on the other system can read it easily. The unix2dos utility converts a Linux text file so that it can be read on a Windows or Macintosh system. Give the following command to convert a file named **memo.txt** (created with a text editor) to a DOS-format file:

```
$ unix2dos memo.txt
```

Without any options unix2dos overwrites the original file. You can now email the file as an attachment to someone on a Windows or Macintosh system.

dos2unix You can use the dos2unix utility to convert Windows or Macintosh files so they can be read on a Linux system:

```
$ dos2unix memo.txt
```

See the unix2dos and dos2unix man pages for more information.

You can also use tr to change a Windows or Macintosh text file into a Linux text file. In the following example, the **–d** option causes tr to remove RETURNs (represented by **\r**) as it makes a copy of the file:

```
$ cat memo | tr -d '\r' > memo.txt
```

The greater than (>) symbol redirects the standard output of tr to the file named **memo.txt**. For more information refer to "Redirecting Standard Output" on page 210. Converting a file the other way without using unix2dos is not as easy.

COMPRESSING AND ARCHIVING FILES

Large files use a lot of disk space and take longer than smaller files to transfer from one system to another over a network. If you do not need to look at the contents of a large file very often, you may want to save it on a CD, DVD, or another medium and remove it from the hard disk. If you have a continuing need for the file, retrieving a copy from a CD may be inconvenient. To reduce the amount of disk space you use without removing the file entirely, you can compress the file without losing any of the information it holds. Similarly a single archive of several files packed into a larger file is easier to manipulate, upload, download, and email than multiple files. You may frequently download compressed, archived files from the Internet. The utilities described in this section compress and decompress files and pack and unpack archives.

bzip2: COMPRESSES A FILE

The bzip2 utility compresses a file by analyzing it and recoding it more efficiently. The new version of the file looks completely different. In fact, because the new file contains many nonprinting characters, you cannot view it directly. The bzip2 utility works particularly well on files that contain a lot of repeated information, such as text and image data, although most image data is already in a compressed format.

The following example shows a boring file. Each of the 8,000 lines of the **letter_e** file contains 72 e's and a NEWLINE character that marks the end of the line. The file occupies more than half a megabyte of disk storage.

```
$ ls -l
-rw-rw-r--  1 sam sam 584000 Mar  1 22:31 letter_e
```

The **–l** (long) option causes ls to display more information about a file. Here it shows that **letter_e** is 584,000 bytes long. The **––verbose** (or **–v**) option causes bzip2 to report how much it was able to reduce the size of the file. In this case, it shrank the file by 99.99 percent:

```
$ bzip2 -v letter_e
letter_e: 11680.00:1, 0.001 bits/byte, 99.99% saved, 584000 in, 50 out.
$ ls -l
-rw-rw-r--  1 sam sam 50 Mar  1 22:31 letter_e.bz2
```

.bz2 filename extension Now the file is only 50 bytes long. The bzip2 utility also renamed the file, appending **.bz2** to its name. This naming convention reminds you that the file is compressed; you would not want to display or print it, for example, without first decompressing it. The bzip2 utility does not change the modification date associated with the file, even though it completely changes the file's contents.

In the following, more realistic example, the file **zach.jpg** contains a computer graphics image:

```
$ ls -l
-rw-r--r--  1 sam sam 33287 Mar  1 22:40 zach.jpg
```

The bzip2 utility can reduce the size of the file by only 28 percent because the image is already in a compressed format:

```
$ bzip2 -v zach.jpg
zach.jpg: 1.391:1, 5.749 bits/byte, 28.13% saved, 33287 in, 23922 out.

$ ls -l
-rw-r--r--  1 sam sam 23922 Mar  1 22:40 zach.jpg.bz2
```

Refer to the bzip2 man page, www.bzip.org, and the *Bzip2 mini-HOWTO* (see page 109) for more information.

bunzip2 AND bzcat: DECOMPRESS A FILE

You can use the bunzip2 utility to restore a file that has been compressed with bzip2:

```
$ bunzip2 letter_e.bz2
$ ls -l
-rw-rw-r--  1 sam sam 584000 Mar  1 22:31 letter_e

$ bunzip2 zach.jpg.bz2
$ ls -l
-rw-r--r--  1 sam sam  33287 Mar  1 22:40 zach.jpg
```

The bzcat utility displays a file that has been compressed with bzip2. The equivalent of cat for **.bz2** files, bzcat decompresses the compressed data and displays the contents of the decompressed file. Like cat, bzcat does not change the source file. The pipe in the following example redirects the output of bzcat so that instead of being displayed on the screen it becomes the input to head, which displays the first two lines of the file:

```
$ bzcat letter_e.bz2 | head -2
eeeeeeeeeeeeeeeeeeeeeeeeeeeeeeeeeeeeeeeeeeeeeeeeeeeeeeeeeeeeeeeeeeeeeeee
eeeeeeeeeeeeeeeeeeeeeeeeeeeeeeeeeeeeeeeeeeeeeeeeeeeeeeeeeeeeeeeeeeeeeeee
```

After bzcat is run, the contents of **letter_e.bz** is unchanged; the file is still stored on the disk in compressed form.

bzip2recover   The bzip2recover utility supports limited data recovery from media errors. Give the command **bzip2recover** followed by the name of the compressed, corrupted file from which you want to try to recover data.

gzip: COMPRESSES A FILE

gunzip and zcat   The gzip (GNU zip) utility is older and less efficient than bzip2. Its flags and operation are very similar to those of bzip2. A file compressed by gzip is marked by a **.gz** filename extension. Linux stores manual pages in gzip format to save disk space; likewise, files you download from the Internet are frequently in gzip format. Use gzip, gunzip, and zcat just as you would use bzip2, bunzip2, and bzcat, respectively. Refer to the gzip info page for more information.

compress   The compress utility can also compress files, albeit not as well as gzip. This utility marks a file it has compressed by adding **.Z** to its name.

gzip **versus** zip

tip   Do not confuse gzip and gunzip with the zip and unzip utilities. These last two are used to pack and unpack zip archives containing several files compressed into a single file that has been imported from or is being exported to a system running Windows. The zip utility constructs a zip archive, whereas unzip unpacks zip archives. The zip and unzip utilities are compatible with PKZIP, a Windows program that compresses and archives files.

tar: PACKS AND UNPACKS ARCHIVES

The tar utility performs many functions. Its name is short for *tape archive,* as its original function was to create and read archive and backup tapes. Today it is used to create a single file (called a *tar file, archive, or tarball*) from multiple files or directory hierarchies and to extract files from a tar file. The cpio utility performs a similar function.

In the following example, the first ls shows the existence and sizes of the files **g, b,** and **d.** Next tar uses the **–c** (create), **–v** (verbose), and **–f** (write to or read from a file) options[2] to create an archive named **all.tar** from these files. Each line output displays the name of the file tar is appending to the archive it is creating.

The tar utility adds overhead when it creates an archive. The next command shows that the archive file **all.tar** occupies about 9,700 bytes, whereas the sum of the sizes of the three files is about 6,000 bytes. This overhead is more appreciable on smaller files, such as the ones in this example.

```
$ ls -l g b d
-rw-r--r--   1 jenny jenny 1302 Aug 20 14:16 g
-rw-r--r--   1 jenny other 1178 Aug 20 14:16 b
-rw-r--r--   1 jenny jenny 3783 Aug 20 14:17 d

$ tar -cvf all.tar g b d
g
b
d
$ ls -l all.tar
-rw-r--r--   1 jenny      jenny        9728 Aug 20 14:17 all.tar
$ tar -tvf all.tar
-rw-r--r-- jenny/jenny    1302 2005-08-20 14:16 g
-rw-r--r-- jenny/other    1178 2005-08-20 14:16 b
-rw-r--r-- jenny/jenny    3783 2005-08-20 14:17 d
```

The final command in the preceding example uses the **–t** option to display a table of contents for the archive. Use **–x** instead of **–t** to extract files from a tar archive. Omit the **–v** option if you want tar to do its work silently.

You can use bzip2, compress, or gzip to compress tar files, making them easier to store and handle. Many files you download from the Internet will already be in one of these formats. Files that have been processed by tar and compressed by bzip2 frequently have a filename extension of **.tar.bz2** or **.tbz.** Those processed by tar and gzip have an extension of **.tar.gz** or **.tz,** whereas files processed by tar and compress use **.tar.Z** as the extension.

You can unpack a tarred and gzipped file in two steps. (Follow the same procedure if the file was compressed by bzip2, but use bunzip2 instead of gunzip.) The next example shows how to unpack the GNU make utility after it has been downloaded (ftp.gnu.org/pub/gnu/make/make-3.80.tar.gz):

```
$ ls -l mak*
-rw-rw-r--  1 sam sam 1211924 Jan 20 11:49 make-3.80.tar.gz

$ gunzip mak*
$ ls -l mak*
-rw-rw-r--  1 sam sam 4823040 Jan 20 11:49 make-3.80.tar
```

2. Although the original UNIX tar did not use a leading hyphen to indicate an option on the command line, it now accepts hyphens. The GNU tar described here will accept tar commands with or without a leading hyphen. This book uses the hyphen for consistency with most other utilities.

```
$ tar -xvf mak*
make-3.80/
make-3.80/po/
make-3.80/po/Makefile.in.in
...
make-3.80/tests/run_make_tests.pl
make-3.80/tests/test_driver.pl
```

The first command lists the downloaded tarred and gzipped file: **make-3.80.tar.gz** (about 1.2 megabytes). The asterisk (∗) in the filename matches any characters in any filenames (page 222), so you end up with a list of files whose names begin with **mak**; in this case there is only one. Using an asterisk saves typing and can improve accuracy with long filenames. The gunzip command decompresses the file and yields **make-3.80.tar** (no **.gz** extension), which is about 4.8 megabytes. The tar command creates the **make-3.80** directory in the working directory and unpacks the files into it.

```
$ ls -ld mak*
drwxrwxr-x  8 sam sam    4096 Oct  3  2002 make-3.80
-rw-rw-r--  1 sam sam 4823040 Jan 20 11:49 make-3.80.tar
$ ls -l make-3.80
total 1816
-rw-r--r--  1 sam sam 24687 Oct  3  2002 ABOUT-NLS
-rw-r--r--  1 sam sam  1554 Jul  8  2002 AUTHORS
-rw-r--r--  1 sam sam 18043 Dec 10  1996 COPYING
-rw-r--r--  1 sam sam 32922 Oct  3  2002 ChangeLog
...
-rw-r--r--  1 sam sam 16520 Jan 21  2000 vmsify.c
-rw-r--r--  1 sam sam 16409 Aug  9  2002 vpath.c
drwxrwxr-x  5 sam sam  4096 Oct  3  2002 w32
```

After tar extracts the files from the archive, the working directory contains two files whose names start with **mak**: **make-3.80.tar** and **make-3.80**. The **–d** (directory) option causes ls to display only file and directory names, not the contents of directories as it normally does. The final ls command shows the files and directories in the **make-3.80** directory. Refer to the tar info page for more information.

tar: the –x option may extract a lot of files

caution   Some tar archives contain many files. To list the files in the archive without unpacking them, run tar with the **–t** option and the name of the tar file. In some cases you may want to create a new directory (mkdir [page 173]), move the tar file into that directory, and expand it there. That way the unpacked files will not mingle with your existing files, and no confusion will occur. This strategy also makes it easier to delete the extracted files. Some tar files automatically create a new directory and put the files into it. Refer to the preceding example.

tar: the –x option can overwrite files

caution   The **–x** option to tar overwrites a file that has the same filename as a file you are extracting. Follow the suggestion in the preceding caution box to avoid overwriting files.

optional   You can combine the gunzip and tar commands on one command line with a pipe (|), which redirects the output of gunzip so that it becomes the input to tar:

```
$ gunzip -c make-3.80.tar.gz | tar -xvf -
```

The –c option causes gunzip to send its output through the pipe instead of creating a file. Refer to "Pipes" (page 216) and gzip (page 141) for more information about how this command line works.

A simpler solution is to use the –z option to tar. This option causes tar to call gunzip (or gzip when you are creating an archive) directly and simplifies the preceding command line to

```
$ tar -xvzf make-3.80.tar.gz
```

In a similar manner, the –j option calls bzip2 or bunzip2.

LOCATING COMMANDS

The whereis and apropos utilities can help you find a command whose name you have forgotten or whose location you do not know. When multiple copies of a utility or program are present, which tells you which copy you will run. The locate utility searches for files on the local system.

which AND whereis: LOCATE A UTILITY

When you give Linux a command, the shell searches a list of directories for a program with that name and runs the first one it finds. This list of directories is called a *search path*. For information on how to change the search path, refer to "PATH: Where the Shell Looks for Programs" on page 292. If you do not change the search path, the shell searches only a standard set of directories and then stops searching. Other directories on the system may also contain useful utilities, however.

which   The which utility locates utilities by displaying the full pathname of the file for the utility. (Chapter 6 contains more information on pathnames and the structure of the Linux filesystem.) The local system may include several commands that have the same name. When you type the name of a command, the shell searches for the command in your search path and runs the first one it finds. You can find out which copy of the program the shell will run by using which. In the following example, which reports the location of the tar command:

```
$ which tar
/bin/tar
```

The which utility can be helpful when a command seems to be working in unexpected ways. By running which, you may discover that you are running a nonstandard version of a tool or a different one than you expected. ("Important Standard Directories and Files" on page 176 provides a list of standard locations for executable files.) For example, if tar is not working properly and you find that you are running **/usr/local/bin/tar** instead of **/bin/tar**, you might suspect that the local version is broken.

which, whereis, **and builtin commands**

caution   Both the which and whereis utilities report only the names for commands as they are found on the disk; they do not report shell builtins (utilities that are built into a shell; see page 225). When you use whereis to try to find where the echo command (which exists as both a utility program and a shell builtin) is kept, you get the following result:

```
$ whereis echo
echo: /bin/echo /usr/share/man/man1/echo.1.gz /usr/share/man/man1p/echo.1p.
gz /usr/share/man/man3/echo.3x.gz
```

The whereis utility does not display the echo builtin. Even the which utility reports the wrong information:

```
$ which echo
/bin/echo
```

Under bash you can use the type builtin (page 927) to determine whether a command is a builtin:

```
$ type echo
echo is a shell builtin
```

whereis   The whereis utility searches for files related to a utility by looking in standard locations instead of using your search path. For example, you can find the locations for files related to tar:

```
$ whereis tar
tar: /bin/tar /usr/include/tar.h /usr/share/man/man1/tar.1.gz
```

In this example whereis finds three references to tar: the tar utility file, a tar header file, and the tar man page.

which **versus** whereis

tip   Given the name of a program, which looks through the directories in your *search path*, in order, and locates the program. If the search path includes more than one program with the specified name, which displays the name of only the first one (the one you would run).

The whereis utility looks through a list of *standard directories* and works independently of your search path. Use whereis to locate a binary (executable) file, any manual pages, and source code for a program you specify; whereis displays all the files it finds.

apropos: SEARCHES FOR A KEYWORD

When you do not know the name of the command you need to carry out a particular task, you can use apropos with a keyword to search for it. This utility searches for the keyword in the short description line (the top line) of all man pages and displays those that contain a match. The man utility, when called with the –k (keyword) option, gives you the same output as apropos (it is the same command).

The database apropos uses, named **whatis**, is not on Red Hat Linux systems when they are first installed, but is built automatically by cron (page 547) using makewhatis. (The cron utility runs the **/etc/cron.weekly/makewhatis.cron** script to build the **whatis** database.) If you turn the system off periodically (as with a laptop), the script may not be run. If apropos does not produce any output, run the command **makewhatis –w** as **root**.

The following example shows the output of apropos when you call it with the **who** keyword. The output includes the name of each command, the section of the manual that contains it, and the brief description from the top of the man page. This list includes the utility that you need (who) and identifies other, related tools that you might find useful:

```
$ apropos who
at.allow [at]          (5)   - determine who can submit jobs via at or batch
at.deny [at]           (5)   - determine who can submit jobs via at or batch
jwhois                 (1)   - client for the whois service
ldapwhoami             (1)   - LDAP who am i? tool
w                      (1)   - Show who is logged on and what they are doing
who                    (1)   - show who is logged on
whoami                 (1)   - print effective userid
```

whatis   The whatis utility is similar to apropos but finds only complete word matches for the name of the utility:

```
$ whatis who
who                    (1)   - show who is logged on
```

locate: SEARCHES FOR A FILE

The locate utility searches for files on the local system:

```
$ locate motd
/etc/motd
/lib/security/pam_motd.so
/usr/share/man/man5/motd.5.gz
```

Before you can use locate the updatedb utility must build or update the locate database. Typically the database is updated once a day by a cron script (page 547).

If you are not on a network, skip the rest of this chapter

tip   If you are the only user on a system that is not connected to a network, you may want to skip the rest of this chapter. If you are not on a network but are set up to send and receive email, read "Email" on page 152.

OBTAINING USER AND SYSTEM INFORMATION

This section covers utilities that provide information about who is using the system, what those users are doing, and how the system is running. To find out who is using

```
$ who
root          console       Mar 27 05:00
alex          pts/4         Mar 27 12:23
alex          pts/5         Mar 27 12:33
jenny         pts/7         Mar 26 08:45
```

Figure 5-10   who lists who is logged in

the local system, you can employ one of several utilities that vary in the details they provide and the options they support. The oldest utility, who, produces a list of users who are logged in on the local system, the device each person is using, and the time each person logged in.

The w and finger utilities show more detail, such as each user's full name and the command line each user is running. You can use the finger utility to retrieve information about users on remote systems if your computer is attached to a network. Table 5-1 on page 150 summarizes the output of these utilities.

who: LISTS USERS ON THE SYSTEM

The who utility displays a list of users who are logged in. In Figure 5-10 the first column that who displays shows that Alex and Jenny are logged in. (Alex is logged in from two locations.) The second column shows the device that each user's terminal, workstation, or terminal emulator is connected to. The third column shows the date and time the user logged in. An optional fourth column shows (in parentheses) the name of the system that a remote user logged in from; this column does not appear in Figure 5-10.

The information that who displays is useful when you want to communicate with a user at your installation. When the user is logged in, you can use write (page 150) to establish communication immediately. If who does not list the user or if you do not need to communicate immediately, you can send email to that person (page 152).

If the output of who scrolls off the screen, you can redirect the output through a pipe (l, page 136) so that it becomes the input to less, which displays the output one page at a time. You can also use a pipe to redirect the output through grep to look for a specific name.

If you need to find out which terminal you are using or what time you logged in, you can use the command **who am i**:

```
$ who am i
alex          pts/5         Mar 27 12:33
```

finger: LISTS USERS ON THE SYSTEM

You can use finger to display a list of the users who are logged in on the system. In addition to usernames, finger supplies each user's full name along with information about which device the user's terminal is connected to, how recently the user typed something on the keyboard, when the user logged in, and what contact information

```
$ finger
Login     Name              Tty    Idle  Login Time    Office  Office Phone
root      root              1      1:35  May 24 08:38
alex      Alex Watson       /0           Jun  7 12:46 (:0)
alex      Alex Watson       /1     19    Jun  7 12:47 (:0)
jenn      Jenny Chen        /2     2:24  Jun  2 05:33 (bravo.example.com)
hls       Helen Simpson     */2    2     Jun  2 05:33 (bravo.example.com)
```

Figure 5-11   finger I: lists who is logged in

is available. If the user has logged in over the network, the name of the remote system is shown as the user's location. For example, in Figure 5-11 **jenny** and **hls** are logged in from the remote system named **bravo**. The asterisk (*) in front of the name of Helen's device (TTY) indicates that she has blocked others from sending messages directly to her terminal (refer to "mesg: Denies or Accepts Messages" on page 151).

finger can be a security risk

security   On systems where security is a concern, the system administrator may disable finger. This utility can reveal information that can help a malicious user break into a system.

You can also use finger to learn more about an individual by specifying the name of that user on the command line. In Figure 5-12, finger displays detailed information about the user named Alex. Alex is logged in and actively using one of his terminals (**pts/1**); he has not used his other terminal (**pts/0**) for 5 minutes and 52 seconds. You also learn from finger that if you want to set up a meeting with Alex, you should contact Jenny at extension 1693.

.plan and .project   Most of the information in Figure 5-12 was collected by finger from system files. The information shown after the heading **Plan:**, however, was supplied by Alex. The finger utility searched for a file named **.plan** in Alex's home directory and displayed its contents. (Filenames that begin with a period, such as **.plan**, are not normally

```
$ finger alex
Login: alex                            Name: Alex Watson
Directory: /home/alex                  Shell: /bin/bash
On since Wed Jun  7 12:46 (PDT) on pts/0 from :0
    5 minutes 52 seconds idle
On since Wed Jun  7 12:47 (PDT) on pts/1 from bravo
Last login Wed Jun  7 12:47 (PDT) on 1 from bravo
New mail received Wed Jun  7 13:16 2006 (PDT)
     Unread since Fri May 26 15:32 2006 (PDT)
Plan:
I will be at a conference in Hawaii all next week.  If you need
to see me, contact Jenny Chen, x1693.
```

Figure 5-12   finger II: lists details about one user

listed by ls and are called hidden filenames [page 170].) You may find it helpful to create a **.plan** file for yourself; it can contain any information you choose, such as your schedule, interests, phone number, or address. In a similar manner, finger displays the contents of the **.project** and **.pgpkey** files in your home directory. If Alex had not been logged in, finger would have reported only his user information, the last time he logged in, the last time he read his email, and his plan.

You can also use finger to display a user's username. For example, on a system with a user named Helen Simpson, you might know that Helen's last name is Simpson but might not guess that her username is **hls**. The finger utility, which is not case sensitive, can search for information on Helen using her first or last name. The following commands find the information you seek as well as information on other users whose names are Helen or Simpson:

```
$ finger HELEN
Login: hls                                      Name: Helen Simpson.
...

$ finger simpson
Login: hls                                      Name: Helen Simpson.
...
```

See page 360 for information about using finger over a network.

w: LISTS USERS ON THE SYSTEM

The w utility displays a list of the users who are logged in. As discussed in the section on who, the information that w displays is useful when you want to communicate with someone at your installation.

The first column in Figure 5-13 shows that Alex, Jenny, and Scott are logged in. The second column shows the designation of the device that each user's terminal is connected to. The third column shows the system that a remote user is logged in from. The fourth column shows the time when each user logged in. The fifth column indicates how long each user has been idle (how much time has elapsed since the user pressed a key on the keyboard). The next two columns identify how much computer processor time each user has used during this login session and on the task that is running. The last column shows the command each user is running.

```
$ w
  8:20am  up 4 days,  2:28, 3 users,  load average: 0.04, 0.04, 0.00
USER      TTY      FROM         LOGIN@    IDLE    JCPU    PCPU   WHAT
alex      pts/4    :0           5:55am   13:45    0.15s   0.07s  w
alex      pts/5    :0           5:55am      27    2:55    1:01   bash
jenny     pts/7    bravo        5:56am   13:44    0.51s    30s   vim 3.txt
scott     pts/12   bravo        7:17pm            1.00s   0:14s  run_bdgt
```

Figure 5-13   The w utility

The first line that the w utility displays includes the time of day, the period of time the computer has been running (in days, hours, and minutes), the number of users logged in, and the load average (how busy the system is). The three load average numbers represent the number of jobs waiting to run, averaged over the past 1, 5, and 15 minutes. Use the uptime utility to display just this line. Table 5-1 compares the w, who, and finger utilities.

Table 5-1   Comparison of w, who, and finger

Information displayed	w	who	finger
Username	x	x	x
Terminal-line identification (tty)	x	x	x
Login day and time	x		
Login date and time		x	x
Idle time	x		x
Program the user is executing	x		
Location the user logged in from			x
CPU time used	x		
Full name (or other information from **/etc/passwd**)			x
User-supplied vanity information			x
System uptime and load average	x		

COMMUNICATING WITH OTHER USERS

The utilities discussed in this section exchange messages and files with other users either interactively or through email.

write: SENDS A MESSAGE

The write utility sends a message to another user who is logged in. When you and another user use write to send messages to each other, you establish two-way communication. Initially a write command (Figure 5-14) displays a banner on the other user's terminal, saying that you are about to send a message.

The syntax of a write command line is

> *write* **username** *[terminal]*

The **username** is the username of the user you want to communicate with. The **terminal** is an optional device name that is useful if the user is logged in more than

```
$ write alex
Hi Alex, are you there? o
```

Figure 5-14   The write utility I

once. You can display the usernames and device names of all users who are logged in on the local system by using who, w, or finger.

To establish two-way communication with another user, you and the other user must each execute write, specifying the other's username as the *username*. The write utility then copies text, line by line, from one keyboard/display to the other (Figure 5-15). Sometimes it helps to establish a convention, such as typing o (for "over") when you are ready for the other person to type and typing oo (for "over and out") when you are ready to end the conversation. When you want to stop communicating with the other user, press CONTROL-D at the beginning of a line. Pressing CONTROL-D tells write to quit, displays **EOF** (end of file) on the other user's terminal, and returns you to the shell. The other user must do the same.

If the **Message from** banner appears on your screen and obscures something you are working on, press CONTROL-L or CONTROL-R to refresh the screen and remove the banner. Then you can clean up, exit from your work, and respond to the person who is writing to you. You have to remember who is writing to you, however, because the banner will no longer appear on the screen.

mesg: DENIES OR ACCEPTS MESSAGES

Give the following command when you do not wish to receive messages from another user:

```
$ mesg n
```

If Alex had given this command before Jenny tried to send him a message, Jenny would have seen the following message:

```
$ write alex
Permission denied
```

You can allow messages again by entering **mesg y**. Give the command **mesg** by itself to display **is y** (for "yes, messages are allowed") or **is n** (for "no, messages are *not* allowed").

```
$ write alex
Hi Alex, are you there? o

Message from alex@bravo.example.com on pts/0 at 16:23 ...
Yes Jenny, I'm here. o
```

Figure 5-15   The write utility II

EMAIL

Email enables you to communicate with users on the local system and, if the installation is part of a network, with other users on the network. If you are connected to the Internet, you can communicate electronically with users around the world.

Email utilities differ from write in that email utilities can send a message when the recipient is not logged in. These utilities can also send the same message to more than one user at a time.

Many email programs are available for Linux, including the original character-based mail program, Mozilla/Thunderbird, pine, mail through emacs, KMail, and evolution. Another popular graphical email program is sylpheed (sylpheed.good-day.net).

Two programs are available that can make any email program easier to use and more secure. The procmail program (www.procmail.org) creates and maintains email servers and mailing lists; preprocesses email by sorting it into appropriate files and directories; starts various programs depending on the characteristics of incoming email; forwards email; and so on. The GNU Privacy Guard (GPG or GNUpg, page 992) encrypts and decrypts email and makes it almost impossible for an unauthorized person to read.

Refer to Chapter 20 for more information on setting email clients and servers. See page 648 for instructions on setting up KMail to send and receive email.

Network addresses   If your system is part of a LAN, you can generally send email to and receive email from users on other systems on the LAN by using their usernames. Someone sending Alex email on the Internet would need to specify his *domain name* (page 1030) along with his username. Use this address to send email to the author of this book: **mgs@sobell.com**.

TUTORIAL: CREATING AND EDITING A FILE WITH vim

This section explains how to start vim, enter text, move the cursor, correct text, save the file to the disk, and exit from vim. The tutorial discusses three of the modes of operation of vim and explains how to switch from one mode to another.

vimtutor   In addition to working with this tutorial, you may want to try vim's tutor, named vimtutor: Give its name as a command to run it.

Specifying a terminal   Because vim takes advantage of features that are specific to various kinds of terminals, you must tell it what type of terminal or terminal emulator you are using. On many systems, and usually when you work on a terminal emulator, your terminal type is set automatically. If you need to specify your terminal type explicitly, refer to "Specifying a Terminal" on page 984.

STARTING vim

Start vim with the following command line to create and edit a file named **practice**:

```
$ vim practice
```

When you press RETURN, the command line disappears, and the screen looks similar to the one shown in Figure 5-16.

The tildes (~) at the left of the screen indicate that the file is empty. They disappear as you add lines of text to the file. If your screen looks like a distorted version of the one shown in Figure 5-16, your terminal type is probably not set correctly.

The vi command runs vim

tip   On Red Hat Linux systems the command **vi** runs a minimal build of vim that is compact and faster to load than vim but includes fewer features. See "The compatible Parameter" on page 159 for information on running vim in vi-compatible mode.

If you start vim with a terminal type that is not in the **terminfo** database, vim displays an error message and the terminal type defaults to **ansi**, which works on many terminals. In the following example, the user mistyped **vt100** and set the terminal type to **vg100**:

```
E558: Terminal entry not found in terminfo
'vg100' not known. Available builtin terminals are:
    builtin_riscos
    builtin_amiga
    builtin_beos-ansi
    builtin_ansi
    builtin_pcansi
    builtin_win32
    builtin_vt320
    builtin_vt52
    builtin_xterm
    builtin_iris-ansi
    builtin_debug
    builtin_dumb
defaulting to 'ansi'
```

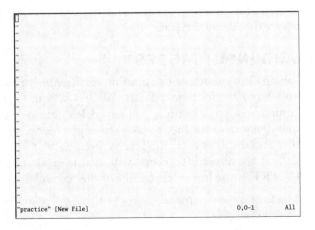

Figure 5-16   Starting vim

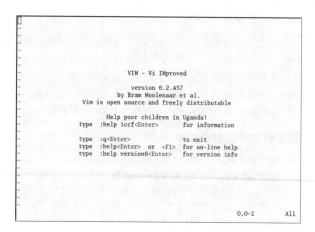

```
                    VIM - Vi IMproved

                       version 6.2.457
                   by Bram Moolenaar et al.
          Vim is open source and freely distributable

                  Help poor children in Uganda!
          type   :help iccf<Enter>       for information

          type   :q<Enter>               to exit
          type   :help<Enter>  or  <F1>  for on-line help
          type   :help version6<Enter>   for version info




                                              0,0-1        All
```

Figure 5-17 Starting vim without a filename

To reset the terminal type, press ESCAPE and then give the following command to exit from vim and get the shell prompt back:

> **:q!**

When you enter the colon (:), vim moves the cursor to the bottom line of the screen. The characters **q!** tell vim to quit without saving your work. (You will not ordinarily exit from vim this way because you typically want to save your work.) You must press RETURN after you give this command. Once you get the shell prompt back, refer to "Specifying a Terminal" on page 984, and then start vim again.

If you start this editor without a filename, vim assumes that you are a novice and tells you how to get started (Figure 5-17).

The **practice** file is new so it does not contain any text. The vim editor displays a message similar to the one shown in Figure 5-16 on the status (bottom) line of the terminal to indicate that you are creating and editing a new file. When you edit an existing file, vim displays the first few lines of the file and gives status information about the file on the status line.

COMMAND AND INPUT MODES

Two of vim's modes of operation are *Command mode* (also called *Normal mode*) and *Input mode* (Figure 5-18). While vim is in Command mode, you can give vim commands. For example, you can delete text or exit from vim. You can also command vim to enter Input mode. In Input mode, vim accepts anything you enter as text and displays it on the screen. Press ESCAPE to return vim to Command mode. By default the vim editor keeps you informed about which mode it is in: It displays **INSERT** at the lower-left corner of the screen while it is in Insert mode.

The following command causes vim to display line numbers next to the text you are editing:

```
:set number RETURN
```

Last Line mode   The colon (:) in the preceding command puts vim into another mode, *Last Line mode*. While in this mode, vim keeps the cursor on the bottom line of the screen. When you finish entering the command by pressing RETURN, vim restores the cursor to its place in the text. Give the command **:set nonumber** RETURN to turn off line numbers.

vim is case sensitive   When you give vim a command, remember that the editor is case sensitive. In other words, vim interprets the same letter as two different commands, depending on whether you enter an uppercase or lowercase character. Beware of the CAPS LOCK (SHIFTLOCK) key. If you set this key to enter uppercase text while you are in Input mode and then exit to Command mode, vim interprets your commands as uppercase letters. It can be confusing when this happens because vim does not appear to be executing the commands you are entering.

ENTERING TEXT

i/a (Input mode)   When you start vim, you must put it in Input mode before you can enter text. To put vim in Input mode, press the **i** key (insert before the cursor) or the **a** key (append after the cursor).

If you are not sure whether vim is currently in Input mode, press the ESCAPE key; vim returns to Command mode if it was in Input mode or beeps, flashes, or does nothing if it is already in Command mode. You can put vim back in Input mode by pressing the **i** or **a** key again.

While vim is in Input mode, you can enter text by typing on the keyboard. If the text does not appear on the screen as you type, vim is not in Input mode.

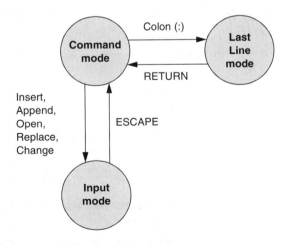

Figure 5-18   Modes in vim

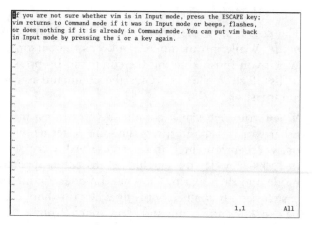

Figure 5-19   Entering text with vim

To continue with this tutorial, enter the sample paragraph shown in Figure 5-19, pressing the RETURN key at the end of each line. If you do not press RETURN before the cursor reaches the right side of the screen or window, vim will wrap the text so that it appears to start a new line. Physical lines will not correspond to programmatic (logical) lines in this situation, so editing will be more difficult. While you are using vim, you can always correct any typing mistakes you make. If you notice a mistake on the line you are entering, you can correct it before you continue (page 157). You can correct other mistakes later. When you finish entering the paragraph, press ESCAPE to return vim to Command mode.

GETTING HELP

To get help while you are using vim, give the command **:help** [*feature*] followed by RETURN (you must be in Command mode when you give this command). The colon

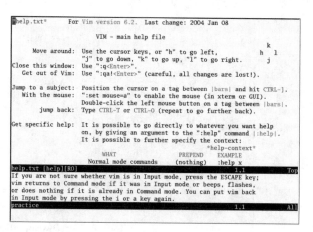

Figure 5-20   The main vim Help screen

moves the cursor to the last line of the screen. If you type **:help**, vim displays an introduction to vim Help (Figure 5-20). Each dark band near the bottom of the screen names the file that is displayed above it. (Each area of the screen that displays a file, such as the two areas shown in Figure 5-20, is a vim "window.") The **help.txt** file occupies most of the screen (the upper window) in Figure 5-20. The file that is being edited (**practice**) occupies a few lines in the lower portion of the screen (the lower window).

Read through the introduction to Help by scrolling the text as you read. Press **j** or the DOWN ARROW key to move the cursor down one line at a time; press CONTROL-D or CONTROL-U to scroll the cursor down or up half a window at a time. Give the command **:q** to close the Help window.

You can get help with the insert commands by giving the command **:help insert** while vim is in Command mode (Figure 5-21).

CORRECTING TEXT AS YOU INSERT IT

The keys that back up and correct a shell command line serve the same functions when vim is in Input mode. These keys include the erase, line kill, and word kill keys (usually CONTROL-H, CONTROL-U, and CONTROL-W, respectively). Although vim may not remove deleted text from the screen as you back up over it using one of these keys, the editor does remove it when you type over the text or press RETURN.

MOVING THE CURSOR

You need to be able to move the cursor on the screen so that you can delete, insert, and correct text. While vim is in Command mode, you can use the RETURN key, the SPACE bar, and the ARROW keys to move the cursor. If you prefer to keep your hand closer to the center of the keyboard, if your terminal does not have ARROW keys, or if the emulator you are using does not support them, you can use the **h**, **j**, **k**, and **l** (lowercase "l") keys to move the cursor left, down, up, and right, respectively.

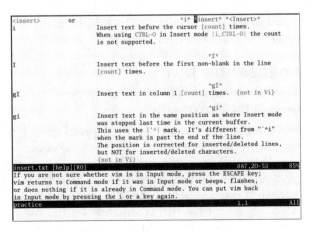

Figure 5-21   Help with insert commands

DELETING TEXT

x (Delete character)
dw (Delete word)
dd (Delete line)

You can delete a single character by moving the cursor until it is over the character you want to delete and then giving the command **x**. You can delete a word by positioning the cursor on the first letter of the word and then giving the command **dw** (Delete word). You can delete a line of text by moving the cursor until it is anywhere on the line and then giving the command **dd**.

UNDOING MISTAKES

u (Undo)

If you delete a character, line, or word by mistake or give any command you want to reverse, give the command **u** (Undo) immediately after the command you want to undo. The vim editor will restore the text to the way it was before you gave the last command. If you give the **u** command again, vim will undo the command you gave before the one it just undid. You can use this technique to back up over many of your actions. With the **compatible** parameter (page 159) set, however, vim can undo only the most recent change.

:redo (Redo)

If you undo a command you did not mean to undo, give a Redo command: CONTROL-R or **:redo** (followed by a RETURN). The vim editor will redo the undone command. As with the Undo command, you can give the Redo command many times in a row.

ENTERING ADDITIONAL TEXT

i (Insert)
a (Append)

When you want to insert new text within existing text, move the cursor so it is on the character that follows the new text you plan to enter. Then give the **i** (Insert) command to put vim in Input mode, enter the new text, and press ESCAPE to return vim to Command mode. Alternatively, you can position the cursor on the character that precedes the new text and use the **a** (Append) command.

o/O (Open)

To enter one or more lines, position the cursor on the line above where you want the new text to go. Give the command **o** (Open). The vim editor opens a blank line, puts the cursor on it, and goes into Input mode. Enter the new text, ending each line with a RETURN. When you are finished entering text, press ESCAPE to return vim to Command mode. The O command works in the same way **o** works, except that it opens a blank line *above* the line the cursor is on.

CORRECTING TEXT

To correct text, use **dd**, **dw**, or **x** to remove the incorrect text. Then use **i**, **a**, **o**, or **O** to insert the correct text.

For example, to change the word **pressing** to **hitting** in Figure 5-19 on page 156, you might use the ARROW keys to move the cursor until it is on top of the **p** in **pressing**. Then give the command **dw** to delete the word **pressing**. Put vim in Input mode by giving an **i** command, enter the word **hitting** followed by a SPACE, and press ESCAPE. The word is changed and vim is in Command mode, waiting for another command. A shorthand for the two commands **dw** followed by the **i** command is **cw** (Change word). The command **cw** puts vim into Input mode.

Page breaks for the printer

tip   CONTROL-L tells the printer to skip to the top of the next page. You can enter this character anywhere in a document by pressing CONTROL-L while you are in Input mode. If **^L** does not appear, press CONTROL-V before CONTROL-L.

ENDING THE EDITING SESSION

While you are editing, vim keeps the edited text in an area named the *Work buffer*. When you finish editing, you must write out the contents of the Work buffer to a disk file so that the edited text is saved and available when you next want it.

Make sure that vim is in Command mode, and then use the **ZZ** command (you must use uppercase Z's) to write your newly entered text to the disk and end the editing session. After you give the **ZZ** command, vim returns control to the shell. You can exit with **:q!** if you do not want to save your work.

Do not confuse ZZ with CONTROL-Z

caution   When you exit from vim with **ZZ**, make sure that you type **ZZ** and not CONTROL-Z (typically the suspend key). When you press CONTROL-Z, vim disappears from your screen, almost as though you had exited from it. In fact, vim will continue running in the background with your work unsaved. Refer to "Job Control" on page 280. If you try to start editing the same file with a new **vim** command, vim displays a message about a swap file.

THE compatible PARAMETER

The **compatible** parameter makes vim more compatible with vi. By default this parameter is not set. From the command line use the **–C** option to set the **compatible** parameter and use the **–N** option to unset it. To get started with vim you can ignore this parameter.

Setting the **compatible** parameter changes many aspects of how vim works. For example, when the **compatible** parameter is set, the Undo command (page 158) can undo only your most recent change; in contrast, with the **compatible** parameter unset, you can call Undo repeatedly to undo many changes. To obtain more details on the **compatible** parameter, give the command **:help compatible** RETURN. To display a complete list of vim's differences from the original vi, use **:help vi-diff** RETURN. See page 156 for a discussion of the **help** command.

CHAPTER SUMMARY

The utilities introduced in this chapter are a small but powerful subset of the many utilities available on a Red Hat Linux system. Because you will use them frequently and because they are integral to the following chapters, it is important that you become comfortable using them.

The utilities listed in Table 5-2 manipulate, display, compare, and print files.

Table 5-2 File utilities

Utility	Function
cp	Copies one or more files (page 129)
diff	Displays the differences between two files (page 135)
file	Displays information about the contents of a file (page 135)
grep	Searches file(s) for a string (page 131)
head	Displays the lines at the beginning of a file (page 132)
lpq	Displays a list of jobs in the print queue (page 131)
lpr	Places file(s) in the print queue (page 131)
lprm	Removes a job from the print queue (page 131)
mv	Renames a file or moves file(s) to another directory (page 130)
sort	Puts a file in order by lines (page 133)
tail	Displays the lines at the end of a file (page 132)
uniq	Displays the contents of a file, skipping successive duplicate lines (page 134)

To reduce the amount of disk space a file occupies, you can compress it with the bzip2 utility. Compression works especially well on files that contain patterns, as do most text files, but reduces the size of almost all files. The inverse of bzip2—bunzip2—restores a file to its original, decompressed form. Table 5-3 lists utilities that compress and decompress files. The bzip2 utility is the most efficient of these.

Table 5-3 (De)compression utilities

Utility	Function
bunzip2	Returns a file compressed with bzip2 to its original size and format (page 140)
bzcat	Displays a file compressed with bzip2 (page 140)
bzip2	Compresses a file (page 140)
compress	Compresses a file (not as well as gzip) (page 141)
gunzip	Returns a file compressed with gzip or compress to its original size and format (page 141)
gzip	Compresses a file (page 141)
zcat	Displays a file compressed with gzip (page 141)

An archive is a file, frequently compressed, that contains a group of files. The tar utility (Table 5-4) packs and unpacks archives. The filename extensions .tar.bz2, .tar.gz, and .tgz identify compressed tar archive files and are often seen on software packages obtained over the Internet.

Table 5-4 Archive utility

Utility	Function
tar	Creates or extracts files from an archive file (page 141)

The utilities listed in Table 5-5 determine the location of a utility on the local system. For example, they can display the pathname of a utility or a list of C++ compilers available on the local system.

Table 5-5 Location utilities

Utility	Function
apropos	Searches the man page one-line descriptions for a keyword (page 145)
locate	Searches for files on the local system (page 146)
whereis	Displays the full pathnames of a utility, source code, or man page (page 144)
which	Displays the full pathname of a command you can run (page 144)

Table 5-6 lists utilities that display information about other users. You can easily learn a user's full name, the user's login status, the login shell of the user, and other items of information maintained by the system.

Table 5-6 User and system information utilities

Utility	Function
finger	Displays detailed information about users, including their full names (page 147)
hostname	Displays the name of the local system (page 129)
w	Displays detailed information about users who are logged in (page 149)
who	Displays information about users who are logged in (page 147)

The utilities shown in Table 5-7 can help you stay in touch with other users on the local network.

Table 5-7 User communication utilities

Utility	Function
mesg	Permits or denies messages sent by write (page 151)
write	Sends a message to another user who is logged in (page 150)

Table 5-8 lists miscellaneous utilities.

Table 5-8   Miscellaneous utilities

Utility	Function
date	Displays the current date and time (page 137)
echo	Copies its *arguments* (page 1019) to the screen (page 137)

Exercises

1. Which commands can you use to determine who is logged in on a specific terminal?

2. How can you keep other users from using write to communicate with you? Why would you want to?

3. What happens when you give the following commands if the file named **done** already exists?

   ```
   $ cp to_do done
   $ mv to_do done
   ```

4. How can you find out which utilities are available on your system for editing files? Which utilities are available for editing on your system?

5. How can you find the phone number for Ace Electronics in a file named **phone** that contains a list of names and phone numbers? Which command can you use to display the entire file in alphabetical order? How can you remove adjacent duplicate lines from the file? How can you remove all duplicates?

6. What happens when you use diff to compare two binary files that are not identical? (You can use gzip to create the binary files.) Explain why the diff output for binary files is different from the diff output for ASCII files.

7. Create a **.plan** file in your home directory. Does finger display the contents of your **.plan** file?

8. What is the result of giving the which utility the name of a command that resides in a directory that is *not* in your search path?

9. Are any of the utilities discussed in this chapter located in more than one directory on your system? If so, which ones?

10. Experiment by calling the file utility with the names of files in **/usr/bin**. How many different types of files are there?

11. Which command can you use to look at the first few lines of a file named **status.report**? Which command can you use to look at the end of the file?

ADVANCED EXERCISES

12. Re-create the **colors.1** and **colors.2** files used in Figure 5-8 on page 135. Test your files by running **diff –u** on them. Do you get the same results as in the figure?

13. Try giving these two commands:

    ```
    $ echo cat
    $ cat echo
    ```

    Explain the differences between them.

14. Repeat exercise 5 using the file **phone.gz,** a compressed version of the list of names and phone numbers. Consider more than one approach to answer each question, and explain how you made your choices.

15. Find existing files or create files that

    a. gzip compresses by more than 80 percent.

    b. gzip compresses by less than 10 percent.

    c. Get larger when compressed with gzip.

    d. Use **ls –l** to determine the sizes of the files in question. Can you characterize the files in a, b, and c?

16. Older email programs were not able to handle binary files. Suppose that you are emailing a file that has been compressed with gzip, which produces a binary file, and the recipient is using an old email program. Refer to the man page on uuencode, which converts a binary file to ASCII. Learn about the utility and how to use it.

    a. Convert a compressed file to ASCII using uuencode. Is the encoded file larger or smaller than the compressed file? Explain. (If uuencode is not on the local system, you can install it using yum [page 476]; it is part of the **sharutils** package.)

    b. Would it ever make sense to use uuencode on a file before compressing it? Explain.

6

THE LINUX FILESYSTEM

A *filesystem* is a set of *data structures* (page 1028) that usually resides on part of a disk and that holds directories of files. Filesystems store user and system data that are the basis of users' work on the system and the system's existence. This chapter discusses the organization and terminology of the Linux filesystem, defines ordinary and directory files, and explains the rules for naming them. It also shows how to create and delete directories, move through the filesystem, and use absolute and relative pathnames to access files in various directories. It includes a discussion of important files and directories as well as file access permissions and Access Control Lists (ACLs), which allow you to share selected files with other users. It concludes with a discussion of hard and symbolic links, which can make a single file appear in more than one directory.

In addition to reading this chapter, you may want to refer to the df info page and to the fsck, mkfs, and tune2fs man pages for more information on filesystems.

165

THE HIERARCHICAL FILESYSTEM

Family tree   A *hierarchical* structure (page 1035) frequently takes the shape of a pyramid. One example of this type of structure is found by tracing a family's lineage: A couple has a child, who may in turn have several children, each of whom may have more children. This hierarchical structure is called a *family tree* (Figure 6-1).

Directory tree   Like the family tree it resembles, the Linux filesystem is called a *tree*. It consists of a set of connected files. This structure allows you to organize files so you can easily find any particular one. On a standard Linux system, each user starts with one directory, to which the user can add subdirectories to any desired level. By creating multiple levels of subdirectories, a user can expand the structure as needed.

Subdirectories   Typically each subdirectory is dedicated to a single subject, such as a person, project, or event. The subject dictates whether a subdirectory should be subdivided further. For example, Figure 6-2 shows a secretary's subdirectory named **correspond**. This directory contains three subdirectories: **business**, **memos**, and **personal**. The **business** directory contains files that store each letter the secretary types. If you expect many letters to go to one client, as is the case with **milk_co**, you can dedicate a subdirectory to that client.

One major strength of the Linux filesystem is its ability to adapt to users' needs. You can take advantage of this strength by strategically organizing your files so they are most convenient and useful for you.

DIRECTORY FILES AND ORDINARY FILES

Like a family tree, the tree representing the filesystem is usually pictured upside down, with its *root* at the top. Figures 6-2 and 6-3 show that the tree "grows"

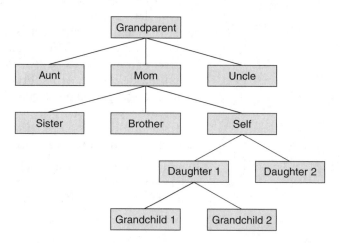

Figure 6-1   A family tree

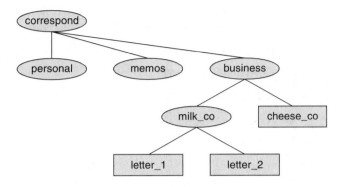

Figure 6-2   A secretary's directories

downward from the root, with paths connecting the root to each of the other files. At the end of each path is either an ordinary file or a directory file. Special files, which can also be at the ends of paths, are described on page 460. *Ordinary files,* or simply *files,* appear at the ends of paths that cannot support other paths. *Directory files,* also referred to as *directories* or *folders,* are the points that other paths can branch off from. (Figures 6-2 and 6-3 show some empty directories.) When you refer to the tree, *up* is toward the root and *down* is away from the root. Directories directly connected by a path are called *parents* (closer to the root) and *children* (farther from the root). A *pathname* is a series of names that trace a path along branches from one file to another. More information about pathnames appears on page 171.

FILENAMES

Every file has a *filename*. The maximum length of a filename varies with the type of filesystem; Linux supports several types of filesystems. Although most of today's filesystems allow you to create files with names up to 255 characters long, some filesystems

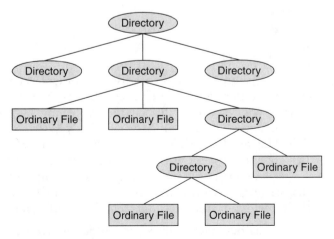

Figure 6-3   Directories and ordinary files

restrict you to shorter names. While you can use almost any character in a filename, you will avoid confusion if you choose characters from the following list:

- Uppercase letters (A–Z)
- Lowercase letters (a–z)
- Numbers (0–9)
- Underscore (_)
- Period (.)
- Comma (,)

/ or root The *root* directory is always named **/** (slash) and referred to by this single character. No other file can use this name or have a **/** in its name. However, in a pathname, which is a string of filenames including directory names, the slash *separates* filenames (page 171).

Like the children of one parent, no two files in the same directory can have the same name. (Parents give their children different names because it makes good sense, but Linux requires it.) Files in different directories, like the children of different parents, can have the same name.

The filenames you choose should mean something. Too often a directory is filled with important files with such unhelpful names as **hold1**, **wombat**, and **junk**, not to mention **foo** and **foobar**. Such names are poor choices because they do not help you recall what you stored in a file. The following filenames conform to the suggested syntax *and* convey information about the contents of the file:

- **correspond**
- **january**
- **davis**
- **reports**
- **2001**
- **acct_payable**

Filename length When you share your files with users on other systems, you may need to make long filenames differ within the first few characters. Systems running DOS or older versions of Windows have an 8-character filename body length and a 3-character filename extension length limit. Some UNIX systems have a 14-character limit and older Macintosh systems have a 31-character limit. If you keep the filenames short, they are easy to type; later you can add extensions to them without exceeding the shorter limits imposed by some filesystems. The disadvantage of short filenames is that they are typically less descriptive than long filenames. See stat on page 420 for a way to determine the maximum length of a filename on the local system.

Long filenames enable you to assign descriptive names to files. To help you select among files without typing entire filenames, shells support filename completion. For more information about this feature, see the "Filename completion" tip on page 129.

Case sensitivity   You can use uppercase and/or lowercase letters within filenames. Linux is case sensitive, so files named **JANUARY, January**, and **january** represent three distinct files.

Do not use SPACEs within filenames

caution   Although you can use SPACEs within filenames, it is a poor idea. Because a SPACE is a special character, you must quote it on a command line. Quoting a character on a command line can be difficult for a novice user and cumbersome for an experienced user. Use periods or underscores instead of SPACEs: **joe.05.04.26, new_stuff**.

If you are working with a filename that includes a SPACE, such as a file from another operating system, you must quote the SPACE on the command line by preceding it with a backslash or by placing quotation marks on either side of the filename. The two following commands send the file named **my file** to the printer.

```
$ lpr my\ file
$ lpr "my file"
```

FILENAME EXTENSIONS

A *filename extension* is the part of the filename following an embedded period. In the filenames listed in Table 6-1, filename extensions help describe the contents of the file. Some programs, such as the C programming language compiler, default to specific filename extensions; in most cases, however, filename extensions are optional. Use extensions freely to make filenames easy to understand. If you like, you can use several periods within the same filename—for example, **notes.4.10.01** or **files.tar.gz**.

Table 6-1   Filename extensions

Filename with extension	Meaning of extension
compute.c	A C programming language source file
compute.o	The object code for the program
compute	The same program as an executable file
memo.0410.txt	A text file
memo.pdf	A PDF file; view with xpdf under a GUI
memo.ps	A PostScript file; view with gs under a GUI
memo.Z	A file compressed with compress (page 141); use uncompress or gunzip (page 141) to decompress
memo.tgz or **memo.tar.gz**	A tar (page 141) archive of files compressed with gzip (page 141)
memo.gz	A file compressed with gzip (page 141); view with zcat or decompress with gunzip (both on page 141)
memo.bz2	A file compressed with bzip2 (page 140); view with bzcat or decompress with bunzip2 (both on page 140)
memo.html	A file meant to be viewed using a Web browser, such as Firefox
photo.gif, photo.jpg, photo.jpeg, photo.bmp, photo.tif, or **photo.tiff**	A file containing graphical information, such as a picture

HIDDEN FILENAMES

A filename that begins with a period is called a *hidden filename* (or a *hidden file* or sometimes an *invisible file*) because ls does not normally display it. The command ls –a displays *all* filenames, even hidden ones. Names of startup files (page 170) usually begin with a period so that they are hidden and do not clutter a directory listing. The **.plan** file (page 148) is also hidden. Two special hidden entries—a single and double period (. and ..)—appear in every directory (page 175).

THE WORKING DIRECTORY

pwd   While you are logged in on a character-based interface to a Linux system, you are always associated with a directory. The directory you are associated with is called the *working directory* or *current directory*. Sometimes this association is referred to in a physical sense: "You are *in* (or *working in*) the **jenny** directory." The pwd (print working directory) utility displays the pathname of the working directory.

YOUR HOME DIRECTORY

When you first log in on a Linux system or start a terminal emulator window, your working directory is your *home directory*. To display the pathname of your home directory, use pwd just after you log in (Figure 6-4).

When used without any arguments, the ls utility displays a list of the files in the working directory. Because your home directory has been the only working directory you have used so far, ls has always displayed a list of files in your home directory. (All the files you have created up to this point were created in your home directory.)

STARTUP FILES

Startup files, which appear in your home directory, give the shell and other programs information about you and your preferences. Frequently one of these files tells the shell what kind of terminal you are using (page 984) and executes the stty (set terminal) utility to establish the erase (page 117) and line kill (page 118) keys.

Either you or the system administrator can put a shell startup file containing shell commands in your home directory. The shell executes the commands in this file each time you log in. Because the startup files have hidden filenames, you must use the ls –a command to see whether one is in your home directory. A GUI has many startup files. Usually you do not need to work with these files directly but can control startup sequences by using icons on the desktop. See page 267 for more information about startup files.

```
login: alex
Password:
Last login: Wed Oct 20 11:14:21 from bravo
$ pwd
/home/alex
```

Figure 6-4   Logging in and displaying the pathname of your home directory

PATHNAMES

This section discusses absolute and relative pathnames and explains how to use them to your advantage.

ABSOLUTE PATHNAMES

Every file has a pathname. Figure 6-5 shows the pathnames of directories and ordinary files in part of a filesystem hierarchy. An absolute pathname always starts with a slash (/), the name of the root directory. You can then build the absolute pathname of a file by tracing a path from the root directory through all the intermediate directories to the file. String all the filenames in the path together, separating each from the next with a slash (/) and preceding the entire group of filenames with a slash (/). This path of filenames is called an *absolute pathname* because it locates a file absolutely by tracing a path from the root directory to the file. The part of a pathname following the final slash is called a *simple filename, filename*, or *basename*.

~ (TILDE) IN PATHNAMES

In another form of absolute pathname, the shell expands the characters ~/ (a tilde followed by a slash) at the start of a pathname into the pathname of your home directory. Using this shortcut, you can display your **.bashrc** startup file (page 267) with the following command, no matter which directory is your working directory:

```
$ less ~/.bashrc
```

A tilde quickly references paths that start with your or someone else's home directory. The shell expands a tilde followed by a username at the beginning of a pathname into the pathname of that user's home directory. For example, assuming he

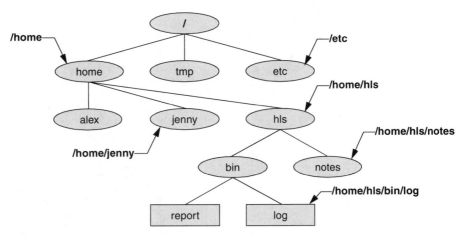

Figure 6-5   Absolute pathnames

has permission to do so, Alex can examine Scott's **.bashrc** file with the following command:

```
$ less ~scott/.bashrc
```

Refer to "Tilde Expansion" on page 331 for more information.

RELATIVE PATHNAMES

A *relative pathname* traces a path from the working directory to a file. The pathname is *relative* to the working directory. Any pathname that does not begin with the root directory (/) or a tilde (~) is a relative pathname. Like absolute pathnames, relative pathnames can trace a path through many directories. The simplest relative pathname is a simple filename, which identifies a file in the working directory. The examples in the next sections use absolute and relative pathnames.

When using a relative pathname, know which directory is the working directory

caution   The location of the file that you are accessing with a relative pathname is dependent on (is relative to) the working directory. Always make sure you know which directory is the working directory before you use a relative pathname. Use **pwd** to verify the directory. If you are using **mkdir** and you are not where you think you are in the file hierarchy, the new directory will end up in an unexpected location.

It does not matter which directory is the working directory when you use an absolute pathname.

SIGNIFICANCE OF THE WORKING DIRECTORY

To access any file in the working directory, you need only a simple filename. To access a file in another directory, you *must* use a pathname. Typing a long pathname is tedious and increases the chance of making a mistake. This possibility is less likely under a GUI, where you click filenames or icons. You can choose a working directory for any particular task to reduce the need for long pathnames. Your choice of a

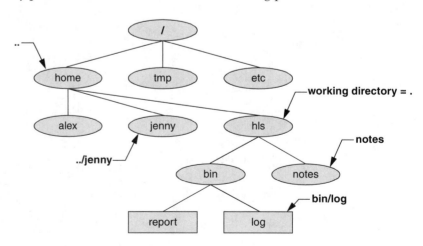

Figure 6-6   Relative pathnames

working directory does not allow you to do anything you could not do otherwise—it just makes some operations easier.

Refer to Figure 6-6 as you read this paragraph. Files that are children of the working directory can be referenced by simple filenames. Grandchildren of the working directory can be referenced by short relative pathnames: two filenames separated by a slash. When you manipulate files in a large directory structure, using short relative pathnames can save you time and aggravation. If you choose a working directory that contains the files used most often for a particular task, you need to use fewer long, cumbersome pathnames.

DIRECTORY COMMANDS

This section discusses how to create directories (mkdir), switch between directories (cd), remove directories (rmdir), use pathnames to make your work easier, and move and copy files and directories between directories.

mkdir: CREATES A DIRECTORY

The mkdir utility creates a directory. The *argument* (page 1019) to mkdir becomes the pathname of the new directory. The following examples develop the directory structure shown in Figure 6-7. In the figure, the directories that are added appear in a lighter shade than the others and are connected by dashes.

In Figure 6-8 (next page), pwd shows that Alex is working in his home directory (**/home/alex**) and ls shows the names of the files in his home directory: **demo, names,** and **temp.** Using mkdir, Alex creates a directory named **literature** as a child of his home directory. He uses a relative pathname (a simple filename) because he wants the **literature** directory to be a child of the working directory. Of course, Alex could have used an absolute pathname to create the same directory: **mkdir /home/alex/literature.**

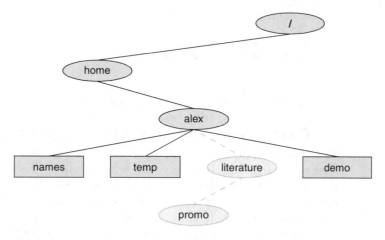

Figure 6-7   The file structure developed in the examples

```
$ pwd
/home/alex
$ ls
demo   names   temp
$ mkdir literature
$ ls
demo   literature   names   temp
$ ls -F
demo   literature/   names   temp
$ ls literature
$
```

Figure 6-8   The mkdir utility

The second ls in Figure 6-8 verifies the presence of the new directory. The **–F** option to ls displays a slash after the name of each directory and an asterisk after each executable file (shell script, utility, or application). When you call it with an argument that is the name of a directory, ls lists the contents of that directory. The final ls does not display anything because there are no files in the **literature** directory.

The following commands show two ways to create the **promo** directory as a child of the newly created **literature** directory. The first way checks that **/home/alex** is the working directory and uses a relative pathname:

```
$ pwd
/home/alex
$ mkdir literature/promo
```

The second way uses an absolute pathname:

```
$ mkdir /home/alex/literature/promo
```

Use the **–p** (parents) option to mkdir to create both the **literature** and **promo** directories with one command:

```
$ pwd
/home/alex
$ ls
demo   names   temp
$ mkdir -p literature/promo
```

or

```
$ mkdir -p /home/alex/literature/promo
```

cd: CHANGES TO ANOTHER WORKING DIRECTORY

The cd (change directory) utility makes another directory the working directory but does *not* change the contents of the working directory. Figure 6-9 shows two ways to make the **/home/alex/literature** directory the working directory, as verified by pwd. First Alex uses cd with an absolute pathname to make **literature** his working directory—it does not matter which is your working directory when you give a command with an absolute pathname. A pwd command confirms the change made

```
$ cd /home/alex/literature
$ pwd
/home/alex/literature
$ cd
$ pwd
/home/alex
$ cd literature
$ pwd
/home/alex/literature
```

Figure 6-9 cd changes your working directory

by Alex. When used without an argument, cd makes your home directory the working directory, as it was when you logged in. The second cd command in Figure 6-9 does not have an argument so it makes Alex's home directory the working directory. Finally, knowing that he is working in his home directory, Alex uses a simple filename to make the **literature** directory his working directory (**cd literature**) and confirms the change with pwd.

The working directory versus your home directory

tip   The working directory is not the same as your home directory. Your home directory remains the same for the duration of your session and usually from session to session. Immediately after you log in, you are always working in the same directory: your home directory.

Unlike your home directory, the working directory can change as often as you like. You have no set working directory, which explains why some people refer to it as the *current directory*. When you log in and until you change directories by using cd, your home directory is your working directory. If you were to change directories to Scott's home directory, then Scott's home directory would be your working directory.

THE . AND .. DIRECTORY ENTRIES

The mkdir utility automatically puts two entries in each directory you create: a single period (.) and a double period (..). The . is synonymous with the pathname of the working directory and can be used in its place; the .. is synonymous with the pathname of the parent of the working directory. These entries are hidden because their filenames begin with a period.

With the **literature** directory as the working directory, the following example uses .. three times: first to list the contents of the parent directory (**/home/alex**), second to copy the **memoA** file to the parent directory, and third to list the contents of the parent directory again.

```
$ pwd
/home/alex/literature
$ ls ..
demo  literature  names  temp
$ cp memoA ..
$ ls ..
demo  literature  memoA  names  temp
```

After using cd to make **promo** (a subdirectory of **literature**) his working directory, Alex can use a relative pathname to call vim to edit a file in his home directory.

```
$ cd promo
$ vim ../../names
```

You can use an absolute or relative pathname or a simple filename virtually anywhere that a utility or program requires a filename or pathname. This usage holds true for ls, vim, mkdir, rm, and most other Linux utilities.

IMPORTANT STANDARD DIRECTORIES AND FILES

Originally files on a Linux system were not located in standard places. The scattered files made it difficult to document and maintain a Linux system and just about impossible for someone to release a software package that would compile and run on all Linux systems. The first standard for the Linux filesystem, the FSSTND (Linux Filesystem Standard), was released on February 14, 1994. In early 1995 work was started on a broader standard covering many UNIX-like systems: FHS (Linux Filesystem Hierarchy Standard, www.pathname.com/fhs). More recently FHS has been incorporated in LSB (Linux Standard Base, www.linuxbase.org), a workgroup of FSG (Free Standards Group, www.freestandards.org). Figure 6-10 shows the locations of some important directories and files as specified by FHS. The significance of many of these directories will become clear as you continue reading.

The following list describes the directories shown in Figure 6-10, some of the directories specified by FHS, and some other directories. Red Hat Linux, however, does not use all the directories specified by FHS. Be aware that you cannot always determine the function of a directory by its name. For example, although **/opt** stores add-on software, **/etc/opt** stores configuration files for the software in **/opt**. See also "Important Files and Directories" on page 448.

/ **Root**   The root directory, present in all Linux filesystem structures, is the ancestor of all files in the filesystem.

/bin **Essential command binaries**   Holds the files needed to bring the system up and run it when it first comes up in single-user mode (page 409).

/boot **Static files of the boot loader**   Contains all of the files needed to boot the system.

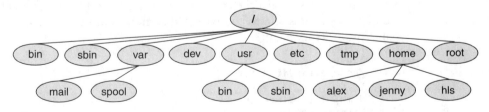

Figure 6-10   A typical FHS-based Linux filesystem structure

/dev **Device files** Contains all files that represent peripheral devices, such as disk drives, terminals, and printers. Previously this directory was filled with all possible devices. As of Fedora Core 3 and RHEL v.4, udev (page 461) provides a dynamic device directory that enables **/dev** to contain only devices that are present on the system.

/etc **Machine–local system configuration files** Holds administrative, configuration, and other system files. One of the most important is **/etc/passwd**, which contains a list of all users who have permission to use the system.

/etc/opt **Configuration files for add-on software packages kept in /opt**

/etc/X11 **Machine–local configuration files for the X Window System**

/home **User home directories** Each user's home directory is typically one of many sub-directories of the **/home** directory. As an example, assuming that users' directories are under **/home**, the absolute pathname of Jenny's home directory is **/home/jenny**. On some systems the users' directories may not be found under **/home** but instead might be spread among other directories such as **/inhouse** and **/clients**.

/lib **Shared libraries**

/lib/modules **Loadable kernel modules**

/mnt **Mount point for temporarily mounting filesystems**

/opt **Add-on software packages (optional packages)**

/proc **Kernel and process information virtual filesystem**

/root **Home directory for root**

/sbin **Essential system binaries** Utilities used for system administration are stored in **/sbin** and **/usr/sbin**. The **/sbin** directory includes utilities needed during the booting process, and **/usr/sbin** holds utilities used after the system is up and running. In older versions of Linux, many system administration utilities were scattered through several directories that often included other system files (**/etc**, **/usr/bin**, **/usr/adm**, **/usr/include**).

/sys **Device pseudofilesystem** See udev on page 461 for more information.

/tmp **Temporary files**

/usr **Second major hierarchy** Traditionally includes subdirectories that contain information used by the system. Files in **/usr** subdirectories do not change often and may be shared by several systems.

/usr/bin **Most user commands** Contains the standard Linux utility programs—that is, binaries that are not needed in single-user mode (page 409).

/usr/games **Games and educational programs**

/usr/include **Header files included by C programs**

/usr/lib **Libraries**

/usr/local **Local hierarchy** Holds locally important files and directories that are added to the system. Subdirectories can include **bin, games, include, lib, sbin, share,** and **src**.

/usr/man	Online manuals
/usr/sbin	Nonvital system administration binaries See /sbin.
/usr/share	Architecture-independent data Subdirectories can include dict, doc, games, info, locale, man, misc, terminfo, and zoneinfo.
/usr/share/doc	Documentation
/usr/share/info	GNU info system's primary directory
/usr/src	Source code
/var	Variable data Files with contents that vary as the system runs are kept in sub-directories under /var. The most common examples are temporary files, system log files, spooled files, and user mailbox files. Subdirectories can include cache, lib, lock, log, opt, run, spool, tmp, and yp. Older versions of Linux scattered such files through several subdirectories of /usr (/usr/adm, /usr/mail, /usr/spool, /usr/tmp).
/var/log	Log files Contains lastlog (a record of the last login by each user), messages (system messages from syslogd), and wtmp (a record of all logins/logouts).
/var/spool	Spooled application data Contains anacron, at, cron, lpd, mail, mqueue, samba, and other directories. The file /var/spool/mail typically has a symbolic link in /var.

WORKING WITH DIRECTORIES

This section covers deleting directories, copying and moving files between directories, and moving directories. It also describes how to use pathnames to make your work with Linux easier.

rmdir: DELETES A DIRECTORY

The rmdir (remove directory) utility deletes a directory. You cannot delete the working directory or a directory that contains files other than the . and .. entries. If you need to delete a directory that has files in it, first use rm to delete the files and then delete the directory. You do not have to (nor can you) delete the . and .. entries; rmdir removes them automatically. The following command deletes the **promo** directory:

```
$ rmdir /home/alex/literature/promo
```

The rm utility has a −r option (rm −r *filename*) that recursively deletes files, including directories, within a directory and also deletes the directory itself.

Use rm −r carefully, if at all

caution   Although **rm −r** is a handy command, you must use it carefully. Do not use it with an ambiguous file reference such as *. It is frighteningly easy to wipe out your entire home directory with a single short command.

USING PATHNAMES

touch Use a text editor to create a file named **letter** if you want to experiment with the examples that follow. Alternatively you can use touch to create an empty file:

```
$ cd
$ pwd
/home/alex
$ touch letter
```

With **/home/alex** as the working directory, the following example uses cp with a relative pathname to copy the file **letter** to the **/home/alex/literature/promo** directory (you will need to create **promo** again if you deleted it earlier). The copy of the file has the simple filename **letter.0610**:

```
$ cp letter literature/promo/letter.0610
```

If Alex does not change to another directory, he can use vim to edit the copy of the file he just made:

```
$ vim literature/promo/letter.0610
```

If Alex does not want to use a long pathname to specify the file, he can use cd to make **promo** the working directory before using vim:

```
$ cd literature/promo
$ pwd
/home/alex/literature/promo
$ vim letter.0610
```

To make the parent of the working directory (named **/home/alex/literature**) the new working directory, Alex can give the following command, which takes advantage of the .. directory entry:

```
$ cd ..
$ pwd
/home/alex/literature
```

mv, cp: MOVE OR COPY FILES

Chapter 5 discussed the use of mv to rename files. However, mv works even more generally: You can use this utility to move files from one directory to another (change the pathname of a file) as well as to change a simple filename. When used to move one or more files to a new directory, the mv command has this syntax:

mv existing-file-list directory

If the working directory is **/home/alex**, Alex can use the following command to move the files **names** and **temp** from the working directory to the **literature** directory:

```
$ mv names temp literature
```

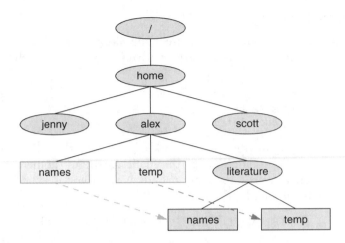

Figure 6-11   Using mv to move **names** and **temp**

This command changes the absolute pathnames of the **names** and **temp** files from **/home/alex/names** and **/home/alex/temp** to **/home/alex/literature/names** and **/home/alex/literature/temp**, respectively (Figure 6-11). Like most Linux commands, mv accepts either absolute or relative pathnames.

As you work with Linux and create more files, you will need to create new directories using mkdir to keep the files organized. The mv utility is a useful tool for moving files from one directory to another as you extend your directory hierarchy.

The cp utility works in the same way as mv does, except that it makes copies of the *existing-file-list* in the specified *directory*.

mv: MOVES A DIRECTORY

Just as it moves ordinary files from one directory to another, so mv can move directories. The syntax is similar except that you specify one or more directories, not ordinary files, to move:

   mv existing-directory-list new-directory

If *new-directory* does not exist, the *existing-directory-list* must contain just one directory name, which mv changes to *new-directory* (mv renames the directory). Although you can rename directories using mv, you cannot copy their contents with cp unless you use the **−r** option. Refer to the tar and cpio man pages for other ways to copy and move directories.

ACCESS PERMISSIONS

In addition to the controls imposed by SELinux (page 400), Red Hat Linux supports two methods of controlling who can access a file and how they can access

Figure 6-12 The columns displayed by the **ls –l** command

it: traditional Linux access permissions and Access Control Lists (ACLs, page 185). ACLs provide finer-grained control of access privileges. This section describes traditional Linux access permissions.

Three types of users can access a file: the owner of the file (*owner*), a member of a group that the file is associated with (*group*; see page 451 for more information on groups), and everyone else (*other*). A user can attempt to access an ordinary file in three ways: by trying to *read from, write to,* or *execute* it.

ls –l: DISPLAYS PERMISSIONS

When you call **ls** with the **–l** option and the name of one or more ordinary files, **ls** displays a line of information about the file. The following example displays information for two files. The file **letter.0610** contains the text of a letter, and **check_spell** contains a shell script, a program written in a high-level shell programming language:

```
$ ls -l letter.0610 check_spell
-rw-r--r-- 1 alex  pubs  3355  May  2 10:52 letter.0610
-rwxr-xr-x 2 alex  pubs   852  May  5 14:03 check_spell
```

From left to right, the lines that an **ls –l** command displays contain the following information (refer to Figure 6-12):

- The type of file (first character)
- The file's access permissions (the next nine characters)
- The ACL flag (present if the file has an ACL, page 185)
- The number of links to the file (page 190)
- The name of the owner of the file (usually the person who created the file)
- The name of the group that the file is associated with
- The size of the file in characters (bytes)
- The date and time the file was created or last modified
- The name of the file

The type of file (first column) for **letter.0610** is a hyphen (–) because it is an ordinary file (directory files have a **d** in this column).

The next three characters specify the access permissions for the *owner* of the file: **r** indicates read permission, **w** indicates write permission, and **x** indicates execute permission. A – in a column indicates that the owner does *not* have the permission that would have appeared in that position.

In a similar manner the next three characters represent permissions for the *group*, and the final three characters represent permissions for *other* (everyone else). In the preceding example, the owner of **letter.0610** can read from and write to the file, whereas the group and others can only read from the file and no one is allowed to execute it. Although execute permission can be allowed for any file, it does not make sense to assign execute permission to a file that contains a document, such as a letter. The **check_spell** file is an executable shell script, so execute permission is appropriate for it. (The owner, group, and others have execute access permission.)

chmod: CHANGES ACCESS PERMISSIONS

The owner of a file controls which users have permission to access the file and how they can access it. When you own a file, you can use the chmod (change mode) utility to change access permissions for that file. In the following example, chmod adds (**+**) read and write permissions (**rw**) for all (**a**) users:

```
$ chmod a+rw letter.0610
$ ls -l letter.0610
-rw-rw-rw- 1 alex pubs 3355  May  2 10:52 letter.0610
```

You must have read permission to execute a shell script

tip Because a shell needs to read a shell script (a text file containing shell commands) before it can execute the commands within that script, you must have read permission for the file containing the script to execute it. You also need execute permission to execute a shell script directly on the command line. In contrast, binary (program) files do not need to be read; they are executed directly. You need only execute permission to run a binary (nonshell) program.

In the next example, chmod removes (–) read (**r**) and execute (**x**) permissions for users other (**o**) than the owner of the file (**alex**) and members of the group the file is associated with (**pubs**):

```
$ chmod o-rx check_spell
$ ls -l check_spell
-rwxr-x--- 2 alex pubs 852  May  5 14:03 check_spell
```

In addition to **a** (*all*) and **o** (*other*), you can use **g** (*group*) and **u** (*user,* although **user** refers to the owner of the file who may or may not be the user of the file at any given time) in the argument to chmod. You can also use absolute, or numeric, arguments with chmod. Refer to page 273 for more information on using chmod to make a file executable and to the chmod man page for information on absolute arguments and chmod in general. Refer to page 451 for more information on groups.

The Linux file access permission scheme lets you give other users access to the files you want to share yet keep your private files confidential. You can allow other users to read from *and* write to a file (handy if you are one of several people working on a joint project). You can allow others only to read from a file (perhaps a project

chmod: **o** for other, **u** for owner

tip   When using chmod, many people assume that the **o** stands for *owner;* it does not. The **o** stands for *other,* whereas **u** stands for *owner* (*user*). The acronym UGO (user-group-other) can help you remember how permissions are named.

specification you are proposing). Or you can allow others only to write to a file (similar to an inbox or mailbox, where you want others to be able to send you mail but do not want them to read your mail). Similarly you can protect entire directories from being scanned (covered shortly).

There is an exception to the access permissions just described. Anyone who knows the **root** password can log in as Superuser (page 391) and gain full access to *all* files, regardless of the file's owner or access permissions.

SETUID AND SETGID PERMISSIONS

When you execute a file that has setuid (set user ID) permission, the process executing the file takes on the privileges of the file's owner. For example, if you run a setuid program that removes all files in a directory, you can remove files in any of the file owner's directories, even if you do not normally have permission to do so.

Minimize use of setuid and setgid programs owned by root

security   Executable files that are setuid and owned by **root** have Superuser privileges when they are run, even if they are not run by **root**. This type of program is very powerful because it can do anything that Superuser can do (and that the program is designed to do). Similarly executable files that are setgid and belong to the group **root** have extensive privileges.

Because of the power they hold and their potential for destruction, it is wise to avoid indiscriminately creating and using setuid and setgid programs owned by or belonging to the group **root**. Because of their inherent dangers, many sites minimize the use of these programs on their systems. One necessary setuid program is passwd. See page 393 for a tip on setuid files owned by **root** and page 399 for a command that lists setuid files on the local system.

In a similar manner, setgid (set group ID) permission means that the process executing the file takes on the privileges of the group the file is associated with. The ls utility shows setuid permission by placing an **s** in the owner's executable position and setgid permission by placing an **s** in the group's executable position:

```
$ ls -l program1
-rwxr-xr-x   1 alex pubs 15828 Nov  5 06:28 program1
$ chmod u+s program1
$ ls -l program1
-rwsr-xr-x   1 alex pubs 15828 Nov  5 06:28 program1
$ chmod g+s program1
$ ls -l program1
-rwsr-sr-x   1 alex pubs 15828 Nov  5 06:28 program1
```

Do not write setuid shell scripts

security   Never give shell scripts setuid permission. Several techniques for subverting them are well known.

DIRECTORY ACCESS PERMISSIONS

Access permissions have slightly different meanings when they are used with directories. Although the three types of users can read from or write to a directory, the directory cannot be executed. Execute access permission is redefined for a directory: It means that you can cd into the directory and/or examine files that you have permission to read from in the directory. It has nothing to do with executing a file.

When you have only execute permission for a directory, you can use ls to list a file in the directory if you know its name. You cannot use ls without an argument to list the entire contents of the directory. In the following exchange, Jenny first verifies that she is logged in as herself. Then she checks the permissions on Alex's **info** directory. You can view the access permissions associated with a directory by running ls with the **–d** (directory) and **–l** (long) options:

```
$ who am i
jenny      pts/7   Aug 21 10:02
$ ls -ld /home/alex/info
drwx-----x  2 alex pubs 512 Aug 21 09:31 /home/alex/info
$ ls -l /home/alex/info
ls: /home/alex/info: Permission denied
```

The **d** at the left end of the line that ls displays indicates that **/home/alex/info** is a directory. Alex has read, write, and execute permissions; members of the pubs group have no access permissions; and other users have execute permission only, as indicated by the **x** at the right end of the permissions. Because Jenny does not have read permission for the directory, the **ls –l** command returns an error.

When Jenny specifies the names of the files she wants information about, she is not reading new directory information but rather searching for specific information, which she is allowed to do with execute access to the directory. She has read permission for **notes** so she has no problem using cat to display the file. She cannot display **financial** because she does not have read permission for it:

```
$ ls -l /home/alex/info/financial /home/alex/info/notes
-rw-------  1 alex pubs 34 Aug 21 09:31 /home/alex/info/financial
-rw-r--r--  1 alex pubs 30 Aug 21 09:32 /home/alex/info/notes

$ cat /home/alex/info/notes
This is the file named notes.
$ cat /home/alex/info/financial
cat: /home/alex/info/financial: Permission denied
```

Next Alex gives others read access to his **info** directory:

```
$ chmod o+r /home/alex/info
```

When Jenny checks her access permissions on **info**, she finds that she has both read and execute access to the directory. Now **ls –l** works just fine without arguments, but she still cannot read **financial**. (This restriction is an issue of file permissions, not directory permissions.) Finally, Jenny tries to create a file named **newfile** by using touch. If Alex were to give her write permission to the **info** directory, Jenny would be able to create new files in it:

```
$ ls -ld /home/alex/info
drwx---r-x   2 alex pubs 512 Aug 21 09:31 /home/alex/info
$ ls -l /home/alex/info
total 8
-rw-------   1 alex pubs 34 Aug 21 09:31 financial
-rw-r--r--   1 alex pubs 30 Aug 21 09:32 notes
$ cat /home/alex/info/financial
cat: financial: Permission denied
$ touch /home/alex/info/newfile
touch: cannot touch '/home/alex/info/newfile': Permission denied
```

ACLs: Access Control Lists

Access Control Lists (ACLs) provide finer-grained control over which users can access specific directories and files than do traditional Linux permissions (page 180). Using ACLs you can specify the ways in which each of several users can access a directory or file. Because ACLs can reduce performance, do not enable them on filesystems that hold system files, where the traditional Linux permissions are sufficient. Also be careful when moving, copying, or archiving files: Not all utilities preserve ACLs. In addition, you cannot copy ACLs to filesystems that do not support ACLs.

Most utilities do not preserve ACLs

caution When used with the **–p** (preserve) or **–a** (archive) option, cp preserves ACLs when it copies files. Another utility that is supplied with Red Hat Linux that preserves ACLs is mv. When you use cp with the **–p** or **–a** option and it is not able to copy ACLs, and in the case where mv is unable to preserve ACLs, the utility performs the operation and issues an error message:

```
$ mv report /tmp
mv: preserving permissions for '/tmp/report': Operation not supported
```

Other utilities, such as tar, cpio, and dump, do not support ACLs. You can use cp with the **–a** option to copy directory hierarchies, including ACLs.

You can never copy ACLs to a filesystem that does not support ACLs or to a filesystem that does not have ACL support turned on.

An ACL comprises a set of rules. A rule specifies how a specific user or group can access the file that the ACL is associated with. There are two kinds of rules: *access rules* and *default rules*. (The documentation refers to *access ACLs* and *default ACLs*, even though there is only one type of ACL: There is one type of list [ACL] and there are two types of rules that an ACL can contain.)

An access rule specifies access information for a single file or directory. A default ACL pertains to a directory only; it specifies default access information (an ACL) for any file in the directory that is not given an explicit ACL.

ENABLING ACLS

Red Hat Linux officially supports ACLs on **ext2** and **ext3** filesystems only, although informal support for ACLs is available on other filesystems. To use ACLs on an **ext2** or **ext3** filesystem, you must mount the device with the **acl** option (**no_acl** is the default). For example, if you want to mount the device represented by **/home** so that you can use ACLs on files in **/home**, you can add **acl** to its options list in **/etc/fstab**:

```
$ grep home /etc/fstab
LABEL=/home              /home            ext3     defaults,acl       1 2
```

After changing **fstab**, you need to remount **/home** before you can use ACLs. If no one else is using the system, you can unmount it and mount it again (working as **root**) as long as your working directory is not in the **/home** hierarchy. Alternatively you can use the **remount** option to mount to remount **/home** while the device is in use:

```
# mount -v -o remount /home
/dev/hda3 on /home type ext3 (rw,acl)
```

See page 469 for information on **fstab** and page 466 for information on mount.

WORKING WITH ACCESS RULES

The setfacl utility modifies a file's ACL and the getfacl utility displays a file's ACL. When you use getfacl to obtain information about a file that does not have an ACL, it displays the same information as an **ls –l** command, albeit in a different format:

```
$ ls -l report
-rw-r--r--  1 max max 9537 Jan 12 23:17 report

$ getfacl report
# file: report
# owner: max
# group: max
user::rw-
group::r--
other::r--
```

The first three lines of the getfacl output are called the header; they specify the name of the file, the owner of the file, and the group the file is associated with. For more information refer to "ls –l: Displays Permissions" on page 181. The **––omit-header** (or just **––omit**) option causes getfacl not to display the header:

```
$ getfacl --omit-header report
user::rw-
group::r--
other::r--
```

In the line that starts with **user,** the two colons (::) with no name between them indicate that the line specifies the permissions for the owner of the file. Similarly, the two colons in the **group** line indicate that the line specifies permissions for the group the file is associated with. The two colons following **other** are there for consistency: No name can be associated with **other**.

The setfacl **--modify** (or **-m**) option adds or modifies one or more rules in a file's ACL using the following format:

*setfacl --modify **ugo:name:permissions file-list***

where *ugo* can be either **u**, **g**, or **o** to indicate that the command sets file permissions for a user, a group, or all other users, respectively; *name* is the name of the user or group that permissions are being set for; *permissions* is the permissions in either symbolic or absolute format; and *file-list* is the list of files that the permissions are to be applied to. You must omit *name* when you specify permissions for other users (**o**). Symbolic permissions use letters to represent file permissions (**rwx**, **r-x**, and so on), whereas absolute permissions use an octal number. While chmod uses three sets of permissions or three octal numbers (one each for the owner, group, and other users), setfacl uses a single set of permissions or a single octal number to represent the permissions being granted to the user or group represented by *ugo* and *name*.

For example, both of the following commands add a rule to the ACL for the **report** file that gives Sam read and write permission to that file:

```
$ setfacl --modify u:sam:rw- report
```

or

```
$ setfacl --modify u:sam:6 report
$ getfacl report
# file: report
# owner: max
# group: max
user::rw-
user:sam:rw-
group::r--
mask::rw-
other::r--
```

The line containing **user:sam:rw-** shows that the user named **sam** has read and write access (**rw-**) to the file. See page 181 for an explanation of how to read symbolic access permissions. See the following optional section for a description of the line that starts with **mask**.

When a file has an ACL, **ls -l** displays a plus sign (**+**) following the permissions, even if the ACL is empty:

```
$ ls -l report
-rw-rw-r--+ 1 max max 9537 Jan 12 23:17 report
```

optional EFFECTIVE RIGHTS MASK

The line that starts with **mask** specifies the *effective rights mask*. This mask limits the effective permissions granted to ACL groups and users. It does not affect the owner of the file or the group the file is associated with. In other words, it does not affect traditional Linux permissions. However, because getfacl always sets the effective rights mask to the least restrictive ACL permissions for the file, the mask has no effect unless you set it explicitly after you set up an ACL for the file. You can set the mask by specifying **mask** in place of *ugo* and by not specifying a *name* in a setfacl command.

The following example sets the effective rights mask to **read** for the **report** file:

```
$ setfacl -m mask::r-- report
```

The **mask** line in the following getfacl output shows the effective rights mask set to read (**r--**). The line that displays Sam's file access permissions shows them still set to read and write. However, the comment at the right end of the line shows that his effective permission is read.

```
$ getfacl report
# file: report
# owner: max
# group: max
user::rw-
user:sam:rw-                              #effective:r--
group::r--
mask::r--
other::r--
```

As the next example shows, setfacl can modify ACL rules and can set more than one ACL rule at a time:

```
$ setfacl -m u:sam:r--,u:zach:rw- report

$ getfacl --omit-header report
user::rw-
user:sam:r--
user:zach:rw-
group::r--
mask::rw-
other::r--
```

The **−x** option removes ACL rules for a user or a group. It has no effect on permissions for the owner of the file or the group that the file is associated with. The next example shows setfacl removing the rule that gives Sam permission to access the file:

```
$ setfacl -x u:sam report

$ getfacl --omit-header report
user::rw-
user:zach:rw-
group::r--
mask::rw-
other::r--
```

You must not specify *permissions* when you use the **–x** option. Instead, specify only the *ugo* and *name*. The **–b** option, followed by a filename only, removes all ACL rules and the ACL itself from the file or directory you specify.

Both setfacl and getfacl have many options. Use the **––help** option to display brief lists of options or refer to the man pages for details.

SETTING DEFAULT RULES FOR A DIRECTORY

The following example shows that the **dir** directory initially has no ACL. The setfacl command uses the **–d** option to add two default rules to the ACL for **dir**. These rules apply to all files in the **dir** directory that do not have explicit ACLs. The rules give members of the **pubs** group read and execute permissions and give members of the **admin** group read, write, and execute permissions.

```
$ ls -ld dir
drwx------ 2 max max 4096 Feb 12 23:15 dir
$ getfacl dir
# file: dir
# owner: max
# group: max
user::rwx
group::---
other::---

$ setfacl -d -m g:pubs:r-x,g:admin:rwx dir
```

The following ls command shows that the **dir** directory now has an ACL, as indicated by the **+** to the right of the permissions. Each of the default rules that getfacl displays starts with **default:**. The first two default rules and the last default rule specify the permissions for the owner of the file, the group that the file is associated with, and all other users. These three rules specify the traditional Linux permissions and take precedence over other ACL rules. The third and fourth rules specify the permissions for the **pubs** and **admin** groups. Next is the default effective rights mask.

```
$ ls -ld dir
drwx------+ 2 max max 4096 Feb 12 23:15 dir
$ getfacl dir
# file: dir
# owner: max
# group: max
user::rwx
group::---
other::---
default:user::rwx
default:group::---
default:group:pubs:r-x
default:group:admin:rwx
default:mask::rwx
default:other::---
```

Remember that the default rules pertain to files held in the directory that are not assigned ACLs explicitly. You can also specify access rules for the directory itself.

When you create a file within a directory that has default rules in its ACL, the effective rights mask for that file is created based on the file's permissions. In some cases the mask may override default ACL rules.

In the next example, touch creates a file named **new** in the **dir** directory. The ls command shows that this file has an ACL. Based on the value of umask (page 420), both the owner and the group that the file is associated with have read and write permissions for the file. The effective rights mask is set to read and write so that the effective permission for **pubs** is read and the effective permissions for **admin** are read and write. Neither group has execute permission.

```
$ cd dir
$ touch new
$ ls -l new
-rw-rw----+ 1 max max 0 Feb 13 00:39 new
$ getfacl --omit new
user::rw-
group::---
group:pubs:r-x                    #effective:r--
group:admin:rwx                   #effective:rw-
mask::rw-
other::---
```

If you change the file's traditional permissions to read, write, and execute for the owner and the group, the effective rights mask changes to read, write, and execute and the groups specified by the default rules gain execute access to the file.

```
$ chmod 770 new
$ ls -l new
-rwxrwx---+ 1 max max 0 Feb 13 00:39 new
$ getfacl --omit new
user::rwx
group::---
group:pubs:r-x
group:admin:rwx
mask::rwx
other::---
```

LINKS

A *link* is a pointer to a file. Every time you create a file by using vim, touch, cp, or any other means, you are putting a pointer in a directory. This pointer associates a filename with a place on the disk. When you specify a filename in a command, you are indirectly pointing to the place on the disk that holds the information you want.

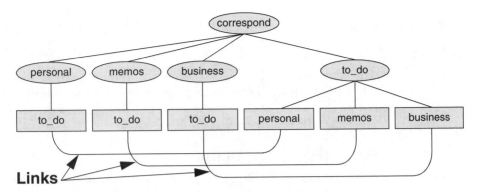

Figure 6-13 Using links to cross-classify files

Sharing files can be useful when two or more people are working on the same project and need to share some information. You can make it easy for other users to access one of your files by creating additional links to the file.

To share a file with another user, first give the user permission to read from and write to the file (page 182). You may also have to change the access permissions of the parent directory of the file to give the user read, write, or execute permission (page 184). Once the permissions are appropriately set, the user can create a link to the file so that each of you can access the file from your separate directory hierarchies.

A link can also be useful to a single user with a large directory hierarchy. You can create links to cross-classify files in your directory hierarchy, using different classifications for different tasks. For example, if you have the file layout depicted in Figure 6-2 on page 167, a file named **to_do** might appear in each subdirectory of the **correspond** directory—that is, in **personal, memos,** and **business.** If you find it difficult to keep track of everything you need to do, you can create a separate directory named **to_do** in the **correspond** directory. You can then link each subdirectory's to-do list into that directory. For example, you could link the file named **to_do** in the **memos** directory to a file named **memos** in the **to_do** directory. This set of links is shown in Figure 6-13.

Although it may sound complicated, this technique keeps all your to-do lists conveniently in one place. The appropriate list is easily accessible in the task-related directory when you are busy composing letters, writing memos, or handling personal business.

About the discussion of hard links

tip Two kinds of links exist: hard links and symbolic (soft) links. Hard links are older and becoming outdated. The section on hard links is marked as optional; you can skip it, although it discusses inodes and gives you insight into the structure of the filesystem.

optional

HARD LINKS

A hard link to a file appears as another file. If the file appears in the same directory as the linked-to file, the links must have different filenames because two files in the same directory cannot have the same name. You can create a hard link to a file only from within the filesystem that holds the file.

ln: CREATES A HARD LINK

The ln (link) utility (without the –s or ––symbolic option) creates a hard link to an existing file using the following syntax:

ln existing-file new-link

The next command makes the link shown in Figure 6-14 by creating a new link named **/home/alex/letter** to an existing file named **draft** in Jenny's home directory:

```
$ pwd
/home/jenny
$ ln draft /home/alex/letter
```

The new link appears in the **/home/alex** directory with the filename **letter**. In practice, Alex may need to change the directory and file permissions so that Jenny will be able to access the file. Even though **/home/alex/letter** appears in Alex's directory, Jenny is the owner of the file because she created it.

The ln utility creates an additional pointer to an existing file but it does *not* make another copy of the file. Because there is only one file, the file status information—such as access permissions, owner, and the time the file was last modified—is the same for all links; only the filenames differ. When Jenny modifies **/home/jenny/draft**, for example, Alex sees the changes in **/home/alex/letter**.

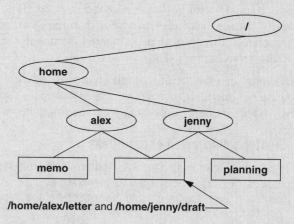

Figure 6-14 Two links to the same file: **/home/alex/letter** and **/home/jenny/draft**

cp VERSUS ln

The following commands verify that ln does not make an additional copy of a file. Create a file, use ln to make an additional link to the file, change the contents of the file through one link, and verify the change through the other link:

```
$ cat file_a
This is file A.
$ ln file_a file_b
$ cat file_b
This is file A.
$ vim file_b
...
$ cat file_b
This is file B after the change.
$ cat file_a
This is file B after the change.
```

If you try the same experiment using cp instead of ln and change a *copy* of the file, the difference between the two utilities will become clearer. Once you change a *copy* of a file, the two files are different:

```
$ cat file_c
This is file C.
$ cp file_c file_d
$ cat file_d
This is file C.
$ vim file_d
...
$ cat file_d
This is file D after the change.
$ cat file_c
This is file C.
```

ls and link counts You can use ls with the –l option, followed by the names of the files you want to compare, to confirm that the status information is the same for two links to the same file and is different for files that are not linked. In the following example, the 2 in the links field (just to the left of **alex**) shows there are two links to **file_a** and **file_b**:

```
$ ls -l file_a file_b file_c file_d
-rw-r--r-- 2 alex pubs 33  May 24 10:52 file_a
-rw-r--r-- 2 alex pubs 33  May 24 10:52 file_b
-rw-r--r-- 1 alex pubs 16  May 24 10:55 file_c
-rw-r--r-- 1 alex pubs 33  May 24 10:57 file_d
```

Although it is easy to guess which files are linked to one another in this example, ls does not explicitly tell you.

ls and inodes Use ls with the –i option to determine without a doubt which files are linked. The –i option lists the *inode* (page 1037) number for each file. An inode is the control structure for a file. If the two filenames have the same inode number, they share the same control structure and are links to the same file. Conversely, when two file-names have different inode numbers, they are different files. The following example shows that **file_a** and **file_b** have the same inode number and that **file_c** and **file_d** have different inode numbers:

```
$ ls -i file_a file_b file_c file_d
3534 file_a    3534 file_b    5800 file_c    7328 file_d
```

All links to a file are of equal value: The operating system cannot distinguish the order in which multiple links were created. When a file has two links, you can remove either one and still access the file through the remaining link. You can remove the link used to create the file, for example, and, as long as one link remains, still access the file through that link.

SYMBOLIC LINKS

In addition to hard links, Linux supports *symbolic links,* also called *soft links* or *symlinks.* A hard link is a pointer to a file (the directory entry points to the inode), whereas a symbolic link is an *indirect* pointer to a file (the directory entry contains the pathname of the pointed-to file—a pointer to the hard link to the file).

Advantages of symbolic links   Symbolic links were developed because of the limitations inherent in hard links. You cannot create a hard link to a directory, but you can create a symbolic link to a directory.

In many cases the Linux file hierarchy encompasses several filesystems. Because each filesystem keeps separate control information (that is, separate inode tables or filesystem structures) for the files it holds, it is not possible to create hard links between files in different filesystems. A symbolic link can point to any file, regardless of where it is located in the file structure, but a hard link to a file must be in the same filesystem as the other hard link(s) to the file. When you create links only among files in your home directory, you will not notice this limitation.

A major advantage of a symbolic link is that it can point to a nonexistent file. This ability is useful if you need a link to a file that is periodically removed and re-created. A hard link keeps pointing to a "removed" file, which the link keeps alive even after a new file is created. In contrast, a symbolic link always points to the newly created file and does not interfere when you delete the old file. For example, a symbolic link could point to a file that gets checked in and out under a source code control system, a .o file that is re-created by the C compiler each time you run make, or a log file that is repeatedly archived.

Although they are more general than hard links, symbolic links have some disadvantages. Whereas all hard links to a file have equal status, symbolic links do not have the same status as hard links. When a file has multiple hard links, it is analogous to a person having multiple full legal names, as many married women do. In contrast, symbolic links are analogous to nicknames. Anyone can have one or more nicknames, but these nicknames have a lesser status than legal names. The following sections describe some of the peculiarities of symbolic links.

ln: CREATES A SYMBOLIC LINK

You use ln with the **--symbolic** (or **-s**) option to create a symbolic link. The following example creates a symbolic link **/tmp/s3** to the file **sum** in Alex's home directory. When you use an ls –l command to look at the symbolic link, ls displays the name of the link and the name of the file it points to. The first character of the listing is l (for link).

```
$ ln --symbolic /home/alex/sum /tmp/s3
$ ls -l /home/alex/sum /tmp/s3
-rw-rw-r--   1 alex alex 38 Jun 12 09:51 /home/alex/sum
lrwxrwxrwx   1 alex alex 14 Jun 12 09:52 /tmp/s3 -> /home/alex/sum
$ cat /tmp/s3
This is sum.
```

The sizes and times of the last modifications of the two files are different. Unlike a hard link, a symbolic link to a file does not have the same status information as the file itself.

You can also use ln to create a symbolic link to a directory. When you use the —symbolic option, ln does not care whether the file you are creating a link to is an ordinary file or a directory.

Use absolute pathnames with symbolic links

tip Symbolic links are literal and are not aware of directories. A link that points to a relative pathname, which includes simple filenames, assumes that the relative pathname is relative to the directory that the link was created *in* (not the directory the link was created *from*). In the following example, the link points to the file named **sum** in the **/tmp** directory. Because no such file exists, cat gives an error message:

```
$ pwd
/home/alex
$ ln --symbolic sum /tmp/s4
$ ls -l sum /tmp/s4
lrwxrwxrwx   1 alex     alex         3 Jun 12 10:13 /tmp/s4 -> sum
-rw-rw-r--   1 alex     alex        38 Jun 12 09:51 sum
$ cat /tmp/s4
cat: /tmp/s4: No such file or directory
```

optional cd AND SYMBOLIC LINKS

When you use a symbolic link as an argument to cd to change directories, the results can be confusing, particularly if you did not realize that you were using a symbolic link.

If you use cd to change to a directory that is represented by a symbolic link, the pwd shell builtin lists the name of the symbolic link. The pwd utility (**/bin/pwd**) lists the name of the linked-to directory, not the link, regardless of how you got there.

```
$ ln -s /home/alex/grades /tmp/grades.old
$ pwd
/home/alex
$ cd /tmp/grades.old
$ pwd
/tmp/grades.old
$ /bin/pwd
/home/alex/grades
```

When you change directories back to the parent, you end up in the directory holding the symbolic link:

```
$ cd ..
$ pwd
/tmp
$ /bin/pwd
/tmp
```

rm: REMOVES A LINK

When you create a file, there is one hard link to it. You can then delete the file or,
using Linux terminology, remove the link with the rm utility. When you remove the
last hard link to a file, you can no longer access the information stored there and the
operating system releases the space the file occupied on the disk for subsequent use
by other files. This space is released even if symbolic links to the file remain. When
there is more than one hard link to a file, you can remove a hard link and still access
the file from any remaining link. Unlike DOS and Windows, Linux does not provide
an easy way to undelete a file once you have removed it. A skilled hacker, however,
can sometimes piece the file together with time and effort.

When you remove all hard links to a file, you will not be able to access the file
through a symbolic link. In the following example, cat reports that the file **total**
does not exist because it is a symbolic link to a file that has been removed:

```
$ ls -l sum
-rw-r--r-- 1 alex pubs 981  May 24 11:05 sum
$ ln -s sum total
$ rm sum
$ cat total
cat: total: No such file or directory
$ ls -l total
lrwxrwxrwx 1 alex pubs 6  May 24 11:09 total -> sum
```

When you remove a file, be sure to remove all symbolic links to it. Remove a symbolic link in the same way you remove other files:

```
$ rm total
```

CHAPTER SUMMARY

Linux has a hierarchical, or treelike, file structure that makes it possible to organize
files so that you can find them quickly and easily. The file structure contains directory files and ordinary files. Directories contain other files, including other directories; ordinary files generally contain text, programs, or images. The ancestor of all
files is the root directory named /.

Most Linux filesystems support 255-character filenames. Nonetheless, it is a good idea to keep filenames simple and intuitive. Filename extensions can help make filenames more meaningful.

When you are logged in, you are always associated with a working directory. Your home directory is your working directory from the time you log in until you use cd to change directories.

An absolute pathname starts with the root directory and contains all the filenames that trace a path to a given file. The pathname starts with a slash, representing the root directory, and contains additional slashes between the other filenames in the path.

A relative pathname is similar to an absolute pathname but traces the path starting from the working directory. A simple filename is the last element of a pathname and is a form of a relative pathname.

A Linux filesystem contains many important directories, including **/usr/bin**, which stores most of the Linux utility commands, and **/dev**, which stores device files, many of which represent physical pieces of hardware. An important standard file is **/etc/passwd**; it contains information about users, such as each user's ID and full name.

Among the attributes associated with each file are access permissions. They determine who can access the file and how the file may be accessed. Three groups of users can potentially access the file: the owner, the members of a group, and all other users. An ordinary file can be accessed in three ways: read, write, and execute. The ls utility with the –l option displays these permissions. For directories, execute access is redefined to mean that the directory can be searched.

The owner of a file or Superuser can use the chmod utility to change the access permissions of a file. This utility specifies read, write, and execute permissions for the file's owner, the group, and all other users on the system.

Access Control Lists (ACLs) provide finer-grained control over which users can access specific directories and files than do traditional Linux permissions. Using ACLs you can specify the ways in which each of several users can access a directory or file. Few utilities preserve ACLs when working with these files.

An ordinary file stores user data, such as textual information, programs, or images. A directory is a standard-format disk file that stores information, including names, about ordinary files and other directory files. An inode is a data structure, stored on disk, that defines a file's existence and is identified by an inode number. A directory relates each of the filenames it stores to a specific inode.

A link is a pointer to a file. You can have several links to a single file so that you can share the file with other users or have the file appear in more than one directory. Because only one copy of a file with multiple links exists, changing the file through any one link causes the changes to appear in all the links. Hard links cannot link directories or span filesystems, whereas symbolic links can.

Table 6-2 summarizes the utilities introduced in this chapter.

Table 6-2   Utilities introduced in Chapter 6

Utility	Function
cd	Associates you with another working directory (page 174)
chmod	Changes the access permissions on a file (page 182)
getfacl	Displays a file's ACL (page 186)
ln	Makes a link to an existing file (page 192)
mkdir	Creates a directory (page 173)
pwd	Displays the pathname of the working directory (page 170)
rmdir	Deletes a directory (page 178)
setfacl	Modifies a file's ACL (page 186)

EXERCISES

1. Is each of the following an absolute pathname, a relative pathname, or a simple filename?

   a. **milk_co**

   b. **correspond/business/milk_co**

   c. **/home/alex**

   d. **/home/alex/literature/promo**

   e. **..**

   f. **letter.0610**

2. List the commands you can use to perform these operations:

   a. Make your home directory the working directory

   b. Identify the working directory

3. If your working directory is **/home/alex** with a subdirectory named **litera-ture**, give three sets of commands that you can use to create a subdirectory named **classics** under **literature**. Also give several sets of commands you can use to remove the **classics** directory and its contents.

4. The df utility displays all mounted filesystems along with information about each. Use the df utility with the **–h** (human-readable) option to answer the following questions.

   a. How many filesystems are mounted on your Linux system?

   b. Which filesystem stores your home directory?

c. Assuming that your answer to exercise 4a is two or more, attempt to create a hard link to a file on another filesystem. What error message do you get? What happens when you attempt to create a symbolic link to the file instead?

5. Suppose that you have a file that is linked to a file owned by another user. How can you ensure that changes to the file are no longer shared?

6. You should have read permission for the **/etc/passwd** file. To answer the following questions, use cat or less to display **/etc/passwd**. Look at the fields of information in **/etc/passwd** for the users on your system.

a. Which character is used to separate fields in **/etc/passwd**?

b. How many fields are used to describe each user?

c. How many users are on your system?

d. How many different login shells are in use on your system? (*Hint:* Look at the last field.)

e. The second field of **/etc/passwd** stores user passwords in encoded form. If the password field contains an **x**, your system uses shadow passwords and stores the encoded passwords elsewhere. Does your system use shadow passwords?

7. If **/home/jenny/draft** and **/home/alex/letter** are links to the same file and the following sequence of events occurs, what will be the date in the opening of the letter?

a. Alex gives the command **vim letter**.

b. Jenny gives the command **vim draft**.

c. Jenny changes the date in the opening of the letter to January 31, 2006, writes the file, and exits from vim.

d. Alex changes the date to February 1, 2006, writes the file, and exits from vim.

8. Suppose that a user belongs to a group that has all permissions on a file named **jobs_list**, but the user, as the owner of the file, has no permissions. Describe which operations, if any, the user/owner can perform on **jobs_list**. Which command can the user/owner give that will grant the user/owner all permissions on the file?

9. Does the root directory have any subdirectories that you cannot search as a regular user? Does the root directory have any subdirectories that you cannot read as a regular user? Explain.

10. Assume that you are given the directory structure shown in Figure 6-2 on page 167 and the following directory permissions:

```
d--x--x---   3 jenny pubs 512 Mar 10 15:16 business
drwxr-xr-x   2 jenny pubs 512 Mar 10 15:16 business/milk_co
```

For each category of permissions—owner, group, and other—what happens when you run each of the following commands? Assume that the working directory is the parent of **correspond** and that the file **cheese_co** is readable by everyone.

a. **cd correspond/business/milk_co**

b. **ls –l correspond/business**

c. **cat correspond/business/cheese_co**

ADVANCED EXERCISES

11. What is an inode? What happens to the inode when you move a file within a filesystem?

12. What does the .. entry in a directory point to? What does this entry point to in the root (/) directory?

13. How can you create a file named **–i**? Which techniques do not work, and why do they not work? How can you remove the file named **–i**?

14. Suppose that the working directory contains a single file named **andor**. What error message do you get when you run the following command line?

    ```
    $ mv andor and\/or
    ```

    Under what circumstances is it possible to run the command without producing an error?

15. The **ls –i** command displays a filename preceded by the inode number of the file (page 193). Write a command to output inode/filename pairs for the files in the working directory, sorted by inode number. (*Hint:* Use a pipe.)

16. Do you think that the system administrator has access to a program that can decode user passwords? Why or why not? (See exercise 6.)

17. Is it possible to distinguish a file from a hard link to a file? That is, given a filename, can you tell whether it was created using an **ln** command? Explain.

18. Explain the error messages displayed in the following sequence of commands:

    ```
    $ ls -l
    total 1
    drwxrwxr-x   2 alex pubs 1024 Mar  2 17:57 dirtmp
    $ ls dirtmp
    $ rmdir dirtmp
    rmdir: dirtmp: Directory not empty
    $ rm dirtmp/*
    rm: No match.
    ```

7

THE SHELL

This chapter takes a close look at the shell and explains how to use some of its features. For example, it discusses command line syntax and also describes how the shell processes a command line and initiates execution of a program. The chapter also explains how to redirect input to and output from a command, construct pipes and filters on the command line, and run a command in the background. The final section covers filename expansion and explains how you can use this feature in your everyday work.

The exact wording of the shell output differs from shell to shell: What your shell displays may differ slightly from what appears in this book. Refer to Chapter 9 for more information on bash and to Chapter 28 for information on writing and executing bash shell scripts.

THE COMMAND LINE

The shell executes a program when you give it a command in response to its prompt. For example, when you give the ls command, the shell executes the utility program named ls. You can cause the shell to execute other types of programs—such as shell scripts, application programs, and programs you have written—in the same way. The line that contains the command, including any arguments, is called the *command line*. In this book the term *command* refers to the characters you type on the command line as well as to the program that action invokes.

SYNTAX

Command line syntax dictates the ordering and separation of the elements on a command line. When you press the RETURN key after entering a command, the shell scans the command line for proper syntax. The syntax for a basic command line is

> *command [arg1] [arg2] ... [argn]* RETURN

One or more SPACEs must separate elements on the command line. The **command** is the name of the command, **arg1** through **argn** are arguments, and RETURN is the keystroke that terminates all command lines. The brackets in the command line syntax indicate that the arguments they enclose are optional. Not all commands require arguments: Some commands do not allow arguments; other commands allow a variable number of arguments; and others require a specific number of arguments. Options, a special kind of argument, are usually preceded by one or two hyphens (also called a dash or minus sign: –).

COMMAND NAME

Usage message   Some useful Linux command lines consist of only the name of the command without any arguments. For example, ls by itself lists the contents of the working directory. Most commands accept one or more arguments. Commands that require arguments typically give a short error message, called a *usage message,* when you use them without arguments, with incorrect arguments, or with the wrong number of arguments.

ARGUMENTS

On the command line each sequence of nonblank characters is called a *token* or *word*. An *argument* is a token, such as a filename, string of text, number, or other object that a command acts on. For example, the argument to a vim or emacs command is the name of the file you want to edit.

The following command line shows cp copying the file named **temp** to **tempcopy**:

```
$ cp temp tempcopy
```

Arguments are numbered starting with the command itself as argument zero. In this example **cp** is argument zero, **temp** is argument one, and **tempcopy** is argument two. The cp utility requires two arguments on the command line. (The utility can take more arguments but not fewer.) Argument one is the name of an existing file. Argument two is the name of the file that cp is creating or overwriting. Here the arguments are not optional; both arguments must be present for the command to work. When you do not supply the right number or kind of arguments, cp displays a usage message. Try typing **cp** and then pressing RETURN.

OPTIONS

An *option* is an argument that modifies the effects of a command. You can frequently specify more than one option, modifying the command in several different ways. Options are specific to and interpreted by the program that the command line calls, not the shell.

By convention options are separate arguments that follow the name of the command and usually precede other arguments, such as filenames. Most utilities require you to prefix options with a single hyphen. However, this requirement is specific to the utility and not the shell. GNU program options are frequently preceded by two hyphens in a row. For example, **––help** generates a (sometimes extensive) usage message.

Figure 7-1 first shows what happens when you give an ls command without any options. By default ls lists the contents of the working directory in alphabetical order, vertically sorted in columns. Next the **–r** (reverse order; because this is a GNU utility, you can also use **––reverse**) option causes the ls utility to display the list of files in reverse alphabetical order, still sorted in columns. The **–x** option causes ls to display the list of files in horizontally sorted rows.

Combining options   When you need to use several options, you can usually group multiple single-letter options into one argument that starts with a single hyphen; do not put SPACES between the options. You cannot combine options that are preceded by two

```
$ ls
alex   house  mark    office    personal  test
hold   jenny  names   oldstuff  temp
$ ls -r
test   personal  office  mark   house  alex
temp   oldstuff  names   jenny  hold
$ ls -x
alex     hold     house     jenny  mark  names
office   oldstuff personal  temp   test
$ ls -rx
test   temp     personal  oldstuff  office  names
mark   jenny    house     hold      alex
```

Figure 7-1   Using options

hyphens in this way, however. Specific rules for combining options depend on the program you are running. Figure 7-1 shows both the **−r** and **−x** options with the ls utility. Together these options generate a list of filenames in horizontally sorted columns, in reverse alphabetical order. Most utilities allow you to list options in any order; thus **ls −xr** produces the same results as **ls −rx**. The command **ls −x −r** also generates the same list.

Displaying readable file sizes: the −h option

tip   Most utilities that report on file sizes specify the size of a file in bytes. Bytes work well when you are dealing with smaller files, but the numbers can be difficult to read when you are working with file sizes that are measured in megabytes or gigabytes. Use the **−h** (or **−−human-readable**) option to display file sizes in kilo-, mega-, and gigabytes. Experiment with **df −h** (disk free) and **ls −lh** commands.

Option arguments   Some utilities have options that themselves require arguments. For example, the gcc utility has a **−o** option that must be followed by the name you want to give the executable file that gcc generates. Typically an argument to an option is separated from its option letter by a SPACE:

```
$ gcc -o prog prog.c
```

Arguments that start with a hyphen   Another convention allows utilities to work with arguments, such as filenames, that start with a hyphen. If a file's name is **−l**, the following command is ambiguous:

```
$ ls -l
```

This command could mean a long listing of all files in the working directory or a listing of the file named **−l**. It is interpreted as the former. You should avoid creating files whose names begin with hyphens. If you do create them, many utilities follow the convention that a **−−** argument (two consecutive hyphens) indicates the end of the options (and the beginning of the arguments). To disambiguate the command, you can type

```
$ ls -- -l
```

You can use an alternative format in which the period refers to the working directory and the slash indicates that the name refers to a file in the working directory:

```
$ ls ./-l
```

Assuming that you are working in the **/home/alex** directory, the preceding command is functionally equivalent to

```
$ ls /home/alex/-l
```

You can give the following command to get a long listing of this file:

```
$ ls -l -- -l
```

These are conventions, not hard-and-fast rules, and a number of utilities do not follow them (e.g., find). Following such conventions is a good idea; it makes it much easier for users to work with your program. When you write shell programs that require options, follow the Linux option conventions.

The --help option

tip Many utilities display a (sometimes extensive) help message when you call them with an argument of **--help**. All utilities developed by the GNU Project (page 2) accept this option. An example follows.

```
$ bzip2 --help
bzip2, a block-sorting file compressor.  Version 1.0.2, 30-Dec-2001.

   usage: bzip2 [flags and input files in any order]

   -h --help           print this message
   -d --decompress     force decompression
   -z --compress       force compression
   -k --keep           keep (don't delete) input files
   -f --force          overwrite existing output files
   -t --test           test compressed file integrity
   -c --stdout         output to standard out
   -q --quiet          suppress noncritical error messages
   -v --verbose        be verbose (a 2nd -v gives more)
   ...
```

PROCESSING THE COMMAND LINE

As you enter a command line, the Linux tty device driver (part of the Linux operating system kernel) examines each character to see whether it must take immediate action. When you press CONTROL-H (to erase a character) or CONTROL-U (to kill a line), the device driver immediately adjusts the command line as required; the shell never sees the character(s) you erased or the line you killed. Often a similar adjustment occurs when you press CONTROL-W (to erase a word). When the character you entered does not require immediate action, the device driver stores the character in a buffer and waits for additional characters. When you press RETURN, the device driver passes the command line to the shell for processing.

Parsing the command line
When the shell processes a command line, it looks at the line as a whole and *parses* (breaks) it into its component parts (Figure 7-2). Next the shell looks for the name of the command. Usually the name of the command is the first item on the command line after the prompt (argument zero). The shell takes the first characters on the command line up to the first blank (TAB or SPACE) and then looks for a command with that name. The command name (the first token) can be specified on the command line either as a simple filename or as a pathname. For example, you can call the ls command in either of the following ways:

```
$ ls

$ /bin/ls
```

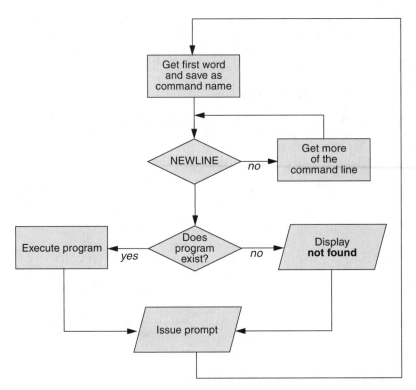

Figure 7-2   Processing the command line

The shell does not require that the name of the program appear first on the command line. Thus you can structure a command line as follows:

```
$ >bb <aa cat
```

This command runs cat with standard input coming from the file named **aa** and standard output going to the file named **bb**. When the shell recognizes the redirect symbols (page 210), it recognizes and processes them and their arguments before finding the name of the program that the command line is calling. This is a properly structured—albeit rarely encountered and possibly confusing—command line.

Absolute versus relative pathnames   When you give an absolute pathname on the command line or a relative pathname that is not a simple filename (i.e., any pathname that includes at least one slash), the shell looks in the specified directory (**/bin** in the case of the **/bin/ls** command) for a file that has the name **ls** and that you have permission to execute. When you give a simple filename, the shell searches through a list of directories for a filename that matches the specified name and that you have execute permission for. The shell does not look through all directories but only the ones specified by the variable named **PATH**. Refer to page 292 for more information on **PATH**. Also refer to the discussion of the which and whereis utilities on page 144.

When it cannot find the executable file, the Bourne Again Shell (bash) displays a message such as the following:

```
$ abc
bash: abc: command not found
```

One reason the shell may not be able to find the executable file is that it is not in a directory in your **PATH**. Under bash the following command temporarily adds the working directory (.) to your **PATH**:

```
$ PATH=$PATH:.
```

For security reasons, you may not want to add the working directory to **PATH** permanently; see the adjacent tip and the one on page 293.

Try giving a command as *./command*

tip You can always execute an executable file in the working directory by prepending ./ to the name of the file. For example, if **myprog** is an executable file in the working directory, you can execute it with the following command, regardless of how **PATH** is set:

```
$ ./myprog
```

When the shell finds the program but cannot execute it (you do not have execute permission for the file that contains the program), it displays a message similar to

```
$ def
bash: ./def: Permission denied
```

See "ls –l: Displays Permissions" on page 181 for information on displaying access permissions for a file and "chmod: Changes Access Permissions" on page 182 for instructions on how to change file access permissions.

EXECUTING THE COMMAND LINE

Process If it finds an executable file with the same name as the command, the shell starts a new process. A *process* is the execution of a command by Linux (page 300). The shell makes each command line argument, including options and the name of the command, available to the called program. While the command is executing, the shell waits for the process to finish. At this point the shell is in an inactive state called *sleep*. When the program finishes execution, it passes its exit status (page 920) to the shell. The shell then returns to an active state (wakes up), issues a prompt, and waits for another command.

The shell does not
process arguments Because the shell does not process command line arguments but only hands them to the called program, the shell has no way of knowing whether a particular option or other argument is valid for a given program. Any error or usage messages about options or arguments come from the program itself. Some utilities ignore bad options.

EDITING THE COMMAND LINE

You can repeat and edit previous commands and edit the current command line. See pages 119 and 304 for more information.

Figure 7-3   The command does not know where standard input comes from or where standard output and standard error go

STANDARD INPUT AND STANDARD OUTPUT

Standard output is a place that a program can send information, such as text. The program never "knows" where the information it sends to standard output is going (Figure 7-3). The information can go to a printer, an ordinary file, or the screen. The following sections show that by default the shell directs standard output from a command to the screen[1] and describe how you can cause the shell to redirect this output to another file.

Standard input is a place that a program gets information from. As with standard output the program never "knows" where the information came from. The following sections also explain how to redirect standard input to a command so that it comes from an ordinary file instead of from the keyboard (the default).

In addition to standard input and standard output, a running program normally has a place to send error messages: *standard error*. Refer to page 270 for more information on handling standard error.

THE SCREEN AS A FILE

Chapter 6 introduced ordinary files, directory files, and hard and soft links. Linux has an additional type of file: a *device file*. A device file resides in the Linux file structure, usually in the **/dev** directory, and represents a peripheral device, such as a terminal emulator window, screen, printer, or disk drive.

The device name that the who utility displays after your username is the filename of your screen. For example, when who displays the device name **pts/4**, the pathname of your screen is **/dev/pts/4**. When you work with multiple windows, each window has its own device name. You can also use the tty utility to display the name of the device that you give the command from. Although you would not normally have occasion to do so, you can read from and write to this file as though it were a text file. Writing to it displays what you wrote on the screen; reading from it reads what you entered on the keyboard.

---

1. The term *screen* is used throughout this book to mean screen, terminal emulator window, or workstation. *Screen* refers to the device that you see the prompt and messages displayed on.

chsh: **changes your login shell**

tip   The person who sets up your account determines which shell you will use when you first log in on the system or when you open a terminal emulator window in a GUI environment. You can run any shell you like once you are logged in. Enter the name of the shell you want to use (bash, tcsh, or another shell) and press RETURN; the next prompt will be that of the new shell. Give an **exit** command to return to the previous shell. Because shells you call in this manner are nested (one runs on top of the other), you will be able to log out only from your original shell. When you have nested several shells, keep giving **exit** commands until you reach your original shell. You will then be able to log out.

Use the chsh utility when you want to change your login shell permanently. First give the command **chsh**. Then in response to the prompts enter your password and the absolute pathname of the shell you want to use (**/bin/bash**, **/bin/tcsh**, or the pathname of another shell). When you change your login shell in this manner using a terminal emulator (page 93) under a GUI, subsequent terminal emulator windows will not reflect the change until you log out of the system and log back in.

THE KEYBOARD AND SCREEN AS STANDARD INPUT AND STANDARD OUTPUT

When you first log in, the shell directs standard output of your commands to the device file that represents your screen (Figure 7-4). Directing output in this manner causes it to appear on your screen. The shell also directs standard input to come from the same file, so that your commands receive as input anything you type on the keyboard.

cat   The cat utility provides a good example of the way the keyboard and the screen function as standard input and standard output, respectively. When you use cat, it copies a file to standard output. Because the shell directs standard output to the screen, cat displays the file on the screen.

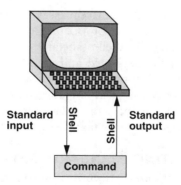

Figure 7-4   By default, standard input comes from the keyboard and standard output goes to the screen

```
$ cat
This is a line of text.
This is a line of text.
Cat keeps copying lines of text
Cat keeps copying lines of text
until you press CONTROL-D at the beginning
until you press CONTROL-D at the beginning
of a line.
of a line.
CONTROL-D
$
```

Figure 7-5   The cat utility copies standard input to standard output

Up to this point cat has taken its input from the filename (argument) you specified on the command line. When you do not give cat an argument (that is, when you give the command cat followed immediately by RETURN), cat takes its input from standard input. Thus, when called without an argument, cat copies standard input to standard output, one line at a time.

To see how cat works, type **cat** and press RETURN in response to the shell prompt. Nothing happens. Enter a line of text and press RETURN. The same line appears just under the one you entered. The cat utility is working. Because the shell associates cat's standard input with the keyboard and cat's standard output with the screen, when you type a line of text cat copies the text from standard input (the keyboard) to standard output (the screen). This exchange is shown in Figure 7-5.

CONTROL-D signals EOF
The cat utility keeps copying text until you enter CONTROL-D on a line by itself. Pressing CONTROL-D sends an EOF (end of file) signal to cat to indicate that it has reached the end of standard input and there is no more text for it to copy. The cat utility then finishes execution and returns control to the shell, which displays a prompt.

REDIRECTION

The term *redirection* encompasses the various ways you can cause the shell to alter where standard input of a command comes from and where standard output goes to. By default the shell associates standard input and standard output of a command with the keyboard and the screen as mentioned earlier. You can cause the shell to redirect standard input or standard output of any command by associating the input or output with a command or file other than the device file representing the keyboard or the screen. This section demonstrates how to redirect input from and output to ordinary text files and utilities.

REDIRECTING STANDARD OUTPUT

The *redirect output symbol* (>) instructs the shell to redirect the output of a command to the specified file instead of to the screen (Figure 7-6). The format of a command line that redirects output is

command [arguments] > filename

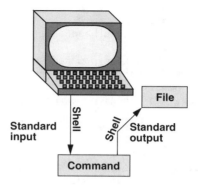

Figure 7-6 Redirecting standard output

where *command* is any executable program (such as an application program or a utility), *arguments* are optional arguments, and *filename* is the name of the ordinary file the shell redirects the output to.

Figure 7-7 uses cat to demonstrate output redirection. This figure contrasts with Figure 7-3 on page 208, where both standard input *and* standard output are associated with the keyboard and the screen. The input in Figure 7-7 comes from the keyboard. The redirect output symbol on the command line causes the shell to associate cat's standard output with the **sample.txt** file specified on the command line.

After giving the command and typing the text shown in Figure 7-7, the **sample.txt** file contains the text you entered. You can use cat with an argument of **sample.txt** to display this file. The next section shows another way to use cat to display the file.

Redirecting output can destroy a file I

caution   Use caution when you redirect output to a file. If the file exists, the shell will overwrite it and destroy its contents. For more information see the tip "Redirecting output can destroy a file II" on page 214.

Figure 7-7 shows that redirecting the output from cat is a handy way to create a file without using an editor. The drawback is that once you enter a line and press RETURN, you cannot edit the text. While you are entering a line, the erase and kill keys work to delete text. This procedure is useful for making short, simple files.

```
$ cat > sample.txt
This text is being entered at the keyboard and
cat is copying it to a file.
Press CONTROL-D to indicate the
end of file.
CONTROL-D
$
```

Figure 7-7 cat with its output redirected

```
$ cat stationery
2,000 sheets letterhead ordered:    10/7/05
$ cat tape
1 box masking tape ordered:         10/14/05
5 boxes filament tape ordered:      10/28/05
$ cat pens
12 doz. black pens ordered:         10/4/05

$ cat stationery tape pens > supply_orders

$ cat supply_orders
2,000 sheets letterhead ordered:    10/7/05
1 box masking tape ordered:         10/14/05
5 boxes filament tape ordered:      10/28/05
12 doz. black pens ordered:         10/4/05
$
```

Figure 7-8   Using cat to catenate files

Figure 7-8 shows how to use cat and the redirect output symbol to *catenate* (join one after the other—the derivation of the name of the cat utility) several files into one larger file. The first three commands display the contents of three files: **stationery, tape,** and **pens.** The next command shows cat with three filenames as arguments. When you call it with more than one filename, cat copies the files, one at a time, to standard output. In this case standard output is redirected to the file **supply_orders.** The final cat command shows that **supply_orders** contains the contents of all three files.

REDIRECTING STANDARD INPUT

Just as you can redirect standard output, so you can redirect standard input. The *redirect input symbol* (<) instructs the shell to redirect a command's input to come from the specified file instead of from the keyboard (Figure 7-9). The format of a command line that redirects input is

> *command [arguments] < filename*

where *command* is any executable program (such as an application program or a utility), *arguments* are optional arguments, and *filename* is the name of the ordinary file the shell redirects the input from.

Figure 7-10 shows cat with its input redirected from the **supply_orders** file that was created in Figure 7-8 and standard output going to the screen. This setup causes cat to display the sample file on the screen. The system automatically supplies an EOF (end of file) signal at the end of an ordinary file.

Utilities that take input from a file or standard input   Giving a cat command with input redirected from a file yields the same result as giving a cat command with the filename as an argument. The cat utility is a member of a class of Linux utilities that function in this manner. Other members of this class of utilities include lpr, sort, and grep. These utilities first examine the command line

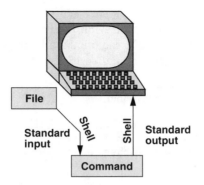

Figure 7-9   Redirecting standard input

that you use to call them. If you include a filename on the command line, the utility takes its input from the file you specify. If you do not specify a filename, the utility takes its input from standard input. It is the utility or program—not the shell or operating system—that functions in this manner.

noclobber: AVOIDS OVERWRITING FILES

The shell provides a feature called **noclobber** that stops you from inadvertently overwriting an existing file using redirection. When you enable this feature by setting the **noclobber** variable and then attempt to redirect output to an existing file, the shell displays an error message and does not execute the command. If the preceding examples result in one of the following messages, the **noclobber** feature has been set. The following examples set **noclobber,** attempt to redirect the output from echo into an existing file, and then unset **noclobber:**

```
$ set -o noclobber
$ echo "hi there" > tmp
bash: tmp: Cannot overwrite existing file
$ set +o noclobber
$ echo "hi there" > tmp
$
```

You can override **noclobber** by putting a pipe symbol after the symbol you use for redirecting output (**>|**).

In the following example, the user first creates a file named **a** by redirecting the output of date to the file. Next the user sets the **noclobber** variable and tries redirecting

```
$ cat < supply_orders
2,000 sheets letterhead ordered:    10/7/05
1 box masking tape ordered:         10/14/05
5 boxes filament tape ordered:      10/28/05
12 doz. black pens ordered:         10/4/05
```

Figure 7-10   cat with its input redirected

output to **a** again. The shell returns an error message. Then the user tries the same thing but using a pipe symbol after the redirect symbol. This time the shell allows the user to overwrite the file. Finally, the user unsets **noclobber** (using a plus sign in place of the hyphen) and verifies that it is no longer set.

```
$ date > a
$ set -o noclobber
$ date > a
bash: a: Cannot overwrite existing file
$ date >| a
$ set +o noclobber
$ date > a
```

Redirecting output can destroy a file II

caution   Depending on which shell you are using and how your environment has been set up, a command such as the following may give you undesired results:

```
$ cat orange pear > orange
cat: orange: input file is output file
```

Although cat displays an error message, the shell goes ahead and destroys the contents of the existing **orange** file. The new **orange** file will have the same contents as **pear** because the first action the shell takes when it sees the redirection symbol (**>**) is to remove the contents of the original **orange** file. If you want to catenate two files into one, use cat to put the two files into a temporary file and then use mv to rename this third file:

```
$ cat orange pear > temp
$ mv temp orange
```

What happens in the next example can be even worse. The user giving the command wants to search through files **a**, **b**, and **c** for the word **apple** and redirect the output from grep (page 131) to the file **a.output**. Unfortunately the user enters the filename as **a output**, omitting the period and inserting a SPACE in its place:

```
$ grep apple a b c > a output
grep: output: No such file or directory
```

The shell obediently removes the contents of **a** and then calls grep. The error message may take a moment to appear, giving you a sense that the command is running correctly. Even after you see the error message, it may take a while to realize that you destroyed the contents of **a**.

APPENDING STANDARD OUTPUT TO A FILE

The *append output symbol* (**>>**) causes the shell to add new information to the end of a file, leaving any existing information intact. This symbol provides a convenient way of catenating two files into one. The following commands demonstrate the action of the append output symbol. The second command accomplishes the catenation described in the preceding caution box:

```
$ cat orange
this is orange
$ cat pear >> orange
$ cat orange
this is orange
this is pear
```

You first see the contents of the **orange** file. Next the contents of the **pear** file is added to the end of (catenated with) the **orange** file. The final cat shows the result.

Do not trust **noclobber**

Appending output is simpler than the two-step procedure described in the preceding caution box but you must be careful to include both greater than signs. If you accidentally use only one and the **noclobber** feature is not on, you will overwrite the **orange** file. Even if you have the **noclobber** feature turned on, it is a good idea to keep backup copies of files you are manipulating in these ways in case you make a mistake.

Although it protects you from making an erroneous redirection, **noclobber** does not stop you from overwriting an existing file using cp or mv. These utilities include the **–i** (interactive) option that helps protect you from this type of mistake by verifying your intentions when you try to overwrite a file. For more information see the tip "cp can destroy a file" on page 130.

The next example shows how to create a file that contains the date and time (the output from date), followed by a list of who is logged in (the output from who). The first line in Figure 7-11 redirects the output from date to the file named **whoson**. Then cat displays the file. Next the example appends the output from who to the **whoson** file. Finally cat displays the file containing the output of both utilities.

/dev/null: MAKING DATA DISAPPEAR

The **/dev/null** device is a *data sink*, commonly referred to as a *bit bucket*. You can redirect output that you do not want to keep or see to **/dev/null**. The output disappears without a trace:

```
$ echo "hi there" > /dev/null
$
```

When you read from **/dev/null**, you get a null string. Give the following cat command to truncate a file named **messages** to zero length while preserving the ownership and permissions of the file:

```
$ ls -l messages
-rw-r--r--  1 alex pubs 25315 Oct 24 10:55 messages
$ cat /dev/null > messages
$ ls -l messages
-rw-r--r--  1 alex pubs 0 Oct 24 11:02 messages
```

```
$ date > whoson
$ cat whoson
Thu Mar 24 14:31:18 PST 2005
$ who >> whoson
$ cat whoson
Thu Mar 24 14:31:18 PST 2005
root        console      Mar 24 05:00(:0)
alex        pts/4        Mar 24 12:23(:0.0)
alex        pts/5        Mar 24 12:33(:0.0)
jenny       pts/7        Mar 23 08:45 (bravo.example.com)
```

Figure 7-11 Redirecting and appending output

PIPES

The shell uses a *pipe* to connect standard output of one command directly to standard input of another command. A pipe (sometimes referred to as a *pipeline*) has the same effect as redirecting standard output of one command to a file and then using that file as standard input to another command. A pipe does away with separate commands and the intermediate file. The symbol for a pipe is a vertical bar (|). The syntax of a command line using a pipe is

> *command_a [arguments]* | *command_b [arguments]*

The preceding command line uses a pipe to generate the same result as the following group of command lines:

> *command_a [arguments]* > *temp*
> *command_b [arguments]* < *temp*
> *rm temp*

In the preceding sequence of commands, the first line redirects standard output from *command_a* to an intermediate file named **temp**. The second line redirects standard input for *command_b* to come from **temp**. The final line deletes **temp**. The command using a pipe is not only easier to type, but is generally more efficient because it does not create a temporary file.

tr   You can use a pipe with any of the Linux utilities that accept input either from a file specified on the command line or from standard input. You can also use pipes with commands that accept input only from standard input. For example, the tr (translate) utility takes its input from standard input only. In its simplest usage tr has the following format:

> *tr string1 string2*

The tr utility accepts input from standard input and looks for characters that match one of the characters in *string1*. Upon finding a match, tr translates the matched character in *string1* to the corresponding character in *string2*. (The first character in *string1* translates into the first character in *string2*, and so forth.) The tr utility sends its output to standard output. In both of the following examples, tr displays the contents of the **abstract** file with the letters **a**, **b**, and **c** translated into **A**, **B**, and **C**, respectively:

```
$ cat abstract | tr abc ABC
$ tr abc ABC < abstract
```

```
$ ls > temp
$ lpr temp
$ rm temp

or

$ ls | lpr
```

Figure 7-12   A pipe

```
$ who > temp
$ sort < temp
alex        pts/4        Mar 24 12:23
alex        pts/5        Mar 24 12:33
jenny       pts/7        Mar 23 08:45
root        console      Mar 24 05:00
$ rm temp
```

Figure 7-13   Using a temporary file to store intermediate results

The tr utility does not change the contents of the original file; it cannot change the original file because it does not "know" the source of its input.

lpr   The lpr (line printer) utility also accepts input from either a file or standard input. When you type the name of a file following lpr on the command line, it places that file in the print queue. When you do not specify a filename on the command line, lpr takes input from standard input. This feature enables you to use a pipe to redirect input to lpr. The first set of commands in Figure 7-12 shows how you can use ls and lpr with an intermediate file (**temp**) to send a list of the files in the working directory to the printer. If the **temp** file exists, the first command overwrites its contents. The second set of commands sends the same list (with the exception of **temp**) to the printer using a pipe.

The commands in Figure 7-13 redirect the output from the who utility to **temp** and then display this file in sorted order. The sort utility (page 133) takes its input from the file specified on the command line or, when a file is not specified, from standard input and sends its output to standard output. The sort command line in Figure 7-13 takes its input from standard input, which is redirected (<) to come from **temp**. The output that sort sends to the screen lists the users in sorted (alphabetical) order.

Because sort can take its input from standard input or from a filename on the command line, omitting the < symbol from Figure 7-13 yields the same result.

Figure 7-14 achieves the same result without creating the **temp** file. Using a pipe the shell redirects the output from who to the input of sort. The sort utility takes input from standard input because no filename follows it on the command line.

When many people are using the system and you want information about only one of them, you can send the output from who to grep (page 131) using a pipe. The grep utility displays the line containing the string you specify—**root** in the following example:

```
$ who | grep 'root'
root        console      Mar 24 05:00
```

```
$ who | sort
alex        pts/4        Mar 24 12:23
alex        pts/5        Mar 24 12:33
jenny       pts/7        Mar 23 08:45
root        console      Mar 24 05:00
```

Figure 7-14   A pipe doing the work of a temporary file

Another way of handling output that is too long to fit on the screen, such as a list of files in a crowded directory, is to use a pipe to send the output through less or more (both on page 128).

```
$ ls | less
```

The less utility displays text one screen at a time. To view another screen, press the SPACE bar. To view one more line, press RETURN. Press **h** for help and **q** to quit.

Some utilities change the format of their output when you redirect it. Compare the output of ls by itself and when you send it through a pipe to less.

Filters

A *filter* is a command that processes an input stream of data to produce an output stream of data. A command line that includes a filter uses a pipe to connect standard output of one command to the filter's standard input. Another pipe connects the filter's standard output to standard input of another command. Not all utilities can be used as filters.

In the following example, sort is a filter, taking standard input from standard output of who and using a pipe to redirect standard output to standard input of lpr. This command line sends the sorted output of who to the printer:

```
$ who | sort | lpr
```

The preceding example demonstrates the power of the shell combined with the versatility of Linux utilities. The three utilities who, sort, and lpr were not specifically designed to work with each other, but they all use standard input and standard output in the conventional way. By using the shell to handle input and output, you can piece standard utilities together on the command line to achieve the results you want.

tee: Sends Output in Two Directions

The tee utility copies its standard input both to a file and to standard output. The utility is aptly named: It takes a single input and sends the output in two directions. In Figure 7-15 the output of who is sent via a pipe to standard input of tee. The tee utility saves a copy of standard input in a file named **who.out** and also sends a copy to standard output. Standard output of tee goes via a pipe to standard input of grep, which displays lines containing the string **root**.

```
$ who | tee who.out | grep root
root        console      Mar 24 05:00
$ cat who.out
root        console      Mar 24 05:00
alex        pts/4        Mar 24 12:23
alex        pts/5        Mar 24 12:33
jenny       pts/7        Mar 23 08:45
```

Figure 7-15 Using tee

RUNNING A PROGRAM IN THE BACKGROUND

Foreground In all the examples so far in this book, commands were run in the foreground. When you run a command in the *foreground,* the shell waits for it to finish before giving you another prompt and allowing you to continue. When you run a command in the *background,* you do not have to wait for the command to finish before you start running another command.

Jobs A *job* is a series of one or more commands that can be connected by pipes. You can have only one foreground job in a window or on a screen, but you can have many background jobs. By running more than one job at a time, you are using one of Linux's important features: multitasking. Running a command in the background can be useful when the command will run for a long time and does not need supervision. It leaves the screen free so that you can use it for other work. Of course, when you are using a GUI, you can open another window to run another job.

Job number, PID number To run a command in the background, type an ampersand (&) just before the RETURN that ends the command line. The shell assigns a small number to the job and displays this *job number* between brackets. Following the job number, the shell displays the *process identification (PID) number*—a larger number assigned by the operating system. Each of these numbers identifies the command running in the background. Then the shell displays another prompt and you can enter another command. When the background job finishes running, the shell displays a message giving both the job number and the command line used to run the command.

The next example runs in the background and sends its output through a pipe to lpr, which sends it to the printer.

```
$ ls -l | lpr &
[1] 22092
$
```

The [1] following the command line indicates that the shell has assigned job number 1 to this job. The **22092** is the PID number of the first command in the job. When this background job completes execution, you see the message

```
[1]+  Done                  ls -l | lpr
```

(In place of **ls –l**, the shell may display something similar to **ls ––color=tty –l**. This difference is due to the fact that ls is aliased [page 318] to ls ––color=tty.)

MOVING A JOB FROM THE FOREGROUND TO THE BACKGROUND

CONTROL-Z You can suspend a foreground job (stop it from running) by pressing the suspend key, usually CONTROL-Z. The shell then stops the process and disconnects standard input from the keyboard. You can put a suspended job in the background and restart it by using the bg command followed by the job number. You do not need to use the job number when there is only one stopped job.

Only the foreground job can take input from the keyboard. To connect the keyboard to a program running in the background, you must bring it into the foreground. Type **fg** without any arguments when only one job is in the background. When more than one job is in the background, type **fg**, or a percent sign (%), followed by the number of the job you want to bring into the foreground. The shell displays the command you used to start the job (**promptme** in the following example), and you can enter any input the program requires to continue:

```
bash $ fg 1
promptme
```

Redirect the output of a job you run in the background to keep it from interfering with whatever you are doing on the screen. Refer to "Separating and Grouping Commands" on page 276 for more detail about background tasks.

kill: ABORTING A BACKGROUND JOB

The interrupt key (usually CONTROL-C) cannot abort a process you are running in the background; you must use kill (page 395) for this purpose. Follow **kill** on the command line with either the PID number of the process you want to abort or a percent sign (%) followed by the job number.

Determining a PID number with ps

If you forget the PID number, you can use the ps (process status) utility (page 300) to display it. The following example runs a **tail –f outfile** command (the –f option causes tail to watch **outfile** and display new lines as they are written to the file) as a background job, uses ps to display the PID number of the process, and aborts the job with kill:

```
$ tail -f outfile &
[1] 18228
$ ps | grep tail
18228 pts/4     00:00:00 tail
$ kill 18228
[1]+  Terminated              tail -f outfile
$
```

If you forget the job number, you can use the jobs command to display a list of job numbers. The next example is similar to the previous one but uses the job number instead of the PID number to kill the job. Sometimes the message saying that the job is terminated does not appear until you press RETURN after the RETURN that ends the kill command:

```
$ tail -f outfile &
[1] 18236
$ bigjob &
[2] 18237
$ jobs
[1]-  Running                 tail -f outfile &
[2]+  Running                 bigjob &
$ kill %1
$ RETURN
[1]-  Terminated              tail -f outfile
$
```

FILENAME GENERATION/PATHNAME EXPANSION

Wildcards, globbing   When you give the shell abbreviated filenames that contain special characters, also called *metacharacters*, the shell can generate filenames that match the names of existing files. These special characters are also referred to as *wildcards* because they act as the jokers do in a deck of cards. When one of these characters appears in an argument on the command line, the shell expands that argument in sorted order into a list of filenames and passes the list to the program that the command line calls. Filenames that contain these special characters are called *ambiguous file references* because they do not refer to any one specific file. The process that the shell performs on these filenames is called *pathname expansion* or *globbing*.

Ambiguous file references refer to a group of files with similar names quickly, saving you the effort of typing the names individually. They can also help you find a file whose name you do not remember in its entirety. If no filename matches the ambiguous file reference, the shell generally passes the unexpanded reference—special characters and all—to the command.

THE ? SPECIAL CHARACTER

The question mark (?) is a special character that causes the shell to generate filenames. It matches any single character in the name of an existing file. The following command uses this special character in an argument to the lpr utility:

```
$ lpr memo?
```

The shell expands the **memo?** argument and generates a list of files in the working directory that have names composed of **memo** followed by any single character. The shell then passes this list to lpr. The lpr utility never "knows" that the shell generated the filenames it was called with. If no filename matches the ambiguous file reference, the shell passes the string itself (**memo?**) to lpr or, if it is set up to do so, passes a null string (see **nullglob** on page 327).

The following example uses ls first to display the names of all files in the working directory and then to display the filenames that **memo?** matches:

```
$ ls
mem     memo12   memo9   memoalex   newmemo5
memo    memo5    memoa   memos
$ ls memo?
memo5   memo9   memoa   memos
```

The **memo?** ambiguous file reference does not match **mem**, **memo**, **memo12**, **memoalex**, or **newmemo5**. You can also use a question mark in the middle of an ambiguous file reference:

```
$ ls
7may4report   may4report      mayqreport   may_report
may14report   may4report.79   mayreport    may.report
$ ls may?report
may.report   may4report   may_report   mayqreport
```

To practice generating filenames, you can use echo and ls. The echo utility displays the arguments that the shell passes to it:

```
$ echo may?report
may.report may4report may_report mayqreport
```

The shell first expands the ambiguous file reference into a list of all files in the working directory that match the string **may?report** and then passes this list to echo, as though you had entered the list of filenames as arguments to echo. Next echo displays the list of filenames.

A question mark does not match a leading period (one that indicates a hidden filename; see page 170). When you want to match filenames that begin with a period, you must explicitly include the period in the ambiguous file reference.

THE * SPECIAL CHARACTER

The asterisk (*) performs a function similar to that of the question mark but matches any number of characters, *including zero characters,* in a filename. The following example shows all of the files in the working directory and then shows three commands that display all the filenames that begin with the string **memo**, end with the string **mo**, and contain the string **alx**:

```
$ ls
amemo      memo         memoalx.0620  memosally  user.memo
mem        memo.0612    memoalx.keep  sallymemo
memalx     memoa        memorandum    typescript
$ echo memo*
memo memo.0612 memoa memoalx.0620 memoalx.keep memorandum memosally
$ echo *mo
amemo memo sallymemo user.memo
$ echo *alx*
memalx memoalx.0620 memoalx.keep
```

The ambiguous file reference **memo*** does not match **amemo, mem, sallymemo,** or **user.memo.** Like the question mark, an asterisk does *not* match a leading period in a filename.

The **–a** option causes ls to display hidden filenames. The command **echo *** does not display . (the working directory), .. (the parent of the working directory), **.aaa,** or **.profile.** In contrast, the command **echo .*** displays only those four names:

```
$ ls
aaa          memo.sally   sally.0612   thurs
memo.0612    report       saturday
$ ls -a
.   .aaa     aaa          memo.sally   sally.0612   thurs
..  .profile memo.0612    report       saturday
$ echo *
aaa memo.0612 memo.sally report sally.0612 saturday thurs
$ echo .*
. .. .aaa .profile
```

In the following example .p* does not match **memo.0612, private, reminder,** or **report.** Next the ls .* command causes ls to list **.private** and **.profile** in addition to the contents of the . directory (the working directory) and the .. directory (the parent of the working directory). When called with the same argument, echo displays the names of files (including directories) in the working directory that begin with a dot (.), but not the contents of directories.

```
$ ls -a
.          .private    memo.0612   reminder
..         .profile    private     report
$ echo .p*
.private .profile
$ ls .*
.private .profile

.:
memo.0612   private     reminder     report

..:
.
.
$ echo .*
. .. .private .profile
```

You can take advantage of ambiguous file references when you establish conventions for naming files. For example, when you end all text filenames with **.txt,** you can reference that group of files with *.txt. The next command uses this convention to send all the text files in the working directory to the printer. The ampersand causes lpr to run in the background.

```
$ lpr *.txt &
```

THE [ ] SPECIAL CHARACTERS

A pair of brackets surrounding a list of characters causes the shell to match filenames containing the individual characters. Whereas **memo?** matches **memo** followed by any character, **memo[17a]** is more restrictive, and matches only **memo1, memo7,** and **memoa.** The brackets define a *character class* that includes all the characters within the brackets. (GNU calls this a *character list;* a GNU *character class* is something different.) The shell expands an argument that includes a character-class definition, by substituting each member of the character class, *one at a time,* in place of the brackets and their contents. The shell then passes the list of matching filenames to the program it is calling.

Each character-class definition can replace only a single character within a filename. The brackets and their contents are like a question mark that substitutes only the members of the character class.

The first of the following commands lists the names of all the files in the working directory that begin with **a, e, i, o,** or **u.** The second command displays the contents of the files named **page2.txt, page4.txt, page6.txt,** and **page8.txt.**

```
$ echo [aeiou]*
...
$ less page[2468].txt
...
```

A hyphen within brackets defines a range of characters within a character-class definition. For example, [6–9] represents [6789], [a–z] represents all lowercase letters in English, and [a–zA–Z] represents all letters, both uppercase and lowercase, in English.

The following command lines show three ways to print the files named **part0**, **part1**, **part2**, **part3**, and **part5**. Each of these command lines causes the shell to call lpr with five filenames:

```
$ lpr part0 part1 part2 part3 part5

$ lpr part[01235]

$ lpr part[0-35]
```

The first command line explicitly specifies the five filenames. The second and third command lines use ambiguous file references, incorporating character-class definitions. The shell expands the argument on the second command line to include all files that have names beginning with **part** and ending with any of the characters in the character class. The character class is explicitly defined as **0, 1, 2, 3,** and **5**. The third command line also uses a character-class definition but defines the character class to be all characters in the range **0–3** plus **5**.

The following command line prints 39 files, **part0** through **part38**:

```
$ lpr part[0-9] part[12][0-9] part3[0-8]
```

The next two examples list the names of some of the files in the working directory. The first lists the files whose names start with **a** through **m**. The second lists files whose names end with **x, y,** or **z**.

```
$ echo [a-m]*
...
$ echo *[x-z]
...
```

optional   When an exclamation point (!) or a caret (^) immediately follows the opening bracket ([) that defines a character class, the string enclosed by the brackets matches any character *not* between the brackets. Thus [^ab]* matches any filename that does not begin with **a** or **b**.

The following examples show that *[^ab] matches filenames that do not end with the letters **a** or **b** and that [b-d]* matches filenames that begin with **b, c,** or **d**.

```
$ ls
aa  ab  ac  ad  ba  bb  bc  bd  cc  dd
```

```
$ ls *[^ab]
ac  ad  bc  bd  cc  ddcc  dd
$ ls [b-d]*
ba  bb  bc  bd  cc  dd
```

You can match a hyphen (–) or a closing bracket (]) by placing it immediately before the final closing bracket.

The next example demonstrates that the ls utility cannot interpret ambiguous file references. First ls is called with an argument of ?old. The shell expands ?old into a matching filename, **hold**, and passes that name to ls. The second command is the same as the first, except the ? is quoted (refer to "Special Characters" on page 126). The shell does not recognize this question mark as a special character and passes it on to ls. The ls utility generates an error message saying that it cannot find a file named ?old (because there is no file named ?old).

```
$ ls ?old
hold
$ ls \?old
ls: ?old: No such file or directory
```

Like most utilities and programs, ls cannot interpret ambiguous file references; that work is left to the shell.

The shell expands ambiguous file references

tip *The shell does the expansion* when it processes an ambiguous file reference, not the program that the shell runs. In the examples in this section, *the utilities* (ls, cat, echo, lpr) *never see the ambiguous file references.* The shell expands the ambiguous file references and passes a list of ordinary filenames to the utility. In the previous examples, echo shows this to be true because it simply displays its arguments; it never displays the ambiguous file reference.

Builtins

A *builtin* is a utility (also called a *command*) that is built into a shell. Each of the shells has its own set of builtins. When it runs a builtin, the shell does not fork a new process. Consequently builtins run more quickly and can affect the environment of the current shell. Because builtins are used in the same way as utilities, you will not typically be aware of whether a utility is built into the shell or is a stand-alone utility.

The echo utility is a shell builtin. The shell always executes a shell builtin before trying to find a command or utility with the same name. See page 926 for an in-depth discussion of builtin commands and page 939 for a list of bash builtins.

Listing bash builtins To get a complete list of bash builtins, give the command **info bash builtin**. To display a page with more information on each builtin, move the cursor to one of the lines listing a builtin command and press RETURN. Alternatively, after typing **info bash**, give the command **/builtin** to search the bash documentation for the string **builtin**. The cursor will rest on the word **Builtin** in a menu; press RETURN to display the builtins menu.

Because bash was written by GNU, the info page has better information than does the man page. If you want to read about builtins in the man page, give the command **man bash** and then search for the section on builtins with the command **/^SHELL BUILTIN COMMANDS** (search for a line that begins with **SHELL . . .**).

CHAPTER SUMMARY

The shell is the Linux command interpreter. It scans the command line for proper syntax, picking out the command name and any arguments. The first argument is argument one, the second is argument two, and so on. The name of the command itself is argument zero. Many programs use options to modify the effects of a command. Most Linux utilities identify an option by its leading one or two hyphens.

When you give it a command, the shell tries to find an executable program with the same name as the command. When it does, the shell executes the program. When it does not, the shell tells you that it cannot find or execute the program. If the command is a simple filename, the shell searches the directories given in the variable **PATH** in an attempt to locate the command.

When it executes a command, the shell assigns one file to the command's standard input and another file to its standard output. By default the shell causes a command's standard input to come from the keyboard and its standard output to go to the screen. You can instruct the shell to redirect a command's standard input from or standard output to any file or device. You can also connect standard output of one command to standard input of another command using a pipe. A filter is a command that reads its standard input from standard output of one command and writes its standard output to standard input of another command.

When a command runs in the foreground, the shell waits for it to finish before it displays a prompt and allows you to continue. When you put an ampersand (**&**) at the end of a command line, the shell executes the command in the background and displays another prompt immediately. Run slow commands in the background when you want to enter other commands at the shell prompt. The jobs builtin displays a list of jobs and includes the job number of each.

The shell interprets special characters on a command line to generate filenames. A question mark represents any single character, and an asterisk represents zero or more characters. A single character may also be represented by a character class: a list of characters within brackets. A reference that uses special characters (wildcards) to abbreviate a list of one or more filenames is called an ambiguous file reference.

A builtin is a utility that is built into a shell. Each shell has its own set of builtins. When it runs a builtin, the shell does not fork a new process. Consequently builtins run more quickly and can affect the environment of the current shell.

UTILITIES AND BUILTINS INTRODUCED IN THIS CHAPTER

Table 7-1 lists the utilities introduced in this chapter.

Table 7-1   New utilities

Utility	Function
tr	Maps one string of characters into another (page 216)
tee	Sends standard input to both a file and standard output (page 218)
bg	Moves a process into the background (page 219)
fg	Moves a process into the foreground (page 220)
jobs	Displays a list of currently running jobs (page 220)

EXERCISES

1. What does the shell ordinarily do while a command is executing? What should you do if you do not want to wait for a command to finish before running another command?

2. Using sort as a filter, rewrite the following sequence of commands:

    ```
    $ sort list > temp
    $ lpr temp
    $ rm temp
    ```

3. What is a PID number? Why are these numbers useful when you run processes in the background? Which utility displays the PID numbers of the commands you are running?

4. Assume that the following files are in the working directory:

    ```
    $ ls
    intro     notesb    ref2      section1   section3   section4b
    notesa    ref1      ref3      section2   section4a  sentrev
    ```

    Give commands for each of the following, using wildcards to express file-names with as few characters as possible.

    a. List all files that begin with **section**.

    b. List the **section1**, **section2**, and **section3** files only.

    c. List the **intro** file only.

    d. List the **section1**, **section3**, **ref1**, and **ref3** files.

5. Refer to the documentation of utilities in the man pages to determine which commands will

   a. Output the number of lines in the standard input that contain the *word* **a** or **A**.

   b. Output only the names of the files in the working directory that contain the pattern **$(**.

   c. List the files in the working directory in their reverse alphabetical order.

   d. Send a list of files in the working directory to the printer, sorted by size.

6. Give a command to

   a. Redirect the standard output from a sort command into a file named **phone_list**. Assume that the input file is named **numbers**.

   b. Translate all occurrences of the characters [and { to the character (, and all occurrences of the characters] and } to the character) in the file **permdemos.c**. (*Hint*: Refer to the tr man page.)

   c. Create a file named **book** that contains the contents of two other files: **part1** and **part2**.

7. The lpr and sort utilities accept input either from a file named on the command line or from standard input.

   a. Name two other utilities that function in a similar manner.

   b. Name a utility that accepts its input only from standard input.

8. Give an example of a command that uses grep

   a. With both input and output redirected.

   b. With only input redirected.

   c. With only output redirected.

   d. Within a pipe.

   In which of the preceding is grep used as a filter?

9. Explain the following error message. What filenames would a subsequent ls display?

```
$ ls
abc   abd   abe   abf   abg   abh
$ rm abc ab*
rm: cannot remove 'abc': No such file or directory
```

ADVANCED EXERCISES

10. When you use the redirect output symbol (>) with a command, the shell creates the output file immediately, before the command is executed. Demonstrate that this is true.

11. In experimenting with shell variables, Alex accidentally deletes his **PATH** variable. He decides that he does not need the **PATH** variable. Discuss some of the problems he may soon encounter and explain the reasons for these problems. How could he *easily* return **PATH** to its original value?

12. Assume that your permissions allow you to write to a file but not to delete it.

    a. Give a command to empty the file without invoking an editor.

    b. Explain how you might have permission to modify a file that you cannot delete.

13. If you accidentally create a filename that contains a nonprinting character, such as a CONTROL character, how can you rename the file?

14. Why does the **noclobber** variable *not* protect you from overwriting an existing file with cp or mv?

15. Why do command names and filenames usually not have embedded SPACEs? How would you create a filename containing a SPACE? How would you remove it? (This is a thought exercise, not recommended practice. If you want to experiment, create and work in a directory that contains only your experimental file.)

16. Create a file named **answer** and give the following command:

```
$ > answers.0102 < answer cat
```

Explain what the command does and why. What is a more conventional way of expressing this command?

PART III

DIGGING INTO RED HAT LINUX

8

LINUX GUIs: X, GNOME, AND KDE

This chapter covers the Linux graphical user interface (GUI). It continues where Chapter 4 left off, going into more detail about the X Window System, the basis for the Linux GUI. It presents a brief history of GNOME and KDE and discusses some of the problems and benefits of having two major Linux desktop environments. The section on GNOME covers the Nautilus file manager, including its spatial interface, and several important GNOME utilities. The final section covers KDE, presenting information about some of the more advanced features of Konqueror, and describing a few KDE utilities.

X Window System

History of X   The X Window System (www.x.org) was created in 1984 at the Massachusetts Institute of Technology (MIT) by researchers working on a distributed computing project and a campuswide distributed environment, called Project Athena. This system was not the first windowing software to run on a UNIX system, but it was the first to become widely available and accepted. In 1985, MIT released X (version 9) to the public, for use without a license. Three years later, a group of vendors formed the X Consortium to support the continued development of X, under the leadership of MIT. By 1998, the X Consortium had become part of the Open Group. In 2001, the Open Group released X version 11, release 6.6 (commonly called X11R6.6).

The X Window System was inspired by the ideas and features found in earlier proprietary window systems but is written to be portable and flexible. X is designed to run on a workstation, typically attached to a LAN. The designers built X with the network in mind. If you can communicate with a remote computer over a network, running an X application on that computer and sending the results to a local display are straightforward.

While the X protocol has remained stable for quite a long time, additions in the form of extensions are quite common. One of the most interesting, albeit one that has not yet made its way into production, is the Media Application Server, which aims to provide the same level of network transparency for sound and video that X does for simple windowing applications.

XFree86 and X.org   Red Hat Linux used the XFree86 X server, which inherited its license from the original MIT X server, through release 4.3. In early 2004, just before the release of XFree86 4.4, the XFree86 license was changed to one that is more restrictive and not compatible with the GPL (page 4). A number of distributions, including Red Hat Linux, abandoned XFree86 and replaced it with an X.org X server that is based on a pre-release version of XFree86 4.4, which predates change in the XFree86 license.

The X.org X server, named Xorg, is functionally equivalent to the one distributed by XFree86 because most of the code is the same. Modules designed to work with one server work with the other.

The X stack   The Linux GUI is built in layers (Figure 8-1). The bottom layer is the kernel, which provides the basic interfaces to the hardware. On top of the kernel is the X server, which is responsible for managing windows and drawing basic graphical primitives such as lines and bitmaps. Rather than directly generating X commands, most programs use Xlib, the next layer, which is a standard library for interfacing with an X server. Xlib is complicated and does not provide high-level abstractions, such as buttons and text boxes. Rather than using Xlib directly, most programs rely on a toolkit that provides high-level abstractions. Using a library not only makes programming easier, but has the added advantage of bringing consistency to applications.

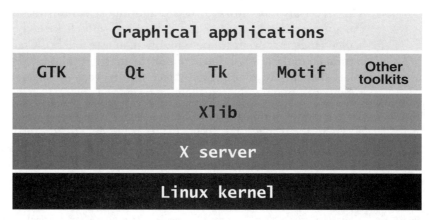

Figure 8-1   The X stack

In recent years, the popularity of X has extended outside the UNIX community and beyond the workstation class of computers it was originally conceived for. Today X is available for Macintosh computers as well as for PCs running Windows. It is also available on a special kind of display terminal, known as an X *terminal,* developed specifically to run X.

Client/server environment
Computer networks are central to the design of X. It is possible to run an application on one computer and display the results on a screen attached to a different computer; the ease with which this can be done distinguishes X from other window systems available today. Thanks to this capability, a scientist can run and manipulate a program on a powerful supercomputer in another building or another country and view the results on a personal workstation or laptop computer. For more information refer to "Remote Computing and Local Displays" on page 237.

When you start an X Window System session, you set up a *client/server environment.* One process, called the *X server,* displays desktops and windows under X. Each application program and utility that makes a request of the X server is a *client* of that server. Examples of X clients include xterm, kwin, xclock, and such general applications as word processing and spreadsheet programs. A typical request from a client is to display an image or open a window.

The roles of X client and server may be counterintuitive

tip   The terms *client* and *server,* when referring to X, have the opposite meanings of how you might think of them intuitively: The server runs the mouse, keyboard, and display; the application program is the client.

This disparity becomes even more apparent when you run an application program on a remote system. You might think of the system running the program as the server and the system providing the display as the client, but in fact it is the other way around. With X, the system providing the display is the server, and the system running the program is the client.

Events   The server also monitors keyboard and mouse actions (*events*) and passes them to the appropriate clients. For example, when you click the border of a window, the server sends this event to the window manager (client). Characters you type into a terminal emulation window are sent to that terminal emulator (client). The client takes appropriate action when it receives an event—for example, making a window active or displaying the typed character on the server.

Separating the physical control of the display (the server) from the processes needing access to the display (the client) makes it possible to run the server on one computer and the client on another computer. In general, this book discusses running the X server and client applications on a single system. Refer to "Remote Computing and Local Displays" for information on using X in a distributed environment.

optional   You can run **xev** (X event) by giving the command **/usr/bin/xev** from a terminal emulation window and then watch the information flow from the client to the server and back again. This utility opens a window with a box in it and asks the X server to send it events each time anything happens, such as moving the mouse pointer, clicking a mouse button, moving the mouse pointer into the box, typing, or resizing the window. The **xev** utility displays information about each event in the window that you opened it from. You can use **xev** as an educational tool: Start it and see how much information is being processed each time you move the mouse. Close the Event Tester window to exit from **xev**.

USING X

This section provides basic information about starting and configuring X from the command line.

Killing a graphical program

caution   When you press CONTROL-ALT-ESCAPE, the mouse pointer changes into a skull and crossbones. When you move this mouse pointer over the window of a misbehaving or frozen application and click, the system kills the program that controls the window.

Use this technique with care. If you decide that you do not want to kill a program, press ESCAPE to return the mouse pointer to its normal mode. Killing the wrong program, such as the desktop, can be problematic.

STARTING X FROM A CHARACTER-BASED DISPLAY

Once you have logged in on a virtual console (page 113), you can start an X Window System server by using **startx**. See page 404 for information on changing the **initdefault** entry in the **/etc/inittab** file so Linux boots into character (and not graphical) mode. When you run **startx**, the X server displays an X screen, using the first available virtual console. The following command causes **startx** to run in the background so that you can switch back to this virtual console and give other commands:

```
$ startx &
```

REMOTE COMPUTING AND LOCAL DISPLAYS

To identify the display that an X application is to use, you can either set a global shell variable or give a command line option.

THE DISPLAY VARIABLE

The most common method of identifying a display is to use the **DISPLAY** shell environment variable. This locally unique identification string is automatically set by xinit when it starts the X server.

The **DISPLAY** variable holds the screen number of a display:

```
$ echo $DISPLAY
:0
```

The format of the complete (globally unique) ID string for a display is

[hostname]:display-number[.screen-number]

where *hostname* is the name of the system running the X server, *display-number* is the number of the logical (physical) display (0 unless multiple monitors or graphical terminals are attached to the system, or if you are running X over ssh), and *screen-number* is the logical number of the (virtual) terminal (0 unless you are running multiple instances of X). When you are working with a single physical screen, you can shorten the identification string. For example, you can use **bravo:0.0** or **bravo:0** to identify the only physical display on the system named **bravo**. When the X server and the X clients are running on the same system, you can shorten this identification string even further to **:0.0** or **:0**. An ssh connection (page 583) shows **DISPLAY** as **localhost:10.0**.

If **DISPLAY** is empty or not set, the screen you are working from is not running X. An application (the X client) uses the value of the **DISPLAY** variable to determine which display, keyboard, and mouse (collectively, the X server) to use. One way to run an X application, such as xclock, on the local system but have it use the X Window System display on a remote system is to change the value of the **DISPLAY** variable on the local system to identify the remote X server. If you get a refused or not authorized error, refer to the tip "xhost grants access to a display" (next page).

```
$ export DISPLAY=bravo:0.0
$ xclock &
```

The preceding example starts xclock with the default X server running on the system named **bravo**. After setting the **DISPLAY** variable to the ID of the **bravo** server, all X programs (clients) you start will use **bravo** as their server (output appears on **bravo's** display and input comes from **bravo's** keyboard and mouse).

When you change the value of DISPLAY

tip When you change the value of the **DISPLAY** variable, all X programs send their output to the display named by **DISPLAY**.

THE −display OPTION

To override the default X server, you can specify the display (and keyboard and mouse) you want to use on the command line:

```
$ xclock -display bravo:0.0
```

Many X programs accept the **−display** option, which affects just the command you use it with. All other X-related commands will send their output to the display specified by the **DISPLAY** variable.

xhost **grants access to a display**

tip   If the system displays an error message when you try to open a window on a remote display, the remote user needs to run xhost to grant you access to that display. For example, if you are logged in on a system named **kudos** and you want to create a window on Alex's display, Alex needs to run the following command:

```
$ xhost +kudos
```

If Alex wants to allow anyone to create windows on his display, he can give the following command, which grants access to all systems:

```
$ xhost +
```

If you frequently work with other users via a network, you may find it convenient to add an xhost line to your **.bash_profile** file (page 267). Be selective in granting access to your X display with xhost, however; if another system has access to your display, you may find that your work is interrupted all too often.

Security and xhost

security   Allowing a remote system access to your display using xhost means that any user on the remote system can watch everything you type in a terminal emulation window, including passwords. For this reason, some software packages, such as the Tcl/Tk development system (www.tcl.tk), restrict their own capabilities when xhost is used. If you are concerned about security or want to take full advantage of systems such as Tcl/Tk, you should use a safer means of granting remote access to your X session. See the xauth man page for information about a more secure replacement for xhost.

RUNNING MULTIPLE X SERVERS

You can start multiple X servers on a single system. The most common reason for starting a second X server is to use a second display that allocates a different number of bits to each screen pixel. The possible values are 8, 16, 24, and 32 bits per pixel. Most X servers available for Linux default to 24 or 32 bits per pixel, permitting the use of millions of colors simultaneously. Starting an X server with 8 bits per pixel permits the use of any combination of 256 colors at the same time. The maximum number of bits per pixel allowed depends on the computer graphics hardware and X server. With fewer bits per pixel, the system has to transfer less data, possibly making it more responsive. In addition, many games work with only 256 colors.

When you start multiple X servers, each must have a different ID string. The following command starts a second X server; do not give this command from a terminal emulator:

```
$ startx -- :1
```

The — option marks the end of the startx options and arguments. Arguments to the left of this option belong to startx. The startx script passes arguments that appear to the right of this option to the X server. The following command starts an X server running at 16 bits per pixel:

```
$ startx -- -depth 16 &
```

Refer to "Using Virtual Consoles" on page 113 for information on how to switch to a virtual console to start a second server.

KDE *FEDORA*   Under KDE you can select **Main menu: Switch User⇨Start a New Session** to start another X server.

X over ssh   See "Tunneling/Port Forwarding" on page 596 for information about running X over an ssh connection.

STOPPING THE X SERVER

How you terminate a window manager depends on which window manager you are running and how it is configured. If X stops responding, switch to a virtual terminal, log in from another terminal or a remote system, or use ssh to gain access to the system. Then kill (page 395) the process running Xorg. You can also press CONTROL-ALT-BACKSPACE to quit the X server. This method may not shut down the X session cleanly, however, so it should be used only as a last resort.

REMAPPING MOUSE BUTTONS

Throughout this book, each description of a mouse click refers to the button by its position (left, middle, or right, with left implied when no button is specified) because the position of a mouse button is more intuitive than an arbitrary name or number. X terminology numbers buttons starting at the left and continuing with the mouse wheel. The buttons on a three-button mouse are numbered 1 (left), 2 (middle), and 3 (right). A mouse wheel, if present, is 4 (rolling it up) and 5 (rolling it down). Clicking the wheel is equivalent to clicking the middle mouse button. The buttons on a two-button mouse are 1 (left) and 2 (right).

If you are right-handed, you can conveniently press the left mouse button with your index finger; X programs take advantage of this fact by relying on button 1 for the most common operations. If you are left-handed, your index finger rests most conveniently on button 2 or 3 (the right button on a two- or three-button mouse).

To exchange the functions of the left and right mouse buttons when you are running GNOME, from the panel at the top of the window select **System: Preferences⇨ Mouse** (*RHEL* uses **Applications: Preferences⇨Mouse**) and put a check mark in the box labeled **Left-handed mouse**. From KDE choose **Main menu: Control Center**⇨ **Peripherals**⇨**Mouse** and select **Left handed** from the General tab.

You can also change how X interprets the mouse buttons by using xmodmap. If you are left-handed and using a three-button mouse with a wheel, the following command causes X to interpret the right button as button 1 and the left button as button 3:

```
$ xmodmap -e 'pointer = 3 2 1 4 5'
```

Omit the 4 and 5 if the mouse does not have a wheel. The following command works for a two-button mouse without a wheel:

```
$ xmodmap -e 'pointer = 2 1'
```

If xmodmap displays an error message complaining about the number of buttons, use the **–pp** option to xmodmap to display the number of buttons that X has defined for the mouse:

```
$ xmodmap -pp
There are 9 pointer buttons defined.
```

Physical Button	Button Code
1	1
2	2
3	3
4	4
5	5
6	6
7	7
8	8
9	9

Then expand the previous command, adding numbers to complete the list. If the **–pp** option shows nine buttons, give the following command:

```
$ xmodmap -e 'pointer = 3 2 1 4 5 6 7 8 9'
```

Changing the order of the first three buttons is critical to making the mouse suitable for a left-handed user. When you remap the mouse buttons, remember to reinterpret the descriptions in this book accordingly. When this book asks you to click the left button, or does not specify a button to click, use the right button, and vice versa.

WINDOW MANAGERS

Conceptually X is very simple and does not provide some of the more common features found in GUIs, such as the ability to drag windows. The UNIX/Linux philosophy is one of modularity: X relies on a window manager, such as Metacity or kwin, to draw window borders and handle moving and resizing operations.

Unlike a window manager, which has a clearly defined task, a desktop environment (manager) does many things. In general, a desktop environment, such as KDE or

GNOME, provides a means of launching applications and utilities, such as a file manager, that a window manager can use.

KDE AND GNOME

The KDE project began in 1996, with the aim of creating a consistent, user-friendly desktop environment for free UNIX-like operating systems. KDE is based on the Qt toolkit made by Trolltech. When KDE development began, the Qt license was not compatible with the GPL (page 4). For this reason the Free Software Foundation decided to support a different project, the GNU Network Object Model Environment (GNOME). More recently Qt has been released under the terms of the GPL, removing part of the rationale for GNOME's existence.

KDE   KDE is written in C++ on top of the Qt framework. KDE tries to use existing technology, if it can be reused, but creates its own if nothing else is available or a superior solution is needed. For example, KDE implemented an HTML rendering engine long before the Mozilla project was born. Similarly, work on KOffice began a long time before StarOffice became the open-source OpenOffice. In contrast, the GNOME office applications are stand-alone programs that originated outside the GNOME project. The GNOME Web browser uses the HTML rendering engine developed by the Mozilla project.

KDE's portability was recently demonstrated when a version of most of the core components, including Konqueror and KOffice, was released for Mac OS X.

KParts   By itself, Konqueror has very little functionality; this application uses other applications to do all its work. Konqueror takes advantage of KDE *i/o slaves* and *components* (KParts). The i/o slaves accept or gather input and change it to a standard format that a component can display. When you open Konqueror to view your home directory, Konqueror calls the File i/o slave, which gathers information about the filesystem and uses the Icon view component (**Konqueror menubar: View⇨View Mode⇨Icon View**) or the Text view component (**Konqueror menubar: View⇨View Mode⇨Text View**) to display the information it gets from the File i/o slave.

The i/o slaves are discrete modules; it is relatively easy to write a new one. Konqueror uses an i/o slave automatically when you put it in the directory structure (**$KDEDIR/lib/kde3/kio_*protocol*.*** and **$KDEDIR/share/services/*protocol*.desktop**, where **$KDEDIR** is **/usr** by default and *protocol* is the name of the protocol). Examples of i/o slaves and their output format include FTP (virtual filesystem), POP3 (each retrieved piece of email appears as a file), and the audio CD browser (**kio_audiocd**; each track appears as a file).

The components display the information they receive from the i/o slaves. One i/o slave can feed several different components, and one component can receive input from several different i/o slaves. Both an i/o slave *and* a component pair must be available to display information within a Konqueror view.

GNOME   GNOME is the default desktop environment for Red Hat Linux. It provides a simple, coherent user interface suitable for corporate use. GNOME uses GTK for drawing widgets. GTK, developed for the GNU Image Manipulation Program (gimp), is written in C, although bindings for C++ and other languages are available.

GNOME does not take much advantage of its component architecture. Instead, it continues to support the traditional UNIX philosophy of having many small programs, each of which is good at doing a specific task.

Interoperability Since version 2, GNOME has focused on simplifying its user interface, removing options where they are deemed unnecessary, and aiming for a set of default settings that the end user will not wish to change. KDE has moved in the opposite direction, emphasizing configurability.

The freedesktop.org group (freedesktop.org), whose members are drawn from the GNOME and KDE projects, is improving interoperability and aims to produce standards that will allow the two environments to work together. One standard released by freedesktop.org allows applications to use the notification area of either the GNOME or KDE panel without being aware of which desktop environment they are running in.

GNUStep

The GNUStep project (www.gnustep.org), which began before both the KDE and GNOME projects, is creating an open-source implementation of the OPENSTEP API and desktop environment. The result is a very clean, fast user interface.

The default look of WindowMaker, the GNUStep window manager, is somewhat dated, but theme support is currently in beta. The user interface is widely regarded as one of the most intuitive of any UNIX platform. GNUStep has less overhead than KDE and GNOME, so it runs better on older hardware. If you are running Linux on hardware that struggles with GNOME and KDE or you would like to try a user interface that does not try to mimic Windows, try GNUStep. WindowMaker is provided in the **WindowMaker** package.

USING GNOME

This section discusses the Nautilus file manager and several GNOME utilities.

THE NAUTILUS FILE MANAGER

Nautilus is a simple, powerful file manager. You can use it to create, open, view, move, and copy files and directories as well as execute programs and scripts. Nautilus gives you two ways to work with files: an innovative spatial view (Figure 8-2) and a traditional File Browser view (Figure 8-4 on page 244).

SPATIAL VIEW

The Nautilus object window presents a spatial view (Figure 8-2). This view has many powerful features but may take some getting used to. The spatial (as in "having the

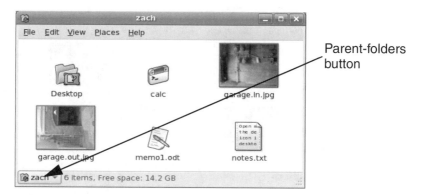

Parent-folders button

Figure 8-2   The Nautilus spatial view

nature of space") view always provides one window per folder. By default, when you open a folder, Nautilus displays a new window.

To open a spatial view of your home directory, double-click the home icon on the desktop and experiment as you read this section. If you double-click the Desktop icon in the spatial view, Nautilus opens a new window that displays the **Desktop** folder.

A spatial view can display icons or a list of filenames; select your preferred format by choosing one of the **View as** selections from View on the menubar. To create files to experiment with, right-click in the window (not on an icon) to display the Nautilus context menu and select **Create Folder** or **Create Document**.

GNOME desktop and Nautilus

tip   The GNOME desktop is run from a back-end process that runs as part of Nautilus. If that process stops running, it usually restarts automatically. If it does not restart, give the command **nautilus** to restore the desktop. You do not have to keep the Nautilus window open to keep the desktop alive.

Use SHIFT to close the current window as you open another window

tip   If you hold the SHIFT key down when you double-click to open a new window, Nautilus closes the current window as it opens the new one. This behavior may be more familiar and can help keep the desktop from becoming overly cluttered. If you do not want to use the keyboard, you can achieve the same result by double-clicking the middle mouse button.

Window memory   Move the window by dragging the titlebar. The spatial view has *window memory*. The next time you open that folder, Nautilus opens it at the same size in the same location. Even the scrollbar will be in the same position.

Parent-folders button   The key to closing the current window and returning to the window of the parent directory is the **Parent-folders** button (Figure 8-2). Click this button to display the

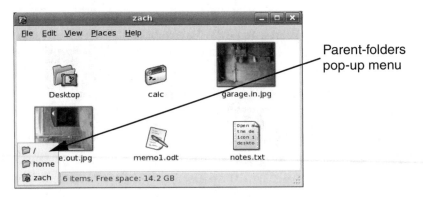

Parent-folders
pop-up menu

Figure 8-3 The Parent-folders pop-up menu

Parent-folders pop-up menu (Figure 8-3). Select the directory you want to open from this menu. Nautilus then displays in a spatial view the directory you specified.

From a spatial view, you can open a folder in a traditional view by right-clicking the folder and selecting **Browse Folder**.

TRADITIONAL VIEW

Figure 8-4 shows the traditional, or file browser, window with a Side pane (sometimes called a *sidebar*), View pane, menubar, toolbar, and location bar. To open a Browser view of your home directory, either right-click the home icon on the desktop and select **Browse Folder** or select **Applications: System Tools⇨File Browser**.

SIDE PANE

Click the button at the top of the Side pane to display the Side pane menu. From this menu select the type of items you want Nautilus to display in the Side pane:

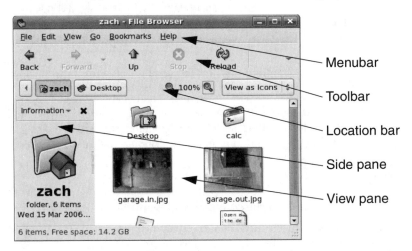

Menubar

Toolbar

Location bar

Side pane

View pane

Figure 8-4 Nautilus traditional (file browser) window

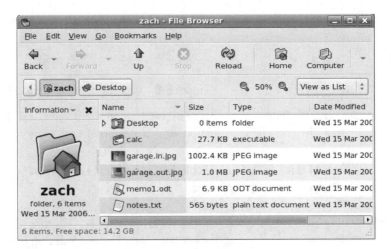

Figure 8-5   Nautilus displaying a List view

Places, Information (information about the folder displayed in the View pane; see Figure 8-4), Tree (directory hierarchy), History (list of recent locations displayed by Nautilus), Notes, or Emblems (drag emblems [page 247] to files in the View pane).

VIEW PANE

You can display icons or a list of filenames in the View pane. Choose your preferred view by making a selection from the drop-down menu that appears at the right end of the location bar. **View as Icons** is shown in Figure 8-4 and **View as List** is shown in Figure 8-5.

CONTROL BARS

This section discusses the three control bars—menubar, toolbar, and location bar—that initially appear at the top of a Nautilus browser window (Figure 8-4).

Menubar   The menubar presents a drop-down menu when you click one of its selections. The menu selections depend on what Nautilus is displaying in the View pane.

Toolbar   The Nautilus toolbar holds navigation tool icons: Back, Forward, Up, Stop, Reload, Home, Computer, and Search. Click the down arrow button at the right end of the toolbar to display and select icons that do not fit on the toolbar.

Location bar   The buttons on the location bar depict the pathname of the directory that is displayed in the View pane and highlighted in the Tree tab, when it is displayed in the Side pane. You can display a text box in the location bar by pressing CONTROL-L. In this text box you can specify a local directory that you want to display in the View pane. When you enter the absolute pathname of the directory and press RETURN, Nautilus displays the contents of the directory.

The location bar also holds the magnification selector and the **View as** drop-down menu. To change the magnification of the display in the View pane, click the plus or minus sign on either side of the magnification percentage; click the magnification

Figure 8-6   Open Location dialog box

percentage itself to return to 100% magnification. Click **View as** (to the right of the magnifying glass) to display and choose from the viewing selections.

FEATURES AVAILABLE FROM BOTH SPATIAL AND TRADITIONAL VIEWS

Open Location dialog box
You can display deeply nested directories quickly by using the Open Location dialog box (Figure 8-6) or the location bar. Press CONTROL-L while the cursor is over a Nautilus window to display the Open Location dialog box (spatial view) or to move the cursor to the location bar (traditional view). Enter the absolute pathname of the directory you want to display. Nautilus provides assistance by completing directory names as you type. Press TAB to accept a suggested completion or keep typing to ignore it.

Zooming images
Use the Open Location dialog box or the location bar to display the directory named **/usr/share/backgrounds/images**. Double-click an image file to display that file in a preview window. Position the mouse pointer over the image and use the mouse wheel to zoom the image. When the image is bigger than the window, you can drag the image to view different parts of it.

Opening files
By default, you double-click a filename or icon to open it, or you can right-click the icon or filename and choose **Open** from the pop-up menu. When you open a file, Nautilus figures out the appropriate tool to use by determining the file's MIME type (page 96). GNOME associates each filename extension with a MIME type and each MIME type with a program. Initially GNOME uses the filename extension to try to determine a file's MIME type. For example, when you open a file with a filename extension of **ps**, Nautilus calls KGhostView, which displays the PostScript file in a readable format. When you open a text file, Nautilus opens a text editor that displays and allows you to edit the file. When you open a directory, Nautilus displays its contents. When you open an executable file such as Firefox, Nautilus runs the executable. When Nautilus cannot determine which tool to use to open a file, it asks you for assistance. See "Open With" on page 248 for information on how to change the program that GNOME associates with a MIME type.

PROPERTIES

You can view information about a file, such as ownership, permissions, size, ways to work with it, and so on, by right-clicking a filename or icon and selecting **Properties** from the drop-down menu. The Properties window initially displays some basic information. Click the tabs at the top of the window to display additional information. Different types of files display different sets of tabs, depending on what is

Figure 8-7 Properties window: Emblems tab (left); Permissions tab (right)

appropriate to the file. You can modify the settings in this window only if you have permission to do so.

Basic | The Basic tab displays information about the file and enables you to select a custom icon for the file or change its name. To change the name of the file, make your changes in the text box. If the filename is not listed in a text box, you do not have permission to change it.

Emblems | The Emblems tab (Figure 8-7, left) allows you to add or remove emblems associated with the file by placing (removing) a check mark in the box next to an emblem. Figure 8-8 shows some emblems on a file icon. Nautilus displays emblems in both its Icon and List views, although there may not be room for more than one icon in the List view. You can also place an emblem on an icon by dragging it from the Side pane Emblems tab to an icon in the View pane. Drag the Erase emblem to an icon to remove all emblems from the icon.

Permissions | The Permissions tab (Figure 8-7, right) allows you to change file permissions (page 181). When the box to the left of the word **Read** in the Owner row (called *user* elsewhere; see the tip "chmod: **o** for other, **u** for owner" on page 183) has a

garage.in.jpg
1002.4 KB

Figure 8-8 Emblems

Figure 8-9   Properties window, Open With tab

check mark in it, the owner has permission to read the file. When you click the boxes in the Owner row so all of them contain check marks, the owner has read, write, and execute permissions. The owner of a file can change the group that the file is associated with to any other group the owner is associated with. When you run as Superuser, you can change the name of the user who owns the file and the group the file is associated with. Directory permissions work as explained on page 184. See page 183 for information on set user ID and set group ID permissions, and page 1057 for a description of the sticky bit.

Open With   When you ask it to open a file that is not executable (by double-clicking its icon or right-clicking and selecting **Open with**), GNOME must figure out which application or utility to use when opening the file. GNOME uses several techniques to determine the MIME type (page 96) of a file and selects an appropriate application based on that determination.

The Open With tab (Figure 8-9) enables you to change which applications GNOME uses to open the current file and other files of the same MIME type (typically files with the same filename extension). Click **Add** to add an application and then click the radio button next to the application to cause GNOME to use that application to open the current file and others of the same MIME type. Highlight an application and click **Remove** to remove an application from the list. You cannot remove the default application.

GNOME UTILITIES

GNOME comes with numerous utilities intended to make your work on the desktop easier and more productive. This section covers several tools that are integral to the use of GNOME.

Figure 8-10   Desktop Search window

beagle: DESKTOP SEARCH (*FEDORA*)

To run beagle, enter **beagle-search** on a command line or select **Places: Search** on the panel at the top of the screen. This utility displays the Desktop Search window (Figure 8-10), from which you can search for a string of characters in a filename and in the contents of a file. To choose the type of files you want to search, make a selection from the menu displayed when you click **Search** on the menubar. By default, beagle searches files in your home directory hierarchy. Click **Search⇨Preferences⇨Indexing** to instruct beagle to search other directories. If, when you start beagle, it displays **Daemon not running,** click **Start the daemon** to start the **beagled** daemon.

To begin a search, enter the word or string of characters you want to search for in the Find text box. The beagle utility starts searching a moment after you stop typing. Click **Find Now** to display additional information about the selected file.

The Sort selection on the menubar allows you to sort the results of a search alphabetically by filename, by the date the file was modified, or by the relevance of each result.

FONT PREFERENCES

To display the GNOME Font Preferences window (Figure 8-11, next page), enter **gnome-font-properties** on a command line. You can also select **System: Preferences⇨Fonts** from the panel at the top of the screen. Click one of the five font bars in the upper part of the window to display the Pick a Font window (discussed in the next section). In this window you can change the font that GNOME uses for applications, documents, the desktop, window titles, or terminal emulators (fixed width).

Examine the four sample boxes in the Font Rendering frame in the lower part of the window and select the one with the best appearance. Subpixel smoothing is usually best for LCD monitors. Click **Details** to refine the font rendering further, again picking the box in each frame that has the best appearance.

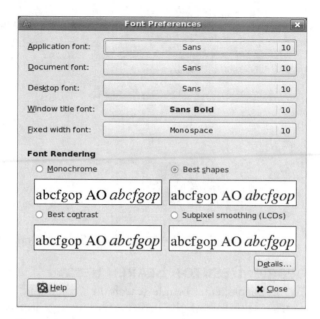

Figure 8-11   Font Preferences window

PICK A FONT WINDOW

The Pick a Font window (Figure 8-12) appears when you need to choose a font. From this window you can select a font family, a style, and a size you want to use. A preview of your choice appears in the Preview frame in the lower part of the window. Click **OK** when you are satisfied with your choice.

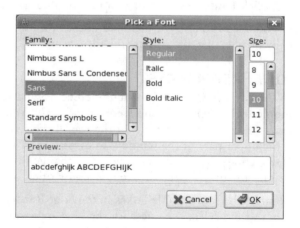

Figure 8-12   Pick a Font window

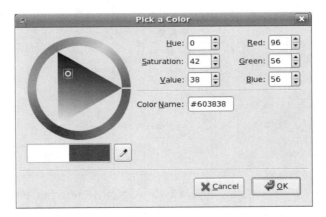

Figure 8-13 Pick a Color window

PICK A COLOR WINDOW

The Pick a Color window (Figure 8-13) appears when you need to choose a color, such as when you choose **Desktop menu: Change Desktop Background** and click the box below and to the right of **Desktop Colors**. When the Pick a Color window opens, the bar below the color circle displays the current color. Click the desired color from the color ring, and click/drag the lightness of that color in the triangle. As you change the color, the right end of the bar previews the color you are selecting, while the left end continues to display the current color. Use the eyedropper to pick up a color from the workspace: Click the eyedropper, and then click the resulting eyedropper mouse pointer on the color you want. The color you choose will appear in the bar.

RUN APPLICATION WINDOW

The Run Application window (Figure 8-14) enables you to run a program as though you had initiated it from a command line. To display the Run Application window, press Alt-F2. Enter a command; click **Run with file** to specify a filename to use as an argument to the command in the text box. Click **Run in terminal** to run textual applications, such as vim, in a terminal emulator window.

Figure 8-14 Run Application window

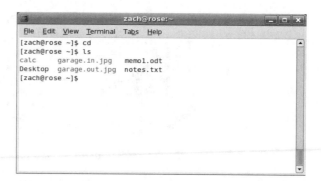

Figure 8-15   GNOME terminal emulator

GNOME TERMINAL EMULATOR/SHELL

The GNOME terminal emulator (gnome-terminal; see Figure 8-15) displays a window that mimics a character-based terminal (page 93). To display the terminal emulator window, select **Applications: Accessories⇨Terminal** from the panel at the top of the screen. When the GNOME terminal emulator is already displayed, select **Menubar: File⇨Open Terminal** to display a different terminal emulator window.

To open an additional terminal session within the same window, right-click the window and select **Open Tab** from the context menu or select **Menubar: File⇨Open Tab**. A row of tabs appears below the menubar as gnome-terminal opens another terminal session on top of the existing one. Add as many terminal sessions as you like; click the tabs to switch between sessions.

A session you add from the context menu uses the same profile as the session you open it from. When you use the menubar to open a session, GNOME gives you a choice of profiles, if more than one is available. You can add and modify profiles, including the Default profile, by selecting **Menubar: Edit⇨Profiles**. Highlight the profile you want to modify or click **New** to design a new profile.

USING KDE

Because KDE has so many features, associated utilities, and programs, this section cannot hope to cover them all. Instead, it attempts to familiarize you with the content and style of KDE; it is up to you to explore and find out more. One of the best ways to learn about KDE is to go through the online documentation and experiment. You can also look through the Main menu and browse www.kde.org.

KONQUEROR BROWSER/FILE MANAGER

Konqueror was introduced on page 94. This section describes additional Konqueror features.

What is a KDE desktop?

tip   In KDE documentation, the term *desktop* refers to a single division of a larger area. This book, in conformance with the GNOME documentation, divides the larger area, called the desktop, into workspaces. You may notice the disparity between the terminology on the KDE desktop and that in this book.

WEB SHORTCUTS

Konqueror Web Shortcuts (different from regular shortcuts [page 258]) enable you to search for a keyword rapidly, using the default or a specified search engine. Search engines can include dictionaries, bug-tracking systems, classic search engines, and more. For example, to look up the word **colocation** in the Free Online Dictionary of Computing, enter the shortcut **foldoc:colocation** in the location bar. To search for discussions about Samba on Google Groups, enter **groups:samba**. Other abbreviations that you may find useful are **gg** for Google (standard search), **webster** (Merriam-Webster Dictionary), and **fm** for Freshmeat.

When you enter a keyword on the location bar without specifying a search engine, Konqueror looks it up using the default search engine. Use **Menubar: Settings⇨ Configure Konqueror**, scroll down the tabs on the right, and click **Web Shortcuts** from the column on the left to specify a default search engine and work with Web Shortcuts.

You can use Web Shortcuts by pressing Alt-F2

tip   You can also use Web Shortcuts from the Run Command dialog box, which you can open by pressing Alt-F2. See page 261 for details.

BOOKMARKS

As with any browser, Konqueror bookmarks give a user-friendly name to a URL or local pathname and allow you to return to the bookmarked location by selecting the name from a menu. Figure 8-16 shows the Konqueror Bookmarks menu, which is available on the menubar. The bookmarks list appears below the standard entries in the Bookmarks menu (Add, Bookmark Tabs as Folder, Edit, and New Bookmark Folder). When you click the bookmark of the location you want to visit, Konqueror displays that location.

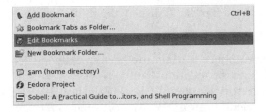

Figure 8-16   Konqueror Bookmarks menu

Figure 8-17   Konqueror menubar and toolbars

Choose **Konqueror menubar: Bookmarks⇨Add Bookmark** (or press CONTROL-B) to add the location displayed in the active view to the bookmarks list. You can also work with bookmarks from the Navigation panel (Figure 4-14, page 97). Click a bookmark entry on the Navigation panel or on the Bookmark toolbar (page 255) to display that entry.

To open, check the status of, or edit the name of or location associated with a bookmark, open the Bookmark Editor window (**Konqueror menubar: Bookmarks⇨Edit Bookmarks**) and right-click the entry you want to work with; choose the appropriate selection from the pop-up menu. You can also use the Bookmark Editor to change the order of the bookmarks: Use the mouse to drag the highlighted bookmark where you want it to appear in the list or use the up and down arrow keys to move the highlighted bookmark within the list. The right and left arrow keys open and close directories and folders containing bookmarks. Click **New Folder** to insert a new folder below the highlighted bookmark.

MENUBAR

The menus on the Konqueror menubar (Figure 8-17) change depending on what Konqueror is displaying. Clicking a selection on the menubar displays a drop-down menu.

TOOLBARS

Konqueror has five toolbars that you can turn on and off from **Konqueror menubar: Settings⇨Toolbars**: Main, Extra, Location, Bookmark, and Speech. These menu entries toggle the toolbars on and off. When a check mark appears to the left of a toolbar name, Konqueror displays that toolbar. Figure 8-17 shows three toolbars. Each toolbar has a handle that you can use to move the toolbar. The handle is the area with hatchmarks, usually at the left end of the toolbar; see Figure 4-17 on page 100 for a closeup picture of a handle. Right-click almost anywhere on a toolbar that has a handle to display the toolbar menu.

MAIN TOOLBAR

The Konqueror Main toolbar typically has left and right arrows that move linearly through the locations you have viewed with Konqueror. The up arrow moves up in a directory hierarchy. Clicking the house icon displays your home directory; clicking the reload button (the arrows going in a circle) reloads a Web page or file structure that may have changed. Clicking the stop button (the **X** that is red when there is an action you can stop) halts the search for or loading of a Web page, and clicking the print button (the printer) sends the image in the active view to the printer.

EXTRA TOOLBAR

Choose **Konqueror menubar: Settings⇨Toolbars⇨Extra Toolbar** to display the Extra toolbar. Use **Konqueror menubar: Settings⇨Configure Toolbars⇨Extra Toolbar** to change which icons appear on this toolbar.

LOCATION TOOLBAR

The Location toolbar has two items you can work with: the text box and the clear button. The clear button (the broom and dustpan at the left end of the toolbar) clears the text box. To display a location, you can enter a local or remote filename or URL, modify the contents of the text box, or click the down arrow at the right of this box and choose from the locations you have visited.

By default, the Search toolbar appears to the right of the Location toolbar. You can remove this toolbar from the Location toolbar by using **Konqueror menubar: Settings⇨Configure Toolbars⇨Location Toolbar.**

BOOKMARK TOOLBAR

The Bookmark toolbar gives you quick access to bookmarks (page 253). Display the Bookmark toolbar with **Konqueror menubar: Settings⇨Toolbars⇨Bookmark Toolbar.**

kfind: FINDS FILES

Start kfind by clicking **Main menu: Find Files/Folders** or by selecting **Konqueror menubar: Tools⇨Find file** (this selection is not active when Konqueror is working as a browser). Konqueror opens a new view that has three tabs: Name/Location, Contents, and Properties. The view opens to the Name/Location tab with a default filename to search for of *, which matches all filenames, *including* those that begin with a period, and your home directory as the place to start the search. If you used kfind previously in the current session, kfind specifies the previous name you searched for instead of the *. In the Named text box, enter the name of the file you want to search for (you can include wildcard characters); in the Look in text box, enter the directory you want to start the search in. Click the **Browse** button to help locate the directory you want to start the search in. Put a check mark in the box next to **Include subfolders** to search through subdirectories. Click **Find** to start the search. The part of the window with the fields you just filled in dims as kfind tabulates and displays the results of the search in the lower part of the window. You can do whatever you want with the found files: copy, move, delete, edit, and display them, among other things.

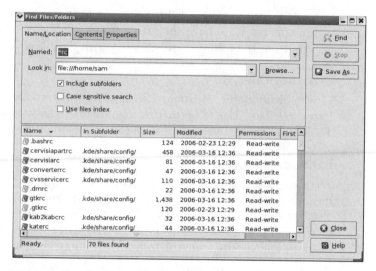

Figure 8-18   Find Files window

Figure 8-18 shows a search for all files whose names end with **rc** (*rc) in Sam's home directory and all subdirectories. The asterisk matches filenames that begin with a period.

In addition to or instead of filling in the Name/Location tab, you can click the **Contents** tab to specify a text string that the files you are looking for contain. Put a check mark in the box next to **Case sensitive** to perform a case-sensitive search for the text in the Containing text box. For a file to be found when you specify a text string, the file must match the Name/Location criteria *and* the Contents criteria.

You can also use the Properties tab to specify the type, creation or modification date, owner, or size of the file you are searching for.

You can save the results of the search to a file by clicking **Save As**, two buttons below the **Find** button on the right side of the window. You will be given a choice of filename, location, and type of file (text or HTML) you want to save.

MORE ABOUT VIEWS

Views, or subwindows, are key to taking advantage of Konqueror's power. This section expands on what was covered in "Views" on page 97 and explores some of the buttons, indicators, and menu choices that work with views.

Figure 8-19 shows two views side-by-side. Two indicators are important when you work with more than one view simultaneously: the Active View indicator and the Link indicator (Figure 4-13, page 96).

ACTIVE VIEW INDICATOR

The small circle at the lower-left corner of each view is green in the active view and gray in other views. The active view has the input focus and is the target of all

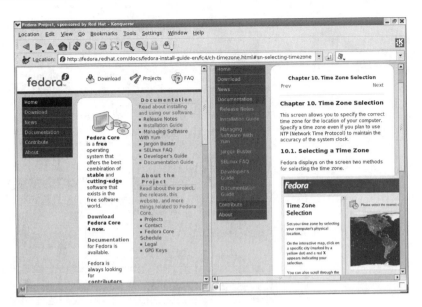

Figure 8-19   Konqueror displaying two views

Konqueror menu commands. The location bar displays the location of the file displayed in the active view. Click within a view to make it the active view.

Konqueror terminology: view versus window

tip   The Konqueror *window* consists of the entire window with four sides adjacent to the root window, the edge of the workspace, or other windows, usually with a menubar, location bar, and toolbar. The Konqueror window can house multiple *views*—that is, subwindows within the Konqueror window. The Navigation panel and terminal emulator are views with special properties. In Figure 8-19, the Konqueror window is displaying two views.

LINK INDICATOR

Click **Konqueror menubar: View⇨Link view** to link the two views that were most recently active. A link of chain appears in the small rectangle at the lower-right corner of each linked view. Two linked views always show the same location, with one useful exception that is covered in the next paragraph. Although linked views display the same information, each may present it differently. For example, one may display an Icon view and the other a List view.

LOCK TO CURRENT LOCATION

Choose **Konqueror menubar: View⇨Lock to Current Location** to place a check mark next to this selection and cause the contents of the active view to remain constant, regardless of which links (URLs) you click in that view. With a normal (not locked) view, when you click a link, the view is replaced by the contents of that link. With two linked views, neither of which is locked, when you click a link in one, both views change to reflect the contents of the link. When a locked view is linked

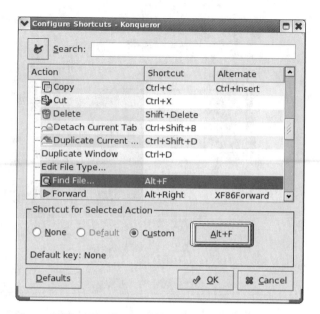

Figure 8-20   Configure Shortcuts window

to an unlocked view and you click a link in the locked view, the contents of the link appears in the unlocked view. Click the same selection to remove the check mark and unlock the active view.

To see how linked views with one view locked can be useful, open Konqueror, hide the Navigation panel if it is present (press F9), maximize the window, enter **fedora.redhat.com/docs** in the location bar, and press RETURN. Konqueror displays the Fedora User Documentation page. Next click **Window⇨Split View Left/Right** to display two identical views side-by-side. Link the views (**View⇨Link View**); a link of chain appears at the lower-right corner of each view. Make the left view active by clicking anywhere in the view that is not a link and then lock the view (**View⇨Lock to Current Location**). Now when you click a link in the left view, the linked-to page appears in the right view. You can view several links from the User Documentation page without constantly returning to this page as you would have to with a single view.

SHORTCUTS

A Konqueror *shortcut* (not a Web Shortcut [page 253]) is the connection between a key or keys (CONTROL-C, for example) that you hold or press at the same time and an action that the system performs when you do so. Open the Configure Shortcuts window (Figure 8-20) by selecting **Konqueror menubar: Settings⇨Configure Shortcuts**. In Figure 8-20 the action Copy, which appears at the top of the list of shortcuts, shows that CONTROL-C (**Ctrl+C**) is a shortcut for *copy* and that CONTROL-Insert is an alternate shortcut. The action Find File is highlighted; it has a shortcut of ALT-F. The bottom frame in the window shows that ALT-F is a Custom shortcut. With Copy highlighted, this frame would show that CONTROL-C is a Default shortcut.

Figure 8-21 Navigation panel, History tab

When you click and highlight an action, you can remove its shortcut by selecting **None** or you can revert to the default shortcut (if one exists) by selecting **Default**. To assign or change a custom binding, click the keycap button (the button labeled **Alt+F** in Figure 8-20) or the **Custom** radio button. A second Configure Shortcuts window opens. To specify a shortcut, clear any existing shortcut by clicking the broom and dustpan icon, press the key(s) you want to use for the shortcut, and click **OK**. The names of the keys that are now bound to the highlighted action appear on the keycap button.

The shortcuts you set in the Configure Shortcuts window apply to actions you take within Konqueror. You can set global and application shortcuts in a similar manner by selecting **Main menu: Control Center⇨Regional & Accessibility⇨Keyboard Shortcuts**). Within Konqueror, the bindings you establish in the Konqueror Configure Shortcuts window take precedence over bindings you set up in the Control Center.

NAVIGATION PANEL

To select the information displayed by the Konqueror Navigation panel, click one of the icons/tabs that appears in a stack at the left of the panel. On the active tab, text replaces the icon. Figure 8-21 shows the Navigation panel with the History tab active.

Toggle the Navigation panel on and off by using **Konqueror menubar: Window⇨ Show Navigation panel** or by pressing F9. Although the Navigation panel is a view, it has a different background than other views and cannot be active. When you click an entry in the Navigation panel, in the active view Konqueror opens the file or directory that that entry points to.

Click one of the icons/tabs in the Navigation panel to display a list of directories and files that corresponds to that icon. In this list, click the plus sign in the small box to expand a directory and click a minus sign in a small box to collapse a directory. Clicking an entry without a box causes Konqueror to display that entry in the active view. When you click a directory in this manner, Konqueror displays a File Manager view of the directory. When you click a URL of a Web site, Konqueror displays the Web site. (The **$KDEHOME/share/apps/konqsidebartng/entries** directory holds files that correspond to the icons in the Navigation panel. **$KDEHOME** defaults to **/usr.**)

Each of the initial icons/tabs in the Navigation panel gives you a different perspective on the system and what you have been doing with it. You can modify, delete, and add to some of these icons by right-clicking the icon. Right-click in the empty space blow the tabs to modify the Navigation panel.

KDE UTILITIES

Many utilities are available on the Main menu and on the KDE Web site. You can also take advantage of utilities, such as the GNOME utilities, that were not specifically designed with KDE in mind. This section lists a few of the most commonly used utilities.

konsole: TERMINAL EMULATOR

The KDE terminal emulator (konsole) displays a window that mimics a character-based terminal. Bring up a terminal emulator by selecting **Main menu: System⇒ Terminal** or by selecting **Konsole** from the Desktop menu.

You can display multiple terminal sessions within a single Konsole window. With the Konsole window open, make a selection from **Menubar: Session⇒New Shell** or click the yellow icon (at the left end of the toolbar, usually at the bottom of the window) to open another session. Click and hold this icon for a few moments to display the Session menu, which offers a choice of sessions to start. Switch between sessions by clicking the terminal icons, also on the toolbar, or by holding SHIFT and pressing the RIGHT or LEFT ARROW key.

kcolorchooser: SELECTS A COLOR

The Select Color window (kcolorchooser; see Figure 8-22) appears when you click a color bar, such as one of the two that appear in the Options frame when you select **Configure Desktop** from the Desktop menu and then click **Background** in the stack of vertical tabs at the left side of the Configure window. The square centered on top of the line above the **OK** and **Cancel** buttons always displays the selected color. When you click the **OK** button, this color returns to the color bar that you initially clicked.

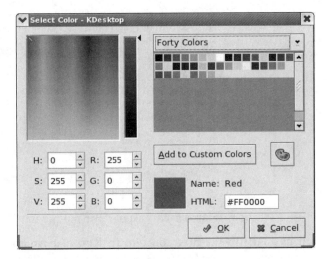

Figure 8-22 Select Color window

There are several ways to select a color:

- Click the color/shade you want on the multicolored box at the upper-left portion of the window.

- Click the palette to the right of the **Add to Custom Colors** button. The mouse pointer turns into crosshairs. Position the crosshairs over the color you want, anywhere on the workspace, and click. The color you click on becomes the selected color.

- Choose a line from the combo box at the upper-right corner of the window (Forty Colors in Figure 8-22). You have a choice of several groups of colors, including Recent Colors (an automatically generated list of colors you have selected) and Custom Colors (colors you have added to the list of custom colors by selecting and then clicking **Add to Custom Colors**). Click a color in the area below the combo box to select it.

- Enter the HTML specification of the color you want.

- Enter the appropriate numbers in the H, S, and V (hue, saturation, value) column of text boxes or in the R, G, and B (red, green, blue) column.

After you select a color, you can adjust its brightness by clicking the vertical bar to the right of the multicolor box or by dragging the pointer on the right side of this bar up or down. Click **OK** when you have selected the color you want.

RUN COMMAND

To run a character-based program, display the Run Command window by selecting **Run Command** from the Main menu or the Desktop menu, or by pressing ALT-F2. Enter the name of the program in the Command text box, click **Options,** put a

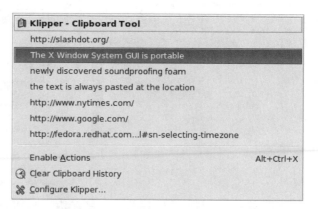

Figure 8-23   klipper pop-up menu

check mark in the box adjacent to **Run in terminal window**, and click **Run**. KDE then runs the program in a Konsole window. When you run who in this manner, for example, KDE displays the output of who in a new window and displays **<Finished>** on the titlebar of the window. Close the window when you are finished viewing the output; you can do no further work in it. If you run a program such as ssh from a Run Command window, the window remains active until you exit from ssh.

You can also use the Run Command window to start graphical programs (enter the name of the program), display Web pages (enter the URL), or enter Web Shortcuts (see page 253).

klipper: CLIPBOARD UTILITY

The klipper utility is a sophisticated multiple-buffer cut-and-paste utility. In addition to cutting and pasting from multiple buffers, klipper can execute a command based on the contents of a buffer. As distributed with Red Hat Linux, klipper is started by default when you log in. If you need to start klipper manually, choose **Main menu: Run Command**, enter **klipper**, and click **Run**. The klipper utility does not start a second occurrence of itself when it is already running. The klipper icon (a clipboard and pencil) appears at the right of the Main panel.

Each time you highlight text, klipper copies the text to one of its buffers. Click the klipper icon or press CONTROL-ALT-V to display the klipper pop-up menu (Figure 8-23). The top part of this menu lists the text that klipper is holding in its buffers. When the lines are too long to fit inside the window, klipper uses ellipses (...) to indicate missing material. To paste the text from a buffer to a document, display the klipper pop-up menu and click the line you want to paste; the pop-up menu closes. Move the mouse pointer to the location where you want to paste the text and middle-click. In a terminal emulator window, the text is always pasted at the location of the text cursor.

CHAPTER SUMMARY

The X Window System GUI is portable and flexible and makes it easy to write applications that work on many different types of systems without having to know low-level details about the individual systems. This GUI can operate in a networked environment, allowing a user to run a program on a remote system and send the results to a local display. The client/server concept is integral to the operation of the X Window System, in which the X server is responsible for fulfilling requests made of X Window System applications or clients. Hundreds of clients are available that can run under X, and programmers can also write their own clients, using tools such as the Qt and KDE libraries to write KDE programs and the GTK+ and GTK+2 GNOME libraries to write GNOME programs.

The window managers, and virtually all X applications, are designed to help users tailor their work environments in simple or complex ways. You can designate applications that start automatically, set such attributes as colors and fonts, and even alter the way keyboard strokes and mouse clicks are interpreted.

Built on top of the X Window System, GNOME is a desktop manager that you can use as is or customize to better suit your needs. It is a graphical user interface to system services (commands), the filesystem, applications, and more. Although not part of it, the Metacity window manager works closely with GNOME and is the default window manager for GNOME under Red Hat Linux. The window manager controls all aspects of the windows: placement, decoration, grouping, minimizing and maximizing, sizing, moving, and so on.

GNOME also provides many graphical utilities that you can use to customize and work with the desktop. It supports MIME types so that when you double-click an icon, it generally knows which tool to use to display the data represented by the icon. In sum, GNOME is a powerful desktop manager that can make your job easier and more fun.

The KDE desktop environment offers an extensive array of tools, including multiple help systems; a flexible file manager and browser; an office package that includes word processing, spreadsheet, presentation, charting, and email applications; numerous panels and menus that you can configure in many ways; and enough options to please the most critical user.

Konqueror, the KDE file manager and browser, has very little functionality of its own. Instead, it depends on other programs to do its work. Konqueror opens these programs within its own window, giving the impression that it is very capable—a good example of seamless program integration. When you ask Konqueror to open a file (which can be a local or remote text, music, picture, or HTML file), it figures out what kind of file it is (the file's MIME type) so it knows which program to use to open or display the file.

Panels and menus, which are closely related, enable you to select an object (which can be just about anything on the system) from a list. On a panel, you generally click an icon from a box of icons (the panel); on a menu, you typically click text in a list.

The KDE environment provides the casual user, the office worker, the power user, and the programmer/system designer a space to work in and a set of tools to work with. KDE also provides off-the-shelf productivity and almost limitless ways to customize its look, feel, and response.

EXERCISES

1. Regarding Konqueror the file manager:

   a. What is Konqueror?

   b. List four things that you can do with Konqueror.

   c. How do you use Konqueror to search for a file?

2. What is a terminal emulator? What does it allow you to do from a GUI that you would not be able to do without one?

3. What is klipper? How do you use it to cut and paste text?

4. a. What is Nautilus?

   b. List two ways that you can you open a file using Nautilus.

   c. How does Nautilus "know" which program to use to open different types of files?

   d. Which are the three common Nautilus control bars? What kinds of tools do you find on each?

   e. Discuss the use of the Nautilus location bar.

ADVANCED EXERCISES

5. Discuss Konqueror's lack of functionality and its ability to perform so many tasks. What is a KPart?

6. Regarding Konqueror the Web browser:

   a. How can you search the Web for a word or phrase without entering it in a search engine?

   b. How would you use Konqueror to transfer local files to a remote FTP site? Describe how you would do this using a Konqueror window with two views.

7. Describe three ways to

   a. Change the size of a window.

   b. Delete a window.

8. Explain the purpose of MIME. How does it facilitate the use of a GUI?

9. Write an xeyes command to display a window that is 600 pixels wide and 400 pixels tall, is located 200 pixels from the right edge of the screen and 300 pixels from the top of the screen, and contains orange eyes outlined in blue with red pupils. (*Hint:* Refer to the xeyes man page.)

9

THE BOURNE AGAIN SHELL

This chapter picks up where Chapter 7 left off. Chapter 28 expands on this chapter, exploring control flow commands and more advanced aspects of programming the Bourne Again Shell. The bash home page is www.gnu.org/software/bash. The bash info page is a complete Bourne Again Shell reference.

The Bourne Again Shell is a command interpreter and high-level programming language. As a command interpreter, it processes commands you enter on the command line in response to a prompt. When you use the shell as a programming language, it processes commands stored in files called *shell scripts*. Like other languages, shells have variables and control flow commands (for example, **for** loops and **if** statements).

When you use a shell as a command interpreter, you can customize the environment you work in. You can make your prompt display the name of the working directory, create a function or alias for cp that keeps it from overwriting certain kinds of files, take advantage of keyword variables to change aspects of how the shell works, and so on. You can also write shell scripts that do your bidding, from a one-line script that

265

stores a long, complex command to a longer script that runs a set of reports, prints them, and mails you a reminder when the job is done. More complex shell scripts are themselves programs; they do not just run other programs. Chapter 28 has some examples of these types of scripts.

Most system shell scripts are written to run under the Bourne Again Shell. If you will ever work in single-user mode—as when you boot your system or do system maintenance, administration, or repair work, for example—it is a good idea to become familiar with this shell.

This chapter expands on the interactive features of the shell described in Chapter 7, explains how to create and run simple shell scripts, discusses job control, introduces the basic aspects of shell programming, talks about history and aliases, and describes command line expansion. Chapter 28 presents some more challenging shell programming problems.

BACKGROUND

The Bourne Again Shell is based on the Bourne Shell (the early UNIX shell; this book refers to it as the *original Bourne Shell* to avoid confusion), which was written by Steve Bourne of AT&T's Bell Laboratories. Over the years the original Bourne Shell has been expanded but it remains the basic shell provided with many commercial versions of UNIX.

sh Shell   Because of its long and successful history, the original Bourne Shell has been used to write many of the shell scripts that help manage UNIX systems. Some of these scripts appear in Linux as Bourne Again Shell scripts. Although the Bourne Again Shell includes many extensions and features not found in the original Bourne Shell, bash maintains compatibility with the original Bourne Shell so you can run Bourne Shell scripts under bash. On UNIX systems the original Bourne Shell is named sh. On Linux systems sh is a symbolic link to bash ensuring that scripts that require the presence of the Bourne Shell still run. When called as sh, bash does its best to emulate the original Bourne Shell.

Korn Shell   System V UNIX introduced the Korn Shell (ksh), written by David Korn. This shell extended many features of the original Bourne Shell and added many new features. Some features of the Bourne Again Shell, such as command aliases and command line editing, are based on similar features from the Korn Shell.

POSIX standards   The POSIX (the Portable Operating System Interface) family of related standards is being developed by PASC (IEEE's Portable Application Standards Committee, www.pasc.org). A comprehensive FAQ on POSIX, including many links, appears at www.opengroup.org/austin/papers/posix_faq.html.

POSIX standard 1003.2 describes shell functionality. The Bourne Again Shell provides the features that match the requirements of this POSIX standard. Efforts are under way to make the Bourne Again Shell fully comply with the POSIX standard. In the meantime, if you invoke bash with the ––posix option, the behavior of the Bourne Again Shell will more closely match the POSIX requirements.

SHELL BASICS

This section covers writing and using startup files, redirecting standard error, writing and executing simple shell scripts, separating and grouping commands, implementing job control, and manipulating the directory stack.

STARTUP FILES

When a shell starts, it runs startup files to initialize itself. Which files the shell runs depends on whether it is a login shell, an interactive shell that is not a login shell (such as you get by giving the command **bash**), or a noninteractive shell (one used to execute a shell script). You must have read access to a startup file to execute the commands in it. Red Hat Linux puts appropriate commands in some of these files. This section covers bash startup files.

LOGIN SHELLS

The files covered in this section are executed by login shells and shells that you start with the **––login** option. Login shells are, by their nature, interactive.

/etc/profile   The shell first executes the commands in **/etc/profile**. Superuser can set up this file to establish systemwide default characteristics for bash users.

.bash_profile .bash_login .profile   Next the shell looks for **~/.bash_profile**, **~/.bash_login**, and **~/.profile** (**~/** is shorthand for your home directory), in that order, executing the commands in the first of these files it finds. You can put commands in one of these files to override the defaults set in **/etc/profile**.

.bash_logout   When you log out, bash executes commands in the **~/.bash_logout** file. Frequently commands that clean up after a session, such as those that remove temporary files, go in this file.

INTERACTIVE NONLOGIN SHELLS

The commands in the preceding startup files are not executed by interactive, nonlogin shells. However, these shells inherit from the login shell variables that are set by these startup files.

/etc/bashrc   Although not called by bash directly, many **~/.bashrc** files call **/etc/bashrc**. This setup allows Superuser to establish systemwide default characteristics for nonlogin bash shells.

.bashrc   An interactive nonlogin shell executes commands in the **~/.bashrc** file. Typically a startup file for a login shell, such as **.bash_profile**, runs this file, so that both login and nonlogin shells benefit from the commands in **.bashrc**.

NONINTERACTIVE SHELLS

The commands in the previously described startup files are not executed by noninteractive shells, such as those that runs shell scripts. However, these shells inherit from the login shell variables that are set by these startup files.

BASH_ENV   Noninteractive shells look for the environment variable **BASH_ENV** (or **ENV**, if the shell is called as sh) and execute commands in the file named by this variable.

SETTING UP STARTUP FILES

Although many startup files and types of shells exist, usually all you need are the **.bash_profile** and **.bashrc** files in your home directory. Commands similar to the following in **.bash_profile** run commands from **.bashrc** for login shells (when **.bashrc** exists). With this setup, the commands in **.bashrc** are executed by login and non-login shells.

```
if [ -f ~/.bashrc ]; then source ~/.bashrc; fi
```

The [**–f ~/.bashrc**] tests whether the file named **.bashrc** in your home directory exists. See pages 879 and 881 for more information on test and its synonym [ ].

Use .bash_profile to set PATH

tip   Because commands in **.bashrc** may be executed many times, and because subshells inherit exported variables, it is a good idea to put commands that add to existing variables in the **.bash_profile** file. For example, the following command adds the **bin** subdirectory of the **home** directory to **PATH** (page 292) and should go in **.bash_profile**:

```
PATH=$PATH:$HOME/bin
```

When you put this command in **.bash_profile** and not in **.bashrc**, the string is added to the **PATH** variable only once, when you log in.

Modifying a variable in **.bash_profile** allows changes you make in an interactive session to propagate to subshells. In contrast, modifying a variable in **.bashrc** overrides changes inherited from a parent shell.

Sample **.bash_profile** and **.bashrc** files follow. Some of the commands used in these files are not covered until later in this chapter. In any startup file, you must export variables and functions that you want to be available to child processes. For more information refer to "Locality of Variables" on page 916.

```
$ cat ~/.bash_profile
if [ -f ~/.bashrc ]; then
    source ~/.bashrc          # read local startup file if it exists
fi
PATH=$PATH:.                   # add the working directory to PATH
export PS1='[\h \W \!]\$ '     # set prompt
```

The first command in the preceding **.bash_profile** file executes the commands in the user's **.bashrc** file if it exists. The next command adds to the **PATH** variable (page 292). Typically **PATH** is set and exported in **/etc/profile** so it does not need to be exported in a user's startup file. The final command sets and exports **PS1** (page 293), which controls the user's prompt.

Next is a sample **.bashrc** file. The first command executes the commands in the **/etc/bashrc** file if it exists. Next the **LANG** (page 298) and **VIMINIT** (for vim initialization) variables are set and exported and several aliases (page 318) are established. The final command defines a function (page 321) that swaps the names of two files.

```
$ cat ~/.bashrc
if [ -f /etc/bashrc ]; then
    source /etc/bashrc          # read global startup file if it exists
fi

set -o noclobber                # prevent overwriting files
unset MAILCHECK                 # turn off "you have new mail" notice
export LANG=C                   # set LANG variable
export VIMINIT='set ai aw'      # set vim options
alias df='df -h'                # set up aliases
alias rm='rm -i'                # always do interactive rm's
alias lt='ls -ltrh | tail'
alias h='history | tail'
alias ch='chmod 755 '

function switch()               # a function to exchange the names
{                               # of two files
    local tmp=$$switch
    mv "$1" $tmp
    mv "$2" "$1"
    mv $tmp "$2"
}
```

. (Dot) or source: Runs a Startup File in the Current Shell

After you edit a startup file such as .bashrc, you do not have to log out and log in again to put the changes into effect. You can run the startup file using the . (dot) or source builtin (they are the same command). As with all other commands, the . must be followed by a SPACE on the command line. Using the . or source builtin is similar to running a shell script, except that these commands run the script as part of the current process. Consequently, when you use . or source to run a script, changes you make to variables from within the script affect the shell that you run the script from. You can use the . or source command to run any shell script—not just a startup file—but undesirable side effects (such as changes in the values of shell variables you rely on) may occur. If you ran a startup file as a regular shell script and did not use the . or source builtin, the variables created in the startup file would remain in effect only in the subshell running the script—not in the shell you ran the script from. For more information refer to "Locality of Variables" on page 916.

In the following example, .bashrc sets several variables and sets PS1, the prompt, to the name of the host. The . builtin puts the new values into effect.

```
$ cat ~/.bashrc
export TERM=vt100               # set the terminal type
export PS1="$(hostname -f): "   # set the prompt string
export CDPATH=:$HOME            # add HOME to CDPATH string
stty kill '^u'                  # set kill line to control-u

$ . ~/.bashrc
bravo.example.com:
```

COMMANDS THAT ARE SYMBOLS

The Bourne Again Shell uses the symbols (,), [,], and $ in a variety of ways. To minimize confusion, Table 9-1 lists the most common use of each of these symbols, even though some of them are not introduced until later.

Table 9-1   Builtin commands that are symbols

Symbol	Command
( )	Subshell (page 279)
$( )	Command substitution (page 334)
(( ))	Arithmetic evaluation; a synonym for let (use when the enclosed value contains an equal sign) (page 940)
$(( ))	Arithmetic expansion (not for use with an enclosed equal sign) (page 332)
[ ]	The test command (pages 879, 881, and 894)
[[ ]]	Conditional expression; similar to [ ] but adds string comparisons (page 941)

REDIRECTING STANDARD ERROR

Chapter 7 covered the concept of standard output and explained how to redirect standard output of a command. In addition to standard output, commands can send output to *standard error*. A command can send error messages to standard error to keep them from getting mixed up with the information it sends to standard output.

Just as it does with standard output, by default the shell sends a command's standard error to the screen. Unless you redirect one or the other, you may not know the difference between the output a command sends to standard output and the output it sends to standard error. This section covers the syntax used by the Bourne Again Shell.

File descriptors   A *file descriptor* is the place a program sends its output to and gets its input from. When you execute a program, the process running the program opens three file descriptors: 0 (standard input), 1 (standard output), and 2 (standard error). The redirect output symbol (> [page 210]) is shorthand for 1>, which tells the shell to redirect standard output. Similarly < (page 212) is short for 0<, which redirects standard input. The symbols 2> redirect standard error. For more information refer to "File Descriptors" on page 911.

The following examples demonstrate how to redirect standard output and standard error to different files and to the same file. When you run the cat utility with the name of a file that does not exist and the name of a file that does exist, cat sends an error message to standard error and copies the file that does exist to standard output. Unless you redirect them, both messages appear on the screen.

```
$ cat y
This is y.
$ cat x
cat: x: No such file or directory
```

```
$ cat x y
cat: x: No such file or directory
This is y.
```

When you redirect standard output of a command, output sent to standard error is not affected and still appears on the screen.

```
$ cat x y > hold
cat: x: No such file or directory
$ cat hold
This is y.
```

Similarly, when you send standard output through a pipe, standard error is not affected. The following example sends standard output of cat through a pipe to tr, which in this example converts lowercase characters to uppercase. (See the tr info page for more information.) The text that cat sends to standard error is not translated because it goes directly to the screen rather than through the pipe.

```
$ cat x y | tr "[a-z]" "[A-Z]"
cat: x: No such file or directory
THIS IS Y.
```

The following example redirects standard output and standard error to different files. The notation **2>** tells the shell where to redirect standard error (file descriptor 2). The **1>** tells the shell where to redirect standard output (file descriptor 1). You can use **>** in place of **1>**.

```
$ cat x y 1> hold1 2> hold2
$ cat hold1
This is y.
$ cat hold2
cat: x: No such file or directory
```

Duplicating a file descriptor In the next example, **1>** redirects standard output to **hold**. Then **2>&1** declares file descriptor 2 to be a duplicate of file descriptor 1. As a result both standard output and standard error are redirected to **hold**.

```
$ cat x y 1> hold 2>&1
$ cat hold
cat: x: No such file or directory
This is y.
```

In the preceding example, **1> hold** precedes **2>&1**. If they had been listed in the opposite order, standard error would have been made a duplicate of standard output before standard output was redirected to **hold**. In that case only standard output would have been redirected to **hold**.

The next example declares file descriptor 2 to be a duplicate of file descriptor 1 and sends the output for file descriptor 1 through a pipe to the tr command.

```
$ cat x y 2>&1 | tr "[a-z]" "[A-Z]"
CAT: X: NO SUCH FILE OR DIRECTORY
THIS IS Y.
```

You can also use **1>&2** to redirect standard output of a command to standard error. This technique is used in shell scripts to send the output of echo to standard error. In the following script, standard output of the first echo is redirected to standard error:

```
$ cat message_demo
echo This is an error message. 1>&2
echo This is not an error message.
```

If you redirect standard output of **message_demo**, error messages such as the one produced by the first echo will still go to the screen because you have not redirected standard error. Because standard output of a shell script is frequently redirected to another file, you can use this technique to display on the screen error messages generated by the script. The **lnks** script (page 886) uses this technique. You can also use the exec builtin to create additional file descriptors and to redirect standard input, standard output, and standard error of a shell script from within the script (page 930).

The Bourne Again Shell supports the redirection operators shown in Table 9-2.

Table 9-2   Redirection operators

Operator	Meaning
< *filename*	Redirects standard input from *filename*.
> *filename*	Redirects standard output to *filename* unless *filename* exists and **noclobber** (page 213) is set. If **noclobber** is not set, this redirection creates *filename* if it does not exist.
>| *filename*	Redirects standard output to *filename*, even if the file exists and **noclobber** (page 213) is set.
>> *filename*	Redirects and appends standard output to *filename* unless *filename* exists and **noclobber** (page 213) is set. If **noclobber** is not set, this redirection creates *filename* if it does not exist.
<&*m*	Duplicates standard input from file descriptor *m* (page 912).
[*n*]>&*m*	Duplicates standard output or file descriptor *n* if specified from file descriptor *m* (page 912).
[*n*]<&–	Closes standard input or file descriptor *n* if specified (page 912).
[*n*]>&–	Closes standard output or file descriptor *n* if specified.

WRITING A SIMPLE SHELL SCRIPT

A *shell script* is a file that contains commands that the shell can execute. The commands in a shell script can be any commands you can enter in response to a shell prompt. For example, a command in a shell script might run a Linux utility, a compiled program, or another shell script. Like the commands you give on the command line, a command in a shell script can use ambiguous file references and can have its input or output redirected from or to a file or sent through a pipe (page 216). You can also use pipes and redirection with the input and output of the script itself.

In addition to the commands you would ordinarily use on the command line, *control flow* commands (also called *control structures*) find most of their use in shell scripts. This group of commands enables you to alter the order of execution of commands in a script just as you would alter the order of execution of statements using a structured programming language. Refer to "Control Structures" on page 878 for specifics.

The shell interprets and executes the commands in a shell script, one after another. Thus a shell script enables you to simply and quickly initiate a complex series of tasks or a repetitive procedure.

chmod: MAKES A FILE EXECUTABLE

To execute a shell script by giving its name as a command, you must have permission to read and execute the file that contains the script (refer to "Access Permissions" on page 180). Read permission enables you to read the file that holds the script. Execute permission tells the shell and the system that the owner, group, and/or public has permission to execute the file; it implies that the content of the file is executable.

When you create a shell script using an editor, the file does not typically have its execute permission set. The following example shows a file named **whoson** that contains a shell script:

```
$ cat whoson
date
echo "Users Currently Logged In"
who

$ whoson
bash: ./whoson: Permission denied
```

You cannot execute **whoson** by giving its name as a command because you do not have execute permission for the file. The shell does not recognize **whoson** as an executable file and issues an error message when you try to execute it. When you give the filename as an argument to bash (**bash whoson**), bash takes the argument to be a shell script and executes it. In this case **bash** is executable and **whoson** is an argument that bash executes so you do not need to have permission to execute **whoson**.

Command not found?

tip If you get the message

```
$ whoson
bash: whoson: command not found
```

the shell is not set up to search for executable files in the working directory. Give this command instead:

```
$ ./whoson
```

The ./ tells the shell explicitly to look for an executable file in the working directory. To change the environment so that the shell searches the working directory automatically, see page 292.

```
$ ls -l whoson
-rw-rw-r--   1 alex group 40 May 24 11:30 whoson

$ chmod u+x whoson
$ ls -l whoson
-rwxrw-r--   1 alex group 40 May 24 11:30 whoson

$ whoson
Tue May 24 11:40:49 PDT 2005
Users Currently Logged In
jenny    pts/7    May 23 18:17
hls      pts/1    May 24 09:59
scott    pts/12   May 24 06:29 (bravo.example.com)
alex     pts/4    May 24 09:08
```

Figure 9-1   Using chmod to make a shell script executable

The chmod utility changes the access privileges associated with a file. Figure 9-1 shows ls with the –l option displaying the access privileges of **whoson** before and after chmod gives execute permission to the file's owner.

The first ls displays a hyphen (–) as the fourth character, indicating that the owner does not have permission to execute the file. Next chmod gives the owner execute permission: The **u+x** causes chmod to add (**+**) execute permission (**x**) for the owner (**u**). (The **u** stands for *user,* although it means the owner of the file who may be the user of the file at any given time.) The second argument is the name of the file. The second ls shows an **x** in the fourth position, indicating that the owner now has execute permission.

If other users will execute the file, you must also change group and/or public access permissions for the file. Any user must have execute access to use the file's name as a command. If the file is a shell script, the user trying to execute the file must also have read access to the file. You do not need read access to execute a binary executable (compiled program).

The final command in Figure 9-1 shows the shell executing the file when its name is given as a command. For more information refer to "Access Permissions" on page 180, ls (page 181), and chmod (page 182).

#! SPECIFIES A SHELL

You can put a special sequence of characters on the first line of a file to tell the operating system which shell should execute the file. Because the operating system checks the initial characters of a program before attempting to **exec** it, these characters save the system from making an unsuccessful attempt. If **#!** are the first two characters of a script, the system interprets the characters that follow as the absolute pathname of the utility that should execute the script. This can be the pathname of any program, not just a shell. The following example specifies that bash should run the script:

```
$ cat bash_script
#!/bin/bash
echo "This is a Bourne Again Shell script."
```

The **#!** characters are useful if you have a script that you want to run with a shell other than the shell you are running the script from. The following example shows a script that should be executed by tcsh:

```
$ cat tcsh_script
#!/bin/tcsh
echo "This is a tcsh script."
set person = jenny
echo "person is $person"
```

Because of the **#!** line, the operating system ensures that tcsh executes the script no matter which shell you run it from.

You can use **ps –f** within a shell script to display the name of the shell that is executing the script. The three lines that ps displays in the following example show the process running the parent bash shell, the process running the tcsh script, and the process running the ps command:

```
$ cat tcsh_script2
#!/bin/tcsh
ps -f

$ tcsh_script2
UID         PID  PPID  C STIME TTY          TIME CMD
alex       3031  3030  0 Nov16 pts/4    00:00:00 -bash
alex       9358  3031  0 21:13 pts/4    00:00:00 /bin/tcsh ./tcsh_script2
alex       9375  9358  0 21:13 pts/4    00:00:00 ps -f
```

If you do not follow **#!** with the name of an executable program, the shell reports that it cannot find the command that you asked it to run. You can optionally follow **#!** with SPACEs. If you omit the **#!** line and try to run, for example, a tcsh script from bash, the shell may generate error messages or the script may not run properly.

BEGINS A COMMENT

Comments make shell scripts and all code easier to read and maintain by you and others. If a pound sign (#) in the first character position of the first line of a script is not immediately followed by an exclamation point (!) or if a pound sign occurs in any other location in a script, the shell interprets it as the beginning of a comment. The shell then ignores everything between the pound sign and the end of the line (the next NEWLINE character).

RUNNING A SHELL SCRIPT

fork and **exec**
system calls
A command on the command line causes the shell to **fork** a new process, creating a duplicate of the shell process (a subshell). The new process attempts to **exec** (execute) the command. Like **fork**, the **exec** routine is executed by the operating system (a system call). If the command is a binary executable program, such as a compiled

C program, **exec** succeeds and the system overlays the newly created subshell with the executable program. If the command is a shell script, **exec** fails. When **exec** fails, the command is assumed to be a shell script, and the subshell runs the commands in the script. Unlike a login shell, which expects input from the command line, the subshell takes its input from a file: the shell script.

As discussed earlier, if you have a shell script in a file that you do not have execute permission for, you can run the commands in the script by using a bash command to **exec** a shell to run the script directly. In the following example, bash creates a new shell that takes its input from the file named **whoson**:

```
$ bash whoson
```

Because the bash command expects to read a file containing commands, you do not need execute permission for **whoson**. (You do need read permission.) Even though bash reads and executes the commands in **whoson**, standard input, standard output, and standard error remain connected to the terminal.

Although you can use bash to execute a shell script, this technique causes the script to run more slowly than giving yourself execute permission and directly invoking the script. Users typically prefer to make the file executable and run the script by typing its name on the command line. It is also easier to type the name, and this practice is consistent with the way other kinds of programs are invoked (so you do not need to know whether you are running a shell script or another kind of program). However, if bash is not your interactive shell or if you want to see how the script runs with different shells, you may want to run a script as an argument to **bash** or **tcsh**.

sh **does not call the original Bourne Shell**

caution   The original Bourne Shell was invoked with the command **sh**. Although you can call bash with an **sh** command, it is not the original Bourne Shell. The **sh** command (**/bin/sh**) is a symbolic link to **/bin/bash**, so it is simply another name for the **bash** command. When you call bash using the command **sh**, bash tries to mimic the behavior of the original Bourne Shell as closely as possible. It does not always succeed.

SEPARATING AND GROUPING COMMANDS

Whether you give the shell commands interactively or write a shell script, you must separate commands from one another. This section reviews the ways to separate commands that were covered in Chapter 7 and introduces a few new ones.

; AND NEWLINE SEPARATE COMMANDS

The NEWLINE character is a unique command separator because it initiates execution of the command preceding it. You have seen this throughout this book each time you press the RETURN key at the end of a command line.

The semicolon (;) is a command separator that *does not* initiate execution of a command and *does not* change any aspect of how the command functions. You can execute a series of commands sequentially by entering them on a single command line and separating each from the next with a semicolon (;). You initiate execution of the sequence of commands by pressing RETURN:

```
$ x ; y ; z
```

If **x**, **y**, and **z** are commands, the preceding command line yields the same results as the next three commands. The difference is that in the next example the shell issues a prompt after each of the commands (**x**, **y**, and **z**) finishes executing, whereas the preceding command line causes the shell to issue a prompt only after **z** is complete:

```
$ x
$ y
$ z
```

Whitespace   Although the whitespace around the semicolons in the earlier example makes the command line easier to read, it is not necessary. None of the command separators needs to be surrounded by SPACEs or TABs.

\ CONTINUES A COMMAND

When you enter a long command line and the cursor reaches the right side of the screen, you can use a backslash (\) character to continue the command on the next line. The backslash quotes, or escapes, the NEWLINE character that follows it so that the shell does not treat the NEWLINE as a command terminator. Enclosing a backslash within single quotation marks turns off the power of a backslash to quote special characters such as NEWLINE. Enclosing a backslash within double quotation marks has no effect on the power of the backslash.

Although you can break a line in the middle of a word (token), it is typically easier to break a line just before or after whitespace.

optional   You can enter a RETURN in the middle of a quoted string on a command line without using a backslash. The NEWLINE (RETURN) that you enter will then be part of the string:

```
$ echo "Please enter the three values
> required to complete the transaction."
Please enter the three values
required to complete the transaction.
```

In the three examples in this section, the shell does not interpret RETURN as a command terminator because it occurs within a quoted string. The **>** is a secondary prompt indicating that the shell is waiting for you to continue the unfinished command. In the next example, the first RETURN is quoted (escaped) so the shell treats it as a separator and does not interpret it literally.

```
$ echo "Please enter the three values \
> required to complete the transaction."
Please enter the three values required to complete the transaction.
```

Single quotation marks cause the shell to interpret a backslash literally:

```
$ echo 'Please enter the three values \
> required to complete the transaction.'
Please enter the three values \
required to complete the transaction.
```

| AND & SEPARATE COMMANDS AND DO SOMETHING ELSE

The pipe symbol (|) and the background task symbol (&) are also command separators. They *do not* start execution of a command but *do* change some aspect of how the command functions. The pipe symbol alters the source of standard input or the destination of standard output. The background task symbol causes the shell to execute the task in the background so you get a prompt immediately and can continue working on other tasks.

Each of the following command lines initiates a single job comprising three tasks:

```
$ x | y | z
$ ls -l | grep tmp | less
```

In the first job, the shell redirects standard output of task **x** to standard input of task **y** and redirects **y**'s standard output to **z**'s standard input. Because it runs the entire job in the foreground, the shell does not display a prompt until task **z** runs to completion: Task **z** does not finish until task **y** finishes, and task **y** does not finish until task **x** finishes. In the second job, task **x** is an **ls –l** command, task **y** is **grep tmp**, and task **z** is the pager **less**. The shell displays a long (wide) listing of the files in the working directory that contain the string **tmp**, piped through less.

The next command line executes tasks **d** and **e** in the background and task **f** in the foreground:

```
$ d & e & f
[1] 14271
[2] 14272
```

The shell displays the job number between brackets and the PID (process identification) number for each process running in the background. You get a prompt as soon as **f** finishes, which may be before **d** or **e** finishes.

Before displaying a prompt for a new command, the shell checks whether any background jobs have completed. For each job that has completed, the shell displays its job number, the word **Done**, and the command line that invoked the job; then the shell displays a prompt. When the job numbers are listed, the number of the last job started is followed by a + character and the job number of the previous job is followed by a – character. Any other jobs listed show a SPACE character. After running the last command, the shell displays the following before issuing a prompt:

```
[1]-  Done                 d
[2]+  Done                 e
```

The next command line executes all three tasks as background jobs. You get a shell prompt immediately:

```
$ d & e & f &
[1] 14290
[2] 14291
[3] 14292
```

You can use pipes to send the output from one task to the next task and an ampersand (&) to run the entire job as a background task. Again the prompt comes back immediately. The shell regards the commands joined by a pipe as being a single job. That is, it treats all pipes as single jobs, no matter how many tasks are connected with the pipe (l) symbol or how complex they are. The Bourne Again Shell shows only one process placed in the background:

```
$ d | e | f &
[1] 14295
```

optional ## () GROUPS COMMANDS

You can use parentheses to group commands. The shell creates a copy of itself, called a *subshell,* for each group. It treats each group of commands as a job and creates a new process to execute each command (refer to "Process Structure" on page 300 for more information on creating subshells). Each subshell (job) has its own environment, meaning that it has its own set of variables with values that can differ from those of other subshells.

The following command line executes commands **a** and **b** sequentially in the background while executing **c** in the background. The shell prompt returns immediately.

```
$ (a ; b) & c &
[1] 15520
[2] 15521
```

The preceding example differs from the earlier example **d** & **e** & **f** & in that tasks **a** and **b** are initiated sequentially, not concurrently.

Similarly the following command line executes **a** and **b** sequentially in the background and, at the same time, executes **c** and **d** sequentially in the background. The subshell running **a** and **b** and the subshell running **c** and **d** run concurrently. The prompt returns immediately.

```
$ (a ; b) & (c ; d) &
[1] 15528
[2] 15529
```

The next script copies one directory to another. The second pair of parentheses creates a subshell to run the commands following the pipe. Because of these parentheses, the output of the first tar command is available for the second tar command despite the intervening cd command. Without the parentheses, the output of the first tar command would be sent to cd and lost because cd does not process input from standard input. The shell variables $1 and $2 represent the first and second command line arguments (page 921), respectively. The first pair of parentheses, which creates a subshell to run the first two commands, allows users to call **cpdir** with relative pathnames. Without them the first cd command would change the working directory of the script (and consequently the working directory of the second cd command). With them only the working directory of the subshell is changed.

```
$ cat cpdir
(cd $1 ; tar -cf - . ) | (cd $2 ; tar -xvf - )
$ cpdir /home/alex/sources /home/alex/memo/biblio
```

The **cpdir** command line copies the files and directories in the **/home/alex/sources** directory to the directory named **/home/alex/memo/biblio**. This shell script is almost the same as using cp with the –r option. Refer to the cp and tar man pages for more information.

JOB CONTROL

A job is a command pipeline. You run a simple job whenever you give the shell a command. For example, type **date** on the command line and press RETURN: You have run a job. You can also create several jobs with multiple commands on a single command line:

```
$ find . -print | sort | lpr & grep -l alex /tmp/* > alexfiles &
[1] 18839
[2] 18876
```

The portion of the command line up to the first & is one job consisting of three processes connected by pipes: find, sort (page 133), and lpr (page 131). The second job is a single process running grep. Both jobs have been put into the background by the trailing & characters, so bash does not wait for them to complete before displaying a prompt.

Using job control you can move commands from the foreground to the background (and vice versa), stop commands temporarily, and list all the commands that are running in the background or stopped.

jobs: LISTS JOBS

The jobs builtin lists all background jobs. The following sequence demonstrates what happens when you give a **jobs** command. Here the sleep command runs in the background and creates a background job that jobs reports on:

```
$ sleep 60 &
[1] 7809
$ jobs
[1] + Running                    sleep 60 &
```

fg: BRINGS A JOB TO THE FOREGROUND

The shell assigns job numbers to commands you run in the background (page 278). Several jobs are started in the background in the next example. For each job the shell lists the job number and PID number immediately, just before it issues a prompt.

```
$ xclock &
[1] 1246
$ date &
[2] 1247
$ Sun Dec 4 11:44:40 PST 2005
[2]+ Done            date
$ find /usr -name ace -print > findout &
[2] 1269
$ jobs
[1]- Running        xclock &
[2]+ Running        find /usr -name ace -print > findout &
```

Job numbers, which are discarded when a job is finished, can be reused. When you start or put a job in the background, the shell assigns a job number that is one more than the highest job number in use.

In the preceding example, the jobs command lists the first job, xclock, as job 1. The date command does not appear in the jobs list because it finished before jobs was run. Because the date command was completed before find was run, the find command became job 2.

To move a background job into the foreground, use the fg builtin followed by the job number. Alternatively, you can give a percent sign (%) followed by the job number as a command. Either of the following commands moves job 2 into the foreground:

```
$ fg 2
```

or

```
$ %2
```

You can also refer to a job by following the percent sign with a string that uniquely identifies the beginning of the command line used to start the job. Instead of the preceding command, you could have used either **fg %find** or **fg %f** because both uniquely identify job 2. If you follow the percent sign with a question mark and a string, the string can match any part of the command line. In the preceding example, **fg %?ace** also brings job 2 into the foreground.

Often the job you wish to bring into the foreground is the only job running in the background or is the job that jobs lists with a plus (+). In these cases you can use fg without an argument.

bg: SENDS A JOB TO THE BACKGROUND

To move the foreground job to the background, you must first suspend (temporarily stop) the job by pressing the suspend key (usually CONTROL-Z). Pressing the suspend key immediately suspends the job in the foreground. You can then use the bg builtin to resume execution of the job in the background.

```
$ bg
```

If a background job attempts to read from the terminal, the shell stops it and notifies you that the job has been stopped and is waiting for input. You must then move the job into the foreground so that it can read from the terminal. The shell displays the command line when it moves the job into the foreground.

```
$ (sleep 5; cat > mytext) &
[1] 1343
$ date
Sun Dec  4 11:58:20 PST 2005
[1]+ Stopped                    ( sleep 5; cat >mytext )
$ fg
( sleep 5; cat >mytext )
Remember to let the cat out!
CONTROL-D
$
```

In the preceding example, the shell displays the job number and PID number of the background job as soon as it starts, followed by a prompt. Demonstrating that you can give a command at this point, the user gives the command date and its output appears on the screen. The shell waits until just before it issues a prompt (after date has finished) to notify you that job 1 is stopped. When you give an **fg** command, the shell puts the job in the foreground and you can enter the input that the command is waiting for. In this case the input needs to be terminated with a CONTROL-D to signify EOF (end of file). The shell then displays another prompt.

The shell keeps you informed about changes in the status of a job, notifying you when a background job starts, completes, or is stopped, perhaps waiting for input from the terminal. The shell also lets you know when a foreground job is suspended. Because notices about a job being run in the background can disrupt your work, the shell delays displaying these notices until just before it displays a prompt. You can set **notify** (page 327) to make the shell display these notices without delay.

If you try to exit from a shell while jobs are stopped, the shell issues a warning and does not allow you to exit. If you then use jobs to review the list of jobs or you immediately try to leave the shell again, the shell allows you to leave and terminates the stopped jobs. Jobs that are running (not stopped) in the background continue to run. In the following example, find (job 1) continues to run after the second **exit** terminates the shell, but cat (job 2) is terminated:

```
$ find / -size +100k > $HOME/bigfiles 2>&1 &
[1] 1426
$ cat > mytest &
[2] 1428
[2]+  Stopped                 cat >mytest
$ exit
exit
There are stopped jobs.
$ exit
exit

login:
```

MANIPULATING THE DIRECTORY STACK

The Bourne Again Shell allows you to store a list of directories you are working with, enabling you to move easily among them. This list is referred to as a *stack*. It is analogous to a stack of dinner plates: You typically add plates to and remove plates from the top of the stack, creating a last-in first-out, (*LIFO*) stack.

dirs: DISPLAYS THE STACK

The dirs builtin displays the contents of the directory stack. If you call dirs when the directory stack is empty, it displays the name of the working directory:

```
$ dirs
~/literature
```

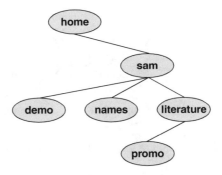

Figure 9-2   The directory structure in the examples

The dirs builtin uses a tilde (~) to represent the name of the home directory. The examples in the next several sections assume that you are referring to the directory structure shown in Figure 9-2.

pushd: PUSHES A DIRECTORY ON THE STACK

To change directories and at the same time add a new directory to the top of the stack, use the pushd (push directory) builtin. In addition to changing directories, the pushd builtin displays the contents of the stack. The following example is illustrated in Figure 9-3:

```
$ pushd ../demo
~/demo ~/literature
$ pwd
/home/sam/demo

$ pushd ../names
~/names ~/demo ~/literature
$ pwd
/home/sam/names
```

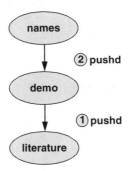

Figure 9-3   Creating a directory stack

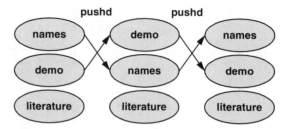

Figure 9-4   Using pushd to change working directories

When you use pushd without an argument, it swaps the top two directories on the stack and makes the new top directory (which was the second directory) become the new working directory (Figure 9-4):

```
$ pushd
~/demo ~/names ~/literature
$ pwd
/home/sam/demo
```

Using pushd in this way, you can easily move back and forth between two directories. You can also use **cd –** to change to the previous directory, whether or not you have explicitly created a directory stack. To access another directory in the stack, call pushd with a numeric argument preceded by a plus sign. The directories in the stack are numbered starting with the top directory, which is number 0. The following pushd command continues with the previous example, changing the working directory to **literature** and moving **literature** to the top of the stack:

```
$ pushd +2
~/literature ~/demo ~/names
$ pwd
/home/sam/literature
```

popd: POPS A DIRECTORY OFF THE STACK

To remove a directory from the stack, use the popd (pop directory) builtin. As the following example and Figure 9-5 show, popd used without an argument removes the top directory from the stack and changes the working directory to the new top directory:

```
$ dirs
~/literature ~/demo ~/names
$ popd
~/demo ~/names
$ pwd
/home/sam/demo
```

To remove a directory other than the top one from the stack, use popd with a numeric argument preceded by a plus sign. The following example removes directory number 1, **demo**:

```
$ dirs
~/literature ~/demo ~/names
$ popd +1
~/literature ~/names
```

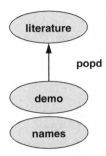

Figure 9-5 Using popd to remove a directory from the stack

Removing a directory other than directory number 0 does not change the working directory.

PARAMETERS AND VARIABLES

Variables   Within a shell, a *shell parameter* is associated with a value that is accessible to the user. There are several kinds of shell parameters. Parameters whose names consist of letters, digits, and underscores are often referred to as *shell variables,* or simply *variables.* A variable name must start with a letter or underscore, not with a number. Thus **A76**, **MY_CAT**, and **___X___** are valid variable names, whereas **69TH_STREET** (starts with a digit) and **MY-NAME** (contains a hyphen) are not.

User-created variables   Shell variables that you name and assign values to are *user-created variables.* You can change the values of user-created variables at any time, or you can make them *readonly* so that their values cannot be changed. You can also make user-created variables *global.* A global variable (also called an *environment variable*) is available to all shells and other programs you fork from the original shell. One naming convention is to use only uppercase letters for global variables and to use mixed-case or lowercase letters for other variables. Refer to "Locality of Variables" on page 916 for more information on global variables.

To assign a value to a variable in the Bourne Again Shell, use the following syntax:

    VARIABLE=value

There can be no whitespace on either side of the equal sign (**=**). An example assignment follows:

    `$ myvar=abc`

The Bourne Again Shell permits you to put variable assignments on a command line. These assignments are local to the command shell—that is, they apply to the command only. The **my_script** shell script displays the value of **TEMPDIR**. The following command runs **my_script** with **TEMPDIR** set to **/home/sam/temp**. The echo builtin shows that the interactive shell has no value for **TEMPDIR** after running **my_script**. If **TEMPDIR** had been set in the interactive shell, running **my_script** in this manner would have had no effect on its value.

```
$ cat my_script
echo $TEMPDIR
$ TEMPDIR=/home/sam/temp my_script
/home/sam/temp
$ echo $TEMPDIR

$
```

Keyword variables   *Keyword shell variables* (or simply *keyword variables*) have special meaning to the shell and usually have short, mnemonic names. When you start a shell (by logging in, for example), the shell inherits several keyword variables from the environment. Among these variables are **HOME**, which identifies your home directory, and **PATH**, which determines which directories the shell searches and in what order to locate commands that you give the shell. The shell creates and initializes (with default values) other keyword variables when you start it. Still other variables do not exist until you set them.

You can change the values of most of the keyword shell variables at any time but it is usually not necessary to change the values of keyword variables initialized in the **/etc/profile** or **/etc/csh.cshrc** systemwide startup files. If you need to change the value of a bash keyword variable, do so in one of your startup files (page 267). Just as you can make user-created variables global, so you can make keyword variables global; this is usually done automatically in the startup files. You can also make a keyword variable readonly.

Positional and special parameters   The names of positional and special parameters do not resemble variable names. Most of these parameters have one-character names (for example, **1**, **?**, and **#**) and are referenced (as are all variables) by preceding the name with a dollar sign (**$1**, **$?**, and **$#**). The values of these parameters reflect different aspects of your ongoing interaction with the shell.

Whenever you give a command, each argument on the command line becomes the value of a *positional parameter*. Positional parameters (page 920) enable you to access command line arguments, a capability that you will often require when you write shell scripts. The set builtin (page 924) enables you to assign values to positional parameters.

Other frequently needed shell script values, such as the name of the last command executed, the number of command line arguments, and the status of the most recently executed command, are available as *special parameters*. You cannot assign values to special parameters.

USER-CREATED VARIABLES

The first line in the following example declares the variable named **person** and initializes it with the value **alex**:

```
$ person=alex
$ echo person
person
$ echo $person
alex
```

Because the echo builtin copies its arguments to standard output, you can use it to display the values of variables. The second line of the preceding example shows that **person** does not represent **alex**. Instead, the string **person** is echoed as **person**. The shell substitutes the value of a variable only when you precede the name of the variable with a dollar sign ($). The command **echo $person** displays the value of the variable **person**; it does not display **$person** because the shell does not pass **$person** to echo as an argument. Because of the leading $, the shell recognizes that **$person** is the name of a variable, *substitutes* the value of the variable, and passes that value to echo. The echo builtin displays the value of the variable—not its name—never knowing that you called it with a variable.

Quoting the $ You can prevent the shell from substituting the value of a variable by quoting the leading $. Double quotation marks do not prevent the substitution; single quotation marks or a backslash (\) do.

```
$ echo $person
alex
$ echo "$person"
alex
$ echo '$person'
$person
$ echo \$person
$person
```

SPACES   Because they do not prevent variable substitution but do turn off the special meanings of most other characters, double quotation marks are useful when you assign values to variables and when you use those values. To assign a value that contains SPACEs or TABs to a variable, use double quotation marks around the value. Although double quotation marks are not required in all cases, using them is a good habit.

```
$ person="alex and jenny"
$ echo $person
alex and jenny

$ person=alex and jenny
bash: and: command not found
```

When you reference a variable that contains TABs or multiple adjacent SPACEs, you need to use quotation marks to preserve the spacing. If you do not quote the variable, the shell collapses each string of blank characters into a single SPACE before passing the variable to the utility:

```
$ person="alex    and    jenny"
$ echo $person
alex and jenny
$ echo "$person"
alex    and    jenny
```

When you execute a command with a variable as an argument, the shell replaces the name of the variable with the value of the variable and passes that value to the program being executed. If the value of the variable contains a special character, such as * or ?, the shell *may* expand that variable.

Pathname
expansion in
assignments

The first line in the following sequence of commands assigns the string **alex✳** to the variable **memo**. The Bourne Again Shell does *not expand the string* because bash does not perform pathname expansion (page 221) when assigning a value to a variable. All shells process a command line in a specific order. Within this order bash expands variables before it interprets commands. In the following echo command line, the double quotation marks quote the asterisk (✳) in the expanded value of **$memo** and prevent bash from performing pathname expansion on the expanded memo variable before passing its value to the echo command:

```
$ memo=alex✳
$ echo "$memo"
alex✳
```

All shells interpret special characters as special when you reference a variable that contains an unquoted special character. In the following example, the shell expands the value of the **memo** variable because it is not quoted:

```
$ ls
alex.report
alex.summary
$ echo $memo
alex.report alex.summary
```

Here the shell expands the **$memo** variable to **alex✳**, expands **alex✳** to **alex.report** and **alex.summary**, and passes these two values to echo.

Braces   The *$VARIABLE* syntax is a special case of the more general syntax *${VARIABLE}*, in which the variable name is enclosed by ${}. The braces insulate the variable name. Braces are necessary when catenating a variable value with a string:

```
$ PREF=counter
$ WAY=$PREFclockwise
$ FAKE=$PREFfeit
$ echo $WAY $FAKE

$
```

The preceding example does not work as planned. Only a blank line is output because, although the symbols **PREFclockwise** and **PREFfeit** are valid variable names, they are not set. By default bash evaluates an unset variable as an empty (null) string and displays this value. To achieve the intent of these statements, refer to the **PREF** variable using braces:

```
$ PREF=counter
$ WAY=${PREF}clockwise
$ FAKE=${PREF}feit
$ echo $WAY $FAKE
counterclockwise counterfeit
```

The Bourne Again Shell refers to the arguments on its command line by position, using the special variables $1, $2, $3, and so forth up to $9. If you wish to refer to arguments past the ninth argument, you must use braces: ${10}. The name of the command is held in $0 (page 921).

unset: REMOVES A VARIABLE

Unless you remove a variable, it exists as long as the shell in which it was created exists. To remove the *value* of a variable but not the variable itself, set the value to null:

```
$ person=
$ echo $person

$
```

You can remove a variable with the unset builtin. To remove the variable **person**, give the following command:

```
$ unset person
```

VARIABLE ATTRIBUTES

This section discusses attributes and explains how to assign them to variables.

readonly: MAKES THE VALUE OF A VARIABLE PERMANENT

You can use the readonly builtin to ensure that the value of a variable cannot be changed. The next example declares the variable **person** to be readonly. You must assign a value to a variable *before* you declare it to be readonly; you cannot change its value after the declaration. When you attempt to unset or change the value of a readonly variable, the shell displays an error message:

```
$ person=jenny
$ echo $person
jenny
$ readonly person
$ person=helen
bash: person: readonly variable
```

If you use the readonly builtin without an argument, it displays a list of all readonly shell variables. This list includes keyword variables that are automatically set as readonly as well as keyword or user-created variables that you have declared as readonly. See "Listing variable attributes" on page 290 for an example (**readonly** and **declare –r** produce the same output).

declare AND typeset: ASSIGN ATTRIBUTES TO VARIABLES

The declare and typeset builtins (two names for the same command) set attributes and values for shell variables. Table 9-3 lists five of these attributes.

Table 9-3   Variable attributes (typeset or declare)

Attribute	Meaning
−a	Declares a variable as an array (page 914)
−f	Declares a variable to be a function name (page 321)
−i	Declares a variable to be of type integer (page 291)
−r	Makes a variable readonly; also readonly (page 289)
−x	Exports a variable (makes it global); also export (page 916)

The following commands declare several variables and set some attributes. The first line declares **person1** and assigns it a value of **alex**. This command has the same effect with or without the word **declare**.

```
$ declare person1=alex
$ declare -r person2=jenny
$ declare -rx person3=helen
$ declare -x person4
```

The readonly and export builtins are synonyms for the commands **declare −r** and **declare −x**, respectively. It is legal to declare a variable without assigning a value to it, as the preceding declaration of the variable **person4** illustrates. This declaration makes **person4** available to all subshells (makes it global). Until an assignment is made to the variable, it has a null value.

You can list the options to declare separately in any order. The following is equivalent to the preceding declaration of **person3**:

```
$ declare -x -r person3=helen
```

Use the **+** character in place of **−** when you want to remove an attribute from a variable. You cannot remove a readonly attribute however. After the following command is given, the variable **person3** is no longer exported but it is still readonly.

```
$ declare +x person3
```

You can also use typeset instead of declare.

Listing variable attributes   Without any arguments or options, the declare builtin lists all shell variables. The same list is output when you run set (page 924) without any arguments.

If you use a declare builtin with options but no variable names as arguments, the command lists all shell variables that have the indicated attributes set. For example, the option **−r** with declare gives a list of all readonly shell variables. This list is the same as that produced by a **readonly** command without any arguments. After the declarations in the preceding example have been given, the results are as follows:

```
$ declare -r
declare -ar BASH_VERSINFO='([0]="2" [1]="05b" [2]="0" [3]="1" ... )'
declare -ir EUID="500"
declare -ir PPID="936"
```

```
declare -r SHELLOPTS="braceexpand:emacs:hashall:histexpand:history:..."
declare -ir UID="500"
declare -r person2="jenny"
declare -rx person3="helen"
```

The first five entries are keyword variables that are automatically declared as read-only. Some of these variables are stored as integers (–i). The –a option indicates that **BASH_VERSINFO** is an array variable; the value of each element of the array is listed to the right of an equal sign.

Integer   By default the values of variables are stored as strings. When you perform arithmetic on a string variable, the shell converts the variable into a number, manipulates it, and then converts it back to a string. A variable with the integer attribute is stored as an integer. Assign the integer attribute as follows:

```
$ typeset -i COUNT
```

KEYWORD VARIABLES

Keyword variables either are inherited or are declared and initialized by the shell when it starts. You can assign values to these variables from the command line or from a startup file. Typically you want these variables to apply to all subshells you start as well as to your login shell. For those variables not automatically exported by the shell, you must use export (page 916) to make them available to child shells.

HOME: YOUR HOME DIRECTORY

By default your home directory is your working directory when you log in. Your home directory is determined when you establish your account; its name is stored in the **/etc/passwd** file.

```
$ grep sam /etc/passwd
sam:x:501:501:Sam S. x301:/home/sam:/bin/bash
```

When you log in, the shell inherits the pathname of your home directory and assigns it to the variable **HOME**. When you give a **cd** command without an argument, cd makes the directory whose name is stored in **HOME** the working directory:

```
$ pwd
/home/alex/laptop
$ echo $HOME
/home/alex
$ cd
$ pwd
/home/alex
```

This example shows the value of the **HOME** variable and the effect of the cd builtin. After you execute cd without an argument, the pathname of the working directory is the same as the value of **HOME**: your home directory.

Tilde (~)   The shell uses the value of **HOME** to expand pathnames that use the shorthand tilde (~) notation (page 171) to denote a user's home directory. The following example uses echo to display the value of this shortcut and then uses ls to list the files in Alex's **laptop** directory, which is a subdirectory of his home directory:

```
$ echo ~
/home/alex
$ ls ~/laptop
tester      count      lineup
```

PATH: WHERE THE SHELL LOOKS FOR PROGRAMS

When you give the shell an absolute or relative pathname rather than a simple file-name as a command, it looks in the specified directory for an executable file with the specified filename. If the file with the pathname you specified does not exist, the shell reports **command not found**. If the file exists as specified but you do not have execute permission for it, or in the case of a shell script you do not have read and execute permission for it, the shell reports **Permission denied**.

If you give a simple filename as a command, the shell searches through certain directories for the program you want to execute. It looks in several directories for a file that has the same name as the command and that you have execute permission for (a compiled program) or read and execute permission for (a shell script). The **PATH** shell variable controls this search.

The default value of **PATH** is determined when bash is compiled. It is not set in a startup file, although it may be modified there. Normally the default specifies that the shell search several system directories used to hold common commands and then search the working directory. These system directories include **/bin** and **/usr/bin** and other directories appropriate to the local system. When you give a command, if the shell does not find the executable—and, in the case of a shell script, readable—file named by the command in any of the directories listed in **PATH**, the shell generates one of the aforementioned error messages.

Working directory | The **PATH** variable specifies the directories in the order the shell should search them. Each directory must be separated from the next by a colon. The following command sets **PATH** so that a search for an executable file starts with the **/usr/local/bin** direc-tory. If it does not find the file in this directory, the shell first looks in **/bin**, and then in **/usr/bin**. If the search fails in those directories, the shell looks in the **bin** directory, a subdirectory of the user's home directory. Finally the shell looks in the working directory. Exporting **PATH** makes its value accessible to subshells:

```
$ export PATH=/usr/local/bin:/bin:/usr/bin:~/bin:
```

A null value in the string indicates the working directory. In the preceding example, a null value (nothing between the colon and the end of the line) appears as the last element of the string. The working directory is represented by a leading colon (not recommended; see the following security tip), a trailing colon (as in the example), or two colons next to each other anywhere in the string. You can also represent the working directory explicitly with a period (.).

Because Linux stores many executable files in directories named **bin** (*binary*), users typically put their own executable files in their own **~/bin** directories. If you put

your own **bin** directory at the end of your **PATH**, as in the preceding example, the shell looks there for any commands that it cannot find in directories listed earlier in **PATH**.

PATH and security

security   Do not put the working directory first in **PATH** when security is a concern. If you are running as Superuser, you should *never* put the working directory first in **PATH**. It is common for Superuser **PATH** to omit the working directory entirely. You can always execute a file in the working directory by prepending **./** to the name: **./ls**.

Putting the working directory first in **PATH** can create a security hole. Most people type **ls** as the first command when entering a directory. If the owner of a directory places an executable file named **ls** in the directory, and the working directory appears first in a user's **PATH**, the user giving an **ls** command from the directory executes the **ls** program in the working directory instead of the system **ls** utility, possibly with undesirable results.

If you want to add directories to **PATH**, you can reference the old value of the **PATH** variable while you are setting **PATH** to a new value (but see the preceding security tip). The following command adds **/usr/local/bin** to the beginning of the current **PATH** and the **bin** directory in the user's home directory (**~/bin**) to the end:

```
$ PATH=/usr/local/bin:$PATH:~/bin
```

MAIL: WHERE YOUR MAIL IS KEPT

The **MAIL** variable contains the pathname of the file that holds your mail (your *mailbox*, usually **/var/spool/mail/***name*, where *name* is your username). If **MAIL** is set and **MAILPATH** (next) is not set, the shell informs you when mail arrives in the file specified by **MAIL**. In a graphical environment you can unset **MAIL** so that the shell does not display mail reminders in a terminal emulator window (assuming you are using a graphical mail program).

The **MAILPATH** variable contains a list of filenames separated by colons. If this variable is set, the shell informs you when any one of the files is modified (for example, when mail arrives). You can follow any of the filenames in the list with a question mark (?), followed by a message. The message replaces the **you have mail** message when you get mail while you are logged in.

The **MAILCHECK** variable specifies how often, in seconds, the shell checks for new mail. The default is 60 seconds. If you set this variable to zero, the shell checks before each prompt.

PS1: USER PROMPT (PRIMARY)

The default Bourne Again Shell prompt is a dollar sign ($). When you run **bash** as **root**, you may have a pound sign (#) prompt. The **PS1** variable holds the prompt string that the shell uses to let you know that it is waiting for a command. When you change the value of **PS1**, you change the appearance of your prompt.

You can customize the prompt displayed by **PS1**. For example, the assignment

```
$ PS1="[\u@\h \W \!]$ "
```

displays the following prompt:

[user@host directory event]$

where **user** is the username, **host** is the hostname up to the first period, **directory** is the basename of the working directory, and **event** is the event number of the current command.

If you are working on more than one system, it can be helpful to incorporate the system name into your prompt. For example, you might change the prompt to the name of the system you are using, followed by a colon and a SPACE (a SPACE at the end of the prompt makes the commands that you enter after the prompt easier to read):

```
$ PS1="$(hostname): "
bravo.example.com: echo test
test
bravo.example.com:
```

The first example that follows changes the prompt to the name of the local host, a SPACE, and a dollar sign (or, if the user is running as **root**, a pound sign). The second example changes the prompt to the time followed by the name of the user. The third example changes the prompt to the one used in this book (a pound sign for **root** and a dollar sign otherwise):

```
$ PS1='\h \$ '
bravo $

$ PS1='\@ \u $ '
09:44 PM alex $

$ PS1='\$ '
$
```

Table 9-4 describes some of the symbols you can use in **PS1**. For a complete list of special characters you can use in the prompt strings, open the bash man page and search for the second occurrence of **PROMPTING** (give the command **/PROMPTING** and then press **n**).

Table 9-4   **PS1** symbols

Symbol	Display in prompt
\$	# if the user is running as **root**; otherwise, $
\w	Pathname of the working directory
\W	Basename of the working directory
\!	Current event (history) number (page 307)
\d	Date in Weekday Month Date format

Table 9-4   **PS1** symbols (continued)

\h	Machine hostname, without the domain
\H	Full machine hostname, including the domain
\u	Username of the current user
\@	Current time of day in 12-hour, AM/PM format
\T	Current time of day in 12-hour HH:MM:SS format
\A	Current time of day in 24-hour HH:MM format
\t	Current time of day in 24-hour HH:MM:SS format

PS2: USER PROMPT (SECONDARY)

Prompt String 2 is a secondary prompt that the shell stores in **PS2**. On the first line of the next example, an unclosed quoted string follows echo. The shell assumes that the command is not finished and, on the second line, gives the default secondary prompt (>). This prompt indicates that the shell is waiting for the user to continue the command line. The shell waits until it receives the quotation mark that closes the string and then executes the command:

```
$ echo "demonstration of prompt string
> 2"
demonstration of prompt string
2
$ PS2="secondary prompt: "
$ echo "this demonstrates
secondary prompt: prompt string 2"
this demonstrates
prompt string 2
```

The second command changes the secondary prompt to **secondary prompt:** followed by a SPACE. A multiline echo demonstrates the new prompt.

PS3: MENU PROMPT

PS3 holds the menu prompt for the **select** control structure (page 908).

PS4: DEBUGGING PROMPT

PS4 holds the bash debugging symbol (page 890).

IFS: SEPARATES INPUT FIELDS (WORD SPLITTING)

The **IFS** (Internal Field Separator) shell variable specifies the characters that you can use to separate arguments on a command line and has the default value of SPACE TAB NEWLINE. Regardless of the value of **IFS**, you can always use one or more SPACE or TAB characters to separate arguments on the command line, provided that these characters are not quoted or escaped. When you assign **IFS** character values, these characters can also separate fields but only if they undergo expansion. This type of interpretation of the command line is called *word splitting*.

Be careful when changing IFS

caution   Changing **IFS** has a variety of side effects so work cautiously. You may find it useful to first save
the value of **IFS** before changing it; you can easily then restore the original value if you get unexpected results. Alternatively, you can fork a new shell with a **bash** command before experimenting
with **IFS**; if you get into trouble, you can **exit** back to the old shell, where **IFS** is working properly.
You can also set **IFS** to its default value with the following command:

```
$ IFS=' \t\n'
```

The following example demonstrates how setting IFS can affect the interpretation
of a command line:

```
$ a=w:x:y:z
$ cat $a
cat: w:x:y:z: No such file or directory
$ IFS=":"
$ cat $a
cat: w: No such file or directory
cat: x: No such file or directory
cat: y: No such file or directory
cat: z: No such file or directory
```

The first time cat is called, the shell expands the variable **a**, interpreting the string
w:x:y:z as a single word to be used as the argument to cat. The cat utility cannot
find a file named **w:x:y:z** and reports an error for that filename. After **IFS** is set to a
colon (:), the shell expands the variable **a** into four words, each of which is an argument to cat. Now cat reports an error for four separate files: **w**, **x**, **y**, and **z**. Word
splitting based on the colon (:) takes place only *after* the variable **a** is expanded.

The shell splits all *expanded* words on a command line according to the separating
characters found in **IFS**. When there is no expansion, there is no splitting. Consider
the following commands:

```
$ IFS="p"
$ export VAR
```

Although **IFS** is set to **p**, the **p** on the **export** command line is not expanded so the
word **export** is not split.

The following example uses variable expansion in an attempt to produce an **export**
command:

```
$ IFS="p"
$ aa=export
$ echo $aa
ex ort
```

This time expansion occurs so that the character **p** in the token **export** is interpreted
as a separator as the preceding echo command shows. Now when you try to use the
value of the **aa** variable to export the **VAR** variable, the shell parses the **$aa VAR**
command line as **ex ort VAR**. The effect is that the command line starts the ex editor with two filenames: **ort** and **VAR**.

```
$ $aa VAR
2 files to edit
"ort" [New File]
Entering Ex mode.  Type "visual" to go to Normal mode.
:q
E173: 1 more file to edit
:q
$
```

If you unset **IFS**, only SPACEs and TABs work as field separators.

Multiple separator characters

tip   Although sequences of multiple SPACE or TAB characters are treated as single separators, *each occurrence* of another field-separator character acts as a separator.

CDPATH: BROADENS THE SCOPE OF cd

The **CDPATH** variable allows you to use a simple filename as an argument to the cd builtin to change the working directory to a directory other than a child of the working directory. If you have several directories you like to work out of, this variable can speed things up and save you the tedium of using cd with longer pathnames to switch among them.

When **CDPATH** is not set and you specify a simple filename as an argument to cd, cd searches the working directory for a subdirectory with the same name as the argument. If the subdirectory does not exist, cd displays an error message. When **CDPATH** is set, cd searches for an appropriately named subdirectory in the directories in the **CDPATH** list. If cd finds one, that directory becomes the working directory. With **CDPATH** set, you can use cd and a simple filename to change the working directory to a child of any of the directories listed in **CDPATH**.

The **CDPATH** variable takes on the value of a colon-separated list of directory pathnames (similar to the **PATH** variable). It is usually set in the **~/.bash_profile** startup file with a command line such as the following:

```
export CDPATH=$HOME:$HOME/literature
```

This command causes cd to search your home directory, the **literature** directory, and then the working directory when you give a cd command. If you do not include the working directory in **CDPATH**, cd searches the working directory if the search of all the other directories in **CDPATH** fails. If you want cd to search the working directory first (which you should never do when you are logged in as **root**—refer to the tip on page 293), include a null string, represented by two colons (::), as the first entry in **CDPATH**:

```
export CDPATH=::$HOME:$HOME/literature
```

If the argument to the cd builtin is an absolute pathname—one starting with a slash (**/**)—the shell does not consult **CDPATH**.

KEYWORD VARIABLES: A SUMMARY

Table 9-5 lists the bash keyword variables.

Table 9-5   bash keyword variables

Variable	Value
BASH_ENV	The pathname of the startup file for noninteractive shells (page 268)
CDPATH	The cd search path (page 297)
COLUMNS	The width of the display used by **select** (page 907)
FCEDIT	The name of the editor that fc uses by default (page 305)
HISTFILE	The pathname of the file that holds the history list (default: ~/**.bash_history**; page 302)
HISTFILESIZE	The maximum number of entries saved in **HISTFILE** (default: 500; page 302)
HISTSIZE	The maximum number of entries saved in the history list (default: 500; page 302)
HOME	The pathname of the user's home directory (page 291); used as the default argument for cd and in tilde expansion (page 171)
IFS	Internal Field Separator (page 295); used for word splitting (page 335)
INPUTRC	The pathname of the Readline startup file (default: ~/**.inputrc**; page 315)
LANG	The locale category when that category is not specifically set with an **LC_*** variable
LC_*	A group of variables that specify locale categories including **LC_COLLATE**, **LC_CTYPE**, **LC_MESSAGES**, and **LC_NUMERIC**; use the locale builtin to display a complete list with values
LINES	The height of the display used by **select** (page 907)
MAIL	The pathname of the file that holds a user's mail (page 293)
MAILCHECK	How often, in seconds, bash checks for mail (page 293)
MAILPATH	A colon-separated list of file pathnames that bash checks for mail in (page 293)
PATH	A colon-separated list of directory pathnames that bash looks for commands in (page 292)
PROMPT_COMMAND	A command that bash executes just before it displays the primary prompt
PS1	Prompt String 1; the primary prompt (default: '**\s–\v\$** '; page 293)
PS2	Prompt String 2; the secondary prompt (default: '**> '**; page 295)
PS3	The prompt issued by **select** (page 907)
PS4	The bash debugging symbol (page 890)
REPLY	Holds the line that read accepts (page 928); also used by **select** (page 907)

SPECIAL CHARACTERS

Table 9-6 lists most of the characters that are special to the bash shell.

Table 9-6   Shell special characters

Character	Use
NEWLINE	Initiates execution of a command (page 276)
;	Separates commands (page 276)
( )	Groups commands (page 279) for execution by a subshell or identifies a function (page 321)
&	Executes a command in the background (pages 219 and 278)
|	Sends standard output of preceding command to standard input of following command (pipe; page 278)
>	Redirects standard output (page 210)
>>	Appends standard output (page 214)
<	Redirects standard input (page 212)
<<	Here document (page 909)
*	Any string of zero or more characters in an ambiguous file reference (page 222)
?	Any single character in an ambiguous file reference (page 221)
\	Quotes the following character (page 126)
'	Quotes a string, preventing all substitution (page 126)
"	Quotes a string, allowing only variable and command substitution (pages 126 and 287)
` ... `	Performs command substitution (page 334)
[ ]	Character class in an ambiguous file reference (page 223)
$	References a variable (page 285)
. (dot builtin)	Executes a command (only at the beginning of a line, page 269)
#	Begins a comment (page 275)
{ }	Used to surround the contents of a function (page 321)
: (null builtin)	Returns *true* (page 935)
&& (Boolean AND)	Executes command on right only if command on left succeeds (returns a zero exit status, page 946)
|| (Boolean OR)	Executes command on right only if command on left fails (returns a nonzero exit status; page 946)
! (Boolean NOT)	Reverses exit status of a command
$()	Performs command substitution (preferred form; page 334)
[ ]	Evaluates an arithmetic expression (page 332)

PROCESSES

A *process* is the execution of a command by Linux. The shell that starts when you log in is a command, or a process, like any other. When you give the name of a Linux utility on the command line, you initiate a process. When you run a shell script, another shell process is started and additional processes are created for each command in the script. Depending on how you invoke the shell script, the script is run either by the current shell or, more typically, by a subshell (child) of the current shell. A process is not started when you run a shell builtin, such as cd.

PROCESS STRUCTURE

fork system call   Like the file structure, the process structure is hierarchical, with parents, children, and even a *root*. A parent process *forks* a child process, which in turn can fork other processes. (The term *fork* indicates that, as with a fork in the road, one process turns into two. Initially the two forks are identical except that one is identified as the parent and one as the child. You can also use the term *spawn;* the words are interchangeable.) The operating system routine, or *system call,* that creates a new process is named **fork**.

When Linux begins execution when a system is started, it starts init, a single process called a *spontaneous process,* with PID number 1. This process holds the same position in the process structure as the root directory does in the file structure: It is the ancestor of all processes that the system and users work with. When the system is in multiuser mode, init runs getty or mingetty processes, which display **login:** prompts on terminals and virtual consoles. When someone responds to the prompt and presses RETURN, getty hands control over to a utility named login, which checks the username and password combination. After the user logs in, the login process becomes the user's shell process.

PROCESS IDENTIFICATION

PID number   Linux assigns a unique PID (process identification) number at the inception of each process. As long as a process exists, it keeps the same PID number. During one session the same process is always executing the login shell. When you fork a new process—for example, when you use an editor—the PID number of the new (child) process is different from that of its parent process. When you return to the login shell, it is still being executed by the same process and has the same PID number as when you logged in.

The following example shows that the process running the shell forked (is the parent of) the process running ps (page 220). When you call it with the –f option, ps displays a full listing of information about each process. The line of the ps display with **bash** in the **CMD** column refers to the process running the shell. The column headed by **PID** identifies the PID number. The column headed **PPID** identifies the PID number of the *parent* of the process. From the PID and PPID columns you can see that the process running the shell (PID 21341) is the parent of the process running sleep

(PID 22789). The parent PID number of sleep is the same as the PID number of the shell (21341).

```
$ sleep 10 &
[1] 22789
$ ps -f
UID        PID  PPID  C STIME TTY          TIME CMD
alex     21341 21340  0 10:42 pts/16    00:00:00 bash
alex     22789 21341  0 17:30 pts/16    00:00:00 sleep 10
alex     22790 21341  0 17:30 pts/16    00:00:00 ps -f
```

Refer to the ps man page for more information on ps and the columns it displays with the –f option. A second pair of **sleep** and **ps –f** commands shows that the shell is still being run by the same process but that it forked another process to run sleep:

```
$ sleep 10 &
[1] 22791
$ ps -f
UID        PID  PPID  C STIME TTY          TIME CMD
alex     21341 21340  0 10:42 pts/16    00:00:00 bash
alex     22791 21341  0 17:31 pts/16    00:00:00 sleep 10
alex     22792 21341  0 17:31 pts/16    00:00:00 ps -f
```

You can also use pstree (or **ps ––forest**, with or without the **–e** option) to see the parent–child relationship of processes. The next example shows the **–p** option to pstree, which causes it to display PID numbers:

```
$ pstree -p
init(1)-+-acpid(1395)
        |-atd(1758)
        |-crond(1702)
        ...
        |-kdeinit(2223)-+-firefox(8914)---run-mozilla.sh(8920)---firefox-bin(8925)
        |               |-gaim(2306)
        |               |-gqview(14062)
        |               |-kdeinit(2228)
        |               |-kdeinit(2294)
        |               |-kdeinit(2314)-+-bash(2329)---ssh(2561)
        |               |               |-bash(2339)
        |               |               '-bash(15821)---bash(16778)
        |               |-kdeinit(16448)
        |               |-kdeinit(20888)
        |               |-oclock(2317)
        |               '-pam-panel-icon(2305)---pam_timestamp_c(2307)
        ...
        |-login(1823)---bash(20986)-+-pstree(21028)
        |                           '-sleep(21026)
        ...
```

The preceding output is abbreviated. The line that starts with **–kdeinit** shows a graphical user running many processes, including **firefox, gaim,** and **oclock**. The line that starts with **–login** shows a textual user running sleep in the background while running pstree in the foreground. Refer to "$$: PID Number" on page 919 for a description of how to instruct the shell to report on PID numbers.

EXECUTING A COMMAND

fork and **sleep**   When you give the shell a command, it usually forks (spawns) a child process to execute the command. While the child process is executing the command, the parent process *sleeps*. While a process is sleeping, it does not use any computer time but remains inactive, waiting to wake up. When the child process finishes executing the command, it tells its parent of its success or failure via its exit status and then dies. The parent process (which is running the shell) wakes up and prompts for another command.

Background process   When you run a process in the background by ending a command with an ampersand (**&**), the shell forks a child process without going to sleep and without waiting for the child process to run to completion. The parent process, which is executing the shell, reports the job number and PID number of the child and prompts for another command. The child process runs in the background, independent of its parent.

Builtins   Although the shell forks a process to run most of the commands you give it, some commands are built into the shell. The shell does not need to fork a process to run builtins. For more information refer to "Builtins" on page 225.

Variables   Within a given process, such as your login shell or a subshell, you can declare, initialize, read, and change variables. By default however, a variable is local to a process. When a process forks a child process, the parent does not pass the value of a variable to the child. You can make the value of a variable available to child processes (global) by using the export builtin (page 916).

HISTORY

The history mechanism, a feature adapted from the C Shell, maintains a list of recently issued command lines, also called *events,* providing a quick way to reexecute any of the events in the list. This mechanism also enables you to execute variations of previous commands and to reuse arguments from them. You can replicate complicated commands and arguments that you used earlier in this login session or in a previous one and enter a series of commands that differ from one another in minor ways. The history list also serves as a record of what you have done. It can prove helpful when you have made a mistake and are not sure what you did or when you want to keep a record of a procedure that involved a series of commands.

The history builtin displays the history list. If it does not, read on—you need to set some variables.

VARIABLES THAT CONTROL HISTORY

The value of the **HISTSIZE** variable determines the number of events preserved in the history list during a session. A value in the range of 100 to 1,000 is normal.

When you exit from the shell, the most recently executed commands are saved in the file given by the **HISTFILE** variable (the default is **~/.bash_history**). The next time you start the shell, this file initializes the history list. The value of the **HISTFILESIZE**

history **can help track down mistakes**

tip When you have made a command line mistake (not an error within a script or program) and are not sure what you did wrong, look at the history list to review your recent commands. Sometimes this list can help you figure out what went wrong and how to fix things.

variable determines the number of lines of history saved in **HISTFILE** (not necessarily the same as **HISTSIZE**). **HISTSIZE** holds the number of events remembered during a session, **HISTFILESIZE** holds the number remembered between sessions, and the file designated by **HISTFILE** holds the history list. See Table 9-7.

Table 9-7 History variables

Variable	Default	Function
HISTSIZE	500 events	Maximum number of events saved during a session
HISTFILE	**~/.bash_history**	Location of the history file
HISTFILESIZE	500 events	Maximum number of events saved between sessions

Event number The Bourne Again Shell assigns a sequential *event number* to each command line. You can display this event number as part of the bash prompt by including \! in **PS1** (page 293). Examples in this section show numbered prompts when they help to illustrate the behavior of a command.

Give the following command manually or place it in **~/.bash_profile** (to affect future sessions) to establish a history list of the 100 most recent events:

    $ HISTSIZE=100

The following command causes bash to save the 100 most recent events across login sessions:

    $ HISTFILESIZE=100

After you set **HISTFILESIZE**, you can log out and log in again, and the 100 most recent events from the previous login session will appear in your history list.

Give the command **history** to display the events in the history list. The list of events is ordered with oldest events at the top of the list. The following history list includes a command to modify the bash prompt so that it displays the history event number. The last event in the history list is the **history** command that displayed the list.

```
32 $ history | tail
   23  PS1="\! bash$ "
   24  ls -l
   25  cat temp
   26  rm temp
   27  vim memo
   28  lpr memo
   29  vim memo
   30  lpr memo
   31  rm memo
   32  history | tail
```

As you run commands and your history list becomes longer, it may run off the top of the screen when you use the history builtin. Pipe the output of history through less to browse through it, or give the command **history 10** to look at the ten most recent commands.

REEXECUTING AND EDITING COMMANDS

You can reexecute any event in the history list. This feature can save you time, effort, and aggravation. Not having to reenter long command lines allows you to reexecute events more easily, quickly, and accurately than you could if you had to retype the entire command line. You can recall, modify, and reexecute previously executed events in three ways: You can use the fc builtin (covered next); the exclamation point commands (page 306); or the Readline Library, which uses a one-line vi- or emacs-like editor to edit and execute events (page 312).

Which method to use?

tip   If you are more familiar with vi or emacs and less familiar with the C or TC Shell, use fc or the Readline Library. If you are more familiar with the C or TC Shell and less familiar with vi and emacs, use the exclamation point commands. If it is a toss-up, try the Readline Library; it will benefit you in other areas of Linux more than learning the exclamation point commands will.

fc: DISPLAYS, EDITS, AND REEXECUTES COMMANDS

The fc (fix command) builtin enables you to display the history list and to edit and reexecute previous commands. It provides many of the same capabilities as the command line editors.

VIEWING THE HISTORY LIST

When you call fc with the –l option, it displays commands from the history list. Without any arguments, fc –l lists the 16 most recent commands in a numbered list, with the oldest appearing first:

```
$ fc -l
1024    cd
1025    view calendar
1026    vim letter.adams01
1027    aspell -c letter.adams01
1028    vim letter.adams01
1029    lpr letter.adams01
1030    cd ../memos
1031    ls
1032    rm *0405
1033    fc -l
1034    cd
1035    whereis aspell
1036    man aspell
1037    cd /usr/share/doc/*aspell*
1038    pwd
1039    ls
1040    ls man-html
```

The fc builtin can take zero, one, or two arguments with the –l option. The arguments specify the part of the history list to be displayed:

fc –l [first [last]]

The fc builtin lists commands beginning with the most recent event that matches *first*. The argument can be an event number, the first few characters of the command line, or a negative number, which is taken to be the *n*th previous command. If you provide *last*, fc displays commands from the most recent event that matches *first* through the most recent event that matches *last*. The next command displays the history list from event 1030 through event 1035:

```
$ fc -l 1030 1035
1030    cd ../memos
1031    ls
1032    rm *0405
1033    fc -l
1034    cd
1035    whereis aspell
```

The following command lists the most recent event that begins with **view** through the most recent command line that begins with **whereis**:

```
$ fc -l view whereis
1025    view calendar
1026    vim letter.adams01
1027    aspell -c letter.adams01
1028    vim letter.adams01
1029    lpr letter.adams01
1030    cd ../memos
1031    ls
1032    rm *0405
1033    fc -l
1034    cd
1035    whereis aspell
```

To list a single command from the history list, use the same identifier for the first and second arguments. The following command lists event 1027:

```
$ fc -l 1027 1027
1027    aspell -c letter.adams01
```

EDITING AND REEXECUTING PREVIOUS COMMANDS

You can use fc to edit and reexecute previous commands.

fc [–e editor] [first [last]]

When you call fc with the –e option followed by the name of an editor, fc calls the editor with event(s) in the Work buffer. Without *first* and *last*, fc defaults to the most recent command. The next example invokes the vi(m) editor to edit the most recent command:

```
$ fc -e vi
```

The fc builtin uses the stand-alone vi(m) editor. If you set the **FCEDIT** variable, you do not need to use the –e option to specify an editor on the command line. Because the value of **FCEDIT** has been changed to **/usr/bin/emacs** and fc has no arguments, the following command edits the most recent command with the emacs editor:

```
$ export FCEDIT=/usr/bin/emacs
$ fc
```

If you call it with a single argument, fc invokes the editor on the specified command. The following example starts the editor with event 21 in the Work buffer. When you exit from the editor, the shell executes the command:

```
$ fc 21
```

Again you can identify commands with numbers or by specifying the first few characters of the command name. The following example calls the editor to work on events from the most recent event that begins with the letters **vim** through event 206:

```
$ fc vim 206
```

Clean up the fc buffer

caution   When you execute an fc command, the shell executes whatever you leave in the editor buffer, possibly with unwanted results. If you decide you do not want to execute a command, delete everything from the buffer before you exit from the editor.

REEXECUTING COMMANDS WITHOUT CALLING THE EDITOR

You can reexecute previous commands without going into an editor. If you call fc with the –s option, it skips the editing phase and reexecutes the command. The following example reexecutes event 1029:

```
$ fc -s 1029
lpr letter.adams01
```

The next example reexecutes the previous command:

```
$ fc -s
```

When you reexecute a command you can tell fc to substitute one string for another. The next example substitutes the string **john** for the string **adams** in event 1029 and executes the modified event:

```
$ fc -s adams=john 1029
lpr letter.john01
```

USING AN EXCLAMATION POINT (!) TO REFERENCE EVENTS

The C Shell history mechanism uses an exclamation point to reference events and is available under bash. It is frequently more cumbersome to use than fc but nevertheless has some useful features. For example, the **!!** command reexecutes the previous event, and the **!$** token represents the last word on the previous command line.

You can reference an event by using its absolute event number, its relative event number, or the text it contains. All references to events, called *event designators*, begin with an exclamation point (!). One or more characters follow the exclamation point to specify an event.

You can put history events anywhere on a command line. To escape an exclamation point so that it is treated literally instead of as the start of a history event, precede it with a backslash (\) or enclose it within single quotation marks.

EVENT DESIGNATORS

An event designator specifies a command in the history list. See Table 9-8 on page 308 for a list of event designators.

!! reexecutes the previous event   You can always reexecute the previous event by giving a **!!** command. In the following example, event 45 reexecutes event 44:

```
44 $ ls -l text
-rw-rw-r--   1 alex group 45 Apr 30 14:53 text
45 $ !!
ls -l text
-rw-rw-r--   1 alex group 45 Apr 30 14:53 text
```

The **!!** command works whether or not your prompt displays an event number. As this example shows, when you use the history mechanism to reexecute an event, the shell displays the command it is reexecuting.

!*n* event number   A number following an exclamation point refers to an event. If that event is in the history list, the shell executes it. Otherwise, the shell displays an error message. A negative number following an exclamation point references an event relative to the current event. For example, the command **!–3** refers to the third preceding event. After you issue a command, the relative event number of a given event changes (event –3 becomes event –4). Both of the following commands reexecute event 44:

```
51 $ !44
ls -l text
-rw-rw-r--   1 alex group 45 Nov 30 14:53 text
52 $ !-8
ls -l text
-rw-rw-r--   1 alex group 45 Nov 30 14:53 text
```

!*string* event text   When a string of text follows an exclamation point, the shell searches for and executes the most recent event that *began* with that string. If you enclose the string between question marks, the shell executes the most recent event that *contained* that string. The final question mark is optional if a RETURN would immediately follow it.

```
68 $ history 10
   59  ls -l text*
   60  tail text5
   61  cat text1 text5 > letter
   62  vim letter
   63  cat letter
   64  cat memo
   65  lpr memo
   66  pine jenny
   67  ls -l
   68  history
69 $ !1
ls -l
...
70 $ !lpr
lpr memo
71 $ !?letter?
cat letter
...
```

Table 9-8   Event designators

Designator	Meaning
!	Starts a history event unless followed immediately by SPACE, NEWLINE, =, or (.
!!	The previous command.
!*n*	Command number *n* in the history list.
!–*n*	The *n*th preceding command.
!*string*	The most recent command line that started with *string*.
!?*string*[?]	The most recent command that contained *string*. The last **?** is optional.
!#	The current command (as you have it typed so far).
!{*event*}	The *event* is an event designator. The braces isolate *event* from the surrounding text. For example, **!{–3}3** is the third most recently executed command followed by a **3**.

optional   WORD DESIGNATORS

A *word designator* specifies a word or series of words from an event. Table 9-9 on page 310 lists word designators.

The words are numbered starting with 0 (the first word on the line—usually the command), continuing with 1 (the first word following the command), and going through *n* (the last word on the line).

To specify a particular word from a previous event, follow the event designator (such as **!14**) with a colon and the number of the word in the previous event. For example, !14:3 specifies the third word following the command from event 14. You can specify the first word following the command (word number 1) by using a caret (^) and the last word by using a dollar sign ($). You can specify a range of words by separating two word designators with a hyphen.

```
72 $ echo apple grape orange pear
apple grape orange pear
73 $ echo !72:2
echo grape
grape
74 $ echo !72:^
echo apple
apple
75 $ !72:0 !72:$
echo pear
pear
76 $ echo !72:2-4
echo grape orange pear
grape orange pear
77 $ !72:0-$
echo apple grape orange pear
apple grape orange pear
```

As the next example shows, !$ refers to the last word of the previous event. You can use this shorthand to edit, for example, a file you just displayed with cat:

```
$ cat report.718
...

$ vim !$
vim report.718
...
```

If an event contains a single command, the word numbers correspond to the argument numbers. If an event contains more than one command, this correspondence does not hold true for commands after the first. In the following example event 78 contains two commands separated by a semicolon so that the shell executes them sequentially; the semicolon is word number 5.

```
78 $ !72 ; echo helen jenny barbara
echo apple grape orange pear ; echo helen jenny barbara
apple grape orange pear
helen jenny barbara
79 $ echo !78:7
echo helen
helen
80 $ echo !78:4-7
echo pear ; echo helen
pear
helen
```

Table 9-9   Word designators

Designator	Meaning
n	The *nth* word. Word 0 is normally the command name.
^	The first word (after the command name).
$	The last word.
m−n	All words from word number *m* through word number *n*; *m* defaults to 0 if you omit it (0−*n*).
n∗	All words from word number *n* through the last word.
∗	All words except the command name. The same as **1**∗.
%	The word matched by the most recent **?***string***?** search.

MODIFIERS

On occasion you may want to change an aspect of an event you are reexecuting. Perhaps you entered a complex command line with a typo or incorrect pathname or you want to specify a different argument. You can modify an event or a word of an event by putting one or more modifiers after the word designator, or after the event designator if there is no word designator. Each modifier must be preceded by a colon (:).

Substitute modifier   The *substitute modifier* is more complex than the other modifiers. The following example shows the substitute modifier correcting a typo in the previous event:

```
$ car /home/jenny/memo.0507 /home/alex/letter.0507
bash: car: command not found
$ !!:s/car/cat
cat /home/jenny/memo.0507 /home/alex/letter.0507
...
```

The substitute modifier has the following syntax:

[g]s/*old*/*new*/

where *old* is the original string (not a regular expression), and *new* is the string that replaces *old*. The substitute modifier substitutes the first occurrence of *old* with *new*. Placing a **g** before the **s** (as in *gs/old/new/*) causes a global substitution, replacing all occurrences of *old*. The **/** is the delimiter in the examples but you can use any character that is not in either *old* or *new*. The final delimiter is optional if a RETURN would immediately follow it. As with the vim Substitute command, the history mechanism replaces an ampersand (&) in *new* with *old*. The shell replaces a null old string (*s//new/*) with the previous old string or string within a command that you searched for with **?***string***?**.

Quick substitution   An abbreviated form of the substitute modifier is *quick substitution*. Use it to reexecute the most recent event while changing some of the event text. The quick substitution character is the caret (^). For example, the command

```
$ ^old^new^
```

produces the same results as

```
$ !!:s/old/new/
```

Thus substituting **cat** for **car** in the previous event could have been entered as

```
$ ^car^cat
cat /home/jenny/memo.0507 /home/alex/letter.0507
...
```

You can omit the final caret if it would be followed immediately by a RETURN. As with other command line substitutions, the shell displays the command line as it appears after the substitution.

Other modifiers   Modifiers (other than the substitute modifier) perform simple edits on the part of the event that has been selected by the event designator and the optional word designators. You can use multiple modifiers, each preceded by a colon (:).

The following series of commands uses ls to list the name of a file, repeats the command without executing it (**p** modifier), and repeats the last command, removing the last part of the pathname (**h** modifier) again without executing it:

```
$ ls /etc/sysconfig/harddisks
/etc/sysconfig/harddisks
$ !!:p
ls /etc/sysconfig/harddisks
$ !!:h:p
ls /etc/sysconfig
$
```

Table 9-10 lists event modifiers other than the substitute modifier.

Table 9-10   Modifiers

Modifier		Function
e	(extension)	Removes all but the filename extension
h	(head)	Removes the last part of a pathname
p	(print-not)	Displays the command, but does not execute it
q	(quote)	Quotes the substitution to prevent further substitutions on it
r	(root)	Removes the filename extension
t	(tail)	Removes all elements of a pathname except the last
x		Like **q** but quotes each word in the substitution individually

THE READLINE LIBRARY

Command line editing under the Bourne Again Shell is implemented through the *Readline Library,* which is available to any application written in C. Any application that uses the Readline Library supports line editing that is consistent with that provided by bash. Programs that use the Readline Library, including bash, read ~/.inputrc (page 315) for key binding information and configuration settings. The --noediting command line option turns off command line editing in bash.

vi mode   You can choose one of two editing modes when using the Readline Library in bash: emacs or vi(m). Both modes provide many of the commands available in the stand-alone versions of the vi(m) and emacs editors. You can also use the ARROW keys to move around. Up and down movements move you backward and forward through the history list. In addition, Readline provides several types of interactive word completion (page 314). The default mode is emacs; you can switch to vi mode with the following command:

```
$ set -o vi
```

emacs mode   The next command switches back to emacs mode:

```
$ set -o emacs
```

vi EDITING MODE

Before you start make sure you are in vi mode.

When you enter bash commands while in vi editing mode, you are in Input mode (page 154). As you enter a command, if you discover an error before you press RETURN, you can press ESCAPE to switch to vi Command mode. This setup is different from the stand-alone vi(m) editor's initial mode. While in Command mode you can use many vi(m) commands to edit the command line. It is as though you were using vi(m) to edit a copy of the history file with a screen that has room for only one command. When you use the k command or the UP ARROW to move up a line, you access the previous command. If you then use the j command or the DOWN ARROW to move down a line, you will return to the original command. To use the k and j keys to move between commands you must be in Command mode; you can use the ARROW keys in both Command and Input modes.

The stand-alone editor starts in Command mode

tip   The stand-alone vim editor starts in Command mode, whereas the command line vi(m) editor starts in Input mode. If commands display characters and do not work properly, you are in Input mode. Press ESCAPE and enter the command again.

In addition to cursor-positioning commands, you can use the search-backward (?) command followed by a search string to look *back* through your history list for the most recent command containing that string. If you have moved back in your history list, use a forward slash (/) to search *forward* toward your most recent command. Unlike the search strings in the stand-alone vi(m) editor, these search strings cannot contain regular expressions. You can, however, start the search string with a caret (^) to force the shell to locate commands that start with the search string. As in vi(m), pressing **n** after a successful search looks for the next occurrence of the same string.

You can also access events in the history list by using event numbers. While you are in Command mode (press ESCAPE), enter the event number followed by a **G** to go to the command with that event number.

When you use **/**, **?**, or **G** to move to a command line, you are in Command mode, not Input mode. Now you can edit the command as you like or press RETURN to execute it.

Once the command you want to edit is displayed, you can modify the command line using vi(m) Command mode editing commands such as **x** (delete character), **r** (replace character), **~** (change case), and **.** (repeat last change). To change to Input mode, use an Insert (**i, I**), Append (**a, A**), Replace (**R**), or Change (**c, C**) command. You do not have to return to Command mode to run a command; simply press RETURN, even if the cursor is in the middle of the command line.

emacs EDITING MODE

Unlike the vi(m) editor, emacs is modeless. You need not switch between Command mode and Input mode because most emacs commands are control characters, allowing emacs to distinguish between input and commands. Like vi(m), the emacs command line editor provides commands for moving the cursor on the command line and through the command history list and for modifying part or all of a command. The emacs command line editor commands differ in a few cases from the commands in the stand-alone emacs editor.

In emacs you perform cursor movement by using both CONTROL and ESCAPE commands. To move the cursor one character backward on the command line, press CONTROL-B. Press CONTROL-F to move one character forward. As in vi, you may precede these movements with counts. To use a count you must first press ESCAPE; otherwise, the numbers you type will appear on the command line.

Like vi(m), emacs provides word and line movement commands. To move backward or forward one word on the command line, press ESCAPE **b** or ESCAPE **f**. To move several words by using a count, press ESCAPE followed by the number and the appropriate escape sequence. To get to the beginning of the line, press CONTROL-A; to the end of the line, press CONTROL-E; and to the next instance of the character *c*, press CONTROL-X CONTROL-F followed by *c*.

You can add text to the command line by moving the cursor to the correct place and typing the desired text. To delete text, move the cursor just to the right of the characters that you want to delete and press the erase key (page 117) once for each character you want to delete.

CONTROL-D **can terminate your screen session**

tip   If you want to delete the character directly under the cursor, press CONTROL-D. If you enter CONTROL-D at the beginning of the line, it may terminate your shell session.

If you want to delete the entire command line, type the line kill character (page 118). You can type this character while the cursor is anywhere in the command line. If you want to delete from the cursor to the end of the line, use CONTROL-K.

READLINE COMPLETION COMMANDS

You can use the TAB key to complete words you are entering on the command line. This facility, called *completion,* works in both vi and emacs editing modes. Several types of completion are possible, and which one you use depends on which part of a command line you are typing when you press TAB.

COMMAND COMPLETION

If you are typing the name of a command (the first word on the command line), pressing TAB results in *command completion.* That is, bash looks for a command whose name starts with the part of the word you have typed. If no command starts with what you have entered, bash beeps. If there is one such command, bash completes the command name for you. If there is more than one choice, bash does nothing in vi mode and beeps in emacs mode. Pressing TAB a second time causes bash to display a list of commands whose names start with the prefix you typed and allows you to finish typing the command name.

In the following example, the user types **bz** and presses TAB. The shell beeps (the user is in emacs mode) to indicate that several commands start with the letters **bz**. The user enters another TAB to cause the shell to display a list of commands that start with **bz** followed by the command line as the user had entered it so far:

```
$ bz —→ TAB (beep) —→ TAB
bzcat          bzdiff        bzip2          bzless
bzcmp          bzgrep        bzip2recover   bzmore
$ bz▮
```

Next the user types **c** and presses TAB twice. The shell displays the two commands that start with **bzc**. The user types **a** followed by TAB and the shell then completes the command because only one command starts with **bzca**.

```
$ bzc —→ TAB (beep) —→ TAB
bzcat bzcmp
$ bzca —→ TAB —→t ▮
```

PATHNAME COMPLETION

Pathname completion, which also uses TABs, allows you to type a portion of a pathname and have bash supply the rest. If the portion of the pathname that you have typed is sufficient to determine a unique pathname, bash displays that pathname. If more than one pathname would match it, bash completes the pathname up to the point where there are choices so that you can type more.

When you are entering a pathname, including a simple filename, and press TAB, the shell beeps (if the shell is in emacs mode—in vi mode there is no beep). It then extends the command line as far as it can.

```
$ cat films/dar  ⟶ TAB (beep) cat films/dark_█
```

In the **films** directory every file that starts with **dar** has **k_** as the next characters, so bash cannot extend the line further without making a choice among files. You are left with the cursor just past the _ character. At this point you can continue typing the pathname or press TAB twice. In the latter case bash beeps, displays your choices, redisplays the command line, and again leaves the cursor just after the _ character.

```
$ cat films/dark_  ⟶ TAB (beep)  ⟶ TAB
dark_passage   dark_victory
$ cat films/dark_█
```

When you add enough information to distinguish between the two possible files and press TAB, bash displays the unique pathname. If you enter **p** followed by TAB after the _ character, the shell completes the command line:

```
$ cat films/dark_p  ⟶ TAB  ⟶ assage
```

Because there is no further ambiguity, the shell appends a SPACE so you can finish typing the command line or just press RETURN to execute the command. If the complete pathname is that of a directory, bash appends a slash (**/**) in place of a SPACE.

VARIABLE COMPLETION

When typing a variable name, pressing TAB results in *variable completion*, where bash tries to complete the name of the variable. In case of an ambiguity, pressing TAB twice displays a list of choices:

```
$ echo $HO  ⟶ TAB  ⟶ TAB
$HOME          $HOSTNAME  $HOSTTYPE
$ echo $HOM  ⟶ TAB  ⟶ E
```

Pressing RETURN executes the command

caution   Pressing RETURN causes the shell to execute the command regardless of where the cursor is on the command line.

.inputrc: CONFIGURING READLINE

The Bourne Again Shell and other programs that use the Readline Library read the file specified by the **INPUTRC** environment variable to obtain initialization information. If **INPUTRC** is not set, these programs read the ~/.inputrc file. They ignore lines of **.inputrc** that are blank or that start with a pound sign (#).

VARIABLES

You can set variables in **.inputrc** to control the behavior of the Readline Library using the following syntax:

set *variable value*

Table 9-11 lists some variables and values you can use. See **Readline Variables** in the bash man or info page for a complete list.

Table 9-11   Readline variables

Variable	Effect
editing-mode	Set to **vi** to start Readline in vi mode. Set to **emacs** to start Readline in emacs mode (the default). Similar to the **set –o vi** and **set –o emacs** shell commands (page 312).
horizontal-scroll-mode	Set to **on** to cause long lines to extend off the right edge of the display area. Moving the cursor to the right when it is at the right edge of the display area shifts the line to the left so you can see more of the line. You can shift the line back by moving the cursor back past the left edge. The default value is **off**, which causes long lines to wrap onto multiple lines of the display.
mark-directories	Set to **off** to cause Readline not to place a slash (/) at the end of directory names it completes. Normally it is **on**.
mark-modified-lines	Set to **on** to cause Readline to precede modified history lines with an asterisk. The default value is **off**.

KEY BINDINGS

You can specify bindings that map keystroke sequences to Readline commands, allowing you to change or extend the default bindings. As in emacs, the Readline Library includes many commands that are not bound to a keystroke sequence. To use an unbound command, you must map it using one of the following forms:

> *keyname: command_name*
> *"keystroke_sequence" : command_name*

In the first form, you spell out the name for a single key. For example, CONTROL-U would be written as **control-u**. This form is useful for binding commands to single keys.

In the second form, you specify a string that describes a sequence of keys that will be bound to the command. You can use the emacs-style backslash escape sequences to represent the special keys CONTROL (\C), META (\M), and ESCAPE (\e). Specify a backslash by escaping it with another backslash: \\. Similarly, a double or single quotation mark can be escaped with a backslash: \" or \'.

The **kill-whole-line** command, available in emacs mode only, deletes the current line. Put the following command in **.inputrc** to bind the **kill-whole-line** command (which is unbound by default) to the keystroke sequence CONTROL-R.

```
control-r: kill-whole-line
```

bind Give the command **bind –P** to display a list of all Readline commands. If a command is bound to a key sequence, that sequence is shown. Commands you can use in vi mode start with **vi**. For example, **vi-next-word** and **vi-prev-word** move the cursor to the beginning of the next and previous words, respectively. Commands that do not begin with **vi** are generally available in emacs mode.

Use **bind –q** to determine which key sequence is bound to a command:

```
$ bind -q kill-whole-line
kill-whole-line can be invoked via "\C-r".
```

You can also bind text by enclosing it within double quotation marks (emacs mode only):

```
"QQ": "The Linux Operating System"
```

This command causes bash to insert the string **The Linux Operating System** when you type **QQ**.

CONDITIONAL CONSTRUCTS

You can conditionally select parts of the .inputrc file using the **$if** directive. The syntax of the conditional construct is

$if test[=value]
      commands
  [$else
      commands]
$endif

where *test* is **mode, term,** or **bash.** If *test* equals *value* or if *test* is *true*, this structure executes the first set of *commands.* If *test* does not equal *value* or if *test* is *false*, it executes the second set of *commands* if they are present or exits from the structure if they are not present.

The power of the **$if** directive lies in the three types of tests it can perform.

1. You can test to see which mode is currently set.

   ```
   $if mode=vi
   ```

   The preceding test is *true* if the current Readline mode is **vi** and *false* otherwise. You can test for **vi** or **emacs.**

2. You can test the type of terminal.

   ```
   $if term=xterm
   ```

   The preceding test is *true* if the **TERM** variable is set to **xterm.** You can test for any value of **TERM.**

3. You can test the application name.

   ```
   $if bash
   ```

   The preceding test is *true* when you are running bash and not another program that uses the Readline Library. You can test for any application name.

These tests can customize the Readline Library based on the current mode, the type of terminal, and the application you are using. They give you a great deal of power and flexibility when using the Readline Library with bash and other programs.

The following commands in **.inputrc** cause CONTROL-Y to move the cursor to the beginning of the next word regardless of whether bash is in vi or emacs mode:

```
$ cat ~/.inputrc
set editing-mode vi
$if mode=vi
        "\C-y": vi-next-word
    $else
        "\C-y": forward-word
$endif
```

Because bash reads the preceding conditional construct when it is started, you must set the editing mode in **.inputrc**. Changing modes interactively using **set** will not change the binding of CONTROL-Y.

For more information on the Readline Library, open the bash man page and give the command **/^READLINE**, which searches for the word **READLINE** at the beginning of a line.

If Readline commands do not work, log out and log in again

tip   The Bourne Again Shell reads **~/.inputrc** when you log in. After you make changes to this file, you should log out and log in again before testing the changes.

ALIASES

An *alias* is a (usually short) name that the shell translates into another (usually longer) name or (complex) command. Aliases allow you to define new commands by substituting a string for the first token of a simple command. They are typically placed in the **~/.bashrc** startup files so that they are available to interactive subshells.

The syntax of the alias builtin is

alias [name[=value]]

No SPACEs are permitted around the equal sign. If *value* contains SPACEs or TABs, you must enclose *value* between quotation marks. An alias does not accept an argument from the command line in *value*. Use a function (page 321) when you need to use an argument.

An alias does not replace itself, which avoids the possibility of infinite recursion in handling an alias such as the following:

```
$ alias ls='ls -F'
```

You can nest aliases. Aliases are disabled for noninteractive shells (that is, shell scripts). To see a list of the current aliases, give the command **alias**. To view the alias for a particular name, use **alias** followed by the name and nothing else. You can use the **unalias** builtin to remove an alias.

When you give an alias builtin command without any arguments, the shell displays a list of all defined aliases:

```
$ alias
alias ll='ls -l'
alias l='ls -ltr'
alias ls='ls -F'
alias zap='rm -i'
```

Red Hat Linux defines some aliases. Give an **alias** command to see which aliases are in effect. You can delete the aliases you do not want from the appropriate startup file.

SINGLE VERSUS DOUBLE QUOTATION MARKS IN ALIASES

The choice of single or double quotation marks is significant in the alias syntax when the alias includes variables. If you enclose *value* within double quotation marks, any variables that appear in *value* are expanded when the alias is created. If you enclose *value* within single quotation marks, variables are not expanded until the alias is used. The following example illustrates the difference.

The **PWD** keyword variable holds the pathname of the working directory. Alex creates two aliases while he is working in his home directory. Because he uses double quotation marks when he creates the **dirA** alias, the shell substitutes the value of the working directory when he creates this alias. The **alias dirA** command displays the **dirA** alias and shows that the substitution has already taken place:

```
$ echo $PWD
/home/alex
$ alias dirA="echo Working directory is $PWD"
$ alias dirA
alias dirA='echo Working directory is /home/alex'
```

When Alex creates the **dirB** alias, he uses single quotation marks, which prevent the shell from expanding the **$PWD** variable. The **alias dirB** command shows that the **dirB** alias still holds the unexpanded **$PWD** variable:

```
$ alias dirB='echo Working directory is $PWD'
$ alias dirB
alias dirB='echo Working directory is $PWD'
```

After creating the **dirA** and **dirB** aliases, Alex uses cd to make **cars** his working directory and gives each of the aliases as commands. The alias that he created with double quotation marks displays the name of the directory that he created the alias in as the working directory (which is wrong) and the **dirB** alias displays the proper name of the working directory:

```
$ cd cars
$ dirA
Working directory is /home/alex
$ dirB
Working directory is /home/alex/cars
```

How to prevent the shell from invoking an alias

tip   The shell checks only simple, unquoted commands to see if they are aliases. Commands given as relative or absolute pathnames and quoted commands are not checked. When you want to give a command that has an alias but do not want to use the alias, precede the command with a backslash, specify the command's absolute pathname, or give the command as ./*command*.

EXAMPLES OF ALIASES

The following alias allows you to type **r** to repeat the previous command or **r abc** to repeat the last command line that began with **abc**:

```
$ alias r='fc -s'
```

If you use the command **ls –ltr** frequently, you can create an alias that substitutes **ls –ltr** when you give the command **l**:

```
$ alias l='ls -ltr'
$ l
total 41
-rw-r--r--  1 alex    group    30015 Mar  1 2004 flute.ps
-rw-r-----  1 alex    group     3089 Feb 11 2005 XTerm.ad
-rw-r--r--  1 alex    group      641 Apr  1 2005 fixtax.icn
-rw-r--r--  1 alex    group      484 Apr  9 2005 maptax.icn
drwxrwxr-x  2 alex    group     1024 Aug  9 17:41 Tiger
drwxrwxr-x  2 alex    group     1024 Sep 10 11:32 testdir
-rwxr-xr-x  1 alex    group      485 Oct 21 08:03 floor
drwxrwxr-x  2 alex    group     1024 Oct 27 20:19 Test_Emacs
```

Another common use of aliases is to protect yourself from mistakes. The following example substitutes the interactive version of the rm utility when you give the command **zap**:

```
$ alias zap='rm -i'
$ zap f*
rm: remove 'fixtax.icn'? n
rm: remove 'flute.ps'? n
rm: remove 'floor'? n
```

The –i option causes rm to ask you to verify each file that would be deleted, to help you avoid accidentally deleting the wrong file. You can also alias rm with the **rm –i** command: **alias rm='rm –i'**.

The aliases in the next example cause the shell to substitute **ls –l** each time you give an **ll** command and **ls –F** when you use **ls**:

```
$ alias ls='ls -F'
$ alias ll='ls -l'
$ ll
total 41
drwxrwxr-x  2 alex    group     1024 Oct 27 20:19 Test_Emacs/
drwxrwxr-x  2 alex    group     1024 Aug 9 17:41 Tiger/
-rw-r-----  1 alex    group     3089 Feb 11 2005 XTerm.ad
-rw-r--r--  1 alex    group      641 Apr 1 2005 fixtax.icn
-rw-r--r--  1 alex    group    30015 Mar 1 2004 flute.ps
-rwxr-xr-x  1 alex    group      485 Oct 21 08:03 floor*
-rw-r--r--  1 alex    group      484 Apr 9 2005 maptax.icn
drwxrwxr-x  2 alex    group     1024 Sep 10 11:32 testdir/
```

The **–F** option causes ls to print a slash (/) at the end of directory names and an asterisk (✳) at the end of the names of executable files. In this example, the string that replaces the alias **ll** (ls –l) itself contains an alias (ls). When it replaces an alias with its value, the shell looks at the first word of the replacement string to see whether it is an alias. In the preceding example, the replacement string contains the alias ls, so a second substitution occurs to produce the final command ls –F –l. (To avoid a *recursive plunge,* the ls in the replacement text, although an alias, is not expanded a second time.)

When given a list of aliases without the *=value* or *value* field, the alias builtin responds by displaying the value of each defined alias. The alias builtin reports an error if an alias has not been defined:

```
$ alias ll l ls zap wx
alias ll='ls -l'
alias l='ls -ltr'
alias ls='ls -F'
alias zap='rm -i'
bash: alias: wx: not found
```

You can avoid alias substitution by preceding the aliased command with a backslash (\):

```
$ \ls
Test_Emacs XTerm.ad  flute.ps  maptax.icn
Tiger      fixtax.icn floor     testdir
```

Because the replacement of an alias name with the alias value does not change the rest of the command line, any arguments are still received by the command that gets executed:

```
$ ll f*
-rw-r--r--  1 alex   group     641 Apr  1 2005 fixtax.icn
-rw-r--r--  1 alex   group   30015 Mar  1 2004 flute.ps
-rwxr-xr-x  1 alex   group     485 Oct 21 08:03 floor*
```

You can remove an alias with the unalias builtin. When the **zap** alias is removed, it is no longer displayed with the alias builtin and its subsequent use results in an error message:

```
$ unalias zap
$ alias
alias ll='ls -l'
alias l='ls -ltr'
alias ls='ls -F'
$ zap maptax.icn
bash: zap: command not found
```

FUNCTIONS

A shell function is similar to a shell script in that it stores a series of commands for execution at a later time. However, because the shell stores a function in the computer's main memory (RAM) instead of in a file on the disk, the shell can access it more quickly than the shell can access a script. The shell also preprocesses (parses) a function so that it starts up more quickly than a script. Finally the shell executes a shell function in the same shell that called it. If you define too many functions, the overhead of starting a subshell (as when you run a script) can become unacceptable.

You can declare a shell function in the ~/.bash_profile startup file, in the script that uses it, or directly from the command line. You can remove functions with the unset builtin. The shell does not keep functions once you log out.

Removing variables and functions

tip   If you have a shell variable and a function with the same name, using unset removes the shell variable. If you then use unset again with the same name, it removes the function.

The syntax that declares a shell function is

[function] function-name ()
{
   commands
}

where the word *function* is optional, *function-name* is the name you use to call the function, and *commands* comprise the list of commands the function executes when you call it. The *commands* can be anything you would include in a shell script, including calls to other functions.

The first brace ({) can appear on the same line as the function name. Aliases and variables are expanded when a function is read, not when it is executed. You can use the **break** statement (page 900) within a function to terminate its execution.

Shell functions are useful as a shorthand as well as to define special commands. The following function starts a process named **process** in the background, with the output normally displayed by **process** being saved in **.process.out**:

```
start_process() {
process > .process.out 2>&1 &
}
```

The next example shows how to create a simple function that displays the date, a header, and a list of the people who are using the system. This function runs the same commands as the **whoson** script described on page 273. In this example the function is being entered from the keyboard. The greater-than (>) signs are secondary shell prompts (**PS2**); do not enter them.

```
$ function whoson ()
> {
>    date
>    echo "Users Currently Logged On"
>    who
> }

$ whoson
Sun Aug  7 15:44:58 PDT 2005
Users Currently Logged On
hls       console      Aug  6 08:59  (:0)
alex      pts/4        Aug  6 09:33  (0.0)
jenny     pts/7        Aug  6 09:23  (bravo.example.com)
```

Functions in startup files If you want to have the **whoson** function always be available without having to enter it each time you log in, put its definition in *~/.bash_profile*. Then run *.bash_profile*, using the **.** (dot) command to put the changes into effect immediately:

```
$ cat ~/.bash_profile
export TERM=vt100
stty kill '^u'
whoson ()
{
    date
    echo "Users Currently Logged On"
    who
}
$ . ~/.bash_profile
```

You can specify arguments when you call a function. Within the function these arguments are available as positional parameters (page 920). The following example shows the **arg1** function entered from the keyboard.

```
$ arg1 ( ) {
> echo "$1"
> }

$ arg1 first_arg
first_arg
```

See the function **switch** () on page 269 for another example of a function. "Functions" on page 917 discusses the use of local and global variables within a function.

optional The following function allows you to export variables using tcsh syntax. The **env** builtin lists all environment variables and their values and verifies that **setenv** worked correctly:

```
$ cat .bash_profile
...
# setenv - keep tcsh users happy
function setenv()
{
    if [ $# -eq 2 ]
        then
            eval $1=$2
            export $1
        else
            echo "Usage: setenv NAME VALUE" 1>&2
    fi
}
$ . ~/.bash_profile
$ setenv TCL_LIBRARY /usr/local/lib/tcl
$ env | grep TCL_LIBRARY
TCL_LIBRARY=/usr/local/lib/tcl
```

eval The **$#** special parameter (page 921) takes on the value of the number of command line arguments. This function uses the **eval** builtin to force bash to scan the command **$1=$2** *twice*. Because **$1=$2** begins with a dollar sign ($), the shell treats the entire string as a single token—a command. With variable substitution performed, the command name becomes **TCL_LIBRARY=/usr/local/lib/tcl**, which results in an error. Using eval, a second scanning splits the string into the three desired tokens, and the correct assignment occurs.

CONTROLLING bash FEATURES AND OPTIONS

This section explains how to control bash features and options using command line options and the set and shopt builtins.

COMMAND LINE OPTIONS

Two kinds of command line options are available: short and long. Short options consist of a hyphen followed by a letter; long options have two hyphens followed by multiple characters. Long options must appear before short options on a command line that calls bash. Table 9-12 lists some commonly used command line options.

Table 9-12   Command line options

Option	Explanation	Syntax
Help	Displays a usage message.	**--help**
No edit	Prevents users from using the Readline Library (page 312) to edit command lines in an interactive shell.	**--noediting**
No profile	Prevents reading these startup files (page 267): **/etc/profile**, **~/.bash_profile**, **~/.bash_login**, and **~/.profile**.	**--noprofile**
No rc	Prevents reading the **~/.bashrc** startup file (page 267). This option is on by default if the shell is called as **sh**.	**--norc**
POSIX	Runs bash in POSIX mode.	**--posix**
Version	Displays bash version information and exits.	**--version**
Login	Causes bash to run as though it were a login shell.	**-l** (lowercase "l")
shopt	Runs a shell with the *opt* shopt option (page 325). A **-O** (uppercase "O") sets the option; **+O** unsets it.	[±]O [*opt*]
End of options	On the command line, signals the end of options. Subsequent tokens are treated as arguments even if they begin with a hyphen (–).	--

SHELL FEATURES

You can control the behavior of the Bourne Again Shell by turning features on and off. Different features use different methods to turn features on and off. The set builtin controls one group of features, while the shopt builtin controls another group. You can also control many features from the command line you use to call bash.

Features, options, variables?

tip To avoid confusing terminology, this book refers to the various shell behaviors that you can control as *features*. The bash info page refers to them as "options" and "values of variables controlling optional shell behavior."

set ±o: TURNS SHELL FEATURES ON AND OFF

The set builtin, when used with the –o or +o option, enables, disables, and lists certain bash features. For example, the following command turns on the **noclobber** feature (page 213):

```
$ set -o noclobber
```

You can turn this feature off (the default) by giving the command

```
$ set +o noclobber
```

The command **set –o** without an option lists each of the features controlled by set followed by its state (on or off). The command **set +o** without an option lists the same features in a form that you can use as input to the shell. Table 9-13 lists bash features.

shopt: TURNS SHELL FEATURES ON AND OFF

The shopt (shell option) builtin enables, disables, and lists certain bash features that control the behavior of the shell. For example, the following command causes bash to include filenames that begin with a period (.) when it expands ambiguous file references (the –s stands for *set*):

```
$ shopt -s dotglob
```

You can turn this feature off (the default) by giving the command (the –**u** stands for *unset*)

```
$ shopt -u dotglob
```

The shell displays how a feature is set if you give the name of the feature as the only argument to shopt:

```
$ shopt dotglob
dotglob         off
```

The command **shopt** without any options or arguments lists the features controlled by shopt and their state. The command **shopt –s** without an argument lists the features controlled by shopt that are set or on. The command **shopt –u** lists the features that are unset or off. Table 9-13 lists bash features.

Setting set ±o features using shopt

tip You can use shopt to set/unset features that are otherwise controlled by **set ±o**. Use the regular shopt syntax with **–s** or **–u** and include the **–o** option. For example, the following command turns on the **noclobber** feature:

```
$ shopt -o -s noclobber
```

Table 9-13   bash features

Feature	Description	Syntax	Alternate syntax
allexport	Automatically exports all variables and functions that you create or modify after giving this command.	**set −o allexport**	**set −a**
braceexpand	Causes bash to perform brace expansion (the default; page 330).	**set −o braceexpand**	**set −B**
cdspell	Corrects minor spelling errors in directory names used as arguments to cd.	**shopt −s cdspell**	
cmdhist	Saves all lines of a multiline command in the same history entry, adding semicolons as needed.	**shopt −s cmdhist**	
dotglob	Causes shell special characters (wildcards; page 221) in an ambiguous file reference to match a leading period in a filename. By default special characters do not to match a leading period. You must always specify the filenames . and .. explicitly because no pattern ever matches them.	**shopt −s dotglob**	
emacs	Specifies emacs editing mode for command line editing (the default; page 313).	**set −o emacs**	
errexit	Causes bash to exit when a simple command (not a control structure) fails.	**set −o errexit**	**set −e**
execfail	Causes a shell script to continue running when it cannot find the file that is given as an argument to exec. By default a script terminates when exec cannot find the file that is given as its argument.	**shopt −s execfail**	
expand_aliases	Causes aliases (page 318) to be expanded (by default it is on for interactive shells and off for noninteractive shells).	**shopt −s expand_alias**	
hashall	Causes bash to remember where commands it has found using **PATH** (page 292) are located (default).	**set −o hashall**	**set −h**
histappend	Causes bash to append the history list to the file named by **HISTFILE** (page 302) when the shell exits. By default bash overwrites this file.	**shopt −s histappend**	
histexpand	Causes the history mechanism (which uses exclamation points; page 306) to work (default). Turn this feature off to turn off history expansion.	**set −o histexpand**	**set −H**

Table 9-13 bash features (continued)

history	Enable command history (on by default; page 302).	**set –o history**	
ignoreeof	Specifies that bash must receive ten EOF characters before it exits. Useful on noisy dial-up lines.	**set –o ignoreeof**	
monitor	Enables job control (on by default, page 280).	**set –o monitor**	**set –m**
nocaseglob	Causes ambiguous file references (page 221) to match filenames without regard to case (off by default).	**shopt –s nocaseglob**	
noclobber	Helps prevent overwriting files (off by default; page 213).	**set –o noclobber**	**set –C**
noglob	Disables pathname expansion (off by default; page 221).	**set –o noglob**	**set –f**
notify	With job control (page 280) enabled, reports the termination status of background jobs immediately. The default behavior is to display the status just before the next prompt.	**set –o notify**	**set –b**
nounset	Displays an error and exits from a shell script when you use an unset variable in an interactive shell. The default is to display a null value for an unset variable.	**set –o nounset**	**set –u**
nullglob	Causes bash to expand ambiguous file references (page 221) that do not match a filename to a null string. By default bash passes these file references without expanding them.	**shopt –s nullglob**	
posix	Runs bash in POSIX mode.	**set –o posix**	
verbose	Displays command lines as bash reads them.	**set –o verbose**	**set –v**
vi	Specifies vi editing mode for command line editing (page 312).	**set –o vi**	
xpg_echo	Causes the echo builtin to expand backslash escape sequences without the need for the **–e** option (page 904).	**shopt –s xpg_echo**	
xtrace	Turns on shell debugging (page 890).	**set –o xtrace**	**set –x**

PROCESSING THE COMMAND LINE

Whether you are working interactively or running a shell script, bash needs to read a command line before it can start processing it—bash always reads at least one line before processing a command. Some bash builtins, such as **if** and **case**, as well as functions and quoted strings, span multiple lines. When bash recognizes a command that covers more than one line, it reads the entire command before processing it. In interactive sessions bash prompts you with the secondary prompt (**PS2**, **>** by default; page 295) as you type each line of a multiline command until it recognizes the end of the command:

```
$ echo 'hi
> end'
hi
end
$ function hello () {
> echo hello there
> }
$
```

After reading a command line, bash applies history expansion and alias substitution to the line.

HISTORY EXPANSION

"Reexecuting and Editing Commands" on page 304 discusses the commands you can give to modify and reexecute command lines from the history list. History expansion is the process that bash uses to turn a history command into an executable command line. For example, when you give the command **!!**, history expansion changes that command line so it is the same as the previous one. History expansion is turned on by default for interactive shells; **set +o histexpand** turns it off. History expansion does not apply to noninteractive shells (shell scripts).

ALIAS SUBSTITUTION

Aliases (page 318) substitute a string for the first word of a simple command. By default aliases are turned on for interactive shells and off for noninteractive shells. Give the command **shopt –u expand_aliases** to turn aliases off.

PARSING AND SCANNING THE COMMAND LINE

After processing history commands and aliases, bash does not execute the command immediately. One of the first things the shell does is to *parse* (isolate strings of characters in) the command line into tokens or words. The shell then scans each token for special characters and patterns that instruct the shell to take certain actions. These actions can involve substituting one word or words for another. When the shell parses the following command line, it breaks it into three tokens (**cp**, **~/letter**, and **.**):

```
$ cp ~/letter .
```

After separating tokens and before executing the command, the shell scans the tokens and performs *command line expansion*.

COMMAND LINE EXPANSION

In both interactive and noninteractive use, the shell transforms the command line using *command line expansion* before passing the command line to the program being called. You can use a shell without knowing much about command line expansion, but you can use what a shell has to offer to a better advantage with an understanding of this topic. This section covers Bourne Again Shell command line expansion.

The Bourne Again Shell scans each token for the various types of expansion and substitution in the following order. Most of these processes expand a word into a single word. Only brace expansion, word splitting, and pathname expansion can change the number of words in a command (except for the expansion of the variable "$@"—page 922).

1. Brace expansion (page 330)

2. Tilde expansion (page 331)

3. Parameter and variable expansion (page 332)

4. Arithmetic expansion (page 332)

5. Command substitution (page 334)

6. Word splitting (page 335)

7. Pathname expansion (page 335)

8. Process substitution (page 337)

Quote removal   After bash finishes with the preceding list, it removes from the command line single quotation marks, double quotation marks, and backslashes that are not a result of an expansion. This process is called *quote removal*.

ORDER OF EXPANSION

The order in which bash carries out these steps affects the interpretation of commands. For example, if you set a variable to a value that looks like the instruction for output redirection and then enter a command that uses the variable's value to perform redirection, you might expect bash to redirect the output.

```
$ SENDIT="> /tmp/saveit"
$ echo xxx $SENDIT
xxx > /tmp/saveit
$ cat /tmp/saveit
cat: /tmp/saveit: No such file or directory
```

In fact, the shell does *not* redirect the output—it recognizes input and output redirection before it evaluates variables. When it executes the command line, the shell checks for redirection and, finding none, evaluates the SENDIT variable. After replacing the variable with **> /tmp/saveit,** bash passes the arguments to echo, which dutifully copies its arguments to standard output. No **/tmp/saveit** file is created.

The following sections provide more detailed descriptions of the steps involved in command processing. Keep in mind that double and single quotation marks cause the shell to behave differently when performing expansions. Double quotation marks permit parameter and variable expansion but suppress other types of expansion. Single quotation marks suppress all types of expansion.

BRACE EXPANSION

Brace expansion, which originated in the C Shell, provides a convenient way to specify filenames when pathname expansion does not apply. Although brace expansion is almost always used to specify filenames, the mechanism can be used to generate arbitrary strings; the shell does not attempt to match the brace notation with the names of existing files.

Brace expansion is turned on in interactive and noninteractive shells by default; you can turn it off with **set +o braceexpand.** The shell also uses braces to isolate variable names (page 288).

The following example illustrates how brace expansion works. The ls command does not display any output because there are no files in the working directory. The echo builtin displays the strings that the shell generates with brace expansion. In this case the strings do not match filenames (there are no files in the working directory.)

```
$ ls
$ echo chap_{one,two,three}.txt
chap_one.txt chap_two.txt chap_three.txt
```

The shell expands the comma-separated strings inside the braces in the echo command into a SPACE-separated list of strings. Each string from the list is prepended with the string **chap_,** called the *preamble,* and appended with the string **.txt,** called the *postscript.* Both the preamble and the postscript are optional. The left-to-right order of the strings within the braces is preserved in the expansion. For the shell to treat the left and right braces specially and for brace expansion to occur, at least one comma and no unquoted whitespace characters must be inside the braces. You can nest brace expansions.

Brace expansion is useful when there is a long preamble or postscript. The following example copies the four files **main.c, f1.c, f2.c,** and **tmp.c** located in the **/usr/local/src/C** directory to the working directory:

```
$ cp /usr/local/src/C/{main,f1,f2,tmp}.c .
```

You can also use brace expansion to create directories with related names:

```
$ ls -F
file1  file2  file3
$ mkdir vrs{A,B,C,D,E}
$ ls -F
file1  file2  file3  vrsA/  vrsB/  vrsC/  vrsD/  vrsE/
```

The **–F** option causes ls to display a slash (/) after a directory and an asterisk (✲) after an executable file.

If you tried to use an ambiguous file reference instead of braces to specify the directories, the result would be different (and not what you wanted):

```
$ rmdir vrs✲
$ mkdir vrs[A-E]
$ ls -F
file1  file2  file3  vrs[A-E]/
```

An ambiguous file reference matches the names of existing files. Because it found no filenames matching **vrs[A–E]**, bash passed the ambiguous file reference to mkdir, which created a directory with that name. Page 223 has a discussion of brackets in ambiguous file references.

TILDE EXPANSION

Chapter 6 showed a shorthand notation to specify your home directory or the home directory of another user. This section provides a more detailed explanation of *tilde expansion*.

The tilde (~) is a special character when it appears at the start of a token on a command line. When it sees a tilde in this position, bash looks at the following string of characters—up to the first slash (/) or to the end of the word if there is no slash—as a possible username. If this possible username is null (that is, if the tilde appears as a word by itself or if it is immediately followed by a slash), the shell substitutes the value of the **HOME** variable for the tilde. The following example demonstrates this expansion, where the last command copies the file named **letter** from Alex's home directory to the working directory:

```
$ echo $HOME
/home/alex
$ echo ~
/home/alex
$ echo ~/letter
/home/alex/letter
$ cp ~/letter .
```

If the string of characters following the tilde forms a valid username, the shell substitutes the path of the home directory associated with that username for the tilde and name. If it is not null and not a valid username, the shell does not make any substitution:

```
$ echo ~jenny
/home/jenny
$ echo ~root
/root
$ echo ~xx
~xx
```

Tildes are also used in directory stack manipulation (page 282). In addition, **~+** is a synonym for **PWD** (the name of the working directory), and **~–** is a synonym for **OLDPWD** (the name of the previous working directory).

PARAMETER AND VARIABLE EXPANSION

On a command line a dollar sign ($) that is not followed by an open parenthesis introduces parameter or variable expansion. *Parameters* include command line, or positional, parameters (page 920) and special parameters (page 918). *Variables* include user-created variables (page 286) and keyword variables (page 291). The bash man and info pages do not make this distinction, however.

Parameters and variables are not expanded if they are enclosed within single quotation marks or if the leading dollar sign is escaped (preceded with a backslash). If they are enclosed within double quotation marks, the shell expands parameters and variables.

ARITHMETIC EXPANSION

The shell performs *arithmetic expansion* by evaluating an arithmetic expression and replacing it with the result. Under bash the syntax for arithmetic expansion is

> *$((expression))*

The shell evaluates *expression* and replaces *$((expression))* with the result of the evaluation. This syntax is similar to the syntax used for command substitution [*$(...)*] and performs a parallel function. You can use *$((expression))* as an argument to a command or in place of any numeric value on a command line.

The rules for forming *expression* are the same as those found in the C programming language; all standard C arithmetic operators are available (see Table 28-8 on page 943). Arithmetic in bash is done using integers. Unless you use variables of type integer (page 291) or actual integers, however, the shell must convert string-valued variables to integers for the purpose of the arithmetic evaluation.

You do not need to precede variable names within *expression* with a dollar sign ($). In the following example, an arithmetic expression determines how many years are left until age 60:

```
$ cat age_check
#!/bin/bash
echo -n "How old are you? "
read age
echo "Wow, in $((60-age)) years, you'll be 60!"

$ age_check
How old are you? 55
Wow, in 5 years, you'll be 60!
```

You do not need to enclose the *expression* within quotation marks because bash does not perform filename expansion on it. This feature makes it easier for you to use an asterisk (✻) for multiplication, as the following example shows:

```
$ echo There are $((60*60*24*365)) seconds in a non-leap year.
There are 31536000 seconds in a non-leap year.
```

The next example uses wc, cut, arithmetic expansion, and command substitution to estimate the number of pages required to print the contents of the file **letter.txt**. The output of the wc (word count) utility used with the **–l** option is the number of lines in the file, in columns 1 through 4, followed by a SPACE and the name of the file (the first command following). The cut utility with the **–c1–4** option extracts the first four columns.

```
$ wc -l letter.txt
351 letter.txt
$ wc -l letter.txt | cut -c1-4
351
```

The dollar sign and single parenthesis instruct the shell to perform command substitution; the dollar sign and double parentheses indicate arithmetic expansion:

```
$ echo $(( $(wc -l letter.txt | cut -c1-4)/66 + 1))
6
```

The preceding example sends standard output from wc to standard input of cut via a pipe. Because of command substitution, the output of both commands replaces the commands between the $(and the matching) on the command line. Arithmetic expansion then divides this number by 66, the number of lines on a page. A 1 is added at the end because the integer division results in any remainder being discarded.

Fewer dollar signs ($)

tip When you use variables within **$((** and **))**, the dollar signs that precede individual variable references are optional:

```
$ x=23 y=37
$ echo $((2*$x + 3*$y))
157
$ echo $((2*x + 3*y))
157
```

Another way to get the same result without using cut is to redirect the input to wc instead of having wc get its input from a file you name on the command line. When you redirect its input, wc does not display the name of the file:

```
$ wc -l < letter.txt
    351
```

It is common practice to assign the result of arithmetic expansion to a variable:

```
$ numpages=$(( $(wc -l < letter.txt)/66 + 1))
```

let builtin The let builtin evaluates arithmetic expressions just as the $(( )) syntax does. The following command is equivalent to the preceding one:

```
$ let "numpages=$(wc -l < letter.txt)/66 + 1"
```

The double quotation marks keep the SPACEs (both those you can see and those that result from the command substitution) from separating the expression into separate arguments to let. The value of the last expression determines the exit status of let. If the value of the last expression is 0, the exit status of let is 1; otherwise, the exit status is 0.

You can give multiple arguments to let on a single command line:

```
$ let a=5+3 b=7+2
$ echo $a $b
8 9
```

When you refer to variables when doing arithmetic expansion with let or $(( )), the shell does not require you to begin the variable name with a dollar sign ($). Nevertheless, it is a good practice to do so, as in most places you must include this symbol.

COMMAND SUBSTITUTION

Command substitution replaces a command with the output of that command. The preferred syntax for command substitution under bash follows:

> $(*command*)

Under bash you can also use the following syntax:

> ` *command* `

The shell executes *command* within a subshell and replaces *command*, along with the surrounding punctuation, with standard output of *command*.

In the following example, the shell executes pwd and substitutes the output of the command for the command and surrounding punctuation. Then the shell passes the output of the command, which is now an argument, to echo, which displays it.

```
$ echo $(pwd)
/home/alex
```

The next script assigns the output of the pwd builtin to the variable **where** and displays a message containing the value of this variable:

```
$ cat where
where=$(pwd)
echo "You are using the $where directory."
$ where
You are using the /home/jenny directory.
```

Although it illustrates how to assign the output of a command to a variable, this example is not realistic. You can more directly display the output of pwd without using a variable:

```
$ cat where2
echo "You are using the $(pwd) directory."
$ where2
You are using the /home/jenny directory.
```

The following command uses find to locate files with the name **README** in the directory tree with its root at the working directory. This list of files is standard output of find and becomes the list of arguments to ls.

```
$ ls -l $(find . -name README -print)
```

The next command line shows the older `*command*` syntax:

```
$ ls -l `find . -name README -print`
```

One advantage of the newer syntax is that it avoids the rather arcane rules for token handling, quotation mark handling, and escaped back ticks within the old syntax. Another advantage of the new syntax is that it can be nested, unlike the old syntax. For example, you can produce a long listing of all **README** files whose size exceeds the size of **./README** with the following command:

```
$ ls -l $(find . -name README -size +$(echo $(cat ./README | wc -c)c ) -print )
```

Try giving this command after giving a **set –x** command (page 890) to see how bash expands it. If there is no **README** file, you just get the output of ls **–l**.

For additional scripts that use command substitution, see pages 886, 905, and 935.

$((Versus $(

tip   The symbols **$((** constitute a separate token. They introduce an arithmetic expression, not a command substitution. Thus, if you want to use a parenthesized subshell (page 279) within **$()**, you must insert a SPACE between the **$(** and the next **(**.

WORD SPLITTING

The results of parameter and variable expansion, command substitution, and arithmetic expansion are candidates for word splitting. Using each character of **IFS** (page 295) as a possible delimiter, bash splits these candidates into words or tokens. If **IFS** is unset, bash uses its default value (SPACE-TAB-NEWLINE). If **IFS** is null, bash does not split words.

PATHNAME EXPANSION

Pathname expansion (page 221), also called *filename generation* or *globbing,* is the process of interpreting ambiguous file references and substituting the appropriate list of filenames. Unless **noglob** (page 327) is set, the shell performs this function when it encounters an ambiguous file reference—a token containing any of the unquoted characters *, ?, [, or]. If bash cannot locate any files that match the specified pattern, the token with the ambiguous file reference is left alone. The shell does not delete the token or replace it with a null string but rather passes it to the program as is (except see **nullglob** on page 327).

In the first echo command in the following example, the shell expands the ambiguous file reference **tmp*** and passes three tokens (**tmp1**, **tmp2**, and **tmp3**) to echo. The echo builtin displays the three filenames it was passed by the shell. After rm removes the three **tmp*** files, the shell finds no filenames that match **tmp*** when it tries to expand it. Thus it passes the unexpanded string to the echo builtin, which displays the string it was passed.

```
$ ls
tmp1 tmp2 tmp3
$ echo tmp*
tmp1 tmp2 tmp3
$ rm tmp*
$ echo tmp*
tmp*
```

A period that either starts a pathname or follows a slash (/) in a pathname must be matched explicitly unless you have set **dotglob** (page 326). The option **nocaseglob** (page 327) causes ambiguous file references to match filenames without regard to case.

Quotation marks Putting double quotation marks around an argument causes the shell to suppress pathname and all other expansion except parameter and variable expansion. Putting single quotation marks around an argument suppresses all types of expansion. The second echo command in the following example shows the variable **$alex** between double quotation marks, which allow variable expansion. As a result the shell expands the variable to its value: **sonar**. This expansion does not occur in the third echo command, which uses single quotation marks. Because neither single nor double quotation marks allow pathname expansion, the last two commands display the unexpanded argument **tmp***.

```
$ echo tmp* $alex
tmp1 tmp2 tmp3 sonar
$ echo "tmp* $alex"
tmp* sonar
$ echo 'tmp* $alex'
tmp* $alex
```

The shell distinguishes between the value of a variable and a reference to the variable and does not expand ambiguous file references if they occur in the value of a variable. As a consequence you can assign to a variable a value that includes special characters, such as an asterisk (*).

Levels of expansion In the next example, the working directory has three files whose names begin with **letter**. When you assign the value **letter*** to the variable **var**, the shell does not expand the ambiguous file reference because it occurs in the value of a variable (in the assignment statement for the variable). No quotation marks surround the string **letter***; context alone prevents the expansion. After the assignment the set builtin (with the help of grep) shows the value of **var** to be **letter***.

The three **echo** commands demonstrate three levels of expansion. When **$var** is quoted with single quotation marks, the shell performs no expansion and passes the character string **$var** to echo, which displays it. When you use double quotation marks, the shell performs variable expansion only and substitutes the value of the **var** variable for its name, preceded by a dollar sign. No pathname expansion is performed on this command because double quotation marks suppress it. In the final command, the shell, without the limitations of quotation marks, performs variable substitution and then pathname expansion before passing the arguments to echo.

```
$ ls letter*
letter1 letter2  letter3
$ var=letter*
$ set | grep var
var='letter*'
$ echo '$var'
$var
$ echo "$var"
letter*
$ echo $var
letter1 letter2 letter3
```

PROCESS SUBSTITUTION

A special feature of the Bourne Again Shell is the ability to replace filename arguments with processes. An argument with the syntax <*(command)* causes **command** to be executed and the output written to a named pipe (FIFO). The shell replaces that argument with the name of the pipe. If that argument is then used as the name of an input file during processing, the output of **command** is read. Similarly an argument with the syntax >*(command)* is replaced by the name of a pipe that **command** reads as standard input.

The following example uses sort (page 133) with the **–m** (merge, which works correctly only if the input files are already sorted) option to combine two word lists into a single list. Each word list is generated by a pipe that extracts words matching a pattern from a file and sorts the words in that list.

```
$ sort -m -f <(grep "[^A-Z]..$" memo1 | sort) <(grep ".*aba.*" memo2 |sort)
```

CHAPTER SUMMARY

The shell is both a command interpreter and a programming language. As a command interpreter, the shell executes commands you enter in response to its prompt. As a programming language, the shell executes commands from files called shell scripts. When you start a shell, it typically runs one or more startup files.

Running a shell script Assuming that the file holding a shell script is in the working directory, there are three basic ways to execute the shell script from the command line.

1. Type the simple filename of the file that holds the script.

2. Type a relative pathname, including the simple filename preceded by ./.

3. Type **bash** followed by the name of the file.

Technique 1 requires that the working directory be in the **PATH** variable. Techniques 1 and 2 require that you have execute and read permission for the file holding the script. Technique 3 requires that you have read permission for the file holding the script.

Job control
A job is one or more commands connected by pipes. You can bring a job running in the background into the foreground by using the fg builtin. You can put a foreground job into the background by using the bg builtin, provided that you first suspend the job by pressing the suspend key (typically CONTROL-Z). Use the jobs builtin to see which jobs are running or suspended.

Variables
The shell allows you to define variables. You can declare and initialize a variable by assigning a value to it; you can remove a variable declaration by using unset. Variables are local to a process unless they are exported using the export builtin to make them available to child processes. Variables you declare are called *user-created* variables. The shell also defines called *keyword* variables. Within a shell script you can work with the command line (*positional*) parameters the script was called with.

Process
Each process has a unique identification (PID) number and is the execution of a single Linux command. When you give it a command, the shell forks a new (child) process to execute the command, unless the command is built into the shell (page 225). While the child process is running, the shell is in a state called sleep. By ending a command line with an ampersand (&), you can run a child process in the background and bypass the sleep state so that the shell prompt returns immediately after you press RETURN. Each command in a shell script forks a separate process, each of which may in turn fork other processes. When a process terminates, it returns its exit status to its parent process. An exit status of zero signifies success and nonzero signifies failure.

History
The history mechanism, a feature adapted from the C Shell, maintains a list of recently issued command lines, also called *events,* that provides a way to reexecute previous commands quickly. There are several ways to work with the history list; one of the easiest is to use a command line editor.

Command line editors
When using an interactive Bourne Again Shell, you can edit your command line and commands from the history file, using either of the Bourne Again Shell's command line editors (vi[m] or emacs). When you use the vi(m) command line editor, you start in Input mode, unlike the way you normally enter vi(m). You can switch between Command and Input modes. The emacs editor is modeless and distinguishes commands from editor input by recognizing control characters as commands.

Aliases
An alias is a name that the shell translates into another name or (complex) command. Aliases allow you to define new commands by substituting a string for the first token of a simple command.

Functions
A shell function is a series of commands that, unlike a shell script, are parsed prior to being stored in memory so that they run faster than shell scripts. Shell scripts are parsed at runtime and are stored on disk. A function can be defined on the command line or within a shell script. If you want the function definition to remain in effect across login sessions, you can define it in a startup file. Like the functions of a

programming language, a shell function is called by giving its name followed by any arguments.

Shell features   There are several ways to customize the shell's behavior. You can use options on the command line when you call bash and you can use the bash set and shopt builtins to turn features on and off.

Command line expansion   When it processes a command line, the Bourne Again Shell may replace some words with expanded text. Most types of command line expansion are invoked by the appearance of a special character within a word (for example, a leading dollar sign denotes a variable). See Table 9-6 on page 299 for a list of special characters. The expansions take place in a specific order. Following the history and alias expansions, the common expansions are parameter and variable expansion, command substitution, and pathname expansion. Surrounding a word with double quotation marks suppresses all types of expansion except parameter and variable expansion. Single quotation marks suppress all types of expansion, as does quoting (escaping) a special character by preceding it with a backslash.

EXERCISES

1. Explain the following unexpected result:

```
$ whereis date
date: /bin/date ...
$ echo $PATH
.:/usr/local/bin:/usr/bin:/bin
$ cat > date
echo "This is my own version of date."
$ date
Tue May 24 11:45:49 PDT 2005
```

2. What are two ways you can execute a shell script when you do not have execute access permission for the file containing the script? Can you execute a shell script if you do not have read access permission for the file containing the script?

3. What is the purpose of the **PATH** variable?

   a. Set the **PATH** variable so that it causes the shell to search the following directories in order:

      • **/usr/local/bin**

      • **/usr/bin**

      • **/bin**

      • **/usr/kerberos/bin**

      • The **bin** directory in your home directory

• The working directory

b. If there is a file named **doit** in **/usr/bin** and another file with the same name in your **~/bin**, which one will be executed? (Assume that you have execute permission for both files.)

c. If your **PATH** variable is not set to search the working directory, how can you execute a program located there?

d. Which command can you use to add the directory **/usr/games** to the end of the list of directories in **PATH**?

4. Assume that you have made the following assignment:

```
$ person=jenny
```

Give the output of each of the following commands:

a. echo $person

b. echo '$person'

c. echo "$person"

5. The following shell script adds entries to a file named **journal-file** in your home directory. This script helps you keep track of phone conversations and meetings.

```
$ cat journal
# journal: add journal entries to the file
# $HOME/journal-file

file=$HOME/journal-file
date >> $file
echo -n "Enter name of person or group: "
read name
echo "$name" >> $file
echo >> $file
cat >> $file
echo "-------------------------------------------------------" >> $file
echo >> $file
```

a. What do you have to do to the script to be able to execute it?

b. Why does the script use the read builtin (page 927) the first time it accepts input from the terminal and the cat utility the second time?

6. Assume that the **/home/jenny/grants/biblios** and **/home/jenny/biblios** directories exist. Give Jenny's working directory after she executes each sequence of commands given. Explain what happens in each case.

a.

```
$ pwd
/home/jenny/grants
$ CDPATH=$(pwd)
```

```
$ cd
$ cd biblios
```

b.

```
$ pwd
/home/jenny/grants
$ CDPATH=$(pwd)
$ cd $HOME/biblios
```

7. Name two ways you can identify the PID number of your login shell.

8. Give the following command:

```
$ sleep 30 | cat /etc/inittab
```

Is there any output from sleep? Where does cat get its input from? What has to happen before the shell displays another prompt?

ADVANCED EXERCISES

9. Write a sequence of commands or a script that demonstrates that variable expansion occurs before pathname expansion.

10. Write a shell script that outputs the name of the shell that is executing it.

11. Explain the behavior of the following shell script:

```
$ cat quote_demo
twoliner="This is line 1.
This is line 2."
echo "$twoliner"
echo $twoliner
```

a. How many arguments does each echo command see in this script? Explain.

b. Redefine the **IFS** shell variable so that the output of the second echo is the same as the first.

12. Add the exit status of the previous command to your prompt so that it behaves similarly to the following:

```
$ [0] ls xxx
ls: xxx: No such file or directory
$ [1]
```

13. The dirname utility treats its argument as a pathname and writes to standard output the path prefix—that is, everything up to but not including the last component:

```
$ dirname a/b/c/d
a/b/c
```

If you give **dirname** a simple filename (no **/** characters) as an argument, **dirname** writes a **.** to standard output:

```
$ dirname simple
.
```

Implement dirname as a bash function. Make sure that it behaves sensibly when given such arguments as **/**.

14. Implement the basename utility, which writes the last component of its pathname argument to standard output, as a bash function. For example, given the pathname **a/b/c/d**, basename writes **d** to standard output:

```
$ basename a/b/c/d
d
```

15. The Linux basename utility has an optional second argument. If you give the command **basename** *path suffix*, basename removes the *suffix* and the prefix from *path*:

```
$ basename src/shellfiles/prog.bash .bash
prog
$ basename src/shellfiles/prog.bash .c
prog.bash
```

Add this feature to the function you wrote for exercise 14.

10

NETWORKING AND THE INTERNET

The communications facilities linking computers are continually improving, allowing faster and more economical connections. The earliest computers were unconnected stand-alone systems. To transfer information from one system to another, you had to store it in some form (usually magnetic tape, paper tape, or punch cards—called IBM or Hollerith cards), carry it to a compatible system, and read it back in. A notable advance occurred when computers began to exchange data over serial lines, although the transfer rate was slow (hundreds of bits per second). People quickly invented new ways to take advantage of this computing power, such as email, news retrieval, and bulletin board services. With the speed of today's networks, a piece of email can cross the country or even travel halfway around the world in a few seconds.

Today it would be difficult to find a computer facility that does not include a LAN to link its systems. Linux systems are typically attached to an *Ethernet* (page 1031) network. Wireless networks are also prevalent. Large computer facilities usually maintain several networks, often of different types, and almost certainly have connections to larger networks (companywide or campuswide and beyond).

Internet   The Internet is a loosely administered network of networks (an *internetwork*) that links computers on diverse LANs around the globe. An internet (small *i*) is a generic network of networks that may share some parts in common with the public Internet. It is the Internet that makes it possible to send an email message to a colleague thousands of miles away and receive a reply within minutes. A related term, *intranet,* refers to the networking infrastructure within a company or other institution. Intranets are usually private; access to them from external networks may be limited and carefully controlled, typically using firewalls (page 349).

Network services   Over the past decade many network services have emerged and become standardized. On Linux and UNIX systems, special processes called *daemons* (page 1027) support such services by exchanging specialized messages with other systems over the network. Several software systems have been created to allow computers to share filesystems with one another, making it appear as though remote files are stored on local disks. Sharing remote filesystems allows users to share information without knowing where the files physically reside, without making unnecessary copies, and without learning a new set of utilities to manipulate them. Because the files appear to be stored locally, you can use standard utilities (such as cat, vim, lpr, mv, or their graphical counterparts) to work with them.

Developers have created new tools and extended existing ones to take advantage of higher network speeds and to work within more crowded networks. The rlogin, rsh, and telnet utilities, which were designed long ago, have largely been supplanted by ssh (secure shell, page 579) in recent years. The ssh utility allows a user to log in on or execute commands securely on a remote computer. Users rely on such utilities as scp and ftp to transfer files from one system to another across the network. Communication utilities, including email utilities and chat programs (e.g., talk, Internet Relay Chat [IRC], ICQ, and instant messenger [IM] programs, such as AOL's AIM and gaim) have become so prevalent that many people with very little computer expertise use them on a daily basis to keep in touch with friends, family, and colleagues.

Intranet   An *intranet* is a network that connects computing resources at a school, company, or other organization but, unlike the Internet, typically restricts access to internal users. An intranet is very similar to a LAN (local area network) but is based on Internet technology. An intranet can provide database, email, and Web page access to a limited group of people, regardless of their geographic location.

The ability of an intranet to connect dissimilar machines is one of its strengths. Think of all the machines you can find on the Internet: Macintosh systems, PCs running different versions of Windows, machines running UNIX and Linux, and so on. Each of these machines can communicate via IP (page 351), a common protocol. So it is with an intranet: Dissimilar machines can all talk to one another.

Another key difference between the Internet and an intranet is that the Internet transmits only one protocol suite: IP. In contrast, an intranet can be set up to use a number of protocols, such as IP, IPX, AppleTalk, DECnet, XNS, or other protocols developed by vendors over the years. Although these protocols cannot be transmitted directly over the Internet, you can set up special gateway boxes at remote sites that tunnel or encapsulate these protocols into IP packets and then use the Internet to pass them.

You can use an *extranet* (also called a *partner net*) or a virtual private network (VPN) to improve security. These terms describe ways to connect remote sites securely to a local site, typically by using the public Internet as a carrier and employing encryption as a means of protecting data in transit.

Following are some terms you may want to become familiar with before you read the rest of this chapter:

ASP (page 1019)	*hub* (page 1036)	*packet* (page 1047)
bridge (page 1022)	*internet* (page 1037)	*router* (page 1053)
extranet (page 1031)	*Internet* (page 1037)	*sneakernet* (page 1055)
firewall (page 1032)	*intranet* (page 1038)	*switch* (page 1058)
gateway (page 1033)	*ISP* (page 1038)	*VPN* (page 1062)

TYPES OF NETWORKS AND HOW THEY WORK

Computers communicate over networks using unique addresses assigned by system software. A computer message, called a *packet, frame,* or *datagram,* includes the address of the destination computer and the sender's return address. The three most common types of networks are *broadcast, point-to-point,* and *switched.* Once popular token-based networks (such as FDDI and token ring) are rarely seen anymore.

Speed is critical to the proper functioning of the Internet. Newer specifications (cat 6 and cat 7) are being standardized for 1000BaseT (1 gigabit per second, called gigabit Ethernet, or GIG-E) and faster networking. Some of the networks that form the backbone of the Internet run at speeds of almost 10 gigabits per second (OC192) to accommodate the ever-increasing demand for network services. Table 10-1 lists some of the specifications in use today.

Table 10-1   Network specifications

Specification	Speed
DS0	64 kilobits per second
ISDN	Two DS0 lines plus signaling (16 kilobits per second) or 128 kilobits per second
T-1	1.544 megabits per second (24 DS0 lines)
T-3	43.232 megabits per second (28 T-1s)
OC3	155 megabits per second (100 T-1s)
OC12	622 megabits per second (4 OC3s)
OC48	2.5 gigabits per seconds (4 OC12s)
OC192	9.6 gigabits per second (4 OC48s)

BROADCAST NETWORKS

On a *broadcast network,* such as Ethernet, any of the many systems attached to the network cable can send a message at any time; each system examines the address in each message and responds only to messages addressed to it. A problem occurs on a broadcast network when multiple systems send data at the same time, resulting in a collision of the messages on the cable. When messages collide, they can become garbled. The sending system notices the garbled message and resends it after waiting a short but random amount of time. Waiting a random amount of time helps prevent those same systems from resending the data at the same moment and experiencing yet another collision. The extra traffic that results from collisions can strain the network; if the collision rate gets too high, retransmissions may result in more collisions. Ultimately the network may become unusable.

POINT-TO-POINT NETWORKS

A point-to-point link does not seem like much of a network because only two endpoints are involved. However, most connections to WANs (wide area networks) go through point-to-point links, using wire cable, radio, or satellite links. The advantage of a point-to-point link is its simplicity: Because only two systems are involved, the traffic on the link is limited and well understood. A disadvantage is that each system can typically be equipped for only a small number of such links; it is impractical and costly to establish point-to-point links that connect each computer to all the rest.

Point-to-point links often use serial lines and modems. The combination of a modem with a point-to-point link allows an isolated system to connect inexpensively to a larger network.

The most common types of point-to-point links are the ones used to connect to the Internet. When you use DSL[1] (digital subscriber line), you are using a point-to-point link to connect to the Internet. Serial lines, such as T-1, T-3, ATM links, and ISDN, are all point-to-point. Although it might seem like a point-to-point link, a cable modem is based on broadcast technology and in that way is similar to Ethernet.

SWITCHED NETWORKS

A *switch* is a device that establishes a virtual path between source and destination hosts in such a way that each path appears to be a point-to-point link, much like a railroad roundhouse. The switch creates and tears down virtual paths as hosts seek to communicate with each other. Each host thinks it has a direct point-to-point path to the host it is talking to. Contrast this approach with a broadcast network, where each host also sees traffic bound for other hosts. The advantage of a switched network over a pure point-to-point network is that each host requires only one connection: the connection to the switch. Using pure point-to-point connections, each host must have a connection to every other host. Scalability is provided by further linking switches.

---

1. The term *DSL* incorporates the xDSL suite of technologies, which includes ADSL, XDSL, SDSL, and HDSL.

LAN: LOCAL AREA NETWORK

Local area networks (LANs) are confined to a relatively small area—a single computer facility, building, or campus. Today most LANs run over copper or fiberoptic (glass or plastic) cable, but other wireless technologies, such as infrared (similar to most television remote control devices) and radio wave (wireless, or Wi-Fi), are becoming more popular.

If its destination address is not on the local network, a packet must be passed on to another network by a router (page 348). A router may be a general-purpose computer or a special-purpose device attached to multiple networks to act as a gateway among them.

ETHERNET

A Linux system connected to a LAN usually connects to a network using Ethernet. A typical Ethernet connection can support data transfer rates from 10 megabits per second to 1 gigabit per second, with further speed enhancements planned for the future. As a result of computer load, competing network traffic, and network overhead, file transfer rates on an Ethernet are always slower than the maximum, theoretical transfer rate.

Cables An Ethernet network transfers data using copper or fiberoptic cable or wireless transmitters and receivers. Originally, each computer was attached to a thick coaxial cable (called *thicknet*) at tap points spaced at six-foot intervals along the cable. The thick cable was awkward to deal with, so other solutions, including a thinner coaxial cable called *thinnet*, or 10Base2,[2] were developed. Today most Ethernet connections are either wireless or made over unshielded twisted pair (referred to as UTP, Category 5 [cat 5], Category 5e [cat 5e], Category 6 [cat 6], 10BaseT, or 100BaseT) wire—similar to the type of wire used for telephone lines and serial data communications.

Switch A *switched Ethernet* network is a special case of a broadcast network that works with a *network switch* (or just *switch*), which is a type of intelligent hub. Instead of having a dumb repeater (passive hub) that broadcasts every packet it receives out of every port, a switch learns which devices are connected to which of its ports. A switch sorts packets and then sends the traffic to only the machine it is intended for. A switch also has buffers for holding and queuing packets.

Some Ethernet switches have enough bandwidth to communicate simultaneously, in full-duplex mode, with all the devices connected to them. A nonswitched (hub-based) broadcast network can run in only half-duplex mode. Full-duplex Ethernet further improves things by eliminating collisions. Each host on a switched network can transmit and receive simultaneously at 10/100/1,000 megabits per second for an effective bandwidth between hosts of 20/200/2,000 megabits per second, depending on the capacity of the switch.

---

2. Versions of Ethernet are classified as **XBaseY**, where *X* is the data rate in megabits per second, **Base** means baseband (as opposed to radio frequency), and *Y* is the category of cabling.

WIRELESS

Wireless networks are becoming increasingly common. They are found in offices, homes, and public places, such as universities, coffee shops, and airports. Wireless access points provide functionality similar to an Ethernet hub. They allow multiple users to interact via a common radio frequency spectrum. A wireless, point-to-point connection allows you to wander about your home or office with a laptop, using an antenna to link to a LAN or to the Internet via an in-house base station. Linux includes drivers for many of the common wireless boards. A wireless access point, or base station, connects a wireless network to a wired network so that no special protocol is required for a wireless connection. Refer to page 572 and to the *Linux Wireless LAN HOWTO* at www.hpl.hp.com/personal/Jean_Tourrilhes/Linux.

WAN: WIDE AREA NETWORK

A wide area network (WAN) covers a large geographic area. In contrast, the technologies (such as Ethernet) used for LANs were designed to work over limited distances and for a certain number of host connections. A WAN may span long distances over dedicated data lines (leased from a telephone company) or radio or satellite links. Such networks are often used to interconnect LANs. Major Internet service providers rely on WANs to connect to their customers within a country and around the globe.

MAN   Some networks do not fit into either the LAN or the WAN designation. A MAN (metropolitan area network) is a network that is contained in a smaller geographic area, such as a city. Like WANs, MANs are typically used to interconnect LANs.

INTERNETWORKING THROUGH GATEWAYS AND ROUTERS

Gateway   A LAN connects to a WAN through a *gateway,* a generic term for a computer or a special device with multiple network connections that passes data from one network to another. A gateway converts the data traffic from the format used on the LAN to that used on the WAN. Data that crosses the country from one Ethernet to another over a WAN, for example, is repackaged from the Ethernet format to a different format that can be processed by the communications equipment that makes up the WAN backbone. When it reaches the end of its journey over the WAN, the data is converted by another gateway to a format appropriate for the receiving network. For the most part, these details are of concern only to the network administrators; the end user does not need to know anything about how the data transfer takes place.

Router   A *router* is the most popular form of gateway. Routers play an important role in internetworking. Just as you might study a map to plan your route when you need to drive to an unfamiliar place, so a computer needs to know how to deliver a message to a system attached to a distant network by passing through intermediary systems and networks along the way. Although you might envision using a giant network road map to choose the route that your data should follow, a static map of computer routes is usually a poor choice for a large network. Computers and networks along the route you choose may be overloaded or down, without providing a detour for your message.

Routers instead communicate dynamically, keeping each other informed about which routes are open for use. To extend the analogy, this situation would be like heading out on a car trip without consulting a map to find a route to your destination; instead you head for a nearby gas station and ask directions. Throughout the journey you continue to stop at one gas station after another, getting directions at each to find the next one. Although it would take a while to make the stops, the owner of each gas station would advise you of bad traffic, closed roads, alternative routes, and shortcuts.

The stops made by the data are much quicker than those you would make in your car, but each message leaves each router on a path chosen based on the most current information. Think of this system as a GPS (global positioning system) setup that automatically gets updates at each intersection and tells you where to go next, based on traffic and highway conditions.

Figure 10-1 (next page) shows an example of how LANs might be set up at three sites interconnected by a WAN (the Internet). In this type of network diagram, Ethernet LANs are drawn as straight lines, with devices attached at right angles; WANs are represented as clouds, indicating that the details have been left out; and wireless connections are drawn as zigzag lines with breaks, indicating that the connection may be intermittent.

In Figure 10-1, a gateway or a router relays messages between each LAN and the Internet. Three of the routers in the Internet are shown (for example, the one closest to each site). Site A has a server, a workstation, a network computer, and a PC sharing a single Ethernet LAN. Site B has an Ethernet LAN that serves a printer and four Linux workstations. A firewall permits only certain traffic to pass between the Internet router and the site's local router. Site C has three LANs linked by a single router, perhaps to reduce the traffic load that would result if the LANs were combined or to keep workgroups or locations on separate networks. Site C also includes a wireless access point that enables wireless communication with nearby computers.

FIREWALL

A firewall in a car separates the engine compartment from the passenger compartment, protecting the driver and passengers from engine fires, noise, and fumes. In much the same way, computer firewalls separate computers from malicious and unwanted users.

A *firewall* prevents certain types of traffic from entering or leaving a network. For example, a firewall might prevent traffic from your IP address from leaving the network and prevent anyone except users from selected domains from using FTP to retrieve data from the network. The implementations of firewalls vary widely—from Linux machines with two *interfaces* (page 1037) running custom software to a *router* (page 1053) with simple access lists to esoteric, vendor-supplied firewall

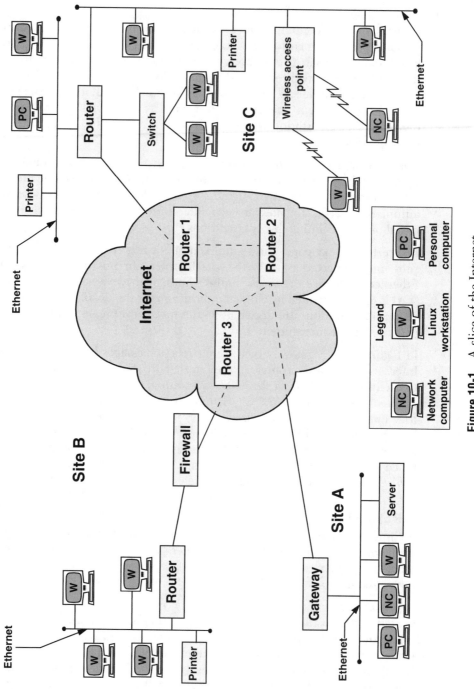

Figure 10-1   A slice of the Internet

appliances. Most larger installations have at least one kind of firewall in place. A firewall is often accompanied by a proxy server/gateway (page 377) that provides an intermediate point between you and the host you are communicating with.

In addition to the firewalls found in multipurpose computers, firewalls are becoming increasingly common in consumer appliances. For example, they are built into cable modems, wireless gateways, routers, and stand-alone devices.

Typically a single Linux machine will include a minimal firewall. A small group of Linux systems may have an inexpensive Linux machine with two network interfaces and packet-filtering software functioning as a dedicated firewall. One of the interfaces connects to the Internet, modems, and other outside data sources. The other connects, normally through a hub or switch, to the local network. Refer to Chapter 25 for information on iptables and setting up a firewall and to Appendix C for a discussion of security.

NETWORK PROTOCOLS

To exchange information over a network, computers must communicate using a common language, or *protocol* (page 1050). The protocol determines the format of message packets. The predominant network protocols used by Linux systems are TCP and IP,[3] collectively referred to as TCP/IP (Transmission Control Protocol and Internet Protocol). Network services that need highly reliable connections, such as ssh and scp, tend to use TCP/IP. Another protocol used for some system services is UDP (User Datagram Protocol). Network services that do not require guaranteed delivery, such as RealAudio and RealVideo, operate satisfactorily with the simpler UDP.[4]

IP: INTERNET PROTOCOL

Layering was introduced to facilitate protocol design: Layers distinguish functional differences between adjacent protocols. A grouping of layers can be standardized into a protocol model. IP has a model that distinguishes protocol layers. The IP model differs from the ISO seven-layer protocol model (also called the OSI model) that is often illustrated in networking textbooks. Specifically IP uses the following simplified five-layer model:

1. The first layer of the IP protocol, called the *physical layer,* describes the physical medium (copper, fiber, wireless) and the data encoding used to transmit signals on that medium (pulses of light, electrical waves, or radio waves, for instance).

---

3. All references to IP imply *IPv4* (page 1038).

4. Voice and video protocols are delay sensitive, not integrity sensitive. The human ear and eye accept and interpolate loss in an audio or video stream but cannot deal with variable delay. The guaranteed delivery that TCP provides introduces a delay on a busy network when packets get retransmitted. This delay is not acceptable for video and audio transmissions, whereas less than 100 percent integrity is acceptable.

2. The second layer, called the *data link layer,* covers media access by network devices and describes how to put data into packets, transmit the data, and check it for errors. Ethernet is found at this layer, as is *802.11* (page 1018) wireless.

3. The third layer, called the *network layer,* frequently uses IP and addresses and routes packets.

4. The fourth layer, called the *transport layer,* is where TCP and UDP exist. This layer provides a means for applications to communicate with each other. Functions commonly performed by the transport layer include guaranteed delivery, delivery of packets in the order of their transmission, flow control, error detection, and error correction. The transport layer is responsible for dividing data streams into packets. In addition, this layer performs port addressing, which allows it to distinguish among different services using the same transport protocol. Port addressing keeps the data from multiple applications using the same protocol (for example, TCP) separate.

5. Anything above the transport layer is the domain of the application and is part of the fifth layer. Unlike the ISO model, the Internet model does not distinguish among application, presentation, and session layers. All of the upper-layer characteristics, such as character encoding, encryption, and GUIs, are part of the application. Applications choose the transport characteristics they require as well as the corresponding transport layer protocol with which to send and receive data.

TCP: TRANSMISSION CONTROL PROTOCOL

TCP is most frequently run on top of IP in a combination referred to as TCP/IP. This protocol provides error recovery and guaranteed delivery in packet transmission order; it also works with multiple ports so that it can handle more than one application. TCP is a *connection-oriented protocol* (page 1026), also known as a stream-based protocol. Once established, a TCP connection looks like a stream of data, not individual IP packets. The connection is assumed to remain up and be uniquely addressable. Every piece of information you write to the connection always goes to the same destination and arrives in the order it was sent. Because TCP is connection oriented and establishes a *virtual circuit* between two systems, this protocol is not suitable for one-to-many transmissions (see the discussion of UDP, following). TCP has builtin mechanisms for dealing with congestion (or flow) control over busy networks and throttles back (slows the speed of data flow) when it has to retransmit dropped packets. TCP can also deal with acknowledgments, wide area links, high-delay links, and other situations.

UDP: USER DATAGRAM PROTOCOL

UDP runs at layer 4 of the IP stack, just as TCP does, but is much simpler. Like TCP, UDP works with multiple ports and multiple applications. It has checksums for error detection but does not automatically retransmit *datagrams* (page 1028) that fail the checksum test. UDP is a datagram-oriented protocol: Each datagram must carry its own address and port information. Each router along the way examines each datagram to determine the destination, one hop at a time. You can broadcast or multicast UDP datagrams to many destinations at the same time by using special addresses.

PPP: POINT-TO-POINT PROTOCOL

PPP provides serial line point-to-point connections that support IP. This protocol compresses data to make the most of the limited bandwidth available on serial connections. PPP, which replaces SLIP[5] (Serial Line IP), acts as a point-to-point layer 2/3 transport that many other types of protocols can ride on. It is used mostly for IP-based services and connections, such as TCP or UDP.

XREMOTE AND LBX

Two protocols that speed up data transfer over serial lines are Xremote and LBX. Xremote compresses the X Window System protocol so that it is more efficient over slower serial lines. LBX (low-bandwidth X) is based on the Xremote technology and is part of X Window System release X11R6 and higher.

HOST ADDRESS

Each computer interface is identified by a unique address, or host number, on its network. A system attached to more than one network has multiple interfaces—one for each network, each with a unique address.

Each packet of information that is broadcast over the network has a destination address. All hosts on the network must process each broadcast packet to see whether it is addressed to that host.[6] If the packet is addressed to a given host, that host continues to process it. If not, the host ignores the packet.

The network address of a machine is an IP address, which, under IPv4, is represented as one number broken into four segments separated by periods (for example, 192.168.184.5). Domain names and IP addresses are assigned through a highly distributed system coordinated by ICANN (Internet Corporation for Assigned Names and Numbers—www.icann.org) via many registrars (see www.internic.net). ICANN is funded by the various domain name registries and registrars and by IP address registries, which supply globally unique identifiers for hosts and services on the Internet. Although you may not deal with any of these agencies directly, your Internet service provider most assuredly does.

How a company uses IP addresses is determined by the system or network administrator. For example, the leftmost two sets of numbers in an IP address might represent

---

5. SLIP was one of the first serial line implementations of IP and has slightly less overhead than PPP. PPP supports multiple protocols (such as AppleTalk and IPX), whereas SLIP supports only IP.

6. Contrast broadcast packets with unicast packets: Ethernet hardware on a computer filters out unicast packets that are not addressed to that machine; the operating system on that machine never sees these packets.

a large network (campuswide or companywide); the third set, a subnetwork (perhaps a department or a single floor in a building); and the rightmost number, an individual computer. The operating system uses the address in a different, lower-level form, converting it to its binary equivalent, a series of 1s and 0s. See the following optional section for more information. Refer to "Private address space" on page 570 for information about addresses you can use on a LAN without registering them.

STATIC VERSUS DYNAMIC IP ADDRESSES

A static IP address is one that always remains the same. A dynamic IP address is one that can change each time you connect to the network. A dynamic address remains the same during a single login session. Any server (mail, Web, and so on) must have a static address so clients can find the machine that is acting as the server. End-user systems usually work well with dynamic addresses. During a given login session, they can function as a client (your Web browser, for example) because they maintain a constant IP address. When you log out and log in again, it does not matter that you have a different IP address because your computer, acting as a client, establishes a new connection with a server. The advantage of dynamic addressing is that it allows inactive addresses to be reused, reducing the total number of IP addresses needed.

optional IP CLASSES

To facilitate routing on the Internet, IP addresses are divided into *classes*. These classes, which are labeled class A through class E, allow the Internet address space to be broken into blocks of small, medium, and large networks that are designed to be assigned based on the number of hosts within a network.

When you need to send a message to an address outside the local network, your system looks up the address block/class in its routing table and sends the message to the next router on the way to the final destination. Every router along the way does a similar lookup and forwards the message accordingly. At the destination, local routers direct the message to the specific address. Without classes and blocks, your host would have to know every network and subnetwork address on the Internet before it could send a message. This setup would be impractical because of the huge number of addresses on the Internet.

Each of the four numbers in the IP address is in the range 0–255 because each segment of the IP address is represented by 8 bits (an *octet*), with each bit being capable of taking on two values; the total number of values is therefore $2^8 = 256$. When you start counting at 0, the range 1–256 becomes 0–255.[7] Each IP address is divided into a net address (*netid*) portion, which is part of the class, and a host address (*hostid*) portion. See Table 10-2.

---

7. Internally, the IP address is represented as a set of four unsigned 8-bit fields or a 32-bit unsigned number, depending on how programs are using it. The most common format in C is to represent it as a union of an unsigned 32-bit long integer, four unsigned chars, and two unsigned short integers.

Table 10-2   IP classes

Class	Start bits	Address range	All bits (including start bits)			
			0–7	8–15	16–23	24–31
Class A	0	001.000.000.000–126.000.000.000	0-netid	========hostid=========		
Class B	10	129.000.000.000–191.255.000.000	10-----netid------		=====hostid=====	
Class C	110	192.000.000.000–223.255.255.000	110----------netid-----------			=hostid=
Class D (multicast)	1110	224.000.000.000–239.255.255.000	1110			
Class E (reserved)	11110	240.000.000.000–255.255.255.000	11110			

The first set of addresses, defining class A networks, is reserved for extremely large corporations, such as General Electric (3.0.0.0) and Hewlett-Packard (15.0.0.0), and for ISPs. One start bit (0) in the first position designates a class A network, 7 bits holds the network portion of the address (netid), and 24 bits holds the host portion of the address (hostid; see Table 10-2). This setup means that GE can have 2^{24}, or approximately 16 million, hosts on its network. Unused address space and *subnets* (page 1057) lower this number quite a bit. The 127.0.0.0 subnet (page 359) is reserved, as are several others (see *private address space* on page 1049).

Two start bits (10) in the first two positions designates a class B network, 14 bits holds the network portion of the address (netid), and 16 bits holds the host portion of the address, for a potential total of 65,534 hosts.[8] A class C network uses 3 start bits (100), 21 netid bits (2 million networks), and 8 hostid bits (254 hosts). Today a new large customer will not receive a class A or B network but is likely to receive a class C or several (usually contiguous) class C networks, if merited.

Several other classes of networks exist. Class D networks are reserved for *multicast* (page 1044) networks. When you run **netstat –nr** on a Linux system, you can see whether the machine is a member of a multicast network. A 224.0.0.0 in the Destination column that netstat displays indicates a class D, multicast address (Table 10-2). A multicast is like a broadcast, but only hosts that subscribe to the

---

8. A 16-bit (class B) address can address $2^{16} = 65,536$ hosts, yet the potential number of hosts is two fewer than that because the first and last addresses on any network are reserved. In a similar manner, an 8-bit (class C) address can address only 254 hosts ($2^8 - 2 = 254$). The 0 host address (for example, 194.16.100.0 for a class C network or 131.204.0.0 for a class B network) is reserved as a designator for the network itself. Several older operating systems use this as a broadcast address. The 255 host address (for example, 194.16.100.255 for a class C network or 131.204.255.255 for a class B network) is reserved as the IP broadcast address. An IP packet (datagram) that is sent to this address is broadcast to all hosts on the network.

The netid portion of a subnet does not have the same limitations. Often you are given the choice of reserving the first and last networks in a range as you would a hostid, but this is rarely done in practice. More often the first and last networks in the netid range provide more usable address space. Refer to "Subnets" on page 357.

multicast group receive the message. To use Web terminology, a broadcast is like a "push." A host pushes a broadcast on the network, and every host on the network must check each packet to see whether it contains relevant data. A multicast is like a "pull." A host will see a multicast only if it registers itself as subscribed to a multicast group or service and pulls the appropriate packets from the network.

Table 10-3 shows some of the computations for the IP address 131.204.027.027. Each address is shown in decimal, hexadecimal, and binary form. Binary is the easiest to work with for bitwise (binary) computations. The first three lines show the IP address. The next three lines show the *subnet mask* (page 1058) in three bases. Next the IP address and the subnet mask are ANDed together bitwise to yield the *subnet number* (page 1058), which is shown in three bases. The last three lines show the *broadcast address* (page 1022), which is computed by taking the subnet number and turning the hostid bits to 1s. The subnet number identifies the local network. The subnet number and the subnet mask determine what range the IP address of the machine must be in. They are also used by routers to segment traffic; see *network segment* (page 1045). A broadcast on this network goes to all hosts in the range 131.204.27.1 through 131.204.27.254 but will be acted on only by hosts that have a use for it.

Table 10-3   Computations for IP address 131.204.027.027

	------Class B------		netid	hostid	
IP address	131	.204	.027	.027	decimal
	83	CC	1B	1B	hexadecimal
	1000 0011	1100 1100	0001 1011	0001 1011	binary
Subnet mask	255	.255	.255	.000	decimal
	FF	FF	FF	00	hexadecimal
	1111 1111	1111 1111	1111 1111	0000 0000	binary
IP address bitwise AND	1000 0011	1100 1100	0001 1011	0001 1011	
Subnet mask	1111 1111	1111 1111	1111 1111	0000 0000	binary
= Subnet number	1000 0011	1100 1100	0001 1011	0000 0000	
Subnet number	131	.204	.027	.000	decimal
	83	CC	1B	00	hexadecimal
	1000 0011	1100 1100	0001 1011	0000 0000	binary
Broadcast address (set host bits to 1)	131	.204	.27	.255	decimal
	83	CC	1B	FF	hexadecimal
	1000 0011	1100 1100	0001 1011	1111 1111	binary

SUBNETS

Each host on a network must process each broadcast packet to determine whether the information in the packet is useful to that host. If the network includes numerous hosts, each host must process many packets. To maintain efficiency—most networks, and particularly shared media networks such as Ethernet—need to be split into subnetworks, or *subnets*.[9] The more hosts on a network, the more dramatically network performance is affected. Organizations use router and switch technology called VLANs (virtual local area networks) to group similar hosts into broadcast domains (subnets) based on function. For example, it is not uncommon to see a switch with different ports being part of different subnets. See page 423 for information on how to specify a subnet.

A *subnet mask* (or *address mask*) is a bit mask that identifies which parts of an IP address correspond to the network address and the subnet portion of the address. This mask has 1s in positions corresponding to the network and subnet numbers and 0s in the host number positions. When you perform a bitwise AND on an IP address and a subnet mask (Table 10-3), the resulting address contains everything except the host address (hostid) portion.

There are several ways to represent a subnet mask: A network could have a subnet mask of 255.255.255.0 (decimal), FFFFFF00 (hexadecimal), or /24 (the number of bits used for the subnet mask). If it were a class B network (of which 16 bits are already fixed), this yields 2^8 (24 total bits − 16 fixed bits = 8 bits, 2^8 = 256) networks[10] with $2^8 − 2$ (256 − 2 = 254) hosts[11] on each network.

For example, when you divide the class C address 192.25.4.0 into eight subnets, you get a subnet mask of 255.255.255.224, FFFFFFE0, or /27 (27 1s). The eight resultant networks are 192.25.4.0, 192.25.4.32, 192.25.4.64, 192.25.4.96, 192.25.4.128, 192.25.4.160, 192.25.4.192, and 192.25.4.224. You can use a Web-based subnet mask calculator to calculate subnet masks (refer to "Network Calculators" on page 983). To use this calculator to determine the preceding subnet mask, start with an IP host address of 192.25.4.0.

CIDR: CLASSLESS INTER-DOMAIN ROUTING

CIDR (pronounced "cider") allows groups of addresses that are smaller than a class C block to be assigned to an organization or ISP and then further subdivided and parceled out. In addition, it helps to alleviate the potential problem of routing tables on major Internet backbone and peering devices becoming too large to manage.

---

9. Splitting a network is also an issue with other protocols, particularly AppleTalk.

10. The first and last networks are reserved in a manner similar to the first and last hosts, although the standard is flexible. You can configure routers to reclaim the first and last networks in a subnet. Different routers have different techniques for reclaiming these networks.

11. Subtract 2 because the first and last host addresses on every network are reserved.

The pool of available IPv4 addresses has been depleted to the point that no one gets a class A address anymore. The trend is to reclaim these huge address blocks, if possible, and recycle them into groups of smaller addresses. Also, as more class C addresses are assigned, routing tables on the Internet are filling up and causing memory overflows. The solution is to aggregate[12] groups of addresses into blocks and allocate them to ISPs, which in turn subdivide these blocks and allocate them to their customers. The address class designations (A, B, and C) described in the previous section are used less often today, although you may still encounter subnets. When you request an address block, your ISP usually gives you as many addresses as you need—and no more. The ISP aggregates several contiguous smaller blocks and routes them to your location. This aggregation is CIDR. Without CIDR, the Internet as we know it would not function.

For example, you might be allocated the 192.168.5.0/22 IP address block, which could support 2^{10} hosts (32 − 22 = 10). Your ISP would set its routers so that any packets going to an address in that block would be sent to your network. Internally, your own routers might further subdivide this block of 1,024 potential hosts into subnets, perhaps into four networks. Four networks require an additional two bits of addressing (2^2 = 4). You could therefore set up your router to support four networks with this allocation: 192.168.5.0/24, 192.168.6.0/24, 192.168.7.0/24, and 192.168.8.0/24. Each of these networks could then have 254 hosts. CIDR lets you arbitrarily divide networks and subnetworks into increasingly smaller blocks along the way. Each router has enough memory to keep track of the addresses it needs to direct and aggregates the rest.

This scheme uses memory and address space efficiently. For example, you could take 192.168.8.0/24 and further divide it into 16 networks with 14 hosts each. The 16 networks require four more bits (2^4 = 16), so you would have 192.168.8.0/28, 192.168.8.16/28, 192.168.8.32/28, and so on, up through the last subnet of 192.168.8.240/16, which would have the hosts 192.168.8.241 through 192.168.8.254.

HOSTNAMES

People generally find it easier to work with names than with numbers, so Linux provides several ways to associate hostnames with IP addresses. The oldest method is to consult a list of names and addresses that are stored in the **/etc/hosts** file:

```
$ cat /etc/hosts
127.0.0.1     localhost
130.128.52.1  gw-example.example.com  gw-example
130.128.52.2  bravo.example.com       bravo
130.128.52.3  hurrah.example.com      hurrah
130.128.52.4  kudos.example.com       kudos
```

---

12. *Aggregate* means to join. In CIDR, the aggregate of 208.178.99.124 and 208.178.99.125 is 208.178.99.124/23 (the aggregation of two class C blocks).

localhost =
127.0.0.1   The address 127.0.0.1 is reserved for the special hostname **localhost**, which serves as a hook for the system's networking software to operate on the local machine without going onto a physical network. The names of the other systems are shown in two forms: in a *fully qualified domain name* (FQDN) format that is unique on the Internet and as a nickname that is locally unique.

NIS   As more hosts joined networks, storing these name-to-address mappings in a text file proved to be inefficient and inconvenient. The **hosts** file grew increasingly larger and became impossible to keep up-to-date. To solve this problem Linux supports NIS (Network Information Service, page 373), which was developed for use on Sun computers. NIS stores information in a database, making it easier to find a specific address, but it is useful only for host information within a single administrative domain. Hosts outside the domain cannot access the information.

DNS   The solution to this dilemma is DNS (Domain Name Service, page 371). DNS effectively addresses the efficiency and update issues by arranging the entire network *namespace* (page 1044) as a hierarchy. Each domain in the DNS manages its own namespace (addressing and name resolution), and each domain can easily query for any host or IP address by following the tree up or down the namespace until it finds the appropriate domain. By providing a hierarchical naming structure, DNS distributes name administration across the entire Internet.

IPv6

The explosive growth of the Internet has uncovered deficiencies in the design of the current address plan—most notably the shortage of addresses. Over the next few years, a revised protocol, named IPng (IP Next Generation), also known as IPv6 (IP version 6),[13] will be phased in. (It may take longer—the phase-in is going quite slowly.) This new scheme is designed to overcome the major limitations of the current approach and can be implemented gradually because it is compatible with the existing address usage. IPv6 makes it possible to assign many more unique Internet addresses (2^{128}, or 340 *undecillion* [10^{36}]). It also supports more advanced security and performance control features:

- IPv6 enables autoconfiguration. With IPv4, autoconfiguration is available using optional DHCP (page 431). With IPv6, autoconfiguration is mandatory, making it easy for hosts to configure their IP addresses automatically.

- IPv6 reserves 24 bits in the header for advanced services, such as resource reservation protocols, better backbone routing, and improved traffic engineering.

- IPv6 makes multicast protocols mandatory and uses them extensively. In IPv4, multicast, which improves scalability, is optional.

---

13. IPv5 referred to an experimental real-time stream protocol named ST—thus the jump from IPv4 to IPv6.

- IPv6 aggregates address blocks more efficiently because of the huge address space. This aggregation makes obsolete *NAT* (page 1044), which decreased scalability and introduced protocol issues.

- IPv6 provides a simplified packet header that allows hardware accelerators to work better.

A sample IPv6 address is fe80::a00:20ff:feff:5be2/10. Each group of four hexadecimal digits is equivalent to a number between 0 and 65,536 (16^4). A pair of adjacent colons indicates a hex value of 0x0000; leading 0s need not be shown. With eight sets of hexadecimal groupings, $65,536^8 = 2^{128}$ addresses are possible. In an IPv6 address on a host with the default autoconfiguration, the first characters in the address are always fe80. The last 64 bits hold an interface ID designation, which is often the *MAC address* (page 1041) of the system's Ethernet controller.

COMMUNICATE OVER A NETWORK

Many commands that you can use to communicate with other users on a single computer system have been extended to work over a network. Examples of extended utilities include electronic mail programs, information-gathering utilities (such as finger, page 147), and communications utilities (such as talk). These utilities are examples of the UNIX philosophy: Instead of creating a new, special-purpose tool, modify an existing one.

Many utilities understand a convention for the format of network addresses: **user@host** (spoken as "user at host"). When you use an @ sign in an argument to one of these utilities, the utility interprets the text that follows as the name of a remote host. When you omit the @ sign, a utility assumes that you are requesting information from or corresponding with someone on the local system.

The prompts shown in the examples in this chapter include the hostname of the system you are using. If you frequently use more than one system over a network, you may find it difficult to keep track of which system you are interacting with at any particular moment. If you set your prompt to include the hostname of the current system, it will always be clear which system you are using. To identify the computer you are using, run hostname or **uname –n**:

```
$ hostname
kudos
```

See page 293 for information on how you can change the prompt.

finger: DISPLAYS INFORMATION ABOUT REMOTE USERS

The finger utility displays information about one or more users on a system. This utility was designed for local use, but when networks became popular, it was obvious that finger should be enhanced to reach out and collect information remotely. In the following examples, finger displays information about all users logged in on the system named **bravo**:

```
[kudos]$ finger @bravo
[bravo.example.com]
Login     Name            Tty   Idle  Login Time    Office     Office Phone
root      root            *1    1:35  Oct 22  5:00
alex      Alex Watson      4          Oct 22 12:23 (kudos)
alex      Alex Watson      5      19  Oct 22 12:33 (:0)
jenny     Jenny Chen       7    2:24  Oct 22  8:45 (:0)
hls       Helen Simpson   11      2d  Oct 20 12:23 (:0)
```

A user's username in front of the @ sign causes finger to display information from the remote system for the specified user only. If the remote system has multiple matches for that name, finger displays the results for all of them:

```
[kudos]$ finger alex@bravo
[bravo.example.com]
Login     Name            Tty   Idle  Login Time    Office     Office Phone
alex      Alex Watson      4          Oct 22 12:23 (kudos)
alex      Alex Watson      5      19  Oct 22 12:33 (:0)
```

The finger utility works by querying a standard network service, the **in.fingerd** daemon, that runs on the system being queried. Although this service is supplied with Red Hat Linux, some sites choose not to run it to minimize the load on their systems, reduce security risks, or maintain privacy. When you use finger to obtain information about someone at such a site, you will see an error message or nothing at all. The remote **in.fingerd** daemon determines how much information to share and in what format. As a result, the report displayed for any given system may differ from that shown in the preceding examples.

The in.fingerd daemon

security   The finger daemon (**in.fingerd**) gives away system account information that can aid a malicious user. Some sites disable finger or randomize user account IDs to make a malicious user's job more difficult. Disable finger by setting **disable = yes** in **/etc/xinetd.d/finger** and restarting **xinetd**. For more information refer to "The xinetd Superserver" on page 425.

The information for remote finger looks much the same as it does when finger runs on the local system, with one difference: Before displaying the results, finger reports the name of the remote system that answered the query (**bravo**, as shown in brackets in the preceding example). The name of the host that answers may be different from the system name you specified on the command line, depending on how the finger daemon service is configured on the remote system. In some cases, several hostnames may be listed if one finger daemon contacts another to retrieve the information.

SENDING MAIL TO A REMOTE USER

Given a user's username on a remote system and the name of the remote system or its domain, you can use an email program to send a message over the network or the Internet, using the @ form of an address:

jenny@bravo

or

jenny@example.com

Although many Linux utilities recognize the @ form of a network address, you may find that you can reach more remote computers with email than with the other networking utilities described in this chapter. This disparity arises because the email system can deliver a message to a host that does not run IP, even though it appears to have an Internet address. The message may be routed over the network, for example, until it reaches a remote system that has a point-to-point, dial-up connection to the destination system. Other utilities, such as talk, rely on IP and operate only between networked hosts.

MAILING LIST SERVERS

A mailing list server (listserv[14]) allows you to create and manage an email list. An electronic mailing list provides a means for people interested in a particular topic to participate in an electronic discussion and for a person to disseminate information periodically to a potentially large mailing list. One of the most powerful features of most list servers is their ability to archive email postings to the list, create an archive index, and allow users to retrieve postings from the archive based on keywords or discussion threads. Typically you can subscribe and unsubscribe from the list with or without human intervention. The owner of the list can restrict who can subscribe, unsubscribe, and post messages to the list. Popular list servers include LISTSERV (www.lsoft.com), Lyris (www.lyris.com), Majordomo (www.greatcircle.com/majordomo), Mailman (www.list.org, page 646), and ListProc (www.listproc.net). Red Hat maintains quite a few mailing lists and list archives for those mailing lists at www.redhat.com/mailman/listinfo. Use Google to search on **linux mailing list** to find other lists.

NETWORK UTILITIES

To realize the full benefits of a networked environment, it made sense to extend certain tools, some of which have already been described. The advent of networks also created a need for new utilities to control and monitor them, spurring the development of new tools that took advantage of network speed and connectivity. This section describes concepts and utilities for systems attached to a network.

TRUSTED HOSTS

Some commands, such as rcp and rsh, work only if the remote system trusts your local computer (that is, if the remote system knows your local computer and believes that it is not pretending to be another system). The **/etc/hosts.equiv** file lists trusted systems. For reasons of security, the Superuser account does not rely on this file to identify trusted Superusers from other systems.

---

14. Although the term *listserv* is sometimes used generically to include many different list server programs, it is a specific product and a registered trademark of L-soft International, Inc.: LISTSERV (for more information go to www.lsoft.com).

Host-based trust is largely obsolete. Because there are many ways to circumvent trusted host security, including subverting DNS systems and *IP spoofing* (page 1038), authentication based on IP address is widely regarded as insecure and obsolete. In a small homogeneous network of machines with local DNS control, it can be "good enough." Its greater ease of use in these situations may outweigh the security concerns.

Do not share your login account

security   You can use a **.rhosts** file to allow another user to log in as you from a remote system without knowing your password. *This setup is not recommended.* Do not compromise the security of your files or the entire system by sharing your login account. Use ssh and scp instead of rsh and rcp whenever possible.

OpenSSH Tools

The OpenSSH project provides a set of tools that replace rcp, rsh, and others with secure equivalents. These tools are installed by default in Red Hat Linux and can be used as drop-in replacements for their insecure counterparts. The OpenSSH tool suite is covered in detail in Chapter 18.

telnet: Logs In on a Remote System

You can use the TELNET protocol to interact with a remote computer. The telnet utility, a user interface to this protocol, is older than ssh and is not secure. Nevertheless, it may work where ssh (page 585) is not available (there is more non-UNIX support for TELNET access than for ssh access). In addition, many legacy devices, such as terminal servers and network devices, do not support ssh.

```
[bravo]$ telnet kudos
Trying 172.19.52.2...
Connected to kudos.example.com
Escape character is '^]'.

Welcome to SuSE Linux 7.3 (i386) - Kernel 2.4.10-4GB (2).
kudos login: watson
Password:
You have old mail in /var/mail/watson.
Last login: Mon Feb 27 14:46:55 from bravo.example.com
watson@kudos:~>
...
watson@kudos:~> logout
Connection closed by foreign host.
[bravo]$
```

telnet versus ssh   When you connect to a remote UNIX or Linux system using telnet, you are presented with a regular, textual **login:** prompt. Unless you specify differently, the ssh utility assumes that your username on the remote system matches that on the local system. Because telnet is designed to work with non-UNIX and non-Linux systems, it makes no such assumptions.

telnet **is not secure**

security Whenever you enter sensitive information, such as your password, while you are using telnet, it is transmitted in cleartext and can be read by someone who is listening in on the session.

Another difference between these two utilities is that telnet allows you to configure many special parameters, such as how RETURNs or interrupts are processed. When using telnet between UNIX and/or Linux systems, you rarely need to change any parameters.

When you do not specify the name of a remote host on the command line, telnet runs in an interactive mode. The following example is equivalent to the previous telnet example:

```
[bravo]$ telnet
telnet> open kudos
Trying 172.19.52.2...
Connected to kudos.example.com
Escape character is '^]'.
...
```

Before connecting you to a remote system, telnet tells you what the *escape character* is; in most cases, it is ^] (where ^ represents the CONTROL key). When you press CONTROL-], you escape to telnet's interactive mode. Continuing the preceding example:

```
[kudos]$ CONTROL-]
telnet> ?
```

(displays help information)

```
telnet> close
Connection closed.
[bravo]$
```

When you enter a question mark in response to the **telnet>** prompt, telnet lists its commands. The **close** command ends the current telnet session, returning you to the local system. To get out of telnet's interactive mode and resume communication with the remote system, press RETURN in response to a prompt.

You can use telnet to access special remote services at sites that have chosen to make such services available. However, many of these services, such as the U.S. Library of Congress Information System (LOCIS), have moved to the Web. As a consequence, you can now obtain the same information using a Web browser.

USING telnet TO CONNECT TO OTHER PORTS

By default telnet connects to port 23, which is used for remote logins. However, you can use telnet to connect to other services by specifying a port number. In addition to standard services, many of the special remote services available on the Internet use unallocated port numbers. For example, you can access some multiplayer text games, called MUDs (Multi-User Dungeons, or Dimensions), using telnet to connect to a specified port, such as 4000 or 8888. Unlike the port numbers for standard protocols, these port numbers can be picked arbitrarily by the administrator of the game.

While telnet is no longer commonly employed to log in on remote systems, it is still used extensively as a debugging tool. This utility allows you to communicate directly with a TCP server. Some standard protocols are simple enough that an experienced user can debug problems by connecting to a remote service directly using telnet. If you are having a problem with a network server, a good first step is to try to connect to it using telnet.

In the following example, a system administrator who is debugging a problem with email delivery uses telnet to connect to the SMTP port (port 25) on a the server at **example.com** to see why it is bouncing mail from the **spammer.com** domain. The first line of output indicates which IP address telnet is trying to connect to. After telnet displays the **Connected to smtpsrv.example.com** message, the user emulates an SMTP dialog, following the standard SMTP protocol. The first line, which starts with **helo,** begins the session and identifies the local system. After the SMTP server responds, the user enters a line that identifies the mail sender as **user@spammer.com**. The SMTP server's response explains why the message is bouncing, so the user ends the session with **quit.**

```
$ telnet smtpsrv 25
Trying 192.168.1.1...
Connected to smtpsrv.example.com.
Escape character is '^]'.
helo example.com
220 smtpsrv.example.com ESMTP Sendmail 8.13.1/8.13.1; Wed, 4 May 2005 00:13:43 -0500 (CDT)
250 smtpsrv.example.com Hello desktop.example.com [192.168.1.97], pleased to meet you
mail from:user@spammer.com
571 5.0.0 Domain banned for spamming
quit
221 2.0.0 smtpsrv.example.com closing connection
```

The telnet utility allows you to use any protocol you want, as long as you know it well enough to type commands manually.

ftp: TRANSFERS FILES OVER A NETWORK

The File Transfer Protocol (FTP) is a method of downloading files from and uploading files to another system using TCP/IP over a network. FTP is not a secure protocol; use it only for downloading public information from a public server. Most Web browsers can download files from FTP servers. Chapter 19 covers FTP clients and servers.

ping: TESTS A NETWORK CONNECTION

The ping[15] utility (http://ftp.arl.mil/~mike/ping.html) sends an ECHO_REQUEST packet to a remote computer. This packet causes the remote system to send back a reply. This exchange is a quick way to verify that a remote system is available and to check how well the network is operating, such as how fast it is or whether it is dropping data packets. The ping utility uses the ICMP (Internet Control Message Protocol) protocol. Without any options, ping tests the connection once per second until you abort execution with CONTROL-C.

```
$ ping tsx-11.mit.edu
PING tsx-11.mit.edu (18.7.14.121) 56(84) bytes of data.
64 bytes from TSX-11.MIT.EDU (18.7.14.121): icmp_seq=0 ttl=45 time=97.2 ms
64 bytes from TSX-11.MIT.EDU (18.7.14.121): icmp_seq=1 ttl=45 time=96.1 ms
64 bytes from TSX-11.MIT.EDU (18.7.14.121): icmp_seq=2 ttl=45 time=95.7 ms
64 bytes from TSX-11.MIT.EDU (18.7.14.121): icmp_seq=3 ttl=45 time=96.3 ms
CONTROL-C

--- tsx-11.mit.edu ping statistics ---
4 packets transmitted, 4 received, 0% packet loss, time 3001ms
rtt min/avg/max/mdev = 95.755/96.361/97.202/0.653 ms
```

This example shows that the remote system named **tsx-11.mit.edu** is up and available over the network.

By default ping sends packets containing 64 bytes (56 data bytes and 8 bytes of protocol header information). In the preceding example, four packets were sent to the system **tsx-11.mit.edu** before the user interrupted ping by pressing CONTROL-C. The four-part number in parentheses on each line is the remote system's IP address. A packet sequence number (called **icmp_seq**) is also given. If a packet is dropped, a gap occurs in the sequence numbers. The round-trip time is listed last; it represents the time (in milliseconds) that elapsed from when the packet was sent from the local system to the remote system until the reply from the remote system was received by the local system. This time is affected by the distance between the two systems, network traffic, and the load on both computers. Before it terminates, ping summarizes the results, indicating how many packets were sent and received as well as the minimum, average, maximum, and mean deviation round-trip times it measured. Use ping6 to test IPv6 networks.

When ping cannot connect

tip   If it is unable to contact the remote system, ping continues trying until you interrupt it with CONTROL-C. A system may not answer for any of several reasons: The remote computer may be down, the network interface or some part of the network between the systems may be broken, a software failure may have occurred, or the remote machine may be set up, for reasons of security, not to return pings (try pinging www.microsoft.com or www.ibm.com).

traceroute: TRACES A ROUTE OVER THE INTERNET

The traceroute utility traces the route that an IP packet follows, including all intermediary points traversed (called *network hops*), to its destination (the argument to traceroute—an Internet host). It displays a numbered list of hostnames, if available, and IP

---

15. The name ping mimics the sound of a sonar burst used by submarines to identify and communicate with each other. The word ping also expands to packet internet groper.

addresses, together with the round-trip time it took for a packet to reach each router along the way and an acknowledgment to get back. You can put this information to good use when you are trying to identify the location of a network bottleneck.

The traceroute utility has no concept of the path from one host to the next; instead, it simply sends out packets with increasing *TTL* (time to live) values. TTL is an IP header field that indicates how many more hops the packet should be allowed to make before being discarded or returned. In the case of a traceroute packet, the packet is returned by the host that has the packet when the TTL value is zero. The result is a list of hosts that the packet traveled through to get to its destination.

The traceroute utility can help you solve routing configuration problems and locate routing path failures. When you cannot reach a host, use traceroute to discover what path the packet follows, how far it gets, and what the delay is.

The next example shows the output of traceroute when it follows a route from a local computer to **www.linux.org**. The first line indicates the IP address of the target, the maximum number of hops that will be traced, and the size of the packets that will be used. Each numbered line contains the name and IP address of the intermediate destination, followed by the time it takes a packet to make a trip to that destination and back again. The traceroute utility sends three packets to each destination; thus three times appear on each line. Line 1 shows the statistics when a packet is sent to the local gateway (less than 3 milliseconds). Lines 4–6 show the packet bouncing around Mountain View (California) before it goes to San Jose. Between hops 13 and 14 the packet travels across the United States (San Francisco to somewhere in the East). By hop 18 the packet has found **www.linux.org**. The traceroute utility displays asterisks when it does not receive a response. Each asterisk indicates that traceroute has waited three seconds. Use traceroute6 to test IPv6 networks.

```
$ /usr/sbin/traceroute www.linux.org
traceroute to www.linux.org (198.182.196.56), 30 hops max, 38 byte packets
 1  gw.localco.com. (204.94.139.65)  2.904 ms   2.425 ms   2.783 ms
 2  covad-gw2.meer.net (209.157.140.1)  19.727 ms   23.287 ms   24.783 ms
 3  gw-mv1.meer.net (140.174.164.1)  18.795 ms   24.973 ms   19.207 ms
 4  d1-4-2.a02.mtvwca01.us.ra.verio.net (206.184.210.241)  59.091 ms d1-10-0-0-200.a03.
      mtvwca01.us.ra.verio.net (206.86.28.5)  54.948 ms   39.485 ms
 5  fa-11-0-0.a01.mtvwca01.us.ra.verio.net (206.184.188.1)  40.182 ms   44.405 ms 49.362 ms
 6  p1-1-0-0.a09.mtvwca01.us.ra.verio.net (205.149.170.66)  78.688 ms   66.266 ms 28.003 ms
 7  p1-12-0-0.a01.snjsca01.us.ra.verio.net (209.157.181.166) 32.424 ms 94.337 ms 54.946 ms
 8  f4-1-0.sjc0.verio.net (129.250.31.81)  38.952 ms   63.111 ms   49.083 ms
 9  sjc0.nuq0.verio.net (129.250.3.98)  45.031 ms   43.496 ms   44.925 ms
10  mae-west1.US.CRL.NET (198.32.136.10)  48.525 ms   66.296 ms   38.996 ms
11  t3-ames.3.sfo.us.crl.net (165.113.0.249)  138.808 ms   78.579 ms   68.699 ms
12  E0-CRL-SFO-02-E0X0.US.CRL.NET (165.113.55.2)  43.023 ms   51.910 ms   42.967 ms
13  sfo2-vva1.ATM.us.crl.net (165.113.0.254)  135.551 ms   154.606 ms   178.632 ms
14  mae-east-02.ix.ai.net (192.41.177.202)  158.351 ms   201.811 ms   204.560 ms
15  oc12-3-0-0.mae-east.ix.ai.net (205.134.161.2)  202.851 ms   155.667 ms   219.116 ms
16  border-ai.invlogic.com (205.134.175.254)  214.622 ms  *  190.423 ms
17  router.invlogic.com (198.182.196.1)  224.378 ms   235.427 ms   228.856 ms
18  www.linux.org (198.182.196.56)  207.964 ms   178.683 ms   179.483 ms
```

host AND dig: QUERY INTERNET NAMESERVERS

The host utility looks up an IP address given a name, or vice versa. The following example shows how to use host to look up the domain name of a machine, given an IP address:

```
$ host 140.174.164.2
2.164.174.140.in-addr.arpa. domain name pointer ns.meer.net.
```

You can also use host to determine the IP address of a domain name:

```
$ host ns.meer.net
ns.meer.net. has address 140.174.164.2
```

The dig (domain information groper) utility queries DNS servers and individual machines for information about a domain. A powerful utility, dig has many features that you may never use. It is more complex than host.

Chapter 24 on DNS has many examples of the use of host and dig.

jwhois: LOOKS UP INFORMATION ABOUT AN INTERNET SITE

The jwhois utility replaces whois and queries a **whois** server for information about an Internet site. This utility returns site contact and InterNIC or other registry information that can help you track down the person who is responsible for a site: Perhaps that person is sending you or your company *spam* (page 1056). Many sites on the Internet are easier to use and faster than jwhois. Use a browser and search engine to search on **whois** or go to www.networksolutions.com/whois or www.ripe.net/perl/whois to get started.

When you do not specify a **whois** server, jwhois defaults to **whois.internic.net.** Use the **–h** option to jwhois to specify a different **whois** server. See the jwhois info page for more options and setup information.

To obtain information on a domain name, specify the complete domain name, as in the following example:

```
$ jwhois sobell.com
[Querying whois.internic.net]
[Redirected to whois.godaddy.com]
[Querying whois.godaddy.com]
[whois.godaddy.com]
The data contained in Go Daddy Software, Inc.'s WhoIs database,
...
Registrant:
    Sobell Associates Inc
    POBox 460068
    San Francisco, California 94146-0068
    United States
```

```
Registered through: GoDaddy.com
Domain Name: SOBELL.COM
    Created on: 07-Apr-95
    Expires on: 08-Apr-13
    Last Updated on: 16-Jan-04

Administrative Contact:
    Sobell, Mark  sobell@meer.net
    Sobell Associates Inc
    PO BOX 460068
    SAN FRANCISCO, California 94146-0068
    United States
    9999999999      Fax -- 9999999999
Technical Contact:
    ,   hostmaster@meer.net
    meer.net
    po box 390804
    Mountain View, California 94039
    United States
    18888446337      Fax -- 18888446337

Domain servers in listed order:
    NS.MEER.NET
    NS2.MEER.NET
```

Several top-level registries serve various regions of the world. You are most likely to use the following ones:

North American registry	**whois.arin.net**
European registry	**www.ripe.net**
Asia-Pacific registry	**www.apnic.net**
U.S. military	**whois.nic.mil**
U.S. government	**www.nic.gov**

DISTRIBUTED COMPUTING

When many similar systems are found on the same network, it is often desirable to share common files and utilities among them. For example, a system administrator might choose to keep a copy of the system documentation on one computer's disk and to make those files available to remote systems. In this case, the system administrator configures the files so users who need to access the online documentation are not aware that the files are stored on a remote system. This type of setup, which is an example of *distributed computing,* not only conserves disk space but also allows you to update one central copy of the documentation rather than tracking down and updating copies scattered throughout the network on many different systems.

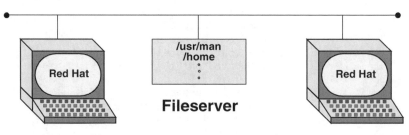

Figure 10-2 A fileserver

Figure 10-2 illustrates a *fileserver* that stores the system manual pages and users' home directories. With this arrangement, a user's files are always available to that user—no matter which system the user logs in on. Each system's disk might contain a directory to hold temporary files as well as a copy of the operating system. Chapter 22 contains instructions for setting up NFS clients and servers in networked configurations.

THE CLIENT/SERVER MODEL

Mainframe model   The client/server model was not the first computational model. First came the mainframe, which follows a one-machine-does-it-all model. That is, all the intelligence resides in one system, including the data and the program that manipulates and reports on the data. Users connect to a mainframe using terminals.

File-sharing model   With the introduction of PCs, file-sharing networks became available. In this scheme data is downloaded from a shared location to a user's PC, where a program then manipulates the data. The file-sharing model ran into problems as networks expanded and more users needed access to the data.

Client/server model   In the client/server model, a client uses a protocol, such as FTP, to request services, and a server provides the services that the client requests. Rather than providing data files as the file-sharing model does, the server in a client/server relationship is a database that provides only those pieces of information that the client needs or requests.

The client/server model dominates UNIX and Linux system networking and underlies most of the network services described in this book. FTP, NFS, DNS, email, and HTTP (the Web browsing protocol) all rely on the client/server model. Some servers, such as Web servers and browser clients, are designed to interact with specific utilities. Other servers, such as those supporting DNS, communicate with one another, in addition to answering queries from a variety of clients. Clients and servers can reside on the same or different systems running the same or different operating systems. The systems can be proximate or thousands of miles apart. A system that is a server to one system can turn around and act as a client to another. A server can reside on a single system or, as is the case with DNS, be distributed among thousands of geographically separated systems running many different operating systems.

Peer-to-peer model   The peer-to-peer (PTP) model, in which either program can initiate a transaction, stands in contrast to the client/server model. PTP protocols are common on small networks. For example, Microsoft's Network Neighborhood and Apple's AppleTalk both rely on broadcast-based PTP protocols for browsing and automatic configuration. The Zeroconf multicast DNS protocol is a PTP alternative DNS for small networks. The highest-profile PTP networks are those used for file sharing, such as Kazaa and GNUtella. Many of these networks are not pure PTP topologies. Pure PTP networks do not scale well, so networks such as Napster and Kazaa employ a hybrid approach.

DNS: Domain Name Service

DNS is a distributed service: Nameservers on thousands of machines around the world cooperate to keep the database up-to-date. The database itself, which maps hundreds of thousands of alphanumeric hostnames to numeric IP addresses, does not exist in one place. That is, no system has a complete copy of the database. Instead, each system that runs DNS knows which hosts are local to that site and understands how to contact other nameservers to learn about other, nonlocal hosts.

Like the Linux filesystem, DNS is organized hierarchically. Each country has an ISO (International Organization for Standardization) country code designation as its domain name. (For example, **AU** represents Australia, **IL** is Israel, and **JP** is Japan; see www.iana.org/cctld/cctld.htm for a complete list.) Although the United States is represented in the same way (**US**) and uses the standard two-letter Postal Service abbreviations to identify the next level of the domain, only governments and a few organizations use these codes. Schools in the **US** domain are represented by a third- (and sometimes second-) level domain: **k12**. For example, the domain name for Myschool in New York state could be www.myschool.k12.ny.us.

Following is a list of the six original top-level domains. These domains are used extensively within the United States and, to a lesser degree, by users in other countries:

COM	Commercial enterprises
EDU	Educational institutions
GOV	Nonmilitary government agencies
MIL	Military government agencies
NET	Networking organizations
ORG	Other (often nonprofit) organizations

As this book was being written, the following additional top-level domains had been approved for use:

AERO	Air-transport industry
BIZ	Business
COOP	Cooperatives
INFO	Unrestricted use
MUSEUM	Museums
NAME	Name registries

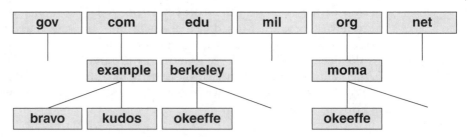

Figure 10-3   U.S. top-level domains

Like Internet addresses, domain names were once assigned by the Network Information Center (NIC, page 353); now they are assigned by several companies. A system's full name, referred to as its *fully qualified domain name* (FQDN), is unambiguous in the way that a simple hostname cannot be. The system **okeeffe.berkeley.edu** at the University of California at Berkeley (Figure 10-3) is not the same as one named **okeeffe.moma.org**, which might represent a host at the Museum of Modern Art. The domain name not only tells you something about where the system is located but also adds enough diversity to the namespace to avoid confusion when different sites choose similar names for their systems.

Unlike the filesystem hierarchy, the top-level domain name appears last (reading from left to right). Also, domain names are not case sensitive, so the names **okeeffe.berkeley.edu**, **okeeffe.Berkeley.edu**, and **okeeffe.Berkeley.EDU** refer to the same computer. Once a domain has been assigned, the local site is free to extend the hierarchy to meet local needs.

With DNS, email addressed to **user@example.com** can be delivered to the computer named **example.com** that handles the corporate mail and knows how to forward messages to user mailboxes on individual machines. As the company grows, its site administrator might decide to create organizational or geographical subdomains. The name **delta.ca.example.com** might refer to a system that supports California offices, for example, while **alpha.co.example.com** is dedicated to Colorado. Functional subdomains might be another choice, with **delta.sales.example.com** and **alpha.dev.example.com** representing the sales and development divisions, respectively.

BIND   On Linux systems, the most common interface to the DNS is BIND (Berkeley Internet Name Domain). BIND follows the client/server model. On any given local network, one or more systems may be running a nameserver, supporting all the local hosts as clients. When it wants to send a message to another host, a system queries the nearest nameserver to learn the remote host's IP address. The client, called a *resolver,* may be a process running on the same computer as the nameserver, or it may pass the request over the network to reach a server. To reduce network traffic and facilitate name lookups, the local nameserver maintains some knowledge of distant hosts. If the local server must contact a remote server to pick up an address, when the answer comes back, the local server adds that address to its internal table and reuses it for a while. The nameserver deletes the nonlocal information before it can become outdated. Refer to "TTL" on page 1060.

The system's translation of symbolic hostnames into addresses is transparent to most users; only the system administrator of a networked system needs to be concerned with the details of name resolution. Systems that use DNS for name resolution are generally capable of communicating with the greatest number of hosts—more than would be practical to maintain in a /etc/hosts file or private NIS database. Chapter 24 covers setting up and running a DNS server.

Three common sources are referenced for hostname resolution: NIS, DNS, and system files (such as /etc/hosts). Linux does not ask you to choose among these sources; rather, the **nsswitch.conf** file (page 435) allows you to choose any of these sources, in any combination, and in any order.

PORTS

Ports are logical channels on a network interface and are numbered from 1 to 65,535. Each network connection is uniquely identified by the IP address and port number of each endpoint.

In a system that has many network connections open simultaneously, the use of ports keeps *packets* (page 1047) flowing to and from the appropriate programs. A program that needs to receive data *binds* to a port and then uses that port for communication.

Privileged ports Services are associated with specific ports, generally with numbers less than 1024. These ports are called *privileged* (or *reserved*) *ports*. For security reasons, only **root** can bind to privileged ports. A service run on a privileged port provides assurance that the service is being provided by someone with authority over the system, with the exception that any user on Windows 98 and earlier Windows systems can bind to any port. Commonly used ports include 22 (SSH), 23 (TELNET), 80 (HTTP), 111 (Sun RPC), and 201–208 (AppleTalk).

NIS: NETWORK INFORMATION SERVICE

NIS (Network Information Service) simplifies the maintenance of frequently used administrative files by keeping them in a central database and having clients contact the database server to retrieve information from the database. Just as DNS addresses the problem of keeping multiple copies of **hosts** files up-to-date, NIS deals with the issue of keeping system-independent configuration files (such as /etc/passwd) current. Refer to Chapter 21 for coverage of NIS.

NFS: NETWORK FILESYSTEM

The NFS (Network Filesystem) protocol allows a server to share selected local directory hierarchies with client systems on a heterogeneous network. Files on the remote fileserver appear as if they are present on the local system. NFS is covered in Chapter 22.

optional

INTERNET SERVICES

Linux Internet services are provided by daemons that run continuously or by a daemon that is started automatically by the **xinetd** daemon (page 376) when a service request comes in. The **/etc/services** file lists network services (for example, **telnet**, **ftp**, and **ssh**) and their associated numbers. Any service that uses TCP/IP or UDP/IP has an entry in this file. IANA (Internet Assigned Numbers Authority) maintains a database of all permanent, registered services. The **/etc/services** file usually lists a small, commonly used subset of services. Visit www.rfc.net/rfc1700.html for more information and a complete list of registered services.

Most of the daemons (the executable files) are stored in **/usr/sbin**. By convention the names of many daemons end with the letter **d** to distinguish them from utilities (one common daemon whose name does not end in **d** is **sendmail**). The prefix **in.** or **rpc.** is often used for daemon names. Look at **/usr/sbin/*d** to see a list of many of the daemon programs on the local system. Refer to "Init Scripts: Start and Stop System Services" on page 404 and "service: Configures Services I" on page 406 for information about starting and stopping these daemons.

To see how a daemon works, consider what happens when you run **ssh**. The local system contacts the **ssh** daemon (**sshd**) on the remote system to establish a connection. The two systems negotiate the connection according to a fixed protocol. Each system identifies itself to the other, and then they take turns asking each other specific questions and waiting for valid replies. Each network service follows its own protocol.

In addition to the daemons that support the utilities described up to this point, many other daemons support system-level network services that you will not typically interact with. Table 10-4 lists some of these daemons.

Table 10-4   Common daemons

Daemon	Used for or by	Function
acpid	Advanced configuration and power interface	Flexible daemon for delivering ACPI events. Replaces **apmd**.
apmd	Advanced power management	Reports and takes action on specified changes in system power, including shutdowns. Useful with machines, such as laptops, that run on batteries.
atd	at	Executes a command once at a specific time and date. See **crond** for periodic execution of a command.
automount	Automatic mounting	Automatically mounts filesystems when they are accessed. Automatic mounting is a way of demand-mounting remote directories without having to hard-configure them into **/etc/fstab**.

Table 10-4   Common daemons *(continued)*

Daemon	Used for or by	Function
crond	cron	Used for periodic execution of tasks. This daemon looks in the **/var/spool/cron** directory for files with filenames that correspond to users' usernames. It also looks at the **/etc/crontab** file and at files in the **/etc/cron.d** directory. When a task comes up for execution, **crond** executes it as the user who owns the file that describes the task.
dhcpcd	DHCP	DHCP client daemon (page 432).
dhcpd	DHCP	Assigns Internet address, subnet mask, default gateway, DNS, and other information to hosts. This protocol answers DHCP requests and, optionally, BOOTP requests. Refer to "DHCP: Configures Hosts" on page 431.
ftpd	FTP	Handles FTP requests. Refer to "ftp: Transfers Files over a Network" on page 365. See also **vsftpd** (page 601). Launched by **xinetd**.
gpm	General-purpose mouse or GNU paste manager	Allows you to use a mouse to cut and paste text on console applications.
httpd	HTTP	The Web server daemon (Apache, page 785).
in.fingerd	finger	Handles requests for user information from the finger utility. Launched by **xinetd**.
inetd		Deprecated in favor of **xinetd**.
lpd	Line printer spooler daemon	Launched by **xinetd** when printing requests come to the machine. Not used with CUPS.
named	DNS	Supports DNS (page 719).
nfsd, statd, lockd, mountd, rquotad	NFS	These five daemons operate together to handle NFS (page 673) operations. The **nfsd** daemon handles file and directory requests. The **statd** and **lockd** daemons implement network file and record locking. The **mountd** daemon converts filesystem name requests from the mount utility into NFS handles and checks access permissions. If disk quotas are enabled, **rquotad** handles those.
ntpd	NTP	Synchronizes time on network computers. Requires a **/etc/ntp.conf** file. For more information go to www.ntp.org.
portmap	RPC	Maps incoming requests for RPC service numbers to TCP or UDP port numbers on the local system. Refer to "RPC Network Services" on page 377.
pppd	PPP	For a modem, this protocol controls the pseudointerface represented by the IP connection between the local computer and a remote computer. Refer to "PPP: Point-to-Point Protocol" on page 353.

Table 10-4 Common daemons (continued)

Daemon	Used for or by	Function
rexecd	rexec	Allows a remote user with a valid username and password to run programs on a system. Its use is generally deprecated for security reasons; certain programs, such as PC-based X servers, may still have it as an option. Launched by **xinetd**.
routed	Routing tables	Manages the routing tables so your system knows where to send messages that are destined for remote networks. If your system does not have a **/etc/defaultrouter** file, **routed** is started automatically to listen to incoming routing messages and to advertise outgoing routes to other systems on the local network. A newer daemon, the gateway daemon (**gated**), offers enhanced configurability and support for more routing protocols and is proportionally more complex.
sendmail	Mail programs	The **sendmail** daemon came from Berkeley UNIX and has been available for a long time. The de facto mail transfer program on the Internet, the **sendmail** daemon always listens on port 25 for incoming mail connections and then calls a local delivery agent, such as **/bin/mail**. Mail user agents, such as KMail and Thunderbird, typically use **sendmail** to deliver mail messages.
smbd, nmbd	Samba	Allow Windows PCs to share files and printers with UNIX and Linux computers (page 695).
sshd	ssh, scp	Enables secure logins between remote systems (page 591).
syslogd	System log	Transcribes important system events and stores them in files and/or forwards them to users or another host running the **syslogd** daemon. This daemon is configured with **/etc/syslog.conf** and used with the syslog utility. See page 562.
talkd	talk	Allows you to have a conversation with another user on the same or a remote machine. The **talkd** daemon handles the connections between the machines. The talk utility on each system contacts the **talkd** daemon on the other system for a bidirectional conversation. Launched by **xinetd**.
telnetd	TELNET	One of the original Internet remote access protocols (page 363). Launched by **xinetd**.
tftpd	TFTP	Used to boot a system or get information from a network. Examples include network computers, routers, and some printers. Launched by **xinetd**.
timed	Time server	On a LAN synchronizes time with other computers that are also running **timed**.
xinetd	Internet superserver	Listens for service requests on network connections and starts up the appropriate daemon to respond to any particular request. Because of **xinetd**, a system does not need the daemons running continually to handle various network requests. For more information refer to "The xinetd Superserver" on page 425.

PROXY SERVERS

A *proxy* is a network service that is authorized to act for a system while not being part of that system. A proxy server or proxy gateway provides proxy services; it is a transparent intermediary, relaying communications back and forth between an application, such as a browser and a server, usually outside of a LAN and frequently on the Internet. When more than one process uses the proxy gateway/server, the proxy must keep track of which processes are connecting to which hosts/servers so that it can route the return messages to the proper process. The most commonly encountered proxies are email and Web proxies.

A proxy server/gateway insulates the local computer from all other computers or from specified domains by using at least two IP addresses: one to communicate with the local computer and one to communicate with a server. The proxy server/gateway examines and changes the header information on all packets it handles so that it can encode, route, and decode them properly. The difference between a proxy gateway and a proxy server is that the proxy server usually includes *cache* (page 1023) to store frequently used Web pages so that the next request for that page is available locally and quickly; a proxy gateway typically does not use cache. The terms "proxy server" and "proxy gateway" are frequently used interchangeably.

Proxy servers/gateways are available for such common Internet services as HTTP, HTTPS, FTP, SMTP, and SNMP. When an HTTP proxy sends queries from local systems, it presents a single organizationwide IP address (the external IP address of the proxy server/gateway) to all servers. It funnels all user requests to the appropriate servers and keeps track of them. When the responses come back, the HTTP proxy fans them out to the appropriate applications using each machine's unique IP address, thereby protecting local addresses from remote/specified servers.

Proxy servers/gateways are generally just one part of an overall firewall strategy to prevent intruders from stealing information or damaging an internal network. Other functions, which can be either combined with or kept separate from the proxy server/gateway, include packet filtering, which blocks traffic based on origin and type, and user activity reporting, which helps management learn how the Internet is being used.

RPC NETWORK SERVICES

Much of the client/server interaction over a network is implemented using the RPC (Remote Procedure Call) protocol, which is implemented as a set of library calls that make network access transparent to the client and server. RPC specifies and interprets messages but does not concern itself with transport protocols; it runs on top of TCP/IP and UDP/IP. Services that use RPC include NFS and NIS. RPC was developed by Sun as ONC RPC (Open Network Computing Remote Procedure Calls) and differs from Microsoft RPC.

In the client/server model, a client contacts a server on a specific port (page 373) to avoid any mixup between services, clients, and servers. To avoid maintaining a long list of port numbers and to enable new clients/servers to start up without registering a port number with a central registry, when a server that uses RPC starts, it specifies the port it expects to be contacted on. RPC servers typically use port numbers that have been defined by Sun. If a server does not use a predefined port number, it picks an arbitrary number.

The server then registers this port with the RPC portmapper (the **portmap** daemon) on the local system. The server tells the daemon which port number it is listening on and which RPC program numbers it serves. Through these exchanges, the **portmap** daemon learns the location of every registered port on the host and the programs that are available on each port. The **portmap** daemon, which always listens on port 111 for both TCP and UDP, must be running to make RPC calls.

Files   The **/etc/rpc** file (page 456) maps RPC services to RPC numbers. The **/etc/services** file (page 456) lists system services.

RPC client/server communication   The sequence of events for communication between an RPC client and server occurs as follows:

1. The client program on the client system makes an RPC call to obtain data from a (remote) server system. (The client issues a "read record from a file" request.)

2. If RPC has not yet established a connection with the server system for the client program, it contacts **portmap** on port 111 of the server and asks which port the desired RPC server is listening on (for example, **rpc.nfsd**).

3. The **portmap** daemon on the remote server looks in its tables and returns a UDP or TCP port number to the local system, the client (typically 2049 for **nfs**).

4. The RPC libraries on the server system receive the call from the client and pass the request to the appropriate server program. The origin of the request is transparent to the server program. (The filesystem receives the "read record from file" request.)

5. The server responds to the request. (The filesystem reads the record.)

6. The RPC libraries on the remote server return the result over the network to the client program. (The read record is returned to the calling program.)

Because standard RPC servers are normally started by the **xinetd** daemon (page 389), the **portmap** daemon must be started before the **xinetd** daemon is invoked. The init scripts (page 404) make sure **portmap** starts before **xinetd**. You can confirm this sequence by looking at the numbers associated with **/etc/rc.d/*/S*portmap** and **/etc/rc.d/*/S*/xinetd**. If the **portmap** daemon stops, you must restart all RPC servers on the local system.

USENET

One of the earliest information services available on the Internet, Usenet is an electronic bulletin board that allows users with common interests to exchange information. Usenet comprises an informal, loosely connected network of systems that exchange email and news items (commonly referred to as *netnews*). It was formed in 1979 when a few sites decided to share some software and information on topics of common interest. They agreed to contact one another and to pass the information along over dial-up telephone lines (at that time running at 1,200 baud at best), using UNIX's uucp utility (UNIX-to-UNIX copy program).

The popularity of Usenet led to major changes in uucp to handle the escalating volume of messages and sites. Today much of the news flows over network links using a sophisticated protocol designed especially for this purpose: NNTP (Network News Transfer Protocol). The news messages are stored in a standard format, and the many public domain programs available let you read them. An old, simple interface is named readnews. Other interfaces, such as rn, its X Window System cousin xrn, tin, nn, and xvnews, have many features that help you browse through and reply to the articles that are available or create articles of your own. In addition, Netscape and Mozilla include an interface that you can use to read news (Netscape/Mozilla News) as part of their Web browsers. One of the easiest ways to read netnews is to go to groups.google.com. The program you select to read netnews is largely a matter of personal taste.

As programs to read netnews articles have been ported to non-UNIX and non-Linux systems, the community of netnews users has become highly diversified. In the UNIX tradition, categories of netnews groups are structured hierarchically. The top level includes such designations as **comp** (computer-related), **misc** (miscellaneous), **rec** (recreation), **sci** (science), **soc** (social issues), and **talk** (ongoing discussions). Usually at least one regional category is at the top level, such as **ba** (San Francisco Bay Area), and includes information about local events. New categories are continually being added to the more than 30,000 newsgroups. The names of newsgroups resemble domain names but are read from left to right (like Linux filenames): **comp.os.unix.misc, comp.lang.c, misc.jobs.offered, rec.skiing, sci.med, soc.singles,** and **talk.politics** are but a few examples. The following article appeared in **linux.redhat.install:**

```
> I have just installed Fedora 5 and when i try to start X I get the
> following error message:
>
> Fatal Server Error.
> no screens found
>
> XIO: Fatal IO err 104 (connection reset by peer) on X server ",0.0" after
> 0 requests (0 known processed) with 0 events remaining.
>
> How can I solve this problem?
>
> Thanks,
> Fred

Fred,

It would appear that your X configuration is incorrect or missing.  You
should run system-config-display and set up the configuration for your
video card and monitor.

Carl
```

A great deal of useful information is available on Usenet, but you need patience and perseverance to find what you are looking for. You can ask a question, as the user did in the previous example, and someone from halfway around the world might answer it. Before posing such a simple question and causing it to appear on thousands of systems around the world, however, first ask yourself whether you can get help in a less invasive way. Try the following:

- Refer to the man pages and info.

- Look through the files in **/usr/share/doc**.

- Ask the system administrator or another user for help.

- All of the popular newsgroups have FAQs (lists of frequently asked questions). Consult these lists and see whether your question has been answered. FAQs are periodically posted to the newsgroups; in addition, all the FAQs are archived at sites around the Internet, including Google groups (groups.google.com).

- Because someone has probably asked the same question earlier, search the netnews archives for an answer. Try looking at groups.google.com, which has a complete netnews archive.

- Use a search engine to find an answer. One good way to get help is to search on an error message.

- Review support documents at **www.redhat.com**.

- Contact a Red Hat Linux users' group.

Post a query to the worldwide Usenet community as a last resort. If you are stuck on a Linux question and cannot find any other help, try submitting it to one of these newsgroups:

- **linux.redhat.install**

- **linux.redhat.misc**

For more generic questions, try these lists:

- **comp.os.linux.misc**

- **comp.os.linux.networking**

- **comp.os.linux.security**

- **comp.os.linux.setup**

- **linux.redhat.rpm**

One way to find out about new tools and services is to read Usenet news. The **comp.os.linux** hierarchy is of particular interest to Linux users; for example, news about newly released software for Linux is posted to **comp.os.linux.announce**. People often announce the availability of free software there, along with instructions on how to get a copy for your own use using anonymous FTP (page 607). Other tools to help you find resources, both old and new, exist on the network; see Appendix B.

WWW: World Wide Web

The World Wide Web (WWW, W3, or the Web) provides a unified, interconnected interface to the vast amount of information stored on computers around the world. The idea that spawned the World Wide Web came from the mind of Tim Berners-Lee (www.w3.org/People/Berners-Lee) of the European Particle Physics Laboratory (CERN) in response to a need to improve communications throughout the high-energy physics community. The first-generation solution consisted of a notebook program named Enquire, short for *Enquire Within Upon Everything* (the name of a book from Berners-Lee's childhood), which he created in 1980 on a NeXT computer and which supported links between named nodes. Not until 1989 was the concept proposed as a global hypertext project to be known as the World Wide Web. In 1990, Berners-Lee wrote a proposal for a hypertext project, which eventually produced HTML (Hypertext Markup Language), the common language of the Web. The World Wide Web program became available on the Internet in the summer of 1991. By designing the tools to work with existing protocols, such as FTP and gopher, the researchers who created the Web produced a system that is generally useful for many types of information and across many types of hardware and operating systems.

The WWW is another example of the client/server paradigm. You use a WWW client application, or *browser,* to retrieve and display information stored on a server that may be located anywhere on your local network or the Internet. WWW clients can interact with many types of servers. For example, you can use a WWW client to contact a remote FTP server and display the list of files it offers for anonymous FTP. Most commonly you use a WWW client to contact a WWW server, which offers support for the special features of the World Wide Web that are described in the remainder of this chapter.

The power of the Web derives from its use of *hypertext,* a way to navigate through information by following cross-references (called *links*) from one piece of information to another. To use the Web effectively, you need to run interactive network applications. The first GUI for browsing the Web was a tool named Mosaic, which was released in February 1993. Designed at the National Center for Supercomputer Applications at the University of Illinois, its introduction sparked a dramatic increase in the number of users of the World Wide Web. Marc Andreessen, who participated in the Mosaic project at the University of Illinois, later cofounded Netscape Communications with the founder of Silicon Graphics, Jim Clark. The pair created Netscape Navigator, a Web client program that was designed to perform better and support more features than the Mosaic browser. Netscape Navigator has enjoyed immense success and has become a popular choice for exploring the World Wide Web. Important for Linux users is the fact that from its inception Netscape has provided versions of its tools that run on Linux. Also, Netscape created Mozilla (mozilla.org) as an open-source browser project.

These browsers provide GUIs that allow you to listen to sounds, watch Web events or live news reports, and display pictures as well as text, giving you access to *hypermedia.* A picture on your screen may be a link to more detailed, nonverbal information, such as a copy of the same picture at a higher resolution or a short animation. If your system can produce audio output, you can listen to audio clips that have been linked to a document.

URL: UNIFORM RESOURCE LOCATOR

Consider the URL http://www.w3.org/Consortium/siteindex. The first component in the URL indicates the type of resource, in this case **http** (HTTP—Hypertext Transfer Protocol). Other valid resource names, such as **https** (HTTPS—secure HTTP) and **ftp** (FTP—File Transfer Protocol), represent information available on the Web using other protocols. Next come a colon and double slash (**://**). Frequently the **http://** string is omitted from a URL in print, as you seldom need to enter it to reach the URL. The next element is the full name of the host that acts as the server for the information (**www.w3.org/**). The rest of the URL consists of a relative pathname to the file that contains the information (**Consortium/siteindex**). If you enter a URL in the location bar of a Web browser, the Web server returns the page, frequently an *HTML* (page 1036) file, pointed to by this URL.

By convention many sites identify their WWW servers by prefixing a host or domain name with **www**. For example, you can reach the Web server at the New Jersey Institute of Technology at www.njit.edu. When you use a browser to explore the World Wide Web, you may never need to enter a URL. However, as more information is published in hypertext form, you cannot help but find URLs everywhere—not just online in email messages and Usenet articles, but also in newspapers, in advertisements, and on product labels.

BROWSERS

Mozilla (www.mozilla.org) is the open-source counterpart to Netscape. Mozilla, which was first released in March 1998, was based on Netscape 4 code. Since then, Mozilla has been under continuous development by employees of Netscape (now a division of AOL), Red Hat, and other companies and by contributors from the community. Firefox is the Web browser component of Mozilla. KDE offers Konqueror, an all-purpose file manager and Web browser (page 94). Other browsers include Epiphany (www.gnome.org/projects/epiphany) and Opera (www.opera.com). Although each Web browser is unique, all of them allow you to move about the Internet, viewing HTML documents, listening to sounds, and retrieving files. If you do not use the X Window System, try a text browser, such as lynx or links. The lynx browser works well with Braille terminals.

SEARCH ENGINES

Search engine is a name that applies to a group of hardware and software tools that help you search for World Wide Web sites that contain specific information. A search engine relies on a database of information collected by a *Web crawler,* a program that regularly looks through the millions of pages that make up the World

Wide Web. A search engine must also have a way of collating the information the Web crawler collects so that you can access it quickly, easily, and in a manner that makes it most useful to you. This part of the search engine, called an *index*, allows you to search for a word, a group of words, or a concept; it returns the URLs of Web pages that pertain to what you are searching for. Many different types of search engines are available on the Internet, each with its own set of strengths and weaknesses.

CHAPTER SUMMARY

A Linux system attached to a network is probably communicating on an Ethernet, which may in turn be linked to other local area networks (LANs) and wide area networks (WANs). Communication between LANs and WANs requires the use of gateways and routers. Gateways translate the local data into a format suitable for the WAN, and routers make decisions about the optimal routing of the data along the way. The most widely used network, by far, is the Internet.

Basic networking tools allow Linux users to log in and run commands on remote systems (ssh, telnet) and copy files quickly from one system to another (scp, ftp/sftp). Many tools that were originally designed to support communication on a single-host computer (for example, finger and talk) have since been extended to recognize network addresses, thus allowing users on different systems to interact with one another. Other features, such as the Network Filesystem (NFS), were created to extend the basic UNIX model and to simplify information sharing.

Concern is growing about our ability to protect the security and privacy of machines connected to networks and of data transmitted over networks. Toward this end, many new tools and protocols have been created: ssh, scp, HTTPS, IPv6, firewall hardware and software, VPN, and so on. Many of these tools take advantage of newer, more impenetrable encryption techniques. In addition, some weaker concepts (such as that of trusted hosts) and some tools (such as finger and rwho) are being discarded in the name of security.

Computer networks offer two major advantages of over other ways of connecting computers: They enable systems to communicate at high speeds and they require few physical interconnections (typically one per system, often on a shared cable). The Internet Protocol (IP), the universal language of the Internet, has made it possible for dissimilar computer systems around the world to readily communicate with one another. Technological advances continue to improve the performance of computer systems and the networks that link them.

One way to gather information on the Internet is via Usenet. Many Linux users routinely peruse Usenet news (netnews) to learn about the latest resources available for their systems. Usenet news is organized into newsgroups that cover a wide range of topics, computer-related and otherwise. To read Usenet news, you need to have access to a news server and the appropriate client software. Many modern email programs, such as Mozilla and Netscape, can display netnews.

The rapid increase of network communication speeds in recent years has encouraged the development of many new applications and services. The World Wide Web provides access to vast information stores on the Internet and makes extensive use of hypertext links to promote efficient searching through related documents. It adheres to the client/server model that is so pervasive in networking. Typically the WWW client is local to a site or is made available through an Internet service provider. WWW servers are responsible for providing the information requested by their many clients.

Mozilla/Firefox is a WWW client program that has enormous popular appeal. Firefox and other browsers use a GUI to give you access to text, picture, and audio information: Making extensive use of these hypermedia simplifies access to and enhances the presentation of information.

EXERCISES

1. Describe the similarities and differences between these utilities:

   a. scp and ftp

   b. ssh and telnet

   c. rsh and ssh

2. Assuming rwho is disabled on the systems on your LAN, describe two ways to find out who is logged in on some of the other machines attached to your network.

3. Explain the client/server model. Give three examples of services on Linux systems that take advantage of this model.

4. A software implementation of chess was developed by GNU and is available for free. How can you use the Internet to find a copy and download it?

5. What is the difference between the World Wide Web and the Internet?

6. If you have access to the World Wide Web, answer the following questions.

   a. Which browser do you use?

   b. What is the URL of the author of this book's home page? How many links does it have?

   c. Does your browser allow you to create bookmarks? If so, how do you create a bookmark? How can you delete one?

7. Give one advantage and two disadvantages of using a wireless network.

ADVANCED EXERCISES

8. Suppose the link between routers 1 and 2 is down in the Internet shown in Figure 10-1 on page 350. What happens if someone at site C sends a message to a user on a workstation attached to the Ethernet cable at site A? What happens if the router at site A is down? What does this tell you about designing network configurations?

9. If you have a class B network and want to divide it into subnets, each with 126 hosts, which subnet mask should you use? How many networks will be available? What are the four addresses (broadcast and network number) for the network starting at 131.204.18?

10. Suppose you have 300 hosts and want to have no more than 50 hosts per subnet. What size of address block should you request from your ISP? How many class C–equivalent addresses would you need? How many subnets would you have left over from your allocation?

11. a. On your system, find two daemons running that are not listed in this chapter and explain what purpose they serve.

    b. Review which services/daemons are automatically started on your system, and consider which you might turn off. Are there any services/daemons in the list in Table 10-4 on page 374 that you would consider adding?

PART IV
SYSTEM ADMINISTRATION

11

SYSTEM ADMINISTRATION: CORE CONCEPTS

The job of a system administrator is to keep one or more systems in a useful and convenient state for users. On a Linux system, the administrator and user may both be you, with you and the computer being separated by only a few feet. Or the system administrator may be halfway around the world, supporting a network of systems, with you being simply one of thousands of users. A system administrator can be one person who works part-time taking care of a system and perhaps is also a user of the system. Or the administrator can be several people, all working full-time to keep many systems running.

389

A well-maintained system

- Runs quickly enough so users do not get too frustrated waiting for the system to respond or complete a task.

- Has enough storage to accommodate users' reasonable needs.

- Provides a working environment appropriate to each user's abilities and requirements.

- Is secure from malicious and accidental acts altering its performance or compromising the security of the data it holds and exchanges with other systems.

- Is backed up regularly, with recently backed-up files readily available to users.

- Has recent copies of the software that users need to get their jobs done.

- Is easier to administer than a poorly maintained system.

In addition, a system administrator should be available to help users with all types of system-related problems—from logging in to obtaining and installing software updates to tracking down and fixing obscure network issues.

Part V of this book breaks system administration into seven chapters:

- Chapter 11 covers the core concepts of system administration, including Superuser, system operation, the Red Hat configuration tools and other useful utilities, general information about setting up and securing a server (including a section on DHCP), and PAM.

- Chapter 12 covers files, directories, and filesystems from an administrator's point of view.

- Chapter 13 covers installing software on the system, including how to use yum, pirut, Red Hat Network (RHN), up2date, BitTorrent, and wget.

- Chapter 14 discusses how to set up local and remote printers that use the CUPS printing system.

- Chapter 15 explains how to rebuild the Linux kernel.

- Chapter 16 covers additional system administrator tasks and tools, including setting up users and groups, backing up files, scheduling tasks, printing system reports, and general problem solving.

- Chapter 17 goes into detail about how to set up a LAN, including setting up and configuring the network hardware and configuring the software.

Because Linux is configurable and runs on a variety of platforms (Sun SPARC, DEC/Compaq Alpha, Intel x86, AMD, PowerPC, and more), this chapter cannot discuss every system configuration or every action you will have to take as a system administrator. Instead, this chapter seeks to familiarize you with the concepts you need to understand and the tools you need to use to maintain a Red Hat Enterprise Linux or Fedora Core system. Where it is not possible to go into depth about a subject, the chapter provides references to other sources.

This chapter assumes that you are familiar with the following terms:

block device (page 1021)   *filesystem* (page 1032)   *root filesystem* (page 1053)

daemon (page 1027)   *fork* (page 1032)   *runlevel* (page 1054)

device (page 1028)   *kernel* (page 1039)   *signal* (page 1055)

device filename (page 1029)   *login shell* (page 1041)   *spawn* (page 1056)

disk partition (page 1029)   *mount* (page 1043)   *system console* (page 1059)

environment (page 1031)   *process* (page 1049)   *X server* (page 1064)

If something does not work, see if the problem is caused by SELinux

tip   If a server or other system software does not work properly, especially if it displays a permissions-related error message, the problem may lie with SELinux. To see if SELinux is the cause of the problem, put SELinux in permissive mode and run the software again. If the problem goes away, you need to modify the SELinux policy. Remember to turn SELinux back on. For more information refer to "Setting the Targeted Policy with system-config-securitylevel" on page 402.

SYSTEM ADMINISTRATOR AND SUPERUSER

Much of what a system administrator does is work that ordinary users do not have permission to do. When performing one of these tasks, the system administrator logs in as **root** (or uses another method; see the list starting on page 392) to have systemwide powers that are beyond those of ordinary users: A user with **root** privileges is referred to as *Superuser*. The username is **root** by default. Superuser has the following powers and more:

- Some commands, such as those that add new users, partition hard drives, and change system configuration, can be executed only by **root**. Superuser can use certain tools, such as sudo, to give specific users permission to perform tasks that are normally reserved for Superuser.

- Read, write, and execute file access and directory access permissions do not affect **root**: Superuser can read from, write to, and execute all files, as well as examine and work in all directories.

- Some restrictions and safeguards that are built into some commands do not apply to **root**. For example, **root** can change any user's password without knowing the old password.

When you are running with **root** (Superuser) privileges, the shell by convention displays a special prompt to remind you of your status. By default this prompt is or ends with a pound sign (#).

To lessen the chance that a user other than Superuser will try to use them by mistake, many of the utilities that Superuser runs are kept in the **/sbin** and **/usr/sbin** directories, rather than in **/bin** and **/usr/bin**. (Many of these utilities can be run by ordinary users.) You can execute these utilities by giving their full pathnames on the command line (for example, **/sbin/runlevel**). When you log in as **root**, these directories are in your **PATH** (page 292) by default.

Least privilege

caution   When you are working on the computer, especially when you are working as the system administrator, perform any task by using the least privilege possible. When you can perform a task logged in as an ordinary user, do so. When you must be logged in as Superuser, do as much as you can as an ordinary user, log in or use su so that you have **root** privileges, complete the part of the task that has to be done as Superuser, and revert to being an ordinary user as soon as you can. Because you are more likely to make a mistake when you are rushing, this concept becomes more important when you have less time to apply it.

You can gain or grant Superuser privileges in a number of ways:

1. When you bring the system up in single-user mode (page 409), you are Superuser.

2. Once the system is up and running in multiuser mode (page 410), you can log in as **root**. When you supply the proper password, you will be Superuser.

3. You can give an su (substitute user) command while you are logged in as yourself and, with the proper password, you will have Superuser privileges. For more information refer to "su: Gives You Another User's Privileges" on page 393.

4. You can use sudo selectively to give users Superuser privileges for a limited amount of time on a per-user and per-command basis. The sudo utility is controlled by the **/etc/sudoers** file, which must be set up by **root**. Refer to the sudo man page for more information.

5. Any user can create a *setuid* (set user ID) file (page 183). Setuid programs run on behalf of the owner of the file and have all the access privileges that the owner has. While you are running as Superuser, you can change the permissions of a file owned by **root** to setuid. When an ordinary user executes a file that is owned by **root** and has setuid permissions, the program has *full root privileges*. In other words, the program can do anything that **root** can do and that the program does or allows the user to do. The user's privileges do not change. When the program finishes running, all user privileges revert to the way they were before the program started. Setuid programs that are owned by **root** are both extremely powerful and extremely dangerous to system security, which is why a system contains very few of them. Examples of setuid programs that are owned by **root** include passwd, at, and crontab. The following example shows two ways for Superuser to give a program setuid privileges:

```
# ls -l my*
-rwxr-xr-x   1 root      other       24152 Apr 29 16:30 myprog
-rwxr-xr-x   1 root      other       24152 Apr 29 16:31 myprog2
# chmod 4755 myprog
# chmod u+s myprog2
# ls -l my*
-rwsr-xr-x   1 root      other       24152 Apr 29 16:30 myprog
-rwsr-xr-x   1 root      other       24152 Apr 29 16:31 myprog2
```

The s in the owner execute position of the ls –l output (page 181) indicates that the file has setuid permission.

root-owned setuid programs are extremely dangerous

security   Because a **root**-owned setuid program allows someone who does not know the **root** password to have the powers of Superuser, it is a tempting target for a malicious user. A system should have as few of these programs as necessary. You can disable setuid programs at the filesystem level by mounting a filesystem with the **nosuid** option (page 467). You can also use SELinux (page 400) to disable setuid programs. See page 399 for a command that lists setuid files on the local system.

6. Some programs ask you for a password (either your password or the **root** password, depending on the particular command and the configuration of the system) when they start. When you provide the **root** password, the program runs with Superuser privileges.

   When a program requests the **root** password when it starts, you stop running as the privileged user when you quit using the program. This setup keeps you from remaining logged in as Superuser when you do not need or intend to be. Refer to "consolehelper: Runs Programs as root" on page 394.

Some techniques limit the number of ways to become Superuser. PAM (page 438) controls the who, when, and how of logging in. The **/etc/securetty** file controls which terminals (ttys) a user can log in on as **root**. The **/etc/security/access.conf** file adds another dimension to login control (see the file for details).

Do not allow root access over the Internet

security   Prohibiting **root** logins using **login** over a network is the default policy of Red Hat Enterprise Linux and Fedora Core and is implemented by the PAM **securetty** module. The **/etc/security/access.conf** file must contain the names of all users and terminals/workstations that you want a user to be able to log in on as **root**. Initially every line in **access.conf** is commented out.

You can, however, log in as **root** over a network using ssh (page 579). As shipped by Red Hat, ssh does not follow the instructions in **securetty** or **access.conf**. Also, in **/etc/ssh/sshd_config**, Red Hat sets **PermitRootLogin** to YES (it is set by default) to permit **root** to log in using ssh (page 594).

SYSTEM ADMINISTRATION TOOLS

Many tools can help you be an efficient and thorough system administrator. A few of these tools/utilities are described in this section, another group of administration utilities is described starting on page 415, and others are scattered throughout Part IV.

su: GIVES YOU ANOTHER USER'S PRIVILEGES

The su (substitute user) utility can create a shell or execute a program with the identity and permissions of a specified user. Follow **su** on the command line with the name of a user; if you are **root** or if you know the user's password, you take on the identity of that user. When you give an su command without an argument, su defaults to Superuser so that you take on the identity of **root** (you have to know the **root** password).

To be sure that you are using the system's official version of su (and not one planted on your system by a malicious user), specify su's absolute pathname (**/bin/su**) when you use it. (Of course, if someone has compromised your system enough that you are running a fake su command, you are in serious trouble anyway—but using an absolute pathname for su is still a good idea.)

When you give an su command to become Superuser, you spawn a new shell, which displays the # prompt. You return to your normal status (and your former shell and prompt) by terminating this shell: Press CONTROL-D, or give an exit command. Giving an su command by itself changes your user and group IDs but makes minimal changes to your environment. You still have the same **PATH** you did when you logged in as yourself. When you run a utility that is normally run by **root** (the utilities in **/sbin** and **/usr/sbin**), you need to specify an absolute pathname for the utility (such as **/sbin/service**). When you give the command **su –** (you can use **–l** or **––login** in place of the hyphen), you get a **root** login shell: It is as though you logged in as **root**. Not only are your user and group IDs those of **root**, but your entire environment is that of **root**. The login shell executes the appropriate startup scripts before displaying a prompt, and your **PATH** is set to what it would be if you had logged in as **root**, typically including **/sbin** and **/usr/sbin**.

Use the id utility to display the changes in your user and group IDs and in the groups you are associated with. In the following example, the information that starts with **context** pertains to SELinux:

```
$ id
uid=500(alex) gid=500(alex) groups=500(alex) context=user_u:system_r:unconfined_t
$ su
Password:
# id
uid=0(root) gid=0(root) groups=0(root),1(bin),2(daemon),3(sys), ...
```

You can use su with the **–c** option to run a single command with **root** privileges, returning to your original shell when the command finishes executing. The following example first shows that a user is not permitted to kill a process. With the use of **su –c** and the **root** password, the user is permitted to kill (page 395) the process. The quotation marks are necessary because **su –c** takes its command as a single argument.

```
$ kill -15 4982
-bash: kill: (4982) - Operation not permitted
$ su -c "kill -15 4982"
Password:
$
```

consolehelper: RUNS PROGRAMS AS root

The consolehelper utility can make it easier for someone who is logged in on the system console but not logged in as **root** to run system programs that normally can be

Superuser, PATH, and security

security The fewer directories you keep in your **PATH** when you are **root**, the less likely you will be to execute an untrusted program as **root**. If possible, keep only the default directories, along with **/sbin** and **/usr/sbin**, in **root**'s **PATH**. *Never include the working directory (as . or : : anywhere in PATH, or : as the last element of PATH).* For more information refer to "PATH: Where the Shell Looks for Programs" on page 292.

run only by **root**. PAM (page 438), which authenticates users, can be set to trust all console users, to require user passwords (not the **root** password), or to require **root** passwords before granting trust. The concept underlying consolehelper is that you may want to consider as trustworthy anyone who has access to the console. For example, Alex can log in on the console as himself and run halt without knowing the **root** password. For more information refer to the discussion of consolehelper on page 413 and to the consolehelper man page.

kill: SENDS A SIGNAL TO A PROCESS

The kill builtin sends a signal to a process. This signal may or may not terminate (kill) the process, depending on which signal is sent and how the process is designed. Refer to "trap: Catches a Signal" on page 933 for a discussion of the various signals and their interaction with a process. Running kill is not the first method a user or system administrator should try when a process needs to be aborted.

kill: Use the kill signal (–KILL or –9) as a method of last resort

caution When you do need to use kill, send the termination signal (**kill –TERM** or **kill –15**) first. Only if that tactic does not work should you attempt to use the kill signal (**kill –KILL** or **kill –9**).

Because of its inherent dangers, using a kill signal is a method of last resort, especially when you are running as Superuser. One kill command issued by **root** can bring the system down without warning.

Usually a user can kill a process by working in another window or by logging in on another terminal. Sometimes you may have to log in as **root** (or use su) to kill a process for a user. To kill a process, you need to know its PID. The ps utility can provide this information once you determine the name of the program the user is running and/or the username of the user. The top utility (page 550) can also be helpful in finding and killing (see top's **k** command) a runaway process.

In the following example, Sam complains that xeyes is stuck and that he cannot do anything from the xeyes window, not even close it. A more experienced user could open another window and kill the process, but in this case, you kill it for Sam. First use ps with the **–u** option, followed by the name of the user and the **–f** (full/wide) option to view all the processes associated with that user.

```
$ ps -u sam -f
UID        PID  PPID  C STIME TTY      TIME CMD
sam       2294  2259  0 09:31 ?    00:00:00 /bin/sh /usr/bin/startkde
sam       2339  2294  0 09:31 ?    00:00:00 /usr/bin/ssh-agent /usr/bin/dbus-launch
sam       2342     1  0 09:31 ?    00:00:00 dbus-daemon --fork --print-pid 8 --prin
sam       2343     1  0 09:31 ?    00:00:00 /usr/bin/dbus-launch --exit-with-sessio
sam       2396     1  0 09:31 ?    00:00:00 kdeinit Running...
sam       2399     1  0 09:31 ?    00:00:00 dcopserver [kdeinit] --nosid
sam       2401  2396  0 09:31 ?    00:00:00 klauncher [kdeinit]
sam       2403     1  0 09:31 ?    00:00:00 kded [kdeinit]
sam       2405     1  0 09:31 ?    00:00:00 /usr/libexec/gam_server
sam       2413  2396  0 09:31 ?    00:00:00 /usr/bin/artsd -F 10 -S 4096 -s 60 -m a
sam       2415     1  0 09:31 ?    00:00:00 kaccess [kdeinit]
sam       2416  2294  0 09:31 ?    00:00:00 kwrapper ksmserver
sam       2418     1  0 09:31 ?    00:00:00 ksmserver [kdeinit]
sam       2421  2396  0 09:31 ?    00:00:00 kwin [kdeinit] -session 1070626e6a00011
sam       2424     1  0 09:31 ?    00:00:01 kdesktop [kdeinit]
sam       2426     1  0 09:31 ?    00:00:01 kicker [kdeinit]
sam       2429  2396  0 09:31 ?    00:00:00 kio_file [kdeinit] file /tmp/ksocket-ma
sam       2434  2396  0 09:31 ?    00:00:00 konsole [kdeinit] -session 1070626e6a00
sam       2435  2396  0 09:31 ?    00:00:00 /bin/sh /usr/lib/firefox-1.5/firefox -U
sam       2446  2435  0 09:31 ?    00:00:00 /bin/sh /usr/lib/firefox-1.5/run-mozill
sam       2451  2446  0 09:31 ?    00:00:01 /usr/lib/firefox-1.5/firefox-bin -UILoc
sam       2453  2434  0 09:31 pts/2 00:00:00 /bin/bash
sam       2474     1  0 09:31 ?    00:00:00 /usr/libexec/gconfd-2 10
sam       2482     1  0 09:32 ?    00:00:00 synergyc jam
sam       3568  3567  0 13:55 pts/3 00:00:00 -bash
sam       3726     1  0 14:07 ?    00:00:00 knotify [kdeinit]
sam       3728     1  0 14:07 ?    00:00:00 /usr/bin/artsd -F 10 -S 4096 -s 60 -m a
sam       3730  2424  0 14:07 ?    00:00:00 xeyes
sam       3731  3568  0 14:07 pts/3 00:00:00 ps -u sam -f
```

This list is fairly short, and the process running xeyes is easy to find. Another way to search for a process is to use ps to produce a long list of all processes and then use grep to find which ones are running xeyes.

```
$ ps -ef | grep xeyes
sam       3730  2424  0 14:07 ?    00:00:00 xeyes
sam       3766  3568  0 14:14 pts/3 00:00:00 grep xeyes
```

If several people are running xeyes, you may need to look in the left column to find the name of the user so you can kill the right process. You can combine the two commands as **ps –u sam –f | grep xeyes**.

Now that you know Sam's process running xeyes has a PID of 3730, you can use kill to terminate it. The safest way to do so is to log in as Sam (perhaps allow him to log in for you or su to sam [**su sam**] if you are logged in as **root**) and give any of the following commands (they all send a termination signal to process 3730):

```
$ kill 3730
```

or

```
$ kill -15 3730
```

or

```
$ kill -TERM 3730
```

Only if this command fails should you send the kill signal:

```
$ kill -KILL 3730
```

The **–KILL** option instructs kill to send a **SIGKILL** signal, which the process cannot ignore. You can give the same command while you are logged in as **root,** but a typing mistake can have much more far-reaching consequences in this circumstance than when you make the mistake while you are logged in as an ordinary user. A user can kill only her own processes, whereas Superuser can kill any process, including system processes.

As a compromise between speed and safety, you can combine the su and kill utilities by using the **–c** option to su. The following command runs the part of the command line following the **–c** with the identity of Sam:

```
# su sam -c "kill -TERM 3730"
```

Two useful utilities related to kill are killall and pidof. The killall utility is very similar to kill but uses a command name instead of a PID number. To kill all your processes that are running xeyes or vi, you can give the following command:

```
$ killall xeyes vi
```

When **root** gives this command, all processes that are running xeyes or vi on the system are killed.

The pidof utility displays the PID number of each process running the command you specify. Because this utility resides in **/sbin,** you must give the absolute pathname if you are not running as **root:**

```
$ /sbin/pidof httpd
567 566 565 564 563 562 561 560 553
```

If it is difficult to find the right process, try using top. Refer to the man pages for these utilities for more information, including lists of options.

RESCUE MODE

Rescue mode is an environment you can use to fix a system that does not boot normally. To bring a system up in rescue mode, boot the system from the rescue CD, the first installation CD, or the installation DVD. From the rescue CD, at the **boot:** prompt press RETURN without entering a command. Give the command **linux rescue** in response the **boot:** prompt from the first installation CD or the installation DVD. The system then comes up in rescue mode. The boot process may take several minutes.

In rescue mode, you can change or replace configuration files, check and repair partitions using fsck (page 470), rewrite boot information, and more. The rescue setup first asks if you want to set up the network interface. This interface is required if you want to copy files from other systems on the LAN or download files from the Internet. When you choose to set up the network interface, you need to choose whether to have DHCP automatically configure the network connection or to manually supply the IP address and netmask of the interface, as well as the IP addresses of the gateway and up to three DNS addresses.

If the rescue setup finds an existing Linux installation, you can choose to mount it under **/mnt/sysimage**, optionally in readonly mode. With the existing installation mounted, once the system displays a shell prompt (similar to **sh-3.1#**), you can give the command **chroot /mnt/sysimage** to mount the existing installation as it would be if you booted normally, with the existing installation's root mounted at **/** (root). (See page 428 for more information on chroot.) If you choose not to mount the existing installation, you are running a rescue system with standard tools mounted in standard locations (**/bin**, **/usr/bin**, and so on). Partitions from your local installation are available for fixing or mounting. When you exit from the rescue shell, the system reboots. Remove the CD or DVD if you want to boot from the hard drive.

AVOIDING A TROJAN HORSE

A *Trojan horse* is a program that does something destructive or disruptive to a system while appearing to be benign. As an example, you could store the following script in an executable file named mkfs:

```
while true
    do
    echo 'Good Morning Mr. Jones. How are you? Ha Ha Ha.' > /dev/console
    done
```

If you are running as Superuser when you run this command, it would continuously write a message to the console. If the programmer were malicious, it could do worse. The only thing missing in this plot is access permissions.

A malicious user could implement this Trojan horse by changing Superuser's **PATH** variable to include a publicly writable directory at the start of the **PATH** string. (The catch is that you need to be able to write to **/etc/profile**—where the **PATH** variable is set for **root**—and only **root** can do that.) Then you would need to put the bogus mkfs program file in that directory. Because the fraudulent version appears in a directory mentioned earlier than the real one in **PATH**, the shell runs it. The next time Superuser tries to run mkfs, the fraudulent version would run.

Trojan horses that lie in wait for and take advantage of the misspellings that most people make are among the most insidious types. For example, you might type **sl** instead of **ls**. Because you do not regularly execute a utility named sl and you may not remember typing the command **sl**, it is more difficult to track down this type of Trojan horse than one that takes the name of a more familiar utility.

A good way to help prevent the execution of a Trojan horse is to make sure that your **PATH** variable does not contain a single colon (:) at the beginning or end of the **PATH** string or a period (.) or double colon (::) anywhere in the **PATH** string. This precaution ensures that you will not execute a file in the working directory by accident. To check for a possible Trojan horse, examine the filesystem periodically for files with setuid (refer to item 5 on page 392) permission. The following command lists these files:

Listing setuid files
```
# find / -perm -4000 -exec ls -lh {} \; 2> /dev/null
-rwsr-xr-x 1 root root 13K Feb 12 00:18 /sbin/pam_timestamp_check
-rwsr-xr-x 1 root root 22K Feb 12 00:18 /sbin/unix_chkpwd
-rwsr-xr-x 1 root root 84K Feb 12 12:38 /bin/mount
-rwsr-xr-x 1 root root 61K Feb 12 12:38 /bin/umount
-rwsr-xr-x 1 root root 25K Feb 10 22:43 /bin/su
-rwsr-xr-x 1 root root 36K Feb 11 15:06 /bin/ping
-rwsr-xr-x 1 root root 32K Feb 11 15:06 /bin/ping6
-rws--x--x 1 root root 37K Feb 12 10:43 /usr/sbin/userhelper
...
```

This command uses find to locate all files that have their setuid bit set (mode 4000). The hyphen preceding the mode causes find to report on any file that has this bit set, regardless of how the other bits are set. The output sent to standard error is redirected to **/dev/null** so that it does not clutter the screen.

You can also set up a program, such as AIDE (Advanced Intrusion Detection Environment), that will take a snapshot of your system and check it periodically as you specify. See sourceforge.net/projects/aide for more information.

GETTING HELP

The Red Hat Linux distribution comes with extensive documentation (page 102). Red Hat maintains a page that points you toward many useful support documents: https://www.redhat.com/apps/support. You can also find help on the System Administrators Guild site (www.sage.org). The Internet is another rich source of information on managing a Linux system; refer to Appendix B (page 977) and to the author's home page (www.sobell.com) for pointers to useful sites.

You do not need to act as a Red Hat system administrator in isolation; a large community of Linux/Red Hat experts is willing to assist you in getting the most out of your system, although you will get better help if you have already tried to solve a problem yourself by reading the available documentation. If you are unable to solve a problem by consulting the documentation, a well-thought-out question to the appropriate newsgroup, such as **comp.os.linux.misc,** or mailing list can often generate useful information. Be sure you describe the problem accurately and identify your system carefully. Include information about your version of Red Hat Enterprise Linux or Fedora Core and any software packages and hardware that you think relate to the problem. The newsgroup **comp.os.linux.answers** contains postings of solutions to common problems and periodic postings of the most up-to-date versions of FAQs and HOWTO documents. See www.catb.org/~esr/faqs/smart-questions.html for a good paper by Eric S. Raymond and Rick Moen titled "How to Ask Questions the Smart Way."

SELINUX

Traditional Linux security, called *Discretionary Access Control* (DAC), is based on users and groups. Because a process run by a user has access to anything the user has access to, fine-grained access control is difficult to achieve. Fine-grained access control is particularly important on servers, which often hold programs that require **root** privileges to run.

SELinux (Security Enhanced Linux), developed by the U.S. National Security Agency (NSA), implements *Mandatory Access Control* (MAC) in the Linux kernel. MAC enforces security policies that limit what a user or program can do. It defines a security policy that controls some or all objects, such as files, devices, sockets, and ports, and some or all subjects, such as processes. Using SELinux, you can grant a process only those permissions it needs to be functional, following the principle of least privilege (page 392). MAC is an important tool for limiting security threats that come from user errors, software flaws, and malicious users. The kernel checks MAC rules after it checks DAC rules.

SELinux can be in one of three states (modes):

- **Enforcing/Active**   The default state, wherein SELinux security policy is enforced. No user or program will be able to do anything not permitted by the security policy.

- **Permissive/Warn**   The diagnostic state, wherein SELinux sends warning messages to a log but does not enforce the security policy. You can use the log to build a security policy that matches your requirements.

- **Disabled**   SELinux does not enforce a security policy because no policy is loaded.

Running SELinux in permissive or enforcing state degrades system performance between 5 and 10 percent. Although SELinux is usually of no benefit on a single-user system, you may want to consider SELinux for a server that connects to the Internet. If you are unsure whether to use SELinux, selecting permissive state allows you to change to disabled or enforcing state easily at a later date.

SELinux implements one of the following policies:

- **Targeted**   Applies SELinux MAC controls only to certain (targeted) processes (default).

- **Strict**   Applies SELinux MAC controls to all processes.

This section discusses the targeted policy. With such a policy, daemons and system processes that do not have a specified policy are controlled by traditional Linux DACs. With the strict policy, all processes are controlled by SELinux (MACs). Setting up a system that runs under strict policy is beyond the scope of this book.

There is always a tradeoff between security and usability. The targeted policy is less secure than the strict policy, but it is much easier to maintain. When you run the strict policy you will likely have to customize the policy so that users can do their work and the system can function as you would like it to.

You can switch from one policy to the other (as explained shortly). However, it is not a good idea to switch from a targeted to a strict policy on a production system. If you do so, some users may not be able to do their work. You would need to customize the policy in such a case. Changing from a strict to a targeted policy should not create any problems.

MORE INFORMATION

Web   NSA: www.nsa.gov/selinux
Fedora SELinux Wiki: fedoraproject.org/wiki/SELinux
Fedora FAQ: fedora.redhat.com/docs/selinux-faq
SELinux News: selinuxnews.org
SELinux for Distributions (Sourceforge):   selinux.sourceforge.net
Unofficial FAQ: www.crypt.gen.nz/selinux/faq.html
Fedora SELinux mailing list: www.redhat.com/mailman/listinfo/fedora-selinux-list

Turning off SELinux

tip   There are two ways to disable SELinux. You can either modify the **/etc/selinux/config** file so that it includes the line **SELINUX=disabled** and reboot the system, or you can use **system-config-securitylevel** (as explained on the next page).

If there is a chance you will want to enable SELinux in the future, putting SELinux in permissive mode is a better choice than disabling it. This strategy allows you to turn on SELinux more quickly when you decide to do so.

config: THE SELINUX CONFIGURATION FILE

The **/etc/selinux/config** file, which has a link at **/etc/sysconfig/selinux**, controls the state of SELinux on the local system. Although you can modify this file, it may be more straightforward to work with system-config-securitylevel (as explained in the next section). In the following example, the policy is set to targeted, but that setting is of no consequence because SELinux is disabled:

```
$ cat /etc/selinux/config
# This file controls the state of SELinux on the system.
# SELINUX= can take one of these three values:
#       enforcing - SELinux security policy is enforced.
#       permissive - SELinux prints warnings instead of enforcing.
#       disabled - SELinux is fully disabled.
SELINUX=disabled
# SELINUXTYPE= type of policy in use. Possible values are:
#       targeted - Only targeted network daemons are protected.
#       strict - Full SELinux protection.
SELINUXTYPE=targeted

# SETLOCALDEFS= Check local definition changes
SETLOCALDEFS=0
```

To put SELinux in enforcing mode, change the line containing the **SELINUX** assignment to **SELINUX=enforcing**. Similarly you can change the policy by setting **SELINUXTYPE**. Always set **SETLOCALDEFS** to 0.

If you will use SELinux in the future

tip   If you will use SELinux in the future but not now, turn it on when you install Linux, and run it in permissive state with the policy set to the policy you will eventually use. Permissive state writes the required extended information to inodes, but it does not stop you from doing anything on the system.

If you turn on SELinux after it has been disabled, when you reboot the system SELinux has to add extended attributes to the files in the filesystem. This process can take a long time on a large filesystem. If you are never going to use SELinux, disable it.

sestatus: DISPLAYS THE STATE OF SELINUX

The sestatus utility displays a summary of the state of SELinux on the local system:

```
# sestatus
SELinux status:              enabled
SELinuxfs mount:             /selinux
Current mode:                permissive
Mode from config file:       permissive
Policy version:              20
Policy from config file:     targeted
```

SETTING THE TARGETED POLICY WITH system-config-securitylevel

The system-config-securitylevel utility displays the Security Level Configuration window (Figure 11-1), which controls SELinux. To run this utility, enter **system-config-securitylevel** from a command line in a graphical environment. From KDE select **Main menu: Administration⇨Security Level and Firewall** or from GNOME select **System: Administration⇨Security Level and Firewall**. From the Security Level Configuration window, click the SELinux tab and choose Enforcing (default), Permissive, or Disabled from the SELinux Setting combo box. See page 768 for information on the Firewall Options tab.

The lower frame, which occupies most of the Security Level Configuration window, holds the Modify SELinux Policy menu. You open and close a list of submenus or options by clicking the triangle adjacent to a submenu.

Click the triangle next to Modify SELinux Policy to display a list of submenus. Some of these submenus are quite simple. For example, open the SpamAssassin (page 640) submenu to display the single choice: **Allow Spam Assassin daemon network access**. By default the targeted policy does not allow the SpamAssassin daemon, **spamd**, to access the network. Click the box next to this choice to display a check mark and allow network access for this daemon.

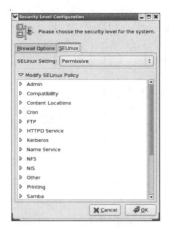

Figure 11-1 Security Level Configuration window,
SELinux tab (system-config-securitylevel)

The NFS submenu presents three choices concerning NFS filesystems. The SELinux Service Protection submenu allows you to disable SELinux protection for a long list of daemons.

The targeted policy works with specific system services (daemons): **crond, ftpd, httpd, named,** NFS, NIS, CUPS, Samba, Spam Assassin, SQUID, and **sshd.** To change the SELinux policy for one of the services listed in the submenu, open that submenu and select from the choices. When you are finished making changes, click **OK.**

SYSTEM OPERATION

This section covers the basics of how the system functions and how you can make intelligent decisions as a system administrator. It does not examine every aspect of system administration in the depth necessary to set up or modify all system functions. Instead, it provides a guide to bringing a system up and keeping it running from day to day.

BOOTING THE SYSTEM

Booting a system is the process of reading the Linux *kernel* (page 1039) into system memory and starting it running. Refer to "Boot Loader" on page 533 for more information on the initial steps of bringing a system up.

As the last step of the boot procedure, Linux runs the init program as PID number 1. The init program is the first genuine process to run after booting and is the parent of all system processes. (That is why when you run as **root** and kill process **1,** the system dies.)

initdefault   The **initdefault** entry in the **/etc/inittab** file (page 452) tells init what runlevel to bring the system to (Table 11-1). Set **initdefault** to 3 to cause the system to present a text login message when it boots; set **initdefault** to 5 to present a graphical login screen (default).

Table 11-1   Runlevels

Number	Name	Login	Network	Filesystems
0	Halt			
1 (not **S** or **s**)	Single user	Textual	Down	Mounted
2	Multiuser without NFS	Textual	Up (partially)	Mounted
3	Multiuser	Textual	Up	Mounted
4	User defined			
5	Multiuser with X	Graphical	Up	Mounted
6	Reboot			

Init Scripts: Start and Stop System Services

The first script that init runs is **/etc/rc.d/rc.sysinit**, which performs basic system configuration, including setting the system clock, hostname, and keyboard mapping; setting up swap partitions; checking the filesystems for errors; and turning on quota management (page 561).

List the kernel boot messages

tip   To save a list of kernel boot messages, give the following command immediately after booting the system and logging in:

```
$ dmesg > dmesg.boot
```

This command saves the kernel messages in a file named **dmesg.boot**. This list can be educational. It can also be useful when you are having a problem with the boot process. For more information refer to "dmesg: Displays Kernel Messages" on page 535.

rc scripts   Next the **/etc/rc.d/rc** init script runs the scripts for the services that need to be started when you first bring the system up and that need to be started or stopped when the system goes from single-user to multiuser mode and back down again. The init (initialization) scripts, also called rc (run command) scripts, are shell scripts located in the **/etc/rc.d/init.d** directory and run via symbolic links in the **/etc/rc.d/rc*n*.d** directories, where *n* is the runlevel the system is entering.

The **/etc/rc.d/rc*n*.d** directories contain scripts whose names begin with **K** (**K15httpd, K72autofs, K30sendmail,** and so on) and scripts whose names begin with **S** (**S05kudzu, S10network, S13portmap,** and so on). When entering a new runlevel, each **K** (kill) script is executed with an argument of **stop**, and then each **S** (start) script is executed with an argument of **start**. Each of the **K** files is run in numerical order. The **S** files are run in similar fashion. This setup allows the person who sets up these files to control which services are stopped and which are started, and in what order, whenever the system enters a given runlevel. Using scripts with **start** and **stop** arguments promotes flexibility because it allows one script to both start and kill a process, depending on the argument it is called with.

To customize system initialization, you can add shell scripts to the **/etc/rc.d/init.d** directory and place links to these files in the **/etc/rc.d/rc*n*.d** directories. The following example shows several links to the **cups** script. These links are called to run the **cups** init script to start or stop the **cupsd** daemon at various runlevels:

```
$ pwd
/etc/rc.d
$ ls -l */*cups
-rwxr-xr-x 1 root root 2312 Jan 17 03:59 init.d/cups
lrwxrwxrwx 1 root root   14 Jan 17 20:38 rc0.d/K10cups -> ../init.d/cups
lrwxrwxrwx 1 root root   14 Jan 17 20:38 rc1.d/K10cups -> ../init.d/cups
lrwxrwxrwx 1 root root   14 Jan 17 20:38 rc2.d/S55cups -> ../init.d/cups
lrwxrwxrwx 1 root root   14 Jan 17 20:38 rc3.d/S55cups -> ../init.d/cups
lrwxrwxrwx 1 root root   14 Jan 17 20:38 rc4.d/S55cups -> ../init.d/cups
lrwxrwxrwx 1 root root   14 Jan 17 20:38 rc5.d/S55cups -> ../init.d/cups
lrwxrwxrwx 1 root root   14 Jan 17 20:38 rc6.d/K10cups -> ../init.d/cups
```

Each link in **/etc/rc.d/rc*n*.d** should point to a file in **/etc/rc.d/init.d**. For example, the file **/etc/rc.d/rc1.d/K10cups** is a link to the file named **cups** in **/etc/rc.d/init.d**. (The numbers that are part of the filenames of the links in the **/etc/rc.d/rc*n*.d** directories may change from one release of the operating system to the next, but the scripts in **/etc/rc.d/init.d** always have the same names.) The names of files in the **/etc/rc.d/init.d** directory are functional. Thus, when you want to turn NFS services on or off, use the **nfs** script. When you want to turn basic network services on or off, run the **network** script. The **cups** script controls the printer daemon. Each script takes an argument of **stop** or **start**, depending on what you want to do. Some scripts also take other arguments, such as **restart**, **reload**, and **status**. Run a script without an argument to display a usage message indicating which arguments it accepts.

Following are three examples of calls to init scripts. You may find it easier to use **service** (discussed next) in place of the pathnames in these commands:

```
# /etc/rc.d/init.d/nfs stop
# /etc/rc.d/init.d/network start
# /etc/rc.d/init.d/network restart
```

The first example stops all NFS processes (processes related to serving filesystems over the network). The second example starts all processes related to basic network services. The third example stops and then restarts these same processes.

Maintain the links in the /etc/rc*.d hierarchy

tip Refer to page 408 for information about using chkconfig to maintain the symbolic links in the /etc/rc*.d hierarchy.

Figure 11-2 The Service Configuration window, Background Services tab

The **/etc/rc.d/rc.local** file is executed after the other init scripts. Put commands that customize the system in **rc.local**. Although you can add any commands you like to **rc.local**, it is best to run them in the background so that if they hang, they do not stop the boot process.

service: CONFIGURES SERVICES I

Red Hat provides service, a handy utility that reports on or changes the status of any of the system services in **/etc/rc.d/init.d**. In place of the commands described at the end of the previous section, you can give the following commands from any directory:

```
# /sbin/service nfs stop
# /sbin/service network start
# /sbin/service network restart
```

The command **/sbin/service --status-all** displays the status of all system services. The next section explores yet another way to configure system services.

system-config-services: CONFIGURES SERVICES II

The system-config-services utility displays the Service Configuration window (Figure 11-2). This utility has two functions: It turns system services on and off, and it controls which services are stopped and started when the system enters and leaves runlevels 3, 4 (not used), and 5.

To run this utility, enter **system-config-services** from a command line in a graphical environment. From KDE select **Main menu: Administration⇨Server Settings⇨ Services** or from GNOME select **System: Administration⇨Server Settings⇨Services**.

The system-config-services utility works with many of the services listed in **/etc/rc.d/init.d** as well as with those controlled by **xinetd** (page 425) and listed in **/etc/xinetd.d** (or as specified in **/etc/xinetd.conf**).

RHEL   The *RHEL* and *FEDORA* versions of this utility arrange the information about services controlled by **xinetd** somewhat differently. The *RHEL* version displays all services in a single list. When you highlight a service that is controlled by **xinetd**, the notice **xinetd is required for this service** appears in the Description frame.

FEDORA   The *FEDORA* version of system-config-services has two tabs. The Background Services tab lists all services except those controlled by **xinetd**, while the On Demand Services tab displays services controlled by **xinetd**. This section describes the *FEDORA* version of the utility.

BACKGROUND SERVICES TAB

When you click the Background Services tab, the line below the note about background services displays the current runlevel (see Table 11-1 on page 404) of the system and the runlevel that you are editing. Services that are turned on at the runlevel you are editing are indicated by a check mark in the box adjacent to the service. To change the runlevel you are editing, click **Edit Runlevel** on the menubar and then select the runlevel you want to edit. When you select **Runlevel All**, system-config-services displays a table listing runlevels 3, 4, and 5.

Scroll to and highlight the service you are interested in. A short description appears in the Description frame and the status of the service appears in the Status frame.

With a background service highlighted, click the toolbar or make a selection from Actions in the menubar to stop, start, or restart (stop and then start) the service. The system turns on (off) the service immediately; the change does not affect whether the service will run the next time you boot the system, enter another runlevel, or reenter the current runlevel. These changes are equivalent to those you would make with the service utility (page 406).

You can also use system-config-services to control the future execution of background services in runlevels 3, 4, and 5. Select the runlevel you want to affect, using the Edit Runlevel selection from the menubar. Click the box next to the service you want to configure. A check mark in the box indicates that the service will be on at the specified runlevel; the absence of a check mark indicates that it will be off. Click the **Save** button. When you enter that runlevel in the future, the service will be on or off as you specified. The current state of the service is not changed.

ON DEMAND SERVICES TAB

The On Demand Services tab allows you to turn **xinetd**-controlled services on or off. As with the Background Services tab, highlight a service to read a description of it. Click the box adjacent to a service to turn it on or off and then click the **Save** button. This action changes the **yes/no** parameter of the **disable** line discussed on page 426. When you click **Save**, the system restarts **xinetd** with the service status change you requested. This change affects all runlevels and will remain in effect through changes in runlevels and reboots unless you change it again. These changes are equivalent to those you would make with the chkconfig utility (see the next section).

chkconfig: Configures Services III

The chkconfig character-based utility duplicates much of what system-config-services does: It makes it easier for a system administrator to maintain the **/etc/rc.d** directory hierarchy. This utility can add, remove, list startup information, and check the state of system services. It changes the configuration only—it does not change the current state of any service. To see a list of all services, give the following command:

```
$ /sbin/chkconfig --list
NetworkManager       0:off   1:off   2:off   3:off   4:off   5:off   6:off
NetworkManagerDispatcher      0:off   1:off   2:off   3:off   4:off   5:off   6:off
acpid                0:off   1:off   2:off   3:on    4:on    5:on    6:off
anacron              0:off   1:off   2:on    3:on    4:on    5:on    6:off
apmd                 0:off   1:off   2:on    3:on    4:on    5:on    6:off
atd                  0:off   1:off   2:off   3:on    4:on    5:on    6:off
auditd               0:off   1:off   2:on    3:on    4:on    5:on    6:off
autofs               0:off   1:off   2:off   3:on    4:on    5:on    6:off
avahi-daemon         0:off   1:off   2:off   3:on    4:on    5:on    6:off
bluetooth            0:off   1:off   2:on    3:on    4:on    5:on    6:off
cpuspeed             0:off   1:on    2:on    3:on    4:on    5:on    6:off
...
xinetd based services:
        chargen:        off
        chargen-udp:    off
        daytime:        off
        daytime-udp:    off
        echo:           off
        echo-udp:       off
...
```

All services that run their own daemons are listed, one to a line, followed by their configured state for each runlevel. Following that list, chkconfig displays each of the **xinetd**-based services and its current status. You can check how a specific daemon is configured by adding its name to the previous command:

```
$ /sbin/chkconfig --list sshd
sshd             0:off   1:off   2:on    3:on    4:on    5:on    6:off
```

In the next example, chkconfig configures the **/etc/rc.d** directory hierarchy so that **sshd** will be off in runlevels **2, 3, 4,** and **5** and then confirms the change. To make changes using chkconfig, you must work as **root**:

```
# /sbin/chkconfig --level 2345 sshd off
# /sbin/chkconfig --list sshd
sshd             0:off   1:off   2:off   3:off   4:off   5:off   6:off
```

For convenience, you can omit the **--level 2345** part. When you specify an init script and **on** or **off**, chkconfig defaults to runlevels **2, 3, 4,** and **5.** The following command is equivalent to the first of the preceding commands:

```
# chkconfig sshd off
```

Both ps and service confirm that even though chkconfig set things up so that **sshd** would be off in all runlevels, this daemon is still running. The chkconfig utility did not shut down **sshd**. In the following example, the second command line shows that when you give a service command followed by the name of an init script, you get the usage message from the script:

```
# ps -ef | grep sshd
root         697     1  0 Oct01 ?        00:00:00 /usr/sbin/sshd
root       17185 21650  0 15:15 pts/4    00:00:00 grep sshd
# /sbin/service sshd
Usage: /etc/init.d/sshd {start|stop|restart|reload|condrestart|status}
# /sbin/service sshd status
sshd (pid 697) is running...
```

With the preceding changes, when you reboot the system, **sshd** will not start. You can stop it more easily using service, however:

```
# /sbin/service sshd stop
Stopping sshd:                                            [  OK  ]
# ps -ef | grep sshd
root       17209 21650  0 15:16 pts/4    00:00:00 grep sshd
# /sbin/service sshd status
sshd is stopped
```

SINGLE-USER MODE

When the system is in single-user mode, only the system console is enabled. You can run programs from the console in single-user mode as you would from any terminal in multiuser mode. The difference is that few of the system daemons will be running. The scripts in **/etc/rc.d/rc1.d** are run as part of single-user initialization. See page 414 for instructions on bringing the system to single-user mode.

With the system in single-user mode, you can perform system maintenance that requires filesystems to be unmounted or that requires just a quiet system—no one except you using it, so that no user programs interfere with disk maintenance and backup programs. The classical UNIX term for this state is *quiescent*. See "Backing Up Files" on page 540 for a discussion of one of the most important and often neglected areas of system administration.

GOING TO MULTIUSER MODE

After you have determined that all is well with the filesystems, you can bring the operating system up to multiuser mode. When you exit from the single-user shell, init brings the system to the default runlevel—usually 5 (page 404). Alternatively you can give the following command in response to the Superuser prompt to bring the system to (textual) multiuser mode (use 5 to go to graphical [multiuser] mode):

```
# /sbin/telinit 3
```

The telinit utility tells init which runlevel to enter. The telinit executable is a symbolic link to the init executable but, by convention, running telinit is preferred to running init directly.

When it goes from single-user to (textual) multiuser mode, the system executes the **K** (kill or stop) scripts and then the **S** (start) scripts in **/etc/rc.d/rc3.d**. For more information refer to "Init Scripts: Start and Stop System Services" on page 404. Use chkconfig (page 408) to stop one of these scripts from running when the system enters the new runlevel.

Runlevel **2** is referred to as multiuser mode, and runlevel **3** is called extended multiuser mode. But because runlevel **2** is rarely used, this chapter uses the term *multiuser* to refer to runlevel **3**. Runlevel **4** is not used, and runlevel **5** is graphics or X11 mode.

MULTIUSER/GRAPHICAL MODE

Multiuser/graphical mode is the default state for a Red Hat Linux system. In this mode all appropriate filesystems are mounted, and users can log in from all connected terminals, dial-up lines, and network connections. All support services and daemons are enabled and running. Once the system is in multiuser/graphical mode, you will see a login screen on the console. Most systems are set up to boot directly to multiuser/graphical mode without stopping at single-user mode.

LOGGING IN

Textual login   With a textual login, the system uses init, mingetty, and login to allow a user to log in; login uses PAM modules (page 438) to authenticate users. Once the system is in multiuser mode, init is responsible for spawning a mingetty process on each of the lines that a user can use to log in.

When you enter your username, mingetty establishes the characteristics of your terminal. It then overlays itself with a login process and passes to the login process whatever you entered in response to the **login:** prompt. The login process uses PAM to consult the **/etc/passwd** file to see whether a username matches the username you entered. PAM then consults the **/etc/shadow** file to see whether a password is associated with the username. If it is, login prompts you for a password; if not, it continues without requiring a password. When your username requires a password, login verifies the password you enter by checking the **/etc/shadow** file again. If either your username or your password is not correct, login displays **Login incorrect** and prompts you to log in again.

All passwords in the **/etc/shadow** file are encrypted or hashed using *MD5* (page 1042). It is not feasible to recover an encrypted password. When you log in, the login process encrypts/hashes the password you type at the prompt and compares it to the encrypted/hashed password in **/etc/shadow**. If the two passwords match, you are authenticated.

Graphical login   With a graphical login, the init process spawns gdm (the GNOME display manager) on the first free virtual terminal, providing features similar to mingetty and login. The gdm utility starts an X server and presents a login window. The gdm display manager then uses PAM to authenticate the user and runs the scripts in the **/etc/gdm/PreSession** directory. These scripts inspect the user's ~/.dmrc file, which stores the user's default session and language, and launch the user's session. Both

GNOME and KDE desktop environments store the state of the last saved session and attempt to restore it when the user logs back in.

With NIS, login compares your username and password with the information in the appropriate naming service instead of (or in addition to) the **passwd** and **shadow** files. If the system is configured to use both methods (**/etc/passwd** and NIS), it checks the **/etc/nsswitch.conf** file (page 435) to see in which order it should consult them.

PAM (page 438), the Pluggable Authentication Module facility, allows you greater control over user logins than the **/etc/passwd** and **/etc/shadow** files do. Using PAM, you can specify multiple levels of authentication, mutually exclusive authentication methods, or parallel methods, each of which is by itself sufficient to grant access to the system. For example, you can have different authentication methods for console logins and for ssh logins. Likewise, you can require that modem users authenticate themselves via two or more methods (such as a smartcard or badge reader and a password). PAM modules also provide security technology vendors with a convenient way to interface their hardware or software products with a system.

When the username and password are correct, login or the scripts in **PreSession** consult the appropriate services to initialize your user and group IDs, establish your home directory, and determine which shell or desktop manager you will be working with.

The login utility/**PreSession** scripts assign values to the **HOME, PATH, LOGNAME, SHELL, TERM,** and **MAIL** variables. They look in the **/etc/group** file (page 451) to identify the groups the user belongs to. When login has finished its work, it overlays itself with the login shell, which inherits the variables set by login. In a graphical environment, the **PreSession** scripts start the desktop manager.

During a textual login, the login shell assigns values to additional shell variables and executes the commands in the system startup shell scripts **/etc/profile** and **/etc/bashrc**. Some systems have additional system startup shell scripts. The actions performed by these scripts are system dependent, but they usually display the contents of the **/etc/motd** (message of the day) and **/etc/issue** files, let you know that you have mail, and set umask (page 420), the file-creation mask.

After executing the system startup commands, the shell executes the commands from the personal startup shell scripts in your home directory. For a list of these scripts, refer to page 267. Because the shell executes the personal startup scripts *after* the system scripts, a sophisticated user can override any variables or conventions that were established by the system, whereas a new user can remain uninvolved in these matters.

LOGGING OUT

When you see a shell prompt, you can either execute a program or exit from the shell. If you exit from the shell, the process running the shell dies and the parent process wakes up. When the shell is a child of another shell, the parent shell wakes up and displays a prompt. Exiting from a login shell causes the operating system to send init a signal that one of its children has died. Upon receiving this signal, init takes action based on the contents of the **/etc/inittab** file. In the case of a process controlling a line for a terminal, init informs mingetty that the line is free for another user.

When you are at runlevel 5 and exit from a GUI, the GNOME display manager, gdm, initiates a new login display.

BRINGING THE SYSTEM DOWN

The shutdown and halt utilities perform the tasks needed to bring the system down safely. These utilities can restart the system, prepare the system to be turned off, put the system in single-user mode, and, on some hardware, power down the system. The poweroff and reboot utilities are linked to halt. If you call halt when the system is not shutting down (runlevel 0) or rebooting (runlevel 6), halt calls shutdown. (When you are running as other than Superuser, the link goes through consolehelper [page 394].)

You must tell shutdown when you would like to bring the system down. This time can be expressed as an absolute time of day, as in 19:15, which causes the shutdown to occur at 7:15 P.M. Alternatively, you can give the number of minutes from the present time, as in +15, which means 15 minutes from now. To bring the system down immediately (recommended for emergency shutdowns only or when you are the only user logged in), you can give the argument +0, or its synonym, **now**. When shutdown times exceed 5 minutes, all non**root** logins are disabled for the last 5 minutes before shutdown.

Calling shutdown with the –r option causes the system to reboot (same as the reboot command except that reboot implies **now**). Adding the –f option forces a fast reboot, in which filesystem checking is disabled (see the shutdown man page for details). Using –h instead of –r forces the system to halt (same as the halt command except that halt implies **now**). A message appears once the system has been safely halted: **System halted.** Most ATX systems turn off automatically after shutdown, however, so you will not see this message.

Because Linux is a multiuser system, shutdown warns all users before taking action. This warning gives users a chance to prepare for the shutdown, perhaps by writing out editor files or exiting from networking applications. You can replace the default shutdown message with one of your own by following the time specification on the command line with a message:

```
# /sbin/shutdown -h 09:30 Going down 9:30 to install disk, up by 10am.
```

CONTROL-ALT-DEL: REBOOTS THE SYSTEM

By default the **/etc/inittab** file on an Intel-based computer contains the entry

```
ca::ctrlaltdel:/sbin/shutdown -t3 -r now
```

Do not turn the power off before bringing the system down

caution Do not turn the power off on a Linux system without first bringing it down as described here. Like UNIX, Linux speeds disk access by keeping an in-memory collection of disk buffers that are written to the disk periodically or when system use is momentarily low. When you turn off or reset the computer without writing the contents of these disk buffers to the disk, you lose any information in the buffers. Running **shutdown** forces these buffers to be written. You can force the buffers to be written at any time by issuing a **sync** command. However, **sync** does not unmount filesystems, nor does it bring the system down.

This entry allows any user[1] to reboot the computer safely by pressing the key sequence CONTROL-ALT-DEL (also referred to as the *three-finger salute* or the *Vulcan death grip*) from a textual login on the console. (Although it is not recommended, you can press CONTROL-ALT-F1 from a graphical session to switch to the system console and then use CONTROL-ALT-DEL.) Because of its hooks into the keyboard driver, this key sequence sends a SIGINT signal to the init process, which in response runs **shutdown**. Because it runs as **root**, init causes **shutdown** to run as **root**, even if an ordinary user initiates the key sequence. You can disable CONTROL-ALT-DEL by deleting the preceding line from **/etc/inittab** (or putting a **#** at the beginning of the line) and then sending init a HUP signal (**kill –HUP 1**), which causes it to reread the **/etc/inittab** file.

consolehelper: ALLOWS AN ORDINARY USER TO RUN A PRIVILEGED COMMAND

Two executable **halt** files exist:

```
$ file /sbin/halt /usr/bin/halt
/sbin/halt:    ELF 32-bit LSB executable, Intel 80386, version 1 (SYSV)...
/usr/bin/halt: symbolic link to 'consolehelper'
```

The file in **/sbin** runs the **halt** utility, whereas the file in **/usr/bin** is a link to console-helper. In **root**'s **PATH** variable, **/sbin** normally precedes **/usr/bin**. Thus, when someone running as **root** gives a **halt** command, the shell executes **/sbin/halt** (the **halt** utility). Normally **/sbin** does not appear in an ordinary user's **PATH**; when an ordinary user gives a **halt** command, the shell follows the link from **/usr/bin/halt** and executes **/usr/bin/consolehelper**.

What consolehelper does depends on how PAM is set up (see **/etc/pam.d/halt** for the modules it calls and **/usr/share/doc/pam-*****/txts/*** for descriptions of the modules). Refer to "PAM" on page 438 for more information. As shipped by Red Hat, con-solehelper does not require the **root** password; any user can give a **halt** command from the system console to shut the system down.

---

1. When you include the **–a** option in the **shutdown** command in **/etc/inittab** and the **/etc/shutdown.allow** file exists, one of the users whose names appear in this file (or **root**) must be logged in on one of the virtual consoles for a non**root** user to run **shutdown** from a virtual console.

GOING TO SINGLE-USER MODE

Because going from multiuser to single-user mode can affect other users, you must be Superuser to make this change. Make sure that you give other users enough warning before switching to single-user mode; otherwise, they may lose whatever they were working on.

The following steps describe a method of manually bringing the system down to single-user mode—the point where it is safe to turn the power off. You must be running as Superuser to perform these tasks.

1. Use wall (write all) to warn everyone who is using the system to log out.

2. If you are sharing files via NFS, use **exportfs –ua** to disable network access to the shared filesystems. (Use **exportfs** without an argument to see which filesystems are being shared.)

3. Confirm that no critical processes are running in the background (someone running an unattended compile or some other job).

4. Give the command **/sbin/telinit 1** to bring the system down to single-user mode.

   The system will display messages about the services it is shutting down and finally display a bash shell prompt similar to **sh-3.1#**. The runlevel utility confirms that the system is in runlevel 1 (S for single-user mode):

   ```
   # /sbin/telinit 1

   sh-3.1# runlevel
   1 S
   ```

5. Use **umount –a** to unmount all mounted devices that are not in use. Use **mount** without an argument to make sure that no devices other than root (/) are mounted before continuing.

TURNING THE POWER OFF

Once the system is in single-user mode, shutting it down is quite straightforward. Give the command **telinit 0** (preferred) or **halt** to bring the system down. You can build a kernel with apm so it turns the machine off at the appropriate time. If your machine is not set up this way, turn the power off when the appropriate prompt appears or when the system starts rebooting.

CRASH

A *crash* occurs when the system suddenly stops or fails when you do not intend it to. A crash may result from software or hardware problems or from a loss of power. As a running system loses power, it may behave in erratic or unpredictable ways. In a fraction of a second, some components are supplied with enough voltage; others are not. Buffers are not flushed, corrupt data may be written to the hard disk, and so on. IDE drives do not behave as predictably as SCSI drives under these circumstances. After a crash, you must bring the operating system up carefully to minimize possible damage to the filesystems. Frequently little or no damage will have occurred.

REPAIRING A FILESYSTEM

Although the filesystems are checked automatically during the boot process if needed, you will have to check them manually if a problem cannot be repaired automatically. To check the filesystems manually after a crash, boot the system up in rescue mode (page 397). *Do not* mount any devices other than root, which Linux mounts automatically. Run fsck (page 470) on all local filesystems that were mounted at the time of the crash, repairing them as needed. Depending on how the system is set up, when fsck cannot repair a filesystem automatically, the system may enter emergency mode so you can run fsck manually. Make note of any ordinary files or directories that you repair (and can identify), and inform their owners that they may not be complete or correct. Look in the **lost+found** directory *in each filesystem* for missing files. After successfully running fsck, type **exit** to exit from the single-user shell and resume booting.

If files are not correct or are missing altogether, you may have to recreate them from a backup copy of the filesystem. For more information refer to "Backing Up Files" on page 540.

WHEN THE SYSTEM DOES NOT BOOT

When you cannot boot the computer from the hard drive, you can try to boot the system into rescue mode. For more information refer to "Rescue Mode" on page 397. If the system comes up in rescue mode, run fsck on the root filesystem and try booting from the hard drive again.

When all else fails, go through the install procedure, and perform an "upgrade" to the current version of Linux. Red Hat Linux systems can perform a nondestructive upgrade and can fix quite a bit in the process. For more information refer to page 27.

SYSTEM ADMINISTRATION UTILITIES

This section briefly describes a few of the many utilities that can help you perform system administration tasks. Some of these utilities are incorporated as part of the Main menu, and some are useful to users other than the system administrator.

RED HAT CONFIGURATION TOOLS

Most of the Red Hat configuration tools are named system-config-*. Many of these tools bring up a graphical display when called from a GUI and a textual display when called from a non-GUI command line. In general, these tools, which are listed in Table 11-2, are simple to use and require little explanation beyond what the tool presents. Some have Help selections on their toolbar; most do not have man pages.

If the tool is not present on your system, use yum (page 476) on *FEDORA* systems or RHN (page 498) on *RHEL* systems to install it.

Table 11-2   Red Hat configuration tools

Tool	Function
system-config-authentication	Displays the Authentication Configuration window with two tabs: User Information and Authentication. The User Information tab allows you to enable NIS, LDAP, Hesiod, and Winbind support. The Authentication tab allows you to use shadow and *MD5* (page 1042) passwords as well as to enable LDAP, Kerberos, SMB, and Winbind support.
system-config-bind (*FEDORA*)	Displays the Domain Name Service window. For more information see page 734.
system-config-boot	Displays the Boot Configuration window, which allows you to specify which boot entry in **/etc/grub.conf** (page 533) the system should boot from.
system-config-date	Displays the Date/Time Properties window with two tabs: Date & Time and Time Zone. You can set the date and time or enable NTP (Network Time Protocol) from the first tab. The Time Zone tab allows you to specify the time zone of the system clock or set the system clock to *UTC* (page 1062).
system-config-display	Brings up the Display Settings window with three tabs: Settings, Hardware, and Dual Head. For more information see page 70.
system-config-httpd	Displays the HTTP window with four tabs: Main, Virtual Hosts, Server, and Performance Tuning. For more information see page 790.
system-config-keyboard	Displays the Keyboard window, which allows you to select the type of keyboard attached to the system. You use this utility to select the keyboard when you install the system.
system-config-kickstart	Displays the Kickstart Configurator window, which allows you to create a Kickstart script. For more information see page 63.

Table 11-2   Red Hat configuration tools (continued)

Tool	Function
system-config-language	Displays the Language Selection window, which allows you to specify the default system language from among those that are installed. You use this utility to select the system language when you install the system.
system-config-lvm	Displays the Logical Volume Management window, which allows you to modify existing logical volumes. For more information see page 32.
system-config-mouse (*RHEL*)	Displays the Mouse Configuration window, which allows you to specify the type of mouse that is attached to the system. You use this utility to select the system mouse when you install the system.
system-config-netboot	Displays the Network Installation and Diskless Environment window, which allows you to configure the network installation or a diskless environment. The first time you run this utility, it displays the First Time Druid window.
system-config-network	Displays the Network Configuration window. For more information see page 571.
system-config-network-cmd	Displays the parameters that system-config-network uses.
system-config-nfs	Displays the NFS Server Configuration window. For more information see page 683.
system-config-packages (*RHEL*)	Displays the Package Management window. You use this utility to customize the list of packages you install when you install the system.
system-config-printer	Displays the Printer Configuration window, which allows you to set up printers and edit printer configurations. For more information see page 505.
system-config-rootpassword	Displays the Root Password window, which allows you to change the **root** password. While logged in as **root**, you can also use passwd from a command line to change the **root** password.
system-config-samba	Displays the Samba Server Configuration window, which can help you configure Samba. For more information see page 699.

Table 11-2   Red Hat configuration tools (continued)

Tool	Function
system-config-securitylevel	Displays the Security Level Configuration window with two tabs: Firewall Options (page 768) and SELinux (page 402).
system-config-services	Displays the Service Configuration window, which allows you to specify which daemons (services) run at each runlevel. For more information see page 406.
system-config-soundcard	Displays the Audio Devices window, which tells you which audio device the system detected and gives you the option of playing a sound to test the device.
system-config-users	Displays the User Manager window, which allows you to work with users and groups. For more information see page 538.
system-logviewer (*RHEL*)	Displays the System Logs window, which can display various system logs.
system-switch-mail	Displays the system-switch-mail window, which allows you to choose between the **sendmail** (page 627) and Postfix (page 652) MTAs.

COMMAND LINE UTILITIES

This section describes a few command line system administration tools you may find useful. To learn more about most of these utilities, read the man pages. For umask and uname, see the info pages.

chsh   Changes the login shell for a user. When you call chsh without an argument, you change your own login shell. Superuser can change the shell for any user by calling chsh with that user's username as an argument. When changing a login shell with chsh, you must specify an installed shell that is listed in the file **/etc/shells**; other entries are rejected. Also, you must give the pathname to the shell exactly as it appears in **/etc/shells**. The **chsh −−list-shells** command displays the list of available shells. In the following example, Superuser changes Sam's shell to tcsh:

```
# chsh sam
Changing shell for sam.
New shell [/bin/bash]: /bin/tcsh
Shell changed.
```

clear   Clears the screen. You can also use CONTROL-L from the bash shell to clear the screen. The value of the environment variable **TERM** (page 984) is used to determine how to clear the screen.

dmesg   Displays recent system log messages (page 535).

e2label   Displays or creates a volume label on an **ext2** or **ext3** disk partition. An e2label command has the following format:

e2label **device** *[newlabel]*

where *device* is the name of the device (**/dev/hda2, /dev/sdb1, /dev/fd0,** and so on) you want to work with. When you include the optional *newlabel* parameter, e2label changes the label on *device* to *newlabel*. Without this parameter, e2label displays the label. You can also create a volume label with the **–L** option of tune2fs (page 471).

kudzu Finds new and changed hardware and configures it. This utility determines which hardware is new by probing all devices on internal and external buses and comparing the results to the **/etc/sysconfig/hwconf** database. In the default configuration, the **/etc/rc.d/init.d/kudzu** script runs and calls kudzu as the machine enters runlevels 3 and 5. When it finds new or changed hardware, kudzu gives you a chance to configure it and permits you to deconfigure any hardware that you have removed.

mkfs Creates a new filesystem on a device. This utility is a front end for many utilities, each of which builds a different type of filesystem. By default, mkfs builds an **ext2** filesystem and works on either a hard disk partition or a floppy diskette. Although it can take many options and arguments, you can use mkfs simply as

```
# mkfs device
```

where *device* is the name of the device (**/dev/hda2, /dev/sdb1, /dev/fd0,** and so on) you want to make a filesystem on. Use the **–t** option to specify a type of filesystem. The following command creates an **ext3** filesystem on *device*:

```
# mkfs -t ext3 device
```

ping Sends packets to a remote system. This utility determines whether you can reach a remote system through the network and determines how much time it takes to exchange messages with the remote system. Refer to "ping: Tests a Network Connection" on page 365.

reset (link to tset) Resets terminal characteristics. The value of the environment variable **TERM** (page 984) determines how to reset the screen. The screen is cleared, the kill and interrupt characters are set to their default values, and character echo is turned on. From a graphical terminal emulator, this command also changes the size of the window to its default. The reset utility is useful to restore your screen to a sane state after it has been corrupted. It is similar to an **stty sane** command.

setserial Gets and sets serial port information. Superuser can use this utility to configure a serial port. The following command sets the input address of **/dev/ttys0** to 0x100, the interrupt (IRQ) to 5, and the baud rate to 115,000 baud:

```
# setserial /dev/ttys0 port 0x100 irq 5 spd_vhi
```

You can also check the configuration of a serial port with setserial:

```
# setserial /dev/ttys0
/dev/ttyS0, UART: 16550A, Port: 0x0100, IRQ: 5, Flags: spd_vhi
```

Normally, setserial is called when the system is booting if a serial port needs custom configuration.

stat Displays information about a file or filesystem. The **–f** (filesystem) option followed
by the device name or mount point of a filesystem displays information about the
filesystem including the maximum length of filenames (**Namelen** in the following
example). See the stat man page for more information.

```
$ stat -f /dev/hda
  File: "/dev/hda"
     ID: 0         Namelen: 255      Type: tmpfs
Block size: 4096      Fundamental block size: 4096
Blocks: Total: 121237    Free: 121206    Available: 121206
Inodes: Total: 121237    Free: 120932
```

umask A shell builtin that specifies a mask the system uses to set up access permissions
when you create a file. A umask command has the following format:

umask [mask]

where *mask* is a three-digit octal number or a symbolic value such as you would use
with chmod (page 182). The *mask* specifies the permissions that are *not* allowed.
When *mask* is an octal number, the digits correspond to the permissions for the
owner of the file, members of the group the file is associated with, and everyone
else. Because *mask* specifies the permissions that are *not* allowed, the system subtracts each of the three digits from 7 when you create a file. The result is three octal
numbers that specify the access permissions for the file (the numbers you would use
with chmod). A *mask* that you specify using symbolic values specifies the permissions that *are* allowed.

Most utilities and applications do not attempt to create files with execute permissions, regardless of the value of *mask*; they assume you do not want an executable
file. As a result, when a utility or application (such as touch) creates a file, the system subtracts each of the three digits in *mask* from 6. An exception is mkdir, which
assumes that you want the execute (access in the case of a directory) bit set.

The following commands set the file-creation permissions mask and display the
mask and its effect when you create a file and a directory. The mask of 022, when
subtracted from 777, gives permissions of 644 (**rw–r––r––**) for a file and 755
(**rwxr–xr–x**) for a directory.

```
$ umask 022
$ umask
0022
$ touch afile
$ mkdir adirectory
$ ls -ld afile adirectory
drwxr-xr-x  2 sam sam 4096 May  2 23:57 adirectory
-rw-r--r--  1 sam sam    0 May  2 23:57 afile
```

The next example sets the same mask using symbolic values. The **–S** option displays
the mask symbolically:

```
$ umask u=rwx,g=rx,o=rx
$ umask
0022
$ umask -S
u=rwx,g=rx,o=rx
```

uname   Displays information about the system. Without any arguments, this utility displays the name of the operating system (**Linux**). With a –a (all) option, it displays the operating system name, hostname, version number and release date of the operating system, and type of hardware you are using:

```
# uname -a
Linux pbnj 2.6.15-1.1871_FC5 #1 Mon Jan 23 15:53:52 EST 2006 i686 athlon i386 GNU/Linux
```

SETTING UP A SERVER

This section discusses issues that you may need to address when setting up a server: how to write configuration files; how to specify hosts and subnets; how to use **port-map**, **rpcinfo**, **xinetd**, and TCP wrappers (**hosts.allow** and **hosts.deny**); and how to set up a chroot jail. Setting up specific servers is covered in Chapters 14 and 18–26. Setting up a LAN is covered in Chapter 17.

STANDARD RULES IN CONFIGURATION FILES

Most configuration files, which are typically named *.conf, rely on the following conventions:

- Blank lines are ignored.

- A # anywhere on a line starts a comment that continues to the end of the line. Comments are ignored.

- When a name contains a SPACE, you must quote the SPACE by preceding it with a backslash (\) or by enclosing the entire name within single or double quotation marks.

- To make long lines easier to read and edit, you can break them into several shorter lines. Break a line by inserting a backslash (\) immediately followed by a NEWLINE (press RETURN in a text editor). When you insert the NEWLINE before or after a SPACE, you can indent the following line to make it easier to read. Do not break lines in this manner while editing on a Windows machine, as the NEWLINEs may not be properly escaped (Windows uses RETURN-LINEFEEDs to end lines).

Configuration files that do not follow these conventions are noted in the text.

SPECIFYING CLIENTS

Table 11-3 shows some common ways to specify a host or a subnet. Most of the time you can specify multiple hosts or subnets by separating the host or subnet specifications with SPACEs.

Table 11-3   Specifying a client

Client name pattern	Matches
n.n.n.n	One IP address.
name	One hostname, either local or remote.
Name that starts with .	Matches a hostname that ends with the specified string. For example, **.tcorp.com** matches the systems **kudos.tcorp.com** and **speedy.tcorp.com**, among others.
IP address that ends with .	Matches a host address that starts with the specified numbers. For example, **192.168.0.** matches **192.168.0.0 – 192.168.0.255**. If you omit the trailing period, this format does not work.
Starts with @	Specifies a netgroup.
n.n.n.n/m.m.m.m *or* n.n.n.n/mm	An IP address and subnet mask specify a subnet.
Starts with /	An absolute pathname of a file containing one or more names or addresses as specified in this table.
Wildcard	**Matches**
* *and* ?	Matches one (**?**) or more (*****) characters in a simple hostname or IP address. These wildcards do not match periods in a domain name.
ALL	Always matches.
LOCAL	Matches any hostname that does not contain a period.
Operator	
EXCEPT	Matches anything in the preceding list that is not in the following list. For example, **a b c d EXCEPT c** matches **a**, **b**, and **d**. Thus you could use **192.168. EXCEPT 192.168.0.1** to match all IP addresses that start with **192.168.** except **192.168.0.1**.

Examples   Each of the following examples specifies one or more systems:

10.10.	Matches all systems with IP addresses that start with **10.10**.
.redhat.com	Matches all named hosts on the Red Hat network
localhost	Matches the local system
127.0.0.1	The loopback address; always resolves to **localhost**
192.168.*.1	Could match all routers on a network of /24 subnets

SPECIFYING A SUBNET

When you set up a server, you frequently need to specify which clients are allowed to connect to the server. Sometimes it is convenient to specify a range of IP addresses, called a subnet. The discussion on page 357 explains what a subnet is and how to use a subnet mask to specify a subnet. Usually, you can specify a subnet as

n.n.n.n/m.m.m.m

or

n.n.n.n/maskbits

where *n.n.n.n* is the base IP address and the subnet is represented by *m.m.m.m* (the subnet mask) or *maskbits* (the number of bits used for the subnet mask). For example, **192.168.0.1/255.255.255.0** represents the same subnet as **192.168.0.1/24**. In binary, decimal **255.255.255.0** is represented by 24 ones followed by 8 zeros. The /24 is shorthand for a subnet mask with 24 ones. Each line in Table 11-4 presents two notations for the same subnet followed by the range of IP addresses that the subnet includes.

Table 11-4   Different ways to represent a subnet

Bits	Mask	Range
10.0.0.0/8	10.0.0.0/255.0.0.0	10.0.0.0 – 10.255.255.255
172.16.0.0/12	172.16.0.0/255.240.0.0	172.16.0.0 – 172.31.255.255
192.168.0.0/16	192.168.0.0/255.255.0.0	192.168.0.0 – 192.168.255.255

rpcinfo: DISPLAYS INFORMATION ABOUT portmap

The rpcinfo utility displays information about programs registered with **portmap** and makes RPC calls to programs to see if they are alive. For more information on **portmap**, refer to "RPC Network Services" on page 377. The rpcinfo utility takes the following options and arguments:

rpcinfo –p [host]
rpcinfo [–n port] –u | –t host program [version]
rpcinfo –b | –d program version

–p   (**probe**)   Lists all RPC programs registered with **portmap** on *host* or on the local system if *host* is not specified.

–n   (**port number**)   With –t or –u, uses the port numbered *port* instead of the port number specified by **portmap**.

–u   (**UDP**)   Makes a UDP RPC call to *version* (if specified) of *program* on *host* and reports whether it received a response.

–t   (**TCP**)   Makes a TCP RPC call to *version* (if specified) of *program* on *host* and reports whether it received a response.

–b (**broadcast**)   Makes an RPC broadcast to *version* of *program* and lists hosts that respond.

–d (**delete**)   Removes local RPC registration for *version* of *program*. Available to Superuser only.

Give the following command to see which RPC programs are registered with the **portmap** daemon on the system named **peach**:

```
$ /usr/sbin/rpcinfo -p peach
   program vers proto   port
    100000   2   tcp    111  portmapper
    100000   2   udp    111  portmapper
    100024   1   udp  32768  status
    100024   1   tcp  32768  status
    100021   1   udp  32769  nlockmgr
    100021   3   udp  32769  nlockmgr
 . . .
```

Use the **–u** option to display a list of versions of a daemon, such as **ypserv**, registered on a remote system (**peach**):

```
$ /usr/sbin/rpcinfo -u peach ypserv
program 100004 version 1 ready and waiting
program 100004 version 2 ready and waiting
```

Specify **localhost** to display a list of versions of a daemon registered on the local system:

```
$ /usr/sbin/rpcinfo -u localhost nfs
program 100003 version 2 ready and waiting
program 100003 version 3 ready and waiting
```

Locking down portmap   Because the **portmap** daemon holds information about which servers are running on the local system and which port each server is running on, only trusted systems should have access to this information. One way to ensure that only selected systems have access to **portmap** is to lock it down in the **/etc/hosts.allow** and **/etc/hosts.deny** files (page 427). Put the following line in **hosts.deny** to prevent all systems from using portmap on the local (server) system:

```
portmap: ALL
```

Test this setup from a remote system with the following command:

```
$ /usr/sbin/rpcinfo -p hostname
No remote programs registered.
```

Replace *hostname* with the name of the remote system that you changed the **hosts.deny** file on. The change is immediate; you do not need to kill/restart a daemon.

Next add the following line to the **hosts.allow** file on the server system:

```
portmap: host-IP
```

where *host-IP* is the IP address of the trusted, remote system that you gave the preceding rpcinfo command from. Use only IP addresses with **portmap** in **hosts.allow**;

do not use system names that **portmap** could get stuck trying to resolve. Give the same rpcinfo command, and you should now see a list of the servers that RPC knows about, including **portmap**. See page 661 for more examples.

Set the clocks

caution   The **portmap** daemon relies on the client's and the server's clocks being synchronized. A simple *DoS attack* (page 1030) can be initiated by setting the server's clock to the wrong time.

THE xinetd SUPERSERVER

The **xinetd** daemon is a more secure replacement for the **inetd** superserver that was originally shipped with 4.3BSD. The **xinetd** superserver listens for network connections. When one is made, it launches a specified server daemon and forwards the data from the socket (page 462) to the daemon's standard input.

The version of **xinetd** distributed with Red Hat Linux is linked against **libwrap.a,** so it can use the **/etc/hosts.allow** and **/etc/hosts.deny** files for access control (see "TCP Wrappers" on page 427 for more information). Using TCP wrappers can simplify configuration but hides some of the more advanced features of **xinetd**.

xinetd may not be installed

tip   Working as **root**, give the following command to install **xinetd** on a *FEDORA* system:

```
# yum install xinetd
```

Use RHN to install it on a *RHEL* system.

The base configuration for **xinetd** is stored in the **/etc/xinetd.conf** file. If this file is not present, **xinetd** is probably not installed. See the preceding tip. The file supplied with Red Hat Linux is shown here:

```
$ cat /etc/xinetd.conf
#
# Simple configuration file for xinetd
#
# Some defaults, and include /etc/xinetd.d/

defaults
{
        instances               = 60
        log_type                = SYSLOG authpriv
        log_on_success          = HOST PID
        log_on_failure          = HOST
        cps                     = 25 30
}

includedir /etc/xinetd.d
```

The **defaults** section specifies the default configuration of **xinetd**; the files in the included directory, **/etc/xinetd.d,** specify server-specific configurations. Defaults can be overridden by server-specific configuration files.

In the preceding file, the **instances** directive specifies that no daemon may run more than 60 copies of itself at one time. The **log_type** directive specifies that **xinetd** send messages to the system log daemon (**syslogd**, page 562) using the **authpriv** facility. The next two lines specify what to log on success and on failure. The **cps** (connections per second) directive specifies that no more than 25 connections to a specific service should be made per second and that the service should be disabled for 30 seconds if this limit is exceeded.

The following **xinetd** configuration file allows telnet connections from the local system and any system with an IP address that starts with **192.168.**. This configuration file does not rely on TCP wrappers, so it does not rely on the **hosts.allow** and **hosts.deny** files.

```
$ cat /etc/xinetd.d/telnet
service telnet
{
        socket_type     = stream
        wait            = no
        user            = root
        server          = /usr/sbin/in.telnetd
        only_from       = 192.168.0.0/16 127.0.0.1
        disable         = no
}
```

The **socket_type** indicates whether the socket uses TCP or UDP. TCP-based protocols establish a connection between the client and the server and are identified by the type **stream**. UDP-based protocols rely on the transmission of individual datagrams and are identified by the type **dgram**.

When **wait** is set to **no, xinetd** handles multiple concurrent connections to this service. Setting **wait** to **yes** causes **xinetd** to wait for the server process to complete before handling the next request for that service. In general, UDP services should be set to **yes** and TCP services to **no**. If you were to set **wait** to **yes** for a service such as telnet, only one person would be able to use the service at any given time.

The **user** specifies which user the server runs as. If this user is a member of multiple groups, you can also specify the group on a separate line with the keyword **group**. The **user** directive is ignored if **xinetd** is run as other than **root**. The **server** provides the pathname of the server program that **xinetd** runs for this service.

The **only_from** specifies which systems **xinetd** allows to use the service. It is a good idea to use IP addresses only—using hostnames can make the service unavailable if DNS fails. Zeros at the right of an IP address are treated as wildcards. For example, **192.168.0.0** allows access from any system in the **192.168** subnet.

The **disable** line can disable a service without removing the configuration file. As shipped by Red Hat, a number of services include an **xinetd** configuration file with **disable** set to **yes**. To run one of these services, change **disable** to **no** in the appropriate file in **xinetd.d** and restart **xinetd**:

```
# /sbin/service xinetd restart
Stopping xinetd:                                        [  OK  ]
Starting xinetd:                                        [  OK  ]
```

SECURING A SERVER

You may secure a server either by using TCP wrappers or by setting up a chroot jail.

TCP WRAPPERS: CLIENT/SERVER SECURITY (hosts.allow AND hosts.deny)

When you open a local system to access from remote systems, you must ensure that the following criteria are met:

- Open the local system only to systems you want to allow to access it.

- Allow each remote system to access only the data you want it to access.

- Allow each remote system to access data only in the appropriate manner (readonly, read/write, write only).

As part of the client/server model, TCP wrappers, which can be used for any daemon that is linked against **libwrap.a**, rely on the **/etc/hosts.allow** and **/etc/hosts.deny** files as the basis of a simple access control language. This access control language defines rules that selectively allow clients to access server daemons on a local system based on the client's address and the daemon the client tries to access.

Each line in the **hosts.allow** and **hosts.deny** files has the following format:

daemon_list : client_list [: command]

where *daemon_list* is a comma-separated list of one or more server daemons (such as **portmap**, **vsftpd**, or **sshd**), *client_list* is a comma-separated list of one or more clients (see Table 11-3, "Specifying a client," on page 422), and the optional *command* is the command that is executed when a client from *client_list* tries to access a server daemon from *daemon_list*.

When a client requests a connection with a local server, the **hosts.allow** and **hosts.deny** files are consulted as follows until a match is found:

1. If the daemon/client pair matches a line in **hosts.allow**, access is granted.

2. If the daemon/client pair matches a line in **hosts.deny**, access is denied.

3. If there is no match in either the **hosts.allow** or the **hosts.deny** files, access is granted.

The first match determines whether the client is allowed to access the server. When either **hosts.allow** or **hosts.deny** does not exist, it is as though that file was empty. Although it is not recommended, you can allow access to all daemons for all clients by removing both files.

Examples   For a more secure system, put the following line in **hosts.deny** to block all access:

```
$ cat /etc/hosts.deny
...
ALL : ALL : echo '%c tried to connect to %d and was blocked' >> /var/log/tcpwrappers.log
```

This line prevents any client from connecting to any service, unless specifically permitted in **hosts.allow**. When this rule is matched, it adds a line to the file named **/var/log/tcpwrappers.log**. The **%c** expands to client information and the **%d** expands to the name of the daemon the client attempted to connect to.

With the preceding **hosts.deny** file in place, you can include lines in **hosts.allow** that explicitly allow access to certain services and systems. For example, the following **hosts.allow** file allows anyone to connect to the OpenSSH daemon (ssh, scp, sftp) but allows telnet connections only from the same network as the local system and users on the 192.168. subnet:

```
$ cat /etc/hosts.allow
sshd : ALL
in.telnet : LOCAL
in.telnet : 192.168.* 127.0.0.1
...
```

The first line allows connection from any system (ALL) to **sshd**. The second line allows connection from any system in the same domain as the server (LOCAL). The third line matches any system whose IP address starts **192.168.** and the local system.

SETTING UP A chroot JAIL

On early UNIX systems, the root directory was a fixed point in the filesystem. On modern UNIX variants, including Linux, you can define the root directory on a perprocess basis. The chroot utility allows you to run a process with a root directory other than /.

The root directory appears at the top of the directory hierarchy and has no parent: A process cannot access any files above the root directory (because they do not exist). If, for example, you run a program (process) and specify its root directory as **/home/sam/jail**, the program would have no concept of any files in **/home/sam** or above: **jail** is the program's root directory and is labeled / (not **jail**).

By creating an artificial root directory, frequently called a (chroot) jail, you prevent a program from accessing or modifying—possibly maliciously—files outside the directory hierarchy starting at its root. You must set up a chroot jail properly to increase security: If you do not set up a chroot jail correctly, you can actually make it easier for a malicious user to gain access to a system than if there were no chroot jail.

USING chroot

Creating a chroot jail is simple: Working as **root**, give the command **/usr/sbin/chroot** *directory*. The *directory* becomes the root directory and the process attempts to run the default shell. Working as **root** from the **/home/sam** directory, the following command sets up a chroot jail in the (existing) **/home/sam/jail** directory:

```
# /usr/sbin/chroot /home/sam/jail
/usr/sbin/chroot: cannot run command '/bin/bash': No such file or directory
```

This example sets up a chroot jail, but when it attempts to run the bash shell, it fails. Once the jail is set up, the directory that was named **jail** takes on the name of the root directory, **/**, so chroot cannot find the file identified by the pathname **/bin/bash**. In this situation the chroot jail is working but is not useful.

Getting a chroot jail to work the way you want is a bit more complicated. To have the preceding example run bash in a chroot jail, you need to create a **bin** directory in **jail** (**/home/sam/jail/bin**) and copy **/bin/bash** to this directory. Because the bash binary is dynamically linked to shared libraries (page 840), you need to copy these libraries into **jail** as well. The libraries go in **lib**. The next example creates the necessary directories, copies **bash**, uses ldd to display the shared library dependencies of bash, and copies the necessary libraries into **lib**. The **linux-gate.so.1** file is a dynamically shared object (DSO) provided by the kernel to speed system calls; you do not need to copy it to the **lib** directory.

```
$ pwd
/home/sam/jail
$ mkdir bin lib
$ cp /bin/bash bin
$ ldd bin/bash
        linux-gate.so.1 =>  (0x0089c000)
        libtermcap.so.2 => /lib/libtermcap.so.2 (0x00cdb000)
        libdl.so.2 => /lib/libdl.so.2 (0x00b1b000)
        libc.so.6 => /lib/libc.so.6 (0x009cb000)
        /lib/ld-linux.so.2 (0x009ae000)
$ cp /lib/{libtermcap.so.2,libdl.so.2,libc.so.6,ld-linux.so.2} lib
```

Now that everything is set up, you can start the chroot jail again. Although all of the setup can be done by an ordinary user, you have to run chroot as Superuser:

```
$ su
Password:
# /usr/sbin/chroot .
bash-3.1# pwd
/
bash-3.1# ls
bash: ls: command not found
bash-3.1#
```

This time the chroot finds and starts **bash**, which displays its default prompt (**bash-3.1#**). The pwd command works because it is a shell builtin (page 225). However, bash cannot find the ls utility (it is not in the chroot jail). You can copy **/bin/ls** and its libraries into the jail if you want users in the jail to be able to use ls.

To set up a useful chroot jail, first determine which utilities the users of the chroot jail will need. Then copy the appropriate binaries and their libraries into the jail. Alternatively you can build static copies of the binaries and put them in the jail without installing separate libraries. (The statically linked binaries are considerably larger than their dynamic counterparts. The base system with bash and the core utilities exceeds 50 megabytes.) You can find the source code for most of the common utilities in the **bash** and **coreutils** SRPMS (source rpm) packages.

Whichever technique you choose, you must put a copy of su in the jail. The su command is required to run programs as a user other than **root**. Because **root** can break out of a chroot jail, it is imperative that you run a program in the chroot jail as a user other than **root**.

The dynamic version of su distributed by Red Hat requires PAM and will not work within a jail. You need to build a copy of su from the source to use in a jail. By default any copy of su you build does not require PAM. Refer to "GNU Configure and Build System" on page 491 for instructions on how to build packages such as **coreutils** (which includes su).

To use su, you must copy the relevant lines from the **/etc/passwd** and **/etc/shadow** files into files with the same names in the **etc** directory inside the jail.

Keeping multiple chroot jails

tip   If you plan to deploy multiple chroot jails, it is a good idea to keep a clean copy of the **bin** and **lib** files somewhere other than in one of the active jails.

RUNNING A SERVICE IN A chroot JAIL

Running a shell inside a jail has limited usefulness. Instead you are more likely to need to run a specific service inside the jail. To run a service inside a jail, you must make sure all files needed by that service are inside the jail. The format of a command to start a service in a chroot jail is

```
# /usr/sbin/chroot jailpath /bin/su user daemonname &
```

where *jailpath* is the pathname of the jail directory, *user* is the username that runs the daemon, and *daemonname* is the path (inside the jail) of the daemon that provides the service.

Some servers are already set up to take advantage of chroot jails. You can set up DNS so that **named** runs in a jail (page 750), and the **vsftpd** FTP server can automatically start chroot jails for clients (page 616).

SECURITY CONSIDERATIONS

Some services need to be run as **root**, but they release their **root** privilege once started (Procmail and **vsftpd** are examples). If you are running such a service, you do not need to put su inside the jail.

A process run as **root** could potentially escape from a chroot jail. For this reason, you should always su to another user before starting a program running inside the jail. Also, be careful about which setuid (page 183) binaries you allow inside a jail—a security hole in one of them could compromise the security of the jail. In addition, make sure the user cannot access executable files that he uploads.

DHCP: CONFIGURES HOSTS

Instead of storing network configuration information in local files on each system, DHCP (Dynamic Host Configuration Protocol) enables client systems to retrieve network configuration information each time they connect to the network. A DHCP server assigns an IP addresses from a pool of addresses to clients as needed. Assigned addresses are typically temporary, but need not be.

This technique has several advantages over storing network configuration information in local files:

- A new user can set up an Internet connection without having to deal with IP addresses, netmasks, DNS addresses, and other technical details. An experienced user can set up a connection more quickly.

- DHCP facilitates assignment and management of IP addresses and related network information by centralizing the process on a server. A system administrator can configure new systems, including laptops that connect to the network from different locations, to use DHCP; DHCP then assigns IP addresses only when each system connects to the network. The pool of IP addresses is managed as a group on the DHCP server.

- IP addresses can be used by more than one system, reducing the total number of IP addresses needed. This conservation of addresses is important because the Internet is quickly running out of IPv4 addresses. Although a particular IP address can be used by only one system at a time, many end-user systems require addresses only occasionally, when they connect to the Internet. By reusing IP addresses, DHCP lengthens the life of the IPv4 protocol. DHCP applies to IPv4 only, as IPv6 forces systems to configure their IP addresses automatically (called autoconfiguration) when they connect to a network (page 359).

DHCP is particularly useful for administrators who are responsible for maintaining a large number of systems because individual systems no longer need to store unique configuration information. With DHCP, the administrator can set up a master system and deploy new systems with a copy of the master's hard disk. In educational establishments and other open access facilities, the hard disk image may be stored on a shared drive, with each workstation automatically restoring itself to pristine condition at the end of each day.

MORE INFORMATION

Web   www.dhcp.org

FAQ   www.dhcp-handbook.com/dhcp_faq.html

HOWTO   *DHCP Mini HOWTO*

HOW DHCP WORKS

The client daemon, **dhclient** (part of the **dhcp** package), contacts the server daemon, **dhcpd**, to obtain the IP address, netmask, broadcast address, nameserver address, and other networking parameters. The server provides a *lease* on the IP address to the client. The client can request the specific terms of the lease, including its duration; the server can, in turn, limit these terms. While connected to the network, a client typically requests extensions of its lease as necessary so its IP address remains the same. The lease can expire once the client is disconnected from the network, with the server giving the client a new IP address when it requests a new lease. You can also set up a DHCP server to provide static IP addresses for specific clients (refer to "Static Versus Dynamic IP Addresses" on page 354).

DHCP is broadcast based, so both client and server must be on the same subnet (page 357).

DHCP CLIENT

A DHCP client requests network configuration parameters from the DHCP server and uses those parameters to configure its network interface.

PREREQUISITES

Install the following package:

• **dhclient**

dhclient: THE DHCP CLIENT

When a DHCP client system connects to the network, dhclient requests a lease from the DHCP server and configures the client's network interface(s). Once a DHCP client has requested and established a lease, it stores information about the lease in a file named **dhclient.leases**, which is stored in **/var/lib/dhcp** (*RHEL*) or **/var/lib/dhclient** (*FEDORA*). This information is used to reestablish a lease when either the server or the client needs to reboot. The DHCP client configuration file, **/etc/dhclient.conf**, is required only for custom configurations. The following **dhclient.conf** file specifies a single interface, eth0:

```
$ cat /etc/dhclient.conf
interface "eth0"
{
send dhcp-client-identifier 1:xx:xx:xx:xx:xx:xx;
send dhcp-lease-time 86400;
}
```

In the preceding file, the 1 in the **dhcp-client-identifier** specifies an Ethernet network and **xx:xx:xx:xx:xx:xx** is the *MAC address* (page 1041) of the device controlling that interface. See page 434 for instructions on how to display a MAC address. The **dhcp-lease-time** is the duration, in seconds, of the lease on the IP address. While the client is connected to the network, dhclient automatically renews the lease each time half of the lease is up. The lease time of 8,6400 seconds (or one day) is a reasonable choice for a workstation.

DHCP Server

The DHCP server maintains a list of IP addresses and other configuration parameters. When requested to do so, the DHCP server provides configuration parameters to a client.

Prerequisites

Install the following package:

- **dhcp**

Run chkconfig to cause **dhcpd** to start when the system enters multiuser mode:

```
# /sbin/chkconfig dhcpd on
```

Start **dhcpd**:

```
# /sbin/service dhcpd start
```

dhcpd: The DHCP Daemon

A simple DCHP server allows you to add clients to a network without maintaining a list of assigned IP addresses. A simple network, such as a home LAN sharing an Internet connection, can use DHCP to assign a dynamic IP address to almost all nodes. The exceptions are servers and routers, which must be at known network locations to be able to receive connections. If servers and routers are configured without DHCP, you can specify a simple DHCP server configuration in **/etc/dhcpd.conf**:

```
$ cat /etc/dhcpd.conf
default-lease-time 600;
max-lease-time 86400;

option subnet-mask 255.255.255.0;
option broadcast-address 192.168.1.255;
option routers 192.168.1.1;
option domain-name-servers 192.168.1.1;

subnet 192.168.1.0 netmask 255.255.255.0 {
    range 192.168.1.2 192.168.1.200;
}
```

The preceding configuration file specifies a LAN where the router and DNS are both located on **192.168.1.1**. The **default-lease-time** specifies the number of seconds the dynamic IP lease will remain valid if the client does not specify a duration. The **max-lease-time** is the maximum time allowed for a lease.

The information in the **option** lines is sent to each client when it connects. The names following the word **option** specify what the following argument represents. For example, the **option broadcast-address** line specifies the broadcast address of the network. The **routers** and **domain-name-servers** options allow multiple values separated by commas.

The **subnet** section includes a **range** line that specifies the range of IP addresses that the DHCP server can assign. If you define multiple subnets, you can define options, such as **subnet-mask**, inside the **subnet** section. Options defined outside all **subnet** sections are global and apply to all subnets.

The preceding configuration file assigns addresses in the range between 192.168.1.2 and 192.168.1.200. The DHCP server starts at the bottom of this range and attempts to assign a new IP address to each new client. Once the DHCP server reaches the top of the range, it starts reassigning IP addresses that have been used in the past, but are not currently in use. If you have fewer systems than IP addresses, the IP address of each system should remain fairly constant. You cannot use the same IP address for more than one system at a time.

Once you have configured a DHCP server, you can start (or restart) it by using the **dhcpd** init script:

```
# /sbin/service dhcpd restart
```

Once the server is running, clients configured to obtain an IP address from the server using DHCP should be able to do so.

STATIC IP ADDRESSES

As mentioned earlier, routers and servers typically require static IP addresses. While you can manually configure IP addresses for these systems, it may be more convenient to have the DHCP server provide them with static IP addresses.

When a system that requires a specific static IP address connects to the network and contacts the DHCP server, the server needs a way to identify the system so the server can assign the proper IP address to the system. The DHCP server uses the *MAC address* (page 1041) of the system's Ethernet card (NIC) as an identifier. When you set up the server, you must know the MAC address of each system that requires a static IP address.

Displaying a MAC address
You can use ifconfig to display the MAC addresses of the Ethernet cards (NICs) in a system. In the following example, the MAC addresses are the colon-separated series of hexadecimal number pairs following **HWaddr**:

```
$ /sbin/ifconfig | grep -i hwaddr
eth0      Link encap:Ethernet   HWaddr BA:DF:00:DF:C0:FF
eth1      Link encap:Ethernet   HWaddr 00:02:B3:41:35:98
```

Run ifconfig on each system that requires a static IP address. Once you have determined the MAC address of each of these systems, you can add a **host** section to the **/etc/dhcpd.conf** file for each system, instructing the DHCP server to assign a specific address to the system. The following **host** section assigns the address **192.168.1.1** to the system with the MAC address of **BA:DF:00:DF:C0:FF**:

```
$ cat /etc/dhcpd.conf
...
host router {
    hardware ethernet BA:DF:00:DF:C0:FF;
    fixed-address 192.168.1.1;
    option host-name router;
}
```

The name following **host** is used internally by **dhcpd**. The name specified after **option host-name** is passed to the client and can be a hostname or an FQDN.

After making changes to **dhcpd.conf**, restart **dhcpd** using service and the **dhcpd** init script (page 433).

nsswitch.conf: WHICH SERVICE TO LOOK AT FIRST

With the advent of NIS and DNS, finding user and system information was no longer a simple matter of searching a local file. Where once you looked in **/etc/passwd** to get user information and in **/etc/hosts** to find system address information, you can now use several methods to find this type of information. The **/etc/nsswitch.conf** (name service switch configuration) file specifies which methods to use and the order in which to use them when looking for a certain type of information. You can also specify what action the system takes based on whether a method works or fails.

Format Each line in **nsswitch.conf** specifies how to search for a piece of information, such as a user's password. A line in **nsswitch.conf** has the following format:

> *info:*   *method [[action]] [method [[action]]...]*

where *info* specifies the type of information that the line describes, *method* is the method used to find the information, and *action* is the response to the return status of the preceding *method*. The action is enclosed within square brackets.

How nsswitch.conf WORKS

When called upon to supply information that **nsswitch.conf** describes, the system examines the line with the appropriate *info* field. It uses the methods specified on the line starting with the method on the left. By default, when it finds the desired information, the system stops searching. Without an *action* specification, when a method fails to return a result, the system tries the next action. It is possible for the search to end without finding the requested information.

INFORMATION

The **nsswitch.conf** file commonly controls searches for users (in **passwd**), passwords (in **shadow**), host IP addresses, and group information. The following list describes most of the types of information (*info* in the format discussed earlier) that **nsswitch.conf** controls searches for.

automount	Automount (**/etc/auto.master** and **/etc/auto.misc**, page 690)
bootparams	Diskless and other booting options (See the **bootparam** man page.)
ethers	MAC address (page 1041)
group	Groups of users (**/etc/group**, page 451)
hosts	System information (**/etc/hosts**, page 452)
netgroup	Netgroup information (**/etc/netgroup**, page 453)
networks	Network information (**/etc/networks**)
passwd	User information (**/etc/passwd**, page 454)
protocols	Protocol information (**/etc/protocols**, page 455)
publickey	Used for NFS running in secure mode
rpc	RPC names and numbers (**/etc/rpc**, page 456)
services	Services information (**/etc/services**, page 456)
shadow	Shadow password information (**/etc/shadow**, page 456)

METHODS

Following is a list of the types of information that **nsswitch.conf** controls searches for (*method* in the format on page 435). For each type of information, you can specify one or more of the following methods:[2]

files	Searches local files such as **/etc/passwd** and **/etc/hosts**
nis	Searches the NIS database; **yp** is an alias for **nis**
dns	Queries the DNS (**hosts** queries only)
compat	± syntax in **passwd**, **group**, and **shadow** files (page 438)

SEARCH ORDER

The information provided by two or more methods may overlap: For example, **files** and **nis** may each provide password information for the same user. With overlapping information, you need to consider which method you want to be authoritative (take precedence), and put that method at the left of the list of methods.

The default **nsswitch.conf** file lists methods without actions, assuming no overlap (which is normal). In this case, the order is not critical: When one method fails, the system goes to the next one; all that is lost is a little time. Order becomes critical when you use actions between methods, or when overlapping entries differ.

The first of the following lines from **nsswitch.conf** causes the system to search for password information in **/etc/passwd** and, if that fails, to use NIS to find the information. If the user you are looking for is listed in both places, the information in the local file would be used and therefore would be authoritative. The second line uses

---

2. There are other, less commonly used methods. See the default **/etc/nsswitch.conf** file and the **nsswitch.conf** man page for more information. Although NIS+ belongs in this list, it is not implemented for Linux and is not discussed in this book.

NIS; if that fails, it searches **/etc/hosts**; if that fails, it checks with DNS to find host information.

```
passwd          files nis
hosts           nis files dns
```

ACTION ITEMS

Each method can optionally be followed by an action item that specifies what to do if the method succeeds or fails for any of a number of reasons. An action item has the following format:

[[!]STATUS=action]

where the opening and closing square brackets are part of the format and do not indicate that the contents are optional; *STATUS* (by convention uppercase although it is not case sensitive) is the status being tested for; and *action* is the action to be taken if *STATUS* matches the status returned by the preceding method. The leading exclamation point (!) is optional and negates the status.

STATUS Values for *STATUS* are as follows:

NOTFOUND The method worked but the value being searched for was not found. Default action is **continue**.

SUCCESS The method worked and the value being searched for was found; no error was returned. Default action is **return**.

UNAVAIL The method failed because it is permanently unavailable. For example, the required file may not be accessible or the required server may be down. Default action is **continue**.

TRYAGAIN The method failed because it was temporarily unavailable. For example, a file may be locked or a server overloaded. Default action is **continue**.

action Values for *action* are as follows:

return Returns to the calling routine with or without a value.

continue Continues with the next method. Any returned value is overwritten by a value found by the next method.

Example For example, the following line from **nsswitch.conf** causes the system first to use DNS to search for the IP address of a given host. The action item following the DNS method tests whether the status returned by the method is not (!) UNAVAIL.

```
hosts           dns [!UNAVAIL=return] files
```

The system takes the action associated with the *STATUS* (**return**) if the DNS method does not return UNAVAIL (!UNAVAIL)—that is, if DNS returns SUCCESS, NOTFOUND, or TRYAGAIN. The result is that the following method (**files**) is used only when the DNS server is unavailable: If the DNS server is *not un*available (read the two negatives as "is available"), the search returns the domain name or reports that the domain name was not found. The search uses the **files** method (check the local **/etc/hosts** file) only if the server is not available.

COMPAT METHOD: ± IN passwd, group, AND shadow FILES

You can put special codes in the **/etc/passwd**, **/etc/group**, and **/etc/shadow** files that cause the system, when you specify the **compat** method in **nsswitch.conf**, to combine and modify entries in the local files and the NIS maps.

A plus sign (**+**) at the beginning of a line in one of these files adds NIS information; a minus sign (**–**) removes information. For example, to use these codes in the **passwd** file, specify **passwd: compat** in **nsswitch.conf**. The system then goes through the **passwd** file in order, adding or removing the appropriate NIS entries when it reaches each line that starts with a **+** or **–**.

Although you can put a plus sign at the end of the **passwd** file, specify **passwd: compat** in **nsswitch.conf** to search the local **passwd** file, and then go through the NIS map, it is more efficient to put **passwd: file nis** in **nsswitch.conf** and not modify the **passwd** file.

PAM

PAM (actually Linux-PAM, or Linux Pluggable Authentication Modules) allows a system administrator to determine how applications use *authentication* (page 1020) to verify the identity of a user. PAM provides shared libraries (page 840) of modules (located in **/lib/security**) that, when called by an application, authenticate a user. The term "Pluggable" in PAM's name refers to the ease with which you can add and remove modules from the authentication stack. The configuration files kept in the **/etc/pam.d** directory determine the method of authentication and contain a list, or stack, of calls to the modules. PAM may also use other files, such as **/etc/passwd**, when necessary.

Instead of building the authentication code into each application, PAM provides shared libraries that keep the authentication code separate from the application code. The techniques of authenticating users stay the same from application to application. PAM enables a system administrator to change the authentication mechanism for a given application without ever touching the application.

PAM provides authentication for a variety of system-entry services (login, ftp, and so on). You can take advantage of PAM's ability to stack authentication modules to integrate system-entry services with different authentication mechanisms, such as RSA, DCE, Kerberos, and smartcards.

From login through using su to shutting the system down, whenever you are asked for a password (or not asked for a password because the system trusts that you are who you say you are), PAM makes it possible for system administrators to configure the authentication process. It also makes the configuration process essentially the same for all applications that use PAM for authentication.

The configuration files stored in **/etc/pam.d** describe the authentication procedure for each application. These files usually have names that are the same as or similar to the name of the application that they authenticate for. For example, authentication for the login utility is configured in **/etc/pam.d/login**. The name of the file is the name of the PAM service[3] that the file configures. Occasionally one file may serve two programs. PAM accepts only lowercase letters in the names of files in the **/etc/pam.d** directory.

Do not lock yourself out of the system

caution   Editing PAM configuration files correctly takes care and attention. It is all too easy to lock yourself out of the computer with a single mistake. To avoid this problem, always keep backup copies of the PAM configuration files you edit, test every change thoroughly, and make sure you can still log in once the change is installed. Keep a Superuser session open until you have finished testing. When a change fails and you cannot log in, use the Superuser session to replace the newly edited files with their backup copies.

PAM warns you about errors it encounters, logging them to the **/var/log/messages** or **/var/log/secure** files. Review these files if you are trying to figure out why a changed PAM file is not working properly. To prevent a malicious user from seeing information about PAM unnecessarily, PAM sends error messages to a file rather than to the screen.

MORE INFORMATION

Local   **/usr/share/doc/pam-**✻**/html/index.html**

Web   *Linux-PAM System Administrators' Guide*
     www.kernel.org/pub/linux/libs/pam/Linux-PAM-html/pam.html

HOWTO   *User Authentication HOWTO*

CONFIGURATION FILES, MODULE TYPES, AND CONTROL FLAGS

Following is an example of a PAM configuration file. Comment lines begin with a pound sign (#).

Login module
```
$ cat /etc/pam.d/login
#%PAM-1.0
auth       required      pam_securetty.so
auth       include       system-auth
account    required      pam_nologin.so
account    include       system-auth
password   include       system-auth
# pam_selinux.so close should be the first session rule
session    required      pam_selinux.so close
session    include       system-auth
session    required      pam_loginuid.so
session    optional      pam_console.so
# pam_selinux.so open should be the last session rule
session    required      pam_selinux.so open
```

---

3. There is no relationship between PAM services and the **/etc/services** file. The name of the PAM service is an arbitrary string that each application gives to PAM; PAM then looks up the configuration file with that name and uses it to control authentication. There is no central registry of PAM service names.

The first line is a special comment; it will become significant only if another PAM format is released. Do not use #% other than in the first line of the preceding example.

The rest of the lines tell PAM to do something as part of the authentication process. Lines that begin with # are comments. The first word on each line is a module type indicator: **account, auth, password,** or **session** (Table 11-5). The second is a control flag (Table 11-6), which indicates the action PAM should take if authentication fails. The rest of the line contains the name of a PAM module (located in **/lib/security**) and any arguments for that module. The PAM library itself uses the **/etc/pam.d** files to determine which modules to delegate work to.

Table 11-5 Module type indicators

Module type	Description	Controls
account	Account management	Determining whether an already authenticated user is allowed to use the service she is trying to use. (That is, has the account expired? Is the user allowed to use this service at this time of day?)
auth	Authentication	Proving that the user is authorized to use the service. This may be done using passwords or another mechanism.
password	Password modification	Updating authentication mechanisms such as user passwords.
session	Session management	Setting things up when the service is started (as when the user logs in) and breaking them down when the service is terminated (as when the user logs out).

You can use one of the control flag keywords listed in Table 11-6 to set the control flags.

Table 11-6 Control flag keywords

Keyword	Flag function
required	Success is required for authentication to succeed. Control and a failure result are returned after all modules in the stack have been executed. The technique of delaying the report to the calling program until all modules have been executed may keep attackers from knowing what caused their authentication attempts to fail and tell them less about the system, making it more difficult for them to break in.
requisite	Success is required for authentication to succeed. Further module processing is aborted, and control is returned immediately after a module fails. This technique may expose information about the system to an attacker. However, if it prevents a user from giving a password over an insecure connection, it might keep information out of the hands of an attacker.

Table 11-6   Control flag keywords (continued)

sufficient	Success indicates that this module type has succeeded, and no subsequent required modules of this type are executed. Failure is not fatal to the stack of this module type. This technique is generally used when one form of authentication or another is good enough: If one fails, PAM tries the other. For example, when you use rsh to connect to another computer, **pam_rhosts** first checks whether your connection can be trusted without a password. If the connection can be trusted, the **pam_rhosts** module reports success, and PAM immediately reports success to the rsh daemon that called it. You will not be asked for a password. If your connection is not considered trustworthy, PAM starts the authentication over, asking for a password. If this second authentication succeeds, PAM ignores the fact that the **pam_rhosts** module reported failure. If both modules fail, you will not be able to log in.
optional	Result is generally ignored. An optional module is relevant only when it is the only module on the stack for a particular service.

PAM uses each of the module types as requested by the application. That is, the application will ask PAM separately to authenticate, check account status, manage sessions, and change the password. PAM will use one or more modules from the **/lib/security** directory to accomplish each of these tasks.

The configuration files in **/etc/pam.d** list the set of modules to be used for each application to perform each task. Each such set of the same module types is called a *stack*. PAM calls the modules one at a time in order, from the top of the stack (the first module listed in the configuration file) to the bottom. Each module reports success or failure back to PAM. When all stacks of modules (with some exceptions) within a configuration file have been called, the PAM library reports success or failure back to the application.

EXAMPLE

Part of the login service's authentication stack follows:

```
$ cat /etc/pam.d/login
#%PAM-1.0
auth        required        pam_securetty.so
auth        include         system-auth
account     required        pam_nologin.so
...
```

The login utility first asks for a username and then asks PAM to run this stack to authenticate the user. Refer to Table 11-5 and Table 11-6 on page 440.

1. PAM first calls the **pam_securetty** (secure tty) module to make sure that the **root** user logs in only from an allowed terminal (by default, **root** is not

allowed to run login over the network; this policy helps prevent security breaches). The **pam_securetty** module is *required* to succeed if the authentication stack is to succeed. The **pam_securetty** module reports failure only if someone is trying to log in as **root** from an unauthorized terminal. Otherwise (if the username being authenticated is not **root** or if the username is **root** and the login attempt is being made from a secure terminal), the **pam_securetty** module reports success.

Success and failure within PAM are opaque concepts that apply only to PAM. They do not equate to true and false as used elsewhere in the operating system.

2. The **system-auth** module checks that the user who is logging in is authorized to do so, including verification of the username and password.

3. The **pam_nologin** module makes sure that if the /etc/nologin.txt file exists, only the **root** user is allowed to log in. (That is, the **pam_nologin** module reports success only if /etc/nologin.txt does not exist or if the **root** user is logging in.) Thus, when a shutdown has been scheduled for some time in the near future, the system administrator can keep users from logging in on the system only to experience a shutdown moments later.

The **account** module type works like the **auth** module type but is called after the user has been authenticated; it acts as an additional security check or requirement for a user to gain access to the system. For example, **account** modules might enforce a policy that a user can log in only during business hours.

The **session** module type sets up and tears down the session (perhaps mounting and unmounting the user's home directory). One common **session** module on a Red Hat Linux system is the **pam_console** module, which sets the system up especially for users who log in at the physical console, rather than remotely. A local user is able to access the floppy and CD drives, the sound card, and sometimes other devices as defined by the system administrator.

The **password** module type is a bit unusual: All modules in the stack are called once; they are told to get all information they need to store the password to persistent memory, such as a disk, but not actually to store it. If it determines that it cannot or should not store the password, a module reports failure. If all **password** modules in the stack report success, they are called a second time and told to store to persistent memory the password they obtained on the first pass. The **password** module is responsible for updating the authentication information (that is, changing the user's password).

Any one module can act as more than one module type; many modules can act as all four module types.

MODIFYING THE PAM CONFIGURATION

Some UNIX systems require that a user be a member of the **wheel** group to use the su command. Although Red Hat Linux is not configured this way by default, PAM allows you to change the default by editing the /etc/pam.d/su file:

```
$ cat /etc/pam.d/su
#%PAM-1.0
auth            sufficient      pam_rootok.so
# Uncomment the following line to implicitly trust users in the "wheel" group.
#auth           sufficient      pam_wheel.so trust use_uid
# Uncomment the following line to require a user to be in the "wheel" group.
#auth           required        pam_wheel.so use_uid
auth            include         system-auth
account         include         system-auth
password        include         system-auth
session         include         system-auth
session         optional        pam_xauth.so
```

The third through sixth lines of the **su** module contain comments that include the lines necessary to permit members of the **wheel** group to run su without supplying a password (sufficient) and to permit only users who are in the **wheel** group to use su (required). Uncomment one of these lines when you want the system to follow one of these rules.

Brackets ([]) in the control flags field

caution   You can set the control flags in a more complex way than described in this section. When you see brackets ([ ]) in the control flags position in a PAM configuration file, the newer, more complex method is in use. Each comma-delimited argument is a *value=action* pair. When the result returned by the function matches *value*, *action* is evaluated. For more information refer to the *PAM System Administrator's Guide* (**/usr/share/doc/pam-✷/txts/pam.txt**).

Do not create /etc/pam.conf

caution   You may have encountered PAM on other systems where all configuration is arranged in a single file (**/etc/pam.conf**). This file does not exist on Red Hat Linux systems. Instead, the **/etc/pam.d** directory contains individual configuration files, one per application that uses PAM. This setup makes it easy to install and uninstall applications that use PAM because you do not have to modify the **/etc/pam.conf** file each time. If you create a **/etc/pam.conf** file on a system that does not use this file, the PAM configuration may become confused. Do not use PAM documentation from a different system. Also, the **requisite** control flag is not available on some systems that support PAM.

CHAPTER SUMMARY

A system administrator is someone who keeps the system useful and convenient for its users. Much of the work you do as the system administrator requires you to log in as **root**. The **root** user, called Superuser, has extensive systemwide powers that normal users do not have. Superuser can read from and write to any file and can execute programs that ordinary users are not permitted to execute.

You can bring up the system in single-user mode. In this mode, only the system console is functional. When the system is in single-user mode, you can back up files and use fsck to check the integrity of filesystems before you mount them. The telinit utility brings the system to its normal multiuser state. With the system running in multiuser mode, you can still perform many administration tasks, such as adding users and printers.

The system administrator controls system operation, which includes many tasks: configuring the system; booting up; running init scripts; setting up servers; working in single-user, multiuser, and rescue modes; bringing the system down; and handling system crashes. Red Hat Linux provides many configuration tools, both graphical and textual. Many of these tools are named system-config-*.

The **xinetd** superserver starts server daemons as needed and can help secure a system by controlling who can use which services. You can also use TCP wrappers to control who can use which system services by editing the **hosts.allow** and **hosts.deny** files in the **/etc** directory. By limiting the portion of the filesystem a user sees, setting up a chroot jail can help control the damage a malicious user can do.

You can set up a DHCP server so you do not have to configure each system on a network manually. This task can entail setting up both static and dynamic IP addresses using DHCP. Whether a system uses NIS, DNS, local files, or a combination (and in what order) as a source of information is determined by **/etc/nsswitch.conf**. Linux-PAM enables you to maintain fine-grained control over who can access the system, how they can access it, and what they can do.

EXERCISES

1. How does single-user mode differ from multiuser mode?

2. How would you communicate each of the following messages?

   a. The system is coming down tomorrow at 6:00 in the evening for periodic maintenance.

   b. The system is coming down in 5 minutes.

   c. Jenny's jobs are slowing the system down drastically, and she should postpone them.

   d. Alex's wife just had a baby girl.

3. What do the letters of the su command stand for? (*Hint:* It is not Superuser.) What can you do with su besides give yourself Superuser privileges? How would you log in as Alex if you did not know his password but knew the **root** password? How would you establish the same environment that Alex has when he first logs in?

4. How would you allow a user to execute privileged commands without giving the user the Superuser password?

5. Assume you are working as Superuser. How do you kill process 1648? How do you kill all processes running kmail?

6. How can you disable SELinux?

7. Develop a strategy for coming up with a password that an intruder would not be likely to guess but that you will be able to remember.

ADVANCED EXERCISES

8. Give the command

```
$ /sbin/fuser -uv /
```

What is this a list of? Why is it so long? Give the same command as **root** (or ask the system administrator to do so and email you the results). How does this list differ from the first? Why is it different?

9. When it puts files in a **lost+found** directory, fsck has lost the directory information for the files and thus has lost the names of the files. Each file is given a new name, which is the same as the inode number for the file:

```
$ ls -lg lost+found
-rw-r--r-- 1 alex pubs   110 Jun 10 10:55 51262
```

What can you do to identify these files and restore them?

10. Take a look at **/usr/bin/lesspipe.sh**. Explain what it does and six ways it works.

11. Why are setuid shell scripts inherently unsafe?

12. When a user logs in, you would like the system to first check the local **/etc/passwd** file for a username and then check NIS. How do you implement this strategy?

13. Some older kernels contain a vulnerability that allows a local user to gain **root** privileges. Explain how this kind of vulnerability negates the value of a chroot jail.

12

FILES, DIRECTORIES, AND FILESYSTEMS

Filesystems hold directories of files. These structures store user data and system data that are the basis of users' work on the system and the system's existence. This chapter discusses important files and directories, various types of files and how to work with them, and the use and maintenance of filesystems.

IMPORTANT FILES AND DIRECTORIES

This section details the most common files used to administer the system. Also refer to "Important Standard Directories and Files" on page 176.

~/.bash_profile Contains an individual user's login shell initialization script. The shell executes the commands in this file in the same environment as the shell each time a user logs in. The file must be located in a user's home directory.

The default Red Hat **.bash_profile** file executes the commands in **~/.bashrc**. You can use **.bash_profile** to specify a terminal type (for vi, terminal emulators, and other programs), run stty to establish the terminal characteristics, set up aliases, and perform other housekeeping functions when a user logs in.

A simple **.bash_profile** file specifying a vt100 terminal and CONTROL-H as the erase key follows:

```
$ cat .bash_profile
export TERM=vt100
stty erase '^h'
```

For more information refer to "Startup Files" on page 267.

~/.bashrc Contains an individual user's interactive, nonlogin shell initialization script. The shell executes the commands in this file in the same environment as the (new) shell each time a user creates a new interactive shell. The **.bashrc** script differs from **.bash_profile** in that it is executed each time a new shell is spawned, not just when a user logs in. The default Red Hat **.bash_profile** file executes the commands in **~/.bashrc** so that these commands are executed when a user logs in. For more information refer to "Startup Files" on page 267.

/dev/null Also called a *bit bucket,* output sent to this file disappears. The **/dev/null** file is a device file and must be created with mknod. Input that you redirect to come from this file appears as nulls, creating an empty file. You can create an empty file named **nothing** by giving the following command:

```
$ cat /dev/null > nothing
```

or

```
$ cp /dev/null nothing
```

or, without explicitly using **/dev/null**,

```
$ > nothing
```

This last command redirects the output of a null command to the file with the same result as the previous commands. You can use any of these commands to truncate an existing file to zero length without changing its permissions. You can also use **/dev/null** to get rid of output that you do not want:

```
$ grep portable * 2>/dev/null
```

This command looks for the string **portable** in all files in the working directory. Any output to standard error (page 270), such as permission or directory errors, is discarded, while output to standard output appears on the screen.

/dev/pts The **/dev/pts** pseudofilesystem is a hook into the Linux kernel; it is part of the pseudoterminal support. Pseudoterminals are used by remote login programs, such as ssh and telnet, and xterm as well as by other graphical terminal emulators. The following sequence of commands demonstrates that the user is logged in on **/dev/pts/1**. After using **who am i** to verify the line the user is logged in on and using ls to show that this line exists, the user redirects the output of an echo command to **/dev/pts/1**, whereupon the output appears on the user's screen:

```
$ who am i
alex       pts/1     2006-02-16 12:30 (bravo.example.com)
$ ls /dev/pts
0  1  2  3  4
$ echo Hi there > /dev/pts/1
Hi there
```

/dev/random and **/dev/urandom** These files are interfaces to the kernel's random number generator. You can use either one with dd to create a file filled with pseudorandom bytes.

```
$ dd if=/dev/urandom of=randfile2 bs=1 count=100
100+0 records in
100+0 records out
100 bytes (100 B) copied, 0.001241 seconds, 80.6 kB/s
```

The preceding command reads from **/dev/urandom** and writes to the file named **randfile**. The block size is 1 and the count is 100 so **randfile** is 100 bytes long. For bytes that are more random, you can read from **/dev/random**. See the **urandom** and **random** man pages for more information.

optional

Wiping a file   You can use a similar technique to wipe data from a file before deleting it, making it almost impossible to recover data from the deleted file. You might want to wipe a file for security reasons.

In the following example, ls shows the size of the file named **secret**. With a block size of 1 and a count corresponding to the number of bytes in **secret**, dd wipes the file. The **conv=notrunc** argument ensures that dd writes over the data in the file and not another place on the disk.

```
$ ls -l secret
-rw-rw-r-- 1 sam sam 3496 Jan 25 21:48 secret
$ dd if=/dev/urandom of=secret bs=1 count=3496 conv=notrunc
3496+0 records in
3496+0 records out
3496 bytes (3.5 kB) copied, 0.029557 seconds, 118 kB/s
$ rm secret
```

For added security, run sync to flush the disk buffers after running dd, and repeat the two commands several times before deleting the file.

/dev/zero   Input you take from this file contains an infinite string of zeros (numerical zeros, not ASCII zeros). You can fill a file (such as a swap file, page 458) or overwrite a file with zeros with a command such as the following:

```
$ dd if=/dev/zero of=zeros bs=1024 count=10
10+0 records in
10+0 records out
10240 bytes (10 kB) copied, 0.000195 seconds, 52.5 MB/s

$ od -c zeros
0000000  \0  \0  \0  \0  \0  \0  \0  \0  \0  \0  \0  \0  \0  \0  \0  \0
*
0024000
```

The od utility shows the contents of the new file.

When you try to do with **/dev/zero** what you can do with **/dev/null,** you fill the partition you are working in:

```
$ cp /dev/zero bigzero
cp: writing 'bigzero': No space left on device
$ rm bigzero
```

/etc/aliases   Used by the mail delivery system (typically **sendmail**) to hold **aliases** for users. Edit this file to suit local needs. For more information refer to "/etc/aliases" on page 633.

/etc/at.allow, /etc/at.deny, /etc/cron.allow, and /etc/cron.deny   By default, users can use the at and crontab utilities. The **at.allow** file lists the users who are allowed to use at. The **cron.allow** file works in the same manner for crontab. The **at.deny** and **cron.deny** files specify users who are not permitted to use the corresponding utilities. As Red Hat Linux is configured, an empty **at.deny** file and the absence of an **at.allow** file allows anyone to use at; the absence of **cron.allow** and **cron.deny** files allows anyone to use crontab. To prevent anyone except Superuser from using at, remove the **at.allow** and **at.deny** files. To prevent anyone except Superuser from using crontab, create a **cron.allow** file with the single entry **root.** For more info on crontab, refer to "Scheduling Tasks" on page 547.

/etc/dumpdates   Contains information about the last execution of dump. For each filesystem, it stores the time of the last dump at a given dump level. The dump utility uses this information to determine which files to back up when executing at a particular dump level. Refer to "Backing Up Files" on page 540 and the dump man page for more information. Following is a sample **/etc/dumpdates** file from a system with four filesystems and a backup schedule that uses three dump levels:

```
/dev/hda1        5 Thu Apr 20 03:53:55 2006
/dev/hda8        2 Sun Apr 16 08:25:24 2006
/dev/hda9        2 Sun Apr 16 08:57:32 2006
/dev/hda10       2 Sun Apr 16 08:58:06 2006
/dev/hda1        2 Sun Apr 16 09:02:27 2006
/dev/hda1        0 Sun Mar 19 22:08:35 2006
/dev/hda8        0 Sun Mar 19 22:33:40 2006
/dev/hda9        0 Sun Mar 19 22:35:22 2006
/dev/hda10       0 Sun Mar 19 22:43:45 2006
```

The first column contains the device name of the dumped filesystem. The second column contains the dump level and the date of the dump.

/etc/fstab   **filesystem (mount) table**   Contains a list of all mountable devices as specified by the system administrator. Programs do not write to this file but only read from it. Refer to "fstab: Keeps Track of Filesystems" on page 469.

/etc/group   Groups allow users to share files or programs without giving all system users access to those files or programs. This scheme is useful when several users are working with files that are not public. The **/etc/group** file associates one or more user names with each group (number). Refer to "ACLs: Access Control Lists" on page 185 for another way to control file access.

An entry in the **/etc/group** file has four fields arranged in the following format:

group-name:password:group-ID:login-name-list

The *group-name* is the name of the group. The *password* is an optional encrypted password. This field frequently contains an **x**, indicating that group passwords are not used. The **group-ID** is a number, with 1–499 reserved for system accounts. The *login-name-list* is a comma-separated list of users who belong to the group. If an entry is too long to fit on one line, end the line with a backslash (\), which quotes the following RETURN, and continue the entry on the next line. A sample entry from a **group** file follows. The group is named **pubs**, has no password, and has a group ID of 503:

```
pubs:x:503:alex,jenny,scott,hls,barbara
```

You can use the groups utility to display the groups that a user belongs to:

```
$ groups alex
alex : alex pubs
```

Each user has a primary group, which is the group that user is assigned in the **/etc/passwd** file. By default, Red Hat Linux has user private groups: Each user's primary group has the same name as the user. In addition, a user can belong to other groups, depending on which *login-name-list*s the user appears on in the **/etc/group** file. In effect, you simultaneously belong both to your primary group and to any groups you are assigned to in **/etc/group**. When you attempt to access a file you do not own, the operating system checks whether you are a member of the group that has access to the file. If you are, you are subject to the group access permissions for the file. If you are not a member of the group that has access to the file and you do not own the file, you are subject to the public access permissions for the file.

When you create a new file, it is assigned to the group associated with the directory the file is being written into, assuming that you belong to that group. If you do not belong to the group that has access to the directory, the file is assigned to your primary group.

Refer to page 539 for information on using system-config-users to work with groups.

/etc/hosts   The **/etc/hosts** file stores the name, IP address, and optional aliases of the other systems that the local system knows about. At the very least, this file must have the hostname and IP address that you have chosen for the local system and a special entry for **localhost**. This entry supports the *loopback service*, which allows the local system to talk to itself (for example, for RPC services). The IP address of the loopback service is always 127.0.0.1. Following is a simple **/etc/hosts** file for the system named **rose** with an IP address of 192.168.0.10:

```
$ cat /etc/hosts
# Do not remove the following line, or various programs
# that require network functionality will fail.
127.0.0.1        rose localhost.localdomain localhost
192.168.0.1      bravo.example.com        bravo
192.168.0.4      mp3server
192.168.0.5      workstation
192.168.0.10     rose
...
```

If you are not using NIS or DNS to look up hostnames (called *hostname resolution*), you must include in **/etc/hosts** all systems that you want the local system to be able to contact. The **hosts** entry in the **/etc/nsswitch.conf** file (page 435) controls the order in which hostname resolution services are checked.

/etc/inittab   **initialization table**   Controls how the init process behaves. Each line in **inittab** contains four colon-separated fields:

> *id:runlevel:action:process*

The *id* uniquely identifies an entry in the **inittab** file. The *runlevel* is the system runlevel(s) at which *process* is executed. The *runlevel* consists of zero or more characters chosen from **0123456S**. If more than one runlevel is listed, the associated *process* is executed at each of the specified runlevels. When you do not specify a runlevel, init executes *process* at all runlevels. When the system changes runlevels, the *processes* specified by all entries in **inittab** that do not include the new runlevel are sent the SIGTERM signal to allow them to terminate gracefully. After 5 seconds, these *processes* are killed with SIGKILL if they are still running. The *process* is any bash command line.

The *action* is one of the following keywords: **respawn, wait, once, boot, bootwait, ondemand, powerfail, powerwait, powerokwait, powerfailnow, ctrlaltdel, kbrequest, off, ondemand, initdefault,** or **sysinit.** This keyword controls how the *process* is treated when it is executed. The most commonly used keywords are **wait** and **respawn.**

The **wait** keyword instructs init to start the *process* and wait for it to terminate. All subsequent scans of **inittab** ignore this **wait** entry. Because a **wait** entry is started only once (on entering *runlevel*) and is not executed again while the system remains at *runlevel*, it is often used to redirect init output to the console.

The **respawn** entry tells init to start the *process* if it does not exist but not to wait for it to terminate. If the *process* does exist, init moves on to the next entry in **inittab.**

The init utility continues to rescan **inittab**, looking for processes that have died. When a *process* dies, a **respawn** entry causes init to restart it.

The **initdefault** entry tells init which runlevel to bring the system to when it boots (see Table 11-1 on page 404). Without this information, init prompts for a runlevel on the system console. The value of the **initdefault** entry is set when you configure the system or when you edit **inittab** directly. By default, Red Hat Linux sets **initdefault** to 5, which causes the system to come up in graphical multiuser mode.

Use caution when you edit inittab

caution   Be careful when you edit **inittab** manually. Always make a backup copy in the same directory before you edit this file. If you make a mistake, you may not be able to boot the system. If you cannot boot the system, refer to "Rescue Mode" on page 397.

Each virtual console (page 113) has in **inittab** a **mingetty** entry that includes a unique terminal identifier (such as **tty1**, which is short for **/dev/tty1**). You can add or remove **mingetty** lines to add or remove virtual consoles. Remember to leave a virtual console for each X window that you want to run. Following is the **mingetty** entry for **/dev/tty2**:

```
2:2345:respawn:/sbin/mingetty tty2
```

The *id* on a **mingetty** line corresponds to the **tty** number.

All of the *actions* are documented in the **inittab** man page. For more information refer to "Booting the System" on page 403.

/etc/motd   Contains the message of the day, which can be displayed each time someone logs in using a textual login. This file typically contains site policy and legal information. Keep this file short because users tend to see the message many times.

/etc/mtab   When you call mount without any arguments, it consults this file and displays a list of mounted devices. Each time you (or an init script) call mount or umount, these utilities make the necessary changes to **mtab**. Although this is an ASCII text file, you should not edit it. See also **/etc/fstab**.

Fixing mtab

tip   The operating system maintains its own internal mount table in **/proc/mounts**. You can use cat to display the contents of **/proc/mounts** so that you can review the internal mount table. Sometimes the list of files in **/etc/mtab** may not be synchronized with the partitions in this table. To bring the **mtab** file in line with the operating system's mount table, you can either reboot the system or replace **/etc/mtab** with a symbolic link to **/proc/mounts** (some information may be lost).

```
# rm /etc/mtab
# ln -s /proc/mounts /etc/mtab
```

/etc/netgroup   Defines netgroups, which are used for checking permissions when performing remote logins and remote mounts and when starting remote shells.

/etc/nsswitch.conf
Specifies whether a system uses as the source of certain information NIS, DNS, local files, or a combination, and in what order it consults these services (page 435).

/etc/pam.d Files in this directory specify the authentication methods used by PAM (page 438) applications.

Be cautious when changing PAM files

caution Unless you understand how to configure PAM, avoid changing the files in **/etc/pam.d**. Mistakes in the configuration of PAM can make the system unusable.

/etc/passwd Describes users to the system. Do not edit this file directly; instead, use one of the utilities discussed in "Configuring User and Group Accounts" on page 538. Each line in **passwd** has seven colon-separated fields that describe one user:

login-name:dummy-password:user-ID:group-ID:info:directory:program

The *login-name* is the user's username—the name you enter in response to the **login:** prompt or GUI login screen. The value of the *dummy-password* is the character **x**. An encrypted/hashed password is stored in **/etc/shadow** (page 456). For security reasons, every account should have a password. By convention, disabled accounts have an asterisk (❋) in this field.

The *user-ID* is a number, with 0 indicating Superuser and 1–499 being reserved for system accounts. The *group-ID* identifies the user as a member of a group. It is a number, with 0–499 being reserved for system accounts; see **/etc/group**. You can change these values and set maximum values in **/etc/login.defs**.

The *info* is information that various programs, such as accounting programs and email, use to identify the user further. Normally it contains at least the first and last names of the user. It is referred to as the *GECOS* (page 1033) field.

The *directory* is the absolute pathname of the user's home directory. The *program* is the program that runs once the user logs in. If *program* is not present, a value of **/bin/bash** is assumed. You can put **/bin/tcsh** here to log in using the TC Shell or **/bin/zsh** to log in using the Z Shell, assuming the shell you specify is installed. The chsh utility (page 418) changes this value.

The *program* is usually a shell, but it can be any program. The following line in the **passwd** file creates a "user" whose only purpose is to execute the who utility:

```
who:x:1000:1000:execute who:/usr:/usr/bin/who
```

Using **who** as a username causes the system to log you in, execute the who utility, and log you out. The output of who flashes by in a hurry because the new login prompt clears the screen immediately after who finishes running. This entry in the **passwd** file does not provide a shell, so you cannot stay logged in after who finishes executing.

This technique is useful for providing special accounts that may do only one thing. For instance, sites may create an FTP (page 601) account to enable anonymous FTP access to their systems. Because no one logs in on this account, the shell is set to **/bin/false** (which returns a false exit status) or to **/sbin/nologin** (which does not permit the user to log in). When you put a message in **/etc/nologin.txt**, nologin displays that message (except it has the same problem as the output of who: It is removed so quickly that you cannot see it).

Do not replace a login shell with a shell script

security Do not use shell scripts as replacements for shells in **/etc/passwd**. A user may be able to interrupt a shell script, giving him or her full shell access when you did not intend to do so. When installing a dummy shell, use a compiled program, not a shell script.

/etc/printcap The printer capability database. This file describes system printers and is derived from 4.3BSD UNIX.

/etc/profile Contains a systemwide interactive shell initialization script for environment and start-up programs. When you log in, the shell immediately executes the commands in this file in the same environment as the shell. (For more information on executing a shell script in this manner, refer to the discussion of the . [dot] command on page 269.) This file allows the system administrator to establish systemwide environment parameters that individual users can override. For example, you can set shell variables, execute utilities, set up aliases, and take care of other housekeeping tasks. See also ~/.bash_profile on page 448.

Following is an example of a **/etc/profile** file that displays the message of the day (the **/etc/motd** file), sets the file-creation mask (umask, page 420), and sets the interrupt character to CONTROL-C:

```
# cat /etc/profile
cat /etc/motd
umask 022
stty intr '^c'
```

See the **/etc/profile** file on the local system for a more complex example.

/etc/protocols Provides protocol numbers, aliases, and brief definitions for DARPA Internet TCP/IP protocols. Do not modify this file.

/etc/rc.d Holds the system init scripts, also called run command (rc) scripts. The init program executes several init scripts each time the system changes state or runlevel. For more information refer to "Init Scripts: Start and Stop System Services" on page 404.

/etc/resolv.conf The resolver (page 722) configuration file, used to provide access to DNS.

The following example shows the **resolv.conf** file for the **example.com** domain. A **resolv.conf** file usually has at least two lines—a domain line and a nameserver line:

```
# cat /etc/resolv.conf
domain example.com
nameserver 10.0.0.50
nameserver 10.0.0.51
```

The first line (optional) specifies the domain name. A **resolv.conf** file may use **search** in place of **domain:** In the simple case, the two perform the same function. In either case, this domain name is appended to all hostnames that are not fully qualified. See *FQDN* on page 1032.

The **domain** keyword takes a single domain name as an argument: This name is appended to all DNS queries, shortening the time needed to query local hosts. When you put **domain example.com** in **resolv.conf**, any reference to a host within the **example.com** domain or a subdomain (such as **marketing.example.com**) can use the abbreviated form of the host. For example, instead of issuing the command **ping speedy.marketing.example.com**, you can use **ping speedy.marketing**.

This **search** keyword is similar to **domain** but can contain up to six domain names. The domains are searched in order in the process of resolving a hostname. The following line in **resolv.conf** causes the **marketing** subdomain to be searched first, followed by **sales**, and finally the entire **example.com** domain:

```
search marketing.example.com sales.example.com example.com
```

It is a good idea to put the most frequently used domain names first to try to outguess possible conflicts. If both **speedy.marketing.example.com** and **speedy.example.com** exist, the order of the search determines which one is selected when you invoke DNS. Do not overuse this feature. The longer the search path, the more network DNS requests generated, and the slower the response. Three or four names are typically sufficient.

The **nameserver** line(s) indicate which systems the local system should query to resolve hostnames to IP addresses, and vice versa. These machines are consulted in the order they appear with a 10-second timeout between queries. The preceding file causes this machine to query 10.0.0.50, followed by 10.0.0.51 when the first machine does not answer within 10 seconds. The **resolv.conf** file may be automatically updated when a PPP- (Point-to-Point Protocol) or DHCP- (Dynamic Host Configuration Protocol) controlled interface is activated. Refer to the **resolv.conf** and **resolver** man pages for more information.

/etc/rpc   Maps RPC services to RPC numbers. The three columns in this file show the name of the server for the RPC program, the RPC program number, and any aliases.

/etc/services   Lists system services. The three columns in this file show the informal name of the service, the port number/protocol the service frequently uses, and any aliases for the service. This file does not specify which services are running on the local system, nor does it map services to port numbers. The **services** file is used internally to map port numbers to services for display purposes.

/etc/shadow   Contains encrypted or *MD5* (page 1042) hashed user passwords. Each entry occupies one line composed of nine fields, separated by colons:

login-name:password:last-mod:min:max:warn:inactive:expire:flag

The *login-name* is the user's username—the name that the user enters in response to the **login:** prompt or GUI login screen. The *password* is an encrypted or hashed password that passwd puts into this file. When setting up new user accounts manually, run passwd as Superuser to assign a password to a new user.

The *last-mod* field indicates when the password was last modified. The *min* is the minimum number of days that must elapse before the password can be changed; the *max* is the maximum number of days before the password must be changed. The *warn* specifies how much advance warning (in days) to give the user before the password expires. The account will be closed if the number of days between login sessions exceeds the number of days specified in the *inactive* field. The account will also be closed as of the date in the *expire* field. The last field in an entry, *flag*, is reserved for future use. You can use the Password Info tab in system-config-users ("Modifying a user" on page 538) to modify these fields.

The **shadow** password file should be owned by **root** and should not be publicly readable or writable. Setting ownership and permissions this way makes it more difficult for someone to break into the system by identifying accounts without passwords or by using specialized programs that try to match hashed passwords.

A number of conventions exist for creating special **shadow** entries. An entry of ∗**LK**∗ or **NP** in the *password* field indicates *locked* or *no password*, respectively. *No password* is different from an empty password, implying that this is an administrative account that no one ever logs in on directly. Occasionally programs will run with the privileges of this account for system maintenance functions. These accounts are set up under the principle of least privilege (page 392).

Entries in the **shadow** file must appear in the same order as in the **passwd** file. There must be exactly one **shadow** entry for each **passwd** entry.

/etc/sysconfig A directory containing a hierarchy of system configuration files. For more information refer to the **/usr/share/doc/initscripts∗/sysconfig.txt** file.

/proc The **/proc** pseudofilesystem provides a window into the Linux kernel. Through **/proc** you can obtain information on any process running on your computer, including its current state, memory usage, CPU usage, terminal, parent, and group. You can extract information directly from the files in **/proc**. An example follows:

```
$ sleep 1000 &
[1] 4567
$ cd /proc/4567
$ ls -l
total 0
dr-xr-xr-x 2 sam sam 0 Jan 25 21:57 attr
-r-------- 1 sam sam 0 Jan 25 21:57 auxv
-r--r--r-- 1 sam sam 0 Jan 25 21:57 cmdline
lrwxrwxrwx 1 sam sam 0 Jan 25 21:57 cwd -> /home/sam
-r-------- 1 sam sam 0 Jan 25 21:57 environ
lrwxrwxrwx 1 sam sam 0 Jan 25 21:57 exe -> /bin/sleep
dr-x------ 2 sam sam 0 Jan 25 21:57 fd
...
-r--r--r-- 1 sam sam 0 Jan 25 21:57 status
dr-xr-xr-x 3 sam sam 0 Jan 25 21:57 task
-r--r--r-- 1 sam sam 0 Jan 25 21:57 wchan
```

```
$ cat status
Name:    sleep
State:   S (sleeping)
SleepAVG:        78%
Tgid:    4567
Pid:     4567
PPid:    4548
TracerPid:       0
Uid:     500     500     500     500
Gid:     500     500     500     500
FDSize: 256
Groups: 500
VmPeak:      3584 kB
VmSize:      3584 kB
...
```

In this example, bash creates a background process (PID 4567) for sleep. Next the user changes directories to the directory in **/proc** that has the same name as the PID of the subject background process (**cd /proc/4567**). This directory holds information about the process for which it is named. In this case, it holds information about the sleep process. The **ls –l** command shows that some entries in this directory are links (**cwd** is a link to the directory the process was started from, and **exe** is a link to the executable file that this process is running) and some appear to be ordinary files. All appear to be empty. When you cat one of these pseudofiles (**status** in the example), you get the output shown. Obviously this is not an ordinary file.

/sbin/shutdown   A utility that brings the system down (see page 412).

swap   Even though **swap** is not a file, swap space can be added and deleted from the system dynamically. Swap space is used by the virtual memory subsystem. When it runs low on real memory (RAM), the system writes memory pages from RAM to the swap space on the disk. Which pages are written and when they are written are controlled by finely tuned algorithms in the Linux kernel. When needed by running programs, these pages are brought back into RAM—a technique is called *paging* (page 1047). When a system is running very short on memory, an entire process may be paged out to disk.

Running an application that requires a large amount of virtual memory may result in the need for additional swap space. If you run out of swap space, you can use mkswap to create a new swap file and swapon to enable it. Normally you use a disk partition as swap space, but you can also use a file. A disk partition provides much better performance than a file.

If you are using a file as swap space, first use df to ensure that the partition has adequate space for the file. In the following sequence of commands, the administrator first uses dd and **/dev/zero** (page 450) to create an empty file (do not use cp as you may create a file with holes, which may not work) in the working directory. Next mkswap takes as an argument the name of the file created in the first step to set up the swap space. For security reasons, change the file so that it cannot be read from or written to by anyone but **root**. Use swapon with the same argument to turn the swap file on; then use **swapon –s** to confirm that the swap space is available. The final two commands turn off the swap file and remove it:

```
# dd if=/dev/zero of=swapfile bs=1024 count=65536
65536+0 records in
65536+0 records out
67108864 bytes (67 MB) copied, 0.684039 seconds, 98.1 MB/s
# mkswap swapfile
Setting up swapspace version 1, size = 67104 kB
# chmod 600 swapfile
# swapon swapfile
# swapon -s
Filename                                Type        Size      Used
Priority
/dev/hda5                               partition   1020088 0      -1
/root/swapfile                          file        65528   0      -2
# swapoff swapfile
# rm swapfile
rm: remove regular file 'swapfile'? y
```

/sys   The **/sys** pseudofilesystem was added in the Linux 2.6 kernel to make it easy for programs running in kernelspace, such as device drivers, to exchange information with programs running in userspace. Refer to udev on page 461.

/usr/share/magic   Most files begin with a unique identifier called a *magic number*. This file is a text database listing all known magic numbers on the system. When you use the file utility, it consults **/usr/share/magic** to determine the type of a file. Occasionally you may acquire a new tool that creates a new type of file that is unrecognized by the file utility. In this situation you need to update the **/usr/share/magic** file; refer to the **magic** man page for details. See also "magic number" on page 1042.

/var/log   Holds system log files.

/var/log/messages

Contains messages from daemons, the Linux kernel, and security programs. For example, you will find **filesystem full** warning messages, error messages from system daemons (NFS, syslog, printer daemons), SCSI and IDE disk error messages, and more in **messages**. Check **/var/log/messages** periodically to keep informed about important system events. Much of the information displayed on the system console is also sent to **messages**. If the system experiences a problem and you cannot access the console, check this file for messages about the problem.

/var/log/secure   Holds messages from security-related programs such as su and the **sshd** daemon.

FILE TYPES

Linux supports many types of files. The following sections discuss these types of files:

- Ordinary files, directories, links, and inodes (discussed next)
- Symbolic links (page 460)
- Special files (page 460)
- FIFO special file (named pipe) (page 462)
- Sockets (page 462)

- Block and character devices (page 463)
- Raw devices (page 464)

ORDINARY FILES, DIRECTORIES, LINKS, AND INODES

Ordinary and directory files An *ordinary* file stores user data, such as textual information, programs, or images, such as a **jpeg** or **tiff** file. A *directory* is a standard-format disk file that stores information, including names, about ordinary files and other directory files.

Inodes An *inode* is a *data structure* (page 1028), stored on disk, that defines a file's existence and is identified by an inode number. An inode contains critical information, such as the name of the owner of the file, where it is physically located on the disk, and how many hard links point to it. In addition, SELinux (page 400) stores extended information about files in inodes. A directory relates each of the filenames it stores to an inode.

When you move (mv) a file within a filesystem, you change the filename portion of the directory entry associated with the inode that describes the file. You do not create a new inode. If you move a file to another filesystem, mv first creates a new inode on the destination filesystem and then deletes the original inode. You can also use mv to move a directory recursively, in which case all files in the directory are copied and deleted.

When you make an additional hard link (ln, page 192) to a file, you create another reference (an additional filename) to the inode that describes the file. You do not create a new inode.

When you remove (rm) a file, you delete the directory entry that describes the file. When you remove the last hard link to a file, the operating system puts all blocks the inode pointed to back in the *free list* (the list of blocks that are available for use on the disk) and frees the inode to be used again.

The . and .. directory entries Every directory contains at least two entries (. and ..). The . entry is a link to the directory itself. The .. entry is a link to the parent directory. In the case of the root directory, there is no parent and the .. entry is a link to the root directory itself. It is not possible to create hard links to directories.

Symbolic links Because each filesystem has a separate set of inodes, you can create hard links to a file only from within the filesystem that holds that file. To get around this limitation, Linux provides symbolic links, which are files that point to other files. Files that are linked by a symbolic link do not share an inode. As a consequence, you can create a symbolic link to a file from any filesystem. You can also create a symbolic link to a directory, device, or other special file. For more information refer to "Symbolic Links" on page 194.

SPECIAL FILES

Special files represent Linux kernel routines that provide access to an operating system feature. FIFO (first in, first out) special files allow unrelated programs to exchange information. Sockets allow unrelated processes on the same or different computers to exchange information. One type of socket, the UNIX domain socket, is a special file. Symbolic links are another type of special file.

Device files   Device files, which include both block and character special files, represent device drivers that let you communicate with peripheral devices, such as terminals, printers, and hard disks. By convention, device files appear in the **/dev** directory and its subdirectories. Each device file represents a device: You read from and write to the file to read from and write to the device it represents. For example, using cat to send an audio file to **/dev/dsp** plays the file. The following example shows part of the output that an ls –l command produces for the **/dev** directory:

```
$ ls -l /dev
total 0
crw-rw----  1 root  root    14,  12 Jan 25 08:33 adsp
crw-------  1 root  root    10, 175 Jan 25 08:33 agpgart
crw-------  1 zach  root    14,   4 Jan 25 08:33 audio
drwxr-xr-x  3 root  root         60 Jan 25 08:33 bus
lrwxrwxrwx  1 root  root          3 Jan 25 08:33 cdrom -> hdb
lrwxrwxrwx  1 root  root          3 Jan 25 08:33 cdwriter -> hdb
crw-------  1 zach  root     5,   1 Jan 25 08:33 console
lrwxrwxrwx  1 root  root         11 Jan 25 08:33 core -> /proc/kcore
drwxr-xr-x  6 root  root        120 Jan 25 08:33 disk
crw-------  1 zach  root    14,   3 Jan 25 08:33 dsp
lrwxrwxrwx  1 root  root         13 Jan 25 08:33 fd -> /proc/self/fd
brw-rw----  1 zach  floppy   2,   0 Jan 25 08:33 fd0
brw-rw----  1 zach  floppy   2,  84 Jan 25 08:33 fd0u1040
brw-rw----  1 zach  floppy   2,  88 Jan 25 08:33 fd0u1120
...
lrwxrwxrwx  1 root  root          3 Jan 25 08:33 floppy -> fd0
crw-rw-rw-  1 root  root     1,   7 Jan 25 08:33 full
brw-r-----  1 root  disk     3,   0 Jan 25 00:33 hda
brw-r-----  1 root  disk     3,   1 Jan 25 08:33 hda1
brw-r-----  1 root  disk     3,   2 Jan 25 08:33 hda2
brw-r-----  1 root  disk     3,   3 Jan 25 00:33 hda3
...
```

The first character of each line is always **–**, **b**, **c**, **d**, **l**, or **p**, representing ordinary (plain), block, character, directory, symbolic link, or named pipe (see the following section), respectively. The next nine characters identify the permissions for the file, followed by the number of hard links and the names of the owner and group. Where the number of bytes in a file would appear for an ordinary or directory file, a device file shows *major* and *minor device numbers* (page 463) separated by a comma. The rest of the line is the same as any other ls –l listing (page 181).

udev   The udev utility manages device naming dynamically. It replaces the earlier **devfs** and moves the device naming functionality from the kernel to userspace. Because devices are added to and removed from a system infrequently, the performance penalty associated with this change is minimal. The benefit of the move is that a bug in udev cannot compromise or crash the kernel.

The udev utility is part of the hotplug system (discussed next). When a device is added to or removed from the system, the kernel creates a device name in the **/sys** pseudofilesystem and notifies hotplug of the event, which is received by udev. The udev utility then creates the device file, usually in the **/dev** directory, or removes the device file from the system. The udev utility can also rename network interfaces. See fedora.redhat.com/docs/udev and www.kernel.org/pub/linux/utils/kernel/hotplug/udev.html for more information.

Hotplug   The hotplug system allows you to plug a device into the system and use it immediately. Although hotplug was available in the Linux 2.4 kernel, the 2.6 kernel integrates hotplug with the unified device driver model framework (the *driver model core*) so that any bus can report an event when a device is added to or removed from the system. User software can be notified of the event so it can take appropriate action. See linux-hotplug.sourceforge.net for more information.

FIFO SPECIAL FILE (NAMED PIPE)

A *FIFO special* file, also called a *named pipe,* represents a pipe: You read from and write to the file to read from and write to the pipe. The term *FIFO* stands for *first in, first out*—the way any pipe works. In other words, the first information that you put in one end is the first information that comes out the other end. When you use a pipe on a command line to send the output of a program to the printer, the printer outputs the information in the same order that the program produced it and sent it to the pipe.

Unless you are writing sophisticated programs, you will not be working with FIFO special files. However, programs that you use on Linux use named pipes for interprocess communication. You can create a pipe using mkfifo:

```
$ mkfifo AA
$ ls -l AA
prw-rw-r--  1 zach zach 0 Apr 26 13:11 AA
```

The **p** at the left end of the output of **ls –l** indicates that the file is a pipe.

The UNIX and Linux systems have included pipes for many generations. Without named pipes, only processes that were children of the same ancestor could use pipes to exchange information. Using named pipes, *any* two processes on a single system can exchange information. When one program writes to a FIFO special file, another program can read from the same file. The programs do not have to run at the same time or be aware of each other's activity. The operating system handles all buffering and information storage. This type of communication is termed *asynchronous* (*async*) because programs on the ends of the pipe do not have to be synchronized.

SOCKETS

Like a FIFO special file, a socket allows asynchronous processes that are not children of the same ancestor to exchange information. Sockets are the central mechanism of the interprocess communication that forms the basis of the networking facility. When you use networking utilities, pairs of cooperating sockets manage the communication between the processes on the local computer and the remote computer. Sockets form the basis of such utilities as ssh and scp.

MAJOR AND MINOR DEVICE NUMBERS

A *major device number* points to a driver in the kernel that works with a class of hardware devices: terminal, printer, tape drive, hard disk, and so on. In the list of the **/dev** directory on page 461, all of the hard disk partitions have a major device number of 3.

A *minor device number* represents a particular piece of hardware within a class. Although all hard disk partitions are grouped together by their major device number, each has a different minor device number (**hda1** is 1, **hda2** is 2, and so on). This setup allows one piece of software (the device driver) to service all similar hardware yet to be able to distinguish among different physical units.

BLOCK AND CHARACTER DEVICES

This section describes typical device drivers. Because device drivers can be changed to suit a particular purpose, the descriptions in this section do not pertain to every system.

A *block device* is an I/O (input/output) device that is characterized by

- Being able to perform random access reads.
- Having a specific block size.
- Handling only single blocks of data at a time.
- Accepting only transactions that involve whole blocks of data.
- Being able to have a filesystem mounted on it.
- Having the Linux kernel buffer its input and output.
- Appearing to the operating system as a series of blocks numbered from 0 through $n - 1$, where n is the number of blocks on the device.

Block devices commonly found on a Linux system include hard disks, floppy diskettes, and CD-ROMs.

A *character device* is any device that is not a block device. Examples of character devices include printers, terminals, tape drives, and modems.

The device driver for a character device determines how a program reads from and writes to that device. For example, the device driver for a terminal allows a program to read the information you type on the terminal in two ways. First, a program can read single characters from a terminal in *raw* mode—that is, without the driver doing any interpretation of the characters. (This mode has nothing to do with the raw device described in the following section.) Alternatively, a program can read one line at a time. When a program reads one line at a time, the driver handles the erase and kill characters so the program never sees typing mistakes that have been corrected. In this case, the program reads everything from the beginning of a line to the RETURN that ends a line; the number of characters in a line can vary.

RAW DEVICES

Device driver programs for block devices usually have two entry points so they can be used in two ways: as block devices or as character devices. The character device form of a block device is called a *raw device*. A raw device is characterized by

- Direct I/O (no buffering through the Linux kernel).

- A one-to-one correspondence between system calls and hardware requests.

- Device-dependent restrictions on I/O.

An example of a utility that uses a raw device is fsck. It is more efficient for fsck to operate on the disk as a raw device, rather than being restricted by the fixed size of blocks in the block device interface. Because it has full knowledge of the underlying filesystem structure, fsck can operate on the raw device using the largest possible units. When a filesystem is mounted, processes normally access the disk through the block device interface, which explains why it is important to allow fsck to modify only an unmounted filesystem. On a mounted filesystem, there is the danger that, while fsck is rearranging the underlying structure through the raw device, another process could change a disk block using the block device, resulting in a corrupted filesystem.

FILESYSTEMS

Table 12-1 lists some of the types of filesystems available under Linux.

Table 12-1   Filesystems

Filesystem	Features
adfs	Advanced Disc Filing System. Used on Acorn computers. The word *Advanced* differentiated this filesystem from its predecessor, DFS, which did not support advanced features such as a hierarchical filesystem.
affs	Amiga Fast Filesystem (FFS).
autofs	Automounting filesystem (page 690).
coda	CODA distributed filesystem (developed at Carnegie Mellon).
devpts	A pseudofilesystem for pseudoterminals (page 449).
ext2	A standard filesystem for Red Hat systems, usually with the **ext3** extension.
ext3	A journaling (page 1039) extension to the **ext2** filesystem. It greatly improves recovery time from crashes (it takes a lot less time to run fsck), promoting increased availability. As with any filesystem, a journaling filesystem can lose data during a system crash or hardware failure.

Table 12-1   Filesystems (continued)

Filesystem	Features
GFS	Global Filesystem. GFS is a journaling, clustering filesystem. It enables a cluster of Linux servers to share a common storage pool.
hfs	Hierarchical Filesystem: used by older Macintosh systems. Newer Macintosh systems use **hfs+**.
hpfs	High-Performance Filesystem: the native filesystem for IBM's OS/2.
iso9660	The standard filesystem for CD-ROMs.
minix	Very similar to Linux, the filesystem of a small operating system that was written for educational purposes by Andrew S. Tanenbaum (www.minix3.org).
msdos	The filesystem used by DOS and subsequent Microsoft operating systems. Do not use **msdos** for mounting Windows filesystems; it does not read VFAT attributes.
ncpfs	Novell NetWare NCP Protocol Filesystem: used to mount remote filesystems under NetWare.
nfs	Network Filesystem. Developed by Sun Microsystems, this protocol allows a computer to access remote files over a network as if they were local (page 673).
ntfs	NT Filesystem: the native filesystem of Windows NT.
proc	An interface to several Linux kernel *data structures* (page 1028) that behaves like a filesystem (page 457).
qnx4	QNX 4 operating system filesystem.
reiserfs	A journaling (page 1039) filesystem, based on balanced-tree algorithms. See **ext3** for more on journaling filesystems.
romfs	A dumb, readonly filesystem used mainly for *RAM disks* (page 1051) during installation.
smbfs	Samba Filesystem (page 695).
software RAID	RAID implemented in software. Refer to "RAID Filesystem" on page 473.
sysv	System V UNIX filesystem.
ufs	Default filesystem under Sun's Solaris operating system and other UNIXs.
umsdos	A full-feature UNIX-like filesystem that runs on top of a DOS FAT filesystem.
vfat	Developed by Microsoft, a standard that allows long filenames on FAT partitions.
xfs	SGI's journaled filesystem (ported from Irix).

mount: MOUNTS A FILESYSTEM

The mount utility connects directory hierarchies—typically filesystems—to the Linux directory hierarchy. These directory hierarchies can be on remote and local disks, CDs, and floppy diskettes. Linux also allows you to mount *virtual filesystems* that have been built inside ordinary files, filesystems built for other operating systems, and the special **/proc** filesystem (page 457), which maps useful Linux kernel information to a pseudodirectory.

Mount point   The *mount point* for the filesystem/directory hierarchy that you are mounting is a directory in the local filesystem. This directory must exist before you can mount a filesystem; its contents disappear as long as a filesystem is mounted on it and reappear when you unmount the filesystem.

Without any arguments, mount lists the currently mounted filesystems, showing the physical device holding each filesystem, the mount point, the type of filesystem, and any options set when each filesystem was mounted:

```
$ mount
proc on /proc type proc (rw)
/dev/hdb1 on / type ext2 (rw)
/dev/hdb4 on /tmp type ext2 (rw)
/dev/hda5 on /usr type ext3 (rw)
/dev/sda1 on /usr/X386 type ext2 (rw)
/dev/sda3 on /usr/local type ext2 (rw)
/dev/hdb3 on /home type ext3 (rw)
/dev/hda1 on /dos type msdos (rw,umask=000)
tuna:/p04 on /p04 type nfs (rw,addr=192.168.0.8)
/dev/scd0 on /mnt/cdrom type iso9660 (ro,noexec,nosuid,nodev)
```

The mount utility gets this information from the **/etc/mtab** file (page 453). This section covers mounting local filesystems; refer to page 673 for information on using NFS to mount remote directory hierarchies.

The first entry in the preceding example shows the **/proc** pseudofilesystem (page 457). The next six entries identify disk partitions holding standard Linux **ext2** and **ext3** filesystems. These partitions are found on three disks: two IDE disks (**hda, hdb**) and one SCSI disk (**sda**). Disk partition **/dev/hda1** has a DOS (**msdos**) filesystem mounted at the directory **/dos** in the Linux filesystem. You can access the DOS files and directories on this partition as if they were Linux files and directories, using Linux utilities and applications. The line starting with **tuna** shows a mounted, remote NFS filesystem. The last line shows a CD mounted on a SCSI CD drive (**/dev/scd0**).

If the list of filesystems in **/etc/mtab** is not correct, see the tip on page 453.

When you add a line for a filesystem to the **/etc/fstab** file (page 451), you can mount that filesystem by giving the associated mount point (or the device) as the argument to mount. For example, the SCSI CD listed earlier was mounted using the following command:

```
$ mount /mnt/cdrom
```

Do not mount anything on root (/)

Always mount network directory hierarchies and removable devices at least one level below the root level of the filesystem. The root filesystem is mounted on /; you cannot mount two filesystems in the same place. If you were to try to mount something on /, all files, directories, and filesystems that were under the root directory would no longer be available, and the system would crash.

This command worked because **/etc/fstab** contains the additional information needed to mount the file:

```
/dev/scd0               /mnt/cdrom                iso9660 user,noauto,ro 0 0
```

You can also mount filesystems that do not appear in **/etc/fstab**. For example, when you insert a floppy diskette that holds a DOS filesystem into the floppy diskette drive, you can mount that filesystem using the following command:

```
# mount -t msdos /dev/fd0 /mnt/floppy
```

The **–t msdos** specifies a filesystem type of **msdos**. You can mount DOS filesystems only if you have configured the Linux kernel (page 525) to accept DOS filesystems. You do not need to mount a DOS filesystem to read from and write to it, such as when you use mcopy (page 139). However, you do need to mount a DOS filesystem to use Linux commands (other than Mtools commands) on files on the filesystem (which may be on a diskette).

MOUNT OPTIONS

The mount utility takes many options, which you can specify on the command line or in the **/etc/fstab** file (page 469). For a complete list of mount options for local filesystems, see the mount man page; for remote directory hierarchies, see the nfs man page.

The **noauto** option causes Linux not to mount the filesystem automatically. The **nosuid** option forces mounted setuid executables to run with regular permissions (no effective user ID change) on the local system (the system that mounted the filesystem).

Mount removable devices with the **nosuid** option

Always mount removable devices with the **nosuid** option so that a malicious user does not, for example, put a setuid copy of bash on a disk and have a **root** shell.

Unless you specify the **user, users,** or **owner** option, only Superuser can mount and unmount a filesystem. The **user** option means that any user can mount the filesystem, but the filesystem can be unmounted only by the same user who mounted it; **users** means that any user can mount and unmount the filesystem. These options are frequently specified for CD and floppy drives. The **owner** option, which is used only under special circumstances, is similar to the **user** option except that the user mounting the device must own the device.

MOUNTING A LINUX FLOPPY DISKETTE

Mounting a Linux floppy diskette is similar to mounting a partition of a hard disk. Put an entry similar to the following in **/etc/fstab** for a diskette in the first floppy drive:

```
/dev/fd0     /mnt/floppy     auto     noauto,users                0 0
```

Specifying a filesystem type of **auto** causes the system to probe the filesystem to determine its type and allows users to mount a variety of diskettes. Create the **/mnt/floppy** directory if necessary. Insert a diskette and try to mount it. The diskette must be formatted (use fdformat). In the following examples, the error message following the first command usually indicates there is no filesystem on the diskette. Use mkfs (page 419) to create a filesystem—but be careful, because mkfs destroys all data on the diskette:

```
# mount /dev/fd0
mount: you must specify the filesystem type

# mkfs /dev/fd0
mke2fs 1.38 (30-Jun-2005)
Filesystem label=
OS type: Linux
Block size=1024 (log=0)
Fragment size=1024 (log=0)
184 inodes, 1440 blocks
72 blocks (5.00%) reserved for the super user
First data block=1
Maximum filesystem blocks=1572864
1 block group
8192 blocks per group, 8192 fragments per group
184 inodes per group

Writing inode tables: done
Writing superblocks and filesystem accounting information: done

This filesystem will be automatically checked every 24 mounts or
180 days, whichever comes first.  Use tune2fs -c or -i to override.
```

Try the mount command again:

```
# mount /dev/fd0
# mount
...
/dev/fd0 on /mnt/floppy type ext2 (rw,noexec,nosuid,nodev)

# df -h /dev/fd0
Filesystem          Size  Used Avail Use% Mounted on
/dev/fd0            1.4M   19K  1.3M   2% /mnt/floppy
```

The mount command without any arguments and **df –h /dev/fd0** show the floppy is mounted and ready for use.

umount: UNMOUNTS A FILESYSTEM

The umount utility unmounts a filesystem as long as it does not contain any files or directories that are in use (open). For example, a logged-in user's working directory must not be on the filesystem you want to unmount. The next command unmounts the CD mounted earlier:

```
$ umount /mnt/cdrom
```

Unmount a floppy or a remote directory hierarchy the same way you would unmount a partition of a hard drive.

The umount utility consults /etc/fstab to get the necessary information and then unmounts the appropriate filesystem from its server. When a process has a file open on the filesystem that you are trying to unmount, umount displays a message similar to the following:

```
umount: /home: device is busy
```

When you cannot unmount a device because it is in use

tip   When a process has a file open on a device you need to unmount, use fuser to determine which process has the file open and to kill it. For example, when you want to unmount the floppy diskette, give the command fuser –ki /mnt/floppy (substitute the mount point for the diskette on the local system for /mnt/floppy). After checking with you, this command kills the process using the diskette.

Use the –a option to umount to unmount all filesystems, except for the one mounted at /, which can never be unmounted. You can combine –a with the –t option to unmount filesystems of a given type (ext3, nfs, or others). For example, the following command unmounts all mounted nfs directory hierarchies that are not being used:

```
# umount -at nfs
```

fstab: KEEPS TRACK OF FILESYSTEMS

The system administrator maintains the /etc/fstab file, which lists local and remote directory hierarchies, most of which the system mounts automatically when it boots. The fstab file has six columns; a hyphen keeps the place of a column that has no value:

1. **Name**   The name of the block device (page 463) or remote directory hierarchy. A remote directory hierarchy appears as *hostname:pathname*, where *hostname* is the name of the host that houses the filesystem, and *pathname* is the absolute pathname of the directory that is to be mounted. You can substitute the volume label of a local filesystem by using the form **LABEL=xx**, where *xx* is the volume label. Refer to e2label on page 418.

2. **Mount point**   The name of a directory file that the filesystem/directory hierarchy is to be mounted on. If it does not already exist, create this directory with mkdir.

3. **Type**   The type of filesystem/directory hierarchy that is to be mounted. Local filesystems are generally of type **ext2** or **ext3**, and remote directory hierarchies are of type **nfs**. Table 12-1 on page 464 provides a list of filesystem types.

4. **Mount options**   A comma-separated list of mount options, such as whether the filesystem is mounted for reading and writing (**rw**, the default) or readonly (**ro**). Refer to the mount and nfs man pages for lists of options.

5. **Dump**   Used by dump (page 545) to determine when to back up the filesystem.

6. **Fsck**   Specifies the order in which fsck checks filesystems. Root (**/**) should have a **1** in this column. Filesystems that are mounted to a directory just below the root directory should have a **2**. Filesystems that are mounted on another mounted filesystem (other than root) should have a **3**. For example, if **local** is a separate filesystem from **/usr** and **local** is mounted on **/usr** (as **/usr/local**), then **local** should have a **3**. Filesystems and directory hierarchies that do not need to be checked (for example, remotely mounted directory hierarchies or a CD) should have a **0**.

The following example shows a typical **fstab** file:

```
# cat /etc/fstab
LABEL=/1                    /               ext3     defaults          1 1
LABEL=/boot1                /boot           ext3     defaults          1 2
devpts                      /dev/pts        devpts   gid=5,mode=620    0 0
tmpfs                       /dev/shm        tmpfs    defaults          0 0
LABEL=/home1                /home           ext3     defaults          1 2
proc                        /proc           proc     defaults          0 0
sysfs                       /sys            sysfs    defaults          0 0
LABEL=SWAP-hda5             swap            swap     defaults          0 0
/dev/hda3                   /oldhome        ext3     defaults          0 0
tuna:/p04                   /p04            nfs      defaults          0 0
/dev/fd0                    /mnt/floppy     auto     noauto,users      0 0
```

fsck: CHECKS FILESYSTEM INTEGRITY

The fsck (filesystem check) utility verifies the integrity of filesystems and, if possible, repairs any problems it finds. Because many filesystem repairs can destroy data, particularly on a non*journaling filesystem* (page 1039), such as **ext2**, by default fsck asks you for confirmation before making each repair.

Do not run fsck on a mounted filesystem

caution   Do not run fsck on a mounted filesystem (except **/**). When you attempt to check a mounted filesystem, fsck warns you and asks you whether you want to continue. Reply **no**. You can run fsck with the **–N** option on a mounted filesystem as it will not write to the filesystem; as a result, no harm can come of running it.

The following command checks all unmounted filesystems that are marked to be checked in **/etc/fstab** (page 451) except for the root filesystem:

```
# fsck -AR
```

You can check a specific filesystem with a command similar to one of the following:

```
# fsck /home
```

or

```
# fsck /dev/hda6
```

Crash flag   The **/etc/rc.d/rc.sysinit** start-up script looks for two flags in the root directory of each partition to determine whether fsck needs to be run on that partition before it is mounted. The **.autofsck** flag (the *crash flag*) indicates that the partition should be checked. By default, the person bringing up the system has 5 seconds to respond to a prompt with a **y**; if no response is made, the check is skipped. When the other flag, **forcefsck**, is set, the user is given no choice; fsck is automatically run on the partition. These checks are in addition to those established by tune2fs (see next section). The **.autofsck** flag is present while the system is running and is removed when the system is properly shut down. When the system crashes, the flag is present when the system is brought up. The **forcefsck** flag is placed on the filesystem when the disk contains an error and must be checked.

tune2fs: CHANGES FILESYSTEM PARAMETERS

The tune2fs utility displays and modifies filesystem parameters on **ext2** filesystems and on **ext3** filesystems, as they are modified **ext2** filesystems. This utility can also set up journaling on an **ext2** filesystem, turning it into an **ext3** filesystem. With the introduction of increasingly more reliable hardware and software, systems are rebooted less frequently, so it is important to check filesystems regularly. By default, fsck is run on each partition while the system is brought up, before the partition is mounted. (The checks scheduled by tune2fs are separate and scheduled differently from the checks that are done following a system crash or hard disk error [see the previous section].) Depending on the flags, fsck may do nothing more than display a message saying that the filesystem is clean. The larger the partition, the more time it takes to check it, assuming a nonjournaling filesystem. These checks are often unnecessary. The tune2fs utility helps you to find a happy medium between checking filesystems each time you reboot the system and never checking them. It does so by scheduling when fsck checks a filesystem (these checks occur only when the system is booted).[1] You can use two scheduling patterns: time elapsed since the last check and number of mounts since the last check. The following command causes **/dev/hda6** to be checked when fsck runs after it has been mounted eight times or after 15 days have elapsed since its last check, whichever happens first:

```
# tune2fs -c 8 -i 15 /dev/hda3
tune2fs 1.38 (30-Jun-2005)
Setting maximal mount count to 8
Setting interval between checks to 1296000 seconds
```

---

1. For systems whose purpose in life is to run continuously, this kind of scheduling does not work. You must develop a schedule that is not based on system reboots but rather on a clock. Each filesystem must be unmounted periodically, checked with fsck (preceding section), and then remounted.

The next tune2fs command is similar but works on a different partition and sets the current mount count to 4. When you do not specify a current mount count, it is set to zero:

```
# tune2fs -c 8 -i 15 -C 4 /dev/hda3
tune2fs 1.38 (30-Jun-2005)
Setting maximal mount count to 8
Setting current mount count to 4
Setting interval between checks to 1296000 seconds
```

The –l option displays a list of information about the partition. You can combine this option with others. Below the **Maximum mount count** is –1, which means that fsck and the kernel ignore the mount count information. A maximum mount count of 0 works the same way:

```
# tune2fs -l /dev/hda3
tune2fs 1.38 (30-Jun-2005)
Filesystem volume name:     /home
Last mounted on:            <not available>
Filesystem UUID:            70929327-f5d2-486a-be44-6f7b677ab6b6
Filesystem magic number:    0xEF53
Filesystem revision #:      1 (dynamic)
Filesystem features:        has_journal ext_attr resize_inode dir_index
          filetype needs_recovery sparse_super large_file
Default mount options:      (none)
Filesystem state:           clean
Errors behavior:            Continue
Filesystem OS type:         Linux
Inode count:                2560864
Block count:                2560359
...
Last mount time:            Wed Jan 25 08:33:30 2006
Last write time:            Wed Jan 25 10:13:27 2006
Mount count:                4
Maximum mount count:        8
Last checked:               Tue Jun 28 03:03:55 2005
Check interval:             1296000 (2 weeks, 1 day)
...
```

Set the filesystem parameters on the local system so that they are appropriate to the way you use it. Using the –C option to stagger the checks ensures that all checks do not occur at the same time. Always check new and upgraded filesystems to make sure that they have checks scheduled as you desire.

To change an **ext2** filesystem to an **ext3** filesystem, you must put a *journal* (page 1039) on the filesystem, and the kernel must support **ext3** filesystems. Use the –j option to set up a journal on an unmounted filesystem:

```
# tune2fs -j /dev/hda7
tune2fs 1.38 (30-Jun-2005)
Creating journal inode: done
This filesystem will be automatically checked every 23 mounts or
180 days, whichever comes first.  Use tune2fs -c or -i to override.
```

Before you can use **fstab** (page 451) to mount the changed filesystem, you must modify its entry in the **fstab** file to reflect its new type. Change the third column to **ext3**.

The following command changes an unmounted **ext3** filesystem to an **ext2** filesystem:

```
# tune2fs -O ^has_journal /dev/hda7
tune2fs 1.38 (30-Jun-2005)
```

Refer to the tune2fs man page for more details.

RAID FILESYSTEM

RAID (Redundant Arrays of Inexpensive/Independent Disks) spreads information across several disks to combine several physical disks into one larger virtual device. RAID improves performance and creates redundancy. More than six types of RAID configurations exist. Using Red Hat tools, you can set up *software* RAID. *Hardware* RAID requires hardware that is designed to implement RAID and is not covered here.

Do not replace backups with RAID

caution Do not use RAID as a replacement for regular backups. If your system experiences a catastrophic failure, RAID will be useless. Earthquake, fire, theft, or another disaster may leave your entire system inaccessible (if your hard drives are destroyed or missing). RAID does not take care of something as simple as replacing a file when you delete it by accident. In these cases a backup on a removable medium (that has been removed) is the only way you will be able to restore a filesystem.

RAID can be an effective *addition* to a backup. Red Hat offers RAID software that you can install either when you install a Red Hat system or as an afterthought. The Linux kernel can automatically detect RAID disk partitions at boot time if the partition ID is set to 0xfd, which fdisk recognizes as Linux **raid autodetect**.

Software RAID, as implemented in the kernel, is much cheaper than hardware RAID. Not only does this software avoid specialized RAID disk controllers, but it also works with the less expensive IDE disks as well as SCSI disks. For more information refer to the *Software-RAID HOWTO*.

CHAPTER SUMMARY

Filesystems hold directories of files. These structures store user data and system data that are the basis of users' work on the system and the system's existence. Linux supports many types of files including ordinary files, directories, links, and special files. Special files provide access to operating system features. The kernel uses major and minor device numbers to identify classes of devices and specific devices within each class. Character and block devices represent I/O devices such as hard disks and printers. Inodes, which are identified by inode numbers, are stored on disk and define a file's existence.

When the system comes up, the **/etc/fstab** file controls which filesystems are mounted and how they are mounted (readonly, read write, and so on). After a system crash, filesystems are automatically verified and repaired if necessary by fsck. You can use tune2fs to force the system to run fsck on a filesystem periodically when the system boots.

EXERCISES

1. What is the function of the **/etc/hosts** file? Which services can you use in place of, or to supplement, the **hosts** file?

2. What does the **/etc/resolv.conf** file do? What does the **nameserver** line in this file do?

3. What is an inode? What happens to the inode when you move a file within a filesystem?

4. What does the **..** entry in a directory point to? What does this entry point to in the root (/) directory?

5. What is a device file? Where are device files located?

6. What is a FIFO? What does FIFO stand for? What is another name for a FIFO? How does a FIFO work?

ADVANCED EXERCISES

7. Write a line for the **/etc/fstab** file that would mount the **/dev/hdb1 ext3** filesystem on **/extra** with the following characteristics: The filesystem will not be mounted automatically when the system boots, and anyone can mount and unmount the filesystem.

8. Without using rm, how can you delete a file? (*Hint:* How do you rename a file?)

9. After burning an ISO image file named **image.iso** to a CD on **/dev/hdc**, how can you can verify the copy from the command line?

10. Why should **/var** reside on a separate partition from **/usr**?

11. Create a FIFO. Using the shell, demonstrate that two users can use this FIFO to communicate asynchronously.

12. How would you mount an ISO image so that you could copy files from it without burning it to a CD?

DOWNLOADING AND INSTALLING SOFTWARE

A software package is the collection of scripts, programs, files, and directories required to run a software application, including utilities and system software. Using packages makes it easier to transfer, install, and uninstall applications. A package contains either executable files or source code files. Executable files are precompiled for a specific processor and operating system, whereas source files need to be compiled but will run on a wide range of machines and operating systems.

Software for your system can come in different kinds of packages, such as rpm (page 487), the GNU Configure and Build System (page 491), tar, compressed tar, and others. The most popular package is rpm. Other packages (such as tar), which were popular before the introduction of rpm, are used less often today because they require more work on the part of the installer (you) and do not provide the depth of prerequisite and compatibility checking that rpm offers. Newer programs such as yum (discussed next) not only check for compatibility but also obtain over the Internet additional software required to install and run a given software package.

yum: KEEPS THE SYSTEM UP-TO-DATE (*FEDORA*)

Early releases of Red Hat Linux did not include a tool for managing updates. Although the rpm utility could install or upgrade individual software packages, it was up to the user to locate a package and any packages it was dependent on. When Terra Soft produced its Red Hat–based Linux distribution for the PowerPC, the company created the Yellow Dog Updater to fill this gap. This program has since been ported to other architectures and distributions. The result, named Yellow Dog Updater, Modified (yum, linux.duke.edu/projects/yum), is included with Fedora Core.

rpm packages   The yum utility works with rpm packages. When yum installs or upgrades a software package, it also installs or upgrades packages that the package is dependent on. Refer to page 487 for more information on rpm.

Repositories   The yum utility downloads package headers and packages from servers called repositories. Although Fedora provides repositories, yum is set up to use copies of these repositories that are kept on mirror sites. The next section covers repository selection.

CONFIGURING yum

You do not need to configure yum: As it is installed, it is ready to use. This section describes the yum configuration files for users who want to modify them. The primary configuration file, **/etc/yum.conf**, holds global settings. As distributed with Fedora, secondary files in the **/etc/yum.repos.d** directory define repositories. The first example shows the Fedora **yum.conf** file:

```
$ cat /etc/yum.conf
[main]
cachedir=/var/cache/yum
keepcache=0
debuglevel=2
logfile=/var/log/yum.log
pkgpolicy=newest
distroverpkg=redhat-release
tolerant=1
exactarch=1
obsoletes=1
gpgcheck=1
plugins=1
metadata_expire=1800

# PUT YOUR REPOS HERE OR IN separate files named file.repo
# in /etc/yum.repos.d
```

The section labeled [**main**] defines global configuration options. The **cachedir** specifies the directory that yum will store downloaded packages in, although with **keepcache** set to 0, yum does not store headers and packages after installing them. The amount of information logged is specified by **debuglevel**, with a value of 10 producing the most information. The **logfile** specifies where yum keeps its log.

The **pkgpolicy** defines which version of a software package yum installs; set it to **newest** to install the most recent versions of packages. You can also configure yum to try to install from a specific server, falling back to other servers in case of failure. The yum utility uses **distroverpkg** to determine which version of the distribution the system is running. You should not need to change this setting.

With **tolerant** set to **1**, yum corrects simple command line errors, such as attempting to install a package that is already present on the system; setting **tolerant** to 0 turns this feature off. Setting **exactarch** to **1** causes yum to update packages only with packages of the same architecture, thereby preventing an i686 package from replacing an i386 package, for example. You can use **retries** to specify the number of times yum will try to retrieve a file before returning an error (the default is 6). Set this parameter to 0 to cause yum to continue trying forever.

Setting **obsoletes** to **1** causes yum to replace obsolete packages when doing an update; it has no effect during an install. When **gpgcheck** is set to **1**, yum checks the GPG (page 992) signatures on packages it installs. This check verifies the authenticity of the packages. Setting **plugins** to **1** enables yum plugins, which extend yum functionality. (See wiki.linux.duke.edu/YumPlugins and yum in section 8 of the man pages for more information on yum plugins.) The **metadata_expire** parameter specifies the number of seconds that yum uses the metadata it downloads from the repository about packages before it downloads the information again.

Although the balance of the yum configuration information, which specifies the yum repositories, can appear in the **yum.conf** file, Fedora Core puts information about each repository in a separate file in the **/etc/yum.repos.d** directory. A parameter set in a repository section overrides the same parameter set in the [**main**] section.

```
$ ls /etc/yum.repos.d
fedora-core.repo                  fedora-legacy.repo
fedora-development.repo           fedora-updates.repo
fedora-extras-development.repo    fedora-updates-testing.repo
fedora-extras.repo
```

Each of these files contains a header, such as [**core**], which provides a unique name for the repository. The name of the file is generally similar to the repository name, with the addition of a **fedora-** prefix and a **.repo** filename extension. Commonly used repositories are **core** (held in the **fedora-core.repo** file), which contains the packages present on the installation CDs; **updates** (held in the **fedora-updates.repo** file), which contains updated versions of the stable packages; and **updates-testing**, which contains updates that are not ready for release. This last repository is not enabled; do not enable it unless you are testing unstable packages. Never enable this repository on a production system.

optional Each *.repo file includes specifications for several related repositories, which are usually disabled. For example, the **fedora-core.repo** file holds [**core-debuginfo**] and [**core-source**] in addition to [**core**]. You cannot download source files using yum. Use yumdownloader (page 482) for this task.

The next example shows part of the **fedora-core.repo** file that specifies the parameters for the **core** repository:

```
$ cat /etc/yum.repos.d/fedora-core.repo
[core]
name=Fedora Core $releasever - $basearch
#baseurl=http://download.fedora.redhat.com/pub/fedora/linux/core/$releasever/$basearch/os/
mirrorlist=http://fedora.redhat.com/download/mirrors/fedora-core-$releasever
enabled=1
gpgcheck=1
gpgkey=file:///etc/pki/rpm-gpg/RPM-GPG-KEY-fedora file:///etc/pki/rpm-gpg/RPM-GPG-KEY
```

Repository specification
Each repository specification contains the name of the repository enclosed in brackets ([]), a **name**, a **baseurl**, and a **mirrorlist**. The **name** provides an informal name for the repository that yum displays. The **baseurl** indicates the location of the main repository; it is commented out by default. The **mirrorlist** specifies the URL of a file that holds a list of **baseurl**s, or mirrors of the main repository. These definitions use two variables: yum sets **$basearch** to the architecture of the system and **$releasever** to the version of the release (such as 5 for Fedora Core 5).

The repository described by the file is enabled (yum will use it) if **enabled** is set to **1** and is disabled if **enabled** is set to 0. As described earlier, **gpgcheck** determines whether yum checks GPG signatures on files it downloads. The **gpgkey** specifies the location of the GPG key. Refer to the **yum.conf** man page for more options.

USING yum TO UPDATE, INSTALL, AND REMOVE PACKAGES

Working as **root**, you can run yum from a command line. The behavior of yum depends on the options you specify. The **update** option, without additional parameters, updates all installed packages. It downloads package headers for installed packages, determines which packages need to be updated, prompts you to continue, and downloads and installs the updated packages.

Updating packages
In the following example, yum determines that two packages, **gok** and **gedit**, need to be updated. The yum utility searches the three enabled repositories: core, extras, and updates. Once it has determined what it needs to do, yum advises you of the action(s) it will take and prompts with **Is this ok [y/N]**.

```
# yum update
Loading "installonlyn" plugin
Setting up Update Process
Setting up repositories
core                                                          [1/3]
extras                                                        [2/3]
updates                                                       [3/3]
Reading repository metadata in from local files
Resolving Dependencies
--> Populating transaction set with selected packages. Please wait.
---> Downloading header for gok to pack into transaction set.
```

```
gok-1.0.7-1.i386.rpm      100% |=========================| 112 kB      00:01
---> Package gok.i386 0:1.0.7-1 set to be updated
---> Downloading header for gedit to pack into transaction set.
gedit-2.14.1-1.i386.rpm    100% |=========================|  62 kB      00:00
---> Package gedit.i386 1:2.14.1-1 set to be updated
--> Running transaction check

Dependencies Resolved

========================================================================
 Package          Arch        Version         Repository        Size
========================================================================
Updating:
 gedit            i386        1:2.14.1-1      updates           3.2 M
 gok              i386        1.0.7-1         updates           1.5 M

Transaction Summary
========================================================================

Install       0 Package(s)
Update        2 Package(s)
Remove        0 Package(s)
Total download size: 4.7 M
Is this ok [y/N]: y
Downloading Packages:
(1/2): gok-1.0.7-1.i386.r 100% |=========================| 1.5 MB      00:06
(2/2): gedit-2.14.1-1.i38 100% |=========================| 3.2 MB      00:14
Running Transaction Test
Finished Transaction Test
Transaction Test Succeeded
Running Transaction
  Updating  : gedit                       ####################### [1/4]
  Updating  : gok                         ####################### [2/4]
  Cleanup   : gok                         ####################### [3/4]
  Cleanup   : gedit                       ####################### [4/4]

Updated: gedit.i386 1:2.14.1-1 gok.i386 0:1.0.7-1
Complete!
```

optional Some packages should only be installed; they should not be updated. The parameter **installonlypkgs** identifies these packages. Packages related to the kernel default to **installonlypkgs**. The **tokeep** parameter specifies the number of versions of **installonlypkgs** packages that yum keeps. The **installonlyn** plugin sets **tokeep** to **2**.

You can update individual packages by specifying the names of the packages on the command line following the word **update**.

Installing packages To install a new package together with the packages it is dependent on, give the command **yum install**, followed by the name of the package. After **yum** determines what it needs to do, it asks for confirmation. The next example installs the **tcsh** package:

```
# yum install tcsh
Loading "installonlyn" plugin
Setting up Install Process
Setting up repositories
core                                                              [1/3]
extras                                                            [2/3]
updates                                                           [3/3]
Reading repository metadata in from local files
Parsing package install arguments
Resolving Dependencies
--> Populating transaction set with selected packages. Please wait.
---> Downloading header for tcsh to pack into transaction set.
tcsh-6.14-6.fc5.1.i386.rp 100% |=========================| 11 kB    00:00
---> Package tcsh.i386 0:6.14-6.fc5.1 set to be updated
--> Running transaction check
...
Is this ok [y/N]: y
Downloading Packages:
(1/1): tcsh-6.14-6.fc5.1. 100% |=========================| 465 kB   00:01
Running Transaction Test
Finished Transaction Test
Transaction Test Succeeded
Running Transaction
  Installing: tcsh                        ####################### [1/1]

Installed: tcsh.i386 0:6.14-6.fc5.1
Complete!
```

You can also use yum to remove packages, using a similar syntax. The following example removes the **tcsh** package:

```
# yum remove tcsh
Loading "installonlyn" plugin
Setting up Remove Process
Resolving Dependencies
--> Populating transaction set with selected packages. Please wait.
---> Package tcsh.i386 0:6.14-6.fc5.1 set to be erased
--> Running transaction check
...
Is this ok [y/N]: y
Downloading Packages:
Running Transaction Test
Finished Transaction Test
Transaction Test Succeeded
Running Transaction
  Removing  : tcsh                        ####################### [1/1]
Removed: tcsh.i386 0:6.14-6.fc5.1
Complete!
```

yum Groups

In addition to working with single packages, yum can work with groups of packages. The next example shows how to display a list of installed and available groups:

```
# yum grouplist
Loading "installonlyn" plugin
Setting up Group Process
Setting up repositories
core                                                        [1/3]
extras                                                      [2/3]
updates                                                     [3/3]
Installed Groups:
   Office/Productivity
   MySQL Database
   Editors
   System Tools
...
   Administration Tools
   Development Tools
   Graphical Internet
Available Groups:
   Engineering and Scientific
   Window Managers
   XFCE Software Development
...
   PostgreSQL Database
   News Server
Done
```

The command **yum groupinfo** followed by the name of a group displays information about the group, including a description of the group and a list of mandatory, default, and optional packages. The next example displays information about the MySQL Database group of packages. If the name of the package includes a SPACE, you must quote it.

```
# yum groupinfo "MySQL Database"
Loading "installonlyn" plugin
Setting up Group Process
Setting up repositories
core                                                        [1/3]
extras                                                      [2/3]
updates                                                     [3/3]

Group: MySQL Database
 Description: This package group contains packages useful for use with MySQL.
 Mandatory Packages:
   mysql
 Default Packages:
   unixODBC
   mysql-server
   MySQL-python
   mysql-connector-odbc
   libdbi-dbd-mysql
   perl-DBD-MySQL
 Optional Packages:
   mod_auth_mysql
   mysql-devel
   qt-MySQL
   mysql-bench
   php-mysql
```

To install a group of packages, give the command **yum groupinstall** followed by the name of the package.

OTHER yum COMMANDS

Many yum commands and options are available. A few of the more useful commands are described here. See the yum man page for a complete list.

check-update   Lists packages that are installed on the local system and have updates available in the yum repositories.

clean all   Removes header files that yum uses for resolving dependencies. Also removes cached packages—yum does not automatically remove packages once they have been downloaded and installed, unless you set **keepcache** to 0.

clean metadata   Removes the files that yum uses to determine remote package availability. Using this option forces yum to download all metadata the next time you run it.

list available   Lists all packages that can be installed from the yum repositories.

search *word*   Searches for *word* in the package description, summary, packager, and name.

RUNNING yum AUTOMATICALLY

Fedora includes a service that will call yum nightly to update the local system. This service relies on a cron script in **/etc/cron.daily/yum.cron**. Use service (page 406) and chkconfig (page 408) to turn on the nightly update service. The log is kept in **/var/log/yum.log** or as specified in **yum.conf**.

```
# /sbin/service yum start
Enabling nightly yum update:                              [  OK  ]

# /sbin/chkconfig yum on
```

UPGRADING A SYSTEM WITH yum

Using yum to upgrade a system from one release to another can be problematic and is not recommended. See fedoraproject.org/wiki/YumUpgradeFaq for more information.

DOWNLOADING rpm PACKAGE FILES WITH yumdownloader

The yumdownloader utility locates and downloads—but does not install—rpm files. If this utility is not available on the local system, use yum to download and install the **yum-utils** package before attempting to run yumdownloader.

The following example downloads the **samba** rpm file into the working directory:

```
$ yumdownloader samba
core                                                            [1/3]
extras                                                          [2/3]
updates                                                         [3/3]
samba-3.0.21b-2.i386.rpm   100% |=========================|  16 MB   06:49
```

Downloading source files   You can use yumdownloader with the **--source** option to download rpm source package files. To download source files, you must enable the source repository in the ***.repo** file you want to use. For example, to download the kernel source code,

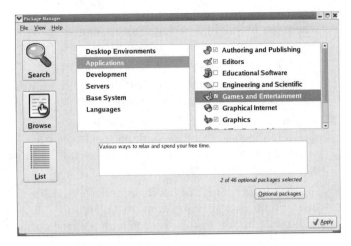

Figure 13-1   The pirut Package Manager window

change **enabled=0** to **enabled=1** in the section of the **fedora-core.repo** file following
the **[core-source]** header. The following example downloads in the working directory
the rpm file for the latest version of the kernel source code for the installed release:

```
# yumdownloader --source kernel
core                                                        [1/4]
core-source                                                 [2/4]
extras                                                      [3/4]
updates                                                     [4/4]
kernel-2.6.15-1.2054_FC5. 100% |=========================| 46 MB   01:18
```

Without the **--source** option, yumdownloader downloads the executable kernel
rpm file.

pirut: ADDS AND REMOVES SOFTWARE PACKAGES (*FEDORA*)

Red Hat Linux makes the process of graphically adding and removing software
packages easier with the pirut package manager utility. This is the same tool you use
during installation when you select packages manually. For closer control over the
packages you install and remove, use yum (page 478). Under *RHEL* use the system-
config-packages utility. To display the Package Manager window (Figure 13-1),
enter **pirut** on a command line. From KDE select **Main menu: Sys-
tem⇨Add/Remove Software** or from GNOME select **Applications: Add/Remove
Software**.

The Package Manager window has three icons on the left: Search, Browse, and List.
With Browse selected (the default), pirut displays two frames toward the top of the
window and a text frame below these frames. The left frame displays six categories
of software: Desktop Environments, Applications, Development, Servers, Base System, and Languages. When you click one of the categories in the left frame, the
right frame displays a list of the package groups in that category.

Figure 13-1 shows seven of the ten package groups in the Applications category. When you highlight a package group, pirut displays information about the group in the text frame.

Initially a check mark in the box adjacent to a package group indicates that the package group is installed. Uninstall package groups by removing the check mark; install them by adding a check mark.

Optional packages   With a check mark in the box adjacent to a highlighted package group, pirut displays the message [*n* of *nn* **optional packages installed**] and activates the **Optional packages** button. Click this button to open a window that lists the optional packages in the package group.

The pirut utility does not list the mandatory packages in a package group. To select the optional packages you want installed on the local system, place check marks in the boxes adjacent to the package names in the optional packages window and then click **Close**.

When you have selected the package groups and packages you want to add and deselected those you want to remove, click **Apply** at the lower-right corner of the Package Manager window. The pirut utility will display progress messages as it proceeds and ask you to click **OK** when it is finished installing and removing packages.

BITTORRENT (*FEDORA*)

The BitTorrent protocol implements a hybrid client/server and *P2P* (page 1047) file transfer mechanism. BitTorrent efficiently distributes large amounts of static data, such as the Fedora installation ISO images (page 35). It can replace protocols such as anonymous FTP, where client authentication is not required. Each BitTorrent client that downloads a file provides additional bandwidth for uploading the file, thereby reducing the load on the initial source. In general, BitTorrent downloads proceed faster than FTP downloads.

Unlike protocols such as FTP, BitTorrent groups multiple files into a single package called a *torrent*. For example, you can download the Fedora Core ISO images, together with the release notes and MD5 values, as a single torrent.

BitTorrent, like other P2P systems, does not use a dedicated server. Instead, the functions of a server are performed by the tracker, peers, and seeds. The *tracker* allows clients to communicate with each other. A client—called a *peer* when it has downloaded part of the torrent and a *seed* once it has downloaded the entire torrent—acts as an additional source for the torrent. As with a P2P network, each peer/seed that downloads a torrent uploads to other clients the sections of the torrent it has already downloaded. There is nothing special about a seed: It can be removed at any time once the torrent is available for download from other seeds.

The first step in downloading a torrent using BitTorrent is to locate or acquire a .torrent file. Such a file contains pertinent information about the torrent, such as its size and the location of the tracker. You can obtain a .torrent file by accessing its *URI* (page 1061), or you can acquire it via the Web, an email attachment, or other means. The BitTorrent client can then connect to the tracker to learn the locations of other clients that it can download the torrent from.

Once you have downloaded a torrent, it is good manners to allow BitTorrent to continue to run so other clients can upload *at least* as much information as you have downloaded.

PREREQUISITES

Use whereis to determine whether bittorrent-curses is installed on the local system. If it is not installed, use yum (page 478) to install the **bittorrent** package. Because BitTorrent is written in Python and runs on any platform with a Python interpreter, it is not dependent on system architecture. (The **noarch** in the name of the rpm file stands for "no architecture.") Python is installed in **/usr/bin/python** and is available in the **python** package.

The BitTorrent program, bittorrent-curses, is a textual client that provides a pseudographical interface. Complementing bittorrent-curses, other clients provide additional features. Some of these clients are available on sourceforge.net.

USING BITTORRENT

Copy the .torrent file for the torrent you want to download to the working directory. For example, to obtain the .torrent file for Fedora Core, point a browser at torrent.fedoraproject.org. (See page 35 for information about burning installation CDs from ISO images.) Select the release (e.g., Fedora Core 5), architecture (e.g., i386), and the format (CD unless DVD is specified in the name of the torrent). Download the .torrent file (it is usually less than 300 kilobytes); it will have a name something like **bordeaux-binary-i386.torrent**. With the .torrent file in the working directory, the simplest command you can use to download the torrent is

```
$ bittorrent-curses bordeaux-binary-i386.torrent
```

The preceding command saves the downloaded files in a directory named **bordeaux** (the name of the Fedora release) as specified by the .torrent file. Figure 13-2 (next page) shows bittorrent-curses running. Depending on the speed of the Internet connection and the number of seeds, downloading a large torrent can take from hours to days.

Make sure you have enough room to download the torrent

caution   Some torrents are huge. Fedora Core comprises files that total more than 3 gigabytes. Make sure the partition you are working in has enough room to hold the files you are downloading.

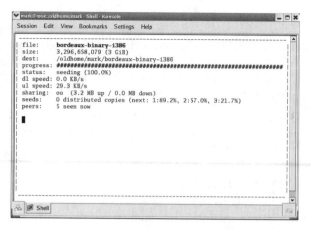

Figure 13-2   bittorrent-curses working with the Fedora Core torrent

For a list of options, give the command **bittorrent-curses --help**. One of the most useful options is **--max_upload_rate**, which limits how much bandwidth other BitTorrent users can use while downloading the torrent *from you*. The default is 20; specify 0 when you do not want to limit the upload bandwidth. The following command prevents BitTorrent from using more than 10 kilobytes per second of upstream bandwidth:

```
$ bittorrent-curses --max_upload_rate 10 bordeaux-binary-i386.torrent
```

BitTorrent usually allows higher download rates for clients that upload more data, so it is to your advantage to increase this value if you have spare bandwidth. You need to leave enough free upstream bandwidth for the acknowledgment packets from your download to get through or else the download will be very slow. By default, the client uploads to a maximum of seven other clients at once. You can change this number by using the **--max_uploads** argument, followed by the number of concurrent uploads you wish to permit. The default value, which can be specified by **-1**, is a reasonable number based on the **--max_upload_rate**. If you are downloading over a modem, try setting **--max_upload_rate** to 3 and **--max_uploads** to 2.

The name of the file or directory that BitTorrent saves a file or files in is specified as part of the **.torrent** file. You can specify a different file or directory name by using the **--save_as** option. The torrentinfo-console utility displays the name of the file or directory that the torrent will be saved in, the sizes of the files, and other information about the torrent:

```
$ torrentinfo-console bordeaux-binary-i386.torrent
torrentinfo-console 4.4.0 - decode BitTorrent metainfo files

metainfo file.......: bordeaux-binary-i386.torrent
info hash...........: 7be29789a9e257a4edaebec3417bf98e3ed459a3
directory name......: bordeaux-binary-i386
files...............:
   FC-5-i386-disc1.iso (687235072)
   FC-5-i386-disc2.iso (700618752)
```

```
      FC-5-i386-disc3.iso (721016832)
      FC-5-i386-disc4.iso (720910336)
      FC-5-i386-disc5.iso (387753984)
      FC-5-i386-rescuecd.iso (79122432)
      SHA1SUM (671)
archive size........: 3296658079 (12575 * 262144 + 197279)
tracker announce url: http://torrent.linux.duke.edu:6969/announce
comment.............:
```

You can abort the download by pressing CONTROL-C. The download will automatically resume from where it left off when you download the same torrent to the same location again.

rpm: RED HAT PACKAGE MANAGER

The rpm (Red Hat Package Manager) utility works only with software packages that have been built for processing by rpm; it installs, uninstalls, upgrades, queries, and verifies rpm packages. Because Red Hat released rpm under the GPL (page 4), rpm is used by several distributions. The rpm utility keeps track of the locations where software packages are installed, the versions of the installed packages, and the dependencies between the packages.

Source rpm packages are frequently found in a directory named **SRPMS** (source rpms), whereas binary rpm packages usually reside in **RPMS**. When you download binary packages, make sure that they are relevant to the local operating system (both distribution and release—for example, **Fedora Core** 5).[1] They should also be compiled for the appropriate architecture:

- **i386** covers all Intel- and most AMD-based systems.
- **i586** covers Pentium-class processors and above.
- **i686** refers to Pentium II or better, and includes MMX extensions.
- **S390** is for IBM System/390.
- **ia64** is for the 64-bit Intel processor.
- **alpha** is for the DEC/Compaq Alpha chip.
- **athlon** denotes the AMD Athlon family including x86_64 and AMD64.
- **ppc** is for the Power PC chip.
- **sparc** covers the Sun Sparc processor).

The name of the rpm file contains almost all the necessary information.

---

1. Many rpm packages run on releases and even distributions other than the ones they were compiled for. However, installing packages intended for other distributions can create problems. In particular, Mandriva packages are rarely compatible with other systems.

yumdownloader See page 482 for instructions on using yumdownloader to download rpm package files.

Fedora download Go to download.fedora.redhat.com/pub/fedora/linux to browse the Fedora Project's
site extensive collection of files that you can download. From this page select **core** for
packages that are part of the Fedora release and **extras** for other packages. Next
select the release of Fedora you want to download a package or updates for. Finally
select the architecture or **SRPMS** if you want to download source files. Select a mirror site from the list at fedora.redhat.com/download/mirrors.html if the Red Hat
site is busy.

rpmfind.net Other sites, such as rpmfind.net, also hold rpm packages. Each of the following lines
from a search for **sendmail** on rpmfind.net provides the information you need to
select the appropriate **sendmail** package:

```
sendmail-8.13.5-2mdk.x86_64.html ...    Mandriva devel cooker amd64    sendmail-8.13.5-2mdk.x86_64.rpm
sendmail-8.13.5-2mdk.i586.html ...      Mandriva devel cooker i586      sendmail-8.13.5-2mdk.i586.rpm
sendmail-8.13.5-2mdk.i586.html ...      Mandriva devel cooker cooker    sendmail-8.13.5-2mdk.i586.rpm
sendmail-8.13.5-2mdk.src.html ...       Mandriva devel cooker SRPMS     sendmail-8.13.5-2mdk.src.rpm
sendmail-8.13.5-2.5.0.amd64.html ...    OpenPKG                         sendmail-8.13.5-2.5.0.amd64.rpm
sendmail-8.13.5-2.5.0.ix86.html ...     OpenPKG                          sendmail-8.13.5-2.5.0.ix86.rpm
sendmail-8.13.5-2.5.0.sparc64.html ...  OpenPKG                      sendmail-8.13.5-2.5.0.sparc64.rpm
sendmail-8.13.5-2.1.ppc.html ...        Fedora Core Development ppc     sendmail-8.13.5-2.1.ppc.rpm
sendmail-8.13.5-2.1.s390.html ...       Fedora Core Development s390    sendmail-8.13.5-2.1.s390.rpm
sendmail-8.13.5-2.1.s390x.html ...      Fedora Core Development s390x   sendmail-8.13.5-2.1.s390x.rpm
sendmail-8.13.5-2.1.ppc64.html ...      Fedora Core Development ppc64   sendmail-8.13.5-2.1.ppc64.rpm
sendmail-8.13.5-2.1.x86_64.html ...     Fedora Core Development x86_64  sendmail-8.13.5-2.1.x86_64.rpm
sendmail-8.13.5-2.1.i386.html ...       Fedora Core Development i386    sendmail-8.13.5-2.1.i386.rpm
sendmail-8.13.5-2.1.ia64.html ...       Fedora Core Development ia64    sendmail-8.13.5-2.1.ia64.rpm
sendmail-8.13.5-2.1.src.html ...        Fedora Core Development Sources sendmail-8.13.5-2.1.src.rpm
```

Click the **html** filename at the left to display more information about the file. (Not
all packages have an HTML description file.) Click the **rpm** filename at the right to
download the file. Both of these names tell you the name of the program, its version
number, and its format (source or compiled for **i386, alpha, ia64,** and so on). The
column to the left of the **rpm** filename tells you which distribution the file is for.

Packages marked **noarch** ("no architecture") contain resources, such as images or
scripts, that are run by an interpreter. You can install and run **noarch** packages on
any architecture.

QUERYING PACKAGES AND FILES

The rpm utility can be run from a command line. Use **rpm –qa** to get a list of one-
line summaries of all packages installed on the system (any user can run this utility).
Use **rpm –q**, followed by the name of the package, to display more information
about a particular package. For instance, **rpm –q nis** tells you whether NIS is
installed and, if so, which version. Use the **–ql** options to list the files in a package:

```
$ rpm -q nis
package nis is not installed

$ rpm -ql logrotate
/etc/cron.daily/logrotate
/etc/logrotate.conf
```

```
/etc/logrotate.d
/usr/sbin/logrotate
/usr/share/doc/logrotate-3.7.3
/usr/share/doc/logrotate-3.7.3/CHANGES
/usr/share/man/man8/logrotate.8.gz
/var/lib/logrotate.status
```

With the **–qi** options, rpm displays information about a package:

```
$ rpm -qi logrotate
Name        : logrotate              Relocations: (not relocatable)
Version     : 3.7.3                      Vendor: Red Hat, Inc.
Release     : 2.2.1                  Build Date: Sat 11 Feb 2006 05:02:04 PM PST
Install Date: Mon 13 Feb 2006 02:29:03 AM PST     Build Host: hs20-bc1-4.build.redhat.com
Group       : System Environment/Base  Source RPM: logrotate-3.7.3-2.2.1.src.rpm
Size        : 53982                     License: GPL
Signature   : (none)
Packager    : Red Hat, Inc. <http://bugzilla.redhat.com/bugzilla>
Summary     : Rotates, compresses, removes and mails system log files.
Description :
The logrotate utility is designed to simplify the administration of
log files on a system which generates a lot of log files.  Logrotate
allows for the automatic rotation compression, removal and mailing of
log files.  Logrotate can be set to handle a log file daily, weekly,
monthly or when the log file gets to a certain size.  Normally,
logrotate runs as a daily cron job.

Install the logrotate package if you need a utility to deal with the
log files on your system.
```

You can use the **–qf** options to determine which package a file belongs to. The following command shows that more is part of the **util-linux** package.

```
$ rpm -qf /bin/more
util-linux-2.13-0.20
```

You can include the **–p** option with other options to query an uninstalled **rpm** file.

INSTALLING, UPGRADING, AND REMOVING PACKAGES

Although it is frequently easier to use yum (page 478) or pirut (page 483), you can use rpm to install, upgrade, or remove a package. Log in as or su to **root**. (Although you can run rpm as a nonprivileged user, you will not have permission to write to the necessary directories during an install or uninstall, and the procedure will fail. During a query, you do not need this permission, so you can and should work as a nonprivileged user.) Give the **–U** option, followed by the name of the file that contains the rpm version of the package you want to install. The **–U** option upgrades existing packages and installs new packages (as though you had used the **–i** option). For kernels, use **–i** (not **–U**) to leave the old kernel intact when you install a new kernel. Add the **–v** (verbose) option to display more information about what is happening and the **–h** (or **––hash**) option to display hash marks as the package is unpacked and installed. For example, while you are logged in as **root**, give the following command to install **samba** on the local system:

```
# rpm -Uvh samba-3.0.21b-2.i386.rpm
Preparing...                ########################################### [100%]
   1:samba                  ########################################### [100%]
```

When you install a package, the rpm file must be in the working directory or you must use a pathname that points to the rpm file.

To remove the same package, give the following command from any directory:

```
# rpm -e samba
error: Failed dependencies:
        samba is needed by (installed) system-config-samba-1.2.34-1.noarch
```

When you run this command, rpm reports that another package, system-config-samba, is dependent on the samba package. To remove the samba package, you have two choices: You can ignore the dependency by including rpm's **--nodeps** option or you can remove the dependent package and then remove the samba package.

```
# rpm -e system-config-samba
# rpm -e samba
```

If you remove the samba package without removing the package that is dependent on it, the utilities within the dependent package will not work. In the preceding example, the system-config-samba utility will not work.

When you use rpm to remove a package, rpm queries its database to find the information it needs to uninstall the package and removes links, unloads device drivers, and stops daemons as necessary. Refer to the rpm man page for more rpm options.

INSTALLING A LINUX KERNEL BINARY

The following steps install a new Linux kernel binary. Refer to Chapter 15 when you want to configure and rebuild a kernel from source files, rather than installing a new, prebuilt kernel binary.

1. Run rpm with the **–i** option to install the new kernel. Do not use the **–U** option: You are installing a new kernel that has a different name than the old kernel; you are not upgrading the existing kernel.

2. Make sure the new kernel works before you remove the old kernel. To verify that the new kernel works, reboot the system using the new kernel.

3. Remove the old kernel by removing files whose names contain the release number (and EXTRAVERSION number [page 530], if applicable) from **/boot** or **/** (root). Remove information about the old kernel from **grub.conf**. You may want to wait a while before removing the old kernel to make sure that no problems arise with the new one. Instead of removing the old kernel manually, you may be able to remove it with the tool you used to install it (rpm, yum, or other).

INSTALLING NON-rpm SOFTWARE

Most software that is not in rpm format comes with detailed instructions on how to configure, build (if necessary), and install it. Some binary distributions (those containing prebuilt executables that run on Red Hat Linux) require you to unpack the software from the root directory.

THE /opt AND /usr/local DIRECTORIES

Some newer application packages include scripts to install themselves automatically into a directory hierarchy under **/opt**, with files in a **/opt** subdirectory that is named after the package and executables in **/opt/bin** or **/opt/*package*/bin**. These scripts are relatively new additions to Red Hat Linux but are familiar to Sun Solaris users.

Other software packages allow you to choose where you unpack them. Because many different people develop software for Linux, there is no consistent method for installing it. As you acquire software, install it on the local system in as consistent and predictable a manner as possible. The standard Linux file structure has a directory hierarchy under **/usr/local** for binaries (**/usr/local/bin**), manual pages (**/usr/local/man**), and so forth. To prevent confusion later and to avoid overwriting or losing the software when you install standard software upgrades in the future, avoid installing nonstandard software in standard system directories (such as **/usr/bin**). On a multiuser system, make sure that users know where to find the local software and make an announcement whenever you install, change, or remove local tools.

GNU CONFIGURE AND BUILD SYSTEM

The GNU Configure and Build System makes it easy to build a program that is distributed as source code (see autoconf at developer.gnome.org/tools/build.html). This two-step process does not require special tools other than a shell, make, and gcc (the GNU C compiler). You do not need to work with **root** privileges for either of these steps.

The following example assumes you have downloaded the GNU chess program (www.gnu.org/software/chess/chess.html) to the working directory. First unpack and decompress the file and cd to the new directory:

```
$ tar -xvzf gnuchess*
gnuchess-5.03/
gnuchess-5.03/book/
gnuchess-5.03/book/README
...
$ cd gnuchess*
```

After reading the **README** and **INSTALL** files, run the configure script, which gathers information about the local system and generates the **Makefile** file:

```
$ ./configure
checking for a BSD compatible install... /usr/bin/install -c
checking whether build environment is sane... yes
```

```
checking for mawk... mawk
checking whether make sets ${MAKE}... yes
checking for gcc... gcc
checking for C compiler default output... a.out
checking whether the C compiler works... yes
...
checking for memset... yes
configure: creating ./config.status
config.status: creating Makefile
config.status: creating src/Makefile
config.status: creating src/config.h
```

Refer to the configure info page, specifically the --**prefix** option, which causes the install phase to place the software in a directory other than **/usr/local**. The second step is to run make:

```
$ make
Making all in src
make[1]: Entering directory '/hdd4/gnuchess-5.03/src'
cd .. \
&& CONFIG_FILES= CONFIG_HEADERS=src/config.h \
/bin/sh ./config.status
config.status: creating src/config.h
config.status: src/config.h is unchanged
make  all-am
make[2]: Entering directory '/hdd4/gnuchess-5.03/src'
source='atak.c' object='atak.o' libtool=no \
depfile='.deps/atak.Po' tmpdepfile='.deps/atak.TPo' \
depmode=gcc3 /bin/sh ../depcomp \
gcc -DHAVE_CONFIG_H -I. -I. -I.      -g -O2 -c 'test -f atak.c || echo './''atak.c
...
gcc   -g -O2   -o gnuchess  atak.o book.o cmd.o epd.o eval.o genmove.o hash.o hung.o init.o
iterate.o main.o move.o null.o output.o players.o pgn.o quiesce.o random.o repeat.o
search.o solve.o sort.o swap.o test.o ttable.o util.o version.o  -lreadline -lncurses -lm
make[2]: Leaving directory '/hdd4/gnuchess-5.03/src'
make[1]: Leaving directory '/hdd4/gnuchess-5.03/src'
make[1]: Entering directory '/hdd4/gnuchess-5.03'
make[1]: Nothing to be done for 'all-am'.
make[1]: Leaving directory '/hdd4/gnuchess-5.03'

$ ls src/gnuchess
src/gnuchess
```

After make finishes, the **gnuchess** executable is found in the **src** directory. If you want to install it, give the following command while running with **root** privileges:

```
# make install
Making install in src
make[1]: Entering directory '/hdd4/gnuchess-5.03/src'
make[2]: Entering directory '/hdd4/gnuchess-5.03/src'
/bin/sh ../mkinstalldirs /usr/local/bin
/usr/bin/install -c gnuchess /usr/local/bin/gnuchess
make[2]: Nothing to be done for 'install-data-am'.
...
```

You can run the two steps and install the software with this command line:

```
# ./configure && make && make install
```

The Boolean AND operator, &&, allows the execution of the second step only if the first step returned a successful exit status.

KEEPING SOFTWARE UP-TO-DATE

Of the many reasons to keep software up-to-date, one of the most important is security. Although you may hear about software-based security breaches after the fact, you rarely hear about the fixes that were available but never installed before the breach occurred. Timely installation of software updates is critical to system security. Linux open-source software is the ideal environment to find and fix bugs and make repaired software available quickly. When you keep the system and application software up-to-date, you keep abreast of bug fixes, new features, support for new hardware, speed enhancements, and more.

BUGS

A *bug* is an unwanted and unintended program property, especially one that causes the program to malfunction (definition courtesy www.foldoc.org). Bugs have been around forever, in many types of systems, machinery, thinking, and so on. All sophisticated software contains bugs. Bugs in system software or application packages can crash the system or cause programs not to run correctly. Security holes (a type of bug) can compromise the security of the system, allowing malicious users to read and write files, send mail to your contacts in your name, or destroy all data on the system, rendering the system useless.

Even if the engineers fixed all the bugs, there would still be feature requests as long as anyone used the software. Bugs, feature requests, and security holes are here to stay. Thus they must be properly tracked if developers are to fix the most dangerous/important bugs first, users are to research and report bugs in a logical manner, and administrators are to apply the developers' fixes quickly and easily.

Bug tracking   Early on, Netscape used an internal bug-tracking system named BugSplat. Later, after Netscape created Mozilla (mozilla.org) as an open-source browser project, the Mozilla team decided that it needed its own bug-tracking system. Netscape's IS department wrote a very short-lived version of Bugzilla. Terry Weissman, who had been maintaining BugSplat, then wrote a new open-source version of Bugzilla in Tcl, rewriting it in Perl a couple of months later.

Bugzilla belongs to a class of programs formally known as *defect tracking systems*, of which Bugzilla is now preeminent. Almost all Linux developers use this tool to track problems and enhancement requests for their software. Red Hat uses Bugzilla to track bugs and bug fixes for its Linux distributions; Red Hat Network takes advantage of Bugzilla to notify users of and distribute these fixes. To use Bugzilla, go to bugzilla.redhat.com.

ERRATA

For both Red Hat Enterprise Linux and Fedora Core, Red Hat processes security, bug fix, and new feature (enhancement) updates. The easiest way to learn about new updates and to obtain and install them is to use up2date (page 494) on *RHEL* systems and yum (page 476) on *FEDORA* systems.

As the Linux community, including Red Hat, finds and fixes operating system and software package bugs, including security holes, Red Hat generates rpm files (page 487) that contain the code that fixes the problems. When you upgrade a system software package, rpm renames modified configuration files with a **.rpmsave** extension. You must manually merge the changes you made to the original files into the new files.

RHEL   If you are running *RHEL*, you probably have a subscription to RHN (page 498) and can use this service to find and download updates.

FEDORA   For information on Fedora Core updates, point a browser at fedora.redhat.com and click **Download** and then **Download Server**. Select **core** and **updates**. Information about updates is posted to www.redhat.com/mailman/listinfo/fedora-announce-list (the Fedora Announce List). You can also use yum to find, download, and install updates.

up2date: KEEPS SOFTWARE UP-TO-DATE (*RHEL*)

The round button on the panel that changes colors to let you know when updates are available is called the Red Hat Network (RHN) Alert Notification Tool (page 497).

Working with the RHN server, the up2date utility downloads and optionally installs rpm packages using yum-like tools. It works with many files and directories, in graphical and character-based modes, and has many options.

The **--configure** option generates **/etc/sysconfig/rhn/up2date**, up2date's system profile file. The up2date-config utility (discussed in the next section) is a link to up2date with the **--configure** option. You do not normally use this option because up2date configures itself (creates the up2date system profile) when necessary. The **--nox** option (also up2date-nox) runs up2date in textual mode. Refer to the up2date man page for more information.

In addition to updating packages on the system, up2date can download and install Red Hat packages that are not on the system. In the following example, Superuser calls links, the character-based browser program, finds links is not on the system, and confirms that finding with whereis. Then up2date, with the **--whatprovides** option, queries the *RHEL* repository to find that the **elinks** package provides links. Finally up2date, with an argument of the name of the rpm package to be installed, downloads the **elinks** package. In this case, up2date installs the package because that is what the up2date profile is set up to do. You must run up2date as Superuser to install or upgrade a package.

```
# links
bash: /usr/bin/links: No such file or directory
# whereis links
links:
# up2date --whatprovides links
elinks-0.9.2-3.2
# up2date elinks
```

```
Fetching Obsoletes list for channel: rhel-i386-es-4...

Fetching rpm headers...
#######################################

Name                              Version      Rel
--------------------------------------------------------
elinks                            0.9.2        3.2            i386


Testing package set / solving RPM inter-dependencies...
#######################################
elinks-0.9.2-3.2.i386.rpm:  ######################## Done.
Preparing                ########################################## [100%]

Installing...
   1:elinks               ########################################### [100%]
```

When you give it a command, up2date determines where to look for the file you requested by looking at the **/etc/sysconfig/rhn/sources** configuration file. Initially the line **up2date default** in this file causes up2date to use the repository specified in the up2date configuration file (**/etc/sysconfig/rhn/up2date**).

up2date-config: CONFIGURES up2date

The up2date-config utility sets parameters in **/etc/sysconfig/rhn/up2date**, the up2date configuration file. Although you can run up2date-config from a command line, you do not usually need to do so because up2date configures itself as necessary the first time you run it. In a graphical environment, this tool displays a window with three tabs: General, Retrieval/Installation (Figure 13-3), and Package Exceptions. See Table 13-1 (next page).

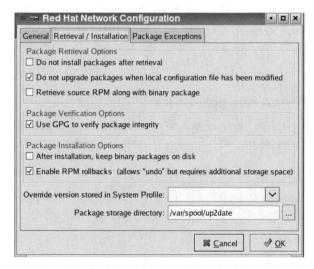

Figure 13-3   Configuring up2date, Retrieval/Installation tab

Table 13-1   Configuring up2date

Text box or check box	Function
General/Network Settings	
Select a Red Hat Network Server to use	This text box is already filled in. Do not change it unless you have reason to do so.
Enable HTTP Proxy	If you need to use a proxy server, enter the HTTP proxy server in the required format.
Use Authentication	Select **Use Authentication** and fill in the Username and Password text boxes when the proxy server requires authentication. These spaces are for the proxy server, *not* for the RHN username and password.
Retrieval/Installation	
Package Retrieval Options	
Do not install packages after retrieval	Download, but do not install packages. You will need to install the new packages manually.
Do not upgrade packages when local configuration file has been modified	Do not download or install packages that have been customized. This option is not necessary unless you are using packages other than the standard Red Hat packages.
Retrieve source **rpm** along with binary package	Download the source code ($*$**.src.rpm**) file in addition to the binary file ($*$.*arch*.**rpm**) that is to be installed. The **up2date** utility does nothing with the source file except download it.
Package Verification Options	
Use GPG to verify package integrity	Use Red Hat's GPG signature to verify the authenticity of the files you are downloading. If the Red Hat signature is not on the local system, **up2date** asks whether you want the system to download it for you. This is a critical security link; it is a good idea to select this option.
Package Installation Options	
After installation, keep binary packages on disk	Normally binary **rpm** files are removed once the files they contain have been installed. Select this option if you want them left on the system in the package storage directory.
Enable **rpm** rollbacks (allows "undo" but requires additional storage space)	By using extra disk space, up2date can store information so it can uninstall a package it has installed and reinstall the version that was installed previously.

Table 13-1   Configuring up2date (continued)

Text box or check box	Function
Override version stored in System Profile	Download and install packages for a version of Red Hat Linux that you specify in the text box, overriding the version number that is stored in the system profile.
Package storage directory	Specify a directory to store the downloaded files in. By default, they are stored in **/var/spool/up2date**.
Package Exceptions	Specify packages and files that you do not want to download. These names can include wildcard characters.
Package Names to Skip	By default, **kernel*** appears in this list box, meaning that no rpm packages whose names begin with the letters **kernel** will be downloaded. Installing a new kernel is an important event, and Red Hat Linux assumes you do not want this to happen without your knowledge. Use the **Add**, **Edit**, and **Remove** buttons to adjust the list box to meet your requirements. Normally you do not have to make any changes here.
File Names to Skip	Similar to Package Names to Skip except you specify filenames you want to skip.

RED HAT NETWORK ALERT NOTIFICATION TOOL

The Red Hat Network (RHN) Alert Notification Tool can take care of everything you need to do from the system to set up and run up2date to keep a system up-to-date. The RHN Alert Notification Tool is represented by a round button on both the GNOME and KDE Main panels. It shows one of four icons:

- Blue with a check mark indicates that all is well: There are no pending downloads.

- Red with an exclamation point indicates that files need to be downloaded.

- Green with half-arrows pointing left and right indicates that the system is communicating with the server.

- Gray with a question mark indicates that an error has occurred. Click the icon to display the error message.

If the button is not on the Main panel, run rhn-applet-gui from **Run Application** on the GNOME Action menu on the panel at the top of the screen or **Run Command** on the KDE Main menu to display it. Table 13-2 (next page) describes the selections on the RHN Alert Notification Tool Icon menu (right-click to display these options).

Table 13-2   Red Hat Network Alert Notification Tool Icon menu

Selection	Function
Check for updates	Runs up2date (page 494) in the background to check for updates. The green icon with arrows on the Red Hat Network Alert Notification button shows that the system is communicating with the server.
Launch up2date	Runs up2date (page 494) in the foreground, opening a series of windows that do not give you many options.
Configuration	Opens a series of windows that display the terms of service, allow you to configure a proxy, and check for updates.
RHN Web site	Opens a Firefox window displaying the RHN Web site.

RED HAT NETWORK (*RHEL*)

Red Hat Network (rhn.redhat.com), a service provided by Red Hat, is an Internet-based system that can keep the software on one or more *RHEL* systems up-to-date with minimal work on your part. You must subscribe to the RHN service to use it. Red Hat uses the term *entitle* to indicate that a system subscribes to RHN: A system must be entitled before it can take advantage of RHN. You can choose to make RHN more or less automated, giving you varying degrees of control over the update process. Red Hat charges a fee for this service.

The entitled systems are the clients; Red Hat maintains the RHN server. The RHN server is much more than a single server: It involves many systems and databases that are replicated and located in different areas. For the purpose of understanding how to use the client tools on the local system, picture the RHN server as a single server. For additional information, refer to the Red Hat Network manuals at www.redhat.com/docs/manuals/RHNetwork.

When Red Hat built RHN, security was its priority. Whenever you allow a remote system to put a program on a system and run it, the setup must be very close to the theoretical ideal of absolutely secure. Toward this end, RHN never initiates communication with a system. Once a program running on a system sends a message to the RHN server, the server can respond and the system can trust the response.

SUBSCRIBING TO RED HAT NETWORK (*RHEL*)

Perform the following tasks to subscribe to and start using RHN:

1. Give the command **up2date ––register** to open the RHN registration window. *RHEL* prompts you for the **root** password.

2. Read the Welcome page and click **Forward**.

3. The Red Hat Login window opens. Choose whether you want to **Create New Account** or **Use Existing Account**. Fill in the requested information. Click **Network Configuration** if you need to enable an HTTP proxy. Click **Read our Privacy Statement** to review Red Hat's privacy policy. Click **Forward**.

4. The Activate window opens. Enter a subscription number or choose to use an existing, active subscription. The window allows you to confirm that you want to include hardware and package information in the profile information that the system will send to RHN at the end of this process. Enter the name you would like RHN to use when referring to the local system. You can put any information to help identify the system in this text box; usually the simple hostname is a good choice. When you click **Forward,** the program compiles a list of the hardware and rpm packages installed on the system and sends the local system's profile to RHN.

5. The Channels window opens. Verify the information in this window. Click **Forward** to display a list of packages on the local system that need to be updated. You can choose to update the system at this time or wait until later. When you finish, the registration window closes.

If necessary, entitle the system. The error **Service not enabled for server profile: "profilename"** means that the system is not entitled. If you get this message, go to rhn.redhat.com, and log in with the username and password you set up in the Red Hat Login window (step 3). Click the Systems tab at the top of the page, and then click the **System Entitlements** box at the left. The system you just registered should be listed. Click the check box adjacent to the system you want to entitle and then click either **Set to Update Entitled** or **Set to Management Entitled.** Follow the instructions on the page if you need more entitlements.

You can check for updates at any time. Run up2date, or choose **RHN Alert Notification Tool Icon menu: Check for updates** (page 498) to see if the RHN server downloads files to or exchanges information with the local system. Alternatively, give the command **up2date --list** to see whether any packages are available for the system, thereby testing the connection with the RHN server.

You can start the flow of updates either from the system or from the Web site. From the system, run up2date. From the Web site, log in, click the Systems tab, click the name of the system in the table, click **update now** if applicable, and click **Apply Errata.** In either case, the next time the **rhnsd** daemon on the local system contacts the RHN server, the system will receive updates per the up2date profile (installed or not, left on the system or not, source code or not, and so on).

rhnsd: RHN DAEMON

The RHN daemon (**rhnsd**) is a background service that periodically queries the RHN server to determine whether any new packages are available to be downloaded. This daemon is one of the keys to RHN security: It initiates contact with the RHN server so the server never has to initiate contact with the local system. Refer to "service: Configures Services I" on page 406 for information on how to start, stop, or display the status of **rhnsd** immediately; refer to "system-config-services: Configures Services II" on page 406 or to "chkconfig: Configures Services III" on page 408 for information on how to start or stop **rhnsd** at specified runlevels.

wget: DOWNLOADS FILES NONINTERACTIVELY

The wget utility is a noninteractive, command line utility that can retrieve files from the Web using HTTP, HTTPS, and FTP.

The following simple example uses wget to download Red Hat's home page, named **index.html**, to a file with the same name:

```
$ wget http://www.redhat.com
--19:42:53--  http://www.redhat.com/
          => 'index.html'
Resolving www.redhat.com... 209.132.177.50
Connecting to www.redhat.com|209.132.177.50|:80... connected.
HTTP request sent, awaiting response... 200 OK
Length: 12,544 (12K) [text/html]

100%[===========================================================>] 12,544          --.--K/s

19:42:54 (102.49 KB/s) - 'index.html' saved [12544/12544]
```

Use the **–b** option to run wget in the background and to redirect its standard error to a file named **wget-log**:

```
$ wget -b http://example.com/big_file.tar.gz
Continuing in background, pid 10752.
Output will be written to 'wget-log'.
```

If you download a file that would overwrite a local file, wget appends a period followed by a number to the filename. Subsequent background downloads are then logged to **wget-log.1**, **wget-log.2**, and so on.

The **–c** option continues an interrupted download. The next command continues the download from the previous example in the background:

```
$ wget -b -c http://example.com/big_file.tar.gz
```

CHAPTER SUMMARY

As a system administrator, you need to keep applications and system software current. Of the many reasons to keep the software on a system up-to-date, one of the most important is system security. The development of rpm packages has made the process of adding and removing the software packages quite easy.

On Fedora Core systems, you can use yum to install and upgrade software packages. The yum utility is installed by default and is easy to configure and use.

In addition, you can use the rpm utility to install, uninstall, upgrade, query, and verify rpm packages. For packages distributed as source code, the GNU Configure and Build System makes it easy to build executable files.

BitTorrent is a handy tool for downloading large static data files such as the Fedora installation ISO images. BitTorrent can replace protocols such as anonymous FTP, where client authentication is not required.

Red Hat Network (RHN), a service provided by Red Hat, is an Internet-based system that can keep the software on one or more Red Hat Enterprise Linux systems up-to-date.

EXERCISES

1. Why would you use HTTP or FTP instead of BitTorrent for downloading large files?

2. Which command would you give to perform a complete upgrade using

   a. up2date?

   b. yum?

3. Why would you build a package from its source code when a (binary) rpm file is available?

4. Suggest two advantages that rpm files have over source distributions.

ADVANCED EXERCISES

5. When you compile a package yourself, rather than from an rpm file, which directory hierarchy should you put it in?

6. What are some steps you should take before performing an upgrade on a mission-critical server?

7. When should you use **rpm –i** instead of **rpm –U**?

14

Printing with CUPS

A *printing system* handles the tasks involved in first getting a
print job from an application (or the command line) through
the appropriate *filters* (page 1032) and into a queue for a suitable printer and then getting it printed. While handling a job, a
printing system can keep track of billing information so that
the proper accounts can be charged for printer use. When a
printer fails, the printing system can redirect jobs to other, similar printers.

INTRODUCTION

LPD and LPR   Traditionally, UNIX had two printing systems: the BSD Line Printer Daemon (LPD) and the System V Line Printer system (LPR). Linux adopted those systems at first, and both UNIX and Linux have seen modifications to and replacements for these systems. Today CUPS is the default printing system under Red Hat Linux.

CUPS   CUPS (Common UNIX Printing System) is a cross-platform print server built around IPP (Internet Printing Protocol), which is itself based on HTTP. CUPS provides a number of printer drivers and can print several different types of files, including PostScript. Because it is built on IPP and written to be portable, CUPS runs under many operating systems, including Linux and Windows. Other UNIX variants, including Mac OS X, use CUPS, and recent versions of Windows include the ability to print to IPP printers, making CUPS an ideal solution for printing in a heterogeneous environment. CUPS provides System V and BSD command line interfaces and, in addition to IPP, supports LPD/LPR, HTTP, SMB, and JetDirect (socket) protocols, among others.

IPP   The IPP project (www.pwg.org/ipp) began in 1996, when Novell and several other companies decided to design a protocol for printing over the Internet. The IPP enables users to

- Determine the capabilities of a printer.
- Submit jobs to a printer.
- Determine the status of a printer.
- Determine the status of a print job.
- Cancel a print job.

IPP is a client/server protocol in which the server side can be a print server or a network-capable stand-alone printer.

Printers and queues   On a modern computing system, when you "send a job to the printer," you actually add the job to the list of jobs waiting their turn to be printed on a printer. The list is called a *print queue* or simply a *queue*. The phrase *configuring* (or *setting up*) *a printer* is often used to mean *configuring a (print) queue*. This chapter uses these phrases interchangeably.

PREREQUISITES

Install the following packages:

- **cups**
- **system-config-printer** (optional)
- **kdebase** (optional, provides kprinter)

Run chkconfig to cause CUPS (the **cupsd** daemon) to start when the system goes into multiuser mode:

```
# /sbin/chkconfig cups on
```

Start CUPS:

```
# /etc/rc.d/init.d/cups start
```

To use the Web interface to CUPS, you need an X server and a Web browser.

MORE INFORMATION

Local CUPS Documentation   With the CUPS Web interface up (page 512), point a local browser at localhost:631/documentation.html.

Web www.linuxprinting.org   Information on printers and printing under Linux; hosts a support database with details about many printers, including notes and driver information; also forums, articles, and a HOWTO document on printing.
CUPS home page   www.cups.org
IPP information   www.pwg.org/ipp

HOWTO *SMB HOWTO* has a section titled "Sharing a Windows Printer with Linux Machines."

NOTES

SELinux When SELinux is set to use a targeted policy, CUPS is protected by SELinux. You can disable this protection if necessary. For more information refer to "Setting the Targeted Policy with system-config-securitylevel" on page 402.

JUMPSTART I: CONFIGURING A LOCAL PRINTER USING system-config-printer

This JumpStart configures a printer that is connected directly to the local system. The fastest way to add a new printer is to use system-config-printer. To display the Printer configuration window (Figure 14-1), enter **system-config-printer** on a command line. From KDE select **Main menu: Administration⇨Printing** or from GNOME select **System: Administration⇨Printing**.

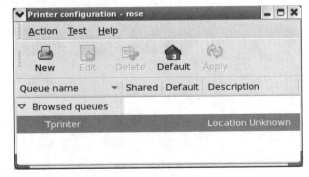

Figure 14-1   The main Printer configuration window

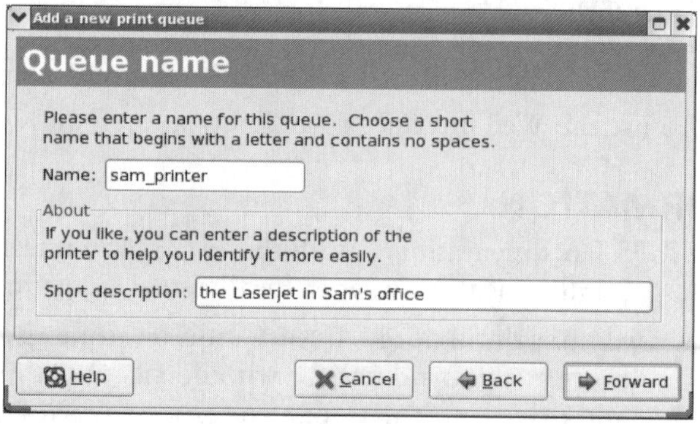

Figure 14-2   The Queue name window

Browsed queues   If the words **Browsed queues** appear in the Printer configuration window, click the adjacent triangle to display a list of queues that CUPS has found. If the printer you want to add is listed here, you are done. To make it the default printer, highlight it, click **Default** and then **Apply** on the toolbar, and close the window. If the printer you want to add is not listed, continue with the next paragraph.

From the Printer configuration window (Figure 14-1), click **New** on the toolbar to open the Add a new print queue wizard. Click **Forward** to display the Queue name window (Figure 14-2). Enter a name for and a short description of the printer. The name is a short identifier that starts with a letter and does not contain any SPACEs. The optional description can be a short sentence. Click **Forward**.

The next window, Queue type, asks you to specify the printer connection (Figure 14-3). By default, the **Locally-connected** queue type is selected in the combo box at the top of the window.

Most printers connect to a parallel or USB port, although older printers may connect to a serial port. The default list in the box in the middle of the window lists the system's parallel ports. Under Linux, a parallel port is identified as **/dev/lp***n*, where *n* is the number that identifies the port. The first parallel port (LPT1 under Windows) is

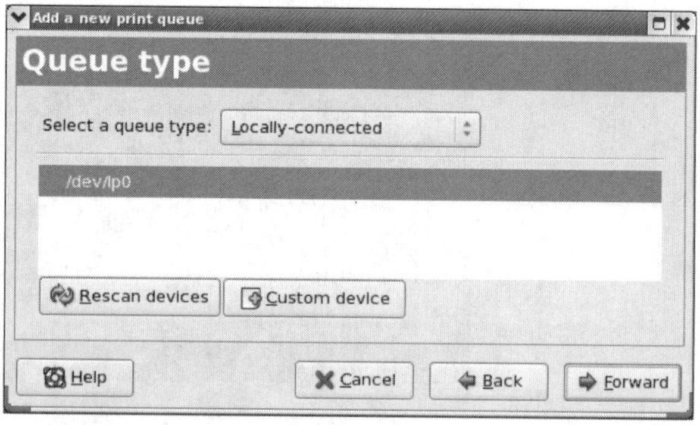

Figure 14-3   The Queue type window

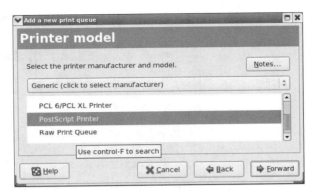

Figure 14-4   The Printer model window

/dev/lp0. Unless the local system has several parallel ports, the printer is probably connected to **/dev/lp0**.

USB devices appear in the **/dev/usb** directory. USB printers appear as standard parallel printers within the **usb** directory hierarchy. The first USB printer port is **/dev/usb/lp0**, with subsequent printers appearing as **lp1, lp2**, and so on, exactly as parallel ports do. The first serial port (COM1 under DOS or Windows) is **/dev/tty0**.

Click to highlight the line that names the port to which the printer you are installing is connected. If the device is not listed, click **Custom device** and enter the pathname of the device as **/dev/***xxx* where *xxx* is the name of the device in the **/dev** directory. Click **Forward**.

The wizard displays the Printer model window (Figure 14-4). Specifying the printer model is a two-step process: First click the bar that has the words **Generic (click to select manufacturer)** on it; the wizard displays a long pop-up menu of manufacturers. Move the mouse pointer over the menu until the manufacturer of the printer is highlighted; then click. The wizard replaces the words in the bar with the name of the manufacturer and displays that manufacturer's known printer models in the frame below the bar. Scroll through these models and click the printer that is attached to the system. Click **Notes** to display notes on the selected printer from the Linux Printing Database.

If the printer is not listed, check whether it can emulate another printer (if it has an *emulation mode*). If it can, check whether the printer it can emulate is listed and set it up that way. If all else fails, reselect **Generic** in the bar and choose a generic printer from the list in the box. Choose **PostScript Printer** if your printer is PostScript capable. If there is no match, select **Text Only Printer**; you will not be able to print graphics, but you should be able to print text. If you are using a winprinter, select **GDI Printer** from the list of generic printers.

Click **Forward** to display the Finish, and create the new print queue window. The wizard has not saved any information up to this point; click **Cancel** to abort the process or click **Finish** to create the new print queue.

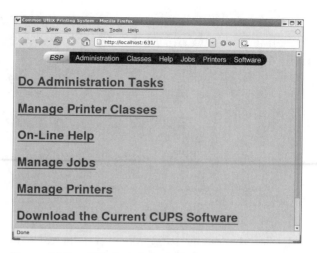

Figure 14-5   CUPS Web interface: main page

Next the wizard asks if you want to print a test page; do so to ensure that the configuration was successful. Printing the test page automatically commits the configuration changes. If you do not print a test page, click **Apply** on the toolbar to commit the changes.

If you have more than one print queue and want to set up the new print queue as the default, highlight the print queue and click **Default** on the toolbar.

JumpStart II: Configuring a Remote Printer Using CUPS

This JumpStart uses the Web interface to CUPS to configure either (1) a printer that is connected to a different UNIX/Linux system that provides IPP support or an LPD/LPR queue or (2) a printer that is connected directly to the network.

If the printer you are configuring is on an older Linux system or another UNIX-like operating system that does not run CUPS, the system is probably running LPD/LPR. Newer versions of Linux and UNIX variants that support CUPS (including Mac OS X) support IPP. Most devices that connect printers directly to a network support LPR/LPD and may support IPP.

Printers connected directly to a network are functionally equivalent to printers connected to a system running a print server: They listen on the same ports as systems running print servers and queue jobs.

Connect to the Web interface to CUPS by pointing a Web browser at **localhost:631** on the system you are configuring the printer on (Figure 14-5).

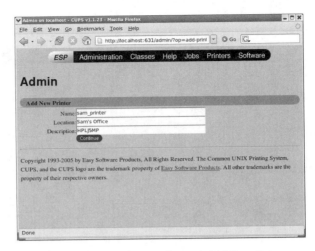

Figure 14-6   CUPS Web interface: Add New Printer page

Click **Printers** on the navigation bar at the top of the page. If the printer you want to add is displayed in the window, you are done. You may need to use system-config-printer as described in JumpStart I (page 505) to establish it as the default printer.

The printer you want to add may already be set up

tip   Follow JumpStart I (page 505) through the paragraph labeled "Browsed queues" (page 506) to see whether the local system already recognizes the printer you want to add. Alternatively you can continue with this section—a printer that is recognized will appear when you click **Printers** on the navigation bar as described shortly.

If the printer you want to add is not displayed, click **Add Printer** to display the Add New Printer page (Figure 14-6). If you are prompted for a username and password, enter **root** and the **root** password on the local system. The **Name** field holds the name of the printer; it must start with a letter and not contain any SPACEs. Fill in the **Location** and **Description** fields with text that will help users identify the printer; then click **Continue**.

The next page asks you to select the device that the printer is attached to. Click the down arrow at the right of the Device combo box to display the list of printer devices. Select **Internet Printing Protocol (ipp)** or **LPD/LPR Host or Printer,** depending on what the printer is attached to. Select **AppSocket/HP JetDirect** for an HP JetDirect-compatible network printer. Click **Continue**.

Click **Administration** to modify a printer

tip   You may not be able to modify a printer when you click **Printers** from the navigation bar because you may not be running with **root** privileges. When you click **Administration** on the navigation bar, the CUPS interface prompts for a username and password. Enter **root** and the **root** password to give yourself **root** privileges. With these privileges you can modify local printers, although you may not be able to modify remote printers.

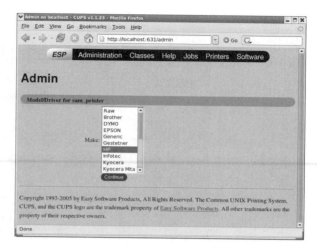

Figure 14-7   CUPS Web interface: Model/Driver page

The next page asks for the URI (location on the network) of the printer. For an LPD printer, use the form **lpd://***hostname***/***queue*; for an IPP printer, use **ipp://***hostname***/ipp**; for an HP JetDirect-compatible network printer, use **socket://***hostname*. Replace *hostname* with the name of the host that the printer is attached to or the name of the printer for a network printer. You can specify an IP address instead of *hostname*. Replace *queue* with the name of the queue on the remote system. Enter the URI of the printer and click **Continue**.

Next is the first of two Model/Driver pages (Figure 14-7). Highlight the brand of printer and click **Continue**. If the printer is PostScript capable but is not listed, select **Postscript**. If the printer is not PostScript capable and is not listed, check whether the printer supports PCL; if it does, select another, similar PCL printer. If all else fails, determine which listed printer is most similar to the one you are configuring and specify that printer. You can also try configuring the printer using system-config-printer (page 505), which offers a different choice of models.

The final step in this process is to complete the second Model/Driver page. Select the model of the printer from the scrollable list and click **Continue**. If the printer was configured properly, CUPS displays a message saying that the printer was added successfully. Click the name of the printer on this page or click **Printers** at the top of the page to display the Printer page (Figure 14-8). Once you have set up the printer, it is a good idea to print a test page.

TRADITIONAL UNIX PRINTING

Before the advent of GUIs and *WYSIWYG* (page 1064) word processors, UNIX users would create documents using an editor such as vi and a typesetting markup language such as TeX or nroff/troff, convert the resulting files to PostScript using an interpreter,

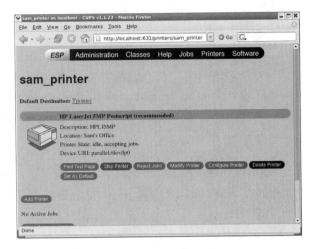

Figure 14-8   CUPS Web interface: Printer page

and send the PostScript files to the printer using lp (System V) or lpr (BSD). Red Hat Linux implements both BSD and System V command line printing utilities for compatibility: These utilities are now wrappers around the equivalent functionality in CUPS rather than core components of the printing system. The corresponding utilities are functionally equivalent; use whichever you prefer (Table 14-1).

Table 14-1   BSD and System V command line utilities

BSD/SysV	Purpose
lpr/lp	Sends job(s) to the printer.
lpq/lpstat	Displays the status of the print queue.
lprm/cancel	Removes job(s) from the print queue.

From the command line, you can print a text or PostScript file using lp:

```
$ lp memo.txt
request id is MainPrinter-25 (1 file(s))
```

The preceding command adds **memo.txt** to the print queue of the default printer as job 25. When this printer is available, it prints the file.

You can specify a printer using the **–d** option:

```
$ lp -d colorprinter graph.ps
request id is ColorPrinter-26 (1 file(s))
```

The **–P** option to lpr is equivalent to the **–d** option to lp.

Without an argument, lp (and lpr) sends its standard input to the printer:

```
$ cat memo2.txt | lp
request id is MainPrinter-27 (1 file(s))
```

The lpq and lpstat commands display information about the print queue:

```
$ lpstat
MainPrinter-25          zach            13312   Sun Feb 26 18:28:38 2006
ColorPrinter-26         zach            75776   Sun Feb 26 18:28:48 2006
MainPrinter-27          zach             8192   Sun Feb 26 18:28:57 2006
```

Use cancel or lprm to remove jobs from the print queue. Only the owner of a print job or **root** can remove a job.

```
$ cancel 27
$ lpstat
MainPrinter-25          zach            13312   Sun Feb 26 18:28:38 2006
ColorPrinter-26         zach            75776   Sun Feb 26 18:28:48 2006
```

Working as **root**, give the command **cancel –a** or **lprm –** to remove all jobs from the print queues.

CONFIGURING PRINTERS USING CUPS

You can use the Web interface or the command line interface to CUPS to manage printers and queues.

THE CUPS WEB INTERFACE

CUPS, which was designed for Internet printing, provides a Web interface to configure printers. To connect to this interface, point a Web browser running on the local system at **localhost:631**.

SETTING UP AND MODIFYING A PRINTER

"JumpStart II: Configuring a Remote Printer Using CUPS" (page 508) discusses how to set up a remote printer using CUPS. The procedure for setting up a local printer is similar. The major difference is the second step: specifying the device that the printer is connected to.

A local printer is generally connected to **USB Port #1** or **Parallel Port #1**. After you specify one of these devices, the Web interface displays the page on which you specify the brand of the printer; you do not specify a URI for a local printer. If you are setting up a serial printer, you will need to specify characteristics of the printer, including its baud rate. After these steps, the procedure is the same as explained in JumpStart II.

To modify a printer, first click **Printers** from the Web interface navigation bar and then click the **Modify Printer** button adjacent to the printer you want to modify. The Web interface takes you through the same steps as when you are setting up a new printer. If the Web interface does not allow you to modify a printer, click **Administration** instead of **Printers** on the navigation bar. Once you supply the username **root** and the **root** password, click **Manage Printers** and continue with the next paragraph.

Click the **Stop Printer** button to pause the printer. Click the **Reject Jobs** button to prevent jobs from being added to the printer's queue.

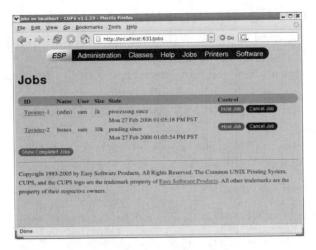

Figure 14-9   CUPS Web interface: Jobs page

JOBS

Click **Jobs** on the navigation bar to display the Jobs page (Figure 14-9), which lists jobs in the print queues. From this page you can hold (pause), release (unpause), and cancel print jobs. Click **Show Complete Jobs** to display a list of recently completed jobs. In some cases, you can restart completed jobs from this page.

CLASSES

CUPS allows you to put similar printers into a group called a *class*. A printer can belong to more than one class. A print job sent to a class will be printed on the first available printer in the class. For example, you may be able to divide your print jobs into black-and-white jobs and color jobs. If more than one printer can fulfill each of these roles, you can allow users to select a printer manually, or you can define two printer classes (black-and-white and color) and have users send their jobs to a certain class of printers.

Plan for the future

tip   If you expect to add printers to the network, you may want to configure classes containing the existing printers when you set up the network. You can then add printers later without having to change printer configurations on client systems.

Adding printers to a class is a two-step process. First, you need to define a class. Second, you need to add existing printers to the class. To define a class, first click **Classes** on the navigation bar at the top of the page and then click **Add Class**. To clients, a class of printers appears as a single printer; for each class, you need to specify a name, location, and description. Once you have defined a class, you can add printers to the class. Repeat this process for each class you want to define.

CUPS ON THE COMMAND LINE

In addition to using the Web interface, you can control CUPS and manage print queues from the command line. This section details utilities that enable you to manage printers and print queues and establish printing quotas.

lpinfo: DISPLAYS AVAILABLE DRIVERS

PPD files   The lpinfo utility provides information about the printer drivers and interfaces available to CUPS. The **−m** option displays the list of available PostScript Printer Definition (PPD) files/drivers.

```
$ /usr/sbin/lpinfo -m | head
raw Raw Queue
foomatic-db-ppds/Brother/BR7025_2_GPL.ppd.gz Brother DCP-7025 BR-Script3
foomatic-db-ppds/Brother/BR8020_2_GPL.ppd.gz Brother DCP-8020 BR-Script3
foomatic-db-ppds/Brother/BR8025_2_GPL.ppd.gz Brother DCP-8025D BR-Script3
foomatic-db-ppds/Brother/BR8040_2_GPL.ppd.gz Brother DCP-8040 BR-Script3
foomatic-db-ppds/Brother/BR8045_2_GPL.ppd.gz Brother DCP-8045D BR-Script3
foomatic-db-ppds/Brother/BRHL14_1_GPL.ppd.gz Brother HL-1450 BR-Script2
foomatic-db-ppds/Brother/BRHL14_2_GPL.ppd.gz Brother HL-1470N BR-Script2
foomatic-db-ppds/Brother/BRHL16_2_GPL.ppd.gz Brother HL-1650/70N BR-Script3
foomatic-db-ppds/Brother/BRHL18_2_GPL.ppd.gz Brother HL-1850/70N BR-Script3
```

CUPS uses *URIs* (page 1061) to identify printer ports by type and location, just as a Web browser identifies documents by protocol and location. A parallel port has a URI with the format **parallel:/dev/lp0**; a remote LPD printer uses the format **lpd://192.168.0.101**. With the **−v** option, lpinfo provides a list of available connections:

```
$ /usr/sbin/lpinfo -v
network socket
network beh
direct hal
direct hp:/no_device_found
network http
network ipp
network lpd
direct parallel:/dev/lp0
direct scsi
serial serial:/dev/ttyS0?baud=115200
...
direct usb:/dev/usb/lp0
direct usb:/dev/usb/lp1
...
network smb
```

The **−v** option to lpinfo does not display every possible network address for the socket, HTTP, IPP, LPD, and SMB protocols because there are more than 4 billion of these addresses in the IPv4 address space.

lpadmin: CONFIGURES PRINTERS

The lpadmin utility can add and remove printers from the system, modify printer configurations, and manage printer classes. It has three major options: **–d** (set the default printer), **–x** (remove a printer), and **–p** (add or modify a printer). The first two options are simple; examples are shown after the next section. Each of the options takes an argument that is the name of a printer. The name of the printer must start with a letter and cannot contain SPACEs.

ADDING OR MODIFYING A PRINTER

You add a printer or modify an existing printer by giving a command in the following format:

/usr/sbin/lpadmin –p printer options

Here *printer* is the name of the printer and ***options*** is a combination of options from the following list:

–c *class* Adds the printer to the class *class*, creating the class if necessary.

–D *info* The *info* is a string that describes the printer for users. This string has no meaning to the system. Enclose *info* within quotation marks if it contains SPACEs.

–E Enables the printer and instructs CUPS to accept jobs into its print queue.

–L *loc* The *loc* is a string that physically locates the printer for users (office, building, floor, and so on). This string has no meaning to the system. Enclose *loc* within quotation marks if it contains SPACEs.

–m *model* The *model* is the name of the PPD file (page 514) that describes the printer. Use **lpinfo –m** to display a list of all of the installed PPD files. If you have a manufacturer-provided PPD file, copy it to **/usr/share/cups/model**. Use the **–P** option to specify the pathname of the file. Specifying **–m postscript.ppd.gz**, for example, is the same as specifying **–P /usr/share/cups/model/postscript.ppd.gz**.

–P *file* The *file* is the absolute pathname of the PPD file (page 514) that holds the printer driver. See **–m** for an alternative way to specify a PPD file.

–r *class* Removes the printer from the class *class*. This option removes the class if, after removing the printer, the class would be left empty.

–v *URI* The *URI* is the device to which the printer is attached. Use **lpinfo –v** to list possible devices.

EXAMPLE lpadmin COMMANDS

At a minimum, you need to provide a device and a model when you add a printer to the system. The following command adds an Epson Stylus Color printer to the system and enables it for use. The printer is connected locally to the first parallel port and is named **ColorPrinter**.

```
# lpadmin -p ColorPrinter -E -v parallel:/dev/lp0 -m stcolor.ppd.gz
```

The printer information generated by the preceding command is stored in the **/etc/cups/printers.conf** file.

```
# cat /etc/cups/printers.conf
# Printer configuration file for CUPS v1.1.23
# Written by cupsd on Fri 27 Jan 2006 05:00:32 PM PST
<Printer ColorPrinter>
Info ColorPrinter
DeviceURI parallel:/dev/lp0
State Idle
Accepting Yes
JobSheets none none
QuotaPeriod 0
PageLimit 0
KLimit 0
Autodetected No
</Printer>
```

The printer driver information from the **/usr/share/cups/model/stcolor.ppd.gz** file is uncompressed and copied to **/etc/cups/ppd**. The resulting file is given the printer's name: **/etc/cups/ppd/ColorPrinter.ppd**.

You can modify a printer configuration with lpadmin using the same options that you used to add it. When you specify the name of an existing printer, lpadmin modifies the printer rather than creating a new one.

The next command configures an HP LaserJet-compatible printer with a JetDirect interface that is connected directly to the LAN at 192.168.1.103 and names this printer HPLJ. Specifying **socket** in the protocol part of the URI instructs CUPS to use the JetDirect protocol, a proprietary protocol developed by HP for printers connected directly to a network.

```
# lpadmin -p HPLJ -E -v socket://192.168.1.103 -m laserjet.ppd.gz
```

The lpstat utility with the **–d** option displays the name of the default printer:

```
$ lpstat -d
system default destination: MainPrinter
```

CUPS automatically makes the first printer you defined the default printer. The following command makes HPLJ the default printer:

```
# lpadmin -d HPLJ
```

The following command removes the configuration for the **ColorPrinter** printer:

```
# lpadmin -x ColorPrinter
```

PRINTING QUOTAS

CUPS provides rudimentary printing quotas. You can define two forms of quotas: page count and file size. File size quotas are almost meaningless because a small PostScript file can take a long time to interpret and can require a lot more ink to print than a large one. Page quotas are more useful, although their implementation is flawed. To determine the number of pages in a document, CUPS examines the PostScript input. If a job is submitted in the printer's native language, such as PCL,

CUPS bypasses this accounting mechanism. Also, if mpage is used to create a Post-Script file with multiple pages printed on each sheet, CUPS counts each page in the original document, rather than each sheet of paper it prints on.

Use the **job-quota-period** and either **job-page-limit** or **job-k-limit** to establish a quota for each user on a given printer. The **job-quota-period** option specifies the number of seconds that the quota remains valid. The following command establishes a quota of 20 pages per day per user for the printer named HPLJ:

```
$ lpadmin -p HPLJ -o job-quota-period=86400 -o job-page-limit=20
```

The **job-k-limit** option works similarly but defines a file size limit in kilobytes. The limit is the total number of kilobytes that each user can print over the quota period. Once a user has exceeded her quota, she will not be allowed to print until the next quota period.

MANAGING PRINT QUEUES

When a printer is operating normally, it accepts jobs into its print queue and prints them in the order they are received. Two factors determine how a printer handles a job: if the printer is accepting jobs and if it is enabled. Table 14-2 shows what happens in each of the four combinations of the two factors.

Table 14-2 Printer status

	Enabled	Disabled
Accepting Jobs	Accepts new jobs into the queue.	Accepts new jobs into the queue.
	Prints jobs from the queue.	Does not print jobs from the queue until the printer is enabled.
Rejecting Jobs	Rejects new jobs.	Rejects new jobs.
	Prints jobs from the queue.	Does not print jobs from the queue until the printer is enabled.

The utilities that change these factors are disable, enable, reject, and accept. Each utility takes the name of a printer as an argument. The following commands first disable and then enable the printer named HPLJ:

```
# /usr/bin/disable HPLJ
# /usr/bin/enable HPLJ
```

The next commands cause HPLJ to reject and then accept jobs:

```
# /usr/sbin/reject HPLJ
# /usr/sbin/accept HPLJ
```

The enable and disable utilities are located in **/usr/bin**, while reject and accept are located in **/usr/sbin**. Depending on how the **PATH** environment variable (page 292) is set, you may need to specify absolute pathnames for disable, reject, and accept.

Because enable is a bash builtin (page 225), you always need to specify the absolute pathname of this utility. You may want to create aliases (page 318) for these commands to make them easier to use.

SHARING CUPS PRINTERS

IPP is designed for remote printing. By default, CUPS binds to **localhost** and accepts connections from the local system only. To allow other systems to connect to CUPS on the local system, you must instruct CUPS to bind to an IP address that the other computers can reach. The Listen directive in the CUPS configuration file, **/etc/cups/cupsd.conf**, specifies which IP address CUPS binds to and accepts requests on. The Listen directive has the following format:

> Listen *IP:port*

where *IP* is the IP address that CUPS accepts connections on and *port* is the port number that CUPS listens on for connections on *IP*. CUPS typically uses port 631. For example, the following directive causes CUPS to listen on IP address 192.168.0.10, port 631:

```
Listen 192.168.0.10:631
```

After you change **cupsd.conf**, you need to restart the CUPS daemon:

```
# /sbin/service cups restart
Stopping cups:                                    [  OK  ]
Starting cups:                                    [  OK  ]
```

Once you restart the CUPS daemon, remote systems can print on the local system's printers using the IP address and port number specified with the Listen directive. Make sure the system's firewall (page 768) allows LAN users to connect to port 631 on the local system and does not allow systems outside the LAN to connect to this port. You may also need to modify the SELinux policy (page 402) depending on the system setup.

Alternatively, you can use CUPS's access control list to permit only selected machines to connect to local printers. An access control list is defined inside a <Location> container. The following example allows only the system at IP 192.168.1.101 and the local system to print to the specified printer:

```
<Location /printers>
Order Deny,Allow
Allow from 192.168.1.101
Allow from @LOCAL
</Location>
```

The **/printers** indicates that this container refers to all local printers. Alternatively, you can control access on a per-printer basis by specifying **/printers/***name*, where *name* is the printer name, or by specifying **/printers/***path*.ppd, where *path*.ppd is the full pathname of the PPD file (page 514) used by the printer.

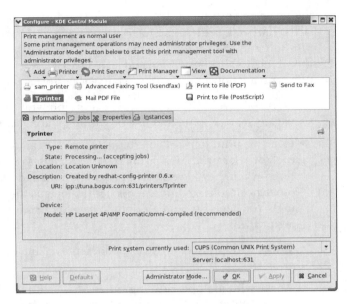

Figure 14-10   The KDE Printing Manager

The **Order Deny,Allow** line denies print requests by default and allows requests only from specified addresses. Specifying **Order Allow,Deny** allows print requests by default and denies requests from specified addresses.

Allow from specifies the IP addresses that CUPS accepts connections from. Use **Deny from** with **Order Allow,Deny** to specify IP addresses that CUPS will not accept connections from.

The @LOCAL macro specifies the local system: It accept jobs from any address that resolves to the local system. Specifying 127.0.0.1 in place of @LOCAL would work as long as no application tried to print to the print server using its external IP address. Do not use the machine's external IP address. Most processes use the loopback device (127.0.0.1) to connect to the printer, and the loopback device does not allow connections to any IP other than itself. You can also use domain names, including wildcards, and IP ranges with either wildcards or netmasks in **Allow from** and **Deny from** directives.

THE KDE PRINTING MANAGER

KDE includes a printing abstraction layer (**kprinter**) that provides the print dialog box for KDE applications and a utility for managing printers (Figure 14-10). To display the Printing Manager window, enter **kcmshell printmgr** on a command line. From KDE select **Main menu: Control Center⇨Peripherals⇨Printers**. You can use the related kprinter utility to print files.

The **kprinter** abstraction layer is not a stand-alone program and does not replace CUPS. Rather, **kprinter** is an interface between an application or a user submitting a print job and the printing system. KDE's Printing Manager provides much of the same functionality as CUPS and can use CUPS as a printing mechanism. With proper permissions, the Printing Manager performs the following tasks:

- **Starts print jobs**   You can start a print job with the Printing Manager, as well as from a command line or within an application.

- **Controls print jobs**   The Printing Manager can display information on each of your print jobs. From these windows, you can cancel print jobs (even when they have started printing), hold and release print jobs, and move print jobs to different queues (as long as they have not started printing). You can also send a print job as a fax or save it as a PDF or Post-Script file.

- **Works with printers**   You can add, remove, and modify printers and their properties.

- **Works with multiple printing systems**   The Printing Manager works with CUPS, LPRng, RLPR, PDQ, and other printing systems.

- **Works with filters**   The Printing Manager allows you to import existing printing *filters* (page 1032) or to install new ones.

Refer to the *KDEPrint Handbook* (click **Help** from the kprinter window) for more information.

INTEGRATION WITH WINDOWS

This section explains how to use Linux printers from Windows computers and how to use Windows printers from Linux systems.

PRINTING FROM WINDOWS

This section assumes that Samba (page 695) is installed and working on the Linux system that controls the printer you want to use from Windows. Samba must be set up so that the Windows user who will be printing is mapped to a Linux user (including mapping the Windows **guest** user to the Linux user **nobody**). Make sure that these users have Samba passwords. Refer to "Samba Users, User Maps, and Passwords" on page 698.

Windows supports printer sharing via SMB, allowing a printer to be shared transparently between Windows systems using the same mechanism as file sharing. Samba allows Windows users to use printers connected to Linux systems just as they would use any other shared printers. Because all Linux printers traditionally appear to be PostScript printers, the Linux print server appears to share a PostScript printer. Windows does not include a generic PostScript printer driver. Instead, Windows users must select a printer driver for a PostScript printer. The Apple Color LaserWriter driver is a good choice.

When you use rpm to install Samba, it creates a directory named **/var/spool/samba** that is owned by **root** and that anyone can read from and write to. The sticky bit (page 1057) is set for this directory, allowing a Windows user who starts a print job as a Linux user to be able to delete that job, but denying users the ability to delete print jobs of other users. Make sure this directory is in place and has the proper ownership and permissions:

```
$ ls -ld /var/spool/samba
drwxrwxrwt 2 root root 4096 Feb 24 12:29 /var/spool/samba
```

Put the following two lines in the [global] section of the **/etc/samba/smb.conf** file:

```
[global]
...
printing = cups
printcap name = cups
```

The printer's share is listed in the [printers] section in **smb.conf**. In the following example, the **path** is the path Samba uses as a spool directory and is not a normal share path. The settings allow anyone, including **guest**, to use the printer. Setting **use client driver** to **yes** causes Windows systems to use their own drivers. Not setting this option, or setting it to **no**, can cause printing from Windows not to work. Make sure the [printers] section in **smb.conf** has the following entries:

```
[printers]
comment = All Printers
path = /var/spool/samba
printer admin = root
guest ok = yes
printable = yes
use client driver = yes
browseable = no
```

Ideally each user who plans to print should have an account. When multiple users share the same account (for example, the **nobody** account), these users can delete one another's print jobs.

Modern versions of Windows (2000 and later) support IPP and, as a result, can communicate directly with CUPS. IPP is easier to manage and can be made more secure than using Samba to print from Windows. To use this feature, you must have CUPS configured on the Linux print server to allow remote IPP printing; you also need to create a new printer on the Windows system that points to the IP address of the Linux print server. The details involved in configuring a Windows machine are beyond the scope of this book. You can use testparm (page 714) and testprns to check the syntax of the Samba setup.

PRINTING TO WINDOWS

CUPS views a printer on a Windows machine exactly the same way it views any other printer. The only difference is the URI you need to specify when connecting it. To configure a printer connected to a Windows machine, go to the Printers page in the CUPS Web interface and select **Add Printer**, as you would for a local printer.

When you are asked to select the device, choose **Windows Printer via SAMBA**. Enter the URI of the printer in the following format: **smb://*windows_system/printer_name*.** Once you have added the printer, you can use it as you would any other printer.

CHAPTER SUMMARY

A printing system such as CUPS sets up printers. It also moves print jobs from an application or the command line through the appropriate filters and into a queue for a suitable printer and then prints those jobs.

CUPS is a cross-platform print server built around the IPP printing protocol. CUPS handles setting up and sending jobs through print queues. The easiest way to work with CUPS is via the Web interface, which you can access by pointing a Web browser at **localhost:631** on the system the printer is connected to. From the Web interface, you can configure print queues and modify print jobs in the queues.

You can use the traditional UNIX commands from a command line to send jobs to a printer (lpr/lp), display a print queue (lpq/lpstat), and remove jobs from a print queue (lprm/cancel). In addition, CUPS provides the lpinfo and lpadmin utilities to configure printers from the command line.

Samba enables you to print on a Linux printer from a Windows system, and vice versa.

EXERCISES

1. Which commands can you use from a command line to send a file to the default printer?

2. Which command would you give to cancel all print jobs on the system?

3. Which commands list your outstanding print jobs?

4. What is the purpose of sharing a Linux printer using Samba?

5. Name three printing protocols that CUPS supports. Which is the CUPS native protocol?

ADVANCED EXERCISES

6. Which command lists the installed printer drivers available to CUPS?

7. How would you send a text file to a printer connected to the first parallel port without using a print queue? Why is doing this not a good idea?

8. Assume you have a USB printer with a manufacturer-supplied PostScript printer definition file named **newprinter.ppd**. Which command would you use to add this printer to the system on the first USB port with the name **USBPrinter**?

9. How would you define a quota that would allow each user to print up to 50 pages per week to the printer named **LaserJet**?

10. Define a set of access control rules for a <Location> container inside **/etc/cups/cupsd.conf** that would allow anyone to print to all printers as long as they were either on the local machine or in the **mydomain.com** domain.

15

REBUILDING THE LINUX KERNEL

Once you have installed Red Hat Enterprise Linux or Fedora Core, you may want to reconfigure and rebuild the Linux kernel. Red Hat Linux comes with a prebuilt kernel that simplifies the installation process. This kernel may not be properly configured for all of your system's features, however. By reconfiguring and rebuilding the kernel, you can create one that is customized for your system and your unique needs.

Because recent releases of the Linux kernel are modular, you do not usually need to rebuild the kernel. Instead, you can dynamically change many things that used to require rebuilding the kernel. Two ways to make these changes are by using boot options or by modifying **/etc/sysctl.conf**, which is used by sysctl when the system is booted.

You can also append a string to the **kernel** line in **/boot/grub/grub.conf** or to its symbolic link, **/etc/grub.conf**. For example, **norelocate** prevents the substitution of CPU-specific optimizations and **acpi=off** prevents **acpid** (the advanced configuration and power interface daemon) from starting.

Maybe you just need to install a new Linux kernel binary

tip Refer to "Installing a Linux Kernel Binary" on page 490 when you want to install a Linux kernel binary that you do not need to configure or build.

sysctl The sysctl utility modifies kernel parameters while the system is running. This utility takes advantage of the facilities of **/proc/sys**, which defines the parameters that sysctl can modify.

The command **sysctl –a** displays a complete list of sysctl parameters. An example of displaying and changing the **domainname** kernel parameter follows. The quotation marks are not required in this example, but you must quote any characters that would otherwise be interpreted by the shell.

```
# /sbin/sysctl kernel.domainname
kernel.domainname = tcorp.com
# /sbin/sysctl -w kernel.domainname="testing.com"
kernel.domainname = testing.com
```

Have the first installation CD or the installation DVD handy when you rebuild the kernel

caution When you rebuild the Linux kernel to install a new version or to change the configuration of the existing version, make sure that you have the first installation CD or the installation DVD handy. You can also use the rescue CD; see page 40. These disks allow you to reboot the system, even when you have destroyed the system software completely. Having this CD or DVD can make the difference between momentary panic and a full-scale nervous breakdown. Refer to "Rescue Mode" on page 397 for instructions on bringing the system up in rescue mode.

PREPARING THE SOURCE CODE

Before you can start rebuilding the kernel, you must locate, install, and clean the source code. If you want to use code that has not been customized (patched) by Red Hat, visit kernel.org.

LOCATING THE SOURCE CODE

When you have the kernel source on the system, the **/usr/src** directory will look similar to the following:

```
$ ls -l /usr/src
total 20
lrwxrwxrwx  1 root root   17 Jan 27 18:25 linux -> linux-2.6.15.i686
drwxr-xr-x 21 root root 4096 Jan 27 22:12 linux-2.6.15.i686
drwxr-xr-x  8 root root 4096 Jan 27 18:20 redhat
```

In the preceding example, the name **linux-2.6.15.i686** means that the directory contains version 2.6 of the Linux kernel, release 15, and is set up for a Pentium Pro (P6 core) architecture.

The **/usr/src** directory is the traditional location for the kernel source. Also check whether the kernel code appears in **/usr/src/redhat**, as that is where it is installed by default. If it is there, see step 4 on page 528.

If the source code is present on the system, skip to "Cleaning the Source Tree" on page 529.

INSTALLING THE SOURCE CODE

When the source is not present on the system, you need to install it.

FEDORA   Before you start, install rpmbuild. You will need this program to unpack and apply patches to the source files. The rpmbuild utility is part of the **fedora-rpmdevtools** package. You can use pirut (page 483) to install this package (the package is an optional package in Developer Tools) or you can issue the following yum command.

Install rpmbuild
```
# yum install fedora-rpmdevtools
```

With rpmbuild installed, follow these steps to install the kernel source code:

1. To download the source code for the Fedora Core 5 kernel, point a browser at

    ```
    download.fedora.redhat.com/pub/fedora/linux/core/5/SRPMS
    ```

    If you want the source code for a version other than the Fedora Core 5 kernel, substitute the release number of the kernel you want for **5** in the preceding URL.

    Download the rpm file for the kernel source code. It will have a name similar to **kernel-2.6.15-1.1955_FC5.src.rpm**. The **src** indicates that the package contains source files. Firefox with its default setup will download the file to **~/Desktop**.

    Alternatively, you can use yumdownloader to download the kernel for the local system. See page 482 for instructions.

2. Working as **root**, use rpm to install the package you just downloaded. You need either to cd to the directory that holds the rpm file or to specify the pathname of the rpm file in the following command:

    ```
    # rpm -Uvh kernel*rpm
    ```

3. The preceding command installs the kernel specification file as **/usr/src/redhat/SPECS/kernel-2.6.spec**. This file holds the instructions that rpmbuild uses to unpack the kernel source files and apply patches to those files. Change directories to **/usr/src/redhat/SPECS** and run rpmbuild:

    ```
    # cd /usr/src/redhat/SPECS
    # rpmbuild -bp --target $(arch) kernel-2.6.spec
    ```

    This command take a few minutes to run and generates a lot of output.

4. Traditionally the source for the kernel that the system is running is kept in
/usr/src/linux. The following commands move the source to the **/usr/src**
directory and create a symbolic link to **linux** there. This example shows
the names of the kernel directories as **kernel-2.6.15** and **linux-2.6.15.i686**.
The names on the system you are working on will be slightly different.

```
# cd /usr/src/redhat/BUILD/kernel-2.6.15
# ls
Config.mk  linux-2.6.15.i686  vanilla  xen
# mv linux-2.6.15.i686 /usr/src
# cd /usr/src
# ln -s /usr/src/linux-2.6.15.i686 /usr/src/linux
```

After you give these commands, the patched kernel source is located in **/usr/src/linux**.
The rest of this chapter assumes that the kernel source is in this location.

RHEL   Installing the kernel source code on a *RHEL* system is similar to installing it on *FEDORA*.
Review the preceding procedure as you read this section for a better understanding
of what each step does.

Before you start, use up2date (page 494) to install two packages that you will need
to install the kernel:

```
# up2date redhat-rpm-config rpm-build
```

Download the kernel source code:

```
# up2date --get-source kernel
```

Use rpm to install the kernel source code:

```
# rpm -ivh /var/spool/up2date/kernel*.src.rpm
```

After you install the code, unpack it and apply the patches:

```
# cd /usr/src/redhat/SPECS
# rpmbuild -bp --target $(arch) kernel-2.6.spec
```

Finally, move the source tree to its classic location. See step 4, substituting the names
of the kernel directories on the *RHEL* system for those in the example.

Now the working directory is /usr/src/linux

tip   All commands in this section on building a kernel are given relative to the top-level directory that
holds the kernel source. Traditionally this directory is **/usr/src/linux**. Make sure that this directory
is your working directory before proceeding. If necessary, link the directory holding the kernel
source in **/usr/src** to **/usr/src/linux** as explained in step 4.

Read the Documentation

The kernel package includes the latest documentation, some of which may not be
available in other documents. Review the **README** file and the relevant files in the

Documentation directory. Read the *Linux Kernel-HOWTO* for an excellent, detailed, generic guide to installing and configuring the Linux kernel.

CONFIGURING AND COMPILING THE LINUX KERNEL

This section describes how to configure the kernel to meet your needs and how to compile it.

CLEANING THE SOURCE TREE

If you want to save an existing configuration file (**/usr/src/linux/.configure**), copy it to another directory (such as your home directory) or rename it before you proceed, because the next command will remove it. Purge the source tree (all subdirectories and files within **/usr/src/linux**) of all configuration and potentially stale ***.o** files by giving the following command:

```
$ make mrproper
```

CONFIGURING THE LINUX KERNEL

Before you can compile the code and create a Linux kernel, you must decide and specify which features you want the kernel to support. You can configure the kernel to support most features in two ways: by building the feature into the kernel or by specifying the feature as a loadable kernel module (page 531), which is loaded into the kernel only as needed. In deciding which method to use, you must weigh the size of the kernel against the time it takes to load a module. Make the kernel as small as possible while minimizing how often modules have to be loaded. Do not make the SCSI driver modular unless you have a reason to do so.

The **configs** directory provides sample configuration files for various processors, multiple processors, and configurations. You may want to look at these files before you get started or even use one of them as your starting point. To use one of these files, copy it from the **configs** directory to the **linux** directory and rename it .config.

Three standard commands are used to configure the Linux kernel:

```
$ make config
$ make menuconfig
$ make xconfig
```

The **make xconfig** command uses Qt (www.trolltech.com), which is normally installed with KDE or GNOME under *FEDORA*. If you prefer to use GTK+ (www.gtk.org) and it is installed on the local system, give the command **make gconfig**.

Under *RHEL* you may need to install the **qt-devel** package. Give the command **up2date qt-devel** to install this package and several packages that it is dependent on.

Each command asks the same questions and produces the same result, given the same responses. The first and second commands work in character-based environments; the

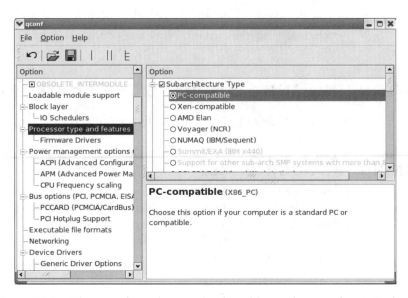

Figure 15-1   The qconf window as displayed by **make xconfig** on Fedora

second and third commands work in graphical environments. For most administrators in most situations, the third (graphical) method is the easiest to use (Figures 15-1 and 15-2). The figures show the windows displayed by *FEDORA*; *RHEL* windows look different but perform the same function.

The **make xconfig** command displays the qconf window. You can view the qconf window in three configurations: single, split, or full view. Choose a view by clicking one of the three icons to the right of the floppy diskette on the toolbar. Figure 15-1 shows the default split view. In this view, the left frame shows the options and the top-right view lists the features for each option. The bottom-right view describes the highlighted option or feature. Figure 15-2 shows the full view.

In any view, you click the boxes and circles next to the choices and subchoices. An empty box/circle indicates the feature is disabled, a check mark indicates it is to be included in the kernel, and a dot means it is to be compiled as a module. Select **Menubar: Option⇨Show All Options** to display all options and features.

Go through the options and mark the features as you would like them to be configured in the new kernel. At any time during the configuration process, you can store the currently defined configuration to a file, load a configuration from a file, or exit with or without saving your changes. See the selections in File on the Menubar. When you are done, select **Menubar: File⇨Save** and close the window.

EXTRAVERSION NUMBER

To prevent overwriting existing kernel files and to identify various compilations of the kernel, you can use the **EXTRAVERSION** variable in **Makefile**. This variable is initially set to **–prep**. Whatever value you assign to this variable is placed at the end of the

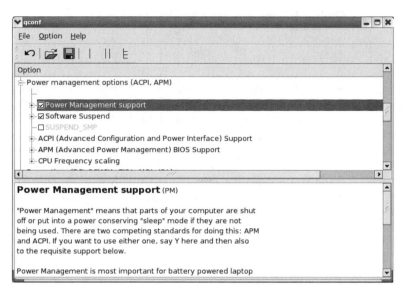

Figure 15-2 The qconf Power Management support submenu

kernel name and release number to identify the kernel. You can make note of patches applied to the kernel in this string to help people track down problems later on.

COMPILING THE LINUX KERNEL

Before compiling the kernel, make sure, once again, that no files are in the source tree from previous work:

```
$ make clean
```

Then give the following command to compile the kernel:

```
$ make bzImage
CHK     include/linux/version.h
UPD     include/linux/version.h
SYMLINK include/asm -> include/asm-i386
HOSTCC  scripts/basic/fixdep
HOSTCC  scripts/basic/split-include
HOSTCC  scripts/basic/docproc
...
```

USING LOADABLE KERNEL MODULES

A *loadable kernel module* (page 1041) (sometimes called a *module* or *loadable module*) is an object file—part of the kernel—that is linked into the kernel at runtime. Modules are compiled separately from the kernel and can be inserted into and removed from a running kernel at almost any time except when the module is being used. This ability gives the kernel the flexibility to be as small as possible at any given time. Modules are a good way to code some kernel features, including drivers that are not used continually (such as a tape driver).

Module filename extensions have changed

tip Filenames of modules in the Linux 2.4 and earlier kernels ended in **.o**. Starting with the 2.6 kernel (introduced in Fedora Core 2 and Red Hat Enterprise LInux version 4), module filenames end in **.ko**.

When you configure the kernel to support loadable modules, you need to build and install the modules. Give the following command to compile the modules that you specified when you configured the kernel:

```
$ make modules
```

Compiling the modules typically takes longer than compiling the kernel. The next command installs the modules in the **/lib/modules/**_kernel-versionEXTRAVERSION_ directory. Run this command as **root** even if you did not build any modules:

```
# make modules_install
```

Table 15-1 lists some of the tools available to help you work with modules. Refer to the corresponding man pages for options and more information.

Table 15-1   Tools for working with modules

Tool/utility	Function
depmod	Works with dependencies for modules.
insmod	Loads modules in a running kernel.
lsmod	Lists information about all loaded modules.
modinfo	Lists information about a module.
modprobe	Loads, unloads, and reports on modules. When it loads a module, it also loads dependencies.
rmmod	Unloads modules from a running kernel.

INSTALLING THE KERNEL AND ASSOCIATED FILES

The next step is to copy the compiled kernel and associated files to the appropriate directory, usually either root (**/**) or **/boot**. When you have a **boot** partition, the files are kept in the root of this partition (**/boot**). Without a **boot** partition, the files are kept in the root directory. Run the following command as **root** to install the new kernel files in the proper directory:

```
# make install
```

REBOOTING

Reboot the computer by selecting **Log Out** from the Main menu or the Desktop menu under KDE and then choosing **Restart Computer** or by selecting **Shut Down** from the System menu under GNOME and then choosing **Reboot**. If you are working at the console, press CONTROL-ALT-DEL. You can also give a **reboot** command from any character-based terminal or terminal emulator.

Boot Loader

A boot loader is a very small program that is used in the *bootstrap* (page 1022) process, which brings a computer from off or reset to a fully functional state. The boot loader frequently resides on the starting sectors of a hard disk called the MBR (Master Boot Record).

The *BIOS* (page 1021), stored in an *EEPROM* (page 1030) on the system's motherboard, gains control of a system when you turn on or reset the computer. After testing the hardware, the BIOS transfers control to the MBR, which usually passes control to the partition boot record. This transfer of control starts the boot loader, which is responsible for locating the operating system kernel (kept in the **/** or **/boot** directory), loading that kernel into memory, and starting it running. Refer to "Booting the System" on page 403 for more information on what happens from this point forward.

You can place the **/boot** directory on a very small filesystem that is located near the beginning of the hard drive, where the BIOS can access it. With this setup, the root (**/**) filesystem can be anywhere on any hard drive that Linux can access and that perhaps the BIOS cannot.

grub: The Linux Loader

The name grub (see the grub info page and www.gnu.org/software/grub) stands for Grand Unified Boot Loader. A product of the GNU project, the grub loader conforms to the *multiboot specification* (page 1044), which allows it to load many free operating systems directly as well as to *chain load* (page 1024) proprietary operating systems. The grub loader can recognize various types of filesystems and kernel executable formats, allowing it to load an arbitrary operating system. You must specify the kernel's filename and location (drive and partition) so that grub knows where to find the kernel. You can pass this information to grub via either the command line or the menu interface. When you boot the system, grub displays a menu of choices that is generated by the **/boot/grub/grub.conf** file (or see its symbolic link, **/etc/grub.conf**). At this point you can modify the menu, choose which operating system to boot, or do nothing and allow grub to boot the default system. When you install grub at the time you install Linux, the installation program configures grub automatically, so you do not have to.

The **/boot/grub/grub.conf** file is the default grub configuration file. The **grub.conf** file in the following example is from a system that had its kernel replaced (there are two versions of **vmlinuz** and **initrd**). The system has a separate **boot** partition so that all kernel and **initrd** (for systems using loadable modules; see page 531) image paths are relative to **/boot** (see the NOTICE in the file). Without a separate **boot** partition, the boot files reside in the root partition (**/**) so that kernel and **initrd** paths are relative to **/**.

The file starts with comments that Anaconda, the graphical installer, puts there, followed by four assignments. The **default** is the section number of the default boot specification. This numbering starts with 0. The example includes two boot specifications: The first, numbered 0, is for the **2.6.15-1.1881_FC5** kernel; the second, numbered 1, is for the **2.6.15-1.1878_FC5** kernel. The **timeout** is the number of seconds that grub waits after it has prompted you for a boot specification before it boots the system with the default boot specification. The **splashimage** is the grub menu interface background that you see when you boot the system. When you specify **hiddenmenu**, grub boots the default entry and does not display the menu interface unless you press ESCAPE while the system is booting.

```
$ cat /etc/grub.conf
# grub.conf generated by anaconda
#
# Note that you do not have to rerun grub after making changes to this file
# NOTICE:  You have a /boot partition.  This means that
#          all kernel and initrd paths are relative to /boot/, eg.
#          root (hd0,0)
#          kernel /vmlinuz-version ro root=/dev/hda2
#          initrd /initrd-version.img
#boot=/dev/hda
default=0
timeout=5
splashimage=(hd0,0)/grub/splash.xpm.gz
hiddenmenu
title Fedora Core (2.6.15-1.1881_FC5)
        root (hd0,0)
        kernel /vmlinuz-2.6.15-1.1881_FC5 ro root=LABEL=/1 rhgb quiet
        initrd /initrd-2.6.15-1.1881_FC5.img
title Fedora Core (2.6.15-1.1878_FC5)
        root (hd0,0)
        kernel /vmlinuz-2.6.15-1.1878_FC5 ro root=LABEL=/1 rhgb quiet
        initrd /initrd-2.6.15-1.1878_FC5.img
```

Following the **hiddenmenu** assignment in the preceding example are two boot specifications, differentiated by the **title** lines as explained previously. The three lines following the title line in each specification specify the location of the **root** (drive 0, partition 0), **kernel**, and **initrd** images. In this case, because there is a **/boot** partition, the pathnames are relative to **/boot**. For the default boot specification (the first one, numbered 0), the absolute pathname of the kernel is **/boot/vmlinuz-2.6.15-1.1881_FC5**, which is specified with the options **ro root=LABEL=/1 rhgb quiet**. These options tell grub that it is to be mounted readonly and that root (**/**) is mounted on the device labeled **/1** in **/etc/fstab** (page 469). The **rhgb** (Red Hat graphical boot) software generates a graphical display that tells you what is happening as the system boots. The **quiet** option produces less debugging output so it is easier to tell what is happening. You specify the **initrd** (initialize *RAM disk*, page 1051) image in a manner similar to the kernel. Substitute the local kernel and **initrd** names and version numbers for the ones in the example. Make sure that when you install a new kernel manually, its **title** line is different from the others in **grub.conf**.

LOADLIN: A DOS-BASED LINUX LOADER

The LOADLIN loader, a DOS utility that loads Linux from DOS and some versions of Windows, can load big kernels (**bzImage**) and RAM disk images (**initrd**). Refer to elserv.ffm.fgan.de/~lermen, where you can find the *LOADLIN Users Guide* and other information. See also the *Loadlin+Win95/98/ME mini-HOWTO.*

dmesg: DISPLAYS KERNEL MESSAGES

The dmesg utility displays the kernel-ring buffer, where the kernel stores messages. When the system boots, the kernel fills this buffer with messages related to hardware and module initialization. Messages in the kernel-ring buffer are often useful for diagnosing system problems. When you run dmesg, it displays a lot of information. It is frequently easier to pipe the output of dmesg through less or grep to find what you are looking for. For example, if you find that your hard disks are performing poorly, you can use dmesg to check that they are running in DMA mode:

```
$ dmesg | grep DMA
...
ide0: BM-DMA at 0xf000-0xf007, BIOS settings: hda:DMA, hdb:DMA
ide1: BM-DMA at 0xf008-0xf00f, BIOS settings: hdc:DMA, hdd:DMA
...
```

The preceding lines tell you which mode each IDE device is operating in. If you are having problems with the Ethernet connection, search the dmesg log for **eth:**

```
$ dmesg | grep eth
forcedeth.c: Reverse Engineered nForce ethernet driver. Version 0.49.
eth0: forcedeth.c: subsystem: 0147b:1c00 bound to 0000:00:04.0
eth0: no IPv6 routers present
```

If everything is working properly, dmesg displays the hardware configuration information for each network card. If you have configured a system service incorrectly, the dmesg log quickly fills up with errors; it is a good place to start when diagnosing faults.

CHAPTER SUMMARY

You can build a Linux kernel from the source code. Sometimes you do not need to build a kernel; you can dynamically change many things by using boot options in **/etc/grub.conf** or by modifying **/etc/sysctl.conf**.

Before you can build a Linux kernel, you must have the kernel source files on the system. These files are located in **/usr/src/linux**. Once you have the source files, you need to clean the source tree, configure the kernel, compile the kernel and the loadable modules, and install the kernel and loadable modules.

The grub boot loader is a very small program that is used in the process of bringing the system up. You must configure the boot loader so that it recognizes the new kernel.

The dmesg utility displays the kernel-ring buffer, where the kernel stores messages. You can use this utility to help diagnose boot-time problems.

EXERCISES

1. What is the purpose of the kernel?

2. How would you display a list of all loaded modules in the current kernel?

3. Which command would you give to upgrade the kernel from an rpm file, and how is this different from upgrading other packages?

4. How would you display information from the kernel about the hard disk on the first IDE channel?

5. The **noreplacement** kernel argument tells the kernel not to use CPU-specific sections of code. How would you use this argument?

6. What is a boot loader?

ADVANCED EXERCISES

7. What is the **EXTRAVERSION** variable? Where is it used and what is it used for?

8. You have just installed an Adaptec SCSI card. How can you find out whether it has been recognized and which entry in **/dev** represents it?

9. When you install an experimental kernel for testing, how do you instruct grub not to load it by default?

10. How would you obtain a list of all network-related kernel parameters?

16

ADMINISTRATION TASKS

The system administrator has many responsibilities. This chapter discusses tasks not covered in Chapter 11, including configuring user and group accounts, backing up files, scheduling tasks, general problem solving, and using the system log daemon, **syslogd**.

CONFIGURING USER AND GROUP ACCOUNTS

More than a username is required for a user to be able to log in and use a system. A user must have the necessary files, directories, permissions, and usually a password to log in. At a minimum a user must have an entry in the **/etc/passwd** and **/etc/shadow** files and a home directory. The following sections describe several ways you can work with user accounts. Refer to page 373 and the *NIS-HOWTO* when you want to run NIS to manage the **passwd** database.

system-config-users: MANAGES USER ACCOUNTS

The system-config-users utility displays the User Manager window and enables you to add, delete, and modify system users and groups. To display the User Manager window, enter **system-config-users** on a command line. From KDE select **Main menu: Administration⇨Users and Groups** or from GNOME select **System: Administration⇨Users and Groups**. This window has two tabs: Users and Groups, where each tab displays information appropriate to its name. Figure 16-1 shows the Users tab.

Search filter   The Search filter, located just below the toolbar, selects users or groups whose names match the string, which can include wildcards, that you enter in the Search filter text box. The string matches the beginning of a name. For example, ***nob** matches **nobody** and **nfsnobody**, whereas **nob** matches only **nobody**. After you enter the string, click **Apply filter** or press RETURN. If you have only a few users, you will not need to use the Search filter.

Adding a user   To create a new user, click the **Add User** button on the toolbar. The User Manager displays the Create New User window, which gathers much of the same information as the User Data tab of the User Properties window (Figure 16-2). Enter the information for the new user and click **OK**. Once you create a user, you can modify the user to add/change/remove information.

Modifying a user   To modify a user, highlight the user in the User Manager window and click **Properties** on the toolbar; the utility displays the User Properties window (Figure 16-2).

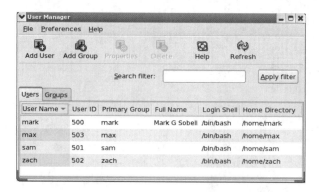

Figure 16-1   The User Manager window, Users tab

The User Properties window has four tabs: User Data, Account Info, Password Info, and Groups. The User Data tab holds basic user information such as name and password. The Account Info tab allows you to specify an expiration date for the account and to lock the account so the user cannot log in. The Password Info tab allows you to turn on password expiration and specify various related parameters. In the Groups tab, you can specify the groups that the user is a member of.

Working with groups
Click the **Groups** tab in the User Manager window to work with groups. To create a group, click **Add Group** on the toolbar and specify the name of the group. To change the name of a group or to add or remove users from a group, highlight the group and click **Properties** on the toolbar. Click the appropriate tab, make the changes you want, and click **OK**. See page 451 for more information on groups.

Help
The User Manager provides extensive help. To access it, click **Help** on the toolbar.

When you are done working with users and groups, close the window.

useradd: ADDS A USER ACCOUNT

The useradd utility (and the link to it, named adduser) adds a new user account to the system. By default, useradd assigns the next highest unused user ID to a new account and specifies bash as the user's login shell. The following example creates the user's home directory (in **/home**), specifies the user's group ID, and puts the user's full name in the comment field:

```
# useradd -g 500 -c "Alex Watson" alex
```

Based on the **/etc/login.defs** file, the system creates a home directory for the new user. When useradd creates a home directory, it copies the contents of **/etc/skel**, which contains bash and other startup files, to that directory. For more information on adding and modifying user information, see the useradd and usermod man pages. Once you have added a user, use passwd to give the user a password.

Figure 16-2   The User Properties window, User Data tab

userdel: Removes a User Account

If appropriate, back up the files belonging to the user before deleting them. The userdel utility deletes user accounts. The following command removes alex's account, his home directory, and all his files:

```
# userdel -r alex
```

To turn off a user's account temporarily, you can use usermod to change the expiration date for the account. Because it specifies that his account expired in the past (December 31, 2005), the following command line prevents alex from logging in:

```
# usermod -e "12/31/05" alex
```

groupadd: Adds a Group

Just as useradd adds a new user to the system, groupadd adds a new group by adding an entry for it in /etc/group (page 451). The following example creates a new group named rtfm:

```
# groupadd -g 1024 rtfm
```

Unless you use the –g option to assign a group ID, the system picks the next available sequential number greater than 500. The –o option allows the group ID to be nonunique if you want to have multiple names for the same group ID.

The analogue of userdel for groups is groupdel, which takes a group name as an argument. You can also use groupmod to change the name or group ID of a group, as in the following examples:

```
# groupmod -g 1025 rtfm
# groupmod -n manuals rtfm
```

The first example gives the previously created rtfm group a new group ID number. The second example renames the rtfm group manuals.

Group ID cautions

caution   The groupmod utility does not change group numbers in /etc/passwd when you renumber a group. You must edit /etc/passwd and change the entries yourself. If you change the number of a group, files that are associated with the group will no longer be associated with the group. Instead, they may be associated with no group or with another group with the old group ID number.

Backing Up Files

One of the most neglected tasks of system administration is making backup copies of files on a regular basis. The backup copies are vital in three instances: when the system malfunctions and files are lost, when a catastrophic disaster (fire, earthquake, and so on) occurs, and when a user or the system administrator deletes or corrupts a file by accident. Even when you set up RAID (page 31), you still need to back up files. Although RAID provides fault tolerance (helpful in the event of disk failure), it does not help when a catastrophic disaster occurs or when a file is corrupted or accidentally removed. It is a good idea to have a written backup policy and to keep copies of backups offsite (in another building, at home, or at a completely different facility or campus) in a fireproof vault or safe.

The time to start thinking about backups is when you partition the disk. Refer to "Partitioning a Disk" on page 29. Make sure the capacity of the backup device and your partition sizes are comparable. Although you can back up a partition onto multiple volumes, it is easier not to and much easier to restore data from a single volume.

You must back up filesystems on a regular basis. Backup files are usually kept on magnetic tape or some other removable media. Exactly how often you should back up which files depends on the system and your needs. Use this criterion when determining a backup schedule: If the system crashes, how much work are you willing to lose? Ideally you would back up all files on the system every few minutes so you would never lose more than a few minutes of work.

Of course, there is a tradeoff: How often are you willing to back up the files? The backup procedure typically slows down the system for other users, takes a certain amount of your time, and requires that you have and store the media (tape or disk) holding the backup. Avoid backing up an active filesystem; the results may be inconsistent, and restoring from the backup may be impossible. This requirement is a function of the backup program and the filesystem you are backing up.

Another question is when to run the backup. Unless you plan to kick users off and bring the system down to single-user mode (not a very user-friendly practice), you want to perform this task when the machine is at its quietest. Depending on the use of the system, sometime in the middle of the night can work well. Then the backup is least likely to affect users, and the files are not likely to change as they are being read for backup.

A *full* backup makes copies of all files, regardless of when they were created or accessed. An *incremental* backup makes copies of those files that have been created or modified since the last (usually full) backup.

The more people using the system, the more often you should back up the filesystems. One popular schedule is to perform an incremental backup one or two times a day and a full backup one or two times a week.

CHOOSING A BACKUP MEDIUM

If the local system is connected to a network, you can write your backups to a tape drive on another system. This technique is often used with networked computers to avoid the cost of having a tape drive on each computer in the network and to simplify management of backing up many computers in a network. Most likely you want to use a tape system for backups. Because tape drives hold many gigabytes of data, using tape simplifies the task of backing up the system, making it more likely that you will take care of this important task regularly. Other options for holding backups are writable CDs, DVDs, and removable hard disks. These devices, although not as cost-effective or able to store as much information as tape systems, offer convenience and improved performance over using tapes.

BACKUP UTILITIES

A number of utilities help you back up the system, and most work with any media. Most Linux backup utilities are based on one of the archive programs—tar or cpio—and augment these basic programs with bookkeeping support for managing backups conveniently.

You can use any of the tar, cpio, or dump/restore utilities to construct full or partial backups of the system. Each utility constructs a large file that contains, or archives, other files. In addition to file contents, an archive includes header information for each file it holds. This header information can be used when extracting files from the archive to restore file permissions and modification dates. An archive file can be saved to disk, written to tape, or shipped across the network while it is being created.

In addition to helping you back up the system, these programs offer a convenient way to bundle files for distribution to other sites. The tar program is often used for this purpose, and some software packages available on the Internet are bundled as tar archive files.

The amanda (Advanced Maryland Automatic Network Disk Archiver, www.amanda.org) utility, one of the more popular backup systems, uses dump or tar and takes advantage of Samba to back up Windows systems. The amanda utility backs up a LAN of heterogeneous hosts to a single tape drive. You can use yum to install amanda; refer to the amanda man page for details.

tar: ARCHIVES FILES

The tar (tape archive) utility stores and retrieves files from an archive and can compress the archive to conserve space. If you do not specify an archive device, tar uses /dev/rmt0 (which may not exist on the local system). With the –f option, tar uses the argument to –f as the name of the archive device. You can use this option to refer to a device on another system on the network. Although tar has many options, you need only a few in most situations. The following command displays a complete list of options:

```
# tar --help | less
```

Most options for tar can be given either in a short form (a single letter) or as a descriptive word. Descriptive-word options are preceded by two hyphens, as in --help. Single-letter options can be combined into a single command line argument and do not need to be preceded by a hyphen (for consistency with other utilities, it is good practice to use the hyphen anyway).

Although the following two commands look quite different, they specify the same tar options in the same order. The first version combines single-letter options into a single command line argument; the second version uses descriptive words for the same options:

```
# tar -ztvf /dev/st0

# tar --gzip --list --verbose --file /dev/st0
```

Both commands tell tar to generate a (**v, verbose**) table of contents (**t, list**) from the tape on /dev/st0 (**f, file**), using gzip (**z, gzip**) to decompress the files. Unlike the original UNIX tar utility, the GNU version strips the leading / from absolute pathnames.

The options in Table 16-1 tell the tar program what to do. You must include exactly one of these options in a tar command.

Table 16-1 The tar utility

Option	Effect
--append (–r)	Appends files to an archive
--catenate (–A)	Adds one or more archives to the end of an existing archive
--create (–c)	Creates a new archive
--delete	Deletes files in an archive (not on tapes)
--dereference (–h)	Follows symbolic links
--diff (–d)	Compares files in an archive with disk files
--extract (–x)	Extracts files from an archive
--help	Displays a help list of tar options
--list (–t)	Lists the files in an archive
--update (–u)	Like the –r option, but the file is not appended if a newer version is already in the archive

The –c, –t, and –x options are used most frequently. You can use many other options to change how tar operates. The –j option, for example, compresses or decompresses the file by filtering it through bzip2 (page 140).

cpio: ARCHIVES FILES

The cpio (copy in/out) program is similar to tar but can use archive files in a variety of formats, including the one used by tar. Normally cpio reads the names of the files to insert into the archive from standard input and produces the archive file as standard output. When extracting files from an archive, cpio reads the archive as standard input.

As with tar, some options can be given in both a short, single-letter form and a more descriptive word form. However, unlike tar, the syntax of the two forms differs when the option must be followed by additional information. In the short form, you must include a SPACE between the option and the additional information; with the word form, you must separate the two with an equal sign and no SPACEs.

Running cpio with --help displays a full list of options.

PERFORMING A SIMPLE BACKUP

When you prepare to make a major change to a system, such as replacing a disk drive or updating the Linux kernel, it is a good idea to archive some or all of the files so you can restore any that become damaged if something goes wrong. For this type of backup, tar or cpio works well. For example, if you have a SCSI tape drive as device /dev/st0 that is capable of holding all the files on a single tape, you can use the following commands to construct a backup tape of the entire system:

```
# cd /
# tar -cf /dev/st0 .
```

All of the commands in this section start by using cd to change to the root directory so you are sure to back up the entire system. The tar command then creates an archive (c) on the device /dev/st0 (f). If you would like to compress the archive, replace the preceding tar command with the following command, which uses j to call bzip2:

```
# tar -cjf /dev/st0 .
```

You can back up the system with a combination of find and cpio. The following commands create an output file and set the I/O block size to 5120 bytes (the default is 512 bytes):

```
# cd /
# find . -depth | cpio -oB > /dev/st0
```

The next command restores the files in the /home directory from the preceding backup. The options extract files from an archive (-i) in verbose mode, keeping the modification times and creating directories as needed.

```
# cd /
# cpio -ivmd /home/\* < /dev/st0
```

Exclude some directories from a backup

tip In practice, you will likely want to exclude some directories from the backup process. For example, not backing up /tmp or /var/tmp (or its link, /usr/tmp) can save room in the archive. Also, do not back up the files in /proc. Because the /proc filesystem is not a disk filesystem but rather a way for the Linux kernel to provide information about the operating system and system memory, you need not back up /proc; you cannot restore it later. You do not need to back up filesystems that are mounted from disks on other systems in the network. Do not back up FIFOs; the results are unpredictable. If you plan on using a simple method, similar to those just discussed, create a file naming the directories to exclude from the backup, and use the appropriate option with the archive program to read the file.

```
# dump -0uf /dev/nst0 /home
# dump -0uf /dev/nst0 /usr
# dump -0uf /dev/st0 /var
```

The preceding example uses the nonrewinding device for the first two dumps. If you use the rewinding device, the tape rewinds after each dump, and you are left with only the last dump on the tape.

You can use mt (magnetic tape), which is part of the **mt-st** package, to manipulate files on a multivolume dump tape. The following mt command positions the tape (**fsf 2** instructs mt to skip forward *past* two files, leaving the tape at the start of the third file). The restore command restores the **/var** filesystem from the previous example:

```
# mt -f /dev/st0 fsf 2
# restore rf /dev/st0
```

SCHEDULING TASKS

It is a good practice to schedule certain routine tasks to run automatically. For example, you may want to remove old core files once a week, summarize accounting data daily, and rotate system log files monthly.

crond AND crontab: SCHEDULE ROUTINE TASKS

Using crontab, you can submit a list of commands in a format that can be read and executed by **crond**. Working as Superuser, you can put commands in one of the **/etc/cron.** directories to be run at intervals specified by the directory name, such as **cron.daily**.

When SELinux is set to use a targeted policy, it protects the **cron** daemon. You can disable this protection if necessary. For more information refer to "Setting the Targeted Policy with system-config-securitylevel" on page 402.

cron **stops for no one; try** anacron

tip   The **crond** daemon assumes the system is always running. A similar utility, anacron, does not make that assumption and is well suited to portable and home computers that are frequently turned off. The anacron utility takes its instructions from the **/etc/anacrontab** file unless you specify otherwise. Refer to the anacron and anacrontab man pages for more information.

at: RUNS OCCASIONAL TASKS

Like the cron utility, at allows you to run a job sometime in the future. Unlike cron, at runs a job only once. For instance, you can schedule an at job that will reboot the system at 3 AM (when all users are probably logged off):

```
# at 3am
at> reboot
at> CONTROL-D <EOT>
job 1 at 2006-02-01 03:00
```

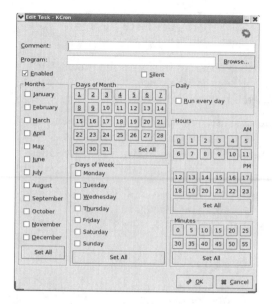

Figure 16-3   The kcron Task Scheduler

It is also possible to run an at job from within an at job. For instance, an at job might check for new patches every 18 days, something that would be more difficult with cron.

kcron: SCHEDULES TASKS

The kcron utility provides a GUI to cron, allowing you to create and modify **crontab** files. Scheduling tasks with kcron is a matter of clicking buttons (Figure 16-3).

Run kcron when you are logged in as yourself to view and modify your personal **crontab** file. When you run kcron as **root**, you can modify any **crontab** file on the system. At first, kcron displays a window that lists Tasks and Variables, and, when you are running as **root**, Users. The Description column of this window is very wide and does not fit in the window. Use the right-left scrollbar to view its contents. If you are running as **root**, you need to double-click a user to display the **Tasks** folder. To create a new **crontab** entry, highlight **Tasks**, and select **New** from **Edit** on the menubar (or from the right-click menu). To modify an entry, highlight the entry, and select **Modify** from **Edit** on the menubar. In the resulting window, enter the name of the program you want to run in the Program text box, and click buttons or place check marks corresponding to the dates and times you want to run the program. Unless you redirect it, output from a program that cron runs is mailed to you.

SYSTEM REPORTS

Many utilities report on one thing or another. The who, finger, ls, ps, and other utilities generate simple end-user reports. In some cases, these reports can help with system administration. This section describes utilities that generate more in-depth reports that can usually provide more assistance with system administration tasks. Linux has many other report utilities, including (from the **sysstat** package) sar (system activity report), iostat (input/output and CPU statistics), and mpstat (processor statistics); (from the **net-tools** package) netstat (network report); and (from the **nfs-utils** package) nfsstat (NFS statistics).

vmstat: REPORTS VIRTUAL MEMORY STATISTICS

The vmstat utility (**procps** package) generates virtual memory information along with (limited) disk and CPU activity data. The following example shows virtual memory statistics in 3-second intervals for seven iterations (from the arguments **3 7**). The first line covers the time since the system was last booted; the rest of the lines cover the period since the previous line.

```
$ vmstat 3 7
procs -----------memory---------- ---swap-- -----io---- --system-- ----cpu----
 r  b   swpd   free   buff   cache   si   so    bi    bo    in   cs us sy id wa
 0  2      0 684328  33924 219916    0    0   430   105  1052  134  2  4 86  8
 0  2      0 654632  34160 248840    0    0  4897  7683  1142  237  0  5  0 95
 0  3      0 623528  34224 279080    0    0  5056  8237  1094  178  0  4  0 95
 0  2      0 603176  34576 298936    0    0  3416   141  1161  255  0  4  0 96
 0  2      0 575912  34792 325616    0    0  4516  7267  1147  231  0  4  0 96
 1  2      0 549032  35164 351464    0    0  4429    77  1120  210  0  4  0 96
 0  2      0 523432  35448 376376    0    0  4173  6577  1135  234  0  4  0 95
```

The following list explains the column heads displayed by vmstat.

- **procs**   Process information
  - ◆ **r**   Number of waiting, runnable processes
  - ◆ **b**   Number of blocked processes (in uninterruptable sleep)
- **memory**   Memory information in kilobytes
  - ◆ **swpd**   Used virtual memory
  - ◆ **free**   Idle memory
  - ◆ **buff**   Memory used as buffers
  - ◆ **cache**   Memory used as cache
- **swap**   System paging activity in kilobytes per second
  - ◆ **si**   Memory swapped in from disk
  - ◆ **so**   Memory swapped out to disk
- **io**   System I/O activity in blocks per second
  - ◆ **bi**   Blocks received from a block device
  - ◆ **bo**   Blocks sent to a block device

- **system** Values are per second
  - ◆ **in** Interrupts (including the clock)
  - ◆ **cs** Context switches
- **cpu** Percentage of total CPU time spent in each of these states
  - ◆ **us** User (nonkernel)
  - ◆ **sy** System (kernel)
  - ◆ **id** Idle
  - ◆ **wa** Waiting for I/O

top: LISTS PROCESSES USING THE MOST RESOURCES

The top utility is a useful supplement to ps. At its simplest, top displays system information at the top and the most CPU-intensive processes below the system information. The top utility updates itself periodically; type **q** to quit. Although you can use command line options, the interactive commands are often more helpful. Refer to Table 16-2 and to the top man page for more information.

```
$ top
top - 21:30:26 up 18 min,  2 users,  load average: 0.95, 0.30, 0.14
Tasks:  63 total,   4 running,  58 sleeping,   1 stopped,   0 zombie
Cpu(s): 30.9% us, 22.9% sy,  0.0% ni,   0.0% id, 45.2% wa, 1.0% hi, 0.0%si
Mem:   1036820k total,  1032276k used,     4544k free,    40908k buffers
Swap:  2048276k total,        0k used,  2048276k free,   846744k cached

  PID USER      PR  NI  VIRT  RES  SHR S %CPU %MEM    TIME+  COMMAND
 1285 root      25   0  9272 6892 1312 R 29.3  0.7  0:00.88 bzip2
 1276 root      18   0  3048  860 1372 R  3.7  0.1  0:05.25 cp
    7 root      15   0     0    0    0 S  0.7  0.0  0:00.27 pdflush
    6 root      15   0     0    0    0 S  0.3  0.0  0:00.11 pdflush
    8 root      15   0     0    0    0 S  0.3  0.0  0:00.06 kswapd0
  300 root      15   0     0    0    0 S  0.3  0.0  0:00.24 kjournald
 1064 mgs2      16   0  8144 2276 6808 S  0.3  0.2  0:00.69 sshd
 1224 root      16   0  4964 1360 3944 S  0.3  0.1  0:00.03 bash
 1275 mgs2      16   0  2840  936 1784 R  0.3  0.1  0:00.15 top
 1284 root      15   0  2736  668 1416 S  0.3  0.1  0:00.01 tar
    1 root      16   0  2624  520 1312 S  0.0  0.1  0:06.51 init
```

Table 16-2 top: interactive commands

Command	Function
A	Sorts processes by age (newest first).
h or **?**	Displays a Help screen.
k	Prompts for a PID number and type of signal and sends the process that signal. Defaults to signal 15 (SIGTERM); specify 9 (SIGKILL) only when 15 does not work.

Table 16-2   top: interactive commands (continued)

M	Sorts processes by memory usage.
P	Sorts processes by CPU usage (default).
q	Quits.
s	Prompts for time between updates in seconds. Use 0 for continuous updates.
SPACE	Updates the display immediately.
T	Sorts tasks by time.
W	Writes a startup file named **~/.toprc** so that next time you start top, it uses the same parameters it is currently using.

KEEPING USERS INFORMED

One of your primary responsibilities as a system administrator is communicating with system users. You need to make announcements, such as when the system will be down for maintenance, when a class on some new software will be held, and how users can access the new system printer. You can even start to fill the role of a small local newspaper, letting users know about new employees, RIFs, births, the company picnic, and so on.

Different communications have different priorities. For example, information about the company picnic in two months is not as time sensitive as the fact that you are bringing the system down in 5 minutes. To meet these differing needs, Linux provides different ways of communicating. The most common methods are described and contrasted in the following list. All of these methods are generally available to everyone, except for the message of the day, which is typically reserved for Superuser.

write Use the write utility (page 150) to communicate with a user who is logged in on the local system. You might use it, for example, to ask a user to stop running a program that is bogging down the system; the user might reply that he will be done in 3 minutes. Users can also use write to ask the system administrator to mount a tape or restore a file. KDE and GNOME open a new window when they receive a message.

wall The wall (write all) utility effectively communicates immediately with all users who are logged in. It works similarly to write, except that users cannot use wall to write back to only you. Use wall when you are about to bring the system down or are in another crisis situation. Users who are not logged in will not get the message.

Use wall while you are Superuser *only* in a crisis situation; it interrupts anything anyone is doing.

Email Email is useful for communicating less urgent information to one or more systems and/or remote users. When you send mail, you have to be willing to wait for each user to read it. The email utilities are useful for reminding users that they are forgetting to log out, their bills are past due, or they are using too much disk space.

Users can easily make permanent records of messages they receive via email, as opposed to messages received via write, so they can keep track of important details. It would be appropriate to use email to inform users about a new, complex procedure, so each user could keep a copy of the information for reference.

Message of the day   Users see the message of the day each time they log in in a textual environment. You can edit the **/etc/motd** file to change this message as necessary. The message of the day can alert users to upcoming periodic maintenance, new system features, or a change in procedures.

CREATING PROBLEMS

Even experienced system administrators make mistakes; new system administrators just make more mistakes. Although you can improve your odds of avoiding problems by carefully reading and following the documentation provided with software, many things can still go wrong. A comprehensive list is not possible, no matter how long, as new and exciting ways to create problems are discovered every day. A few of the more common techniques are described here.

FAILING TO PERFORM REGULAR BACKUPS

Few feelings are more painful to a system administrator than realizing that important information is lost forever. If your system supports multiple users, having a recent backup may be your only protection from a public lynching. If it is a single-user system, having a recent backup certainly keeps you happier when you lose a hard disk.

NOT READING AND FOLLOWING INSTRUCTIONS

Software developers provide documentation for a reason. Even when you have installed a software package before, carefully read the instructions again. They may have changed, or you may simply remember them incorrectly. Software changes more quickly than books are revised, so no book should be taken as offering foolproof advice. Instead, look for the latest documentation online.

FAILING TO ASK FOR HELP WHEN INSTRUCTIONS ARE NOT CLEAR

If something does not seem to make sense, try to find out what does make sense—do not guess. Refer to "Help" on page 977.

DELETING OR MISTYPING A CRITICAL FILE

One sure way to give yourself nightmares is to execute the command

```
# rm -rf /etc
```
← *do not do this*

Perhaps no other command renders a Linux system useless so quickly. The only recourse is to reboot into rescue mode (page 397) using the first installation CD and restore the missing files from a recent backup. Although this example depicts an extreme case, many files are critical to proper operation of a system. Deleting one of these files or mistyping information in one of them is almost certain to cause problems. If you directly edit **/etc/passwd**, for example, entering the wrong information in a field can make it impossible for one or more users to log in. Do not use **rm –rf** with an argument that includes wildcard characters; do pause after typing the command, and read it before you press RETURN. Check everything you do carefully, and make a copy of a critical file before you edit it.

Be careful when using a wildcard character with rm

caution   When you must use a wildcard character, such as ∗, in an argument to an rm command, first use echo with the same argument to see exactly which files you will be deleting. This check is especially important when you are working as **root**.

SOLVING PROBLEMS

As the system administrator, it is your responsibility to keep the system secure and running smoothly. When a user is having a problem, it usually falls to the administrator to help the user get back on track. This section suggests ways to keep users happy and the system functioning at peak performance.

HELPING WHEN A USER CANNOT LOG IN

When a user has trouble logging in on the system, the source may be a user error or a problem with the system software or hardware. The following steps can help determine where the problem is:

- Determine whether only that one user or only that one user's terminal/workstation has a problem or whether the problem is more widespread.

- Check that the user's Caps Lock key is not on.

- Make sure the user's home directory exists and corresponds to that user's entry in the **/etc/passwd** file. Verify that the user owns his or her home directory and startup files and that they are readable (and, in the case of the home directory, executable). Confirm that the entry for the user's login shell in the **/etc/passwd** file is valid (that is, the entry is accurate and the shell exists as specified).

- Change the user's password if there is a chance that he or she has forgotten the correct password.

- Check the user's startup files (**.profile**, **.login**, **.bashrc**, and so on). The user may have edited one of these files and introduced a syntax error that prevents login.

- Check the terminal or monitor data cable from where it plugs into the terminal to where it plugs into the computer (or as far as you can follow it). Try turning the terminal or monitor off and then turning it back on.

- When the problem appears to be widespread, check whether you can log in from the system console. If you can, make sure that the system is in multiuser mode. If you cannot log in, the system may have crashed; reboot it and perform any necessary recovery steps (the system usually does quite a bit automatically).

- Check that the **/etc/inittab** file is set up to start mingetty at runlevels 2–5.

- Check the **/var/log/messages** file. This file accumulates system errors, messages from daemon processes, and other important information. It may indicate the cause or more symptoms of a problem. Also, check the system console. Occasionally messages about system problems that are not written to **/var/log/messages** (for instance, a full disk) are displayed on the system console.

- If the user is logging in over a network connection, run system-config-services (page 406) to make sure that the service the user is trying to use (such as telnet or ssh) is enabled.

- Use df to check for full filesystems. If the **/tmp** filesystem or the user's home directory is full, login sometimes fails in unexpected ways. In some cases you may be able to log in to a textual environment but not a graphical one. When applications that start when the user logs in cannot create temporary files or cannot update files in the user's home directory, the login process itself may terminate.

SPEEDING UP THE SYSTEM

When the system is running slowly for no apparent reason, perhaps a process did not exit when a user logged out. Symptoms of this problem include poor response time and a system load, as shown by w or uptime, that is greater than 1.0. Running top (page 550) is an excellent way to quickly find rogue processes. Use **ps –ef** to list all processes. One thing to look for in **ps –ef** output is a large number in the **TIME** column. For example, if a Firefox process has a **TIME** field over 100.0, this process has likely run amok. However, if the user is doing a lot of Java work and has not logged out for a long time, this value may be normal. Look at the **STIME** field to see when the process was started. If the process has been running for longer than the user has been logged in, it is a good candidate to be killed.

When a user gets stuck and leaves her terminal unattended without notifying anyone, it is convenient to kill (page 395) all processes owned by that user. If the user is running a window system, such as GNOME or KDE on the console, kill the window manager process. Manager processes to look for include **startkde, gnome-session,** or another process name that ends in **wm.** Usually the window manager is either the first or the last thing to be run, and exiting from the window manager logs the user out. If killing the window manager does not work, try killing the X server process itself. This process is typically listed as **/usr/bin/Xorg**. If that fails, you can kill all processes owned by a user by giving the command **kill –1 –1**, or equivalently **kill –TERM –1** *while you are logged in as that user*. Using **–1** (one) in place of the process ID tells kill that it should send the signal to all processes that are owned by that user. For example, as **root** you could give the following command:

```
# su jenny -c 'kill -TERM -1'
```

If this does not kill all processes (sometimes TERM does not kill a process), you can use the KILL signal. The following line will definitely kill all processes owned by Jenny and will not be friendly about it:

```
# su jenny -c 'kill -KILL -1'
```

(If you do not use **su jenny –c**, the same command brings the system down.)

lsof: FINDS OPEN FILES

The lsof (ls open files) utility locates open files. Its options display only certain processes, only certain file descriptors of a process, or only certain network connections (network connections use file descriptors just as normal files do and lsof can show these as well). Once you have identified a suspect process using **ps –ef**, give the following command:

```
# lsof -sp pid
```

Replace *pid* with the process ID of the suspect process; lsof displays a list of file descriptors that process *pid* has open. The **–s** option displays the sizes of all open files. This size information is helpful in determining whether the process has a very large file open. If it does, contact the owner of the process or, if necessary, kill the process. The **–r***n* option redisplays the output of lsof every *n* seconds.

KEEPING A MACHINE LOG

A machine log that includes the information shown in Table 16-3 (next page) can help you find and fix system problems. Note the time and date for each entry in the log. Avoid the temptation to keep the log *only* on the computer—it will be most useful to you when the system is down. Another good idea is to keep a record of all email about user problems. One strategy is to save this mail to a separate file or folder as you read it. Another approach is to set up a mail alias that users can send mail to when they have problems. This alias can then forward mail to you and also store a copy in an archive file. Following is an example of an entry in the **/etc/aliases** file (page 633) that sets up this type of alias:

```
trouble: admin,/var/spool/mail/admin.archive
```

Email sent to the **trouble** alias will be forwarded to the **admin** user and also stored in the file **/var/mail/admin.archive**.

Table 16-3   Machine log

Entry	Function
Hardware modifications	Keep track of the system hardware configuration: which devices hold which partitions, the model of the new NIC you added, and so on.
System software modifications	Keep track of the options used when building Linux. Print such files as **/usr/src/linux/.config** (Linux kernel configuration) and the X11 configuration file **/etc/X11/xorg.conf**. The file hierarchy under **/etc/sysconfig** contains valuable information about network configuration, among other things.
Hardware malfunctions	Keep as accurate a list as possible of any problems with the system. Make note of any error messages or numbers that the system displays on the system console and identify what users were doing when the problem occurred.
User complaints	Make a list of all reasonable complaints made by knowledgeable users (for example, "machine is abnormally slow").

KEEPING THE SYSTEM SECURE

No system with dial-in lines or public access to terminals is absolutely secure. You can make a system as secure as possible by changing the Superuser password frequently and choosing passwords that are difficult to guess. Do not tell anyone who does not *absolutely* need to know the Superuser password. You can also encourage system users to choose difficult passwords and to change them periodically.

By default, passwords on Red Hat Linux use *MD5* (page 1042) hashing, which makes them more difficult to break than passwords encrypted with DES (page 990). It makes little difference how well encrypted your password is if you make it easy for someone to find out or guess what it is.

A password that is difficult to guess is one that someone else would not be likely to think you would have chosen. Do not use words from the dictionary (spelled forward or backward); names of relatives, pets, or friends; or words from a foreign language. A good strategy is to choose a couple of short words, include some punctuation (for example, put a ^ between them), mix the case, and replace some of the letters in the words with numbers. If it were not printed in this book, an example of a good password would be **C&yGram5** (candygrams). Ideally you would use a random combination of ASCII characters, but that would be difficult to remember.

You can use one of several excellent password-cracking programs to find users who have chosen poor passwords. These programs work by repeatedly encrypting words from dictionaries, phrases, names, and other sources. If the encrypted password matches the output of the program, then the program has found the password of the user. A program that cracks passwords is crack. It and many other programs and security tips are available from CERT (www.cert.org), which was originally called the Computer Emergency Response Team. Specifically look at www.cert.org/tech_tips.

Make sure that no one except Superuser can write to files containing programs that are owned by **root** and run in setuid mode (for example, mail and su). Also make sure that users do not transfer programs that run in setuid mode and are owned by **root** onto the system by means of mounting tapes or disks. These programs can be used to circumvent system security. One technique that prevents users from having setuid files is to use the **–nosuid** flag to mount, which you can set in the flags section in the **fstab** file. Refer to "fstab: Keeps Track of Filesystems" on page 469.

The BIOS in many machines gives you some degree of protection from an unauthorized person modifying the BIOS or rebooting the system. When you set up the BIOS, look for a section named Security. You can probably add a BIOS password. If you depend on the BIOS password, lock the computer case. It is usually a simple matter to reset the BIOS password by using a jumper on the motherboard.

LOG FILES AND MAIL FOR root

Users frequently email **root** and **postmaster** to communicate with the system administrator. If you do not forward **root**'s mail to yourself (**/etc/aliases** on page 633), remember to check **root**'s mail periodically. You will not receive reminders about mail that arrives for **root** when you use su to perform system administration tasks. However, after you use su to become **root**, you can give the command **mail –u root** to look at **root**'s mail.

Review the system log files regularly for evidence of problems. Two important files are **/var/log/messages**, where the operating system and some applications record errors, and **/var/log/maillog**, which contains errors from the mail system.

The logwatch utility (**/usr/sbin/logwatch** points to the Perl script named **/usr/share/logwatch/scripts/logwatch.pl**) is a report writer that sends email reports on log files. By default, this script is run daily (**/etc/cron.daily/0logwatch** points to the same Perl script) and emails its output to **root**. Refer to the logwatch man page and to the script itself for more information.

MONITORING DISK USAGE

Sooner or later you will probably start to run out of disk space. Do not fill up a disk; Linux can write to files significantly faster if at least 5 to 30 percent of the disk space in a given filesystem remains free. Using more than the maximum optimal disk space in a filesystem can degrade system performance.

Fragmentation As a filesystem becomes full, it can become fragmented. This is similar to the DOS concept of fragmentation but is not nearly as pronounced and is typically rare on modern Linux filesystems; by design Linux filesystems are resistant to fragmentation. Keep filesystems from running near full capacity, and you may never need to worry about fragmentation. If there is no space on a filesystem, you cannot write to it at all.

To check for filesystem fragmentation, unmount the filesystem and run fsck on it. The output of fsck includes a percent fragmentation figure for the filesystem. You can defragment a filesystem by backing it up, using mkfs (page 419) to make a clean, empty image, and then restoring the filesystem. Which utility you use to do the backup and restore—dump/restore, tar, cpio, or a third-party backup program—is irrelevant.

Reports   Linux provides several programs that report on who is using how much disk space on which filesystems. Refer to the du, quota, and df man pages and the **–size** option in the find utility man page. In addition to these utilities, you can use the disk quota system to manage disk space.

Four strategies to increase the amount of free space on a filesystem are to compress files, delete files, grow LVM-based filesystems, and condense directories. This section contains some ideas on ways to maintain a filesystem so that it does not become overloaded.

Files that grow quickly   Some files, such as log files and temporary files, grow over time. Core dump files, for example, take up substantial space and are rarely needed. Also, users occasionally run programs that accidentally generate huge files. As the system administrator, you must review these files periodically so that they do not get out of hand.

If a filesystem is running out of space quickly (that is, over a period of an hour rather than weeks or months), first figure out why it is running out of space. Use a **ps –ef** command to determine whether a user has created a runaway process that is creating a huge file. When evaluating the output of ps, look for a process that has consumed a large amount of CPU time. If such a process is running and creating a large file, the file will continue to grow as you free up space. If you remove the huge file, the space it occupied will not be freed until the process terminates, so you need to kill the process. Try to contact the user running the process, and ask the user to kill it. If you cannot contact the user, log in as **root** and kill the process yourself. Refer to kill on page 395 for more information.

You can also truncate a large log file rather than removing it, although you can better deal with this recurring situation with logrotate (discussed in the next section). For example, if the **/var/log/messages** file has become very large because a system daemon is misconfigured, you can use **/dev/null** to truncate it:

```
# cp /dev/null /var/log/messages
```

or

```
# cat /dev/null > /var/log/messages
```

or, without spawning a new process,

```
# : > /var/log/messages
```

If you remove **/var/log/messages**, you have to restart the **syslogd** daemon. If you do not restart **syslogd**, the space on the filesystem is not released.

When no single process is consuming the disk space but capacity has instead been used up gradually, locate unneeded files and delete them. You can archive these files by using cpio, dump, or tar before you delete them. You can safely remove most files named **core** that have not been accessed for several days. The following command line performs this function without removing necessary files named **core** (such as **/dev/core**):

```
# find / -type f -name core | xargs file | grep 'B core file' | sed 's/:ELF.*//g' | xargs rm -f
```

The find command lists all ordinary files named **core** and sends its output to xargs, which runs file on each of the files in the list. The file utility displays a string that includes **B core file** for files created as the result of a core dump. These files need to be removed. The grep command filters out from file lines that do not contain this string. Finally sed removes everything following the colon so that all that is left on the line is the pathname of the **core** file; xargs removes the file.

To free up more disk space, look through the **/tmp** and **/var/tmp** directories for old temporary files and remove them. Keep track of disk usage in **/var/mail**, **/var/spool**, and **/var/log**.

logrotate: MANAGES LOG FILES

Rather than deleting or truncating log files, you may want to keep these files for a while in case you need to refer to them. The logrotate utility helps you manage system log (and other) files automatically by *rotating* (page 1053), compressing, mailing, and removing each as you specify. The logrotate utility is controlled by the **/etc/logrotate.conf** file, which sets default values and can optionally specify files to be rotated. Typically, **logrotate.conf** has an **include** statement that points to utility-specific specification files in **/etc/logrotate.d**. Following is the default **logrotate.conf** file:

```
$ cat /etc/logrotate.conf
# see "man logrotate" for details
# rotate log files weekly
weekly

# keep 4 weeks worth of backlogs
rotate 4

# create new (empty) log files after rotating old ones
create

# uncomment this if you want your log files compressed
#compress

# RPM packages drop log rotation information into this directory
include /etc/logrotate.d

# no packages own wtmp -- we'll rotate them here
/var/log/wtmp {
    monthly
    create 0664 root utmp
    rotate 1
}

# system-specific logs may be also be configured here.
```

The **logrotate.conf** file sets default values for common parameters. Whenever logrotate reads another value for one of these parameters, it resets the default value. You have a choice of rotating files **daily, weekly,** or **monthly**. The number following the **rotate** keyword specifies the number of rotated log files that you want to keep. The

create keyword causes logrotate to create a new log file with the same name and attributes as the newly rotated log file. The **compress** keyword (commented out in the default file) causes log files to be compressed using gzip. The **include** keyword specifies the standard **/etc/logrotate.d** directory for program-specific logrotate specification files. When you install a program using rpm (page 487) or an rpm-based utility such as yum (page 476), rpm puts the logrotate specification file in this directory.

The last set of instructions in **logrotate.conf** takes care of the **/var/log/wtmp** log file (**wtmp** holds login records; you can view this file with the command **who /var/log/wtmp**). The keyword **monthly** overrides the default value of **weekly** *for this utility only* (because the value is within brackets). The **create** keyword is followed by the arguments establishing the permissions, owner, and group for the new file. Finally **rotate** establishes that one rotated log file should be kept.

The **/etc/logrotate.d/cups** file is an example of a utility-specific logrotate specification file:

```
$ cat /etc/logrotate.d/cups
/var/log/cups/*_log {
    missingok
    notifempty
    sharedscripts
    postrotate
        /etc/init.d/cups condrestart >/dev/null 2>&1 || true
    endscript
}
```

This file, which is incorporated in **/etc/logrotate.d** because of the **include** statement in **logrotate.conf**, works with each of the files in **/var/log/cups** that has a filename that ends in **_log** (***_log**). The **missingok** keyword means that no error will be issued when the file is missing. The **notifempty** keyword causes logrotate not to rotate the log file if it is empty, overriding the default action of rotating empty log files. The **sharedscripts** keyword causes logrotate to execute the command(s) in the **prerotate** and **postrotate** sections one time only—not one time for each log that is rotated. Although it does not appear in this example, the **copytruncate** keyword causes logrotate to truncate the original log file immediately after it copies it. This keyword is useful for programs that cannot be instructed to close and reopen their log files because they might continue writing to the original file even after it has been moved. The logrotate utility executes the commands between **prerotate** and **endscript** before the rotation begins. Similarly, commands between **postrotate** and **endscript** are executed after the rotation is complete.

The logrotate utility has many keywords, many of which take arguments and have side effects. Refer to the logrotate man page for details.

REMOVING UNUSED SPACE FROM DIRECTORIES

A directory that contains too many filenames is inefficient. The point at which a directory on an **ext2** or **ext3** filesystem becomes inefficient varies, depending partly on the length of the filenames it contains. Keep directories relatively small. Having fewer than several hundred files (or directories) in a directory is generally a good idea, and having more than several thousand is generally a bad idea. Additionally, Linux uses a caching mechanism for frequently accessed files to speed the process of locating an inode from a filename. This caching mechanism works only on filenames of up to 30 characters in length, so avoid giving extremely long filenames to frequently accessed files.

When a directory becomes too large, you can usually break it into several smaller directories by moving its contents to those new directories. Make sure that you remove the original directory once you have moved all of its contents.

Because Linux directories do not shrink automatically, removing a file from a directory does not shrink the directory, even though it frees up space on the disk. To remove unused space and make a directory smaller, you must copy or move all the files to a new directory *and* remove the original directory.

The following procedure removes unused directory space. First remove all unneeded files from the large directory. Then create a new, empty directory. Next move or copy all remaining files from the old large directory to the new empty directory. Remember to copy hidden files. Finally, delete the old directory and rename the new directory.

```
# mkdir /home/alex/new
# mv /home/alex/large/* /home/alex/large/.[A-z]* /home/alex/new
# rmdir /home/alex/large
# mv /home/alex/new /home/alex/large
```

optional

DISK QUOTA SYSTEM

The disk quota system limits the disk space and number of files owned by individual users. You can choose to limit each user's disk space, the number of files each user can own, or both. Each resource that is limited has two limits. The lower limit, or *quota*, can be exceeded by the user, although a warning is given each time the user logs in when he is above the quota. After a certain number of warnings (set by the system administrator), the system will behave as if the user had reached the upper limit. Once the upper limit is reached or the user has received the specified number of warnings, the user will not be allowed to create any more files or use any more disk space. The user's only recourse at that point is to remove some files.

Users can review their usage and limits with the quota utility. Superuser can use quota to obtain information about any user.

First you must decide which filesystems to limit and how to allocate space among users. Typically only filesystems that contain users' home directories, such as **/home**, are limited. Use the edquota utility to set the quotas, and then use quotaon to start the quota system. You will probably want to put a quotaon command into the appropriate init script so that the quota system will be enabled when you bring up the system (page 404). Unmounting a filesystem automatically disables the quota system for that filesystem.

syslogd: LOGS SYSTEM MESSAGES

Traditionally UNIX programs sent log messages to standard error. If a more permanent log was required, the output was redirected to a file. Because of the limitations of this approach, 4.3BSD introduced the system log daemon (**syslogd**) now used by Linux. This daemon listens for log messages and stores them in the **/var/log** hierarchy. In addition to providing logging facilities, **syslogd** allows a single machine to serve as a log repository for a network and allows arbitrary programs to process specific log messages.

syslog.conf   The **/etc/syslog.conf** file stores configuration information for **syslogd**. Each line in this file contains one or more *selectors* and an *action*, separated by whitespace. The selectors define the origin and type of the messages; the action specifies how **syslogd** is to process the message. Sample lines from **syslog.conf** follow (a # indicates a comment):

```
# Log all kernel messages to the console.
kern.*                                  /dev/console
# Log all the mail messages in one place.
mail.*                                  /var/log/maillog
# Log cron stuff
cron.*                                  /var/log/cron
# Everybody gets emergency messages
*.emerg                                 *
# Save boot messages also to boot.log
local7.*                                /var/log/boot.log
```

Selectors   A selector is split into two parts, a *facility* and a *priority,* which are separated by a period. The facility indicates the origin of the message. For example, **kern** messages come from the kernel and **mail** messages come from the mail subsystem. Following is a list of facility names used by **syslogd** and the systems that generate these messages:

auth	Authorization and security systems including login
authpriv	Same as **auth**, but should be logged to a secure location
cron	cron
daemon	System and network daemons without their own categories
kern	Kernel
lpr	Printing subsystem
mail	Mail subsystem
news	Network news subsystem
user	Default facility; all user programs use this facility
uucp	The UNIX-to-UNIX copy protocol subsystem
local0 to **local7**	Reserved for local use

The priority indicates the severity of the message. The following list of the priority names and the conditions they represent is in priority order:

debug	Debugging information
info	Information that does not require intervention

notice	Conditions that may require intervention
warning	Warnings
err	Errors
crit	Critical conditions such as hardware failures
alert	Conditions that require immediate attention
emerg	Emergency conditions

A selector consisting of a single facility and priority, such as **kern.info**, causes the corresponding action to be applied to every message from that facility with that priority *or higher* (more urgent). Use **.=** to specify a single priority; for example, **kern.=info** applies the action to kernel messages of **info** priority. An exclamation point specifies that a priority is not matched, so **kern.!info** matches kernel messages with a priority lower than **info** and **kern.!=info** matches kernel messages with a priority other than **info**.

A line with multiple selectors, separated by semicolons, applies the action if any of the selectors is matched. Each of the selectors on a line with multiple selectors constrains the match, with subsequent selectors frequently tightening the constraints. For example, the selectors **mail.info;mail.!err** match mail subsystem messages with **info**, **notice**, or **warning** priorities.

You can replace either part of the selector with an asterisk to match anything. The keyword **none** in either part of the selector indicates no match is possible. The selector ***.crit;kern.none** matches all critical or higher-priority messages, except those from the kernel.

Actions   The action specifies how **syslogd** processes a message that matches the selector. The simplest actions are ordinary files, which are specified by their absolute pathnames; **syslogd** appends messages to these files. Specify **/dev/console** if you want messages sent to the system console. If you want a hardcopy record of messages, you can specify a device file that represents a dedicated printer.

You can write important messages to a specific user's terminal by specifying a username, such as **root**, or a comma-separated list of usernames. Very important messages can be written to every logged-in terminal by using an asterisk.

To forward messages to **syslogd** on a remote system, specify the name of the system preceded by @. It is a good idea to forward critical messages from the kernel to another system because these messages often precede a system crash and may not be saved to the local disk. The following line from **syslog.conf** sends critical kernel messages to **grape**:

```
kern.crit        @grape
```

Because **syslogd** is not configured by default to enable logging over the network, you must edit the **/etc/sysconfig/syslog** file on the remote system (**grape** in this case) so that **syslogd** is started with the **–r** option. After you modify the **syslog** file, restart **syslogd** using the **syslog** init script.

CHAPTER SUMMARY

The system-config-users utility adds new users and groups to the system and modifies existing users' accounts. You can also use the equivalent command line tools (useradd, usermod, userdel, groupadd, and groupmod) to work with user accounts. Backing up files on the system is a critical and often overlooked part of system administration. Linux includes the tar, cpio, dump, and restore utilities to back up and restore files. You can also use more sophisticated packages such as amanda and various commercial products.

The system scheduling daemon, **cron**, periodically executes scheduled tasks. You can schedule tasks using crontab, at, and KDE's kcron. System reports present information on the health of the system. Two useful tools that generate these reports are vmstat, which details virtual memory, I/O, and CPU statistics, and top, which reports on how the system is performing from moment to moment and can help you figure out what might be slowing it down.

Another aspect of system administration is solving problems. Linux includes several tools that can help you track down system problems. One of the most important of these tools is **syslogd**, the system log daemon. Using **/etc/syslogd.conf**, you can control which error messages appear on the console, which are sent as email, and which go to one of several log files.

EXERCISES

1. How would you list all the processes running vi?

2. How would you use kill to cause a server process to reread its configuration files?

3. From the command line, how would you create a user named John Doe who has the username **jd** and who belongs to group 65535?

4. How would you notify the users of the system that you are going to reboot the system in 10 minutes?

5. Give a command that will create a level 0 dump of the **/usr** filesystem on the first tape device on the system. Which command would you use to take advantage of a drive that supports compression? Which command would place a level 3 dump of the **/var** filesystem immediately after the level 0 dump on the tape?

ADVANCED EXERCISES

6. If the system is less responsive than normal, what is a good first step in figuring out where the problem is?

7. A process stores its PID in a file named **process.pid**. Write a command line that will terminate the process.

8. Working as **root**, you are planning to delete some files but want to make sure that the wildcard expression you will use is correct. Suggest two ways you could make sure that you deleted the correct files.

9. Create a cron file that will regularly perform the following backups:

   a. Performs a level 0 backup once per month.

   b. Performs a level 2 dump one day per week.

   c. Performs a level 5 dump every day that neither a level 0 nor a level 2 dump is performed.

   In the worst case, how many restores would you have to perform to recover a file that was dumped using the preceding schedule?

17

Configuring a LAN

Networks allow computers to communicate and share resources. A local area network (LAN) connects computers at one site, such as an office, home, or library, and can allow the connected computers to share an Internet connection and a printer. Of course, one of the most important reasons to set up a LAN is to allow systems to communicate while users enjoy multiplayer games.

This chapter covers the two aspects of configuring a LAN: setting up the hardware and configuring the software. This chapter is not necessarily organized in the order you will perform the tasks involved in setting up a particular LAN: Read the chapter through, figure out how you will set up your LAN, and then read the parts of the chapter in the order appropriate to your setup.

SETTING UP THE HARDWARE

Each system, or node, on a LAN must have a network interface card (NIC). NICs can be connected to the network with cables or radio waves (wireless); in either case, each system must connect to a central hub. If the network is connected to another network, such as the Internet, it must also have a router, or gateway. The router can be either one of the systems on the LAN or a dedicated piece of hardware.

CONNECTING THE COMPUTERS

A modern Ethernet-based LAN has a connection between each computer and a central hub. Two kinds of hubs exist: passive (sometimes just called a *hub*) and switching (called a *switch*). A passive hub simply connects all systems together and shares the network bandwidth among the systems. A switching hub puts each system on its own network with the switch and routes packets between those networks, providing each system with the full network bandwidth.

In the simple network shown in Figure 17-1, four computers are connected to a single hub. Assuming the hub is passive, when computers 1 and 2 are communicating at the same time as computers 3 and 4, each conversation is limited to a maximum of half the network bandwidth. If the hub were a switch, each conversation could use the full network bandwidth.

Usually hubs are less expensive than switches. If you plan to use the network for sharing an Internet connection and light file sharing, a hub is likely to be fast enough. If systems on the network will exchange files regularly, a switch may be more appropriate. Refer to "Ethernet" on page 347 for a discussion of switches, hubs, and cables.

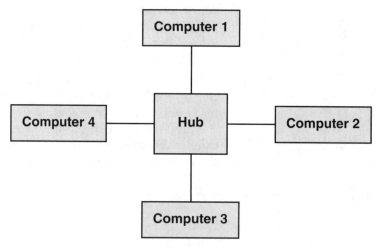

Figure 17-1   A simple network

Each computer on a LAN must be connected to the hub. If you are using use more than one hub, connect the port labeled **uplink** on one to a normal port on another.

Wireless access point (WAP) A wireless access point (WAP) connects a wireless network to a wired one. Typically a WAP acts as a transparent bridge, forwarding packets between the two networks as if they were one. If you connect multiple WAPs in different locations to the same wired network, wireless clients can roam transparently between the WAPs.

Wireless networks do not require a hub, although a WAP can optionally fill a similar role. In a wireless network, the bandwidth is shared among all nodes within range of one another; the maximum speed is limited by the slowest node.

GATEWAYS AND ROUTERS

If the LAN you are setting up is connected to another network, such as the Internet, you need a router, sometimes called a gateway. A router can perform several functions, the most common of which is allowing several systems to share a single Internet connection and IP address (NAT, page 764). When a router uses NAT, the packets from each system on the LAN appear to come from a single IP address; return packets are passed back to the correct system.

You have several choices for routers:

- A simple hardware router is relatively cheap and does most things required by a small network.
- You can set up a Red Hat Linux system as a router. The Linux kernel can use iptables (page 763) to route packets between network adapters.
- You can use a Linux distribution tailored for use as a router. For example, SmoothWall (www.smoothwall.org) provides a browser-based configuration in the style of a hardware router.

NIC: NETWORK INTERFACE CARD

Each system's NIC may be a separate Ethernet card (wired or wireless) or it may be built into the motherboard.

Supported NICs Linux supports most wired Ethernet NICs. Fewer wireless NICs are supported. See "More Information" on page 575 for references.

Unsupported wireless NICs If a wireless network card is not supported under Linux directly, you may be able to get it to work with NdisWrapper (ndiswrapper.sourceforge.net), which uses Win32 drivers. NdisWrapper is a kernel module that provides a subset of the Windows network driver API. No Red Hat package contains this program.

Wireless bridge An alternative to a wireless NIC is a wireless bridge. A wireless bridge forwards packets between wired and wireless interfaces, eliminating the need for wireless drivers. This simple device has an Ethernet port that plugs into a NIC and an 802.11 (wireless) controller. While carrying a bridge around is usually not feasible for mobile users, it is an easy way to migrate a desktop computer to a wireless configuration.

Mode   Wireless networks operate in either ad hoc or infrastructure mode. In ad hoc mode, individual nodes in the network communicate directly with each other. In infrastructure mode, nodes communicate via a WAP (page 569). Infrastructure mode is generally more reliable if the wireless LAN communicates with a wired LAN.

If you do not want to use a WAP, it may be possible to set up a WLAN card so it acts as a WAP; consult the NIC/driver documentation for more information.

CONFIGURING THE SYSTEMS

kudzu   Once the hardware is in place, you need to configure each system so that it knows about the NIC that connects it to the network. Normally kudzu, the Red Hat utility that detects and configures new hardware, gives the system the information it needs about the NIC. The kudzu utility probes the NIC when you install Red Hat Linux or the first time you boot the system after you install a NIC.

You can use system-config-network (discussed in the next section) to augment the information kudzu collects and to activate the NIC. When it prompts you for information, kudzu allows you to specify only one nameserver. It is a good idea to specify at least two or three nameservers; you can use system-config-network to add additional nameservers.

System information   In addition to information about the NIC, each system needs the following information:

- The system's IP address
- The netmask (subnet mask) for the system's address (pages 357 and 423)
- The IP address of the gateway
- The IP addresses of the nameservers (DNS addresses)
- The system's hostname (set when you install Red Hat Linux)

If you set up a DHCP server (page 431) to distribute network configuration information to systems on the LAN, you do not need to specify the preceding information on each system; you just specify that the system is using DHCP to obtain this information. You need to specify this information when you set up the DHCP server.

Private address space   When you set up a LAN, the IP addresses of the systems on the LAN are generally not made public on the Internet. Some special IP addresses, part of the *private address space* defined by *IANA* (page 1036), are reserved for private use and are appropriate to use on a LAN (Table 17-1). Unless you have been assigned IP addresses for the systems on the LAN, choose addresses from the private address space.

Table 17-1   Private IP ranges (defined in RFC 1918)

Range of IP addresses	From IP address	To IP address
10.0.0.0/8	10.0.0.1	10.255.255.254
172.16.0.0/12	172.16.0.1	172.31.255.254
192.168.0.0/16	192.168.0.1	192.168.255.254

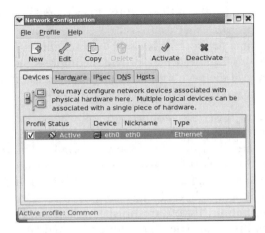

Figure 17-2   The Network Configuration window, Devices tab

system-config-network: CONFIGURES THE HARDWARE

The system-config-network utility configures network hardware. To display the Network Configuration window (Figure 17-2), enter **system-config-network** on a command line. From KDE select **Main menu: System⇨Administration⇨Network** or from GNOME select **System: Administration⇨Network**. The Network Configuration window has tabs to specify hosts (**/etc/hosts**, page 452) and DNS servers (**/etc/resolv.conf**, page 455), as well as to configure network hardware and logical devices associated with the hardware.

Adding a device   Normally kudzu identifies and adds new hardware to the system. You can then use system-config-network to edit the configuration information. If you need to add a NIC to the system manually, click the Devices tab; then click **New** on the toolbar. The utility displays the Select Device Type window (Figure 17-3).

The Select Device Type window can set up six types of connections (most of which do not pertain to setting up a LAN): Ethernet (page 347), *ISDN* (page 1038), modem, *token ring* (page 1060), wireless, and *xDSL* (page 1064). ISDN, modem,

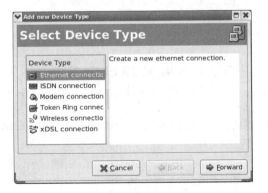

Figure 17-3   The Select Device Type window

wireless, and xDSL are PPP (Point-to-Point Protocol) connections. PPP is a serial line protocol that establishes a connection between two systems, putting them on the same network. It is capable of handling several protocols, the most common of which is TCP/IP, which provides compression for increased efficiency. The two systems can then run ssh, X, or any other network application between them. Ethernet and token ring are used to connect to LANs.

Choose the type of connection you want to establish and click **Forward**. Some selections probe for information at this point. You can accept entries in the text boxes that are filled in in the following window. Fill in blank text boxes as appropriate. When you have finished setting up the device, click **Apply**. The Select Device Type window closes, and the Network Configuration window displays the device you just added. Follow the instructions in the next paragraph to edit the configuration information. If you are finished, click the Devices tab, highlight the new device, click **Menubar: File⇨Save**, and click **Activate** to bring the new device on line.

Editing a device   The Network Configuration window (Figure 17-2) has four tabs, two of which pertain to hardware devices and two of which relate to the system. The Hosts tab modifies the **/etc/hosts** file (page 452) and the DNS tab modifies the system's hostname and the **/etc/resolv.conf** file (page 455). Make changes in these tabs as necessary.

To modify the configuration of network hardware, such as a NIC, click the Hardware tab, highlight the description of the hardware, and click **Edit** on the toolbar. The utility displays the Network Adapters Configuration window. In this window, you can change the name of the device (**eth0, eth1,** and so on) and the resources it uses. Typically you will change only the name. Click **OK** to accept the changes and close the window.

To modify the device represented by a piece of hardware, click the Devices tab, highlight the device, and click **Edit** on the toolbar. The utility displays a window appropriate to the device you are editing. For example, if you are working with an Ethernet NIC, system-config-network displays the Ethernet Device window (Figure 17-4).

From this window, you can set up the device to use DHCP or manually specify the necessary IP addresses. The Hardware Device tab allows you to associate the device with a piece of hardware and specify a *MAC address* (page 1041). When you are finished making changes, click **OK**, click the Devices tab, highlight the new device, and click **Menubar: File⇨Save**. Activate the device if necessary.

iwconfig: CONFIGURES A WIRELESS NIC

You can configure a wireless NIC using either system-config-network (page 571) or iwconfig. The iwconfig utility is based on ifconfig and configures elements of a wireless NIC not supported by ifconfig, such as setting up Master mode and binding a card to a WAP.

The most common parameters you will change with iwconfig are the encryption key, the mode, and the name of the network. Most devices support a minimum of 40-bit

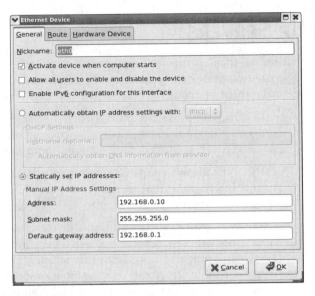

Figure 17-4 The Ethernet Device window

Wired Equivalent Privacy (WEP) encryption. The encryption key is defined by a string of 10 hexadecimal digits. The contents of the string are arbitrary, but must be the same on all nodes:

```
# iwconfig eth1 key 19FEB47A5B
```

The algorithm used by WEP is known to be flawed; using it does not give much protection. If you require privacy, use an encrypted protocol, such as SSH or HTTPS. If you have difficulty connecting, disable encryption on all nodes:

```
# iwconfig eth1 key off
```

The **mode** defines whether you are connecting to an ad hoc or an infrastructure network. Normally you can set **mode** to **Auto**, which selects the correct mode automatically:

```
# iwconfig eth1 mode Auto
```

The exception is if you want to use the NIC as a WAP, in which case you need to set **mode** to **Master**:

```
# iwconfig eth1 mode Master
```

Not all wireless NICs are capable of acting as masters.

The network name is defined by the ESSID (Extended Service Set ID), an arbitrary string. With the ESSID set (it must be the same on every node, including the WAP), you should be able to roam between any set of nodes with the same network name:

```
# iwconfig eth1 essid "My Wireless Network"
```

See the iwconfig man page for more information.

SETTING UP SERVERS

Setting up local clients and servers can make a LAN easier to use and more useful. The following list briefly describes some of these tools and references the pages that describe them in detail.

- **NIS**   NIS can provide a uniform login regardless of which system you log in on. The NIS authentication server is covered on page 663 and the client on page 659. NIS is often combined with home directories mounted using NFS.

- **NFS**   NFS allows you to share directory hierarchies. Sharing directories using NFS requires that the server export the directory hierarchy (page 684) and the clients mount the hierarchy (page 676).

  Using NFS, you can store all home directories on one system and mount them from other systems as needed. This configuration works well with NIS login authentication. With this setup, it can be convenient to create a world-writable directory—for example **/home/shared**—which users can use to exchange files. If you set the sticky bit (page 1057) on this directory (**chmod 1777 /home/shared**), users can delete only files they created. If you do not set the sticky bit, any user can delete any file.

- **OpenSSH**   OpenSSH tools include ssh (logs in on a remote system, page 585) and scp (copies files to/from a remote system, page 588). You can also set up automatic logins with OpenSSH: If you set up a shared home directory with NFS, each user's ~/.ssh directory (page 581) is the same on each system; a user who sets up a personal authentication key (page 592) will be able to use OpenSSH tools between systems without entering a password. See page 591 for information on how to set up an OpenSSH server. You can just use the ssh and scp clients; you do not have to set them up.

- **DNS cache**   Setting up a local cache can reduce the traffic between the LAN and the outside world and can improve response times. For more information refer to "JumpStart I: Setting Up a DNS Cache" on page 733.

- **DHCP**   DHCP enables a client system to retrieve network configuration information from a server each time it connects to a network. See page 431 for more information.

- **Samba**   Samba allows Linux systems to participate in a Windows network, sharing directories and printers, and accessing those shared by Windows systems. Samba includes a special share for accessing users' home directories. For more information refer to "The [homes] Share: Sharing Users' Home Directories" on page 711.

You can also use Samba to set up a shared directory similar to the one described under "NFS." To share a Linux directory with Windows computers, place the following code in **/etc/smb.conf** (page 706):

```
[public]
    comment = Public file space
    path = /home/shared
    read only = no
    public = yes
    browseable = yes
```

Any Windows user can access this share; it can be used to exchange files between users and between Linux and Windows systems.

MORE INFORMATION

Web   SmoothWall Linux distribution   www.smoothwall.org
NdisWrapper   ndiswrapper.sourceforge.net
Hardware compatibility list   hardware.redhat.com

HOWTOs   *Linux Wireless Lan HOWTO*   www.hpl.hp.com/personal/Jean_Tourrilhes/Linux *Wireless HOWTO*

CHAPTER SUMMARY

A local area network (LAN) connects computers at one site and can allow the connected computers to share an Internet connection and a printer. Each system, or node, on a LAN must have a network interface card (NIC). NICs can be connected to the network via cables or radio waves (wireless).

An Ethernet-based LAN has a connection between each computer and a central hub. Two kinds of hubs exist: passive (sometimes just called a *hub*) and switching (faster, called a *switch*). A wireless access point (WAP) connects a wireless network to a wired one. If the LAN you are setting up is connected to another network, such as the Internet, you need a router (gateway). A router can perform several functions, the most common of which is allowing several systems to share a single Internet connection and IP address, called NAT.

You can configure the LAN to use NIS as a login server so that you do not have to set up accounts on each system. You can use NFS, which allows you to mount remote directory hierarchies, to set up a universal home directory. Samba is an important part of many LANs: It allows Linux systems to participate in a Windows network, sharing directories and printers, and accessing those shared by Windows systems.

EXERCISES

1. What advantage does a switch have over a passive hub?

2. Which server would you set up to allow users to log in with the same user-name and password on all computers on a LAN?

3. Name two servers that allow you to share directories between systems.

4. What is a WAP and what does it do?

5. What is a common function of a router? What is this function called?

6. What does a wireless bridge do?

7. What is kudzu? What does it do when you install a new NIC?

8. What is the private address space? When would you use a private address?

ADVANCED EXERCISES

9. If you set a system's subnet mask to 255.255.255.0, how many computers can you put on the network without using a router?

10. Which file stores information about which DNS servers the system uses?

PART V

## CHAPTER 26

USING CLIENTS AND SETTING UP SERVERS

18

OpenSSH: Secure Network Communication

OpenSSH is a suite of secure network connectivity tools that replaces telnet, rcp, rsh/**rshd**, rlogin/**rlogind**, and ftp/**ftpd**. Unlike the tools it replaces, OpenSSH tools encrypt all traffic, including passwords. In this way they thwart malicious users who would eavesdrop, hijack connections, and steal passwords.

This chapter covers the following OpenSSH tools:

- scp   Copies files to/from another system
- sftp   Copies files to/from other systems (a secure replacement for ftp)
- ssh   Runs a command on or logs in on another system
- **sshd**   The OpenSSH daemon (runs on the server)
- ssh-keygen   Creates RSA or DSA host/user authentication keys

INTRODUCTION

Using public key encryption (page 989), OpenSSH provides two levels of authentication: server and client/user. First the client verifies that it is connected to the correct server. Then OpenSSH encrypts communication between the systems. Once a secure, encrypted connection has been established, OpenSSH makes sure that the user is authorized to log in on or copy files from/to the server. After verifying the system and user, OpenSSH allows different services to be passed through the connection. These services include interactive shell sessions (ssh), remote command execution (ssh and scp), X11 client/server connections, and TCP/IP port tunneling.

SSH1 versus SSH2   SSH protocol version 2 (SSH2) is a complete rewrite of SSH protocol version 1 (SSH1) that offers improved security, performance, and portability. The two protocols are not compatible. Because SSH1 is being rapidly supplanted by SSH2 and because SSH1 is vulnerable to a man-in-the-middle attack (footnote 3 on page 992), this chapter does not discuss SSH1. Because version 2 is floating-point intensive, version 1 does have a place on systems without FPUs (floating-point units or accelerators), such as old 486SX systems. As initially installed, the OpenSSH tools supplied with Red Hat Linux support both protocols; you need run only one server to communicate with systems using either protocol.

ssh   The ssh utility allows you to log in on a remote system over a network. You might choose to use a remote system to access a special-purpose application or to use a device that is available only on that system, or you might use a remote system because you know that it is faster or not as busy as the local computer. While traveling, many business-people use ssh on a laptop to log in on a system at company headquarters. From a GUI you can use several systems simultaneously by logging in on each from a different terminal emulator window.

X11 forwarding   With X11 forwarding turned on, as it is when you install Red Hat Linux, it is a simple matter to run an X11 program over an ssh connection: Run ssh from a terminal emulator running on a GUI and give an X11 command such as **xclock**; the graphical output appears on the local display. For more information refer to "Forwarding X11" on page 596.

ABOUT OpenSSH

This section discusses configuration files used by OpenSSH clients and servers, describes how OpenSSH works, and highlights additional OpenSSH resources.

FILES

OpenSSH clients and servers rely on many files. Global files are kept in **/etc/ssh** and user files in **~/.ssh**. In the description of each file, the first word indicates whether the client or the server uses the file.

rhost authentication is a security risk

caution   Although OpenSSH can get authentication information from **/etc/hosts.equiv**, **/etc/shosts.equiv**, **~/.rhosts**, and **~/.shosts**, this chapter does not cover the use of these files because they are security risks. The default settings in the **/etc/ssh/sshd_config** configuration file prevent their use.

/etc/ssh: GLOBAL FILES

Global files listed in this section affect all users but can be overridden by files in a user's **~/.ssh** directory.

moduli   client and server   Contains key exchange information that OpenSSH uses to establish a secure connection. Do not modify this file.

ssh_config   client   The global OpenSSH configuration file (page 589). Entries here can be overridden by entries in a user's **~/.ssh/config** file.

sshd_config   server   The configuration file for **sshd** (page 593).

ssh_host_dsa_key,
ssh_host_dsa_key.pub

server   SSH protocol version 2 DSA host keys. Both files should be owned by **root**. The **ssh_host_dsa_key.pub** public file should be readable by anyone but writable only by its owner (644 permissions). The **ssh_host_dsa_key** private file should not be readable or writable by anyone except its owner (600 permissions).

ssh_host_rsa_key,
ssh_host_rsa_key.pub

server   SSH protocol version 2 RSA host keys. Both files should be owned by **root**. The **ssh_host_rsa_key.pub** public file should be readable by anyone but writable only by its owner (644 permissions). The **ssh_host_rsa_key** private file should not be readable or writable by anyone except its owner (600 permissions).

ssh_known_hosts   client   Contains public RSA (by default) keys of hosts that users on the local system can connect to. This file contains information similar to **~/.ssh/known_hosts**, except it is set up by the administrator and is available to all users. This file should be owned by **root** and should be readable by anyone but writable only by its owner (644 permissions).

sshrc   server   Contains initialization routines. If **~/.ssh/rc** is not present, this script runs after **~/.ssh/environment** and before the user's shell starts.

~/.ssh: USER FILES

OpenSSH creates the **~/.ssh** directory and the **known_hosts** file therein automatically when you connect to a remote system.

authorized_keys   server   Enables you to log in on or copy files from/to another system without supplying a password (page 592). No one except the owner should be able to write to this file.

config   client   A user's private OpenSSH configuration file (page 589). Entries here override those in **/etc/ssh/ssh_config**.

environment server   Contains commands that are executed when a user logs in with ssh. Similar in function to **~/.bashrc** for a local bash shell.

id_dsa, client   User authentication DSA keys generated by ssh-keygen (page 592). Both
id_dsa.pub files should be owned by the user in whose home directory they appear. The **id_dsa.pub** public file should be readable by anyone but writable only by its owner (644 permissions). The **id_dsa** private file should not be readable or writable by anyone except its owner (600 permissions).

id_rsa, client   User authentication RSA keys generated by ssh-keygen (page 592). Both
id_rsa.pub files should be owned by the user in whose home directory they appear. The **id_rsa.pub** public file should be readable by anyone but writable only by its owner (644 permissions). The **id_rsa** private file should not be readable or writable by anyone except its owner (600 permissions).

known_hosts client   Contains public RSA keys (by default) of hosts that the user has connected to. OpenSSH automatically adds entries each time the user connects to a new server (page 584). Refer to "HostKeyAlgorithms" (page 590) for information on using DSA keys.

rc server   Contains initialization routines. This script runs after **environment** and before the user's shell starts. If this file is not present, OpenSSH runs **/etc/ssh/sshrc**; if that file does not exist, OpenSSH runs xauth.

HOW OPENSSH WORKS

When OpenSSH starts, it first establishes an encrypted connection and then authenticates the user. Once these two tasks are completed, OpenSSH allows the two systems to send information back and forth.

OpenSSH uses two key pairs to negotiate an encrypted session: a *host key* pair and a *session key* pair. The host key pair is a set of public/private keys that is established the first time the server system runs **sshd** (page 592), typically the first time the system boots. The session key pair is a set of public/private keys that changes hourly.

The first time an OpenSSH client connects with an OpenSSH server, you are asked to verify that it is connected to the correct server (see "First-time authentication" on page 584). After verification, the client makes a copy of the server's public host key. On subsequent connections, the client compares the key provided by the server with the key it stored. Although this test is not foolproof, the next one is quite secure.

The client then generates a random key, which it encrypts with both the server's public host key and the session key. The client sends this encrypted key to the server. The server, in turn, uses its private keys to decrypt the encrypted key. This process creates a key that is known only to the client and server and is used to encrypt the rest of the session.

MORE INFORMATION

Local   man pages   ssh, scp, ssh-keygen, ssh_config, sshd, sshd_config

Web   OpenSSH home page   www.openssh.com
      Search tldp.org for **ssh** for various HOWTOs and other documents.

Books   *Implementing SSH: Strategies for Optimizing the Secure Shell*
        by Dwivedi; John Wiley & Sons (October 2003)
        SSH, The Secure Shell: The Definitive Guide by Barrett & Silverman;
        O'Reilly & Associates (February 2001)

OpenSSH Clients

This section covers setting up and using the ssh, scp, and sftp clients.

Prerequisites

Install the following packages:

- **openssh**
- **openssh-clients**

There are no startup commands for OpenSSH clients.

JumpStart: Using ssh and scp

The ssh and scp clients do not require setup beyond installing the requisite packages, although you can create and edit files that facilitate their use. To run a secure shell on or securely copy a file to/from a remote system, the following criteria must be met: The remote system must be running the OpenSSH daemon (**sshd**), you must have an account on the remote system, and the server must positively identify itself to the client. The following example shows a user logging in on **grape** as **zach** and then giving an **exit** command to return to the shell on the local system:

```
$ ssh zach@grape
zach@grape's password:
[zach@grape zach]$ exit
Connection to grape closed.
$
```

You can omit *user@* (**zach@** in the preceding example) from the command line if you want to log in as yourself and you have the same username on both systems. The first time you connect to a remote OpenSSH server, ssh or scp asks you to confirm that you are connected to the right system. Refer to "First-time authentication" on page 584.

The following example copies **ty1** from the working directory on the local system to Zach's home directory on **grape**:

```
$ scp ty1 zach@grape:
zach@grape's password:
ty1                    100% |*****************************|  1311      00:00
```

SETUP

This section describes how to set up OpenSSH on the client side.

RECOMMENDED SETTINGS

X11 forwarding   The configuration files provided by Red Hat establish a mostly secure system and may or may not meet your needs. The important OpenSSH default value that the Red Hat configuration files override is ForwardX11Trusted, which is set to **yes** in the Red Hat **/etc/ssh/ssh_config** configuration file (page 595). See page 596 for more information on X11 forwarding.

SERVER AUTHENTICATION/KNOWN HOSTS

known_hosts,   Two files list the hosts the local system has connected to and positively identified:
ssh_known_hosts   **~/.ssh/known_hosts** (user) and **/etc/ssh/ssh_known_hosts** (global). No one except the owner (**root** in the case of the second file) should be able to write to either of these files. No one except the owner should have any access to a **~/.ssh** directory.

First-time   When you connect to an OpenSSH server for the first time, the OpenSSH client
authentication   prompts you to confirm that you are connected to the right system. This checking can help prevent a man-in-the-middle attack (footnote 3 on page 992):

```
The authenticity of host 'grape (192.168.0.3)' can't be established.
RSA key fingerprint is c9:03:c1:9d:c2:91:55:50:e8:19:2b:f4:36:ef:73:78.
Are you sure you want to continue connecting (yes/no)? yes
Warning: Permanently added 'grape,192.168.0.3' (RSA) to the list of
known hosts.
```

Before you respond to the preceding query, make sure you are logging in on the correct system and not on an imposter. If you are not sure, a telephone call to someone who logs in on that system locally can help verify that you are on the intended system. When you answer **yes** (you must spell it out), the client appends the server's public host key (the single line in the **/etc/ssh/ssh_host_rsa_key.pub** or **/etc/ssh/ssh_host_dsa_key.pub** file on the server) to the user's **~/.ssh/known_hosts** file on the local client, creating the **~/.ssh** directory if necessary. So that it can keep track of which line in **known_hosts** applies to which server, OpenSSH prepends the name of the server and the server's IP address (by default) to the line.

When you subsequently use OpenSSH to connect to that server, the client verifies that it is connected to the correct server by comparing this key to the one the server supplies.

known_hosts file   The **known_hosts** file uses one very long line to identify each host it keeps track of. Each line starts with the hostname and IP address of the system the line corresponds to, followed by the type of encryption being used and the server's public host key. The following line (it is one logical line wrapped on to four physical lines) from **known_hosts** is used to connect to **grape** at 192.168.0.3 using *RSA* (page 1053) encryption:

```
$ cat ~/.ssh/known_hosts
grape,192.168.0.3 ssh-rsa AAAAB3NzaC1yc2EAAAABIwAAAIEArinPGsaLUtnSL4V7b
T51ksF7KoScsIk7wqm+2sJEC43rxVNS5+MO/O64UXp5qQOHBmeLCCFCsIJg8xseuVkg9iwO
BKKOdlZdBNVqFS7tnJdBQTFf+ofPIDDip8w6ftHOdM8hZ/diQq5gXqMH+Mpac31pQXAxXgY
SP8NYIgb3X18=
```

OpenSSH automatically stores keys from servers it has connected to in user-private files (**~/.ssh/known_hosts**). These files work only for the user whose directory they appear in. Working as **root** and using a text editor, you can copy lines from a user's private list of known hosts to the public list in **/etc/ssh/ssh_known_hosts** to make a server known globally on the local system.

If, after a remote system's public key is stored in one of the known hosts files, the remote system supplies a different fingerprint when the systems connect, OpenSSH displays the following message and does not complete the connection:

```
@@@@@@@@@@@@@@@@@@@@@@@@@@@@@@@@@@@@@@@@@@@@@@@@@@@@@@@@@@@
@    WARNING: REMOTE HOST IDENTIFICATION HAS CHANGED!    @
@@@@@@@@@@@@@@@@@@@@@@@@@@@@@@@@@@@@@@@@@@@@@@@@@@@@@@@@@@@
IT IS POSSIBLE THAT SOMEONE IS DOING SOMETHING NASTY!
Someone could be eavesdropping on you right now (man-in-the-middle attack)!
It is also possible that the RSA host key has just been changed.
The fingerprint for the RSA key sent by the remote host is
f1:6f:ea:87:bb:1b:df:cd:e3:45:24:60:d3:25:b1:0a.
Please contact your system administrator.
Add correct host key in /home/sam/.ssh/known_hosts to get rid of this message.
Offending key in /home/sam/.ssh/known_hosts:1
RSA host key for grape has changed and you have requested strict checking.
Host key verification failed.
```

If you see this message, you may be the subject of a man-in-the-middle attack. It is more likely, however, that something on the remote system has changed, causing it to supply a new fingerprint. Check with the remote system's administrator. If all is well, remove the offending key from the specified file (the third line from the bottom in the preceding example points to the line you need to remove) and try connecting again. You will see the first-time authentication (page 584) again as OpenSSH verifies that you are connecting to the correct system. Follow the same steps as when you initially connected to the remote host.

ssh: Connects to or Executes Commands on a Remote System

The format of an ssh command line is

ssh [options] [user@]host [command]

where *host,* the name of the OpenSSH server you want to connect to, is the only required argument. The *host* can be a local system name, an FQDN of a system on the Internet, or an IP address. Give the command **ssh** *host* to log in on the remote system *host* with the same username that you are using on the local system. Include *user@* when you want to log in with a username other than the one you are using on the local system. Depending on how things are set up, you may need to supply your password.

Opening a remote shell   Without *command*, ssh logs you in on *host*. The remote system displays a shell prompt and you can run commands on *host*. Give the command **exit** to close the connection to *host* and return to the local system's prompt:

```
[bravo]$ ssh speedy
alex@speedy's password:
Last login: Sat Sep 16 06:51:59 from bravo
Have a lot of fun...
You have new mail.
[speedy]$
...
[speedy]$ exit
Connection to speedy closed.
[bravo]$
```

Running a remote command   When you include *command*, ssh logs in on *host,* executes *command,* closes the connection to *host,* and returns control to the local system. The remote system never displays a prompt.

The following example runs ls in the **memos** directory on the remote system **speedy**. The example assumes that the user running the command (Alex) has a login on **speedy** and that the **memos** directory is in Alex's home directory on **speedy**:

```
[bravo]$ ssh speedy ls memos
alex@speedy's password:
memo.0921
memo.draft
[bravo]$
```

For the next example, assume a file named **memo.new** is in the working directory on the local system (**bravo**). You cannot remember whether this file contains certain changes or whether you made these changes to the file named **memo.draft** on **speedy**. You could copy **memo.draft** to the local system and run diff (page 135) on the two files, but then you would have three similar copies of the file spread across two systems. If you are not careful about removing the old copies when you are done, you may just become confused again in a few days. Instead of copying the file, you can use ssh:

```
[bravo]$ ssh speedy cat memos/memo.draft | diff memos.new -
```

When you run ssh, standard output of the command run on the remote system is passed to the local shell as though the command had been run in place on the local system. As with all shell commands, you must quote special characters that you do not want the local system to interpret. In the preceding example, the output of the cat command on **speedy** is sent through a pipe on **bravo** to diff (running on **bravo**), which compares the local file **memos.new** to standard input (–). The following command line has the same effect but causes diff to run on the remote system:

```
[bravo]$ cat memos.new | ssh speedy diff - memos/memo.draft
```

Standard output from diff on the remote system is sent to the local shell, which displays it on the screen (because it is not redirected).

OPTIONS

This section describes some of the options you can use with ssh.

–C (**compression**) Enables compression. (In the commercial version of ssh, –C disables compression and **+C** enables compression.)

–f (**not foreground**) Sends ssh to the background after asking for a password and before executing the *command*. Useful when you want to run the *command* in the background but must supply a password. Implies **–n**.

–L Forwards a port on the local client to a remote system. For more information refer to "Tunneling/Port Forwarding" on page 596.

–l *user* (**login**) Attempts to log in as *user*.

–n (**null**) Redirects standard input to ssh to come from **/dev/null**. Required when running ssh in the background.

–o *option* (**option**) Specifies *option* in the format used in configuration files (page 589).

–p (**port**) Specifies the port on the remote host that the connection is made to. Using the **host** declaration (page 590) in the configuration file, you can specify a different port for each system you connect to.

–R Forwards a port on the remote system to the local client. For more information refer to "Tunneling/Port Forwarding" on page 596.

–t (**tty**) Allocates a pseudo-tty to the ssh process on the remote system. Without this option, when you run a command on a remote system, ssh does not allocate a tty (terminal) to the process. Instead, ssh attaches standard input and standard output of the remote process to the ssh session—that is normally, but not always, what you want. This option forces ssh to allocate a tty on the remote system so programs that require a tty will work.

–v (**verbose**) Displays debugging messages about the connection and transfer. Useful if things are not going as expected.

–X (**X11**) Turns on nontrusted X11 forwarding. This option is not necessary if you turn on X11 nontrusted forwarding in the configuration file. For more information refer to "Forwarding X11" on page 596.

–x (**X11**) Turns off X11 forwarding.

–Y (**X11trusted**) Turns on trusted X11 forwarding. This option is not necessary if you turn on trusted X11 forwarding in the configuration file. For more information refer to "Forwarding X11" on page 596.

scp: COPIES FILES FROM/TO A REMOTE SYSTEM

The scp (secure copy) utility copies an ordinary or directory file from one system to another on a network. This utility uses ssh to transfer files and employs the same authentication mechanism as ssh; thus it provides the same security as ssh. The scp utility asks you for a password when one is required. The format of an scp command is

scp [[user@]from-host:]source-file [[user@]to-host:][destination-file]

where *from-host* is the name of the system you are copying files from and *to-host* is the system you are copying to. The *from-host* and *to-host* arguments can be local system names, *FQDNs* (page 1032) of systems on the Internet, or IP addresses. When you do not specify a host, scp assumes the local system. The *user* on either system defaults to the user on the local system who is giving the command; you can specify a different user with *user@*. The scp utility can copy between two remote systems.

The *source-file* is the file you are copying, and the *destination-file* is the resulting copy. Make sure that you have read permission for the file you are copying and write permission for the directory you are copying it into. You can specify plain or directory files as relative or absolute pathnames. (A relative pathname is relative to the specified or implicit user's home directory.) When the *source-file* is a directory, you must use the –r option to copy its contents. When the *destination-file* is a directory, each of the source files maintains its simple filename. When the *destination-file* is missing, scp assumes the user's home directory.

Sam has an alternate username, **sls**, on **grape**. In the following example, Sam uses scp to copy **memo.txt** from the home directory of his **sls** account on **grape** to the **allmemos** directory in the working directory on the local system. If **allmemos** was not the name of a directory, **memo.txt** would be copied to a file named **allmemos** in the working directory.

```
$ scp sls@grape:memo.txt allmemos
sls@grape's password:
memo.txt              100% |*********************************| 14664        00:00
```

As the transfer progresses, the percent and number of bytes transferred increase and the time remaining decreases. The asterisks provide a visual representation of the progress of the transfer.

In the next example, Sam, while working from **peach**, copies the same file as in the previous example to the directory named **old** in Sam's home directory on **speedy**. For this example to work, Sam must be able to use ssh to log in on **speedy** from **grape** without using a password. For more information refer to "Authorized Keys: Automatic Login" on page 592.

```
$ [sam@peach] scp sls@grape:memo.txt speedy:old
sam@grape's password:
```

Options

This section describes some of the options you can use with scp.

−C (**compression**) Enables compression.

−o *option* (**option**) Specifies *option* in the format used in configuration files (discussed shortly).

−P *port* (**port**) Connects to port *port* on the remote host.

−p (**preserve**) Preserves the modification and access times as well as the modes of the original file.

−q (**quiet**) Does not display the progress meter.

−r (**recursive**) Recursively copies a directory hierarchy.

−v (**verbose**) Displays debugging messages about the connection and transfer. Useful if things are not going as expected.

sftp: A Secure FTP Client

As part of OpenSSH, Red Hat Linux provides sftp, a secure alternative to ftp (page 601). Functionally the same as ftp, sftp maps ftp commands into OpenSSH commands. You can replace ftp with sftp when you are logging in on a server that is running the OpenSSH daemon, **sshd**. Once you are connected to a system with sftp, give the command ? to display a list of commands. For secure communication, use sftp or scp to perform all file transfers requiring authentication. Refer to the sftp man page for more information.

~/.ssh/config and /etc/ssh/ssh_config Configuration Files

It is rarely necessary to modify OpenSSH client configuration files. For a given user there may be two configuration files: **~/.ssh/config** (user) and **/etc/ssh/ssh_config** (global). These files are read in this order and, for a given parameter, the first one found is the one that is used. A user can override a global parameter setting by setting the same parameter in his user configuration file. Parameters given on the ssh or scp command line take precedence over parameters set in either of these files.

A user's **~/.ssh/config** file must be owned by the user (the owner of the **~/** directory) and must not be writable by anyone except the owner; if it is, the client will exit with an error message. This file is typically set to mode 600 as there is no reason for anyone except its owner to be able to read it.

Lines in the configuration files contain declarations that start with a keyword, which is not case sensitive, followed by whitespace, and end with case-sensitive arguments.

You can use the **Host** keyword to cause declarations to apply to a specific system. A Host declaration applies to all the lines between it and the next Host declaration. You can use * and ? wildcards within a hostname.

Host *hostnames* Specifies that the following declarations, until the next Host declaration, apply to *hostnames* only. The *hostnames* should be in the same form you would use on a command line and can contain ? and * wildcards. A single * specifies all hosts.

CheckHostIP yes | no

Uses an IP address in addition to a hostname to identify a system in the **known_hosts** file when set to **yes** (default). Set to **no** to use a hostname only.

ForwardX11 yes | no

When set to **yes**, automatically forwards X11 connections over a secure channel in nontrusted mode and sets the **DISPLAY** shell variable . Alternatively, you can use –**X** on the command line to redirect X11 connections in nontrusted mode. The default value for this parameter is **no**. For X11 forwarding to work, X11Forwarding must also be set to **yes** in the **/etc/sshd_config** file on the server (page 595). For more information refer to "Forwarding X11" on page 596.

ForwardX11Trusted yes | no

When set to **yes**, automatically forwards X11 connections over a secure channel in trusted mode and sets the **DISPLAY** shell variable. Alternatively, you can use –**Y** on the command line to redirect X11 connections in trusted mode. The default value for this parameter is **no** but Red Hat Linux sets it to **yes**. For X11 forwarding to work, X11Forwarding must also be set to **yes** in the **/etc/sshd_config** file on the server (page 595). For more information refer to "Forwarding X11" on page 596.

HostbasedAuthentication yes | no

Tries **rhosts** authentication when set to **yes**. For a more secure system, set to **no** (default).

HostKeyAlgorithms *algorithms*

The *algorithms* is a comma-separated list of algorithms that the client uses in order of preference. Choose *algorithms* from **ssh-rsa** or **ssh-dss** (default is **ssh-rsa,ssh-dss**).

TCPKeepAlive yes | no

Periodically checks whether a connection is alive when set to **yes** (default). This checking causes the ssh or scp connection to be dropped when the server crashes or the connection dies for another reason, even if it is only temporary. Setting this parameter to **no** causes the client not to check whether the connection is alive.

This declaration uses the TCP **keepalive** option, which is not encrypted and is susceptible to *IP spoofing* (page 1038). Refer to "ClientAliveInterval" on page 594 for a server-based nonspoofable alternative.

StrictHostKeyChecking yes | no | ask

Determines whether and how OpenSSH adds host keys to a user's **known_hosts** file. Set to **ask** (default) to ask whether to add a host key when connecting to a new system, set to **no** to add a host key automatically, and set to **yes** to require that host keys be added manually. The **yes** and **ask** arguments cause OpenSSH to refuse to connect to a system whose host key has changed. For a more secure system, set to **yes** or **ask**.

User *name*   Specifies a username to use when logging in on a system. Specify systems with the Host declaration. This option means that you do not have to enter a username on the command line when you are using a username that differs from your username on the local system.

sshd: OpenSSH Server

This section discusses how to set up an OpenSSH server.

Prerequisites

Install the following packages:

- **openssh**
- **openssh-server**

Run chkconfig to cause **sshd** to start when the system enters multiuser mode:

```
# /sbin/chkconfig sshd on
```

See "Starting **sshd** for the First Time" (page 592) for information on starting the server for the first time.

Notes

Firewall   An OpenSSH server normally uses TCP port 22. If the OpenSSH server system is running a firewall, you need to open this port. Using the Red Hat graphical firewall tool (page 768), select **SSH** from the Trusted Services frame to open this port. For more general information see Chapter 25, which details iptables.

SELinux   When SELinux is set to use a targeted policy, **sshd** is protected by SELinux. You can disable this protection if necessary. For more information refer to "Setting the Targeted Policy with system-config-securitylevel" on page 402.

JumpStart: Starting the sshd Daemon

Install the requisite packages and start the **sshd** daemon as described following. Look in **/var/log/secure** to make sure everything is working properly.

Recommended Settings

The configuration files provided by Red Hat establish a mostly secure system and may or may not meet your needs. The Red Hat **/etc/ssh/sshd_config** file turns on X11 forwarding (page 596). For a more secure system, you can set PermitRootLogin to **no**, thereby removing a known-name, privileged account that is exposed to the outside world with only password protection.

STARTING sshd FOR THE FIRST TIME

When you start the **sshd** OpenSSH daemon for the first time, generally when you first boot the system after installation, it automatically creates host key files (page 581) in **/etc/ssh**:

```
# /sbin/service sshd start
Generating SSH1 RSA host key:                              [  OK  ]
Generating SSH2 RSA host key:                              [  OK  ]
Generating SSH2 DSA host key:                              [  OK  ]
Starting sshd:                                             [  OK  ]
```

OpenSSH uses the files it creates to identify the server.

AUTHORIZED KEYS: AUTOMATIC LOGIN

You can configure OpenSSH so you do not have to enter a password each time you connect to a remote system. To set things up, you need to generate a personal authentication key, place the public part of the key on the remote server, and keep the private part of the key on the local client. When you connect, the remote system issues a challenge based on the public part of the key. The private part of the key is required to respond properly to the challenge. If the local system provides the appropriate response, the remote system logs you in.

The first step in setting up an automatic login is to generate your personal authentication keys. Check whether these authentication keys already exist: Look in **~/.ssh** for either **id_dsa** and **id_dsa.pub** or **id_rsa** and **id_rsa.pub**. If one of these pairs of files is present, skip the next step (do not create a new key).

The **ssh-keygen** utility creates the public and private parts of an RSA key:

ssh-keygen

```
$ ssh-keygen -t rsa
Generating public/private rsa key pair.
Enter file in which to save the key (/home/sam/.ssh/id_rsa):RETURN
Created directory '/home/sam/.ssh'.
Enter passphrase (empty for no passphrase):RETURN
Enter same passphrase again:RETURN
Your identification has been saved in /home/sam/.ssh/id_rsa.
Your public key has been saved in /home/sam/.ssh/id_rsa.pub.
The key fingerprint is:
f2:eb:c8:fe:ed:fd:32:98:e8:24:5a:76:1d:0e:fd:1d sam@peach
```

Replace **rsa** with **dsa** to generate DSA keys. In this example, the user pressed RETURN in response to each query. You have the option of specifying a passphrase (10–30 characters is a good length) to encrypt the private part of the key. There is no way to recover a lost passphrase. See the following security tip for more information about the passphrase.

The **ssh-keygen** utility generates two keys: a private key or identification in **~/.ssh/id_rsa** and a public key in **~/.ssh/id_rsa.pub**. No one except the owner should be able to write to either of these files. Only the owner should be able to read from the private key file.

authorized_keys   To enable you to log in on or copy files from/to another system without supplying a password, first create a ~/.ssh directory with permissions set to 700 on the remote system. Next copy ~/.ssh/id_rsa.pub on the local system to a file named ~/.ssh/authorized_keys on the remote system. No one except the owner should be able to read from or write to this file. Now when you run ssh or scp to access the remote system, you do not have to supply a password. To make the system even more secure, you can disable password authentication by setting PasswordAuthentication to **no** in /etc/sshd_config.

When you encrypt your personal key

security   The private part of the key is kept in a file that only you can read. If a malicious user compromises either your account or the **root** account on the local system, that user then has access to your account on the remote system because she can read the private part of your personal key.

Encrypting the private part of your personal key protects the key and, therefore, restricts access to the remote system should someone compromise your local account. However, if you encrypt your personal key, you must supply the passphrase you used to encrypt the key each time you use the key, negating the benefit of not having to type a password when logging in on the remote system. Also, most passphrases that you can remember can be cracked quite quickly by a powerful computer.

A better idea is to store the private keys on a removable medium, such as a USB flash drive, and have your ~/.ssh directory as the mount point for the filesystem stored on this drive.

COMMAND LINE OPTIONS

Command line options override declarations in the configuration files. Following are descriptions of some of the more useful **sshd** options.

−d   (**debug**) Sets debug mode wherein **sshd** sends debugging messages to the system log and the server stays in the foreground. You can specify this option up to three times to increase the verbosity of the output. See also −e. (The ssh client uses −v for debugging; see page 587.)

−e   (**error**) Sends output to standard error, not to the system log. Useful with −d.

−f *file*   (**file**) Specifies the file with the pathname *file* as the default configuration file instead of /etc/ssh/sshd_config.

−t   (**test**) Checks the configuration file syntax and the sanity of the key files.

−D   (**noDetach**) Keeps **sshd** in the foreground. Useful for debugging; implied by −d.

/etc/ssh/sshd_config CONFIGURATION FILE

The /etc/ssh/sshd_config configuration file contains one-line declarations that start with a keyword, which is not case sensitive, followed by whitespace, and end with case-sensitive arguments.

AllowUsers *userlist*

The *userlist* is a SPACE-separated list of usernames that specifies users who are allowed to log in using **sshd**. This list can include * and ? wildcards. You can specify a user as *user* or *user@host*. If you use the second format, make sure that you specify the host as returned by hostname. Without this declaration, any user who can log in locally can log in using an OpenSSH client.

ClientAliveCountMax *n*

The *n* specifies the number of client-alive messages that can be sent without receiving a response before **sshd** disconnects from the client. See ClientAliveInterval. Default is 3.

ClientAliveInterval *n*

Sends a message through the encrypted channel after *n* seconds of not receiving a message from the client. See ClientAliveCountMax. Default is 0, meaning that no messages are sent.

This declaration passes messages over the encrypted channel and is not susceptible to *IP spoofing* (page 1038). It differs from TCPKeepAlive, which uses the TCP **keepalive** option and is susceptible to IP spoofing.

HostbasedAuthentication yes | no

Tries **rhosts** authentication when set to **yes**. For a more secure system, set to **no** (default).

IgnoreRhosts yes | no

Ignores **.rhosts** and **.shosts** files for authentication. Does not affect the use of **/etc/hosts.equiv** and **/etc/ssh/shosts.equiv** files for authentication. For a more secure system, set to **yes** (default).

LoginGraceTime *n*

Waits *n* seconds for a user to log in on the server before disconnecting. A value of 0 means there is no time limit. The default is 120.

LogLevel *val*   Specifies how detailed the log messages are. Choose *val* from QUIET, FATAL, ERROR, INFO, and VERBOSE. The default is INFO.

PasswordAuthentication

Permits a user to use a password for authentication. Default is **yes**.

PermitEmptyPasswords

Permits a user to log in to an account that has an empty password. Default is **no**.

PermitRootLogin   Permits **root** to log in using an OpenSSH client. For a more secure system, set to **no**. The default is **yes**.

StrictModes yes | no

Checks modes and ownership of user's home directory and files. Login fails if the directories and/or files can be written to by anyone. For security, set to **yes** (default).

TCPKeepAlive yes | no

Periodically checks whether a connection is alive when set to **yes** (default). Checking causes the ssh or scp connection to be dropped when the client crashes or the connection dies for another reason, even if it is only temporary. Setting this parameter to **no** causes the server not to check whether the connection is alive.

This declaration uses the TCP **keepalive** option, which is not encrypted and is susceptible to *IP spoofing* (page 1038). Refer to ClientAliveInterval (page 594) for a nonspoofable alternative.

X11Forwarding yes | no

Allows X11 forwarding when set to **yes**. The default is **no**, but Red Hat Linux sets X11Forwarding to **yes**. For X11 forwarding to work, the ForwardX11 declaration or the ForwardX11Trusted declaration must also be set to **yes** in either the **~/.ssh/config** or **/etc/ssh/ssh_config** client configuration file (page 590). For more information refer to "Forwarding X11" on page 596.

TROUBLESHOOTING

Log files There are several places to look for clues when you have a problem connecting with ssh or scp. First look for **sshd** entries in **/var/log/secure** and **/var/log/messages** on the server. Following are messages you may see when you are using an AllowUsers declaration but have not included the user who is trying to log in (page 593):

```
# grep sshd /var/log/secure
grape sshd[16]: User sam not allowed because not listed in AllowUsers
grape sshd[16]: Failed password for illegal user sam from 192.168.0.6 port 59276 ssh2
```

The next messages originate with PAM (page 438) and indicate that the user is not known to the system:

```
# grep sshd /var/log/messages
grape sshd(pam_unix)[2817]: check pass; user unknown
grape sshd(pam_unix)[2817]: authentication failure; logname= uid=0
euid=0 tty=NODEVssh ruser= rhost=peach.sobell.com
```

Debug the client If entries in these files do not help solve the problem, try connecting with the **−v** option (either ssh or scp—the results should be the same). OpenSSH displays a lot of messages and one of them may help you figure out what the problem is.

```
$ ssh -v grape
OpenSSH_4.2p1, OpenSSL 0.9.8a 11 Oct 2005
debug1: Reading configuration data /etc/ssh/ssh_config
debug1: Applying options for *
debug1: Connecting to grape [192.168.0.3] port 22.
debug1: Connection established.
debug1: identity file /home/sam/.ssh/identity type -1
debug1: identity file /home/sam/.ssh/id_rsa type 1
...
debug1: Host 'grape' is known and matches the RSA host key.
debug1: Found key in /home/sam/.ssh/known_hosts:2
debug1: ssh_rsa_verify: signature correct
...
debug1: Authentications that can continue: publickey,password,keyboard-interactive
debug1: Trying private key: /home/sam/.ssh/id_dsa
debug1: Next authentication method: keyboard-interactive
debug1: Authentications that can continue: publickey,password,keyboard-interactive
debug1: Next authentication method: password
sam@grape's password:
```

Debug the server You can debug from the server side by running **sshd** with the **−de** options. The server will run in the foreground and its display may help you solve the problem.

TUNNELING/PORT FORWARDING

The ssh utility allows you to forward a port (*port forwarding,* page 1049) through the encrypted connection it establishes. Because the data sent across the forwarded port uses the encrypted ssh connection as its data link layer (page 351), the term *tunneling* (page 1061) is applied to this type of connection: "The connection is tunneled through ssh." You can secure protocols—including POP, X, IMAP, and WWW—by tunneling them through ssh.

Forwarding X11   The ssh utility makes it easy to tunnel the X11 protocol. For X11 tunneling to work, you must enable it on both the server and the client. On the server, you enable X11 forwarding by setting the X11Forwarding declaration to **yes** in the **/etc/ssh/sshd_config** file (page 595).

Trusted clients   In the past there was only one way for a client to enable X11 forwarding; today there are two ways. Previously, when you enabled X11 forwarding (by setting ForwardX11 to **yes** in a configuration file or by using the –X option on the ssh command line) on a client, the client connected as a trusted client, which meant that the client trusted the server, and was given full access to the X11 display. With full access to the X11 display, in some situations a client may be able to modify other clients of the X display. Make a secure connection only when you trust the remote system. (You do not want someone tampering with your client.) If this concept is confusing, see the tip "The roles of X client and server may be counterintuitive" on page 235.

Nontrusted clients   As of Fedora Core 3 and RHEL version 4 (OpenSSH 3.8 and later), an ssh client can connect to an ssh server as a trusted client or as a nontrusted client. A nontrusted client is given limited access to the X11 display and cannot modify other clients of the X display.

Few clients work properly when they are run in nontrusted mode. If you are running an X client in nontrusted mode and you encounter problems, try running in trusted mode (assuming you trust the remote system). Red Hat Linux sets up ssh clients to run in trusted mode by default.

Running ssh   When you start an ssh client, you can use the –Y option (page 587) on the command line to start the client in trusted mode. This option performs the same function as the –X option did in earlier versions of ssh. Or you can set the ForwardX11trusted declaration to **yes** in a user's **~/.ssh/config** configuration file (page 590) or, working as **root**, you can set ForwardX11trusted to **yes** in the global **/etc/ssh/ssh_config** file (page 590) to enable trusted X11 tunneling.

To use nontrusted tunneling you can use the –X option (page 587) or set the ForwardX11 declaration to **yes** in one of the configuration files (page 590).

With X11 forwarding turned on, ssh tunnels the X11 protocol, setting the **DISPLAY** environment variable on the system it connects to and forwarding the required port. You must have the **DISPLAY** variable set. Typically you will be running from a GUI, which usually means that you are using ssh on a terminal emulator to connect to a remote system. When you give an X11 command from an ssh prompt, OpenSSH creates a new secure channel that carries the X11 data. The graphical output from the X11 program appears on your screen.

```
[peach] $ ssh speedy
[speedy] $ echo $DISPLAY
localhost:10.0
```

By default, ssh uses X Window System display numbers 10 and higher (port numbers 6010 and higher) for forwarded X sessions. Once you connect to a remote system using ssh, you can give a command to run an X application. The application will then run on the remote system with its display appearing on the local system, so that it appears to run locally.

Port forwarding You can forward arbitrary ports using the –L and –R options. The –L option forwards a local port to a remote system, so that a program that tries to connect to the forwarded port on the local system transparently connects to the remote system. The –R option does the reverse: It forwards remote ports to the local system. The –N option, which prevents ssh from executing remote commands, is generally used with –L and –R. When you specify –N, ssh works only as a private network to forward ports. An ssh command line using one of these options has the following format:

$ *ssh –N –L | –R local-port:remote-host:remote-port target*

where *local-port* is the number of the local port that is being forwarded to or from *remote-host*, *remote-host* is the name or IP address of the system that *local-port* gets forwarded to or from, *remote-port* is the number of the port on *remote-host* that is being forwarded from or to the local system, and *target* is the name or IP address of the system ssh connects to.

As an example, assume that there is a POP mail client on the local system and that the POP server is on a remote network, on a system named **pophost**. POP is not a secure protocol; passwords are sent in cleartext each time the client connects to the server. You can make it more secure by tunneling POP through ssh (POP-3 connects on port 110; port 1550 is an arbitrary port on the local system):

```
$ ssh -N -L 1550:pophost:110 pophost
```

After giving the preceding command, you can point the POP client at **localhost:1550**, and the connection between the client and the server will be encrypted. (When you set up an account on the POP client, specify the location of the server as **localhost, port 1550**; details vary with different mail clients.) In this example, *remote-host* and *target* are the same system.

Firewalls The system specified for port forwarding (*remote-host*) does not have to be the same as the destination of the ssh connection (*target*). As an example, assume the POP server is behind a firewall and you cannot connect to it via ssh. If you can connect to the firewall via the Internet using ssh, you can encrypt the part of the connection over the Internet:

```
$ ssh -N -L 1550:pophost:110 firewall
```

Here *remote-host,* the system receiving the port forwarding, is **pophost,** and *target,* the system that ssh connects to, is **firewall.**

You can also use ssh when you are behind a firewall (that is running **sshd**) and want to forward a port into your system without modifying the firewall settings:

```
$ ssh -R 1678:localhost:80 firewall
```

The preceding command forwards connections from the outside to port 1678 on the firewall to the local Web server. Forwarding connections in this manner allows you to use a Web browser to connect to port 1678 on the firewall in order to connect to the Web server on the local system. This setup would be useful if you ran a Webmail program (page 644) on the local system because it would allow you to check your mail from anywhere using an Internet connection.

Compression   Compression, which is enabled with the **–C** option, can speed up communication over a low-bandwidth connection. This option is commonly used with port forwarding. Compression can increase latency to an extent that may not be desirable for an X session forwarded over a high-bandwidth connection.

Chapter Summary

OpenSSH is a suite of secure network connectivity tools that encrypts all traffic, including passwords, thereby thwarting malicious users who might otherwise eavesdrop, hijack connections, and steal passwords. The components discussed in this chapter are **sshd** (the server daemon), ssh (runs a command on or logs in on another system), scp (copies files to/from another system), sftp (securely replaces ftp), and ssh-keygen (creates authentication keys).

To ensure secure communications, when an OpenSSH client opens a connection, it first verifies that it is connected to the correct server. Then OpenSSH encrypts communication between the systems. Finally OpenSSH makes sure that the user is authorized to log in on or copy files from/to the server.

OpenSSH also enables secure X11 forwarding. With this feature, you can run securely a graphical program on a remote system and have the display appear on the local system.

Exercises

1. What is the difference between the scp and sftp utilities?

2. How can you use ssh to find out who is logged in on a remote system?

3. How would you use scp to copy your **~/.bashrc** file from **bravo** to the local system?

4. How would you use ssh to run xterm on **bravo** and show the display on the local system?

5. What problem can enabling compression present when using ssh to run remote X11 applications on a local display?

6. When you try to connect to another system using an OpenSSH client and you see a message warning you that the remote host identification has changed, what has happened? What should you do?

ADVANCED EXERCISES

7. Which scp command would you use to copy your home directory from **bravo** to the local system?

8. Which single command could you give to log in as **root** on the remote system named **bravo,** if **bravo** has remote **root** logins disabled?

9. How could you use ssh to compare the contents of the **~/memos** directories on **bravo** and the local system?

19

FTP: Transferring Files Across a Network

File Transfer Protocol is a method of downloading files from and uploading files to another system using TCP/IP over a network. File Transfer Protocol is the name of a client/server protocol (FTP) and a client utility (ftp) that invokes the protocol. In addition to the original ftp utility, there are many textual and graphical FTP client programs, including most browsers, that run under many different operating systems. There are also many FTP server programs.

INTRODUCTION

First implemented under 4.2BSD, FTP has played an essential role in the propagation of Linux; this protocol/program is frequently used to distribute free software. The term *FTP site* refers to an FTP server that is connected to a network, usually the Internet. FTP sites can be public, allowing anonymous users to log in and download software and documentation. In contrast, private FTP sites require you to log in with a username and password. Some sites allow you to upload programs.

ftp and **vsftpd**   Although most FTP clients are similar, the servers differ quite a bit. This chapter describes the ftp client with references to sftp, a secure FTP client. It also covers the FTP server that Red Hat uses internally and offers as part of its distribution, **vsftpd** (very secure FTP).

Security   FTP is not a secure protocol. All usernames and passwords exchanged in setting up an FTP connection are sent in cleartext, data exchanged over an FTP connection is not encrypted, and the connection is subject to hijacking. FTP is best used for downloading public files. In most cases, the OpenSSH clients, ssh (page 585), scp (page 588), and sftp (page 589), offer secure alternatives to FTP.

Use FTP only to download public information

security   FTP is not secure. You can use scp for almost all FTP functions other than allowing anonymous users to download information. Because scp uses an encrypted connection, user passwords and data cannot be sniffed. See page 585 for more information on scp.

The **vsftpd** server does *not* make usernames, passwords, data, and connections more secure. The **vsftpd** server is secure in that a malicious user finds it more difficult to compromise directly the system running it, even if **vsftpd** is poorly implemented. One feature that makes **vsftpd** more secure than **ftpd** is that it does not run with **root** privileges. See also "Security" on page 613.

ftp utility   The ftp utility is a user interface to File Transfer Protocol (FTP), the standard protocol used to transfer files between systems that can communicate over a network.

sftp utility   Part of the OpenSSH suite, sftp is a secure alternative to ftp. See page 589 for more information.

FTP connections   FTP uses two connections: one for control (you establish this connection when you log in on an FTP server) and one for data transfer (FTP sets up this connection when you ask it to transfer a file). An FTP server listens for incoming connections on port 21 by default and handles user authentication and file exchange.

Passive versus active connections   A client can ask an FTP server to establish either a PASV (passive—the default) or a PORT (active) connection for data transfer. Some servers are limited to only one type of connection. The difference between a passive and an active FTP connection lies in whether the client or server initiates the data connection. In passive mode, the client initiates the connection to the server (on port 20 by default); in active mode, the server initiates the connection (there is no default port; see "Connection Parameters" on page 622 for the parameters that determine which ports are used). Neither is inherently more secure than the other. Passive connections are more common because a client behind a NAT (page 764) can connect to a passive server and it is simpler to program a scalable passive server.

The parameters that control the type of connection that a **vsftpd** server allows are discussed under "Connection Parameters" on page 622.

MORE INFORMATION

Local   Type **help** or **?** at an **ftp>** prompt to display a list of commands. Follow the **?** with a SPACE and an **ftp** command to display information about that command.
Files   **/usr/share/doc/vsftpd**✻
man pages   **ftp, netrc, vsftpd.conf**

Web   **vsftpd** home page   vsftpd.beasts.org

HOWTO   *FTP mini-HOWTO*

FTP CLIENT

ftp   Red Hat supplies several FTP clients including ftp (an older version of the BSD ftp utility). This section discusses ftp because most other FTP clients provide a superset of ftp commands.

sftp   Part of the OpenSSH suite, sftp is a secure alternative to ftp. See page 589 for more information.

gftp   The gftp utility (**gftp** package) is a graphical client that works with FTP, SSH, and HTTP servers. This client has many useful features, including the ability to resume an interrupted file transfer. See the gftp man page for more information.

ncftp   The ncftp utility (**ncftp** package) is a textual client that offers many more features than ftp, including filename completion and command line editing. See the ncftp man page for details.

PREREQUISITES

The ftp and sftp utilities are installed on most Red Hat systems. You can check for their presence by giving either of these utilities' names as commands:

```
$ ftp
ftp> quit

$ sftp
usage: sftp [-1Cv] [-B buffer_size] [-b batchfile] [-F ssh_config]
            [-o ssh_option] [-P sftp_server_path] [-R num_requests]
            [-S program] [-s subsystem | sftp_server] host
       sftp [[user@]host[:file [file]]]
       sftp [[user@]host[:dir[/]]]
       sftp -b batchfile [user@]host
```

Install the **ftp** or **openssh-clients** (contains sftp) package if needed.

JUMPSTART: DOWNLOADING FILES USING ftp

This JumpStart section is broken into two parts: a description of the basic commands and a tutorial session that shows a user working with ftp.

BASIC COMMANDS

Give the command

```
$ ftp hostname
```

where *hostname* is the name of the FTP server you want to connect to. If you have an account on the server, log in with your username and password. If it is a public system, log in as the user **anonymous** (or **ftp**) and give your email address as your password. Use the **ls** and **cd** ftp commands on the server as you would use the corresponding utilities from a shell. The command **get** *file* copies *file* from the server to the local system, **put** *file* copies *file* from the local system to the server, **status** displays information about the FTP connection, and **help** displays a list of commands.

The preceding instructions, except for **status**, also work from sftp and ncftp.

TUTORIAL SESSION

Following are two ftp sessions wherein Alex transfers files from and to a **vsftpd** server named **bravo**. When Alex gives the command **ftp bravo**, the local ftp client connects to the server, which asks for a username and password. Because he is logged in on his local system as **alex**, ftp suggests that Alex log in on **bravo** as **alex**. To log in as **alex**, he could just press RETURN. Because his username on **bravo** is **watson**, however, he types **watson** in response to the **Name (bravo:alex):** prompt. Alex responds to the **Password:** prompt with his normal system password, and the **vsftpd** server greets him and informs him that it is **Using binary mode to transfer files**. With ftp in binary mode, Alex can transfer ASCII and binary files (page 608).

Connect and log in

```
$ ftp bravo
Connected to bravo.
220 (vsFTPd 2.0.4)
530 Please login with USER and PASS.
530 Please login with USER and PASS.
KERBEROS_V4 rejected as an authentication type
Name (bravo:alex): watson
331 Please specify the password.
Password:
230 Login successful.
Remote system type is UNIX.
Using binary mode to transfer files.
ftp>
```

After logging in, Alex uses the ftp **ls** command to see what is in his remote working directory, which is his home directory on **bravo**. Then he **cd**s to the **memos** directory and displays the files there.

ls and cd

```
ftp> ls
227 Entering Passive Mode (192,168,0,6,79,105)
150 Here comes the directory listing.
drwxr-xr-x    2 500        500          4096 Oct 10 23:52 expenses
```

```
drwxr-xr-x    2 500        500           4096 Oct 10 23:59 memos
drwxrwxr-x   22 500        500           4096 Oct 10 23:32 tech
226 Directory send OK.

ftp> cd memos
250 Directory successfully changed.

ftp> ls
227 Entering Passive Mode (192,168,0,6,114,210)
150 Here comes the directory listing.
-rw-r--r--    1 500        500           4770 Oct 10 23:58 memo.0514
-rw-r--r--    1 500        500           7134 Oct 10 23:58 memo.0628
-rw-r--r--    1 500        500           9453 Oct 10 23:58 memo.0905
-rw-r--r--    1 500        500           3466 Oct 10 23:59 memo.0921
-rw-r--r--    1 500        500           1945 Oct 10 23:59 memo.1102
226 Directory send OK.
```

Next Alex uses the ftp **get** command to copy **memo.1102** from the server to the local system. Binary mode ensures that he will get a good copy of the file regardless of whether it is binary or ASCII. The server confirms that this file was copied successfully and reports on the size of the file and how long it took to copy. Alex then copies the local file **memo.1114** to the remote system. The file is copied into his remote working directory, **memos**.

get and **put**
```
ftp> get memo.1102
local: memo.1102 remote: memo.1102
227 Entering Passive Mode (192,168,0,6,194,214)
150 Opening BINARY mode data connection for memo.1102 (1945 bytes).
226 File send OK.
1945 bytes received in 7.1e-05 secs (2.7e+04 Kbytes/sec)

ftp> put memo.1114
local: memo.1114 remote: memo.1114
227 Entering Passive Mode (192,168,0,6,174,97)
150 Ok to send data.
226 File receive OK.
1945 bytes sent in 2.8e-05 secs (6.8e+04 Kbytes/sec)
```

Now Alex decides he wants to copy all the files in the **memo** directory on **bravo** to a new directory on his local system. He gives an **ls** command to make sure he will copy the right files, but ftp has timed out. Instead of exiting from ftp and giving another ftp command from the shell, he gives ftp an **open bravo** command to reconnect to the server. After logging in, he uses the ftp **cd** command to change directories to **memos** on the server.

Timeout and **open**
```
ftp> ls
No control connection for command: Bad file descriptor
Passive mode refused.  Turning off passive mode.
No control connection for command: Bad file descriptor
ftp> open bravo
Connected to bravo (192.168.0.6).
220 (vsFTPd 1.1.3)
...
ftp> cd memos
250 Directory successfully changed.
```

Local cd (**lcd**)   At this point, Alex realizes he has not created the new directory to hold the files he wants to download. Giving an ftp **mkdir** command would create a new directory on the server, but Alex wants a new directory on his local system. He uses an exclamation point (**!**) followed by a **mkdir memos.hold** command to invoke a shell and run mkdir on the local system, creating a directory named **memos.hold** in his working directory on the local system. (You can display the name of your working directory on the local system with **!pwd**.) Next, because Alex wants to copy files from the server to the **memos.hold** directory on his local system, he has to change his working directory on the local system. Giving the command **!cd memos.hold** will not accomplish what Alex wants to do because the exclamation point will spawn a new shell on the local system and the **cd** command would be effective only in the new shell, which is not the shell that ftp is running under. For this situation, ftp provides the **lcd** (local **cd**) command, which changes the working directory for ftp and reports on the new local working directory:

```
ftp> !mkdir memos.hold

ftp> lcd memos.hold
Local directory now /home/alex/memos.hold
```

Alex uses the ftp **mget** (multiple get) command followed by the asterisk (*****) wildcard to copy all files from the remote **memos** directory to the **memos.hold** directory on the local system. When ftp prompts him for the first file, Alex realizes that he forgot to turn off prompts, so he responds with **n** and presses CONTROL-C to stop copying files in response to the second prompt. The server checks whether he wants to continue with his **mget** command.

Next Alex gives the ftp **prompt** command, which toggles the prompt action (turns it off if it is on and turns it on if it is off). Now when he gives a **mget *** command, ftp copies all the files without prompting him. After getting the desired files, Alex gives a **quit** command to close the connection with the server, exit from ftp, and return to the local shell prompt.

mget and **prompt**

```
ftp> mget *
mget memo.0514? n
mget memo.0628? CONTROL-C
Continue with mget? n

ftp> prompt
Interactive mode off.

ftp> mget *
local: memo.0514 remote: memo.0514
227 Entering Passive Mode (192,168,0,6,53,55)
150 Opening BINARY mode data connection for memo.0514 (4770 bytes).
226 File send OK.
4770 bytes received in 8.8e-05 secs (5.3e+04 Kbytes/sec)
local: memo.0628 remote: memo.0628
227 Entering Passive Mode (192,168,0,6,65,102)
150 Opening BINARY mode data connection for memo.0628 (7134 bytes).
226 File send OK.
```

```
...
150 Opening BINARY mode data connection for memo.1114 (1945 bytes).
226 File send OK.
1945 bytes received in 3.9e-05 secs (4.9e+04 Kbytes/sec)
ftp> quit
221 Goodbye.
```

NOTES

A Linux system running ftp can exchange files with any of the many operating systems that support FTP. Many sites offer archives of free information on an FTP server, although for many it is just an alternative to an easier-to-access Web site (see, for example, ftp://ftp.ibiblio.org/pub/Linux and http://www.ibiblio.org/pub/Linux). Most browsers can connect to and download files from FTP servers.

The ftp utility makes no assumptions about filesystem naming or structure because you can use ftp to exchange files with non-UNIX/Linux systems (which may use different filenaming conventions).

ANONYMOUS FTP

Many systems—most notably those from which you can download free software—allow you to log in as **anonymous**. Most systems that support anonymous logins accept the name **ftp** as an easier-to-spell and quicker-to-enter synonym for **anonymous**. An anonymous user is usually restricted to a portion of a filesystem set aside to hold files that are to be shared with remote users. When you log in as an anonymous user, the server prompts you to enter a password. Although any password may be accepted, by convention you are expected to supply your email address. Many systems that permit anonymous access store interesting files in the **pub** directory. Most browsers, such as Firefox, log in on an anonymous FTP site and transfer a file when you click on the filename.

AUTOMATIC LOGIN

You can store server-specific FTP username and password information so that you do not have to enter it each time you visit an FTP site. Each line of ~/.netrc identifies a server. When you connect to an FTP server, ftp reads the ~/.netrc file to determine whether you have an automatic login set up for that server. The format of a line in ~/.netrc is

   machine **server** *login* **username** *password* **passwd**

where **server** is the name of the server, **username** is your username, and **passwd** is your password on **server**. Replace **machine** with **default** on the last line of the file to specify a username and password for systems not listed in ~/.netrc. The **default** line is useful for logging in on anonymous servers. A sample ~/.netrc file follows:

```
$ cat ~/.netrc
machine bravo login alex password mypassword
default login anonymous password alex@tcorp.com
```

To protect the account information in **.netrc**, make it readable by only the user whose home directory it appears in. Refer to the **netrc** man page for more information.

BINARY VERSUS ASCII TRANSFER MODE

The **vsftpd** FTP server can—but does not always—provide two modes to transfer files. Binary mode transfers always copy an exact, byte-for-byte image of a file and never change line endings. Transfer all binary files using binary mode. Unless you need to convert line endings, use binary mode to transfer ASCII files as well.

ASCII files, such as text or program source code, when created under Linux with a text editor such as vi, use a single NEWLINE character (CONTROL-J, written as **\n**) to mark the end of each line. Other operating systems mark the ends of lines differently. Windows marks the end of each such line with a RETURN (CONTROL-M, written as **\r**) followed by a NEWLINE (two characters). Macintosh uses a RETURN by itself. These descriptions do not apply to files created by word processors such as Word or OpenOffice because those programs generate binary files.

The **vsftpd** FTP server can map Linux line endings to Windows line endings as you upload files and Windows line endings to Linux line endings as you download files. Although you could argue that these features should be on the client and not the server, they are incorporated in **vsftpd**, where the ASCII download feature can be a security risk.

To use ASCII mode on an FTP server that allows it, give an **ascii** command (page 610) after you log in and set **cr** to ON (the default, page 610). If the server does not allow you to change line endings as you transfer a file, you can use the unix2dos (page 139) or dos2unix (page 139) utility before or after you transfer a file in binary mode.

Security   When run against a very large file, the ftp **size** command, which displays the size of a file, consumes a lot of server resources and can be used to initiate a *DoS attack* (page 1030). To enhance security, by default **vsftpd** transfers every file in binary mode, even when it appears to be using ASCII mode. On the server side, you can enable *real* ASCII mode transfers by setting the **ascii_upload_enable** and **ascii_download_enable** parameters (page 619) to YES. With the server set to allow ASCII transfers, the client controls whether line endings are mapped by using the **ascii**, **binary**, and **cr** commands (page 610).

ftp SPECIFICS

This section covers the details of using ftp.

FORMAT

An ftp command line has the following format:

ftp [options] [ftp-server]

where *options* is one or more options from the list in the next section and *ftp-server* is the name or network address of the FTP server that you want to exchange files with. If you do not specify an *ftp-server*, you will need to use the ftp **open** command to connect to a server once ftp is running.

COMMAND LINE OPTIONS

–g (**globbing**) Turns off globbing. See **glob** (page 610).

–i (**interactive**) Turns off prompts during file transfers with **mget** (page 610) and **mput** (page 610). See also **prompt** (page 611).

–n (**no automatic login**) Disables automatic logins (page 607).

–v (**verbose**) Tells you more about how ftp is working. Responses from the remote computer are displayed, and ftp reports information on how quickly files are transferred. See also **verbose** (page 612).

ftp COMMANDS

The ftp utility is interactive: After you start ftp, it prompts you to enter commands to set parameters or transfer files. You can abbreviate commands as long as the abbreviations are unique. Enter a question mark (**?**) in response to the **ftp>** prompt to display a list of commands. Follow the question mark by a SPACE and a command to display a brief description of what the command does:

```
ftp> ? mget
mget            get multiple files
```

SHELL COMMAND

![*command*] Without *command*, escapes to (spawns) a shell on the local system. Use CONTROL-D or **exit** to return to ftp when you are finished using the local shell. Follow the exclamation point with *command* to execute that command only; ftp displays an **ftp>** prompt when execution of the command finishes. Because the shell that ftp spawns with this command is a child of the shell that is running ftp, no changes you make in this shell are preserved when you return to ftp. Specifically, when you want to copy files to a local directory other than the directory that you started ftp from, you need to use the ftp **lcd** command to change your local working directory: Issuing a **cd** command in the spawned shell will not make the change you desire. See "Local cd (lcd)" on page 606 for an example.

TRANSFER FILES

In the following descriptions, *remote-file* and *local-file* can be pathnames.

append *local-file* [*remote-file*]
Appends *local-file* to the file of the same name on the remote system or to *remote-file* if specified.

get *remote-file* [*local-file*]
Copies *remote-file* to the local system under the name *local-file*. Without *local-file*, ftp uses *remote-file* as the filename on the local system.

mget *remote-file-list*

> (**multiple get**) Copies several files to the local system, each maintaining its original filename. You can name the remote files literally or use wildcards (see **glob**). Use **prompt** (page 611) to turn off prompts during transfers.

mput *local-file-list*

> (**multiple put**) Copies several files to the server, each maintaining its original filename. You can name the local files literally or use wildcards (see **glob**). Use **prompt** (page 611) to turn off prompts during transfers.

newer *remote-file* [*local-file*]

> If the modification time of *remote-file* is more recent than that of *local-file* or if *local-file* does not exist, copies *remote-file* to the local system under the name *local-file*. Without *local-file*, ftp uses *remote-file* as the filename on the local system. Similar to **get**, but does not overwrite a newer file with an older one.

put *local-file* [*remote-file*]

> Copies *local-file* to the remote system under the name *remote-file*. Without *remote-file*, ftp uses *local-file* as the filename on the remote system.

reget *remote-file* [*local-file*]

> If *local-file* exists and is smaller than *remote-file*, assumes that a previous **get** of *local-file* was interrupted and continues from where the previous **get** left off. This command can save time when a **get** of a large file fails partway through the transfer.

STATUS

ascii Sets the file transfer type to ASCII. The **cr** command must be ON for **ascii** to work (page 608).

binary Sets the file transfer type to binary (page 608).

bye Closes the connection to the server and terminates ftp. Same as **quit**.

case Toggles and displays case mapping status. Default is OFF. When ON, for **get** and **mget** commands, maps filenames that are all uppercase on the server to all lowercase on the local system.

close Closes the connection to the server without exiting from ftp.

cr (**carriage** RETURN) Toggles and displays (carriage) RETURN stripping status. Effective only when the file transfer type is **ascii**. Set **cr** to ON (default) to remove RETURN characters from RETURN/LINEFEED line termination sequences used by Windows, yielding the standard Linux line termination of LINEFEED. Set **cr** to OFF to leave line endings unmapped (page 608).

debug [*n*] Toggles/sets and displays debugging status/level, where *n* is the debugging level. OFF or 0 (zero) is the default. When *n* > 0, displays each command ftp sends to the server.

glob Toggles and displays filename expansion (page 221) status for **mdelete** (page 611), **mget** (page 610), and **mput** (page 610) commands.

hash   Toggles and displays pound sign (#, also called a hash mark) display status. When ON, ftp displays one pound sign for each 1024-byte data block it transfers.

open [*hostname*]

Specifies *hostname* as the name of the server to connect to. Without *hostname*, prompts for the name of the server. Useful when a connection times out or otherwise fails.

passive   Toggles between active (PORT—the default) and passive (PASV) transfer modes and displays the transfer mode. For more information refer to "Passive versus active connections" on page 602.

prompt   Toggles and displays the prompt status. When ON (default), **mdelete** (page 611), **mget** (page 610), and **mput** (page 610) ask for verification before transferring each file. Set to OFF to turn off these prompts.

quit   Closes the connection to the server and terminates ftp. Same as **bye**.

umask [*nnn*]   Changes the umask (page 420) applied to files created on the server to *nnn*. Without *nnn*, displays the umask.

user [*username*] [*password*]

Prompts for or accepts the *username* and *password* that enable you to log in on the server. When you call it with the –n option, ftp prompts you for a username and password automatically. For more information refer to "Automatic Login" on page 607.

DIRECTORIES

cd *remote-directory*

Changes the working directory on the server to *remote-directory*.

cdup   Changes the working directory on the server to the parent of the working directory.

lcd [*local_directory*]

(**local change directory**) Changes the working directory on the local system to *local_directory*. Without an argument, this command changes the working directory on the local system to your home directory (just as the cd shell builtin does without an argument). See "Local cd (lcd)" on page 606 for an example.

FILES

chmod *mode remote-file*

Changes the access permissions of *remote-file* on the server to *mode*. See chmod on page 182 for more information on how to specify the *mode*.

delete *remote-file*   Removes *remote-file* from the server.

mdelete *remote-file-list*

(**multiple delete**) Deletes the files specified by *remote-file-list* from the server.

DISPLAY INFORMATION

dir [*remote-directory*] [*file*]

    Displays a listing of **remote-directory** from the server. When you do not specify **remote-directory**, displays the working directory. When you specify *file*, the listing is saved on the local system in a file named *file*.

help [*command*] Displays information about **command**. Without **command**, displays a list of local ftp commands.

ls [*remote-directory*] [*file*]

    Similar to **dir** but produces a more concise listing from some servers. When you specify *file*, the listing is saved on the local system in a file named *file*.

pwd Displays the pathname of the working directory on the server. Use **!pwd** to display the pathname of the local working directory.

status Displays ftp connection and status information.

verbose Toggles and displays verbose mode, which displays responses from the server and reports on how quickly files are transferred. Same as specifying the **–v** option on the command line.

FTP SERVER (vsftpd)

    This section discusses the **vsftpd** server as supplied by Red Hat.

PREREQUISITES

    Install the following package:

- **vsftpd**

    Run chkconfig to cause **vsftpd** to start when the system enters multiuser mode.

        `# /sbin/chkconfig vsftpd on`

    Start **vsftpd**:

        `# /sbin/service vsftpd start`

    If you change the **vsftpd.conf** configuration file, you need to restart **vsftpd**.

NOTES

    The **vsftpd** server can run in normal mode (the **xinetd** daemon [page 425] calls **vsftpd** each time a client tries to make a connection) or it can run in stand-alone mode (**vsftpd** runs as a daemon and handles connections directly).

Stand-alone mode Although by default **vsftpd** runs in normal mode, Red Hat sets it up to run in stand-alone mode by setting the **listen** parameter (page 615) to YES in the **vsftpd.conf** file. Under Red Hat Linux, with **vsftpd** running in stand-alone mode, you start and stop the server using service and the **vsftpd** init script.

Normal mode   You must install an **xinetd** control file (page 425) if you want to run **vsftpd** in normal mode. A sample file can be found at **/usr/share/doc/vsftpd*/vsftpd.xinetd**. Copy the sample file to the **/etc/xinetd.d** directory, rename it **vsftpd**, and edit the file to change the **disable** parameter to **no**. With the **listen** parameter in **vsftpd.conf** set to NO, **xinetd** will take care of starting **vsftpd** as needed.

Security   The safest policy is not to allow users to authenticate against FTP: Use FTP for anonymous access only. If you do allow local users to authenticate and upload files to the server, be sure to put local users in a chroot jail (page 616). Because FTP sends usernames and passwords in cleartext, a malicious user can easily *sniff* (page 1056) them. With a username and password, the same user can impersonate a local user, upload a *Trojan horse* (page 1060), and compromise the system.

Firewall   An FTP server normally uses TCP port 21. If the FTP server system is running a firewall, you need to open this port. Using the Red Hat graphical firewall tool (page 768), select **FTP** from the Trusted Services frame to open this port. For more general information see Chapter 25, which details iptables.

SELinux   When SELinux is set to use a targeted policy, FTP is protected by SELinux. You can disable this protection if necessary. For more information refer to "Setting the Targeted Policy with system-config-securitylevel" on page 402.

JumpStart: Starting a vsftpd Server

By default, under Red Hat Linux **vsftpd** allows local and anonymous users to log in on the server and does not set up a guest account. When someone logs in as an anonymous user, that person is working in the **/var/ftp** directory. You do not have to configure anything.

Testing the Setup

Make sure **vsftpd** is working by logging in from the system running the server. You can refer to the server as **localhost** or by using its hostname on the command line. Log in as **anonymous**; use any password.

```
$ ftp localhost
Connected to localhost.localdomain.
220 (vsFTPd 2.0.4)
530 Please login with USER and PASS.
530 Please login with USER and PASS.
KERBEROS_V4 rejected as an authentication type
Name (bravo:alex): anonymous
331 Please specify the password.
Password:
230 Login successful.
Remote system type is UNIX.
Using binary mode to transfer files.
ftp> quit
221 Goodbye.
```

If you are not able to connect to the server, first make sure the server is running:

```
$ /sbin/service vsftpd status
vsftpd (pid 3091) is running...
```

Next check that permissions on **/var/ftp**, or the home directory of ftp as specified in **/etc/passwd**, are set to 755. If the **ftp** user can write to **/var/ftp**, connections will fail.

```
# ls -ld /var/ftp
drwxr-xr-x 4 root root 4096 Aug 27 23:54 /var/ftp
```

Once you are able to log in from the local system, log in from another system—either one on the LAN or another system with access to the server. On the command line, use the hostname from within the LAN or the *FQDN* (page 1032) from outside the LAN. The dialog should appear the same as in the previous example. If you cannot log in from a system that is not on your LAN, use ping (page 365) to test the connection and make sure the firewall is set up to allow FTP access. See "FTP connections" on page 602 for a discussion of active and passive modes and the ports that each mode uses.

vsftpd.conf: THE vsftpd CONFIGURATION FILE

The configuration file for **vsftpd**, **/etc/vsftpd/vsftpd.conf**, lists Boolean, numeric, and string name-value pairs of configuration parameters, called directives. Each name-value pair is joined by an equal sign with no SPACEs on either side. Red Hat Linux provides a well-commented **/etc/vsftpd/vsftpd.conf** file that changes many of the compiled-in defaults. This section covers most of the options, noting their default values and their values as specified in the **vsftpd.conf** file supplied with Red Hat Linux.

Set Boolean options to YES or NO and numeric options to a nonnegative integer. Octal numbers, which are useful for setting umask options, must have a leading 0 (zero). Numbers without a leading zero are treated as base 10 numbers. Following are examples from **vsftpd.conf** of setting each type of option:

```
anonymous_enable=YES
local_umask=022
xferlog_file=/var/log/vsftpd.log
```

Descriptions of the directives are broken into the following groups:

- Stand-alone mode (page 615)
- Logging in (page 615)
- Working directory and the chroot jail (page 616)
- Downloading and uploading files (page 618)
- Messages (page 620)
- Display (page 620)
- Logs (page 621)
- Connection parameters (page 622)

STAND-ALONE MODE

Refer to "Notes" on page 607 for a discussion of normal and stand-alone modes. This section describes the parameters that affect stand-alone mode.

listen   YES runs **vsftpd** in stand-alone mode; NO runs it in normal mode.

Default: NO
Red Hat: YES

listen_address   In stand-alone mode, specifies the IP address of the local interface that **vsftpd** listens on for incoming connections. When not set, **vsftpd** uses the default network interface.

Default: none

listen_port   In stand-alone mode, specifies the port that **vsftpd** listens on for incoming connections.

Default: 21

max_clients   In stand-alone mode, specifies the maximum number of clients. Zero (0) indicates unlimited clients.

Default: 0

max_per_ip   In stand-alone mode, specifies the maximum number of clients from the same IP address. Zero (0) indicates unlimited clients from the same IP address.

Default: 0

LOGGING IN

Three classes of users can log in on a **vsftpd** server: anonymous, local, and guest. The guest user is rarely used and is not covered in this chapter. Local users log in with their system username and password. Anonymous users log in with **anonymous** or **ftp**, using their email address as a password. You can control whether each of these classes of users can log in on the server and what they can do once they log in. You can also specify what a local user can do on a per-user basis; refer to **user_config_dir** on page 624.

LOCAL USERS

userlist_enable   The **/etc/vsftpd/user_list** file (page 624), or another file specified by **userlist_file**, contains a list of zero or more users. YES consults this list and takes action based on **userlist_deny**, either granting or denying users in the list permission to log in on the server. To prevent the transmission of cleartext passwords, access is denied immediately after the user enters her username. NO does not consult the list. For a more secure system, set to NO.

Default: NO
Red Hat: YES

userlist_deny   YES prevents users listed in **/etc/vsftpd/user_list** (page 624) from logging in on the server. NO allows *only* users listed in **/etc/vsftpd/user_list** to log in on the server.

Use **userlist_file** to change the name of the file that this parameter consults. This parameter is checked only when **userlist_enable** is set to YES.

Default: YES

userlist_file   The name of the file consulted when **userlist_enable** is set to YES.

Default: **/etc/vsftpd/user_list**

local_enable   YES permits local users (users listed in **/etc/passwd**) to log in on the server.

Default: NO
Red Hat: YES

ANONYMOUS USERS

anonymous_enable

YES allows anonymous logins.

Default: YES

no_anon_password

YES skips asking anonymous users for passwords.

Default: NO

deny_email_enable

YES checks whether the password (email address) that an anonymous user enters is listed in **/etc/vsftpd/banned_emails** or other file specified by **banned_email_file**. If it is, the user is not allowed to log in on the system. NO does not perform this check. Using iptables (page 763) to block specific hosts is generally more productive than using this parameter.

Default: NO

banned_email_file

The name of the file consulted when **deny_email_enable** is set to YES.

Default: **/etc/vsftpd/banned_emails**

WORKING DIRECTORY AND THE chroot JAIL

When a user logs in on a **vsftpd** server, standard filesystem access permissions control which directories and files the user can access and how the user can access them. Three basic parameters control a user who is logged in on a **vsftpd** server:

- User ID (UID)
- Initial working directory
- Root directory

By default, the **vsftpd** server sets the user ID of a local user to that user's username and sets the user ID of an anonymous user to **ftp**. A local user starts in her home directory and an anonymous user starts in **/var/ftp**.

By default, anonymous users are placed in a chroot jail for security; local users are not. For example, when an anonymous user logs in on a **vsftpd** server, his home directory is **/var/ftp**. All that user sees, however, is that his home directory is **/**. The user sees the directory at **/var/ftp/upload** as **/upload**. The user cannot see, or work with, for example, the **/home**, **/usr/local**, or **/tmp** directories. The user is in a chroot jail. For more information refer to "Setting Up a chroot Jail" on page 428.

You can use the **chroot_local_user** option to put each local user in a chroot jail whose root is the user's home directory. You can use **chroot_list_enable** to put selected local users in chroot jails.

chroot_list_enable

Upon login, YES checks whether a local user is listed in **/etc/vsftpd/chroot_list** (page 624) or another file specified by **chroot_list_file**.

When a user is in the list and **chroot_local_user** is set to NO, the user is put in a chroot jail in his home directory. Only users listed in **/etc/vsftpd/chroot_list** are put in chroot jails.

When a user is in the list and **chroot_local_user** is set to YES, that user is not put in a chroot jail. Users not listed in **/etc/vsftpd/chroot_list** are put in chroot jails.

Default: NO

chroot_local_user

See **chroot_list_enable**. Set to NO for a more open system, but remember to add new users to the **chroot_list_file** as needed when you add users to the system. Set to YES for a more secure system. New users are automatically restricted unless you add them to **chroot_list_file**.

Default: NO

chroot_list_file The name of the file consulted when **chroot_list_enable** is set to YES.

Default: **/etc/vsftpd/chroot_list**

passwd_chroot_enable

YES enables you to change the location of the chroot jail that the **chroot_list_enable** and **chroot_local_user** settings impose on a local user.

The location of the chroot jail can be moved up the directory structure by including a **/./** within the home directory string for that user in **/etc/passwd**. This change has no effect on the standard system login, just as a **cd .** command has no effect on the working directory.

For example, changing the home directory field in **/etc/passwd** (page 454) for Sam from **/home/sam** to **/home/./sam** allows Sam to cd to **/home** after logging in using **vsftpd**. Given the proper permissions, Sam can now view files and possibly collaborate with another user.

Default: NO

secure_chroot_dir The name of an empty directory that is not writable by the user **ftp**. The **vsftpd** server uses this directory as a secure chroot jail when the user does not need access to the filesystem.

Default: **/usr/share/empty**

local_root After a local user logs in on the server, this directory becomes the user's working directory. No error results if the specified directory does not exist.

Default: none

DOWNLOADING AND UPLOADING FILES

By default, any user—whether local or anonymous—can download files from the **vsftpd** server, assuming proper filesystem access and permissions. You must change **write_enable** from NO (default) to YES to permit local users to upload files. By default, **local_umask** is set to 022, giving uploaded files 644 permissions (page 180).

Security Refer to "Security" on page 613 for information on the security hole that is created when you allow local users to upload files.

The following actions set up **vsftpd** to allow anonymous users to upload files:

1. Set **write_enable** (page 619) to YES.

2. Create a directory under **/var/ftp** that an anonymous user can write to but not read from (mode 333). You do not want a malicious user to be able to see, download, modify, and upload a file that another user originally uploaded. The following commands create a **/var/ftp/uploads** directory that anyone can write to but no one can read from:

```
# mkdir /var/ftp/uploads
# chmod 333 /var/ftp/uploads
```

Because of the security risk, **vsftpd** prevents anonymous connections when an anonymous user (**ftp**) can write to **/var/ftp**.

3. Set **anon_upload_enable** (page 619) to YES.

4. See the other options in this section.

DOWNLOAD/UPLOAD FOR LOCAL USERS

local_umask The umask (page 420) setting for local users.

Default: 077
Red Hat: 022

file_open_mode Uploaded file permissions for local users. The umask (page 420) is applied to this value. Change to 0777 to make uploaded files executable.

Default: 0666

write_enable
: YES permits users to create and delete files and directories (assuming appropriate filesystem permissions). NO prevents users from making changes to the filesystem.

> Default: NO
> Red Hat: YES

Anonymous Users

anon_mkdir_write_enable
: YES permits an anonymous user to create new directories when **write_enable**=YES and the anonymous user has permission to write to the parent directory.

> Default: NO

anon_other_write_enable
: YES grants an anonymous user write permission in addition to the permissions granted by **anon_mkdir_write_enable** and **anon_upload_enable**. For example, YES allows an anonymous user to delete and rename files, assuming permission to write to the parent directory. Not recommended for secure sites.

> Default: NO

anon_root
: After an anonymous user logs in on the server, this directory becomes the user's working directory. No error results if the specified directory does not exist.

> Default: none

anon_umask
: The umask (page 420) setting for anonymous users. The default setting gives only anonymous users access to files uploaded by anonymous users; set to 022 to give everyone read access to these files.

> Default: 077

anon_upload_enable
: YES allows anonymous users to upload files when **write_enable**=YES and the anonymous user has permission to write to the directory.

> Default: NO

anon_world_readable_only
: YES limits the files that a user can download to those that are readable by the owner of the file, members of the group the file is associated with, and others. It may not be desirable to allow one anonymous user to download a file that another anonymous user uploaded. Setting this parameter to YES can avoid this scenario.

> Default: YES

ascii_download_enable
: YES allows a user to download files using ASCII mode. Setting this parameter to YES can create a security risk (page 608).

> Default: NO

ascii_upload_enable
YES allows a user to upload files using ASCII mode (page 608).

Default: NO

chown_uploads   YES causes files uploaded by anonymous users to be owned by **root** (or another user specified by **chown_username**).

Default: NO

chown_username   See **chown_uploads**.

Default: **root**

ftp_username   The username of anonymous users.

Default: **ftp**

nopriv_user   The name of the user with minimal privileges, as used by **vsftpd**. To enhance security, because other programs use **nobody**, replace **nobody** with the name of a dedicated user such as **ftp**.

Default: **nobody**

MESSAGES

You can replace the standard greeting banner that **vsftpd** displays when a user logs in on the system (**banner_file** and **ftpd_banner**). You can also display a message each time a user enters a directory (**dirmessage_enable** and **message_file**). When you set **dirmessage_enable=YES**, each time a user enters a directory using cd, **vsftpd** displays the contents of the file in that directory named **.message** (or other file specified by **message_file**).

dirmessage_enable
YES displays **.message** or another file specified by **message_file** as an ftp user enters a new directory by giving a **cd** command.

Default: NO
Red Hat: YES

message_file   See **dirmessage_enable**.

Default: **.message**

banner_file   The absolute pathname of the file that is displayed when a user connects to the server. Overrides **ftpd_banner**.

Default: none

ftpd_banner   This string overrides the standard **vsftpd** greeting banner displayed when a user connects to the server.

Default: none; uses standard **vsftpd** banner

DISPLAY

This section describes parameters that can improve security and performance by controlling how **vsftpd** displays information.

hide_ids   YES lists all users and groups in directory listings as **ftp**. NO lists the real owners.

Default: NO

setproctitle_enable

NO causes ps to display the process running **vsftpd** as **vsftpd**. YES causes ps to display what **vsftpd** is currently doing (uploading and so on). Set to NO to provide a more secure system.

Default: NO

text_userdb_names

NO improves performance by displaying numeric UIDs and GIDs in directory listings. YES displays names.

Default: NO

use_localtime   NO causes **ls, mls,** and **modtime** FTP commands to display *UTC* (page 1062); YES causes these commands to display the local time.

Default: NO

ls_recurse_enable   YES permits users to give **ls –R** commands. Setting this parameter to YES may pose a security risk because giving an **ls –R** command at the top of a large directory hierarchy can consume a lot of system resources.

Default: NO

Logs

By default, logging is turned off. However, the **vsftpd.conf** file distributed with Red Hat Linux turns it on. This section describes parameters that control the details and locations of logs.

log_ftp_protocol   YES logs FTP requests and responses, provided that **xferlog_std_format** is set to NO.

Default: NO

xferlog_enable   YES maintains a transfer log in **/var/log/vsftpd.log** (or another file specified by **xferlog_file**). NO does not create a log.

Default: NO
Red Hat: YES

xferlog_std_format

YES causes a transfer log (not covering connections) to be written in standard **xferlog** format, as used by wu-ftpd, as long as **xferlog_file** is explicitly set. The default **vsftpd** log format is more readable than **xferlog** format, but it cannot be processed by programs that generate statistical summaries of **xferlog** files. Search for **xferlog** on the Internet for more information.

Default: NO
Red Hat: YES

xferlog_file   See **xferlog_enable** and **xferlog_std_format**.

Default: **/var/log/vsftpd.log**

CONNECTION PARAMETERS

You can allow clients to establish passive and/or active connections (page 602). Setting timeouts and maximum transfer rates can improve server security and performance. This section describes parameters that control the types of connections that a client can establish, the length of time **vsftpd** will wait while establishing a connection, and the speeds of connections for different types of users.

PASSIVE (PASV) CONNECTIONS

pasv_enable   NO prevents the use of PASV connections.

Default: YES

pasv_promiscuous

NO causes PASV to perform a security check that ensures that the data and control connections originate from a single IP address. YES disables this check; it is not recommended for a secure system.

Default: NO

pasv_max_port   The highest port number that **vsftpd** will allocate for a PASV data connection; useful in setting up a firewall.

Default: 0 (use any port)

pasv_min_port   The lowest port number that **vsftpd** will allocate for a PASV data connection; useful in setting up a firewall.

Default: 0 (use any port)

pasv_address   Specifies an IP address other than the one used by the client to contact the server.

Default: none; the address is the one used by the client

ACTIVE (PORT) CONNECTIONS

port_enable   NO prevents the use of PORT connections.

Default: YES

port_promiscuous

NO causes PORT to perform a security check that ensures that outgoing data connections connect only to the client. YES disables this check; it is not recommended for a secure system.

Default: NO

connect_from_port_20

YES specifies port 20 (**ftp-data**, a privileged port) on the server for PORT connections, as required by some clients. NO allows **vsftpd** to run with fewer privileges (on a nonprivileged port).

Default: NO
Red Hat: YES

ftp_data_port   With **connect_from_port_20** set to NO, specifies the port that **vsftpd** uses for PORT connections.

Default: 20

TIMEOUTS
accept_timeout   The number of seconds the server waits for a client to establish a PASV data connection.

Default: 60

connect_timeout   The number of seconds the server waits for a client to respond to a PORT data connection.

Default: 60

data_connection_timeout

The number of seconds the server waits for a stalled data transfer to resume before disconnecting.

Default: 300

idle_session_timeout

The number of seconds the server waits between FTP commands before disconnecting.

Default: 300

local_max_rate   For local users, the maximum data transfer rate in bytes per second. Zero (0) indicates no limit.

Default: 0

anon_max_rate   For anonymous users, the maximum data transfer rate in bytes per second. Zero indicates no limit.

Default: 0

one_process_model

YES establishes one process per connection, which improves performance but degrades security. NO allows multiple processes per connection. NO is recommended for a more secure system.

Default: NO

MISCELLANEOUS

This section describes parameters not discussed elsewhere.

pam_service_name

The name of the PAM service used by **vsftpd**.

Default: **ftp**
Red Hat: **vsftpd**

tcp_wrappers   YES causes incoming connections to use **tcp_wrappers** (page 427) if **vsftpd** was compiled with **tcp_wrappers** support. When **tcp_wrappers** sets the environment variable **VSFTPD_LOAD_CONF**, **vsftpd** loads the configuration file specified by this variable, allowing per-IP configuration.

Default: NO
Red Hat: YES

user_config_dir   Specifies a directory that contains files named for local users. Each of these files, which mimic **vsftpd.conf**, contains parameters that override, on a per-user basis, default parameters and parameters specified in **vsftpd.conf**. For example, assume that **user_config_dir** is set to **/etc/vsftpd/user_conf**. If the default configuration file, **/etc/vsftpd/vsftpd.conf**, sets **idlesession_timeout=300** and Sam's individual configuration file, **/etc/vsftpd/user_conf/sam**, sets **idlesession_timeout=1200**, all users' sessions, except for Sam's, will time out after 300 seconds of inactivity. Sam's sessions will time out after 1,200 seconds.

Default: none

FILES

In addition to **/etc/vsftpd/vsftpd.conf**, the following files control the functioning of **vsftpd**. The directory hierarchy that **user_config_dir** points to is not included in this list as it has no default name.

/etc/vsftpd/ftpusers
Lists users, one per line, who are never allowed to log in on the FTP server, regardless of how **userlist_enable** (page 615) is set and regardless of the users listed in the **user_list** file. The default file lists **root, bin, daemon**, and others.

/etc/vsftpd/user_list
Lists either the only users who can log in on the server or the users who are not allowed to log in on the server. The **userlist_enable** (page 615) option must be set to YES for **vsftpd** to examine the list of users in this file. Setting **userlist_enable** to YES and **userlist_deny** (page 615) to YES (or not setting it) prevents listed users from logging in on the server. Setting **userlist_enable** to YES and **userlist_deny** to NO permits only the listed users to log in on the server.

/etc/vsftpd/chroot_list
Depending on the **chroot_list_enable** (page 617) and **chroot_local_user** (page 617) settings, this file lists either users who are forced into a chroot jail in their home directories or users who are not placed in a chroot jail.

/var/log/vsftpd.log
Log file. For more information refer to "Logs" on page 621.

CHAPTER SUMMARY

FTP is a protocol for downloading files from and uploading files to another system over a network. FTP is the name of both a client/server protocol (FTP) and a client utility (ftp) that invokes this protocol. Because FTP is not a secure protocol, it should be used only to download public information. You can run the **vsftpd** FTP server in the restricted environment of a chroot jail to make it significantly less likely that a malicious user can compromise the system.

Many servers and clients implement the FTP protocol. The ftp utility is the original client implementation; sftp is a secure implementation that uses OpenSSH facilities to encrypt the connection. The **vsftpd** daemon is a secure FTP server; it better protects the server from malicious users than do other FTP servers.

Public FTP servers allow you to log in as **anonymous** or **ftp**. By convention, you supply your email address as a password when you log in as an anonymous user. Public servers frequently have interesting files in the **pub** directory.

FTP provides two modes of transferring files: binary and ASCII. It is safe to use binary mode to transfer all types of files, including ASCII files. If you transfer a binary file using ASCII mode, the transfer will fail.

EXERCISES

1. What changes does FTP make to an ASCII file when you download it in ASCII mode to a Windows machine from a Linux server? What changes are made when you download the file to a Mac?

2. What happens if you transfer an executable program file in ASCII mode?

3. When would ftp be a better choice than sftp?

4. How would you prevent local users from logging in on a **vsftpd** server using their system username and password?

5. What advantage does sftp have over ftp?

6. What is the difference between cd and lcd in ftp?

ADVANCED EXERCISES

7. Why might you have problems connecting to an FTP server in PORT mode?

8. Why is it advantageous to run **vsftpd** in a chroot jail?

9. After downloading a file, you find that it does not match the MD5 checksum provided. Downloading the file again gives the same incorrect checksum. What have you done wrong and how would you fix it?

10. How would you configure **vsftpd** to run through **xinetd**, and what would be the main advantage of this approach?

20

sendmail: SETTING UP MAIL CLIENTS, SERVERS, AND MORE

Sending and receiving email require three pieces of software. At each end, there is a client, called an MUA (Mail User Agent), which is a bridge between a user and the mail system. Common MUAs are mutt, KMail, Thunderbird, and Outlook. When you send an email, the MUA hands it to an MTA (a Mail Transfer Agent such as **sendmail**), which transfers it to the destination server. At the destination, an MDA (a Mail Delivery Agent such as **procmail**) puts the mail in the recipient's mailbox file. On Linux systems, the MUA on the receiving system either reads the mailbox file or retrieves mail from a remote MUA or MTA, such as an ISP's SMTP (mail) server, using POP (Post Office Protocol) or IMAP (Internet Message Access Protocol).

Most Linux MUAs expect a local copy of **sendmail** to deliver outgoing email. On some systems, including those with a dial-up connection to the Internet, **sendmail** relays email to an ISP's mail server. Because **sendmail** uses SMTP (Simple Mail Transfer Protocol) to deliver email, **sendmail** is often referred to as an SMTP server.

In the default Red Hat Linux setup, the **sendmail** MTA uses **procmail** as the local MDA. In turn, **procmail** writes email to the end of the recipient's mailbox file. You can also use **procmail** to sort email according to a set of rules, either on a per-user basis or globally. The global filtering function is useful for systemwide filtering to detect spam and for other tasks, but the per-user feature is largely superfluous on a modern system. Traditional UNIX MUAs were simple programs that could not filter mail and thus delegated this function to MDAs such as **procmail**. Modern MUAs, by contrast, incorporate this functionality.

You do not need to set up sendmail to send and receive email

tip Most MUAs can use POP or IMAP for receiving email. These protocols do not require an MTA such as **sendmail**. As a consequence, you do not need to install or configure **sendmail** (or another MTA) to receive email. You still need SMTP to send email. However, the SMTP server can be at a remote location, such as your ISP, so you do not need to concern yourself with it.

Introduction

When the network that was to evolve into the Internet was first set up, it connected a few computers, each serving a large number of users and running several services. Each computer was capable of sending and receiving email and had a unique hostname, which was used as a destination for email.

Today the Internet has a large number of transient clients. Because these clients do not have fixed IP addresses or hostnames, they cannot receive email directly. Users on these systems usually maintain an account on an email server run by their employer or an ISP, and they collect email from this account using POP or IMAP. Unless you own a domain that you want to receive email at, you will not need to set up **sendmail** as an incoming SMTP server.

You can set up **sendmail** on a client system so that it simply relays outbound mail to an SMTP server. This configuration is required by organizations that use firewalls to prevent email from being sent out on the Internet from any system other than the company's official mail servers. As a partial defense against spreading viruses, some ISPs block outbound port 25 to prevent their customers from sending email directly to a remote computer. This configuration is required by these ISPs.

You can also set up **sendmail** as an outbound server that does not use an ISP as a relay. In this configuration, **sendmail** connects directly to the SMTP servers for the domains receiving the email. An ISP set up as a relay is configured this way.

You can set up **sendmail** to accept email for a registered domain name as specified in the domain's DNS MX record (page 726). However, most mail clients (MUAs) do not interact directly with **sendmail** to receive email. Instead, they use POP or IMAP—protocols that include features for managing mail folders, leaving messages on the server, and reading only the subject of an email without downloading the entire message. If you want to collect your email from a system other than the one running the incoming mail server, you may need to set up a POP or IMAP server, as discussed on page 647.

PREREQUISITES

Install the following packages:

- **sendmail** (required)
- **sendmail-cf** (required to configure **sendmail**)
- **squirrelmail** (optional; provides Webmail, page 644)
- **spamassassin** (optional; provides spam filtering, page 640)
- **mailman** (optional; provides mailing list support, page 646)
- **dovecot** (optional; provides IMAP and POP incoming mail server daemons)

Run chkconfig to cause **sendmail** to start when the system goes multiuser (by default, **sendmail** does not run in single-user mode):

```
# /sbin/chkconfig sendmail on
```

Start **sendmail**. Because **sendmail** is normally running, you need to restart it to cause **sendmail** to reread its configuration files. The following restart command works even when **sendmail** is not running—it just fails to shut down **sendmail**:

```
# /sbin/service sendmail restart
Shutting down sendmail:                        [  OK  ]
Shutting down sm-client:                        [  OK  ]
Starting sendmail:                              [  OK  ]
Starting sm-client:                             [  OK  ]
```

Run chkconfig to cause the SpamAssassin daemon, **spamd,** to start when the system enters multiuser mode (SpamAssassin is normally installed in this configuration):

```
# /sbin/chkconfig spamassassin on
```

As with **sendmail**, SpamAssassin is normally running. Restart it to cause **spamd** to reread its configuration files:

```
# /sbin/service spamassassin restart
Stopping spamd:                                 [  OK  ]
Starting spamd:                                 [  OK  ]
```

The IMAP and POP protocols are implemented as several daemons. See page 647 for information on these daemons and how to start them.

NOTES

Firewall An SMTP server normally uses TCP port 25. If the SMTP server system is running a firewall, you need to open this port. Using the Red Hat graphical firewall tool (page 768), select **Mail (SMTP)** from the Trusted Services frame to open this port. For more general information see Chapter 25, which details iptables.

cyrus This chapter covers the IMAP and POP3 servers included in the **dovecot** package. Red Hat Linux also provides IMAP and POP3 servers in the **cyrus-imapd** package.

MORE INFORMATION

Web **sendmail**   www.sendmail.org
IMAP   www.imap.org
IMAP and POP3   www.dovecot.org
IMAP and POP3   cyrusimap.web.cmu.edu
SquirrelMail   www.squirrelmail.org
Postfix   www.postfix.org/docs.html (alternative MTA, page 652)
Qmail   qmail.area.com
Mailman   www.list.org
procmail   www.procmail.org
SpamAssassin   spamassassin.org
Spam database   razor.sourceforge.net

JUMPSTART I: CONFIGURING sendmail ON A CLIENT

You may not need to configure sendmail to send email

tip   With **sendmail** running, give the command described under "Test" on page 631. As long as **sendmail** can connect to port 25 outbound, you should not need to set up **sendmail** to use an SMTP relay as described in this section. If you receive the mail sent by the test, you can skip this section.

This JumpStart configures an outbound **sendmail** server. This server

- Uses a remote SMTP server—typically an ISP—to relay outbound email to its destination (an SMTP relay).

- Sends to the SMTP server email originating from the local system only. It does not forward email originating from other systems.

- Does not handle inbound email. As is frequently the case, you need to use POP or IMAP to receive email.

To set up this server, you must edit **/etc/mail/sendmail.mc** and restart **sendmail**.

Change **sendmail.mc**   The **dnl** at the start of the following line in **sendmail.mc** indicates that this line is a comment:

```
dnl define('SMART_HOST', 'smtp.your.provider')
```

To specify a remote SMTP server, you must open **sendmail.mc** in an editor and change the preceding line, deleting **dnl** from the beginning of the line and replacing **smtp.your.provider** with the FQDN of your ISP's SMTP server (obtain this name from your ISP). Be careful not to alter the back ticks (`) and the single quotation marks (') in this line. If your ISP's SMTP server is at **smtp.myisp.com**, you would change the line to

```
define('SMART_HOST', 'smtp.myisp.com')
```

Do not alter the back ticks (`) or the single quotation marks (')

tip Be careful not to alter the back ticks (`) or the single quotation marks (') in any line in **send-mail.mc**. These symbols control the way the m4 preprocessor converts **sendmail.mc** to **send-mail.cf**; **sendmail** will not work properly if you do not preserve these symbols.

Restart sendmail When you restart it, **sendmail** regenerates the **sendmail.cf** file from the **sendmail.mc** file you edited:

```
# /sbin/service sendmail restart
```

Test Test **sendmail** with the following command:

```
$ echo "my sendmail test" | /usr/sbin/sendmail user@remote.host
```

Replace *user@remote.host* with an email address on *another system* where you receive email. You need to send email to a remote system to make sure that **send-mail** is relaying your email.

JUMPSTART II: CONFIGURING sendmail ON A SERVER

If you want to receive inbound email sent to a registered domain that you own, you need to set up **sendmail** as an incoming mail server. This JumpStart describes how to set up such a server. This server

- Accepts outbound email from the local system only.
- Delivers outbound email directly to the recipient's system, without using a relay.
- Accepts inbound email from any system.

This server does not relay outbound email originating on other systems. Refer to "access: Sets Up a Relay Host" on page 638 if you want the local system to act as a relay. For this configuration to work, you must be able to make outbound connections from and receive inbound connections to port 25.

The line in **sendmail.mc** that limits **sendmail** to accepting inbound email from the local system only is

```
DAEMON_OPTIONS(`Port=smtp,Addr=127.0.0.1, Name=MTA')dnl
```

To allow **sendmail** to accept inbound email from other systems, remove the parameter **Addr=127.0.0.1,** from the preceding line:

```
DAEMON_OPTIONS(`Port=smtp, Name=MTA')dnl
```

By default, **sendmail** does not use a remote SMTP server to relay email, so there is nothing to change to cause **sendmail** to send email directly to recipients' systems. (JumpStart I set up a SMART_HOST to relay email.)

Once you have restarted **sendmail**, it will accept mail addressed to the local system, as long as a DNS MX record (page 726) points at the local system. If you are not running a DNS server, you must ask your ISP to set up an MX record.

How sendmail WORKS

Outbound email When you send email, the MUA passes the email to **sendmail**, which creates in the **/var/spool/mqueue** (mail queue) directory two files that hold the message while **sendmail** processes it. To create a unique filename for a particular piece of email, **sendmail** generates a random string and uses that string in filenames pertaining to the email. The **sendmail** daemon stores the body of the message in a file named **df** (data file) followed by the generated string. It stores the headers and other information in a file named **qf** (queue file) followed by the generated string.

If a delivery error occurs, **sendmail** creates a temporary copy of the message that it stores in a file whose name starts with **tf** (temporary file) and logs errors in a file whose name starts **xf**. Once an email has been sent successfully, **sendmail** removes all files pertaining to that email from **/var/spool/mqueue**.

Incoming email By default, the MDA stores incoming messages in users' files in the mail spool directory, **/var/spool/mail**, in **mbox** format. Within this directory, each user has a mail file named with the user's username. Mail remains in these files until it is collected, typically by an MUA. Once an MUA collects the mail from the mail spool, the MUA stores the mail as directed by the user, usually in the user's home directory hierarchy.

mbox versus maildir The **mbox** format stores all messages for a user in a single file. To prevent corruption, the file must be locked while a process is adding messages to or deleting messages from the file; you cannot delete a message at the same time the MTA is adding messages. A competing format, **maildir**, stores each message in a separate file. This format does not use locks, allowing an MUA to read and delete messages at the same time as new mail is delivered. In addition, the **maildir** format is better able to handle larger mailboxes. The downside is that the **maildir** format adds overhead when you are using a protocol such as IMAP to check messages. The **dovecot** package supports both **mbox** and **maildir** formats. Qmail (page 652), a **sendmail** alternative, uses **maildir**-format mailboxes.

MAIL LOGS

The **sendmail** daemon stores log messages in **/var/log/maillog**. Other mail servers, such as the dovecot **imap-login** and **pop3-login** daemons, may also log information to this file. Following is a sample log entry:

/var/log/maillog
```
# cat /var/log/maillog
...
Mar  3 16:25:33 MACHINENAME sendmail[7225]: i23GPXvm007224:
to=<user@localhost.localdomain>, ctladdr=<root@localhost.localdomain>
(0/0), delay=00:00:00, xdelay=00:00:00, mailer=local, pri=30514,
dsn=2.0.0, stat=Sent
```

Each log entry starts with a timestamp, the name of the system sending the email, the name of the mail server (**sendmail**), and a unique identification number. The address of the recipient follows the **to=** label and the address of the sender follows **ctladdr=**. Additional fields provide the name of the mailer and the time it took to send the message. If a message is sent correctly, the **stat=** label is followed by **Sent**.

A message is marked **Sent** when **sendmail** sends it; **Sent** does not indicate that the message has been delivered. If a message is not delivered because an error occurred farther down the line, the sender usually receives an email saying that it was not delivered and giving a reason why.

If you send and receive a lot of email, the **maillog** file can grow quite large. The **syslog** logrotate (page 559) entry is set up to archive and rotate the **maillog** files regularly.

ALIASES AND FORWARDING

Three files can forward email: **.forward** (page 634), **aliases** (discussed next), and **virtusertable** (page 640). Table 20-1 on page 640 compares the three files.

/etc/aliases Most of the time when you send email, it goes to a specific person; the recipient, **user@system**, maps to a specific, real user on the specified system. Sometimes you may want email to go to a class of users and not to a specific recipient. Examples of classes of users include **postmaster, webmaster, root,** and **tech_support**. Different users may receive this email at different times or the email may be answered by a group of users. You can use the **/etc/aliases** file to map inbound addresses to local users, files, commands, and remote addresses.

Each line in **/etc/aliases** contains the name of a local pseudouser, followed by a colon, whitespace, and a comma-separated list of destinations. The default installation includes a number of aliases that redirect messages for certain pseudousers to **root**. These have the form

```
system:      root
```

Sending messages to the **root** account is a good way of making them easy to review. However, because **root**'s email is rarely checked, you may want to send copies to a real user. The following line forwards mail sent to **abuse** on the local system to **root** and **alex**:

```
abuse:       root, alex
```

You can create simple mailing lists with this type of alias. For example, the following alias sends copies of all email sent to **admin** on the local system to several users, including Zach, who is on a different system:

```
admin:       sam, helen, mark, zach@tcorp.com
```

You can direct email to a file by specifying an absolute pathname in place of a destination address. The following alias, which is quite popular among less conscientious system administrators, redirects email sent to **complaints** to **/dev/null** (page 448), where they disappear:

```
complaints:  /dev/null
```

You can also send email to standard input of a command by preceding the command with a pipe character (|). This technique is commonly used with mailing list software such as Mailman (page 646). For each list it maintains, Mailman has entries, such as the following entry for **mylist**, in the **aliases** file:

```
mylist:                "|/usr/lib/mailman/mail/mailman post mylist"
```

newaliases   After you edit **/etc/aliases**, you must either run newaliases as **root** or restart **sendmail** to recreate the **aliases.db** file that **sendmail** reads.

praliases   You can use praliases to list aliases currently loaded by **sendmail**:

```
# /usr/sbin/praliases | head -5
postmaster:root
daemon:root
adm:root
lp:root
shutdown:root
```

~/.forward   Systemwide aliases are useful in many cases, but non**root** users cannot make or change them. Sometimes you may want to forward your own mail: Maybe you want mail from several systems to go to one address or perhaps you just want to forward your mail while you are working at another office for a week. The **~/.forward** file allows ordinary users to forward their email.

Lines in a **.forward** file are the same as the right column of the **aliases** file explained previously: Destinations are listed one per line and can be a local user, a remote email address, a filename, or a command preceded by a pipe character (|).

Mail that you forward does not go to your local mailbox. If you want to forward mail and keep a copy in your local mailbox, you must specify your local username preceded by a backslash to prevent an infinite loop. The following example sends Sam's email to himself on the local system and on the system at **tcorp.com**:

```
$cat ~sam/.forward
sams@tcorp.com
\sam
```

RELATED PROGRAMS

sendmail   The **sendmail** package includes several programs. The primary program, **sendmail**, reads from standard input and sends an email to the recipient specified by its argument. You can use **sendmail** from the command line to check that the mail delivery system is working and to email the output of scripts. See page 631 for an example.

mailq   The mailq utility displays the status of the outgoing mail queue and normally reports there are no messages in the queue. Messages in the queue usually indicate a problem with the local or remote **sendmail** configuration or a network problem.

```
# /usr/bin/mailq
/var/spool/mqueue is empty
                Total requests: 0
```

mailstats   The mailstats utility reports on the number and sizes of messages **sendmail** has sent and received since the date it displays on the first line:

```
# /usr/sbin/mailstats
Statistics from Sat Dec 24 16:02:34 2005
M   msgsfr   bytes_from    msgsto    bytes_to  msgsrej msgsdis  Mailer
0        0           0K     17181      103904K       0       0  prog
4   368386     4216614K    136456     1568314K   20616       0  esmtp
9   226151    26101362K    479025    12776528K    4590       0  local
=========================================================
T   594537    30317976K    632662    14448746K   25206       0
C   694638                 499700                146185
```

In the preceding output, each mailer is identified by the first column, which displays the mailer number, and by the last column, which displays the name of the mailer. The second through fifth columns display the number and total sizes of messages sent and received by the mailer. The sixth and seventh columns display the number of messages rejected and discarded respectively. The row that starts with T lists the column totals, and the row that starts with C lists the number of TCP connections.

CONFIGURING sendmail

The **sendmail** configuration files reside in **/etc/mail**, where the primary configuration file is **sendmail.cf**. This directory contains other text configuration files, such as **access**, **mailertable**, and **virtusertable**. The **sendmail** daemon does not read these files but instead reads the corresponding ✱.db files in the same directory.

makemap You can use makemap or give the command **make** from the **/etc/mail** directory to generate the ✱.db files, although this step is not usually necessary. The **sendmail** init script automatically generates these files when you start or restart **sendmail**:

```
# /sbin/service sendmail restart
```

THE sendmail.mc AND sendmail.cf FILES

This **sendmail.cf** file is not intended to be edited by hand and contains a large warning to this effect:

```
$ cat /etc/mail/sendmail.cf
...
######################################################################
#####
#####    DO NOT EDIT THIS FILE!  Only edit the source .mc file.
#####
######################################################################
...
```

EDITING sendmail.mc AND GENERATING sendmail.cf

The **sendmail.cf** file is generated from **sendmail.mc** using the m4 macro processor. It can be helpful to use a text editor that supports syntax highlighting, such as vim, to edit **sendmail.mc**.

dnl   Many of the lines in **sendmail.mc** start with **dnl**, which stands for **delete to new line**; this token causes m4 to delete from the **dnl** to the end of the line (the next NEWLINE character). Because m4 ignores anything on a line after a **dnl** instruction, you can use **dnl** to introduce comments; it works the same way as **#** does in a shell script.

Many of the lines in **sendmail.mc** *end* with **dnl**. Because NEWLINEs immediately follow these **dnls**, these **dnls** are superfluous; you can remove them if you like.

After you edit **sendmail.mc**, you need to regenerate **sendmail.cf** to make your changes take effect. When you restart **sendmail**, the **sendmail** init script regenerates **sendmail.cf**.

ABOUT sendmail.mc

Lines near the beginning of **sendmail.mc** provide basic configuration information:

```
divert(-1)dnl
include(`/usr/share/sendmail-cf/m4/cf.m4')dnl
VERSIONID(`setup for Red Hat Linux')dnl
OSTYPE(`linux')dnl
```

The line that starts with **divert** tells m4 to discard extraneous output it may generate when processing this file.

The **include** statement tells m4 where to find the macro definition file that it will use to process the rest of this file; it points to the file named **cf.m4**. The **cf.m4** file contains other **include** statements that include parts of the **sendmail** configuration rule sets.

The **VERSIONID** statement defines a string that indicates the version of this configuration. You can change this string to include a brief comment about changes you have made to this file or other information. The value of this string is not significant to **sendmail**.

Do not change the **OSTYPE** statement unless you are migrating a **sendmail.mc** file from another operating system.

Other statements you may want to change are explained in the following sections and in the **sendmail** documentation.

Quoting m4 strings

tip   The m4 macro processor, which converts **sendmail.mc** to **sendmail.cf**, requires strings to be preceded by a back tick (`) and closed with a single quotation mark (').

MASQUERADING

Typically you want your email to appear to come from the user and the domain where you receive email; sometimes the outbound server is in a different domain than the inbound server. You can cause **sendmail** to alter outbound messages so that they appear to come from a user and/or domain other than the one they are sent from: In other words, you *masquerade* (page 1042) the message.

Several lines in **sendmail.mc** pertain to this type of masquerading. Each is commented out in the file that Red Hat distributes:

```
dnl MASQUERADE_AS(`mydomain.com')dnl
dnl MASQUERADE_DOMAIN(localhost)dnl
dnl FEATURE(masquerade_entire_domain)dnl
```

The MASQUERADE_AS statement causes email that you send from the local system to appear to come from the specified domain (**mydomain.com** in the commented-out line in the distributed file). Remove the leading **dnl** and change **mydomain.com** to the domain name that you want mail to appear to come from.

The MASQUERADE_DOMAIN statement causes email from the specified system or domain to be masqueraded, just as local email is. That is, email from the system specified in this statement is treated as though it came from the local system: It is changed so that it appears to come from the domain specified in the MASQUERADE_AS statement. Remove the leading **dnl** and change **localhost** to the name of the system or domain that sends the email that you want to masquerade. If the name you specify has a leading period, it specifies a domain. If there is no leading period, the name specifies a system or host. The **sendmail.mc** file can include as many MASQUERADE_DOMAIN statements as necessary.

The **masquerade_entire_domain** feature statement causes **sendmail** also to masquerade subdomains of the domain specified in the MASQUERADE_DOMAIN statement. Remove the leading **dnl** to masquerade entire domains.

ACCEPTING EMAIL FROM UNKNOWN HOSTS

As configured by Red Hat, **sendmail** accepts email from domains that it cannot resolve (and that may not exist). To turn this feature off and cut down the amount of spam you receive, add **dnl** to the beginning of the following line:

```
FEATURE(`accept_unresolvable_domains')dnl
```

When this feature is off, **sendmail** uses DNS to look up the domains of all email it receives. If it cannot resolve the domain, it rejects the email.

SETTING UP A BACKUP SERVER

You can set up a backup mail server to hold email when the primary mail server experiences problems. For maximum coverage, the backup server should be on a different connection to the Internet from the primary server.

Setting up a backup server is easy. Just remove the leading **dnl** from the following line in the *backup* mail server's **sendmail.mc** file:

```
dnl FEATURE(`relay_based_on_MX')dnl
```

DNS MX records (page 726) specify where email for a domain should be sent. You can have multiple MX records for a domain, each pointing to a different mail server. When a domain has multiple MX records, each record usually has a different priority; the priority is specified by a two-digit number, where lower numbers specify higher priorities.

When attempting to deliver email, an MTA first tries to deliver email to the highest-priority server. If that delivery attempt fails, it tries to deliver to a lower-priority server. If you activate the **relay_based_on_MX** feature and point a low-priority MX record at a secondary mail server, the mail server will accept email for the domain. The mail server will then forward email to the server identified by the highest-priority MX record for the domain when that server becomes available.

OTHER FILES IN /etc/mail

The **/etc/mail** directory holds most of the files that control **sendmail**. This section discusses three of those files: **mailertable**, **access**, and **virtusertable**.

mailertable: FORWARDS EMAIL FROM ONE DOMAIN TO ANOTHER

When you run a mail server, you may want to send mail destined for one domain to a different location. The **sendmail** daemon uses the **/etc/mail/mailertable** file for this purpose. Each line in **mailertable** holds the name of a domain and a destination mailer separated by whitespace; when **sendmail** receives email for the specified domain, it forwards it to the mailer specified on the same line. Red Hat enables this feature by default: Put an entry in the **mailertable** file and restart **sendmail** to use it.

The following line in **mailertable** forwards email sent to **tcorp.com** to the mailer at **bravo.com**:

```
$ cat /etc/mail/mailertable
tcorp.com           smtp:[bravo.com]
```

The square brackets in the example instruct **sendmail** not to use MX records but rather to send email directly to the SMTP server. Without the brackets, email could enter an infinite loop.

A period in front of a domain name acts as a wildcard and causes the name to match any domain that ends in the specified name. For example, **.tcorp.com** matches **sales.tcorp.com**, **mktg.tcrop.com**, and so on.

The **sendmail** init script regenerates **mailertable.db** from **mailertable** each time you run it, as when you restart **sendmail**.

access: SETS UP A RELAY HOST

On a LAN, you may want to set up a single server to process outbound mail, keeping local mail inside the network. A system that processes outbound mail for other systems is called a *relay host*. The **/etc/mail/access** file specifies which systems the local server relays email for. As configured by Red Hat, this file lists only the local system:

```
$ cat /etc/mail/access
...
```

```
# by default we allow relaying from localhost...
localhost.localdomain        RELAY
localhost                    RELAY
127.0.0.1                    RELAY
```

You can add systems to the list in **access** by adding an IP address followed by whitespace and the word **RELAY**. The following line adds the 192.168. subnet to the list of hosts that the local system relays mail for:

```
192.168.                     RELAY
```

The **sendmail** init script regenerates **access.db** from **access** each time you run it, as when you restart **sendmail**.

virtusertable: SERVES EMAIL TO MULTIPLE DOMAINS

When the DNS MX records are set up properly, a single system can serve email to multiple domains. On a system that serves mail to many domains, you need a way to sort the incoming mail so that it goes to the right places. The **virtusertable** file can forward inbound email addressed to different domains (**aliases** cannot do this).

As **sendmail** is configured by Red Hat, **virtusertable** is enabled. You need to put forwarding instructions in the **/etc/mail/virtusertable** file and restart **sendmail** to serve the specified domains. The **virtusertable** file is similar to the **aliases** file (page 633), except the left column contains full email addresses, not just local ones. Each line in **virtusertable** starts with the address that the email was sent to, followed by whitespace and the address **sendmail** will forward the email to. As with **aliases**, the destination can be a local user, an email address, a file, or a pipe symbol (|), followed by a command.

The following line from **virtusertable** forwards mail addressed to **zach@tcorp.com** to **zcs**, a local user:

```
zach@tcorp.com        zcs
```

You can also forward email for a user to a remote email address:

```
sams@bravo.com        sams@tcorp.com
```

You can forward all email destined for a domain to another domain without specifying each user individually. To forward email for every user at **bravo.com** to **tcorp.com**, specify **@bravo.com** as the first address on the line. When **sendmail** forwards email, it replaces the **%1** in the destination address with the name of the recipient. The next line forwards all email addressed to **bravo.com** to **tcorp.com**, keeping the original recipients' names:

```
@bravo.com        %1@tcorp.com
```

Finally you can specify that email intended for a specific user should be rejected by using the **error** namespace in the destination. The next example bounces email addressed to **spam@tcorp.com** with the message **5.7.0:550 Invalid address**:

```
spam@tcorp.com           error:5.7.0:550 Invalid address
```

.forward, aliases, and virtusertable   The **.forward** (page 634), **aliases** (page 633), and **virtusertable** files all do the same thing: They forward email addressed to one user to another user. They can also redirect email to a file or to serve as input to a program. The difference between them is scope and ownership; see Table 20-1.

Table 20-1   Comparison of forwarding techniques

	.forward	**aliases**	**virtusertable**
Controlled by	non**root** user	**root**	**root**
Forwards email addressed to	non**root** user	Any real or virtual user on the local system	Any real or virtual user on any domain recognized by **sendmail**
Order of precedence	Third	Second	First

ADDITIONAL EMAIL TOOLS

This section covers SpamAssassin, Webmail, and mailing lists. In addition, it discusses how to set up IMAP and POP3 servers and a KMail client.

SPAMASSASSIN

Spam—or more correctly, UCE (unsolicited commercial email)—accounts for more than three-quarters of all email. SpamAssassin evaluates each piece of incoming email and assigns it a number that indicates the likelihood that the email is spam. The higher the number, the more likely that the email is spam. You can filter email based on its rating. SpamAssassin is effective as installed, but you can modify its configuration files to make it better fit your needs.

How SpamAssassin works   You can set up SpamAssassin (**spamassassin** package) on a mail server so that it rates all inbound email before it is sent to users. Alternatively, individual users can run it from their mail clients. Either way, you run the SpamAssassin **spamd** daemon and filter email through this daemon using the **spamc** client.

SpamAssassin uses several techniques to identify spam:

- **Header analysis**   Checks for tricks that people who send spam use to make you think email is legitimate

- **Text analysis**   Checks the body of an email for characteristics of spam

- **Blacklists**   Checks various lists to see if the sender is known for sending spam

- **Database**   Checks the signature of the message against Vipul's Razor (razor.sourceforge.net), a spam-tracking database

With **spamd** running, you can see how **spamc** works by sending a simple string to it:

```
$ echo "hi there" | spamc
X-Spam-Flag: YES
X-Spam-Checker-Version: SpamAssassin 3.1.0 (2005-09-13) on pbnj
X-Spam-Level: *****
X-Spam-Status: Yes, score=5.7 required=5.0 tests=EMPTY_MESSAGE,MISSING_HB_SEP,
        MISSING_HEADERS,MISSING_SUBJECT,NO_RECEIVED,NO_RELAYS,TO_CC_NONE
        autolearn=no version=3.1.0
X-Spam-Report:
        *  -0.0 NO_RELAYS Informational: message was not relayed via SMTP
        *   2.5 MISSING_HB_SEP Missing blank line between message header and body
        *   0.2 MISSING_HEADERS Missing To: header
        *   1.3 MISSING_SUBJECT Missing Subject: header
        *   1.5 EMPTY_MESSAGE Message appears to be empty with no Subject: text
        *  -0.0 NO_RECEIVED Informational: message has no Received headers
        *   0.1 TO_CC_NONE No To: or Cc: header
hi there
Subject: [SPAM]
X-Spam-Prev-Subject: (nonexistent)
```

Of course, SpamAssassin complains because the string you gave it did not contain standard email headers. The logical line that starts with X-Spam-Status contains the heart of the report on the string **hi there**. First it says **Yes** (it considers the message to be spam). SpamAssassin uses a rating system that assigns a number of hits to a piece of email. If the email receives more than the required number of hits (5.0 by default), SpamAssassin marks it as spam. The string failed for many reasons that are enumerated on this status line. The reasons are detailed in the following X-Spam-Report. The following listing is from a real piece of spam processed by SpamAssassin. It received 24.5 hits, indicating that it is almost certainly spam.

```
X-Spam-Status: Yes, hits=24.5 required=5.0
        tests=DATE_IN_FUTURE_06_12,INVALID_DATE_TZ_ABSURD,
            MSGID_OE_SPAM_4ZERO,MSGID_OUTLOOK_TIME,
            MSGID_SPAMSIGN_ZEROES,RCVD_IN_DSBL,RCVD_IN_NJABL,
            RCVD_IN_UNCONFIRMED_DSBL,REMOVE_PAGE,VACATION_SCAM,
            X_NJABL_OPEN_PROXY
        version=2.55
X-Spam-Level: ************************
X-Spam-Checker-Version: SpamAssassin 2.55 (1.174.2.19-2003-05-19-exp)
X-Spam-Report:   This mail is probably spam.  The original message has been attached
    along with this report, so you can recognize or block similar unwanted
    mail in future.  See http://spamassassin.org/tag/ for more details.
    Content preview:  Paradise SEX Island Awaits! Tropical 1 week vacations
    where anything goes! We have lots of WOMEN, SEX, ALCOHOL, ETC! Every
    man's dream awaits on this island of pleasure. [...]
    Content analysis details:   (24.50 points, 5 required)
    MSGID_SPAMSIGN_ZEROES (4.3 points)  Message-Id generated by spam tool (zeroes variant)
    INVALID_DATE_TZ_ABSURD (4.3 points)  Invalid Date: header (timezone does not exist)
    MSGID_OE_SPAM_4ZERO (3.5 points)  Message-Id generated by spam tool (4-zeroes variant)
    VACATION_SCAM       (1.9 points)  BODY: Vacation Offers
    REMOVE_PAGE         (0.3 points)  URI: URL of page called "remove"
    MSGID_OUTLOOK_TIME (4.4 points)  Message-Id is fake (in Outlook Express format)
    DATE_IN_FUTURE_06_12 (1.3 points)  Date: is 6 to 12 hours after Received: date
    RCVD_IN_NJABL       (0.9 points)  RBL: Received via a relay in dnsbl.njabl.org
    [RBL check: found 94.99.190.200.dnsbl.njabl.org.]
    RCVD_IN_UNCONFIRMED_DSBL (0.5 points)  RBL: Received via a relay in unconfirmed.dsbl.org
    [RBL check: found 94.99.190.200.unconfirmed.dsbl.org.]
    X_NJABL_OPEN_PROXY (0.5 points)  RBL: NJABL: sender is proxy/relay/formmail/spam-source
    RCVD_IN_DSBL        (2.6 points)  RBL: Received via a relay in list.dsbl.org
    [RBL check: found 211.157.63.200.list.dsbl.org.]
    X-Spam-Flag: YES
    Subject: [SPAM] re: statement
```

Because SpamAssassin considered the preceding email to be spam, it modified the Subject line by adding [SPAM] at the beginning of the line.

Configuration   Edit **/etc/mail/spamassassin/local.cf** to configure SpamAssassin globally. Users can override the global options and add their own options in **~/.spamassassin/user_prefs**. You can put the options discussed in this section in either of these files. Use **perldoc** to display the configuration document that lists all the options:

Documentation   `$ perldoc Mail::SpamAssassin::Conf`

As shown in the preceding example, SpamAssassin rewrites the Subject line of email that it rates as spam. The **rewrite_subject** keyword in the configuration files controls this behavior. A **1** following this keyword indicates that SpamAssassin will rewrite Subject lines. Change the **1** to a **0** (zero) to turn off this behavior:

```
rewrite_subject 0
```

The **required_hits** keyword specifies the minimum number of hits a piece of email must receive before SpamAssassin considers it to be spam. The default is 5.0. With a higher number, SpamAssassin marks fewer pieces of email as spam.

```
required_hits 5.00
```

Sometimes mail from addresses that should be marked as spam is not, or mail from addresses that should not be marked as spam is. Use the **whitelist_from** keyword to specify addresses that should never be marked as spam and **blacklist_from** to specify addresses that should always be marked as spam:

```
whitelist_from sams@tcorp.com
blacklist_from spammer.net
```

You can specify multiple addresses, separated by SPACEs, on the **whitelist_from** and **blacklist_from** lines. Each address can include wildcards. You can also use multiple lines.

USING SPAMASSASSIN WITH A MAIL SERVER

To add SpamAssassin headers to each email that arrives on the system, you need to configure your MDA to pipe email through the **spamc**. The first step is to make sure you have **procmail** configured as your MDA. The first of the following lines in **sendmail.mc** specifies the **procmail** command, its path, and flags. The MAILER line defines **procmail** as the mailer. You should not have to change either of these lines.

```
FEATURE(local_procmail,`',`procmail -t -Y -a $h -d $u')dnl
MAILER(procmail)dnl
```

The **procmail** configuration file, **/etc/procmailrc**, may not exist on the server. If the file does not exist, create it so that it is owned by **root** and has 644 permissions and the following contents. If it does exist, append the last two lines from the following file to it:

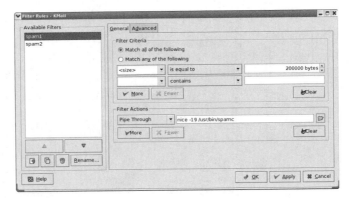

Figure 20-1   The first rule passes messages through SpamAssassin

```
$ cat /etc/procmailrc
DROPPRIVS=yes
:0 fw
| /usr/bin/spamc
```

The first line of this file ensures that **procmail** runs with the least possible privileges. The next two lines implement a rule that pipes each user's incoming email through spamc. The :0 tells **procmail** that a rule follows. The **f** flag indicates a filter; the **w** flag causes **procmail** to wait for the filter to complete and check the exit code. The last line specifies the **/usr/bin/spamc** file as the filter.

With the preceding changes in place, all email that comes into the system passes through SpamAssassin, which rates it according to the options in the global configuration file. For users who have home directories on the server system, SpamAssassin allows users' configuration files to override the global file.

When you run SpamAssassin on a server, you typically want to rate the email more conservatively so that fewer pieces of good email are marked as spam. Setting **required_hits** in the range of 6–10 is generally appropriate. Also, you do not want to remove any email automatically because you could prevent a user from getting a piece of nonspam email. When the server marks email as possibly being spam, users can manually or automatically filter the spam and decide what to do with it.

USING SPAMASSASSIN WITH A MAIL CLIENT

With the SpamAssassin (**spamd**) daemon running and the configuration files set up, you are ready to have SpamAssassin filter your email. To do so, you need to set up two rules in your mail client: The first passes each piece of email through SpamAssassin using spamc (page 640) and the second filters email based on whether the X-Spam-Flag line has a YES or NO on it.

In general, you do not want to pass very large pieces of email through SpamAssassin. The following example, which uses KMail, passes messages smaller than 200,000 bytes through SpamAssassin. The first filter rule (Figure 20-1) processes all messages

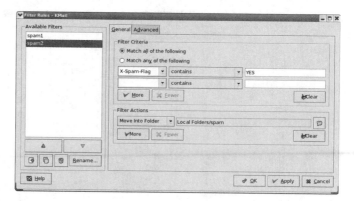

Figure 20-2   The second rule checks the X-Spam-Flag

where the size is less than 200,000 bytes. The rule pipes messages through **/usr/bin/spamc**. This rule uses nice to conserve system resources. The Advanced tab specifies that the rule is applied to incoming messages and filtering does not stop if the message matches this rule.

The first rule adds an X-Spam-Flag line to each piece of email it processes. The second rule checks the value of the flag on this line. If the X-Spam-Flag line contains YES, the second rule moves the email to a folder named **spam** (Figure 20-2). Because the **If this filter matches, stop processing here** box is checked in the Advanced tab, KMail does not further process messages marked as spam. Messages not marked as spam can be processed by other rules.

SELinux   When SELinux is set to use a targeted policy, the SpamAssassin daemon, **spamd**, is protected by SELinux. You can disable this protection if necessary. For more information refer to "Setting the Targeted Policy with system-config-securitylevel" on page 402.

WEBMAIL

Traditionally you read email using a dedicated email client such as KMail. Recently it has become more common to use a Web application to read email. If you have an email account with a commercial provider such as Gmail, HotMail, or Yahoo! Mail, you use a Web browser to read email. Email read in this manner is called *Webmail*. Unlike email you read on a dedicated client, you can read Webmail from anywhere you can open a browser on the Internet: You can check your email from an Internet cafe or a friend's computer, for example.

SquirrelMail (**squirrelmail** package) provides Webmail services; the SquirrelMail files reside in **/usr/share/squirrelmail**. If you want to run SquirrelMail, you must run IMAP (page 647) because SquirrelMail uses IMAP to receive and authenticate email. You must also run Apache (Chapter 26) so a user can use a browser to connect to SquirrelMail.

SquirrelMail is modular: You can easily add functionality using plugins. There are plugins that allow you to share a calendar and plugins that give you the ability to

Figure 20-3   SquirrelMail login page

change passwords using the Webmail interface. See the plugins section of the SquirrelMail Web site for more information.

Create the following link to make SquirrelMail accessible from the Web:

```
# ln -s /usr/share/squirrelmail /var/www/html/mail
```

With this link in place, you can point a Web browser at **http://localhost/mail** to display the SquirrelMail login page (Figure 20-3).

Next use the **conf.pl** script in **/usr/share/squirrelmail/config** to configure SquirrelMail:

```
# cd /usr/share/squirrelmail/config
# ./conf.pl
SquirrelMail Configuration : Read: config_default.php (1.4.0)
--------------------------------------------------------
Main Menu --
1.  Organization Preferences
2.  Server Settings
3.  Folder Defaults
4.  General Options
5.  Themes
6.  Address Books
7.  Message of the Day (MOTD)
8.  Plugins
9.  Database
10. Languages

D.  Set pre-defined settings for specific IMAP servers

C   Turn color on
S   Save data
Q   Quit

Command >>
```

The only item that you must set to get SquirrelMail to work is the server's domain name (from the Server Settings page). SquirrelMail provides several themes; if you do not like the way SquirrelMail looks, choose another theme from the Themes page.

MAILING LISTS

A mailing list can be an asset if you regularly send email to the same large group of people. A mailing list provides several advantages over listing numerous recipients in the To or Cc field of an email or sending the same email individually to many people:

- **Anonymity** None of the recipients of the email can see the addresses of the other recipients.

- **Archiving** Email sent to the list is stored in a central location where list members or the public, as specified by the list administrator, can browse through it.

- **Access control** You can easily specify who can send email to the list.

- **Consistency** When you send mail to a group of people using To or Cc, it is all too easy to leave people who want to be on the list off and to leave people who want to be off the list on.

- **Efficiency** A mailing list application spreads email transmissions over time so it does not overload the mail server.

Mailman provides mailing list support. The bulk of Mailman resides in **/usr/lib/mailman**. The configuration file is **/etc/mailman/mm_cfg.py**, which is a link to **/usr/lib/mailman/Mailman/mm_cfg.py**. Before you can use Mailman, you need to replace **fqdn** in the two following lines in **mm_cfg.py** with the name of the local domain enclosed within single quotation marks:

```
DEFAULT_URL_HOST   = fqdn
DEFAULT_EMAIL_HOST = fqdn
```

After making these changes, create a new mailing list with the newlist utility:

```
# /usr/lib/mailman/bin/newlist
Enter the name of the list: painting_class
Enter the email of the person running the list: helen@tcorp.com
Initial painting_class password:
To finish creating your mailing list, you must edit your /etc/aliases (or
equivalent) file by adding the following lines, and possibly running the
'newaliases' program:

## painting_class mailing list
painting_class:                "|/usr/lib/mailman/mail/mailman post painting_class"
painting_class-admin:          "|/usr/lib/mailman/mail/mailman admin painting_class"
painting_class-bounces:        "|/usr/lib/mailman/mail/mailman bounces painting_class"
painting_class-confirm:        "|/usr/lib/mailman/mail/mailman confirm painting_class"
painting_class-join:           "|/usr/lib/mailman/mail/mailman join painting_class"
painting_class-leave:          "|/usr/lib/mailman/mail/mailman leave painting_class"
```

```
painting_class-owner:         "|/usr/lib/mailman/mail/mailman owner painting_class"
painting_class-request:       "|/usr/lib/mailman/mail/mailman request painting_class"
painting_class-subscribe:     "|/usr/lib/mailman/mail/mailman subscribe painting_class"
painting_class-unsubscribe:   "|/usr/lib/mailman/mail/mailman unsubscribe painting_class"

Hit enter to notify painting_class owner...
```

Before the list can receive email, you need to copy the lines generated by newlist to the end of **/etc/aliases** (page 633) and run newaliases.

Mailman includes a Web configuration interface that you can enable by configuring a Web server to run the scripts in **/usr/lib/mailman/cgi-bin**. Refer to the file **/etc/httpd/conf.d/mailman.conf** for a sample entry that you can put in **/etc/httpd/conf/httpd.conf** (page 794) to set up this interface (pipermail is the archive manager that Mailman uses).

SETTING UP AN IMAP OR POP3 SERVER

Two protocols allow users to retrieve email remotely: IMAP (Internet Message Access Protocol) and POP (Post Office Protocol). The **dovecot** package (www.dovecot.org) includes the **imap-login** and **pop3-login** daemons that implement these protocols. Typically you do not have to modify the **dovecot** configuration file (**/etc/dovecot.conf**). See **/usr/share/doc/dovecot*** for more information.

The **dovecot** self-signed certificate   The following commands generate and install the self-signed certificates that **dovecot** requires:

FEDORA
```
# export SSLDIR=/etc/pki/dovecot
# cd /etc/pki/dovecot
# /usr/share/doc/dovecot-1.0/examples/mkcert.sh
```

RHEL   First edit **/usr/share/doc/dovecot*/dovecot-openssl.cnf** as necessary. Typically no changes are needed. Then give the following commands to generate and install the self-signed certificates that **dovecot** requires:

```
# mkdir -p /etc/ssl/certs /etc/ssl/private
# cd /usr/share/doc/dovecot*
# sh mkcert.sh
```

The **mkcert.sh** script writes the certificates to the directories you created with the first command.

RHEL+FEDORA   Run chkconfig to cause the **dovecot** daemons to start when the system enters multiuser mode:

```
# /sbin/chkconfig dovecot on
```

Start the daemons with the following command:

```
# /sbin/service dovecot start
Starting Dovecot Imap:                                        [  OK  ]
```

Despite **dovecot** reporting that it started the IMAP server only, it also starts the POP3 server.

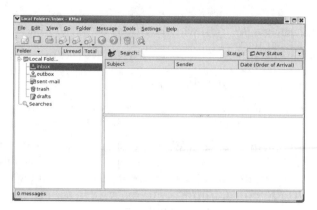

Figure 20-4   The initial KMail window

SETTING UP KMAIL

KMail is the graphical email client for KDE that is compatible with the MIME, SMTP, POP3, and IMAP standards. To start KMail, give the command **kmail** from a terminal emulator window or from a Run Command window (press ALT-F2 to open this window). You can also choose **Internet⇨KMail** from the KDE main menu. You can run KMail from any desktop environment, including GNOME. Figure 20-4 shows the initial KMail window.

When you start KMail for the first time, it takes you through the steps necessary to configure it. Alternatively, you can configure KMail by selecting **Configure KMail** from the Settings menu on the menubar to display the Configure KMail window (Figure 20-5). This window has buttons along the left side; click the buttons to display different configuration pages on the right.

Identity   KMail sets up a minimal identity for you. Click the **Identities** button to display the Identities page. From this page you can create new identities and modify existing ones, such as the default identity that KMail created for you. You can specify your email address, a reply-to address (if it differs from your email address), a signature that KMail automatically appends to your outgoing email messages, and more.

Help   KMail provides help in setting up KMail to send and receive email. Click the **Help** button at the lower-left corner of any KMail window to display the appropriate page of the online Configure KMail manual (part of the KDE Help Center).

Accounts   Once you have an identity, you need to set up incoming and outgoing accounts. Click the **Accounts** button to display the Accounts page where you can set up accounts for sending and receiving messages. This page has two tabs: Sending and Receiving.

Outgoing account   Click the **Sending** tab on the Accounts page to display the outgoing accounts. The outgoing account defaults to **sendmail** on the local system. If you use the local **sendmail**, you need to configure it as explained in "JumpStart I: Configuring sendmail on a Client" on page 630. If you are using SMTP, you need to remove the **sendmail** account and add an SMTP account. To do so, highlight the **sendmail** account and

Figure 20-5   The Configure KMail window

click **Remove**; then click **Add** to display the Add Transport window where you can select **sendmail** or SMTP.

Incoming account   Click the **Receiving** tab on the Accounts page to display the incoming accounts; there is no default incoming account. Click **Add** to display the Add Account window where you can select a type of account such as Local mailbox, POP3, or IMAP. If you receive mail both locally and from an ISP, you need to set up two accounts. For a POP3 or IMAP account you need to specify the server (host) and your username and password on the server. If you want KMail to check for mail periodically, turn on **Enable interval mail checking** and specify how often KMail should check for mail.

You do not have to change any settings on other pages. Following is a summary of what you will find on each of the Configure KMail pages:

- **Identities**   Specify one or more email identities including a name and email address in the General tab, a signature in the Signature tab, and use of PGP or GnuPG (page 992) and your OpenPGP key in the Cryptography tab.

- **Accounts**   Specify outgoing and incoming email accounts.

- **Appearance**   Specify how KMail looks, including fonts, colors, layout, and headers.

- **Composer**   Specify what outgoing messages look like and which headers are included when you reply to or forward a message.

- **Security**   Specify security features including whether you want to receive HTML messages in HTML or plain text. Receiving HTML messages in HTML can make a system less secure.

- **Misc**   Specify KMail options including which warnings you receive, how messages you read are marked, and what happens when you exit from KMail.

KMail has a lot of options and features. Use the **Help** button to get assistance. It is easy to set up KMail for basic use. As you become more comfortable using it, you can configure KMail to a greater extent to take care of more tasks for you.

AUTHENTICATED RELAYING

If you travel with a portable computer such as a laptop, you may connect to the Internet through a different connection at each location where you work. Perhaps you travel for work, or maybe you just bring your laptop home at night.

This section does not apply if you always dial in to the network through your ISP. In that case, you are always connected to your ISP's network and it is as though you never moved your computer.

On a laptop you do not use a local instance of **sendmail** to send email. Instead you use SMTP to connect to an ISP or to a company's SMTP server, which relays the outgoing mail. To avoid relaying email for anyone, including malicious users who would send spam, SMTP servers restrict who they relay email for, based on IP address. By implementing authenticated relaying, you can cause the SMTP server to authenticate, based on user identification. In addition, SMTP can encrypt communication when you send mail from your email client and use the SMTP server.

An authenticated relay provides these advantages over a plain connection:

- You can send email from any Internet connection.
- The secure connection makes it more difficult to intercept email as it traverses the Internet.
- The outgoing mail server requires authentication, preventing it from being used for spam.

You set up authenticated relaying by creating an SSL certificate or using an existing one, enabling SSL in **sendmail**, and telling your email client to connect to the SMTP server using SSL. If you have an SSL certificate from a company such as Verisign, you can skip the next section, in which you create a self-signed certificate.

CREATING A SELF-SIGNED CERTIFICATE FOR sendmail

FEDORA The default location for SSL certificates is **/etc/pki/tls/certs** (PKI stands for public key infrastructure). Working as **root**, use mkdir to create this directory if necessary and then use the **Makefile** in this directory to generate the required certificates. Apache uses a similar procedure for creating a certificate (page 822).

```
# cd /etc/pki/tls/certs
# make sendmail.pem
...
Generating a 1024 bit RSA private key
........................++++++
........................++++++
```

```
writing new private key to '/tmp/openssl.q15963'
-----
You are about to be asked to enter information that will be incorporated
into your certificate request.
What you are about to enter is what is called a Distinguished Name or a DN.
There are quite a few fields but you can leave some blank
For some fields there will be a default value,
If you enter '.', the field will be left blank.
-----
Country Name (2 letter code) [GB]:US
State or Province Name (full name) [Berkshire]:California
Locality Name (eg, city) [Newbury]:San Francisco
Organization Name (eg, company) [My Company Ltd]:Sobell Associates Inc.
Organizational Unit Name (eg, section) []:
Common Name (eg, your name or your server's hostname) []:sobell.com
Email Address []:mgs@sobell.com
```

You can enter any information you wish in the certificate.

RHEL The default location for SSL certificates is **/usr/share/ssl/certs**. Before giving the **make sendmail.pem** command as explained above, use mkdir to create this directory if necessary and then cd to it.

ENABLING SSL IN sendmail

Once you have a certificate, instruct **sendmail** to use it by adding the following lines to **sendmail.mc**:

```
define('confAUTH_OPTIONS', 'A p')
TRUST_AUTH_MECH('EXTERNAL DIGEST-MD5 CRAM-MD5 LOGIN PLAIN')
define('confAUTH_MECHANISMS', 'EXTERNAL GSSAPI DIGEST-MD5 CRAM-MD5 LOGIN PLAIN')
```

The first of these lines tells **sendmail** to allow authenticated users to relay. The next two lines specify the authentication mechanisms.

The first option for confAUTH_OPTIONS, **A**, instructs **sendmail** to use the AUTH parameter when sending mail only if authentication succeeded. The second option, **p**, instructs **sendmail**, for connections that are not secure, not to allow authentication methods that could be cracked by a packet sniffer.

Now add the following lines to **sendmail.mc** to tell **sendmail** where the certificate is:

```
define('CERT_DIR', '/etc/pki/tls/certs')
define('confCACERT_PATH', 'CERT_DIR')
define('confCACERT', 'CERT_DIR/sendmail.pem')
define('confSERVER_CERT', 'CERT_DIR/sendmail.pem')
define('confSERVER_KEY', 'CERT_DIR/sendmail.pem')
define('confCLIENT_CERT', 'CERT_DIR/sendmail.pem')
define('confCLIENT_KEY', 'CERT_DIR/sendmail.pem')
```

Encrypted connections are made in one of two ways: SSL (simpler) or TLS. SSL requires a dedicated port and has the client and the server negotiate a secure connection and continue the transaction as if the connection were not encrypted. TLS has the client connect to the server using an insecure connection and then issue a

STARTTLS command to negotiate a secure connection. TLS runs over the same port as an unencrypted connection. Because many clients support only SSL, it is a good idea to instruct **sendmail** to listen on the SMTPS port. The final line that you add to **sendmail.mc** instructs **sendmail** to listen on the SSL port:

```
DAEMON_OPTIONS( 'Port=smtps, Name=TLSMTA, M=s')
```

ENABLING SSL IN THE MAIL CLIENT

Enabling SSL in a mail client is usually quite simple. For example, KMail provides **Settings⇨Configure KMail⇨Accounts⇨Receiving⇨Add/Modify⇨Extras** that allows you to choose the type of encryption you want to use: **None, SSL,** or **TLS.**

ALTERNATIVES TO sendmail

Over the years, **sendmail** has grown to be enormously complex. Its complexity makes it challenging to configure if you want to set up something more than a simple mail server. Its size and complexity also add to its vulnerability. For optimal security, make sure you run the latest version of **sendmail** and always keep **sendmail** up-to-date. You might consider using one of the following alternatives.

Postfix   Postfix (**postfix** package) is an alternative MTA. Postfix attempts to be fast and easy to administer, while also being **sendmail** compatible enough to not upset **sendmail** users. Postfix has a good reputation for ease of use and security and is a drop-in replacement for **sendmail.** Documentation for Postfix can be found at www.postfix.org/docs.html.

Qmail   Qmail is a direct competitor of Postfix and has the same objectives. By default, Qmail stores email using the **maildir** format as opposed to the **mbox** format that other MTAs use (page 632). The Qmail Web site is www.qmail.org.

CHAPTER SUMMARY

The **sendmail** daemon is an MTA (Mail Transfer Agent). When you send a message, **sendmail** works with other software to get it to the proper recipients. You can set up **sendmail** to relay email to an SMTP server that sends the email on to its ultimate destination or you can have **sendmail** send email directly to the SMTP servers for the domains receiving the email. By default, **sendmail** stores incoming messages in the mail spool directory, **/var/spool/mail.**

The file that controls many aspects of how **sendmail** works is **sendmail.cf.** If you edit **sendmail.mc,** when you restart **sendmail,** the **sendmail** init script generates **sendmail.cf.** The system administrator can use the **/etc/aliases** file and ordinary users can use **~/.forward** files to reroute email to one or more local or remote addresses, to files, or as input to programs.

You can use a program such as SpamAssassin to grade and mark email as to the likelihood of it being spam. You can then decide what to do with the marked email: You can look at each piece of potential spam and decide where to put it, or you can have your MUA automatically put potential spam in a special mailbox for spam.

Other programs that can help with email include SquirrelMail, which provides Webmail services, and Mailman, which provides mailing list support.

EXERCISES

1. By default, email addressed to **system** goes to **root**. How would you also save a copy in **/var/logs/systemmail**?

2. How would Max store a copy of his email in **~/mbox** and send a copy to **max@bravo.com**?

3. If your firewall allowed only the machine with the IP address 192.168.1.1 to send email outside the network, how would you instruct your local copy of **sendmail** to use this server as a relay?

4. What does **dnl** stand for in the m4 macro language? What are **dnl** commands used for?

5. SpamAssassin is installed on your mail server, with the threshold set to an unusually low value of 3, resulting in a lot of false positives. What rule could you give to your mail client to allow it to identify spam with a score of 5 or higher?

6. Describe the software and protocols used when Max sends an email to Sam on a remote Linux system.

ADVANCED EXERCISES

7. Your company's current mail server runs on a commercial UNIX server, and you are planning to migrate it to Linux. After copying the configuration files across to the Linux system, you find that it does not work. What might you have forgotten to change?

8. Assume you have a script that sends its output to standard output. How would you modify the script to send the output in an email to a user specified by the first argument on the command line? (You may assume that the data is stored in **$RESULT**.)

9. Give a simple way of reading your email that does not involve the use of an MUA.

10. If you accidentally delete the **/etc/aliases** file, how could you easily re-create it (assuming that you had not restarted **sendmail**)?

NIS: NETWORK INFORMATION SERVICE

NIS (Network Information Service) simplifies the maintenance of common administrative files by keeping them in a central database and having clients contact the database server to retrieve information from the database. Developed by Sun Microsystems, NIS is an example of the client/server paradigm.

Just as DNS addresses the problem of keeping multiple copies of **/etc/hosts** files up-to-date, NIS deals with the issue of keeping system-independent configuration files (such as **/etc/passwd**) current. Most networks today are *heterogeneous* (page 1035); even though they run different varieties of UNIX or Linux, they have certain common attributes, such as a **passwd** file.

INTRODUCTION TO NIS

A primary goal of a LAN administrator is to make the network transparent to users. One aspect of this transparency is presenting users with similar environments, including username and password, when they log in on different machines. From the administrator's perspective, the information that supports a user's environment should not be replicated but rather should be kept in a central location and distributed as requested. NIS simplifies this task.

As with DNS, users need not be aware that NIS is managing system configuration files. Setting up and maintaining NIS databases are tasks for the system administrator; individual users and users on single-user Linux systems rarely need to work directly with NIS.

Yellow Pages   NIS used to be called the *Yellow Pages,* and some people still refer to it by this name. Sun renamed the service because another corporation holds the trademark to that name. The names of NIS utilities and files, however, are reminiscent of the old name: ypcat displays and ypmatch searches an NIS file, and the server daemon is named **ypserv**.

HOW NIS WORKS

NIS domain   NIS makes a common set of information available to systems on a network. The network, referred to as an *NIS domain,* is characterized by each system having the same *NIS domain name* (different than a (DNS) *domain name* [page 1030]). Technically, an NIS domain is a set of NIS maps, or database files.

Master and slave servers   Each NIS domain must have exactly one master server; larger networks may have slave servers. Each slave server holds a copy of the NIS database from the master. The need for slave servers is based on the size of the NIS domain and the reliability of the systems and network. A system can belong to only one NIS domain at a time.

When a client determines that a server is down or is not responding fast enough, it selects another server, as specified in the configuration file. If it cannot reach a server, **ypbind** terminates with an error.

nsswitch.conf   Whether a system uses NIS, DNS, local files, or a combination as the source of certain information, and in what order, is determined by **/etc/nsswitch.conf** (page 435). When it needs information from the NIS database, a client requests the information from the NIS server. For example, when a user attempts to log in, the client system may authenticate the user with name and password information from the NIS server.

You can configure **nsswitch.conf** to cause **/etc/passwd** to override NIS password information for the local system. When you do not export the **root** account to NIS (and you should not), this setup allows you to have a unique **root** password for each system.

Source files   Under Red Hat Linux, NIS derives the information it offers—such as usernames, passwords, and local system names and IP addresses—from local ASCII configuration files such as **/etc/passwd** and **/etc/hosts**. These files are called *source files* or *master files*. (Some administrators avoid confusion by using different files for local configuration and NIS source information.) An NIS server can include information from as many of the following source files as is appropriate:

/etc/group	Defines groups and their members
/etc/gshadow	Provides shadow passwords for groups
/etc/hosts	Maps local systems and IP addresses
/etc/passwd	Lists user information
/etc/printcap	Lists printer information
/etc/rpc	Maps RPC program names and numbers
/etc/services	Maps system service names and port numbers
/etc/shadow	Provides shadow passwords for users

The information that NIS offers is based on files that change from time to time; NIS is responsible for making this changing information available in a timely manner to all systems in the NIS domain.

NIS maps   Before NIS can store the information contained in a source file, it must be converted to a *dbm* (page 1028) format file called a *map*. Each map is indexed on one field (column). Records (rows) from a map can be retrieved by specifying a value from the indexed field. Some files generate two maps, each indexed on a different field. For example, the **/etc/passwd** file generates two maps: one indexed by username, the other indexed by UID. These maps are named **passwd.byname** and **passwd.byuid**.

optional   NIS maps correspond to C library functions. The **getpwnam**() and **getpwuid**() functions obtain username and UID information from **/etc/passwd** on non-NIS systems. On NIS systems, these functions place RPC calls to the NIS server in a process that is transparent to the application calling the function.

Map names   The names of the maps that NIS uses correspond to the files in the **/var/yp/***nisdomainname* directory on the master server, where *nisdomainname* is the name of the NIS domain:

```
$ ls /var/yp/mgs
group.bygid    mail.aliases     protocols.byname    services.byname
group.byname   netid.byname     protocols.bynumber  services.byservicename
hosts.byaddr   passwd.byname    rpc.byname          ypservers
hosts.byname   passwd.byuid     rpc.bynumber
```

Map nicknames To make it easier to refer to NIS maps, you can assign nicknames to maps. The **/var/yp/nicknames** file contains a list of commonly used nicknames. View the **nicknames** file or give the command **ypcat –x** to display the list of nicknames:

```
$ cat /var/yp/nicknames
passwd          passwd.byname
group           group.byname
networks        networks.byaddr
hosts           hosts.byname
protocols       protocols.bynumber
services        services.byname
aliases         mail.aliases
ethers          ethers.byname
```

Each line in **nicknames** contains a nickname followed by whitespace and the name of the map the nickname refers to. You can add, remove, or modify nicknames by changing the **nicknames** file.

Displaying maps The ypcat and ypmatch utilities display information from the NIS maps. Using the nickname **passwd**, the following command displays the information contained in the **passwd.byname** map:

```
$ ypcat passwd
mark:$1$X4JAzD0.$c.64fRCLPvQNSmq9qrfYv/:500:500:Mark Sobell:/home/mark:/bin/bash
...
```

By default, NIS stores passwords only for users with UIDs less than 500 (see MINUID, on page 666). Thus ypcat does not display lines for **root, bin,** and other system entries. You can display password information for a single user with ypmatch:

```
$ ypmatch mark passwd
mark:$1$X4JAzD0.$c.64fRCLPvQNSmq9qrfYv/:500:500:Mark Sobell:/home/mark:/bin/bash
```

You can retrieve the same information by filtering the output of ypcat through grep, but ypmatch is more efficient because it searches the map directly, using a single process. The ypmatch utility works on the key for the map only. To match members of the group or other fields not in a map, such as the *GECOS* (page 1033) field in **passwd,** you need to use ypcat with grep:

```
$ ypcat passwd | grep -i sobell
mark:$1$X4JAzD0.$c.64fRCLP9qrfYv/:500:500:Mark Sobell:/home/mark:/bin/bash
```

Terminology This chapter uses the following definitions:

NIS source files The ASCII files that NIS obtains information from
NIS maps The dbm-format files created from NIS source files
NIS database The collection of NIS maps

MORE INFORMATION

Local man pages   domainname, makedbm, **netgroup**, revnetgroup, **ypbind**, ypcat, ypinit, ypmatch, yppasswd, yppoll, yppush, ypset, **ypserv**, **ypserv.conf**, ypwhich, ypxfr, ypxfrd (Some of these are installed only when you install **ypserv**, which is needed when you run an NIS server [page 663].)

Web   www.linux-nis.org

SETTING UP AN NIS CLIENT

This section discusses how to set up an NIS client on the local system.

PREREQUISITES

Install the following packages:

- **yp-tools**
- **ypbind**

Run chkconfig to cause **ypbind** to start when the system enters multiuser mode:

```
# /sbin/chkconfig ypbind on
```

After you have configured **ypbind**, start it with service:

```
# /sbin/service ypbind start
Binding to the NIS domain:                              [  OK  ]
Listening for an NIS domain server.
```

NOTES

If there is no NIS server for the local system's NIS domain, you need to set one up (page 663). If there is an NIS server, you need to know the name of the NIS domain the system belongs to and (optionally) the name or IP address of one or more NIS servers for the NIS domain.

An NIS client can run on the same system as an NIS server.

SELinux   When SELinux is set to use a targeted policy, NIS is protected by SELinux. You can disable this protection if necessary. For more information refer to "Setting the Targeted Policy with system-config-securitylevel" on page 402.

STEP-BY-STEP SETUP

This section lists the steps involved in setting up and starting an NIS client.

SPECIFYING THE SYSTEM'S NIS DOMAIN NAME

Specify the system's NIS domain name in the **/etc/sysconfig/network** file by adding the following line:

NISDOMAIN=nisdomainname

where ***nisdomainname*** is the name of the NIS domain that the local system belongs to. The **ypbind** and **ypserv** init scripts execute the **network** file so that the name of

A DNS domain name is different from an NIS domain name

tip The DNS domain name is used throughout the Internet to refer to a group of systems. DNS maps these names to IP addresses to enable systems to communicate with one another.

The NIS domain name is used strictly to identify systems that share an NIS server and is normally not seen or used by users and other programs. Some administrators use one name as both a DNS domain name and an NIS domain name, although this practice can degrade security.

the system's NIS domain is set just before it is needed. You can use the nisdomain-name utility to set or view the NIS domain name, but setting it in this manner does not maintain the name when the system is rebooted:

```
# nisdomainname
(none)
# nisdomainname mgs
# nisdomainname
mgs
```

To avoid confusion, use **nisdomainname**, not **domainname**

caution The domainname and nisdomainname utilities do the same thing: They display or set the system's NIS domain name. Use nisdomainname to avoid confusion when you are also working with DNS domain names.

You must set the local system's NIS domain name

caution If you do not set the local system's NIS domain name, when you start **ypbind**, it sends a message to **syslogd** (page 562) and quits.

EDIT /etc/yp.conf TO SPECIFY AN NIS SERVER

Edit **/etc/yp.conf** to specify one or more NIS servers (masters and/or slaves). As explained by comments in the file, you can use one of three formats to specify each server:

*domain **nisdomain** server **server_name***

*domain **nisdomain** broadcast* (**do not use**)

*ypserver **server_name***

where ***nisdomain*** is the name of the NIS domain that the local (client) system belongs to and ***server_name*** is the hostname of the NIS server that the local system queries. The second format is less secure than the first and third formats because it exposes the system to rogue servers by broadcasting a request for a server to identify itself.

You can use multiple lines to specify multiple servers for one or more domains. Specifying multiple servers for a single domain allows the system to change to another server when its current server is slow or down.

When you specify more than one NIS domain, you must set the system's NIS domain name before starting **ypbind** so the client queries the proper server. Specifying the NIS domain name in **/etc/sysconfig/network** before running the **ypbind** init script takes care of this issue. See "Specifying the System's NIS Domain Name" on page 659.

START ypbind

The Red Hat Linux **ypbind** daemon is **ypbind-mt** renamed—that is, a newer, multi-threaded version of the older **ypbind** daemon. Use chkconfig to cause **ypbind** to start each time the system enters multiuser mode and service to start **ypbind** immediately. For more information refer to "Prerequisites" on page 659.

TESTING THE SETUP

After starting **ypbind**, use nisdomainname to make sure the correct NIS domain name is set. Refer to "Specifying the System's NIS Domain Name" on page 659 if you need to set the NIS domain name. Next check that the system is set up to connect to the proper server. The name of the server is set in **/etc/yp.conf** (page 660).

```
$ ypwhich
peach
```

Make sure the NIS server is up and running (replace *server* with the name of the server that ypwhich returned):

```
$ /usr/sbin/rpcinfo -u server ypserv
program 100004 version 1 ready and waiting
program 100004 version 2 ready and waiting
```

After starting **ypbind**, check that it has registered with **portmap**:

```
$ /usr/sbin/rpcinfo -u localhost ypbind
program 100007 version 1 ready and waiting
program 100007 version 2 ready and waiting
```

If rpcinfo does not report that **ypbind** is **ready and waiting**, check that **ypbind** is running:

```
$ /sbin/service ypbind status
ypbind (pid 28689) is running...
```

If NIS is still not working properly, use the init script to stop **ypbind**. Start it again with debugging turned on:

```
# /sbin/service ypbind stop
Shutting down NIS services:                          [ OK ]
# /sbin/ypbind -debug
...
```

The **–debug** option keeps **ypbind** in the foreground and causes it to send error messages and debugging output to standard error.

yppasswd: CHANGES NIS PASSWORDS

The yppasswd utility—not to be confused with the **yppasswdd** daemon (two **d**'s; see page 669) that runs on the NIS server—replaces the functionality of passwd on clients when you are using NIS for passwords. Where passwd changes password information in the **/etc/shadow** file on the local system, yppasswd changes password information in the **/etc/shadow** file on the NIS master server *and* in the NIS **shadow.byname** map. Optionally, yppasswd can also change user information in the **/etc/passwd** file and **passwd.byname** map.

The yppasswd utility changes the way you log in on all systems in the NIS domain that use NIS to authenticate passwords. The yppasswd utility cannot change **root** and system passwords; by default, NIS does not store passwords of users with UIDs less than 500. You have to use passwd to change these users' passwords locally.

To use yppasswd, the **yppasswdd** daemon must be running on the NIS master server.

passwd VERSUS yppasswd

When a user who is authenticated using NIS passwords runs passwd to change her password, all appears to work properly, yet the user's password is not changed: The user needs to use yppasswd. The **root** and system accounts, in contrast, must use passwd to change their passwords. A common solution to this problem is first to rename passwd, for example, to rootpasswd, and then to change its permissions so only **root** can execute it.[1] Second, create a link to yppasswd named passwd:

```
# ls -l /usr/bin/passwd
-r-s--x--x 1 root root 16336 Feb 13 2006 /usr/bin/passwd
# mv /usr/bin/passwd /usr/bin/rootpasswd
# chmod 700 /usr/bin/rootpasswd
# ln -s /usr/bin/yppasswd /usr/bin/passwd
# ls -l /usr/bin/{yppasswd,passwd,rootpasswd}
lrwxrwxrwx 1 root root    17 Oct  8 15:32 /usr/bin/passwd -> /usr/bin/yppasswd
-rwx------ 1 root root 16336 Feb 13 2006 /usr/bin/rootpasswd
-r-xr-xr-x 3 root root 18544 Jan 25 2006 /usr/bin/yppasswd
```

With this setup, a non**root** user changing his password using passwd will run yppasswd, which is appropriate. If **root** or a system account user runs passwd (really yppasswd), yppasswd displays an error that will ideally remind the administrator to run rootpasswd.

MODIFYING USER INFORMATION

As long as **yppasswdd** is running on the NIS master server, a user can use yppasswd from an NIS client to change her NIS password and **root** can change any user's password (except that of **root** or a system account user). A user can also use yppasswd to

---

1. The passwd utility has setuid permission with execute permission for all users. If, after changing its name and permissions, you want to restore its original name and permissions, first change its name and then give the command **chmod 4511 /usr/bin/passwd**.

change his login shell and *GECOS* (page 1033) information if the **yppasswdd** daemon is set up to permit these changes. Refer to "**yppasswdd:** The NIS Password Update Daemon" on page 669 for information on how to configure **yppasswdd** to permit users to change these fields. Use the **–l** option with yppasswd to change the login shell. Use **–f** to change GECOS information:

```
$ yppasswd -f
Changing NIS account information for mark on peach.
Please enter password:

Changing full name for mark on peach.
To accept the default, simply press return. To enter an empty
field, type the word "none".
Name [MSobell]: Mark G Sobell
Location []: SF
Office Phone []:
Home Phone []:

The GECOS information has been changed on peach.

$ ypmatch mark passwd
mark:$1$X49qrfYv/:500:500:Mark G Sobell,SF:/home/mark:/bin/bash
```

ADDING AND REMOVING USERS

There are several ways to add and remove users from the NIS **passwd** map. The easiest approach is to keep the **/etc/passwd** file on the NIS master server synchronized with the **passwd** map. You can keep these files synchronized by making changes to the **passwd** file using standard tools such as passwd and running ypinit to update the map (page 668).

SETTING UP AN NIS SERVER

This section discusses how to set up an NIS server.

PREREQUISITES

Decide on an NIS domain name. Some sites use their DNS domain name as the NIS domain name. Choosing a different name is more secure.

Install the following package:

• ypserv

Run chkconfig to cause **ypserv** to start when the system enters multiuser mode:

```
# /sbin/chkconfig ypserv on
```

On the master server only, run chkconfig to cause the map server, **ypxfrd** (page 668), to start when the system enters multiuser mode:

```
# /sbin/chkconfig ypxfrd on
```

In addition, on the master server only, run chkconfig to cause the NIS password update daemon, **yppasswdd** (page 669), to start when the system enters multiuser mode:

```
# /sbin/chkconfig yppasswdd on
```

After configuring **ypserv**, start it with the **ypserv** init script:

```
# /sbin/service ypserv start
Starting YP server services:
```

Next start the **ypxfrd** daemon (page 668) on the system running the master server:

```
# /sbin/service ypxfrd start
Starting YP map server:                                    [  OK  ]
```

Now start the **yppasswdd** daemon (page 669) on the master server:

```
# /sbin/service yppasswdd start
Starting YP passwd service:                                [  OK  ]
```

NOTES

An NIS client can run on the same system as an NIS server.

There must be only one master server for each domain.

You can run multiple NIS domain servers (for different domains) on a single system.

An NIS server serves the NIS domains listed in **/var/yp**. For a more secure system, remove the maps directories from **/var/yp** when disabling an NIS server.

SELinux   When SELinux is set to use a targeted policy, NIS is protected by SELinux. You can disable this protection if necessary. For more information refer to "Setting the Targeted Policy with system-config-securitylevel" on page 402.

STEP-BY-STEP SETUP

This section lists the steps involved in setting up and starting an NIS server.

SPECIFY THE SYSTEM'S NIS DOMAIN NAME

Specify the system's NIS domain name by adding the following line to the **/etc/sysconfig/network** file:

NISDOMAIN=nisdomainname

where ***nisdomainname*** is the name of the NIS domain that the local system belongs to. For more information refer to "Specifying the System's NIS Domain Name" on page 659.

EDIT /etc/ypserv.conf TO CONFIGURE THE NIS SERVER

The **/etc/ypserv.conf** file, which holds NIS server configuration information, specifies options and access rules. Option rules specify server options and have the following format:

option: value

OPTIONS

Following is a list of *option*s and their default *value*s:

files Specifies the maximum number of map files that **ypserv** caches. Set to 0 to turn off caching. Default is 30.

trusted_master On a slave server, the name/IP address of the master server that new maps will be accepted from. Default is no master server, meaning no new maps are accepted.

xfer_check_port YES (default) requires the master server to run on a *privileged port* (page 1049). NO allows it to run on any port.

ACCESS RULES

Access rules, which specify which hosts and domains can access which maps, have the following format:

host:domain:map:security

where *host* and *domain* specify the IP address and NIS domain this rule applies to; *map* is the name of the map that this rule applies to; and *security* is either **none** (always allow access), **port** (allow access from a privileged port), or **deny** (never allow access).

The following lines appear in the **ypserv.conf** file supplied with Red Hat Linux:

```
$ cat /etc/ypserv.conf
...
# Not everybody should see the shadow passwords, not secure, since
# under MSDOG everbody is root and can access ports < 1024 !!!
*                            : *      : shadow.byname     : port
*                            : *      : passwd.adjunct.byname : port
...
```

These lines restrict the **shadow.byname** and **passwd.adjunct.byname** (the **passwd** map with shadow [asterisk] entries) maps to access from ports numbered less than 1024. As the comment points out, however, anyone using a DOS or early Windows system on the network can read the maps because they can access ports numbered less than 1024.

The following example describes a LAN with some addresses that you want to grant NIS access from and some that you do not; perhaps you have a wireless segment or some public network connections that you do not want to expose to NIS. You can list the systems or an IP subnet that you want to grant access to in **ypserv.conf**. Anyone logging in on another IP address will then be denied NIS services. The following line from **ypserv.conf** grants access to anyone logging in from an IP address in the range of 192.168.0.1 to 192.168.0.255 (specified as 192.168.0.1 with a subnet mask [page 423] of /24):

```
$ cat /etc/ypserv.conf
...
  192.168.0.1/24 : * : * : none
```

CREATE /var/yp/securenets TO ENHANCE SECURITY

To enhance system security, create the **/var/yp/securenets** file, which prevents unauthorized systems from sending RPC requests to the NIS server and retrieving NIS maps. Notably **securenets** prevents unauthorized users from retrieving the **shadow** map, which contains encrypted passwords. When **securenets** does not exist or is empty, an NIS server accepts requests from any system.

Each line of **securenets** lists a netmask and IP address. NIS accepts requests from systems whose IP addresses are specified in **securenets** and ignores and logs requests from other addresses. You must include the (local) server system as **localhost** (127.0.0.1) in **securenets**. A simple **securenets** file follows:

```
$ cat /var/yp/securenets
# you must accept requests from localhost
255.255.255.255        127.0.0.1
#
# accept requests from IP addresses 192.168.0.1 - 192.168.0.62
255.255.255.192        192.168.0.0
#
# accept requests from IP addresses starting with 192.168.14
255.255.255.0          192.168.14.0
```

EDIT /var/yp/Makefile TO SPECIFY MAPS

The make utility (page 842), controlled by **/var/yp/Makefile**, uses makedbm to create the NIS maps that hold the information that NIS distributes. When you run ypinit on the master server, ypinit calls make: You do not need to run make manually.

Edit **/var/yp/Makefile** to set options and specify which maps to create. The following sections discuss **/var/yp/Makefile** in more detail.

VARIABLES

Following is a list of variables you can set in **/var/yp/Makefile**. The values following the words **Red Hat** are the values set in the file distributed by Red Hat.

B   Do not change.

Red Hat: not set

NOPUSH   Specifies that **ypserv** is not to copy (push) maps to slave servers. Set to TRUE if you do not have any slave NIS servers; set to FALSE to cause NIS to copy maps to slave servers.

Red Hat: TRUE

MINUID, MINGID   Specifies the lowest UID and GID numbers to include in NIS maps. In the **/etc/passwd** and **/etc/group** files, lower ID numbers belong to **root** and system accounts and groups. To enhance security, NIS does not distribute password and group information about these users and groups. Set MINUID to the lowest UID number you want to include in the NIS maps and set MINGID to the lowest GID number you want to include.

Red Hat: 500/500

NFSNOBODYUID,
NFSNOBODYGID

Specifies the UID and GID of the user named **nfsnobody**. NIS does not export values for this user. Set to 0 to export maps for **nfsnobody**.

Red Hat: 65534/65534

MERGE_PASSWD,
MERGE_GROUP

TRUE merges the **/etc/shadow** and **/etc/passwd** files and the **/etc/gshadow** and **/etc/group** files in the **passwd** and **group** maps, enabling shadow user passwords and group passwords.

Red Hat: TRUE/TRUE

FILE LOCATIONS

The next sections of **/var/yp/Makefile** specify the standard file locations; you do not normally need to change them. This part of the makefile is broken into the following groups:

Commands   Locates gawk and make and sets a value for umask (page 420)
Source directories   Locates directories that contain NIS source files
NIS source files   Locates NIS source files used to build the NIS database
Servers   Locates the file that lists NIS servers

THE all: TARGET

The **all:** target in **/var/yp/Makefile** specifies the maps that make is to build for NIS:

```
all:  passwd group hosts rpc services netid protocols mail \
        # netgrp shadow publickey networks ethers bootparams printcap \
        # amd.home auto.master auto.home auto.local passwd.adjunct \
        # timezone locale netmasks
```

The first line of the **all:** target lists the maps that make builds by default. This line starts with the word **all**, followed by a colon (:) and a TAB. Because each of the first three lines of the **all:** target ends with a backslash, each of the four physical lines in the **all:** target is part of one long logical line. The last three physical lines are commented out. Uncomment lines and delete or move map names until the list matches your needs.

As your needs change, you can edit the **all:** target in **Makefile** and run make in the **/var/yp** directory to modify the list of maps that NIS distributes.

START THE SERVERS

Start the master server and then the slave servers after completing the preceding steps. Use chkconfig to cause **ypserv** to start each time the system enters multiuser mode and service to start **ypserv** immediately. For more information refer to "Prerequisites" on page 663.

ypxfrd: the map server

The **ypxfrd** daemon speeds up the process of copying large NIS databases from servers to slaves. It allows slaves to copy the maps, thereby avoiding the need for each slave to copy the raw data and then compile the maps. When an NIS slave receives a message from the server stating that there is a new map, it starts ypxfr, which reads the map from the server.

The **ypxfrd** daemon runs on the master server only; it is not necessary to run it on slave servers. Use chkconfig to cause **ypxfrd** to start each time the system enters multiuser mode and service to start **ypxfrd** immediately. For more information refer to "Prerequisites" on page 663.

ypinit: BUILDS OR IMPORTS THE MAPS

The ypinit utility builds or imports and then installs the NIS database. On the master server, ypinit gathers information from the **passwd, group, hosts, networks, services, protocols, netgroup**, and **rpc** files in /etc and builds the database. On a slave server, ypinit copies the database from the master server.

You must run ypinit by giving its absolute pathname (**/usr/lib/yp/ypinit**). Use the **–m** option to create the domain subdirectory under **/var/yp** and build the maps that go in it on the master server; use the **–s** *master* option on slave servers to import maps from *master* (the master server). In the following example, ypinit asks for the names of each of the slave servers; it already has the name of the master server because this command is run on that system (**peach** in the example). Terminate the list with CONTROL-D on a line by itself. After you respond to the query about the list of servers being correct, ypinit builds the **ypservers** map and calls make with **/var/yp/Makefile**, which builds the maps specified in **Makefile**.

```
# /usr/lib/yp/ypinit -m

At this point, we have to construct a list of the hosts which will run NIS
servers.  peach is in the list of NIS server hosts.  Please continue to add
the names for the other hosts, one per line.  When you are done with the
list, type a <control D>.
next host to add:  peach
next host to add:  speedy
next host to add: CONTROL-D
The current list of NIS servers looks like this:

peach
speedy

Is this correct?  [y/n: y]  y
We need a few minutes to build the databases...
Building /var/yp/mgs/ypservers...
Running /var/yp/Makefile...
gmake[1]: Entering directory `/var/yp/mgs'
Updating passwd.byname...
Updating passwd.byuid...
Updating group.byname...
Updating group.bygid...
```

```
Updating hosts.byname...
Updating hosts.byaddr...
Updating rpc.byname...
Updating rpc.bynumber...
Updating services.byname...
Updating services.byservicename...
Updating netid.byname...
Updating protocols.bynumber...
Updating protocols.byname...
Updating mail.aliases...
gmake[1]: Leaving directory `/var/yp/mgs'

peach has been set up as a NIS master server.

Now you can run ypinit -s peach on all slave server.
```

TESTING

From the server, check that **ypserv** is connected to **portmap**:

```
# rpcinfo -p | grep ypserv
    100004    2    udp    849    ypserv
    100004    1    udp    849    ypserv
    100004    2    tcp    852    ypserv
    100004    1    tcp    852    ypserv
```

Again from the server system, make sure the NIS server is up and running:

```
$ /usr/sbin/rpcinfo -u localhost ypserv
program 100004 version 1 ready and waiting
program 100004 version 2 ready and waiting
```

If the server is not working properly, use service to stop **ypserv**. Start it again with debugging turned on:

```
# /sbin/service ypserv stop
Stopping YP server services:                                    [  OK  ]
# /usr/sbin/ypserv --debug
...
```

The **--debug** option keeps **ypserv** in the foreground and causes it to send error messages and debugging output to standard error.

yppasswdd: THE NIS PASSWORD UPDATE DAEMON

The NIS password update daemon, **yppasswdd**, runs only on the master server; it is not necessary to run it on slave servers. (If the master server is down and you try to change your password from a client, you get an error message.) When a user runs yppasswd (page 662) on a client, yppasswd exchanges information with the **yppasswdd** daemon to update the user's password (and optionally other) information in the NIS **shadow** (and optionally **passwd**) map and in the **/etc/shadow** (and optionally **/etc/passwd**) file on the NIS master server. Password change requests are sent to **syslogd** (page 562).

START yppasswdd

Use chkconfig to cause **yppasswdd** to start each time the system enters multiuser mode and service to start **yppasswdd** immediately. For more information refer to "Prerequisites" on page 663.

ALLOW GECOS AND LOGIN SHELL MODIFICATION

By default, **yppasswdd** does not allow users to change *GECOS* (page 1033) information or the login shell when they run yppasswd. You can allow users to change this information with options on the command line when you start **yppasswdd** or, more conveniently, by modifying the **/etc/sysconfig/yppasswdd** configuration file. The **–e chfn** option to **yppasswdd** allows users to change their GECOS information; **–e chsh** allows users to change their login shell. When you set the options in the **/etc/sysconfig/yppasswdd** file, they are set automatically each time the **yppasswdd** init file is run.

```
$ cat /etc/sysconfig/yppasswdd
...
YPPASSWDD_ARGS=" -e chfn -e chsh"
```

CHAPTER SUMMARY

NIS (Network Information Service) simplifies the management of common administrative files by maintaining them in a central database and having clients contact the database server to retrieve information from the database. The network that NIS serves is called an NIS domain. Each NIS domain has one master server; larger networks may have slave servers.

NIS derives the information it offers from local configuration files, such as **/etc/passwd** and **/etc/hosts**. These files are called source files or master files. Before NIS can store the information contained in a source file, it must be converted to dbm-format files, called maps. The ypcat and ypmatch utilities display information from NIS maps.

The yppasswd utility replaces the functionality of passwd on clients when you are using NIS to authenticate passwords. The **/etc/ypserv.conf** file, which holds NIS server configuration information, specifies options and access rules for the NIS server. To enhance system security, you can create a **/var/yp/securenets** file, which prevents unauthorized systems from sending RPC requests to the NIS server and retrieving NIS maps.

EXERCISES

1. What is the difference between the passwd and yppasswd utilities?

2. How would you prevent NIS from exporting the **root** user and other system users to clients?

3. How would you make NIS user information override local user information on client systems?

4. Why does the **/etc/passwd** file need two NIS maps?

ADVANCED EXERCISES

5. How can you use NIS to mirror the functionality of a private DNS server for a small network? Why should NIS not be used this way on a large network?

6. How can you find out if the working directory is the home directory of an NIS user?

7. What advantage does NIS provide when you use it with NFS?

8. Suggest a way to implement NIS maps so they can be indexed on more than one field.

22

NFS: SHARING FILESYSTEMS

The NFS (Network Filesystem) protocol, a UNIX de facto standard originally developed by Sun Microsystems, allows a server to share selected local directory hierarchies with client systems on a heterogeneous network. NFS runs on UNIX, DOS, Windows, VMS, Linux, and more. Files on the remote computer (the *fileserver*) appear as if they are present on the local system (the client). The physical location of a file is irrelevant to an NFS user.

NFS reduces storage needs and system administration workload. As an example, each system in a company traditionally holds its own copy of an application program. To upgrade the program, the administrator needs to upgrade it on each system. NFS allows you to store a copy of a program on a single system and give other users access to it over the network. This scenario minimizes storage requirements by reducing the number of locations that need to maintain the same data. In addition to boosting efficiency, NFS gives users on the network access to the same data (not just application programs), thereby improving data consistency and reliability. By consolidating data, NFS reduces administrative overhead and provides a convenience to users.

INTRODUCTION

Figure 22-1 shows the flow of data from a client to a server in a typical NFS client/server setup. An NFS directory hierarchy appears to users and application programs as just another directory hierarchy. By looking at it, you cannot tell that a given directory holds a remotely mounted NFS directory hierarchy and not a local **ext3** filesystem. The NFS server translates commands from the client into operations on the server's filesystem.

Diskless systems In many computer facilities, user files are stored on a central fileserver equipped with many large-capacity disk drives and devices that quickly and easily make backup copies of the data. A *diskless* system boots from a fileserver (netboots, discussed next), a CD, or a floppy diskette and loads system software from a fileserver. The Linux Terminal Server Project (LTSP.org) Web site says it all: "Linux makes a great platform for deploying diskless workstations that boot from a network server.

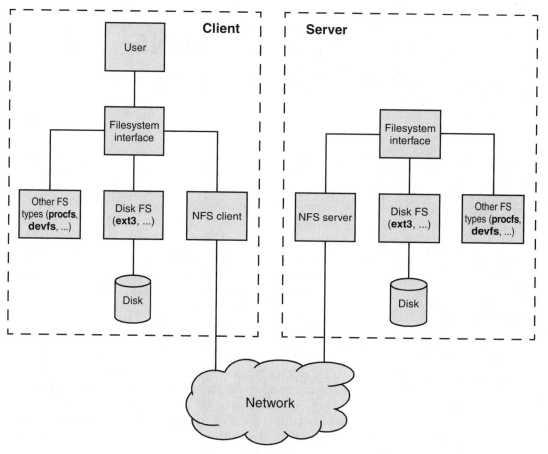

Figure 22-1 Flow of data in a typical NFS client/server setup

The LTSP is all about running thin client computers in a Linux environment."
Because a diskless workstation does not require a lot of computing power, you can
give older, retired computers a second life by using them as diskless systems.

Netboot/PXE You can *netboot* (page 1044) systems that are appropriately set up. Red Hat Linux
includes the PXE (Preboot Execution Environment) server package for netbooting
Intel systems. Older systems sometimes use tftp (Trivial File Transfer Protocol) for
netbooting. Non-Intel architectures have historically included netboot capabilities,
which Red Hat Linux also supports. You can build the Linux kernel so that it
mounts **root** (**/**) using NFS. Given the many ways to set up a system, the one you
choose depends on what you want to do. See the *Remote-Boot mini-HOWTO* for
more information.

Dataless systems Another type of Linux system is a *dataless* system, in which the client has a disk but
stores no user data (only Linux and the applications are kept on the disk). Setting
up this type of system is a matter of choosing which directory hierarchies are
mounted remotely.

df: shows where The df utility displays a list of the directory hierarchies available on the system,
directory hierarchies along with the amount of disk space, free and used, on each. The **–h** (human)
are mounted option makes the output more intelligible. Directory hierarchy names that are
prepended with **hostname:** are available through NFS.

```
[bravo]$ cd;pwd
/speedy.home/jenny
[bravo]$ df -h
Filesystem      Size  Used Avail Use% Mounted on
/dev/hda1       981M  287M  645M  31% /
/dev/hda6        20G  2.7G   16G  15% /usr
/dev/hda7       9.7G  384M  8.8G   5% /home
grape:/gc1      985M   92M  844M  10% /grape.gc1
grape:/gc5      3.9G  3.0G  738M  81% /grape.gc5
speedy:/home    3.9G  2.4G  1.4G  64% /speedy.home
```

In the preceding example, Jenny's home directory, **/home/jenny**, is on the remote
system **speedy**. Using NFS, the **/home** filesystem on **speedy** is mounted on **bravo**; to
make it easy to recognize, it is mounted as **/speedy.home**. The **/gc1** and **/gc5** filesystems on **grape** are mounted on **bravo** as **/grape.gc1** and **/grape.gc5**, respectively.

You can use the **–T** option to df to add a Type column to the display. The following
command uses **–t nfs** to display NFS filesystems only:

```
[grape]$ df -ht nfs
Filesystem      Size  Used Avail Use% Mounted on
grape:/gc1      985M   92M  844M  10% /grape.gc1
grape:/gc5      3.9G  3.0G  738M  81% /grape.gc5
speedy:/home    3.9G  2.4G  1.4G  64% /speedy.home
```

Errors Sometimes you may lose access to remote files. For example, a network problem or a
remote system crash may make these files temporarily unavailable. When you try to
access a remote file in these circumstances, you get an error message, such as **NFS
server speedy not responding**. When the local system can contact the remote server

again, you see another message, such as **NFS server speedy OK**. Setting up a stable network and server (or not using NFS) is the best defense against these kinds of problems.

Security NFS is based on the trusted-host paradigm (page 362) and therefore has all the security shortcomings that plague other services based on this paradigm. In addition, NFS is not encrypted. Because of these issues, you should implement NFS on a single LAN segment only, where you can be (reasonably) sure that systems on a LAN segment are what they claim to be. Make sure a firewall blocks NFS traffic from outside the LAN and never use NFS over the Internet.

To improve security, make sure UIDs and GIDs are the same on the server and clients (page 687).

MORE INFORMATION

Web nfs.sourceforge.net

HOWTO *NFS HOWTO*
Netboot and PXE   *Remote-Boot mini-HOWTO*

Book *NFS Illustrated* by Callaghan, Addison-Wesley (December 1999)

SETTING UP AN NFS CLIENT

This section covers setting up an NFS client, mounting remote directory hierarchies, and improving NFS performance.

PREREQUISITES

Install the following packages:

* **nfs-utils**

* **system-config-nfs** (optional)

The portmap utility (part of the **portmap** package; refer to "RPC Network Services" on page 377) must be running to enable reliable file locking.

There are no daemons to start for NFS clients.

JUMPSTART: MOUNTING A REMOTE DIRECTORY HIERARCHY

To set up an NFS client, mount the remote directory hierarchy the same way you mount a local directory hierarchy (page 466). The following sections detail this process.

mount: MOUNTS A REMOTE DIRECTORY HIERARCHY

The following examples show two ways to mount a remote directory hierarchy, assuming that **speedy** is on the same network as the local system and is sharing **/home** and **/export** with the local system. The **/export** directory on **speedy** holds two directory hierarchies that you want to mount: **/export/progs** and **/export/oracle**.

The example mounts **speedy**'s **/home** directory on **/speedy.home** on the local system, **/export/progs** on **/apps**, and **/export/oracle** on **/oracle**.

First use mkdir to create the directories that are the mount points for the remote directory hierarchies:

```
# mkdir /speedy.home /apps /oracle
```

You can mount any directory from an exported directory hierarchy. In this example, **speedy** exports **/export** and the local system mounts **/export/progs** and **/export/oracle**. The following commands manually mount the directory hierarchies one time:

```
# mount speedy:/home /speedy.home
# mount -o ro,nosuid speedy:/export/progs /apps
# mount -o ro speedy:/export/oracle /oracle
```

If you receive the error **mount: RPC: Program not registered**, it may mean NFS is not running on the server.

By default, directory hierarchies are mounted read-write, assuming the NFS server is exporting them with read-write permissions. The first of the preceding commands mounts the **/home** directory hierarchy from **speedy** on the local directory **/speedy.home**. The second and third commands use the **–o ro** option to force a readonly mount. The second command adds the **nosuid** option, which forces setuid (page 183) executables in the mounted directory hierarchy to run with regular permissions on the local system.

nosuid option If a user has the ability to run a setuid program, that user has the power of Superuser. This ability should be limited. Unless you know that a user will need to run a program with setuid permissions from a mounted directory hierarchy, always mount a directory hierarchy with the **nosuid** option. For example, you would need to mount a directory hierarchy with setuid privileges when a diskless workstation has its root partition mounted using NFS.

nodev option Mounting a device file creates another potential security hole. Although the best policy is not to mount untrustworthy directory hierarchies, it is not always possible to implement this policy. Unless a user needs to use a device on a mounted directory hierarchy, mount directory hierarchies with the **nodev** option, which prevents character and block special files (page 463) on the mounted directory hierarchy from being used as devices.

fstab file If you mount directory hierarchies frequently, you can add entries for the directory hierarchies to the **/etc/fstab** file (page 681). (Alternatively, you can use **automount**; see page 690.) The following **/etc/fstab** entries automatically mount the same directory hierarchies as in the previous example at the same time as the system mounts the local filesystems:

```
$ cat /etc/fstab
...
speedy:/home            /speedy.home    nfs     -           0  0
speedy:/export/progs    /apps           nfs     r,nosuid    0  0
speedy:/export/oracle   /oracle         nfs     r           0  0
```

A file that is mounted using NFS is always type **nfs** on the local system, regardless of what type it is on the remote system. Typically you do not run fsck on or back up an NFS directory hierarchy. The entries in the third, fifth, and sixth columns of **fstab** are usually **nfs** (filesystem type), **0** (do not back up this directory hierarchy with dump [page 545]), and **0** (do not run fsck [page 470] on this directory hierarchy). The options for mounting an NFS directory hierarchy differ from those for mounting an **ext3** or other type of filesystem. See the next section for details.

umount: UNMOUNTS A REMOTE DIRECTORY HIERARCHY

Use umount to unmount a remote directory hierarchy the same way you would unmount a local filesystem (page 469).

mount: MOUNTS A DIRECTORY HIERARCHY

The mount utility (page 466) associates a directory hierarchy with a mount point (a directory). You can use mount to mount an NFS (remote) directory hierarchy. This section describes some mount options. It lists default options first, followed by non-default options (enclosed in parentheses). You can use these options on the command line or in **/etc/fstab** (page 681). For a complete list of options, refer to the mount and nfs man pages.

ATTRIBUTE CACHING

File attributes, which are stored in a file's inode (page 460), provide information about a file, such as file modification time, size, links, and owner. File attributes do not include the data stored in a file. Typically file attributes do not change very often for an ordinary file; they change even less often for a directory file. Even the size attribute does not change with every write instruction: When a client is writing to an NFS-mounted file, several write instructions may be given before the data is actually transferred to the server. In addition, many file accesses, such as that performed by ls, are readonly operations and do not change the file's attributes or its contents. Thus a client can cache attributes and avoid costly network reads.

The kernel uses the modification time of the file to determine when its cache is out-of-date. If the time the attribute cache was saved is later than the modification time of the file itself, the data in the cache is current. The attribute cache of an NFS-mounted file must be periodically refreshed from the server to determine whether another process has modified the file. This period is specified as a minimum and maximum number of seconds for ordinary and directory files. Following is a list of options that affect attribute caching:

ac (noac) (**attribute cache**) Permits attribute caching (default). The **noac** option disables attribute caching. Although **noac** slows the server, it avoids stale attributes when two NFS clients actively write to a common directory hierarchy.

acdirmax=*n* (**attribute cache directory file maximum**) The *n* is the number of seconds, at a maximum, that NFS waits before refreshing directory file attributes (default is 60 seconds).

acdirmin=*n* (**attribute cache directory file minimum**) The *n* is the number of seconds, at a minimum, that NFS waits before refreshing directory file attributes (default is 30 seconds).

acregmax=*n* (**attribute cache regular file maximum**) The *n* is the number of seconds, at a maximum, that NFS waits before refreshing regular file attributes (default is 60 seconds).

acregmin=*n* (**attribute cache regular file minimum**) The *n* is the number of seconds, at a minimum, that NFS waits before refreshing regular file attributes (default is 3 seconds).

actimeo=*n* (**attribute cache timeout**) Sets **acregmin**, **acregmax**, **acdirmin**, and **acdirmax** to *n* seconds (without this option, each individual option takes on its assigned or default value).

ERROR HANDLING

The following options control what NFS does when the server does not respond or when an I/O error occurs. To allow for a mount point located on a mounted device, a missing mount point is treated as a timeout.

fg (bg) (**foreground**) Retries failed NFS mount attempts in the foreground (default). The **bg** (background) option retries failed NFS mount attempts in the background.

hard (soft) Displays **server not responding** on the console on a major timeout and keeps retrying (default). The **soft** option reports an I/O error to the calling program on a major timeout. In general, it is not advisable to use **soft**. As the mount man page says of **soft**, "Usually it just causes lots of trouble." For more information refer to "Improving Performance" on page 680.

nointr (intr) (**no interrupt**) Does not allow a signal to interrupt a file operation on a **hard**-mounted directory hierarchy when a major timeout occurs (default). The **intr** option allows this type of interrupt.

retrans=*n* (**retransmission value**) After *n* minor timeouts, NFS generates a major timeout (default is 3). A major timeout aborts the operation or displays **server not responding** on the console, depending on whether **hard** or **soft** is set.

retry=*n* (**retry value**) The number of minutes that NFS retries a mount operation before giving up (default is 10,000).

timeo=*n* (**timeout value**) The *n* is the number of tenths of a second that NFS waits before retransmitting following an RPC, or minor, timeout (default is 7). The value is increased at each timeout to a maximum of 60 seconds or until a major timeout occurs (see **retrans**). On a busy network, in case of a slow server, or when the request passes through multiple routers/gateways, increasing this value may improve performance.

MISCELLANEOUS OPTIONS

Following are additional useful options:

lock (nolock) Permits NFS locking (default). The **nolock** option disables NFS locking (does not start the **lockd** daemon) and is useful with older servers that do not support NFS locking.

mounthost=*name* The name of the host running **mountd**, the NFS mount daemon.

mountport=*n*   The port used by **mountd**.

nodev   (**no device**) Causes mounted device files not to function as devices (page 677).

port=*n*   The port used to connect to the NFS server (defaults to 2049 if the NFS daemon is not registered with **portmap**). When **n=0** (default), NFS queries **portmap** on the server to determine the port.

rsize=*n*   (**read block size**) The number of bytes read at one time from an NFS server. The default block size is 4096. Refer to "Improving Performance."

wsize=*n*   (**write block size**) The number of bytes written at one time to an NFS server. The default block size is 4096. Refer to "Improving Performance."

tcp   Use TCP in place of the default UDP protocol for an NFS mount. This option may improve performance on a congested network; however, some NFS servers support UDP only.

udp   Use the default UDP protocol for an NFS mount.

IMPROVING PERFORMANCE

hard/soft   Several parameters can affect the performance of NFS, especially over slow connections such as a line with a lot of traffic or one controlled by a modem. If you have a slow connection, make sure **hard** (page 679) is set (this is the default) so that timeouts do not abort program execution.

Block size   One of the easiest ways to improve NFS performance is to increase the block size—that is, the number of bytes NFS transfers at a time. The default of 4096 is low for a fast connection using modern hardware. Try increasing **rsize** and **wsize** to 8192 or higher. Experiment until you find the optimal block size. Unmount and mount the directory hierarchy each time you change an option. See the *NFS HOWTO* for more information on testing different block sizes.

Timeouts   NFS waits the amount of time specified by the **timeo** (timeout, page 679) option for a response to a transmission. If it does not receive a response in this amount of time, it sends another transmission. The second transmission uses bandwidth that, over a slow connection, may slow things down further. You may be able to increase performance by increasing **timeo**.

The default value of **timeo** is seven-tenths of a second (700 milliseconds). After a timeout, NFS doubles the time it waits to 1400 milliseconds. On each timeout it doubles the amount of time it waits to a maximum of 60 seconds. You can test the speed of a connection with the size packets you are sending (**rsize** and **wsize**) by using ping with the **–s** (size) option:

```
$ ping -s 4096 speedy
PING speedy.tcorp.com (192.168.0.1) 4096(4124) bytes of data.
4104 bytes from speedy.tcorp.com (192.168.0.1): icmp_seq=0 ttl=64 time=1.43 ms
4104 bytes from speedy.tcorp.com (192.168.0.1): icmp_seq=1 ttl=64 time=1.17 ms
4104 bytes from speedy.tcorp.com (192.168.0.1): icmp_seq=2 ttl=64 time=1.17 ms
...
```

```
4104 bytes from speedy.tcorp.com (192.168.0.1): icmp_seq=26 ttl=64 time=1.16 ms
4104 bytes from speedy.tcorp.com (192.168.0.1): icmp_seq=27 ttl=64 time=1.16 ms
4104 bytes from speedy.tcorp.com (192.168.0.1): icmp_seq=28 ttl=64 time=1.16 ms
4104 bytes from speedy.tcorp.com (192.168.0.1): icmp_seq=29 ttl=64 time=1.26 ms

--- speedy.tcorp.com ping statistics ---
30 packets transmitted, 30 received, 0% packet loss, time 29281ms
rtt min/avg/max/mdev = 1.154/1.192/1.431/0.067 ms
```

The preceding example uses Red Hat Linux's default packet size of 4096 bytes and shows a fast average packet round-trip time of slightly more than 1 millisecond. Over a modem line, you can expect times of several seconds. If the connection is dealing with other traffic, the time will be longer. Run the test during a period of heavy traffic. Try increasing **timeo** to three or four times the average round-trip time (to allow for unusually bad network conditions, as when the connection is made) and see whether performance improves. Remember that the **timeo** value is given in tenths of a second (100 milliseconds = one-tenth of a second).

/etc/fstab: MOUNTS DIRECTORY HIERARCHIES AUTOMATICALLY

The **/etc/fstab** file (page 469) lists directory hierarchies that the system mounts automatically as it comes up. You can use the options discussed in the preceding section on the command line or in the **fstab** file.

The first example line from **fstab** mounts **grape**'s **/gc1** filesystem on the **/grape.gc1** mount point:

```
grape:/gc1              /grape.gc1      nfs     rsize=8192,wsize=8192         0 0
```

A mount point should be an empty, local directory. (Files in a mount point are hidden when a directory hierarchy is mounted on it.) The type of a filesystem mounted using NFS is always **nfs**, regardless of its type on the local system. You can increase the **rsize** and **wsize** options to improve performance. Refer to "Improving Performance" on page 680.

The next example from **fstab** mounts a filesystem from **speedy**:

```
speedy:/export          /speedy.export  nfs     timeo=50,hard                0 0
```

Because the local system connects to **speedy** over a slow connection, **timeo** is increased to 5 seconds (50 tenths of a second). Refer to "Timeouts" on page 680. In addition, **hard** is set to make sure that NFS keeps trying to communicate with the server after a major timeout. Refer to "hard/soft" on page 680.

The final example from **fstab** shows a remote-mounted home directory. Because **speedy** is a local server and is connected via a reliable, high-speed connection, **timeo** is decreased and **rsize** and **wsize** are increased substantially:

```
speedy:/export/home     /home           nfs     timeo=4,rsize=16384,wsize=16384  0 0
```

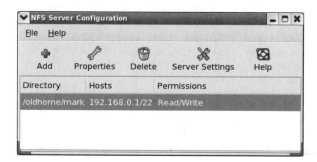

Figure 22-2   NFS Server Configuration window

SETTING UP AN NFS SERVER

PREREQUISITES

Install the following package:

• **nfs-utils**

Run chkconfig to cause nfs to start when the system enters multiuser mode:

```
# /sbin/chkconfig nfs on
```

Start **nfs**:

```
# /etc/rc.d/init.d/nfs start
```

The **nfs** init script starts **mountd, nfsd,** and **rquotad**.

The portmap utility (part of the **portmap** package; refer to "RPC Network Services" on page 377) must be running to enable reliable file locking.

NOTES

SELinux   When SELinux is set to use a targeted policy, NFS is protected by SELinux. You can disable this protection if necessary. For more information refer to "Setting the Targeted Policy with system-config-securitylevel" on page 402.

Firewall   If the system is running a firewall, you generally need to open TCP port 111 for **portmap**, TCP ports 1013 and 1016 for **mountd**, and TCP port 2049 for **nfs**. If these ports do not allow NFS access, use **rpcinfo –p** (page 423) to determine the TCP ports that the local server uses for these services and then open those ports. For information on using the Red Hat Linux graphical firewall tool, see "Opening other ports" on page 768. For more general information, see Chapter 25, which details iptables.

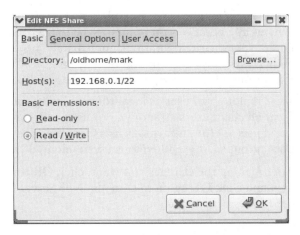

Figure 22-3   Edit NFS Share window

JumpStart: Configuring an NFS Server
Using system-config-nfs

To display the NFS Server Configuration window (Figure 22-2), enter the command **system-config-nfs**. From KDE select **Main menu: Administration⇨Server Settings⇨NFS** or from GNOME select **System: Administration⇨Server Settings⇨NFS**. From this window you can generate an **/etc/exports** file, which is almost all there is to setting up an NFS server. If the system is running a firewall, see "Notes" in the preceding section. The system-config-nfs utility allows you to specify which directory hierarchies are shared and how they are shared using NFS. Each exported hierarchy is called a *share*.

To add a share, click **Add** on the toolbar. To modify a share, highlight the share and click **Properties** on the toolbar. Clicking **Add** displays the Add NFS Share window, while clicking **Properties** displays the Edit NFS Share window. These windows are identical except for their titles.

The Add/Edit NFS Share window has three tabs: Basic, General Options, and User Access. On the Basic tab (Figure 22-3) you can specify the pathname of the root of the shared directory hierarchy, the names or IP addresses of the systems (hosts) that the hierarchy will be shared with, and whether users from the specified systems will be able to write to the shared files.

The selections in the other two tabs correspond to options that you can specify in the **/etc/exports** file. Following is a list of the check box descriptions in these tabs and the option each corresponds to:

General Options tab   Allow connections from ports 1023 and higher: **insecure** (page 686)
Allow insecure file locking: **no_auth_nlm** or **insecure_locks** (page 686)

Disable subtree checking: **no_subtree_check** (page 686)
Sync write operations on request: **sync** (page 686)
Force sync of write operations immediately: **no_wdelay** (page 686)
Hide filesystems beneath: **nohide** (page 686)
Export only if mounted: **mountpoint** (page 686)

User Access tab   Treat remote root user as local root: **no_root_squash** (page 687)
Treat all client users as anonymous users: **all_squash** (page 688)
Local user ID for anonymous users: **anonuid** (page 688)
Local group ID for anonymous users: **anongid** (page 688)

After making the changes you want, click **OK** to close the Add/Edit NFS Share window and click **OK** again to close the NFS Server Configuration window. There is no need to restart any daemons.

EXPORTING A DIRECTORY HIERARCHY

Exporting a directory hierarchy makes the directory hierarchy *available* for mounting by designated systems via a network. "Exported" does not mean "mounted": When a directory hierarchy is exported, it is placed in the list of directory hierarchies that can be mounted by other systems. An exported directory hierarchy may be mounted (or not) at any given time. A server holds three lists of exported directory hierarchies:

- **/etc/exports**   Access control list for exported directory hierarchies (discussed in the next section). The system administrator can modify this file by editing it or by running system-config-nfs.

- **/var/lib/nfs/xtab**   Access control list for exported directory hierarchies. Initialized from **/etc/exports** when the system is brought up. Read by mountd when a client asks to mount a directory hierarchy. Modified by exportfs (page 688) as directory hierarchies are mounted and unmounted by NFS.

- Kernel's export table   List of active exported directory hierarchies. The kernel obtains this information from **/var/lib/nfs/xtab**. You can display this table by giving the command **cat /proc/fs/nfs/exports**.

Exporting symbolic links and device files

tip   When you export a directory hierarchy that contains a symbolic link, make sure the object of the link is available on the client (remote) system. If the object of the link does not exist on a client system, you must export and mount it along with the exported link. Otherwise, the link will not point to the file it points to on the server.

A device file refers to a Linux kernel interface. When you export a device file, you export that interface. If the client system does not have the same type of device, the exported device will not work. From a client, you can use mount's **nodev** option (page 677) to prevent device files on mounted directory hierarchies from being used as devices.

A mounted filesystem with a mount point within an exported filesystem will not be exported with the exported filesystem. You need to explicitly export each filesystem that you want exported, even if it resides within an already exported filesystem. For example, when you have two filesystems, **/opt/apps** and **/opt/apps/oracle**, residing on two partitions to export, you must export each explicitly, even though **oracle** is a subdirectory of **apps**. Most other subdirectories and files are exported automatically.

/etc/exports: HOLDS A LIST OF EXPORTED DIRECTORY HIERARCHIES

The **/etc/exports** file is the access control list for exported directory hierarchies that NFS clients can mount; it is the only file you need to edit to set up an NFS server. The **exports** file controls the following aspects:

- Which clients can access files on the server

- Which directory hierarchies on the server each client can access

- How each client can access each directory hierarchy

- How client usernames are mapped to server usernames

- Various NFS parameters

Each line in the **exports** file has the following format:

> *export-point client1(options) [client2(options) ...]*

where *export-point* is the absolute pathname of the root directory of the directory hierarchy to be exported, *client1-n* is the name of one or more clients or is one or more IP addresses, separated by SPACEs, that are allowed to mount the *export-point*. The *options*, which are described in the next section, apply to the preceding *client*.

Either you can use system-config-nfs (page 683) to make changes to **exports** or you can edit this file directly. The following simple **exports** file gives **grape** read and write access and gives **speedy** readonly access to the files in **/home**:

```
# cat /etc/exports
/home grape(rw,sync)
/home speedy(ro,sync)
```

In each case, access is implicitly granted for all subdirectories. For historical reasons, exportfs complains when you do not specify either **sync** or **async**. You can use IP addresses and include more than one system on a line:

```
# cat /etc/exports
/home grape(rw,sync) speedy(ro,sync) 192.168.0.22(rw,sync)
```

GENERAL OPTIONS

This section lists default options first, followed by nondefault options (enclosed in parentheses). Refer to the **exports** man page for more information.

auth_nlm (no_auth_nlm) or secure_locks (insecure_locks)
Causes the server to require authentication of lock requests (using the NLM [NFS Lock Manager] protocol). Use **no_auth_nlm** for older clients when you find that only files that anyone can read can be locked.

mountpoint[=*path*]
Allows a directory to be exported only if it has been mounted. This option prevents a mount point that does not have a directory hierarchy mounted on it from being exported and prevents the underlying mount point from being exported. Also **mp**.

nohide (hide) When a server exports two directory hierarchies, one of which is mounted on the other, a client has to mount both directory hierarchies explicitly to access both. When the second (child) directory hierarchy is not explicitly mounted, its mount point appears as an empty directory and the directory hierarchy is hidden. The **nohide** option causes the underlying second directory hierarchy to appear when it is not explicitly mounted, but this option does not work in all cases.

ro (rw) (**readonly**) Permits only read requests on an NFS directory hierarchy. Use **rw** to permit read and write requests.

secure (insecure) Requires that NFS requests originate on a *privileged port* (page 1049) so that a program without **root** permissions cannot mount a directory hierarchy. This option does not guarantee a secure connection.

subtree_check (no_subtree_check)
Checks subtrees for valid files. Assume that you have an exported directory hierarchy that has its root below the root of the filesystem that holds it (that is, an exported subdirectory of a filesystem). When the NFS server receives a request for a file in that directory hierarchy, it performs a subtree check to confirm the file is in the exported directory hierarchy.

Subtree checking can cause problems with files that are renamed while opened and, when **no_root_squash** is used, files that only **root** can access. The **no_subtree_check** option disables subtree checking and can improve reliability in some cases.

For example, you may need to disable subtree checking for home directories. Home directories are frequently subtrees (of **/home**), are written to often, and can have files within them frequently renamed. You would probably not need to disable subtree checking for directory hierarchies that contain files that are mostly read, such as **/usr.**

sync (async) (**synchronize**) Specifies that the server is to reply to requests only after disk changes made by the request are written to disk. The **async** option specifies that the server does not have to wait for information to be written to disk and can improve performance, albeit at the cost of possible data corruption if the server crashes or the connection is interrupted.

Because the default changed with release 1.0.0 of **nfs-utils**, exportfs displays a warning when you do not specify either **sync** or **async**.

wdelay (**write delay**) Causes the server to delay committing write requests when it anticipates
(no_wdelay) that another, related request follows, thereby improving performance by committing multiple write requests within a single operation. The **no_wdelay** option does not

delay committing write requests and can improve performance when the server receives multiple, small, unrelated requests.

USER ID MAPPING OPTIONS

Each user has a UID number and a primary GID number on the local system. The local **/etc/passwd** and **/etc/group** files map these numbers to names. When a user makes a request of an NFS server, the server uses these numbers to identify the user on the remote system, raising several issues:

- The user may not have the same ID numbers on both systems and may therefore have owner access to files of another user (see "NIS and NFS" for a solution).

- You may not want the **root** user on the client system to have owner access to **root**-owned files on the server.

- You may not want a remote user to have owner access to some important system files that are not owned by **root** (such as those owned by **bin**).

Critical files in NFS-mounted directories should be owned by root

security   Despite the mapping done by the **root-squash** option, the **root** user on a client system can use su to assume the identity of any user on the system and then access that user's files on the server. Thus, without resorting to **all-squash**, you can protect only files owned by **root** on an NFS server. Make sure that **root**—and not **bin** or another user—owns and is the only user who can modify or delete all critical files within any NFS-mounted directory hierarchy.

Taking this precaution does not completely protect against an attacker with **root** privileges, but it can help protect a system from less experienced malicious users.

Owner access means that the remote user can execute, remove, or—worse—modify the file. NFS gives you two ways to deal with these cases:

- You can use the **root_squash** option to map the ID number of the **root** user on a client to the **nfsnobody** user on the server.

- You can use the **all-squash** option to map all NFS users on the client to **nfsnobody** on the server.

The **/etc/passwd** file shows that **nfsnobody** has a UID and GID of 65534. You can use the **anonuid** and **anongid** options to override these values.

NIS and NFS   When you use NIS (page 655) for user authorization, users automatically have the same UIDs on both systems. If you are using NFS on a large network, it is a good idea to use a directory service such as *LDAP* (page 1040) or NIS for authorization. Without such a service, you must synchronize the **passwd** files on all the systems manually.

root_squash (no_root_squash)

Maps requests from **root** on a remote system so that they appear to come from the UID for **nfsnobody**, an unprivileged user on the local system, or as specified by **anonuid**. Does not affect other sensitive UIDs such as **bin**. The **no_root_squash** option turns off this mapping so that requests from **root** appear to come from **root**.

no_all_squash (all_squash)   Does not change the mapping of users making requests of the NFS server. The **all_squash** option maps requests from all users, not just **root,** on remote systems to appear to come from the UID for **nfsnobody,** an unprivileged user on the local system, or as specified by **anonuid.** This option is useful for controlling access to exported public FTP, news, and other directories.

anonuid=*un* and anongid=*gn*   Set the UID or the GID of the anonymous account to *un* or *gn,* respectively. NFS uses these accounts when it does not recognize an incoming UID or GID and when instructed to do so by **root_squash** or **all_squash.**

showmount: DISPLAYS NFS STATUS INFORMATION

Without any options, the showmount utility displays a list of systems that are allowed to mount local directories. To display information for a remote system, give the name of the remote system as an argument. You typically use showmount to display a list of directory hierarchies that a server is exporting. The information that showmount provides may not be complete, however, because it depends on **mountd** and trusts that remote servers are reporting accurately.

In the following example, **bravo** and **grape** can mount local directories, but you do not know which ones:

```
# /usr/sbin/showmount
Hosts on localhost:
bravo.tcorp.com
grape.tcorp.com
```

If showmount displays an error such as **RPC: Program not registered,** NFS is not running on the server. Start NFS on the server with the **nfs** init script (page 682).

–a   (**all**) Tells which directories are mounted by which remote systems. This information is stored in **/etc/exports.**

```
# /usr/sbin/showmount -a
All mount points on localhost:
bravo.tcorp.com:/home
grape.tcorp.com:/home
```

–e   (**exports**) Displays a list of exported directories.

```
# /usr/sbin/showmount -e
Export list for localhost:
/home bravo.tcorp.com,grape.tcorp.com
```

exportfs: MAINTAINS THE LIST OF EXPORTED DIRECTORY HIERARCHIES

The exportfs utility maintains the kernel's list of exported directory hierarchies. Without changing **/etc/exports,** exportfs can add to or remove from the list of exported directory hierarchies. An exportfs command has the following format:

/usr/sbin/exportfs [options] [client:dir ...]

where *options* is one or more options (as detailed in the next section), *client* is the name of the system that *dir* is exported to, and *dir* is the absolute pathname of the directory at the root of the directory hierarchy being exported.

The system executes the following command when it comes up (it is in the **nfs** init script). This command reexports the entries in **/etc/exports** and removes invalid entries from **/var/lib/nfs/xtab** (page 684) so that **/var/lib/nfs/xtab** is synchronized with **/etc/exports**:

```
# exportfs -r
```

Replace the **–r** with **–a** to export only the entries in **/etc/exports**. Remove an exported directory hierarchy with the **–u** option; remove all exported directory hierarchies with the **–ua** options.

OPTIONS

–a (**all**) Exports directory hierarchies specified in **/etc/exports**. This option does not *unexport* entries you have removed from **exports** (that is, it does not remove invalid entries from **/var/lib/nfs/xtab**); use **–r** to perform this task.

–i (**ignore**) Ignores **/etc/exports**; uses what is specified on the command line only.

–o (**options**) Specifies options. You can specify options following **–o** the same way you do in the **exports** file. For example, **exportfs –i –o ro speedy:/home/sam** exports **/home/sam** on the local system to **speedy** for readonly access.

–r (**reexport**) Reexports the entries in **/etc/exports** and removes invalid entries from **/var/lib/nfs/xtab** so that **/var/lib/nfs/xtab** is synchronized with **/etc/exports**.

–u (**unexport**) Makes an exported directory hierarchy no longer exported. If a directory hierarchy is mounted when you unexport it, you will see the message **Stale NFS file handle** if you try to access the directory hierarchy from the remote system.

–v (**verbose**) Provides more information. Displays export options when you use exportfs to display export information.

TESTING THE SERVER SETUP

From the server, run the **nfs** init script with an argument of **status**. If all is well, the system displays something similar to the following:

```
# /sbin/service nfs status
rpc.mountd (pid 15795) is running...
nfsd (pid 15813 15812 15811 15810 15809 15808 15807 15806) is running...
rpc.rquotad (pid 15784) is running...
```

Next, from the server, use rpcinfo to make sure NFS is registered with portmap:

```
$ /usr/sbin/rpcinfo -p localhost | grep nfs
    100003    2    udp    2049    nfs
    100003    3    udp    2049    nfs
```

Repeat the preceding command from the client, replacing **localhost** with the name of the server. The results should be the same.

Finally, try mounting directory hierarchies from remote systems and verify access.

automount: Automatically Mounts Directory Hierarchies

With distributed computing, when you log in on any system on the network, all of your files, including startup scripts, are available. In a distributed computing environment, all systems are commonly able to mount all directory hierarchies on all servers: Whichever system you log in on, your home directory is waiting for you.

As an example, assume that **/home/alex** is a remote directory hierarchy that is mounted on demand. When you issue the command **ls /home/alex**, autofs goes to work: It looks in the **/etc/auto.home** map, finds that **alex** is a key that says to mount **bravo:/export/home/alex**, and mounts the remote directory hierarchy. Once the directory hierarchy is mounted, ls displays the list of files you want to see. If you give the command **ls /home** after this mounting sequence, ls shows that **alex** is present within the **/home** directory. The df utility shows that **alex** is mounted from **bravo**.

Prerequisites

Install the following package:

- **autofs**

Run chkconfig to cause **autofs** to start when the system enters multiuser mode:

```
# /sbin/chkconfig autofs on
```

Start **autofs**:

```
# /sbin/service nfs start
```

More Information

Local   man pages   autofs, **automount**, **auto.master**

Web   tutorial   www.linuxhq.com/lg/issue24/nielsen.html

HOWTO   *Automount mini-HOWTO*

autofs: Automatically Mounted Directory Hierarchies

An **autofs** directory hierarchy is like any other directory hierarchy, but remains unmounted until it is needed, at which time the system mounts it automatically (*demand mounting*). The system unmounts an **autofs** directory hierarchy when it is no longer needed—by default after five minutes of inactivity. Automatically mounted directory hierarchies are an important part of administrating a large collection of systems in a consistent way. The **automount** daemon is particularly useful when an installation includes a large number of servers or a large number of directory hierarchies. It also helps to remove server–server dependencies (discussed next).

When you boot a system that uses traditional **fstab**-based mounts and an NFS server is down, the system can take a long time to come up as it waits for the server to time out. Similarly, when you have two servers, each mounting directory hierarchies from the other, and both systems are down, both may hang as they are brought up and each tries to mount a directory hierarchy from the other. This situation is called a *server–server dependency*. The **automount** facility gets around these issues by mounting a directory hierarchy from another system only when a process tries to access it.

When a process attempts to access one of the directories within an unmounted **autofs** directory hierarchy, the kernel notifies the **automount** daemon, which mounts the directory hierarchy. You have to give a command, such as **cd /home/alex**, that accesses the **autofs** mount point (in this case **/home/alex**) so as to create the demand that causes **automount** to mount the **autofs** directory hierarchy so you can see it. Before you issue the **cd** command, **alex** does not appear to be in **/home**.

The main file that controls the behavior of **automount** is **/etc/auto.master**. A simple example follows:

```
# cat /etc/auto.master
/free1 /etc/auto.misc   --timeout 60
/free2 /etc/auto.misc2 --timeout 60
```

The **auto.master** file has three columns. The first column names the parent of the **autofs** *mount point*—the location where the **autofs** directory hierarchy is to be mounted (**/free1** and **/free2** in the example are not mount points but will hold the mount points when the directory hierarchies are mounted). The second column names the files, called *map files,* that store supplemental configuration information. The optional third column holds mount options for map entries that do not specify an option.

Although the map files can have any names, one is traditionally named **auto.misc**. Following are the two map files specified in **auto.master**:

```
# cat /etc/auto.misc
sam                -fstype=ext3              :/dev/hda8

# cat /etc/auto.misc2
helen              -fstype=ext3              :/dev/hda9
```

The first column of a map file holds the relative **autofs** mount point (**sam** and **helen**). This mount point is appended to the corresponding **autofs** mount point from column 1 of the **auto.master** file to create the absolute **autofs** mount point. In this example, **sam** (from **auto.misc**) is appended to **/free1** (from **auto.master**) to make **/free1/sam**. The second column holds the options, and the third column shows the server and directory hierarchy to be mounted. This example shows local drives; for an NFS-mounted device, the hostname of the remote system would appear before the colon (for example, **grape:/home/sam**).

Before the new setup can work, you must create directories for the parents of the mount points (**/free1** and **/free2** in the preceding example) and start (or restart) the **automount** daemon using the **autofs** init script. The following command displays information about configured and active **autofs** mount points:

```
# /sbin/service autofs status
```

CHAPTER SUMMARY

NFS allows a server to share selected local directory hierarchies with client systems on a heterogeneous network, reducing storage needs and administrative overhead. NFS defines a client/server relationship in which a server provides directory hierarchies that clients can mount.

On the server, the **/etc/exports** file lists the directory hierarchies that the system exports. Each line in **exports** lists the systems that are allowed to mount the hierarchy and specifies the options for each hierarchy (readonly, read-write, and so on). Give an **exportfs –r** command to cause NFS to reread this file.

From a client, you can give a **mount** command to mount an exported NFS directory hierarchy. Alternatively you can put an entry in **/etc/fstab** to have the system automatically mount the directory hierarchy when it comes up.

Automatically mounted directory hierarchies help manage large groups of systems with many servers and filesystems in a consistent way and can help remove server–server dependencies. The **automount** daemon automatically mounts **autofs** directory hierarchies when they are needed and unmounts them when they are no longer needed.

EXERCISES

1. List three reasons to use NFS.

2. Which command would you give to mount on the local system the **/home** directory hierarchy that resides on the file server named **bravo**? Assume the mounted directory hierarchy will appear as **/bravo.home** on the local system. How would you mount the same directory hierarchy if it resided on the fileserver at 192.168.1.1? How would you unmount **/home**?

3. How would you list the mount points on the remote system named **bravo** that the local system named **grape** can mount?

4. Which command line lists the currently mounted NFS directory hierarchies?

5. What does the **/etc/fstab** file do?

6. From a server, how would you allow readonly access to **/opt** for any system in **example.com**?

ADVANCED EXERCISES

7. When is it a good idea to disable attribute caching?

8. Describe the difference between the **root_squash** and the **all_squash** options in **/etc/exports**.

9. Why does the **secure** option in **/etc/exports** not really provide any security?

10. Some diskless workstations use NFS as swap space. Why is this useful? What is the downside?

11. NFS maps client users to users on the server. Explain why this mapping is a security risk.

12. What does the mount **nosuid** option do? Why would you want to do this?

23

SAMBA: INTEGRATING LINUX AND WINDOWS

Samba is a free suite of programs that enables UNIX-like operating systems, including Linux, Solaris, FreeBSD, and Mac OS X, to work with other operating systems, such as OS/2 and Windows, as both a server and a client.

As a server, Samba shares Linux files and printers with Windows systems. As a client, Samba gives Linux users access to files on Windows systems. Its ability to share files across operating systems makes Samba an ideal tool in a heterogeneous computing environment.

Refer to "Integration with Windows" on page 520 for information about printing using Samba.

INTRODUCTION

This chapter starts by providing a list of Samba tools followed by some basic information. The JumpStart section discusses how to set up a Samba server using system-config-samba, a minimal GUI. The next section covers how to use swat, a Web-based advanced configuration tool, to set up a Samba server. The final server section discusses how to set up a Samba server by hand, using a text editor to manually edit the files that control Samba. The next two sections, "Accessing Linux Shares from Windows" (page 711) and "Accessing Windows Shares from Linux" (page 712), explain how to work with Linux and Windows files and printers. The final section of the chapter, "Troubleshooting" (page 714), offers tips on what to do when you have a problem setting up or using Samba.

Table 23-1 lists the utilities and daemons that make up the Samba suite of programs.

Table 23-1   Samba utilities and daemons

Utility or daemon	Function
net	This utility has the same syntax as the DOS net command and, over time, will eventually replace other Samba utilities such as smbpasswd.
nmbd	The *NetBIOS* (page 1044) nameserver program, run as a daemon by default. Provides NetBIOS over IP naming services for Samba clients. Also provides browsing (as in the Windows Network Neighborhood or My Network Places view) support.
nmblookup	Makes *NetBIOS* (page 1044) name queries (page 715).
smbclient	Displays shares on a Samba server such as a Windows machine (page 713).
smbd	The Samba program, run as a daemon by default. Provides file and print services for Samba clients.
smbpasswd	Changes Windows NT password hashes on Samba and Windows NT servers (page 698).
smbstatus	Displays information about current **smbd** connections.
smbtree	Displays a hierarchical diagram of available shares (page 712).
swat	Samba Web Administration Tool. A graphical editor for the **smb.conf** file (page 701).
testparm	Checks syntax of the **smb.conf** file (page 714).
testprns	Checks printer names in the **printcap** file.

ABOUT SAMBA

This section covers the packages you need to install to run Samba, sources of more information on Samba, and users and passwords under Samba.

PREREQUISITES

Install the following packages:

- **samba**
- **samba-client**
- **samba-common**
- **system-config-samba** (optional)
- **samba-swat** (optional, but a good idea)

Run chkconfig to cause **smb** to start when the system enters multiuser mode:

```
# /sbin/chkconfig smb on
```

Start **smb**:

```
# /sbin/service smb start
```

If you want to use swat, modify **/etc/xinetd.d/swat**, as explained in "swat: Configures a Samba Server" on page 701, and restart **xinetd**:

```
# /sbin/service xinetd restart
```

MORE INFORMATION

Local Documentation   Samba/swat home page has links to local Samba documentation (page 701) **/usr/share/doc/samba-***

Web   Samba   www.samba.org (mailing lists, documentation, downloads, and more) CIFS   www.samba.org/cifs

HOWTO   *Unofficial Samba HOWTO* hr.uoregon.edu/davidrl/samba.html *Samba HOWTO Collection*   Point a browser at the following pathname on the local system (after replacing the * with the value, such as **3.0.21b**, from the local filesystem): **/usr/share/doc/samba-*/htmldocs/index.html**

NOTES

Firewall   The Samba server normally uses UDP ports 137 and 138 and TCP ports 139 and 445. If the Samba server system is running a firewall, you need to open these ports. Using the Red Hat graphical firewall tool (page 768), select Samba from the Trusted Services frame to open these ports. For more general information, see Chapter 25, which details iptables.

SELinux   When SELinux is set to use a targeted policy, Samba is protected by SELinux. You can disable this protection if necessary. For more information refer to "Setting the Targeted Policy with system-config-securitylevel" on page 402.

Share   Under Samba, an exported directory hierarchy is called a *share*.

Samba   The name *Samba* is derived from *SMB* (page 1055), the protocol that is the native method of file and printer sharing for Windows.

SAMBA USERS, USER MAPS, AND PASSWORDS

For a Windows user to gain access to Samba services on a Linux system, the user must provide a Windows username and a Samba password. In some cases, Windows supplies the username and password for you. It is also possible to authenticate using other methods. For example, Samba can use *LDAP* (page 1040) or PAM (page 438) instead of the default password file. Refer to the Samba documentation for more information on authentication methods.

Usernames   The supplied username must be the same as a Linux username or must map to a Linux username. Samba keeps the username maps in **/etc/samba/smbusers**. Users with the same username on Linux and Samba do not need to appear in this file, but they still need a Samba password.

When you install Samba, **smbusers** has two entries:

```
$ cat /etc/samba/smbusers
# Unix_name = SMB_name1 SMB_name2 ...
root = administrator admin
nobody = guest pcguest smbguest
```

The first entry maps the two Windows usernames (**administrator** and **admin**) to the Linux username **root**. The second entry maps three Windows usernames, including **guest,** to the Linux username **nobody:** When a Windows user attempts to log in on the Samba server as **guest**, Samba authenticates the Linux user named **nobody**.

Passwords   Samba uses Samba passwords—not Linux passwords—to authenticate users. By default, Samba keeps passwords in **/etc/samba/smbpasswd**. As Samba is installed, authentication for **root** or **nobody** would fail because Samba is installed without passwords: The **smbpasswd** file does not exist.

Each of the configuration techniques described in this chapter allows you to add users to **smbusers** and passwords to **smbpasswd**. You can always use smbpasswd as discussed later in this section to add and change passwords in **smbpasswd**.

Note   When you attempt to connect from Windows to a Samba server, Windows presents your Windows username and password to Samba. If your Windows username is the same as or maps to your Linux username, and if your Windows and Samba passwords are the same, you do not have to enter a username or password to connect to the Samba server.

Example   You can add the following line to **smbusers** to map the Windows username **sam** to the Linux username **sls**:

```
sls = sam
```

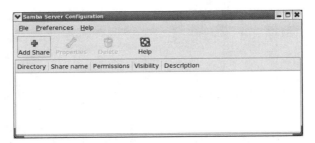

Figure 23-1   Samba Server Configuration window

You can add a password for **sls** to **smbpasswd** with the following command:

```
# smbpasswd -a sls
New SMB password:
Retype new SMB password:
Added user sls.
```

Now when Sam uses the username **sam** to log in on the Samba server, Samba maps **sam** to **sls** and looks up **sls** in **smbpasswd**. Assuming Sam provides the correct password, he logs in on the Samba server as **sls**.

JUMPSTART: CONFIGURING A SAMBA SERVER USING system-config-samba

The system-config-samba utility can set up only basic features of a Samba server. It is, however, the best tool to use if you are not familiar with Samba and you want to set up a simple Samba server quickly. The system-config-samba utility performs three basic functions: configuring the server, configuring users, and setting up shares (directory hierarchies) that are exported to the Windows machines.

Make a copy of **smb.conf**

tip   As installed, the **/etc/samba/smb.conf** file has extensive comments (page 705). The system-config-samba utility overwrites this file. Make a copy of **smb.conf** for safekeeping before you run this utility for the first time.

To display the Samba Server Configuration window (Figure 23-1), enter **system-config-samba** on a command line. From KDE select **Main menu: System⇨Samba** or from GNOME select **System: Administration⇨Server Settings⇨Samba**.

Select **Menubar: Preferences⇨Server Settings** to display the Server Settings window Basic tab (Figure 23-2, next page). Change the workgroup to the one in use on the Windows machines. Change the description of the server if you like. Click the **Security** tab and make sure Authentication Mode is set to **User**; you do not need to specify an Authentication Server or a Kerberos Realm. If you are using Windows 98 or

Figure 23-2   Server Settings window, Basic tab

later, set Encrypt Passwords to **Yes**. When you specify a username in the Guest Account, anyone logging in on the Samba server as **guest** maps to that user's ID. Typically the **guest** account maps to the UID of the Linux user named **nobody**. Click **OK**.

Samba users   Select **Menubar: Preferences⇨Samba Users** to display the Samba Users window (Figure 23-3). If the user you want to log in as is not already specified in this window, click **Add User**. When you have the proper permissions, the Create New Samba User window displays a combo box next to Unix Username that allows you to select a Linux user; otherwise, your username is displayed as the Unix Username. The Windows Username is the Windows username that you want to map to the specified Linux (UNIX) username. The Samba Password is the password this user or Windows enters to gain access to the Samba server.

If Sam has accounts named **sam** on both the Windows and Linux systems, you would select **sam** from the Unix Username combo box, enter **sam** in the Windows Username text box, and enter Sam's Windows password in the two Samba Password text boxes. Click **OK** to close the Create New Samba User window and click **OK** to close the Samba Users window.

Adding a Samba password for the Linux user nobody

tip   Because the user **nobody** exists in **smbusers** when you install Samba, you cannot add the user **nobody**, nor can you add a password for **nobody** from system-config-samba. Instead, you must use smbpasswd from the command line as follows:

```
# smbpasswd -a nobody
New SMB password:
Retype new SMB password:
```

Normally the user **nobody** does not have a password because it is the guest login. Press RETURN (without typing any characters) in response to each of the **SMB password** prompts to add **nobody** to the Samba password file without a password.

Linux shares   Next you need to add a *share,* which is the directory hierarchy you export from the Linux system to the Windows system. Click **Add Share** on the toolbar to display the Basic tab in the Create Samba Share window (Figure 23-4). In the Directory text box, enter the absolute pathname of the directory you want to share (**/tmp** is an easy directory to practice with). Enter a description if you like. It can be useful to

Figure 23-3   Samba Users window

enter the Linux hostname and the pathname of the directory you are sharing here. Specify Writable if you want to be able to write to the directory from the Windows machine; Visible allows the share to be seen from the Windows machine. Click the Access tab and specify whether you want to limit access to specified users or whether you want to allow anyone to access this share. Click **OK**. Close the Samba Server Configuration window.

You should now be able to access the share from a Windows machine (page 711). There is no need to restart the Samba server.

swat: CONFIGURES A SAMBA SERVER

Make a copy of smb.conf

tip As installed, the **/etc/samba/smb.conf** file contains extensive comments (page 705). The **swat** utility overwrites this file. Make a copy of **smb.conf** for safekeeping before you run this utility for the first time.

The swat (Samba Web Administration Tool) utility is a browser-based graphical editor for the **smb.conf** file. It is part of the **samba-swat** package. For each of the configurable parameters, it provides help links, default values, and a text box to change

Figure 23-4   Create Samba Share window, Basic tab

the value. The swat utility is a well-designed tool in that it remains true to the lines in the **smb.conf** file you edit: You can use and learn from swat, so that making the transition to using a text editor to modify **smb.conf** will be straightforward.

The swat utility is run from **xinetd** (page 425). Before you can run swat, you need to edit **/etc/xinetd.d/swat** (as discussed next):

```
$ cat /etc/xinetd.d/swat
# Default: off
# description: SWAT is the Samba Web Admin Tool. Use swat \
#              to configure your Samba server. To use SWAT, \
#              connect to port 901 with your favorite web browser.
service swat
{
        port            = 901
        socket_type     = stream
        wait            = no
        only_from       = 127.0.0.1
        user            = root
        server          = /usr/sbin/swat
        log_on_failure  += USERID
        disable         = yes
}
```

First you must turn swat on by changing the **yes** that follows **disable =** to **no**. If you want to access swat from other than the local system, add the names or IP addresses of the other systems you want to access swat from on the line that starts with **only_from**. Separate the system names or IP addresses with SPACEs. If you want to access swat only from the local system, giving the command **chkconfig swat on** is an easier way of making this change. Then restart **xinetd** so that it rereads its configuration files:

```
# /sbin/service xinetd restart
Stopping xinetd:                                        [  OK  ]
Starting xinetd:                                        [  OK  ]
```

After making these changes and restarting **xinetd**, you should be able to run swat. From the local system, open a browser, enter either **http://127.0.0.1:901** or **http://localhost:901** in the location bar, and enter the username **root** and the **root** password in response to swat's request for a username and password. From a remote system, replace **127.0.0.1** with the IP address of the server (but see the adjacent security tip). If a firewall is running on the local system and you want to access swat from a remote system, open TCP port 901 (page 768).

Do not allow remote access to swat

security Do not allow access to swat from a remote system on an insecure network. When you do so and log in, your password is sent in cleartext over whatever connection you are using and can easily be sniffed.

The browser displays the local Samba/swat home page (Figure 23-5). This page includes links to local Samba documentation and the following buttons:

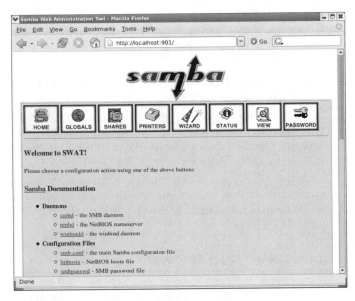

Figure 23-5   The local swat home page

HOME   Links to local Samba documentation. When you click the word **Samba** (not the logo, but the one just before the word **Documentation** in the HOME window), swat displays the Samba man page, which defines each Samba program.

GLOBALS   Edits global variables (parameters) in **smb.conf.**

SHARES   Edits share information in **smb.conf.**

PRINTERS   Edits printer information in **smb.conf.**

WIZARD   Rewrites the **smb.conf** file, removing all comment lines and lines that specify default values.

STATUS   Shows the active connections, active shares, and open files. Stops and restarts **smbd** and **nmbd.**

VIEW   Displays a subset or all of the configuration parameters as determined by default values and settings in **smb.conf.**

PASSWORD   Manages passwords.

It is quite easy to establish a basic Samba setup so that you can see a Linux directory from a Windows system (Windows 3.1 or later). More work is required to set up a secure connection or one with special features. The following example creates a basic setup based on the sample **smb.conf** file that is included with Red Hat Linux.

swat Help and defaults   Each of the variables/parameters in swat has a link named **Help** next to it. If you click **Help,** a new browser window containing an explanation of the parameter appears. Each variable/parameter also has a **Set Default** button that you can click to reset the variable/parameter to its default value.

For this example, do not click any of the **Set Default** buttons. Make sure to click **Commit Changes** at the top of each page after you finish making changes on a page but before you click a menu button at the top of the window. Otherwise, swat will not keep your changes.

GLOBALS page   First click **GLOBALS** at the top of the Samba/swat home page. Leave everything at its current setting with three exceptions: **workgroup, hosts allow**, and **hosts deny**. Set **workgroup** to the workgroup used on the Windows systems. (If you followed the preceding JumpStart, the workgroup is already set.) Scroll to the bottom of the Security Options and set **hosts allow** to the names or IP addresses of machines that you want to be able to access the local system's shares and printers (including localhost [127.0.0.1]). Separate the entries with SPACEs or commas. See page 707 for more information on various ways you can set **hosts allow**. Set **hosts deny** to **ALL**. Click **Commit Changes** (near the top of the page) when you are done with the GLOBALS page.

If you can no longer use swat

tip   If you can no longer use swat, you probably changed the **hosts allow** setting incorrectly. In this case, you need to edit **/etc/samba/smb.conf** and fix the line with the words **hosts allow** in it:

```
# grep hosts smb.conf
        hosts allow = 127.0.0.1, 192.168.0.8
        hosts deny = ALL
```

The preceding entries allow access from the local system and from 192.168.0.8 only.

SHARES page   Next click **SHARES** at the top of the page. Three buttons and two text boxes appear in addition to the two **Change View To** buttons (Figure 23-6). In the box adjacent to the **Create Share** button, enter the name you want to assign to the share you are setting up. This name can be anything you want; it is the name that Windows displays and a user selects when working with the share. Click **Create Share**. When you want to modify an existing share, bring up the name of the share in the combo box adjacent to **Choose Share**, and click **Choose Share**. Either of these actions expands the Share Parameters window so that it displays information about the selected share.

Leave everything at its default setting except **path**, which specifies the absolute pathname on the local Linux system of the share, and optionally **comment**, which you can use to specify the Linux system and directory that this share points to. The values for **hosts allow** and **hosts deny** are taken from the global variables that you set previously. Click **Commit Changes** when you are done with the SHARES page. If you want to see how many parameters there really are, click **Advanced** near the top of the page.

Now, from a Windows machine, you should be able to access the share you just created (page 711).

You do not need to restart Samba when you change smb.conf

tip   Samba rereads its configuration files each time a client connects. Unless you change the **security** parameter (page 708), you do not need to restart Samba when you change **smb.conf**.

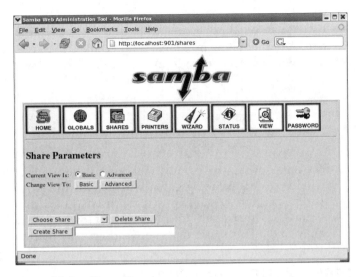

Figure 23-6   Share Parameters page

MANUALLY CONFIGURING A SAMBA SERVER

The **/etc/samba/smb.conf** file controls most aspects of how Samba works and is divided into sections. Each section begins with a line that starts with an open bracket ([), includes some text, and ends with a close bracket (]). The text within the brackets identifies the section. Typical sections are

[globals]	Defines global parameters
[printers]	Defines printers
[homes]	Defines shares in the **homes** directory
[*share name*]	Defines a share (you can have more than one of these sections)

smb.conf
comments
As installed on a Red Hat Linux system, the **/etc/samba/smb.conf** sample configuration file contains extensive comments and commented-out examples. Comment lines in **smb.conf** can start with either a pound sign (#) or a semicolon (;). The sample file uses pound signs to begin lines that are intended to remain as comments and semicolons to begin lines that you may want to mimic or use as is by removing the semicolons. The following segment of **smb.conf** contains two lines of true comments and seven lines beginning with semicolons that you may want to uncomment and make changes to:

```
# A private directory, usable only by fred. Note that fred requires
# write access to the directory.
;[fredsdir]
;    comment = Fred's Service
;    path = /usr/somewhere/private
;    valid users = fred
;    public = no
;    writable = yes
;    printable = no
```

Assuming the global parameters in **smb.conf** are set properly, you need to add a share for a Windows system to be able to access a directory on the local Linux system. Add the following simple share to the end of the **smb.conf** file to enable a user on a Windows system to be able to read from and write to the local **/tmp** directory:

```
[tmp]
            comment = temporary directory
            path = /tmp
            writable = yes
            guest ok = yes
```

The name of the share under Windows is **tmp**; the path under Linux is **/tmp**. Any Windows user, including **guest**, who can log in on Samba, can read from and write to this directory, assuming that the user's Linux permissions allow it. The Linux permissions that apply to a Windows user using Samba are the permissions that apply to the Linux user that the Windows user maps to.

PARAMETERS IN THE smbd.conf FILE

The the **smb.conf** man page and the Help feature of swat list all the parameters you can set in **smb.conf**. The following sections identify some of the parameters you are likely to want to change.

GLOBAL PARAMETERS

interfaces   A SPACE-separated list of the networks that Samba uses. Specify as interface names (such as **eth0**) or as IP address/net mask pairs (page 423).

Default: all active interfaces except 127.0.0.1

server string   The string that is displayed in various places on the Windows machine. Within the string, Samba replaces **%v** with the Samba version number and **%h** with the hostname.

Default: Samba %v
Red Hat: Samba Server

workgroup   The workgroup that the server belongs to. Set to the same workgroup as the Windows clients that use the server. This parameter controls the domain name that Samba uses when **security** (page 708) is set to DOMAIN.

Default: WORKGROUP
Red Hat: MYGROUP

SECURITY PARAMETERS

encrypt   YES accepts only encrypted passwords from clients. Windows 98 and Windows NT
passwords   4.0 Service Pack 3 and later use encrypted passwords by default. This parameter uses **smbpasswd** to authenticate passwords unless you set **security** to SERVER or DOMAIN, in which case Samba authenticates using another server.

Default: YES

Samba defaults to storing encrypted passwords in the **smbpasswd** file if you do not set up **passdb** (a password database). Storing passwords in the **smbpasswd** file is sensible on servers with fewer than 250 users. For high-load servers, consult the Samba HOWTO collection for information about configuring a database back end.

guest account   The username that is assigned to users logging in as **guest** or mapped to **guest**; applicable only when **guest ok** (page 711) is set to YES. This username should be present in **/etc/passwd** but should not be able to log in on the system. Typically **guest account** is assigned a value of **nobody** because the user **nobody** can access only files that any user can access. If you are using the **nobody** account for other purposes on the Linux system, set this variable to a name other than **nobody**.

Default: **nobody**

hosts allow   Analogous to the **/etc/hosts.allow** file (page 427), this parameter specifies hosts that are allowed to connect to the server. Overrides hosts specified in **hosts deny**. A good strategy is to specify ALL in **hosts deny** and to specify the hosts you want to grant access to in this file. Specify hosts in the same manner as in **hosts.allow**.

Default: none (all hosts permitted access)

hosts deny   Analogous to the **/etc/hosts.deny** file (page 427), this parameter specifies hosts that are not allowed to connect to the server. Overridden by hosts specified in **hosts allow**. If you specify ALL in this file, remember to include the local system (127.0.0.1) in **hosts allow**. Specify hosts in the same manner as in **hosts.deny**.

Default: none (no hosts excluded)

map to guest   Defines when a failed login is mapped to the **guest account**. Useful only when **security** is not set to **SHARE**.

Never: Allows **guest** to log in only when the user explicitly provides **guest** as the username and a blank password.

Bad User: Treats any attempt to log in as a user who does not exist as a **guest** login. This parameter is a security risk because it allows a malicious user to retrieve a list of users on the system quickly.

Bad Password: Silently logs in as **guest** any user who incorrectly enters his or her password. This parameter may confuse a user when she mistypes her password and is unknowingly logged in as **guest** because she will suddenly see fewer shares than she is used to.

Default: Never

passwd chat   The chat script that Samba uses to converse with the passwd program. If this script is not followed, Samba does not change the password. Used only when **unix password sync** is set to YES.

Default: *new*password* %n\n*new*password* %n\n *changed*

passwd program   The program Samba uses to set Linux passwords. Samba replaces **%u** with the user's username.

Default: **/usr/bin/passwd %u**

security   Specifies if and how clients transfer user and password information to the server. Choose one of the following:

USER: Causes Samba to require a username and password from users or Windows when logging in on the Samba server. With this setting you can use

- **username map** to map usernames to other names
- **encrypt passwords** (page 706) to encrypt passwords (recommended)
- **guest account** (page 707) to map users to the **guest** account

SHARE: Causes Samba not to authenticate clients on a per-user basis. Instead, Samba uses the system found in Windows 9x, in which each share can have an individual password for either read or full access. This option is not compatible with more recent versions of Windows.

SERVER: Causes Samba to use another SMB server to validate usernames and passwords. Failing remote validation, the local Samba server tries to validate as though **security** were set to USER.

DOMAIN: Samba passes an encrypted password to a Windows NT domain controller for validation.

ADS: Instructs Samba to use an Active Directory server for authentication, allowing a Samba server to participate as a native Active Directory member. (Active Directory is the centralized information system that Windows 2000 and later use. It replaces Windows Domains, which was used by Windows NT and earlier.)

Default: USER

unix password   YES causes Samba to change a user's Linux password when the associated user
sync   changes the encrypted Samba password.

Default: NO

update   YES allows users to migrate from cleartext passwords to encrypted passwords without
encrypted   logging in on the server and using smbpasswd. To migrate users, set to YES and set **encrypt passwords** to NO. As each user logs in on the server with a cleartext Linux password, smbpasswd encrypts and stores the password in **/etc/samba/smbpasswd**. Set to NO and set **encrypt passwords** to YES after all users have been converted.

Default: NO

username map   The name of the file that maps usernames from a client to usernames on the server. Each line of the map file starts with a server username, followed by a SPACE, an equal sign, another SPACE, and one or more SPACE-separated client usernames. An asterisk (*) on the client side matches any client username. This file frequently maps Windows usernames to Linux usernames and/or maps multiple Windows usernames to a single Linux username to facilitate file sharing. A sample map file is shown here:

```
$ cat /etc/samba/smbusers
# Unix_name = SMB_name1 SMB_name2 ...
root = administrator admin
```

```
nobody = guest
sam = sams
```

Default: no map
Red Hat /etc/samba/smbusers

LOGGING PARAMETERS

log file   The name of the Samba log file. Samba replaces **%m** with the name of the client system, allowing you to generate a separate log file for each client.

Default: none
Red Hat: **/var/log/samba/%m.log**

log level   Sets the log level, with 0 (zero) being off and higher numbers being more verbose.

Default: 0 (off)

max log size   An integer specifying the maximum size of the log file in kilobytes. A 0 (zero) specifies no limit. When a file reaches this size, Samba appends a **.old** to the filename and starts a new log, deleting any old log file.

Default: 5000
Red Hat: 50

BROWSER PARAMETERS

The *domain master browser* is the system that is responsible for maintaining the list of machines on a network used when browsing a Windows Network Neighborhood or My Network Places. *SMB* (page 1055) uses weighted elections every 11–15 minutes to determine which machine will be the domain master browser.

Whether a Samba server wins this election depends on two parameters: First, setting **domain master** to YES instructs the Samba server to enter the election. Second, the **os level** determines how much weight the Samba server's vote receives. Setting **os level** to 2 should cause the Samba server to win against any Windows 9*x* machines. NT Server series domain controllers, including Windows 2000, XP, and 2003, use an **os level** of 32. The maximum setting for **os level** is 255, although setting it to 65 should ensure that the Samba server wins.

domain master   YES causes **nmbd** to attempt to be the domain master browser. If a domain master browser exists, then local master browsers will forward copies of their browse lists to it. If there is no domain master browser, then browse queries may not be able to cross subnet boundaries. A Windows PDC (Primary Domain Controller) will always try to become the domain master and may behave in unexpected ways if it fails. Refer to the preceding discussion.

Default: AUTO

local master   YES causes **nmbd** to enter elections for the local master browser on a subnet. A local master browser stores a cache of the *NetBIOS* (page 1044) names of entities on the local subnet, allowing browsing. Windows machines automatically enter elections; for browsing to work, the network must have at least one Windows machine or one Samba server with **local master** set to YES. It is poor practice to set **local master** to NO. If you do not want a computer to act as a local master, set its **os level** to a lower number, allowing it to be used as the local master if all else fails.

Default: YES

os level An integer that controls how much Samba advertises itself for browser elections and how likely **nmbd** is to become the local master browser for its workgroup. A higher number increases the chances of the local server becoming the local master browser. Refer to the discussion at the beginning of this section.

Default: 20

preferred master YES forces **nmbd** to hold an election for local master and enters the local system with a slight advantage. With **domain master** set to YES, this parameter helps ensure that the local Samba server becomes the domain master. Setting this parameter to YES on more than one server causes the servers to compete to become master, generating a lot of network traffic and sometimes leading to unpredictable results. A Windows PDC (Primary Domain Controller) automatically acts as if this parameter is set.

Default: AUTO

COMMUNICATION PARAMETERS

dns proxy When acting as a *WINS server* (page 1063), YES causes **nmbd** to use DNS if *Net-BIOS* (page 1044) resolution fails.

Default: YES
Red Hat: NO

socket options Tunes the network parameters used when exchanging data with a client. The Red Hat Linux setting is appropriate in most cases.

Default: TCP_NODELAY
Red Hat: TCP_NODELAY SO_RCVBUF=8192 SO_SNDBUF=8192

wins server The IP address of the WINS server that **nmbd** should register with.

Default: not enabled

wins support YES specifies that **nmbd** act as a WINS server.

Default: NO

SHARE PARAMETERS

Each of the following parameters can appear many times in **smb.conf**, once in each share definition.

available YES specifies the share as active. Set this parameter to NO to disable the share, but continue logging requests for it.

Default: YES

browseable   Determines whether the share can be browsed, for example, in Windows My Network Places.

Default: YES
Red Hat: NO

comment   A description of the share, shown when browsing the network from Windows.

Default: none
Red Hat: varies

guest ok   Allows a user who logs in as **guest** to access this share.

Default: NO

path   The path of the directory that is being shared.

Default: none
Red Hat: various

read only   Does not allow write access.

Default: YES

THE [HOMES] SHARE: SHARING USERS' HOME DIRECTORIES

Frequently users want to share their Linux home directories with a Windows machine. To make this task easier, Samba provides the **[homes]** share. When you define this share, each user's home directory is shared with the specified parameters. In most cases, the following parameters are adequate:

```
[homes]
        comment = Home Directories
        browseable = no
        writable = yes
```

These settings prevent users other than the owners from browsing home directories, while allowing logged-in owners full access.

SELinux   If the system is running SELinux with a targeted policy and you want to allow users to share their home directories as explained in this section, you must turn on the SELinux setting **Samba⇨Allow Samba to share users home directories** as displayed by system-config-securitylevel (page 402).

ACCESSING LINUX SHARES FROM WINDOWS

BROWSING SHARES

To access a share on a Samba server from Windows, open My Computer or Explorer on the Windows system and, in the Address text box, enter \\ followed by the NetBIOS name (or just the hostname if you have not assigned a different NetBIOS name) of the Samba server. Windows then displays the directories that the Linux system is sharing. To view the shares on the Linux system named **bravo**, for example, you would enter **\\bravo**. From this window, you can view and browse the shares available on the Linux system. If you set a share so that it is not browseable, you need to enter the path of the share using the format ***servername**sharename*.

MAPPING A SHARE

Another way to access a share on a Samba server is by mapping a share. Open My Computer or Explorer on the Windows system and click **Map Network Drive** from one of the drop-down menus on the menubar (found on the **Tools** menu on Windows XP). Windows displays the Map Network Drive window. Select an unused Windows drive letter from the Drive combo box and enter the Windows path to the share you just created. (When you use system-config-samba to create a share, the share has the same name as the name of the directory you are sharing.) The format of the windows path is ***hostname**sharename*. For example, to map **/tmp** on **bravo** to Windows drive J, assuming the share is named **tmp** on the Linux system, select **J** in the Drive combo box, enter **\\bravo\tmp** in the Folder text box, and click **Finish**. You should be able to access the **/tmp** directory from **bravo** as **J** (**tmp**) on the Windows machine. If you cannot map the drive, refer to "Troubleshooting" on page 714.

ACCESSING WINDOWS SHARES FROM LINUX

As a client, Samba enables you to view and work with files on a Windows system from a Linux system. This section discusses several ways of accessing Windows files from Linux.

smbtree: DISPLAYS WINDOWS SHARES

The smbtree utility displays a hierarchical diagram of available shares. When you run smbtree, it prompts you for a password; do not enter a password if you want to browse shares that are visible to the **guest** user. The password allows you to view restricted shares, such as a user's home directory in the **[homes]** share. Following is sample output from smbtree:

```
$ smbtree
Password:
MGS
        \\PB                            pb Samba
                \\PB\mark               Home Directories
                \\PB\MainPrinter        MainPrinter
                \\PB\ADMIN$             IPC Service (pb Samba)
                \\PB\IPC$               IPC Service (pb Samba)
                \\PB\tmp                mgs temp
```

In the preceding output, **MGS** is the name of the workgroup, **PB** is the name of the Windows machine, **mark** and **tmp** are directory shares, and **MainPrinter** is a shared printer. Workgroup and machine names are always shown in capitals. Refer to the smbtree man page for more information.

smbclient: CONNECTS TO WINDOWS SHARES

The smbclient utility functions similarly to ftp (page 601) and connects to a Windows share; however, smbclient uses Linux-style forward slashes (/) as path separators rather than Windows-style backslashes (\). The next example connects to one of the shares displayed in the preceding example:

```
$ smbclient //PB/mark
Password:
Domain=[PB] OS=[Unix] Server=[Samba 3.0.10-1.fc2]
smb: \> ls
  .                      D        0   Wed Feb 22 15:10:03 2006
  ..                     D        0   Mon Feb  6 12:40:17 2006
  .kde                   DH       0   Tue Feb  7 22:24:17 2006
  .xemacs                DH       0   Mon Feb  6 10:12:45 2006
  .bash_logout           H       24   Tue Oct 25 06:15:04 2005
  .bash_profile          H      191   Tue Oct 25 06:15:04 2005
  .bashrc                H      124   Tue Oct 25 06:15:04 2005
  ...
```

You can use most ftp commands from smbclient. Refer to "Tutorial Session" on page 604 for some examples or give the command **help** to display a list of commands.

BROWSING WINDOWS NETWORKS

Browsing Windows shares using smbtree and smbclient is quite awkward compared with the ease of browsing a network from Windows; Gnome and KDE provide more user-friendly alternatives. From either Konqueror or Nautilus (the KDE and Gnome file managers), enter **smb:/** in the location bar to browse the Windows shares on the network.

Both Konqueror and Nautilus use virtual filesystem add-ons, which are part of the respective desktop environments and not part of the native Linux system. As a consequence, only native Gnome or KDE applications can open files on remote shares; normal Linux programs cannot. For example, gedit and kedit will be able to open files on remote shares, while OpenOffice, mplayer, and xedit cannot.

MOUNTING WINDOWS SHARES

The mount utility (page 466) with a **–t cifs** option mounts a Windows share as if it were a Linux directory hierarchy. See page 1024 for more information on the CIFS protocol. When you mount a Windows share, you can write to the files on the share; you cannot write to files on a share using smbclient.

A mount command that mounts a Windows share has the following syntax:

mount -t cifs //host/share dir

where *host* is the name of the system that the share is on, *share* is the name of the Windows share that you want to mount, and *dir* is the absolute pathname of the Linux directory that you are mounting the share on (the mount point).

The following command, when run as **root**, mounts on the **/share** directory the share used in the preceding example. If you omit the **password** argument (which you may want to do for security reasons), **mount** prompts for it.

```
# mount -t cifs //PB/mark /share -o username=mark,password=pizza
# ls /share
Desktop      mansmbconf                          smb.conf   smbout
httpd.conf   NVIDIA-Linux-x86-1.0-5336-pkg1.run  smbhold    x
```

You can use the **uid, file_mode,** and **dir_mode** mount options with type **cifs** filesystems to establish ownership and permissions of mounted files.

```
# mount -t cifs //PB/mark /share -o username=mark,uid=mark,file_mode=0644,dir_mode=0755
```

Permissions must be expressed as octal numbers preceded by a zero. For more information refer to the **mount.cifs** man page.

TROUBLESHOOTING

Samba provides three utilities that can help you troubleshoot a connection: The smbstatus utility displays a report on open Samba connections; testparm checks the syntax of **/etc/samba/smb.conf** and displays its contents; and testprns checks the validity of the name of a printer.

The following steps can help you narrow down the problem when you cannot get Samba to work.

1. Restart the **smbd** and **nmbd** daemons. Make sure the last two lines of output end with **OK**.

```
# /sbin/service smb restart
Shutting down SMB services:                             [  OK  ]
Shutting down NMB services:                             [  OK  ]
Starting SMB services:                                  [  OK  ]
Starting NMB services:                                  [  OK  ]
```

testparm   2. Run testparm to check that the **smb.conf** file is syntactically correct:

```
$ testparm
Load smb config files from /etc/samba/smb.conf
Processing section "[homes]"
Processing section "[printers]"
Processing section "[tmp]"
Loaded services file OK.
```

```
Server role: ROLE_STANDALONE
Press enter to see a dump of your service definitions
...
```

If you misspell a keyword in **smb.conf**, you get an error such as the following:

```
# testparm
Load smb config files from /etc/samba/smb.conf
Unknown parameter encountered: "workgruop"
Ignoring unknown parameter "workgruop"
...
```

ping   3. Use ping (page 365) from both sides of the connection to make sure the network is up.

net view   4. From a Windows command prompt, use net view to display a list of shares available from the server (**pb** in this example):

```
C:>net view \\pb
Shared resources at \\pb

pb Samba

Share name   Type   Used as   Comment

-------------------------------------------------------------------
MainPrinter  Print            MainPrinter
mark         Disk   (UNC)     Home Directories
tmp          Disk             mgs temp
The command completed successfully.
```

net use   5. Try to map the drive from a Windows command prompt. The following command attempts to mount the share named **tmp** on **pb** as drive X:

```
C:>net use x: \\pb\tmp
The command completed successfully.
```

nmblookup   6. From the server, query the **nmbd** server, using the special name __SAMBA__ for the server's NetBIOS name. The **–d 2** option turns the debugger on at level 2, which generates a moderate amount of output:

```
$ nmblookup -d 2 -B pb __SAMBA__
added interface ip=192.168.0.10 bcast=192.168.0.255
nmask=255.255.255.0
querying __SAMBA__ on 192.168.0.10
Got a positive name query response from 192.168.0.10 ( 192.168.0.10 )
192.168.0.10 __SAMBA__<00>
```

nmblookup   7. From the server, query the **nmbd** server for the client's NetBIOS name. (The machine named **jam** is the Windows client.)

```
$ nmblookup -B jam \*
querying * on 192.168.0.9
192.168.0.9 *<00>
```

Omit the **–B jam** option to query for all NetBIOS names.

smbclient

8. From the server, use smbclient with the **−L** option to generate a list of shares offered by the server:

```
$ smbclient -L pb
Password:
Domain=[PB] OS=[Unix] Server=[Samba 3.0.10-1.fc2]

        Sharename      Type       Comment
        ---------      ----       -------
        tmp            Disk       mgs temp
        IPC$           IPC        IPC Service (pb Samba)
        ADMIN$         IPC        IPC Service (pb Samba)
        MainPrinter    Printer    MainPrinter
        mark           Disk       Home Directories
Domain=[PB] OS=[Unix] Server=[Samba 3.0.10-1.fc2]

        Server         Comment
        ---------      -------


        Workgroup      Master
        ---------      -------
        MGS            TUNAER
```

nmblookup

9. To query for the master browser from the server, run nmblookup with the **−M** option followed by the name of the workgroup:

```
$ nmblookup -M MGS
querying MGS on 192.168.0.255
192.168.0.8 MGS<1d>
```

CHAPTER SUMMARY

Samba is a suite of programs that enables Linux and Windows to share directories and printers. A directory or printer that is shared between Linux and Windows systems is called a *share*. To access a share on a Linux system, a Windows user must supply a username and password. Usernames must correspond to Linux usernames either directly or as mapped by the **/etc/samba/smbusers** file. Samba passwords are generated by smbpasswd and kept in **/etc/samba/smbpasswd**.

The main Samba configuration file is **/etc/samba/smb.conf**, which you can edit using a text editor, swat (a Web-based administration utility), or system-config-samba (a minimal-configuration GUI). The swat utility is a powerful configuration tool that provides integrated online documentation and clickable default values to help you set up Samba.

From a Windows machine, you can access a share on a Linux Samba server by opening My Computer or Explorer and, in the Address text box, entering \\ followed by the name of the server. Windows displays the shares on the server and you can work with them as though they were Windows files.

From a Linux system, you can use any of several Samba tools to access Windows shares. These tools include smbtree (displays shares), smbclient (similar to ftp), and mount with the **–t cifs** option (mounts shares). In addition, you can enter **smb:/** in the location bar of Konqueror or Nautilus and browse the shares.

EXERCISES

1. Which two daemons are part of the Samba suite? What does each do?

2. What steps are required for mapping a Windows user to a Linux user?

3. How would you allow access to swat only from machines on the 192.168.1.0/8 subnet?

4. What is the purpose of the [homes] share?

ADVANCED EXERCISES

5. Describe how Samba's handling of users differs from that of NFS.

6. Which configuration changes would you need to apply to routers if you wanted to allow SMB/CIFS browsing across multiple subnets without configuring master browsers?

7. How could you use swat securely from a remote location?

8. WINS resolution allows hosts to define their own names. Suggest a way to use Samba to assign names from a centralized list.

24

DNS/BIND: TRACKING DOMAIN NAMES AND ADDRESSES

DNS (Domain Name System) maps domain names to IP addresses, and vice versa. It reduces the need for humans to work with IP addresses, which, with the introduction of IPv6, are complex. The DNS specification defines a secure, general-purpose database that holds Internet host information. It also specifies a protocol that is used to exchange this information. Further, DNS defines library routines that implement the protocol. Finally, DNS provides a means for routing email. Under DNS, *nameservers* work with clients, called *resolvers,* to distribute host information in the form of *resource records* in a timely manner as needed.

This chapter describes BIND (Berkeley Internet Name Domain) version 9, a popular open-source implementation of DNS. Part of the Red Hat Linux distribution, BIND includes the DNS server daemon (**named**), a DNS resolver library, and tools for working with DNS. Although DNS can be used for private networks, this chapter covers DNS as used by the Internet.

719

INTRODUCTION TO DNS

You normally use DNS when you display a Web page. For example, to display Red Hat's home page, you enter its name, www.redhat.com, in a browser and the browser displays the page you want. You never enter or see the IP address for the displayed page. However, without the IP address, the browser could not display the page. DNS works behind the scenes to find the IP address when you enter the name in the browser. The DNS database is

- **Hierarchical**, so that it provides quick responses to queries: DNS has a root, branches, and nodes.

- **Distributed**, so that it offers fast access to servers. The DNS database is spread across thousands of systems worldwide; each system is referred to as a *DNS server* (or a *domain server* or *nameserver*).

- **Replicated**, to enhance reliability. Because many systems hold the same information, when some systems fail, DNS does not stop functioning.

As implemented, DNS is

- **Secure**, so that your browser or email is directed to the correct location.

- **Flexible**, so that it can adapt to new names, deleted names, and names whose information changes.

- **Fast**, so that Internet connections are not delayed by slow DNS lookups.

History The mapping that DNS does was originally done statically in a **/etc/hosts** file (page 452) on each system on a network. Small LANs still make use of this file. As networks—specifically the Internet—grew, a dynamic mapping system was required. DNS was specified in 1983 and BIND became part of BSD in 1985.

Security BIND is by far the most popular implementation of a DNS. However, recently concerns about its security have arisen. You may want to run BIND inside a **chroot** jail (page 750) or under SELinux (page 400) and use transaction signatures (TSIG, page 748) to improve security.

host and dig The **host** and **dig** utilities (page 368) query DNS servers. The **host** utility is simpler, is easier to use, and returns less information than **dig**. This chapter uses both tools to explore DNS.

NODES, DOMAINS, AND SUBDOMAINS

Each node in the hierarchical DNS database is called a *domain* and is labeled with a (domain) name. As with the Linux file structure, the node at the top of the DNS hierarchy is called the *root node* or *root domain*. While the Linux file structure separates the nodes (directory and ordinary files) with slashes (**/**) and labels the root node (directory) with a slash, the DNS structure uses periods (Figure 24-1).

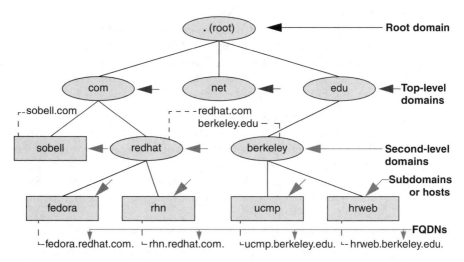

Figure 24-1   The DNS domain structure

You read an absolute pathname in a Linux filesystem from left to right: It starts with the root directory (**/**) at the left and, as you read to the right, describes the path to the file being identified (for example, **/var/named/named.ca**). Unlike a Linux pathname, you read a DNS domain name from right to left: It starts with the root domain at the right (represented by a period [**.**]) and, as you read to the left, works its way down through the top-level and second-level domains to a subdomain or host. Frequently the name of the root domain (the period at the right) is omitted from a domain name. The term *domain* refers both to a single node in the DNS domain structure and to a catenated, period-separated list (path) of domain names that describes the location of a domain.

FQDN A fully qualified domain name (FQDN) is the DNS equivalent of a filesystem's absolute pathname: It is a pointer that positively locates a domain on the Internet. Just as you (and Linux) can identify an absolute pathname by its leading slash (**/**) that names the root directory, so an FQDN can be identified by its trailing period (.) that names the root domain (Figure 24-2).

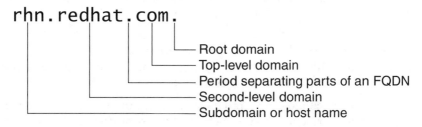

Figure 24-2   A fully qualified domain name (FQDN)

Resolver   The resolver comprises the routines that turn an unqualified domain name into an FQDN that is passed to DNS to be mapped to an IP address. The resolver can append several domains, one at a time, to an unqualified domain name, producing several FQDNs that it passes, one at a time, to DNS. For each FQDN, DNS reports success (it found the FQDN and is returning the corresponding IP address) or failure (the FQDN does not exist).

The resolver always appends the root domain (.) to an unqualified domain name first, allowing you to type **www.redhat.com** instead of **www.redhat.com.** (including the trailing period) in a browser. You can specify other domains for the resolver to try if the root domain fails. Put the domain names, in the order you want them tried, after the **search** keyword in **/etc/resolv.conf** (page 455). For example, if your search domains include **redhat.com.**, then the domains **rhn** and **rhn.redhat.com.** resolve to the same address.

Subdomains   Each node in the domain hierarchy is a domain. Each domain that has a parent (that is, every domain except the root domain) is also a subdomain, regardless of whether it has children. All subdomains *can* resolve to hosts—even those with children. For example, the **redhat.com.** domain resolves to the host that serves the Red Hat Web site, without preventing its children—domains such as **fedora.redhat.com.**—from resolving. The leftmost part of an FQDN is often called the *hostname*.

Hostnames   In the past, hostnames could contain only characters from the set a–z, A–Z, 0–9, and –. As of March 2004, however, hostnames can include various accents, umlauts, and so on (www.switch.ch/id/idn). DNS considers uppercase and lowercase letters to be the same (it is not case sensitive), so www.sobell.com is the same as WWW.sObEll.coM.

ZONES

For administrative purposes, domains are grouped into zones that extend downward from a domain (Figure 24-3). A single DNS server is responsible for (holds the information required to resolve) all domains within a zone. The DNS server for a zone also holds pointers to DNS servers that are responsible for the zones immediately below the zone it is responsible for. Information about zones originates in zone files, one zone per file.

Root domain   The highest zone, the one containing the root domain, does not contain any hosts. Instead, this domain delegates to the DNS servers for the top-level domains (Figure 24-1, page 721).

Authority   Each zone has at least one authoritative DNS server. This server holds all information about the zone. A DNS query returns information about a domain and specifies which DNS server is authoritative for that domain.

DNS employs a hierarchical structure to keep track of names and authority. At the top or root of the structure is the root domain, which employs 13 authoritative nameservers. These are the only servers that are authoritative for the root and top-level domains.

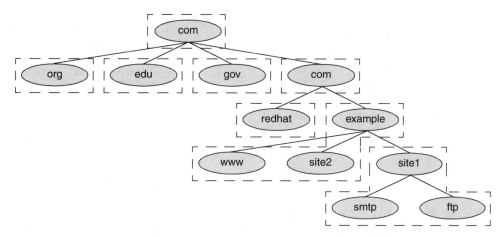

Figure 24-3   DNS structure showing zones

Delegation of
authority
When referring to DNS, the term *delegation* means *delegation of authority*. ICANN (Internet Corporation for Assigned Names and Numbers, www.icann.org) delegates authority to the root and top-level domains. In other words, ICANN says which servers are authoritative for these domains. Authority is delegated to each domain below the top-level domains by the authoritative server at the next-higher-level domain. ICANN is not authoritative for most second-level domains. For example, Red Hat is authoritative for the redhat.com domain. This scheme of delegating authority allows for local control over segments of the DNS database while making all segments available to the public.

QUERIES

Iterative query
There are two types of DNS queries: *iterative* and *recursive*.[1] An iterative query sends a domain name to a DNS server and asks the server to return either the IP address of the domain or the name of the DNS server that is authoritative for the domain or one of its parents: The server does not query other servers when seeking an answer. Nameservers typically send each other iterative queries.

Recursive query
A recursive query sends a domain name to a DNS server and asks the server to return the IP address of the domain: The server may need to query other servers to get the answer. Both types of queries can fail, in which case the server returns a message saying it is unable to locate the domain.

When a client, such as a browser, needs the IP address that corresponds to a domain name, the client queries a resolver. Most resolvers are quite simple and require a DNS server to do most of the work: That is, they send recursive queries. The

---

1. There is a third type of query that is not covered in this book: *inverse*. An inverse query provides a domain name given a resource record. Reverse name resolution (page 729), not an inverse query, is used to query for a domain name given an IP address.

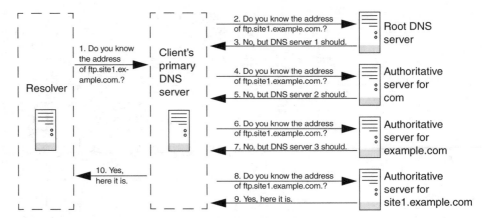

Figure 24-4 A recursive query that starts several iterative queries to find the answer

resolver communicates with a single DNS server, which can perform multiple iterative queries in response to the resolver's recursive query.

All DNS servers must answer iterative queries. DNS servers can also be set up to answer recursive queries. A DNS server that is not set up to answer recursive queries treats a recursive query as though it is an iterative query.

In Figure 24-4, the resolver on a client system is trying to discover the address of the server ftp.site1.example.com. on the network with the DNS layout shown in Figure 24-3 on page 723. The resolver on the client sends a recursive query to its primary DNS server. This server interrogates the root server and one additional server for each zone until it receives an answer, which it returns to the resolver on the client. In practice, the query would not start with the root server because most servers usually have the location of the authoritative nameserver for the **com**. domain stored in cache (memory).

SERVERS

There are three main types of DNS servers: primary (master), secondary (slave), and caching-only.

- A *primary master server*, also called a *primary server* or *master server*, is the authoritative server that holds the master copy of zone data. It copies information from the *zone* or *master file*, a local file that the server administrator maintains. For security and efficiency, a primary master server should provide iterative answers only. A primary master server that provides recursive answers is more easily subverted by a *DoS attack* (page 1030) than one that provides iterative answers only.

- *Slave servers*, also called *secondary servers*, are authoritative and copy zone information from the primary master server or another slave server.

On some systems, when information on the primary master server changes, the primary master server sends a message to the slave servers. When a slave receives such a message, it uses a process called *zone transfer* to copy the new zone information from the master server to itself.

- *DNS caches,* also called *caching-only servers,* are not authoritative. These servers store answers to previous queries in cache (memory). When a DNS cache receives a query, it answers it from cache if it can. If the DNS cache does not have the answer in cache, it forwards the query to an authoritative server.

It is possible—but for reasons of security not recommended—for the same server to be the primary master server (authoritative) for some zones and a DNS cache for others. When the same server acts as both a DNS cache and a master server, if a malicious local user or malfunctioning resolver on the local network floods the DNS cache with more traffic than it can handle (a DoS attack), users may be prevented from accessing the public servers that the primary master server handles. Conversely, if the authoritative server is compromised, the attacker can subvert all traffic leaving the network.

RESOURCE RECORDS

Information about nodes (domains) in the DNS database is stored in resource records. Resource records are kept in zone files (page 741). The zone that a resource record pertains to is defined by the zone file that contains the resource record. The zone is named in the **named.conf** file (page 739) that references the zone file.

A resource record has the following fields:

- **Name**   The domain name or IP address
- **TTL**   Time to live (not in all resource records; see page 1060)
- **Class** Always IN for Internet (the only class that DNS supports)
- **Type**   Record type (discussed in the next section)
- **Data**   Varies with record type

If the Name field is missing, the resource record inherits the name from the previous resource record in the same file. Cached resource records become out-of-date when the information in the record changes on the authoritative server. The TTL field indicates the maximum time a server may keep a record in cache before checking whether a newer one is available. Typically, the TTL is on the order of days. A TTL of 0 means that the resource record should not be cached.

More than 30 types of resource records exist, ranging from common types, such as address records that store the address of a host, to those that contain geographical information. The following paragraphs describe the types of resource records you are most likely to encounter.

A   IPv4 Address   Maps a domain name to the IPv4 address of a host. There must be at least one address record for each domain; multiple address records can point to the same IP address. The Name field holds the domain name, which is assumed to be in the same zone as the domain. The Data field holds the IP address associated with the name. The following address resource record maps the **ns** domain in the zone to 192.168.0.1:

```
ns      IN      A       192.168.0.1
```

AAAA   IPv6 Address   Maps a domain name to the IPv6 address of a host. The following address resource record maps the **ns** domain in the zone to an IPv6 address:

```
ns      IN      AAAA    2001:630:d0:131:a00:20ff:feb5:ef1e
```

CNAME   Canonical Name   Maps an alias or nickname to a domain name. The Name field holds the alias or nickname; the Data field holds the official or canonical name. CNAME is useful for specifying an easy-to-remember name or multiple names for the same domain. It is also useful when a system changes names or IP addresses. In this case the alias can point to the real name that must resolve to an IP address.

When a query returns a CNAME, a client or DNS tool performs a DNS lookup on the domain name returned with the CNAME. It is acceptable to provide multiple levels of CNAME records. The following resource record maps **ftp** in the zone to www.sam.net.:

```
ftp     IN      CNAME   www.sam.net.
```

MX   Mail Exchange   Specifies a destination for mail addressed to the domain. MX records must always point to A (or AAAA) records. The Name field holds the domain name, which is assumed to be in the zone; the Data field holds the name of a mail server preceded by its priority. Unlike A records, MX records contain a priority number that allows mail delivery agents to fall back to a backup server in case the primary server is down. Several mail servers can be ranked in priority order, where the lowest number has the highest priority. DNS selects randomly from among mail servers with the same priority. The following resource records forward mail sent to **speedy** in the zone first to **mail** in the zone and then, if that fails, to **mail.sam.net.**. The value of **speedy** in the Name field on the second line is implicit.

```
speedy          MX      10 mail
                MX      20 mail.sam.net.
```

NS   Nameserver   Specifies the name of the system that provides domain service (DNS records) for the domain. The Name field holds the domain name; the Data field holds the name of the DNS server. Each domain must have at least one NS record. DNS servers do not need to reside in the domain and, in fact, it is better if at least one does not. The system name **ns** is frequently used to specify a nameserver, but this name is not required and does not have any significance beyond assisting humans in identifying a nameserver. The following resource record specifies **ns.max.net.** as a nameserver for **peach** in the zone:

```
peach           NS      ns.max.net.
```

PTR **Pointer**   Maps an IP address to a domain name and is used for reverse name resolution. The Name field holds the IP address; the Data field holds the domain name. Do not use PTR resource records with aliases. The following resource record maps 3 in a reverse zone (for example, 3 in the 0.168.192.in-addr.arpa zone is 192.168.0.3) to **grape** in the zone:

```
3       IN      PTR     grape
```

For more information refer to "Reverse Name Resolution" on page 729.

SOA **Start of Authority**   Designates the start of a zone. Each zone must have exactly one SOA record. An authoritative server maintains the SOA record for the zone it is authoritative for.

All zone files must have one SOA resource record, which must be the first resource record in the file. The Name field holds the name of the domain at the start of the zone. The Data field holds the name of the host the data was created on, the email address of the person responsible for the zone, and the following information enclosed within parentheses (the opening parenthesis must appear on the first physical line of an SOA record):

serial   A value in the range 1–2,147,483,647. A change in this number indicates that the zone data has changed. By convention, this field is set to the string **yyyymmddnn** (year, month, day, change number). Along with the date, the final two digits—that is, the change number—should be incremented each time you change the SOA record.

refresh   The elapsed time after which the primary master server notifies slave (secondary) servers to refresh the record; the time between updates.

retry   The time to wait after a refresh fails before trying to refresh again.

expiry   The elapsed time after which the zone is no longer authoritative and the root servers must be queried. The expiry applies to slave servers only.

minimum   The negative caching TTL, which is the amount of time that a nonexistent domain error (NXDOMAIN) can be held in a slave server's cache. A negative caching TTL is the same as a normal TTL except that it applies to domains that do not exist rather than to domains that do exist.

The $TTL directive (page 742) specifies the default zone TTL (the maximum amount of time that data stays in a slave server's cache). Jointly, the default zone TTL and the negative caching TTL encompass all types of replies the server can generate.

The following two SOA resource records are equivalent:

```
@ IN SOA ns.zach.net. mgs@sobell.com. ( 2005111247 8H 2H 4W 1D )

@       IN      SOA     ns.zach.net. mgs@sobell.com. (
                        2005111247      ; serial
                        8H              ; refresh
                        2H              ; retry
                        4W              ; expire
                        1D )            ; minimum
```

The second format is more readable because of its layout and the comments. The at symbol (**@**) at the start of the SOA resource record stands for the zone name, also called the origin, as specified in the **named.conf** file. Because the **named.conf** file specifies the zone name to be **zach.net**, you could rewrite the first line as follows:

```
zach.net.  IN  SOA     ns.zach.net. mgs@sobell.com. (
```

The host utility returns something closer to the first format with each of the times specified in seconds:

```
$ host -t soa zach.net
zach.net. SOA ns.zach.net. mgs\@sobell.com. 03111 28800 7200 2419200 86400
```

TXT **Text**   Associates a character string with a domain. The Name field holds the domain name. The data field can contain up to 256 characters and must be enclosed within quotation marks. TXT records can contain any arbitrary text value. As well as general information, they can be used for things such as public key distribution. Following is a TXT resource record that specifies a company name:

```
zach.net   IN  TXT     "Sobell Associates Inc."
```

DNS QUERY AND RESPONSE

Query   A DNS query has three parts:

1. Name   Domain name, FQDN, or IP address for reverse name resolution

2. Type   Type of record requested (page 725)

3. Class   Always IN for Internet class

Cache   Most DNS servers store in cache memory the query responses from other DNS servers. When a DNS server receives a query, it first tries to resolve the query from its cache. Failing that, the server may query other servers to get an answer.

Because DNS uses cache, when you make a change to a DNS record, the change takes time—sometimes a matter of days—to propagate through the DNS hierarchy.

Response   A DNS message that is sent in response to a query has the following structure:

- Header record   Information about this message

- Query record   Repeats the query

- Answer records   Resource records that answer the query

- Authority records   Resource records for servers that have authority for the answers

- Additional records   Additional resource records, such as NS records

The dig utility does not consult **/etc/nsswitch.conf** (page 435) to determine which server to query. The following example uses dig to query a DNS server:

```
$ dig fedora.redhat.com
...
;; QUESTION SECTION:
;fedora.redhat.com.              IN      A

;; ANSWER SECTION:
fedora.redhat.com.      600     IN      CNAME    www.redhat.com.
www.redhat.com.         330     IN      A        209.132.177.50

;; AUTHORITY SECTION:
redhat.com.             409     IN      NS       ns1.redhat.com.
redhat.com.             409     IN      NS       ns2.redhat.com.
redhat.com.             409     IN      NS       ns3.redhat.com.

;; ADDITIONAL SECTION:
ns1.redhat.com.         300     IN      A        66.187.233.210
ns2.redhat.com.         600     IN      A        66.187.224.210
ns3.redhat.com.         600     IN      A        66.187.229.10
...
```

REVERSE NAME RESOLUTION

In addition to normal or forward name resolution, DNS provides *reverse name resolution*, also referred to as *inverse mapping* or *reverse mapping*, so that you can look up domain names given an IP address. Because resource records in the forward DNS database are indexed hierarchically by domain name, DNS cannot perform an efficient search by IP address on this database.

DNS implements reverse name resolution by means of a special domain named **in-addr.arpa** (IPv4) or **ip6.arpa** (IPv6). Resource records in these domains have Name fields that hold IP addresses; the records are indexed hierarchically by IP address. The Data fields hold the FQDN that corresponds to the IP address.

Reverse name resolution can verify that someone is who he says he is or at least is from the domain he says he is from. In general, it allows a server to retrieve and record the domain names of the clients it provides services to. For example, legitimate mail contains the domain of the sender and the IP address of the sending machine. A mail server can verify the stated domain of a sender by checking the domain associated with the IP address. Reverse name resolution is also used by anonymous FTP servers to verify that a domain specified in an email address used as a password is legitimate.

For example, to determine the domain name that corresponds to an IP address of 209.132.177.110, a resolver would query DNS for information about the domain named 110.177.132.209.in-addr.arpa (Figure 24-5, next page).

The following example uses dig to query DNS for the IP address that corresponds to rhn.redhat.com, which is 209.132.177.110. The second command line uses the dig utility to query the same IP address, reversed, and appended with **.in-addr.arpa**:

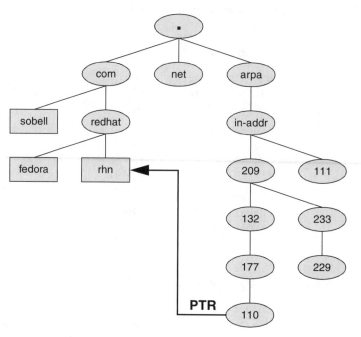

Figure 24-5   Reverse name resolution and the **in-addr.arpa** domain

110.177.132.209.in-addr.arpa to display a PTR resource record (page 727). The data portion of the resultant resource record is the domain name from the original query: rhn.redhat.com.

```
$ dig rhn.redhat.com
...
;; QUESTION SECTION:
;rhn.redhat.com.                         IN      A

;; ANSWER SECTION:
rhn.redhat.com.          60      IN      A       209.132.177.110
...

$ dig 110.177.132.209.in-addr.arpa PTR
...
;; QUESTION SECTION:
;110.177.132.209.in-addr.arpa.   IN      PTR

;; ANSWER SECTION:
110.177.132.209.in-addr.arpa. 600 IN    PTR     rhn.redhat.com.
...
```

Instead of reformatting the IP address as in the preceding example, you can use the –x option to dig to perform a reverse query:

```
$ dig -x 209.132.177.110
...
;; QUESTION SECTION:
;110.177.132.209.in-addr.arpa.   IN      PTR
```

```
;; ANSWER SECTION:
110.177.132.209.in-addr.arpa. 456 IN     PTR      rhn.redhat.com.
...
```

Or you can just use host:

```
$ host 209.132.177.110
110.177.132.209.in-addr.arpa domain name pointer rhn.redhat.com.
```

ABOUT DNS

This section discusses how DNS works and provides resources for additional information on DNS.

How DNS Works

Application programs do not issue DNS queries directly but rather use the **gethostbyname**() system call. How the system comes up with the corresponding IP address is transparent to the calling program. The **gethostbyname**() call examines the **hosts** line in **/etc/nsswitch.conf** file (page 435) to determine which files it should examine and/or which services it should query and in what order to obtain the IP address corresponding to a domain name. When it needs to query DNS, the local system (i.e., the DNS client) queries the DNS database by calling the resolver library on the local system. This call returns the required information to the application program.

PREREQUISITES

Install the following packages:

- **bind**
- **bind-utils**
- **bind-config** (*FEDORA*, optional, used to set up a caching-only nameserver; see the following caution box for an important note)
- **caching-nameserver** (*RHEL*, optional, used to set up a caching-only nameserver)
- **system-config-bind** (*FEDORA*, optional)
- **bind-chroot** (optional, used to set up BIND to run in a chroot jail)

Run chkconfig to cause **named** to start when the system enters multiuser mode:

```
# /sbin/chkconfig named on
```

After you have configured **named**, start it with service:

```
# /sbin/service named start
Starting named:                                              [  OK  ]
```

Remove caching-nameserver and install bind-config

caution   The released version of Fedora Core 5, including the version on the DVD enclosed with this book, includes the **caching-nameserver** package.

Shortly after Fedora Core 5 was released, the **caching-nameserver** package was replaced by the **bind-config** package.

To follow the examples in this chapter, you must remove the **caching-nameserver** package and install the **bind-config** package. The following commands use yum (page 478) to accomplish these tasks. In addition, it may be helpful to remove or rename **/etc/named.conf** as shown below.

```
# yum remove caching-nameserver
...
# yum install bind-config
...
# mv /etc/named.conf /etc/named.conf.old
```

If you cannot or do not want to replace the **caching-nameserver** package, read the parts of this chapter that are labeled *RHEL* and that describe the **named.caching-nameserver.conf** file.

RHEL includes the **caching-nameserver** package.

MORE INFORMATION

DNS for Rocket Scientists is an excellent site that makes good use of links to present information on DNS in a very digestible form.

Local   *Bind Administrator Reference Manual*   **/usr/share/doc/bind*/arm/Bv9ARM.html** or see the tip "Using this JumpStart" on page 735.

Web   DNS for Rocket Scientists   www.zytrax.com/books/dns
BIND   www.isc.org/products/BIND
DNS security   www.sans.org/rr/papers/index.php?id=1069

HOWTO   *DNS HOWTO*

Book   *DNS & BIND,* fourth edition, by Albitz & Liu, O'Reilly & Associates (April 2001)

NOTES

Firewall   The **named** server normally accepts queries on TCP and UDP port 53. If the server system is running a firewall, you need to open these ports. For information on using the Red Hat graphical firewall tool, see "Opening Other Ports" on page 768. For more general information, see Chapter 25, which details iptables.

SELinux   According to the Red Hat **named** man page, the default Red Hat SELinux policy for **named** is very secure and prevents known BIND security vulnerabilities from being exploited. This setup has some limitations, however. Refer to the **named** man page for more information.

If the system is running SELinux with a targeted policy and you want to modify the SELinux **named** settings, you must turn on one or more of the SELinux settings under the **Name Service** section as displayed by system-config-securitylevel (page 402).

chroot jail   The **bind-chroot** package sets up **named** to run in a chroot jail. With this package installed, all files that control BIND are located within this jail. In this case the filenames used in this chapter are symbolic links to the files in the chroot jail. See page 750 for more information.

named options   See the comments in the **/etc/sysconfig/named** file for information about **named** options that you can set there. One of the most important of these options sets the value of the **ROOTDIR** variable that controls the location of the chroot jail (page 750) that BIND runs in.

named.conf
(FEDORA)   Traditionally, **named** looks for configuration information in the **/etc/named.conf** file. The caching-only nameserver, which is part of the **bind-config** package, places **named** configuration information in **/etc/named.caching-nameserver.conf**.

For the caching-only nameserver to work without any setup, and so that **named** will work normally if you create a **/etc/named.conf** file, the Red Hat Linux **named** init script (**/etc/rc.d/init.d/named**) first looks for configuration information in **/etc/named.conf**. If that file does not exist, it looks for configuration information in **/etc/named.caching-nameserver.conf**.

JUMPSTART I: SETTING UP A DNS CACHE

As explained earlier, a DNS cache is a bridge between a resolver and authoritative DNS servers: It is not authoritative; it simply stores the results of its queries in memory. Most ISPs provide a DNS cache for the use of their customers. Setting up a local cache can reduce the traffic between the LAN and the outside world and can improve response times. While it is possible to set up a DNS cache on each system on a LAN, setting up a single DNS cache on a LAN prevents multiple systems on the LAN from having to query a remote server for the same information.

After installing BIND, including the **bind-config** package (see the caution box on page 732), you have most of a caching-only nameserver ready to run. Refer to "A DNS Cache" (page 742) for an explanation of which files this nameserver uses and how it works. Before you start the DNS cache, put the following line in **/etc/resolv.conf** (page 455), before any other nameserver lines:

```
nameserver 127.0.0.1
```

This line tells the resolver to use the local system (**localhost** or 127.0.0.1) as the primary nameserver. To experiment with using the local system as the only nameserver, comment out other nameserver lines in **resolv.conf** by preceding each with a pound sign (#).

Finally, start the **named** daemon using service as explained in the "Prerequisites" section (page 731). Refer to "Troubleshooting" on page 751 for ways to check that the DNS cache is working. Once **named** is running, you can see the effect of the cache by using dig to look up the IP address of www.redhat.com, a remote system:

```
$ dig www.redhat.com

; <<>> DiG 9.3.2 <<>> www.redhat.com
;; global options:  printcmd
;; Got answer:
;; ->>HEADER<<- opcode: QUERY, status: NOERROR, id: 38263
;; flags: qr rd ra; QUERY: 1, ANSWER: 1, AUTHORITY: 3, ADDITIONAL: 0

;; QUESTION SECTION:
;www.redhat.com.                            IN       A

;; ANSWER SECTION:
www.redhat.com.            60       IN       A        209.132.177.50

;; AUTHORITY SECTION:
redhat.com.                600      IN       NS       ns1.redhat.com.
redhat.com.                600      IN       NS       ns2.redhat.com.
redhat.com.                600      IN       NS       ns3.redhat.com.

;; Query time: 496 msec
;; SERVER: 127.0.0.1#53(127.0.0.1)
;; WHEN: Wed Mar 29 18:55:37 2006
;; MSG SIZE  rcvd: 102
```

The fourth line from the bottom shows that the query took 496 milliseconds (about one-half of a second). When you run the same query again, it runs more quickly because the DNS cache has saved the information in memory:

```
$ dig www.redhat.com
...
;; Query time: 2 msec
;; SERVER: 127.0.0.1#53(127.0.0.1)
;; WHEN: Wed Mar 29 18:55:43 2006
;; MSG SIZE  rcvd: 102
```

JUMPSTART II: SETTING UP A DOMAIN USING system-config-bind (*FEDORA*)

To display the BIND Configuration GUI window, enter **system-config-bind** on a command line (Figure 24-6). From KDE select **Main menu: Administration⇨Server Settings⇨Domain Name System** or from GNOME select **System: Administration⇨ Server Settings⇨Domain Name System**.

If */etc/named.conf* does not exist, system-config-bind displays a dialog box that informs you that it is installing a default configuration. Click **OK**.

NOTES

The */etc/named.caching-nameserver.conf* file, which is installed with the *FEDORA* bind-config package, is not recognized by system-config-bind as a **named** configuration file. See "named.conf" on page 733 for more information about this file.

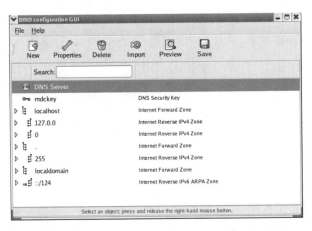

Figure 24-6   The BIND Configuration GUI window

Using this JumpStart

tip | The system-config-bind utility is a complex tool that you may find helpful for setting up BIND. Run this utility and click **Help⇨Manual** on the menubar to display the Red Hat manual for this utility. Click **Help⇨ISC ARM** to display the BIND 9 Administrator Reference Manual. You may want to experiment with this utility after you have set up one of the servers described at the end of this chapter, as its configuration information may make more sense after you go through the process of manually configuring BIND.

This section explains how to use system-config-bind but does not go into detail about what each of the files and settings does; that information is covered elsewhere in this chapter.

Each zone file that system-config-bind creates has a filename extension of **.db**.

Because the windows displayed by system-config-bind contain a lot of information, you may find it helpful to expand or maximize these windows so that you can view the information more easily.

The system-config-bind utility creates files in the **/var/named/chroot** directory hierarchy so that you can run **named** in a chroot jail. See page 750 for more information.

USING THE BIND CONFIGURATION GUI WINDOW

Right-click on an object (line) in the BIND Configuration GUI window to display a pop-up context menu. This menu always has an Edit selection, which displays a window in which you can edit information pertaining to the object you clicked on. You can display the same window by double-clicking on the object or by highlighting the object and clicking **Properties** on the Icon menu. This pop-up menu also always has an Add selection that displays a submenu with choices appropriate to the object you are working with. Figure 24-7 (next page) shows the pop-up menu for the DNS Server object along with the Add submenu.

In the BIND Configuration GUI window, a triangle at the left end of a line indicates that the object holds other objects. Click a triangle so that it points down to expand an entry. Click it so that it points to the right to collapse an entry.

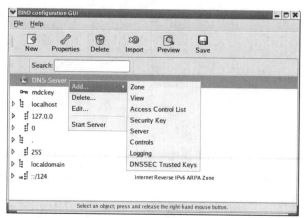

Figure 24-7   The BIND Configuration GUI window with a right-click menu

SETTING UP A DOMAIN SERVER

Highlight DNS Server in the BIND Configuration GUI window and click **New⇨ Zone** on the toolbar (or right-click and select **Add⇨Zone**) to add a new zone (page 722) and its associated nameserver. In response, system-config-bind displays the first New Zone window (Figure 24-8), which allows you to specify information about the zone you are setting up.

With the Class combo box displaying **IN Internet,** click **OK** under this box.

Next select the origin type from the combo box under Origin Type. The most common choices are Forward or IPV4 Reverse. Click **OK** under this box. Assuming you selected a forward zone, the Forward Zone Origin text box replaces the origin type information. Enter the domain name of the zone, including a trailing period, in the text box.

Finally select the type of zone you want to set up by clicking the combo box in the Zone Type frame. You can select from master, slave, forward, hint, and other types of zones. Refer to "Servers" on page 724 and **type** on page 741 for information on types of zones.

Figure 24-8   The first New Zone window

After you make your selections and click **OK**, system-config-bind displays the second New Zone window (Figure 24-9). This window enables you to set up SOA information for the zone. Refer to "SOA" on page 727 for information about the fields in the SOA record, including the serial number and the various times (refresh intervals). In this window, the authoritative (primary) nameserver (page 724) defaults to the local system and the email address of the person responsible for the zone defaults to **root** on the local system. If you enter names that do not end with a period in these text boxes, system-config-bind appends the domain name of the zone to the name you have entered. Change the values in this window as necessary. All zone files that system-config-bind creates have a filename extension of **.db** by default. The default filename for the zone file is the name of the domain you are setting up with an extension of **.db**. Click **OK** to close the window when you are done making changes.

After you add a new zone, the information about this zone appears in the BIND Configuration GUI window (Figure 24-6, page 735). Click **Save** on the toolbar to save the changes you made before you close the window.

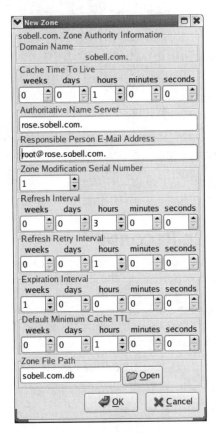

Figure 24-9   The second New Zone window

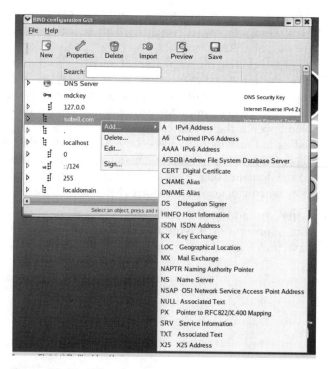

Figure 24-10   The domain Add drop-down menu

To view information about the new zone, you can by expand the object that holds the name of the new zone. You can further expand the Zone Authority Information and Name Server objects that appear when you expand the new zone object. Right-click any object to add to or modify the information in the object or to delete the object.

ADDING RESOURCE RECORDS

You can add any of an extensive list of resource records to a domain. Right-click on the object representing the domain you just added to display a pop-up menu. Slide the mouse pointer over **Add** to display the domain Add menu (Figure 24-10). The uppercase letters at the left end of each selection specify the type of resource record (page 725) that the selection adds to the domain. Following are some of the choices available on this menu:

- **A**   IPv4 Address record (page 726)
- **CNAME**   Alias record (page 726)
- **MX**   Mail Exchange record (page 726)
- **NS**   Nameserver record (page 726)
- **TXT**   Text record (page 728)

To add a reverse zone (a PTR record [page 727]), add a new zone as before, but this time select **IPv4** (or **IPv6**) **Reverse** as the origin type. For more information refer to "Reverse Name Resolution" on page 729.

Click **Save** when you are done, close the BIND Configuration GUI window, and start the **named** daemon as explained on page 731.

SETTING UP BIND

This section discusses the **/etc/named.conf** file, zone files, implementation of a DNS cache, and running DNS inside a chroot jail.

named.conf: THE named CONFIGURATION FILE

Configuration information for **named**, including zone names and the names and locations of zone files, is kept in **/etc/named.conf**. By default, the zone files are kept in **/var/named**. If you are running **named** in a chroot jail, these files are kept in **/var/named/chroot/var/named** (page 750).

RHEL A sample **named.conf** configuration file is included with the **caching-nameserver** package.

FEDORA A sample configuration file, named **named.caching-nameserver.conf**, is included with the **bind-config** package. See the caution box on page 732 and "named.conf" on page 733 for information about this file and its relationship to **named.conf**. If you want to make changes to this file, copy it to **named.conf** and then make changes to the copy. This way your changes will not be overwritten when the **caching-nameserver** package is updated.

IP-LIST

In the descriptions in this section, *IP-list* is a semicolon-separated list of IP addresses, each optionally followed by a slash and subnet mask length (page 423). You can prefix an *IP-list* with an exclamation point (!) to negate it. Builtin names that you can use in *IP-list* include **any**, **none**, and **localhost**. You must enclose builtin names within double quotation marks.

COMMENTS

Within **named.conf**, you can specify a comment by preceding it with a pound sign (#) as in a Perl or shell program, preceding it with a double slash (//) as in a C++ program, or enclosing it between /* and */ as in a C program.

OPTIONS SECTION

Option statements can appear within two sections of **named.conf**: Options and Zone. Option statements within the Options section apply globally. When an option statement appears in a Zone section, the option applies to the zone and overrides any corresponding global option within that zone. An Options section starts with the keyword **options** and continues with braces surrounding the statements. Following is a list of some option statements. Statements that can appear only in an Options section are so noted.

allow-query {*IP-list*}

Allows queries from *IP-list* only. Without this option, the server responds to all queries.

allow-recursion {*IP-list*}

Specifies systems that this server will perform recursive queries (page 723) for. For systems not in *IP-list*, the server performs iterative queries only. Without this option, the server performs recursive queries for any system. This statement may be overridden by the **recursion** statement.

allow-transfer {*IP-list*}

Specifies systems that are allowed to perform zone transfers from this server. Specify an *IP-list* of "**none**" (include the quotation marks) to prevent zone transfers.

directory *path*   Specifies the absolute pathname of the directory containing the zone files; under Red Hat Linux, this directory is initially **/var/named**. Filenames specified in this **named.conf** file are relative to this directory. Options section only.

forward ONLY|FIRST

ONLY forwards all queries and fails if it does not receive an answer. **FIRST** forwards all queries and, if a query does not receive an answer, attempts to find an answer using additional queries. Valid with the **forwarders** statement only.

forwarders {*IP* [*port*] [; ...]}

Specifies IP addresses and optionally port numbers that queries are forwarded to. See the **forward** statement.

notify YES|NO   **YES** sends a message to slave servers for the zone when zone information changes. Master servers only.

recursion YES|NO

YES (default) provides recursive queries (page 723) if the client requests. **NO** provides iterative queries only (page 723). An answer is always returned if it appears in the server's cache. This statement overrides the **allow-recursion** statement. Options section only.

ZONE SECTION

A Zone section defines a zone and can include any of the statements listed for the Options section except as noted. A Zone section is introduced by the keyword **zone**, the name of the zone enclosed within double quotation marks, and the class (always IN). The body of the Zone section consists of a pair of braces surrounding one or more zone statements. See the listing of **named.rfc1912.zones** on page 743 for examples of Zone sections. Following is a list of some zone statements:

allow-update {*IP-list*}

Specifies systems that are allowed to update this zone dynamically. This statement may be useful when hosting a master DNS server for a domain owned by someone other than the local administrator because it allows a remote user to update the DNS entry without granting the user access to the server.

file *filename*   Specifies the *zone file*, the file that specifies the characteristics of the zone. The *filename* is relative to the directory specified by the **directory** statement in the Options section. The **file** statement is mandatory for master and hint zones and is a good idea for slave zones (see **type**).

masters (*IP-list*)   Specifies systems that a slave zone can use to update zone files. Slave zones only.

type *ztype*   Specifies the type of zone that this section defines. Specify *ztype* from the following list:

- **forward**   Specifies a forward zone, which forwards queries directed to this zone. See the **forward** and/or **forwarders** statements in the Options section.

- **hint**   Specifies a hint zone. A hint zone lists root servers that the local server queries when it starts and when it cannot find an answer in its cache.

- **master**   Specifies the local system as a primary master server (page 724) for this zone.

- **slave**   Specifies the local system as a slave server (page 724) for this zone.

ZONE FILES

Zone files define zone characteristics. The name of the zone is typically specified in **named.conf** (or **named.caching-nameserver.conf**). Contrasted with **named.conf**, zone files use periods at the ends of domain names. See page 745 for sample zone files. To improve security, master and hint zone files should be kept in **/var/named**, which is owned by **root** and is not writable by processes running with a UID of **named**. Slave zone files should be kept in **/var/named/slaves**, which is owned by **named** and is writable by processes running with a UID of **named**. This configuration enables SELinux to offer better security. When you set up a chroot jail, the slaves directory is not put in the jail. Both of these setups ensure that master and hint zone files cannot be updated by dynamic DNS updates or by zone transfers. See the **named** man page for more information.

TIME FORMATS

All times in BIND files are given in seconds, unless they are followed by one of these letters (uppercase or lowercase): S (seconds), M (minutes), H (hours), D (days), or W (weeks). You can combine formats: The time 2h25m30s means 2 hours, 25 minutes, and 30 seconds and is the same as 8,730 seconds.

DOMAIN QUALIFICATION

An unqualified domain in a zone file is assumed to be in the current zone (the zone being defined by the zone file and named by the **named.conf** file that refers to the zone file). The name **zach** in the zone file for **myzone.com**, for example, would be expanded to the FQDN **zach.myzone.com.**. Use an FQDN (include the trailing period) to specify a domain that is not in the current zone. Any name that does not end with a period is regarded as a subdomain of the current zone.

ZONE NAME

Within a zone file, an @ is replaced with the zone name as specified by the **named.conf** file that refers to the zone file. The zone name is also used to complete unqualified domain names. The zone name is also referred to as the *origin*. See "$ORIGIN," in the next section.

ZONE FILE DIRECTIVES

The following directives can appear within a zone file. Each directive is identified by a leading dollar sign. The $TTL directive is mandatory and must be the first entry in a zone file.

$TTL   Defines the default time to live for all resource records in the zone. This directive must appear in a zone file before any resource records that it applies to. Any resource record can include a TTL value to override this value, except for the resource record in the root zone (.).

$ORIGIN   Changes the zone name from that specified in the **named.conf** file. This name, or the zone name if this directive does not appear in the zone file, replaces an @ sign in the Name field of a resource record.

$INCLUDE   Includes a file as though it were part of the zone file. The scope of an $ORIGIN directive within an included file is the included file. That is, an $ORIGIN directive within an included file does not affect the file that holds the $INCLUDE directive.

A DNS CACHE

You install a DNS cache, also called a resolving, caching nameserver, when you install the **bind-config** package (see the caution box on page 732). The section "JumpStart I: Setting Up a DNS Cache" (page 733) explains how to run this server. This section explains how the files Red Hat Linux provides implement this server.

named.caching-nameserver.conf: THE named CONFIGURATION FILE (*FEDORA*)

See the caution box on page 732 for more information about this file. The default **named.caching-nameserver.conf** file is shown here:

```
# cat /etc/named.caching-nameserver.conf
//
// named.caching-nameserver.conf
//
// Provided by Red Hat bind-config package to configure the
// ISC BIND named(8) DNS server as a caching only nameserver
// (as a localhost DNS resolver only).
//
// DO NOT EDIT THIS FILE - use system-config-bind or an editor
```

```
// to create named.conf - edits to this file will be lost on
// bind-config package upgrade.
//
options {
        listen-on port 53 { 127.0.0.1; };
        listen-on-v6 port 53 { ::1; };
        directory       "/var/named";
        dump-file       "/var/named/data/cache_dump.db";
        statistics-file "/var/named/data/named_stats.txt";
        memstatistics-file "/var/named/data/named_mem_stats.txt";
        query-source    port 53;
        query-source-v6 port 53;
        allow-query     { localhost; };
};
logging {
        channel default_debug {
                file "data/named.run";
                severity dynamic;
        };
};
view localhost_resolver {
        match-clients      { localhost; };
        match-destinations { localhost; };
        recursion yes;
        include "/etc/named.rfc1912.zones";
};
```

Options section   The first two lines of the Options section instruct **named** to listen on port 53 (the default **named** port) on the local system for incoming queries. The **directory** statement specifies the directory that all relative pathnames in this file are relative to. Specifically, the files named in the Zone sections (of the included **named.rfc1912.zones** file) are in the **/var/named** directory. If you are running **named** in a chroot jail, this directory is located under **/var/named/chroot** (page 750). The file also specifies the locations of the **dump-file** (cache dump), **statistics-file** (statistics file), and **memstatistics-file** (memory statistics file). The **query-source** statement specifies the (address and) port from which the server issues queries. The **allow-query** statement specifies the IP addresses that are allowed to query the server. This file specifies that only **localhost** can query the server.

Logging section   The Logging section causes debugging messages to be sent to **data/named.run**. For more information refer to "Logging" on page 753.

View section   The single View section specifies that this server respond to queries from the local system (**localhost**) and perform recursive queries. The **include** statement includes the **/etc/named.rfc1912.zones** file (discussed in the next section) as though it were present in the View section. For more information refer to "View sections" on page 757.

named.rfc1912.zones: THE ZONE CONFIGURATION FILE (*FEDORA*)

As explained in the previous section, the **named.caching-nameserver.conf** file incorporates the **/etc/named.rfc1912.zones** file by naming it in an **include** statement:

```
# cat /etc/named.rfc1912.zones
// named.rfc1912.zones:
//
// Provided by Red Hat bind-config package
//
// ISC BIND named zone configuration for zones recommended by
// RFC 1912 section 4.1 : localhost TLDs and address zones
//

zone "." IN {
        type hint;
        file "named.ca";
};

zone "localdomain" IN {
        type master;
        file "localdomain.zone";
        allow-update { none; };
};

zone "localhost" IN {
        type master;
        file "localhost.zone";
        allow-update { none; };
};

zone "0.0.127.in-addr.arpa" IN {
        type master;
        file "named.local";
        allow-update { none; };
};

zone "0.0.0.0.0.0.0. ... .0.0.0.0.0.0.0.0.0.ip6.arpa" IN {
        type master;
        file "named.ip6.local";
        allow-update { none; };
};

zone "255.in-addr.arpa" IN {
        type master;
        file "named.broadcast";
        allow-update { none; };
};

zone "0.in-addr.arpa" IN {
        type master;
        file "named.zero";
        allow-update { none; };
};
```

Zone sections   This file holds seven Zone sections, each of which has an **allow-update** statement that specifies dynamic updates of the zone are not allowed. All filenames in this file are relative to the **directory** statement in the Options section of **named.caching-nameserver.conf.**

- **.** (The name of the zone is a period.) The hint zone. Specifies that when the server starts or when it does not know which server to query, it should look in the **/var/named/named.ca** (ca stands for cache) file to find the addresses of authoritative servers for the root domain.

- **localdomain**   Specifies that **localhost.localdomain** points to 127.0.0.1, preventing the local server from looking upstream for this information.

- **localhost**   Sets up the normal server on the local system.

- **0.0.127.in-addr.arpa**   Sets up IPv4 reverse name resolution.

- **0.0 ... 0.0.ip6.arpa**   Sets up IPv6 reverse name resolution.

- **255.in-addr.arpa**   Specifies that IP addresses that start with 255 have their reverse lookup handled by the local server, preventing the local server from looking upstream for this information.

- **0.in-addr.arpa**   Specifies that IP addresses that start with 0 have their reverse lookup handled by the local server, preventing the local server from looking upstream for this information.

ZONE FILES

There are seven zone files in **/var/named**, each corresponding to one of the Zone sections in **named.rfc1912.zones**. This section describes three of these zone files.

The root zone:
named.ca

The hint zone file, **named.ca**, is a copy of ftp.internic.net/domain/named.cache, which does not change frequently. The **named.ca** file specifies authoritative servers for the root domain. The DNS server initializes its cache from this file and can determine an authoritative server for any domain from this information.

The root zone is required only for servers that answer recursive queries: If a server responds to recursive queries, it needs to perform a series of iterative queries starting at the root domain. Without the root domain hint file, it would not know the location of the root domain servers.

```
$ cat /var/named/named.ca
;       This file holds the information on root name servers needed to
;       initialize cache of Internet domain name servers
;       (e.g. reference this file in the "cache  .  <file>"
;       configuration file of BIND domain name servers).
;
;       This file is made available by InterNIC
;       under anonymous FTP as
;           file                /domain/named.cache
;           on server           FTP.INTERNIC.NET
;       -OR-                    RS.INTERNIC.NET
;
;       last update:    Jan 29, 2004
;       related version of root zone:    2004012900
;
;
; formerly NS.INTERNIC.NET
```

```
;
.                                 3600000   IN  NS      A.ROOT-SERVERS.NET.
A.ROOT-SERVERS.NET.               3600000       A       198.41.0.4
;
; formerly NS1.ISI.EDU
;
.                                 3600000       NS      B.ROOT-SERVERS.NET.
B.ROOT-SERVERS.NET.               3600000       A       192.228.79.201
;
; formerly C.PSI.NET
;
.                                 3600000       NS      C.ROOT-SERVERS.NET.
C.ROOT-SERVERS.NET.               3600000       A       192.33.4.12
;
...
; End of File
```

localhost.zone The **localhost.zone** zone file defines the **localhost** zone, the normal server on the
local system. It starts with a $TTL directive and holds three resource records: SOA,
NS, and A. The $TTL directive in the following file specifies that the default time to
live for the resource records specified in this file is 86,400 seconds (24 hours):

```
# cat /var/named/localhost.zone
$TTL    86400
@           IN  SOA     @       root (
                                        42              ; serial (d. adams)
                                        3H              ; refresh
                                        15M             ; retry
                                        1W              ; expiry
                                        1D )            ; minimum

            IN NS               @
            IN A                127.0.0.1
            IN AAAA             ::1
```

As explained earlier, the **@** at the start of the SOA resource record stands for the origin (the name of the zone), which is **localhost**. The last three lines in the preceding
file are the NS resource record that specifies the nameserver for the zone as **localhost (@)**, the A resource record that specifies the IPv4 address of the host as
127.0.0.1, and the AAAA resource record that specifies the IPv6 address of the host
as ::1. Because these three records have blank Name fields, each inherits this value
from the preceding resource record—in this case, **@**.

named.local The **named.local** zone file provides information about the 0.0.127.in-addr.arpa
reverse lookup zone. It follows the same pattern as the **localhost** zone file, except
that instead of the A resource record, this file has a PTR record that provides the
name that the zone associates with the IP address. The PTR resource record specifies the name 1, which equates the system at address 1 in the zone (0.0.127.in-
addr.arpa) with the name **localhost**, which has an IP address of 127.0.0.1:

```
$ cat /var/named/named.local
$TTL    86400
@       IN      SOA     localhost. root.localhost.   (
                                1997022700      ; Serial
                                28800           ; Refresh
                                14400           ; Retry
                                3600000         ; Expire
                                86400)          ; Minimum
        IN      NS      localhost.
1       IN      PTR     localhost.
```

The other zone files perform similar functions as described under "Zone sections" on page 744. Once you start **named** (page 731), you can use the tests described under "Troubleshooting" on page 751 to make sure the server is working.

THE named.conf CONFIGURATION FILE (*RHEL*)

The **named.conf** file holds the same zones as the **named.caching-nameserver.conf** file described in the previous section. The comments in the Options section of the **named.conf** file are dated and do not apply in most cases. In addition, the **named.conf** file has a Controls section and an Include section that includes the file **/etc/rndc.key**.

Controls section   The Controls section contains two statements that set up rndc control: **inet** and **keys**. The **inet** statement opens a control channel on 127.0.0.1, allowing local, non-privileged users to manage the nameserver. The **keys** statement allows a key to be defined so as to secure rndc communications.

include/rndc   The rndc (Remote Name Daemon Control) utility allows the system administrator to control BIND remotely (from the local or a remote system). You can use rndc to start and stop the daemon, force the daemon to reread the configuration files, and view diagnostic information. See the rndc man page for more information.

The Include section of **named.conf** on the nameserver incorporates the **/etc/rndc.key** file as though it appeared within **named.conf**. By putting the rndc key information in a file kept separate from the **named.conf** file, the rndc key information can be kept private using file permissions, while the **named.conf** file can be read by anyone. The rndc key is a secret shared between the nameserver and the remote control program. The **/etc/rndc.key** file must also be included in the **/etc/rndc.conf** file on the controlling system. If you wish to use rndc on a system other than the local one, you must copy **rndc.key** to the remote system and add the remote host to the Controls section in the **named.conf** file on the server.

DNS GLUE RECORDS

It is common practice to put the nameserver for a zone inside the zone it serves. For example, you might put the nameserver for the zone starting at site1.example.com (Figure 24-3, page 723) in ns.site1.example.com. When a DNS cache tries to resolve www.site1.example.com, the authoritative server for example.com gives it the NS record pointing to ns.site1.example.com. In an attempt to resolve ns.site1.example.com, the DNS cache again queries the authoritative server for example.com, which points back to ns.site1.example.com. This loop does not allow ns.site1.example.com to be resolved.

The simplest solution to this problem is not to allow any nameserver to reside inside the zone it points to. Because every zone is a child of the root zone, this solution means that every domain would be served by the root server and would not scale at all. A better solution is *glue* records. A glue record is an A record for a nameserver that is returned in addition to the NS record when an NS query is performed. Because the A record provides an IP address for the nameserver, it does not need to be resolved and does not create the problematic loop.

The nameserver setup for redhat.com illustrates the use of glue records. When you query for NS records for redhat.com, DNS returns three NS records. In addition, it returns three A records that provide the IP addresses for the hosts that the NS records point to:

```
$ dig -t NS redhat.com
...
;; QUESTION SECTION:
;redhat.com.                    IN      NS

;; ANSWER SECTION:
redhat.com.           28       IN      NS      ns2.redhat.com.
redhat.com.           28       IN      NS      ns3.redhat.com.
redhat.com.           28       IN      NS      ns1.redhat.com.

;; ADDITIONAL SECTION:
ns1.redhat.com.       5633     IN      A       66.187.233.210
ns2.redhat.com.       151369   IN      A       66.187.224.210
ns3.redhat.com.       80180    IN      A       66.187.229.10
...
```

You can create a glue record by providing an A record for the nameserver inside the delegating domain's zone file:

```
site1.example.com              IN      NS      ns.site1.example.com
ns.site1.example.com           IN      A       1.2.3.4
```

TSIGs: Transaction Signatures

Interaction between DNS components is based on the query–response model: One part queries another and receives a reply. Traditionally a server determines whether and how to reply to a query based on the IP client's address. *IP spoofing* (page 1038) is relatively easy to carry out, making this situation less than ideal. Recent versions of BIND support transaction signatures (TSIGs), which allow two systems to establish a trust relationship by using a shared secret key.

TSIGs provide an additional layer of authentication between master and slave servers for a zone. When a slave server is located at a different site than the master server (as it should be), a malicious person operating a router between the sites can spoof the IP address of the master server and change the DNS data on the slave (a man-in-the-middle scenario). With TSIGs, this person would need to know the secret key to change the DNS data on the slave.

CREATING A SECRET KEY

A secret key is an encoded string of up to 512 bits. The dnssec-keygen utility, included with BIND, generates this key. The following command generates a 512-bit random key using MD5, a *one-way hash function* (page 1046):

```
$ /usr/sbin/dnssec-keygen -a hmac-md5 -b 512 -n HOST keyname
Kkeyname.+157+47586
```

In the preceding command, replace **keyname** with something unique yet meaningful. This command creates a key in a file whose name is similar to **Kkeyname.+157+47586.private**, where **keyname** is replaced by the name of the key, **+157** indicates the algorithm used, and **+47586** is a hash of the key. If you run the same command again, the hash part will be different. The key file is not used directly. Use cat with an argument of the private filename to display the algorithm and key information you will need in the next step:

```
$ cat Kkeyname.+157+47586.private
Private-key-format: v1.2
Algorithm: 157 (HMAC_MD5)
Key: uNPDouqVwR7fvo/zFyjkqKbQhcTd6Prm...
```

USING THE SHARED SECRET

The next step is to tell the nameservers about the shared secret by inserting the following code in the **/etc/named.conf** file on both servers. This code is a top-level section in **named.conf**; insert it following the Options section:

```
key keyname {
    algorithm "hmac-md5";
    secret "uNPDouqVwR7fvo/zFyjkqKbQhcTd6Prm...";
};
```

The **keyname** is the name of the key you created. The **algorithm** is the string that appears within parentheses in the output from cat. The **secret** is the string that follows **Key:** in the preceding output. You must enclose each string within double quotation marks. Be careful when you copy the key; although it is long, do not break it into multiple lines.

Because key names are unique, you can insert any number of key sections into **named.conf**. To keep the key a secret, make sure users other than **root** cannot read it: Either give **named.conf** permissions such that no one except **root** has access to it or put the key in a file that only **root** can read and incorporate it in **named.conf** using an **include** statement.

Once both servers know about the key, use the **server** statement in **named.conf** to tell them when to use it:

```
server 1.2.3.4 {
# 1.2.3.4 is the IP address of the other server using this key
    keys {
        "keyname";
    };
};
```

Each server must have a server section, each containing the IP address of the other server. The servers will now communicate with each other only if they first authenticate each other using the secret key.

RUNNING BIND IN A chroot JAIL

To increase security, you can run BIND in a chroot jail. See page 428 for information about the security advantages of and ways to set up a chroot jail. See also the note about SELinux on page 732 and the **named** man page for information about BIND, SELinux, and chroot jails. The **bind-chroot** package, which sets up BIND to run in a chroot jail, creates a directory named **/var/named/chroot** that takes the place of the root directory (**/**) for all BIND files. With this package installed, all files that control BIND are located within this chroot jail and the filenames used in this chapter are symbolic links to the files in the chroot jail:

```
# ls -l /var/named /etc/named
... /etc/named.caching-nameserver.conf -> /var/named/chroot//etc/named.caching
nameserver.conf
... /etc/named.rfc1912.zones -> /var/named/chroot//etc/named.rfc1912.zones

/var/named:
total 52
... chroot
... data
... localdomain.zone -> /var/named/chroot//var/named/localdomain.zone
... localhost.zone -> /var/named/chroot//var/named/localhost.zone
... named.broadcast -> /var/named/chroot//var/named/named.broadcast
... named.ca -> /var/named/chroot//var/named/named.ca
... named.ip6.local -> /var/named/chroot//var/named/named.ip6.local
... named.local -> /var/named/chroot//var/named/named.local
... named.zero -> /var/named/chroot//var/named/named.zero
... slaves
```

With the **bind-chroot** package installed, the **ROOTDIR** shell variable is set to **/var/named/chroot** in the **/etc/sysconfig/named** file, which is executed by the **named** init script.

TROUBLESHOOTING

When you start a DNS cache, the **/var/log/messages** file contains lines similar to the following. Other types of DNS servers display similar messages.

```
# cat /var/log/messages
...
18:45:18 peach named[10003]: starting BIND 9.3.2 -u named -t /var/named/chroot
18:45:18 peach named[10003]: found 1 CPU, using 1 worker thread
18:45:18 peach named[10003]: loading configuration from '/etc/named.conf'
18:45:18 peach named[10003]: listening on IPv6 interface lo, ::1#53
18:45:18 peach named[10003]: listening on IPv4 interface lo, 127.0.0.1#53
18:45:18 peach named[10003]: command channel listening on 127.0.0.1#953
18:45:18 peach named[10003]: command channel listening on ::1#953
18:45:18 peach named[10003]: zone 0.in-addr.arpa/IN/localhost_resolver: loaded serial 42
18:45:18 peach named[10003]: zone 0.0.127.in-addr.arpa/IN/localhost_resolver: loaded
    serial 1997022700
18:45:18 peach named[10003]: zone 255.in-addr.arpa/IN/localhost_resolver: loaded serial 42
18:45:18 peach named[10003]: zone 0.0.0.0.0.0.0.0.0.0.0.0.0.0.0.0.0.0.0.0.0.0.0.0.0.0.0.0.0.
    0.0.0.ip6.arpa/IN/localhost_resolver: loaded serial 1997022700
18:45:18 peach named[10003]: zone localdomain/IN/localhost_resolver: loaded serial 42
18:45:18 peach named[10003]: zone localhost/IN/localhost_resolver: loaded serial 42
18:45:18 peach named[10003]: running
```

With an argument of **status**, the **named** init script displays useful information:

```
# /sbin/service named status
number of zones: 6
debug level: 0
xfers running: 0
xfers deferred: 0
soa queries in progress: 0
query logging is OFF
recursive clients: 0/1000
tcp clients: 0/100
server is up and running
```

When you create or update DNS information, you can use dig or host to test that the server works the way you planned. The most useful part of the output from dig is usually the answer section, which gives the nameserver's reply to your query:

```
$ dig example.com
...
;; ANSWER SECTION:
example.com.          172800  IN      A       192.0.34.166
...
```

The preceding output shows that the **example.com.** domain has a single A record and that record points to 192.0.34.166. The TTL of this record, which tells you how long the record can be held in cache, is 172,800 seconds (2 days). You can also use dig to query other record types by using **–t** option followed by the type of record you want to query for (**–t** works with host, too):

```
$ dig -t MX redhat.com
...
;; ANSWER SECTION:
redhat.com.                    600      IN      MX      10 mx1.redhat.com.
redhat.com.                    600      IN      MX      10 mx3.redhat.com.
redhat.com.                    600      IN      MX      20 mx2.redhat.com.
...
```

If you query for a domain that does not exist, dig returns the SOA record for the authority section of the highest-level domain in your query that does exist:

```
$ dig domaindoesnotexist.info
...
;; AUTHORITY SECTION:
info. 7200    IN        SOA        tld1.ultradns.net.domadmin.ultradns.net. ...
...
```

Because it tells you the last zone that was queried correctly, this information can be useful in tracing faults.

TSIGs   If two servers using TSIGs (page 748) fail to communicate, check that the time is the same on both servers. The TSIG authentication mechanism is dependent on the current time. If the clocks on the two servers are not synchronized, TSIG will fail. Consider setting up *NTP* (page 1046) on the servers to prevent this problem.

A FULL-FUNCTIONED NAMESERVER

Because the IP addresses used in this example are part of the *private address space* (page 1049) you can copy the example and run the server without affecting global DNS. Also, to prevent contamination of the global DNS, each zone has the **notify** option set to NO. When you build a nameserver that is integrated with the Internet, you will want to use IP addresses that are unique to your installation. You may want to change the settings of the **notify** statements.

named.conf   The **named.conf** file in this example limits the IP addresses that **named** answers queries from and sets up logging:

```
$ cat /etc/named.conf
options {
    directory "/var/named";
    allow-query {127.0.0.1; 192.168.0.0/24;};};

zone "." IN {
    type    hint;
    file    "named.ca";};
```

```
zone "0.168.192.in-addr.arpa" IN {
    type    master;
    file    "named.local";
    notify  NO;
};

zone "sam.net" IN {
    type    master;
    file    "sam.net";
    notify  NO;
};

logging{
    channel "misc" {
        file "/var/log/bind/misc.log" versions 4 size 4m;
        print-time YES;
        print-severity YES;
        print-category YES;
    };
    channel "query" {
        file "/var/log/bind/query.log" versions 4 size 4m;
        print-time YES;
        print-severity NO;
        print-category NO;
    };
    category default {
        "misc";
    };
    category queries {
        "query";
    };
};
```

The **allow-query** statement in the Options section specifies the IP addresses of the systems that the server will answer queries from. You must include the local system as 127.0.0.1 if it will be querying the server. The zone that this server is authoritative for is **sam.net**; the zone file for sam.net is **/var/named/sam.net**.

Logging   Logging is turned on by the Logging section. This section opens two logging channels: one that logs information to **/var/log/bind/misc.log** and one that logs information to **/var/log/bind/query.log**. When one of these logs grows to 4 megabytes (**size 4m** in the **file** statement), it is renamed by appending **.1** to its filename and a new log is started. The numbers at the ends of other, similarly named logs are incremented. Any log that would have a larger number than that specified by the **versions** clause (**4** in the example) is removed. See logrotate (page 559) for another way to maintain log files. The **print** statements determine whether the time, severity, and category of the information are sent to the log; specify each as YES or NO. The category determines what information is logged to the channel. In the example, default information is sent to the **misc** channel and queries are sent to the **query** channel. Refer to the **named.conf** man page for more choices.

named.local   The origin for the reverse zone file (**named.local**) is 0.168.192.in-addr.arpa (as specified in the Zone section that refers to this file in **named.conf**). Following the SOA and NS resource records, the first three PTR resource records equate address 1 in the subnet 0.168.192.in-addr.arpa (192.168.0.1) with the names **gw.sam.net.**, **www.sam.net.**, and **ftp.sam.net.**, respectively. The next three PTR resource records equate 192.168.0.3 with **mark.sam.net.**, 192.168.0.4 with **mail.sam.net.**, and 192.168.0.6 with **ns.sam.net.**.

```
$ cat named.local
; zone "0.168.192.in-addr.arpa"
;
$TTL    3D
@       IN      SOA     ns.sam.net. mgs@sobell.com. (
                                2005110501      ; serial
                                8H              ; refresh
                                2H              ; retry
                                4W              ; expire
                                1D)             ; minimum
        IN      NS      ns.sam.net.
1       IN      PTR     gw.sam.net.
1       IN      PTR     www.sam.net.
1       IN      PTR     ftp.sam.net.
3       IN      PTR     mark.sam.net.
4       IN      PTR     mail.sam.net.
6       IN      PTR     ns.sam.net.
```

sam.net   The zone file for sam.net takes advantage of many BIND features and includes TXT (page 728), CNAME (page 726), and MX (page 726) resource records. When you query for resource records, **named** returns the TXT resource record along with the records you requested. The first of the two NS records specifies an unqualified name (**ns**) to which BIND appends the zone name (**sam.net**), yielding an FQDN of **ns.sam.net**. The second nameserver is specified with an FQDN name that BIND does not alter. The MX records specify mail servers in a similar manner and include a priority number at the start of the data field; lower numbers indicate preferred servers.

```
$ cat sam.net
; zone "sam.net"
;
$TTL    3D
@       IN      SOA     ns.sam.net. mgs@sobell.com. (
                                200511051       ; serial
                                8H              ; refresh
                                2H              ; retry
                                4W              ; expire
                                1D )            ; minimum

        TXT     "Sobell Associates Inc."
        NS      ns              ; Nameserver address(unqualified)
        NS      ns.max.net.; Nameserver address (qualified)
        MX      10 mail     ; Mail exchange (primary/unqualified)
        MX      20 mail.max.net.; Mail exchange (2nd/qualified)
```

```
        localhost IN   A        127.0.0.1

        www     IN     CNAME    ns
        ftp     IN     CNAME    ns

        gw      IN     A        192.168.0.1
                       TXT      "Router"

        ns      IN     A        192.168.0.6
                       MX       10 mail
                       MX       20 mail.max.net.

        mark    IN     A        192.168.0.3
                       MX       10 mail
                       MX       20 mail.max.net.
                       TXT      "MGS"

        mail    IN     A        192.168.0.4
                       MX       10 mail
                       MX       20 mail.max.net.
```

Some resource records have a value in the Name field; those without a name inherit the name from the previous resource record. In a similar manner, the previous resource record may have an inherited name value, and so on. The five resource records following the SOA resource record inherit the @, or zone name, from the SOA resource record. These resource records pertain to the zone as a whole. In the preceding example, the first TXT resource record inherits its name from the SOA resource record; it is the TXT resource record for the sam.net zone (give the command **host –t TXT sam.net** to display the TXT resource record).

Following these five resource records are resource records that pertain to a domain within the zone. For example, the MX resource records that follow the A resource record with the Name field set to **mark** are resource records for the **mark.sam.net.** domain.

The A resource record for **localhost** is followed by two CNAME resource records that specify www(.sam.net.) and ftp(.sam.net.) as aliases for the nameserver **ns.sam.net.**. For example, a user connecting to ftp.sam.net will connect to 192.168.0.6. The resource records named **gw**, **ns**, **mark**, and **mail** are resource records for domains within the sam.net zone.

Log files Before restarting **named**, create the directory for the log files and give it permissions and ownership as shown below. If you are running **named** in a chroot jail, create the **bind** directory in **/var/named/chroot/var/log**.

```
# mkdir /var/log/bind
# chmod 744 /var/log/bind
# chown named /var/log/bind
# ls -ld /var/log/bind
drwxr--r-- 2 named root 4096 Nov  5 19:41 /var/log/bind
```

With the log directory in place, **named.conf** in **/etc** (or in **/var/named/chroot/etc** if you are running **named** in a chroot jail), and the **named.ca, named.local,** and **sam.net** zone files in **/var/named** (or in **/var/named/chroot/var/named** if you are running **named** in a chroot jail), restart **named** and check the log files. The file **/var/log/messages** should show something like the following:

```
# cat /var/log/messages
...
19:25:48 peach named[22416]: starting BIND 9.3.2 -u named -t /var/named/chroot
19:25:48 peach named[22416]: found 1 CPU, using 1 worker thread
19:25:48 peach named[22416]: loading configuration from '/etc/named.conf'
19:25:48 peach named[22416]: listening on IPv4 interface lo, 127.0.0.1#53
19:25:48 peach named[22416]: listening on IPv4 interface eth0, 192.168.0.10#53
19:25:48 peach named[22416]: command channel listening on 127.0.0.1#953
19:25:48 peach named[22416]: command channel listening on ::1#953
```

The **misc.log** file may show errors that do not appear in the **messages** file:

```
# cat /var/log/bind/misc.log
19:25:48.077 general: info: zone 0.168.192.in-addr.arpa/IN: loaded serial 2005110501
19:25:48.079 general: info: zone sam.net/IN: loaded serial 200511051
19:25:48.097 general: notice: running
```

A SLAVE SERVER

To set up a slave server, copy the **/etc/named.conf** file from the master server to the slave server, replacing the **type master** statement with **type slave.** Remove any zones that the slave server will not be acting as a slave for, including the root (.) zone, if the slave server will not respond to recursive queries. Create the **/var/log/bind** directory for log files as explained at the end of the previous section.

notify statement Slave servers copy zone information from the primary master server or another slave server. The **notify** statement specifies whether you want a master server to notify slave servers when information on the master server changes. Set the (global) value of **notify** in the Options section or set it within a Zone section, which overrides a global setting for a given zone. The format is

> *notify YES | NO | EXPLICIT*

YES causes the master server to notify all slaves listed in NS resource records for the zone as well as servers at IP addresses listed in an **also-notify** statement. When you set **notify** to *EXPLICIT*, the server notifies servers listed in the **also-notify** statement only. *NO* turns off notification.

When you start **named**, it copies the zone files to **/var/named**. If you specify **notify YES** on the master server, the zone files on the slave server will be updated each time you change the serial field of the SOA resource record in a zone. You must manually distribute changes to the **/etc/named.conf** file.

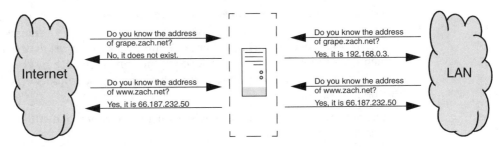

Figure 24-11   A split horizon DNS server

A SPLIT HORIZON SERVER

Assume you want to set up a LAN that provides all its systems and services to local users on internal systems, which may be behind a firewall, and only certain public services—such as Web, FTP, and mail—to Internet (public) users. A *split horizon* (also called *DMZ*) DNS server takes care of this situation by treating queries from internal systems differently from queries from public systems (systems on the Internet).

View sections   BIND 9 introduced View sections in **named.conf**. View sections facilitate the implementation of a split DNS server. Each view provides a different perspective of the DNS namespace to a group of clients. When there is no View section, all zones specified in **named.conf** are part of the implicit default view.

Assume that an office has several systems on a LAN and public Web, FTP, DNS, and mail servers. The single connection to the Internet is NATed (page 1044) so that it is shared by the local systems and the servers. The gateway system—the one connected directly to the Internet—is a router, firewall, and server. This scenario takes advantage of the View sections in **named.conf** and supports separate secondary nameservers for local and public users. Although public users need access to the DNS server as the authority on the domain that supports the servers, they do not require the DNS server to support recursive queries. Not supporting recursion for public users limits the load on the DNS server and the Internet connection. For security reasons, public users must not have access to information about local systems other than the servers. Local users should have access to information about local systems and should be able to use the DNS server recursively.

Figure 24-11 shows that the server responds differently to queries from the LAN and the Internet.

The iptables utility (page 763) controls which ports on which systems users on internal and external systems can access. DNS controls which systems are advertised to which users.

The **named.conf** file has four sections: Options, two View sections, and Logging. The Options section specifies that the zone files are in the **/var/named** directory. The View sections specify the characteristics and zones that a resolver is given access to, which depend on the resolver's address. One zone is for use by the LAN/local users and the other by Internet/public users. The Logging section sets up the **misc2.log** file for default messages.

There are several ways to specify which clients see a view. The following **named.conf** file uses **match-clients** statements:

```
$ cat /etc/named.conf
options {
    directory "/var/named";
}; //end options


view "local" IN {                       // start local view
match-clients { 127.0.0.1; 192.168.0.0/24;};
recursion YES;

zone"zach.net" IN {
    type    master;
    file    "local.net";
    notify YES;
};

zone "0.168.192.in-addr.arpa" IN {
    type    master;
    file    "named.local";
    notify YES;
};

zone "." IN {
    type    hint;
    file    "named.ca";
};

};               // end local view

view "public" IN {                      // start public view
match-clients { "all";};
recursion NO;

zone"zach.net" IN {
    type    master;
    file    "public.net";
    notify YES;
};

zone "0.168.192.in-addr.arpa" IN {
    type    master;
    file    "named.public";
    notify YES;
};
```

```
zone "." IN {
    type    hint;
    file    "named.ca";
};

};                                      // end public view

logging{
    channel "misc" {
        file "/var/log/bind/misc2.log" versions 2 size 1m;
        print-time YES;
        print-severity YES;
        print-category YES;
    };
    category default {
        "misc";
    };
};                                      //end logging
```

The ordering of View sections within **named.conf** is critical: The view that is presented to a client is the first view that the client matches. The preceding **named.conf** file holds two View sections: one for local users and one for public users, in that order. Local users are defined to be those on the 192.168.0.0/24 subnet or **localhost** (127.0.0.1); public users are defined to be any users. If you reversed the order of the View sections, all users—including local users—would get the view intended for the public and no users would see the local view.

Many statements from the Options section can be used within View sections, where they override statements in the (global) Options section. The **recursion** statement, which can appear within an Options section, appears in each View section. This **named.conf** file sets up a server that provides recursive answers to queries that originate locally and iterative answers to queries from the public. This setup provides quick, complete answers to local users, limiting the network and processor bandwidth that is devoted to other users while still providing authoritative name service for the local servers.

To make **named.conf** easier to understand and maintain, zones in different View sections can have the same name while having different zone files. Both the local and public View sections in the example have zones named **zach.net**: The public **zach.net** zone file is named **public.net**, while the local one is named **local.net**.

The Logging section is described on page 753.

The zone files defining **zach.net** are similar to the ones in the previous examples; the public file is a subset of the local one. Following the SOA resource record in both files is a TXT, two NS, and two MX resource records. Next are three CNAME resource records that direct queries addressed to www.zach.net, ftp.zach.net, and mail.zach.net to the system named **ns.zach.net**. The next four resource records specify two nameserver addresses and two mail servers for the ns.zach.net domain.

The final four resource records appear in the local **zach.net** zone file and not in the public zone file; they are address (A) resource records for local systems. Instead of keeping this information in **/etc/hosts** files on each system, you can keep it on the DNS server, where it can be updated easily. When you use DNS instead of **/etc/hosts**, you must change the **hosts** line in **/etc/nsswitch.conf** (page 435).

```
$ cat local.net
; zach.net local zone file
;
$TTL    3D
@       IN      SOA     ns.zach.net. mgs@sobell.com. (
                                200511118      ; serial
                                8H             ; refresh
                                2H             ; retry
                                4W             ; expire
                                1D )           ; minimum

        IN      TXT     "Sobell Associates Inc."
        IN      NS      ns          ; Nameserver address (unqualified)
        IN      NS      ns.speedy.net.; Nameserver address (qualified)
        IN      MX      10 mail     ; Mail exchange (primary/unqualified)
        IN      MX      20 mail.max.net.; Mail exchange (2nd/qualified)

www     IN      CNAME   ns
ftp     IN      CNAME   ns
mail    IN      CNAME   ns

ns      IN      A       192.168.0.1
        IN      A       192.168.0.6
        IN      MX      10 mail
        IN      MX      20 mail.max.net.

speedy  IN      A       192.168.0.1
grape   IN      A       192.168.0.3
potato  IN      A       192.168.0.4
peach   IN      A       192.168.0.6
```

The public version of the **zach.net** zone file follows:

```
$ cat public.net
; zach.net public zone file
;
$TTL    3D
@       IN      SOA     ns.zach.net. mgs@sobell.com. (
                                200511118      ; serial
                                8H             ; refresh
                                2H             ; retry
                                4W             ; expire
                                1D )           ; minimum

        IN      TXT     "Sobell Associates Inc."
        IN      NS      ns          ; Nameserver address(unqualified)
        IN      NS      ns.speedy.net.; Nameserver address (qualified)

        IN      MX      10 mail ; Mail exchange (primary/unqualified)
        IN      MX      20 mail.max.net.; Mail exchange (2nd/qualified)
```

```
www      IN      CNAME    ns
ftp      IN      CNAME    ns
mail     IN      CNAME    ns

ns       IN      A        192.168.0.1
         IN      A        192.168.0.6
         IN      MX       10 mail
         IN      MX       20 mail.max.net.
```

There are two reverse zone files, each of which starts with SOA and NS resource records followed by PTR resource records for each of the names of the servers. The local version of this file also lists the names of the local systems:

```
$ cat named.local
;"0.168.192.in-addr.arpa" reverse zone file
;
$TTL    3D
@        IN      SOA      ns.zach.net. mgs@sobell.com. (
                                2005110501    ; serial
                                8H            ; refresh
                                2H            ; retry
                                4W            ; expire
                                1D)           ; minimum
         IN      NS       ns.zach.net.
         IN      NS       ns.speedy.net.
1        IN      PTR      gw.zach.net.
1        IN      PTR      www.zach.net.
1        IN      PTR      ftp.zach.net.
1        IN      PTR      mail.zach.net.
1        IN      PTR      speedy.zach.net.
3        IN      PTR      grape.zach.net.
4        IN      PTR      potato.zach.net.
6        IN      PTR      peach.zach.net.
```

CHAPTER SUMMARY

DNS, which maps domain names to IP addresses, and vice versa, is implemented as a hierarchical, distributed, and replicated database on the Internet. Although BIND, which implements DNS, has security issues, you can improve its security by running it inside a chroot jail and using transaction signatures (TSIGs) and SELinux.

When a program on the local system needs to look up an IP address that corresponds to a domain name, it calls the resolver. The resolver queries the local DNS cache, if available, and then queries DNS servers on the LAN or Internet. There are two types of queries: iterative and recursive. When a server responds to an iterative query, it returns whatever information it has at hand; it does not query other servers. Recursive queries cause a server to query other servers if necessary to respond with an answer.

There are three types of servers. Master servers, which hold the master copy of zone data, are authoritative for a zone. Slave servers are also authoritative and copy their data from a master server or other slave servers. DNS caches are not authoritative and either answer queries from cache or forward queries to another server.

The DNS database holds resource records for domains. Many types of resource records exist, including A (address), MX (mail exchange), NS (nameserver), PTR (pointer for performing reverse name resolution), and SOA (start of authority, which describes the zone).

EXERCISES

1. What kind of server responds to recursive queries?

2. What kind of DNS record is likely to be returned when a Web browser tries to resolve the domain part of a URI?

3. What are MX resource records for?

4. How would you find the IP address of example.com from the command line?

5. How would you instruct a Linux system to use the local network's DNS cache, located at 192.168.1.254, or the ISP's DNS cache, located on 1.2.3.4, if the LAN nameserver is unavailable?

6. How would you instruct a DNS server to respond only to queries from the **137.44.**∗ IP range?

7. How might a resolver attempt to find the IP address of the **example** domain?

ADVANCED EXERCISES

8. How would you set up a private domain name hierarchy that does not include any of the official InterNIC-assigned domain names?

9. Which part of DNS is most vulnerable to an attack from a malicious user and why?

10. It is often irritating to have to wait for DNS records to update around the world when you change DNS entries. You could prevent this delay by setting the TTL to a small number. Why is setting the TTL to a small number a bad idea?

11. Outline a method by which DNS could be used to support encryption.

25

iptables: Setting Up a Firewall

The iptables utility builds and manipulates network packet filtering rules in the Linux kernel. You can use iptables to create a firewall that protects a system from malicious users and to set up *NAT* (Network Address Translation, page 1044), which can allow multiple systems to share a single Internet connection. The iptables utility is flexible and extensible, allowing you to set up both simple and complex network packet filtering solutions. It provides connection tracking (stateful packet filtering), allowing you to handle packets based on the state of their connection. For example, you can set up rules that reject inbound packets trying to open a new connection and accept inbound packets that are responses to locally initiated connections. Features not included in the base iptables package are available as patches via the patch-o-matic program.

Some of the concepts required to fully understand iptables are beyond the scope of this book. Although you can use iptables at several different levels, this chapter presents only the fundamentals. There are, however, some sections of this chapter that delve into areas that may require additional understanding or explanation. If a concept is not clear, refer to one of the resources in "More Information" on page 766.

How iptables WORKS

netfilter and iptables The functionality frequently referred to as iptables is actually composed of two components: **netfilter** and **iptables**. Running in *kernelspace* (page 1039), the **netfilter** component is a set of tables that hold rules that the kernel uses to control network packet filtering. Running in *userspace* (page 1062), the iptables utility sets up, maintains, and displays the rules stored by **netfilter**.

Rules, matches, targets, and chains A *rule* comprises one or more criteria (*matches* or *classifiers*) and a single action (a *target*). If, when a rule is applied to a network packet, the packet matches all of the criteria, the action is applied to the packet. Rules are stored in *chains*. Each rule in a chain is applied, in order, to a packet, until a match is found. If there is no match, the chain's *policy*, or default action, is applied to the packet (page 771).

History In the kernel, iptables replaces the earlier ipchains as a method of filtering network packets and provides multiple chains for increased filtration flexibility. The iptables utility also provides stateful packet inspection (page 766).

Example rules As an example of how rules work, assume that a chain has two rules (Figure 25-1). The first rule tests whether a packet's destination is port 23 (FTP) and drops the packet if it is. The second rule tests whether a packet was received from the IP address 192.168.1.1 and alters the packet's destination if it was. When a packet is processed by the example chain, the kernel applies the first rule in the chain to see if the packet arrived on port 23. If the answer is yes, the packet is dropped and that is the end of processing for that packet. If the answer is no, the kernel applies the second rule in the chain to see if the packet came from the specified IP address. If yes, the destination in the packet's header is changed and the modified packet is sent on its way. If no, the packet is sent on without being changed.

Chains are collected in three tables: Filter, NAT, and Mangle. Each of the tables has builtin chains (described next). You can create additional, user-defined chains in Filter, the default table.

Filter The default table. This table is mostly used to DROP or ACCEPT packets based on their content; it does not alter packets. Builtin chains are INPUT, FORWARD, and OUTPUT. All user-defined chains go in this table.

NAT The Network Address Translation table. Packets that create new connections are routed through this table, which is used exclusively to translate the source or destination field

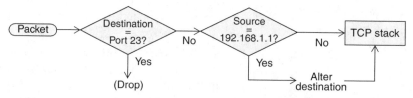

Figure 25-1 Example of how rules work

of the packet. Builtin chains are PREROUTING, OUTPUT, and POSTROUTING. Use this table with DNAT, SNAT, and MASQUERADE targets only.

- **DNAT** (destination NAT) alters the destination IP address of the first inbound packet in a connection so it is rerouted to another host. Subsequent packets in the connection are automatically DNATed. Useful for redirecting packets from the Internet that are bound for a firewall or a NATed server (page 782).

- **SNAT** (source NAT) alters the source IP address of the first outbound packet in a connection so that it appears to come from a fixed IP address—for example, a firewall or router. Subsequent packets in the connection are automatically SNATed. Replies to SNATed packets are automatically de-SNATed so they go back to the original sender. SNAT is useful for hiding LAN addresses from systems outside the LAN and using a single IP address to serve multiple local hosts. See also MASQUERADE (next).

- **MASQUERADE** differs from SNAT only in that it checks for an IP address to apply to each outbound packet, making it suitable for use with dynamic IP addresses such as those provided by DHCP (page 431). MASQUERADE is slightly slower than SNAT.

Mangle Used exclusively to alter the TOS (type of service), TTL (time to live), and MARK fields in a packet. Builtin chains are PREROUTING and OUTPUT.

Network packet When a packet from the network enters the kernel's network protocol stack, it is given some basic sanity tests, including checksum verification. After passing these tests, the packet goes through the PREROUTING chain, where its destination address may be changed (Figure 25-2).

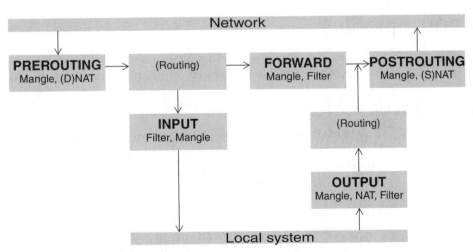

Figure 25-2 Filtering a packet in the kernel

Next the packet is routed based on its destination address. If it is bound for the local system, it first goes through the INPUT chain, where it can be filtered (accepted, dropped, or sent to another chain) or altered. If the packet is not addressed to the local system (the local system is forwarding the packet), it goes through the FORWARD and POSTROUTING chains, where it can again be filtered or altered.

Packets that are created locally pass through the OUTPUT and POSTROUTING chains, where they can be filtered or altered before being sent to the network.

State   The connection tracking machine (sometimes called the state machine) provides information on the state of a packet, allowing you to define rules that match criteria based on the state of the connection the packet is part of. For example, when a connection is opened, the first packet is part of a NEW connection, whereas subsequent packets are part of an ESTABLISHED connection. Connection tracking is handled by the **conntrack** module.

The OUTPUT chain handles connection tracking for locally generated packets. The PREROUTING chain handles connection tracking for all other packets. For more information refer to "State" on page 774.

Before the advent of connection tracking, it was sometimes necessary to open many or all nonprivileged ports to make sure that you accepted all RETURN and RELATED traffic. Because connection tracking allows you to identify these kinds of traffic, you can keep many more ports closed to general traffic, thereby increasing system security.

Jumps and targets   A *jump* or *target* specifies the action the kernel takes if a packet matches all the match criteria for the rule being processed (page 775).

ABOUT iptables

This section contains information about iptables: resources to consult for more information on this utility, prerequisites for running iptables, and notes.

MORE INFORMATION

Web   Documentation, HOWTOs, FAQs, patch-o-matic,
    security information   www.netfilter.org
Tutorial   www.faqs.org/docs/iptables
Scripts and more   www.linuxguruz.com/iptables

HOWTO   *KernelAnalysis-HOWTO*
    IP Masquerade HOWTO (contains useful scripts)
    Netfilter Extensions HOWTO at netfilter.org and
        www.iptables.org/documentation/HOWTO/netfilter-extensions-HOWTO.html

Book   *TCP Illustrated* by W. Richard Stevens, Addison-Wesley, December 1993

PREREQUISITES

Install the following package:

- **iptables**

Run chkconfig to cause iptables to start when the system comes up:

```
# /sbin/chkconfig iptables on
```

To ensure maximum protection, the **iptables** init script starts packet filtering by running iptables very soon after the system enters runlevels 2–5; in contrast, this script does not stop packet filtering almost until the system leaves runlevels 0, 1, and 6. See page 404 for more information on init scripts.

NOTES

The iptables utility differs from most other Linux utilities in its setup and use. Whereas other Linux utilities such as Apache, **vsftpd**, and **sshd** read the data that controls their operation from a configuration file, iptables requires you to give a series of iptables commands to build a set of packet filtering rules that are kept in the kernel.

There are two ways to set up the same set of rules each time you bring the system up. First, you can put iptables commands in a script and run that script each time the system boots. You can call this script from **/etc/rc.d/rc.local**.

Second, you can put the arguments to the iptables commands you want to execute in **/etc/sysconfig/iptables**. The system-config-securitylevel utility (page 777) and the Anaconda installer (page 47) both use this technique, building sets of rules and storing the corresponding iptables command arguments in **/etc/sysconfig/iptables**. The command **service iptables save** stores the iptables rules currently in effect to this file. If you use the **/etc/sysconfig/iptables** file in this manner, be aware that system-config-securitylevel and **service iptables save** overwrite this file.

For information on copying packet filtering rules to and from the kernel, refer to "Copying Rules to and from the Kernel" on page 776. You can run iptables with the –L option or you can run **service iptables status** to display the packet filtering rules the kernel is using.

The **iptables** init script executes the **/etc/sysconfig/iptables-config** file. Refer to the comments in this file for options you can set in it.

Resetting iptables   If you encounter problems related to the firewall rules, you can return packet processing rules in the kernel to their default state without rebooting by giving the following commands:

```
# iptables --flush && iptables --delete-chain
```

These commands flush all chains and delete any user-defined chains, leaving the system without a firewall. In an emergency you can give the following command to unload all iptables modules from the kernel and set a policy of DROP for all tables:

```
# /sbin/service iptables panic
```

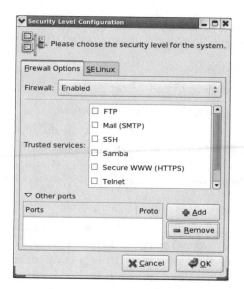

Figure 25-3   Security Level Configuration window, Firewall Options tab

JUMPSTART: BUILDING A FIREWALL USING
system-config-securitylevel

To run this utility, enter **system-config-securitylevel** on a command line. From KDE select **Main menu: Administration⇨Security Level and Firewall** or from GNOME select **System: Administration⇨Security Level and Firewall**. The system-config-securitylevel utility builds an extremely simple firewall but struggles with complex setups. The system-config-securitylevel utility displays the Security Level Configuration window (Figure 25-3), which has two tabs. The SELinux tab is discussed on page 402 and the Firewall Options tab is discussed here.

From the Firewall combo box, select **Enabled**. The firewall automatically allows packets that originate locally through to the outside (generally the Internet) and allows responses to those packets back in.

Opening Trusted services   Click the check boxes next to the services that the local system provides. These boxes set up a firewall that allows the local system to function as one or more of the following types of servers: FTP, mail (SMTP), SSH, Samba, Secure WWW (HTTPS), TELNET, and WWW (HTTP).

Opening other ports   Enter other ports you want to open by clicking the triangle next to **Other ports** and then clicking **Add** to open the Add Port window. This window allows you to specify a port to open and the protocol that each port uses (TCP or UDP).

Opened ports are not maintained when you disable the firewall

caution When you enable a firewall using system-config-securitylevel, specify Trusted services and/or open Other ports, and then disable the firewall, the system does not maintain the list of services and ports you specified. When you reenable the firewall, you need to specify the services and ports again. See page 776 for information on how you can save and reload a list of rules.

Click **OK**, and system-config-securitylevel sets up and turns on the firewall. For more information refer to "system-config-securitylevel: Generates a Set of Rules" on page 777.

ANATOMY OF AN iptables COMMAND

Command line   This section lists the components of an iptables command line that follow the name of the utility, iptables. Except as noted, the iptables utility is not sensitive to the position of arguments on the command line. The examples in this chapter reflect a generally accepted syntax that allows commands to be easily read, understood, and maintained. Not all commands have all components.

Many tokens on an iptables command line have two forms: a short form, consisting of a single letter preceded by a single hyphen, and a long form, consisting of a word preceded by two hyphens. Most scripts use the short forms for brevity; lines using the long forms can get unwieldy. The following iptables command lines are equivalent and are used as examples in this section:

```
# iptables --append FORWARD --in-interface eth1 --out-interface eth0 --jump ACCEPT
# iptables -A FORWARD -i eth1 -o eth0 -j ACCEPT
```

Table   Specifies the name of the table the command operates on: Filter, NAT, or Mangle. You can specify a table name in any iptables command. When you do not specify a table name, the command operates on the Filter table. Most of the examples in this chapter do not specify table names and, therefore, work on the Filter table. Specify a table as **-t** *tablename* or **--table** *tablename*.

Command   Tells iptables what to do with the rest of the command line—for example, add or delete a rule, display rules, or add a chain. The example commands, **-A** and **--append**, append the rule specified by the command line to the specified table and chain. See page 771 for a list of commands.

Chain   Specifies the name of the chain that this rule belongs to or that this command works on. The chain is INPUT, OUTPUT, FORWARD, PREROUTING, POSTROUTING, or the name of a user-defined chain. Specify a chain by putting the name of the chain on the command line without any preceding hyphens. The examples at the beginning of this section work with the FORWARD chain.

There are two kinds of match criteria: *packet match* criteria, which match a network packet, and *rule match* criteria, which match an existing rule.

Rule specifications   Packet match criteria identify network packets and implement rules that take action on packets that match the criteria. The combination of packet match criteria and an action is called a *rule specification*. Rule specifications form the basis for packet filtering. The first example at the beginning of this section uses the **--in-interface eth1 --out-interface eth0** rule match criteria. The second example uses the short form of the same criteria: **-i eth1 -o eth0**. Both of these rules forward packets that come in on device **eth1** and go out on device **eth0**.

Rule match criteria   Rule match criteria identify existing rules. An iptables command can modify, remove, or position a new rule adjacent to a rule specified by a rule match criterion. There are two ways to identify an existing rule: You can use the same rule specification that was used to create the rule or you can use the rule's ordinal number, called a *rule number*. Rule numbers begin with 1, signifying the first rule in a chain, and can be displayed with **iptables –L** (or **--line-numbers**). The first command below deletes the rule listed at the beginning of this section; the second replaces rule number 3 in the INPUT chain with a rule that rejects all packets from IP address 192.168.0.10:

```
# iptables --delete -A FORWARD -i eth1 -o eth0 -j ACCEPT
# iptables -R INPUT 3 --source 192.168.0.10 --jump REJECT
```

A *jump* or *target* specifies what action the kernel takes on packets that match all match criteria for a rule. Specify a jump or target as **–j** *target* or **--jump** *target*. The examples at the beginning of this section specify the ACCEPT target using the following commands: **--jump ACCEPT** and **–j ACCEPT**.

Jumps   A jump transfers control to a different chain within the same table. The following command adds (**--append**) a rule to the INPUT chain that transfers packets that use the TCP protocol (**--protocol tcp**) to a user-defined chain named **tcp_rules** (**--jump tcp_rules**):

```
# iptables --append INPUT --protocol tcp --jump tcp_rules
```

When the packet finishes traversing the **tcp_rules** chain, assuming it has not been dropped or rejected, it continues traversing the INPUT chain from the rule following the one it jumped from.

Targets   A target specifies an action the kernel takes on the packet; the simplest actions are ACCEPT, DROP, and REJECT. The following command adds a rule to the FORWARD chain that rejects packets coming from the FTP port (**/etc/services**, the file iptables consults to determine which port to use, shows that FTP uses port 21):

```
# iptables --append FORWARD --sport ftp --jump REJECT
```

Some targets, such as LOG, are *nonterminating*: Control passes to the next rule after the target is executed. See page 775 for information on how to use targets.

BUILDING A SET OF RULES

To specify a table, it is common practice to put the table declaration on the command line immediately following **iptables**. For example, the following command flushes (deletes all the rules from) the NAT table:

```
# iptables -t NAT -F
```

COMMANDS

Following is a list of iptables commands:

--append –A Adds rule(s) specified by *rule-specifications* to the end of *chain*. When a packet matches one of the *rule-specifications, target* processes it.

    iptables –A chain rule-specifications --jump target

--delete –D Removes one or more rules from *chain*, as specified by the *rule-numbers* or *rule-specifications.*

    iptables –D chain rule-numbers | rule-specifications

--insert –I Adds rule(s) specified by *rule-specifications* and *target* to the location in *chain* specified by *rule-number*. If you do not specify *rule-number*, it defaults to 1, the head of the chain.

    iptables –I chain rule-number rule-specifications --jump target

--replace –R Replaces rule number *rule-number* in *chain* with *rule-specification* and *target*. The command fails if *rule-number* or *rule-specification* resolves to more than one address.

    iptables –R chain rule-number rule-specification --jump target

--list –L Displays the rules in *chain*. Omit *chain* to display rules for all chains. Use **--line-numbers** to display rule numbers or select other display criteria from the list on page 772.

    iptables –L [chain] display-criteria

--flush –F Deletes all rules from *chain*. Omit *chain* to delete all rules from all chains.

    iptables –F [chain]

--zero –Z Change to zero the value of all packet and byte counters in *chain* or in all chains when you do not specify *chain*. Use with –L to display the counters before clearing them.

    iptables –Z [–L] [chain]

--delete-chain –X Removes the user-defined chain named *chain*. If you do not specify *chain*, removes all user-defined chains. You cannot delete a chain that a target points to.

    iptables –X chain

--policy –P Sets the default target or policy *builtin-target* for the builtin chain *builtin-chain*. This policy is applied to packets that do not match any rule in the chain. If a chain does not have a policy, unmatched packets are ACCEPTed.

    iptables –P builtin-chain builtin-target

--rename-chain –E Changes the name of the chain *old* to *new*.

    iptables –E old new

--help **-h** Displays a summary of iptables command syntax.

> *iptables -h*

Follow a match extension protocol with **-h** to display options you can use with that protocol. For more information refer to "Help with extensions" on page 773.

PACKET MATCH CRITERIA

The following criteria match network packets. When you precede a criterion with an exclamation point (!), the rule matches packets that do not match the criterion.

--protocol [!] *proto*

> **-p** Matches if the packet uses the *proto* protocol. This criterion is a match extension (page 773).

--source [!] *address[/mask]*

> **-s** or **--src** Matches if the packet came from *address*. The *address* can be a name or IP address. See page 423 for formats of the optional *mask* (only with an IP address).

--destination [!] *address[/mask]*

> **-d** or **--dst** Matches if the packet is going to *address*. The *address* can be a name or IP address. See page 423 for formats of the optional *mask* (only with an IP address).

--in-interface [!] *iface[+]*

> **-i** For the INPUT, FORWARD, and PREROUTING chains, matches if *iface* is the name of the interface the packet was received from. Append a plus sign (+) to *iface* to match any interface whose name begins with *iface*. When you do not specify **in-interface**, the rule matches packets coming from any interface.

--out-interface [!] *iface[+]*

> **-o** For the FORWARD, OUTPUT, and POSTROUTING chains, matches if *iface* is the interface the packet will be sent to. Append a plus sign (+) to *iface* to match any interface whose name begins with *iface*. When you do not specify **out-interface**, the rule matches packets going to any interface.

[!] --fragment **-f** Matches the second and subsequent fragments of fragmented packets. Because these packets do not contain source or destination information, they do not match any other rules.

DISPLAY CRITERIA

The following criteria display information. All packets match these criteria.

--verbose **-v** Displays additional output.

--numeric **-n** Displays IP addresses and port numbers as numbers, not names.

--exact **-x** Use with **-L** to display exact packet and byte counts instead of rounded values.

--line-numbers Display line numbers when listing rules. The line numbers are also the rule numbers that you can use in rule match criteria (page 770).

MATCH EXTENSIONS

Rule specification (packet match criteria) extensions, called *match extensions,* add matches based on protocols and state to the matches described previously. Each of the protocol extensions is kept in a module that must be loaded before that match extension can be used. The command that loads the module must appear in the same rule specification as, and to the left of, the command that uses the module. There are two types of match extensions: implicit and explicit.

IMPLICIT MATCH EXTENSIONS

Help with extensions   Implicit extensions are loaded (somewhat) automatically when you use a **--protocol** command (following). Each protocol has its own extensions. Follow the protocol with **-h** to display extensions you can use with that protocol. For example, the following command displays TCP extensions *at the end* of the Help output:

```
# iptables -p tcp -h
...
TCP v1.3.5 options:
  --tcp-flags [!] mask comp    match when TCP flags & mask == comp
                               (Flags: SYN ACK FIN RST URG PSH ALL NONE)
  [!] --syn                    match when only SYN flag set
                               (equivalent to --tcp-flags SYN,RST,ACK SYN)
  --source-port [!] port[:port]
  --sport ...
                               match source port(s)
  --destination-port [!] port[:port]
  --dport ...
                               match destination port(s)
  --tcp-option [!] number      match if TCP option set
```

This section does not describe all extensions. Use **-h,** as described in the preceding example, to display a complete list.

--protocol [!] *proto*

-p   Loads the *proto* module and matches if the packet uses the *proto* protocol. The *proto* can be a name or number from **/etc/protocols,** including **tcp, udp,** and **icmp** (page 1036). Specifying **all** or **0** (zero) matches any of all protocols and is the same as not including this match in a rule.

The following criteria load the TCP module and match TCP protocol packets coming from port 22 (ssh packets):

```
--protocol tcp --source-port 22
```

The following command expands the preceding match to cause the kernel to drop all incoming ssh packets. This command uses **ssh,** which iptables looks up in **/etc/services,** in place of **22:**

```
# iptables --protocol tcp --source-port ssh --jump DROP
```

TCP

The extensions in this section are loaded when you specify --**protocol tcp**.

--destination-port [!] [*port*][:*port*]]

--**dport**   Matches a destination port number or service name (see **/etc/services**). You can also specify a range of port numbers. Specifically, :*port* specifies ports 0 through *port,* and *port:* specifies ports *port* through 65535.

--source-port [!] [*port*][:*port*]]

--**sport**   Matches a source port number or service name (see **/etc/services**). You can also specify a range of port numbers. Specifically, :*port* specifies ports 0 through *port,* and *port:* specifies ports *port* through 65535.

[!] --**syn**   Matches packets with the SYN bit set and the ACK and FIN bits cleared. This match extension is shorthand for --**tcp-flags SYN,RST,ACK SYN**.

--tcp-flags [!] *mask comp*

Defines TCP flag settings that constitute a match. Valid flags are SYN, ACK, FIN, RST, URG, PSH, ALL, and NONE. The *mask* is a comma-separated list of flags to be examined; *comp* is a comma-separated subset of *mask* that specifies the flags that must be set for a match to occur. Flags not specified in *mask* must be unset.

--tcp-option [!] *n* Matches a TCP option with a decimal value of *n*.

UDP

When you specify --**protocol udp**, you can specify a source and/or destination port in the same manner as described earlier under "TCP."

ICMP

The extension in this section is loaded when you specify --**protocol icmp**. *ICMP* (page 1036) packets carry messages only.

--icmp-type [!] *name*

Matches when the packet is an ICMP packet of type *name*. The *name* can be a numeric ICMP type or one of the names returned by

```
# iptables -p icmp -h
```

EXPLICIT MATCH EXTENSIONS

Explicit match extensions differ from implicit match extensions in that you must use a –**m** or --**match** option to specify a module before you can use the extension. Many explicit match extension modules are available; this section covers **state**, one of the most important.

STATE

The **state** extension matches criteria based on the state of the connection the packet is part of (page 766).

--state *state* Matches a packet whose state is defined by *state,* a comma-separated list of states from the following list:

- **ESTABLISHED**   Any packet, within a specific connection, following the exchange of packets in both directions for that connection.

- **INVALID**   A stateless or unidentifiable packet.

- **NEW**   The first packet within a specific connection, typically a SYN packet.

- **RELATED**   Any packets exchanged in a connection spawned from an ESTABLISHED connection. For example, an FTP data connection might be related to the FTP control connection. (You need the **ip_conntrack_ftp** module for FTP connection tracking.)

The following command loads the **state** extension and establishes a rule that matches and drops both invalid packets and packets from new connections:

```
# iptables --match state --state INVALID,NEW --jump DROP
```

TARGETS

All targets are built in; there are no user-defined targets. This section lists some of the targets available with iptables. Applicable target options are listed following each target.

ACCEPT   Continues processing the packet.

DNAT   **Destination Network Address Translation**   Rewrites the destination address of the packet (page 765).

--to-destination *ip[-ip][:port-port]*
Same as SNAT with **to-source**, except that it changes the destination addresses of packets to the specified address(es) and port(s) and is valid only in the PREROUTING or OUTPUT chains of the NAT table and any user-defined chains called from those chains. The following command adds to the PREROUTING chain of the NAT table a rule that changes the destination in the headers of TCP packets with a destination of 66.187.232.50 to 192.168.0.10:

```
# iptables -t NAT -A PREROUTING -p tcp -d 66.187.232.50 -j DNAT --to-destination 192.168.0.10
```

DROP   Ends the packet's life without notice.

LOG   Turns on logging for the packet being processed. The kernel uses **syslogd** (page 562) to process output generated by this target. LOG is a nonterminating target; processing continues with the next rule. Use two rules to LOG packets that you REJECT, one each with the targets LOG and REJECT, with the same matching criteria.

--log-level *n*   Specifies logging level *n* as per **syslog.conf** (page 562).

--log-prefix *string*
Prefixes log entries with *string*, which can be up to 14 characters long.

--log-tcp-options   Logs options from the TCP packet header.

--log-ip-options   Logs options from the IP packet header.

MASQUERADE   Similar to SNAT with −−to-source, except that the IP information is grabbed from the interface on the specified port. For use on systems with dynamically assigned IP addresses, such as those that use DHCP, including most dial-up lines. Valid only in rules in the POSTROUTING chain of the NAT table.

−−to-ports *port[-port]*
Specifies the port for the interface you want to masquerade. Forgets connections when the interface goes down, as is appropriate for dial-up lines. You must specify the TCP or UDP protocol (−−protocol tcp or udp) with this target.

REJECT   Similar to DROP, except that it notifies the sending system that the packet was blocked.

−−reject-with *type*   Returns the error *type* to the originating system. The *type* can be any of the following, all of which return the appropriate *ICMP* (page 1036) error: icmp-net-unreachable, icmp-host-unreachable, icmp-port-unreachable, icmp-proto-unreachable, icmp-net-prohibited, or icmp-host-prohibited. You can specify *type* as echo-reply from rules that require an ICMP ping (page 365) packet to return a ping reply. You can specify tcp-reset from rules in or called from the INPUT chain to return a TCP RST packet. This parameter is valid in the INPUT, FORWARD, and OUTPUT chains and user-defined chains called from these chains.

RETURN   Stops traversing this chain and returns the packet to the calling chain.

SNAT   **Source Network Address Translation**   Rewrites the source address of the packet. Appropriate for hosts on a LAN that share an Internet connection.

−−to-source *ip[-ip][:port-port]*
Alters the source IP address of an outbound packet, and the source IP addresses of all future packets in this connection, to *ip*. Skips additional rules, if any. Returning packets are automatically de-SNATed so they return to the originating host. Valid only in the POSTROUTING chain of the NAT table.

When you specify a range of IP addresses (*ip-ip*) or use multiple to-source targets, iptables assigns the addresses in a round-robin fashion, cycling through the addresses, one for each new connection.

When the rule specifies the TCP or UDP protocol (−p tcp or −p udp), you can specify a range of ports. When you do not specify a range of ports, the rule matches all ports. Every connection on a NATed subnet must have a unique IP address and port combination. If two computers on a NATed subnet try to use the same port, the kernel maps one of the ports to another (unused) one. Ports less than 512 are mapped to other ports less than 512, ports from 512 to 1024 are mapped to other ports from 512 to 1024, and ports above 1024 are mapped to other ports above 1024.

COPYING RULES TO AND FROM THE KERNEL

The iptables-save utility copies packet filtering rules from the kernel to standard output so you can save them in a file. The iptables-restore utility copies rules from standard input, as written by iptables-save, to the kernel. Sample output from iptables-save follows:

```
# iptables-save
# Generated by iptables-save v1.3.5 on Tue Mar  7 20:52:04 2006
*filter
:INPUT ACCEPT [0:0]
:FORWARD ACCEPT [0:0]
:OUTPUT ACCEPT [4779:2823599]
:RH-Firewall-1-INPUT - [0:0]
-A INPUT -j RH-Firewall-1-INPUT
-A FORWARD -j RH-Firewall-1-INPUT
-A RH-Firewall-1-INPUT -i lo -j ACCEPT
...
COMMIT
```

Most of the lines that iptables-save writes are iptables command lines without the **iptables** at the beginning. Lines that begin with a pound sign (#) are comments. Lines that begin with an asterisk are names of tables that the following commands work on; all of the commands in the preceding example work on the Filter table. The COMMIT line must appear at the end of all commands for a table; it executes the preceding commands. Lines that begin with colons specify chains in the following format:

:chain policy [packets:bytes]

where *chain* is the name of the chain, *policy* is the policy (default target) for the chain, and *packets* and *bytes* are the packet and byte counters, respectively. The square brackets must appear in the line; they do not indicate optional parameters. Refer to the next section and visit www.faqs.org/docs/iptables/iptables-save.html for more information.

system-config-securitylevel: GENERATES A SET OF RULES

This section describes the set of rules generated by system-config-securitylevel (page 768) when you ask it to create a firewall with only ssh running as a trusted service and no other ports specified. The system-config-securitylevel utility writes the rules in the format used by iptables-save (see the preceding section) to the **/etc/sysconfig/iptables** file, which is read by the **iptables** init script so that the firewall is implemented each time the system boots. See the tip on page 769 about disabling the firewall using this utility.

In the following listing, *filter indicates that the commands appearing after it work on the Filter table. The first line that begins with a colon specifies that the policy for the INPUT chain in the Filter table is ACCEPT. FORWARD and OUTPUT chains are specified similarly. Because the counters for all the chains are zero, the counters will be reset to zero each time the system boots and initializes iptables from this file.

The system-config-securitylevel utility creates a user-defined chain named RH-Firewall-1-INPUT. No policy is specified because user-defined chains cannot have policies.

```
# cat /etc/sysconfig/iptables
# Firewall configuration written by system-config-securitylevel
# Manual customization of this file is not recommended.
*filter
:INPUT ACCEPT [0:0]
:FORWARD ACCEPT [0:0]
:OUTPUT ACCEPT [0:0]
:RH-Firewall-1-INPUT - [0:0]
-A INPUT -j RH-Firewall-1-INPUT
-A FORWARD -j RH-Firewall-1-INPUT
-A RH-Firewall-1-INPUT -i lo -j ACCEPT
-A RH-Firewall-1-INPUT -p icmp --icmp-type any -j ACCEPT
-A RH-Firewall-1-INPUT -p 50 -j ACCEPT
-A RH-Firewall-1-INPUT -p 51 -j ACCEPT
-A RH-Firewall-1-INPUT -p udp --dport 5353 -d 224.0.0.251 -j ACCEPT
-A RH-Firewall-1-INPUT -p udp -m udp --dport 631 -j ACCEPT
-A RH-Firewall-1-INPUT -p tcp -m tcp --dport 631 -j ACCEPT
-A RH-Firewall-1-INPUT -m state --state ESTABLISHED,RELATED -j ACCEPT
-A RH-Firewall-1-INPUT -m state --state NEW -m tcp -p tcp --dport 22 -j ACCEPT
-A RH-Firewall-1-INPUT -j REJECT --reject-with icmp-host-prohibited
COMMIT
```

The first two lines that begin with **−A** add rules to the INPUT and FORWARD chains that cause control to transfer to the RH-Firewall-1-INPUT chain. The subsequent lines append rules to the RH-Firewall-1-INPUT chain. Following is a description of what the rest of the lines do.

This line accepts packets from the local interface:

```
-A RH-Firewall-1-INPUT -i lo -j ACCEPT
```

This line accepts all ICMP packets:

```
-A RH-Firewall-1-INPUT -p icmp --icmp-type any -j ACCEPT
```

These lines accept packets that match protocols 50 and 51, which **/etc/protocols** lists as IPv6-Crypt and IPv6-Auth, both encryption headers for IPv6:

```
-A RH-Firewall-1-INPUT -p 50 -j ACCEPT
-A RH-Firewall-1-INPUT -p 51 -j ACCEPT
```

The next line accepts multicast DNS (www.multicastdns.org) packets:

```
-A RH-Firewall-1-INPUT -p udp --dport 5353 -d 224.0.0.251 -j ACCEPT
```

These lines allow IPP (page 504) UDP and TCP packets through:

```
-A RH-Firewall-1-INPUT -p udp -m udp --dport 631 -j ACCEPT
-A RH-Firewall-1-INPUT -p tcp -m tcp --dport 631 -j ACCEPT
```

This line uses **−m** to specify the **state** module and accepts ESTABLISHED and RELATED packets:

```
-A RH-Firewall-1-INPUT -m state --state ESTABLISHED,RELATED -j ACCEPT
```

This line allows TCP packets through on port 22 (**ssh**):

```
-A RH-Firewall-1-INPUT -m state --state NEW -m tcp -p tcp --dport 22 -j ACCEPT
```

This line rejects all packets that have not been accepted and returns ICMP error **icmp-host-prohibited** to the system that sent the packet:

```
-A RH-Firewall-1-INPUT -j REJECT --reject-with icmp-host-prohibited
```

COMMIT executes the preceding commands. With the preceding rules loaded, you can use iptables to list the rules and see the defaults that iptables puts in place:

```
# iptables -L
Chain INPUT (policy ACCEPT)
target         prot opt source                destination
RH-Firewall-1-INPUT  all  --  anywhere              anywhere

Chain FORWARD (policy ACCEPT)
target         prot opt source                destination
RH-Firewall-1-INPUT  all  --  anywhere              anywhere

Chain OUTPUT (policy ACCEPT)
target         prot opt source                destination

Chain RH-Firewall-1-INPUT (2 references)
target         prot opt source                destination
ACCEPT         all  --  anywhere              anywhere
ACCEPT         icmp --  anywhere              anywhere              icmp any
ACCEPT         ipv6-crypt--  anywhere              anywhere
ACCEPT         ipv6-auth--  anywhere              anywhere
ACCEPT         udp  --  anywhere              224.0.0.251           udp dpt:5353
ACCEPT         udp  --  anywhere              anywhere              udp dpt:ipp
ACCEPT         tcp  --  anywhere              anywhere              tcp dpt:ipp
ACCEPT         all  --  anywhere              anywhere              state RELATED,ESTABLISHED
ACCEPT         tcp  --  anywhere              anywhere              state NEW tcp dpt:ssh
REJECT         all  --  anywhere              anywhere              reject-with icmp-host-prohibited
```

SHARING AN INTERNET CONNECTION USING NAT

On the Internet there are many scripts available that set up Internet connection sharing using iptables. Each of these scripts boils down to the same few basic iptables commands, albeit with minor differences. This section discusses those few statements to explain how a connection can be shared. You can use the statements presented in this section or refer to the *Linux IP Masquerade HOWTO* for complete scripts. The tldp.org/HOWTO/IP-Masquerade-HOWTO/firewall-examples.html Web page holds the simplest of these scripts.

There are two ways you can share a single connection to the Internet (one IP address). Both involve setting up NAT to alter addresses in packets and then forward them. The first allows clients (browsers, mail readers, and so on) on several systems on a LAN to share a single IP address to connect to servers on the Internet. The second allows servers (mail, Web, FTP, and so on) on different systems on a LAN to provide their services over a single connection to the Internet. You can use iptables to set up one or both of these configurations. In both cases, you need to set up a system that is a router: It must have two network connections—one connected to the Internet and the other to the LAN.

For optimal security, use a dedicated system as a router. Because data transmission over a connection to the Internet—even over a broadband connection—is relatively slow, using a slower, older system as a router does not generally slow down a LAN. This setup also gives you some defense against intrusion from the Internet. A workstation on the LAN can also function as a router, but this setup means that you maintain data on a system that is directly connected to the Internet. The following sections discuss the security of each setup.

The examples in this section assume that the device named **eth0** connects to the Internet on 10.255.255.255 and that **eth1** connects to the LAN on 192.168.0.1. Substitute the devices and IP addresses that your systems use. If you use a modem to connect to the Internet, you need to substitute **ppp0** (or another device) for **eth0** in the examples.

For the examples in this section to work, you must turn on IP forwarding. First give the following command and make sure everything is working:

```
# /sbin/sysctl -w net.ipv4.ip_forward=1
net.ipv4.ip_forward = 1
```

Once you know that iptables is working correctly, change the **0** to a **1** in the following line in **/etc/sysctl.conf** to make the kernel always perform IP forwarding:

```
net.ipv4.ip_forward = 0
```

After making this change, give the command **/sbin/sysctl –p** to apply the change and to make sure that there are no typographical errors in the configuration file.

CONNECTING SEVERAL CLIENTS TO A SINGLE INTERNET CONNECTION

Configuring the kernel of the router system to allow clients on multiple local systems on the LAN to connect to the Internet requires you to set up *IP masquerading*, or *SNAT* (source NAT). IP masquerading translates the source and destination addresses in the headers of network packets that originate on local systems and the packets that remote servers send in response to those packets. These packets are part of connections that originate on a local system. The example in this section does nothing to packets that are part of connections that originate on the remote systems (on the Internet): These packets cannot get past the router system, which provides some degree of security.

The point of rewriting the packet headers is to allow systems with different local IP addresses to share a single IP address on the Internet. The router system translates the source or origin address of packets from local systems to that of the Internet connection, so that all packets passing from the router to the Internet appear to come from a single system—10.255.255.255 in the example. All packets sent in response by remote systems on the Internet to the router system have the address of the Internet connection—10.255.255.255 in the example—as their destination address. The router system remembers each connection and alters the destination address of each response packet to become that of the local, originating system.

The router system is established by four iptables commands, one of which sets up a log of masqueraded connections. The first command puts the first rule in the FOR-WARD chain of the Filter (default) table (–A FORWARD):

```
# iptables -A FORWARD -i eth0 -o eth1 -m state --state ESTABLISHED,RELATED -j ACCEPT
```

To match this rule, a packet must be

1. Received on **eth0** (coming in from the Internet): **–i eth0**.

2. Going to be sent out on **eth1** (going out to the LAN): **–o eth1**.

3. Part of an established connection or a connection that is related to an established connection: **––state ESTABLISHED,RELATED**.

The kernel accepts (**–j ACCEPT**) packets that meet these three criteria. Accepted packets pass to the next appropriate chain or table. Packets from the Internet that attempt to create a new connection are not matched and therefore not accepted by this rule. Packets that are not accepted pass to the next rule in the FORWARD chain.

The second command puts the second rule in the FORWARD chain of the Filter table:

```
# iptables -A FORWARD -i eth1 -o eth0 -j ACCEPT
```

To match this rule, a packet must be

1. Received on **eth1** (coming in from the LAN): **–i eth1**.

2. Going to be sent out on **eth0** (going out to the Internet): **–o eth0**.

The kernel accepts packets that meet these two criteria, which means that all packets that originate locally and are going to the Internet are accepted. Accepted packets pass to the next appropriate chain/table. Packets that are not accepted pass to the next rule in the FORWARD chain.

The third command puts the third rule in the FORWARD chain of the Filter table:

```
# iptables -A FORWARD -j LOG
```

Because this rule has no match criteria, it acts on all packets it processes. This rule's action is to log packets—that is, it logs packets from the Internet that attempt to create a new connection.

Packets that get to the end of the FORWARD chain of the Filter table are done with the rules set up by iptables and are handled by the local TCP stack. Packets from the Internet that attempt to create a new connection on the router system are accepted or returned, depending on whether the service they are trying to connect to is available on the router system.

The fourth command puts the first rule in the POSTROUTING chain of the NAT table. Only packets that are establishing a new connection are passed to the NAT table. Once a connection has been set up for SNAT or MASQUERADE, the headers on all subsequent ESTABLISHED and RELATED packets are altered the same way as the first packet. Packets that are sent in response to these packets automatically have their headers adjusted so that they return to the originating local system.

```
# iptables -t NAT -A POSTROUTING -o eth0 -j MASQUERADE
```

To match this rule, a packet must be

1. Establishing a new connection (otherwise it would not have come to the NAT table).

2. Going to be sent out on **eth0** (going out to the Internet): **–o eth0**.

The kernel MASQUERADEs all packets that meet these criteria. In other words, all locally originating packets that are establishing new connections have their source address changed to the address that is associated with **eth0** (10.255.255.255 in the example).

Following are the four commands together:

```
# iptables -A FORWARD -i eth0 -o eth1 -m state --state ESTABLISHED,RELATED -j ACCEPT
# iptables -A FORWARD -i eth1 -o eth0 -j ACCEPT
# iptables -A FORWARD -j LOG
# iptables -t NAT -A POSTROUTING -o eth0 -j MASQUERADE
```

You can put these commands in **/etc/rc.local** or in a script called by this file on the router system to have them executed each time the system boots. Alternatively, you can put them in **/etc/sysconfig/iptables**, leaving off the iptables command at the beginning of each line and adding a final line with the word **COMMIT** on it. When you put the commands in the **iptables** file, they are executed by the **iptables** init script each time it is called. For more information refer to "Copying Rules to and from the Kernel" on page 776.

To limit the local systems that can connect to the Internet, you can add a **–s** (source) match criterion to the last command:

```
# iptables -t NAT -A POSTROUTING -o eth0 -s 192.168.0.0-192.168.0.32 -j MASQUERADE
```

In the preceding command, **–s 192.168.0.0-192.168.0.32** causes only packets from an IP address in the specified range to be MASQUERADEd.

CONNECTING SEVERAL SERVERS TO A SINGLE INTERNET CONNECTION

DNAT (destination NAT) can set up rules to allow clients from the Internet to send packets to servers on the LAN. This example sets up an SMTP mail server on 192.168.1.33 and an HTTP (Web) server on 192.168.1.34. Both protocols use TCP. SMTP uses port 25 and HTTP uses port 80, so the rules match TCP packets with destination ports of 25 and 80. The example assumes the mail server does not make outgoing connections and uses another server on the LAN for DNS and mail relaying. Both commands put rules in the PREROUTING chain of the NAT table (**–A PREROUTING –t NAT**):

```
# iptables -A PREROUTING -t NAT -p tcp --dport 25 --to-source 192.168.0.33:25 -j DNAT
# iptables -A PREROUTING -t NAT -p tcp --dport 80 --to-source 192.168.0.34:80 -j DNAT
```

To match these rules, the packet must use the TCP protocol (**-p tcp**) and have a destination port of 25 (first rule, **--dport 25**) or 80 (second rule, **--dport 80**).

The **--to-source** is a target specific to the PREROUTING and OUTPUT chains of the NAT table; it alters the destination address and port of matched packets as specified. As with MASQUERADE and SNAT, subsequent packets in the same and related connections are altered appropriately.

The fact that the servers cannot originate connections means that neither server can be exploited to participate in a *DDoS attack* (page 1028) on systems on the Internet and cannot send private data from the local system back to a malicious user's system.

CHAPTER SUMMARY

The iptables utility creates firewalls intended to prevent unauthorized access to a system or network. An iptables command sets up or maintains in the kernel rules that control the flow of network packets; rules are stored in chains. Each rule has a criteria part and an action part, called a target. When the criteria part matches a network packet, the kernel applies the action from the rule to the packet.

Chains are collected in three tables: Filter, NAT, and Mangle. Filter, the default table, DROPs or ACCEPTs packets based on their content. NAT, the Network Address Translation table, translates the source or destination field of packets. Mangle is used exclusively to alter TOS (type of service), TTL (time to live), and MARK fields in a packet. The connection tracking machine, which is handled by the **conntrack** module, defines rules that match criteria based on the state of the connection a packet is part of.

In an emergency you can give the following command to unload all iptables modules from the kernel and set a policy of DROP for all tables:

```
# /sbin/service iptables panic
```

EXERCISES

1. How would you remove all iptables rules and chains?

2. How would you list all current iptables rules?

3. How is configuring iptables different from configuring most Linux services?

4. Define an iptables rule that will reject incoming connections on the TELNET port.

5. What does NAT stand for? What does the NAT table do?

ADVANCED EXERCISES

6. What does the **conntrack** module do?

7. What do rule match criteria do? What are they used for?

8. What do packet match criteria do? What are they used for?

9. Which utilities copy packet filtering rules to and from the kernel? How do they work?

10. Define a rule that will silently block incoming SMTP connections from **spmr.com.**

26

APACHE (httpd): SETTING UP A WEB SERVER

IN THIS CHAPTER

The World Wide Web (WWW or Web for short), is a collection of servers that hold material, called *content,* that Web browsers (or just browsers) can display. Each of the servers on the Web is connected to the Internet, a network of networks (an *internetwork*). Much of the content on the Web is coded in HTML (Hypertext Markup Language, page 1036). *Hypertext,* the code behind the links that you click on a Web page, allows browsers to display and react to links that point to other Web pages on the Internet.

Apache is the most popular Web server on the Internet today. It is both robust and extensible. The ease with which you can install, configure, and run it in the Linux environment makes it an obvious choice for publishing content on the World Wide Web. The Apache server and related projects are developed and maintained by the Apache Software Foundation (ASF), a not-for-profit corporation formed in June 1999. The ASF grew out of the Apache Group, which was established in 1995 to develop the Apache server.

This chapter starts by providing introductory information about Apache. This information is followed by the first JumpStart section, which describes the minimum steps needed to get Apache up and running. The second JumpStart section covers the use of the Red Hat system-config-httpd configuration script. Following these sections is "Filesystem Layout," which tells you where the various Apache files are located.

Configuration directives, a key part of Apache, are discussed starting on page 794. This section includes coverage of contexts and containers, two features/concepts that are critical to understanding Apache. The next section explains the main Apache configuration file, **/etc/httpd/conf/httpd.conf**, as modified by Red Hat. The final pages of the chapter cover virtual hosts, troubleshooting, and modules you can use with Apache, including CGI and SSL.

INTRODUCTION

Apache is a server that responds to requests from Web browsers, or *clients,* such as Firefox, Netscape, lynx, and Internet Explorer. When you enter the address of a Web page (a *URI,* page 1061) in a Web browser's location bar, the browser sends a request over the Internet to the (Apache) server at that address. In response, the server sends the requested content back to the browser. The browser then displays or plays the content, which might be a song, picture, video clip, or other information.

Content   Aside from add-on modules that can interact with the content, Apache remains oblivious to the content itself. Server administration and content creation are two different aspects of bringing up a Web site. This chapter concentrates on setting up and running an Apache server; it spends little time discussing content creation.

Modules   Apache, like the Linux kernel, uses external modules to increase load-time flexibility and allow parts of its code to be recompiled without recompiling the whole program. Rather than being part of the Apache binary, modules are stored as separate files that can be loaded when Apache is started.

Apache uses external modules, called dynamic shared objects (DSOs), for basic and advanced functions; there is not much to Apache without these modules. Apache also uses modules to extend its functionality: Modules can process scripts written in Perl, PHP, Python, and other languages; use several different methods to authenticate users; facilitate publishing content; and process nontextual content, such as audio. The list of modules written by the Apache Group and third-party developers is always growing. For more information refer to "Modules" on page 820.

ABOUT APACHE

This section describes the packages you need to install and provides references for the programs covered in this chapter. The "Notes" section on page 788 introduces terminology and other topics that will help you make better sense of this chapter. "JumpStart I" (page 789) gets Apache up and running as quickly as possible.

PREREQUISITES

Minimal installation   Install the following packages:

- **httpd**
- **apr** (Apache portable runtime)
- **apr-util**

Starting Apache   Run chkconfig to cause **httpd** to start when the system enters multiuser mode:

```
# /sbin/chkconfig httpd on
```

After you configure Apache, use service to start **httpd**:

```
# /sbin/service httpd start
```

After changing the Apache configuration, restart **httpd** with the following command, which will not disturb clients connected to the server:

```
# /sbin/service httpd graceful
```

Optional packages   You can install the following optional packages:

- **httpd-manual**   The Apache manual
- **webalizer**   Web server log analyzer (page 825)
- **mod_perl**   Embedded Perl scripting language
- **mod_python**   Embedded Python scripting language
- **mod_ssl**   Secure Sockets Layer extension (page 821)
- **php**   Embedded PHP scripting language, including IMAP & LDAP support
- **mrtg**   MRTG traffic monitor (page 826)
- **net-snmp** and **net-snmp-utils**   SNMP, required for MRTG (page 826).

MORE INFORMATION

Local   The Apache *Reference Manual* and *Users' Guide*   **/var/www/manual**
Point a browser at **http://localhost/manual** if **httpd** is running or at **/var/www/manual/index.html** if **httpd** is not running. The manual is available online only if the **httpd-manual** package is installed.

Web   Apache documentation   *RHEL* httpd.apache.org/docs/2.0,
FEDORA httpd.apache.org/docs/2.2

Apache directives list   *RHEL* httpd.apache.org/docs/2.0/mod/directives.html,
FEDORA httpd.apache.org/docs/2.2/mod/directives.html

Apache Software Foundation (newsletters, mailing lists, projects, module registry, and more)   www.apache.org

mod_perl   perl.apache.org

mod_php   www.php.net

mod_python   www.modpython.org

mod_ssl   www.modssl.org

MRTG   mrtg.hdl.com/mrtg.html

SNMP   net-snmp.sourceforge.net

SSI   *RHEL* httpd.apache.org/docs/2.0/howto/ssi.html,
        FEDORA httpd.apache.org/docs/2.2/howto/ssi.html

webalizer   www.mrunix.net/webalizer

NOTES

Terms: Apache and httpd   Apache is the name of a server that serves HTTP and other content. The Apache daemon is named **httpd** because it is an HTTP server daemon. This chapter uses the terms *Apache* and ***httpd*** interchangeably.

Terms: server and process   An Apache *server* is the same thing as an Apache *process*. An Apache child process exists to handle incoming client requests, hence it is referred to as a server.

Firewall   An Apache server normally uses TCP port 80; a secure server uses TCP port 443. If the Apache server system is running a firewall, you need to open one or both of these ports. To get started you just need to open port 80 (HTTP). Using the Red Hat graphical firewall tool (page 768), select **WWW (HTTPD)** and/or **Secure WWW (HTTPS)** from the Trusted services frame to open these ports. For more general information, see Chapter 25, which details iptables.

SELinux   When SELinux is set to use a targeted policy, **httpd** is protected by SELinux. You can disable this protection if necessary. For more information refer to "Setting the Targeted Policy with system-config-securitylevel" on page 402.

Running as root   Because Apache serves content on privileged ports, you must start it as **root**. For security reasons, the processes that Apache spawns run as the user and group **apache**.

Locale   The **httpd** daemon is started using the C locale by default. You can modify this behavior, for example, to use the configured system locale, by setting the **HTTPD_LANG** variable in the **/etc/sysconfig/httpd** file.

Document root   The root of the directory hierarchy that Apache serves content from is called the *document root*. As shipped by Red Hat, the document root is **/var/www/html**. You can use the DocumentRoot directive (page 796) to change the location of the document root.

Modifying content   As shipped by Red Hat, only **root** can add or modify content in **/var/www/html**. To avoid having people work as **root** when they are manipulating content, create a group (**webwork**, for example), put people who need to work with Web content in this group, and make the directory hierarchy starting at **/var/www/html** (or another document root) writable by that group. In addition, if you make the directory hierarchy setgid (**chmod g+s** *filename*), all new files created within this hierarchy will belong to the group, which facilitates sharing files. See page 539 for more information about working with groups.

Versions   *RHEL* runs Apache version 2.0. *FEDORA* runs version 2.2.

JUMPSTART I: GETTING APACHE UP AND RUNNING

To get Apache up and running, modify the **/etc/httpd/conf/httpd.conf** configuration file. "Directives I: Directives You May Want to Modify as You Get Started" on page 794 explains more about this file and explores other changes you may want to make to it.

MODIFYING THE httpd.conf CONFIGURATION FILE

Apache runs as installed, but it is a good idea to add the three lines described in this section to the **/etc/httpd/conf/httpd.conf** configuration file before starting Apache. If you do not add these lines, Apache assigns values that may not work for you.

The ServerName line establishes a name for the server. Add one of the following lines to **httpd.conf** to set the name of the server to the domain name of the server or, if you do not have a domain name, to the IP address of the server:

> ServerName **example.com**

or

> ServerName **IP_address**

where *example.com* is the domain name of the server and *IP_address* is the IP address of the server. If you are not connected to a network, you can use the **local-host** address, 127.0.0.1, so that you can start the server and experiment with it.

When a client has trouble getting information from a server, the server frequently displays an error page that identifies the problem. For example, when Apache cannot find a requested page, it displays a page that says **Error 404: Not Found**. Each error page has a link that the user can click to send mail to the server's administrator. ServerSignature can specify that you want an email link on error pages and ServerAdmin specifies the email address that the server displays on error pages. Add these two lines to **httpd.conf**:

> ServerAdmin **email_address**
> ServerSignature EMail

where *email_address* is the email address of the person who needs to know if people are having trouble using the server. Make sure that someone checks this email account frequently.

After making the changes to **httpd.conf**, start or restart **httpd** as explained on page 787.

TESTING APACHE

Once you start the **httpd** daemon, you can confirm that Apache is working correctly by pointing a browser on the local system to **http://localhost/**. From a remote system, point a browser to **http://** followed by the ServerName you specified in **httpd.conf**.

For example, you might use either of these URI formats: **http://192.168.0.16** or **http://example.org**. The browser should display the Red Hat/Apache test page. This test page is actually an error page that says there is no content. For more information refer to "Red Hat test page" on page 816.

If the server is behind a firewall, open TCP port 80 (page 788). If you are having problems getting Apache to work, see "Troubleshooting" on page 819.

PUTTING YOUR CONTENT IN PLACE

Place the content you want Apache to serve in **/var/www/html**. Apache automatically displays the file named **index.html** in this directory. Working as **root** (or as a member of the group you set up for this purpose [e.g., **webwork**]), give the following command to create such a page:

```
# cat > /var/www/html/index.html
<html><body><p>This is my test page.</p></body></html>
CONTROL-D
```

After creating this file, either refresh the browser if it is still running or start it again and point it at the server. The browser should display the page you just created.

JUMPSTART II: SETTING UP APACHE
USING system-config-httpd

Make a copy of **httpd.conf**

tip As installed, the **/etc/httpd/conf/httpd.conf** file contains extensive comments and is set up as explained in this chapter. The system-config-httpd utility overwrites this file. Make a copy of **httpd.conf** for safekeeping before you run this utility for the first time.

You can use the system-config-httpd utility to display the HTTP window, which allows you to edit the **/etc/httpd/conf/httpd.conf** file to set up Apache. To run this utility, enter **system-config-httpd** on a command line. From KDE select **Main menu: Administration⇨Server Settings⇨HTTP** or from GNOME select **System: Administration⇨Server Settings⇨HTTP**.

The HTTP window has four tabs: Main, Virtual Hosts, Server, and Performance Tuning. Each field in these tabs/windows corresponds to a directive in the **/etc/httpd/conf/httpd.conf** file. This section discusses some of the basic directives you can change with system-config-httpd. For more information click **Help** at the bottom of the HTTP window.

Main tab   The Main tab (Figure 26-1) allows you to establish an *FQDN* (page 1032) as the name of the server (ServerName, page 796), an email address for the server administrator (ServerAdmin, page 795), and the ports and addresses that Apache listens on for requests (Listen, page 795). Highlight an entry in the Available Addresses subwindow, and click **Edit** to edit that entry or **Add** to add a new entry. Both

Figure 26-1   HTTP window, Main tab

actions bring up a window that allows you to specify a port and select whether you want to listen to all IP addresses on that port or listen to a specific address. To get started, set up Apache to listen to all available addresses on port 80.

Virtual Hosts   The Virtual Hosts tab allows you to establish default settings for Apache and set up virtual hosts (page 818). Click the Virtual Hosts tab, and then click **Edit** to edit the settings for the highlighted virtual host or **Add** to add a new virtual host. Both actions open the Virtual Host Properties window, General Options tab (Figure 26-2).

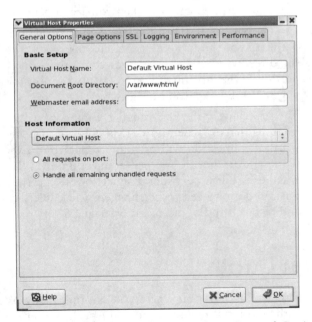

Figure 26-2   Virtual Host Properties window, General Options tab

Figure 26-3   Virtual Host Properties window, Page Options tab

The other tabs in the Virtual Host Properties window are Page Options (Figure 26-3), SSL, Logging, Environment, and Performance. This window is similar to the one you used to establish default settings, except that it pertains to a specific virtual host and has more tabs. You do not have to change most of the values in this window. Click **OK** when you are done making changes.

Server tab   Usually you do not need to change the values in the Server tab. You can specify the pathname of the lock file (LockFile directive), the PID file (PidFile directive), and the directory that Apache stores core dumps in (CoreDumpDirectory). The lower portion of the tab allows you to specify the user (User, page 812) and group (Group, page 810) that Apache runs as.

Performance   The selections in the Performance Tuning tab control the maximum number of con-
Tuning tab   nections that Apache allows (MaxClients, page 802), the number of seconds after which a connection will disconnect (Timeout, page 804), the maximum number of requests Apache allows per connection (MaxRequestsPerChild, page 803), and whether to allow persistent connections (KeepAlive directive). Initially, the values in this tab do not need to be changed. Click **OK** when you are done making changes and restart **httpd** as discussed on page 787.

FILESYSTEM LAYOUT

This section tells you where you can find many of the files you may need to work with as you set up and modify an Apache server.

Binaries, scripts, and modules   The Apache server and related binary files are kept in several directories:

/usr/sbin/httpd   The Apache server (daemon).

/usr/sbin/apachectl   Starts and stops Apache. The **httpd** init script calls apachectl.

/usr/bin/htpasswd   Creates and maintains password files used by the Apache authentication module (page 824).

/usr/sbin/rotatelogs   Rotates Apache log files so the files do not get too large. See logrotate (page 559) for more information about rotating log files.

/etc/httpd/modules   Holds module binaries. Two of the most frequently used module binary files are **mod_perl.so** and **mod_python.so**. This directory is a symbolic link to **/usr/lib/httpd/modules** (page 820).

Configuration files   Apache configuration files are kept in the **/etc/httpd/conf** and **/etc/httpd/conf.d** directories.

/etc/httpd/conf/httpd.conf   Holds configuration directives. This file is the main Apache configuration file. The discussion of configuration directives starts on page 794. Refer to "The Red Hat **httpd.conf** File" on page 814 for a description of the **httpd.conf** file.

/etc/httpd/conf/magic   Provides *MIME* (page 1043) file type identification (the MIME hints file). It is not normally changed. See *magic number* (page 1042) for more information.

/etc/httpd/conf/ssl.✲   *RHEL* Holds files and directories used by **mod_ssl** (page 821).

/etc/pki/tls/certs   *FEDORA* Holds files and directories used by **mod_ssl** (page 821).

/etc/httpd/conf.d   Holds configuration files for modules including **php** and **mod_perl**.

Logs   Logs are kept in **/var/log/httpd** (there is a symbolic link at **/etc/httpd/logs**):

/var/log/httpd/access_log   Logs requests made to the server.

/var/log/httpd/error_log   Logs request and runtime server errors.

/var/log/httpd/ssl_✲_log   Holds **mod_ssl** logs.

Web documents   Web documents (including the Web pages displayed by client browsers), custom error messages, and CGI scripts are kept in **/var/www** by default:

/var/www/cgi-bin   Holds CGI scripts (page 821).

/var/www/error   Holds default error documents. You can modify these documents to conform to the style of your Web site. See ErrorDocument (page 807).

/var/www/icons   Holds icons used to display directory entries.

/var/www/manual   Holds the Apache *Reference Manual* and *Users' Guide*. *FEDORA* Present only if the **httpd-manual** package is installed.

Document root   By default, the document root (page 788) is **/var/www/html**. You can change this location with the DocumentRoot directive (page 796). In addition to content for the

Web pages that Apache serves, this directory can house the **usage** directory, which holds **webalizer** (page 825) output.

.htaccess files   A **.htaccess** file contains configuration directives and can appear in any directory in the document root hierarchy. The location of a **.htaccess** file is critical: The directives in a **.htaccess** file apply to all files in the hierarchy rooted at the directory that holds the **.htaccess** file. You must use the AllowOverride directive (page 813) to cause Apache to examine **.htaccess** files. Based on the Red Hat **httpd.conf** file, Apache does not answer requests for files whose names start with **.ht**, so clients cannot read **.htaccess** files.

CONFIGURATION DIRECTIVES

Configuration directives, or simply *directives,* are lines in a configuration file that control some aspect of how Apache functions. A configuration directive is composed of a keyword followed by one or more arguments (values) separated by SPACEs. For example, the following configuration directive sets **Timeout** to 300 (seconds):

```
Timeout 300
```

You must enclose arguments that contain SPACEs within double quotation marks. Keywords are not case sensitive, but arguments (pathnames, filenames, and so on) often are.

httpd.conf   The most important file that holds Apache configuration directives is, by default, **/etc/httpd/conf/httpd.conf**. This file holds global directives that affect all content served by Apache. An Include directive (page 810) within **httpd.conf** can incorporate the contents of another file as though it were part of **httpd.conf**.

.htaccess   Local directives can appear in **.htaccess** files (above). A **.htaccess** file can appear in any directory within the document root hierarchy; it affects files in the directory hierarchy rooted at the directory the **.htaccess** file appears in.

Pathnames   When you specify an absolute pathname in a configuration directive, the directive uses that pathname without modifying it. When you specify a relative pathname, such as a simple filename or the name of a directory, Apache prepends to the name the value specified by the ServerRoot (page 809) directive (**/etc/httpd** by default).

DIRECTIVES I: DIRECTIVES YOU MAY WANT TO MODIFY AS YOU GET STARTED

When it starts, Apache reads the **/etc/httpd/conf/httpd.conf** configuration file (by default) for instructions governing every aspect of how Apache runs and delivers content. The **httpd.conf** file shipped by Red Hat is more than 1,000 lines long. This section details some lines you may want to change as you are getting started with Apache. You can use each of the following directives in **httpd.conf**; the Context line in each explanation shows which other files the directives can appear in. Context is explained on page 798. The section titled "Directives II: Advanced Directives" on page 802 describes more directives.

Listen *Specifies the port(s) that Apache listens for requests on.*

Listen [IP-address:]portnumber

where **IP-address** is the IP address that Apache listens on and **portnumber** is the number of the port that Apache listens on for the given **IP-address**. When **IP-address** is absent or is set to 0.0.0.0, Apache listens on all network interfaces. At least one Listen directive must appear in **httpd.conf** or Apache will not work.

FEDORA The following minimal directive from the **httpd.conf** file listens for requests on all interfaces on port 80:

```
Listen 80
```

RHEL The following Listen directive from **httpd.conf** is equivalent to the preceding one:

```
Listen 0.0.0.0:80
```

The next directive changes the port from the default value of 80 to 8080:

```
Listen 8080
```

When you specify a port other than 80, each request to the server must include a port number (as in **www.example.org:8080**) or the kernel will return a **Connection Refused** message. Use multiple Listen directives to cause Apache to listen on multiple IP addresses and ports. For example,

```
Listen 80
Listen 192.168.1.1:8080
Listen 192.168.1.2:443
```

accepts connections on all network interfaces on port 80, on 192.168.1.1 on port 8080, and on 192.168.1.2 on port 443.

Context: **server config**
Default: none (Apache will not start without this directive)
Red Hat: Listen 80

ServerAdmin *Sets the email address displayed on error pages.*

ServerAdmin email-address

where **email-address** is the email address of the person responsible for managing the Web content. Under most versions of Apache, this address appears on Apache-generated error pages. However, Red Hat Linux sets ServerSignature (page 810) to **On** which causes Apache to display information about the server, not an email address, on error pages. If you want to display an email address on error pages set ServerSignature to **EMail**. Make sure **email-address** points to an email account that someone checks frequently. Users can use this address to get help with the Web site or to inform the administrator of problems. There is no default value for ServerAdmin; if you do not use this directive, the value is undefined and no email address appears on error pages.

Because **webmaster** is a common name, you can use **webmaster** at your domain and use the **/etc/aliases** file (page 633) to forward mail that is sent to **webmaster** to the person who is responsible for maintaining the Web site.

Contexts: **server config, virtual host**
Default: none
Red Hat: *RHEL* none, *FEDORA* **root@localhost**

ServerName   *Specifies the server's name and the port it listens on.*

ServerName **FQDN** [:*port*]

where **FQDN** is the fully qualified domain name or IP address of the server and **port** is the optional port number Apache listens on. The domain name of the server must be able to be resolved by DNS and may differ from the hostname of the system running the server. If you do not specify a ServerName, Apache performs a DNS reverse name resolution (page 729) on the system's IP address and assigns that value to ServerName. If the reverse lookup fails, Apache assigns the system's IP address to ServerName.

Red Hat Linux provides the following ServerName template in the **httpd.conf** file:

```
#ServerName www.example.com:80
```

Copy this line, remove the #, and substitute the FQDN or IP address of the server in place of **www.example.com**. Change the 80 to the port number Apache listens on if it is not port 80.

The ports specified by ServerName and Listen (page 795) must be the same if you want the FQDN specified by ServerName tied to the IP address specified by the Listen directive.

Apache uses ServerName to construct a URI when it redirects a client (page 817).

Contexts: **server config, virtual host**
Default: none
Red Hat: none

DocumentRoot   *Points to the root of the directory hierarchy that holds the server's content.*

DocumentRoot **dirname**

where **dirname** is the absolute pathname of the directory at the root of the directory hierarchy that holds the content Apache serves. Do not use a trailing slash. You can put the document root wherever you like, as long as the user **apache** has read access to the ordinary files and execute access to the directory files in the directory hierarchy. The FHS (page 176) specifies **/srv** as the top-level directory for this purpose. The following directive puts the document root at **/home/www**:

```
DocumentRoot /home/www
```

Contexts: **server config, virtual host**
Default: **/usr/local/apache/htdocs**
Red Hat: **/var/www/html**

UserDir *Allows users to publish content from their home directories.*

*UserDir **dirname** | disabled | enabled **user-list***

where **dirname** is the name of a directory that, if it appears in a local user's home directory, Apache publishes to the Web. The **disabled** keyword prevents content from being published from users' home directories; **enabled** causes content to be published from the home directories of users specified in the SPACE-separated **user-list**. When you do not specify a **dirname**, Apache publishes content to **~/public_html**.

Apache can combine the effects of multiple UserDir directives. Suppose you have the following directives:

```
UserDir disabled
UserDir enabled user1 user2 user3
UserDir web
```

The first directive turns off user publishing for all users. The second directive enables user publishing for three users. The third directive makes **web** the name of the directory that, if it appears in one of the specified users' home directories, Apache publishes to the Web.

To cause a browser to display the content published by a user, specify in the location bar the name of the Web site followed by a **/~** and the user's username. For example, if Sam published content in the **public_html** directory in his home directory and the URI of the Web site was **www.example.com**, you would enter **http://www.example.com/~sam** to display Sam's Web page. To display a user's Web page, Apache must have execute permission (as user **apache**) for the user's home directory and the directory holding the content, and read permission for the content files.

Red Hat Linux provides the following ServerName directive and template in the **httpd.conf** file:

```
UserDir disable
#UserDir public_html
```

Put a pound sign (#) in front of the first line and remove the pound sign from the second line to allow users to publish content from directories named **public_html** in their home directories.

Contexts: **server config, virtual host**
Default: *RHEL* **public_html**, *FEDORA* none
Red Hat: disabled

DirectoryIndex *Specifies which file to display when a user asks for a directory.*

*DirectoryIndex **filename** [**filename** ...]*

where **filename** is the name of the file that Apache serves.

This directive specifies a list of filenames. When a client requests a directory, Apache attempts to find a file in the specified directory whose name matches a file in the list. When Apache finds a match, it returns that file. When this directive is absent or when none of the files specified by this directive exists in the specified directory, Apache displays a directory listing as specified by the IndexOptions directive (page 807).

FEDORA provides the following DirectoryIndex directive in the **httpd.conf** file:

```
DirectoryIndex  index.php index.html index.htm index.shtml
```

This directive causes Apache to return from the specified directory the file named **index.php, index.html, index.htm,** or **index.shtml.**

The **index.php** is the name of a PHP document; **index.html** and **index.htm** are the names of the standard, default HTML documents; and **index.shtml** is a secure HTML document. If you supply CGI documents, you may want to add the **index.cgi** value to this directive. The name **index** is standard but arbitrary.

A **.var** filename extension denotes a content-negotiated document that allows Apache to serve the Apache manual and other documents in one of several languages as specified by the client. If you are not providing content in different languages, you can omit this filename extension from the DirectoryIndex directive.

Contexts: **server config, virtual host**
Default: index.html
Red Hat: *RHEL* **index.html index.html.var**
     FEDORA **index.php index.html index.htm index.shtml**

CONTEXTS AND CONTAINERS

To make it flexible and easy to customize, Apache uses configuration directives, contexts, and containers. Configuration directives were covered in the previous section. This section discusses contexts and containers, which are critical to managing an Apache server.

CONTEXTS

Four locations, called *contexts,* define where a configuration directive can appear. This chapter marks each configuration directive to indicate which context(s) it can appear in. Table 26-1 describes each of these contexts.

Table 26-1   Contexts

Context	Location(s) directives can appear in
server config	Directive can appear in the **httpd.conf** file only, but not inside <VirtualHost> or <Directory> containers (next section) unless so marked
virtual host	Directive can appear inside <VirtualHost> containers in the **httpd.conf** file only
directory	Directive can appear inside <Directory>, <Location>, and <Files> containers in the **httpd.conf** file only
.htaccess	Directive can appear in **.htaccess** files (page 794) only

Directives in files incorporated by means of the Include directive (page 810) are part of the context they are included in and must be allowed in that context.

Putting a directive in the wrong context generates a configuration error and can cause Apache not to serve content correctly or not to start.

CONTAINERS

Containers, or *special directives,* are directives that group other directives. Containers are delimited by XML-style tags. Three examples are shown here:

```
<Directory> ... </Directory>

<Location> ... </Location>

<VirtualHost> ... </VirtualHost>
```

Look in **httpd.conf** for examples of containers. Like other directives, containers are limited to use within specified contexts. This section describes some of the more frequently used containers.

<Directory> *Applies directives to directories within specified directory hierarchies.*

*<Directory **directory**> ... </Directory>*

where **directory** is an absolute pathname specifying the root of the directory hierarchy that holds the directories the directives in the container apply to. The **directory** can include wildcards; a * does not match a /.

A <Directory> container provides the same functionality as a **.htaccess** file. While an administrator can use a <Directory> container in the **httpd.conf** file, regular users cannot. Regular users can use **.htaccess** files to control access to their own directories.

The directives in the <Directory> container shown in the following example apply to the **/var/www/html/corp** directory hierarchy: The Deny directive denies access to all clients, the Allow directive grants clients from the 192.168.10. subnet access, and the AllowOverride directive (page 813) enables the use of **.htaccess** files in the hierarchy:

```
<Directory /var/www/html/corp>
    Deny from all
    Allow from 192.168.10.
    AllowOverride All
</Directory>
```

Contexts: **server config, virtual host**

<Files> *Applies directives to specified ordinary files.*

*<Files **directory**> ... </Files>*

where **directory** is an absolute pathname specifying the root of the directory hierarchy that holds the ordinary files the directives in the container apply to. The **directory** can include wildcards; a * does not match a /. This container is similar to <Directory> but applies to ordinary files and not to directories.

The following directive, from the Red Hat **httpd.conf** file, denies access to all files whose filenames start with **.ht**. The tilde (~) changes how Apache interprets the following string. Without a tilde, the string is a simple shell match that interprets shell special characters (page 221). With a tilde, Apache interprets the string as a regular expression (page 967):

```
<Files ~ "^\.ht">
    Order allow,deny
    Deny from all
</Files>
```

Contexts: **server config, virtual host, directory, .htaccess**

<IfModule>   *Applies directives if a specified module is loaded.*

<IfModule [!]module-name> ... </IfModule>

where **module-name** is the name of the module (page 820) that is tested for. Apache executes the directives in this container if **module-name** is loaded or with **!** if **module-name** is not loaded.

Apache will not start if you specify a configuration directive that is specific to a module that is not loaded.

The following <IfModule> container from the Red Hat **httpd.conf** file depends on the **mod_mime_magic.c** module being loaded. If this module is loaded, Apache runs the MIMEMagicFile directive, which tells the **mod_mime_magic.c** module where its hints file is located.

```
<IfModule mod_mime_magic.c>
    MIMEMagicFile conf/magic
</IfModule>
```

See page 815 for another example of the <IfModule> container.

Contexts: **server config, virtual host, directory, .htaccess**

<Limit>   *Limits access-control directives to specified HTTP methods.*

<Limit method [method] ... > ... </Limit>

where **method** is an HTTP method. An HTTP method specifies which action is to be performed on a URI. The most frequently used methods are GET, PUT, POST, and OPTIONS; method names are case sensitive. GET, the default method, sends any data indicated by the URI. PUT stores data from the body section of the communication at the specified URI. POST creates a new document containing the body of the request at the specified URI. OPTIONS requests information about the capability of the server.

This container binds a group of access-control directives to specified HTTP methods: Only methods named by the <Limit> container are affected by this group of directives.

The following example disables HTTP uploads (PUTs) from systems that are not in a subdomain of **example.com**:

```
<Limit PUT>
order deny,allow
deny from all
allow from .example.com
</Limit>
```

Use <LimitExcept> instead of <Limit>

caution   It is safer to use the <LimitExcept> container instead of the <Limit> container, as the former protects against arbitrary methods. When you use <Limit>, you must be careful to name explicitly all possible methods that the group of directives could affect.

It is safer still not to put access-control directives in any container.

Contexts: **server config, virtual host, directory, .htaccess**

<LimitExcept>   *Limits access-control directives to all except specified HTTP methods.*

<LimitExcept method [method] ... > ... </LimitExcept>

where ***method*** is an HTTP method. See <Limit> for a discussion of methods.

This container causes a group of access-control directives *not* to be bound to specified HTTP methods: Methods *not* named in <LimitExcept> are affected by this group of directives.

The access-control directives within the following <LimitExcept> container affect HTTP methods other than GET and POST. You could put this container in a <Directory> container to limit its scope:

```
<LimitExcept GET POST OPTIONS>
        Order deny,allow
        Deny from all
    </LimitExcept>
```

Contexts: **server config, virtual host, directory, .htaccess**

<Location>   *Applies directives to specified URIs.*

<Location URI> ... </Location>

where ***URI*** points to content and specifies a file or the root of the directory hierarchy that the directives in the container apply to. While the <Directory> container points within the local filesystem, <Location> points outside the local filesystem. The ***URI*** can include wildcards; a ✻ does not match a /.

The following <Location> container limits access to **http://*server*/pop** to clients from the **example.net** domain, where *server* is the FQDN of the server:

```
<Location /pop>
    Order deny,allow
    Deny from all
    Allow from .example.net
</Location>
```

Contexts: **server config, virtual host**

Use <Location> with care

caution   Use this powerful container with care. Do not use it to replace the <Directory> container: When several URIs point to the same location in a filesystem, a client may be able to circumvent the desired access control by using a URI not specified by this container.

<LocationMatch> *Applies directives to matched URIs.*

<LocationMatch regexp> ... </LocationMatch>

where **regexp** is a regular expression that matches one or more URIs. This container works the same way as <Location>, except that it applies to any URIs that **regexp** matches:

```
# Disable autoindex for the root directory and present a
# default welcome page if no other index page is present.
#
<LocationMatch "^/$">
Options -Indexes
ErrorDocument 403 /error/noindex.html
</LocationMatch>
```

Contexts: **server config, virtual host**

<VirtualHost> *Applies directives to a specified virtual host.*

<VirtualHost addr[:port] [addr[:port]] ... > ... </VirtualHost>

where **addr** is an FQDN or IP address of the virtual host and **port** is the port that Apache listens on for the virtual host. This container holds commands that Apache applies to a virtual host. For an example and more information, refer to "Virtual Hosts" on page 818.

Context: **server config**

DIRECTIVES II: ADVANCED DIRECTIVES

This section discusses configuration directives that you may want to use after you have gained some experience with Apache.

DIRECTIVES THAT CONTROL PROCESSES

MaxClients *Specifies the maximum number of child processes.*

MaxClients num

where *num* is the maximum number of child processes (servers) Apache runs at one time, including idle processes and those serving requests. When Apache is running *num* processes and there are no idle processes, Apache issues **Server too busy** errors to new connections; it does not start new child processes. A value of 150 is usually sufficient, even for moderately busy sites.

Context: **server config**
Default: 256
Red Hat: 150

MaxRequestsPerChild

Specifies the maximum number of requests a child process can serve.

*MaxRequestsPerChild **num***

where *num* is the maximum number of requests a child process (server) can serve during its lifetime. After a child process serves *num* requests, it does not process any more requests but dies after it finishes processing its current requests. At this point additional requests are processed by other processes from the server pool.

Set *num* to 0 to not set a limit on the number of requests a child can process, except for the effects of MinSpareServers. By limiting the life of processes, this directive can prevent memory leaks from consuming too much system memory. However, setting MaxRequestsPerChild to a small value can hurt performance by causing Apache to create new child servers constantly.

Context: **server config**
Default: 10000
Red Hat: 4000

MaxSpareServers
Specifies the maximum number of idle processes.

*MaxSpareServers **num***

where *num* is the maximum number of idle processes (servers) Apache keeps running to serve requests as they come in. Do not set this number too high, as each process consumes system resources.

Context: **server config**
Default: 10
Red Hat: 20

MinSpareServers
Specifies the minimum number of idle processes.

*MinSpareServers **num***

where *num* is the minimum number of idle processes (servers) Apache keeps running to serve requests as they come in. More idle processes occupy more computer resources; increase this value for busy sites only.

Context: **server config**
Default: 5
Red Hat: 5

StartServers   *Specifies the number of child processes that Apache starts with.*

StartServers **num**

where **num** is the number of child processes, or servers, that Apache starts when it is brought up. This value is significant only when Apache starts; MinSpareServers and MaxSpareServers control the number of idle processes once Apache is up and running. Starting Apache with multiple servers ensures that a pool of servers is waiting to serve requests immediately.

Context: **server config**
Default: 5
Red Hat: 8

NETWORKING DIRECTIVES

HostnameLookups

Specifies whether Apache puts a client's hostname or its IP address in the logs.

HostnameLookups On | Off | Double

On: Performs DNS reverse name resolution (page 729) to determine the hostname of each client for logging purposes.

Off: Logs each client's IP address.

Double: To provide greater security, performs DNS reverse name resolution (page 729) to determine the hostname of each client, performs a forward DNS lookup to verify the original IP address, and logs the hostname.

Contexts: **server config, virtual host, directory**
Default: Off
Red Hat: Off

Lookups can consume a lot of system resources

tip   Use the **On** and **Double** options with caution: They can consume a lot of resources on a busy system. You can use a program such as logresolve to perform reverse name resolution offline for statistical purposes.

If you perform hostname resolution offline, you run the risk that the name may have changed; you usually want the name that was current at the time of the request. To minimize this problem, perform the hostname resolution as soon as possible after writing the log.

Timeout   *Specifies the time Apache waits for network operations to complete.*

Timeout **num**

where **num** is the number of seconds that Apache waits for network operations to finish. You can usually set this directive to a lower value; five minutes is a long time to wait on a busy server. The Apache documentation says that the default is not lower "because there may still be odd places in the code where the timer is not reset when a packet is sent."

Context: **server config**
Default: 300
Red Hat: 120

UseCanonicalName

Specifies the method the server uses to identify itself.

UseCanonicalName On | Off | DNS

On: Apache uses the value of the ServerName directive (page 796) as its identity.

Off: Apache uses the name and port from the incoming request as its identity.

DNS: Apache performs a DNS reverse name resolution (page 729) on the IP address from the incoming request and uses the result as its identity. Rarely used.

This directive is important when a server has more than one name and needs to perform a redirect. Red Hat sets this directive to Off because the ServerName directive (page 796) is commented out. Once you set ServerName, change UseCanonicalName to On. See page 817 for a discussion of redirects and this directive.

Contexts: **server config, virtual host, directory**
Default: *RHEL* On, *FEDORA* Off
Red Hat: *RHEL* Off, *FEDORA* On

LOGGING DIRECTIVES

ErrorLog *Specifies where Apache sends error messages.*

ErrorLog filename | syslog[:facility]

where *filename* specifies the name of the file, relative to ServerRoot (page 809), that Apache sends error messages to; *syslog* specifies that Apache send errors to **syslogd** (page 562); and *facility* specifies which **syslogd** facility to use. The default facility is local7.

Contexts: **server config, virtual host**
Default: **logs/error_log**
Red Hat: **logs/error_log**

LogLevel *Specifies the level of error messages that Apache logs.*

LogLevel level

where *level* specifies that Apache log errors of that level and higher (more urgent). Choose *level* from the following list, which is presented here in order of decreasing urgency and increasing verbosity:

emerg	System unusable messages
alert	Need for immediate action messages

crit	Critical condition messages
error	Error condition messages
warn	Nonfatal warning messages
notice	Normal but significant messages
info	Operational messages and recommendations
debug	Messages for finding and solving problems

Contexts: **server config, virtual host**
Default: warn
Red Hat: warn

DIRECTIVES THAT CONTROL CONTENT

AddHandler   *Creates a mapping between filename extensions and a builtin Apache handler.*

*AddHandler **handler extension** [extension] ...*

where ***handler*** is the name of a builtin handler and ***extension*** is a filename extension that maps to the ***handler***. Handlers are actions that are built into Apache and are directly related to loaded modules. Apache uses a handler when a client requests a file with a specified filename extension.

For example, the following AddHandler directive causes Apache to process files that have a filename extension of **.cgi** with the **cgi-script** handler:

```
AddHandler cgi-script .cgi
```

Contexts: **server config, virtual host, directory, .htaccess**
Default: none
Red Hat: type-map var

Alias   *Maps a URI to a directory or file.*

*Alias **alias pathname***

where ***alias*** must match part of the URI that the client requested to invoke the alias and ***pathname*** is the absolute pathname of the target of the alias, usually a directory.

For example, the following alias causes Apache to serve **/usr/local/pix/milk.jpg** when a client requests **http://www.example.com/pix/milk.jpg**:

```
Alias /pix /usr/local/pix
```

In some cases, you need to use a <Directory> container (page 799) to grant access to aliased content.

Contexts: **server config, virtual host**
Default: None
Red Hat: provides two aliases, one for **/icons/** and one for **/error/**

ErrorDocument   *Specifies the action Apache takes when the specified error occurs.*

*ErrorDocument **code action***

where ***code*** is the error code (page 826) that this directive defines a response for and ***action*** is one of the following:

string: Defines the message that Apache returns to the client.

absolute pathname: Points to a local script or other content that Apache redirects the client to.

URI: Points to an external script or other content that Apache redirects the client to.

When you do not specify this directive for a given error code, Apache returns a hardcoded error message when that error occurs. See page 816 for an explanation of how an ErrorDocument directive returns the Red Hat test page when the system is first installed.

Some examples of ErrorDocument directives follow:

```
ErrorDocument 403 "Sorry, access is forbidden."
ErrorDocument 403 /cgi-bin/uh-uh.pl
ErrorDocument 403 http://errors.example.com/not_allowed.html
```

Contexts: **server config, virtual host, directory, .htaccess**
Default: none; Apache returns hardcoded error messages
Red Hat: 403 /error/noindex.html; refer to "Red Hat test page" on page 816.

IndexOptions   Specifies how Apache displays directory listings.

*IndexOptions [±]**option** [[±]**option**]* ...

where ***option*** can be any combination of the following:

DescriptionWidth=*n*: Sets the width of the description column to *n* characters. Use ✲ in place of *n* to accommodate the widest description.

FancyIndexing: In directory listings, displays column headers that are links. When you click one of these links, Apache sorts the display based on the content of the column. Clicking a second time reverses the order.

FoldersFirst: Sorts the listing so that directories come before plain files. Use only with FancyIndexing.

HTMLTable: *FEDORA* Displays a directory listing in a table.

IconsAreLinks: Makes the icons clickable. Use only with FancyIndexing.

IconHeight=*n*: Sets the height of icons to *n* pixels. Use only with IconWidth.

IconWidth=*n*: Sets the width of icons to *n* pixels. Use only with IconHeight.

IgnoreCase: Ignores case when sorting names.

IgnoreClient: Ignores options the client supplied in the URI.

NameWidth=*n*: Sets the width of the filename column to *n* characters. Use * in place of *n* to accommodate the widest filename.

ScanHTMLTitles: Extracts and displays titles from HTML documents. Use only with FancyIndexing. Not normally used because it is CPU and disk intensive.

SuppressColumnSorting: Suppresses clickable column headings that can be used for sorting columns. Use only with FancyIndexing.

SuppressDescription: Suppresses file descriptions. Use only with FancyIndexing.

SuppressHTMLPreamble: Suppresses the contents of the file specified by the HeaderName directive, even if that file exists.

SuppressIcon: Suppresses icons. Use only with FancyIndexing.

SuppressLastModified: Suppresses the modification date. Use only with FancyIndexing.

SuppressRules: Suppresses horizontal lines. Use only with FancyIndexing.

SuppressSize: Suppresses file sizes. Use only with FancyIndexing.

VersionSort: Sorts version numbers (in filenames) in a natural way; character strings, except for substrings of digits, are not affected.

As an example, suppose a client requests a URI that points to a directory (such as **http://www.example.com/support/**) and none of the files specified by the Directory-Index directive (page 797) is present in that directory. If the directory hierarchy is controlled by a **.htaccess** file and AllowOverride (page 813) has been set to allow indexing, then Apache displays a directory listing according to the options specified by this directive.

When this directive appears more than once within a directory, Apache merges the options from the directives. Use + and – to merge options with options from higher-level directories. (Unless you use + or – with all options, Apache discards any options set in higher-level directories.) For example, the following directives and containers set the options for **/custsup/download** to VersionSort; Apache discards FancyIndexing and IgnoreCase in the **download** directory because there is no + or – before VersionSort in the second <Directory> container:

```
<Directory /custsup>
    IndexOptions FancyIndexing
    IndexOptions IgnoreCase
</Directory>

<Directory /custsup/download>
    IndexOptions VersionSort
</Directory>
```

Because + appears before VersionSort, the next directives and containers set the options for **/custsup/download** to FancyIndexing, IgnoreCase, and VersionSort:

```
<Directory /custsup>
    IndexOptions FancyIndexing
    IndexOptions IgnoreCase
</Directory>

<Directory /custsup/download>
    IndexOptions +VersionSort
</Directory>
```

Contexts: **server config, virtual host, directory, .htaccess**
Default: none; lists only filenames
Red Hat: FancyIndexing VersionSort NameWidth=*

ServerRoot *Specifies the root directory for server files (not content).*

*ServerRoot **directory***

where ***directory*** specifies the pathname of the root directory for files that make up the server. Apache prepends ***directory*** to relative pathnames in **httpd.conf**. This directive does not specify the location of the content that Apache serves; the DocumentRoot directive (page 796) performs that function. Do not change this value unless you move the server files.

Context: **server config**
Default: **/usr/local/apache**
Red Hat: **/etc/httpd**

ServerTokens *Specifies the server information that Apache returns to a client.*

ServerTokens Prod | Major | Minor | Min | OS | Full

Prod: Returns the product name (**Apache**). Also ***ProductOnly***.

Major: Returns the major release number of the server (**Apache/2**).

Minor: Returns the major and minor release numbers of the server (**Apache/2.2**).

Minimal: Returns the complete version (**Apache/2.2.0**). Also ***Min***.

OS: Returns the name of the operating system and the complete version (**Apache/2.2.0 (Red Hat Linux)**). Provides less information that might help a malicious user than *Full* does.

Full: Same as *OS*, plus sends the names and versions of non-Apache group modules (**Apache/2.2.0 (Red Hat Linux) PHP/5.1.2**).

Unless you want clients to know the details of the software you are running for some reason, set ServerTokens to reveal as little as possible.

Context: **server config**
Default: Full
Red Hat: OS

ServerSignature   *Adds a line to server-generated pages.*

ServerSignature On | Off | EMail

On: Turns the signature line on. The signature line contains the server version as specified by the ServerTokens directive (page 809) and the name specified by the <VirtualHost> container (page 802).

Off: Turns the signature line off.

EMail: To the signature line, adds a **mailto:** link to the server email address. This option produces output that can attract spam. See ServerAdmin (page 795) for information on specifying an email address.

Contexts: **server config, virtual host, directory, .htaccess**
Default: Off
Red Hat: On

CONFIGURATION DIRECTIVES

Group   *Sets the GID of the processes that run the servers.*

Group #groupid | groupname

where *groupid* is a GID value, preceded by a **#**, and *groupname* is the name of a group. The processes (servers) that Apache spawns are run as the group specified by this directive. See the User directive (page 812) for more information.

Context: **server config**
Default: #–1
Red Hat: apache

Include   *Loads directives from files.*

Include filename | directory

where *filename* is the relative pathname of a file that contains directives. Apache prepends ServerRoot (page 809) to *filename*. The directives in *filename* are included in the file holding this directive at the location of the directive. Because *filename* can include wildcards, it can specify more than one file.

The *directory* is the relative pathname that specifies the root of a directory hierarchy that holds files containing directives. Apache prepends ServerRoot to *directory*. The directives in ordinary files in this hierarchy are included in the file holding this directive at the location of the directive. The *directory* can include wildcards.

When you install Apache and its modules, rpm puts configuration files, which have a filename extension of **conf**, in the **conf.d** directory within the ServerRoot directory. The Include directive in the Red Hat **httpd.conf** file incorporates module configuration files for whichever modules are installed.

Contexts: **server config, virtual host, directory**
Default: none
Red Hat: **conf.d/*.conf**

LoadModule *Loads a module.*

LoadModule module filename

where **module** is the name of an external DSO module and **filename** is the relative pathname of the named module. Apache prepends ServerRoot (page 809) to **filename**. Apache loads the external module specified by this directive. For more information refer to "Modules" on page 820.

Context: **server config**
Default: none; nothing is loaded by default if this directive is omitted
Red Hat: loads more than 40 modules; refer to **httpd.conf** for the list

Options *Controls server features by directory.*

Options [±]option [[±]option ...]

This directive controls which server features are enabled for a directory hierarchy. The directory hierarchy is specified by the container this directive appears in. A + or the absence of a – turns an option on and a – turns it off.

The **option** may be one of the following:

None None of the features this directive can control are enabled.

All All of the features this directive can control are enabled, except for Multi-Views, which you must explicitly enable.

ExecCGI Apache can execute CGI scripts (page 821).

FollowSymLinks Apache follows symbolic links.

Includes Permits SSIs (server-side includes, page 821). SSIs are containers embedded in HTML pages that are evaluated on the server before the content is passed to the client.

IncludesNOEXEC The same as Includes but disables the **#exec** and **#exec cgi** commands that are part of SSIs. Does *not* prevent the **#include** command from referencing CGI scripts.

Indexes Generates a directory listing if DirectoryIndex (page 797) is not set.

MultiViews Allows multiviews (page 818).

SymLinksIfOwnerMatch The same as FollowSymLinks but follows the link only if the file or directory being pointed to has the same owner as the link.

The following Options directive from the Red Hat **httpd.conf** file sets the Indexes and FollowSymLinks options and, because the <Directory> container specifies the **/var/www/html** directory hierarchy (the document root), affects all content:

```
<Directory "/var/www/html">
    Options Indexes FollowSymLinks
...
<Directory>
```

Context: **directory**
Default: All
Red Hat: None

ScriptAlias   *Maps a URI to a directory or file and declares the target to be a server (CGI) script.*

ScriptAlias alias pathname

where ***alias*** must match part of the URI the client requested to invoke the Script-Alias and ***pathname*** is the absolute pathname of the target of the alias, usually a directory. Similar to the Alias directive, this directive specifies that the target is a CGI script (page 821).

The following ScriptAlias directive from the Red Hat **httpd.conf** file maps client requests that include **/cgi-bin/** to the **/var/www/cgi-bin** directory (and indicates that these requests will be treated as CGI requests):

```
ScriptAlias /cgi-bin/ "/var/www/cgi-bin/"
```

Contexts: **server config, virtual host**
Default: none
Red Hat: /cgi-bin/ "/var/www/cgi-bin"

User   *Sets the UID of the processes that run the servers.*

User #userid | username

where ***userid*** is a UID value, preceded by a **#**, and ***username*** is the name of a local user. The processes (servers) that Apache spawns are run as the user specified by this directive.

Apache must start as **root** to listen on a privileged port. For reasons of security, Apache's child processes (servers) run as nonprivileged users. The default UID of −1 does not map to a user under Red Hat Linux. Instead, Red Hat's **httpd** package creates a user named **apache** during installation and sets User to that user.

Context: **server config**
Default: #−1
Red Hat: **apache**

Do not set User to **root** or **0**

security   For a more secure system, do not set User to **root** or **0** (zero) and do not allow the **apache** user to have write access to the DocumentRoot directory hierarchy (except as needed for storing data), especially not to configuration files.

Security Directives

Allow   *Specifies which clients can access specified content.*

Allow from All | host [host ...] | env=var [env=var ...]

This directive, which must be written as **Allow from**, grants access to a directory hierarchy to the specified clients. The directory hierarchy is specified by the container or **.htaccess** file this directive appears in.

All: Serves content to any client.

host: Serves content to the client(s) specified by *host,* which can take several forms: *host* can be an FQDN, a partial domain name (such as **example.com**), an IP address, a partial IP address, or a network/netmask pair.

var: Serves content when the environment variable named *var* is set. You can set a variable with the SetEnvIf directive. See the Order directive (page 814) for an example.

Contexts: **directory, .htaccess**
Default: none; default behavior depends on the Order directive
Red Hat: All

AllowOverride *Specifies the classes of directives that are allowed in .htaccess files.*

*AllowOverride All | None | **directive-class** [**directive-class** ...]*

This directive specifies whether Apache read **.htaccess** files in the directory hierarchy specified by its container. If Apache does reads **.htaccess** files, this directive specifies which kinds of directives are valid within **.htaccess** files.

None: Ignores **.htaccess** files.

All: Allows all classes of directives in **.htaccess** files.

The **directive-class** is one of the following directive class identifiers:

AuthConfig: Class of directives that control authorization (AuthName, AuthType, Require, and so on). This class is used mostly in **.htaccess** files to require a username and password to access the content. For more information refer to "Authentication Modules and .htaccess" on page 824.

FileInfo: Class of directives that controls document types (DefaultType, ErrorDocument, SetHandler, and so on).

Indexes: Class of directives relating to directory indexing (DirectoryIndex, FancyIndexing, IndexOptions, and so on).

Limit: Class of client access directives (Allow, Deny, and Order).

Options: Class of directives controlling directory features.

Context: **directory**
Default: All
Red Hat: None

Deny *Specifies which clients are not allowed to access specified content.*

*Deny from All | **host** [**host** ...] | env=var [env=var ...]*

This directive, which must be written as **Deny from,** denies access to a directory hierarchy to the specified clients. The directory hierarchy is specified by the container or **.htaccess** file this directive appears in. See the Order directive (page 814) for an example.

All: Denies content to all clients.

host: Denies content to the client(s) specified by *host,* which can take several forms: *host* can be an FQDN, a partial domain name (such as **example.com**), an IP address, a partial IP address, or a network/netmask pair.

var: Denies content when the environment variable named *var* is set. You can set a variable with the SetEnvIf directive.

Contexts: **directory, .htaccess**
Default: none
Red Hat: none

Order   *Specifies default access and the order in which Allow and Deny directives are evaluated.*

Order Deny,Allow | Allow,Deny

Deny,Allow: Allows access by default; denies access only to clients specified in Deny directives. (First evaluates Deny directives, then evaluates Allow directives.)

Allow,Deny: Denies access by default; allows access only to clients specified in Allow directives. (First evaluates Allow directives, then evaluates Deny directives.)

Access granted or denied by this directive applies to the directory hierarchy specified by the container or **.htaccess** file this directive appears in.

There must not be SPACEs on either side of the comma. Although Red Hat Linux has a default of Allow,Deny, which denies access to all clients not specified by Allow directives, the next directive in **httpd.conf**, **Allow from all**, grants access to all clients:

```
Order allow,deny
Allow from all
```

You can restrict access by specifying Deny,Allow to deny all access and then specifying only those clients you want to grant access to in an Allow directive. The following directives grant access to clients from the **example.net** domain only and would typically appear within a <Directory> container (page 799):

```
Order deny,allow
Deny from all
Allow from .example.net
```

Contexts: **directory, .htaccess**
Default: Deny,Allow
Red Hat: Allow,Deny

THE RED HAT httpd.conf FILE

This section highlights some of the important features of the Red Hat **httpd.conf** file, which is based on the **httpd.conf** file distributed by Apache. This heavily commented file is broken into the following parts (as is this section):

1. **Global Environment**: Controls the overall functioning of the Apache server.

2. **Main Server Configuration**: Configures the default server (as opposed to virtual hosts) and provides default configuration information for virtual hosts.

3. **Virtual Hosts**: Configures virtual hosts. For more information refer to "Virtual Hosts" on page 818.

SECTION 1: GLOBAL ENVIRONMENT

ServerTokens   The ServerTokens directive (page 809) is set to **OS**, which causes Apache, when queried, to return the name of the operating system and the complete version number of Apache:

```
ServerTokens OS
```

ServerRoot   The ServerRoot directive (page 809) is set to **/etc/httpd**, which is the pathname that Apache prepends to relative pathnames in **httpd.conf**:   .

```
ServerRoot "/etc/httpd"
```

<IfModule>   Multiprocessing modules (MPMs) allow you to change the way Apache works by changing the modules it uses. The <IfModule> containers (page 800) allow you to use the same **httpd.conf** file with different modules: The directives in an <IfModule> container are executed only if the specified module is loaded.

The section of **httpd.conf** that starts with the comment

```
## Server-Pool Size Regulation (MPM specific)
```

holds two <IfModule> containers (page 800) that configure Apache, depending on which module, **prefork** or **worker**, is loaded. Red Hat ships Apache with the **prefork** module loaded; this section does not discuss the <IfModule> container for the **worker** module. (See the comments in the **/etc/sysconfig/httpd** file if you want to load the **worker** module.)

The **prefork** <IfModule> container, shown below, holds directives that control the functioning of Apache when it starts and as it runs:

```
<IfModule prefork.c>
StartServers        8
MinSpareServers     5
MaxSpareServers    20
ServerLimit       256
MaxClients        256
MaxRequestsPerChild  4000
</IfModule>
```

Listen   *FEDORA* The Listen directive (page 795) does not specify an IP address.

RHEL The Listen directive specifies an IP address of 0.0.0.0, which is the same as not specifying an IP address, so Apache listens on all network interfaces.

```
Listen 80
```

LoadModule   There are quite a few LoadModule directives (page 811); these directives load the Apache DSO modules (page 820).

Include   The Include directive (page 810) includes the files that match *.conf in the /etc/httpd/conf.d directory, as though they were part of httpd.conf:

```
Include conf.d/*.conf
```

Red Hat test page   When you first install Apache, there is no index.html file in /var/www/html; when you point a browser at the local Web server, Apache generates error 403, which returns the Red Hat test page. The mechanism by which this page is returned is convoluted: The Red Hat httpd.conf file holds an Include directive that includes all files in the conf.d directory that is in the ServerRoot directory (page 809). The welcome.conf file in this directory contains an ErrorDocument 403 directive (page 807) that redirects users who receive this error to error/noindex.html in the DocumentRoot directory (page 796). The noindex.html file is the Red Hat test page that confirms the server is working but there is no content to display.

SECTION 2: MAIN SERVER CONFIGURATION

ServerAdmin,   As Red Hat Linux is shipped, the ServerAdmin and ServerName directives are com-
ServerName   mented out. Change them to useful values as suggested in the ServerAdmin (page 795) and ServerName (page 796) sections.

DocumentRoot   The DocumentRoot directive (page 796) appears as follows:

```
DocumentRoot "/var/www/html"
```

You need to modify this directive only if you want to put your content somewhere other than /var/www/html.

<Directory>   The following <Directory> container (page 799) sets up a restrictive environment for the entire local filesystem (specified by /):

```
<Directory />
    Options FollowSymLinks
    AllowOverride None
</Directory>
```

The Options directive (page 811) allows Apache to follow symbolic links but disallows many options. The AllowOverride directive (page 813) causes Apache to ignore .htaccess files. You must explicitly enable less restrictive options if you want them, but be aware that doing so can expose the root filesystem and compromise system security.

Next another <Directory> container sets up less restrictive options for the DocumentRoot (/var/www/html). The code in httpd.conf is interspersed with many comments. Without the comments it looks like this:

```
<Directory "/var/www/html">
    Options Indexes FollowSymLinks
    AllowOverride None
    Order allow,deny
    Allow from all
</Directory>
```

The Indexes option in the Options directive allows Apache to display directory listings. The Order (page 814) and Allow (page 812) directives combine to allow requests from all clients. This container is slightly less restrictive than the preceding one, although it still does not allow Apache to follow directives in **.htaccess** files.

DirectoryIndex As explained on page 797, the DirectoryIndex directive causes Apache to return the file named **index.php**, **index.html**, **index.htm**, or **index.shtml** from a requested directory. Because Options Indexes is specified in the preceding <Directory> container, if none of these files exists in a queried directory, Apache returns a directory listing:

```
DirectoryIndex  index.php index.html index.htm index.shtml
```

There are many more directives in this part of the **httpd.conf** file. The comments in the file provide a guide as to what they do. There is nothing here you need to change as you get started using Apache.

Section 3: Virtual Hosts

All lines in this section are comments or commented-out directives. If you want to set up virtual hosts, see page 818.

Redirects

Apache can respond to a request for a URI by asking the client to request a different URI. This response is called a *redirect*. A redirect works because redirection is part of the HTTP implementation: Apache sends the appropriate response code and the new URI, and a compliant browser requests the new location.

The Redirect directive can establish an explicit redirect that sends a client to a different page when a Web site is moved. Or, when a user enters the URI of a directory in a browser but leaves off the trailing slash, Apache can automatically redirect the client to the same URI terminated with a slash.

UseCanonicalName The ServerName directive (page 796), which establishes the name of the server, and the UseCanonicalName directive (page 805) are both important when a server has more than one name and needs to perform an automatic redirect. For example, assume the server with the name **zach.example.com** and the alias **www.example.com** has ServerName set to **www.example.com**. When a client specifies a URI of a directory but leaves off the trailing slash (**zach.example.com/dir**), Apache has to perform a redirect to determine the URI of the requested directory. When UseCanonicalName is set to On, Apache uses the value of ServerName and returns **www.example.com/dir/**. With UseCanonicalName set to Off, Apache uses the name from the incoming request and returns **zach.example.com/dir/**.

MULTIVIEWS

Multiviews is a way to represent a page in different ways, most commonly in different languages. Using request headers, a browser can request a specific language from a server. Servers that cannot handle these requests ignore them.

RHEL Multiviews is demonstrated by the Apache manual, which can be installed locally in **/var/www/manual** (**httpd-manual** package). When you point a browser to **http://**server**/manual/index.html**, the browser displays the page in the browser's default language. If you change the browser's default language setting and reload the page, the browser displays the page in the new language. The browser can display the pages in different languages because the server has a copy of the page for each language. For example, the files **index.html.en** and **index.html.de** both exist in the **/var/www/manual** directory.

SERVER-GENERATED DIRECTORY LISTINGS (INDEXING)

When a client requests a directory, the Apache configuration determines what is returned to the client. Apache can return a file as specified by the DirectoryIndex directive (page 797), a directory listing if no file matches DirectoryIndex and the Options Indexes directive (page 811) is set, or an error message if no file matches DirectoryIndex and Options Indexes is not set.

VIRTUAL HOSTS

Apache supports *virtual hosts,* which means that one instance of Apache can respond to requests directed to multiple IP addresses or hostnames as though it were multiple servers. Each IP address or hostname can then provide different content and be configured differently.

There are two types of virtual hosts: *host-by-name* and *host-by-IP*. Host-by-name relies on the FQDN the client uses in its request to Apache—for example, **www.example.com** versus **www2.example.com**. Host-by-IP examines the IP address the host resolves as and responds according to that match.

Host-by-name is handy if there is only one IP address, but Apache must support multiple FQDNs. Although you can use host-by-IP if a given Web server has aliases, Apache should serve the same content regardless of which name is used.

Virtual hosts inherit their configurations from **httpd.conf** Section 1 (page 815) and Section 2 (page 816). In Section 3, <VirtualHost> containers create the virtual hosts and specify directives that override inherited and default values. You can specify many virtual hosts for a single instance of Apache.

The following <VirtualHost> container sets up a host-by-name for the site named **intranet.example.com**. This virtual host handles requests that are directed to **intranet.example.com**.

```
<VirtualHost intranet.example.com>
    ServerName intranet.example.com
    DocumentRoot /usr/local/www
    ErrorLog /var/log/httpd/intra.error_log
    CustomLog /var/log/httpd/intra.server_log
    <Directory /usr/local/www>
        Order deny,allow
        Deny from all
        Allow from 192.168.  # allow from private subnet only
    </Directory>
</VirtualHost>
```

TROUBLESHOOTING

You can use service and the **httpd** init script to check the syntax of the Apache configuration files:

```
# service httpd configtest
Syntax OK
```

Once you start the **httpd** daemon, you can confirm that Apache is working correctly by pointing a browser on the local system at **http://localhost/**. From a remote system, use **http://*server/***, substituting the hostname of the server for *server*. In response, Apache displays the Red Hat test page.

If the browser does not display the test page, it will display one of two errors: **Connection refused** or an error page. If you get a **Connection refused** error, make sure that port 80 is not blocked by a firewall (page 788) and check that the server is running:

```
# /sbin/service httpd status
httpd (pid 21406 21405 21404 21403 21402 21401 13622) is running...
```

If the server is running, check that you did not specify a port other than 80 in a Listen directive. If you did, the URI you specify in the browser must reflect this port number (**http://localhost:*port*** specifies port *port*). Otherwise, check the error log (**/var/log/httpd/error_log**) for information on what is not working.

To verify that the browser is not at fault, use telnet to try to connect to port 80 of the server:

```
$ telnet www.example.com 80
Trying 192.0.34.166...
Connected to www.example.com.
Escape character is '^]'.
CONTROL-]
telnet> quit
Connection closed.
```

If **Connection refused** is displayed, you have verified that you cannot get through to the server.

Modules

Apache is a skeletal program that relies on external modules, called dynamic shared objects (DSOs), to provide most of its functionality. This section lists these modules and discusses some of the more important ones. In addition to the modules included with Red Hat Linux, many other modules are available. See httpd.apache.org/modules for more information.

Module List

Following is a list of some of the modules that are available under Apache:

access   (mod_access.so) Controls access based on client characteristics.
actions   (mod_actions.so) Allows execution of CGI scripts based on the request method.
alias   (mod_alias.so) Allows outside directories to be mapped to DocumentRoot.
asis   (mod_asis.so) Allows sending files that contain their own headers.
auth   (mod_auth.so) Provides user authentication via **.htaccess**.
auth_anon   (mod_auth_anon.so) Provides anonymous user access to restricted areas.
auth_dbm   (mod_auth_dbm.so) Uses DBM files for authentication.
auth_digest   (mod_auth_digest.so) Uses MD5 digest for authentication.
autoindex   (mod_autoindex.so) Allows directory indexes to be generated.
cern_meta   (mod_cern_meta.so) Allows the use of CERN **httpd** metafile semantics.
cgi   (mod_cgi.so) Allows the execution of CGI scripts.
dav   (mod_dav.so) Allows Distributed Authoring and Versioning.
dav_fs   (mod_dav_fs.so) Provides a filesystem for mod_dav.
dir   (mod_dir.so) Allows directory redirects and listings as index files.
env   (mod_env.so) Allows CGI scripts to access environment variables.
expires   (mod_expires.so) Allows generation of Expires HTTP headers.
headers   (mod_headers.so) Allows customization of request and response headers.
imap   (mod_imap.so) Allows image maps to be processed on the server side.
include   (mod_include.so) Provides server-side includes (SSIs).
info   (mod_info.so) Allows the server configuration to be viewed.
log_config   (mod_log_config.so) Allows logging of requests made to the server.
mime   (mod_mime.so) Allows association of file extensions with content.
mime_magic   (mod_mime_magic.so) Determines MIME types of files.
negotiation   (mod_negotiation.so) Allows content negotiation.
proxy   (mod_proxy.so) Allows Apache to act as a proxy server.
proxy_connect   (mod_proxy_connect.so) Allows connect request handling.
proxy_ftp   (mod_proxy_ftp.so) Provides an FTP extension proxy.
proxy_http   (mod_proxy_http.so) Provides an HTTP extension proxy.
rewrite   (mod_rewrite.so) Allows on-the-fly URI rewriting based on rules.
setenvif   (mod_setenvif.so) Sets environment variables based on a request.
speling   (mod_speling.so) Auto-corrects spelling if the requested URI has incorrect capitalization and one spelling mistake.
status   (mod_status.so) Allows the server status to be queried and viewed.

unique_id (mod_unique_id.so) Generates a unique ID for each request.
userdir (mod_userdir.so) Allows users to have content directories (public_html).
usertrack (mod_usertrack.so) Allows tracking of user activity on a site.
vhost_alias (mod_vhost_alias.so) Allows the configuration of virtual hosting.

mod_cgi AND CGI SCRIPTS

The CGI (Common Gateway Interface) allows external application programs to interface with Web servers. Any program can be a CGI program if it runs in real time (at the time of the request) and relays its output to the requesting client. Various kinds of scripts, including shell, Perl, Python, and PHP, are the most commonly encountered CGI programs because a script can call a program and reformat its output in HTML for a client.

Apache can handle requests for CGI programs in several different ways. The most common method is to put a CGI program in the **cgi-bin** directory and then enable its execution from that directory only. The location of the **cgi-bin** directory, as specified by the ScriptAlias directive (page 812), is **/var/www/cgi-bin**. Alternatively, an AddHandler directive (page 806) can identify filename extensions of scripts, such as **.cgi** or **.pl**, within the regular content (for example, **AddHandler cgi-script .cgi**). If you use AddHandler, you must also specify the ExecCGI option in an Options directive within the appropriate <Directory> container. The **mod_cgi** module must be loaded to access and execute CGI scripts.

The following Perl CGI script displays the Apache environment. This script should be used for debugging only because it presents a security risk if outside clients can access it:

```perl
#!/usr/bin/perl
##
##  printenv -- demo CGI program that prints its environment
##

print "Content-type: text/plain\n\n";
foreach $var (sort(keys(%ENV))) {
    $val = $ENV{$var};
    $val =~ s|\n|\\n|g;
    $val =~ s|"|\\"|g;
    print "${var}=\"${val}\"\n";
}
```

mod_ssl

SSL (Secure Sockets Layer), which is implemented by the **mod_ssl** module, has two functions: It allows a client to verify the identity of a server and it enables secure two-way communication between a client and a server. SSL is used on Web pages with forms that require passwords, credit card numbers, or other sensitive data.

Apache uses the HTTPS protocol—not HTTP—for SSL communication. When Apache uses SSL, it listens on a second port (443 by default) for a connection and performs a handshaking sequence before sending the requested content to the client.

Server verification is critical for financial transactions. After all, you do not want to give your credit card number to a fraudulent Web site posing as a known company. SSL uses a certificate to positively identify a server. Over a public network such as the Internet, the identification is reliable only if the certificate contains a digital signature from an authoritative source such as VeriSign or Thawte. SSL Web pages are denoted by a URI beginning with **https://**.

Data encryption prevents malicious users from eavesdropping on Internet connections and copying personal information. To encrypt communication, SSL sits between the network and an application and encrypts communication between the server and the client.

SETTING UP mod_ssl

The **/etc/httpd/conf.d/ssl.conf** file configures **mod_ssl**. The first few directives in this file load the **mod_ssl** module, instruct Apache to listen on port 443, and set various parameters for SSL operation. About a third of the way through the file is a section labeled **SSL Virtual Host Context** that sets up virtual hosts (page 818).

A <VirtualHost> container in **ssl.conf** is similar to one in **httpd.conf**. As with any <VirtualHost> container, it holds directives such as ServerName and ServerAdmin that need to be configured. In addition, it holds some SSL-related directives.

USING A SELF-SIGNED CERTIFICATE FOR ENCRYPTION

If you require SSL for encryption and not verification—that is, if the client already trusts the server—you can generate and use a self-signed certificate, bypassing the time and expense involved in obtaining a digitally signed certificate. Self-signed certificates generate a warning when you connect to the server: Most browsers display a dialog box that allows you to examine and accept the certificate. The **sendmail** daemon also uses certificates (page 650).

The self-signed certificate depends on two files: a private key and the certificate. The location of each file is specified in **/etc/httpd/conf.d/ssl.conf**. The files have different names and are stored in different locations under *FEDORA* and *RHEL*.

FEDORA
```
# grep '^SSLCertificate' /etc/httpd/conf.d/ssl.conf
SSLCertificateFile /etc/pki/tls/certs/localhost.crt
SSLCertificateKeyFile /etc/pki/tls/private/localhost.key
```

To generate the private key that the encryption relies on, cd to **/etc/pki/tls/certs** and enter a make command:

```
# cd /etc/pki/tls/certs
# make localhost.key
umask 77 ; \
/usr/bin/openssl genrsa -des3 1024 > localhost.key
Generating RSA private key, 1024 bit long modulus
...............++++++
.........++++++
e is 65537 (0x10001)
Enter pass phrase:
Verifying - Enter pass phrase:
```

The preceding command generates a file named **localhost.key** that is protected by the pass phrase you entered: *You will need this pass phrase to start the server.* Keep the **server.key** file secret.

The next command generates the certificate. This process uses the private key you just created. You need to supply the same pass phrase you entered when you created the private key.

```
# make localhost.crt
umask 77 ; \
/usr/bin/openssl req -utf8 -new -key localhost.key -x509 -days 365 -out
localhost.crt -set_serial 0
Enter pass phrase for localhost.key:
You are about to be asked to enter information that will be incorporated
into your certificate request.
What you are about to enter is what is called a Distinguished Name or a DN.
There are quite a few fields but you can leave some blank
For some fields there will be a default value,
If you enter '.', the field will be left blank.
-----
Country Name (2 letter code) [GB]:US
State or Province Name (full name) [Berkshire]:California
Locality Name (eg, city) [Newbury]:San Francisco
Organization Name (eg, company) [My Company Ltd]:Sobell Associates Inc.
Organizational Unit Name (eg, section) []:
Common Name (eg, your name or your server's hostname) []:www.sobell.com
Email Address []:mgs@sobell.com
```

The answers to the first five questions are arbitrary: They can help clients identify a site when they examine the certificate. The answer to the sixth question (**Common Name**) is critical. Because certificates are tied to the name of the server, you must enter the server's FQDN accurately. If you mistype this information, the server name and that of the certificate will not match. The browser will then generate a warning message each time a connection is made.

As specified by **ssl.conf**, Apache looks for the files in the directory that you created them in. Do not move these files. After you restart Apache, the new certificate will be in use.

RHEL   The process of creating the key and certificate is similar under *RHEL*. The following output shows the location of the two files:

```
# grep '^SSLCertificate' /etc/httpd/conf.d/ssl.conf
SSLCertificateFile /etc/httpd/conf/ssl.crt/server.crt
SSLCertificateKeyFile /etc/httpd/conf/ssl.key/server.key
```

To generate the private key, **cd** to **/etc/httpd/conf** and give the command **make server.key**. From the same directory, give the command **make server.crt** to generate the certificate. These commands create files in the working directory. Next move **server.key** into the **ssl.key** directory, and **server.crt** into the **ssl.crt** directory. After you restart Apache, the new certificate will be in use.

NOTES ON CERTIFICATES

- Although the server name is part of the certificate, the SSL connection is tied to the IP address of the server: You can have only one certificate per IP address. For multiple virtual hosts to have separate certificates, you must specify host-by-IP rather than host-by-name virtual hosts (page 818).

- As long as the server is identified by the name for which the certificate was issued, you can use the certificate on another server and/or IP address.

- A root certificate (root CA) is the certificate that signs the server certificate. Every browser contains a database of the public keys for the root certificates of the major signing authorities, including VeriSign and Thawte.

- It is possible to generate a root certificate (root CA) and sign all your server certificates with this root CA. Regular clients can import the public key of the root CA so that they recognize every certificate signed by that root CA. This setup is convenient for a server with multiple SSL-enabled virtual hosts and no commercial certificates. For more information see www.modssl.org/docs/2.8/ssl_faq.html#ToC29.

- You cannot use a self-signed certificate if clients need to verify the identity of the server.

AUTHENTICATION MODULES AND .htaccess

To restrict access to a Web page, Apache and third parties provide authentication modules and methods that can verify a user's credentials, such as a username and password. Some modules enable authentication against various databases including *LDAP* (page 1040) and NIS (page 655).

User authentication directives are commonly placed in a **.htaccess** file. A basic **.htaccess** file that uses the Apache default authentication module (**mod_auth**) follows. Substitute appropriate values for the local server.

```
# cat .htaccess
AuthUserFile /var/www/.htpasswd
AuthGroupFile /dev/null
AuthName "Browser dialog box query"
AuthType Basic
require valid-user
```

The **/var/www/.htpasswd** is a typical absolute pathname of a **.htpasswd** file and **Browser dialog box query** is the string that the user will see as part of the dialog box that requests a username and password.

The second line of the preceding **.htaccess** file turns off the group function. The fourth line specifies the user authentication type **Basic**, which is implemented by the default **mod_auth** module. The last line tells Apache which users can access the protected directory. The entry **valid-user** grants access to the directory to any user who is in the Apache password file and who enters the correct password. You can also specify Apache usernames separated by SPACEs.

You can put the Apache password file anywhere on the system, as long as Apache can read it. It is safe to put this file in the same directory as the **.htaccess** file because, by default, Apache will not answer any requests for files whose names start with **.ht**.

The following command creates a **.htpasswd** file for Sam:

```
$ htpasswd -c .htpasswd sam
New password:
Re-type new password:
Adding password for user sam
```

Omit the **–c** option to add a user or to change a password in an existing **.htpasswd** file. Remember to use an AllowOverride directive (page 813) to permit Apache to read the **.htaccess** file.

SCRIPTING MODULES

Apache can process content before serving it to a client. In earlier versions of Apache, only CGI scripts could process content. In the current version, *scripting modules* can work with scripts that are embedded in HTML documents.

Scripting modules manipulate content before Apache serves it to a client. Because they are built into Apache, they are fast. Scripting modules are especially efficient at working with external data sources such as relational databases. Clients can pass data to a scripting module that modifies the information that Apache serves.

Contrast scripting modules with CGI scripts that are run externally to Apache: CGI scripts do not allow client interaction and are slow because they must make external calls.

Red Hat provides packages that allow you to embed Perl, Python, and PHP code in HTML content. Perl and Python, which are general-purpose scripting languages, are encapsulated for use directly in Apache and are implemented in the **mod_perl** and **mod_python** modules, respectively.

PHP, which was developed for manipulating Web content, outputs HTML by default. Implemented in the **mod_php** module, this language is easy to set up, has a syntax similar to Perl and C, and comes with a large number of Web-related functions.

webalizer: ANALYZES WEB TRAFFIC

The **webalizer** package, which is typically installed as part of Apache, creates a directory at **/var/www/usage** and a cron file (page 547) at **/etc/cron.daily/00webalizer**. Once a day, the cron file generates usage data and puts it in the **usage** directory; you can view this data by pointing a browser at **http://***server***/usage/**, where *server* is the hostname of the server.

The **/etc/webalizer.conf** file controls the behavior of the webalizer utility. If you change the location of the DocumentRoot or log files, you must edit this file to reflect those changes. For more information on webalizer, refer to the webalizer man page and the sites listed under "More Information" on page 787.

MRTG: MONITORS TRAFFIC LOADS

Multi Router Traffic Grapher (MRTG) is an open-source application that graphs statistics available through SNMP (Simple Network Management Protocol). SNMP information is available on all high-end routers and switches, as well as on some other networked equipment, such as printers and wireless access points. You can use the **net-snmp** and **net-snmp-utils** packages supplied by Red Hat to install SNMP on a system. You also need to install the **mrtg** package.

Once MRTG and SNMP are installed and running, you can view the reports at **http://*server*/mrtg**, where *server* is the FQDN of the server. For more information see the mrtg man page and the sites listed under "More Information" on page 787.

ERROR CODES

Following is a list of Apache error codes:

100 Continue
101 Switching Protocols
200 OK
201 Created
202 Accepted
203 Non-Authoritative Information
204 No Content
205 Reset Content
206 Partial Content
300 Multiple Choices
301 Moved Permanently
302 Moved Temporarily
303 See Other
304 Not Modified
305 Use Proxy
400 Bad Request
401 Unauthorized
402 Payment Required
403 Forbidden
404 Not Found
405 Method Not Allowed
406 Not Acceptable

407 Proxy Authentication Required
408 Request Time-out
409 Conflict
410 Gone
411 Length Required
412 Precondition Failed
413 Request Entity Too Large
414 Request-URI Too Large
415 Unsupported Media Type
500 Internal Server Error
501 Not Implemented
502 Bad Gateway
503 Service Unavailable
504 Gateway Time-out
505 HTTP Version not supported

CHAPTER SUMMARY

Apache is the most popular Web server on the Internet today. It is both robust and extensible. The **/etc/httpd/conf/httpd.conf** configuration file controls many aspects of how Apache runs. The Red Hat **httpd.conf** file, which is based on the **httpd.conf** file distributed by Apache, is heavily commented and broken into three parts: Global Environment, Main Server Configuration, and Virtual Hosts. You can use the system-config-httpd utility to modify **httpd.conf**.

Content to be served must be placed in **/var/www/html**, called the document root. Apache automatically displays the file named **index.html** in this directory.

Configuration directives, or simply directives, are lines in a configuration file that control some aspect of how Apache functions. Four locations, called contexts, define where a configuration directive can appear: **server config**, **virtual host**, **directory**, and **.htaccess**. Containers, or special directives, are directives that group other directives.

To restrict access to a Web page, Apache and third parties provide authentication modules and methods that can verify a user's credentials, such as a username and password. Some modules enable authentication against various databases, including LDAP and NIS.

Apache can respond to a request for a URI by asking the client to request a different URI. This response is called a redirect. Apache can also process content before serving it to a client using scripting modules that work with scripts embedded in HTML documents.

Apache supports virtual hosts, which means that one instance of Apache can respond to requests directed to multiple IP addresses or hostnames as though it were multiple servers. Each IP address or hostname can provide different content and be configured differently.

The CGI (Common Gateway Interface) allows external application programs to interface with Web servers. Any program can be a CGI program if it runs in real time and relays its output to the requesting client.

SSL (Secure Sockets Layer) has two functions: It allows a client to verify the identity of a server and it enables secure two-way communication between a client and server.

EXERCISES

1. How would you tell Apache that your content is in **/usr/local/www**?

2. How would you instruct an Apache server to listen on port 81 instead of port 80?

3. How would you enable Sam to publish Web pages from his **~/website** directory but not allow anyone else to publish to the Web?

4. Apache must be started as **root**. Why? Why does this action not present a security risk?

ADVANCED EXERCISES

5. If you are running Apache on a firewall system, perhaps to display a Web front end for firewall configuration, how would you make sure that it is accessible only from inside the local network?

6. Why is it more efficient to run scripts using **mod_php** or **mod_perl** than through CGI?

7. What two things does SSL provide and how does this differ if the certificate is self-signed?

8. Some Web sites generate content by retrieving data from a database and inserting it into a template using PHP or CGI each time the site is accessed. Why is this practice often a poor idea?

9. Assume you want to provide Webmail access for employees on the same server that hosts the corporate Web site. The Web site address is example.com, you want to use mail.example.com for Webmail, and the Webmail application is located in **/var/www/webmail**. Describe two ways you can set this up this configuration.

10. Part of a Web site is a private intranet and is accessed as http://example.com/intranet. Describe how you would prevent people outside the company from accessing this site. Assume the company uses the 192.168.0.0/16 subnet internally.

PART VI
Programming

27

PROGRAMMING TOOLS

With its rich set of languages and development tools, the Linux operating system provides an outstanding environment for programming. C is one of the most popular system programming languages to use in conjunction with Linux, in part because the operating system itself is written mostly in C. Using C, programmers can easily access system services using function libraries and system calls. In addition, a variety of helpful tools can facilitate the development and maintenance of programs.

This chapter explains how to compile and link C programs. It introduces the GNU gdb debugger and tools that provide feedback about memory, disk, and CPU resources. It also covers some of the most useful software development tools: the make utility and CVS (Concurrent Versions System). The make utility helps you keep track of which program modules have been updated and helps ensure that you use the latest versions of all program modules when you compile a program. CVS is a source code management system that tracks the versions of files involved in a project.

PROGRAMMING IN C

A major reason that the Linux system provides an excellent C programming environment is that C programs can easily access the services of the operating system. System calls—the routines that make operating system services available to programmers—can be made from C programs. These system calls provide such services as creating files, reading from and writing to files, collecting information about files, and sending signals to processes. When you write a C program, you can use system calls in the same way you use ordinary C program modules, or *functions*, that you have written. For more information refer to "System Calls" on page 861.

Several *libraries* of functions have been developed to support programming in C. These libraries are collections of related functions that you can use just as you use your own functions and the system calls. Many of the library functions access basic operating system services through system calls, providing the services in ways that are better suited to typical programming tasks. Other library functions, such as the math library functions, serve special purposes.

This chapter describes the processes of writing and compiling C programs. However, it will *not* teach you to program in C.

CHECKING YOUR COMPILER

The C compiler in common use on Linux is GNU gcc, which comes as part of Red Hat Linux distributions (www.gnu.org/software/gcc/gcc.html). If it is not already present on the system you are working on, you need to install the **gcc** package. Give the following command to determine whether you have access to the gcc compiler:

```
$ gcc --version
bash: gcc: command not found
```

If you get a response other than version information, either the compiler is not installed or your **PATH** variable does not contain the necessary pathname (usually gcc is installed in **/usr/bin**). If you get version information from the gcc command, the GNU C compiler is installed.

Next make sure that the compiler is functioning. As a simple test, create a file named **Makefile** with the following lines. The line that starts with **gcc** must be indented by using a TAB, not SPACES.

```
$ cat Makefile
morning: morning.c
TAB gcc -o morning morning.c
```

Now create a source file named **morning.c** with the following lines:

```
$ cat morning.c
#include <stdio.h>
int main(int argc, char** argv) {
    printf("Good Morning\n");
    return 0;
}
```

Compile the file with the command **make morning**. When it compiles successfully, the resulting file will be executable; you can run the program by giving the command **morning** or **./morning**. When you get output from this program, you know that you have a working C compiler.

```
$ make morning
gcc -o morning morning.c
$ morning
Good Morning
```

A C PROGRAMMING EXAMPLE

To create or modify a C program, you must use an editor, such as emacs or vim. The name of the C program file must end in **.c**. Entering the source code for a program is similar to typing a memo or shell script. Although emacs and vim "know" that you are editing a C program, other editors may not know whether your file is a C program, a shell script, or an ordinary text document. You are responsible for making the contents of the file syntactically suitable for the C compiler to process.

Figure 27-1 (next page) illustrates the structure of a simple C program named **tabs.c**. The first two lines of the program are comments that describe what the program does. The string /* identifies the beginning of the comment, and the string */ identifies the end of the comment; the C compiler ignores all characters between them. Because a comment can span two or more lines, the */ at the end of the first line and the /* at the beginning of the second line are not necessary but are included for clarity. As the comment explains, the program reads standard input, converts TAB characters into the appropriate number of SPACEs, and writes the transformed input to standard output. Like many Linux utilities, this program is a filter.

The comments at the top of **tabs.c** are followed by *preprocessor directives,* which are instructions for the C preprocessor. During the initial phase of compilation the C preprocessor expands these directives, readying the program for the later stages of the compilation process. Preprocessor directives begin with the pound sign (#) and may optionally be preceded by SPACE and TAB characters.

Symbolic constants   You can use the #define preprocessor directive to define symbolic constants and macros. *Symbolic constants* are names that you can use in a program in place of constant values. For example, **tabs.c** uses a #define preprocessor directive to associate the symbolic constant TABSIZE with the constant 8. The preprocessor then uses TABSIZE in place of the constant 8 as the distance between TAB stops. By convention the names of symbolic constants consist of all uppercase letters.

By defining symbolic names for constant values, you can make a program both easier to read and easier to modify. If you later decide to change a constant, you need to change only the preprocessor directive; you do not need to change the value everywhere it occurs in the program. If you replace the #define directive for TABSIZE in Figure 27-1 with the following directive, the program will place TAB stops every four columns rather than every eight:

```
#define    TABSIZE    4
```

```
 1  /* convert tabs in standard input to spaces in */
 2  /* standard output while maintaining columns */
 3
 4  #include        <stdio.h>
 5  #define         TABSIZE        8
 6
 7  /* prototype for function findstop */
 8  int findstop(int *);
 9
10  int main()
11  {
12  int c;          /* character read from stdin */
13  int posn = 0;   /* column position of character */
14  int inc;        /* column increment to tab stop */
15
16  while ((c = getchar()) != EOF)
17          switch(c)
18                  {
19                  case '\t':              /* c is a tab */
20                          inc = findstop(&posn);
21                          for( ; inc > 0; inc-- )
22                                  putchar(' ');
23                          break;
24                  case '\n':              /* c is a newline */
25                          putchar(c);
26                          posn = 0;
27                          break;
28                  default:                /* c is anything else */
29                          putchar(c);
30                          posn++;
31                          break;
32                  }
33  return 0;
34  }
35
36  /* compute size of increment to next tab stop */
37
38  int findstop(int *col)
39  {
40  int retval;
41  retval = (TABSIZE - (*col % TABSIZE));
42
43  /* increment argument (current column position) to next tabstop */
44  *col += retval;
45
46  return retval;          /* main gets how many blanks for filling */
47  }
```

Comments

Preprocessor directives

Function prototype

Main function

Function

Figure 27-1   A simple C program: **tabs.c** (The line numbers are not part of the source code.)

Macros   A symbolic constant, which is a type of *macro,* maps a symbolic name to *replacement text.* Macros are handy when the replacement text is needed at multiple points throughout the source code or when the definition of the macro is subject to change. The process of substituting the replacement text for the symbolic name is called *macro expansion.*

You can also use #define directives to define macros with arguments. Use of such a macro resembles a function call. Unlike C functions, however, macros are replaced with C code prior to compilation into object files.

The NEXTTAB macro computes the distance to the next TAB stop, given the current column position **curcol**:

```
#define NEXTTAB(curcol) (TABSIZE - ((curcol) % TABSIZE))
```

This definition uses the symbolic constant TABSIZE, whose definition must appear prior to NEXTTAB in the source code. The macro NEXTTAB could be used in **tabs.c** to assign a value to **retval** in the function **findstop**:

```
retval = NEXTTAB(*col);
```

Headers (include files) When modules of a program use several macro definitions, the definitions are typically collected together in a single file called a *header file* or an *include file*. Although the C compiler does not place constraints on the names of header files, by convention they end in **.h**. The name of the header file is listed in an #include preprocessor directive in each program source file that uses any of the macros. The program in Figure 27-1 uses **getchar** and **putchar**, which are functions defined in **stdio.h**. The **stdio.h** header file, which defines a variety of general-purpose macros, is used by many C library functions.

The angle brackets (< and >) that surround **stdio.h** in **tabs.c** instruct the C preprocessor to look for the header file in a standard list of directories (such as **/usr/include**). To include a header file from another directory, enclose its pathname between double quotation marks. You can specify an absolute pathname within the double quotation marks or you can give a relative pathname. If you give a relative pathname, searching begins with the working directory and then moves to the same directories that are searched when the header file is surrounded by angle brackets. By convention header files that you supply are surrounded by double quotation marks.

You can also specify directories to be searched for header files by using the –I option to the C compiler. Assume that you want to compile the program **deriv.c**, which contains the following preprocessor directive:

```
#include "eqns.h"
```

If the header file **eqns.h** is located in the subdirectory **myincludes**, you can compile **deriv.c** with the –I option to tell the C preprocessor to look for **eqns.h** there:

```
$ gcc -I./myincludes deriv.c
```

When the C preprocessor encounters the #include directive in the **deriv.c** file, it will look for **eqns.h** in the **myincludes** subdirectory of the working directory.

Use relative pathnames for include files

tip Using absolute pathnames for include files does not work if the location of the header file within the filesystem changes. Using relative pathnames for header files works as long as the location of the header file relative to the working directory remains the same. Relative pathnames also work with the **–I** option on the gcc command line and allow header files to be moved.

Function prototype Preceding the definition of the function **main** is a *function prototype*. This declaration tells the compiler what type a function returns, how many arguments a function expects, and what the types of those arguments are. In **tabs.c** the prototype for the function **findstop** informs the compiler that **findstop** returns type *int* and that it expects a single argument of type *pointer to int*:

```
int findstop(int *);
```

Once the compiler has seen this declaration, it can detect and flag inconsistencies in the definition and the uses of the function. As an example, suppose that you replaced the reference to **findstop** in **tabs.c** with the following statement:

```
inc = findstop();
```

The prototype for **findstop** would cause the compiler to detect a missing argument and issue an error message. You could then easily fix the problem. When a function is present in a separate source file or is defined after it is referenced in a source file (as **findstop** is in the example), the function prototype helps the compiler check that the function is being called properly. Without the prototype, the compiler would not issue an error message and the problem might manifest itself as unexpected behavior during execution. At this late point, finding the bug might be difficult and time-consuming.

Functions   Although you can name most C functions anything you want, each program must have exactly one function named **main**. The function **main** is the control module: A program begins execution with the function **main**, which typically calls other functions, which in turn may call still other functions, and so forth. By putting different operations into separate functions, you can make a program easier to read and maintain. For example, the program in Figure 27-1 uses the function **findstop** to compute the distance to the next TAB stop. Although the few statements of **findstop** could easily have been included in the **main** function, isolating them in a separate function draws attention to a key computation.

Functions can make both development and maintenance of the program more efficient. By putting a frequently used code segment into a function, you avoid entering the same code into the program over and over again. When you later want to modify the code, you need change it only once.

If a program is long and includes several functions, you may want to split it into two or more files. Regardless of its size, you may want to place logically distinct parts of a program in separate files. A C program can be split into any number of different files; however, each function must be wholly contained within a single file.

Use a header file for multiple source files

tip   When you are creating a program that takes advantage of multiple source files, put #define preprocessor directives into a header file. Then use an include statement with the name of the header file in any source file that uses those directives.

COMPILING AND LINKING A C PROGRAM

To compile **tabs.c** and create an executable file named **a.out**, give the following command:

```
$ gcc tabs.c
```

The gcc utility calls the C preprocessor, the C compiler, the assembler, and the linker. Figure 27-2 shows these four components of the compilation process. The C

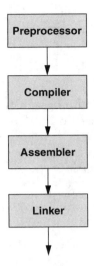

Figure 27-2   The compilation process

preprocessor expands macro definitions and includes header files. The compilation phase creates assembly language code corresponding to the instructions in the source file. Next the assembler creates machine-readable object code. One object file is created for each source file. Each object file has the same name as the source file, except that the .c extension is replaced with .o. After successfully completing all phases of the compilation process for a program, the C compiler creates the executable file and removes any .o files.

During the final phase of the compilation process, the linker searches specified libraries for functions the program uses and combines object modules for those functions with the program's object modules. By default, the C compiler links the standard C library **libc.so** (usually found in **/lib**), which contains functions that handle input and output and provides many other general-purpose capabilities. If you want the linker to search other libraries, you must use the –l (lowercase "l") option to specify the libraries on the command line. Unlike most options to Linux system utilities, the –l option does not precede all filenames on the command line but rather appears after the filenames of all modules that it applies to. In the next example, the C compiler searches the math library **libm.so** (usually found in **/lib**):

```
$ gcc calc.c -lm
```

The –l option uses abbreviations for library names, appending the letter following –l to **lib** and adding a .so or .a extension. The **m** in the example stands for **libm.so**.

Using the same naming mechanism, you can have a graphics library named **libgraphics.a**, which can be linked with the following command:

```
$ gcc pgm.c -lgraphics
```

When you use this convention to name libraries, gcc knows to search for them in **/usr/lib** and **/lib**. You can also have gcc search other directories by using the –L option:

```
$ gcc pgm.c -L. -L/opt/libgraphics/lib/ -lgraphics
```

The preceding command causes gcc to search for library files in the working directory and in the **/opt/libgraphics/lib** directory before searching in the default locations (typically **/usr/lib** and **/lib**). A library might be installed in one of these special locations if it were built from source and not installed using rpm. The final part of the command line instructs the linker to search for and link **libgraphics.a** with the executable file created by gcc.

As the last step of the compilation process, the linker creates an executable file named **a.out** unless you specify a different filename with the –o option. Object files are deleted after the executable is created.

ELF format | You may occasionally encounter references to the **a.out** format, an old UNIX binary format. Linux uses the Executable and Linking Format (ELF) for binaries; recent versions of gcc produce this format—not the **a.out** format, despite the filename. Use the file utility (page 135) to display the format of the executable that gcc generates:

```
$ file a.out
a.out: ELF 32-bit LSB executable, Intel 80386, version 1 (SYSV), for
GNU/Linux 2.6.9, dynamically linked (uses shared libs), for GNU/Linux
2.6.9, not stripped
```

In the next example, the –O3 option causes gcc to use the C compiler *optimizer*. The optimizer makes object code more efficient so that the executable program runs more quickly. Optimization has many facets, including locating frequently used variables and taking advantage of processor-specific features. The number after the –O indicates the level of optimization, where a higher number specifies more optimization. See the gcc info page for specifics. The following example also shows that the **.o** files are no longer present after **a.out** is created:

```
$ ls
acctspay.c  acctsrec.c  ledger.c
$ gcc -O3 ledger.c acctspay.c acctsrec.c
$ ls
a.out  acctspay.c  acctsrec.c  ledger.c
```

You can use the executable **a.out** in the same way you use shell scripts and other programs: by typing its name on the command line. The program in Figure 27-1 on page 834 expects to read from standard input. Thus, once you have created the executable **a.out**, you can use a command such as the following to run it:

```
$ ./a.out < mymemo
```

If you want to save the **a.out** file, you should change its name to a more descriptive one. Otherwise, you might accidentally overwrite it during a later compilation.

```
$ mv a.out accounting
```

To save yourself the trouble of renaming an **a.out** file, you can specify the name of the executable file on the gcc command line. The −o option causes the C compiler to give the executable the name you specify rather than **a.out**. In the next example, the executable is named **accounting**:

```
$ gcc -o accounting ledger.c acctspay.c acctsrec.c
```

If **accounting** does not require arguments, you can run it with the following command:

```
$ accounting
```

You can suppress the linking phase of compilation by using the −c option with the gcc command. Because the −c option does not treat unresolved external references as errors, it allows you to compile and debug the syntax of the modules of a program as you create them. Once you have compiled and debugged all of the modules, you can run gcc again with the object files as arguments to produce an executable program. In the next example, gcc produces three object files but no executable:

```
$ gcc -c ledger.c acctspay.c acctsrec.c
$ ls
acctspay.c  acctspay.o  acctsrec.c  acctsrec.o  ledger.c  ledger.o
```

Now if you run gcc again and name the object files on the command line, gcc will produce the executable. Because it recognizes the filename extension .o, the C compiler knows that the files need only to be linked. You can also include both .c and .o files on a single command line:

```
$ gcc -o accounting ledger.o acctspay.c acctsrec.o
```

The C compiler recognizes that the .c file needs to be preprocessed and compiled, whereas the .o files do not. The C compiler also accepts assembly language files ending in .s and assembles and links them. This feature makes it easy to modify and recompile a program.

You can create a series of files to divide a project into functional groups. For instance, you might put graphics routines in one file, string functions in another file, and database calls in a third file. Having multiple files can enable several engineers to work on the same project concurrently and can speed up compilation. For example, if all functions are in one file and you change one of the functions, the compiler must recompile all of the functions in the file. Recompiling the entire program may take considerable time even if you made only a small change. When you separate functions into different files, only the file that you change must be recompiled. For large programs with many source files (for example, the C compiler or emacs), the time lost by recompiling one huge file for every small change would be enormous. For more information refer to "make: Keeps a Set of Programs Current" on page 842.

What not to name a program

tip   Do not name a program **test** or any other name of a builtin or other executable on the local system. If you do, you will likely execute the builtin or other program instead of the program you intend to run. Use which (page 144) to determine which program you will run when you give a command.

USING SHARED LIBRARIES

Most modern operating systems use *shared* libraries, also called *dynamic* libraries. These libraries are not linked into a program at compile time but rather are loaded when the program starts (or later in some cases). The names of files housing shared libraries have filename extensions of **.so** (shared object)—for example, **libc.so**. Usually **libaaa.so** is a symbolic link to **libaaa.so.x**, where *x* is a small number representing the version of the library. Many of these libraries are kept in **/usr/lib**. A typical Linux installation has more than 300 shared libraries in **/usr/lib**. Applications can have their own shared libraries. For example, the gcc compiler might keep its libraries in **/usr/lib/gcc-lib/i386-redhat-linux/3.4.0**.

Archived libraries

In contrast to shared libraries are the older, *statically linked* libraries (with a **.a** filename extension), also called *archived* libraries. Archived libraries are added to the executable file during the last (linking) phase of compilation. Their addition can make a program run slightly faster the first time it is run, albeit at the expense of program maintainability and size. Taken together, the combined size of several executables that use a shared library and the size of the shared library are smaller than the combined size of the same executables with static libraries. When a running program has already loaded a dynamic library, a second program that requires the same dynamic library starts slightly faster.

Reducing memory usage and increasing maintainability are the primary reasons for using shared object libraries; thanks to these advantages, they have largely replaced statically linked libraries as the library type of choice. Consider what happens when you discover an error in a library. With a static library, you must relink every program that uses the library once the library has been fixed and recompiled. In contrast, with a dynamic library, you need to fix and recompile only the library itself.

Shared object libraries also make dynamic loading of program libraries on the fly possible (for example, perl, python, and tcl extensions and modules). For example, the Apache (HTTP) Web server specifies modules in the **httpd.conf** file and loads them as needed.

ldd

The ldd (list dynamic dependencies) utility tells you which shared libraries a program needs. The following example shows that cp uses **libacl**, the Access Control Lists library; **libc**, the C library; **libattr**, the Extended Attributes library; and **ld-linux**, the runtime linker:

```
$ ldd /bin/cp
        linux-gate.so.1 => (0x00ef8000)
        libacl.so.1 => /lib/libacl.so.1 (0x00c81000)
        libselinux.so.1 => /lib/libselinux.so.1 (0x00570000)
        libc.so.6 => /lib/libc.so.6 (0x0027b000)
        libattr.so.1 => /lib/libattr.so.1 (0x00b92000)
        libdl.so.2 => /lib/libdl.so.2 (0x003ce000)
        libsepol.so.1 => /lib/libsepol.so.1 (0x00aed000)
        /lib/ld-linux.so.2 (0x0025e000)
```

Running ldd on **/usr/bin/gnome-session** (a program that starts a graphical GNOME session) lists 69 libraries from **/usr/lib** and **/lib**.

The program that does the dynamic runtime linking, ld-linux.so, always looks in **/usr/lib** for libraries. The other directories that ld searches vary depending on how ld is set up. You can add directories for ld to look in by specifying a search path at compile (actually link) time, using the –r option followed by a colon-separated list of directories (do not put a SPACE after –r). Use only absolute pathnames in this search path. Although you use this option on the gcc command line, it is passed to the linker (ld). The gnome-session desktop manager was likely linked with a command such as the following:

> gcc *flags* –o gnome-session *objects* –r/lib *libraries*

This command line allows ld.so (and ldd) to search **/lib** in addition to the standard **/usr/lib** for the libraries needed by the executable.

The compiler needs to see the shared libraries at link time to confirm that the needed functions and procedures are present as promised by the header (**.h**) files. Use the –L option to tell the compile-time linker to look in the directory **mylib** for shared or static libraries: –L **mylib**. Unlike the search path, –L can use relative pathnames such as –L **../lib**—a handy feature when a program builds its own shared library. The library can be in one location at build time (–L) but in another location at runtime after it is installed (–**rpath**). The SPACE after –L is optional and is usually omitted; –r must not be followed by a SPACE. You can repeat the –L and the –r options multiple times on the link line.

FIXING BROKEN BINARIES

The command line search path is a fairly new idea. The search path was traditionally specified by using the **LD_LIBRARY_PATH** and, more recently, **LD_RUN_PATH** environment variables. These variables have the same format as **PATH** (page 292). The directories in **LD_LIBRARY_PATH** are normally searched before the usual library locations. Newer Linux releases extend the function of **LD_LIBRARY_PATH** to specify directories to be searched either before or after the normal locations. See the ld man page for details. The **LD_RUN_PATH** variable behaves similarly to **LD_LIBRARY_PATH**. If you use –r, however, **LD_LIBRARY_PATH** supersedes anything in **LD_RUN_PATH**.

The use of **LD_LIBRARY_PATH** brings up several problems. Because only one environment variable exists, it must be shared among all programs. If two programs have the same name for a library or use different, incompatible versions of the same library, only the first will be found. As a result one of the programs will not run or—even worse—will not run correctly.

Wrappers   **LD_LIBRARY_PATH** still has its place in the scripts, called *wrappers,* that are used to fix broken binaries. Suppose that the broken binary **bb** uses the shared library **libbb.so**, which you want to put in **/opt/bb/lib** and not in **/usr/lib**, as the **bb** programmer requested. The command **ldd bb** will tell you which libraries are missing.

LD_LIBRARY_PATH

security   Under certain circumstances a malicious user can create a Trojan horse named **libc.so** and place it in a directory that is searched before **/usr/lib** (any directory that appears in **LD_LIBRARY_PATH** before **/usr/lib**). The fake **libc** will then be used instead of the real **libc**.

This is not a problem: Rename **bb** to **bb.broken**, and create a **/bin/sh** wrapper named **bb**.

```
#!/bin/sh
LD_LIBRARY_PATH=/opt/bb/lib
export LD_LIBRARY_PATH
exec bb.broken "$@"
```

Using **$@** rather than **$*** preserves SPACEs in the parameters; see page 922.

A wrapper can also allow you to install programs in arbitrary locations.

CREATING SHARED LIBRARIES

Building a dynamically loadable shared library is not a trivial matter: It involves setting up reentrant function calls, defining a library entrance routine, and performing other tasks. When you want to create a shared object library, you must compile the source files with the **–fPIC** (position-independent code) option to gcc and link the resulting object files into the **lib*xx*.so** file using the **–shared –x** options to the linker (for example, ld **–shared –x –o libmylib.so *.o**). The best resource for investigating shared library construction and usage is existing code on the Internet. For example, you can look at the source files for zlib at www.gzip.org/zlib.

C++   C++ files have special needs, and libraries (shared or not) often have to be made by the compiler rather than ld or ar. Shared libraries can depend on other shared libraries and have their own search paths. If you set **LD_LIBRARY_PATH**, add the **–i** flag to the link phase when compiling to ignore the current **LD_LIBRARY_PATH** or you may have unexpected results. Ideally you would not have **LD_LIBRARY_PATH** set on a global level but would use it only in wrappers as needed.

make: KEEPS A SET OF PROGRAMS CURRENT

This section covers the GNU make program

tip   This section describes the GNU make program. Other make tools (BSN make, GNUstep make, Borland make, and so on) are available as well as similar tools such as ant (the Apache build tool). Makefiles created for GNU make are often incompatible with other make tools, which can be problematic if you are trying to compile code targeted for another platform.

In a large program with many source and header files, the files typically depend on one another in complex ways. When you change a file that other files depend on, you *must* recompile all dependent files. For example, you might have several source

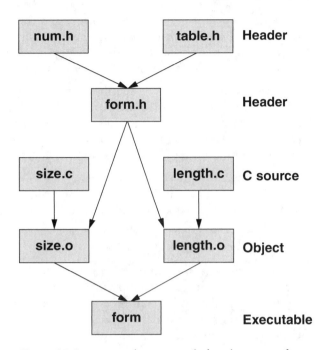

Figure 27-3   Dependency graph for the target **form**

files, all of which use a single header file. When you change the header file, you must recompile each of the source files. The header file might depend on other header files, and so forth. Figure 27-3 shows a simple example of these kinds of dependency relationships. Each arrow in this figure points from a file to another file that depends on it.

When you are working on a large program, it can be difficult, time-consuming, and tedious to determine which modules need to be recompiled because of their dependency relationships. The make utility automates this process.

Dependency lines: target files and prerequisite files At its simplest, make looks at *dependency lines* in a file named **makefile** or **Makefile** in the working directory. The dependency lines indicate relationships among files, specifying a *target file* that depends on one or more *prerequisite files*. If you have modified any of the prerequisite files more recently than their target file, make updates the target file based on construction commands that follow the dependency line. The make utility normally stops if it encounters an error during the construction process.

The file containing the updating information for the make utility is called a *makefile*. (See page 832 for a trivial example.) A simple makefile has the following syntax:

> *target: prerequisite-list*
> TAB *construction-commands*

The dependency line consists of the *target* and the *prerequisite-list*, separated by a colon. Each *construction-commands* line (you may have more than one) must start with a TAB and must follow the dependency line. Long lines can be continued by placing a BACKSLASH (\) as the last character on the line.

The *target* is the name of the file that depends on the files in the *prerequisite-list*. The *construction-commands* are regular shell commands that construct (usually compile and/or link) the target file. The make utility executes the *construction-commands* when the modification time of one or more files in the *prerequisite-list* is more recent than that of the target file.

The following example shows the dependency line and construction commands for the file named **form** in Figure 27-3. The **form** file depends on the prerequisites **size.o** and **length.o**. An appropriate gcc command constructs the **target**:

```
form: size.o length.o
TAB     gcc -o form size.o length.o
```

Each of the prerequisites on one dependency line can be a target on another dependency line. For example, both **size.o** and **length.o** are targets on other dependency lines. Although the example in Figure 27-3 illustrates a simple case, in other situations the nesting of dependency specifications can create a complex hierarchy that dictates relationships among many files.

The following makefile (named **Makefile**) corresponds to the complete dependency structure shown in Figure 27-3. The executable file **form** depends on two object files, and each of these object files depends on its respective source file and a header file, **form.h**. In turn, **form.h** depends on two other header files.

```
$ cat Makefile
form: size.o length.o
        gcc -o form size.o length.o
size.o: size.c form.h
        gcc -c size.c
length.o: length.c form.h
        gcc -c length.c
form.h: num.h table.h
        cat num.h table.h > form.h
```

Although the last line would not normally be seen in a makefile, it illustrates the point that you can put any shell command on a construction line. Because the shell processes makefiles, the command line should be one that you could enter in response to a shell prompt.

The following command builds the default target **form** if any of its prerequisites are more recent than their corresponding targets or if any of the targets do not exist:

```
$ make
```

Thus, if the file **form** has been deleted, make will rebuild it, regardless of the modification dates of its prerequisite files. The first target in a makefile is the default and is built when you call make without any arguments.

If you want make to rebuild a target other than the first one in the makefile, you must provide that target as an argument to make. The following command rebuilds only **form.h** if it does not exist or if its prerequisites were more recently modified than the target:

```
$ make form.h
```

IMPLIED DEPENDENCIES

You can rely on *implied* dependencies and construction commands to facilitate the job of writing a makefile. For instance, if you do not include a dependency line for an object file, make assumes that the object file depends on a compiler or assembler source code file. Thus, if a prerequisite for a target file is **xxx.o** and no dependency line identifies **xxx.o** as a target, make looks at the filename extension to determine how to build the .o file. If it finds an appropriate source file, make provides a default construction command line that calls the proper compiler or the assembler to create the object file. Table 27-1 lists some filename extensions that make recognizes and the type of file that corresponds to each filename extension.

Table 27-1   Filename extensions

Filename with extension	Type of file
filename.c	C programming language source code
filename.C, filename.cc, filename.cxx, filename.c++, filename.cpp	C++ programming language source code
filename.f	Fortran programming language source code
filename.h	Header file
filename.l	flex, lex lexical analyzer generator source code
filename.m	Objective-C programming language source code
filename.o	Object module
filename.s	Assembler code
filename.sh	Shell script
filename.y	bison, yacc parser generator source code

C and C++ are traditional programming languages that are available with Red Hat many other Linux distributions. The bison and flex tools create command languages.

In the next example, a makefile keeps the file named **compute** up-to-date. The make utility ignores any line that begins with a pound sign (#), so the first three lines of the following makefile are comment lines. The first dependency line shows that **compute** depends on two object files: **compute.o** and **calc.o**. The corresponding construction line gives the command that make needs to produce **compute**. The second dependency line shows that **compute.o** depends not only on its C source file but also on the **compute.h** header file. The construction line for **compute.o** uses the C compiler optimizer (**–O3** option). The third set of dependency and construction lines is not required. In their absence, make infers that **calc.o** depends on **calc.c** and produces the command line needed for the compilation:

```
$ cat Makefile
#
# Makefile for compute
#
compute: compute.o calc.o
        gcc -o compute compute.o calc.o

compute.o: compute.c compute.h
        gcc -c -O3 compute.c

calc.o: calc.c
        gcc -c calc.c

clean:
        rm *.o *core* *~
```

There are no prerequisites for **clean**, the last target. This target is commonly used to get rid of extraneous files that may be out-of-date or no longer needed, such as **.o** files.

Below are some sample executions of make based on the previous makefile. As the ls command shows, **compute.o**, **calc.o**, and **compute** are not up-to-date. Consequently the make command runs the construction commands that re-create them.

```
$ ls -ltr
total 22
-rw-rw----  1 alex  pubs   311 Jun 21 15:56 makefile
-rw-rw----  1 alex  pubs   354 Jun 21 16:02 calc.o
-rwxrwx---  1 alex  pubs  6337 Jun 21 16:04 compute
-rw-rw----  1 alex  pubs    49 Jun 21 16:04 compute.h
-rw-rw----  1 alex  pubs   880 Jun 21 16:04 compute.o
-rw-rw----  1 alex  pubs   780 Jun 21 18:20 compute.c
-rw-rw----  1 alex  pubs   179 Jun 21 18:20 calc.c

$ make
gcc -c -O3 compute.c
gcc -c calc.c
gcc -o compute compute.o calc.o
```

If you run make once and then run it again without making any changes to the prerequisite files, make indicates that the program is up-to-date and does not execute any commands:

```
$ make
make: 'compute' is up to date.
```

touch   The next example uses the touch utility to change the modification time of a prerequisite file. This simulation shows what happens when you alter the file. The make utility executes only the commands necessary to bring the out-of-date targets up-to-date:

```
$ touch calc.c
$ make
gcc -c calc.c
gcc -o compute compute.o calc.o
```

In the next example, touch changes the modification time of **compute.h**. The make utility re-creates **compute.o** because it depends on **compute.h** and re-creates the executable because it depends on **compute.o**:

```
$ touch compute.h
$ make
gcc -c -O3 compute.c
gcc -o compute compute.o calc.o
```

-n If you want to see what make *would* do if you ran it, run it with the **–n** (no execute) option. This option displays the commands that make would execute but it does not execute them.

-t As these examples illustrate, touch is useful when you want to fool make either into recompiling programs or into *not* recompiling them. You can use touch to update the modification times of all source files so that make considers nothing to be up-to-date; make will then recompile everything. Alternatively, you can use touch or the **–t** option to make to touch all relevant files; make then considers everything to be up-to-date. Using touch in this manner is useful if the modification times of files have changed yet the files remain up-to-date (as can happen when you copy a set of files from one directory to another).

The following example uses **make –n** several times to see what make *would* do if you gave a **make** command. The first command shows that the target, **compute**, is up-to-date. Next touch makes the modification dates on all ***.c** files more recent than their targets, and **make –n** shows what make would do if you called it without the **–n** option. The **make –t** command then brings all targets up-to-date. The final **make –n** command confirms that **compute** is up-to-date.

```
$ make -n
make: 'compute' is up to date.
$ touch *.c
$ make -n
gcc -c -O3 compute.c
gcc -c calc.c
gcc -o compute compute.o calc.o
$ make -t
touch compute.o
touch calc.o
touch compute
$ make -n
make: 'compute' is up to date.
```

-j The **–j** (jobs) option performs a number of tasks in parallel; the numeric argument to **–j** specifies the number of jobs or processes. Most make tasks hit the disk first and the CPU second, resulting in CPU usage dropping between compilations. On a multiprocessor system, you can reduce CPU usage by issuing the command **make –j** *n*, where *n* is the number of CPUs plus 1. Running tasks in parallel can significantly reduce the build time for a large project.

It is a good idea to keep intermediate files around while you are writing and debugging a program so that you need to rebuild only the ones that change. Once you are satisfied with the program you have created, you can use the makefile to release the disk space occupied by the extra files. Using a **clean** target in a makefile means that you do not have to remember all the little pieces that can safely be deleted. The next example simply removes all object (**.o**) files and all files with filenames that end with a tilde (**~**):

```
$ make clean
rm *.o *.~
```

MACROS

The make utility's macro facility enables you to create and use macros within a makefile. The syntax of a macro definition is

   ID = *list*

where *ID* is an identifying name and *list* is a list of filenames. After this macro definition, **$(ID)** represents *list* in the makefile.

With a macro you can compile a program with any of several C compilers by making only a minor change to the makefile. By using the CC macro and replacing all occurrences of **gcc** in the makefile on page 846 with **$(CC)**, for example, you need to assign a value only to CC to use the compiler of your choice:

```
$ cat Makefile
#
# Makefile for compute
#
CC=gcc
compute: compute.o calc.o
        $(CC) -o compute compute.o calc.o

compute.o: compute.c compute.h
        $(CC) -c -O3 compute.c

calc.o: calc.c
        $(CC) -c calc.c

clean:
        rm *.o
```

This example assumes that the compiler/loader flags are the same across compilers/loaders. In a more complex situation, you may need to create macros for these flags or use the default values.

Several commercial, high-performance compilers are available for Linux. You could specify the compiler from the Portland Group, pgcc, by replacing the **CC=gcc** assignment with **CC=pgcc**. If you do not assign a value to the CC macro, it defaults to gcc under Linux. The CC macro invokes the C compiler with only the options that you specify.

Several other macro definitions are commonly used. The CFLAGS macro sends arguments to the C compiler, LDFLAGS sends arguments to the linker (ld, or **gcc** –o), and CPPFLAGS sends arguments to the C preprocessor and programs that use it, including gcc. The COMPILE.c macro expands to **$(CC) –c $(CFLAGS) $(CPP-FLAGS)**. The LINK.c macro expands to **$(CC) $(CFLAGS) $(CPPFLAGS) $(LDFLAGS)**.

By default, make invokes the C compiler without any options (except the –c option when it is appropriate to compile but not link a file). You can use the CFLAGS macro definition to cause make to call the C compiler with specific options. In the following syntax, replace *options* with the options you want to use:

   CFLAGS = options

The following makefile uses macros as well as implied dependencies and constructions:

```
# makefile: report, print, printf, printh
#
CC=gcc
CFLAGS = -O3
# comment out the two lines above and uncomment the
# two below when you are using the Portland Group's compiler
#CC=pgcc
#CFLAGS = -fast
FILES = in.c out.c ratio.c process.c tally.c
OBJECTS = in.o out.o ratio.o process.o tally.o
HEADERS = names.h companies.h conventions.h

report: $(OBJECTS)
        $(LINK.c) -o report $(OBJECTS)

ratio.o: $(HEADERS)

process.o: $(HEADERS)

tally.o: $(HEADERS)

print:
    pr $(FILES) $(HEADERS) | lpr

printf:
    pr $(FILES) | lpr

printh:
    pr $(HEADERS) | lpr
```

Following the comment lines in this example, the makefile uses the CFLAGS macro to cause make always to use the optimizer (–O3 option) when it invokes the C compiler as the result of an implied construction. (The CC and CFLAGS definitions for the pgcc C compiler perform the same functions when they are uncommented and you are working with pgcc, except that you use –fast with pgcc and –O3 with gcc.) A construction line in a makefile overrides the corresponding implied construction line, if one exists. If you want to apply a macro to a construction command, you must include the macro in that command; see OBJECTS in the construction command for the **report** target. Following CFLAGS, the makefile defines the FILES, OBJECTS, and HEADERS macros. Each of these macros defines a list of files.

The first dependency line in the preceding example shows that **report** depends on the list of files defined by OBJECTS. The corresponding construction line uses the LINK.c macro to link the files defined by OBJECTS and create an executable file named **report**. If you specify any LDFLAGS, they are used in this step.

The next three dependency lines show that three object files depend on the list of files defined by HEADERS. Because there are no construction lines, make looks for a source code file corresponding to each object file and compiles it. These three dependency lines ensure that the object files are recompiled if any header files change.

You can combine several targets on one dependency line, so these three dependency lines could have been combined into one line:

```
ratio.o process.o tally.o: $(HEADERS)
```

The three final dependency lines in the preceding example send source and header files to the printer. These lines have nothing to do with compiling the **report** file; none of these targets (**print, printf,** and **printh**) depends on anything. When you call one of these targets from the command line, make executes the construction line following it. The following command prints all source files defined by FILES:

```
$ make printf
```

You can override macros in a makefile by specifying them on the command line. The following command adds debugging symbols to all object files:

```
$ make CFLAGS=-g ...
```

DEBUGGING C PROGRAMS

The C compiler is liberal about the kinds of constructs it allows in programs. In keeping with the UNIX philosophy that "no news is good news" and that the user knows what is best, gcc, like many other Linux utilities, accepts almost any construct that is logically possible according to the definition of the language. Although this approach gives the programmer a great deal of flexibility and control, it can make debugging difficult.

```
1   /* convert tabs in standard input to spaces in */      │ Comments
2   /* standard output while maintaining columns */         │
3                                                           │
4   #include        <stdio.h>                               │ Preprocessor
5   #define         TABSIZE         8                       │ directives
6                                                           │
7   /* prototype for function findstop */                   │ Function
8   int findstop(int *);                                    │ prototype
9                                                           │
10  main()                                                  │
11  {                                                       │ Main
12  int c;          /* character read from stdin */         │ function
13  int posn = 0;   /* column position of character */      │
14  int inc;        /* column increment to tab stop */      │
15                                                          │
16  while ((c = getchar()) != EOF)                          │
17          switch(c)                                       │
18                  {                                       │
19                  case '\t':              /* c is a tab */│
20                          inc = findstop(&posn);          │
21                          for( ; inc > 0; inc-- )         │
22                                  putchar(' ');           │
23                          break;                          │
24                  case '\n':              /* c is a newline */│
25                          putchar(c);                     │
26                          posn = 0;                       │
27                          break;                          │
28                  default:                /* c is anything else */│
29                          putchar(c);                     │
30                          posn++;                         │
31                          break;                          │
32                  }                                       │
33                                                          │
34  }                                                       │
35                                                          │
36  /* compute size of increment to next tab stop */        │ Function
37                                                          │
38  int findstop(int *col)                                  │
39  {                                                       │
40  int colindex, retval;                                   │
41  retval = (TABSIZE - (*col % TABSIZE));                  │
42                                                          │
43  /* increment argument (current column position) to next tabstop */│
44  *col += retval;                                         │
45                                                          │
46  return retval;          /* main gets how many blanks for filling */│
47  }                                                       │
```

Figure 27-4   The **badtabs.c** program (The line numbers are not part of the source code; the arrows point to errors in the program.)

Figure 27-4 shows **badtabs.c,** a flawed version of the **tabs.c** program discussed earlier. It contains some errors and does not run properly. This section uses this program to illustrate some debugging techniques.

In the following example, **badtabs.c** is compiled and then run with input from the **testtabs** file. Inspection of the output shows that the TAB character has not been replaced with the proper number of SPACEs:

```
$ gcc -o badtabs badtabs.c
$ cat testtabs
abcTABxyz
$ badtabs < testtabs
abc   xyz
```

One way to debug a C program is to insert print statements at critical points throughout the source code. To learn more about the behavior of **badtabs.c** when it runs, you can replace the contents of the **switch** statement as follows:

```
case '\t':                    /* c is a tab */
    fprintf(stderr, "before call to findstop, posn is %d\n", posn);
    inc = findstop(&posn);
    fprintf(stderr, "after call to findstop, posn is %d\n", posn);
    for( ; inc > 0; inc-- )
        putchar(' ');
    break;
case '\n':                    /* c is a newline */
    fprintf(stderr, "got a newline\n");
    putchar(c);
    posn = 0;
    break;
default:                      /* c is anything else */
    fprintf(stderr, "got another character\n");
    putchar(c);
    posn++;
    break;
```

The **fprintf** statements in this code send their messages to standard error. Thus, if you redirect standard output of this program, it will not be interspersed with the output sent to standard error. The next example demonstrates the operation of this program on the input file **testtabs**:

```
$ gcc -o badtabs badtabs.c
$ badtabs < testtabs > testspaces
got another character
got another character
got another character
before call to findstop, posn is 3
after call to findstop, posn is 3
got another character
got another character
got another character
got a newline
$ cat testspaces
abcTABxyz
```

The **fprintf** statements provide additional information about the execution of **tabs.c**. The value of the variable **posn** is not incremented in **findstop**, as it should be. This clue might be enough to lead you to the bug in the program. If not, you might attempt to "corner" the offending code by inserting print statements in **findstop**.

For simple programs or when you have an idea of what is wrong with a program, adding print statements that trace the execution of the code can often help you discover the problem quickly. A better strategy may be to take advantage of the tools that Linux provides to help you debug programs.

gcc COMPILER WARNING OPTIONS

The gcc compiler includes many of the features of lint, the classic C program verifier, and then some. (The lint utility is not available under Linux; use splint [secure programming lint; www.splint.org] instead.) The gcc compiler can identify many C program constructs that pose potential problems, even for programs that conform to the language's syntax rules. For instance, you can request that the compiler report a variable that is declared but not used, a comment that is not properly terminated, or a function that returns a type not permitted in older versions of C. Options that enable this stricter compiler behavior all begin with the uppercase letter **W** (Warning).

Among the **–W** options is a class of warnings that typically result from programmer carelessness or inexperience (see Table 27-2). The constructs that generate these warnings are generally easy to fix and easy to avoid.

Table 27-2   gcc –W options

Option	Reports an error when
–Wimplicit	A function or parameter is not explicitly declared
–Wreturn-type	A function that is not void does not return a value or the type of a function defaults to **int**
–Wunused	A variable is declared but not used
–Wcomment	The characters /*, which normally begin a comment, occur within a comment
–Wformat	Certain input/output statements contain format specifications that do not match the arguments

The **–Wall** option displays warnings about all of the errors listed in Table 27-2, along with other, similar errors.

The example program **badtabs.c** is syntactically correct: It compiles without generating an error. However, if you compile it (**–c** causes gcc to compile but not to link) with the **–Wall** option, gcc identifies several problems. (Warning messages do not stop the program from compiling, whereas error messages do.)

```
$ gcc -c -Wall badtabs.c
badtabs.c:11: warning: return type defaults to 'int'
badtabs.c: In function 'main':
badtabs.c:34: warning: control reaches end of non-void function
badtabs.c:46:25: warning: "/*" within comment
badtabs.c: In function 'findstop':
badtabs.c:40: warning: unused variable 'colindex'
badtabs.c:47: warning: control reaches end of non-void function
```

The fourth warning message references line 46, column 25. Inspection of the code for **badtabs.c** around that line reveals a comment that is not properly terminated. The compiler sees the string /* in the following line as the beginning of a comment:

```
/* increment argument (current column position) to next tabstop * /
```

However, because the characters * and / at the end of the line are separated by a SPACE, they do not signify the end of the comment to the compiler. Instead the compiler interprets all of the statements—including the statement that increments the argument—through the string ✳/ at the very end of the **findstop** function as part of the comment. After you remove the SPACE between the characters ✳ and /, **badtabs** produces the correct output.

The next few paragraphs discuss the remaining warning messages. Although most do not cause problems in the execution of **badtabs**, you can generally improve a program by rewriting those parts of the code that produce such warnings.

Because the definition of the function **main** does not include an explicit type, the compiler assumes type **int**, the default. This results in the warning message referencing line 11 in **badtabs.c**, the top of the function **main**. An additional warning is given when the compiler encounters the end of the function **main** (line 34) without seeing a value returned.

If a program runs successfully, by convention it should return a zero value; if no value is returned, the exit code is undefined. Although many C programs do not return a value, this oversight can cause problems when the program is executed. When you add the following statement at the end of the function **main** in **badtabs.c**, the warning referencing line 34 disappears:

```
return 0;
```

Line 40 of **badtabs.c** contains the definition for the local variable **colindex** in the function **findstop**. A warning message references this line because the **colindex** variable is never used. Removing its declaration eliminates the warning message.

The final warning message, referencing line 47, results from the improperly terminated comment discussed earlier. The compiler issues the warning message because it never sees a **return** statement in **findstop**. (The compiler ignores commented text.) Because the function **findstop** returns type **int**, the compiler expects to find a **return** statement before reaching the end of the function. This warning disappears when the comment is properly terminated.

Many other **–W** options are available with the gcc compiler. The ones not covered in the **–Wall** class often deal with portability differences; modifying the code causing these warnings may not be appropriate. These warnings usually result when programs are written in different C dialects or when constructs may not work well with other (especially older) C compilers. The **–pedantic-errors** option turns warnings into errors, causing a build to fail if it contains items that would generate warnings. To learn more about these and other warning options, refer to the gcc info page.

SYMBOLIC DEBUGGERS

Many debuggers are available to tackle problems that evade simpler debugging methods such as print statements and compiler warning options. These debuggers include gdb, kdbg, xxgdb mxgdb, ddd, and ups, all of which are available on the Web (refer to Appendix B). Such high-level symbolic debuggers enable you to analyze the execution of a program in terms of C language statements. They also provide a lower-level view for analyzing the execution of a program in terms of the machine instructions. Except for gdb, each of these debuggers provides a GUI.

A debugger enables you to monitor and control the execution of a program. You can step through a program line by line while you examine the state of the execution environment.

Core dumps   A debugger also allows you to examine *core* files (which are named **core**). When a serious error occurs during the execution of a program, the operating system can create a core file containing information about the state of the program and the system when the error occurred. This file comprises a dump of the computer's memory (it was previously called *core memory*—hence the term *core dump*) that was being used by the program. To conserve disk space, your system may not save core files automatically. You can use the ulimit builtin to allow core files to be saved. If you are running bash, the following command allows core files of unlimited size to be saved to disk:

```
$ ulimit -c unlimited
```

The operating system advises you whenever it dumps core. You can use a symbolic debugger to read information from a core file to identify the line in the program where the error occurred, to check the values of variables at that point, and so forth. Because core files tend to be large and take up disk space, be sure to remove these files when you no longer need them.

gdb: SYMBOLIC DEBUGGER

This section explains how to use the GNU gdb debugger. Other symbolic debuggers offer a different interface but operate in a similar manner. To take full advantage of a symbolic debugger with a program, you must compile the program with the **–g** option, which causes gcc to generate additional information that the debugger uses. This information includes a *symbol table*—a list of variable names used in the program and their associated values. Without the symbol table information, the debugger cannot display the values and types of variables. If a program is compiled without the **–g** option, gdb cannot identify source code lines by number, as many gdb commands require.

Always use –g

tip   It is a good idea to use the **–g** option even when you are releasing software. Including debugging symbols makes a binary a bit larger. Debugging symbols do not make a program run more slowly, but they do make it much easier to find problems identified by users.

Avoid using optimization flags with the debugger

tip   Limit the optimization flags to **–O** or **–O2** when you compile a program for debugging. Because debugging and optimizing inherently have different goals, it may be best to avoid combining the two operations.

Optimization should work

tip Turning optimization off completely can sometimes eliminate errors. Eliminating errors in this way should not be seen as a permanent solution, however. When optimization is not enabled, the compiler may automatically initialize variables and perform certain other checks for you, resulting in more stable code. Correct code should work correctly when compiled with at least the **–O** option and almost certainly with the **–O2** option. The **–O3** option often includes experimental optimizations: It may not generate correct code in all cases.

The following example uses the **–g** option when creating the executable file **tabs** from the C program **tabs.c**, which was discussed at the beginning of this chapter:

```
$ gcc -g tabs.c -o tabs
```

Input for **tabs** is contained in the file **testtabs**, which consists of a single line:

```
$ cat testtabs
xyzTABabc
```

You cannot specify the input file to **tabs** when you call the debugger. Instead, you must call the debugger and then specify the input file when you start execution with the **run** command.

To run the debugger on the sample executable, give the name of the executable file on the command line when you run gdb. You will see some introductory statements about gdb, followed by the gdb prompt [(**gdb**)]. At this point the debugger is ready to accept commands. The **list** command displays the first ten lines of source code. A subsequent **list** command displays the next ten lines of source code.

```
$ gdb tabs
GNU gdb Red Hat Linux (6.3.0.0-1.114rh)
Copyright 2004 Free Software Foundation, Inc.
...
(gdb) list
2           /* standard output while maintaining columns */
3
4           #include        <stdio.h>
5           #define         TABSIZE         8
6
7           /* prototype for function findstop */
8           int findstop(int *);
9
10          int main()
11          {
(gdb) list
12          int c;          /* character read from stdin */
13          int posn = 0;   /* column position of character */
14          int inc;        /* column increment to tab stop */
15
16          while ((c = getchar()) != EOF)
17                  switch(c)
18                          {
19                          case '\t':                  /* c is a tab */
20                              inc = findstop(&posn);
21                              for( ; inc > 0; inc-- )
(gdb)
```

One of the most important features of a debugger is its ability to run a program in a controlled environment. You can stop the program from running whenever you want. While it is stopped, you can check the state of an argument or variable. For example, you can give the **break** command a source code line number, an actual memory address, or a function name as an argument. The following command tells gdb to stop the process whenever the function **findstop** is called:

```
(gdb) break findstop
Breakpoint 1 at 0x8048454: file tabs.c, line 41.
(gdb)
```

The debugger acknowledges the request by displaying the breakpoint number, the hexadecimal memory address of the breakpoint, and the corresponding source code line number (41). The debugger numbers breakpoints in ascending order as you create them, starting with 1.

After setting a breakpoint you can issue a **run** command to start execution of **tabs** under the control of the debugger. The **run** command syntax allows you to use angle brackets to redirect input and output (just as the shells do). In the following example, the **testtabs** file is specified as input. When the process stops (at the breakpoint), you can use the **print** command to check the value of ***col**. The **backtrace** (or **bt**) command displays the function stack. In this example, the currently active function has been assigned the number 0. The function that called **findstop** (**main**) has been assigned the number 1.

```
(gdb) run < testtabs
Starting program: /home/mark/book/10/tabs < testtabs
Reading symbols from shared object read from target memory...done.
Loaded system supplied DSO at 0x28a000

Breakpoint 1, findstop (col=0xbf93ae78) at tabs.c:41
41        retval = (TABSIZE - (*col % TABSIZE));
(gdb) print *col
$1 = 3
(gdb) backtrace
#0  findstop (col=0xbf93ae78) at tabs.c:41
#1  0x080483ed in main () at tabs.c:20
(gdb)
```

You can examine anything in the current scope—variables and arguments in the active function as well as global variables. In the next example, the request to examine the value of the variable **posn** at breakpoint 1 results in an error. The error is generated because the variable **posn** is defined locally in the function **main**, not in the function **findstop**.

```
(gdb) print posn
No symbol "posn" in current context.
```

The **up** command changes the active function to the caller of the currently active function. Because **main** calls the function **findstop**, the function **main** becomes the active function when you give the **up** command. (The **down** command does the inverse.) The **up** command may be given an integer argument specifying the number of levels in the function stack to backtrack, with **up 1** having the same meaning as **up**. (You can use the **backtrace** command to determine which argument to use with **up**.)

```
(gdb) up
#1  0x080483ed in main () at tabs.c:20
20                              inc = findstop(&posn);
(gdb) print posn
$2 = 3
(gdb) print *col
No symbol "col" in current context.
(gdb)
```

The **cont** (continue) command causes the process to continue running from where it left off. The **testtabs** file contains only one line, so the process finishes executing and the results appear on the screen. The debugger reports the exit code of the program. A **cont** command given after a program has finished executing reminds you that execution of the program is complete. The debugging session is then ended with a **quit** command.

```
(gdb) cont
Continuing.
abc     xyz

Program exited normally.
(gdb) cont
The program is not being run.
(gdb) quit
$
```

The gdb debugger supports many commands that are designed to facilitate debugging. Type **help** at the **(gdb)** prompt to get a list of the command classes available under gdb:

```
(gdb) help
List of classes of commands:

aliases -- Aliases of other commands
breakpoints -- Making program stop at certain points
data -- Examining data
files -- Specifying and examining files
internals -- Maintenance commands
obscure -- Obscure features
running -- Running the program
stack -- Examining the stack
status -- Status inquiries
support -- Support facilities
tracepoints -- Tracing of program execution without stopping the program
user-defined -- User-defined commands

Type "help" followed by a class name for a list of commands in that class.
Type "help" followed by command name for full documentation.
Command name abbreviations are allowed if unambiguous.
(gdb)
```

As explained in the instructions following the list, entering **help** followed by the name of a command class or command name will display even more information. The following listing shows the commands in the class **data**:

```
(gdb) help data
Examining data.

List of commands:

append -- Append target code/data to a local file
call -- Call a function in the program
delete display -- Cancel some expressions to be displayed when program stops
delete mem -- Delete memory region
disable display -- Disable some expressions to be displayed when program stops
disable mem -- Disable memory region
disassemble -- Disassemble a specified section of memory
display -- Print value of expression EXP each time the program stops
...
print -- Print value of expression EXP
print-object -- Ask an Objective-C object to print itself
printf -- Printf "printf format string"
ptype -- Print definition of type TYPE
restore -- Restore the contents of FILE to target memory
set -- Evaluate expression EXP and assign result to variable VAR
set variable -- Evaluate expression EXP and assign result to variable VAR
undisplay -- Cancel some expressions to be displayed when program stops
whatis -- Print data type of expression EXP
x -- Examine memory: x/FMT ADDRESS
...
(gdb)
```

The following command requests information on the command **whatis**, which takes a variable name or other expression as an argument:

```
(gdb) help whatis
Print data type of expression EXP.
```

GRAPHICAL SYMBOLIC DEBUGGERS

Several graphical interfaces to gdb exist. For instance, the xxgdb graphical version of gdb provides a number of windows, including a Source Listing window, a Command window that contains a set of commonly used commands, and a Display window for viewing the values of variables. The left mouse button selects commands from the Command window. You can click the desired line in the Source Listing window to set a breakpoint, and you can select variables by clicking them in the Source Listing window. Selecting a variable and clicking **print** in the Command window will display the value of the variable in the Display window. You can view lines of source code by scrolling (and resizing) the Source Listing window.

Figure 27-5 The ddd debugger

The GNU ddd debugger (www.gnu.org/software/ddd; see Figure 27-5) also provides a GUI to gdb. Unlike xxgdb, ddd can display complex C structures and the links between them in graphical form. This display makes it easier to see errors in these structures. Otherwise, the ddd interface is very similar to that of xxgdb.

Unlike xxgdb, ups (ups.sourceforge.net) was designed from the ground up to work as a graphical debugger; the graphical interface was not added after the debugger was complete. The resulting interface is simple yet powerful. For example, ups automatically displays the value of a variable when you click it and provides a built-in C interpreter that allows you to attach C code to the program you are debugging. Because this attached code has access to the variables and values in the program, you can use it to perform sophisticated checks, such as following and displaying the links in a complex *data structure* (page 1028).

THREADS

A *thread* is a single sequential flow of control within a process. Threads are the basis for multithreaded programs, in which multiple independent but related threads cooperate to accomplish a larger task. Threads are lightweight processes that reduce scheduling overhead in several ways. The most significant way is that threads reduce the need to swap in new memory segments on a context switch, because threads share the same memory space.

Multithreaded programs generally use *reentrant* code (code that multiple threads can use simultaneously) and are most valuable when run on multiple-CPU machines. Under Linux, multithreaded servers, such as NFS, may be easier to write and maintain than multiple server processes. When applied judiciously, multithreading can also serve as a lower-overhead replacement for the traditional fork–exec idiom for spawning processes.

Fedora Core 5 and Red Hat Enterprise Linux 5 no longer support LinuxThreads (linas.org/linux/threads-faq.html). Instead they support the Native POSIX Thread Library (NPTL). NPTL implements POSIX threads and improves performance and scalability over LinuxThreads. See tldp.org/FAQ/Threads-FAQ and page 1012 for more information about threads.

Multiple threads are not always better

tip   If you write a multithreaded program with no clear goal or division of effort for a single-CPU system (for example, a parallel-server process), the resulting program will likely run more slowly than a nonthreaded program would on the same system.

SYSTEM CALLS

The Linux kernel has three fundamental responsibilities: to control processes, to manage the filesystem, and to operate peripheral devices. As a programmer you have access to these kernel operations through system calls and library functions. This section discusses system calls at a general level; a detailed treatment is beyond the scope of this book.

As the name implies, a system call instructs the system (kernel) to perform some work directly on your behalf. The request tells the kernel what work needs to be done and includes the necessary arguments. For example, a system call to open a file includes the name of the file. A library routine is less direct: It issues system calls on your behalf. The advantages of a library routine are that it may insulate you from the low-level details of kernel operations and that it has been written carefully to make sure that it performs efficiently.

For example, it is straightforward to use the standard I/O library function **fprintf()** to send text to standard output or standard error. Without this function, you would need to issue several system calls to achieve the same result. The calls to the library routines **putchar()** and **getchar()** in Figure 27-1 on page 834 ultimately use the **write()** and **read()** system calls to perform the I/O operations.

strace: TRACES SYSTEM CALLS

The strace utility is a debugging tool that displays a trace of all system calls made by a process or program. Because you do not need to recompile the program that you want to trace, you can use strace on binaries that you do not have source for.

System calls are events that take place at the interface (boundary) between user code and kernel code. Examining this boundary can help you isolate bugs, track down race conditions, and perform sanity checking. For more information refer to the strace home page (www.liacs.nl/~wichert/strace and sourceforge.net/projects/strace).

CONTROLLING PROCESSES

When you enter a command at a shell prompt, the shell process calls the **fork**() system call to create a copy of itself (spawn a child) and then uses an **exec**() system call to overlay that copy in memory with a different program (the command you asked it to run). Table 27-3 lists system calls that affect processes.

Table 27-3   System calls: process control

System call	Function
fork()	Creates a copy of a process
exec()	Overlays a program in memory with another program
getpid()	Returns the PID number of the calling process
getppid()	Returns the PID number of the calling process's parent process
wait()	Causes the parent process to wait for the child process to finish running before it resumes execution
exit()	Causes a process to exit
nice()	Changes the priority of a process
kill()	Sends a signal to a process

ACCESSING THE FILESYSTEM

Many operations take place when a program reads from or writes to a file. Because the program needs to know where the file is located, the filename must be converted to an inode number on the correct filesystem. Your access permissions must be checked not only for the file itself but also for all intervening directories in the path to the file. Because the file is not stored in one continuous piece on the disk, all disk blocks that contain pieces of the file must be located. The appropriate kernel device driver must be called to control the operation of the disk. Once the file has been found, the program may need to find a particular location within the file rather than working with it sequentially from beginning to end. Table 27-4 lists some of the most common system calls for filesystem operations.

Table 27-4   System calls: filesystem

System call	Function
stat()	Gets status information from an inode, such as the inode number, the device on which it is located, owner and group information, and the size of the file

Table 27-4   System calls: filesystem (continued)

lseek( )	Moves to a position in the file
creat( )	Creates a new file
open( )	Opens an existing file
read( )	Reads a file
write( )	Writes a file
close( )	Closes a file
unlink( )	Unlinks a file (deletes a name reference to the inode)
chmod( )	Changes file access permissions
chown( )	Changes file ownership

Access to peripheral devices on a Linux system is handled through the filesystem interface. Peripheral devices are represented by one or more special files, usually located under **/dev**. When you read from or write to one of these special files, the kernel passes your request to the appropriate kernel device driver. As a result you can use the standard system calls and library routines to interact with these devices; you do not need to learn a new set of specialized functions. This ability is one of the most powerful features of a Linux system because it allows users to use the same basic utilities on a wide range of devices.

The availability of standard system calls and library routines is the key to the portability of Linux tools. For example, as an applications programmer, you can rely on the **read**() and **write**() system calls working the same way on different versions of the Linux system and on different types of computers. The systems programmer who writes a device driver or ports the kernel to run on a new computer, however, must understand the details at their lowest level.

SOURCE CODE MANAGEMENT

When you work on a project involving many files that evolve over long periods of time, it can be difficult to keep track of the different versions of the files, particularly if several people are updating the files. This problem crops up regularly in large software development projects. Source code and documentation files change frequently as you fix bugs, enhance programs, and release new versions of the software. The task becomes even more complex when more than one version of each file is active. In many situations developers may be using one version of a file while a newer version is being modified. In these circumstances you can easily lose track of the versions and accidentally undo changes or duplicate earlier work.

To help avoid these kinds of problems, Linux includes CVS (Concurrent Versions System; www.nongnu.org/cvs) for managing and tracking changes to files. Although

CVS can be used on any set of files, it is most often employed to manage source code and software documentation. CVS is based on RCS (GNU's Revision Control System) and is designed to control the concurrent access and modification of source files by multiple users.

A graphical front end to CVS named TkCVS (page 872) simplifies the use of CVS, especially if you do not use it frequently enough to memorize its many commands and options.

CVS controls who is allowed to update files. For each update, CVS records who made the changes and why the changes were made. Because CVS stores the most recent version of a file and the information needed to re-create all previous versions, it is possible to regenerate any version of a file.

A set of versions for several files may be grouped together to form a *release*. An entire release can be re-created from the change information stored with each file. Saving the changes for a file rather than saving a complete copy of the file generally conserves a lot of disk space—well in excess of the space required to store each update in the CVS files themselves.

This section provides an overview of CVS and TkCVS. See the *CVS-RCS-HOW-TO Document for Linux* for more information.

CVS: CONCURRENT VERSIONS SYSTEM

CVS treats collections of files as single units, making it easy to work on large projects and permitting multiple users to work on the same file simultaneously. CVS also provides valuable self-documenting features for its utilities.

BUILTIN CVS HELP

CVS uses a single utility, cvs, for all its functions. To display the instructions for getting help, use the **--help** option:

```
$ cvs --help
Usage: cvs [cvs-options] command [command-options-and-arguments]
  where cvs-options are -q, -n, etc.
    (specify --help-options for a list of options)
  where command is add, admin, etc.
    (specify --help-commands for a list of commands
    or --help-synonyms for a list of command synonyms)
  where command-options-and-arguments depend on the specific command
    (specify -H followed by a command name for command-specific help)
  Specify --help to receive this message

The Concurrent Versions System (CVS) is a tool for version control.
For CVS updates and additional information, see
    the CVS home page at http://www.cvshome.org/
```

To get help with a cvs command, use the **--help** option followed by the name of the command. The following example shows help information for the log command:

```
$ cvs --help log
Usage: cvs log [-lRhtNb] [-r[revisions]] [-d dates] [-s states]
    [-w[logins]] [files...]
        -l        Local directory only, no recursion.
        -b        Only list revisions on the default branch.
        -h        Only print header.
        -R        Only print name of RCS file.
        -t        Only print header and descriptive text.
        -N        Do not list tags.
        -S        Do not print name/header if no revisions selected.  -d, -r,
                  -s, & -w have little effect in conjunction with -b, -h, -R, and
                  -t without this option.
    -r[revisions]    A comma-separated list of revisions to print:
        rev1:rev2 Between rev1 and rev2, including rev1 and rev2.
        rev1::rev2 Between rev1 and rev2, excluding rev1.
        rev:      rev and following revisions on the same branch.
        rev::     After rev on the same branch.
        :rev      rev and previous revisions on the same branch.
        ::rev     rev and previous revisions on the same branch.
        rev       Just rev.
        branch    All revisions on the branch.
        branch.   The last revision on the branch.
    -d dates      A semicolon-separated list of dates
                  (D1<D2 for range, D for latest before).
    -s states     Only list revisions with specified states.
    -w[logins]    Only list revisions checked in by specified logins.
(Specify the --help global option for a list of other help options)
```

Options for individual cvs commands (command options) go to the *right* of the individual command names. Options to the cvs utility itself, such as the **--help** option to the **log** command, go to the *left* of all individual command names (that is, they follow the word **cvs** on the command line). The two types of options sometimes use the same letter yet may have an entirely different meaning.

How CVS Stores Revision Files

CVSROOT With CVS, revision files are kept in a common area called a *source repository*. The environment variable **CVSROOT** holds the absolute pathname of this repository. The system administrator can tell you what value to use for **CVSROOT**, or you can create your own private repository and have **CVSROOT** point to it.

The source repository is organized as a hierarchical collection of files and directories. CVS does not limit you to checking out one file at a time; you can check out an entire subdirectory containing many files—typically all the files for a particular project. A subdirectory of **CVSROOT** that can be checked out as a single unit is called a *module*. Several people can check out and simultaneously modify the files within a single module.

CVS users typically store the modules they are currently working on in a special directory. If you want to follow this practice, you must use cd to make that special directory the working directory before you check out a module. When you check out a module, CVS replicates the module's tree structure in the working directory. Multiple developers can therefore check out and edit CVS files simultaneously because the originals are retained in the source repository; the files in the repository undergo relatively infrequent modification in a controlled manner.

BASIC CVS COMMANDS

Although many cvs commands are available, knowledge of just a handful of commands allows a software developer to use CVS and to contribute changes to a module. A discussion of some useful commands follows. All examples assume that the appropriate modules have been installed in the CVS source repository. "Adding a Module to the Repository" (page 869) explains how to install a module.

Of the commands discussed in this section, **cvs commit** is the only one that changes the source repository. The other commands affect only the files in the working directory.

To simplify examples in the following sections, the pathname of the working directory is given by the variable **CVSWORK**; all modules can be assumed to be subdirectories of **CVSWORK**. Although this variable has no special meaning to CVS, you may find it helpful to define such a variable for your own work.

CHECKING OUT FILES FROM THE SOURCE REPOSITORY

To check out a module from the CVS source repository, use the **cvs checkout** command. The following example checks out the **Project2** module, which consists of four source files. First use cd to make the directory you want the module copied into (**CVSWORK** in this case) the working directory. The cvs utility always copies into the working directory.

```
$ cd $CVSWORK
$ ls
Project1
$ cvs checkout Project2
cvs checkout: Updating Project2
U Project2/adata.h
U Project2/compute.c
U Project2/randomfile.h
U Project2/shuffle.c
$ ls
Project1 Project2
$ ls Project2
CVS adata.h compute.c randomfile.h shuffle.c
```

The name of the module, **Project2**, is given as an argument to **cvs checkout**. Because the **Project2** directory does not already exist, cvs creates it in the working directory and places copies of all source files for the **Project2** module into it: The name of the module and the name of the directory holding the module are the same. The **checkout** command preserves the tree structure of the cvs module, creating subdirectories as needed.

The second ls command after **checkout** reveals, in addition to the four source files for **Project2**, a directory named **CVS**. The CVS system uses this directory for administrative purposes; you do not normally access it.

Once you have your own copies of the source files, you can edit them as you see fit. You can change files within the module even if other developers are modifying the same files at the same time.

MAKING YOUR CHANGES AVAILABLE TO OTHERS

To check in your changes so that other users can access them, you need to run the **cvs commit** command. When you give this command, cvs prompts you to provide a brief log message describing the changes, unless you use the **–m** option. With this option, cvs uses the string following the option as the log message. The file or files that you want to commit follow the optional log message on the command line:

```
$ cvs commit -m "function shuffle inserted" compute.c
cvs commit: Up-to-date check failed for 'compute.c'
cvs [commit aborted]: correct above errors first!
```

Here the cvs utility reports an error because the version of **compute.c** that you modified is not up-to-date. That is, a newer version of **compute.c** has been committed by someone else since you last checked it out of the source repository. After informing you of the problem, cvs exits without storing your changes in the source repository.

To make your version of **compute.c** current, you need to run the update command. A subsequent **commit** will then succeed, and your changes will apply to the latest revision in the source repository.

UPDATING YOUR COPIES WITH CHANGES BY OTHERS

As the preceding example shows, CVS does not notify you when another developer checks in a new revision of a file after you have checked out your working copy. You learn this fact only when you attempt to commit your changes to the source repository. To incorporate up-to-date revisions of a CVS source file, use the **cvs update** command:

```
$ cvs update compute.c
RCS file: /usr/local/src/master/Project2/compute.c,v
retrieving revision 1.9
retrieving revision 1.10
Merging differences between 1.9 and 1.10 into compute.c
M compute.c
```

Here the changes made to the working copy of **compute.c** remain intact because the **update** command merges the latest revision in the source repository with the version specified on the **update** command line. The result of the merge is not always perfect, however. For this reason, the **cvs update** command informs you if it detects overlapping changes.

ADDING NEW FILES TO THE REPOSITORY

You can use the **cvs add** command to schedule new files to be added to the source repository as part of the module you are working on. With the directory containing the files as the working directory, give the **cvs add** command, listing the files you want to add as arguments:

```
$ cd $CVSWORK/Project2
$ ls
CVS compute.c shuffle.c tabout2.c
adata.h randomfile.h tabout1.c
$ cvs add tabout[1-2].c
cvs add: scheduling file 'tabout1.c' for addition
cvs add: scheduling file 'tabout2.c' for addition
cvs add: use 'cvs commit' to add these files permanently
```

This **add** command marks the files **tabout1.c** and **tabout2.c** for entry into the repository. However, these files will not be available to other users until you give a **commit** command. This staging allows you to prepare several files before others incorporate the changes into their working copies with the **cvs update** command.

REMOVING FILES FROM THE REPOSITORY

The **cvs remove** command records the fact that you wish to remove a file from the source repository. Like the **add** command, it does not affect the source repository. To delete a file from the repository, you must first delete your working copy of the file, as the following example shows:

```
$ cvs remove shuffle.c
cvs remove: file 'shuffle.c' still in working directory
cvs remove: 1 file exists; use 'rm' to remove it first
$ rm shuffle.c
$ cvs remove shuffle.c
cvs remove: scheduling 'shuffle.c' for removal
cvs remove: use 'cvs commit' to remove this file permanently
```

In this example, after using rm to delete the working copy of **shuffle.c**, a **cvs remove** command is given. Again, you must give the **commit** command before the file is actually removed from the source repository.

OTHER CVS COMMANDS

Although the commands described earlier are sufficient for most work on a module, you may find some other commands to be useful.

TAGGING A RELEASE

You can apply a common label, or *tag,* to the files in a module as they currently exist. Once you have tagged files of a module, you can re-create them in exactly the same form even if they have been modified, added, or deleted since they were tagged. This ability enables you to *freeze* a release yet allows development to continue on the next release:

```
$ cvs rtag Release_1 Project1
cvs rtag: Tagging Project1
```

Here the **Project1** module has been tagged with the label **Release_1**. You can use this tag with the **cvs export** command to extract the files as they existed when they were frozen.

Extracting a Release

The **cvs export** command lets you extract files as they were frozen and tagged:

```
$ cvs export -r Release_1 -d R1 Project1
cvs export: Updating R1
U R1/scm.txt
```

This command works like the **cvs checkout** command but does not create the CVS support files. You must give either the **–r** option to identify the release (as shown above) or a date with the **–D** option. The **–d R1** option instructs cvs to place the files for the module into the directory **R1** instead of using the module name as the directory.

Removing Working Files

When you are finished making changes to the files you have checked out of the repository, you may decide to remove your copy of the module from your working directory. One simple approach is to cd to the working directory and recursively remove the module. For example, if you want to remove your working copy of **Project2**, you could give the following commands:

```
$ cd $CVSWORK
$ rm -rf Project2
```

The repository will not be affected by the removal of these files. However, if you had made changes to the files but had not yet committed those changes, the changes would be lost if you used this approach. The **cvs release** command is helpful in this situation:

```
$ cd $CVSWORK
$ cvs release -d Project2
```

The **release** command also removes the working files but first checks each one to see whether it has been marked for addition into the repository but has not yet been committed. If that is the case, the **release** command warns you and asks you to verify your intention to delete the file. You can fix the problem at this point if you like and redo the **release** command. The **release** command also warns you if the repository holds a newer version of the file than the one found in the working directory. Thus you have the opportunity to update and commit your file before deleting it. (Without the **–d** option, your working files will not be deleted but you will receive the same sequence of warning messages.)

Adding a Module to the Repository

The discussion of CVS to this point has assumed that the module is already present in the CVS source repository. If you want to install a directory hierarchy as a new module in the repository or update an existing module with a new release that was developed elsewhere, go to the directory that holds the files for the project and run the **cvs import** command. The following example installs the files for **Project1** in the source repository:

```
$ cvs import -m "My first project" Project1 ventag reltag
```

The **–m** option allows you to enter a brief description of the module on the command line. Following the description is the directory or the pathname of the directory under **CVSROOT** that you want to hold the module. The last two fields are symbolic names for the vendor branch and the release. Although they are not significant here, they can be useful when releases of software are supplied by outside sources.

You can now use the **cvs checkout** command to check out the **Project1** module:

```
$ cvs checkout Project1
```

CVS ADMINISTRATION

Before you install a CVS repository, think about how you would like to administer it. Many installations maintain a single repository in which separate projects are kept as separate modules. You may choose to have more than one repository. The CVS system supports a single repository that is shared across several computer systems using NFS.

Inside a repository is a module named CVSROOT that contains administrative files (here CVSROOT is the name of a module and is different from the **CVSROOT** directory). Although the files in this module are not required to use CVS, they can simplify access to the repository.

Do not change any files in the CVSROOT module by editing them directly. Instead, check out the file you want to change, edit the checked-out copy, and then check it back in, just as you would with files in any other module in the repository. For example, to check out the **modules** file from the CVSROOT module, give the following command:

```
$ cvs checkout CVSROOT/modules
```

This command creates the directory **CVSROOT** in your working directory and places a checked-out copy of **modules** in that directory. After checking it out, you can edit the **modules** file in the **CVSROOT** directory:

```
$ cd CVSROOT
$ vim modules
```

After you edit the **modules** file, check it back into the repository:

```
$ cd ..
$ cvs checkin CVSROOT/modules
```

Of all the administrative files in the CVSROOT module, the **modules** file is the most important. You can use this file to attach symbolic names to modules in the repository, allow access to subdirectories of a module as if they were themselves modules, and specify actions to take when checking specific files in or out.

Most repositories start with a **modules** file that allows you to check out the **modules** file with the following command, instead of the one shown earlier:

```
$ cvs checkout modules
```

With the preceding command CVS creates a subdirectory named **modules** within the working directory, instead of one named **CVSROOT**. The **modules** file is then checked out into this directory.

The following example shows a **modules** file (the lines that start with # are comment lines and, along with blank lines, are ignored by CVS):

```
# The CVS modules file
#
# Three different line formats are valid:
#    key -a aliases...
#    key [options] directory
#    key [options] directory files...
#
# Where "options" are composed of:
#    -i prog     Run "prog" on "cvs commit" from top-level of module.
#    -o prog     Run "prog" on "cvs checkout" of module.
#    -t prog     Run "prog" on "cvs rtag" of module.
#    -u prog     Run "prog" on "cvs update" of module.
#    -d dir      Place module in directory "dir" instead of module name.
#    -l          Top-level directory only -- do not recurse.
#
# And "directory" is a path to a directory relative to $CVSROOT.
#
# The "-a" option specifies an alias.  An alias is interpreted as if
# everything on the right of the "-a" had been typed on the command line.
#
#
# You can encode a module within a module by using the special '&'
# character to interpose another module into the current module.  This
# can be useful for creating a module that consists of many directories
# spread out over the entire source repository.


# Convenient aliases
world       -a .

# CVSROOT support; run mkmodules whenever anything changes.
CVSROOT     -i mkmodules CVSROOT
modules     -i mkmodules CVSROOT modules
loginfo     -i mkmodules CVSROOT loginfo
commitinfo  -i mkmodules CVSROOT commitinfo
rcsinfo     -i mkmodules CVSROOT rcsinfo
editinfo    -i mkmodules CVSROOT editinfo
# Add other modules here...
testgen     testgen
testdata1   testdata1
testdata2   testdata2
testdata3   testdata3
testdata4   testdata4
testcode    testgen/_code
cvs         cvs
```

The lines after the comment and blank lines define symbolic names for many modules. For example, the following line defines **world** to be an alias for the root of the CVS repository:

```
world       -a .
```

You can use such names in CVS commands as the names of modules. For example, the following command checks out the entire repository (probably not a good idea):

```
$ cvs checkout world
```

In the sample **modules** file, the administrative files contain definitions that attach both a symbolic name to the file and an action (**–i mkmodules**) to take when each file is checked into the repository. The **–i mkmodules** action causes CVS to run the **mkmodules** program when the file is checked in. This program ensures that a copy of the checked-in file exists in a location where CVS can locate it.

Following the action is the name of the subdirectory in **CVSROOT** that holds files associated with the symbolic name. Any remaining arguments on the line are the names of specific files within that directory.

The following line identifies CVSROOT as the name of the module in the directory **$CVSROOT/CVSROOT**—that is, for all the administrative files for CVS:

```
CVSROOT     -i mkmodules CVSROOT
```

Similarly the following line associates the **modules** module with the **modules** file within the **CVSROOT** directory:

```
modules     -i mkmodules CVSROOT modules
```

Now the following command can find and check out the **modules** file:

```
$ cvs checkout modules
```

The last set of lines in the sample **modules** file associates symbolic module names with directories and files in the repository.

USING TkCVS

The cvs utility is useful enough that a graphical interface, TkCVS, has been written for it using the Tk extension to the Tcl programming language (tcl.sourceforge.net). TkCVS is part of the **tkcvs** package. It provides a convenient point-and-click interface to CVS (Figure 27-6). After you have downloaded and installed TkCVS (www.twobarleycorns.net/tkcvs.html), you can start the utility by using cd to change to the directory you want to work in and then entering the following command:

```
$ tkcvs &
```

All operations are available through the pull-down menus found at the top of the window. Along the bottom of the window are buttons for accessing the most common actions. A description of the action bound to a button (a *tooltip,* page 1060) appears when you allow the mouse pointer to hover over a button.

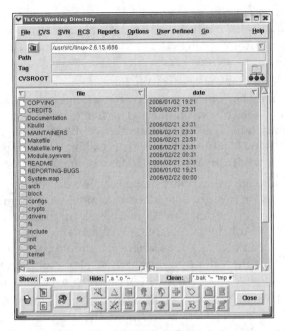

Figure 27-6   The TkCVS utility

In the middle of the window is a *browse list*. To move into a subdirectory, double-click the left mouse button while the mouse pointer is on the directory name in this list. To edit a file double-click the filename. To select more than one file, hold down the left mouse button and drag the mouse pointer across several names. Clicking the right mouse button will *mark* all selected files. Some of the operations (such as viewing the revision log messages) will work on all marked files.

The Help pull-down menu in the upper-right corner of the window is an excellent way to learn how TkCVS works. For example, when you select the Help menu item **CVS modules file**, an explanation of the lines that you can add to the CVS **modules** file to better support TkCVS appears in a window. If you choose not to add these lines to the **modules** file, some TkCVS commands, such as those for browsing the repository, may not display all available modules.

CHAPTER SUMMARY

The operating system interface to C programs and a variety of software development tools render the Linux system well suited to programming in C. The C libraries provide general-purpose C functions that make operating system services and other functionality available to C programmers. The standard C library **libc** is always accessible to C programs, and you can specify other libraries by using the –l option to the **gcc** compiler.

You can write a C program by using a text editor, such as vim or emacs. C programs always have a function named **main** and often include several other functions. Preprocessor directives define symbolic constants and macros and instruct the preprocessor to include header files.

gcc   When you use gcc, it calls the C preprocessor followed by the C compiler and the assembler. The compiler creates assembly language code, which the assembler uses to create object modules. The linker then combines these object modules into an executable file. You can use the –**Wall** option to gcc to detect *risky* constructs—ones that are legal but suggest the possibility of later problems. Other options to gcc can help locate areas of your code that might not be portable.

gdb   Although using **printf** statements and the –**Wall** option can help in locating program bugs, it is a good practice to compile C programs routinely with the –**g** option. Information that can be interpreted by gdb, a symbolic debugger, is then generated as part of the executable file. When you run a program under the control of gdb, you can specify points where gdb should pause the program so that you can inquire about the values of variables, display the program stack, or use a wide range of commands to learn about many other aspects of the program's behavior.

make   The make utility uses a file named **makefile** (or **Makefile**) that documents the relationships among files. It determines which modules of a program are out-of-date and compiles files so that all modules are up-to-date. The dependency line, which specifies the exact relationships between target and prerequisite files, is the key to the operation of a makefile. Following the dependency line are construction commands that can bring the target up-to-date. Implied dependencies, construction commands, and the make macro facility are available to simplify the writing of complex makefiles.

CVS   The Linux system includes several utilities that assist in keeping track of groups of files that undergo multiple revisions, often at the hands of multiple developers. One of these source code management systems is CVS (Concurrent Versions System). CVS is built on top of RCS but provides a much more extensive set of operations for managing directories of files that may be accessed and modified by many users. It is a good choice for managing large-scale projects and for maintaining software releases that are sent to and from other sites.

EXERCISES

1. What function does every C program have? Why should you split large programs into several functions?

2. What command could you give to compile **prog.c** and **func.c** into an executable named **cprog**?

3. Show two ways to instruct the C preprocessor to include the header file **/usr/include/math.h** in your C program. Assuming that the **declar.h** header file is located in the subdirectory named **headers** of your home directory,

describe two ways to instruct the C preprocessor to include this header file in your C program.

4. How are the names of system libraries abbreviated on the gcc command line? Where does gcc search for libraries named in this manner? Describe how to specify your own library on the gcc command line.

5. Write a makefile that reflects the following relationships:

    a. The C source files **transactions.c** and **reports.c** are compiled to produce an executable file named **accts**.

    b. Both **transactions.c** and **reports.c** include a header file named **accts.h**.

    c. The header file **accts.h** is composed of two other header files: **trans.h** and **reps.h**.

6. If you retrieve version 4.1 of the file **answer** for editing and then attempt to retrieve the same version again, what will CVS do? Why is CVS set up this way?

ADVANCED EXERCISES

7. Modify the **badtabs.c** program (page 851) so that it exits cleanly (with a specific return value). Compile the program and run it using gdb or another debugger. What values does the debugger report when the program finishes executing?

8. For the makefile

```
$ cat Makefile
leads: menu.o users.o resellers.o prospects.o
            gcc -o leads menu.o users.o resellers.o prospects.o

menu.o: menu.h dialog.h inquiry.h

users.o: menu.h dialog.h

prospects.o: dialog.h
```

identify:

a. Targets.

b. Construction commands.

c. Prerequisites.

9. Refer to **Makefile** in exercise 8 to answer the following questions:

    a. If the target **leads** is up-to-date and you then change **users.c**, what happens when you run make again? Be specific.

b. Rewrite the makefile to include the following macros:

```
OBJECTS = menu.o users.o resellers.o prospects.o
HFILES = menu.h dialog.h
```

10. Review the make info page to answer the following questions:

a. What does the –t option do?

b. If you have files named **makefile** and **Makefile** in the working directory, how can you instruct make to use **Makefile**?

c. Give two ways to define a variable so that you can use it inside a makefile.

11. Refer to the makefile for **compute** on page 846.

a. Suppose that a file in the working directory is named **clean**. What is the effect of giving the following command? Explain.

```
$ make clean
```

b. The discussion on page 844 states that the following command is not normally seen in makefiles:

```
cat num.h table.h > form.h
```

What is the effect of removing this construction command from the makefile while retaining the dependency line?

c. The preceding construction command works only because the file **form.h** is made up of **num.h** and **table.h**. More often #include directives in the target define the dependencies. Suggest a more general technique that updates **form.h** whenever **num.h** or **table.h** has a more recent modification date.

28

PROGRAMMING THE BOURNE AGAIN SHELL

Chapter 7 introduced the shells and Chapter 9 went into detail about the Bourne Again Shell. This chapter introduces additional Bourne Again Shell commands, builtins, and concepts that carry shell programming to a point where it can be useful. The first part of this chapter covers programming control structures, which are also known as control flow constructs. These structures allow you to write scripts that can loop over command line arguments, make decisions based on the value of a variable, set up menus, and more. The Bourne Again Shell uses the same constructs found in such high-level programming languages as C.

The next part of this chapter discusses parameters and variables, going into detail about array variables, local versus global variables, special parameters, and positional parameters. The exploration of builtin commands covers type, which displays information about a command, and read, which allows you to accept user input in a shell script. The section on the exec builtin demonstrates how exec provides an efficient way to execute a command by replacing a process and explains how you can use it to redirect input and output from within a script. The next section covers the trap builtin, which provides a way to detect and respond to operating system signals (such as that which is generated when you press CONTROL-C). The discussion of builtins concludes with a discussion of kill, which can abort a process, and getopts, which makes it easy to parse options for a shell script. (Table 28-6 on page 939 lists some of the more commonly used builtins.)

Next the chapter examines arithmetic and logical expressions and the operators that work with them. The final section walks through the design and implementation of two major shell scripts.

This chapter contains many examples of shell programs. Although they illustrate certain concepts, most use information from earlier examples as well. This overlap not only reinforces your overall knowledge of shell programming but also demonstrates how you can combine commands to solve complex tasks. Running, modifying, and experimenting with the examples in this book is a good way to become comfortable with the underlying concepts.

Do not name a shell script test

tip You can unwittingly create a problem if you give a shell script the name **test** because a Linux utility has the same name. Depending on how the **PATH** variable is set up and how you call the program, you may run your script or the utility, leading to confusing results.

This chapter illustrates concepts with simple examples, which are followed by more complex ones in sections marked "Optional." The more complex scripts illustrate traditional shell programming practices and introduce some Linux utilities often used in scripts. You can skip these sections without loss of continuity the first time you read the chapter. Return to them later when you feel comfortable with the basic concepts.

CONTROL STRUCTURES

The *control flow* commands alter the order of execution of commands within a shell script. Control structures include the **if...then**, **for...in**, **while**, **until**, and **case** statements. In addition, the **break** and **continue** statements work in conjunction with the control structures to alter the order of execution of commands within a script.

if...then

The **if...then** control structure has the following syntax:

> *if test-command*
> > *then*
> > > *commands*
> > *fi*

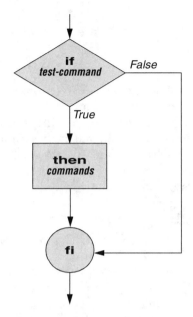

Figure 28-1 An **if...then** flowchart

The *bold* words in the syntax description are the items you supply to cause the structure to have the desired effect. The *nonbold* words are the keywords the shell uses to identify the control structure.

test builtin Figure 28-1 shows that the **if** statement tests the status returned by the ***test-command*** and transfers control based on this status. The end of the **if** structure is marked by a **fi** statement, (*if* spelled backward). The following script prompts for two words, reads them, and then uses an **if** structure to execute commands based on the result returned by the test builtin when it compares the two words. (See the test info page for information on the test utility, which is similar to the test builtin.) The test builtin returns a status of *true* if the two words are the same and *false* if they are not. Double quotation marks around **$word1** and **$word2** make sure that test works properly if you enter a string that contains a SPACE or other special character:

```
$ cat if1
echo -n "word 1: "
read word1
echo -n "word 2: "
read word2

if test "$word1" = "$word2"
    then
        echo "Match"
fi
echo "End of program."
```

```
$ if1
word 1: peach
word 2: peach
Match
End of program.
```

In the preceding example the *test-command* is **test** "**$word1**" = "**$word2**". The **test** builtin returns a *true* status if its first and third arguments have the relationship specified by its second argument. If this command returns a *true* status (= 0), the shell executes the commands between the **then** and **fi** statements. If the command returns a *false* status (not = 0), the shell passes control to the statement following **fi** without executing the statements between **then** and **fi**. The effect of this **if** statement is to display **Match** if the two words are the same. The script always displays **End of program**.

Builtins   In the Bourne Again Shell, **test** is a builtin—part of the shell. It is also a stand-alone utility kept in **/usr/bin/test**. This chapter discusses and demonstrates many Bourne Again Shell builtins. You usually use the builtin version if it is available and the utility if it is not. Each version of a command may vary slightly from one shell to the next and from the utility to any of the shell builtins. See page 926 for more information on shell builtins.

Checking arguments   The next program uses an **if** structure at the beginning of a script to check that you have supplied at least one argument on the command line. The **–eq** test operator compares two integers, where the **$#** special parameter (page 921) takes on the value of the number of command line arguments. This structure displays a message and exits from the script with an exit status of 1 if you do not supply at least one argument:

```
$ cat chkargs
if test $# -eq 0
    then
        echo "You must supply at least one argument."
        exit 1
fi
echo "Program running."
$ chkargs
You must supply at least one argument.
$ chkargs abc
Program running.
```

A test like the one shown in **chkargs** is a key component of any script that requires arguments. To prevent the user from receiving meaningless or confusing information from the script, the script needs to check whether the user has supplied the appropriate arguments. Sometimes the script simply tests whether arguments exist (as in **chkargs**). Other scripts test for a specific number or specific kinds of arguments.

You can use **test** to ask a question about the status of a file argument or the relationship between two file arguments. After verifying that at least one argument has been given on the command line, the following script tests whether the argument is the name of an ordinary file (not a directory or other type of file) in the working directory. The test builtin with the **–f** option and the first command line argument (**$1**) check the file:

```
$ cat is_ordfile
if test $# -eq 0
    then
        echo "You must supply at least one argument."
        exit 1
fi
if test -f "$1"
    then
        echo "$1 is an ordinary file in the working directory"
    else
        echo "$1 is NOT an ordinary file in the working directory"
fi
```

You can test many other characteristics of a file with test and various options. Table 28-1 lists some of these options.

Table 28-1 Options to the test builtin

Option	Tests file to see if it
–d	Exists and is a directory file
–e	Exists
–f	Exists and is an ordinary file (not a directory)
–r	Exists and is readable
–s	Exists and has a size greater than 0 bytes
–w	Exists and is writable
–x	Exists and is executable

Other test options provide ways to test relationships between two files, such as whether one file is newer than another. Refer to later examples in this chapter for more detailed information.

Always test the arguments

tip   To keep the examples in this book short and focused on specific concepts, the code to verify arguments is often omitted or abbreviated. It is a good practice to test arguments in shell programs that other people will use. Doing so results in scripts that are easier to run and debug.

[] is a synonym   The following example—another version of **chkargs**—checks for arguments in a
for test   way that is more traditional for Linux shell scripts. The example uses the bracket ([]) synonym for test. Rather than using the word test in scripts, you can surround the arguments to test with brackets. The brackets must be surrounded by whitespace (SPACEs or TABs).

```
$ cat chkargs2
if [ $# -eq 0 ]
    then
        echo "Usage: chkargs2 argument..." 1>&2
        exit 1
fi
echo "Program running."
exit 0
$ chkargs2
Usage: chkargs2 arguments
$ chkargs2 abc
Program running.
```

Usage message   The error message that **chkargs2** displays is called a *usage message* and uses the **1>&2** notation to redirect its output to standard error (page 270). After issuing the usage message, **chkargs2** exits with an exit status of 1, indicating that an error has occurred. The **exit 0** command at the end of the script causes **chkargs2** to exit with a 0 status after the program runs without an error. The Bourne Again Shell returns a 0 status if you omit the status code.

The usage message is commonly employed to specify the type and number of arguments the script takes. Many Linux utilities provide usage messages similar to the one in **chkargs2**. If you call a utility or other program with the wrong number or kind of arguments, you will often see a usage message. Following is the usage message that cp displays when you call it without any arguments:

```
$ cp
cp: missing file argument
Try 'cp --help' for more information.
```

if...then...else

The introduction of an **else** statement turns the **if** structure into the two-way branch shown in Figure 28-2. The **if...then...else** control structure has the following syntax:

> if *test-command*
> > then
> > > *commands*
> > else
> > > *commands*
> fi

Because a semicolon (;) ends a command just as a NEWLINE does, you can place **then** on the same line as **if** by preceding it with a semicolon. (Because **if** and **then** are separate builtins, they require a command separator between them; a semicolon and NEWLINE work equally well.) Some people prefer this notation for aesthetic reasons, while others like it because it saves space:

> if *test-command;* then
> > *commands*
> > else
> > > *commands*
> fi

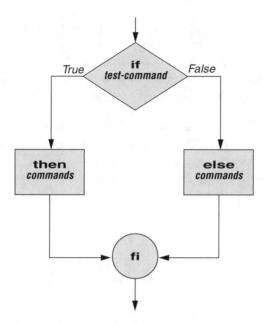

Figure 28-2 An if...then...else flowchart

If the *test-command* returns a *true* status, the **if** structure executes the commands between the **then** and **else** statements and then diverts control to the statement following **fi**. If the *test-command* returns a *false* status, the **if** structure executes the commands following the **else** statement.

When you run the next script, named **out**, with arguments that are filenames, it displays the files on the terminal. If the first argument is –v (called an option in this case), **out** uses less (page 128) to display the files one page at a time. After determining that it was called with at least one argument, **out** tests its first argument to see whether it is –v. If the result of the test is *true* (if the first argument is –v), **out** uses the shift builtin to shift the arguments to get rid of the –v and displays the files using less. If the result of the test is *false* (if the first argument is *not* –v), the script uses cat to display the files:

```
$ cat out
if [ $# -eq 0 ]
    then
        echo "Usage: out [-v] filenames..." 1>&2
        exit 1
fi
if [ "$1" = "-v" ]
    then
        shift
        less -- "$@"
    else
        cat -- "$@"
fi
```

optional In out the -- argument to cat and less tells these utilities that no more options follow on the command line and not to consider leading hyphens (–) in the following
list as indicating options. Thus -- allows you to view a file with a name that starts
with a hyphen. Although not common, filenames beginning with a hyphen do occasionally occur. (You can create such a file by using the command **cat > –fname.**) The
-- argument works with all Linux utilities that use the getopts builtin (page 936) to
parse their options; it does not work with more and a few other utilities. This argument is particularly useful when used in conjunction with rm to remove a file whose
name starts with a hyphen (**rm -- –fname**), including any that you create while
experimenting with the -- argument.

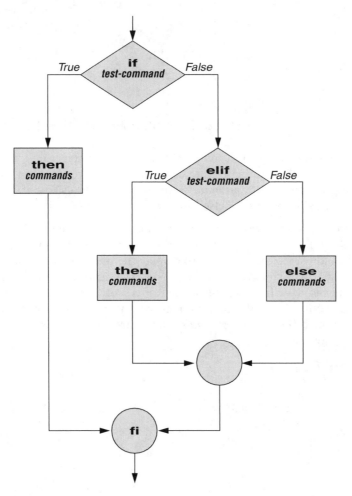

Figure 28-3   An if…then…elif flowchart

if...then...elif

The **if...then...elif** control structure (Figure 28-3) has the following syntax:

if test-command
    then
        commands
    elif test-command
        then
            commands

. . .

    else
        commands
fi

The **elif** statement combines the **else** statement and the **if** statement and allows you to construct a nested set of **if...then...else** structures (Figure 28-3). The difference between the **else** statement and the **elif** statement is that each **else** statement must be paired with a **fi** statement, whereas multiple nested **elif** statements require only a single closing **fi** statement.

The following example shows an **if...then...elif** control structure. This shell script compares three words that the user enters. The first **if** statement uses the Boolean operator AND (**–a**) as an argument to test. The test builtin returns a *true* status only if the first and second logical comparisons are *true* (that is, if **word1** matches **word2** and **word2** matches **word3**). If test returns a *true* status, the script executes the command following the next **then** statement, passes control to the statement following **fi**, and terminates:

```
$ cat if3
echo -n "word 1: "
read word1
echo -n "word 2: "
read word2
echo -n "word 3: "
read word3

if [ "$word1" = "$word2" -a "$word2" = "$word3" ]
    then
        echo "Match: words 1, 2, & 3"
    elif [ "$word1" = "$word2" ]
    then
        echo "Match: words 1 & 2"
    elif [ "$word1" = "$word3" ]
    then
        echo "Match: words 1 & 3"
    elif [ "$word2" = "$word3" ]
    then
        echo "Match: words 2 & 3"
    else
        echo "No match"
    fi
```

```
$ if3
word 1: apple
word 2: orange
word 3: pear
No match
$ if3
word 1: apple
word 2: orange
word 3: apple
Match: words 1 & 3
$ if3
word 1: apple
word 2: apple
word 3: apple
Match: words 1, 2, & 3
```

If the three words are not the same, the structure passes control to the first **elif**, which begins a series of tests to see if any pair of words is the same. As the nesting continues, if any one of the **if** statements is satisfied, the structure passes control to the next **then** statement and subsequently to the statement following **fi**. Each time an **elif** statement is not satisfied, the structure passes control to the next **elif** statement. The double quotation marks around the arguments to echo that contain ampersands (&) prevent the shell from interpreting the ampersands as special characters.

optional THE lnks SCRIPT

The following script, named **lnks**, demonstrates the **if...then** and **if...then...elif** control structures. This script finds hard links to its first argument, a filename. If you provide the name of a directory as the second argument, **lnks** searches for links in that directory and all subdirectories. If you do not specify a directory, **lnks** searches the working directory and its subdirectories. This script does not locate symbolic links.

```
$ cat lnks
#!/bin/bash
# Identify links to a file
# Usage: lnks file [directory]

if [ $# -eq 0 -o $# -gt 2 ]; then
    echo "Usage: lnks file [directory]" 1>&2
    exit 1
fi
if [ -d "$1" ]; then
    echo "First argument cannot be a directory." 1>&2
    echo "Usage: lnks file [directory]" 1>&2
    exit 1
else
    file="$1"
fi
```

```
       if [ $# -eq 1 ]; then
            directory="."
       elif [ -d "$2" ]; then
            directory="$2"
       else
            echo "Optional second argument must be a directory." 1>&2
            echo "Usage: lnks file [directory]" 1>&2
            exit 1
fi

# Check that file exists and is an ordinary file:
if [ ! -f "$file" ]; then
    echo "lnks: $file not found or special file" 1>&2
    exit 1
fi
# Check link count on file
set -- $(ls -l "$file")
linkcnt=$2
if [ "$linkcnt" -eq 1 ]; then
    echo "lnks: no other hard links to $file" 1>&2
    exit 0
fi

# Get the inode of the given file
set $(ls -i "$file")

inode=$1

# Find and print the files with that inode number
echo "lnks: using find to search for links..." 1>&2
find "$directory" -xdev -inum $inode -print
```

Alex has a file named **letter** in his home directory. He wants to find links to this file in his and other users' home directory file trees. In the following example, Alex calls **lnks** from his home directory to perform the search. The second argument to **lnks**, **/home**, is the pathname of the directory he wants to start the search in. The **lnks** script reports that **/home/alex/letter** and **/home/jenny/draft** are links to the same file:

```
$ lnks letter /home
lnks: using find to search for links...
/home/alex/letter
/home/jenny/draft
```

In addition to the **if...then...elif** control structure, **lnks** introduces other features that are commonly used in shell programs. The following discussion describes **lnks** section by section.

Specify the shell   The first line of the **lnks** script uses **#!** (page 274) to specify the shell that will execute the script:

```
#!/bin/bash
```

In this chapter the **#!** notation appears only in more complex examples. It ensures that the proper shell executes the script, even when the user is running a different shell or the script is called from another shell script.

Comments The second and third lines of **lnks** are comments; the shell ignores the text that follows a pound sign up to the next NEWLINE character. These comments in **lnks** briefly identify what the file does and how to use it:

```
# Identify links to a file
# Usage: lnks file [directory]
```

Usage messages The first **if** statement tests whether **lnks** was called with zero arguments or more than two arguments:

```
if [ $# -eq 0 -o $# -gt 2 ]; then
    echo "Usage: lnks file [directory]" 1>&2
    exit 1
fi
```

If either of these conditions is *true*, **lnks** sends a usage message to standard error and exits with a status of 1. The double quotation marks around the usage message prevent the shell from interpreting the brackets as special characters. The brackets in the usage message indicate that the **directory** argument is optional.

The second **if** statement tests whether the first command line argument (**$1**) is a directory (the **–d** argument to test returns a *true* value if the file exists and is a directory):

```
if [ -d "$1" ]; then
    echo "First argument cannot be a directory." 1>&2
    echo "Usage: lnks file [directory]" 1>&2
    exit 1
else
    file="$1"
fi
```

If the first argument is a directory, **lnks** displays a usage message and exits. If it is not a directory, **lnks** saves the value of **$1** in the **file** variable because later in the script **set** resets the command line arguments. If the value of **$1** is not saved before the **set** command is issued, its value will be lost.

Test the arguments The next section of **lnks** is an **if...then...elif** statement:

```
if [ $# -eq 1 ]; then
    directory="."
    elif [ -d "$2" ]; then
    directory="$2"
    else
        echo "Optional second argument must be a directory." 1>&2
        echo "Usage: lnks file [directory]" 1>&2
        exit 1
fi
```

The first *test-command* determines whether the user specified a single argument on the command line. If the *test-command* returns 0 (*true*), the user-created variable named **directory** is assigned the value of the working directory (.). If the *test-command* returns *false*, the **elif** statement tests whether the second argument is a directory. If it is a directory, the **directory** variable is set equal to the second command line argument, **$2**. If **$2** is not a directory, **lnks** sends a usage message to standard error and exits with a status of 1.

The next **if** statement in **lnks** tests whether **$file** does not exist. This test keeps **lnks** from wasting time looking for links to a nonexistent file.

The **test** builtin with the three arguments **!**, **–f**, and **$file** evaluates to *true* if the file **$file** does *not* exist:

```
[ ! -f "$file" ]
```

The **!** operator preceding the **–f** argument to **test** negates its result, yielding *false* if the file **$file** *does* exist and is an ordinary file.

Next **lnks** uses **set** and **ls –l** to check the number of links **$file** has:

```
# Check link count on file
set -- $(ls -l "$file")
linkcnt=$2
if [ "$linkcnt" -eq 1 ]; then
    echo "lnks: no other hard links to $file" 1>&2
    exit 0
fi
```

The **set** builtin uses command substitution (page 334) to set the positional parameters to the output of **ls –l**. The second field in this output is the link count, so the user-created variable **linkcnt** is set equal to **$2**. The **––** used with **set** prevents **set** from interpreting as an option the first argument produced by **ls –l** (the first argument is the access permissions for the file and typically begins with –). The **if** statement checks whether **$linkcnt** is equal to 1; if it is, **lnks** displays a message and exits. Although this message is not truly an error message, it is redirected to standard error. The way **lnks** has been written, all informational messages are sent to standard error. Only the final product of **lnks**—the pathnames of links to the specified file—is sent to standard output, so you can redirect the output as you please.

If the link count is greater than one, **lnks** goes on to identify the *inode* (page 1037) for **$file**. As explained on page 193, comparing the inodes associated with filenames is a good way to determine whether the filenames are links to the same file. The **lnks** script uses **set** to set the positional parameters to the output of **ls –i**. The first argument to **set** is the inode number for the file, so the user-created variable named **inode** is assigned the value of **$1**:

```
# Get the inode of the given file
set $(ls -i "$file")

inode=$1
```

Finally **lnks** uses the find utility to search for files having inode numbers that match **$inode**:

```
# Find and print the files with that inode number
echo "lnks: using find to search for links..." 1>&2
find "$directory" -xdev -inum $inode -print
```

The find utility searches for files that meet the criteria specified by its arguments, beginning its search with the directory specified by its first argument (**$directory**) and searching all subdirectories. The remaining arguments specify that the file-names of files having inodes matching **$inode** should be sent to standard output. Because files in different filesystems can have the same inode number and not be linked, find must search only directories in the same filesystem as **$directory**. The **–xdev** argument prevents find from searching directories on other filesystems. Refer to page 190 for more information about filesystems and links.

The echo command preceding the find command in **lnks**, which tells the user that find is running, is included because find frequently takes a long time to run. Because **lnks** does not include a final exit statement, the exit status of **lnks** is that of the last command it runs, find.

DEBUGGING SHELL SCRIPTS

When you are writing a script such as **lnks**, it is easy to make mistakes. You can use the shell's **–x** option to help debug a script. This option causes the shell to display each command before it runs the command. Tracing a script's execution in this way can give you information about where a problem lies.

You can run **lnks** as in the previous example and cause the shell to display each command before it is executed. Either set the **–x** option for the current shell (**set –x**) so that all scripts display commands as they are run or use the **–x** option to affect only the shell that is running the script called by the command line.

```
$ bash -x lnks letter /home
+ '[' 2 -eq 0 -o 2 -gt 2 ']'
+ '[' -d letter ']'
+ file=letter
+ '[' 2 -eq 1 ']'
+ '[' -d /home ']'
+ directory=/home
+ '[' '!' -f letter ']'
...
```

PS4   Each command that the script executes is preceded by the value of the **PS4** variable—a plus sign (**+**) by default, so you can distinguish debugging output from script-produced output. You must export **PS4** if you set it in the shell that calls the script. The next command sets **PS4** to **>>>>** followed by a SPACE and exports it:

```
$ export PS4='>>>> '
```

You can also set the **–x** option of the shell running the script by putting the following **set** command at the top of the script:

```
set -x
```

Put **set –x** anywhere in the script you want to turn debugging on. Turn the debugging option off with a plus sign.

```
set +x
```

The **set –o xtrace** and **set +o xtrace** commands do the same things as **set –x** and **set +x**, respectively.

for...in

The **for...in** control structure has the following syntax:

for loop-index in argument-list
do
     commands
done

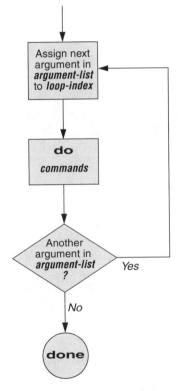

Figure 28-4   A **for...in** flowchart

The **for...in** structure (Figure 28-4) assigns the value of the first argument in the *argument-list* to the *loop-index* and executes the *commands* between the **do** and **done** statements. The **do** and **done** statements mark the beginning and end of the **for** loop.

After it passes control to the **done** statement, the structure assigns the value of the second argument in the *argument-list* to the *loop-index* and repeats the *commands*. The structure repeats the *commands* between the **do** and **done** statements one time for each argument in the *argument-list*. When the structure exhausts the *argument-list*, it passes control to the statement following **done**.

The following **for...in** structure assigns **apples** to the user-created variable **fruit** and then displays the value of **fruit**, which is **apples**. Next the structure assigns **oranges** to **fruit** and repeats the process. When it exhausts the argument list, the structure transfers control to the statement following **done**, which displays a message.

```
$ cat fruit
for fruit in apples oranges pears bananas
do
    echo "$fruit"
done
echo "Task complete."

$ fruit
apples
oranges
pears
bananas
Task complete.
```

The next script lists the names of the directory files in the working directory by looping over all the files, using test to determine which files are directories:

```
$ cat dirfiles
for i in *
do
    if [ -d "$i" ]
        then
            echo "$i"
    fi
done
```

The ambiguous file reference character * matches the names of all files (except hidden files) in the working directory. Prior to executing the **for** loop, the shell expands the * and uses the resulting list to assign successive values to the index variable **i**.

for

The **for** control structure has the following syntax:

for loop-index
do
    commands
done

In the **for** structure the *loop-index* takes on the value of each of the command line arguments, one at a time. It is the same as the **for...in** structure (Figure 28-4) except for where it gets values for the *loop-index*. The **for** structure performs a sequence of commands, usually involving each argument in turn.

The following shell script shows a **for** structure displaying each command line argument. The first line of the script, **for arg**, implies **for arg in "$@"**, where the shell expands **"$@"** into a list of quoted command line arguments **"$1" "$2" "$3"** and so on. The balance of the script corresponds to the **for...in** structure.

```
$ cat for_test
for arg
do
    echo "$arg"
done
$ for_test candy gum chocolate
candy
gum
chocolate
```

optional **THE whos SCRIPT**

The following script, named **whos**, demonstrates the usefulness of the implied **"$@"** in the **for** structure. You give **whos** one or more users' full names or usernames as arguments, and **whos** displays information about the users. The **whos** script gets the information it displays from the first and fifth fields in the **/etc/passwd** file. The first field always contains a username, and the fifth field typically contains the user's full name. You can provide a username as an argument to **whos** to identify the user's name or provide a name as an argument to identify the username. The **whos** script is similar to the finger utility, although **whos** delivers less information.

```
$ cat whos
#!/bin/bash
# adapted from finger.sh by Lee Sailer
# UNIX/WORLD, III:11, p. 67, Fig. 2

if [ $# -eq 0 ]
    then
        echo "Usage: whos id..." 1>&2
        exit 1
fi
for id
do
    gawk -F: '{print $1, $5}' /etc/passwd |
    grep -i "$id"
done
```

Below **whos** identifies the user whose username is **chas** and the user whose name is **Marilou Smith**:

```
$ whos chas "Marilou Smith"
chas Charles Casey
msmith Marilou Smith
```

Use of "$@" The **whos** script uses a **for** statement to loop through the command line arguments. In this script the implied use of "$@" in the **for** loop is particularly beneficial because it causes the **for** loop to treat an argument that contains a SPACE as a single argument. This example quotes **Marilou Smith**, which causes the shell to pass it to the script as a single argument. Then the implied "$@" in the **for** statement causes the shell to regenerate the quoted argument **Marilou Smith** so that it is again treated as a single argument.

gawk For each command line argument, **whos** searches the /etc/passwd file. Inside the **for** loop the gawk utility extracts the first ($1) and fifth ($5) fields from the lines in /etc/passwd. The –F: option causes gawk to use a colon (:) as a field separator when it reads /etc/passwd, allowing it to break each line into fields. The gawk command sets and uses the $1 and $5 arguments; they are included within single quotation marks and are not interpreted by the shell. Do not confuse these arguments with positional parameters, which correspond to command line arguments. The first and fifth fields are sent to grep (page 131) via a pipe. The grep utility searches for $id (which has taken on the value of a command line argument) in its input. The –i option causes grep to ignore case as it searches; grep displays each line in its input that contains $id.

| at the end of a line An interesting syntactical exception that bash gives the pipe symbol (|) appears on the line with the gawk command: You do not have to quote a NEWLINE that immediately follows a pipe symbol (that is, a pipe symbol that is the last thing on a line) to keep the NEWLINE from executing a command. Try giving the command **who |** and pressing RETURN. The shell displays a secondary prompt. If you then enter **sort** followed by another RETURN, you see a sorted who list. The pipe works even though a NEWLINE follows the pipe symbol.

while

The **while** control structure has the following syntax:

while test-command
do
    commands
done

As long as the *test-command* (Figure 28-5) returns a *true* exit status, the **while** structure continues to execute the series of *commands* delimited by the **do** and **done** statements. Before each loop through the *commands*, the structure executes the *test-command*. When the exit status of the *test-command* is *false*, the structure passes control to the statement after the **done** statement.

test builtin The following shell script first initializes the **number** variable to zero. The test builtin then determines whether **number** is less than 10. The script uses test with the –lt argument to perform a numerical test. For numerical comparisons, you must use –ne (not equal), –eq (equal), –gt (greater than), –ge (greater than or equal to), –lt (less than), or –le (less than or equal to). For string comparisons use = (equal) or != (not equal) when you are working with test. In this example, test has an exit status

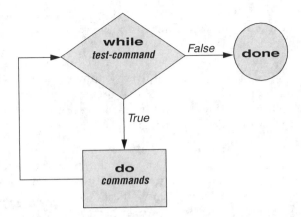

Figure 28-5 A while flowchart

of 0 (*true*) as long as **number** is less than 10. As long as test returns *true*, the structure executes the commands between the **do** and **done** statements. See page 879 for information on the test utility, which is very similar to the test builtin.

```
$ cat count
#!/bin/bash
number=0
while [ "$number" -lt 10 ]
    do
        echo -n "$number"
        ((number +=1))
    done
echo
$ count
0123456789
$
```

The echo command following **do** displays **number**. The **–n** prevents echo from issuing a NEWLINE following its output. The next command uses arithmetic evaluation [((...)); page 940] to increment the value of **number** by 1. The **done** statement terminates the loop and returns control to the **while** statement to start the loop over again. The final echo causes **count** to send a NEWLINE character to standard output, so that the next prompt occurs in the leftmost column on the display (rather than immediately following 9).

---

optional THE spell_check SCRIPT

The aspell utility checks the words in a file against a dictionary of correctly spelled words. With the **–l** option, aspell runs in list mode: Input comes from standard input and aspell sends each potentially misspelled word to standard output. The following command produces a list of possible misspellings in the file **letter.txt**:

```
$ aspell -l < letter.txt
quikly
portible
frendly
```

The next shell script, named **spell_check**, shows another use of a **while** structure. To find the incorrect spellings in a file, you can use **spell_check**, which calls aspell to check a file against a system dictionary but goes a step further: It enables you to specify a list of correctly spelled words and removes these words from the output of aspell. This script is useful for removing words that you use frequently, such as names and technical terms, that are not in a standard dictionary. Although you can duplicate the functionality of **spell_check** by using additional aspell dictionaries, the script is included here for its instructive value.

The **spell_check** script requires two filename arguments: a file containing the list of correctly spelled words and a file that you want to check. The first **if** statement verifies that the user specified two arguments. The next two **if** statements verify that both arguments are readable files. (The exclamation point negates the sense of the following operator; the –r operator causes test to determine whether a file is readable. The result is a test that determines whether a file is *not readable*.)

```
$ cat spell_check
#!/bin/bash
# remove correct spellings from aspell output
if [ $# -ne 2 ]
    then
        echo "Usage: spell_check file1 file2" 1>&2
        echo "file1: list of correct spellings" 1>&2
        echo "file2: file to be checked" 1>&2
        exit 1
fi

if [ ! -r "$1" ]
    then
        echo "spell_check: $1 is not readable" 1>&2
        exit 1
fi

if [ ! -r "$2" ]
    then
        echo "spell_check: $2 is not readable" 1>&2
        exit 1
fi

aspell -l < "$2" |
while read line
do
    if ! grep "^$line$" "$1" > /dev/null
        then
            echo $line
    fi
done
```

The **spell_check** script sends the output from aspell (with the –l option so that it produces a list of misspelled words on standard output) through a pipe to standard input of a **while** structure, which reads one line at a time (each line has one word on it) from standard input. The *test-command* (that is, **read line**) returns a *true* exit status as long as it receives a line from standard input.

Inside the **while** loop an **if** statement[1] monitors the return value of grep, which determines whether the line that was read is in the user's list of correctly spelled words. The pattern that grep searches for (the value of **$line**) is preceded and followed by special characters that specify the beginning and end of a line (**^** and **$**, respectively). These special characters ensure that grep finds a match only if the **$line** variable matches an entire line in the file of correctly spelled words. (Otherwise, grep would match a string, such as **paul**, in the output of aspell if the file of correctly spelled words contained the word **paulson**.) These special characters, together with the value of the **$line** variable, form a regular expression (Appendix A).

The output of grep is redirected to **/dev/null** (page 215) because the output is not needed; only the exit code is important. The **if** statement checks the negated exit status of grep (the leading exclamation point negates or changes the sense of the exit status—*true* becomes *false*, and vice versa), which is 0 or *true* (*false* when negated) when a matching line is found. If the exit status is *not* 0 or *false* (*true* when negated), the word was *not* in the file of correctly spelled words. The echo builtin sends a list of words that are not in the file of correctly spelled words to standard output.

Once it detects the EOF (end of file), the read builtin returns a *false* exit status. Control then passes out of the **while** structure, and the script terminates.

Before you use **spell_check**, create a file of correct spellings containing words that you use frequently but that are not in a standard dictionary. For example, if you work for a company named **Blinkenship and Klimowski, Attorneys**, you would put **Blinkenship** and **Klimowski** into the file. The following example shows how spell_check checks the spelling in a file named **memo** and removes **Blinkenship** and **Klimowski** from the output list of incorrectly spelled words:

```
$ aspell -l < memo
Blinkenship
Klimowski
targat
hte
$ cat word_list
Blinkenship
Klimowski
$ spell_check word_list memo
targat
hte
```

Refer to the aspell manual (in the **/usr/share/doc/aspell** directory or at aspell.net) for more information.

---

1. This **if** statement can also be written as

```
if ! grep -qw "$line" "$1"
```

The **–q** option suppresses the output from grep so that only an exit code is returned. The **–w** option causes grep to match only a whole word.

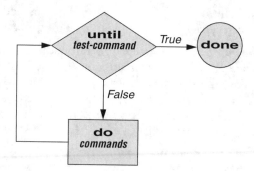

Figure 28-6   An **until** flowchart

until

The **until** and **while** structures are very similar, differing only in the sense of the test performed at the top of the loop. Figure 28-6 shows that **until** continues to loop *until* the *test-command* returns a *true* exit status. The **while** structure loops *while* the *test-command* continues to return a *true* or nonerror condition. The **until** control structure has the following syntax:

*until **test-command***
do
        commands
done

The following script demonstrates an **until** structure that includes read. When the user enters the correct string of characters, the *test-command* is satisfied and the structure passes control out of the loop.

```
$ cat until1
secretname=jenny
name=noname
echo "Try to guess the secret name!"
echo
until [ "$name" = "$secretname" ]
do
    echo -n "Your guess: "
    read name
done
echo "Very good."

$ until1
Try to guess the secret name!

Your guess: helen
Your guess: barbara
Your guess: rachael
Your guess: jenny
Very good
```

The following **locktty** script is similar to the lock command on Berkeley UNIX and the **Lock Screen** menu selection in GNOME. The script prompts you for a key (password) and uses an **until** control structure to lock the terminal. The **until** statement causes the system to ignore any characters typed at the keyboard until the user types in the key on a line by itself, which unlocks the terminal. The **locktty** script can keep people from using your terminal while you are away from it for short periods of time. It saves you from having to log out if you are concerned about other users using your login.

```
$ cat locktty
#! /bin/bash
# UNIX/WORLD, III:4

trap '' 1 2 3 18
stty -echo
echo -n "Key: "
read key_1
echo
echo -n "Again: "
read key_2
echo
key_3=
if [ "$key_1" = "$key_2" ]
    then
        tput clear
        until [ "$key_3" = "$key_2" ]
        do
            read key_3
        done
    else
        echo "locktty: keys do not match" 1>&2
fi
stty echo
```

Forget your password for **locktty**?

tip   If you forget your key (password), you will need to log in from another (virtual) terminal and kill the process running **locktty**.

trap builtin   The trap builtin (page 933) at the beginning of the **locktty** script stops a user from being able to terminate the script by sending it a signal (for example, by pressing the interrupt key). Trapping signal 18 means that no one can use CONTROL-Z (job control, a stop from a tty) to defeat the lock. (See Table 28-5 on page 933 for a list of signals.) The **stty -echo** command causes the terminal not to display characters typed at the keyboard, thereby preventing the key that the user enters from appearing on the screen. After turning off keyboard echo, the script prompts the user for a key, reads it into the user-created variable **key_1**, prompts the user to enter the same key again, and saves it in **key_2**. The statement **key_3=** creates a variable with a NULL value. If **key_1** and **key_2** match, **locktty** clears the screen (with the tput command) and starts an **until** loop. The **until** loop keeps attempting to read from the terminal and assigning the input to the **key_3** variable. Once the user types in a string that matches one of the original keys (**key_2**), the **until** loop terminates and keyboard echo is turned on again.

break **AND** continue

You can interrupt a **for, while,** or **until** loop by using a **break** or **continue** statement. The **break** statement transfers control to the statement after the **done** statement, which terminates execution of the loop. The **continue** command transfers control to the **done** statement, which continues execution of the loop.

The following script demonstrates the use of these two statements. The **for...in** structure loops through the values 1–10. The first **if** statement executes its commands when the value of the index is less than or equal to 3 (**$index –le 3**). The second **if** statement executes its commands when the value of the index is greater than or equal to 8 (**$index –ge 8**). In between the two **if**s, echo displays the value of the index. For all values up to and including 3, the first **if** statement displays **continue** and executes a **continue** statement that skips echo **$index** and the second **if** statement and continues with the next **for** statement. For the value of 8, the second **if** statement displays **break** and executes a **break** statement that exits from the **for** loop:

```
$ cat brk
for index in 1 2 3 4 5 6 7 8 9 10
    do
        if [ $index -le 3 ] ; then
            echo "continue"
            continue
        fi
#
    echo $index
#
    if [ $index -ge 8 ] ; then
        echo "break"
        break
    fi
done

$ brk
continue
continue
continue
4
5
6
7
8
break
```

case

The **case** structure (Figure 28-7, page 902) is a multiple-branch decision mechanism. The path taken through the structure depends on a match or lack of a match between the *test-string* and one of the *patterns*. The **case** control structure has the following syntax:

```
case test-string in
    pattern-1)
        commands-1
        ;;
    pattern-2)
        commands-2
        ;;
    pattern-3)
        commands-3
        ;;
    . . .
esac
```

The following **case** structure examines the character that the user enters as the *test-string*. This value is held in the variable **letter**. If the *test-string* has a value of **A**, the structure executes the command following the *pattern* **A**. The right parenthesis is part of the **case** control structure, not part of the *pattern*. If the *test-string* has a value of **B** or **C**, the structure executes the command following the matching *pattern*. The asterisk (*) indicates *any string of characters* and serves as a catchall in case there is no match. If no *pattern* matches the *test-string* and if there is no catchall (*) *pattern*, control passes to the command following the **esac** statement, without the **case** structure taking any action.

```
$ cat case1
echo -n "Enter A, B, or C: "
read letter
case "$letter" in
    A)
        echo "You entered A"
        ;;
    B)
        echo "You entered B"
        ;;
    C)
        echo "You entered C"
        ;;
    *)
        echo "You did not enter A, B, or C"
        ;;
esac

$ case1
Enter A, B, or C: B
You entered B
```

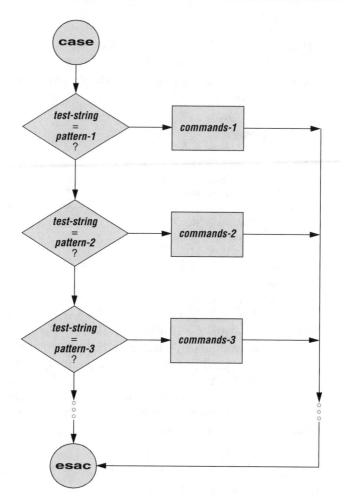

Figure 28-7   A case flowchart

The next execution of **case1** shows the user entering a lowercase **b**. Because the *test-string* **b** does not match the uppercase **B** *pattern* (or any other *pattern* in the **case** statement), the program executes the commands following the catchall *pattern* and displays a message:

```
$ case1
Enter A, B, or C: b
You did not enter A, B, or C
```

The *pattern* in the **case** structure is analogous to an ambiguous file reference. It can include any of the special characters and strings shown in Table 28-2.

The next script accepts both uppercase and lowercase letters:

```
$ cat case2
echo -n "Enter A, B, or C: "
read letter
case "$letter" in
    a|A)
        echo "You entered A"
        ;;
    b|B)
        echo "You entered B"
        ;;
    c|C)
        echo "You entered C"
        ;;
    *)
        echo "You did not enter A, B, or C"
        ;;
esac

$ case2
Enter A, B, or C: b
You entered B
```

Table 28-2 Patterns

Pattern	Function
*	Matches any string of characters. Use for the default case.
?	Matches any single character.
[...]	Defines a character class. Any characters enclosed within brackets are tried, one at a time, in an attempt to match a single character. A hyphen between two characters specifies a range of characters.
|	Separates alternative choices that satisfy a particular branch of the **case** structure.

optional The following example shows how you can use the **case** structure to create a simple menu. The **command_menu** script uses echo to present menu items and prompt the user for a selection. (The **select** control structure [page 907] makes it much easier to code a menu.) The **case** structure then executes the appropriate utility depending on the user's selection.

```
$ cat command_menu
#!/bin/bash
# menu interface to simple commands

echo -e "\n        COMMAND MENU\n"
echo "  a.  Current date and time"
echo "  b.  Users currently logged in"
echo "  c.  Name of the working directory"
echo -e "  d.  Contents of the working directory\n"
echo -n "Enter a, b, c, or d: "
read answer
echo
```

```
        #
        case "$answer" in
            a)
                date
                ;;
            b)
                who
                ;;
            c)
                pwd
                ;;
            d)
                ls
                ;;
            *)
                echo "There is no selection: $answer"
                ;;
        esac
```

```
$ command_menu
```

```
            COMMAND MENU

        a.  Current date and time
        b.  Users currently logged in
        c.  Name of the working directory
        d.  Contents of the working directory

    Enter a, b, c, or d: a

    Wed Jan  5 12:31:12 PST 2005
```

echo –e The –e option causes echo to interpret \n as a NEWLINE character. If you do not include this option, echo does not output the extra blank lines that make the menu easy to read but instead outputs the (literal) two-character sequence \n. The –e option causes echo to interpret several other backslash-quoted characters (Table 28-3). Remember to quote (i.e., place double quotation marks around the string) the backslash-quoted character so that the shell does not interpret it but passes the backslash and the character to echo. See **xpg_echo** (page 327) for a way to avoid using the –e option.

Table 28-3   Special characters in echo (must use –e)

Quoted character	echo **displays**
\a	Alert (bell)
\b	BACKSPACE
\c	Suppress trailing NEWLINE
\f	FORMFEED
\n	NEWLINE
\r	RETURN

Table 28-3	Special characters in echo (must use –e) (continued)
\t	Horizontal TAB
\v	Vertical TAB
\\	Backslash
\nnn	The character with the ASCII octal code nnn; if nnn is not valid, echo displays the string literally

You can also use the **case** control structure to take various actions in a script, depending on how many arguments the script is called with. The following script, named **safedit**, uses a **case** structure that branches based on the number of command line arguments ($#). It saves a backup copy of a file you are editing with vim.

```
$ cat safedit
#!/bin/bash
# UNIX/WORLD, IV:11

PATH=/bin:/usr/bin
script=$(basename $0)
case $# in

    0)
        vim
        exit 0
        ;;

    1)
        if [ ! -f "$1" ]
            then
                vim "$1"
                exit 0
            fi
        if [ ! -r "$1" -o ! -w "$1" ]
            then
                echo "$script: check permissions on $1" 1>&2
                exit 1
            else
                editfile=$1
            fi
        if [ ! -w "." ]
            then
                echo "$script: backup cannot be " \
                    "created in the working directory" 1>&2
                exit 1
            fi
        ;;
    *)
        echo "Usage: $script [file-to-edit]" 1>&2
        exit 1
        ;;
esac
```

```
        tempfile=/tmp/$$.$script
        cp $editfile $tempfile
        if vim $editfile
           then
                mv $tempfile bak.$(basename $editfile)
                echo "$script: backup file created"
           else
                mv $tempfile editerr
                echo "$script: edit error--copy of " \
                     "original file is in editerr" 1>&2
    fi
```

If you call **safedit** without any arguments, the **case** structure executes its first branch and calls vim without a filename argument. Because an existing file is not being edited, **safedit** does not create a backup file. If you call **safedit** with one argument, it runs the commands in the second branch of the **case** structure and verifies that the file specified by **$1** does not yet exist or is the name of a file for which the user has read and write permission. The **safedit** script also verifies that the user has write permission for the working directory. If the user calls **safedit** with more than one argument, the third branch of the **case** structure presents a usage message and exits with a status of 1.

Set **PATH**   In addition to using a **case** structure for branching based on the number of command line arguments, the **safedit** script introduces several other features. First, at the beginning of the script, the **PATH** variable is set to search **/bin** and **/usr/bin**. Setting **PATH** in this way ensures that the commands executed by the script are standard utilities, which are kept in those directories. By setting **PATH** inside a script, you can avoid the problems that might occur if users have set **PATH** to search their own directories first and have scripts or programs with the same names as the utilities the script calls. You can also include absolute pathnames within a script to achieve this end, but this practice can make a script less portable.

Name of the   In a second **safedit** feature, the following line creates a variable named **script** and
program   assigns the simple filename of the script to it:

```
        script=$(basename $0)
```

The basename utility sends the simple filename component of its argument to standard output, which is assigned to the **script** variable, using command substitution. The **$0** holds the command the script was called with (page 921). No matter which of the following commands the user calls the script with, the output of basename is the simple filename **safedit**:

```
$ /home/alex/bin/safedit memo
$ ./safedit memo
$ safedit memo
```

After the **script** variable is set, it replaces the filename of the script in usage and error messages. By using a variable that is derived from the command that invoked the script rather than a filename that is hardcoded into the script, you can create links to the script or rename it, and the usage and error messages will still provide accurate information.

Naming temporary files
A third significant feature of **safedit** relates to the use of the **$$** variable in the name of a temporary file. The statement following the **esac** statement creates and assigns a value to the **tempfile** variable. This variable contains the name of a temporary file that is stored in the **/tmp** directory, as are many temporary files. The temporary filename begins with the PID number of the shell and ends with the name of the script. Use of the PID number ensures that the filename is unique, and **safedit** will not attempt to overwrite an existing file, as might happen if two people were using **safedit** at the same time. The name of the script is appended so that, should the file be left in **/tmp** for some reason, you can figure out where it came from.

The PID number is used in front of—rather than after—**$script** in the filename because of the 14-character limit placed on filenames by some older versions of UNIX. Linux systems do not have this limitation. Because the PID number ensures the uniqueness of the filename, it is placed first so that it cannot be truncated. (If the **$script** component is truncated, the filename is still unique.) For the same reason, when a backup file is created inside the **if** control structure a few lines down in the script, the filename is composed of the string **bak.** followed by the name of the file being edited. On an older system, if **bak** were used as a suffix rather than a prefix and the original filename were 14 characters long, **.bak** might be lost and the original file would be overwritten. The **basename** utility extracts the simple filename of **$editfile** before it is prefixed with **bak.**

Fourth, **safedit** uses an unusual *test-command* in the **if** structure: **vim $editfile**. The *test-command* calls vim to edit **$editfile**. When you finish editing the file and exit from vim, vim returns an exit code. The **if** control structure uses that exit code to determine which branch to take. If the editing session completed successfully, vim returns 0 and the statements following the **then** statement are executed. If vim does not terminate normally (as would occur if the user killed [page 395] the vim process), vim returns a nonzero exit status and the script executes the statements following **else**.

select

The **select** control structure is based on the one found in the Korn Shell. It displays a menu, assigns a value to a variable based on the user's choice of items, and executes a series of commands. The **select** control structure has the following syntax:

```
select varname [in arg . . . ]
do
    commands
done
```

The **select** structure displays a menu of the *arg* items. If you omit the keyword **in** and the list of arguments, **select** uses the positional parameters in place of the *arg* items. The menu is formatted with numbers before each item. For example, a **select** structure that begins with

```
select fruit in apple banana blueberry kiwi orange watermelon STOP
```

displays the following menu:

```
1) apple      3) blueberry   5) orange      7) STOP
2) banana     4) kiwi        6) watermelon
```

The **select** structure uses the values of the **LINES** and **COLUMNS** variables to determine the size of the display. (**LINES** has a default value of 24; **COLUMNS** has a default value of 80.) With **COLUMNS** set to 20, the menu looks like this:

```
1) apple
2) banana
3) blueberry
4) kiwi
5) orange
6) watermelon
7) STOP
```

PS3   After displaying the menu **select** displays the value of **PS3**, the special **select** prompt. The default value of **PS3** is **?#** but you typically set **PS3** to a more meaningful value. When you enter a valid number (one in the menu range) in response to the **PS3** prompt, **select** sets *varname* to the argument corresponding to the number you entered. If you make an invalid entry, *varname* is set to null. Either way **select** stores your response in the keyword variable **REPLY** and then executes the *commands* between **do** and **done**. If you press RETURN without entering a choice, the shell redisplays the menu and the **PS3** prompt.

The **select** structure continues to issue the **PS3** prompt and execute the *commands* until something causes it to exit—typically a **break** or **exit** statement. A **break** statement exits from the loop and an **exit** statement exits from the script.

The following script illustrates the use of **select**:

```
$ cat fruit2
#!/bin/bash
PS3="Choose your favorite fruit from these possibilities: "
select FRUIT in apple banana blueberry kiwi orange watermelon STOP
do
    if [ "$FRUIT" == "" ]; then
        echo -e "Invalid entry.\n"
        continue
    elif [ $FRUIT = STOP ]; then
        echo "Thanks for playing!"
        break
    fi
echo "You chose $FRUIT as your favorite."
echo -e "That is choice number $REPLY.\n"
done
```

```
$ fruit2
1) apple       3) blueberry   5) orange      7) STOP
2) banana      4) kiwi        6) watermelon
Choose your favorite fruit from these possibilities: 3
You chose blueberry as your favorite.
That is choice number 3.

Choose your favorite fruit from these possibilities: 99
Invalid entry.

Choose your favorite fruit from these possibilities: 7
Thanks for playing!
```

After setting the **PS3** prompt and establishing the menu with the **select** statement, **fruit2** executes the *commands* between **do** and **done**. If the user makes an invalid entry, the shell sets *varname* (**$FRUIT**) to a null value, so **fruit2** first tests whether **$FRUIT** is null. If it is, echo displays an error and **continue** causes the shell to redisplay the **PS3** prompt. If the entry is valid, the script tests whether the user wants to stop. If so, echo displays a message and **break** exits from the **select** structure (and from the script). If the user entered a valid response and does not want to stop, the script displays the name and number of the user's response. (See page 904 for information about the –e option to echo.)

HERE DOCUMENT

A Here document allows you to redirect input to a shell script from within the shell script itself. A Here document is so called because it is *here*—immediately accessible in the shell script—instead of *there,* perhaps in another file.

The following script, named **birthday,** contains a Here document. The two less than (<<) symbols in the first line indicate that a Here document follows. One or more characters that delimit the Here document follow the less than symbols—this example uses a plus sign. Whereas the opening delimiter must appear adjacent to the less than symbols, the closing delimiter must be on a line by itself. The shell sends everything between the two delimiters to the process as standard input. In the example it is as though you had redirected standard input to grep from a file, except that the file is embedded in the shell script:

```
$ cat birthday
grep -i "$1" <<+
Alex     June 22
Barbara  February 3
Darlene  May 8
Helen    March 13
Jenny    January 23
Nancy    June 26
+
$ birthday Jenny
Jenny    January 23
$ birthday june
Alex     June 22
Nancy    June 26
```

When you run **birthday**, it lists all the Here document lines that contain the argument you called it with. In this case the first time **birthday** is run, it displays Jenny's birthday because it is called with an argument of **Jenny**. The second run displays all the birthdays in June. The –i argument causes grep's search not to be case sensitive.

optional The next script, named **bundle**,[2] includes a clever use of a Here document. The **bundle** script is an elegant example of a script that creates a shell archive (**shar**) file. The script, shown following, creates a file that is itself a shell script containing several other files as well as the code to re-create the original files.

```
$ cat bundle
#!/bin/bash
# bundle:  group files into distribution package

echo "# To unbundle, bash this file"
for i
do
    echo "echo $i 1>&2"
    echo "cat >$i <<'End of $i'"
    cat $i
    echo "End of $i"
done
```

Just as the shell does not treat special characters that occur in standard input of a shell script as special, so the shell does not treat the special characters that occur between the delimiters in a Here document as special.

As the following example shows, the output of **bundle** is a shell script, which is redirected to a file named **bothfiles**. It contains the contents of each file given as an argument to **bundle** (**file1** and **file2** in this case) inside a Here document. To extract the original files from **bothfiles**, you simply run it as an argument to a bash command. Before each Here document is a cat command that causes the Here document to be written to a new file when **bothfiles** is run:

```
$ cat file1
This is a file.
It contains two lines.
$ cat file2
This is another file.
It contains
three lines.

$ bundle file1 file2 > bothfiles
$ cat bothfiles
# To unbundle, bash this file
echo file1 1>&2
cat >file1 <<'End of file1'
```

---

2. Thanks to Brian W. Kernighan and Rob Pike, *The Unix Programming Environment* (Englewood Cliffs, N.J.: Prentice-Hall, 1984), 98. Reprinted with permission.

```
This is a file.
It contains two lines.
End of file1
echo file2 1>&2
cat >file2 <<'End of file2'
This is another file.
It contains
three lines.
End of file2
```

In the next example, **file1** and **file2** are removed before **bothfiles** is run. The **bothfiles** script echoes the names of the files it creates as it creates them. The ls command then shows that **bothfiles** has re-created **file1** and **file2**:

```
$ rm file1 file2
$ bash bothfiles
file1
file2
$ ls
bothfiles
file1
file2
```

FILE DESCRIPTORS

As discussed on page 270, before a process can read from or write to a file it must open that file. When a process opens a file, Linux associates a number (called a *file descriptor*) with the file. Each process has its own set of open files and its own file descriptors. After opening a file, a process reads from and writes to that file by referring to its file descriptor. When it no longer needs the file, the process closes the file, freeing the file descriptor.

A typical Linux process starts with three open files: standard input (file descriptor 0), standard output (file descriptor 1), and standard error (file descriptor 2). Often those are the only files the process needs. Recall that you redirect standard output with the symbol > or the symbol **1>** and that you redirect standard error with the symbol **2>**. Although you can redirect other file descriptors, because file descriptors other than 0, 1, and 2 do not have any special conventional meaning, it is rarely useful to do so. The exception is in programs that you write yourself, in which case you control the meaning of the file descriptors and can take advantage of redirection.

Opening a file descriptor   The Bourne Again Shell opens files using the exec builtin as follows:

exec n> outfile
exec m< infile

The first line opens *outfile* for output and holds it open, associating it with file descriptor *n*. The second line opens *infile* for input and holds it open, associating it with file descriptor *m*.

Duplicating a file
descriptor
The **<&** token duplicates an input file descriptor; use **>&** to duplicate an output file descriptor. You can duplicate a file descriptor by making it refer to the same file as another open file descriptor, such as standard input or output. Use the following format to open or redirect file descriptor *n* as a duplicate of file descriptor *m*:

> *exec n<&m*

Once you have opened a file, you can use it for input and output in two different ways. First, you can use I/O redirection on any command line, redirecting standard output to a file descriptor with **>&***n* or redirecting standard input from a file descriptor with **<&***n*. Second, you can use the read (page 927) and echo builtins. If you invoke other commands, including functions (page 321), they inherit these open files and file descriptors. When you have finished using a file, you can close it with

> *exec n<&–*

When you invoke the shell function in the next example, named **mycp**, with two arguments, it copies the file named by the first argument to the file named by the second argument. If you supply only one argument, the script copies the file named by the argument to standard output. If you invoke **mycp** with no arguments, it copies standard input to standard output.

A function is not a shell script

tip   The **mycp** example is a shell function; it will not work as you expect if you execute it as a shell script. (It will work: The function will be created in a very short-lived subshell, which is probably of little use.) You can enter this function from the keyboard. If you put the function in a file, you can run it as an argument to the . (dot) builtin (page 269). You can also put the function in a startup file if you want it to be always available (page 323).

```
function mycp ()
{
case $# in
    0)
        # zero arguments
        # file descriptor 3 duplicates standard input
        # file descriptor 4 duplicates standard output
        exec 3<&0 4<&1
        ;;
    1)
        # one argument
        # open the file named by the argument for input
        # and associate it with file descriptor 3
        # file descriptor 4 duplicates standard output
        exec 3< $1 4<&1
        ;;
    2)
        # two arguments
        # open the file named by the first argument for input
        # and associate it with file descriptor 3
        # open the file named by the second argument for output
        # and associate it with file descriptor 4
        exec 3< $1 4> $2
        ;;
```

```
      *)
            echo "Usage: mycp [source [dest]]"
            return 1
            ;;
esac

# call cat with input coming from file descriptor 3
# and output going to file descriptor 4
cat <&3 >&4

# close file descriptors 3 and 4
exec 3<&- 4<&-
}
```

The real work of this function is done in the line that begins with cat. The rest of the
script arranges for file descriptors 3 and 4, which are the input and output of the cat
command, to be associated with the appropriate files.

optional   The next program takes two filenames on the command line, sorts both, and sends
the output to temporary files. The program then merges the sorted files to standard
output, preceding each line by a number that indicates which file it came from.

```
$ cat sortmerg
#!/bin/bash
usage ()
{
if [ $# -ne 2 ]; then
    echo "Usage: $0 file1 file2" 2>&1
    exit 1
    fi
}

# Default temporary directory
: ${TEMPDIR:=/tmp}

# Check argument count
usage "$@"

# Set up temporary files for sorting
file1=$TEMPDIR/$$.file1
file2=$TEMPDIR/$$.file2

# Sort
sort $1 > $file1
sort $2 > $file2

# Open $file1 and $file2 for reading. Use file descriptors 3 and 4.
exec 3<$file1
exec 4<$file2

# Read the first line from each file to figure out how to start.
read Line1 <&3
status1=$?
read Line2 <&4
status2=$?
```

```
# Strategy: while there is still input left in both files:
#    Output the line that should come first.
#    Read a new line from the file that line came from.
while [ $status1 -eq 0 -a $status2 -eq 0 ]
    do
        if [[ "$Line2" > "$Line1" ]]; then
            echo -e "1.\t$Line1"
            read -u3 Line1
            status1=$?
        else
            echo -e "2.\t$Line2"
            read -u4 Line2
            status2=$?
        fi
    done

# Now one of the files is at end-of-file.
# Read from each file until the end.
# First file1:
while [ $status1 -eq 0 ]
    do
        echo -e "1.\t$Line1"
        read Line1 <&3
        status1=$?
    done
# Next file2:
while [[ $status2 -eq 0 ]]
    do
        echo -e "2.\t$Line2"
        read Line2 <&4
        status2=$?
    done

# Close and remove both input files
exec 3<&- 4<&-
rm -f $file1 $file2
exit 0
```

PARAMETERS AND VARIABLES

Shell parameters and variables were introduced on page 285. This section adds to the previous coverage with a discussion of array variables, global versus local variables, special and positional parameters, and expanding null and unset variables.

ARRAY VARIABLES

The Bourne Again Shell supports one-dimensional array variables. The subscripts are integers with zero-based indexing (i.e., the first element of the array has the subscript 0). The following format declares and assigns values to an array:

name=(element1 element2 ...)

The following example assigns four values to the array **NAMES**:

```
$ NAMES=(max helen sam zach)
```

You reference a single element of an array as follows:

```
$ echo ${NAMES[2]}
sam
```

The subscripts [*] and [@] both extract the entire array but work differently when used within double quotation marks. An @ produces an array that is a duplicate of the original array; an * produces a single element of an array (or a plain variable) that holds all the elements of the array separated by the first character in IFS (normally a SPACE). In the following example, the array **A** is filled with the elements of the **NAMES** variable using an *, and **B** is filled using an @. The declare builtin with the –a option displays the values of the arrays (and reminds you that bash uses zero-based indexing for arrays):

```
$ A=("${NAMES[*]}")
$ B=("${NAMES[@]}")

$ declare -a
declare -a A='([0]="max helen sam zach")'
declare -a B='([0]="max" [1]="helen" [2]="sam" [3]="zach")'
...
declare -a NAMES='([0]="max" [1]="helen" [2]="sam" [3]="zach")'
```

From the output of declare, you can see that **NAMES** and **B** have multiple elements. In contrast, **A**, which was assigned its value with an * within double quotation marks, has only one element: **A** has all its elements enclosed between double quotation marks.

In the next example, echo attempts to display element 1 of array **A**. Nothing is displayed because **A** has only one element and that element has an index of 0. Element 0 of array **A** holds all four names. Element 1 of **B** holds the second item in the array and element 0 holds the first item.

```
$ echo ${A[1]}

$ echo ${A[0]}
max helen sam zach
$ echo ${B[1]}
helen
$ echo ${B[0]}
max
```

You can apply the ${#*name*[*]} operator to array variables, returning the number of elements in the array:

```
$ echo ${#NAMES[*]}
4
```

The same operator, when given the index of an element of an array in place of *, returns the length of the element:

```
$ echo ${#NAMES[1]}
5
```

You can use subscripts on the left side of an assignment statement to replace selected elements of the array:

```
$ NAMES[1]=alex
$ echo ${NAMES[*]}
max alex sam zach
```

LOCALITY OF VARIABLES

By default variables are local to the process in which they are declared. Thus a shell script does not have access to variables declared in your login shell unless you explicitly make the variables available (global). Under bash, export makes a variable available to child processes.

Once you use the export builtin with a variable name as an argument, the shell places the value of the variable in the calling environment of child processes. This *call by value* gives each child process a copy of the variable for its own use.

The following **extest1** shell script assigns a value of **american** to the variable named **cheese** and then displays its filename (**extest1**) and the value of **cheese**. The **extest1** script then calls **subtest**, which attempts to display the same information. Next **subtest** declares a **cheese** variable and displays its value. When **subtest** finishes, it returns control to the parent process, which is executing **extest1**. At this point **extest1** again displays the value of the original **cheese** variable.

```
$ cat extest1
cheese=american
echo "extest1 1: $cheese"
subtest
echo "extest1 2: $cheese"
$ cat subtest
echo "subtest 1: $cheese"
cheese=swiss
echo "subtest 2: $cheese"
$ extest1
extest1 1: american
subtest 1:
subtest 2: swiss
extest1 2: american
```

The **subtest** script never receives the value of **cheese** from **extest1**, and **extest1** never loses the value. Unlike in the real world, a child can never affect its parent's attributes. When a process attempts to display the value of a variable that has not been declared, as is the case with **subtest**, the process displays nothing; the value of an undeclared variable is that of a null string.

The following **extest2** script is the same as **extest1** except that it uses export to make **cheese** available to the **subtest** script:

```
$ cat extest2
export cheese=american
echo "extest2 1: $cheese"
subtest
echo "extest2 2: $cheese"
$ extest2
extest2 1: american
subtest 1: american
subtest 2: swiss
extest2 2: american
```

Here the child process inherits the value of **cheese** as **american** and, after displaying this value, changes *its copy* to **swiss**. When control is returned to the parent, the parent's copy of **cheese** retains its original value: **american.**

An export builtin can optionally include an assignment:

```
export cheese=american
```

The preceding statement is equivalent to the following two statements:

```
cheese=american
export cheese
```

Although it is rarely done, you can export a variable before you assign a value to it. You do not need to export an already-exported variable a second time after you change its value. For example, you do not usually need to export **PATH** when you assign a value to it in **~/.bash_profile** because it is typically exported in the **/etc/profile** global startup file.

FUNCTIONS

Because functions run in the same environment as the shell that calls them, variables are implicitly shared by a shell and a function it calls.

```
$ function nam () {
> echo $myname
> myname=zach
> }

$ myname=sam
$ nam
sam
$ echo $myname
zach
```

In the preceding example, the **myname** variable is set to **sam** in the interactive shell. Then the **nam** function is called. It displays the value of **myname** it has (**sam**) and sets **myname** to **zach**. The final echo shows that, in the interactive shell, the value of **myname** has been changed to **zach**.

Function local variables

Local variables are helpful in a function written for general use. Because the function is called by many scripts that may be written by different programmers, you need to make sure that the names of the variables used within the function do not interact with variables of the same name in the programs that call the function. Local variables eliminate this problem. When used within a function, the typeset builtin declares a variable to be local to the function it is defined in.

The next example shows the use of a local variable in a function. It uses two variables named **count**. The first is declared and assigned a value of 10 in the interactive shell. Its value never changes, as echo verifies after **count_down** is run. The other **count** is declared, using typeset, to be local to the function. Its value, which is unknown outside the function, ranges from 4 to 1, as the echo command within the function confirms.

The example shows the function being entered from the keyboard; it is not a shell script. (See the tip "A function is not a shell script" on page 912).

```
$ function count_down () {
> typeset count
> count=$1
> while [ $count -gt 0 ]
> do
> echo "$count..."
> ((count=count-1))
> sleep 1
> done
> echo "Blast Off."
> }
$ count=10
$ count_down 4
4...
3...
2...
1...
Blast Off\!
$ echo $count
10
```

The ((**count=count–1**)) assignment is enclosed between double parentheses, which cause the shell to perform an arithmetic evaluation (page 940). Within the double parentheses you can reference shell variables without the leading dollar sign ($).

SPECIAL PARAMETERS

Special parameters enable you to access useful values pertaining to command line arguments and the execution of shell commands. You reference a shell special parameter by preceding a special character with a dollar sign ($). As with positional parameters, it is not possible to modify the value of a special parameter by assignment.

$$: PID NUMBER

The shell stores in the **$$** parameter the PID number of the process that is executing it. In the following interaction, echo displays the value of this variable and the ps utility confirms its value. Both commands show that the shell has a PID number of 5209:

```
$ echo $$
5209
$ ps
   PID TTY          TIME CMD
  5209 pts/1    00:00:00 bash
  6015 pts/1    00:00:00 ps
```

Because echo is built into the shell, the shell does not have to create another process when you give an echo command. However, the results are the same whether echo is a builtin or not, because the shell substitutes the value of **$$** *before* it forks a new process to run a command. Try using the echo utility (**/bin/echo**), which is run by another process, and see what happens. In the following example, the shell substitutes the value of **$$** and passes that value to cp as a prefix for a filename:

```
$ echo $$
8232
$ cp memo $$.memo
$ ls
8232.memo memo
```

Incorporating a PID number in a filename is useful for creating unique filenames when the meanings of the names do not matter; it is often used in shell scripts for creating names of temporary files. When two people are running the same shell script, these unique filenames keep them from inadvertently sharing the same temporary file.

The following example demonstrates that the shell creates a new shell process when it runs a shell script. The **id2** script displays the PID number of the process running it (not the process that called it—the substitution for **$$** is performed by the shell that is forked to run **id2**):

```
$ cat id2
echo "$0 PID= $$"
$ echo $$
8232
$ id2
./id2 PID= 8362
$ echo $$
8232
```

The first echo displays the PID number of the interactive shell. Then **id2** displays its name (**$0**) and the PID of the subshell that it is running in. The last echo shows that the PID number of the interactive shell has not changed.

$! The value of the PID number of the last process that you ran in the background is stored in $!. The following example executes sleep as a background task and uses echo to display the value of $!:

```
$ sleep 60 &
[1] 8376
$ echo $!
8376
```

$?: EXIT STATUS

When a process stops executing for any reason, it returns an *exit status* to the parent process. The exit status is also referred to as a *condition code* or a *return code*. The $? variable stores the exit status of the last command.

By convention a nonzero exit status represents a *false* value and means that the command failed. A zero is *true* and indicates that the command was successful. In the following example, the first ls command succeeds and the second fails:

```
$ ls es
es
$ echo $?
0
$ ls xxx
ls: xxx: No such file or directory
$ echo $?
1
```

You can specify the exit status that a shell script returns by using the exit builtin, followed by a number, to terminate the script. If you do not use exit with a number to terminate a script, the exit status of the script is that of the last command the script ran.

```
$ cat es
echo This program returns an exit status of 7.
exit 7
$ es
This program returns an exit status of 7.
$ echo $?
7
$ echo $?
0
```

The es shell script displays a message and terminates execution with an exit command that returns an exit status of 7, the user-defined exit status in this script. The first echo then displays the value of the exit status of es. The second echo displays the value of the exit status of the first echo. The value is 0 because the first echo was successful.

POSITIONAL PARAMETERS

The *positional* parameters comprise the command name and command line arguments. They are called *positional* because within a shell script, you refer to them by their position on the command line. Only the set builtin (page 924) allows you to change the values of positional parameters with one exception: You cannot change the value of the command name from within a script.

$#: Number of Command Line Arguments

The $# parameter holds the number of arguments on the command line (positional parameters), not counting the command itself:

```
$ cat num_args
echo "This script was called with $# arguments."
$ num_args sam max zach
This script was called with 3 arguments.
```

$0: Name of the Calling Program

The shell stores the name of the command you used to call a program in parameter $0. This parameter is numbered zero because it appears before the first argument on the command line:

```
$ cat abc
echo "The command used to run this script is $0"
$ abc
The command used to run this script is ./abc
$ /home/sam/abc
The command used to run this script is /home/sam/abc
```

The preceding shell script uses echo to verify the name of the script you are executing. You can use the basename utility and command substitution to extract and display the simple filename of the command:

```
$ cat abc2
echo "The command used to run this script is $(basename $0)"
$ /home/sam/abc2
The command used to run this script is abc2
```

$1–$*n*: Command Line Arguments

The first argument on the command line is represented by parameter $1, the second argument by $2, and so on up to $*n*. For values of *n* over 9, the number must be enclosed within braces. For example, the twelfth command line argument is represented by ${12}. The following script displays positional parameters that hold command line arguments:

```
$ cat display_5args
echo First 5 arguments are $1 $2 $3 $4 $5

$ display_5args jenny alex helen
First 5 arguments are jenny alex helen
```

The display_5args script displays the first five command line arguments. The shell assigns a null value to each parameter that represents an argument that is not present on the command line. Thus the **$4** and **$5** variables have null values in this example.

$***   The **$* variable represents all the command line arguments, as the **display_all** program demonstrates:

```
$ cat display_all
echo All arguments are $*

$ display_all a b c d e f g h i j k l m n o p
All arguments are a b c d e f g h i j k l m n o p
```

Enclose references to positional parameters between double quotation marks. The quotation marks are particularly important when you are using positional parameters as arguments to commands. Without double quotation marks, a positional parameter that is not set or that has a null value disappears:

```
$ cat showargs
echo "$0 was called with $# arguments, the first is :$1:."

$ showargs a b c
./showargs was called with 3 arguments, the first is :a:.
$ echo $xx

$ showargs $xx a b c
./showargs was called with 3 arguments, the first is :a:.
$ showargs "$xx" a b c
./showargs was called with 4 arguments, the first is ::.
```

The **showargs** script displays the number of arguments (**$#**) followed by the value of the first argument enclosed between colons. The preceding example first calls **showargs** with three simple arguments. Next the echo command demonstrates that the **$xx** variable, which is not set, has a null value. In the final two calls to **showargs**, the first argument is **$xx**. In the first case the command line becomes **showargs a b c**; the shell passes **showargs** three arguments. In the second case the command line becomes **showargs "" a b c**, which results in calling **showargs** with four arguments. The difference in the two calls to **showargs** illustrates a subtle potential problem that you should keep in mind when using positional parameters that may not be set or that may have a null value.

"$*" versus "$@"   The **$*** and **$@** parameters work the same way except when they are enclosed within double quotation marks. Using **"$*"** yields a single argument (with SPACEs or the value of **IFS** [page 295] between the positional parameters), whereas **"$@"** produces a list wherein each positional parameter is a separate argument. This difference typically makes **"$@"** more useful than **"$*"** in shell scripts.

The following scripts help to explain the difference between these two special parameters. In the second line of both scripts, the single quotation marks keep the shell from interpreting the enclosed special characters so they can be displayed as themselves. The **bb1** script shows that **set "$*"** assigns multiple arguments to the first command line parameter:

```
$ cat bb1
set "$*"
echo $# parameters with '"$*"'
echo 1: $1
echo 2: $2
echo 3: $3

$ bb1 a b c
1 parameters with "$*"
1: a b c
2:
3:
```

The **bb2** script shows that **set "$@"** assigns each argument to a different command line parameter:

```
$ cat bb2
set "$@"
echo $# parameters with '"$@"'
echo 1: $1
echo 2: $2
echo 3: $3

$ bb2 a b c
3 parameters with "$@"
1: a
2: b
3: c
```

shift: PROMOTES COMMAND LINE ARGUMENTS

The shift builtin promotes each command line argument. The first argument (which was **$1**) is discarded. The second argument (which was **$2**) becomes the first argument (now **$1**), the third becomes the second, and so on. Because no "unshift" command exists, you cannot bring back arguments that have been discarded. An optional argument to shift specifies the number of positions to shift (and the number of arguments to discard); the default is 1.

The following **demo_shift** script is called with three arguments. Double quotation marks around the arguments to echo preserve the spacing of the output. The program displays the arguments and shifts them repeatedly until there are no more arguments left to shift:

```
$ cat demo_shift
echo "arg1= $1    arg2= $2    arg3= $3"
shift
echo "arg1= $1    arg2= $2    arg3= $3"
shift
echo "arg1= $1    arg2= $2    arg3= $3"
shift
echo "arg1= $1    arg2= $2    arg3= $3"
shift
```

```
$ demo_shift alice helen jenny
arg1= alice     arg2= helen     arg3= jenny
arg1= helen     arg2= jenny     arg3=
arg1= jenny     arg2=     arg3=
arg1=     arg2=     arg3=
```

Repeatedly using shift is a convenient way to loop over all the command line arguments in shell scripts that expect an arbitrary number of arguments. See page 883 for a shell script that uses shift.

set: INITIALIZES COMMAND LINE ARGUMENTS

When you call the set builtin with one or more arguments, it assigns the values of the arguments to the positional parameters, starting with $1. The following script uses set to assign values to the positional parameters $1, $2, and $3:

```
$ cat set_it
set this is it
echo $3 $2 $1
$ set_it
it is this
```

Combining command substitution (page 334) with the set builtin is a convenient way to get standard output of a command in a form that can be easily manipulated in a shell script. The following script shows how to use date and set to provide the date in a useful format. The first command shows the output of date. Then cat displays the contents of the **dateset** script. The first command in this script uses command substitution to set the positional parameters to the output of the date utility. The next command, echo $*, displays all positional parameters resulting from the previous set. Subsequent commands display the values of parameters $1, $2, $3, and $4. The final command displays the date in a format you can use in a letter or report:

```
$ date
Wed Jan  5 23:39:18 PST 2005
$ cat dateset
set $(date)
echo $*
echo
echo "Argument 1: $1"
echo "Argument 2: $2"
echo "Argument 3: $3"
echo "Argument 6: $6"
echo
echo "$2 $3, $6"

$ dateset
Wed Jan 5 23:39:25 PST 2005

Argument 1: Wed
Argument 2: Jan
Argument 3: 5
Argument 6: 2005

Jan 5, 2005
```

You can also use the *+format* argument to date to modify the format of its output.

When used without any arguments, set displays a list of the shell variables that are set, including user-created variables and keyword variables. Under bash, this list is the same as that displayed by declare and typeset when they are called without any arguments.

The set builtin also accepts options that let you customize the behavior of the shell. For more information refer to "set ±o: Turns Shell Features On and Off" on page 325.

EXPANDING NULL AND UNSET VARIABLES

The expression ${name} (or just $name if it is not ambiguous) expands to the value of the **name** variable. If **name** is null or not set, bash expands ${name} to a null string. The Bourne Again Shell provides the following alternatives to accepting the expanded null string as the value of the variable:

- Use a default value for the variable.
- Use a default value and assign that value to the variable.
- Display an error.

You can choose one of these alternatives by using a modifier with the variable name. In addition, you can use **set –o nounset** (page 327) to cause bash to display an error and exit from a script whenever an unset variable is referenced.

:– USES A DEFAULT VALUE

The :– modifier uses a default value in place of a null or unset variable while allowing a nonnull variable to represent itself:

${name:–default}

The shell interprets :– as "If *name* is null or unset, expand *default* and use the expanded value in place of *name*; else use *name*." The following command lists the contents of the directory named by the **LIT** variable. If **LIT** is null or unset, it lists the contents of **/home/alex/literature**:

```
$ ls ${LIT:-/home/alex/literature}
```

The default can itself have variable references that are expanded:

```
$ ls ${LIT:-$HOME/literature}
```

:= ASSIGNS A DEFAULT VALUE

The :– modifier does not change the value of a variable. You may want to change the value of a null or unset variable to its default in a script, however. You can do so with the := modifier:

${name:=default}

The shell expands the expression *${name:=default}* in the same manner as it expands *${name:–default}* but also sets the value of **name** to the expanded value of **default**. If a script contains a line such as the following and **LIT** is unset or null at the time this line is executed, **LIT** is assigned the value **/home/alex/literature**:

```
$ ls ${LIT:=/home/alex/literature}
```

: builtin   Shell scripts frequently start with the : (colon) builtin followed on the same line by the := expansion modifier to set any variables that may be null or unset. The : builtin evaluates each token in the remainder of the command line but does not execute any commands. Without the leading colon (:), the shell evaluates and attempts to execute the "command" that results from the evaluation.

Use the following syntax to set a default for a null or unset variable in a shell script (there is a SPACE following the first colon):

: *${name:=default}*

When a script needs a directory for temporary files and uses the value of **TEMPDIR** for the name of this directory, the following line makes **TEMPDIR** default to **/tmp**:

```
: ${TEMPDIR:=/tmp}
```

:? DISPLAYS AN ERROR MESSAGE

Sometimes a script needs the value of a variable but you cannot supply a reasonable default at the time you write the script. If the variable is null or unset, the :? modifier causes the script to display an error message and terminate with an exit status of 1:

${name:?message}

You must quote **message** if it contains SPACEs. If you omit **message**, the shell displays the default error message (**parameter null or not set**). Interactive shells do not exit when you use :?. In the following command, **TESTDIR** is not set so the shell displays on standard error the expanded value of the string following :?. In this case the string includes command substitution for date, with the %T format being followed by the string **error, variable not set**.

```
cd ${TESTDIR:?$(date +%T) error, variable not set.}
bash: TESTDIR: 16:16:14 error, variable not set.
```

BUILTIN COMMANDS

Builtin commands were introduced in Chapter 7. Commands that are built into a shell do not fork a new process when you execute them. This section discusses the type, read, exec, trap, kill, and getopts builtins and concludes with Table 28-6 on page 939, which lists many bash builtins.

type: Displays Information About a Command

The type builtin provides information about a command:

```
$ type cat echo who if lt
cat is hashed (/bin/cat)
echo is a shell builtin
who is /usr/bin/who
if is a shell keyword
lt is aliased to 'ls -ltrh | tail'
```

The preceding output shows the files that would be executed if you gave **cat** or **who** as a command. Because cat has already been called from the current shell, it is in the *hash table* (page 1034) and type reports that **cat is hashed**. The output also shows that a call to **echo** runs the echo builtin, **if** is a keyword, and **lt** is an alias.

read: Accepts User Input

When you begin writing shell scripts, you soon realize that one of the most common tasks for user-created variables is storing information a user enters in response to a prompt. Using read, scripts can accept input from the user and store that input in variables. The read builtin reads one line from standard input and assigns the words on the line to one or more variables:

```
$ cat read1
echo -n "Go ahead: "
read firstline
echo "You entered: $firstline"
$ read1
Go ahead: This is a line.
You entered: This is a line.
```

The first line of the **read1** script uses echo to prompt you to enter a line of text. The **–n** option suppresses the following NEWLINE, allowing you to enter a line of text on the same line as the prompt. The second line reads the text into the variable **firstline**. The third line verifies the action of read by displaying the value of **firstline**. The variable is quoted (along with the text string) in this example because you, as the script writer, cannot anticipate which characters the user might enter in response to the prompt. Consider what would happen if the variable were not quoted and the user entered * in response to the prompt:

```
$ cat read1_no_quote
echo -n "Go ahead: "
read firstline
echo You entered: $firstline
$ read1_no_quote
Go ahead: *
You entered: read1 read1_no_quote script.1
$ ls
read1    read1_no_quote    script.1
```

The ls command lists the same words as the script, demonstrating that the shell expands the asterisk into a list of files in the working directory. When the variable **$firstline** is surrounded by double quotation marks, the shell does not expand the asterisk. Thus the **read1** script behaves correctly:

```
$ read1
Go ahead: *
You entered: *
```

If you want the shell to interpret the special meanings of special characters, do not use quotation marks.

REPLY   The read builtin has features that can make it easier to use. When you do not specify a variable to receive read's input, bash puts the input into the variable named **REPLY**. You can use the **–p** option to prompt the user instead of using a separate echo command. The following **read1a** script performs exactly the same task as **read1**:

```
$ cat read1a
read -p "Go ahead: "
echo "You entered: $REPLY"
```

The **read2** script prompts for a command line and reads the user's response into the variable **cmd**. The script then attempts to execute the command line that results from the expansion of the **cmd** variable:

```
$ cat read2
read -p "Enter a command: " cmd
$cmd
echo "Thanks"
```

In the following example, **read2** reads a command line that calls the echo builtin. The shell executes the command and then displays **Thanks**. Next **read2** reads a command line that executes the who utility:

```
$ read2
Enter a command: echo Please display this message.
Please display this message.
Thanks
$ read2
Enter a command: who
alex      pts/4        Jun 17 07:50  (:0.0)
scott     pts/12       Jun 17 11:54  (bravo.example.com)
Thanks
```

If **cmd** does not expand into a valid command line, the shell issues an error message:

```
$ read2
Enter a command: xxx
./read2: line 2: xxx: command not found
Thanks
```

The **read3** script reads values into three variables. The read builtin assigns one word (a sequence of nonblank characters) to each variable:

```
$ cat read3
read -p "Enter something: " word1 word2 word3
echo "Word 1 is: $word1"
echo "Word 2 is: $word2"
echo "Word 3 is: $word3"

$ read3
Enter something: this is something
Word 1 is: this
Word 2 is: is
Word 3 is: something
```

When you enter more words than read has variables, read assigns one word to each variable, with all leftover words going to the last variable. Both **read1** and **read2** assigned the first word and all leftover words to the one variable they each had to work with. In the following example, read accepts five words into three variables, assigning the first word to the first variable, the second word to the second variable, and the third through fifth words to the third variable:

```
$ read3
Enter something: this is something else, really.
Word 1 is:  this
Word 2 is:  is
Word 3 is:  something else, really.
```

Table 28-4 lists some of the options supported by the read builtin.

Table 28-4 read options

Option	Function
–a *aname* (array)	Assigns each word of input to an element of array *aname*.
–d *delim* (delimiter)	Uses *delim* to terminate the input instead of NEWLINE.
–e (Readline)	If input is coming from a keyboard, use the Readline Library (page 312) to get input.
–n *num* (number of characters)	Reads *num* characters and returns. As soon as the user types *num* characters, read returns; there is no need to press RETURN.
–p *prompt* (prompt)	Displays *prompt* on standard error without a terminating NEWLINE before reading input. Displays *prompt* only when input comes from the keyboard.
–s (silent)	Does not echo characters.

–u *n* (file descriptor)	Uses the integer *n* as the file descriptor that read takes its input from.
	
	`read –u4 arg1 arg2`
	
	is equivalent to
	
	`read arg1 arg2 <&4`
	
	See "File Descriptors" (page 911) for a discussion of redirection and file descriptors.

The **read** builtin returns an exit status of 0 if it successfully reads any data. It has a nonzero exit status when it reaches the EOF (end of file). The following example runs a **while** loop from the command line. It takes its input from the **names** file and terminates after reading the last line from **names**.

```
$ cat names
Alice Jones
Robert Smith
Alice Paulson
John Q. Public

$ while read first rest
> do
> echo $rest, $first
> done < names
Jones, Alice
Smith, Robert
Paulson, Alice
Q. Public, John
$
```

The placement of the redirection symbol (**<**) for the **while** structure is critical. It is important that you place the redirection symbol at the **done** statement and not at the call to **read**.

optional Each time you redirect input, the shell opens the input file and repositions the read pointer at the start of the file:

```
$ read line1 < names; echo $line1; read line2 < names; echo $line2
Alice Jones
Alice Jones
```

Here each **read** opens **names** and starts at the beginning of the **names** file. In the following example, **names** is opened once, as standard input of the subshell created by the parentheses. Each **read** then reads successive lines of standard input.

```
$ (read line1; echo $line1; read line2; echo $line2) < names
Alice Jones
Robert Smith
```

Another way to get the same effect is to open the input file with **exec** and hold it open (refer to "File Descriptors" on page 911):

```
$ exec 3< names
$ read -u3 line1; echo $line1; read -u3 line2; echo $line2
Alice Jones
Robert Smith
$ exec 3<&-
```

exec: EXECUTES A COMMAND

The **exec** builtin has two primary purposes: to run a command without creating a new process and to redirect a file descriptor—including standard input, output, or error—of a shell script from within the script (page 911). When the shell executes a command that is not built into the shell, it typically creates a new process. The new process inherits environment (global or exported) variables from its parent but does not inherit variables that are not exported by the parent. (For more information refer to "Locality of Variables" on page 916.) In contrast, exec executes a command in place of (overlays) the current process.

exec versus . (dot) Insofar as exec runs a command in the environment of the original process, it is similar to the . (dot) command (page 269). However, unlike the . command, which can run only shell scripts, exec can run both scripts and compiled programs. Also, whereas the . command returns control to the original script when it finishes running, exec does not. Finally, the . command gives the new program access to local variables, whereas exec does not.

exec runs a command The exec builtin used for running a command has the following syntax:

*exec **command arguments***

exec does not return control Because the shell does not create a new process when you use exec, the command runs more quickly. However, because exec does not return control to the original program, it can be used only as the last command that you want to run in a script. The following script shows that control is not returned to the script:

```
$ cat exec_demo
who
exec date
echo "This line is never displayed."

$ exec_demo
jenny    pts/7    May 30   7:05 (bravo.example.com)
hls      pts/1    May 30   6:59 (:0.0)
Mon May 30 11:42:56 PDT 2005
```

The next example, a modified version of the **out** script (page 883), uses exec to execute the final command the script runs. Because **out** runs either cat or less and then terminates, the new version, named **out2**, uses exec with both cat and less:

```
$ cat out2
if [ $# -eq 0 ]
    then
        echo "Usage: out2 [-v] filenames" 1>&2
        exit 1
fi
if [ "$1" = "-v" ]
    then
        shift
        exec less "$@"
    else
        exec cat -- "$@"
fi
```

exec redirects input and output The second major use of exec is to redirect a file descriptor—including standard input, output, or error—from within a script. The next command causes all subsequent input to a script that would have come from standard input to come from the file named **infile**:

```
exec < infile
```

Similarly the following command redirects standard output and standard error to **outfile** and **errfile**, respectively:

```
exec > outfile 2> errfile
```

When you use **exec** in this manner, the current process is not replaced with a new process, and **exec** can be followed by other commands in the script.

/dev/tty   When you redirect the output from a script to a file, you must make sure that the user sees any prompts the script displays. The **/dev/tty** device is a pseudonym for the screen the user is working on; you can use this device to refer to the user's screen without knowing which device it is. (The **tty** utility displays the name of the device you are using.) By redirecting the output from a script to **/dev/tty**, you ensure that prompts and messages go to the user's terminal, regardless of which terminal the user is logged in on. Messages sent to **/dev/tty** are also not diverted if standard output and standard error from the script are redirected.

The **to_screen1** script sends output to three places: standard output, standard error, and the user's screen. When it is run with standard output and standard error redirected, **to_screen1** still displays the message sent to **/dev/tty** on the user's screen. The **out** and **err** files hold the output sent to standard output and standard error.

```
$ cat to_screen1
echo "message to standard output"
echo "message to standard error" 1>&2
echo "message to the user" > /dev/tty

$ to_screen1 > out 2> err
message to the user
$ cat out
message to standard output
$ cat err
message to standard error
```

The following command redirects the output from a script to the user's screen:

```
exec > /dev/tty
```

Putting this command at the beginning of the previous script changes where the output goes. In **to_screen2**, **exec** redirects standard output to the user's screen so the > **/dev/tty** is superfluous. Following the **exec** command, all output sent to standard output goes to **/dev/tty** (the screen). Output to standard error is not affected.

```
$ cat to_screen2
exec > /dev/tty
echo "message to standard output"
echo "message to standard error" 1>&2
echo "message to the user" > /dev/tty

$ to_screen2 > out 2> err
message to standard output
message to the user
```

One disadvantage of using **exec** to redirect the output to **/dev/tty** is that all subsequent output is redirected unless you use **exec** again in the script.

You can also redirect the input to read (standard input) so that it comes from **/dev/tty** (the keyboard):

```
read name < /dev/tty
```

or

```
exec < /dev/tty
```

trap: CATCHES A SIGNAL

A *signal* is a report to a process about a condition. Linux uses signals to report interrupts generated by the user (for example, pressing the interrupt key) as well as bad system calls, broken pipes, illegal instructions, and other conditions. The trap builtin catches, or traps, one or more signals, allowing you to direct the actions a script takes when it receives a specified signal.

This discussion covers six signals that are significant when you work with shell scripts. Table 28-5 lists these signals, the signal numbers that systems often ascribe to them, and the conditions that usually generate each signal. Give the command **kill –l**, **trap –l**, or **man 7 signal** for a list of signal names.

Table 28-5   Signals

Type	Name	Number	Generating condition
Not a real signal	EXIT	0	Exit because of exit command or reaching the end of the program (not an actual signal but useful in trap)
Hang up	SIGHUP or HUP	1	Disconnect the line
Terminal interrupt	SIGINT or INT	2	Press the interrupt key (usually CONTROL-C)
Quit	SIGQUIT or QUIT	3	Press the quit key (usually CONTROL-SHIFT-| or CONTROL-SHIFT-\)
Kill	SIGKILL or KILL	9	The kill command with the **–9** option (cannot be trapped; use only as a last resort)
Software termination	SIGTERM or TERM	15	Default of the kill command
Stop	SIGTSTP or TSTP	20	Press the suspend key (usually CONTROL-Z)
Debug	DEBUG		Executes *commands* specified in the trap statement after each command (not an actual signal but useful in trap)
Error	ERR		Executes *commands* specified in the trap statement after each command that returns a nonzero exit status (not an actual signal but useful in trap)

When it traps a signal, a script takes whatever action you specify: It can remove files or finish any other processing as needed, display a message, terminate execution immediately, or ignore the signal. If you do not use trap in a script, any of the six actual signals listed in Table 28-5 (not EXIT, DEBUG, or ERR) terminates the script. Because a process cannot trap a KILL signal, you can use **kill –KILL** (or **kill –9**) as a last resort to terminate a script or any other process. (See page 936 for more information on kill.)

The trap command has the following syntax:

trap ['commands'] [signal]

The optional *commands* part specifies the commands that the shell executes when it catches one of the signals specified by *signal*. The *signal* can be a signal name or number—for example, INT or 2. If *commands* is not present, trap resets the trap to its initial condition, which is usually to exit from the script.

The trap builtin does not require single quotation marks around *commands* as shown in the preceding syntax, but it is a good practice to use them. The single quotation marks cause shell variables within the *commands* to be expanded when the signal occurs, not when the shell evaluates the arguments to trap. Even if you do not use any shell variables in the *commands,* you need to enclose any command that takes arguments within either single or double quotation marks. Quoting the *commands* causes the shell to pass to trap the entire command as a single argument.

After executing the *commands,* the shell resumes executing the script where it left off. If you want trap to prevent a script from exiting when it receives a signal but not to run any commands explicitly, you can specify a null (empty) *commands* string, as shown in the **locktty** script (page 899). The following command traps signal number 15 after which the script continues.

```
trap '' 15
```

The following script demonstrates how the trap builtin can catch the terminal interrupt signal (2). You can use SIGINT, INT, or 2 to specify this signal. The script returns an exit status of 1:

```
$ cat inter
#!/bin/bash
trap 'echo PROGRAM INTERRUPTED; exit 1' INT
while true
do
    echo "Program running."
    sleep 1
done
$ inter
Program running.
Program running.
Program running.
CONTROL-C
PROGRAM INTERRUPTED
$
```

: (null) builtin The second line of **inter** sets up a trap for the terminal interrupt signal using INT. When trap catches the signal, the shell executes the two commands between the single quotation marks in the trap command. The echo builtin displays the message **PROGRAM INTERRUPTED**, exit terminates the shell running the script, and the parent shell displays a prompt. If exit were not there, the shell would return control to the **while** loop after displaying the message. The **while** loop repeats continuously until the script receives a signal because the true utility always returns a *true* exit status. In place of true you can use the : (null) builtin, which is written as a colon and always returns a 0 (*true*) status.

The trap builtin frequently removes temporary files when a script is terminated prematurely so that the files are not left to clutter the filesystem. The following shell script, named **addbanner**, uses two traps to remove a temporary file when the script terminates normally or owing to a hangup, software interrupt, quit, or software termination signal:

```
$ cat addbanner
#!/bin/bash
script=$(basename $0)

if [ ! -r "$HOME/banner" ]
    then
        echo "$script: need readable $HOME/banner file" 1>&2
        exit 1
fi

trap 'exit 1' 1 2 3 15
trap 'rm /tmp/$$.$script 2> /dev/null' 0

for file
do
    if [ -r "$file" -a -w "$file" ]
        then
            cat $HOME/banner $file > /tmp/$$.$script
            cp /tmp/$$.$script $file
            echo "$script: banner added to $file" 1>&2
        else
            echo "$script: need read and write permission for $file" 1>&2
        fi
done
```

When called with one or more filename arguments, **addbanner** loops through the files, adding a header to the top of each. This script is useful when you use a standard format at the top of your documents, such as a standard layout for memos, or when you want to add a standard header to shell scripts. The header is kept in a file named **~/banner**. Because **addbanner** uses the **HOME** variable, which contains the pathname of the user's home directory, the script can be used by several users without modification. If Alex had written the script with **/home/alex** in place of **$HOME** and then given the script to Jenny, either she would have had to change it or **addbanner** would have used Alex's **banner** file when Jenny ran it (assuming Jenny had read permission for the file).

The first trap in **addbanner** causes it to exit with a status of 1 when it receives a hangup, software interrupt (terminal interrupt or quit signal), or software termination signal. The second trap uses a 0 in place of **signal-number,** which causes trap to execute its command argument *whenever* the script exits because it receives an exit command or reaches its end. Together these traps remove a temporary file whether the script terminates normally or prematurely. Standard error of the second trap is sent to **/dev/null** for cases in which trap attempts to remove a nonexistent temporary file. In those cases rm sends an error message to standard error; because standard error is redirected, the user does not see this message.

See page 899 for another example that uses trap.

kill: ABORTS A PROCESS

The kill builtin sends a signal to a process or job. The kill command has the following syntax:

> *kill [–signal] PID*

where *signal* is the signal name or number (for example, INT or 2) and *PID* is the process identification number of the process that is to receive the signal. You can specify a job number (page 219) as *%n* in place of *PID*. If you omit *signal,* kill sends a TERM (software termination, number 15) signal. For more information on signal names and numbers see Table 28-5 on page 933.

The following command sends the TERM signal to job number 1:

```
$ kill -TERM %1
```

Because TERM is the default signal for kill, you can also give this command as **kill %1**. Give the command **kill –l** (lowercase "l") to display a list of signal names.

A program that is interrupted often leaves matters in an unpredictable state: Temporary files may be left behind (when they are normally removed), and permissions may be changed. A well-written application traps, or detects, signals and cleans up before exiting. Most carefully written applications trap the INT, QUIT, and TERM signals.

To terminate a program, first try INT (press CONTROL-C, if the job is in the foreground). Because an application can be written to ignore these signals, you may need to use the KILL signal, which cannot be trapped or ignored; it is a "sure kill." For more information refer to "kill: Sends a Signal to a Process" on page 395.

getopts: PARSES OPTIONS

The getopts builtin parses command line arguments, thereby making it easier to write programs that follow the Linux argument conventions. The syntax for getopts is

> *getopts optstring varname [arg ...]*

where *optstring* is a list of the valid option letters, *varname* is the variable that receives the options one at a time, and *arg* is the optional list of parameters to be processed. If *arg* is not present, getopts processes the command line arguments. If *optstring* starts with a colon (:), the script takes care of generating error messages; otherwise, getopts generates error messages.

The getopts builtin uses the **OPTIND** (option index) and **OPTARG** (option argument) variables to store option-related values. When a shell script starts, the value of **OPTIND** is 1. Each time getopts locates an argument, it increments **OPTIND** to the index of the next option to be processed. If the option takes an argument, bash assigns the value of the argument to **OPTARG**.

To indicate that an option takes an argument, follow the corresponding letter in *optstring* with a colon (:). The option string **dxo:lt:r** indicates that getopts should search for –d, –x, –o, –l, –t, and –r options and that the –o and –t options take arguments.

Using getopts as the *test-command* in a **while** control structure allows you to loop over the options one at a time. The getopts builtin checks the option list for options that are in *optstring*. Each time through the loop, getopts stores the option letter it finds in *varname*.

Suppose that you want to write a program that can take three options:

1. A **–b** option indicates that the program should ignore whitespace at the start of input lines.

2. A **–t** option followed by the name of a directory indicates that the program should use that directory for temporary files. Otherwise, it should use **/tmp**.

3. A **–u** option indicates that the program should translate all its output to uppercase.

In addition, the program should ignore all other options and end option processing when it encounters two hyphens (––).

The problem is to write the portion of the program that determines which options the user has supplied. The following solution does not use getopts:

```
SKIPBLANKS=
TMPDIR=/tmp
CASE=lower
while [[ "$1" = -* ]] # [[ = ]] does pattern match
do
    case $1 in
        -b)     SKIPBLANKS=TRUE ;;
        -t)     if [ -d "$2" ]
                then
                    TMPDIR=$2
                    shift
                else
                    echo "$0: -t takes a directory argument." >&2
                    exit 1
                fi ;;
        -u)     CASE=upper ;;
        --)     break   ;;      # Stop processing options
        *)      echo "$0: Invalid option $1 ignored." >&2 ;;
        esac
    shift
done
```

This program fragment uses a loop to check and shift arguments while the argument is not ––. As long as the argument is not two hyphens, the program continues to loop through a **case** statement that checks for possible options. The –– **case** label breaks out of the **while** loop. The * **case** label recognizes any option; it appears as the last **case** label to catch any unknown options, displays an error message, and allows processing to continue. On each pass through the loop, the program does a shift to get to the next argument. If an option takes an argument, the program does an extra shift to get past that argument.

The following program fragment processes the same options, but uses getopts:

```
SKIPBLANKS=
TMPDIR=/tmp
CASE=lower

while getopts :bt:u arg
do
    case $arg in
        b)      SKIPBLANKS=TRUE ;;
        t)      if [ -d "$OPTARG" ]
                then
                    TMPDIR=$OPTARG
                else
                    echo "$0: $OPTARG is not a directory." >&2
                    exit 1
                fi ;;
        u)      CASE=upper ;;
        :)      echo "$0: Must supply an argument to -$OPTARG." >&2
                exit 1 ;;
        \?)     echo "Invalid option -$OPTARG ignored." >&2 ;;
    esac
done
```

In this version of the code, the **while** structure evaluates the getopts builtin each time it comes to the top of the loop. The getopts builtin uses the **OPTIND** variable to keep track of the index of the argument it is to process the next time it is called. There is no need to call shift in this example.

In the getopts version of the script the **case** patterns do not start with a hyphen because the value of **arg** is just the option letter (getopts strips off the hyphen). Also, getopts recognizes –– as the end of the options, so you do not have to specify it explicitly as in the **case** statement in the first example.

Because you tell getopts which options are valid and which require arguments, it can detect errors in the command line and handle them in two ways. This example uses a leading colon in *optstring* to specify that you check for and handle errors in your code; when getopts finds an invalid option, it sets *varname* to ? and **OPTARG** to the option letter. When it finds an option that is missing an argument, getopts sets *varname* to : and **OPTARG** to the option lacking an argument.

The \? **case** pattern specifies the action to take when getopts detects an invalid option. The : **case** pattern specifies the action to take when getopts detects a missing option argument. In both cases getopts does not write any error message; it leaves that task to you.

If you omit the leading colon from *optstring*, both an invalid option and a missing option argument cause *varname* to be assigned the string ?. OPTARG is not set and getopts writes its own diagnostic message to standard error. Generally this method is less desirable because you have less control over what the user sees when an error is made.

Using getopts will not necessarily make your programs shorter. Its principal advantages are that it provides a uniform programming interface and it enforces standard option handling.

A PARTIAL LIST OF BUILTINS

Table 28-6 lists some of the bash builtins. See "Listing bash builtins" on page 225 for instructions on how to display complete lists of builtins.

Table 28-6   bash builtins

Builtin	Function
:	Returns 0 or *true* (the null builtin; page 935)
. (dot)	Executes a shell script as part of the current process (page 269)
bg	Puts a suspended job in the background (page 281)
break	Exits from a looping control structure (page 900)
cd	Changes to another working directory (page 174)
continue	Starts with the next iteration of a looping control structure (page 900)
echo	Displays its arguments (page 137)
eval	Scans and evaluates the command line (page 323)
exec	Executes a shell script or program in place of the current process (page 930)
exit	Exits from the current shell (usually the same as CONTROL-D from an interactive shell; page 920)
export	Places the value of a variable in the calling environment (makes it global; page 916)
fg	Brings a job from the background into the foreground (page 280)
getopts	Parses arguments to a shell script (page 936)
jobs	Displays list of background jobs (page 280)
kill	Sends a signal to a process or job (page 395)
pwd	Displays the name of the working directory (page 170)

Table 28-6   bash builtins (continued)

read	Reads a line from standard input (page 927)
readonly	Declares a variable to be readonly (page 289)
set	Sets shell flags or command line argument variables; with no argument, lists all variables (pages 325 and 924)
shift	Promotes each command line argument (page 923)
test	Compares arguments (page 879)
times	Displays total times for the current shell and its children
trap	Traps a signal (page 933)
type	Displays how each argument would be interpreted as a command (page 927)
umask	Returns the value of the file-creation mask (page 420)
unset	Removes a variable or function (page 289)
wait	Waits for a background process to terminate

EXPRESSIONS

An expression is composed of constants, variables, and operators that can be processed to return a value. This section covers arithmetic, logical, and conditional expressions as well as operators. Table 28-8 on page 943 lists the bash operators.

ARITHMETIC EVALUATION

The Bourne Again Shell can perform arithmetic assignments and evaluate many different types of arithmetic expressions, all using integers. The shell performs arithmetic assignments in a number of ways. One is with arguments to the let builtin:

```
$ let "VALUE=VALUE * 10 + NEW"
```

In the preceding example, the variables **VALUE** and **NEW** contain integer values. Within a let statement you do not need to use dollar signs (**$**) in front of variable names. Double quotation marks must enclose a single argument, or expression, that contains SPACEs. Because most expressions contain SPACEs and need to be quoted, bash accepts *((expression))* as a synonym for *let "expression"*, obviating the need for both quotation marks and dollar signs:

```
$ ((VALUE=VALUE * 10 + NEW))
```

You can use either form wherever a command is allowed and can remove the SPACEs if you like. In the following example, the asterisk (*****) does not need to be quoted because the shell does not perform pathname expansion on the right side of an assignment (page 288):

```
$ let VALUE=VALUE*10+NEW
```

Because each argument to let is evaluated as a separate expression, you can assign values to more than one variable on a single line:

```
$ let "COUNT = COUNT + 1" VALUE=VALUE*10+NEW
```

You need to use commas to separate multiple assignments within a set of double parentheses:

```
$ ((COUNT = COUNT + 1, VALUE=VALUE*10+NEW))
```

Arithmetic evaluation versus arithmetic expansion

tip   Arithmetic evaluation differs from arithmetic expansion. As explained on page 332, arithmetic expansion uses the syntax *$((expression))*, evaluates *expression*, and replaces *$((expression))* with the result. You can use arithmetic expansion to display the value of an expression or to assign that value to a variable.

Arithmetic evaluation uses the *let expression* or *((expression))* syntax, evaluates *expression*, and returns a status code. You can use arithmetic evaluation to perform a logical comparison or an assignment.

Logical expressions   You can use the *((expression))* syntax for logical expressions, although that task is frequently left to *[[expression]]*. The next example expands the **age_check** script (page 332) to include logical arithmetic evaluation in addition to arithmetic expansion:

```
$ cat age2
#!/bin/bash
echo -n "How old are you? "
read age
if ((30 < age && age < 60)); then
        echo "Wow, in $((60-age)) years, you'll be 60!"
    else
        echo "You are too young or too old to play."
fi

$ age2
How old are you? 25
You are too young or too old to play.
```

The *test-statement* for the **if** structure evaluates two logical comparisons joined by a Boolean AND and returns 0 (*true*) if they are both *true* or 1 (*false*) otherwise.

LOGICAL EVALUATION (CONDITIONAL EXPRESSIONS)

The syntax of a conditional expression is

[[expression]]

where *expression* is a Boolean (logical) expression. You must precede a variable name with a dollar sign ($) within *expression*. The result of executing this builtin, like the test builtin, is a return status. The *conditions* allowed within the brackets are almost a superset of those accepted by test (page 879). Where the test builtin uses **–a** as a Boolean AND operator, *[[expression]]* uses &&. Similarly, where test uses **–o** as a Boolean OR operator, *[[expression]]* uses ||.

You can replace the line that tests **age** in the **age2** script (preceding) with the following conditional expression. You must surround the [[and]] tokens with whitespace or a command terminator, and place dollar signs before the variables:

```
if [[ 30 < $age && $age < 60 ]]; then
```

You can also use test's relational operators –gt, –ge, –lt, –le, −eq, and −ne:

```
if [[ 30 -lt $age && $age -lt 60 ]]; then
```

String comparisons The test builtin tests whether strings are equal or unequal. The *[[expression]]* syntax adds comparison tests for string operators. The > and < operators compare strings for order (for example, "aa" < "bbb"). The = operator tests for pattern match, not just equality: *[[string = pattern]]* is *true* if **string** matches **pattern**. This operator is not symmetrical; the **pattern** must appear on the right side of the equal sign. For example, [[**artist** = a*]] is *true* (= 0), whereas [[a* = **artist**]] is *false* (= 1):

```
$ [[ artist = a* ]]
$ echo $?
0
$ [[ a* = artist ]]
$ echo $?
1
```

The next example uses a command list that starts with a compound condition. The condition tests that the directory **bin** and the file **src/myscript.bash** exist. If this is *true,* cp copies **src/myscript.bash** to **bin/myscript.** If the copy succeeds, chmod makes **myscript** executable. If any of these steps fails, echo displays a message.

```
$ [[ -d bin && -f src/myscript.bash ]] && cp src/myscript.bash \
bin/myscript && chmod +x bin/myscript || echo "Cannot make \
executable version of myscript"
```

STRING PATTERN MATCHING

The Bourne Again Shell provides string pattern-matching operators that can manipulate pathnames and other strings. These operators can delete from strings prefixes or suffixes that match patterns. The four operators are listed in Table 28-7.

Table 28-7 String operators

Operator	Function
#	Removes minimal matching prefixes
##	Removes maximal matching prefixes
%	Removes minimal matching suffixes
%%	Removes maximal matching suffixes

The syntax for these operators is

${varname op pattern}

where *op* is one of the operators listed in Table 28-7 and ***pattern*** is a match pattern similar to that used for filename generation. These operators are commonly used to manipulate pathnames so as to extract or remove components or to change suffixes:

```
$ SOURCEFILE=/usr/local/src/prog.c
$ echo ${SOURCEFILE#/*/}
local/src/prog.c
$ echo ${SOURCEFILE##/*/}
prog.c
$ echo ${SOURCEFILE%/*}
/usr/local/src
$ echo ${SOURCEFILE%%/*}

$ echo ${SOURCEFILE%.c}
/usr/local/src/prog
$ CHOPFIRST=${SOURCEFILE#/*/}
$ echo $CHOPFIRST
local/src/prog.c
$ NEXT=${CHOPFIRST%%/*}
$ echo $NEXT
local
```

Here the string-length operator, ${#*name*}, is replaced by the number of characters in the value of **name**:

```
$ echo $SOURCEFILE
/usr/local/src/prog.c
$ echo ${#SOURCEFILE}
21
```

OPERATORS

Arithmetic expansion and arithmetic evaluation use the same syntax, precedence, and associativity of expressions as the C language. Table 28-8 lists operators in order of decreasing precedence (priority of evaluation); each group of operators has equal precedence. Within an expression you can use parentheses to change the order of evaluation.

Table 28-8   Operators

Type of operator/operator	Function
Post	
var++	Postincrement
var--	Postdecrement
Pre	
++*var*	Preincrement
--*var*	Predecrement

Table 28-8 Operators (continued)

Unary	
	− Unary minus
	+ Unary plus

Negation	
	! Boolean NOT (logical negation)
	~ Complement (bitwise negation)

Exponentiation	
	** Exponent

Multiplication, division, remainder	
	* Multiplication
	/ Division
	% Remainder

Addition, subtraction	
	− Subtraction
	+ Addition

Bitwise shifts	
	<< Left bitwise shift
	>> Right bitwise shift

Comparison	
	<= Less than or equal
	>= Greater than or equal
	< Less than
	> Greater than

Equality, inequality	
	== Equality
	!= Inequality

Bitwise	
	& Bitwise AND
	^ Bitwise XOR (exclusive OR)
	| Bitwise OR

Table 28-8 Operators (continued)

Boolean (logical)

&&	Boolean AND
||	Boolean OR

Conditional evaluation

? :	Ternary operator

Assignment

=, *=, /=, %=, +=, −=,	Assignment
<<=, >>=, &=, ^=, |=	

Comma

,	Comma

Pipe   The pipe token has higher precedence than operators. You can use pipes anywhere in a command that you can use simple commands. For example, the command line

```
$ cmd1 | cmd2 || cmd3 | cmd4 && cmd5 | cmd6
```

is interpreted as if you had typed

```
$ ((cmd1 | cmd2) || (cmd3 | cmd4)) && (cmd5 | cmd6)
```

Do not rely on rules of precedence: use parentheses

tip   Do not rely on the precedence rules when you use compound commands. Instead, use parentheses to explicitly state the order in which you want the shell to interpret the commands.

Increment and decrement operators   The postincrement, postdecrement, preincrement, and predecrement operators work with variables. The pre- operators, which appear in front of the variable name as in **++COUNT** and **−−VALUE**, first change the value of the variable (**++** adds 1; **−−** subtracts 1) and then provide the result for use in the expression. The post- operators appear after the variable name as in **COUNT++** and **VALUE−−**; they first provide the unchanged value of the variable for use in the expression and then change the value of the variable.

```
$ N=10
$ echo $N
10
$ echo $((--N+3))
12
$ echo $N
9
$ echo $((N++ - 3))
6
$ echo $N
10
```

Remainder   The remainder operator (%) gives the remainder when its first operand is divided by its second. For example, the expression $((15\%7))$ has the value 1.

Boolean   The result of a Boolean operation is either 0 (*false*) or 1 (*true*).

The && (AND) and || (OR) Boolean operators are called *short-circuiting* operators. If the result of using one of these operators can be decided by looking only at the left operand, the right operand is not evaluated. The && operator causes the shell to test the exit status of the command preceding it. If the command succeeded, bash executes the next command; otherwise, it skips the remaining commands on the command line. You can use this construct to execute commands conditionally:

```
$ mkdir bkup && cp -r src bkup
```

This compound command creates the directory **bkup**. If mkdir succeeds, the contents of directory **src** is copied recursively to **bkup**.

The || separator also causes bash to test the exit status of the first command but has the opposite effect: The remaining command(s) are executed only if the first one failed (that is, exited with nonzero status):

```
$ mkdir bkup || echo "mkdir of bkup failed" >> /tmp/log
```

The exit status of a command list is the exit status of the last command in the list. You can group lists with parentheses. For example, you could combine the previous two examples as

```
$ (mkdir bkup && cp -r src bkup) || echo "mkdir failed" >> /tmp/log
```

In the absence of parentheses, && and || have equal precedence and are grouped from left to right. The following examples use the true and false utilities. These utilities do nothing and return *true* (0) and *false* (1) exit statuses, respectively:

```
$ false; echo $?
1
```

The $? variable holds the exit status of the preceding command (page 920). The next two commands yield an exit status of 1 (*false*):

```
$ true || false && false
$ echo $?
1
$ (true || false) && false
$ echo $?
1
```

Similarly the next two commands yield an exit status of 0 (*true*):

```
$ false && false || true
$ echo $?
0
$ (false && false) || true
$ echo $?
0
```

Because || and && have equal precedence, the parentheses in the two preceding pairs of examples do nothing to change the order of operations.

Because the expression on the right side of a short-circuiting operator may never get executed, you must be careful with assignment statements in that location. The following example demonstrates what can happen:

```
$ ((N=10,Z=0))
$ echo $((N || ((Z+=1)) ))
1
$ echo $Z
0
```

Because the value of **N** is nonzero, the result of the || (OR) operation is 1 (*true*), no matter what the value of the right side is. As a consequence ((**Z+=1**)) is never evaluated and **Z** is not incremented.

Ternary   The ternary operator, **? :**, decides which of two expressions should be evaluated, based on the value returned from a third expression:

expression1 ? expression2 : expression3

If *expression1* produces a *false* (0) value, *expression3* is evaluated; otherwise, *expression2* is evaluated. The value of the entire expression is the value of *expression2* or *expression3*, depending on which one is evaluated. If *expression1* is *true*, *expression3* is not evaluated. If *expression1* is *false expression2* is not evaluated:

```
$ ((N=10,Z=0,COUNT=1))
$ ((T=N>COUNT?++Z:--Z))
$ echo $T
1
$ echo $Z
1
```

Assignment   The assignment operators, such as **+=**, are shorthand notations. For example, **N+=3** is the same as ((**N=N+3**)).

Other bases   The following commands use the syntax *base#n* to assign base 2 (binary) values. First **v1** is assigned a value of 0101 (5 decimal) and **v2** is assigned a value of 0110 (6 decimal). The echo utility verifies the decimal values.

```
$ ((v1=2#0101))
$ ((v2=2#0110))
$ echo "$v1 and $v2"
5 and 6
```

Next the bitwise AND operator (**&**) selects the bits that are on in both 5 (0101 binary) and 6 (0110 binary). The result is binary 0100, which is 4 decimal.

```
$ echo $(( v1 & v2 ))
4
```

The Boolean AND operator (&&) produces a result of 1 if both of its operands are nonzero and a result of 0 otherwise. The bitwise inclusive OR operator (|) selects the bits that are on in either 0101 or 0110, resulting in 0111, which is 7 decimal. The Boolean OR operator (||) produces a result of 1 if either of its operands is non-zero and a result of 0 otherwise.

```
$ echo $(( v1 && v2 ))
1
$ echo $(( v1 | v2 ))
7
$ echo $(( v1 || v2 ))
1
```

Next the bitwise exclusive OR operator (^) selects the bits that are on in either, but not both, of the operands 0101 and 0110, yielding 0011, which is 3 decimal. The Boolean NOT operator (!) produces a result of 1 if its operand is 0 and a result of 0 otherwise. Because the exclamation point in $((! v1)) is enclosed within double parentheses, it does not need to be escaped to prevent the shell from interpreting the exclamation point as a history event. The comparison operators produce a result of 1 if the comparison is *true* and a result of 0 otherwise.

```
$ echo $(( v1 ^ v2 ))
3
$ echo $(( ! v1 ))
0
$ echo $(( v1 < v2 ))
1
$ echo $(( v1 > v2 ))
0
```

SHELL PROGRAMS

The Bourne Again Shell has many features that make it a good programming language. The structures that bash provides are not a random assortment. Rather, they have been chosen to provide most of the structural features that are in other procedural languages, such as C or Pascal. A procedural language provides the ability to

- Declare, assign, and manipulate variables and constant data. The Bourne Again Shell provides string variables, together with powerful string operators, and integer variables, along with a complete set of arithmetic operators.

- Break large problems into small ones by creating subprograms. The Bourne Again Shell allows you to create functions and call scripts from other scripts. Shell functions can be called recursively; that is, a Bourne Again Shell function can call itself. You may not need to use recursion often, but it may allow you to solve some apparently difficult problems with ease.

- Execute statements conditionally, using statements such as **if**.

- Execute statements iteratively, using statements such as **while** and **for**.

- Transfer data to and from the program, communicating with both data files and users.

Programming languages implement these capabilities in different ways but with the same ideas in mind. When you want to solve a problem by writing a program, you must first figure out a procedure that leads you to a solution—that is, an *algorithm*. Typically you can implement the same algorithm in roughly the same way in different programming languages, using the same kinds of constructs in each language.

Chapter 9 and this chapter have introduced numerous bash features, many of which are useful for interactive use as well as for shell programming. This section develops two complete shell programs, demonstrating how to combine some of these features effectively. The programs are presented as problems for you to solve along with sample solutions.

A RECURSIVE SHELL SCRIPT

A recursive construct is one that is defined in terms of itself. Alternatively, you might say that a recursive program is one that can call itself. This may seem circular, but it need not be. To avoid circularity a recursive definition must have a special case that is not self-referential. Recursive ideas occur in everyday life. For example, you can define an ancestor as your mother, your father, or one of their ancestors. This definition is not circular; it specifies unambiguously who your ancestors are: your mother or your father, or your mother's mother or father or your father's mother or father, and so on.

A number of Linux system utilities can operate recursively. See the **–R** option to the chmod, chown, and cp utilities for examples.

Solve the following problem by using a recursive shell function:

Write a shell function named **makepath** that, given a pathname, creates all components in that pathname as directories. For example, the command **makepath a/b/c/d** should create directories **a**, **a/b**, **a/b/c**, and **a/b/c/d**. (The mkdir utility supports a **–p** option that does exactly this. Solve the problem without using **mkdir –p**.)

One algorithm for a recursive solution follows:

1. Examine the path argument. If it is a null string or if it names an existing directory, do nothing and return.

2. If it is a simple path component, create it (using mkdir) and return.

3. Otherwise, call **makepath** using the path prefix of the original argument. This step eventually creates all the directories up to the last component, which you can then create with mkdir.

In general, a recursive function must invoke itself with a simpler version of the problem than it was given until it is finally called with a simple case that does not need to call itself. Following is one possible solution based on this algorithm:

makepath

```
# this is a function
# enter it at the keyboard, do not run it as a shell script
#
function makepath()
{
    if [[ ${#1} -eq 0 || -d "$1" ]]
        then
            return 0         # Do nothing
    fi
    if [[ "${1%/*}" = "$1" ]]
        then
            mkdir $1
            return $?
    fi
    makepath ${1%/*} || return 1
    mkdir $1
    return $?
}
```

In the test for a simple component (the **if** statement in the middle of the function), the left expression is the argument after the shortest suffix that starts with a **/** character has been stripped away (page 942). If there is no such character (for example, if **$1** is **alex**), nothing is stripped off and the two sides are equal. If the argument is a simple filename preceded by a slash, such as **/usr**, the expression **${1%/*}** evaluates to a null string. To make the function work in this case, you must take two precautions: Put the left expression within quotation marks and ensure that the recursive function behaves sensibly when it is passed a null string as an argument. In general, good programs are robust: They should be prepared for borderline, invalid, or meaningless input and behave appropriately in such cases.

By giving the following command from the shell you are working in, you turn on debugging tracing so that you can watch the recursion work:

```
$ set -o xtrace
```

(Give the same command, but replace the hyphen with a plus sign (**+**) to turn debugging off.) With debugging turned on, the shell displays each line in its expanded form as it executes the line. A **+** precedes each line of debugging output. In the following example, the first line that starts with **+** shows the shell calling **makepath**. The **makepath** function is called from the command line with arguments of **a/b/c**. Subsequently it calls itself with arguments of **a/b** and finally **a**. All the work is done (using mkdir) as each call to **makepath** returns.

```
$ makepath a/b/c
+ makepath a/b/c
+ [[ 5 -eq 0 ]]
+ [[ -d a/b/c ]]
+ [[ a/b = \a\/\b\/\c ]]
+ makepath a/b
+ [[ 3 -eq 0 ]]
+ [[ -d a/b ]]
+ [[ a = \a\/\b ]]
```

```
+ makepath a
+ [[ 1 -eq 0 ]]
+ [[ -d a ]]
+ [[ a = \a ]]
+ mkdir a
+ return 0
+ mkdir a/b
+ return 0
+ mkdir a/b/c
+ return 0
```

The function works its way down the recursive path and back up again.

It is instructive to invoke **makepath** with an invalid path and see what happens. The following example, run with debugging turned on, tries to create the path **/a/b**, which requires that you create directory **a** in the root directory. Unless you have permission to write to the root directory, you are not permitted to create this directory.

```
$ makepath /a/b
+ makepath /a/b
+ [[ 4 -eq 0 ]]
+ [[ -d /a/b ]]
+ [[ /a = \/\a\/\b ]]
+ makepath /a
+ [[ 2 -eq 0 ]]
+ [[ -d /a ]]
+ [[ '' = \/\a ]]
+ makepath
+ [[ 0 -eq 0 ]]
+ return 0
+ mkdir /a
mkdir: cannot create directory '/a': Permission denied
+ return 1
+ return 1
```

The recursion stops when **makepath** is denied permission to create the **/a** directory. The error return is passed all the way back, so the original **makepath** exits with nonzero status.

Use local variables with recursive functions

tip The preceding example glossed over a potential problem that you may encounter when you use a recursive function. During the execution of a recursive function, many separate instances of that function may be active simultaneously. All but one of them are waiting for their child invocation to complete.

Because functions run in the same environment as the shell that calls them, variables are implicitly shared by a shell and a function it calls so that all instances of the function share a single copy of each variable. Sharing variables can give rise to side effects that are rarely what you want. As a rule, you should use **typeset** to make all variables of a recursive function be local variables. See page 917 for more information.

THE quiz SHELL SCRIPT

Solve the following problem using a bash script:

Write a generic multiple-choice quiz program. The program should get its questions from data files, present them to the user, and keep track of the number of correct and incorrect answers. The user must be able to exit from the program at any time with a summary of results to that point.

The detailed design of this program and even the detailed description of the problem depend on a number of choices: How will the program know which subjects are available for quizzes? How will the user choose a subject? How will the program know when the quiz is over? Should the program present the same questions (for a given subject) in the same order each time, or should it scramble them?

Of course, you can make many perfectly good choices that implement the specification of the problem. The following details narrow the problem specification:

- Each subject will correspond to a subdirectory of a master quiz directory. This directory will be named in the environment variable **QUIZDIR**, whose default will be **~/quiz**. For example, you could have the following directories correspond to the subjects engineering, art, and politics: **~/quiz/engineering**, **~/quiz/art**, and **~/quiz/politics**. Put the **quiz** directory in **/usr/games** if you want all users to have access to it (requires root privileges).

- Each subject can have several questions. Each question is represented by a file in its subject's directory.

- The first line of each file that represents a question is the text of the question. If it takes more than one line, you must escape the NEWLINE with a backslash. (This setup makes it easy to read a single question with the read builtin.) The second line of the file is an integer that specifies the number of choices. The next lines are the choices themselves. The last line is the correct answer. Following is a sample question file:

```
Who discovered the principle of the lever?
4
Euclid
Archimedes
Thomas Edison
The Lever Brothers
Archimedes
```

- The program presents all the questions in a subject directory. At any point the user can interrupt the quiz with CONTROL-C, whereupon the program will summarize the results so far and exit. If the user does not interrupt, the program summarizes the results and exits when it has asked all questions for the chosen subject.

- The program scrambles the questions in a subject before presenting them.

Following is a top-level design for this program:

1. Initialize. This involves a number of steps, such as setting the counts of the number of questions asked so far and the number of correct and wrong answers to zero. Sets up to trap CONTROL-C.

2. Present the user with a choice of subjects and get the user's response.

3. Change to the corresponding subject directory.

4. Determine the questions to be asked (that is, the filenames in that directory). Arrange them in random order.

5. Repeatedly present questions and ask for answers until the quiz is over or is interrupted by the user.

6. Present the results and exit.

Clearly some of these steps (such as step 3) are simple, whereas others (such as step 4) are complex and worthy of analysis on their own. Use shell functions for any complex step, and use the trap builtin to handle a user interrupt.

Here is a skeleton version of the program with empty shell functions:

```
function initialize
{
# Initializes variables.
}
function choose_subj
{
# Writes choice to standard output.
}

function scramble
{
# Stores names of question files, scrambled,
# in an array variable named questions.
}

function ask
{
# Reads a question file, asks the question, and checks the
# answer. Returns 1 if the answer was correct, 0 otherwise. If it
# encounters an invalid question file, exit with status 2.
}

function summarize
{
# Presents the user's score.
}

# Main program
initialize                     # Step 1 in top-level design

subject=$(choose_subj)         # Step 2
[[ $? -eq 0 ]] || exit 2       # If no valid choice, exit
```

```
cd $subject || exit 2                # Step 3
echo                                 # Skip a line
scramble                             # Step 4

for ques in ${questions[*]}; do      # Step 5
    ask $ques
    result=$?
    (( num_ques=num_ques+1 ))
    if [[ $result == 1 ]]; then
        (( num_correct += 1 ))
    fi
    echo                             # Skip a line between questions
    sleep ${QUIZDELAY:=1}
done

summarize                            # Step 6
exit 0
```

To make reading the results a bit easier for the user, a sleep call appears inside the question loop. It delays **$QUIZDELAY** seconds (default = 1) between questions.

Now the task is to fill in the missing pieces of the program. In a sense this program is being written backward. The details (the shell functions) come first in the file but come last in the development process. This common programming practice is called top-down design. In top-down design you fill in the broad outline of the program first and supply the details later. In this way you break the problem up into smaller problems, each of which you can work on independently. Shell functions are a great help in using the top-down approach.

One way to write the **initialize** function follows. The cd command causes **QUIZDIR** to be the working directory for the rest of the script and defaults to **~/quiz** if **QUIZDIR** is not set.

```
function initialize ()
{
trap 'summarize ; exit 0' INT        # Handle user interrupts
num_ques=0                           # Number of questions asked so far
num_correct=0                        # Number answered correctly so far
first_time=true                      # true until first question is asked
cd ${QUIZDIR:=~/quiz} || exit 2
}
```

Be prepared for the cd command to fail. The directory may be unsearchable or conceivably another user may have removed it. The preceding function exits with a status code of 2 if cd fails.

The next function, **choose_subj**, is a bit more complicated. It displays a menu using a **select** statement:

```
function choose_subj ()
{
subjects=($(ls))
PS3="Choose a subject for the quiz from the preceding list: "
select Subject in ${subjects[*]}; do
    if [[ -z "$Subject" ]]; then
        echo "No subject chosen.  Bye." >&2
        exit 1
    fi
    echo $Subject
    return 0
done
}
```

The function first uses an **ls** command and command substitution to put a list of subject directories in the **subjects** array. Next the **select** structure (page 907) presents the user with a list of subjects (the directories found by **ls**) and assigns the chosen directory name to the **Subject** variable. Finally the function writes the name of the subject directory to standard output. The main program uses command substitution to assign this value to the **subject** variable [**subject=$(choose_subj)**].

The **scramble** function presents a number of difficulties. In this solution it uses an array variable (**questions**) to hold the names of the questions. It scrambles the entries in an array using the **RANDOM** variable (each time you reference **RANDOM** it has the value of a [random] integer between 0 and 32767):

```
function scramble ()
{
typeset -i index quescount
questions=($(ls))
quescount=${#questions[*]}          # Number of elements
((index=quescount-1))
while [[ $index > 0 ]]; do
    ((target=RANDOM % index))
    exchange $target $index
    ((index -= 1))
done
}
```

This function initializes the array variable **questions** to the list of filenames (questions) in the working directory. The variable **quescount** is set to the number of such files. Then the following algorithm is used: Let the variable index count down from **quescount – 1** (the index of the last entry in the array variable). For each value of **index**, the function chooses a random value target between 0 and **index**, inclusive. The command

```
((target=RANDOM % index))
```

produces a random value between 0 and **index – 1** by taking the remainder (the **%** operator) when **$RANDOM** is divided by **index**. The function then exchanges the elements of **questions** at positions **target** and **index**. It is convenient to do this in another function named **exchange**:

```
function exchange ()
{
temp_value=${questions[$1]}
questions[$1]=${questions[$2]}
questions[$2]=$temp_value
}
```

The **ask** function also uses the **select** structure. It reads the question file named in its argument and uses the contents of that file to present the question, accept the answer, and determine whether the answer is correct. (See the code that follows.)

The **ask** function uses file descriptor 3 to read successive lines from the question file, whose name was passed as an argument and is represented by **$1** in the function. It reads the question into the **ques** variable and the number of questions into **num_opts**. The function constructs the variable **choices** by initializing it to a null string and successively appending the next choice. Then it sets **PS3** to the value of **ques** and uses a **select** structure to prompt the user with **ques**. The **select** structure places the user's answer in **answer**, and the function then checks it against the correct answer from the file.

The construction of the **choices** variable is done with an eye toward avoiding a potential problem. Suppose that one answer has some whitespace in it. Then it might appear as two or more arguments in **choices**. To avoid this problem, make sure that **choices** is an array variable. The **select** statement does the rest of the work:

quiz
```
$ cat quiz
#!/bin/bash

# remove the # on the following line to turn on debugging
# set -o xtrace

#==================
function initialize ()
{
trap 'summarize ; exit 0' INT      # Handle user interrupts
num_ques=0                          # Number of questions asked so far
num_correct=0                       # Number answered correctly so far
first_time=true                     # true until first question is asked
cd ${QUIZDIR:=~/quiz} || exit 2
}

#==================
function choose_subj ()
{
subjects=($(ls))
PS3="Choose a subject for the quiz from the preceding list: "
select Subject in ${subjects[*]}; do
    if [[ -z "$Subject" ]]; then
        echo "No subject chosen.  Bye." >&2
        exit 1
    fi
    echo $Subject
    return 0
done
}
```

```
#==================
function exchange ()
{
temp_value=${questions[$1]}
questions[$1]=${questions[$2]}
questions[$2]=$temp_value
}


#==================
function scramble ()
{
typeset -i index quescount
questions=($(ls))
quescount=${#questions[*]}            # Number of elements
((index=quescount-1))
while [[ $index > 0 ]]; do
    ((target=RANDOM % index))
    exchange $target $index
    ((index -= 1))
done
}


#==================
function ask ()
{
exec 3<$1
read -u3 ques || exit 2
read -u3 num_opts || exit 2

index=0
choices=()
while (( index < num_opts )) ; do
    read -u3 next_choice || exit 2
    choices=("${choices[@]}" "$next_choice")
    ((index += 1))
done
read -u3 correct_answer || exit 2
exec 3<&-

if [[ $first_time = true ]]; then
    first_time=false
    echo -e "You may press the interrupt key at any time to quit.\n"
fi

PS3=$ques" "                         # Make $ques the prompt for select
                                     # and add some spaces for legibility.
select answer in "${choices[@]}"; do
    if [[ -z "$answer" ]]; then
            echo  Not a valid choice. Please choose again.
        elif [[ "$answer" = "$correct_answer" ]]; then
            echo "Correct!"
            return 1
        else
            echo "No, the answer is $correct_answer."
            return 0
    fi
done
}
```

```
#==================
function summarize ()
{
echo                                # Skip a line
if (( num_ques == 0 )); then
    echo "You did not answer any questions"
    exit 0
fi

(( percent=num_correct*100/num_ques ))
echo "You answered $num_correct questions correctly, out of \
$num_ques total questions."
echo "Your score is $percent percent."
}

#==================
# Main program
initialize                          # Step 1 in top-level design

subject=$(choose_subj)              # Step 2
[[ $? -eq 0 ]] || exit 2            # If no valid choice, exit

cd $subject || exit 2               # Step 3
echo                                # Skip a line
scramble                            # Step 4

for ques in ${questions[*]}; do     # Step 5
    ask $ques
    result=$?
    (( num_ques=num_ques+1 ))
    if [[ $result == 1 ]]; then
        (( num_correct += 1 ))
    fi
    echo                            # Skip a line between questions
    sleep ${QUIZDELAY:=1}
done

summarize                           # Step 6
exit 0
```

CHAPTER SUMMARY

The shell is a programming language. Programs written in this language are called shell scripts, or simply scripts. Shell scripts provide the decision and looping control structures present in high-level programming languages while allowing easy access to system utilities and user programs. Shell scripts can use functions to modularize and simplify complex tasks.

Control structures   The control structures that use decisions to select alternatives are **if...then**, **if...then...else**, and **if...then...elif**. The **case** control structure provides a multiway branch and can be used when you want to express alternatives using a simple pattern-matching syntax.

The looping control structures are **for...in**, **for**, **until**, and **while**. These structures perform one or more tasks repetitively.

The **break** and **continue** control structures alter control within loops: **break** transfers control out of a loop, and **continue** transfers control immediately to the top of a loop.

The Here document allows input to a command in a shell script to come from within the script itself.

File descriptors   The Bourne Again Shell provides the ability to manipulate file descriptors. Coupled with the read and echo builtins, file descriptors allow shell scripts to have as much control over input and output as programs written in lower-level languages.

Variables   You assign attributes, such as readonly, to bash variables using the typeset builtin. The Bourne Again Shell provides operators to perform pattern matching on variables, provide default values for variables, and evaluate the length of variables. This shell also supports array variables and local variables for functions and provides built-in integer arithmetic capability, using the let builtin and an expression syntax similar to the C programming language.

Builtins   Bourne Again Shell builtins include type, read, exec, trap, kill, and getopts. The type builtin displays information about a command, including its location; read allows a script to accept user input.

The exec builtin executes a command without creating a new process. The new command overlays the current process, assuming the same environment and PID number of that process. This builtin executes user programs and other Linux commands when it is *not* necessary to return control to the calling process.

The trap builtin catches a signal sent by Linux to the process running the script and allows you to specify actions to be taken upon receipt of one or more signals. You can use this builtin to cause a script to ignore the signal that is sent when the user presses the interrupt key.

The kill builtin allows you to terminate a running program. The getopts builtin parses command line arguments, making it easier to write programs that follow standard Linux conventions for command line arguments and options.

Utilities in scripts   In addition to using control structures, builtins, and functions, shell scripts generally call Linux utilities. The find utility, for instance, is commonplace in shell scripts that search for files in the system hierarchy and can perform a vast range of tasks, from simple to complex.

A well-written shell script adheres to standard programming practices, such as specifying the shell to execute the script on the first line of the script, verifying the number and type of arguments that the script is called with, displaying a standard usage message to report command line errors, and redirecting all informational messages to standard error.

Expressions   There are two basic types of expressions: arithmetic and logical. Arithmetic expressions allow you to do arithmetic on constants and variables, yielding a numeric result. Logical (Boolean) expressions compare expressions or strings, or test conditions to yield a *true* or *false* result. As with all decisions within Linux shell scripts, a *true* status is represented by the value zero; *false,* by any nonzero value.

EXERCISES

1. Rewrite the **journal** script of Chapter 9 (question 5, page 340) by adding commands to verify that the user has write permission for a file named **journal-file** in the user's home directory, if such a file exists. The script should take appropriate actions if **journal-file** exists and the user does not have write permission to the file. Verify that the modified script works.

2. The special parameter "$@" is referenced twice in the **out** script (page 883). Explain what would be different if the parameter "$*" were used in its place.

3. Write a filter that takes a list of files as input and outputs the basename (page 906) of each file in the list.

4. Write a function that takes a single filename as an argument and adds execute permission to the file for the user.

   a. When might such a function be useful?

   b. Revise the script so that it takes one or more filenames as arguments and adds execute permission for the user for each file argument.

   c. What can you do to make the function available every time you log in?

   d. Suppose that, in addition to having the function available on subsequent login sessions, you want to make the function available now in your current shell. How would you do so?

5. When might it be necessary or advisable to write a shell script instead of a shell function? Give as many reasons as you can think of.

6. Write a shell script that displays the names of all directory files, but no other types of files, in the working directory.

7. Write a script to display the time every 15 seconds. Read the date man page and display the time, using the **%r** field descriptor. Clear the window (using the clear command) each time before you display the time.

8. Enter the following script named **savefiles**, and give yourself execute permission to the file:

```
$ cat savefiles
#! /bin/bash
echo "Saving files in current directory in file savethem."
exec > savethem
for i in *
        do
        echo "================================================"
        echo "File: $i"
        echo "================================================"
        cat "$i"
        done
```

    a. What error message do you get when you execute this script? Rewrite the script so that the error does not occur, making sure the output still goes to **savethem**.

    b. What might be a problem with running this script twice in the same directory? Discuss a solution to this problem.

9. Read the bash man or info page, try some experiments, and answer the following questions:

    a. How do you export a function?

    b. What does the hash builtin do?

    c. What happens if the argument to exec is not executable?

10. Using the find utility, perform the following tasks:

    a. List all files in the working directory and all subdirectories that have been modified within the last day.

    b. List all files that you have read access to on the system that are larger than 1 megabyte.

    c. Remove all files named **core** from the directory structure rooted at your home directory.

    d. List the inode numbers of all files in the working directory whose filenames end in **.c**.

    e. List all files that you have read access to on the root filesystem that have been modified in the last 30 days.

11. Write a short script that tells you whether the permissions for two files, whose names are given as arguments to the script, are identical. If the permissions for the two files are identical, output the common permission field. Otherwise, output each filename followed by its permission field. (*Hint*: Try using the cut utility.)

12. Write a script that takes the name of a directory as an argument and searches the file hierarchy rooted at that directory for zero-length files. Write the names of all zero-length files to standard output. If there is no option on the command line, have the script delete the file after displaying its name, asking the user for confirmation, and receiving positive confirmation. A –f (force) option on the command line indicates that the script should display the filename but not ask for confirmation before deleting the file.

ADVANCED EXERCISES

13. Write a script that takes a colon-separated list of items and outputs the items, one per line, to standard output (without the colons).

14. Generalize the script written in exercise 13 so that the character separating the list items is given as an argument to the function. If this argument is absent, the separator should default to a colon.

15. Write a function named **funload** that takes as its single argument the name of a file containing other functions. The purpose of **funload** is to make all functions in the named file available in the current shell; that is, **funload** loads the functions from the named file. To locate the file, **funload** searches the colon-separated list of directories given by the environment variable **FUNPATH**. Assume that the format of **FUNPATH** is the same as **PATH** and that searching **FUNPATH** is similar to the shell's search of the **PATH** variable.

16. Rewrite **bundle** (page 910) so that the script it creates takes an optional list of filenames as arguments. If one or more filenames are given on the command line, only those files should be re-created; otherwise, all files in the shell archive should be re-created. For example, suppose that all files with the filename extension .c are bundled into an archive named **srcshell**, and you want to unbundle just the files **test1.c** and **test2.c**. The following command will unbundle just these two files:

    $ **bash srcshell test1.c test2.c**

17. What kind of links will the **lnks** script (page 886) not find? Why?

18. In principle, recursion is never necessary. It can always be replaced by an iterative construct, such as **while** or **until**. Rewrite **makepath** (page 950) as a nonrecursive function. Which version do you prefer? Why?

19. Lists are commonly stored in environment variables by putting a colon (:) between each of the list elements. (The value of the **PATH** variable is a good example.) You can add an element to such a list by catenating the new element to the front of the list, as in

    PATH=/opt/bin:$PATH

If the element you add is already in the list, you now have two copies of it in the list. Write a shell function named **addenv** that takes two arguments: (1) the name of a shell variable and (2) a string to prepend to the list that is the value of the shell variable only if that string is not already an element of the list. For example, the call

    addenv PATH /opt/bin

would add **/opt/bin** to **PATH** only if that pathname is not already in **PATH**. Be sure that your solution works even if the shell variable starts out empty. Also make sure that you check the list elements carefully. If **/usr/opt/bin** is in **PATH** but **/opt/bin** is not, the example just given should still add **/opt/bin** to **PATH**. (*Hint:* You may find this exercise easier to complete if you first write a function **locate_field** that tells you whether a string is an element in the value of a variable.)

20. Write a function that takes a directory name as an argument and writes to standard output the maximum of the lengths of all filenames in that directory. If the function's argument is not a directory name, write an error message to standard output and exit with nonzero status.

21. Modify the function you wrote for exercise 20 to descend all subdirectories of the named directory recursively and to find the maximum length of any filename in that hierarchy.

22. Write a function that lists the number of ordinary files, directories, block special files, character special files, FIFOs, and symbolic links in the working directory. Do this in two different ways:

    a. Use the first letter of the output of **ls –l** to determine a file's type.

    b. Use the file type condition tests of the *[[expression]]* syntax to determine a file's type.

23. Modify the **quiz** program (page 956) so that the choices for a question are randomly arranged.

PART VII

APPENDIXES

REGULAR EXPRESSIONS

A regular expression defines a set of one or more strings of characters. A simple string of characters is a regular expression that defines one string of characters: itself. A more complex regular expression uses letters, numbers, and special characters to define many different strings of characters. A regular expression is said to *match* any string it defines.

This appendix describes the regular expressions used by ed, vim, emacs, grep, gawk, sed, and other utilities. The regular expressions used in shell ambiguous file references are different and are described in "Filename Generation/Pathname Expansion" on page 221.

CHARACTERS

As used in this appendix, a *character* is any character *except* a NEWLINE. Most characters represent themselves within a regular expression. A *special character* is one that does not represent itself. If you need to use a special character to represent itself, you must quote it as explained on page 971.

DELIMITERS

A character called a *delimiter* usually marks the beginning and end of a regular expression. The delimiter is always a special character for the regular expression it delimits (that is, it does not represent itself but marks the beginning and end of the expression). Although vim permits the use of other characters as a delimiter and grep does not use delimiters at all, the regular expressions in this appendix use a forward slash (/) as a delimiter. In some unambiguous cases, the second delimiter is not required. For example, you can sometimes omit the second delimiter when it would be followed immediately by RETURN.

SIMPLE STRINGS

The most basic regular expression is a simple string that contains no special characters except the delimiters. A simple string matches only itself (Table A-1). In the examples in this appendix, the strings that are matched are underlined and look like this.

Table A-1   Simple strings

Regular expression	Matches	Examples
/ring/	ring	ring, spring, ringing, stringing
/Thursday/	Thursday	Thursday, Thursday's
/or not/	or not	or not, poor nothing

SPECIAL CHARACTERS

You can use special characters within a regular expression to cause the regular expression to match more than one string. A regular expression that includes a special character always matches the longest possible string, starting as far toward the beginning (left) of the line as possible.

Periods

A period (.) matches any character (Table A-2).

Table A-2   Period

Regular expression	Matches	Examples
/ .alk/	All strings consisting of a SPACE followed by any character followed by alk	will talk, may balk
/.ing/	All strings consisting of any character preceding ing	sing song, ping, before inglenook

Brackets

Brackets ([]) define a *character class*[1] that matches any single character within the brackets (Table A-3). If the first character following the left bracket is a caret (^), the brackets define a character class that matches any single character not within the brackets. You can use a hyphen to indicate a range of characters. Within a character-class definition, backslashes and asterisks (described in the following sections) lose their special meanings. A right bracket (appearing as a member of the character class) can appear only as the first character following the left bracket. A caret is special only if it is the first character following the left bracket. A dollar sign is special only if it is followed immediately by the right bracket.

Table A-3   Brackets

Regular expression	Matches	Examples
/[bB]ill/	Member of the character class b and B followed by ill	bill, Bill, billed
/t[aeiou].k/	t followed by a lowercase vowel, any character, and a k	talkative, stink, teak, tanker
/# [6–9]/	# followed by a SPACE and a member of the character class 6 through 9	# 60, # 8:, get # 9
/[^a–zA–Z]/	Any character that is not a letter (ASCII character set only)	1, 7, @, ., }, Stop!

1. GNU documentation calls these List Operators and defines Character Class operators as expressions that match a predefined group of characters, such as all numbers (page 1024).

ASTERISKS

An asterisk can follow a regular expression that represents a single character (Table A-4). The asterisk represents *zero* or more occurrences of a match of the regular expression. An asterisk following a period matches any string of characters. (A period matches any character, and an asterisk matches zero or more occurrences of the preceding regular expression.) A character-class definition followed by an asterisk matches any string of characters that are members of the character class.

Table A-4   Asterisks

Regular expression	Matches	Examples
/ab*c/	<u>a</u> followed by zero or more <u>b</u>'s followed by a <u>c</u>	<u>ac</u>, <u>abc</u>, <u>abbc</u>, debbca<u>abbc</u>
/ab.*c/	<u>ab</u> followed by zero or more characters followed by <u>c</u>	<u>abc</u>, <u>abxc</u>, <u>ab45c</u>, x<u>ab 756.345 x c</u>at
/t.*ing/	<u>t</u> followed by zero or more characters followed by <u>ing</u>	<u>thing</u>, <u>ting</u>, I <u>thought of going</u>
/[a–zA–Z]*/	A string composed only of letters and SPACES	1.<u> any string without numbers or punctuation</u>!
/(.*)/	As long a string as possible between (and)	Get <u>(this) and (that)</u>;
/([^)]*)/	The shortest string possible that starts with (and ends with)	<u>(this)</u>, Get <u>(this and that)</u>

CARETS AND DOLLAR SIGNS

A regular expression that begins with a caret (^) can match a string only at the beginning of a line. In a similar manner, a dollar sign ($) at the end of a regular expression matches the end of a line. The caret and dollar sign are called anchors because they force (anchor) a match to the beginning or end of a line (Table A-5).

Table A-5   Carets and dollar signs

Regular expression	Matches	Examples
/^T/	A <u>T</u> at the beginning of a line	<u>T</u>his line..., <u>T</u>hat Time..., In Time
/^+[0–9]/	A plus sign followed by a digit at the beginning of a line	<u>+5</u> +45.72, <u>+7</u>59 Keep this...
/:$/	A colon that ends a line	...below<u>:</u>

QUOTING SPECIAL CHARACTERS

You can quote any special character (but not a digit or a parenthesis) by preceding it with a backslash (Table A-6). Quoting a special character makes it represent itself.

Table A-6   Quoted special characters

Regular expression	Matches	Examples
/end\./	All strings that contain <u>end</u> followed by a period	The <u>end.</u>, s<u>end.</u>, pret<u>end.</u>mail
/ \\/	A single backslash	\
/ */	An asterisk	<u>*</u>.c, an asterisk (<u>*</u>)
/ \[5\]/	<u>[5]</u>	it was five <u>[5]</u>
/and\/or/	<u>and/or</u>	<u>and/or</u>

RULES

The following rules govern the application of regular expressions.

LONGEST MATCH POSSIBLE

A regular expression always matches the longest possible string, starting as far toward the beginning of the line as possible. For example, given the string

```
This (rug) is not what it once was (a long time ago), is it?
```

the expression /Th.*is/ matches

```
This (rug) is not what it once was (a long time ago), is
```

and /(.*)/ matches

```
(rug) is not what it once was (a long time ago)
```

However, /([^)]*)/ matches

```
(rug)
```

Given the string

```
singing songs, singing more and more
```

the expression /s.*ing/ matches

```
singing songs, singing
```

and /s.*ing song/ matches

```
singing song
```

EMPTY REGULAR EXPRESSIONS

Within some utilities, such as vim and less (but not grep), an empty regular expression represents the last regular expression that you used. For example, suppose you give vim the following Substitute command:

```
:s/mike/robert/
```

If you then want to make the same substitution again, you can use the following command:

```
:s//robert/
```

Alternatively, you can use the following commands to search for the string **mike** and then make the substitution

```
/mike/
:s//robert/
```

The empty regular expression (**//**) represents the last regular expression you used (**/mike/**).

BRACKETING EXPRESSIONS

You can use quoted parentheses, \(and \), to *bracket* a regular expression. The string that the bracketed regular expression matches can be recalled, as explained in "Quoted Digit." A regular expression does not attempt to match quoted parentheses. Thus a regular expression enclosed within quoted parentheses matches what the same regular expression without the parentheses would match. The expression /\(rexp\)/ matches what **/rexp/** would match; **/a\(b✲\)c/** matches what **/ab✲c/** would match.

You can nest quoted parentheses. The bracketed expressions are identified only by the opening \(, so no ambiguity arises in identifying them. The expression /\([a–z]\([A–Z]✲\)x\)/ consists of two bracketed expressions, one nested within the other. In the string **3 t dMNORx7 l u**, the preceding regular expression matches **dMNORx**, with the first bracketed expression matching **dMNORx** and the second matching **MNOR**.

THE REPLACEMENT STRING

The vim and sed editors use regular expressions as search strings within Substitute commands. You can use the ampersand (**&**) and quoted digits (**\\n**) special characters to represent the matched strings within the corresponding replacement string.

AMPERSAND

Within a replacement string, an ampersand (&) takes on the value of the string that the search string (regular expression) matched. For example, the following vim Substitute command surrounds a string of one or more digits with **NN**. The ampersand in the replacement string matches whatever string of digits the regular expression (search string) matched:

> **:s/[0-9][0-9]*/NN&NN/**

Two character-class definitions are required because the regular expression [0–9]* matches *zero* or more occurrences of a digit, and *any* character string constitutes zero or more occurrences of a digit.

QUOTED DIGIT

Within the search string, a bracketed regular expression, \(**xxx**\), matches what the regular expression would have matched without the quoted parentheses, **xxx**. Within the replacement string, a quoted digit, *n,* represents the string that the bracketed regular expression (portion of the search string) beginning with the *n*th \(matched. For example, you can take a list of people in the form

> `last-name, first-name initial`

and put it in the form

> `first-name initial last-name`

with the following vim command:

> **:1,$s/\([^,]*\), \(.*\)/\2 \1/**

This command addresses all the lines in the file (**1,$**). The Substitute command (**s**) uses a search string and a replacement string delimited by forward slashes. The first bracketed regular expression within the search string, \([^,]*\), matches what the same unbracketed regular expression, [^,]*, would match: zero or more characters not containing a comma (the **last-name**). Following the first bracketed regular expression are a comma and a SPACE that match themselves. The second bracketed expression, \(.*\), matches any string of characters (the **first-name** and **initial**).

The replacement string consists of what the second bracketed regular expression matched (\2), followed by a SPACE and what the first bracketed regular expression matched (\1).

EXTENDED REGULAR EXPRESSIONS

The three utilities egrep, grep when run with the –E option (similar to egrep), and gawk provide all the special characters that are included in ordinary regular expressions, except for \(and \), as well as several others. The vim editor includes the additional characters as well as \(and \). Patterns using the extended set of special characters are called *full regular expressions* or *extended regular expressions.*

Two of the additional special characters are the plus sign (+) and the question mark (?). They are similar to *, which matches *zero* or more occurrences of the previous character. The plus sign matches *one* or more occurrences of the previous character, whereas the question mark matches *zero* or *one* occurrence. You can use any one of the special characters *, +, and ? following parentheses, causing the special character to apply to the string surrounded by the parentheses. Unlike the parentheses in bracketed regular expressions, these parentheses are not quoted (Table A-7).

Table A-7   Extended regular expressions

Regular expression	Matches	Examples
/ab+c/	<u>a</u> followed by one or more <u>b</u>'s followed by a <u>c</u>	y<u>abc</u>w, <u>abbc</u>57
/ab?c/	<u>a</u> followed by zero or one <u>b</u> followed by <u>c</u>	b<u>ac</u>k, <u>abc</u>def
/(ab)+c/	One or more occurrences of the string <u>ab</u> followed by <u>c</u>	z<u>abc</u>d, <u>ababc</u>!
/(ab)?c/	Zero or one occurrence of the string <u>ab</u> followed by <u>c</u>	x<u>c</u>, <u>abc</u>c

In full regular expressions, the vertical bar (|) special character is a Boolean OR operator. Within vim, you must quote the vertical bar by preceding it with a backslash to make it special (\|). A vertical bar between two regular expressions causes a match with strings that match the first expression, the second expression, or both. You can use the vertical bar with parentheses to separate from the rest of the regular expression the two expressions that are being ORed (Table A-8).

Table A-8   Full regular expressions

Regular expression	Meaning	Examples
/ab|ac/	Either <u>ab</u> or <u>ac</u>	<u>ab</u>, <u>ac</u>, <u>abac</u> *(**abac** is two matches of the regular expression)*
/^Exit|^Quit/	Lines that begin with <u>Exit</u> or <u>Quit</u>	<u>Exit</u>, <u>Quit</u>, No Exit
/(D|N)\. Jones/	<u>D. Jones</u> or <u>N. Jones</u>	P.<u>D. Jones</u>, <u>N. Jones</u>

APPENDIX SUMMARY

A regular expression defines a set of one or more strings of characters. A regular expression is said to match any string it defines.

In a regular expression, a special character is one that does not represent itself. Table A-9 lists special characters.

Table A-9   Special characters

Character	Meaning
.	Matches any single character
*	Matches zero or more occurrences of a match of the preceding character
^	Forces a match to the beginning of a line
$	A match to the end of a line
\	Quotes special characters
\<	Forces a match to the beginning of a word
\>	Forces a match to the end of a word

Table A-10 lists ways of representing character classes and bracketed regular expressions.

Table A-10   Character classes and bracketed regular expressions

Class	Defines
[*xyz*]	Defines a character class that matches *x*, *y*, or *z*
[^*xyz*]	Defines a character class that matches any character except *x*, *y*, or *z*
[*x–z*]	Defines a character class that matches any character *x* through *z* inclusive
\(*xyz*\)	Matches what *xyz* matches (a bracketed regular expression)

In addition to the preceding special characters and strings (excluding quoted parentheses, except in vim), the characters in Table A-11 are special within full, or extended, regular expressions.

Table A-11   Extended regular expressions

Expression	Matches
+	Matches one or more occurrences of the preceding character
?	Matches zero or one occurrence of the preceding character
(*xyz*)+	Matches one or more occurrences of what *xyz* matches

Table A-11   Extended regular expressions (continued)

(*xyz*)?	Matches zero or one occurrence of what *xyz* matches
(*xyz*)*	Matches zero or more occurrences of what *xyz* matches
xyz|*abc*	Matches either what *xyz* or what *abc* matches (use \\\| in vim)
(*xy*|*ab*)*c*	Matches either what *xyc* or what *abc* matches (use \\\| in vim)

Table A-12 lists characters that are special within a replacement string in sed and vim.

Table A-12   Replacement strings

String	Represents
&	Represents what the regular expression (search string) matched
n	A quoted number, *n*, represents what the *n*th bracketed regular expression in the search string matched

B

Help

You need not act as a user or system administrator in isolation. A large community of Linux experts is willing to assist you in learning about, helping you solve problems with, and getting the most out of a Linux system. Before you ask for help, however, make sure you have done everything you can to solve the problem yourself. No doubt, someone has experienced the same problem before you and the answer to your question can be found somewhere on the Internet. Your job is to find it. This appendix lists resources and describes methods that can help you in that task.

SOLVING A PROBLEM

Following is a list of steps that can help you solve a problem without asking someone for help. Depending on your understanding of and experience with the hardware and software involved, these steps may lead to a solution.

1. Red Hat Linux comes with extensive documentation. Read the documentation on the specific hardware or software you are having a problem with. If it is a GNU product, use info; otherwise, use man to find local information. Also look in **/usr/share/doc** for documentation on specific tools. For more information refer to "Getting the Facts: Where to Find Documentation" on page 102.

2. When the problem involves some type of error or other message, use a search engine, such as Google (www.google.com/linux) or Google Groups (groups.google.com), to look up the message on the Internet. If the message is long, pick a unique part of the message to search for; 10 to 20 characters should be enough. Enclose the search string within double quotation marks.

3. Check whether the Linux Documentation Project (www.tldp.org) has a HOWTO or mini-HOWTO on the subject in question. Search on keywords that relate directly to the product and problem. Read the FAQs.

4. See Table B-1 for other sources of documentation.

5. Use Google or Google Groups to search on keywords that relate directly to the product and problem.

6. When all else fails (or perhaps before you try anything else), examine the system logs in **/var/log**. Running as Superuser, first look at the end of the **messages** file using the following command:

    # `tail -20 /var/log/messages`

   If **messages** contains nothing useful, run the following command. It displays the names of the log files in chronological order, with the most recently modified files appearing at the bottom of the list:

    $ `ls -ltr /var/log`

   If the problem involves a network connection, review the **secure** log file on the local and remote systems. Also look at **messages** on the remote system.

7. The **/var/spool** directory contains subdirectories with useful information: **cups** holds the print queues, **mail** holds the user's mail files, and so on.

If you are unable to solve a problem yourself, a thoughtful question to an appropriate newsgroup (page 981) or mailing list (page 981) can elicit useful information.

When you send or post a question, make sure you describe the problem and identify the local system carefully. Include the version numbers of Red Hat Linux and any software packages that relate to the problem. Describe the hardware, if appropriate. For a fee, Red Hat provides many types of support.

The author's home page (www.sobell.com) contains corrections to this book, answers to selected chapter exercises, and pointers to other Linux sites.

FINDING LINUX-RELATED INFORMATION

Red Hat Linux comes with reference pages stored online. You can read these documents by using the info (page 106) or man (page 104) utilities. You can read man and info pages to get more information about specific topics while reading this book or to determine which features are available with Linux. You can search for topics using apropos (see page 145 or give the command **man apropos**).

DOCUMENTATION

Good books are available on various aspects of using and managing UNIX systems in general and Linux systems in particular. In addition, you may find the sites listed in Table B-1 useful.[1]

Table B-1   Documentation

Site	About the site	URL
freedesktop.org	Creates standards for interoperability between open-source desktop environments.	freedesktop.org
GNOME	GNOME home page.	www.gnome.org
GNU Manuals	GNU manuals.	www.gnu.org/manual
Internet FAQ Archives	Searchable FAQ archives.	www.faqs.org
info	Instructions for using the info utility.	www.gnu.org/software/texinfo/manual/info
KDE Documentation	KDE documentation.	kde.org/documentation
KDE News	KDE news.	dot.kde.org

---

1. The right-hand columns of most of the tables in this appendix show Internet addresses (URLs). All sites have an implicit http:// prefix unless ftp:// or https:// is shown. Refer to "URLs (Web addresses)" on page 18.

Table B-1 Documentation (continued)

The Linux Documentation Project	All things related to Linux documentation (in many languages): HOWTOs, guides, FAQs, man pages, and magazines. This is the best overall source for Linux documentation. Make sure to visit the Links page.	www.tldp.org
Red Hat Documentation and Support	This site has a link to the Red Hat Knowledgebase that can help answer questions. It also has links to online documentation for Red Hat products and to a support guide.	www.redhat.com/apps/support
RFCs	Request for comments; see *RFC* (page 1052).	www.rfc-editor.org
System Administrators Guild (SAGE)	SAGE is a group for system administrators.	www.sage.org

USEFUL LINUX SITES

Sometimes the sites listed in Table B-2 are so busy that you cannot connect to them. In this case, you are usually given a list of alternative, or *mirror,* sites to try.

Table B-2 Useful Linux sites

Site	About the site	URL
DistroWatch	A survey of many Linux distributions, including news, reviews, and articles.	distrowatch.com
GNU	GNU Project Web server.	www.gnu.org
ibiblio	A large library and digital archive. Formerly Metalab; formerly Sunsite.	www.ibiblio.org www.ibiblio.org/pub/linux www.ibiblio.org/pub/historic-linux
LinuxHQ.org	An administrator and power user resource site.	www.linuxhq.org
Linux Standard Base (LSB)	A group dedicated to standardizing Linux.	www.linuxbase.org
Rpmfind.Net	A good source for rpm files, especially when you need a specific version.	rpmfind.net

Table B-2   Useful Linux sites (continued)

Sobell	The author's home page contains useful links, errata for this book, code for many of the examples in this book, and answers to selected exercises.	www.sobell.com
USENIX	A large, well-established UNIX group. This site has many links, including a list of conferences.	www.usenix.org
X.Org	The X Window System home.	www.x.org

LINUX NEWSGROUPS

One of the best ways of getting specific information is through a newsgroup (refer to "Usenet" on page 378). Frequently you can find the answer to a question by reading postings to the newsgroup. Try using Google Groups (groups.google.com) to search through newsgroups to see whether the question has already been asked and answered. Or open a newsreader program and subscribe to appropriate newsgroups. If necessary, you can post a question for someone to answer. Before you do so, make sure you are posting to the correct group and that your question has not already been answered. There is an etiquette to posting questions—see www.catb.org/~esr/faqs/smart-questions.html for a good paper by Eric S. Raymond and Rick Moen titled "How To Ask Questions the Smart Way."

The newsgroup **comp.os.linux.answers** provides postings of solutions to common problems and periodic postings of the most up-to-date versions of the FAQ and HOWTO documents. The **comp.os.linux.misc** newsgroup has answers to miscellaneous Linux-related questions.

MAILING LISTS

Subscribing to a mailing list (page 646) allows you to participate in an electronic discussion. With most lists, you can send and receive email dedicated to a specific topic to and from a group of users. Moderated lists do not tend to stray as much as unmoderated lists, assuming the list has a good moderator. The disadvantage of a moderated list is that some discussions may be cut off when they get interesting if the moderator deems that the discussion has gone on for too long. Mailing lists described as bulletins are strictly unidirectional: You cannot post information to these lists but can only receive periodic bulletins. If you have the subscription address for a mailing list but are not sure how to subscribe, put the word **help** in the body and/or header of email that you send to the address. You will usually receive instructions via return email. Red Hat hosts several mailing lists; go to www.redhat.com/mailman/listinfo for more information. You can also use a search engine to search for **mailing list linux**.

WORDS

Many dictionaries, thesauruses, and glossaries are available online. Table B-3 lists a few of them.

Table B-3   Looking up words

Site	About the site	URL
ROGET'S Thesaurus	Thesaurus	humanities.uchicago.edu/forms_unrest/ROGET.html
DICT.org	Multiple-database search for words	www.dict.org
Dictionary.com	Everything related to words	dictionary.reference.com
DNS Glossary	DNS glossary	www.menandmice.com/online_docs_and_faq/glossary/glossarytoc.htm
FOLDOC (The Free On-Line Dictionary of Computing)	Computer terms	www.foldoc.org
The Jargon File	An online version of *The New Hacker's Dictionary*	www.catb.org/~esr/jargon
Merriam-Webster	English language	www.m-w.com
OneLook	Multiple-site word search with a single query	www.onelook.com
Webopedia	Commercial technical dictionary	www.webopedia.com
Wikipedia	An open-source (user-contributed) encyclopedia project	wikipedia.org
Wordsmyth	Dictionary and thesaurus	www.wordsmyth.net
Yahoo Reference	Search multiple sources at the same time	education.yahoo.com/reference

SOFTWARE

There are many ways to learn about interesting software packages and their availability on the Internet. Table B-4 lists sites that you can download software from. For security-related programs, refer to Table C-1 on page 1002. Another way to learn about software packages is through a newsgroup (page 981).

Table B-4   Software

Site	About the site	URL
Apt	Apt installs, removes, and updates system software packages	apt.freshrpms.net

Table B-4   Software (continued)

BitTorrent	BitTorrent efficiently distributes large amounts of static data	www.bittorrent.com
CVS	CVS (Concurrent Versions System) is a version control system	www.nongnu.org/cvs
ddd	The ddd utility is a graphical front end for command line debuggers such as gdb	www.gnu.org/software/ddd
Firefox	Web browser	www.mozilla.com/firefox
Free Software Directory	Categorized, searchable lists of free software	directory.fsf.org
Freshmeat	A large index of UNIX and cross-platform software and themes	freshmeat.net
gdb	The gdb utility is a command line debugger	www.gnu.org/software/gdb
GNOME Project	Links to all GNOME projects	www.gnome.org/projects
IceWALKERS	Categorized, searchable lists of free software	www.icewalkers.com
kdbg	The kdbg utility is a graphical user interface to gdb	freshmeat.net/projects/kdbg
Linux Software Map	A database of packages written for, ported to, or compiled for Linux	www.boutell.com/lsm
Mtools	A collection of utilities to access DOS floppy diskettes from Linux without mounting the diskettes	mtools.linux.lu
Network Calculators	Subnet mask calculator	www.subnetmask.info
rpmfind.net	Searchable list of rpm files for various Linux distributions and versions	rpmfind.net/linux/RPM
Savannah	Central point for development, distribution, and maintenance of free software	savannah.gnu.org
SourceForge	A development Web site with a large repository of open-source code and applications	sourceforge.net
strace	The strace utility is a system call trace debugging tool	www.liacs.nl/~wichert/strace sourceforge.net/projects/strace

Table B-4   Software (continued)

Thunderbird	Mail application	www.mozilla.com/thunderbird
Tucows-Linux	Commercial, categorized, searchable list of software	www.tucows.com/Linux
ups	The ups utility is a graphical source-level debugger	ups.sourceforge.net
yum	The yum utility installs, removes, and updates system software packages	linux.duke.edu/projects/yum apt.freshrpms.net

OFFICE SUITES AND WORD PROCESSORS

Several office suites and many word processors are available for Linux. Table B-5 lists a few of them. If you are exchanging documents with people using Windows, make sure the import from/export to MS Word functionality covers your needs.

Table B-5   Office suites and word processors

Product name	What it does	URL
AbiWord	Word processor	www.abisource.com
KOffice	Integrated suite of office applications including the KWord word processing program	www.koffice.org
OpenOffice	A multiplatform and multilingual office suite	www.openoffice.org www.gnome.org/projects/ooo
Xcoral	A programmer's multiwindow mouse-based editor that runs under X	xcoral.free.fr

SPECIFYING A TERMINAL

Because vim, emacs, konsole, and other programs take advantage of features that are specific to various kinds of terminals and terminal emulators, you must tell these programs the name of the terminal you are using or the terminal that your terminal emulator is emulating. On many systems the terminal name is set for you. If the terminal name is not specified or is not specified correctly, the characters on the screen will be garbled or, when you start a program, the program will ask what type of terminal you are using.

Terminal names describe the functional characteristics of a terminal or terminal emulator to programs that require this information. Although terminal names are referred to as either Terminfo or Termcap names, the difference relates to the method that each system uses to store the terminal characteristics internally, not the manner that you specify the name of a terminal. Terminal names that are often used with Linux terminal emulators and with graphical monitors while they are run in text mode include **ansi, linux, vt100, vt102, vt220,** and **xterm.**

When you are running a terminal emulator, you can specify the type of terminal you want to emulate. Set the emulator to either **vt100** or **vt220,** and then set **TERM** to the same value.

When you log in, you may be prompted to identify the type of terminal you are using:

```
TERM = (vt100)
```

You can respond to this prompt in one of two ways. First you can press RETURN to set your terminal type to the name in parentheses. If that name does not describe the terminal you are using, you can enter the correct name and then press RETURN.

```
TERM = (vt100) ansi
```

You may also receive the following prompt:

```
TERM = (unknown)
```

This prompt indicates that the system does not know what type of terminal you are using. If you plan to run programs that require this information, enter the name of the terminal or terminal emulator you are using before you press RETURN.

TERM If you do not receive a prompt, you can give the following command to display the value of the **TERM** variable and check whether the terminal type has been set:

```
$ echo $TERM
```

If the system responds with the wrong name, a blank line, or an error message, set or change the terminal name. From the Bourne Again Shell (bash), enter a command similar to the following to set the **TERM** variable so that the system knows which type of terminal you are using:

export TERM=name

Replace *name* with the terminal name for the terminal you are using, making sure that you do not put a SPACE before or after the equal sign. If you always use the same type of terminal, you can place this command in your ~/.**bashrc** file (page 267), causing the shell to set the terminal type each time you log in. For example, give the following command to set your terminal name to **vt100:**

```
$ export TERM=vt100
```

LANG For some programs to display information correctly you may need to set the **LANG** variable (page 298). Frequently you can set this variable to C. Under bash use the command

```
$ export LANG=C
```

C

SECURITY

Security is a major part of the foundation of any system that is not totally cut off from other machines and users. Some aspects of security have a place even on isolated machines. Examples of these measures include periodic system backups, BIOS or power-on passwords, and self-locking screensavers.

A system that is connected to the outside world requires other mechanisms to secure it: tools to check files (tripwire), audit tools (tiger/cops), secure access methods (kerberos/ssh), services that monitor logs and machine states (swatch/watcher), packet-filtering and routing tools (ipfwadm/iptables/ipchains), and more.

System security has many dimensions. The security of your system as a whole depends on the security of individual components, such as your email, files, network, login, and remote access policies, as well as the physical security of the host itself. These dimensions frequently overlap, and their borders are not always static or clear. For instance, email security is affected by the security of files and your network. If the medium (the network) over which you send and receive your email is not secure, then you must take extra steps to ensure the security of your

987

messages. If you save your secure email into a file on your local system, then you rely on the filesystem and host access policies for file security. A failure in any one of these areas can start a domino effect, diminishing reliability and integrity in other areas and potentially compromising system security as a whole.

This short appendix cannot cover all facets of system security in depth, but it does provide an overview of the complexity of setting up and maintaining a secure system. This appendix provides some specifics, concepts, guidelines to consider, and many pointers to security resources (Table C-1 on page 1002).

Other sources of system security information

security   Depending on how important system security is to you, you may want to purchase one or more of the books dedicated to system security, visit some of the Internet sites that are dedicated to security, or hire someone who is an expert in the field.

Do not rely on this appendix as your sole source of information on system security.

ENCRYPTION

One of the building blocks of security is encryption, which provides a means of scrambling data for secure transmission to other parties. In cryptographic terms, the data or message to be encrypted is referred to as *plaintext,* and the resulting encrypted block of text as *ciphertext.* Processes exist for converting plaintext into ciphertext through the use of *keys,* which are essentially random numbers of a specified length used to *lock* and *unlock* data. This conversion is achieved by applying the keys to the plaintext according to a set of mathematical instructions, referred to as the *encryption algorithm.*

Developing and analyzing strong encryption software is extremely difficult. Many nuances exist, many standards govern encryption algorithms, and a background in mathematics is requisite. Also, unless an algorithm has undergone public scrutiny for a significant period of time, it is generally not considered secure; it is often impossible to know that an algorithm is completely secure but possible to know that one is not secure. Time is the best test of any algorithm. Also, a solid algorithm does not guarantee an effective encryption mechanism, as the fallibility of an encryption scheme frequently lies in problems with its implementation and distribution.

An encryption algorithm uses a key that is a certain number of bits long. Each bit you add to the length of a key effectively doubles the *key space* (the number of combinations allowed by the number of bits in the key—2 to the power of the length of the key in bits[1]) and means that it will take twice as long for an attacker to decrypt your message (assuming that the scheme lacks any inherent weaknesses or vulnerabilities to exploit). However, it is a mistake to compare algorithms based only on

---

1. A 2-bit key would have a key space of 4 (2^2), a 3-bit key would have a key space of 8 (2^3), and so on.

the number of bits used. In some cases an algorithm that uses a 64-bit key can be more secure than an algorithm that uses a 128-bit key.

The two primary classifications of encryption schemes are *public key encryption* and *symmetric key encryption*. Public key encryption, also called *asymmetric encryption*, uses two keys: a public key and a private key. These keys are uniquely associated with a specific individual user. Public key encryption schemes are used mostly to exchange keys and signatures. Symmetric key encryption, also called *symmetric encryption* or *secret key encryption*, uses one key that you and the person you are communicating with (hereafter referred to as your *friend*) share as a secret. Symmetric key encryption is typically used to encrypt large amounts of data. Public key algorithm keys typically have a length of 512 bits to 2,048 bits, whereas symmetric key algorithms use keys in the range of 64 bits to 512 bits.

When you are choosing an encryption scheme, realize that security comes at a price. There is usually a tradeoff between resilience of the cryptosystem and ease of administration.

Hard to break? Hard to use!

security | The more difficult an algorithm is to crack, the more difficult it is to maintain and to get people to use properly. The paramount limitations of most respectable cryptosystems lie not in weak algorithms but rather in users' failure to transmit and store keys in a secure manner.

The practicality of a security solution is a far greater factor in encryption, and in security in general, than most people realize. With enough time and effort, nearly every algorithm can be broken. In fact, you can often unearth the mathematical instructions for a widely used algorithm by flipping through a cryptography book, reviewing a vendor's product specifications, or performing a quick search on the Internet. The challenge is to ensure that the effort required to follow the twists and turns taken by an encryption algorithm and its resulting encryption solution outweighs the worth of the information it is protecting.

How much time and money should you spend on encryption?

tip | When the cost of obtaining the information exceeds the value realized by its possession, the solution is an effective one.

PUBLIC KEY ENCRYPTION

To use public key encryption, you must generate two keys: a public key and a private key. You keep the private key for yourself and give the public key to the world. In a similar manner, your friends will generate a pair of keys and give you their public keys. Public key encryption is marked by two distinct features:

1. When you encrypt data with someone's public key, only that person's private key can decrypt it.

2. When you encrypt data with your private key, anyone else can decrypt it with your public key.

You may wonder why the second point is useful: Why would you want everybody else to be able to decrypt something you just encrypted? The answer lies in the purpose of the encryption. Although encryption changes the original message into unreadable ciphertext, its purpose is to provide a *digital signature*. If the message can be properly decrypted with your public key, *only you* could have encrypted it with your private key, proving that the message is authentic. Combining these two modes of operation yields privacy and authenticity. You can sign something with your private key so that it is verified as authentic, and then you can encrypt it with your friend's public key so that only your friend can decrypt it.

Public key encryption has three major shortcomings:

1. Public key encryption algorithms are generally much slower than symmetric key algorithms and usually require a much larger key size and a way to generate large prime numbers to use as components of the key, making them more resource intensive.

2. The private key must be stored securely and its integrity safeguarded. If a person's private key is obtained by another party, that party can encrypt, decrypt, and sign messages while impersonating the original owner of the key. If the private key is lost or becomes corrupted, any messages previously encrypted with it are also lost, and a new keypair must be generated.

3. It is difficult to authenticate the origin of a key—that is, to prove whom it originally came from. This so-called key-distribution problem is the raison d'être for such companies as VeriSign (www.verisign.com).

Algorithms such as RSA, Diffie-Hellman, and El-Gamal implement public key encryption methodology. Today a 512-bit key is considered barely adequate for RSA encryption and offers marginal protection; 1,024-bit keys are expected to withhold determined attackers for several more years. Keys that are 2,048 bits long are now becoming commonplace and are rated as *espionage strength*. A mathematical paper published in late 2001 and reexamined in spring 2002 describes how a machine can be built—for a very large sum of money—that could break 1,024-bit RSA encryption in seconds to minutes (this point is debated in an article at www.schneier.com/crypto-gram-0203.html#6). Although the cost of such a machine exceeds the resources available to most individuals and smaller corporations, it is well within the reach of large corporations and governments.

SYMMETRIC KEY ENCRYPTION

Symmetric key encryption is generally fast and simple to deploy. First you and your friend agree on which algorithm to use and a key that you will share. Then either of you can decrypt or encrypt a file with the same key. Behind the scenes, symmetric key encryption algorithms are most often implemented as a network of black boxes, which can involve hardware components, software, or a combination of the two. Each box imposes a reversible transformation on the plaintext and passes it on to the next box, where another reversible transformation further alters the data. The security of a symmetric key algorithm relies on the difficulty of determining which boxes were used and the number of times the data was fed through the set of boxes. A good algorithm will cycle the plaintext through a given set of boxes many times before yielding the result, and there will be no obvious mapping from plaintext to ciphertext.

The disadvantage of symmetric key encryption is that it depends heavily on the availability of a secure channel through which to send the key to your friend. For example, you would not use email to send your key; if your email is intercepted, a third party is in possession of your secret key, and your encryption is useless. You could relay the key over the phone, but your call could be intercepted if your phone were tapped or someone overheard your conversation.

Common implementations of symmetric key algorithms include DES (Data Encryption Standard), 3-DES (triple DES), IDEA, RC5, Blowfish, and AES (Advanced Encryption Standard). AES is the new Federal Information Processing Standard (FIPS-197) algorithm endorsed for governmental use and has been selected to replace DES as the de facto encryption algorithm. AES uses the Rijndael algorithm (www.rijndael.com), chosen after a thorough evaluation of 15 candidate algorithms by the cryptographic research community.

None of the aforementioned algorithms has undergone more scrutiny than DES, which has been in use since the late 1970s. However, the use of DES has drawbacks and it is no longer considered secure, as the weakness of its 56-bit key makes it unreasonably easy to break. Because of the advances in computing power and speed since DES was developed, the small size of this algorithm's key renders it inadequate for operations requiring more than basic security for a relatively short period of time. For a few thousand dollars, you can link off-the-shelf computer systems so that they can crack DES keys in a few hours.

The 3-DES application of DES is intended to combat its degenerating resilience by running the encryption three times; it is projected to be secure for years to come. DES is probably sufficient for such tasks as sending email to a friend when you need it to be confidential or secure for only a few days (for example, to send a notice of a meeting that will take place in a few hours). It is unlikely that anyone is sufficiently interested in your email to invest the time and money to decrypt it. Because of 3-DES's wide availability and ease of use, it is advisable to use it instead of DES.

ENCRYPTION IMPLEMENTATION

Most of today's commercial software packages use both public and symmetric key encryption algorithms, taking advantage of the strengths of each and avoiding their weaknesses. The public key algorithm is used first, as a means of negotiating a randomly generated secret key and providing for message authenticity. Then a secret key algorithm, such as 3-DES, IDEA, AES, or Blowfish, encrypts and decrypts the data on both ends for speed. Finally a hash algorithm, such as DSA (Digital Signature Algorithm), generates a message digest that provides a signature that can alert you to tampering. The digest is digitally signed with the sender's private key.

GNuPG/PGP

The most popular personal encryption packages available today are GnuPG (GNU Privacy Guard, also called GPG; www.gnupg.org) and PGP (Pretty Good Privacy; www.pgp.com). GNU Privacy Guard was designed as a free replacement for PGP, a security tool that made its debut during the early 1990s. Phil Zimmerman developed PGP as a Public Key Infrastructure (PKI), featuring a convenient interface, ease of use and management, and the security of digital certificates. One critical characteristic set PGP apart from the majority of cryptosystems then available: PGP functions entirely without certification authorities (CAs). Until the introduction of PGP, PKI implementations were built around the concept of CAs and centralized key management controls.

PGP and GnuPG rely on the notion of a ring of trust:[2] If you trust someone and that person trusts someone else, the person you trust can provide an introduction to the third party. When you trust someone, you perform an operation called *key signing*. By signing someone else's key, you verify that the person's public key is authentic and safe for you to use to send email. When you sign a key, you are asked whether you trust this person to introduce other keys to you. It is common practice to assign this trust based on several criteria, including your knowledge of a person's character or a lasting professional relationship with the person. The best practice is to sign someone's key only after you have met face to face to avert any chance of a man-in-the-middle[3] scenario. The disadvantage of this scheme is the lack of a central registry for associating with people you do not already know.

PGP is available without cost for personal use, but its deployment in a commercial environment requires the purchase of a license. This was not always the case: Soon after its introduction, PGP was available on many bulletin board systems, and users could implement it in any manner they chose. PGP rapidly gained popularity in the networking community, which capitalized on its encryption and key management capabilities for secure transmission of email.

After a time, attention turned to the two robust cryptographic algorithms, RSA and IDEA, which form an integral part of PGP's code. These algorithms are privately owned. The wide distribution of and growing user base for PGP sparked battles over patent violation and licenses, resulting in the eventual restriction of PGP's use.

Enter GnuPG, which supports most of the features and implementations made available by PGP and complies with the OpenPGP Message Format standard.

---

2. For more information, see the section of *The GNU Privacy Handbook* (www.gnupg.org/docs.html) titled "Validating Other Keys on Your Public Keyring."

3. Man-in-the-middle: If Alex and Jenny try to carry on a secure email exchange over a network, Alex first sends Jenny his public key. However, suppose that Mr. X sits between Alex and Jenny on the network and intercepts Alex's public key. Mr. X then sends *his own* public key to Jenny. Jenny then sends her public key to Alex, but once again Mr. X intercepts it and substitutes *his own* public key and sends that to Alex. Without some kind of active protection (a piece of shared information), Mr. X, the *man-in-the-middle*, can decrypt all traffic between Alex and Jenny, reencrypt it, and send it on to the other party.

Because GnuPG does not use the patented IDEA algorithm but rather relies on BUGS (www.gnu.org/directory/bugs.html), you can use it almost without restriction: It is released under the GNU GPL (refer to "The Code Is Free" on page 4). PGP and GnuPG are considered to be interchangeable and interoperable. The command sequences for and internal workings of these two tools are very similar.

The GnuPG system includes the gpg program

tip   GnuPG is frequently referred to as gpg, but gpg is actually the main program for the GnuPG system.

GNU offers a good introduction to privacy, *The GNU Privacy Handbook*, which is available in several languages and listed at www.gnupg.org (click **Documentation⇨Guides**). Click **Documentation⇨HOWTOs** on the same Web page to view the *GNU Privacy Guard (GnuPG) Mini Howto*, which steps through the setup and use of gpg. And, of course, there is a gpg info page.

In addition to encryption, gpg is useful for authentication. For example, you can use it to verify that the person who signed a piece of email is the person who actually sent it.

FILE SECURITY

From an end user's perspective, file security is one of the most critical areas of security. Some file security is built into Linux: chmod (page 182) gives you basic security control. ACLs (Access Control Lists) allow for more fine-grained control of file access permissions. ACLs are part of Solaris, Windows NT/2000/XP, VAX/VMS, and mainframe operating systems. Red Hat Linux supports ACLs (page 185). Even these tools are insufficient, however, when your account is compromised (for example, by someone watching your fingers on the keyboard as you type your password). To provide maximum file security, you must encrypt your files. Then even someone who knows your password cannot read your files. (Of course, if someone knows your key, that person can decrypt your files if he or she can get to them.)

EMAIL SECURITY

Email security overlaps with file security and, as discussed later, with network security. GnuPG is the tool most frequently used for email security, although you can also use PGP. PEM (Privacy Enhanced Mail) is a standard rather than an algorithm and is used less frequently.

MTAs (MAIL TRANSFER AGENTS)

An increasingly commonplace MTA is STARTTLS (Start Transport Layer Security; www.sendmail.org/~ca/email/starttls.html). TLS itself usually refers to SSL (Secure

Sockets Layer) and has become the de facto method for encrypting TCP/IP traffic on the Internet. The **sendmail** daemon can be built to support STARTTLS, and much documentation exists on how to do so. STARTTLS enhancements also exist for qmail and postfix and other popular MTAs. It is important to recognize that this capability provides encryption between two mail servers but not necessarily between your machine and the mail server. Also, the advantages of using TLS are negated if the email must pass through a relay that does not support TLS.

MUAS (MAIL USER AGENTS)

Many popular mail user agents, such as mutt, elm, and emacs, include the ability to use PGP or GnuPG for encryption. This approach has become the default way to exchange secure email.

NETWORK SECURITY

Network security is a vital component for ensuring the security of a computing site. However, without the right infrastructure, providing network security is difficult, if not impossible. For example, if you run a shared network topology,[4] such as Ethernet, and have in public locations jacks that allow anyone to plug in to the network at will, how can you prevent someone from plugging in a machine and capturing all the *packets* (page 1047) that traverse the network?[5] You cannot, so you have a potential security hole. Another common security hole relates to the use of telnet for logins. Because telnet sends and receives cleartext, anyone "listening in" on the line can easily capture usernames and passwords, compromising security.

Do not allow any unauthenticated PC (any PC that does not require users to supply a local name and password) on your network. With a Windows 9*x* PC, any user on the network is effectively Superuser for the following reasons:

- A PC does not recognize the concept of **root**. All users, by default, have access to and can watch the network, capture packets, and send packets.

- On UNIX/Linux, only Superuser can put the network interface in promiscuous mode and collect packets. On UNIX and Linux, ports numbered less than 1024[6] are privileged—that is, normal user protocols cannot bind to these ports. This is an important but regrettable means of security for some protocols, such as NIS, NFS, RSH, and LPD. Normally a data switch on your LAN automatically protects your machines from people snooping

---

4. Shared network topology: A network in which each packet may be seen by machines other than its destination. "Shared" means that the 100 megabits per second bandwidth is shared by all users.

5. Do not make the mistake of assuming that you have security just because you have a switch. Switches are designed to allocate bandwidth, not to guarantee security.

6. The term *port* has many meanings. Here it is a number assigned to a program. The number links incoming data with a specific service. For example, port 21 is used by ftp traffic, and port 23 is used by telnet.

on your network for data. In high-load situations, switches have been known to behave unpredictably, directing packets to the wrong ports. Certain programs can overload the switch tables that hold information about which machine is on which port. When these tables are overloaded, the switch becomes a repeater and broadcasts all packets to all ports. The attacker on the same switch as you can potentially see all the traffic your system sends and receives.

NETWORK SECURITY SOLUTIONS

One solution to shared-network problems is to encrypt messages that travel between machines. IPSec (Internet Protocol Security Protocol) provides just such a technology. IPSec is commonly used to establish a secure point-to-point virtual network (*VPN*, page 1062) that allows two hosts to communicate securely over an insecure channel, such as the Internet. This protocol provides integrity, confidentiality, authenticity, and flexibility of implementation that supports multiple vendors.

IPSec is an amalgamation of protocols (IPSec = AH + ESP + IPComp + IKE):

- **Authentication Header**   (AH) A cryptographically secure, irreversible *checksum* (page 1024) for an entire packet. AH guarantees that the packet is authentic.

- **Encapsulating Security Payload**   (ESP) Encrypts a packet to make the data unreadable.

- **IP Payload Compression**   (IPComp) Compresses a packet. Encryption can increase the size of a packet, and IPComp counteracts this increase in size.

- **Internet Key Exchange**   (IKE) Provides a way for the endpoints to negotiate a common key securely. For AH to work, both ends of the exchange must use the same key to prevent a "man-in-the-middle" (see footnote 3 on page 992) from spoofing the connection.

While IPSec is an optional part of IPv4, IPv6 (page 359) mandates its use. However, it may be quite some time before IPv6 is widely implemented. See page 1012 for information about the implementation of IPSec in the Linux 2.6 kernel.

NETWORK SECURITY GUIDELINES

Some general guidelines for establishing and maintaining a secure system follow. This list is not complete but meant rather only as a guide.

- Fiberoptic cable is more secure than copper cable. Copper is subject to both active and passive eavesdropping. With access to copper cable, all a data thief needs to monitor your network traffic is a passive device for measuring magnetic fields. In contrast, it is much more difficult to tap a fiberoptic cable without interrupting the signal. Sites requiring top security keep fiberoptic cable in pressurized conduits, where a change in pressure signals that the physical security of the cable has been breached.

- Avoid leaving unused ports available in public areas. If a malicious user can plug a laptop into the network without being detected, you are at risk of a serious security problem. Network drops that will remain unused for extended periods should be disabled at the switch, preventing them from accepting or passing network traffic.

- Many network switches have provisions for binding a hardware address to a port for enhanced security. If someone unplugs one machine and plugs in another machine to capture traffic, chances are that the second machine will have a different hardware address. When it detects a device with a different hardware address, the switch can disable the port. Even this solution is no guarantee, however, as there are programs that enable you to change or mask the hardware address of a network interface.

Install a small kernel and run only the programs you need

security   Linux systems contain a huge number of programs that, although useful, significantly reduce the security of the host. Install the smallest operating system kernel that meets your needs. For Web and FTP servers, install only the needed components. Users usually require additional packages.

- Do not allow NFS or NIS access outside of your network. Otherwise, it is a simple matter for a malicious user to steal your entire password map. Default NFS security is marginal to nonexistent (a common joke is that NFS stands for No File Security) so such access should not be allowed outside your network to machines that you do not trust. Experimental versions of NFS for Linux that support much better authentication algorithms are now becoming available. Use IPSec, an experimental NFSv4 with improved authentication, or firewalls to provide access outside of your domain.

- Support for VPN configuration is often built into new firewalls or provided as a separate product, enabling your system to join securely with those of your customers or partners. If you must allow business partners, contractors, or other outside parties to access your files, consider using a secure filesystem, such as NFS with *Kerberos* (page 1039), secure NFS (encrypts authentication, not traffic), NFS over a VPN such as IPSec, or cfs (cryptographic filesystem).

- Specify **/usr** as readonly (**ro**) in **/etc/fstab**. Following is an example of such a configuration.

```
/dev/hda6     /usr     ext2     ro     0     0
```

This approach may make your machine difficult to update, so use this tactic with care.

- Mount filesystems other than **/** and **/usr nosuid** to prevent setuid programs from executing on this filesystem. For example,

```
/dev/hda4     /var        ext3     nosuid     0     0
/dev/hda5     /usr/local  ext3     nosuid     0     0
```

- Use a barrier or firewall product between your network and the Internet. Several valuable mailing lists cover firewalls, including the **comp.security.firewalls** newsgroup and the free firewalls Web site, www.freefire.org. Red Hat Linux includes iptables (page 763), which allows you to implement a firewall.

HOST SECURITY

Your host must be secure. Simple security steps include preventing remote logins and leaving the **/etc/hosts.equiv** and individual users' **~/.rhosts** files empty (or not having them at all). Complex security steps include installing IPSec for VPNs between hosts. Many common security measures fall somewhere in between these two extremes. A few of these follow. See Table C-1 on page 1002 for relevant URLs.

- Although potentially tricky to implement and manage, intrusion detection systems (IDSs) are an excellent way to keep an eye on the integrity of a device. An IDS can warn of possible attempts to subvert security on the host on which it runs. The great-granddaddy of intrusion detection systems is tripwire. This host-based system checks modification times and integrity of files by using strong algorithms (cryptographic checksums or signatures) that can detect even the most minor modifications. A commercial version of tripwire is also available. Another commercial IDS is DragonSquire. Other free, popular, and flexible IDSs include samhain and AIDE. The last two IDSs offer even more features and means of remaining invisible to users than tripwire does. Commercial IDSs that are popular in enterprise environments include Cisco Secure IDS (formerly NetRanger), Enterasys Dragon, and ISS RealSecure.

- Keep Fedora systems up-to-date by downloading and installing the latest updates. Use yum to update the system regularly (page 478) or set up the system to update itself every night automatically (page 482). Go to fedora.redhat.com/download/updates.html for more information.

- Red Hat Network (RHN, page 498) can automatically or semiautomatically keep one or more systems up-to-date, preventing the system from becoming prey to fixed security bugs.

- Complementing host-based IDSs are network-based IDSs. The latter programs monitor the network and nodes on the network and report suspicious occurrences (attack signatures) via user-defined alerts. These signatures can be matched based on known worms, overflow attacks against programs, or unauthorized scans of network ports. Such programs as snort, klaxon, and NFR are used in this capacity. Commercial programs, such as DragonSentry, also fill this role.

- Provided with Red Hat Linux is PAM, which allows you to set up different methods and levels of authentication in many ways (page 438).

- Process accounting—a good supplement to system security—can provide a continuous record of user actions on your system. See the accton man page for more information.

- Emerging standards for such things as Role Based Access Control (RBAC) allow tighter delegation of privileges along defined organizational boundaries. You can delegate a role or roles to each user as appropriate to the access required.

- General mailing lists and archives are extremely useful repositories of security information, statistics, and papers. The most useful are the bugtraq mailing list and CERT.[7] The bugtraq site and email service offer immediate notifications about specific vulnerabilities, whereas CERT provides notice of widespread vulnerabilities and useful techniques to fix them, as well as links to vendor patches.

- The syslog facility (provided with Red Hat Linux) can direct messages from system daemons to specific files such as those in **/var/log**. On larger groups of systems, you can send all important syslog information to a secure host, where that host's only function is to store syslog data so that it cannot be tampered with. See page 376 and the **syslogd** man page for more information.

LOGIN SECURITY

Without a secure host, good login security cannot add much protection. Table C-1 lists some of the best login security tools, including replacement daemons for **telnetd, rlogind,** and **rshd.** The current choice of most sites is ssh, which comes as both freeware and a commercially supported package that works on UNIX/Linux, Windows, and Macintosh platforms.

The PAM facility (page 438) allows you to set up multiple authentication methods for users in series or in parallel. In-series PAM requires multiple methods of authentication for a user. In-parallel PAM uses any one of a number of methods for authentication.

Although it is not the most popular choice, you can configure your system to take advantage of one-time passwords. S/Key is the original implementation of one-time passwords by Bellcore. OPIE (one-time passwords in everything), which was developed by the U.S. Naval Research Labs, is an improvement over the original Bellcore system. In one permutation of one-time passwords, the user gets a piece of paper listing a set of one-time passwords. Each time a user logs in, she enters a password from the piece of paper. Once used, a password becomes obsolete, and the next password in the list is the only one that will work. Even if a malicious user compromises the network and sees your password, the information will be of no use

---

7. CERT is slow but useful as a medium for coordination between sites. It acts as a tracking agency to document the spread of security problems.

because the password can be used only once. This setup makes it very difficult for someone to log in as you but does nothing to protect the data you type at the keyboard. One-time passwords are a good solution if you are at a site where no encrypted login is available. A truly secure (or paranoid) site will combine one-time passwords and encrypted logins.

Another type of secure login that is becoming more common is facilitated by a token or a *smartcard*. Smartcards are credit-card-like devices that use a challenge–response method of authentication. Smartcard and token authentication rely on something you have (the card) and something you know (a pass phrase, user ID, or PIN). For example, you might enter your username in response to the login prompt and get a password prompt. You would then enter your PIN and the number displayed on the access token. The token has a unique serial number that is stored in a database on the authentication server. The token and the authentication server use this serial number as a means of computing a challenge every 30 to 60 seconds. If the PIN and token number you enter match what they should be as computed by the access server, you are granted access to the system.

REMOTE ACCESS SECURITY

Issues and solutions surrounding remote access security overlap with those pertaining to login and host security. Local logins may be secure with simply a username and password, whereas remote logins (and all remote access) should be made more secure. Many breakins can be traced back to reusable passwords. It is a good idea to use an encrypted authentication client, such as ssh or kerberos. You can also use smartcards for remote access authentication.

Modem pools can also be an entry point into a system. Most people are aware of how easy it is to monitor a network line. However, they may take for granted the security of the public switched telephone network (PSTN, also known as POTS—plain old telephone service). You may want to set up an encrypted channel after dialing in to a modem pool. One way to do so is by running ssh over PPP.

There are ways to implement stringent modem authentication policies so that unauthorized users are not able to use your modems. The most common techniques are PAP (Password Authentication Protocol), CHAP (Challenge Handshake Authentication Protocol), and Radius. PAP and CHAP are relatively weak when compared with Radius, so the latter has rapidly gained in popularity. Cisco also provides a method of authentication called TACACS/TACACS+ (Terminal Access Controller Access Control System).

One or more of these authentication techniques are available in a RAS (remote access server—in a network a computer that provides network access to remote users via modem). Before purchasing a RAS, check what kind of security it provides and decide whether that level of security meets your needs.

Two other techniques for remote access security can be built into a modem (or RAS if it has integrated modems). One is callback: After you dial in, you get a password prompt. Once you type in your password, the modem hangs up and calls you back at a phone number it has stored internally. Unfortunately this technique is not foolproof. Some modems have a built-in callback table that holds about ten entries, so this strategy works for small sites with only a few modems. If you use more modems, the RAS software must provide the callback.

The second technique is to use CLID (caller line ID) or ANI (automatic number identification) to decide whether to answer the call. Depending on your wiring and the local phone company, you may or may not be able to use ANI. ANI information is provided before the call, whereas CLID information is provided along with the call.

VIRUSES AND WORMS

Examples of UNIX/Linux viruses include the Bliss virus/worm released in 1997 and the RST.b virus discovered in December 2001. Both are discussed in detail in articles on the Web. Viruses spread through systems by infecting executable files. In the cases of Bliss and RST.b, the Linux native executable format, ELF, was used as a propagation vector.

Just after 5 PM on November 2, 1988, Robert T. Morris, Jr., a graduate student at Cornell University, released the first big virus onto the Internet. Called an Internet worm, this virus was designed to propagate copies of itself over many machines on the Internet. The worm was a piece of code that exploited four vulnerabilities, including one in finger, to get a buffer to overflow on a system. Once the buffer overflowed, the code was able to get a shell and then recompile itself on the remote machine. The worm spread around the Internet very quickly and was not disabled, despite many people's efforts, for 36 hours.

The chief characteristic of any worm is propagation over a public network, such as the Internet. A virus propagates by infecting executables on the machine, whereas a worm tends to prefer exploiting known security holes in network servers to gain **root** access and then tries to infect other machines in the same way.

UNIX/Linux file permissions help to inoculate systems against many viruses. Windows NT is resistant for similar reasons. You can easily protect your system against many viruses and worms by keeping your system patches up-to-date, not executing untrusted binaries from the Internet, limiting your path to include only necessary system directories, and doing as little as possible while enabled with Superuser privileges. You can prevent a disaster in case a virus strikes by backing up your system frequently.

PHYSICAL SECURITY

Often overlooked as a defense against intrusion, physical security covers access to the computer itself and to the console or terminal attached to the machine. If the machine is unprotected in an unlocked room, there is very little hope for physical security. (A simple example of physical vulnerability is someone walking into the room where the computer is, removing the hard drive from the computer, taking it home, and analyzing it.) You can take certain steps to improve the physical security of your computer.

- Keep servers in a locked room with limited access. A key, a combination, or a swipe card should be required to gain access. Protect windows as well as doors. Maintain a single point of entry. (Safety codes may require multiple exits, but only one must be an entry.)

- For public machines, use a security system, such as a fiberoptic security system, that can secure a lab full of machines. With such a system, you run a fiberoptic cable through each machine such that the machine cannot be removed (or opened) without cutting the cable. When the cable is cut, an alarm goes off. Some machines—for example, PCs with plastic cases—are much more difficult to secure than others. Although it is not a perfect solution, a fiberoptic security system may improve local security enough to persuade a would-be thief to go somewhere else.

- Most modern PCs have a BIOS password. You can set the order in which a PC searches for a boot device, preventing the PC from being booted from a floppy disk or CD. Some BIOSs can prevent the machine from booting altogether without a proper password. The password protects the BIOS from unauthorized modification. Beware, however: Many BIOSs have well-known *back doors* (page 1020). Research this issue if the BIOS password is an important feature for you. In addition, you can blank the BIOS password by setting the clear-CMOS jumper on a PC motherboard; if you are relying on a BIOS password, lock the case.

- Run only fiberoptic cable between buildings. This strategy is not only more secure but also safer in the event of lightning strikes and is required by many commercial building codes.

- Maintain logs of who goes in and out of secure areas. Sign-in/out sheets are useful only if everyone uses them. Sometimes a guard is warranted. Often a simple proximity badge or smartcard can tell when anyone has entered or left an area and keep logs of these events, although these can be expensive to procure and install.

- Anyone who has access to the physical hardware has the keys to the palace. Someone with direct access to a computer system can do such things as swap components and insert boot media, all of which are security threats.

- Avoid having activated, unused network jacks in public places. Such jacks provide unnecessary risk.

- Many modern switches can lock a particular switch port so that it accepts only traffic from an NIC (network interface card) with a particular hardware address and shuts down the port if another address is seen. However, commonly available programs can enable someone to reset this address.

- Make periodic security sweeps. Check doors for proper locking. If you must have windows, make sure that they are locked or are permanently sealed.

- Waste receptacles are often a source of information for intruders. Have policies for containment and disposal of sensitive documents.

- Use a UPS (uninterruptable power supply). Without a clean source of power, your system is vulnerable to corruption.

SECURITY RESOURCES

Many free and commercial programs can enhance system security. Some of these are listed in Table C-1. Many of these sites have links to other, interesting sites that are worth looking at.

Table C-1   Security resources

Tool	What it does	Where to get it
AIDE	Advanced Intrusion Detection Environment. Similar to trip-wire with extensible verification algorithms.	sourceforge.net/projects/aide
bugtraq	A moderated mailing list for the announcement and detailed discussion of all aspects of computer security vulnerabilities.	www.securityfocus.com/archive/1
CERT	Computer Emergency Response Team. A repository of papers and data about major security events and a list of security tools.	www.cert.org
chkrootkit	Checks for signs of a rootkit indicating that the machine has been compromised.	www.chkrootkit.org
dsniff	Sniffing and network audit tool suite. Free.	naughty.monkey.org/~dugsong/dsniff/
ethereal	Network protocol analyzer. Free.	www.ethereal.com
freefire	Supplies free security solutions and supports developers of free security solutions.	www.freefire.org

Table C-1   Security resources (continued)

fwtk	Firewall toolkit. A set of proxies that can be used to construct a firewall.	www.fwtk.org
GIAC	A security certification and training Web site.	www.giac.org
hping	Multipurpose network auditing and packet analysis tool. Free.	www.hping.org
ISC^2	Educates and certifies industry professionals and practitioners under an international standard.	www.isc2.org
John	John the Ripper: a fast, flexible, weak password detector.	www.openwall.com/john
Kerberos	Complete, secure network authentication system.	web.mit.edu/kerberos/www
L6	Verifies file integrity; similar to tripwire.	www.pgci.ca/l6.html
LIDS	Intrusion detection and active defense system.	www.lids.org
LinuxSecurity.com	A solid news site dedicated to Linux security issues.	www.linuxsecurity.com
LWN.net	Security alert database for all major Linux distributions.	lwn.net/Alerts
Microsoft Security	Microsoft security information.	www.microsoft.com/security
nessus	A plugin-based remote security scanner that can perform more than 370 security checks. Free.	www.nessus.org
netcat	Explores, tests, and diagnoses networks.	freshmeat.net/projects/netcat
nmap	Scans hosts to see which ports are available. It can perform stealth scans, determine operating system type, find open ports, and more.	www.insecure.org/nmap
OPIE	Provides one-time passwords for system access.	inner.net/opie

Table C-1 Security resources (continued)

RBAC	Role Based Access Control. Assigns roles and privileges associated with the roles.	csrc.nist.gov/rbac
Red Hat Security	Red Hat security information.	www.redhat.com/security
SAINT	Security Administrator's Integrated Network Tool. Assesses and analyzes network vulnerabilities. This tool follows **satan**.	www.wwdsi.com/saint
samhain	A file integrity checker. Has a GUI configurator, client/server capability, and real-time reporting capability.	samhain.sourceforge.net
SANS	Security training and certification.	www.sans.org
SARA	The Security Auditor's Research Assistant security analysis tool.	www-arc.com/sara
Schneier, Bruce	Security visionary.	www.schneier.com
Secunia	Monitors a broad spectrum of vulnerabilities.	secunia.com
SecurityFocus	Home for security tools, mail lists, libraries, and cogent analysis.	www.securityfocus.com
snort	A flexible IDS.	www.snort.org
srp	Secure Remote Password. Upgrades common protocols, such as TELNET and FTP, to use secure password exchange.	srp.stanford.edu
ssh	A secure **rsh**, **ftp**, and **rlogin** replacement with encrypted sessions and other options. Supplied with Red Hat Linux.	www.ssh.org openssh.org
swatch	A Perl-based log parser and analyzer.	swatch.sourceforge.net
Treachery	A collection of tools for security and auditing.	www.treachery.net/tools
tripwire	Checks for possible signs of intruder activity. Supplied with Red Hat Linux.	www.tripwire.com

APPENDIX SUMMARY

Security is inversely proportional to usability. There must be a balance between your users' requirements to get their work done and the amount of security that is implemented. It is often unnecessary to provide top security for a small business with only a few employees. By contrast, if you work for a government military contractor, you are bound to have extreme security constraints and an official audit policy to determine whether your security policies are being implemented correctly.

Review your own security requirements periodically. Several of the tools mentioned in this appendix are designed to help you monitor your system's security measures. Such tools as nessus, samhain, and SAINT all provide auditing mechanisms.

Some companies specialize in security and auditing. Hiring one of them to examine your site can be costly but may yield specific recommendations for areas that you may have overlooked in your initial setup. When you hire someone to audit your security, recognize that you may be providing both physical and Superuser access to your systems. Make sure the company that you hire has a good history, has been in business for several years, and has impeccable references. Check up on the company periodically: Things change over time. Avoid the temptation to hire former system crackers as consultants. Security consultants should have an irreproachable ethical background, or you will always have doubts about their intentions.

Your total security package is based on your risk assessment of your vulnerabilities. Strengthen those areas that are most important for your business. For example, many sites rely on a firewall to protect them from the Internet, whereas internal hosts receive little or no security attention. Crackers refer to this setup as "the crunchy outside surrounding the soft chewy middle." Yet this is entirely sufficient to protect some sites. Perform your own risk assessment and address your needs accordingly. If need be, hire a full-time security administrator whose job it is to design and audit your security policies.

D

THE FREE SOFTWARE DEFINITION[1]

We maintain this free software definition to show clearly what must be true about a particular software program for it to be considered free software.

"Free software" is a matter of liberty, not price. To understand the concept, you should think of "free" as in "free speech," not as in "free beer."

Free software is a matter of the users' freedom to run, copy, distribute, study, change and improve the software. More precisely, it refers to four kinds of freedom, for the users of the software:

- The freedom to run the program, for any purpose (freedom 0).

---

1. This material is at www.gnu.org/philosophy/free-sw.html on the GNU Web site. Because GNU requests a verbatim copy, links remain in place (underlined). View the document on the Web to ensure you are reading the latest copy and to follow the links.

- The freedom to study how the program works, and adapt it to your needs (freedom 1). Access to the source code is a precondition for this.

- The freedom to redistribute copies so you can help your neighbor (freedom 2).

- The freedom to improve the program, and release your improvements to the public, so that the whole community benefits (freedom 3). Access to the source code is a precondition for this.

A program is free software if users have all of these freedoms. Thus, you should be free to redistribute copies, either with or without modifications, either gratis or charging a fee for distribution, to <u>anyone anywhere</u>. Being free to do these things means (among other things) that you do not have to ask or pay for permission.

You should also have the freedom to make modifications and use them privately in your own work or play, without even mentioning that they exist. If you do publish your changes, you should not be required to notify anyone in particular, or in any particular way.

The freedom to use a program means the freedom for any kind of person or organization to use it on any kind of computer system, for any kind of overall job, and without being required to communicate subsequently with the developer or any other specific entity.

The freedom to redistribute copies must include binary or executable forms of the program, as well as source code, for both modified and unmodified versions. (Distributing programs in runnable form is necessary for conveniently installable free operating systems.) It is ok if there is no way to produce a binary or executable form for a certain program (since some languages don't support that feature), but you must have the freedom to redistribute such forms should you find or develop a way to make them.

In order for the freedoms to make changes, and to publish improved versions, to be meaningful, you must have access to the source code of the program. Therefore, accessibility of source code is a necessary condition for free software.

One important way to modify a program is by merging in available free subroutines and modules. If the program's license says that you cannot merge in an existing module, such as if it requires you to be the copyright holder of any code you add, then the license is too restrictive to qualify as free.

In order for these freedoms to be real, they must be irrevocable as long as you do nothing wrong; if the developer of the software has the power to revoke the license, without your doing anything to give cause, the software is not free.

However, certain kinds of rules about the manner of distributing free software are acceptable, when they don't conflict with the central freedoms. For example, copyleft (very simply stated) is the rule that when redistributing the program, you cannot add restrictions to deny other people the central freedoms. This rule does not conflict with the central freedoms; rather it protects them.

You may have paid money to get copies of free software, or you may have obtained copies at no charge. But regardless of how you got your copies, you always have the freedom to copy and change the software, even to <u>sell copies</u>.

"Free software" does not mean "non-commercial". A free program must be available for commercial use, commercial development, and commercial distribution. Commercial development of free software is no longer unusual; such free commercial software is very important.

Rules about how to package a modified version are acceptable, if they don't substantively block your freedom to release modified versions, or your freedom to make and use modified versions privately. Rules that "if you make your version available in this way, you must make it available in that way also" can be acceptable too, on the same condition. (Note that such a rule still leaves you the choice of whether to publish your version at all.) Rules that require release of source code to the users for versions that you put into public use are also acceptable. It is also acceptable for the license to require that, if you have distributed a modified version and a previous developer asks for a copy of it, you must send one, or that you identify yourself on your modifications.

In the GNU project, we use "<u>copyleft</u>" to protect these freedoms legally for everyone. But <u>non-copylefted free software</u> also exists. We believe there are important reasons why <u>it is better to use copyleft</u>, but if your program is non-copylefted free software, we can still use it.

See <u>Categories of Free Software</u> for a description of how "free software," "copylefted software" and other categories of software relate to each other.

Sometimes government <u>export control regulations</u> and trade sanctions can constrain your freedom to distribute copies of programs internationally. Software developers do not have the power to eliminate or override these restrictions, but what they can and must do is refuse to impose them as conditions of use of the program. In this way, the restrictions will not affect activities and people outside the jurisdictions of these governments.

Most free software licenses are based on copyright, and there are limits on what kinds of requirements can be imposed through copyright. If a copyright-based license respects freedom in the ways described above, it is unlikely to have some other sort of problem that we never anticipated (though this does happen occasionally). However, some free software licenses are based on contracts, and contracts can impose a much larger range of possible restrictions. That means there are many possible ways such a license could be unacceptably restrictive and non-free.

We can't possibly list all the ways that might happen. If a contract-based license restricts the user in an unusual way that copyright-based licenses cannot, and which isn't mentioned here as legitimate, we will have to think about it, and we will probably conclude it is non-free.

When talking about free software, it is best to avoid using terms like "give away" or "for free", because those terms imply that the issue is about price, not freedom. Some common terms such as "piracy" embody opinions we hope you won't endorse. See <u>Confusing Words and Phrases that are Worth Avoiding</u> for a discussion of these terms. We also have a list of <u>translations of "free software"</u> into various languages.

Finally, note that criteria such as those stated in this free software definition require careful thought for their interpretation. To decide whether a specific software license qualifies as a free software license, we judge it based on these criteria to determine whether it fits their spirit as well as the precise words. If a license includes unconscionable restrictions, we reject it, even if we did not anticipate the issue in these criteria. Sometimes a license requirement raises an issue that calls for extensive thought, including discussions with a lawyer, before we can decide if the requirement is acceptable. When we reach a conclusion about a new issue, we often update these criteria to make it easier to see why certain licenses do or don't qualify.

If you are interested in whether a specific license qualifies as a free software license, see our list of licenses. If the license you are concerned with is not listed there, you can ask us about it by sending us email at licensing@gnu.org.

If you are contemplating writing a new license, please contact the FSF by writing to that address. The proliferation of different free software licenses means increased work for users in understanding the licenses; we may be able to help you find an existing Free Software license that meets your needs.

If that isn't possible, if you really need a new license, with our help you can ensure that the license really is a Free Software license and avoid various practical problems.

Another group has started using the term "open source" to mean something close (but not identical) to "free software". We prefer the term "free software" because, once you have heard it refers to freedom rather than price, it calls to mind freedom. The word "open" never does that.

Other Texts to Read

Translations of this page:

[Català | Chinese (Simplified) | Chinese (Traditional) | Czech | Dansk | Deutsch | English | Español | Persian/Farsi | Français | Galego | Hebrew | Hrvatski | Bahasa Indonesia | Italiano | Japanese | Korean | Magyar | Nederlands | Norsk | Polski | Português | Româna | Russian | Slovinsko | Serbian | Tagalog | Türkçe]

Return to the GNU Project home page.

Please send FSF & GNU inquiries to gnu@gnu.org. There are also other ways to contact the FSF.

Please send broken links and other corrections (or suggestions) to webmasters@gnu.org

Please see the Translations README for information on coordinating and submitting translations of this article.

Copyright (C) 1996, 1997, 1998, 1999, 2000, 2001, 2002, 2003, 2004 Free Software Foundation, Inc., 51 Franklin St, Fifth Floor, Boston, MA 02110, USA

Verbatim copying and distribution of this entire article is permitted in any medium without royalty provided this notice is preserved.

• Updated: $Date: 2005/11/26 13:16:40 $ $Author: rms $

E

THE LINUX 2.6 KERNEL

The Linux 2.6 kernel was released on December 17, 2003. A major release of a Linux kernel is not an everyday occurrence: The last kernel, Linux 2.4, was released in January 2001. This appendix lists features that are new to the 2.6 kernel.

Linux kernel revisions alternate between stable and unstable versions: 2.4 was the previous stable version, so 2.5 was the development branch, which later became 2.6. For each of the major revisions, there is a series of minor revisions. Usually, minor revisions do not contain major changes, although one minor revision to the 2.4 kernel replaced the entire virtual memory subsystem, a major part of the kernel.

Fedora Core 2 and above and Red Hat Enterprise Linux v.4 and above include the 2.6 kernel.

See www.kniggit.net/wwol26.html if you want more information on the Linux 2.6 kernel than this appendix provides.

NATIVE POSIX THREAD LIBRARY (NPTL)

Classically programs start execution at the beginning of a series of instructions and execute them in sequence. While this technique works well for simple programs running on single CPU systems, it is often better to allow a program to execute different parts of itself simultaneously in parallel. Most programs with a GUI benefit from this functionality as it can prevent the user interface from freezing while the program performs computations.

The traditional way of writing parallel code under UNIX is to execute a **fork**() system call (page 861), which creates a copy of the running program in memory and starts it executing at the same point as the original. At the point **fork**() is called, the two copies of the program are indistinguishable, except for the fact that they receive different return values from their **fork**() call. One disadvantage of this approach is that each time **fork**() is called, the system must create a complete copy of the process. This copying takes a relatively long time and causes parallel applications to use a lot of memory. (This description is not quite accurate: Copy-on-write functionality in a modern operating system copies only those parts of memory that would be different.)

A more efficient solution to this problem is to allow a single process to run multiple threads. A thread exists in the same memory space as other threads and so has a much smaller overhead than a single program running multiple processes. The disadvantage of this strategy is that multithreaded applications must be designed more carefully and thus take more time to write than multiprocessor ones. Operating systems, such as Solaris, rely heavily on threads to provide scalability to very large SMP (symmetric multiprocessing) systems. The new threading support in the Linux 2.6 kernel uses the same industry standard POSIX APIs as Solaris for implementing threads and provides high-performance processing.

IPSECURITY (IPSEC)

IPSec is a network layer protocol suite that secures Internet connections by encrypting IP packets. IPSec is an optional part of IPv4 (page 1038) and a required part of IPv6 (page 1038). See page 995 for more information on IPSec.

Kernel integration of IPSec means that any kernel module or application can use IPSec in the same way that it would use unsecured IP.

ASYNCHRONOUS I/O (AIO)

Without AIO, when an application needs to get data from a hardware device or a network connection, it can either poll the connection until the data becomes available or spawn a thread for the connection that waits for the data. Neither of these techniques is particularly efficient.

Asynchronous I/O allows the kernel to notify an application when it has data ready to be read. This feature is most useful to large servers but can provide moderate performance gains in almost any application.

O(1) SCHEDULER

One of the responsibilities of the kernel is to make sure that each execution thread gets a reasonable amount of time on the CPU(s). The scheduling algorithm used in the Linux 2.4 kernel gradually decreased performance as more processes were added and additional CPUs were brought online, making it hard to use Linux on large SMP systems. The 2.6 scheduling algorithm runs in O(1) time, a term that indicates that a process takes the same time to run under all conditions, making Linux better able to run large numbers of processes and scale to large systems.

OPROFILE

It is often said that a program spends 90 percent of its time executing 10 percent of the code. Programmers use profiling tools to identify bottlenecks in code and target this 10 percent for optimization. OProfile is an advanced profiling tool that identifies common programming inefficiencies. Thanks to its close relationship with the kernel, OProfile is able to identify hardware-specific efficiency problems, such as cache misses, which are often not possible to identify from source code.

kksymoops

When something goes wrong in the kernel, it generates an error message called an *OOPS*. This message is an in-joke from the Linux Kernel Mailing List, where developers would start bug reports with "Oops, we've found a bug in the kernel." An OOPS provides debugging information that can help kernel developers track down the offending code or indicate that the OOPS was caused by hardware failure.

The **kksymoops** functionality provides detailed debugging information, allowing a developer to determine the line of code in the kernel that caused the OOPS. While this feature does not directly benefit the end user, it allows developers to find kernel bugs more quickly, resulting in a more stable kernel.

REVERSE MAP VIRTUAL MEMORY (RMAP VM)

Virtual memory (VM) allows each process to exist in its own memory space. Every time a process attempts to access a portion of memory, the kernel translates the memory location from an address in the process's own address space to one in real memory. The reverse map enables the kernel to perform this process in reverse: Given a location in physical memory, the kernel can determine which process owns it. The reverse map allows pages to be unallocated quickly, giving the system more free memory, fewer page faults, and less overhead when quitting a program.

HugeTLBFS: Translation Look-Aside Buffer Filesystem

The kernel allocates memory in units of pages. Virtual memory uses these pages to map between the virtual and real memory address spaces. Older versions of the Linux kernel set the size of these pages to 4 kilobytes. In cases where a lot of virtual memory is used, such as in large database servers, this small size can place a heavy load on the VM subsystem. HugeTLBFS allows for much larger pages, which significantly improves performance under heavy VM load conditions.

remap_file_pages

When retrieving data from or writing data to a file, it is common practice to map the file on disk to an area of memory. The system then translates accesses to that area of memory directly into accesses to disk.

For additional flexibility, large database systems map different parts of a file to different parts of memory. Each mapping results in an additional load on the kernel and VM subsystems. The **remap_file_pages**() system call can perform a nonuniform mapping, meaning that a file needs to be mapped only once, which significantly improves the performance of large database servers.

2.6 Network Stack Features (IGMPv3, IPv6, and Others)

The Linux 2.6 kernel includes a large number of improvements in the area of networking, including support for IPv6 (page 1038) and enhanced multicast (page 1044) support. Although these features do not immediately benefit end users, they do permit the development and deployment of network services that will not require significant modification for integration with future technologies.

Internet Protocol Virtual Server (IPVS)

IPVS implements transport layer switching inside the kernel for load balancing. This feature enables a single machine to distribute connections to a server farm, allowing transparent load balancing.

ACCESS CONTROL LISTS (ACLs)

The traditional UNIX permission system allows three permissions to be assigned to each file: controlling access by the owner, by a single group, and by everyone else. ACLs provide much finer-grained access control. In theory, ACLs can increase security. However, they make setting correct permissions more complicated, which may encourage administrators to establish weaker controls than they should.

4GB-4GB MEMORY SPLIT: PHYSICAL ADDRESS EXTENSION (PAE)

Although Red Hat speaks of the 4GB-4GB Memory Split in its discussion of the 2.6 kernel, this terminology has nothing to do with the new kernel. The memory split is a Red Hat enhancement to the Enterprise and Fedora kernels; it is not integrated into the main source tree (it is not part of the 2.6 kernel).

The 32-bit CPUs are limited in that they can address only 2^{32} bytes (4 gigabytes) of memory. With the Pentium Pro, Intel introduced a work-around to this limitation called Physical Address Extension (PAE), which permits the operating system to address up to 64 gigabytes of memory. Because they are limited to addressing 4 gigabytes each, 32-bit programs cannot access this much memory. A Linux kernel from the main tree is able to allocate up to 1 gigabyte for the kernel and 3 gigabytes for each *userspace* (page 1062) process.

The kernels shipped with Red Hat Linux are patched to allow the kernel to allocate up to 4 gigabytes for itself and 3.7 gigabytes for each userspace process. These limitations affect Linux on 32-bit architectures only. A 64-bit Linux kernel on a 64-bit CPU, such as a SPARC64, UltraSparc, Alpha, or Opteron, is able to access up to 16 *exabytes* (16×2^{60} bytes) of RAM.

SCHEDULER SUPPORT FOR HYPERTHREADED CPUs

The Linux 2.6 kernel supports Intel's HyperThreading. The 2.6 kernel treats each virtual CPU as the equivalent of a physical CPU.

BLOCK I/O (BIO) BLOCK LAYER

The 2.6 kernel includes a completely redesigned interface to drivers for block devices (page 463). While this conveys a number of benefits, it also means that these device drivers need to be rewritten and tested.

SUPPORT FOR FILESYSTEMS LARGER THAN 2 TERABYTES

The Linux 2.6 kernel includes SGI's XFS journaling filesystem, which supports filesystems of up to 9 exabytes (9×2^{60} bytes).

NEW I/O ELEVATORS

I/O elevators control how long I/O requests can be queued to allow them to be re-ordered for optimal device performance. The Linux 2.6 kernel includes some additional settings that allow I/O elevators to be tuned for specific high-device-load situations.

INTERACTIVE SCHEDULER RESPONSE TUNING

The new scheduler in the Linux 2.6 kernel prioritizes I/O bound processes. Because most user interface processes spend most of their time waiting for input from the user, this tuning should result in a more responsive system under high system load.

GLOSSARY

All entries marked with ^{FOLDOC} are based on definitions in the Free Online Dictionary of Computing (www.foldoc.org), Denis Howe, editor. Used with permission.

10.0.0.0   See *private address space* on page 1049.

172.16.0.0   See *private address space* on page 1049.

192.168.0.0   See *private address space* on page 1049.

802.11   A family of specifications developed by IEEE for wireless LAN technology, including 802.11 (1–2 megabits per second), 802.11a (54 megabits per second), 802.11b (11 megabits per second), and 802.11g (54 megabits per second).

absolute pathname   A pathname that starts with the root directory (/). An absolute pathname locates a file without regard to the working directory.

access   In computer jargon, a verb meaning to use, read from, or write to. To access a file means to read from or write to the file.

Access Control List See *ACL*.

access permission   Permission to read from, write to, or execute a file. If you have write access permission to a file, you can write to the file. Also *access privilege*.

ACL   Access Control List. A system that performs a function similar to file permissions but with much finer-grain control.

active window   On a desktop, the window that receives the characters you type on the keyboard. Same as *focus, desktop* (page 1032).

address mask   See *subnet mask* on page 1058.

alias   A mechanism of a shell that enables you to define new commands.

alphanumeric character One of the characters, either uppercase or lowercase, from A to Z and 0 to 9, inclusive.

ambiguous file reference A reference to a file that does not necessarily specify any one file but can be used to specify a group of files. The shell expands an ambiguous file reference into a list of filenames. Special characters represent single characters (?), strings of zero or more characters (*), and character classes ([]) within ambiguous file references. An ambiguous file reference is a type of *regular expression* (page 1052).

angle bracket   A left angle bracket (<) and a right angle bracket (>). The shell uses < to redirect a command's standard input to come from a file and > to redirect the standard output. The shell uses the characters << to signify the start of a Here document and >> to append output to a file.

animate   When referring to a window action, means that the action is slowed down so the user can view it. For example, when you minimize a window, it can disappear all at once (not animated) or it can slowly telescope into the panel so you can get a visual feel for what is happening (animated).

anti-aliasing   Adding gray pixels at the edge of a diagonal line to get rid of the jagged appearance and thereby make the line look smoother. Anti-aliasing sometimes makes type on a screen look better and sometimes worse; it works best on small and large fonts and is less effective on fonts from 8 to 15 points. See also *subpixel hinting* (page 1058).

API   Application program interface. The interface (calling conventions) by which an application program accesses an operating system and other services. An API is defined at the source code level and provides a level of abstraction between the application and the kernel (or other privileged utilities) to ensure the portability of the code._{FOLDOC}

append   To add something to the end of something else. To append text to a file means to add the text to the end of the file. The shell uses >> to append a command's output to a file.

applet   A small program that runs within a larger program. Examples are Java applets that run in a browser and panel applets that run from a desktop panel.

archive   A file that contains a group of smaller, typically related, files. Also, to create such a file. The tar and cpio utilities can create and read archives.

argument   A number, letter, filename, or another string that gives some information to a command and is passed to the command when it is called. A command line argument is anything on a command line following the command name that is passed to the command. An option is a kind of argument.

arithmetic expression   A group of numbers, operators, and parentheses that can be evaluated. When you evaluate an arithmetic expression, you end up with a number. The Bourne Again Shell uses the expr command to evaluate arithmetic expressions; the TC Shell uses @, and the Z Shell uses let.

array   An arrangement of elements (numbers or strings of characters) in one or more dimensions. The Bourne Again, TC, and Z Shells and gawk can store and process arrays.

ASCII   American Standard Code for Information Interchange. A code that uses seven bits to represent both graphic (letters, numbers, and punctuation) and CONTROL characters. You can represent textual information, including program source code and English text, in ASCII code. Because ASCII is a standard, it is frequently used when exchanging information between computers. See the file **/usr/pub/ascii** or give the command **man ascii** to see a list of ASCII codes.

Extensions of the ASCII character set use eight bits. The seven-bit set is common; the eight-bit extensions are still coming into popular use. The eighth bit is sometimes referred to as the metabit.

ASCII terminal   A textual terminal. Contrast with *graphical display* (page 1033).

ASP   Application service provider. A company that provides applications over the Internet.

asynchronous event An event that does not occur regularly or synchronously with another event. Linux system signals are asynchronous; they can occur at any time because they can be initiated by any number of nonregular events.

attachment A file that is attached to, but is not part of, a piece of email. Attachments are frequently opened by programs (including your Internet browser) that are called by your mail program so you may not be aware that they are not an integral part of an email message.

authentication The verification of the identity of a person or process. In a communication system, authentication verifies that a message comes from its stated source. Methods of authentication on a Linux system include the **/etc/passwd** and **/etc/shadow** files, LDAP, Kerberos 5, and SMB authentication.FOLDOC

automatic mounting A way of demand mounting directories from remote hosts without having them hard configured into **/etc/fstab**. Also called *automounting*.

avoided An object, such as a panel, that should not normally be covered by another object, such as a window.

back door A security hole deliberately left in place by the designers or maintainers of a system. The motivation for creating such holes is not always sinister; some operating systems, for example, come out of the box with privileged accounts intended for use by field service technicians or the vendor's maintenance programmers.

Ken Thompson's 1983 Turing Award lecture to the ACM revealed the existence, in early UNIX versions, of a back door that may be the most fiendishly clever security hack of all time. The C compiler contained code that would recognize when the **login** command was being recompiled and would insert some code recognizing a password chosen by Thompson, giving him entry to the system whether or not an account had been created for him.

Normally such a back door could be removed by removing it from the source code for the compiler and recompiling the compiler. But to recompile the compiler, you have to *use* the compiler, so Thompson arranged that the compiler would *recognize when it was compiling a version of itself*. It would insert into the recompiled compiler the code to insert into the recompiled **login** the code to allow Thompson entry, and, of course, the code to recognize itself and do the whole thing again the next time around. Having done this once, he was then able to recompile the compiler from the original sources; the hack perpetuated itself invisibly, leaving the back door in place and active but with no trace in the sources.

Sometimes called a wormhole. Also *trap door*.FOLDOC

background process A process that is not run in the foreground. Also called a *detached process,* a background process is initiated by a command line that ends with an ampersand (&). You do not have to wait for a background process to run to completion before giving the shell additional commands. If you have job control, you can move background processes to the foreground, and vice versa.

basename   The name of a file that, in contrast with a pathname, does not mention any of the directories containing the file (and therefore does not contain any slashes [/]). For example, **hosts** is the basename of **/etc/hosts**.^{FOLDOC}

baud   The maximum information-carrying capacity of a communication channel in symbols (state transitions or level transitions) per second. It coincides with bits per second only for two-level modulation with no framing or stop bits. A symbol is a unique state of the communication channel, distinguishable by the receiver from all other possible states. For example, it may be one of two voltage levels on a wire for a direct digital connection, or it might be the phase or frequency of a carrier.^{FOLDOC}

Baud is often mistakenly used as a synonym for bits per second.

baud rate   Transmission speed. Usually used to measure terminal or modem speed. Common baud rates range from 110 to 38,400 baud. See *baud.*

Berkeley UNIX   One of the two major versions of the UNIX operating system. Berkeley UNIX was developed at the University of California at Berkeley by the Computer Systems Research Group and is often referred to as *BSD* (Berkeley Software Distribution).

BIND   Berkeley Internet Name Domain. An implementation of a *DNS* (page 1029) server developed and distributed by the University of California at Berkeley

BIOS   Basic Input/Output System. On PCs, *EEPROM*-based (page 1030) system software that provides the lowest-level interface to peripheral devices and controls the first stage of the *bootstrap* (page 1022) process, which loads the operating system. The BIOS can be stored in different types of memory. The memory must be nonvolatile so that it remembers the system settings even when the system is turned off. Also BIOS ROM. Refer to page 26 for instructions on how to open the BIOS screens for maintenance.

bit   The smallest piece of information a computer can handle. A *bit* is a binary digit: either 1 or 0 (*on* or *off*).

bit depth   Same as *color depth* (page 1025).

bit-mapped display   A graphical display device in which each pixel on the screen is controlled by an underlying representation of zeros and ones.

blank character   Either a SPACE or a TAB character, also called *whitespace* (page 1063). In some contexts, NEWLINEs are considered blank characters.

block   A section of a disk or tape (usually 1,024 bytes long but shorter or longer on some systems) that is written at one time.

block device   A disk or tape drive. A block device stores information in blocks of characters. A block device is represented by a block device (block special) file. Contrast with *character device* (page 1024).

block number   Disk and tape *blocks* are numbered so that Linux can keep track of the data on the device.

blocking factor The number of logical blocks that make up a physical block on a tape or disk. When you write 1K logical blocks to a tape with a physical block size of 30K, the blocking factor is 30.

Boolean The type of an expression with two possible values: *true* and *false*. Also, a variable of Boolean type or a function with Boolean arguments or result. The most common Boolean functions are AND, OR, and NOT.FOLDOC

boot See *bootstrap*.

boot loader A very small program that takes its place in the *bootstrap* process that brings a computer from off or reset to a fully functional state. See "Boot Loader" on page 533.

bootstrap Derived from "Pull oneself up by one's own bootstraps," the incremental process of loading an operating system kernel into memory and starting it running without any outside assistance. Frequently shortened to *boot*.

Bourne Again Shell bash. GNU's command interpreter for UNIX, bash is a POSIX-compliant shell with full Bourne Shell syntax and some C Shell commands built in. The Bourne Again Shell supports emacs-style command line editing, job control, functions, and online help.FOLDOC

Bourne Shell sh. This UNIX command processor was developed by Steve Bourne at AT&T Bell Laboratories.

brace A left brace ({) and a right brace (}). Braces have special meanings to the shell.

bracket A *square bracket* (page 1057) or an *angle bracket* (page 1018).

branch In a tree structure, a branch connects nodes, leaves, and the root. The Linux filesystem hierarchy is often conceptualized as an upside-down tree. The branches connect files and directories. In a source code control system, such as SCCS or RCS, a branch occurs when a revision is made to a file and is not included in subsequent revisions to the file.

bridge Typically a two-port device originally used for extending networks at layer 2 (data link) of the Internet Protocol model.

broadcast A transmission to multiple, unspecified recipients. On Ethernet a broadcast packet is a special type of multicast packet that has a special address indicating that all devices that receive it should process it. Broadcast traffic exists at several layers of the network stack, including Ethernet and IP. Broadcast traffic has one source but indeterminate destinations (all hosts on the local network).

broadcast address The last address on a subnet (usually 255), reserved as shorthand to mean all hosts.

broadcast network A type of network, such as Ethernet, in which any system can transmit information at any time, and all systems receive every message.

BSD See *Berkeley UNIX* on page 1021.

buffer An area of memory that stores data until it can be used. When you write information to a file on a disk, Linux stores the information in a disk buffer until there is enough to write to the disk or until the disk is ready to receive the information.

bug An unwanted and unintended program property, especially one that causes the program to malfunction.^{FOLDOC}

builtin (command) A command that is built into a shell. Each of the three major shells—the Bourne Again, TC, and Z Shells—has its own set of builtins. Refer to "Builtins" on page 225.

byte A component in the machine data hierarchy, usually larger than a bit and smaller than a word; now most often eight bits and the smallest addressable unit of storage. A byte typically holds one character.^{FOLDOC}

C programming language A modern systems language that has high-level features for efficient, modular programming as well as lower-level features that make it suitable for use as a systems programming language. It is machine independent so that carefully written C programs can be easily transported to run on different machines. Most of the Linux operating system is written in C, and Linux provides an ideal environment for programming in C.

C Shell csh. The C Shell command processor was developed by Bill Joy for BSD UNIX. It was named for the C programming language because its programming constructs are similar to those of C. See *shell* on page 1055.

cable modem A type of modem that allows you to access the Internet by using your cable television connection.

cache Holding recently accessed data, a small, fast memory designed to speed up subsequent access to the same data. Most often applied to processor-memory access but also used for a local copy of data accessible over a network, from a hard disk, and so on.^{FOLDOC}

calling environment A list of variables and their values that is made available to a called program. Refer to "Executing a Command" on page 302.

cascading stylesheet See *CSS* on page 1027.

cascading windows An arrangement of windows such that they overlap, generally with at least part of the title bar visible. Opposite of *tiled windows* (page 1060).

case sensitive Able to distinguish between uppercase and lowercase characters. Unless you set the **ignorecase** parameter, vim performs case-sensitive searches. The grep utility performs case-sensitive searches unless you use the –i option.

catenate To join sequentially, or end to end. The Linux cat utility catenates files: It displays them one after the other. Also *concatenate*.

chain loading	The technique used by a boot loader to load unsupported operating systems. Used for loading such operating systems as DOS or Windows, it works by loading another boot loader.
character-based	A program, utility, or interface that works only with *ASCII* (page 1019) characters. This set of characters includes some simple graphics, such as lines and corners, and can display colored characters. It cannot display true graphics. Contrast with *GUI* (page 1034).
character-based terminal	A terminal that displays only characters and very limited graphics. See *character-based*.
character class	In a regular expression, a group of characters that defines which characters can occupy a single character position. A character-class definition is usually surrounded by square brackets. The character class defined by [abcr] represents a character position that can be occupied by **a**, **b**, **c**, or **r**. Also *list operator*.

In POSIX, used to refer to sets of characters with a common characteristic, denoted by the notation [:*class*:]; for example, [:upper:] denotes the set of uppercase letters.

This book uses the term character class as explained under "Brackets" on page 969. |
| **character device** | A terminal, printer, or modem. A character device stores or displays characters one at a time. A character device is represented by a character device (character special) file. Contrast with *block device* (page 1021). |
| **checksum** | A computed value that depends on the contents of a block of data and is transmitted or stored along with the data to detect corruption of the data. The receiving system recomputes the checksum based on the received data and compares this value with the one sent with the data. If the two values are the same, the receiver has some confidence that the data was received correctly.

The checksum may be 8, 16, or 32 bits, or some other size. It is computed by summing the bytes or words of the data block, ignoring overflow. The checksum may be negated so that the total of the data words plus the checksum is zero.

Internet packets use a 32-bit checksum.ᶠᵒˡᴰᴼᶜ |
child process	A process that is created by another process, the parent process. Every process is a child process except for the first process, which is started when Linux begins execution. When you run a command from the shell, the shell spawns a child process to run the command. See *process* on page 1049.
CIDR	Classless Inter-Domain Routing. A scheme that allocates blocks of Internet addresses in a way that allows summarization into a smaller number of routing table entries. A CIDR block is a block of Internet addresses assigned to an ISP by the Internic. Refer to "CIDR: Classless Inter-Domain Routing" on page 357.ᶠᵒˡᴰᴼᶜ
CIFS	Common Internet File System. An Internet filesystem protocol based on *SMB* (page 1055). CIFS runs on top of TCP/IP, uses DNS, and is optimized to support slower dial-up Internet connections. SMB and CIFS are used interchangeably.ᶠᵒˡᴰᴼᶜ

CIPE   Crypto IP *Encapsulation* (page 1031). This *protocol* (page 1050) *tunnels* (page 1061) IP packets within encrypted *UDP* (page 1061) packets, is lightweight and simple, and works over dynamic addresses, *NAT* (page 1044), and *SOCKS* (page 1056) *proxies* (page 1050).

cipher (cypher)   A cryptographic system that uses a key to transpose/substitute characters within a message, the key itself, or the message.

ciphertext   Text that is encrypted. Contrast with *plaintext* (page 1048). See also "Encryption" on page 988.

Classless Inter-Domain Routing   See *CIDR* on page 1024.

cleartext   Text that is not encrypted. Also *plaintext*. Contrast with *ciphertext*. See also "Encryption" on page 988.

CLI   Command line interface. See also *character-based* (page 1024).

client   A computer or program that requests one or more services from a server.

CODEC   Coder/decoder or compressor/decompressor. A hardware and/or software technology that codes and decodes data. MPEG is a popular CODEC for computer video.

color depth   The number of bits used to generate a pixel—usually 8, 16, 24, or 32. The color depth is directly related to the number of colors that can be generated. The number of colors that can be generated is 2 raised to the color-depth power. Thus a 24-bit video adapter can generate about 16.7 million colors.

color quality   See *color depth*.

combo box   A combination of a list and text entry box. A user can either select an option from a provided list or enter his own option.

command   What you give the shell in response to a prompt. When you give the shell a command, it executes a utility, another program, a builtin command, or a shell script. Utilities are often referred to as commands. When you are using an interactive utility, such as vim or mail, you use commands that are appropriate to that utility.

command line   A line containing instructions and arguments that executes a command. This term usually refers to a line that you enter in response to a shell prompt on a character-based terminal or terminal emulator (page 93).

command substitution   Replacing a command with its output. The shells perform command substitution when you enclose a command between $(and) or between a pair of back ticks (` `), also called grave accent marks.

component architecture   A notion in object-oriented programming where "components" of a program are completely generic. Instead of having a specialized set of methods and fields, they have generic methods through which the component can advertise the functionality it supports to the system into which it is loaded. This strategy enables completely dynamic loading of objects. JavaBeans is an example of a component architecture.[FOLDOC]

concatenate	See *catenate* on page 1023.
condition code	See *exit status* on page 1031.
connection-oriented protocol	A type of transport layer data communication service that allows a host to send data in a continuous stream to another host. The transport service guarantees that all data will be delivered to the other end in the same order as sent and without duplication. Communication proceeds through three well-defined phases: connection establishment, data transfer, and connection release. The most common example is *TCP* (page 1059).
	Also called connection-based protocol and stream-oriented protocol. Contrast with *connectionless protocol* and *datagram* (page 1028).FOLDOC
connectionless protocol	The data communication method in which communication occurs between hosts with no previous setup. Packets sent between two hosts may take different routes. There is no guarantee that packets will arrive as transmitted or even that they will arrive at the destination at all. *UDP* (page 1061) is a connectionless protocol. Also called packet switching. Contrast with circuit switching and *connection-oriented protocol.*FOLDOC
console	See *system console* on page 1059.
console terminal	See *system console* on page 1059.
control character	A character that is not a graphic character, such as a letter, number, or punctuation mark. Such characters are called control characters because they frequently act to control a peripheral device. RETURN and FORMFEED are control characters that control a terminal or printer.
	The word CONTROL is shown in this book in THIS FONT because it is a key that appears on most terminal keyboards. Control characters are represented by ASCII codes less than 32 (decimal). See also *nonprinting character* on page 1046.
control structure	A statement used to change the order of execution of commands in a shell script or other program. Each shell provides control structures (for example, **if** and **while**) as well as other commands that alter the order of execution (for example, **exec**). Also *control flow commands.*
cookie	Data stored on a client system by a server. The client system browser sends the cookie back to the server each time it accesses that server. For example, a catalog shopping service may store a cookie on your system when you place your first order. When you return to the site, it knows who you are and can supply your name and address for subsequent orders. You may consider cookies to be an invasion of privacy.
CPU	Central processing unit. The part of a computer that controls all the other parts. The CPU includes the control unit and the arithmetic and logic unit (ALU). The control unit fetches instructions from memory and decodes them to produce signals that control the other parts of the computer. These signals can cause data to be

transferred between memory and ALU or peripherals to perform input or output. A CPU that is housed on a single chip is called a microprocessor. Also *processor* and *central processor.*

cracker An individual who attempts to gain unauthorized access to a computer system. These individuals are often malicious and have many means at their disposal for breaking into a system. Contrast with *hacker* (page 1034).^{FOLDOC}

crash The system suddenly and unexpectedly stops or fails. Derived from the action of the hard disk heads on the surface of the disk when the air gap between the two collapses.

cryptography The practice and study of encryption and decryption—encoding data so that only a specific individual or machine can decode it. A system for encrypting and decrypting data is a cryptosystem. Such systems usually rely on an algorithm for combining the original data (plaintext) with one or more keys—numbers or strings of characters known only to the sender and/or recipient. The resulting output is called *ciphertext* (page 1025).

The security of a cryptosystem usually depends on the secrecy of keys rather than on the supposed secrecy of an algorithm. Because a strong cryptosystem has a large range of keys, it is not possible to try all of them. Ciphertext appears random to standard statistical tests and resists known methods for breaking codes.^{FOLDOC}

.cshrc file In your home directory, a file that the TC Shell executes each time you invoke a new TC Shell. You can use this file to establish variables and aliases.

CSS Cascading stylesheet. Describes how documents are presented on screen and in print. Attaching a stylesheet to a structured document can affect the way it looks without adding new HTML (or other) tags and without giving up device independence. Also *stylesheet.*

current (process, line, character, directory, event, and so on) The item that is immediately available, working, or being used. The current process is the program you are running, the current line or character is the one the cursor is on, and the current directory is the working directory.

cursor A small lighted rectangle, underscore, or vertical bar that appears on the terminal screen and indicates where the next character will appear. Differs from the *mouse pointer* (page 1043).

daemon A program that is not invoked explicitly but lies dormant, waiting for some condition(s) to occur. The perpetrator of the condition need not be aware that a daemon is lurking (although often a program will commit an action only because it knows that it will implicitly invoke a daemon). From the mythological meaning, later rationalized as the acronym Disk And Execution MONitor. See Table 10-4 on page 374 for a list of daemons.^{FOLDOC}

data structure   A particular format for storing, organizing, working with, and retrieving data. Frequently, data structures are designed to work with specific algorithms that facilitate these tasks. Common data structures include trees, files, records, tables, arrays, and so on.

datagram   A self-contained, independent entity of data carrying sufficient information to be routed from the source to the destination computer without reliance on earlier exchanges between this source and destination computer and the transporting network. *UDP* (page 1061) uses datagrams; *IP* (page 1038) uses *packets* (page 1047). Packets are indivisible at the network layer; datagrams are not.ᶠᴼᴸᴰᴼᶜ See also *frame* (page 1033).

dataless   A computer, usually a workstation, that uses a local disk to boot a copy of the operating system and access system files but does not use a local disk to store user files.

dbm   A standard, simple database manager. Implemented as **gdbm** (GNU database manager), it uses hashes to speed searching. The most common versions of the **dbm** database are **dbm**, **ndbm**, and **gdbm**.

DDoS attack   Distributed denial of service attack. A *DoS attack* (page 1030) from many systems that do not belong to the perpetrator of the attack.

debug   To correct a program by removing its bugs (that is, errors).

default   Something that is selected without being explicitly specified. For example, when used without an argument, ls displays a list of the files in the working directory by default.

delta   A set of changes made to a file that has been encoded by the Source Code Control System (SCCS).

denial of service   *See DoS attack* on page 1030.

dereference   When speaking of symbolic links, follow the link rather than working with the reference to the link. For example, the –L or ––dereference option causes ls to list the entry that a symbolic link points to rather than the symbolic link (the reference) itself.

desktop   A collection of windows, toolbars, icons, and buttons, some or all of which appear on your display. A desktop comprises one or more *workspaces* (page 1064). Refer to "Getting the Most from the Desktop" on page 85.

desktop manager   An icon- and menu-based user interface to system services that allows you to run applications and use the filesystem without using the system's command line interface.

detached process   See *background process* on page 1020.

device   A disk drive, printer, terminal, plotter, or other input/output unit that can be attached to the computer. Short for *peripheral device*.

device driver   Part of the Linux kernel that controls a device, such as a terminal, disk drive, or printer.

device file   A file that represents a device. Also *special file*.

device filename   The pathname of a device file. All Linux systems have two kinds of device files: block and character device files. Linux also has FIFOs (named pipes) and sockets. Device files are traditionally located in the **/dev** directory.

device number   See *major device number* (page 1042) and *minor device number* (page 1043).

DHCP   Dynamic Host Configuration Protocol. A protocol that dynamically allocates IP addresses to computers on a LAN. Refer to "DHCP: Configures Hosts" on page 431.FOLDOC

directory   Short for *directory file*. A file that contains a list of other files.

directory hierarchy   A directory, called the root of the directory hierarchy, and all the directory and ordinary files below it (its children).

directory service   A structured repository of information on people and resources within an organization, facilitating management and communication.FOLDOC

disk partition   See *partition* on page 1047.

diskless   A computer, usually a workstation, that has no disk and must contact another computer (a server) to boot a copy of the operating system and access the necessary system files.

distributed computing   A style of computing in which tasks or services are performed by a network of cooperating systems, some of which may be specialized.

DMZ   Demilitarized zone. A host or small network that is a neutral zone between a LAN and the Internet. It can serve Web pages and other data to the Internet and allow local systems access to the Internet while preventing LAN access to unauthorized Internet users. Even if a DMZ is compromised, it holds no data that is private and none that cannot be easily reproduced.

DNS   Domain Name Service. A distributed service that manages the correspondence of full hostnames (those that include a domain name) to IP addresses and other system characteristics.

DNS domain name   See *domain name*.

document object model   See *DOM*.

DOM   Document Object Model. A platform-/language-independent interface that enables a program to update the content, structure, and style of a document dynamically. The changes can then be made part of the displayed document. Go to www.w3.org/DOM for more information.

domain name	A name associated with an organization, or part of an organization, to help identify systems uniquely. Technically, the part of the *FQDN* (page 1032) to the right of the leftmost period. Domain names are assigned hierarchically. The domain berkeley.edu refers to the University of California at Berkeley, for example; it is part of the top-level edu (education) domain. Also DNS domain name. Different than *NIS domain name* (page 1046).
Domain Name Service	See *DNS*.
door	An evolving filesystem-based *RPC* (page 1053) mechanism.
DoS attack	Denial of service attack. An attack that attempts to make the target host or network unusable by flooding it with spurious traffic.
DPMS	Display Power Management Signaling. A standard that can extend the life of CRT monitors and conserve energy. DPMS supports four modes for a monitor: Normal, Standby (power supply on, monitor ready to come to display images almost instantly), Suspend (power supply off, monitor takes up to ten seconds to display an image), and Off.
drag	To move an icon from one position or application to another, usually in the context of a window manager. The motion part of drag-and-drop.
druid	In role-playing games, a character that represents a magical user. Red Hat uses the term *druid* at the ends of names of programs that guide you through a task-driven chain of steps. Other operating systems call these types of programs *wizards*.
DSA	Digital Signature Algorithm. A public key cipher used to generate digital signatures.
DSL	Digital Subscriber Line/Loop. Provides high-speed digital communication over a specialized, conditioned telephone line. See also *xDSL* (page 1064).
Dynamic Host Configuration Protocol	See *DHCP* on page 1029.
editor	A utility, such as vim or emacs, that creates and modifies text files.
EEPROM	Electrically erasable, programmable, readonly memory. A *PROM* (page 1049) that can be written to.
effective user ID	The user ID that a process appears to have; usually the same as the user ID. For example, while you are running a setuid program, the effective user ID of the process running the program is that of the owner of the program.
element	One thing; usually a basic part of a group of things. An element of a numeric array is one of the numbers stored in the array.
emoticon	See *smiley* on page 1055.

encapsulation   See *tunneling* on page 1061.

environment   See *calling environment* on page 1023.

EOF   End of file.

EPROM   Erasable programmable readonly memory. A *PROM* (page 1049) that can be written to by applying a higher than normal voltage.

escape   See *quote* on page 1050.

Ethernet   A type of *LAN* (page 1040) capable of transfer rates as high as 1,000 megabits per second. Refer to "Ethernet" on page 347.

event   An occurrence, or happening, of significance to a task or program—for example, the completion of an asynchronous input/output operation, such as a keypress or mouse click.^{FOLDOC}

exabyte 2^{60} bytes or about 10^{18} bytes. See also *large number* (page 1040).

exit status   The status returned by a process; either successful (usually 0) or unsuccessful (usually 1).

exploit   A security hole or an instance of taking advantage of a security hole.^{FOLDOC}

expression   See *logical expression* (page 1041) and *arithmetic expression* (page 1019).

extranet   A network extension for a subset of users (such as students at a particular school or engineers working for the same company). An extranet limits access to private information even though it travels on the public Internet.

failsafe session   A session that allows you to log in on a minimal desktop in case your standard login does not work well enough to allow you to log in to fix a login problem.

FDDI   Fiber Distributed Data Interface. A type of *LAN* (page 1040) designed to transport data at the rate of 100 million bits per second over fiberoptic cable.

file   A collection of related information referred to with a *filename* and frequently stored on a disk. Text files typically contain memos, reports, messages, program source code, lists, or manuscripts. Binary or executable files contain utilities or programs that you can run. Refer to "Directory Files and Ordinary Files" on page 166.

filename   The name of a file. A filename refers to a file.

filename completion   Automatic completion of a filename after you specify a unique prefix.

filename extension   The part of a filename following a period.

filename generation   What occurs when the shell expands ambiguous file references. See *ambiguous file reference* on page 1018.

filesystem	A *data structure* (page 1028) that usually resides on part of a disk. All Linux systems have a root filesystem, and many have other filesystems. Each filesystem is composed of some number of blocks, depending on the size of the disk partition that has been assigned to the filesystem. Each filesystem has a control block, named the superblock, that contains information about the filesystem. The other blocks in a filesystem are inodes, which contain control information about individual files, and data blocks, which contain the information in the files.
filling	A variant of maximizing in which window edges are pushed out as far as they can go without overlapping another window.
filter	A command that can take its input from standard input and send its output to standard output. A filter transforms the input stream of data and sends it to standard output. A pipe usually connects a filter's input to standard output of one command, and a second pipe connects the filter's output to standard input of another command. The grep and sort utilities are commonly used as filters.
firewall	A device for policy-based traffic management used to keep a network secure. A firewall can be implemented in a single router that filters out unwanted packets, or it can rely on a combination of routers, proxy servers, and other devices. Firewalls are widely used to give users access to the Internet in a secure fashion and to separate a company's public WWW server from its internal network. They are also employed to keep internal network segments more secure.
	Recently the term has come to be defined more loosely to include a simple packet filter running on an endpoint machine.
	See also *proxy server* on page 1050.
firmware	Software built into a computer, often in *ROM* (page 1053). May be used as part of the *bootstrap* (page 1022) procedure.
focus, desktop	On a desktop, the window that is active. The window with the desktop focus receives the characters you type on the keyboard. Same as *active window* (page 1018).
footer	The part of a format that goes at the bottom (or foot) of a page. Contrast with *header* (page 1034).
foreground process	When you run a command in the foreground, the shell waits for the command to finish before giving you another prompt. You must wait for a foreground process to run to completion before you can give the shell another command. If you have job control, you can move background processes to the foreground, and vice versa. See *job control* on page 1039. Contrast with *background process* (page 1020).
fork	To create a process. When one process creates another process, it forks a process. Also *spawn*.
FQDN	Fully qualified domain name. The full name of a system, consisting of its hostname and its domain name, including the top-level domain. Technically the name that **gethostbyname**(2) returns for the host named by **gethostname**(2). For example,

speedy is a hostname and **speedy.example.com** is an FQDN. An FQDN is sufficient to determine a unique Internet address for a machine on the Internet.ꜰᴏʟᴅᴏᴄ

frame   A data link layer packet that contains, in addition to data, the header and trailer information required by the physical medium. Network layer packets are encapsulated to become frames.ꜰᴏʟᴅᴏᴄ See also *datagram* (page 1028) and *packet* (page 1047).

free list   In a filesystem, the list of blocks that are available for use. Information about the free list is kept in the superblock of the filesystem.

free software   Refer to Appendix D, "The Free Software Definition."

free space   The portion of a hard disk that is not within a partition. A new hard disk has no partitions and contains all free space.

full duplex   The ability to receive and transmit data simultaneously. A *network switch* (page 1045) is typically a full-duplex device. Contrast with *half-duplex* (page 1034).

fully qualified   See *FQDN* on page 1032.
domain name

function   See *shell function* on page 1055.

gateway   A generic term for a computer or a special device connected to more than one dissimilar type of network to pass data between them. Unlike a router, a gateway often must convert the information into a different format before passing it on. The historical usage of gateway to designate a router is deprecated.

GCOS   See *GECOS*.

GECOS   General Electric Comprehensive Operating System. For historical reasons, the user information field in the **/etc/passwd** file is called the GECOS field. Also GCOS.

giga-   In the binary system, the prefix *giga-* multiplies by 2^{30} (i.e., 1,073,741,824). Gigabit and gigabyte are common uses of this prefix. Abbreviated as G. See also *large number* on page 1040.

glyph   A symbol that communicates a specific piece of information nonverbally. A *smiley* (page 1055) is a glyph.

GMT   Greenwich Mean Time. See *UTC* on page 1062.

graphical   A bitmapped monitor that can display graphical images. Contrast with *ASCII terminal* (page 1019).
display

graphical user   See *GUI* on page 1034.
interface

group (of   A collection of users. Groups are used as a basis for determining file access permissions. If you are not the owner of a file and you belong to the group the file is assigned to, you are subject to the group access permissions for the file. A user can simultaneously belong to several groups.
users)

group (of windows)   A way to identify similar windows so they can be displayed and acted on similarly. Typically windows started by a given application belong to the same group.

group ID   A unique number that identifies a set of users. It is stored in the password and group databases (**/etc/passwd** and **/etc/group** files or their NIS equivalents). The group database associates group IDs with group names.

GUI   Graphical user interface. A GUI provides a way to interact with a computer system by choosing items from menus or manipulating pictures drawn on a display screen instead of by typing command lines. Under Linux, the X Window System provides a graphical display and mouse/keyboard input. GNOME and KDE are two popular desktop managers that run under X. Contrast with *character-based* (page 1024).

hacker   A person who enjoys exploring the details of programmable systems and learning how to stretch their capabilities, as opposed to users, who prefer to learn only the minimum necessary. One who programs enthusiastically (even obsessively) or who enjoys programming rather than just theorizing about programming.ᶠᵒˡᵈᵒᶜ Contrast with *cracker* (page 1027).

half-duplex   A half-duplex device can only receive or transmit at a given moment; it cannot do both. A *hub* (page 1036) is typically a half-duplex device. Contrast with *full duplex* (page 1033).

hard link   A directory entry that contains the filename and inode number for a file. The inode number identifies the location of control information for the file on the disk, which in turn identifies the location of the file's contents on the disk. Every file has at least one hard link, which locates the file in a directory. When you remove the last hard link to a file, you can no longer access the file. See *link* (page 1040) and *symbolic link* (page 1058).

hash   A string that is generated from another string. See *one-way hash function* on page 1046. When used for security, a hash can prove, almost to a certainty, that a message has not been tampered with during transmission: The sender generates a hash of a message, encrypts the message and hash, and sends the encrypted message and hash to the recipient. The recipient decrypts the message and hash, generates a second hash from the message, and compares the hash that the sender generated to the new hash. When they are the same, the message has probably not been tampered with. A hash can also be used to create an index called a *hash table*. Also *hash value*.

hash table   An index created from hashes of the items to be indexed. The hash function makes it highly unlikely that two items will create the same hash. To look up an item in the index, create a hash of the item and search for the hash. Because the hash is typically shorter than the item, the search is more efficient.

header   When you are formatting a document, the header goes at the top, or head, of a page. In electronic mail the header identifies who sent the message, when it was sent, what the subject of the message is, and so forth.

Here document	A shell script that takes its input from the file that contains the script.
hesiod	The nameserver of project Athena. Hesiod is a name service library that is derived from *BIND* (page 1021) and leverages a DNS infrastructure.
heterogeneous	Consisting of different parts. A heterogeneous network includes systems produced by different manufacturers and/or running different operating systems.
hexadecimal number	A base 16 number. Hexadecimal (or *hex*) numbers are composed of the hexadecimal digits 0–9 and A–F. See Table G-1.

Table G-1   Decimal, octal, and hexadecimal numbers

Decimal	Octal	Hex	Decimal	Octal	Hex
1	1	1	17	21	11
2	2	2	18	22	12
3	3	3	19	23	13
4	4	4	20	24	14
5	5	5	21	25	15
6	6	6	31	37	1F
7	7	7	32	40	20
8	10	8	33	41	21
9	11	9	64	100	40
10	12	A	96	140	60
11	13	B	100	144	64
12	14	C	128	200	80
13	15	D	254	376	FE
14	16	E	255	377	FF
15	17	F	256	400	100
16	20	10	257	401	101

hidden file	A file whose filename starts with a period. These files are called hidden because the ls utility does not normally list them. Use the –a option of ls to list all files, including hidden ones. The shell does not expand a leading asterisk (*) in an ambiguous file reference to match the filename of a hidden file. Also *invisible file*.
hierarchy	An organization with a few things, or thing—one at the top—and with several things below each other thing. An inverted tree structure. Examples in computing include a file tree where each directory may contain files or other directories, a hierarchical network, and a class hierarchy in object-oriented programming.[FOLDOC] Refer to "The Hierarchical Filesystem" on page 166.
history	A shell mechanism that enables you to modify and reexecute recent commands.

home directory	The directory that is your working directory when you first log in. The pathname of this directory is stored in the **HOME** shell variable.
hover	To leave the mouse pointer stationary for a moment over an object. In many cases hovering displays a *tooltip* (page 1060).
HTML	Hypertext Markup Language. A *hypertext* document format used on the World Wide Web. Tags, which are embedded in the text, consist of a less than sign (<), a directive, zero or more parameters, and a greater than sign (>). Matched pairs of directives, such as <TITLE> and </TITLE>, delimit text that is to appear in a special place or style.^{FOLDOC} For more information on HTML, go to www.htmlhelp.com/faq/html/all.html.
HTTP	Hypertext Transfer Protocol. The client/server TCP/IP protocol used on the World Wide Web for the exchange of *HTML* documents.
hub	A multiport repeater. A hub rebroadcasts all packets it receives on all ports. This term is frequently used to refer to small hubs and switches, regardless of the device's intelligence. It is a generic term for a layer 2 shared-media networking device. Today the term *hub* is sometimes used to refer to small intelligent devices, although that was not its original meaning. Contrast with *network switch* (page 1045).
hypertext	A collection of documents/nodes containing (usually highlighted or underlined) cross-references or links, which, with the aid of an interactive browser program, allow the reader to move easily from one document to another.^{FOLDOC}
Hypertext Markup Language	See *HTML*.
Hypertext Transfer Protocol	See *HTTP*.
i/o device	Input/output device. See *device* on page 1028.
IANA	Internet Assigned Numbers Authority. A group that maintains a database of all permanent, registered system services (www.iana.org).
ICMP	Internet Control Message Protocol. A type of network packet that carries only messages, no data.
icon	In a GUI, a small picture representing a file, directory, action, program, and so on. When you click an icon, an action, such as opening a window and starting a program or displaying a directory or Web site, takes place. From miniature religious statues.^{FOLDOC}
iconify	The process of changing a window into an *icon*. Contrast with *restore* (page 1052).
ignored window	A state in which a window has no decoration and therefore no buttons or titlebar to control it with.

indentation   See *indention*.

indention   The blank space between the margin and the beginning of a line that is set in from the margin.

inode   A *data structure* (page 1028) that contains information about a file. An inode for a file contains the file's length, the times the file was last accessed and modified, the time the inode was last modified, owner and group IDs, access privileges, number of links, and pointers to the data blocks that contain the file itself. Each directory entry associates a filename with an inode. Although a single file may have several filenames (one for each link), it has only one inode.

input   Information that is fed to a program from a terminal or other file. See *standard input* on page 1057.

installation   A computer at a specific location. Some aspects of the Linux system are installation dependent. Also *site*.

interactive   A program that allows ongoing dialog with the user. When you give commands in response to shell prompts, you are using the shell interactively. Also, when you give commands to utilities, such as vim and mail, you are using the utilities interactively.

interface   The meeting point of two subsystems. When two programs work together, their interface includes every aspect of either program that the other deals with. The *user interface* (page 1062) of a program includes every program aspect the user comes into contact with: the syntax and semantics involved in invoking the program, the input and output of the program, and its error and informational messages. The shell and each of the utilities and built-in commands have a user interface.

International Organization for Standardization   See *ISO* on page 1038.

internet   A large network that encompasses other, smaller networks.

Internet   The largest internet in the world. The Internet (uppercase "I") is a multilevel hierarchy composed of backbone networks (ARPANET, NSFNET, MILNET, and others), midlevel networks, and stub networks. These include commercial (**.com** or **.co**), university (**.ac** or **.edu**), research (**.org** or **.net**), and military (**.mil**) networks and span many different physical networks around the world with various protocols, including the Internet Protocol (IP). Outside the United States, country code domains are popular (**.us, .es, .mx, .de**, and so forth), although you will see them used within the United States as well.

Internet Protocol   See *IP*.

Internet service provider	See *ISP*.
intranet	An inhouse network designed to serve a group of people such as a corporation or school. The general public on the Internet does not have access to the intranet. See page 344.
invisible file	See *hidden file* on page 1035.
IP	Internet Protocol. The network layer for TCP/IP. IP is a best-effort, packet-switching, *connectionless protocol* (page 1026) that provides packet routing, fragmentation, and reassembly through the data link layer. IPv4 is slowly giving way to *IPv6*.FOLDOC
IP address	Internet Protocol address. A four-part address associated with a particular network connection for a system using the Internet Protocol (IP). A system that is attached to multiple networks that use the IP will have a different IP address for each network interface.
IP multicast	See *multicast* on page 1044.
IP spoofing	A technique used to gain unauthorized access to a computer. The would-be intruder sends messages to the target machine. These messages contain an IP address indicating that the messages are coming from a trusted host (page 362). The target machine responds to the messages, giving the intruder (privileged) access to the target.
IPC	Interprocess communication. A method to communicate specific information between programs.
IPv4	*IP* version 4. See *IP* and *IPv6*.
IPv6	*IP* version 6. The next generation of Internet Protocol, which provides a much larger address space (2^{128} bits versus 2^{32} bits for IPv4) that is designed to accommodate the rapidly growing number of Internet addressable devices. IPv6 also has built-in autoconfiguration, enhanced security, better multicast support, and many other features.
ISDN	Integrated Services Digital Network. A set of communications standards that allows a single pair of digital or standard telephone wires to carry voice, data, and video at a rate of 64 kilobits per second.
ISO	International Organization for Standardization. A voluntary, nontreaty organization founded in 1946. It is responsible for creating international standards in many areas, including computers and communications. Its members are the national standards organizations of 89 countries, including the American National Standards Institute.FOLDOC
ISO9660	The *ISO* standard defining a filesystem for CD-ROMs.
ISP	Internet service provider. Provides Internet access to its customers.

job control   A facility that enables you to move commands from the foreground to the background and vice versa. Job control enables you to stop commands temporarily.

journaling   A filesystem that maintains a noncached log file, or journal, which records all trans-
filesystem   actions involving the filesystem. When a transaction is complete, it is marked as complete in the log file.

               The log file results in greatly reduced time spent recovering a filesystem after a crash, making it particularly valuable in systems where high availability is an issue.

JPEG   Joint Photographic Experts Group. This committee designed the standard image-compression algorithm. JPEG is intended for compressing either full-color or gray-scale digital images of natural, real-world scenes and does not work as well on nonrealistic images, such as cartoons or line drawings. Filename extensions: **.jpg, .jpeg**.^{FOLDOC}

justify   To expand a line of type in the process of formatting text. A justified line has even margins. A line is justified by increasing the space between words and sometimes between letters on the line.

Kerberos   An MIT-developed security system that authenticates users and machines. It does not provide authorization to services or databases; it establishes identity at logon, which is used throughout the session. Once you are authenticated, you can open as many terminals, windows, services, or other network accesses as you like until your session expires.

kernel   The part of the operating system that allocates machine resources, including memory, disk space, and *CPU* (page 1026) cycles, to all other programs that run on a computer. The kernel includes the low-level hardware interfaces (drivers) and manages *processes* (page 1049), the means by which Linux executes programs. The kernel is the part of the Linux system that Linus Torvalds originally wrote (see the beginning of Chapter 1).

kernelspace   The part of memory (RAM) where the kernel resides. Code running in kernelspace has full access to hardware and all other processes in memory. See the *KernelAnalysis-HOWTO*.

key binding   A *keyboard* key is said to be bound to the action that results from pressing it. Typically keys are bound to the letters that appear on the keycaps: When you press **A**, an **A** appears on the screen. Key binding usually refers to what happens when you press a combination of keys, one of which is CONTROL, ALT, META, or SHIFT, or when you press a series of keys, the first of which is typically ESCAPE.

keyboard   A hardware input device consisting of a number of mechanical buttons (keys) that the user presses to input characters to a computer. By default a keyboard is connected to standard input of a shell.^{FOLDOC}

kilo-   In the binary system, the prefix *kilo-* multiplies by 2^{10} (i.e., 1,024). Kilobit and kilobyte are common uses of this prefix. Abbreviated as *k*.

Korn Shell   ksh. A command processor, developed by David Korn at AT&T Bell Laboratories, that is compatible with the Bourne Shell but includes many extensions. See also *shell* on page 1055.

LAN   Local area network. A network that connects computers within a localized area (such as a single site, building, or department).

large number   Go to mathworld.wolfram.com/LargeNumber.html for a comprehensive list.

LDAP   Lightweight Directory Access Protocol. A simple protocol for accessing online directory services. LDAP is a lightweight alternative to the X.500 Directory Access Protocol (DAP). It can be used to access information about people, system users, network devices, email directories, and systems. In some cases, it can be used as an alternative for services such as NIS. Given a name, many mail clients can use LDAP to discover the corresponding email address. See *directory service* on page 1029.

leaf   In a tree structure, the end of a branch that cannot support other branches. When the Linux filesystem hierarchy is conceptualized as a tree, files that are not directories are leaves. See *node* on page 1046.

least privilege, concept of   Mistakes that Superuser makes can be much more devastating than those made by an ordinary user. When you are working on the computer, especially when you are working as the system administrator, always perform any task using the least privilege possible. If you can perform a task logged in as an ordinary user, do so. If you must be logged in as Superuser, do as much as you can as an ordinary user, log in as **root** or give an **su** or **sudo** command so that you have Superuser privileges, do as much of the task that has to be done as Superuser, and revert to being an ordinary user as soon as you can.

Because you are more likely to make a mistake when you are rushing, this concept becomes more important when you have less time to apply it.

Lightweight Directory Access Protocol   See *LDAP*.

link   A pointer to a file. Two kinds of links exist: hard links and symbolic (soft) links. A hard link associates a filename with a place on the disk where the contents of the file is located. A symbolic link associates a filename with the pathname of a hard link to a file. See *hard link* (page 1034) and *symbolic link* (page 1058).

Linux-PAM   See *PAM* on page 1047.

Linux-Pluggable Authentication Modules   See *PAM* on page 1047.

loadable kernel module	See *loadable module*.
loadable module	A portion of the operating system that controls a special device and that can be loaded automatically into a running kernel as needed to access that device. See "Using Loadable Kernel Modules" on page 531.
local area network	See *LAN* on page 1040.
locale	The language; date, time, and currency formats; character sets; and so forth that pertain to a geopolitical place or area. For example, en_US specifies English as spoken in the United States and dollars; en_UK specifies English as spoken in the United Kingdom and pounds. See the **locale** man page in section 5 of the system manual for more information. Also the **locale** utility.
log in	To gain access to a computer system by responding correctly to the **login:** and **Password:** prompts. Also *log on, login*.
log out	To end your session by exiting from your login shell. Also *log off*.
logical expression	A collection of strings separated by logical operators (>, >=, =, !=, <=, and <) that can be evaluated as *true* or *false*. Also *Boolean* (page 1022) *expression*.
.login file	A file in a user's home directory that the TC Shell executes when you log in. You can use this file to set environment variables and to run commands that you want executed at the beginning of each session.
login name	See *username* on page 1062.
login shell	The shell that you are using when you log in. The login shell can fork other processes that can run other shells, utilities, and programs.
.logout file	A file in a user's home directory that the TC Shell executes when you log out, assuming that the TC Shell is your login shell. You can put in the **.logout** file commands that you want run each time you log out.
MAC address	Media Access Control address. The unique hardware address of a device connected to a shared network medium. Each Ethernet adapter has a globally unique MAC address in ROM. MAC addresses are 6 bytes long, enabling 256^6 (about 300 trillion) possible addresses or 65,536 addresses for each possible IPv4 address.
	A MAC address performs the same role for Ethernet that an IP address performs for TCP/IP: It provides a unique way to identify a host.
machine collating sequence	The sequence in which the computer orders characters. The machine collating sequence affects the outcome of sorts and other procedures that put lists in alphabetical order. Many computers use ASCII codes so their machine collating sequences correspond to the ordering of the ASCII codes for characters.

macro A single instruction that a program replaces by several (usually more complex) instructions. The C compiler recognizes macros, which are defined using a #define instruction to the preprocessor.

magic number A magic number, which occurs in the first 512 bytes of a binary file, is a 1-, 2-, or 4-byte numeric value or character string that uniquely identifies the type of file (much like a DOS 3-character filename extension). See **/usr/share/magic** and the **magic** man page for more information.

main memory Random access memory (RAM), an integral part of the computer. Although disk storage is sometimes referred to as memory, it is never referred to as main memory.

major device number A number assigned to a class of devices, such as terminals, printers, or disk drives. Using the ls utility with the –l option to list the contents of the **/dev** directory displays the major and minor device numbers of many devices (as major, minor).

MAN Metropolitan area network. A network that connects computers and *LANs* (page 1040) at multiple sites in a small regional area, such as a city.

masquerade To appear to come from one domain or IP address when actually coming from another. Said of a packet (iptables) or message (**sendmail**). See also *NAT* on page 1044.

MD5 Message Digest 5. A *one-way hash function* (page 1046). The *SHA1* (page 1054) algorithm has supplanted MD5 in many applications.

MDA Mail delivery agent. One of the three components of a mail system; the other two are the *MTA* (page 1043) and *MUA* (page 1044). An MDA accepts inbound mail from an MTA and delivers it to a local user.

mega- In the binary system, the prefix *mega-* multiplies by 2^{20} (i.e., 1,048,576). Megabit and megabyte are common uses of this prefix. Abbreviated as *M*.

menu A list from which the user may select an operation to be performed. This selection is often made with a mouse or other pointing device under a GUI but may also be controlled from the keyboard. Very convenient for beginners, menus show which commands are available and facilitate experimenting with a new program, often reducing the need for user documentation. Experienced users usually prefer keyboard commands, especially for frequently used operations, because they are faster to use.[FOLDOC]

merge To combine two ordered lists so that the resulting list is still in order. The sort utility can merge files.

META key On the keyboard, a key that is labeled META or ALT. Use this key as you would the SHIFT key. While holding it down, press another key. The emacs editor makes extensive use of the META key.

metacharacter A character that has a special meaning to the shell or another program in a particular context. Metacharacters are used in the ambiguous file references recognized by the shell and in the regular expressions recognized by several utilities. You must quote a metacharacter if you want to use it without invoking its special meaning. See *regular character* (page 1052) and *special character* (page 1056).

metadata   Data about data. In data processing, metadata is definitional data that provides information about, or documentation of, other data managed within an application or environment.

For example, metadata can document data about data elements or attributes (name, size, data type, and so on), records or *data structures* (page 1028) (length, fields, columns, and so on), and data itself (where it is located, how it is associated, who owns it, and so on). Metadata can include descriptive information about the context, quality and condition, or characteristics of the data.^{FOLDOC}

metropolitan area network   See *MAN* on page 1042.

MIME   Multipurpose Internet Mail Extension. Originally used to describe how specific types of files that were attached to email were to be handled. Today MIME types describe how a file is to be opened or worked with, based on its filename extension.

minimize   See *iconify* on page 1036.

minor device number   A number assigned to a specific device within a class of devices. See *major device number* on page 1042.

modem   Modulator/demodulator. A peripheral device that modulates digital data into analog data for transmission over a voice-grade telephone line. Another modem demodulates the data at the other end.

module   See *loadable module* on page 1041.

mount   To make a filesystem accessible to system users. When a filesystem is not mounted, you cannot read from or write to files it contains.

mount point   A directory that you mount a local or remote filesystem (page 466) on.

mouse   A device you use to point to a particular location on a display screen, typically so you can choose a menu item, draw a line, or highlight some text. You control a pointer on the screen by sliding a mouse around on a flat surface; the position of the pointer moves relative to the movement of the mouse. You select items by pressing one or more buttons on the mouse.

mouse pointer   In a GUI, a marker that moves in correspondence with the mouse. It is usually a small black **X** with a white border or an arrow. Differs from the *cursor* (page 1027).

mouseover   The action of passing the mouse pointer over an icon or other object on the screen.

MTA   Mail transfer agent. One of the three components of a mail system; the other two are the *MDA* (page 1042) and *MUA* (page 1044). An MTA accepts mail from users and MTAs.

MUA	Mail user agent. One of the three components of a mail system; the other two are the *MDA* (page 1042) and *MTA* (page 1043). An MUA is an end-user mail program such as KMail, mutt, or Outlook.
multiboot specification	Specifies an interface between a boot loader and an operating system. With compliant boot loaders and operating systems, any boot loader should be able to load any operating system. The object of this specification is to ensure that different operating systems will work on a single machine. For more information, go to odin-os.sourceforge.net/guides/multiboot.html.
multicast	A multicast packet has one source and multiple destinations. In multicast, source hosts register at a special address to transmit data. Destination hosts register at the same address to receive data. In contrast to *broadcast* (page 1022), which is LAN-based, multicast traffic is designed to work across routed networks on a subscription basis. Multicast reduces network traffic by transmitting a packet one time, with the router at the end of the path breaking it apart as needed for multiple recipients.
multitasking	A computer system that allows a user to run more than one job at a time. A multitasking system, such as Linux, allows you to run a job in the background while running a job in the foreground.
multiuser system	A computer system that can be used by more than one person at a time. Linux is a multiuser operating system. Contrast with *single-user system* (page 1055).
namespace	A set of names in which all names are unique.FOLDOC
NAT	Network Address Translation. A scheme that enables a LAN to use one set of IP addresses internally and a different set externally. The internal set is for LAN (private) use. The external set is typically used on the Internet and is Internet unique. NAT provides some privacy by hiding internal IP addresses and allows multiple internal addresses to connect to the Internet through a single external IP address. See also *masquerade* on page 1042.
NBT	NetBIOS over TCP/IP. A protocol that supports NetBIOS services in a TCP/IP environment. Also *NetBT*.
NetBIOS	Network Basic Input/Output System. An *API* (page 1019) for writing network-aware applications.
netboot	To boot a computer over the network (as opposed to booting from a local disk).
netiquette	The conventions of etiquette—that is, polite behavior—recognized on Usenet and in mailing lists, such as not (cross-)posting to inappropriate groups and refraining from commercial advertising outside the business groups.
	The most important rule of netiquette is "Think before you post." If what you intend to post will not make a positive contribution to the newsgroup and be of interest to several readers, do not post it. Personal messages to one or two individuals should not be posted to newsgroups; use private email instead.FOLDOC

netmask
A 32-bit mask (for IPv4), that shows how an Internet address is to be divided into network, subnet, and host parts. The netmask has ones in the bit positions in the 32-bit address that are to be used for the network and subnet parts and zeros for the host part. The mask should contain at least the standard network portion (as determined by the address class). The subnet field should be contiguous with the network portion.<small>FOLDOC</small>

network address
The network portion (**netid**) of an IP address. For a class A network, it is the first byte, or segment, of the IP address; for a class B network, it is the first two bytes; and for a class C network, it is the first three bytes. In each case the balance of the IP address is the host address (**hostid**). Assigned network addresses are globally unique within the Internet. Also *network number*. See also "Host Address" on page 353.

Network Filesystem
See *NFS*.

Network Information Service
See *NIS*.

network number
See *network address*.

network segment
A part of an Ethernet or other network on which all message traffic is common to all nodes; that is, it is broadcast from one node on the segment and received by all others. This commonality normally occurs because the segment is a single continuous conductor. Communication between nodes on different segments is via one or more routers.<small>FOLDOC</small>

network switch
A connecting device in networks. Switches are increasingly replacing shared media hubs in an effort to increase bandwidth. For example, a 16-port 10BaseT hub shares the total 10 megabits per second bandwidth with all 16 attached nodes. By replacing the hub with a switch, both sender and receiver can take advantage of the full 10 megabits per second capacity. Each port on the switch can give full bandwidth to a single server or client station or to a hub with several stations. Network switch refers to a device with intelligence. Contrast with *hub* (page 1036).

Network Time Protocol
See *NTP* on page 1046.

NFS
Network Filesystem. A remote filesystem designed by Sun Microsystems, available on computers from most UNIX system vendors.

NIC
Network interface card (or controller). An adapter circuit board installed in a computer to provide a physical connection to a network.<small>FOLDOC</small>

NIS
Network Information Service. A distributed service built on a shared database to manage system-independent information (such as usernames and passwords).

NIS domain name	A name that describes a group of systems that share a set of NIS files. Different from *domain name* (page 1030).
NNTP	Network News Transfer Protocol. Refer to "Usenet" on page 378.
node	In a tree structure, the end of a branch that can support other branches. When the Linux filesystem hierarchy is conceptualized as a tree, directories are nodes. See *leaf* on page 1040.
nonprinting character	See *control character* on page 1026. Also *nonprintable character*.
nonvolatile storage	A storage device whose contents are preserved when its power is off. Also NVS and persistent storage. Some examples are CD-ROM, paper punch tape, hard disk, *ROM* (page 1053), *PROM* (page 1049), *EPROM* (page 1031), and *EEPROM* (page 1030). Contrast with *RAM* (page 1051).
NTP	Network Time Protocol. Built on top of TCP/IP, NTP maintains accurate local time by referring to known accurate clocks on the Internet.
null string	A string that could contain characters but does not. A string of zero length.
octal number	A base 8 number. Octal numbers are composed of the digits 0–7, inclusive. Refer to Table G-1 on page 1035.
one-way hash function	A one-way function that takes a variable-length message and produces a fixed-length hash. Given the hash, it is computationally infeasible to find a message with that hash; in fact, you cannot determine any usable information about a message with that hash. Also *message digest function*. See also *hash* (page 1034).
OpenSSH	A free version of the SSH (secure shell) protocol suite that replaces TELNET, rlogin, and more with secure programs that encrypt all communication—even passwords—over a network. Refer to "OpenSSH: Secure Network Communication" on page 579.
operating system	A control program for a computer that allocates computer resources, schedules tasks, and provides the user with a way to access resources.
option	A command line argument that modifies the effects of a command. Options are usually preceded by hyphens on the command line and traditionally have single-character names (such as –h or –n). Some commands allow you to group options following a single hyphen (for example, –hn). GNU utilities frequently have two arguments that do the same thing: a single-character argument and a longer, more descriptive argument that is preceded by two hyphens (such as −−show-all and −−invert-match).
ordinary file	A file that is used to store a program, text, or other user data. See *directory* (page 1029) and *device file* (page 1029).
output	Information that a program sends to the terminal or another file. See *standard output* on page 1057.

P2P
Peer-to-Peer. A network that does not divide nodes into clients and servers. Each computer on a P2P network can fulfill the roles of client and server. In the context of a file-sharing network, this ability means that once a node has downloaded (part of) a file, it can act as a server. BitTorrent implements a P2P network.

packet
A unit of data sent across a network. *Packet* is a generic term used to describe a unit of data at any layer of the OSI protocol stack, but it is most correctly used to describe network or application layer (page 352) data units ("application protocol data unit," APDU).FOLDOC See also *frame* (page 1033) and *datagram* (page 1028).

packet filtering
A technique used to block network traffic based on specified criteria, such as the origin, destination, or type of each packet. See also *firewall* (page 1032).

packet sniffer
A program or device that monitors packets on a network. See *sniff* on page 1056.

pager
A utility that allows you to view a file one screen at a time (for example, less and more).

paging
The process by which virtual memory is maintained by the operating system. The contents of process memory is moved (paged out) to the *swap space* (page 1058) as needed to make room for other processes.

PAM
Linux-PAM or Linux-Pluggable Authentication Modules. These modules allow a system administrator to determine how various applications authenticate users. Refer to "PAM" on page 438.

parent process
A process that forks other processes. See *process* (page 1049) and *child process* (page 1024).

partition
A section of a (hard) disk that has a name so you can address it separately from other sections. A disk partition can hold a filesystem or another structure, such as the swap area. Under DOS and Windows, partitions (and sometimes whole disks) are labeled C:, D:, and so on. Also *disk partition* and *slice*.

passive FTP
Allows FTP to work through a firewall by allowing the flow of data to be initiated and controlled by the client FTP program instead of the server. Also called PASV FTP because it uses the FTP PASV command.

passphrase
A string of words and characters that you type in to authenticate yourself. A passphrase differs from a *password* only in length. A password is usually short—6 to 10 characters. A passphrase is usually much longer—up to 100 characters or more. The greater length makes a passphrase harder to guess or reproduce than a password and therefore more secure.FOLDOC

password
To prevent unauthorized access to a user's account, an arbitrary string of characters chosen by the user or system administrator and used to authenticate the user when attempting to log in.FOLDOC See also *passphrase*.

PASV FTP
See *passive FTP*.

pathname	A list of directories separated by slashes (/) and ending with the name of a file, which can be a directory. A pathname is used to trace a path through the file structure to locate or identify a file.
pathname, last element of a	The part of a pathname following the final /, or the whole filename if there is no /. A simple filename. Also *basename*.
pathname element	One of the filenames that forms a pathname.
peripheral device	See *device* on page 1028.
persistent	Data that is stored on nonvolatile media, such as a hard disk.
phish	An attempt to trick users into revealing or sharing private information, especially passwords or financial information. The most common form is email purporting to be from a bank or vendor that requests that a user fill out a form to "update" an account on a phoney Web site disguised to appear legitimate. Generally sent as *spam* (page 1056).
physical device	A tangible device, such as a disk drive, that is physically separate from other, similar devices.
PID	Process identification, usually followed by the word *number*. Linux assigns a unique PID number as each process is initiated.
pipe	A connection between programs such that standard output of one program is connected to standard input of the next. Also *pipeline*.
pixel	The smallest element of a picture, typically a single dot on a display screen.
plaintext	Text that is not encrypted. Also *cleartext*. Contrast with *ciphertext* (page 1025). See also "Encryption" on page 988.
Pluggable Authentication Modules	See *PAM* on page 1047.
point-to-point link	A connection limited to two endpoints, such as the connection between a pair of modems.
port	A logical channel or channel endpoint in a communications system. The *TCP* (page 1059) and *UDP* (page 1061) transport layer protocols used on Ethernet use port numbers to distinguish between different logical channels on the same network interface on the same computer.
	The **/etc/services** file (see the beginning of this file for more information) or the *NIS* (page 1045) **services** database specifies a unique port number for each application program. The number links incoming data to the correct service (program). Standard, well-known ports are used by everyone: Port 80 is used for HTTP (Web) traffic. Some

protocols, such as TELNET and HTTP (which is a special form of TELNET), have default ports specified as mentioned earlier but can use other ports as well.[FOLDOC]

port forwarding
The process by which a network *port* on one computer is transparently connected to a port on another computer. If port X is forwarded from system A to system B, any data sent to port X on system A is sent to system B automatically. The connection can be between different ports on the two systems. See also *tunneling* (page 1061).

portmapper
A server that converts TCP/IP port numbers into *RPC* (page 1053) program numbers. See "RPC Network Services" on page 377.

printable character
One of the graphic characters: a letter, number, or punctuation mark. Contrast with a nonprintable, or CONTROL, character. Also *printing character*.

private address space
IANA (page 1036) has reserved three blocks of IP addresses for private internets or LANs:

```
10.0.0.0 - 10.255.255.255
172.16.0.0 - 172.31.255.255
192.168.0.0 - 192.168.255.255
```

You can use these addresses without coordinating with anyone outside of your LAN (you do not have to register the system name or address). Systems using these IP addresses cannot communicate directly with hosts using the global address space but must go through a gateway. Because private addresses have no global meaning, routing information is not stored by DNSs and most ISPs reject privately addressed packets. Make sure that your router is set up not to forward these packets onto the Internet.

privileged port
A *port* (page 1048) with a number less than 1024. On Linux and other UNIX-like systems, only **root** can bind to a privileged port. Any user on Windows 98 and earlier Windows systems can bind to any *port*. Also *reserved port*.

procedure
A sequence of instructions for performing a particular task. Most programming languages, including machine languages, enable a programmer to define procedures that allow the procedure code to be called from multiple places. Also *subroutine*.[FOLDOC]

process
The execution of a command by Linux. See "Processes" on page 300.

.profile file
A startup file in a user's home directory that the Bourne Again or Z Shell executes when you log in. The TC Shell executes **.login** instead. You can use the **.profile** file to run commands, set variables, and define functions.

program
A sequence of executable computer instructions contained in a file. Linux utilities, applications, and shell scripts are all programs. Whenever you run a command that is not built into a shell, you are executing a program.

PROM
Programmable readonly memory. A kind of nonvolatile storage. *ROM* (page 1053) that can be written to using a PROM programmer.

prompt   A cue from a program, usually displayed on the screen, indicating that it is waiting for input. The shell displays a prompt, as do some of the interactive utilities, such as mail. By default the Bourne Again and Z Shells use a dollar sign ($) as a prompt, and the TC Shell uses a percent sign (%).

protocol   A set of formal rules describing how to transmit data, especially across a network. Low-level protocols define the electrical and physical standards, bit and byte ordering, and transmission, error detection, and correction of the bit stream. High-level protocols deal with data formatting, including message syntax, terminal-to-computer dialog, character sets, and sequencing of messages.ᶠᴼᴸᴰᴼᶜ

proxy   A service that is authorized to act for a system while not being part of that system. See also *proxy gateway* and *proxy server*.

proxy gateway A computer that separates clients (such as browsers) from the Internet, working as a trusted agent that accesses the Internet on their behalf. A proxy gateway passes a request for data from an Internet service, such as HTTP from a browser/client, to a remote server. The data that the server returns goes back through the proxy gateway to the requesting service. A proxy gateway should be transparent to the user.

A proxy gateway often runs on a *firewall* (page 1032) system and acts as a barrier to malicious users. It hides the IP addresses of the local computers inside the firewall from Internet users outside the firewall.

You can configure browsers, such as Mozilla/Firefox and Netscape, to use a different proxy gateway or to use no proxy for each URL access method including FTP, netnews, SNMP, HTTPS, and HTTP. See also *proxy*.

proxy server A *proxy gateway* that usually includes a *cache* (page 1023) that holds frequently used Web pages so that the next request for that page is available locally (and therefore more quickly). The terms proxy server and proxy gateway are frequently interchanged so that the use of cache does not rest exclusively with the proxy server. See also *proxy*.

Python   A simple, high-level, interpreted, object-oriented, interactive language that bridges the gap between C and shell programming. Suitable for rapid prototyping or as an extension language for C applications, Python supports packages, modules, classes, user-defined exceptions, a good C interface, and dynamic loading of C modules. It has no arbitrary restrictions. For more information, see www.python.orgᶠᴼᴸᴰᴼᶜ

quote   When you quote a character, you take away any special meaning that it has in the current context. You can quote a character by preceding it with a backslash. When you are interacting with the shell, you can also quote a character by surrounding it with single quotation marks. For example, the command **echo *** or **echo '*'** displays *. The command **echo *** displays a list of the files in the working directory. See *ambiguous file reference* (page 1018), *metacharacter* (page 1042), *regular character* (page 1052), *regular expression* (page 1052), and *special character* (page 1056). See also *escape* on page 1031.

radio button   One of a group of buttons similar to those used to select the station on a radio. Only one button can be selected at a time.

RAID   Redundant array of inexpensive/independent disks. Two or more (hard) disk drives used in combination to improve fault tolerance and performance. RAID can be implemented in hardware or software.

RAM   Random access memory. A kind of volatile storage. A data storage device for which the order of access to different locations does not affect the speed of access. Contrast with a hard disk or tape drive, which provides quicker access to sequential data because accessing a nonsequential location requires physical movement of the storage medium and/or read/write head rather than just electronic switching. Contrast with *nonvolatile storage* (page 1046).ꜰᴏʟᴅᴏᴄ

RAM disk   *RAM* that is made to look like a floppy diskette or hard disk. A RAM disk is frequently used as part of the *boot* (page 1022) process.

RAS   Remote access server. In a network, a computer that provides access to remote users via analog modem or ISDN connections. RAS includes the dial-up protocols and access control (authentication). It may be a regular fileserver with remote access software or a proprietary system, such as Shiva's LANRover. The modems may be internal or external to the device.

RDF   Resource Description Framework. Being developed by W3C (the main standards body for the World Wide Web), a standard that specifies a mechanism for encoding and transferring *metadata* (page 1043). RDF does not specify what the metadata should or can be. It can integrate many kinds of applications and data, using XML as an interchange syntax. Examples of the data that can be integrated include library catalogs and worldwide directories; syndication and aggregation of news, software, and content; and collections of music and photographs. Go to www.w3.org/RDF for more information.

redirection   The process of directing standard input for a program to come from a file rather than from the keyboard. Also, directing standard output or standard error to go to a file rather than to the screen.

reentrant   Code that can have multiple simultaneous, interleaved, or nested invocations that do not interfere with one another. Noninterference is important for parallel processing, recursive programming, and interrupt handling.

It is usually easy to arrange for multiple invocations (that is, calls to a subroutine) to share one copy of the code and any readonly data. For the code to be reentrant, however, each invocation must use its own copy of any modifiable data (or synchronized access to shared data). This goal is most often achieved by using a stack and allocating local variables in a new stack frame for each invocation. Alternatively, the caller may pass in a pointer to a block of memory that that invocation can use (usually for output), or the code may allocate some memory on a heap, especially if the data must survive after the routine returns.

Reentrant code is often found in system software, such as operating systems and teleprocessing monitors. It is also a crucial component of multithreaded programs, where the term *thread-safe* is often used instead of reentrant.FOLDOC

regular character
A character that always represents itself in an ambiguous file reference or another type of regular expression. Contrast with *special character*.

regular expression
A string—composed of letters, numbers, and special symbols—that defines one or more strings. See Appendix A.

relative pathname
A pathname that starts from the working directory. Contrast with *absolute pathname* (page 1018).

remote access server
See *RAS* on page 1051.

remote filesystem
A filesystem on a remote computer that has been set up so that you can access (usually over a network) its files as though they were stored on your local computer's disks. An example of a remote filesystem is NFS.

remote procedure call
See *RPC* on page 1053.

resolver
The TCP/IP library software that formats requests to be sent to the *DNS* (page 1029) for hostname-to-Internet address conversion.FOLDOC

Resource Description Framework
See *RDF* on page 1051.

restore
The process of turning an icon into a window. Contrast with *iconify* (page 1036)

return code
See *exit status* on page 1031.

RFC
Request for comments. Begun in 1969, one of a series of numbered Internet informational documents and standards widely followed by commercial software and freeware in the Internet and UNIX/Linux communities. Few RFCs are standards but all Internet standards are recorded in RFCs. Perhaps the single most influential RFC has been RFC 822, the Internet electronic mail format standard.

The RFCs are unusual in that they are floated by technical experts acting on their own initiative and reviewed by the Internet at large rather than being formally promulgated through an institution such as ANSI. For this reason they remain known as RFCs, even after they are adopted as standards. The RFC tradition of pragmatic, experience-driven, after-the-fact standard writing done by individuals or small working groups has important advantages over the more formal, committee-driven process typical of ANSI or ISO. For a complete list of RFCs, go to www.rfc-editor.org.FOLDOC

roam
To move a computer between *wireless access points* (page 1063) on a wireless network without the user or applications being aware of the transition. Moving

between access points typically results in some packet loss, although this loss is transparent to programs that use TCP.

ROM   Readonly memory. A kind of nonvolatile storage. A data storage device that is manufactured with fixed contents. In general, ROM describes any storage system whose contents cannot be altered, such as a phonograph record or printed book. When used in reference to electronics and computers, ROM describes semiconductor integrated circuit memories, of which several types exist, and CD-ROM.

ROM is nonvolatile storage—it retains its contents even after power has been removed. ROM is often used to hold programs for embedded systems, as these usually have a fixed purpose. ROM is also used for storage of the *BIOS* (page 1021) in a computer. Contrast with *RAM* (page 1051).^{FOLDOC}

root directory   The ancestor of all directories and the start of all absolute pathnames. The name of the root directory is */*.

root filesystem   The filesystem that is available when the system is brought up in single-user mode. The name of this filesystem is always */*. You cannot unmount or mount the root filesystem. You can remount root to change its mount options.

root login   Usually the username of *Superuser* (page 1058).

root (user)   Another name for *Superuser* (page 1058).

rotate   When a file, such as a log file, gets indefinitely larger, you must keep it from taking up too much space on the disk. Because you may need to refer to the information in the log files in the near future, it is generally not a good idea to delete the contents of the file until it has aged. Instead you can periodically save the current log file under a new name and create a new, empty file as the current log file. You can keep a series of these files, renaming each as a new one is saved. You will then *rotate* the files. For example, you might remove **xyzlog.4**, **xyzlog.3**→ **xyzlog.4**, **xyzlog.2**→ **xyzlog.3**, **xyzlog.1**→ **xyzlog.2**, **xyzlog**→ **xyzlog.1**, and create a new **xyzlog** file. By the time you remove **xyzlog.4**, it will not contain any information more recent than you want to remove.

router   A device (often a computer) that is connected to more than one similar type of network to pass data between them. See *gateway* on page 1033.

RPC   Remote procedure call. A call to a *procedure* (page 1049) that acts transparently across a network. The procedure itself is responsible for accessing and using the network. The RPC libraries make sure that network access is transparent to the application. RPC runs on top of TCP/IP or UDP/IP.

RSA   A public key encryption (page 989) technology that is based on the lack of an efficient way to factor very large numbers. Because of this lack, it takes an extraordinary amount of computer processing time and power to deduce an RSA key. The RSA algorithm is the de facto standard for data sent over the Internet.

run	To execute a program.
runlevel	The mode that Linux is running in. Runlevels include single-user and multiuser. See Table 11-1 on page 404 for a complete list of runlevels.
Samba	A free suite of programs that implement the Server Message Block (SMB) protocol. See *SMB* (page 1055).
schema	Within a GUI, a pattern that helps you see and interpret the information that is presented in a window, making it easier to understand new information that is presented using the same schema.
scroll	To move lines on a terminal or window up and down or left and right.
scrollbar	A widget found in graphical user interfaces that controls (scrolls) which part of a document is visible in the window. A window can have a horizontal scrollbar, a vertical scrollbar (more common), or both.ᶠᴼᴸᴰᴼᶜ
server	A powerful centralized computer (or program) designed to provide information to clients (smaller computers or programs) on request.
session	The lifetime of a process. For a desktop, it is the desktop session manager. For a character-based terminal, it is the user's login shell process. In KDE, it is launched by kdeinit. A session may also be the sequence of events between when you start using a program, such as an editor, and when you finish.
setgid	When you execute a file that has setgid (set group ID) permission, the process executing the file takes on the privileges of the group the file belongs to. The ls utility shows setgid permission as an **s** in the group's executable position. See also *setuid*.
setuid	When you execute a file that has setuid (set user ID) permission, the process executing the file takes on the privileges of the owner of the file. As an example, if you run a setuid program that removes all the files in a directory, you can remove files in any of the file owner's directories, even if you do not normally have permission to do so. When the program is owned by **root**, you can remove files in any directory that **root** can remove files from. The ls utility shows setuid permission as an **s** in the owner's executable position. See also *setgid*.
sexillion	In the British system, 10^{36}. In the American system, this number is named *undecillion*. See also *large number* (page 1040).
SHA1	Secure Hash Algorithm 1. The SHA family is a set of cryptographic *hash* (page 1034) algorithms that were designed by the National Security Agency (NSA). The second member of this family is SHA1, a successor to *MD5* (page 1042). See also *cryptography* on page 1027.
share	A filesystem hierarchy that is shared with another system using *SMB* (page 1055). Also *Windows share* (page 1063).

shared network topology A network, such as Ethernet, in which each packet may be seen by systems other than its destination system. *Shared* means that the network bandwidth is shared by all users.

shell A Linux system command processor. The three major shells are the *Bourne Again Shell* (page 1022), the *TC Shell* (page 1059), and the *Z Shell* (page 1064).

shell function A series of commands that the shell stores for execution at a later time. Shell functions are like shell scripts but run more quickly because they are stored in the computer's main memory rather than in files. Also, a shell function is run in the environment of the shell that calls it (unlike a shell script, which is typically run in a subshell).

shell script An ASCII file containing shell commands. Also *shell program*.

signal A very brief message that the UNIX system can send to a process, apart from the process's standard input. Refer to "trap: Catches a Signal" on page 933.

simple filename A single filename containing no slashes (*/*). A simple filename is the simplest form of pathname. Also the last element of a pathname. Also *basename* (page 1021).

single-user system A computer system that only one person can use at a time. Contrast with *multiuser system* (page 1044).

SMB Server Message Block. Developed in the early 1980s by Intel, Microsoft, and IBM, SMB is a client/server protocol that is the native method of file and printer sharing for Windows. In addition, SMB can share serial ports and communications abstractions, such as named pipes and mail slots. SMB is similar to a remote procedure call (*RPC*, page 1053) that has been customized for filesystem access. Also *Microsoft Networking*.FOLDOC

smiley A character-based *glyph* (page 1033), typically used in email, that conveys an emotion. The characters :-) in a message portray a smiley face (look at it sideways). Because it can be difficult to tell when the writer of an electronic message is saying something in jest or in seriousness, email users often use :-) to indicate humor. The two original smileys, designed by Scott Fahlman, were :-) and :-(. Also *emoticon*, *smileys*, and *smilies*. For more information search on **smiley** on the Internet.

smilies See *smiley*.

SMTP Simple Mail Transfer Protocol. A protocol used to transfer electronic mail between computers. It is a server-to-server protocol, so other protocols are used to access the messages. The SMTP dialog usually happens in the background under the control of a message transport system such as sendmail.FOLDOC

snap (windows) As you drag a window toward another window or edge of the workspace, it can move suddenly so that it is adjacent to the other window/edge. Thus the window *snaps* into position.

sneakernet Using hand-carried magnetic media to transfer files between machines.

sniff   To monitor packets on a network. A system administrator can legitimately sniff packets and a malicious user can sniff packets to obtain information such as usernames and passwords. See also *packet sniffer* (page 1047).

SOCKS   A networking proxy protocol embodied in a SOCKS server, which performs the same functions as a *proxy gateway* (page 1050) or *proxy server* (page 1050). SOCKS works at the application level, requiring that an application be modified to work with the SOCKS protocol, whereas a *proxy* (page 1050) makes no demands on the application.

SOCKSv4 does not support authentication or UDP proxy. SOCKSv5 supports a variety of authentication methods and UDP proxy.

sort   To put in a specified order, usually alphabetic or numeric.

SPACE character   A character that appears as the absence of a visible character. Even though you cannot see it, a SPACE is a printable character. It is represented by the ASCII code 32 (decimal). A SPACE character is considered a *blank* or *whitespace* (page 1063).

spam   Posting irrelevant or inappropriate messages to one or more Usenet newsgroups or mailing lists in deliberate or accidental violation of *netiquette* (page 1044). Also, sending large amounts of unsolicited email indiscriminately. This email usually promotes a product or service. Another common purpose of spam is to *phish* (page 1048). Spam is the electronic equivalent of junk mail. From the Monty Python "Spam" song.ᶠᴼᴸᴰᴼᶜ

sparse file   A file that is large but takes up little disk space. The data in a sparse file is not dense (thus its name). Examples of sparse files are core files and dbm files.

spawn   See *fork* on page 1032.

special character   A character that has a special meaning when it occurs in an ambiguous file reference or another type of regular expression, unless it is quoted. The special characters most commonly used with the shell are * and ?. Also *metacharacter* (page 1042) and *wildcard*.

special file   See *device file* on page 1029.

spinner   In a GUI, a type of *text box* (page 1059) that holds a number you can change by typing over it or using the up and down arrows at the end of the box.

spoofing   See *IP spoofing* on page 1038.

spool   To place items in a queue, each waiting its turn for some action. Often used when speaking about printers. Also used to describe the queue.

SQL   Structured Query Language. A language that provides a user interface to relational database management systems (RDBMS). SQL, the de facto standard, is also an ISO and ANSI standard and is often embedded in other programming languages.ᶠᴼᴸᴰᴼᶜ

square bracket   A left square bracket ([) or a right square bracket (]). These special characters define character classes in ambiguous file references and other regular expressions.

SSH Communications Security   The company that created the original SSH (secure shell) protocol suite (www.ssh.com). Linux uses *OpenSSH* (page 1046).

standard error   A file to which a program can send output. Usually only error messages are sent to this file. Unless you instruct the shell otherwise, it directs this output to the screen (that is, to the device file that represents the screen).

standard input   A file from which a program can receive input. Unless you instruct the shell otherwise, it directs this input so that it comes from the keyboard (that is, from the device file that represents the keyboard).

standard output   A file to which a program can send output. Unless you instruct the shell otherwise, it directs this output to the screen (that is, to the device file that represents the screen).

startup file   A file that the login shell runs when you log in. The Bourne Again and Z Shells run **.profile**, and the TC Shell runs **.login**. The TC Shell also runs **.cshrc** whenever a new TC Shell or a subshell is invoked. The Z Shell runs an analogous file whose name is identified by the **ENV** variable.

status line   The bottom (usually the twenty-fourth) line of the terminal. The vim editor uses the status line to display information about what is happening during an editing session.

sticky bit   An access permission bit that causes an executable program to remain on the swap area of the disk. It takes less time to load a program that has its sticky bit set than one that does not. Only Superuser can set the sticky bit. If the sticky bit is set on a directory that is publicly writable, only the owner of a file in that directory can remove the file.

streaming tape   A tape that moves at a constant speed past the read/write heads rather than speeding up and slowing down, which can slow the process of writing to or reading from the tape. A proper blocking factor helps ensure that the tape device will be kept streaming.

streams   See *connection-oriented protocol* on page 1026.

string   A sequence of characters.

stylesheet   *See CSS* on page 1027.

subdirectory   A directory that is located within another directory. Every directory except the root directory is a subdirectory.

subnet   Subnetwork. A portion of a network, which may be a physically independent network segment, that shares a network address with other portions of the network and is distinguished by a subnet number. A subnet is to a network as a network is to an internet.[FOLDOC]

subnet address The subnet portion of an IP address. In a subnetted network, the host portion of an IP address is split into a subnet portion and a host portion using a subnet mask (also address mask). See also *subnet number*.

subnet mask A bit mask used to identify which bits in an IP address correspond to the network address and subnet portions of the address. Called a subnet mask because the network portion of the address is determined by the number of bits that are set in the mask. The subnet mask has ones in positions corresponding to the network and subnet numbers and zeros in the host number positions. Also *address mask*.

subnet number The subnet portion of an IP address. In a subnetted network, the host portion of an IP address is split into a subnet portion and a host portion using a *subnet mask*. Also *address mask*. See also *subnet address*.

subpixel hinting Similar to *anti-aliasing* (page 1019) but takes advantage of colors to do the anti-aliasing. Particularly useful on LCD screens.

subroutine See *procedure* on page 1049.

subshell A shell that is forked as a duplicate of its parent shell. When you run an executable file that contains a shell script by using its filename on the command line, the shell forks a subshell to run the script. Also, commands surrounded with parentheses are run in a subshell.

superblock A block that contains control information for a filesystem. The superblock contains housekeeping information, such as the number of inodes in the filesystem and free list information.

superserver The extended Internet services daemon. Refer to xinetd on page 376.

Superuser A privileged user having access to anything any other system user has access to and more. The system administrator must be able to become Superuser to establish new accounts, change passwords, and perform other administrative tasks. The username of Superuser is usually **root**. Also *root* or *root user*.

swap The operating system moving a process from main memory to a disk, or vice versa. Swapping a process to the disk allows another process to begin or continue execution. Refer to "swap" on page 458.

swap space An area of a disk (that is, a swap file) used to store the portion of a process's memory that has been paged out. Under a virtual memory system, the amount of swap space—rather than the amount of physical memory—determines the maximum size of a single process and the maximum total size of all active processes. Also *swap area* or *swapping area*.FOLDOC

switch See *network switch* on page 1045.

symbolic link A directory entry that points to the pathname of another file. In most cases a symbolic link to a file can be used in the same ways a hard link can be used. Unlike a hard link, a symbolic link can span filesystems and can connect to a directory.

system administrator The person responsible for the upkeep of the system. The system administrator has the ability to log in as Superuser. See also *Superuser*.

system console The main system terminal, usually directly connected to the computer and the one that receives system error messages. Also *console* and *console terminal.*

system mode The designation for the state of the system while it is doing system work. Some examples are making system calls, running NFS and autofs, processing network traffic, and performing kernel operations on behalf of the system. Contrast with *user mode* (page 1062).

System V One of the two major versions of the UNIX system.

TC Shell tcsh. An enhanced but completely compatible version of the BSD UNIX C shell, csh.

TCP Transmission Control Protocol. The most common transport layer protocol used on the Internet. This connection-oriented protocol is built on top of *IP* (page 1038) and is nearly always seen in the combination TCP/IP (TCP over *IP*). TCP adds reliable communication, sequencing, and flow control and provides full-duplex, process-to-process connections. *UDP* (page 1061), although connectionless, is the other proto-col that runs on top of *IP*.^{FOLDOC}

tera- In the binary system, the prefix *tera-* multiplies by 2^{40} (1,099,511,627,776). Ter-abyte is a common use of this prefix. Abbreviated as *T*. See also *large number* on page 1040.

termcap Terminal capability. The **/etc/termcap** file contains a list of various types of termi-nals and their characteristics. *System V* replaced the function of this file with the *terminfo* system.

terminal Differentiated from a *workstation* (page 1064) by its lack of intelligence, a terminal connects to a computer that runs Linux. A workstation runs Linux on itself.

terminfo Terminal information. The **/usr/lib/terminfo** directory contains many subdirecto-ries, each containing several files. Each of those files is named for and holds a sum-mary of the functional characteristics of a particular terminal. Visually oriented textual programs, such as vim, use these files. An alternative to the **termcap** file.

text box In a GUI, a box you can type in.

theme Defined as an implicit or recurrent idea, *theme* is used in a GUI to describe a look that is consistent for all elements of a desktop. Go to themes.freshmeat.net for examples.

thicknet A type of coaxial cable (thick) used for an Ethernet network. Devices are attached to thicknet by tapping the cable at fixed points.

thinnet A type of coaxial cable (thin) used for an Ethernet network. Thinnet cable is smaller in diameter and more flexible than *thicknet* cable. Each device is typically attached to two separate cable segments by using a T-shaped connector; one segment leads to the device ahead of it on the network and one to the device that follows it.

thread-safe See *reentrant* on page 1051.

thumb The movable button in the scrollbar that positions the image in the window. The size of the thumb reflects the amount of information in the buffer. Also *bubble.*

TIFF	Tagged Image File Format. A file format used for still-image bitmaps, stored in tagged fields. Application programs can use the tags to accept or ignore fields, depending on their capabilities. FOLDOC
tiled windows	An arrangement of windows such that no window overlaps another. The opposite of *cascading windows* (page 1023).
time to live	See *TTL*.
toggle	To switch between one of two positions. For example, the ftp **glob** command toggles the **glob** feature: Give the command once, and it turns the feature on or off; give the command again, and it sets the feature back to its original state.
token	A basic, grammatically indivisible unit of a language, such as a keyword, operator, or identifier. FOLDOC
token ring	A type of *LAN* (page 1040) in which computers are attached to a ring of cable. A token packet circulates continuously around the ring. A computer can transmit information only when it holds the token.
tooltip	A minicontext help system that you activate by allowing your mouse pointer to *hover* (page 1036) over a button, icon, or applet (such as those on a panel).
transient window	A dialog or other window that is displayed for only a short time.
Transmission Control Protocol	See *TCP* on page 1059.
Trojan horse	A program that does something destructive or disruptive to your system. Its action is not documented, and the system administrator would not approve of it if she were aware of it. See "Avoiding a Trojan Horse" on page 398.
	The term *Trojan horse* was coined by MIT-hacker-turned-NSA-spook Dan Edwards. It refers to a malicious security-breaking program that is disguised as something benign, such as a directory lister, archive utility, game, or (in one notorious 1990 case on the Mac) a program to find and destroy viruses. Similar to *back door* (page 1020). FOLDOC
TTL	Time to live.
	1. All DNS records specify how long they are good for—usually up to a week at most. This time is called the record's *time to live*. When a DNS server or an application stores this record in *cache* (page 1023), it decrements the TTL value and removes the record from cache when the value reaches zero. A DNS server passes a cached record to another server with the current (decremented) TTL guaranteeing the proper TTL, no matter how many servers the record passes through.
	2. In the IP header, a field that indicates how many more hops the packet should be allowed to make before being discarded or returned.

TTY   Teletypewriter. The terminal device that UNIX was first run from. Today TTY refers to the screen (or window, in the case of a terminal emulator), keyboard, and mouse that are connected to a computer. This term appears in UNIX, and Linux has kept the term for the sake of consistency and tradition.

tunneling   Encapsulation of protocol A within packets carried by protocol B, such that A treats B as though it were a data link layer. Tunneling is used to transfer data between administrative domains that use a protocol not supported by the internet connecting those domains. It can also be used to encrypt data sent over a public internet, as when you use ssh to tunnel a protocol over the Internet.FOLDOC See also *VPN* (page 1062) and *port forwarding* (page 1049).

UDP   User Datagram Protocol. The Internet standard transport layer protocol that provides simple but unreliable datagram services. UDP is a *connectionless protocol* (page 1026) that, like *TCP* (page 1059), is layered on top of *IP* (page 1038).

Unlike *TCP*, UDP neither guarantees delivery nor requires a connection. As a result it is lightweight and efficient, but the application program must handle all error processing and retransmission. UDP is often used for sending time-sensitive data that is not particularly sensitive to minor loss, such as audio and video data.FOLDOC

UID   User ID. A number that the **passwd** database associates with a username.

undecillion   In the American system, 10^{36}. In the British system, this number is named *sexillion*. See also *large number* (page 1040).

unicast   A packet sent from one host to another host. Unicast means one source and one destination.

Unicode   A character encoding standard that was designed to cover all major modern written languages with each character having exactly one encoding and being represented by a fixed number of bits.

unmanaged window   See *ignored window* on page 1036.

URI   Universal Resource Identifier. The generic set of all names and addresses that are short strings referring to objects (typically on the Internet). The most common kinds of URIs are *URLs*.FOLDOC

URL   Uniform (was Universal) Resource Locator. A standard way of specifying the location of an object, typically a Web page, on the Internet. URLs are a subset of *URIs*.

usage message   A message displayed by a command when you call the command using incorrect command line arguments.

User Datagram Protocol   See *UDP*.

User ID   See *UID*.

user interface	See *interface* on page 1037.
user mode	The designation for the state of the system while it is doing user work, such as running a user program (but not the system calls made by the program). Contrast with *system mode* (page 1059).
username	The name you enter in response to the **login:** prompt. Other users use your username when they send you mail or write to you. Each username has a corresponding user ID, which is the numeric identifier for the user. Both the username and the user ID are stored in the **passwd** database (**/etc/passwd** or the NIS equivalent). Also *login name*.
userspace	The part of memory (RAM) where applications reside. Code running in userspace cannot access hardware directly and cannot access memory allocated to other applications. Also *userland*. See the *KernelAnalysis-HOWTO*.
UTC	Coordinated Universal Time. UTC is the equivalent to the mean solar time at the prime meridian (0 degrees longitude). Also called Zulu time (Z stands for longitude zero) and GMT (Greenwich Mean Time).
UTF-8	An encoding that allows *Unicode* (page 1061) characters to be represented using sequences of 8-bit bytes.
utility	A program included as a standard part of Linux. You typically invoke a utility either by giving a command in response to a shell prompt or by calling it from within a shell script. Utilities are often referred to as commands. Contrast with *builtin (command)* (page 1023).
variable	A name and an associated value. The shell allows you to create variables and use them in shell scripts. Also, the shell inherits several variables when it is invoked, and it maintains those and other variables while it is running. Some shell variables establish characteristics of the shell environment; others have values that reflect different aspects of your ongoing interaction with the shell.
viewport	Same as *workspace* (page 1064).
virtual console	Additional consoles, or displays, that you can view on the system, or physical, console. See page 113 for more information.
virus	A *cracker* (page 1027) program that searches out other programs and "infects" them by embedding a copy of itself in them, so that they become *Trojan horses* (page 1060). When these programs are executed, the embedded virus is executed as well, propagating the "infection," usually without the user's knowledge. By analogy with biological viruses. FOLDOC
VLAN	Virtual LAN. A logical grouping of two or more nodes that are not necessarily on the same physical network segment but that share the same network number. A VLAN is often associated with switched Ethernet. FOLDOC
VPN	Virtual private network. A private network that exists on a public network, such as the Internet. A VPN is a less expensive substitute for company-owned/leased lines and uses encryption (page 988) to ensure privacy. A nice side effect is that you can send non-Internet protocols, such as AppleTalk, IPX, or *NetBIOS* (page 1044), over the VPN connection by *tunneling* (page 1061) them through the VPN IP stream.

W2K	Windows 2000 Professional or Server.
W3C	World Wide Web Consortium (www.w3.org).
WAN	Wide area network. A network that interconnects *LANs* (page 1040) and *MANs* (page 1042), spanning a large geographic area (typically states or countries).
WAP	Wireless access point. A bridge or router between wired and wireless networks. WAPs typically support some form of access control to prevent unauthorized clients from connecting to the network.
Web ring	A collection of Web sites that provide information on a single topic or group of related topics. Each home page that is part of the Web ring has a series of links that let you go from site to site.
whitespace	A collective name for SPACEs and/or TABs and occasionally NEWLINEs. Also *white space*.
wide area network	See *WAN*.
widget	The basic objects of a graphical user interface. Buttons, text fields, and scrollbars are examples of widgets.
wildcard	See *metacharacter* on page 1042.
Wi-Fi	Wireless Fidelity. A generic term that refers to any type of *802.11* (page 1018) wireless network.
window	On a display screen, a region that runs or is controlled by a particular program.
window manager	A program that controls how windows appear on a display screen and how you manipulate them.
Windows share	See *share* on page 1054.
WINS	Windows Internet Naming Service. The service responsible for mapping NetBIOS names to IP addresses. WINS has the same relationship to NetBIOS names that DNS has to Internet domain names.
WINS server	The program responsible for handling WINS requests. This program caches name information about hosts on a local network and resolves them to IP addresses.
wireless access point	See *WAP*.
word	A sequence of one or more nonblank characters separated from other words by TABs, SPACEs, or NEWLINEs. Used to refer to individual command line arguments. In vim, a word is similar to a word in the English language—a string of one or more characters bounded by a punctuation mark, a numeral, a TAB, a SPACE, or a NEWLINE.
Work buffer	A location where vim stores text while it is being edited. The information in the Work buffer is not written to the file on the disk until you give the editor a command to write it.

working directory	The directory that you are associated with at any given time. The relative pathnames you use are *relative to* the working directory. Also *current directory*.
workspace	A subdivision of a *desktop* (page 1028) that occupies the entire display. Refer to "Getting the Most from the Desktop" on page 85.
workstation	A small computer, typically designed to fit in an office and be used by one person and usually equipped with a bit-mapped graphical display, keyboard, and mouse. Differentiated from a *terminal* (page 1059) by its intelligence. A workstation runs Linux on itself while a terminal connects to a computer that runs Linux.
worm	A program that propagates itself over a network, reproducing itself as it goes. Today the term has negative connotations, as it is assumed that only *crackers* (page 1027) write worms. Compare to *virus* (page 1062) and *Trojan horse* (page 1060). From **Tapeworm** in John Brunner's novel, *The Shockwave Rider*, Ballantine Books, 1990 (via XEROX PARC).FOLDOC
WYSIWYG	What You See Is What You Get. A graphical application, such as a word processor, whose display is similar to its printed output.
X server	The X server is the part of the *X Window System* that runs the mouse, keyboard, and display. (The application program is the client.)
X terminal	A graphics terminal designed to run the X Window System.
X Window System	A design and set of tools for writing flexible, portable windowing applications, created jointly by researchers at MIT and several leading computer manufacturers.
XDMCP	X Display Manager Control Protocol. XDMCP allows the login server to accept requests from network displays. XDMCP is built into many X terminals.
***x*DSL**	Different types of *DSL* (page 1030) are identified by a prefix, for example, ADSL, HDSL, SDSL, and VDSL.
Xinerama	An extension to X.org. Xinerama allows window managers and applications to use the two or more physical displays as one large virtual display. Refer to the Xinerama-HOWTO.
XML	Extensible Markup Language. A universal format for structured documents and data on the Web. Developed by *W3C* (page 1063), XML is a pared-down version of SGML. See www.w3.org/XML and www.w3.org/XML/1999/XML-in-10-points.
XSM	X Session Manager. This program allows you to create a session that includes certain applications. While the session is running, you can perform a *checkpoint* (saves the application state) or a *shutdown* (saves the state and exits from the session). When you log back in, you can load your session so that everything in your session is running just as it was when you logged off.
Z Shell	zsh. A *shell* (page 1055) that incorporates many of the features of the *Bourne Again Shell* (page 1022), *Korn Shell* (page 1040), and *TC Shell* (page 1059), as well as many original features.
Zulu time	See *UTC* on page 1062.

INDEX

Note: Only variables that must always appear with a leading dollar sign are indexed with a leading dollar sign. Other variables are indexed without a leading dollar sign.

NUMERICS

B

B language, 9
Back door, 1020
Back tick, 335, 1025
Background
  command grouping, 279
  defined, 219
  desktop, 91
  foreground, versus, 219
  job control, 13, 280
  PID stored in $!, 920
  process, 302, 1020
  running a command in, 219
  symbol (&), 278
BACKSLASH escape character, 126,
    277, 287
BACKSLASH in replacement strings,
    973
BACKSPACE key, 117
Backup
  active filesystem, 541
  amanda, 542
  cpio utility, 543
  dump level, 545
  failing to perform, 552
  file, 540, 545
  full, 541
  incremental, 541
  media, 541
  offsite, 541
  policy, 541
  simple, 544
  tar utility, 542
  utilities, 542
badtabs.c program, 851
Basename, 171, 1021
basename utility, 905, 906, 935
bash, 1022
  <& duplicate input file
      descriptor, 912
  >& duplicate output file
      descriptor, 912
  alias, 318
  arguments, 922
  arithmetic evaluation, 940
    example, 895, 918, 941
    operators, 943
  arithmetic expansion, 332
    operators, 943
  array variables, 914

attribute
  array, 290
  export, 290
  function, 290
  integer, 290, 291
  readonly, 289, 290
background, 266
builtin
  exec, 911
  getopts, 936
  typeset, 918
close file, 912
command
  process, 328
  substitution, 334
command line, order of
    expansion, 287
conditional expression, 941
  example, 913, 937
control structure. *See Control,*
    structure
directory stack manipulation,
    282
editing previous commands,
    304, 305
emacs command line editor,
    313
event number, 303
expand null variable, 925
expand unset variable, 925
expression, 943
features, 324
file descriptor, 911
globbing, 335
history mechanism, 302, 306
makepath shell script, 949
menu, 907
open file, 911
operator, 943
  bitwise, 947
  remainder, 946
  short-circuiting, 946
  ternary, 947
options. *See bash, features*
overlay, 276
pathname completion, 314
process substitution, 337
program structures, 948
programming, 948
prompt, 293
PS3 prompt, 908

quick substitution, 311
quiz shell script, 952
quotation mark removal, 329
recursion, 949
redirection operators, 272
reexecuting events, 304, 305
REPLY keyword variable, 908
signal names, 933, 936
special characters, 126
standard error. *See Standard,*
    error
standard input. *See Standard,*
    input
standard output. *See Standard,*
    output
startup files, 267
string pattern matching, 942
substitution, quick, 311
symbolic link, 195
ternary operator, 945
tilde substitution, 331
variable. *See also Variable*
  array, 914
  assign default value, 925
  BASH_ENV, 268
  COLUMNS, 908
  display error message, 926
  expansion, 925
  LINES, 908
  modifier, 925
  OPTARG, 937
  OPTIND, 937
  PS3, 908
  REPLY, 908, 928
  substitute default value, 925
vi command line editor, 312
vim command line editor, 312
−x option, 890
BASH_ENV variable, 268
bashrc file, 411
Baud, 1021
Baud rate, 1021
BCPL language, 9
beagle utility, 249
beagled daemon, 249
Bell Laboratories. *See AT&T*
    Bell Laboratories
Berkeley
  Internet Name Domain. *See*
    DNS
  UNIX, 6, 14, 1021

Also Available from Mark G. Sobell

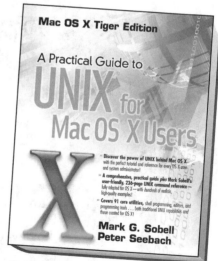

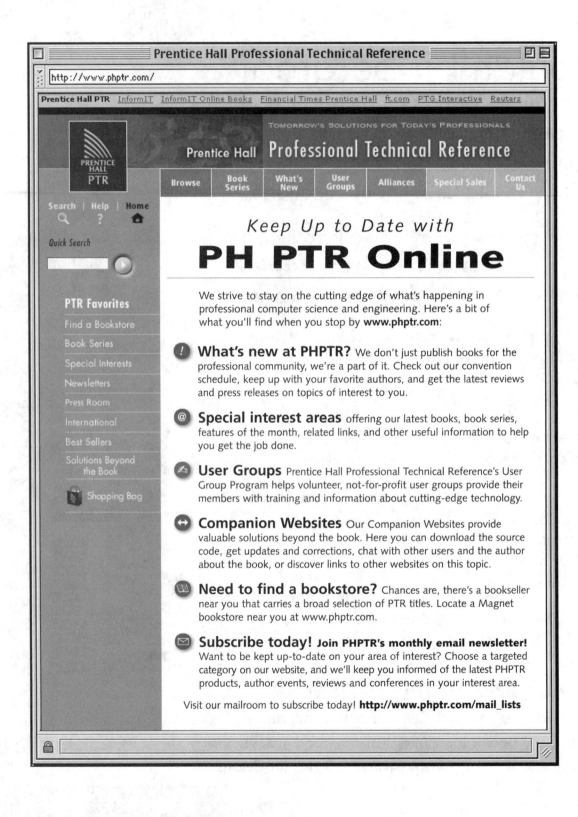

Safari
BOOKS ONLINE
ENABLED

THIS BOOK IS SAFARI ENABLED

INCLUDES FREE 45-DAY ACCESS TO THE ONLINE EDITION

The Safari® Enabled icon on the cover of your favorite technology book means the book is available through Safari Bookshelf. When you buy this book, you get free access to the online edition for 45 days.

Safari Bookshelf is an electronic reference library that lets you easily search thousands of technical books, find code samples, download chapters, and access technical information whenever and wherever you need it.

TO GAIN 45-DAY SAFARI ENABLED ACCESS TO THIS BOOK:

- Go to **http://www.prenhallprofessional.com/safarienabled**
- Complete the brief registration form
- Enter the coupon code found in the front of this book on the "Copyright" page

If you have difficulty registering on Safari Bookshelf or accessing the online edition, please e-mail customer-service@safaribooksonline.com.

PRENTICE
HALL

DVD-ROM Warranty

Prentice Hall warrants the enclosed DVD-ROM to be free of defects in materials and faulty workmanship under normal use for a period of ninety days after purchase (when purchased new). If a defect is discovered in the DVD during this warranty period, a replacement DVD-ROM can be obtained at no charge by sending the defective DVD-ROM, postage prepaid, with proof of purchase to:

Disc Exchange
Prentice Hall
Pearson Technology Group
75 Arlington Street, Suite 300
Boston, MA 02116
Email: AWPro@aw.com

Prentice Hall makes no warranty or representation, either expressed or implied, with respect to this software, its quality, performance, merchantability, or fitness for a particular purpose. In no event will Prentice Hall, its distributors, or dealers be liable for direct, indirect, special, incidental, or consequential damages arising out of the use or inability to use the software. The exclusion of implied warranties is not permitted in some states. Therefore, the above exclusion may not apply to you. This warranty provides you with specific legal rights. There may be other rights that you may have that vary from state to state. The contents of this DVD-ROM are intended for personal use only.

More information and updates are available at www.prenhallprofessional.com